BIOGRAPHICAL
DICTIONARIES

ROBERT B. SLOCUM

BIOGRAPHICAL

DICTIONARIES

AND

RELATED WORKS

An International Bibliography of Collective Biographies,
Bio-bibliographies, Collections of Epitaphs, Selected
Genealogical Works, Dictionaries of Anonyms and Pseudonyms,
Historical and Specialized Dictionaries, Biographical
Materials in Government Manuals, Bibliographies of Biography,
Biographical Indexes, and Selected Portrait Catalogs

GALE RESEARCH COMPANY   THE BOOK TOWER   DETROIT, MICHIGAN 48226

PAPER USED IN THIS EDITION IS
A FINE ACID FREE PERMANENT/DURABLE PAPER
COMMONLY REFERRED TO AS "300-YEAR" PAPER

Copyright 1967 by

GALE RESEARCH COMPANY

1400 Book Tower, Detroit, Michigan 48226

Library of Congress Card No. 67-27789

$20.00

Printed in the United States of America

CONTENTS

PREFACE ix

HISTORICAL NOTE xv

BIBLIOGRAPHICAL NOTE xix

UNIVERSAL BIOGRAPHY
    Bibliography, Indexes, Portrait Catalogs 1
    Anonyms and Pseudonyms 4
    Dictionaries, Bio-bibliographies, etc. 6

NATIONAL OR AREA BIOGRAPHY
    Africa 42
    Africa, South 42
    Americas 43
    Argentine Republic 44
    Armenia 47
    Asia 47
    Australasia 47
    Australia 47
    Austria 49
    Balkan Peninsula 52
    Baltic Provinces 52
    Belgium 53
    Bolivia 60
    Brazil 60
    British Guiana 62
    Bulgaria 62
    Burma 62
    Cambodia 63
    Canada 63

Contents

Central America 66
Chile 66
China 68
Colombia 76
Congo (Leopoldville) 77
Cuba 77
Cyprus 78
Czechoslovakia 78
Denmark 80
Dominican Republic 82
Dutch Guiana. SEE: Surinam.
Dutch East Indies. SEE: Indonesia.
Dutch West Indies. SEE under West Indies.
Ecuador 83
England. SEE: Great Britain.
Europe 84
Finland 86
France 87
Germany 133
Great Britain 155
Greece, Ancient 179
Greece, Modern 179
Hong Kong 179
Hungary 179
Iceland 181
India 181
Indonesia 185
Ireland 186
Islamic countries 187
Israel. SEE: Entries under Jews.
Italy 191
Jamaica 204
Japan 205
Jews 208
Korea 213
Laos 214
Latin America 214
Lebanon 217
Luxemburg 217
Malaya 217
Malta 217
Mauritius 218
Mexico 218

Middle East. SEE under Islamic countries.
Near East. SEE under Islamic countries.
Netherlands 223
New Caledonia 227
New Hebrides 227
New Zealand 227
Nigeria 228
Norway 228
Pacific Islands 229
Pakistan 230
Palestine. SEE: Entries under Jews.
Panama 230
Paraguay 231
Peru 231
Philippine Islands 232
Poland 234
Portugal 236
Puerto Rico 238
Rhodesia 239
Roman Empire 239
Rumania 239
Russia 240
Salvador 254
Santo Domingo. SEE: Dominican Republic.
Sarawak 254
Scandinavia 254
Scotland. SEE under Great Britain.
Siam. SEE: Thailand.
Singapore 255
Slavs 255
South Africa. SEE: Africa, South.
South America. SEE: Central America; Latin
     America; Individual Countries. ....
Spain 256
Spanish America. SEE: Latin America.
Sudan 264
Surinam 264
Sweden 265
Switzerland 268
Thailand 273
Turkey 274
United Arab Republic. SEE under Islamic
     countries.

Contents

United States 275
Uruguay 342
Venezuela 342
Vietnam 343
Wales. SEE under Great Britain.
West Indies 344
Yugoslavia 344

BIOGRAPHY BY VOCATION
Arts 348
    Bibliography, Indexes, Artists' Marks,
      etc. 348
    General Works 349
    Architecture 381
    Sculpture 383
    Applied Arts 384
    Music 388
    Theater 440
Athletics and Games 452
Education 456
Language and Literature 467
Law 562
Library Science and Book Arts 570
Medicine 579
Philosophy and Psychology 605
Religion 609
Science 655
    General Works 655
    Biology and Geology 663
    Chemistry 667
    Mathematics 669
    Physics 670
Social Sciences 671
    General Works 671
    Economics and Commerce 673
    Geography and Travel 678
    History, Archaeology, Anthropology,
      etc. 680
    Political Science 683
Technology and Applied Science 684

AUTHOR INDEX 694
TITLE INDEX 832
SUBJECT INDEX 994

PREFACE

The search for basic facts about personalities of the past and present is a task that involves librarians, genealogists, and many others who are interested in the human condition, and however overwhelmed by <u>other</u> kinds of printed matter we may feel, we suspect that there is a shortage of biographical reference tools whenever our quest fails. The bibliography which follows, therefore, is an attempt to tabulate the labors of compilers of biographical dictionaries through several centuries and to suggest additional sources for searchers after biographical data in brief form, in the hope that more quests can thereby be successful.

The attempt to organize works of collective biography has been made before. Two examples come immediately to mind: (1) E. M. Oettinger's bibliography of bio-bibliographical works at the end of the second volume of his *Bibliographie Biographique Universelle* (1854), and (2) *A Handbook to the Literature of Collective Biography* (1885), by Edward Edwards and Charles Hole, which ceased after the publication of a first small "part." These are products of the nineteenth century; the twentieth century has produced a number of bibliographies of national biography, yet it seems to lack any comprehensive publication devoted entirely to the topic Edwards and Hole chose for themselves (their "collective biography" being more or less synonymous with what we now call a "biographical dictionary").

Although my concern in this bibliography is primarily the biographical dictionary, closely related

materials have not been neglected--bio-bibliographies;
collections of epitaphs; those genealogical works that
have great biographical value; dictionaries of anonyms
and pseudonyms; portrait volumes (hopefully accompanied
by biographical sketches); historical and specialized
subject dictionaries; government and legislative manuals that include substantial biographical material;
bibliographies of individual and collective biography;
biographical indexes; and selected portrait catalogs.
General encyclopedias, with very few exceptions, have
been excluded, because they seemed such obvious and
available choices for consultation on major figures in
world civilization. "Analytical entries" in catalogs
and bibliographies (i.e., entries identifying biographical material which is a part of a larger work) are
particularly difficult to locate; references of this
type contained in this bibliography were chanced upon
and are not the result of concentrated effort.

In regard to virtually all the above-mentioned
types of sources, I realize that the listings of individual specimens in this volume are incomplete; however, those that are enumerated should point out to
the user the possibilities of materials of a similar
nature listed in other sources.

A word about "collective biographies." It has
not been my intention to list collections of biography
as such--and by this I mean rather lengthy biographical studies of a comparatively small number of person-
alities--unless they also fit into the category of
biographical dictionaries (e.g., the *Dictionary of
American Biography* and the *Dictionary of National Biography*). Nevertheless, I have included some collective
biographies that treat relatively obscure areas or subjects. The numeral "100" has been used as a criterion,
too; i.e., it seemed worthwhile to include works which
do not have the format of biographical dictionaries
(alphabetical arrangement of concise biographical data)
but which do contain material on a large number of individuals (ca. 100 or more) and in many cases offer alphabetical approaches through indexes. Again, the figure "100" has been disregarded when a subject's or

area's obscurity so warranted.

Directories posed problems of choice. Many of
them are merely listings of members of specific professions and organizations with their addresses and
present positions; they were not selected for this
bibliography. Accepted were directories and registers which yielded (even if in capsule or much-abbre-
viated format) basic facts--e.g., birth and/or death
dates, educational background and training, present
position, address and/or other identifying data. If
these criteria fail to apply to a few wayward pieces
in the bibliography the fault rests solely with the
compiler whose "informed" guesses were in lieu of di-
rect examination of these pieces because of their un-
availability at a particular place or time.

Another limitation in this bibliography must be
mentioned, and it may be an unfortunate one. At the
outset the compiler decided to omit biographical dictionaries which dealt with the several smaller units
of government or relatively limited geographical ar-
eas--for example, towns, villages, the counties of
the states of the United States of America, and the
like. In the last-mentioned case, especially, there
exists a long line of local histories with sizable
biographical sections. The thought was that their
inclusion would contribute towards an unwieldy tool--
and that they might better be left to a separate bibliography of their own. Biographical dictionaries
concentrating on particular professions or vocations
in some small localities will be found in the bibliography, however; their presence accounts for the entries for smaller cities, towns, etc. in the subject
index.

After the final arrangement of the text had been
made, several omissions and dislocations came to
light--among them: (1) Items 3178 and 3179 (Poidras,
Critical & Documentary Dictionary of Violin Makers--
English and French versions) are under the subject
"Theater," when they, of course, correctly belong
under "Music." (2) Item 2367 (Stacey, firm, publisher, *Men of the West)* is in "American Biography,"

when in reality it is a collection of sketches of notable figures from the West Country of England. (3) Item 2597 Quatremère de Quincy, *Histoire de la vie ... de Plus Célèbres Architectes ...*) slipped into the section on fine arts in general; (4) Item 2981 (*Deutsches Musiker-Lexikon*) is misfiled under "M," because it was at one time entered under the editor, E. H. Müller; (5) Item 2013 (Shoemaker, F. C., *Missouri and Missourians*) is far from its proper niche, "Missouri-Biography."

One omission I especially regret is the *Biographical Encyclopedia of American Jews;* it was planned for inclusion, but lost its way somewhere along the line. May this and other omissions find their way into future supplements or editions.

Do not be perturbed should you note missing numbers at various places in the text. Constant rechecking and similarities uncovered in subject indexing revealed duplicates or doubtful entries which were deleted in the last stages of revision; reassignment of numbers at this point would have been a difficult and expensive venture at best.

All entries in the bibliography are in Latin letters. Entries for materials converted from non-European alphabets are abbreviated. Transliteration and romanization schemes, with rare exceptions, are those of the Library of Congress.

In the collation statement you will note occasional variations in the statement of size; in several cases size is not given. The explanation for these inconsistencies rests with the bibliographies employed in the compilation of the text; e.g., the *Library of Congress Catalog of Printed Books* gives size in centimeters, while the comparable publications of the British Museum and Bibliothèque Nationale (France) use quartos (4°), octavos (8°), etc.; some bibliographies make no mention of size.

Entries, with the exceptions noted above, are as complete as possible. Authors' birth and/or death dates are included whenever possible, because I feel that they often tell us something about the limitations or nature of the books under their names. Some works require few or no explanatory notes; others, especially works in the lesser known languages, or books with obscure titles, demand fuller informative comments and translations of titles.

The first reaction of the user of a bibliography or library catalog to "open entry" listings (i.e., an entry that indicates an incomplete or continuing work, because the volume statement and imprint date are not closed) is that the works are still in progress. This is not necessarily true. Complete information may be lacking and extremely difficult to find. Such is often the case in this bibliography. It contains a number of open entries which might have better been closed had the compiler made a more intensive investigation of them; I preferred to spend available time on the accumulation of entries and accept the statements of incompleteness given by various bibliographical sources.

The table of contents points out the simplicity of arrangement in the body of the work. A detailed approach is offered by the author, title, and subject indexes at the back of the volume.

When using the indexes the reader must keep in mind the following points: The references are to item numbers, not to pages. Certain liberties have been taken in filing words with very similar spellings--*cyclopaedia* or *encyclopaedia* are filed as if spelled *cyclopedia* or *encyclopedia; Verzeichnis* and *Verzeichniss* are interfiled, etc. However, umlauts and other diacritical marks in various foreign languages have been taken into consideration so that: ä, ö, ü in Finnish, German, Hungarian, Scandinavian and modern Turkish are filed as if written: ae, oe, ue. The Hungarian ő and ű and the Danish-Norwegian ø are similarly treated. The Scandinavian å is filed as aa; the Icelandic letters ð and þ = d and th, respectively. Arabic names or words are filed by

Preface

the term following the article al and its equivalents. Thus *al-Ansari̅* is filed under *Ansari̅*.

Incidentally, the edition of an individual title listed in this bibliography is by no means invariably the first or only edition. When a title has gone through many editions, the most comprehensive edition or the best translation into a well-known language has often been selected with the assumption that the interested reader will use mentioned bibliographical tools to work his way back or forward to the other editions.

The bibliography would not have progressed as far as it did without the assistance of my colleagues in the Cornell University Libraries who were readily and cheerfully on hand for consultation on many important points. I owe special thanks to Richard S. Howard, curator of Cornell's Wason (East Asian) Collection; John T. Ma, former bibliographer for Chinese materials at Cornell, and now with the Hoover Institution, Stanford University; and Vilhjalmur T. Bjarnar, curator of Cornell's Icelandic Collection. James M. Ethridge and Rosemary Dolinski of the Gale Research Company were always available for editorial assistance and suggestions. Mrs. Betty Rush (ably assisted by her husband William and daughter Suzanne) was the most faithful and consistent of a battery of typists who converted my manuscript cards into legible copy. My wife, son, and daughter displayed commendable patience and forebearance, even as I threatened to engulf them with numerous card files and notes. And I am grateful to those indefatigable searchers after biographical data whose industry has been responsible for dictionaries and related works that keep alive the memory of figures of the past; without their spadework this bibliography would not have been possible. All errors and sins of omission are, of course, the responsibility of the compiler.

HISTORICAL NOTE

How far back in time must we reach before we come upon anything resembling our "biographical dictionary"? The Western tradition of biographical dictionaries has its true beginnings in the sixteenth and seventeenth centuries. To be sure, antiquity offers Plutarch's 46 *Lives* and extant fragments from Cornelius Nepos's *De Viris Illustribus* and Suetonius' work of the same title (as well as his *De Vita Caesarum*). The Middle Ages yield numerous collected lives of the saints and churchmen and biographical compilations within various chronicles. But none of these is a biographical dictionary; they are collected biographies whose chief aim is didactic--biographical information is subordinate. Two "exceptions" remain: (1) the so-called *Suidas, Suidae,* or *Suda Lexicon,* compiled circa 1000 A.D. This work is primarily a dictionary of the Greek language, yet it also contains bio-bibliographical data on many classical (chiefly Greek) and Byzantine authors. Limited in scope though it may be, the *Suidas Lexicon* still has a claim to being one of the earliest Western examples of a "biographical" dictionary (perhaps the <u>earliest</u>). (2) *Las Vidas dels Trobadors,* succinct sketches of 101 Provençal poets composed in the thirteenth and fourteenth centuries, but collected and printed much later (the best modern editions stem from the early nineteenth century).

The sixteenth century offers several works that closely approach the desiderata of our "biographical dictionary." Books 2-4 of Bernardus de Lutzenburgo's *Catalogus Hereticorum* (1522?) include in alphabetical arrangement the names of heretics with a few words about them and their "errors." Konrad Gesner's *Bibliotheca Universalis* (1545) is a monumental bio-bibliography of writers in Latin, Greek and Hebrew. Vasari's famous *Le Vite de Più Eccellenti Architetti, Pittori et Scultori Italiani* contains circa 200 biographies of varying lengths; it is collective biography on a large scale for its day (Vasari started his compilation in the 1550's), as is André Thevet's *Les Vrais Pourtraits et Vies des Hommes Illustres Grecz, Latins et Payens* (1584); the latter was reissued in 1671 under the title: *Histoire de Plus Illustres Scavans Hommes de Leur Siècles.*

In terms of numbers, this bibliography lists 16 biographical dictionaries and/or extensive collective biographies for the sixteenth century. For the seventeenth century this figure is quadrupled--64 items. Among the most prominent of these are: Du Verdier's *Prosopographia* (1603); Melchior Adam's German biographies (*Vitae Germanorum Theologorum, Medicorum, Philosophorum, etc.*, 1615-1653?); the Bollandists' *Acta Sanctorum* (began 1643); Thomas Fuller's *The History of the Worthies of England* (1662); Nicolás Antonio's *Bibliotheca Hispana* (1672); Louis Moreri's *Le Grand Dictionnaire Historique* (1674); Henning Witte's *Memoriae Jurisconsultorum* (and *Memoriae Medicorum*) *Nostri Saeculi Clarissimorum* (1676) and *Diarium Biographicum* (1688-1691); and Pierre Bayle's *Dictionnaire Historique et Critique* (1697).

Publication of biographical dictionaries gathered momentum during the eighteenth century. Among the 346 works listed for the Century of the Enlightenment, the following are prominent and perhaps familiar: Mencke's *Compendiöses Gelehrten-Lexicon*, a forerunner of the great Jöcher *Allgemeines Gelehrten-Lexicon*; Le Neve's *Fasti Ecclesiae Anglicanae* and *Monumenta Anglicana;* Ward's *Athenae Oxonienses;* Nicéron's *Mémoires pour Servir à l'Histoire des Hommes dans la République de Lettres;* Barbosa Machado's *Biblioteca Lusitana;* the *Biographia Britannica;* Ladvocat's *Dictionnaire Historique et Bibliographique;* Azulai's *Shem ha-Gedolim;* Butler's *Lives of the Saints;*

Pilkington's *A General Dictionary of Painters*; Feller's *Biographie Universelle*; and Hutchinson's *Biographia Medica*.

The flood-gates opened in the nineteenth century. In an era of heightened patriotism it seemed natural for several huge national biographical dictionaries to have their beginnings--e.g., the *Belgian Biographie Nationale*; the *Allgemeine Deutsche Biographie*; the *Dictionary of National Biography*; the *Russkii Biograficheskii Slovar'*; Aa's *Biographisch Woordenboek der Nederlanden*; the *Biografiskt Lexicon öfver Namnkunnige Svenske Män* and its continuation *Svenskt Biografiskt Lexikon (Ny följd)*; Wurzbach's *Biographisches Lexikon des Kaiserthums Oesterreich*; and Bricka's *Dansk Biografisk Leksikon*. This too was the century of the "universal" biographical dictionary--the Michaud *Biographie Universelle*, with its many editions and imitations; Chalmer's *General Biographical Dictionary*; Vapereau's *Dictionnaire Universel des Contemporains*; Joseph Thomas's *Universal Pronouncing Dictionary of Biography and Mythology* and Oettinger's *Moniteur des Dates*.

The twentieth century intensified the output of national and other biographical dictionaries, but it also fathered the "Who's Who." The "Who's Who" gave brief pertinent facts about many persons (generally those living at the time of the compilation of the dictionary) in alphabetical arrangement. Not only did it cover nations or geographical areas--it also spilled over into every conceivable human activity, vocational and social. The "Who's Who" covered many of the gaps left by the national and universal biographies, especially in the field of contemporary biography.

Non-Western materials--In the medieval period (as conceived by Western historians) biographical compilations formed a large part of the flourishing Arabic and Persian literatures; Islamic civilization, much more than its Christian contemporary, evinced interest in the activities of its prominent figures, secular and religious, or so the volume of its biographical literature indicated. In fact, one of the few analo-

Historical Note

gies to these works in other literatures of this and
earlier periods are the biographical sections of the
Chinese dynastic histories. No attempt has been made
in this bibliography to enter either area in any great
depth. Nevertheless, a few of the major Arabic and
Persian writings of the genre have been cited. Those
omissions in a bibliography that had hoped to approach
"comprehensive world coverage" can be attributed solely
to the compiler's insufficient knowledge, linguistic
and subject, of the available materials. A number of
indexes to old Chinese biographical collections have
been included in the expectation that they might serve
as a back door for those who have minimal familiarity
with this literature. Coverage of Asia is at best
sketchy and scant. India and Southeastern Asia offer
native and Western biographical sources; Central Asia,
Afghanistan, Tibet, and the Himalayan principalities
yield virtually nothing, unless one is qualified to
mine the myriad dialects of those areas. Somewhat the
same statement must be made about portions of Africa,
large pockets of which are perhaps lacking in written
records dating back to the early modern period of history.

BIBLIOGRAPHICAL NOTE

Invaluable aids for checking out the various biographical dictionaries and related materials were the
Library of Congress Printed Catalog (now the *National
Union Catalog*), the *British Museum General Catalogue
of Printed Books* and the *Catalogue Général des Livres
Imprimés de la Bibliothèque Nationale*, as well as the
more specialized tools like Palau y Dulcet's *Manual
del Librero Hispanoamericana* and national bibliographies like Kayser's *Bücherlexikon*, the *English Catalogue of Books*, the *Bibliographie de la France*, etc.
In addition to the more specific bibliographies scattered through the main body of the work the following
books (or sections thereof) were helpful:

Arnold, Robert Franz. *Allgemeine Bücherkunde zer
Neueren Deutschen Literaturgeschichte*. 3., neu
bearb. und stark verm. Aufl. Berlin, W. de
Gruyter, 1931.

Balys, Jonas. *Lithuania and Lithuanians; a Selected Bibliography*. New York, Published for
the Lithuanian Research Institute by F. A.
Praeger, 1961.

Barth, Hans. *Bibliographie der Schweizer Geschichte
Enthaltend die Selbständig Erschienenen Druck-
werke zur Geschichte der Schweiz bis Ende 1912*.
Basel, Basler Buch- und Antiquariatshandlung,
1914-15 (3v.)

Bibliografia Historii Polski XIX Wieku. Wrocław,

Bibliographical Note

Zaklad Narodowy im. Ossoliñskich, 1958-

British Museum. Dept. of Printed Books. *Subject Index of Modern Books Acquired*. London, 1881-1900--

Chamberlin, Mary W. *Guide to Art Reference Books*. Chicago, American Library Association, 1959.

Duckles, Vincent Harris. *Music Reference and Research Materials; an Annotated Bibliography*. London, Free Press of Glencoe, 1964.

Elahi, Khwaja Nur. *A Guide to Works of Reference Published in Pakistan*. by Khwaja Nur Elahi, A. Moid and Akhtar H. Siddiqui. Karachi, Pakistan Bibliographical Working Group, 1953.

Fomin, Aleksandr Grigor'evich. *Putevoditel'Bibliografii, Biobibliografii, Istoriografii, Khronologii i Entsiklopedii Literatury* ... Leningrad, Gos. izd-vo khudozhestvennoi lit-ry, Leningradskoe otd-nie, 1934.

Garde, P. K. *Directory of Reference Works Published in Asia*. Paris, Unesco, 1956.

Greene, Katrine R. C. *Institutions and Individuals; an Annotated List of Directories Useful in International Administration*. Chicago, Public Administration Clearing House, 1953.

Guide to American Directories. 1954- New York, McGraw-Hill, etc.

Guide to American Educational Directories. 1st- ed.; 1963- New York, McGraw-Hill.

Hall, John Whitney. *Japanese History; a Guide to Japanese Reference and Research Materials*. Ann Arbor, University of Michigan Press, 1954.

Jones, Cecil Knight. *A Bibliography of Latin American Bibliographies*. 2d ed. Washington, U.S.

Govt. Print. Off., 1942.

London Library. *Subject-index of the London Library*. London, 1900-

Lewis, Bernard, ed. *Historians of the Middle East*. Edited by Bernard Lewis and P. M. Holt. London, New York, Oxford University Press, 1962--"Islamic biographical literature," by Sir Hamilton Gibb (p. 54-58); and "Persian biographical literature," by Ann K. S. Lambton (p. 141-151).

Maichel, Karol. *Guide to Russian Reference Books*. Stanford, Calif., Hoover Institution on War, Revolution, and Peace, Stanford University, 1962-

Malclès, Louis Noëlle. *Les Sources du Travail Bibliographique*. Genève, E. Droz, 1950-58 (3v.)

Minto, John. *Reference Books; a Classified and Annotated Guide* ... London, Library Association, 1929; and Supplement (1931).

Mitchell, Phillip Marshall. *A Bibliographical Guide to Danish Literature*. Copenhagen, Munksgaard, 1951.

Morley, Charles. *Guide to Research in Russian History*. Syracuse, N.Y., Syracuse University Press, 1951.

Mudge, Isadore Gilbert. *Guide to Reference Books*. 6th ed. Chicago, American Library Association; and Supplements, 1935/37-

Murphey, Robert W. *How and Where to Look It Up*. New York, McGraw-Hill, 1958.

Musiker, Reuben. *Guide to South African Reference Books*. 2d rev. ed. Rondebosch, Cape Town, University of Cape Town, School of Librarianship, 1958.

Bibliographical Note

Paris. Bibliothèque nationale. Département des Imprimés. *Catalogue de l'Histoire de France.* Tome 9 (1865) and Supplément (1884) Paris, Firmin Didot frères.

Peddie, Robert Alexander. *Subject Index of Books ...* London, Grafton, 1933-48 (4v.)

Petzholdt, Julius. *Bibliotheca Bibliographica.* Leipzig, W. Engelmann, 1866.

Sabor, Josefa Emilia. *Manuel de Fuentes de Información ...* Buenos Aires, Editorial Kapelusz, 1957.

Schneider, Georg. *Handbuch der Bibliographie.* 4., gänzlich veränderte und stark verm. Aufl. Leipzig, K. W. Hiersemann, 1930.

Seris, Homero. *Manual de Bibliografía de la Literatura Española.* 1. pt.: Obras generales. Syracuse, N.Y., Centro de Estudios Hispánicos, 1948.

Shunami, Shlomo. *Bibliography of Jewish Bibliographies.* 2d ed. enl. Jerusalem, Magnus Press, Hebrew University, 1965.

Sjögren, Paul. *Svensk Historisk Bibliografi.* Uppsala, Almqvist & Wiksell, 1956-

Têng, Ssŭ-yü. *An Annotated Bibliography of Selected Chinese Reference Works.* Rev. ed. Cambridge, Mass., Harvard University Press, 1950.

Tezla, Albert. *An Introductory Bibliography to the Study of Hungarian Literature.* Cambridge, Mass., Harvard University Press, 1964.

Totok, Wilhelm. *Handbuch der Bibliographischen Nachschlagewerke.* von Wilhelm Totok und Rolf Weitzel. Frankfurt a. M., V. Klostermann, 1954.

U.S. Library of Congress. Science and Technology Division. *Directories in Science and Technology; a Provisional Checklist.* Washington, 1963.

U.S. Library of Congress. *Library of Congress Catalog--Books: Subjects...* Jan./Mar. 1950- .
Washington.

Walter, Gérard. *Répertoire de l'Histoire de la Révolution Française...* Paris, Bibliothèque nationale, 1941- .

Winchell, Constance Mabel. *Guide to Reference Books.* 7th ed. Chicago, American Library Association, 1951; and Supplements (1950-52--)

Bibliographical note

UNIVERSAL BIOGRAPHY

BIBLIOGRAPHY, INDEXES, PORTRAIT CATALOGS

1   A. L. A. PORTRAIT INDEX;
Index to portraits contained in printed books and periodicals, compiled with the co-operation of many librarians and
others for the Publishing Board of the American Library
Association. Edited by William Coolidge Lane and Nina E.
Browne. Washington, Govt. Print. Off., 1906. lxxiv, 1600p.
25cm. At head of title: Library of Congress.

2   ANNUALS, DIRECTORIES, WHO'S WHO, PRESS GUIDES.
London. v. 22cm. Cover title: Directories, who's who,
press guides and year books. 12th issue, 1960, the latest?

3   ARNIM, MAX, 1889-
Internationale Personalbibliographie, 1800-1959. 2., verb.
und stark verm. Aufl. Leipzig, K. W. Hiersemann, 1944-63.
3 v. 29cm. A bibliography of bio-bibliographical literature.
Gives name, epithet (profession, etc.) and dates.

4   BELTRÁN Y DE TORRES, FRANCISCO
Biblioteca bio-bibliográfica. Catálogo de una importante
colección de libros y folletos españoles y extranjeros
referentes a bibliografía, biografía, bibliogía, bibliofilia,
la imprenta y sus auxiliares... Precedido de una introd. por
el marqués de Villa-Urrutia. Madrid, Librería Española y
Extranjera [1927] 498p. illus. 25cm. A bibliography of
bio-bibliography.

5   BIOGRAPHY INDEX;
A cumulative index to biographical material in books and
magazines. Jan. 1946/June 1947-   v. 1-   New York,
H. W. Wilson Co.   v. 27cm.

6   BROWN, STEPHEN JAMES MEREDIT H, 1881-
International index of Catholic biographies. 2d ed., rev.
and greatly enl. London, Burns, Oates and Washbourne,
1935. xix, 287 p. 22cm. (Catholic bibliographical series,
no. 3 (i. e. 2)) First ed. (1930) published under title: An
index of Catholic biographies.

7   DIEPENBROICK-GRÜTER, HANS DIETRICH VON, firm,
Hamburg.
Allgemeiner Porträt-Katalog; Verzeichnis einer Sammlung
von 3000 Porträts der sechzehnten bis neunzehnten Jahrhunderts in Holzschnitt, Kupferstich, Schabkunst und Lithographie,
mit biographischen Notizen. Hamburg, 1931. xxxiii, xxxii,
xxxiii, xxxii, xxviii, 902, xvii p. 23cm. Portrait catalog of
historical persons of the 16th to the 19th century.

8   DIMPFEL, RUDOLF A
        Biographische Nachschlagwerke, Adelslexika, Wappenbü-
        cher; systematische Zusammenstellung für Historiker und
        Genealogen. Leipzig, W. Heims, 1922. 128 p. 24cm.
        A bibliography of biographical reference works, dictionaries
        of noble families and books of heraldry, with some biobibli-
        ographical material for Germany.

9   DRUGULIN, WILHELM EDUARD, 1822-1879.
        Allgemeiner Portrait-Katalog... Verzeichniss einer ge-
        wählten Sammlung von 24,000 Portraits berühmter Personen
        aller Länder und Zeiten (mit biographischen und chalko -
        graphischen Notizen) welche zu den beigesetzten billigen
        Preisen von dem Leipziger Kunst-Comptoir zu beziehen sind.
        Leipzig, Kunst-Comptoir, 1859-60. 2v. in 1. 22cm.

10   --- ----Supplement... Juni 1881. Leipzig, 1861. 52 p. 22cm.

        A portrait catalog (24,000 in all) with biographical notes.

11   ERRERA, Mme. ISABELLE, d. 1929.
        Répertoire abrégé d'iconographie. Wetteren, Impr. J.
        de Meester, 1929-   v. 25cm. Abridged iconography list-
        ing. A catalog of portraits.

12   HAYDN, JOSEPH TIMOTHY, 1786 or 7-1856.
        Universal index of biography from the creation to the
        present time, for the use of the statesman, the historian,
        and the journalist. Edited by J. Bertrand Payne. London,
        E. Moxon, 1870. [76], 586p. geneal. tables. 22cm. A
        companion volume to the author's Dictionary of dates.

13   HEFLING, HELEN
        Hefling & Richards' Index to contemporary biography and
        criticism. A new ed. rev. and enl. by Helen Hefling and
        Jessie W. Dyde. With an introd. by Mary Emogene Hazel-
        tine. Boston, F. W. Faxon Co., 1934. 229p. 25cm.
        (Useful reference series, no. 50) First edition published
        in 1929.

14   ITALY. PARLAMENTO. CAMERA DEI DEPUTATI.
        BIBLIOTECA.
        Catalogo metodico degli scritti contenuti nelle pubblica-
        zioni periodiche italiane e straniere. Parte 1: Scritti bio-
        grafici e critici. Roma, Tip. della Camera dei deputati,
        1885. xvii, 517p. 28cm.

        Methodical catalogue of the writings contained in Italian &
        foreign periodical publications. Part 1: Biographical and
        critical writings.

15   -----1.-5. supplemento. Roma, Tip. della Camera dei
        deputati, 1889-1907. 5 v. 28cm.

2

16   -----Parte 1.: Scritti bibliografici [i. e. biografici] e critici.
Indice generale a tutto l'anno 1906. Roma, Tip. della Camera
dei deputati, 1909. 117p. 28cm.

17   -----Parte 1.: Scritti biografici e critici. Nuova serie.
v. 1-   Roma, Tip della Camera dei deputati, 1914-   v.
28cm.

18   LAWÄTZ, HEINRICH WILHELM, 1748-1825.
Verzeichnis einzelner Lebensbeschreibungen berühmter
Gelehrten und Schriftsteller älterer und neuerer Zeiten.
Halle, 1790. 2 v. (viii, 788, v, 606p.) Also forms the 4th
volume (in 2 parts) of the 1st section of Lawätz's Handbuch
für Bücherfreunde. A list of individual biographies of famous
scholars and authors of olden and modern times.

19   LOGASA, HANNAH, 1879-
Biography in collections, suitable for junior and senior high
schools. 3d ed., rev. and enl. New York, H. W. Wilson Co.,
1940. 152 p. 27cm.

20   OETTINGER, EDUARD MARIA, 1808-1872.
Bibliographie biographique universelle. Dictionnaire des
ouvrages relatifs à l'histoire de la vie publique et privée des
personnages célèbres de tous les temps et de toutes les nations, depuis le commencement du monde jusqu'à nos jours...
enrichi du répertoire des bio-bibliographies générales, nationales et spéciales. Bruxelles, J. J. Stienon, 1854. 2 v.
29cm. Includes bibliography of bio-bibliographical works.
Gives birth-death dates and professions of biographees.

21   O'NEILL, EDWARD HAYES
Biography by Americans, 1658-1936; a subject bibliography.
Philadelphia, University of Pennsylvania Press, 1939.
x, 465 p. 24cm.

22   RICHES, PHYLLIS M
Analytical bibliography of universal collected biography,
comprising books published in the English tongue in Great
Britain and Ireland, America and the British dominions.
With an introd. by Sir Frederick Kenyon. London, Library
Association, 1934. ix, 709p. 30cm. Gives dates and pro-
fession.

23   ROYAL COMMONWEALTH SOCIETY. LIBRARY.
Biography catalogue of the Library of the Royal Common-
wealth Society, by Donald H. Simpson, librarian. London,
Royal Commonwealth Society, 1961. xxiii, 511p. 30cm.

24   SHAW, THOMAS SHULER, 1906-
Index to profile sketches in New Yorker magazine. Boston,
F. W. Faxon, 1946. 100 p. 23cm. (Useful reference series,
no. 72) Covers sketches in vol. 1, no. 1, Feb. 21, 1925 to

vol. 16, no. 1, Feb. 17, 1940, when Reader's guide ... began indexing the periodical.

25   SINGER, HANS WOLFGANG, 1867-
Allgemeiner Bildniskatalog ... Leipzig, K. W. Hiersemann, 1930-36. 14 v. 28cm. A general catalog of portraits.

26   SINGER, HANS WOLFGANG, 1867-
Neuer Bildniskatalog ... Leipzig, Hiersemann, 1937-38.
5 v. 28cm. A newer catalog of portraits.

27   SONNENSCHEIN, WILLIAM SWAN, 1855-1931.
A bibliography of history and historical biography. (In
his The best books; a reader's guide ... London, 1923. 24cm.
pt. III [section] F)

28   U. S. LIBRARY OF CONGRESS. GENERAL REFERENCE
AND BIBLIOGRAPHY DIVISION.
Biographical sources for foreign countries. Compiled by
Helen Dudenbostel Jones. Washington, 1944-45. 4 v. 26cm.
No more published? Contents. -- 1. General. -- 2. Germany
and Austria, compiled by N. R. Burr. -- 3. The Philippines.
-- 4. The Japanese Empire, compiled by N. R. Burr.

29   YALE UNIVERSITY.
Yale University portrait index, 1701-1951. New Haven,
Yale University Press, 1951. vii, 185p. illus. 29cm.

ANONYMS AND PSEUDONYMS

30   [BAILLET, ADRIEN] 1649-1706.
Auteurs deguisez. Sous des noms etrangers; empruntez,
supposez, feints a plaisir, chiffrez, renversez, retournez,
ou changez d'une langue en une autre. Paris, A. Dezallier,
1690. xxvi, 615p. 17cm. Disguised authors; anonyms &
pseudonyms.

31   BERLIN. DEUTSCHE STAATSBIBLIOTHEK.
Namenschlüssel, die Verweisungen der Berliner
Titeldrucke zu Pseudonymen, Doppelnamen und Namensab-
wandlungen, 1892-1935. [2. Aufl.] Berlin, Staatsbibliothek,
1936. 780p. 1st ed. published in 1932. A key to pseudonyms,
double names and changes of name for the period 1892-1935.

32   DAHLMANN, PETER
Schauplatz der masquirten und demasquirten Gelehrten
bey ihren verdeckten und nunmehro entdeckten Schrifften
aus gewissen Anzeigungen/glaubwürdigen Nachrichten/und
wahrscheinlichen Conjecturen bewährter Männer/nach ihren
vornehmsten Denckwürdigkeiten/samt Beyfügung neuer Raison-
nements und Autoritäten kürtzlich dargestellet. Leipzig, J.
L. Gleiditsch, 1710. 16, 923, [84] p. 17cm. An early dictionary of anonyms and pseudonyms.

33   DECKHERR, JOHANN

De scriptis adespotis, pseudoepigraphis et supposititiis conjecturae, cum additionibus variorum. Ed. 3. altera parte auctior. Amstelaedami, 1686. 41lp. 12.º A treatise on pseudonymous writers and writing.

34   GEISSLER, FRIEDRICH, 1636-1679.

De nominum mutatione et anonymis scriptoribus... dispp. F. Geislerus... et D. Schröck. Lipsiae [1669] 1 v. 4.º About change of names and anonymous writers.

35   HEUMANN, CHRISTOPH AUGUST, 1681-1764.

De libris anonymis ac pseudonymis schediasma, complectens observationes generales et spicilegium ad V. Placcii Theatrum anonymorum et pseudonymorum. Jenae, Apud J. F. Bielckium, 1711. xvi, 206p. 8.º Anonymous and pseudonymous works, remarks concerning their probable authors; supplementary to Placcius' Theatrum anonymorum et pseudonymorum.

36   MYLIUS, JOHANN CHRISTOPH, 1710-1757.

Bibliotheca anonymorum et pseudonymorum ad supplendum et continuandum Vincentii Placii Theatrum et Christoph. Aug. Heumanni Schediasma de anonymis et pseudonymis, collecta et adornata à M. Joh. Christoph. Mylio. Cum prefatione M. Gottlieb Stollii. Hamburgi, C. W. Brandt, 1740. 2 pts. in 1 v. 18cm. Library of anonyms and pseudonyms to supplement and continue Placcius's Theatrum & Heumann's Schediasma...

37   PLACCIUS, VINCENT, 1642-1699.

Theatrum anonymorum et pseudonymorum ex symbolis & collatione virorum per Europam doctissimorum ac celeberrimorum, post syntagma dudum editum, summa beati auctoris cura reclusum, & benignis auspiciis summe reverendi ac consultissimi viri, dn. Matthiae Dreyeri... cujus & commentatio, de summa & scopo hujus operis accedit, luci publicae redditum. Praemissa est praefatio & vita auctoris, scriptore Jo. Alberto Fabricio... cum indicibus necessariis. Hamburgi, Sumptibus Viduae G. Liebernickelii, 1708. 722, [4], 623, 195p. front. 34cm. A famous early dictionary of anonyms & pseudonyms.

38   [THOMAS, RALPH] 1840-

Handbook of fictitious names: being a guide to authors, chiefly in the lighter literature of the XIXth century, who have written under assumed names; and to literary forgers, impostors, plagiarists, and imitators, by Olphar Hamst, Esq. [pseud.] London, J. R. Smith, 1868. xiv, 235p. 22cm.

39   VIRORUM ERUDITORUM ONOMATOMORPHOSIS;

Dass ist, Etlicher gelehrter Männer gebrauchte Nahmens-

Veränderung, insonderheit aber derjenigen, welche ihre
Namen mit griechischen und lateinischen Wörtern ver-
wechselt haben. Welche aus Curiosität zusam̃en tragen, und
guten Freunden zu Gefallen in den Druck geben wollen C. W.
P. G. [Zürich, 1720] 1 v. 8.º Learned men who changed
their names, especially those who exchanged their names
for Greek & Latin terms—anonyms and pseudonyms.

DICTIONARIES, BIO-BIBLIOGRAPHIES, ETC.

40 A'BECKETT, Sir WILLIAM, 1806-1869.
A universal biography; including Scriptural, classical
and mythological memoirs, together with accounts of many
eminent living characters. The whole newly compiled and
composed from the most recent and authentic sources.
London, Isaac, Tuckey, 1836. 4v. 25cm.

41 ABERCONWAY, CHRISTABEL MARY MELVILLE
(MACNAGHTEN) MCLAREN, baroness, 1890-
A dictionary of cat lovers, XV century B. C.-XX century
A. D.; with five legends concerning cats and with notes on the
cat in ancient Egypt, etc. London, M. Joseph [1949] 446p.
illus., ports. 26cm.

42 ACADÉMIE DIPLOMATIQUE INTERNATIONALE.
Dictionnaire diplomatique, comprenant les biographies des
diplomates, du Moyen Age à nos jours, constituant un traité
d'histoire diplomatique sur six siècles. Publié sous la direction de A.-F. Frangulis. Genève [etc., 1954?] 1261p.
Comprises vol. 5 of the Dictionnaire diplomatique; biographies of diplomats of all nations from the Middle Ages to the
present era.

43 ADAMS, HENRY GARDINER, 1811 or 12-1881.
Cyclopaedia of female biography; consisting of sketches of
all women who have been distinguished by great talents,
strength of character, piety, benovolence, or moral virtue of
any kind. London, G. Routledge, 1869. iv,788p. 17cm.

44 ADELMAN, JOSEPH FERDINAND GOTTLIEB, 1862-
Famous women; an outline of feminine achievement
through the ages with life stories of five hundred noted women.
New York, E. M. Lonow [c1926] 328p. plates, ports. 20cm.

45 AGRAMONTE Y CORTIJO, FRANCISCO, 1880-
Diccionario cronológico biográfico universal; con 4,400
biografiás, cronológicas y esquemáticas, de las mas notables
personalidades de la historia. [2. ed. corr. y muy aumentada]
Madrid, Aguilar [1952] 1226p. 25cm. First published 1942
under title: Ensayo de un diccionario biográfico-cronológico
de los siglos XV al XX. A universal biographical dictionary
in chronological arrangement; 4,400 biographies.

46 AGRICOLA, PETER FRANZ
Saeculi XVIII. bibliotheca ecclesiastica authorumque
notitiae biographicae. Hannoverae, Typ. H. M. Pockwitzii,
1781-82. 4 v. 8.º Ecclesiastical library of the 18th century
and biographical notices of authors.

47 AIKIN, JOHN, 1747-1822.
General biography; or, Lives critical and historical, of
the most eminent persons of all ages, countries, conditions,
and professions, arranged according to the alphabetical order.
Chiefly composed by John Aikin and William Enfield. London,
Printed for G. G. and J. Robinson [etc.] 1799-1815. 10v. 27cm.
Vols. 2-10 by Aikin, "Mr." Nicholson, Thomas Morgan,
William Johnston, and others.

48 AN ALMANAC OF CURRENT WORLD LEADERS.
v.1-   ; Sept. 1957-   Palo Alto, Calif., Los Angeles
[etc.]   v. Issued Sept. 1957-   by Stanford Scholastic
Associates.

49 ALTEN, GEORG KARL FRIEDRICH VIKTOR VON, 1846-1912.
Handbuch für Heer und Flotte; Enzyklopädie der Kriegs-
wissenschaften und verwandten Gebiete, unter Mitwirkung von
zahlreichen Offizieren, Sanitätsoffizieren, Beamten, Ge-
lehrten, Technikern, Künstlern, usw. Hrsg. von Georg von
Alten. Berlin, Bong, 1909-14.   v. illus., maps. 26cm.
Handbook for army and navy; encyclopedia of military sciences.
Includes many biographical articles.

50 THE AMERICANA;
A universal reference library comprising the arts and
sciences, literature, history, biography, geography, commerce, etc., of the world. Biographies.   New York, Americana Corp. [1929]   202 p. ports. 26cm.

51 ANNALES BIOGRAPHIQUES;
Ou, Complément annuel et Continuation de toutes les biographies et dictionnaires historiques...1820-1828.   Paris,
Baudouin [etc.] 9 v.   Title varies: 1821-1826, Annuaire
nécrologique. Edited by A. J. Mahul, and others. Universal
biographical annals.

52 ANTOINE, A   , de Saint-Gervais, 1776-1836.
Les jeunes personnes devenues célèbres par leur piété
filiale, leur courage, leurs talents. Rouen, Mégard, 1860.
215p. 12.º Rev. ed. (1st published 1852) of his earlier work:
Dictionnaire historique de la jeunesse (1822) Young people who
became famous for their filial piety, their courage, their
talents (chiefly Frenchmen)

53 ARA, MASATO
Sekai jimmei hyakka jiten. Tokyo, Seikei Shōin, 1951.
918 p. World biographical encyclopedia, by Masato Ara and
Masayuki Murakami.

54   LES ARCHIVES INTERNATIONALES CONTEMPORAINES.
1944-   Paris, Agence internationale de documenta-
tion "Pharos."   v. in   28cm. No. in 3 parts: pt. [A]
Archives biographiques contemporaines. Contemporary universal biography.

55   -----Index général analytique et systématique, Oct. 1944-
mars 1950. Paris. 64 p.

56   AYGUALS DE IZCO, WENCESLAO, 1801-1873.
El panteón universal; diccionario histórico de vidas
interesantes... Con la colaboración de B. S. Castellanos
[et al.] Madrid, 1853-54. 4v. A universal biographical
dictionary. In Spanish.

57   [BALDWIN, CHARLES N   ]
A universal biographical dictionary containing the lives of
the most celebrated characters of every age and nation...
To which is added, a dictionary of the principal divinities and
heroes of Grecian and Roman mythology, and a biographical
dictionary of eminent living characters. New ed. Hartford,
S. Andrus, 1852. 444p. 20cm.

58   [BARRAL, PIERRE] abbé, d. 1772.
Dictionnaire historique, littéraire et critique, contenant
une idée abrégée de la vie et des ouvrages des hommes illustres en tout genre. [Avignon, 1758- 59] 6 v. 8.º By
Barral, E. Guibaud and J. Valla. An historical, literary &
critical dictionary that contains biographical sketches of famous men of all times and vocations.

59   [BATES, WILLIAM] 1625-1699, ed.
Vitae selectorum aliquot virorum, qui doctrina, dignitate
aut pietate inclaruere. Londini, Typis A. G. & J. P. &
prostant venales apud G. Wells, 1681. 749p. 4.º Lives of
men famed for their piety, dignity or doctrinal purity.

60   BAUR, SAMUEL, 1768-1832.
Neues historisch-biographisch-literarisches Handwörterbuch, von der Schöpfung der Welt bis zum Schlusse des
achtzehnten Jahrhunderts. Enthaltend das Leben, den
Charakter und die Verdienste der grossten und denkwürdigsten Personen aller Zeiten, Länder und Stände. Nach den
zuverlässigsten Quellen bearb. Ein Handbuch für Kenner
und Liebhaber der Geschichte, besonders für studierende
Junglinge. Ulm, Stettinische Buchhandlung, 1807-16. 7 v.
port. 21cm. Vols. 6 and 7 have titles respectively: Neues
historisches Handlexikon... bis zu Ende des Jahrs 1810
fortgesetzt [and] Neues historisch-biographisch-literarisches
Handwörterbuch, von der Schöpfung der Welt bis zum Schlusse
des Jahres 1810. Vols. 6-7 also issued separately under title:
Allgemeines historisch-biographisches Handwörterbuch merkwürdigen Personen die in dem ersten Jahrzehend des neunzehnten Jahrhunderts gestorben sind (Ulm, 1816. 2 v.) and as

v. 3-4 of His Kleines historisch-literarisches Handwörterbuch (Ulm, 1813-16)   A universal biographical dictionary to
the end of the 18th century.

61   BAYLE, PIERRE, 1647-1706.
Dictionnaire historique et critique. Nouv. éd. augm. de
notes extraites de Chaufepié [et al.] Paris, Desoer, 1820-
[24] 16v. 21cm. Many French and English editions have been
published, beginning with the 1st French ed. of 1697.

62   BAYLE, PIERRE, 1647-1706.
A general dictionary, historical and critical: in which a
new and accurate translation of that of the celebrated Mr.
Bayle, with the corrections and observations printed in the
late edition at Paris is included; and interspersed with several
thousand lives never before published. The whole containing
the history of the most illustrious persons of all ages and
nations particularly those of Great Britain and Ireland, distinguished by their rank, actions, learning and other accom-
plishments. With reflections on such passages of Bayle, as
seem to favor scepticism and the Manichee system. By John
Peter Bernard, Mr. Thomas Birch...and other hands.   London, Printed by J. Bettenham [etc.] 1734-41. 10 v. 39cm.
A different translation from that published in 1710 (4 v.) and,
second edition, 1734-38 (5 v.)

63   BEARD, JOHN RELLY, 1800-1876.
The people's biographical dictionary; a picture gallery of
great men of all ages and countries. London, J. Cassell,
1851. 4v. in 1. 17cm.

64   BEETON, SAMUEL ORCHART, 1831-1877.
Beeton's dictionary of universal biography; being the lives
of eminent persons of all times. With the pronunciation of
every name. 2d ed., rev. and corr. Brought down to the
present period, 1870; and containing an additional number of
modern biographies. London, Ward, Lock, and Tyler [1870]
iv, 1116p. ports. 20cm.

65   BELLCHAMBERS, EDMUND.
A general biographical dictionary, containing lives of the
most eminent persons of all ages and nations. London, A.
Bell, 1835. 4v. ports. 11cm.

66   BIOGRAFIA UNIVERSALE ANTICA E MODERNA;
ossia, Storia per alfabeto della vita pubblica e privata di
tutte le persone che si distinsero per opere, azioni, talenti,
virtù e delitti. Opera affatto nuova, compilata in Francia da
una società di dotti ed ora per la prima volta recata in italiano con aggiunte e correzioni. Venezia, presso G. B.
Missiaglia, 1822-41. 77 v. 25cm. An Italian translation of
the famous Universal biography (Michaud)

67   BIOGRAFIJE.
        [Beograd] Sedma sila.   v.   24-27cm.   monthly.   Vols. –
        also called no.– A periodical devoted to biography.

68   THE BIOGRAPHER.
        Illustrated.   v. 1, no. 1; May 1883.   New York [1883]
        64p.   illus. (ports.)   24cm.   Cover title.   No more published.
        "Short sketches of eminent persons, selected... because of
        a present public interest felt in them. " Universal in cover-
        age.

69   THE BIOGRAPHER AND REVIEW.
        [A monthly (fortnightly) journal] v. 1-4; 1894-1901.
        London.   4 v.   4.º   Title varies; v. 1-2, The Biographer.
        Universal in coverage.

70   THE BIOGRAPHICAL AND IMPERIAL MAGAZINE .
        Containing history, philosophy, etc.   1789-1792.   London.
        5v.   8°.   Edited by John Thelwall.

71   LE BIOGRAPHE UNIVERSELLE.
        Revue générale biographique et littéraire, par une société
        des hommes de lettres francais et étrangers sous la direction
        de M. E. Pascallet.   année 1-6; 1841-46.   Paris.   6 v.   8.º
        Universal biography; a general biographical and literary re-
        view.   Title varies.

72   THE BIOGRAPHICAL MAGAZINE.
        Containing portraits & characters of eminent and ingenious
        persons, of every age & nation.   [v. 1]   London, Harrison,
        1794.   138 1.   ports.   23cm.   No more published.

73   THE BIOGRAPHICAL QUARTERLY...
        Recording biographical data of noteworthy citizens of the
        English-speaking countries.   v. 1-2, no. 2; 1935-1936.   Lon-
        don.   v. 8.º

74   BIOGRAPHIE DES HOMMES VIVANTS;
        Ou, Histoire par ordre alphabétique de la vie publique de
        tous les hommes qui se sont fait remarquer par leurs actions
        ou leurs écrits.   Ouvrage entièrement neuf, rédigé par un
        société de gens de lettres et savants.   Paris, Michaud, 1816-
        19.   5 v.   21cm.   Sequel and complement to the Biographie
        universelle of Michaud.   Edited by L. G. Michaud and others.
        An alphabetical biographical dictionary of famous men living
        in the early years of the 19th century.

75   LE BIOGRAPHE ET L'HISTORIEN;
        Revue générale historique, biographique, nécrologique.
        1. -4. vol. ; 1854-55.   Paris.   4 v. in 2.   8.º   Edited by E.
        Pascallet.   A periodical for general history, biography and
        necrology.

76   BIOGRAPHIE ÉTRANGERE;
        Ou, Galerie universelle, historique, civile, militaire, poli-
        tique et littéraire contenant les portraits politiques de plus de
        trois mille personnages célèbres, étrangers à la France.   Par

une société des gens de lettres.   Paris, 1819. 2 v. 8.°   Universal biography, excluding France.

77   BIOGRAPHIE POLITIQUE DU DIX-NEUVIÈME SIÈCLE.
Paris, Société française d'Éditions d'art, L. -H. May, 1899.
2 v. in 1. illus. 20cm. (Encyclopédie populaire illustrée du vingtième siècle) Universal biography of the 19th century, chiefly statesmen.

78   BIOGRAPHIE UNIVERSELLE, ANCIENNE ET MODERNE; ou,
Histoire, par ordre alphabétique, de la vie publique et privée de tous les hommes qui se sont fait remarquer par leurs écrits, leurs actions, leurs talents, leurs vertus ou leurs crimes. Ouvrage entièrement neuf, rédigé par une société de gens de lettres et des savants. Tome 1-   [52 et Supplément] Paris, Michaud frères [etc.] 1811-62. 85 v. 21cm. Founded by J. F. Michaud and his brother L. G. Michaud; chiefly the work of the latter. Vols. 54-85, Supplément [A-Vil]

79   BIOGRAPHIE UNIVERSELLE CLASSIQUE;
Ou, Dictionnaire historique portatif. Par une société de gens de lettres... Ouvrage entièrement neuf, contenant...des articles sur l'histoire générale des peuples...et particulière-ment la nécrologie des personnages célèbres de tous les pays et de tous les temps...Paris, 1829. 3 pts. Another edition (?) published in 1833 (6 vols.) By Jean Augustin Amar du Rivier, Charles Theodore Beauvais, and others. British Museum enters the work under the first named. A universal biographical dictionary.

80   BIOGRAPHIE UNIVERSELLE (MICHAUD) ANCIENNE ET
MODERNE...Nouv. éd., publiée sous la direction de M. Michaud, rev., corr. et considérablement augm. d'articles omis ou nouveaux. Ouvrage rédigé par une société de gens de lettres et de savants. Paris, Madame C. Desplaces [etc.] 1854-[65] 45 v. 28cm. 2d ed. of the work founded by J. F. Michaud and his brother L. G. Michaud; v. 13-45 edited by E. E. Desplaces.

81   BIOGRAPHIUM FAEMINUM.
The female worthies; or, Memoirs of the most illustrious ladies of all ages and nations... London, S. Crowder, 1766. 2 v. 8.°

82   BITARD, ADOLPHE LOUIS ÉMILE
Dictionnaire de biographie contemporaine francaise et étrangère, contenant les noms, prénoms, pseudonymes de tous les personnages célèbres du temps présent, l'histoire de leur vie, de leurs actes et de leurs oeuvres, la date de leur naissance et des principaux évènements de leur carrière. Augmenté d'un supplément. Paris, L. Vanier, 1880. 1198 p. 25cm. First published 1878. General bio-bibliographical dictionary of the 19th century.

83 BLAKE, JOHN LAURIS, 1788-1857.
A biographical dictionary: comprising a summary account
of the lives of the most distinguished persons of all ages,
nations, and professions; including more than two thousand
articles of American biography. 13th ed. Philadelphia,
H. Cowperthwait, 1856. 1366 p. 28cm.

84 BOLM, AUGUST, ed.
Tagebuch der Geschichte und Biographie über alle wichtigen
Ereignisse und Persönlichkeiten für alle Tage des Jahres.
Bearb. unter Mitwirkung anderer von H. Preiss und H. Tod.
Berlin, Bolm, 1881. 2 v. 8.° (Handlexikon der Geschichte
und Biographie) Journal of the history and biography of all
important events and personalities for every day of the year.

85 BONNEGARDE,   abbé de
Dictionnaire historique et critique; ou, Recherches sur la
vie, le caractère, les moeurs et les opinions de plusieurs
hommes célèbres, tirés des dictionnaires de MM.Bayle et
Chauffepié. Lyon, Barret; Paris, Delalain, 1771. 4 v. 8.°
Historical and critical dictionary; or, Inquiries into the life...
of several famous men, drawn from the dictionaries of
Bayle & Chauffepie.

86 BORNEMANN, JOHANN GOTTFRIED, d. 1825.
Gelehrten-Almanach; oder, Verzeichniss der vorzüglichsten
Gelehrten alter und neuer Zeit. Leipzig, Glück, 1825. lv. (?)
Almanach of scholars; or, List of the foremost scholars of
ancient and modern times.

87 BRUCE, JOHN EDWARD, comp.
Short biographical sketches of eminent Negro men and
women in Europe and the United States, with brief extracts
from their writings and public utterances. Yonkers, N. Y.
[Gazette Press] 1940-   v. 24 cm.

88 BULLART, ISAAC, 1599-1672.
Académie des sciences et des arts, contenant les vies, &
les eloges historiques des hommes illustres... A Brusselle,
Chez F. Foppens, 1695. 2 v. illus., ports. 35cm. First
published at Amsterdam, 1642. Academy of the sciences &
the arts, containing the lives & praises of famous men.

89 BÜSCHING, ANTON FRIEDRICH, 1724-1793.
Beyträge zu der Lebensgeschichte denkwürdiger Personen,
insonderheit gelehrter Männer. Halle, Verlegt von J. J.
Curts Witwe, 1783-86. 6 v. 8.° Contributions to the lives
of memorable persons, particularly of learned men.

90 CARNOY, HENRY, 1861-   ed.
Dictionnaire biographique international des écrivains, des
artistes, des membres des sociétés savantes, du clergé, du
monde diplomatique, politique et administratif, du barreau
de la magistrature, de la haute société, des folkloristes,

voyageurs et géographes, des médecins, chirurgiens chimistes et naturalistes, etc. Paris, Chez l'auteur [1902]- 09. 4 v. illus. 28 cm. (Collection des grands dictionnaires biographiques internationaux, t. 5-6, 14, 16) A collected edition of Carnoy's individual volumes, q. v. International biographical dictionary; contemporary.

91 CASSELL'S BIOGRAPHICAL DICTIONARY.
Containing original memoirs of the most eminent men and women of all ages and countries. London, New York, Cassell, Petter and Galpin [1867-69] viii, 1160 p. 28cm. Edited by T. T. Shore.

92 CATES, WILLIAM LEIST READWIN, 1821-1895.
A dictionary of general biography. 4th ed., with supplement brought down to the end of 1884. London, Longmans, Green, 1885. viii, 1551 p. 24 cm.

93 CÉLÉBRITÉS D'AUJOURD'HUI.
Revue mensuelle et internationale de biographie. 1-   ; 1954-   Bruxelles.   v.   Celebrities of the day; a monthly & international review of biography.

94 CELEBRITIES MONTHLY.
Actual photographs with biographical sketches. v. 1-   ; Apr. 1895-   New York, Automatic Photograph Co.   v. ports. 19 x 30cm.

95 CELEBRITIES OF THE DAY: BRITISH AND FOREIGN.
A monthly repertoire of contemporary biography. Edited by S. E. Thomas. Vol. 1-3; 1881-1882. London. 3 v. 8.º

96 THE CENTURY CYCLOPEDIA OF NAMES;
A pronouncing and etymological dictionary of names in geography, biography, mythology, history, art, archaeology, fiction, etc. Edited by Benjamin E. Smith, assisted by a number of specialists. Rev. and enl. New York, Century Co. [c1911] 1085, [158] p. 31cm.

97 CHALMERS, ALEXANDER, 1759-1834.
The general biographical dictionary; containing an historical and critical account of the lives and writings of the most eminent persons in every nation, particularly the British and Irish; from the earliest accounts to the present time. New ed., rev. and enl. London, Nichols, 1812-17. 32 v.

98 CHAMBER'S BIOGRAPHICAL DICTIONARY.
Edited by J. O. Thorne. New ed. New York, St. Martin's Press [1962] v. 1432p. 22cm. English ed. published in 1961 (Edinburgh, W. & R. Chambers)

99 CHAUDON, LOUIS MAYEUL, 1737-1817, ed.
Dictionnaire universel, historique, critique, et bibliographique; ou, Histoire abrégée et impartiale des hommes de toutes les nations qui se sont rendus célèbres, illustres ou fameux depuis la plus haute antiquité jusqu'a nos

jours; avec les dieux et les héros de toutes les mythologies;
enrichie des notes et additions des abbés Brotier et Mercier
de Saint-Leger, etc., etc. D'après la 8. éd. publié par MM.
Chaudon et Delandine. 9. éd., rev., corr. et augm. de
16,000 articles environ, par une société de savons francais
étrangers. Suivie de tables chronologiques, pour réduire en
corps d'histoire les articles répandus dans ce dictionnaire...
Paris, Impr. de Mame frères, 1810-12. 20 v. port. Title
varies slightly. 1st published ca. 1769 under title: Nouveau
dictionnaire historique-portatif, or Nouveau dictionnaire
historique? A general biographical compilation.

100   CHAUFFEPIÉ, JACQUES GEORGES DE, 1702-1786.
Nouveau dictionnaire historique et critique pour servir de
supplement ou de continuation au Dictionnaire historique et
critique de Mr. Pierre Bayle. Par Jacques George de
Chaufepié. Amsterdam, Z. Chatelain [etc.] 1750-56. 4 v.
40 cm. An historical dictionary with emphasis on biography.

101   CHESUROLLES, DÉSIRÉ
Petit dictionnaire biographique, contenant les noms des
personnages célèbres de tous les temps et de tous les pays,
extrait du Complément du grand dictionnaire de Napoléon
Landais. Paris, Didier, 1853. 603p. 32.° A universal
biographical dictionary.

102   CHEVALIER, CYR ULYSSE JOSEPH, 1841-1923.
Répertoire des sources historiques du moyen age. Bio-
bibliographie. Nouv. éd. refondue, corr. et considérablement
augm. Paris, A. Picard, 1905-07. 2 v. 28 cm. Issued in
9 parts, 1903-07. Gives dates when possible, occupation, etc.
of medieval historical figures.

103   THE COMPREHENSIVE DICTIONARY OF BIOGRAPHY;
Embracing a series of original memoirs of the most distinguished persons of all countries, living and dead. To which
is added, a classified list of the most distinguished persons
of all times, arranged chronologically... London, R. Griffin,
1860. 911, 70, 63 p. illus., ports. 8.° Issued in parts.

104   COOPER, THOMPSON, 1837-1904.
A New biographical dictionary: containing concise notices
of eminent persons of all ages and countries: and more particularly of all distinguished natives of Great Britain and
Ireland. New York, Macmillan, 1874. 1211p. 20cm.

105   CURRENT BIOGRAPHY YEARBOOK.
1940-   New York, H. W. Wilson Co.   v. illus.
26cm. Cumulated from monthly issues. Title varies: 1940-
54, Current biography; who's news and why.

106   DAIJIMMEI JITEN.
[Tokyo] Heibon Sha [1953-56] 10 v. ports. 26cm. Biographical dictionary of famous men; universal. First ed.
published 1937-1941 under title: Shinsen daijimmei jiten.

107   DANTÈS, ALFRED LANGUE, 1830-1891.
      Dictionnaire biographique et bibliographique, alphabétique
et méthodique des hommes les plus remarquables dans les
lettres, les sciences et les artes, chez tous les peuples, à
toutes les époques. Paris, A. Boyer, 1875. 1423,154 p.
24cm. A general bio-bibliographical dictionary.

108   DAVENPORT, RICHARD ALFRED, 1777?-1852.
      A dictionary of biography; comprising the most eminent
characters of all ages, nations, and professions. 1st American ed., with numerous additions, corrections and improvements. And illustrated by two hundred fine portraits, on wood.
Boston, Otis, Broaders, 1846. 527 p. ports. 26cm. First
published in Great Britain in 1831.

109   DEWAMIN, ÉMILE, ed.
      Collection encyclopédique des notabilités du XIXe siècle;
ou, Nouveau dictionnaire des contemporains...tom 1. Paris,
1901. viii,335 p. 8.$^{\circ}$ Biographical dictionary of prominent
people of the 19th century.

110   DEZOBRY, LOUIS CHARLES, 1798-1871.
      Dictionnaire général de biographie et d'histoire, de mythol-
ogie, de géographie ancienne et moderne comparée, des an-
tiquités et des institutions grecques, romaines, françaises et
étrangères, par Ch. Dezobry [et] Th. Bachelet. Éd. rev.
par E. Darsy avec le concours d'une société de littérateurs, de
professeurs et de savants. Paris, Delagrave [1922] 3v.
28cm. On t.p. of v. 3 (Supplément): 14. éd. refondue et
augm.... A general dictionary of biography & history [etc.]

111   DÍAZ DOIN, GUILLERMO
      236 [i. e. Doscientos treintiseis] biografías sintéticas, po-
líticos y militares. Buenos Aires, Editorial Mundo Atlántico
[1943] 235 p. 21cm. Biographical sketches of men prominent in the years 1910-1943.

112   DICCIONARIO BIOGRÁFICO UNIVERSAL,
      Que contiene la vida de los personajes históricos de todos
los países y de todos los tiempos; santos o mártires, sabios,
artistas, escritores, héroes o personajes fabulosos de todos
los pueblos, por D. J. R. Gerona, Grases, 1855. 15 pts. A
Spanish universal biographical dictionary.

113   DICCIONARIO HISTÓRICO;
      O, Biografía universal compendiada, por G. Mh. L. y S.
Barcelona, Impr. de J. Verdaguer, 1830-36. 13 v. 160 ports.
4.$^{\circ}$ Historical dictionary; or, Abridged universal biography.

114   A DICTIONARY OF CONTEMPORARY BIOGRAPHY.
      A handbook of the peerage of rank, worth and intellect.
Containing memoirs of nearly one thousand eminent living
individuals. London, R. Griffin, 1861. xvi, 416 p. 20cm.
Issued also under title: The rank and talent of our time.

115 DÍEZ CANSECO, VICENTE
Diccionario biográfico universal de mujeres célebres;
6, Compendio de la vida de todas las mujeres que han adquiri-
do celebridad en las naciones antiguas y modernas, desde los
tiempos remotos hasta nuestros dias. Madrid, Impr. de J.
F. Palacios, 1844-46. 3v. 4.° Universal biographical
dictionary of celebrated women, ancient & modern.

116 DIPLOMATISCHESKII SLOVAR'.
[Glav. red. A. A. Gromyko, S. A. Golunskii, V. M.
Khvostov] Moskva, Gos izd-vo polit. lit-ry, 1960-64. 3 v.
23cm. A generous amount of biography is included in this
dictionary of diplomacy.

117 DUNKEL, JOHANN GOTTLOB WILHELM, 1720-1759.
Historisch-critische Nachrichten von verstorbenen Gelehrten und deren Schriften, insonderheit aber denenjenigen,
welche in der allerneusten Ausgabe des Jocherischen Allgemeinen Gelehrten-Lexicons entweder gänzlich mit Stillschweig-
en übergangen oder doch mangellhaft und unrichtig angefuhret
werden. Cöthen, Cörner, 1753-60. 3v. 18cm. Bio-bibliographical notices of deceased scholars, especially those not
mentioned or mentioned only briefly or incorrectly in Jöcher's
Allgemeines Gelehrten-Lexicon.

118 DU VERDIER, ANTOINE, 1544-1600.
Prosopographia; ou, Description des hommes illustres,
et autres renommez, divisee en trois tomes... Avec un
ample indice à la fin de chaque volume. À Lyon, Par Paul
Frelon, 1603. 3 v. illus., ports. 34cm. Title pages vary
slightly. Universal biography.

119 ELLIOTT, FLORENCE.
A dictionary of politics, by Florence Elliott and Michael
Summerskill. [3d ed.] Baltimore, Penguin Books [1961]
372 p. 18 cm. (Penguin reference books, R 10) With
biographies of living statesmen.

120 THE ENGLISH CYCLOPAEDIA.
A new dictionary of universal knowledge. Conducted by
Charles Knight. [Division III] Biography. London, Bradbury
and Evans, 1856-72. 7 v. illus. 29cm. Vol. 7: Supplement.

121 FELLER, FRANCOIS XAVIER DE, 1753-1802.
Biographie universelle; ou, Dictionnaire historique des
hommes qui se sont fait un nom par leur génie, leurs talents,
leurs vertus... Revue et continuée par l'abbé Simonin [avec le
concours de Collombet et Delgamier] Lyon, J.-B. Pélagaud,
1867. 8 v. Many editions were published, beginning with the
1st ed. of 1781-1794 (?) A universal biographical dictionary.

122 FITZHUGH, HARRIET LLOYD LEPORTE
The concise biographical dictionary of famous men and
women, by Harriet Lloyd Fitzhugh and Percy K. Fitzhugh.

Rev. and enl. New York, Grosset & Dunlap [c1949] xiii,
830 p. 22 cm. First ed. published in 1935.

123 FLLOYD, THOMAS.
Bibliotheca biographica; a synopsis of universal biography,
ancient and modern, the whole affording a comprehensive
abstract of universal history. London, Printed for J. Hinton
[etc.] 1760. 3 v. 21 cm.

124 FULLER, MURIEL, 1901-   ed.
More junior authors. New York, H. W. Wilson Co. , 1963.
vi, 235 p. ports. 27 cm. (The Authors series) 268 authors
and illustrators of books for children and young people.
Companion volume to Junior book of authors, 2d ed. , 1951,
edited by Stanley J. Kunitz and Howard Haycraft.

125 GALERÍA UNIVERSAL DE BIOGRAFÍAS
y retratos de los personas mas distinguidos en política,
armas, religion, letras, ciencias y artes, y de las familias
reinantes en las cinco partes del globo desde 1848 hasta nuestros días, redactada por conocidos autores nacionales y extranjeros. Madrid, Elizalde [1867-70] 2 v. 200 ports. A universal biography for the 19th century, but with special emphasis on Spain.

126 GALERIE CHOISIE D'HOMMES ET DE FEMMES CÉLÈBRES
DE TOUS LES TEMPS ET DE TOUTES LES NATIONS...
Amsterdam, 1822-23. 5 v. 12.° Famous people, universal.

127 GALERIE HISTORIQUE DES CONTEMPORAINS;
Ou, Nouvelle biographie dans laquelle se trouvent réunis
les hommes morts ou vivans, de toutes les nations, qui ont
acquis de la célébrité à la fin du XVIIIᵉ siècle et au commencement de celui-ci... Bruxelles, A. Wahlen, 1817-20. 8 v.
Edited by P. L. P. de Jullian. A universal biography of contemporaries, living and dead, who acquired fame at the turn of
the 19th century.

128 --- ----Supplément à la Galerie historique... et complément
de toutes les autres biographies. Mons, 1826-[28] 3 v.

129 THE GALLERY OF CELEBRITIES.
v. 1, no. 1-12; new ser. , v. 1, no. 1-2. 1891. London. 2 v.
4. ° No more published? The old series (v. 1, no. 1-12) was
published under title: The Weekly gallery of Celebrities, with
biographical sketches. Universal biography; emphasis on
Great Britain.

130 GAROLLO, GOTTARDO, 1850-1917.
Dizionario biografico universale. Milano, U. Hoepli, 1907.
2 v. 16cm. (Manuali Hoepli) A universal biographical dictionary.

131 GAUHE, JOHANN FRIEDRICH
Historisches Helden- und Heldinnen- Lexicon. Leipzig,
1716. 1 v. 8.° Dictionary of historical heroes and heroines.

132   GENDAI KOKUSAI JIMMEI JITEN.
      Tōkyō, Kōjunsha, 1957.   280, 26 p.   International bio-
      graphical dictionary of the present age (Japanese not included)
133   GENDAI SEKAI JIMMEI JITEN.
      Tôkyô, Heibon-sha, 1949.   5, 447, 4, 20 p.   21cm.
      Current world biographical dictionary.
134   GERRITS, GERRIT ENGELBERTS
      Biographisch handwoordenboek.   Levensbeschrijvingen
      der meist beroemde personen uit alle eeuwen en volken.
      Amsterdam, 1848-50.   2 v.   8.º   A general biographical dic-
      tionary covering all nations and all times.
135   GIDEL, CHARLES ANTOINE, 1827-1899.
      Dictionnaire-manuel-illustré des écrivains et des littéra-
      tures.   Par Charles Gidel [et] Frédéric Loliée.   Paris, A.
      Colin, 1898.   908 p.   illus.   19cm.   (Bibliothèque de diction-
      naires-manuels-illustrés)   A general bio-bibliographical dic-
      tionary.
136   GIRARD DE PROPRIAC, CATHERINE JOSPEH FERDINAND
      Le Plutarque des jeunes demoiselles; ou, Abrégé des vies
      des femmes illustres de tous les pays... 2. éd.   Paris,
      Gérard, 1810.   2 v.   12.º   The Plutarch of young women; or,
      Brief lives of illustrious women of all countries.
137   GODWIN, PARKE, 1816-1904.
      The cyclopaedia of biography; a record of the lives of
      eminent persons.   New ed.   With a supplement, brought down
      to August, 1877.   New York, G. P. Putnam, 1878.   821,332 p.
      22cm.   1st published under title: Hand-book of universal biog-
      raphy.   Another ed. appeared in 1866, with a supplement to
      1865 or 6 by George Sheppard.
138   [GOODRICH, SAMUEL GRISWOLD] 1793-1860.
      Popular biography, by Peter Parley [pseud.]   Embracing
      the most eminent characters of every age, nation and profes-
      sion; including painters, poets, philosophers, politicians,
      heroes, warriors, & c., & c., illustrated with 200 fine por-
      traits.   New York, Leavitt & Allen, 1854 [c1832]   527 p.   illus.
      20cm.   Actually a reprint of the American edition of R. A.
      Davenport's Dictionary of biography (q. v.)   Goodrich (whose
      name also appears in the copyright notice of the aforementioned
      work) purports to have made alterations and improvements and
      to have added several European and ca. 300 American names
      to 'his' edition.
139   GORDON, WILLIAM JOHN
      The Bijou biography of the world; a reference book of the
      names, dates, and vocations of distinguished men and women
      of every age and nation, including living celebrities.   London,
      F. Warne [1881]   640 p.   32.
140   GORTON, JOHN, d. 1835.
      A general biographical dictionary.   New ed.   London, H.

G. Bohn, 1851. 4v. 23cm. 1st ed. published in 3 vols. in 1838 by Whittaker, London.

141 GREGOIRE, LOUIS, 1819-1892.
Dictionnaire encyclopédique d'histoire, de biographie, de mythologie et de géographie. Nouv. éd., revue, corrigée et augm. Paris, Garnier frères, 1877. iv,2074,58 p. 28cm. Includes general biography.

142 GRIGSON, GEOFFREY, 1905-   ed.
People; a volume of the good, bad, great & eccentric who illustrate the admirable diversity of man. General editors: Geoffrey Grigson & Charles Harvard Gibbs-Smith. London, Grosvenor Press, 1954. 469 p. illus., ports. 26cm. (People, places, and things, v. 1) 750 persons of all times & countries are sketched.

143 GRIMAL, PIERRE, ed.
Dictionnaire des biographies. Publié sous la direction de Pierre Grimal, avec la collaboration de J. Ardoino [et al. 1. éd.] Paris, Presses universitaires de France, 1958. 2 v. (xii, 1563 p.) ports. 24cm. A general biographical dictionary.

144 HALE, SARA JOSEPHA (BUELL) 1788-1879.
Woman's record; or, Sketches of all distinguished women, from the creation to A. D. 1868. Arranged in four eras. With selections from authoresses of each era. Illustrated by two hundred and thirty portraits, engraved on wood by Lossing and Barritt. 3d ed., rev., with additions. New York, Harper, 1870. xlviii, 17-918p. ports. 27cm.

145 HAMMERTON, SIR JOHN ALEXANDER, 1871-   ed.
Concise universal biography; a dictionary of the famous men and women of all countries and all times, recording the lives of more than 20,000 persons and arranged for reading or reference. London, Amalgamated Press [1934-35] 4 v. in 2. Based upon the biographical section of the Universal encyclopedia.

146 HARDIE, JAMES, 1750?-1826?
The new universal biographical dictionary, and American remembrancer of departed merit: containing complete and impartial accounts of the lives and writings of the most eminent persons in every station, but more particularly those who have signalized themselves in America. New York, Printed for T. Kirk, 1805. 4 v. ports. 22cm.

147 HARRISON, FREDERIC, 1831-1923, ed.
New calendar of great men: biographies of the 559 worthies of all ages and nations in the positivist calendar of August Comte. Edited by Frederic Harrison, S. H. Swinny and F. S. Marvin. New ed., rev. and enl. New York, London, Macmillan, 1921. xx, 708p. 23cm.

148 HAYS, FRANCES.
Women of the day; a biographical dictionary of notable

contemporaries. London, Chatto and Windus, 1885. xiv, 224p. 19cm.

149   HEILPRIN, LOUIS, 1851-1912.

The historical reference book; comprising a chronological table of universal history; a biographical dictionary with geographical notes; for the use of students, teachers and readers. Rev. to 1899; 6th ed., with a supplement. New York, D. Appleton, 1902. xi, 592p. 21cm. (The Concise knowledge library)

150   HEINZEL, ERWIN

Lexikon historischer Ereignisse und Personen in Kunst, Literatur und Musik. Wien, Brüder Hollinek, 1956. xxvi, 728p. 17 plates. 22cm. Dictionary of historical events and persons in art, literature and music.

151   HIRSCHING, FRIEDRICH CARL GOTTLOB, 1762-1800.

Historisch-literarisches Handbuch berühmter und denkwürdiger Personen, welche in dem 18. Jahrhunderte gestorben sind; oder, Kurzgefasste biographische und historische Nachrichten von berühmten Kaisern, Königen, Fürsten, grossen Feldherren, Staatsmännern, Pabsten, Erz- und Bischöffen, Cardinälen, Gelehrten aller Wissenschaften, Malern, Bildhauern, Mechanikern, Künstlern und anderen merkwürdigen Personen beyderley Geschlechts. Leipzig, Schwickert, 1794- v. in 21cm. Vol. 8, pt. 1- "Fortgesetzt und herausgegeben von Johann Heinrich Martin Ernesti." Historical-literary handbook of famous and memorable persons who died in the 18th century.

152   HISTORICAL BIOGRAPHY.

1923- London, H. Marshall. Edited by Clara L. Thomson. v. 8.°

153   HOLE, CHARLES

A brief biographical dictionary. With additions and corrections by William A. Wheeler. Thoroughly rev. to Jan. 1, 1800, by J. W. Abernethy. New York, Hurst [1883] xv, 497p. 20cm.

154   HUNT, CECIL, 1902-

A dictionary of word makers; pen pictures of the people behind our language. With illustrations by John Nicolson. London, H. Jenkins [1949] 176p. illus. 22cm.

155   HUTCHINSON'S WOMAN'S WHO'S WHO.

1908- London, Hutchinson. v. 19cm. Title varies: 1908-1918, The Ladies' court book --1919-1930, The Ladies' who's who.

156   HYAMSON, ALBERT MONTEFIORE.

A dictionary of universal biography of all ages and of all peoples. 2d ed. entirely rewritten. New York, Dutton, 1951. xii, 679p. 25cm. "Not a biographical dictionary.. but an

index to the persons appearing in some 24 standard biographical dictionaries. Most of the entries consist of a
single line, giving name, dates, nationality, profession and
symbol for source. "

157   THE IMPERIAL DICTIONARY OF UNIVERSAL BIOGRAPHY.
A series of original memoirs of distinguished men, of all
ages and all nations. By writers of eminence in the various
branches of literature, science, and art. Conducted by John
Eadie [and others] John Francis Waller, editor. London,
W. Mackenzie [1863] 3v. ports. 28cm. Issued in parts,
1857-1863.

158   THE INTERNATIONAL BLUE BOOK.
Who's who in the world. A biographical dictionary of the
world's notable living men and women. 1926-   London,
New York, H. Ringrose [etc.]   v.   22-25cm. On cover,
1951-52: World notables. Americans predominate in the
listings.

159   INTERNATIONAL CELEBRITY REGISTRY.
U. S. edition. 1st-   ed. ; 1959-   New York,
Celebrity Register.   v. ports. 27cm. Editor: 1959-
C. Amory.

160   THE INTERNATIONAL WHO'S WHO. 1935-
London, Europa Publications and Allen and Unwin.
v. 26 x 30cm. Supersedes the loose-leaf European who's
who, formerly published as vol. 2 of Europa.

161   INTERNATIONAL WORLD WHO'S WHO. 1947-
New York, American Universities Medical Research
Publications. v. 23cm.

162   THE INTERNATIONAL YEAR BOOK AND STATESMEN'S
WHO'S WHO.
1953-   London, Burke's Peerage. v. 26cm. annual.

163   IWANAMI SEIYŌ JIMMEI JITEN.
Tōkyō, Iwanami, 1965. 1962 p. Iwanami's world biographical dictionary. Edited by Shinoda, Hideo. An earlier edition (1932) was edited by Kamei, Takayoshi.

164   JAL, AUGUSTE, 1795-1873.
Dictionnaire critique de biographie et d'histoire; errata et
supplément pour tous les dictionnaires historique, d'après
des documents authentiques inédits. 2. éd. corr. et augm.
d'articles nouveaux et renfermant 218 facsimilés
d'autographes. Paris, H. Plon, 1872. iv, 1357p. facsims.
25cm. Critical dictionary of biography and history; errata
and supplement for all historical dictionaries. . .

165   JOÃO DE SÃO PEDRO, Brother, d. 1692.
Theatro heroino, abecedario historico, e catalogo das
mulheres illustres em armas, lettras, accões heroicas, e
artes liberaes, por Damião de Froés Perim [pseud.] Lisboa,
Officina da Musica de T. A. Lima, puis Officina Silviana,

1736-40. 2 v. Women famous in arms, letters, heroic actions and the liberal arts (with emphasis on Portuguese women)

166 JÖCHER, CHRISTIAN GOTTLIEB, 1694-1758.
Allgemeines Gelehrten-Lexicon, darinne die Gelehrten alle Stände sowohl mann- als weiblichen Geschlechts, welche vom Anfange der Welt bis auf ietzige Zeit gelebt... Leipzig, Gleditsch, 1750-51. 4 v. 28cm.

167 ---- ----Fortsetzungen und Ergänzungen... Leipzig, Gleditsch, 1784-87; Delmenhorst, Jöntzen, 1810; Bremen, Heyse, 1813-19; Leipzig, Selbstverlag der Deutschen Gesellschaft, 1897. 7 v. 28cm. Continued by J. C. Adelung, and others. Reprinted 1960-   by G. Olms, Hildesheim.

General dictionary of scholars from the world's beginning to the 'present' time.

168 JOHNSON, STANLEY CURRIE, 1878-
Who are they? A biographical reference book for young and old. Exeter [Eng.] A. Wheaton [1945] 252p. illus. 19cm.

169 JONES, STEPHEN, 1763-1827.
A new biographical dictionary: containing a brief account of the most eminent persons and remarkable characters in every age and nation. 8th ed. , with additions and improvements. London, Longman, Orme [etc.] 1840. 464p. 15cm. First published ca. 1799.

170 KEITNER, ÁRPÂD, ed.
Menschen und Menschenwerke. Men of today and their works. Hommes et oeuvres du temps présent. Wien, Verlag "Menschen und Menschenwerke," 1924-26. 3 v. illus., ports. 33 x 26cm. German, English, and French.

171 ---- ----Menschen und Menschenwerke; an index to the 434 personal and 240 institutional biographies in Menschen und Menschenwerke. Compiled by Herbert Kleist. Chicago, John Crerar Library, 1944. 16 p. (Reference list no. 54)

172 KNAPP, SAMUEL LORENZO, 1783-1838.
Female biography; containing notices of distinguished women, in different ages and nations. Philadelphia, T. Wardle, 1842. xii, [13], 501, [3] p. 20cm.

173 KOKUSAI JIJO KENKYŪKAI.
Gendai kokusai jimmei jiten. [Tokyo] Taimusu Shuppan-sha, 1937. 1 v. Current international who's who.

174 LABARRE DE RAILLICOURT, DOMINIQUE
Nouveau dictionnaire des biographies françaises et étrangères. Publié sous la direction de Dominique Labarre de Raillicourt avec la collaboration de Marie-Teresa Candela y Sapieha. Blasons de Maria-Teresa Labarre de Raillicourt. Paris [1961-   v. illus. 22cm. Issued in fascicles. Universal biography, with particular emphasis on Frenchmen.

175   [LACOMBE DE PREZEL, HONORÉ] b. 1725
    Dictionnaire des portraits historiques, anecdotes, et traits remarquables des hommes illustres. Paris, Chez Lacombe, 1768. 3 v. 19cm. Universal biography.

176   LADVOCAT, JEAN BAPTISTE, 1709-1765.
    Dictionnaire historique et bibliographique. Contenant l'histoire abrégée de toutes les personnes de l'un et de l'autre sexe qui se sont fait un nom par leurs talens, leurs vertus ou leurs crimes, depuis le commencement du monde... Nouv. éd., rev., corr. et augm., et ou l'on a fondu le Supplément de Le Clerc. Paris, E. Ledoux, 1822. 5 v. 21cm. 1st ed., 1752, has title: Dictionnaire historique portatif des grands hommes. An English translation in 4 vols. (2d ed.) was published in 1799-1801 under title: An historical and biographical dictionary. A Spanish ed. (2 v. only--A-Du) was published in 1753 under title: Diccionario histórico abreviado...

177   LANTEIRES, JEAN
    Tableau abrégé de l'antiquité littéraire, mis à la portée de tout le monde; ou, Dictionnaire historique et littéraire des poètes grecs et latins, suivi de quelques directions pour conduire à la lecture des traductions francaises que nous en avons, et de courtes notices des philosophes, auteurs, musiciens... femmes célèbres et autres personnages renommés chez les anciens. Lausanne, L. Luquiens, 1791. xvi, 359p. 8.º A dictionary of classical biography.

178   LARNED, JOSEPHUS NELSON, 1836-1913.
    The new Larned history for ready reference, reading and research; the actual words of the world's best historians, biographers and specialists; a complete system of history for all uses, extending to all countries and subjects and representing the better and newer literature of history, based on the work of the late J. N. Larned. New completely rev., enl. and brought up to date. Donald E. Smith, editor-in-chief. Charles Seymour, Augustus H. Shearer [and] Daniel C. Knowlton, associate editors. Springfield, Mass., C. A. Nichols Pub. Co. [1928?] 12 v. illus., ports. 27cm. An alphabetically arranged historical dictionary with many biographical entries.

179   LATHAM, EDWARD
    Who was he? A concise dictionary of general biography. London, G. Routledge [1905] 161p. 32.º

180   LECTUUR-REPERTORIUM,
    Bewerkt door A. S. K. B. [2. en definitieve uitg. Antwerpen, Vlaamsche Boekcentrale, 1952-54] 3 v. ports. 21cm. Cover title. Includes general bio-bibliography, anonyms, and pseudonyms, and Dutch bio-bibliography.

181   LEIDENFROST, CARL FLORENTIN
Historisch-biographisches Handwörterbuch der denkwürdigsten, berühmtesten und berüchtigsten Menschen aller Stände, Zeiten und Nationen. Ilmenau, 1824-27. 5 v. 8.°
A universal biographical dictionary.

182   LEMPRIERE, JOHN, 1765?-1824.
Lempriere's Universal biography; containing a critical and historical account of the lives, characters and labours of eminent persons, in all ages and countries. Together with selections of foreign biography from Watkin's dictionary, recently published, and about 800 original articles of American biography. By Eleazar Lord. New York, R. Lockwood, 1825. 2 v. 22cm. An earlier ed. (in 2 v.) was published in 1810.

183   LEVENSBESCHRYVING VAN BEROEMDE EN GELEERDE
MANNEN. Met hedendaagsche sterfgevallen en andere nieuwigheden. 1. [-6.] stuk. Te Amsterdam, By A. Wor, 1730-33. 6 v. ports. 21cm. Lives of famous and learned men [especially Hollanders]

184   LEXIKON DER ALTEN WELT.
Zürich, Artemis Verlag [1965] xv p., 3524 columns. illus., maps. 27cm. A dictionary of the ancient world which includes many biographies.

185   LEXIKON DER FRAU.
Zürich, Encyclios Verlag, 1953-54. 2 v. illus., ports. 27cm. Includes many bio-bibliographical sketches of famous women of all times and nationalities. 'Dictionary of the woman.'

186   THE LINCOLN LIBRARY OF ESSENTIAL INFORMATION;
An up-to-date manual for daily reference, for self-instruction, and for general culture. [1st]- ed.; 1024- Buffalo, Frontier Press Co. v. plates, ports. 25cm. The 25th ed. (1961) has a section: "Biography," of some 300 pages--2 columns to the page--in alphabetical arrangement with over 3600 sketches of famous persons.

187   THE LIVES AND PORTRAITS OF REMARKABLE CHARAC-
TERS, drawn from the most authentic sources. A new ed. v. 1-2. London, Printed and published by W. Lewis, 1819. 2 v. in 1. ports. 25cm. A new ed. of the Eccentric magazine; or, Lives and portraits of remarkable persons, originally compiled and edited successively by Henry Lemoine and James Caulfield and published by G. Smeeton, London, 1812-13. A reissue was printed and sold by G. Smeeton and J. Caulfield, London, 1814. Cf. Brit. Mus. Cat.

188   MACCALLUM, THOMAS WATSON, 1881-   ed.
The Nobel prize-winners and the Nobel Foundation, 1901-1937, edited by T. W. MacCallum and Stephen Taylor. With an introd. by Gilbert Murray. Zurich, Central European Times Pub. Co., 1938. xi, 599 p. plates, ports. 24cm.

189   MÄNNER DER ZEIT.
     Biographisches Lexikon der Gegenwart. Mit Supplement:
     Frauen der Zeit.   Leipzig, C. B. Lorck, 1862.   3 v. in l.
     29cm.   2 columns to the page.   Published in parts, 1858-1862.
     Men of the time; biographical dictionary of the present (19th
     century)

190   MARTIN, FREDERICK, 1830-1883.
     Handbook of contemporary biography.   London, Macmillan,
     1870.   287 p.   18cm.

191   MARCHAND, PROSPER, d. 1756.
     Dictionnaire historique; ou, Memoires critiques et litter-
     aires, concernant la vie et les ouvrages de divers personnages
     distingués, particulierement dans la republique des lettres.
     La Haye, P. de Hondt, 1758-59.   2 v. in l.   42cm.   Designed
     as a supplement to Bayle's Dictionnaire historique.   A
     general bio-bibliographical dictionary.

192   MAUNDER, SAMUEL, 1785-1849.
     The biographical treasury; a dictionary of universal biog-
     raphy.   11th ed. , rev. , corr. and extended to the present time.
     With a supplement.   London, Longman, Green, Longman, and
     Roberts, 1859.   iv, 962p.   front.   17cm.   A later edition was
     issued in 1873?

193   MEE, ARTHUR, 1875-
     Arthur Mee's 1000 heroes.   Immortal men & women of ev-
     ery age & every land.   London, Amalgamated Press, 1933-34.
     2 v. (1828p.) illus.   8.º

194   MEN AND WOMEN OF THE TIME;
     A dictionary of contemporaries.   15th ed. , rev. and brought
     down to the present time, by Victor G. Plarr.   London, G.
     Routledge, 1899.   x, 1300p.   24cm.   1st-12th editions publish-
     ed under title: Men of the time.

195   MEN IN THE NEWS;
     Personality sketches from the New York times.   1958-
     Philadelphia, Lippincott.   v.   22cm.   Editor: 1958-
     R. H. Phelps.

196   MEN OF THE MOMENT.
     1902-   London, A. Treherne.   v.   8.º

197   MEN OF THE TIME;
     A dictionary of contemporaries, containing biographical
     notices of eminent characters of both sexes.   [1st]-12th ed. ;
     1852-1887.   London, D. Bogue.   12 v.   15-20cm.   Title and
     subtitle vary.   Imprint varies: 7th-12th editions, London,
     New York, G. Routledge.

198   MENCKE, JOHANN BURKHARD, 1674-1732.
     Compendiöses Gelehrten-Lexicon, darinnen die Gelehrten,
     als Fürsten und Staats-Leute, die in der Literatur erfahren,
     Theologi, Prediger, Juristen, Politici, Medici, Philologi,
     Philosophi... so wohl männ - als weiblichen Geschlechts,

welche vom Anfang der Welt grössten Theils in gantz Europa biss auf jetzige Zeit gelebet, und sich durch Schrifften oder sonst der gelehrten Welt bekant gemacht, an der Zahl über 20 000 nach ihrer Geburth, absterben, vornehmsten Schrifften, Leben und merckwürdigsten Geschichten, aus denen glaubwürdigsten Scribenten, die man jedesmahl fleissig angemerckt, kurtz und deutlich nach alphabetischer Ordnung beschrieben werden, denen Liebhabern der Historie der Gelehrten... zu nützlichen Gebrauch zum Druck befordert. Nebst einer Vorrede. Leipzig, J. F. Gleditsch, 1715. 2682, [6] columns. front. 22cm. A general bio-bibliography. The 2d and 3d editions, 1726 and 1733, were edited by C. G. Jöcher and may be regarded as forerunners of Jöcher's Allgemeines Gelehrten-Lexicon, 1750-51, 4 vols. (with continuation by Adelung and Rotermund, 1784-1819)

199 MENCKE, JOHANN BURKHARD, 1674-1732.
Joannis Burchardi et Friderici Ottonis Menckeniorum Bibliotheca virorum militia aeque ac scriptis illustrium. Lipsiae, Apud Haeredes Lankisios, 1734. 480p. 8.° Library of men illustrious for military and literary activities.

200 THE MONTHLY RECORD OF EMINENT MEN.
With portraits and autographs. Edited by G. Potter. v. 1-4; 1890-1891. London. 4 v. ports. 8.° No more published.

201 MORÉRI, LOUIS, 1643-1680.
Le grand dictionnaire historique; ou, Le mélange curieux de l'histoire sacrée et profane, qui contient en abrégé l'histoire fabuleuse des dieux & des héros de l'antiquité païenne: les vies et les actions remarquables des patriarches; des empereurs; des rois, des princes illustres, des grands capitaines; des papes... l'établissement et le progrès des ordres religieux & militaires; & la vie de leurs fondateurs: les généalogies des familles illustres de France, & des autres pays de l'Europe... Nouv. éd. dans laquelle on a refondu les supplemens de M. l'abbé Goujet. Le tout rev., corr. & augm. par M. Drouet. Paris, Libraires associés, 1759. 10 v. port. 41cm. 1st ed. published in 1674 in Lyon in 1 vol. Abbreviated English editions were issued in 1694 and 1701 under title: The great historical, geographical and poetical dictionary... [by Jeremy Collier] A Spanish ed. was published in Paris in 1753 (8 v. in 10) under title: El gran diccionario historico...

202 MORRIS, CHARLES, 1833-1922.
The handy dictionary of biography. New and rev. ed. Philadelphia, J. C. Winston [1905] 607p. 22cm.

203 MORRIS, DAVID K
Notes of a thousand men, and some things they did in art,

literature, war, government, science, and industry, arranged in groups, and in order of time. London, Cassell, 1891. 67p. 8.°

204   MORTIMER, THOMAS, 1730-1810.

The students' pocket dictionary; or, Compendium of universal history, chronology, and biography. From the earliest accounts to the present time. With authorities. In two parts. Pt. I containing a compendium of universal history. Pt. II containing a compendium of biography. London, Printed for J. Johnson, 1777. 2 pts. in 1 v. 18cm.

205   MOURRE, MICHEL, 1928-   ed.

Dictionnaire des idées contemporaines [par] Pierre de Boisdeffre [et al.] Paris, Editions universitaires [1964] 718 p. ports. 22 x 11cm. This dictionary of "ideas" includes 177 bio-bibliographies of philosophers, religious figures, writers, statesmen, etc. , prominent in the intellectual history of the 20th century; alphabetical.

206   LE NÉCROLOGE UNIVERSEL DU XIXe SIÈCLE.

1-10; 1845-54. Paris. 10 v. 8.° Universal necrology of the 19th century. Edited by Saint-Maurice Cabany (J. Maurice Cabany, called E. de Saint-Maurice Cabany)

207   NELSON'S BIOGRAPHICAL DICTIONARY,

With a short dictionary of mythology. Edited by John Gunn. London, New York, T. Nelson [1936] 592 p. 18cm.

208   A NEW AND GENERAL BIOGRAPHICAL DICTIONARY;

Containing an historical and critical account of the lives and writings of the most eminent persons in every nation; particularly the British and Irish; from the earliest accounts of time to the present period. New ed. , in fifteen volumes, greatly enl. and improved. London, Printed for G. G. and J. Robinson [etc.] 1798. 15v. ports. 23cm.

209   A NEW BIOGRAPHICAL DICTIONARY;

or, Pocket compendium; containing a brief account of the lives and writings of the most eminent persons in every age and nation. London, Printed for G. G. and J. Robinson, 1794. 1 v. (unpaged) 13cm. Preface signed: S. J.

210   A NEW BIOGRAPHICAL DICTIONARY OF 3000 CONTEMPORARY PUBLIC CHARACTERS, British and foreign, of all ranks and professions. 2d ed. London, G. B. Whittaker, 1825. 3 v. in 6 pts. ports. 18cm.

211   THE NEW CENTURY CLASSICAL HANDBOOK.

Edited by Catherine B. Avery. Editorial consultant: Jotham Johnson. New York, Appleton-Century-Crofts, 1962. xiii, 1162 p. illus. 26cm.

212   THE NEW CENTURY CYCLOPEDIA OF NAMES.

Edited by Clarence L. Barnhart with the assistance of William D. Halsey and a staff of more than 350 consulting scholars,

special editors, and other contributors.   New York, Appleton-
Century-Crofts, 1954.   3 v. (xxviii, 4342 p.) 28cm.

213   [NICÉRON, JEAN PIERRE] 1685-1738.
     Mémoires pour servir à l'histoire des hommes dans la
république des lettres, avec un catalogue raisonné de leurs
ouvrages.   Paris, Briasson, 1729-45.   43 v. in 44. 17cm.
A universal bio-bibliography. By Nicéron and others. Beginning with vol. 30 Nicéron's name appears on t. p.   A German
version appeared 1749-1777 (Halle) under title: Nachrichten
von den Begebenheiten und Schriften berühmter Gelehrten(?)

214   NISENSON, SAMUEL
     Minute biographies; intimate glimpses into the lives of 150
famous men and women, by Samuel Nisenson and Alfred Parker. [New York] Grosset & Dunlap [1931] 160 p. illus. 26cm.

215   NISENSON, SAMUEL
     More minute biographies; intimate glimpses into the lives
of 150 famous men and women, by Samuel Nisenson and Alfred
Parker.   [New York] Grosset & Dunlap [1933] 160 p. illus.
26cm.

216   NISENSON, SAMUEL
     Pictured biographies, wherein the spotlight is thrown upon
the careers of 150 great men and women of history, by Samuel
Nisenson and Alfred Parker.   New York, Literary Club [1932]
160 p. illus. 26cm.   Published in part in 1931 under title:
Minute biographies.

217   NOËL, FRANÇOIS JOSEPH MICHEL, 1755-1841.
     Dictionnaire historique des personnages célèbres de l'anti-
quité, princes, généraux, philosophes, poetes, artistes, etc. ;
des dieux, héros de la fable; des villes, fleuves, etc.; avec
l'étymologie et la valeur de leurs noms et surnoms: précédé
d'un essai sur les noms propres chez les peuples anciens et
modernes. 2. éd., rev., corr., et augm.   Paris, Le Nor-
mant père, 1824.   581 p. 22cm.   Historical dictionary of
famous persons of antiquity.

218   NOORTHOUCK, JOHN, 1746?-1816.
     An historical and classical dictionary, containing the lives
and characters of the most eminent and learned persons in
every age and nation, from the earliest period to the present
time.   London, 1776.   2 v. 8.°

219   NOTABLE WOMEN OF AFFAIRS.
     New York, Women's Syndicate Press, 1925.   138 p. illus.
(incl. ports.) 26cm.

220   NOUVELLE BIOGRAPHIE GÉNÉRALE DEPUIS LES TEMPS LE
     PLUS RECULÉS JUSQU'À NOS JOURS, avec les renseigne-
ments bibliographiques de l'indication des sources à consulter.
Publiée par Firmin Didot frères sous la direction de M. le Dr.
Hoefer.   Paris, Firmin Didot frères, 1853-66 [v. 1, 1857]

46 v. 24cm. A universal biographical dictionary, but with emphasis on France.

221   OETTINGER, EDUARD MARIA, 1808-1872.
Moniteur des dates. Biographisch-genealogisch-historisches Welt-Register enthaltend die Personal-Akten der Menshheit, d. h. den Heimaths- und Geburts-Schein, den Heirathsakt und Todestag von mehr als 100,000 geschichtlichen Persönlichkeiten aller Zeiten und Nationen von Erschaffung der Welt bis auf den heutigen Tag, mit zahlreich eingestreuten Noten aus allen Zweigen der Curiosität. Leipzig, L. Denicke, 1869. 6 v. in 1. 32cm. Published in 33 monthly parts, Dresden, 1866-68. Very brief information on ca. 100,000 famous persons.

222   --- ----Moniteur des dates, contenant un million de reseignements biographiques, genéalogiques et historiques. Supplément, commencé par Edouard-Marie Oettinger, considérablement augm. et continué jusqu'à nos jours, rédigé et édité par Hugo Schramm. t. 7[-9] de l'ouvrage entier. t. 1-[3] du supplément. Leipzig, B. Hermann, 1873-82. 3 v. in 1. 32cm. Published in 19 parts numbered 34-52.

223   OLIVIER-POLI, GIOACCHINO MARIA
Continuazione al Nuovo dizionario istórico degli uomini che si sono renduti più celebri per talenti, virtù, scelleratezze, errori, ec., la quale abbraccia il periodo degli ultimi 40 anni dell'era volgare. Napoli, R. Marotta e Vanspandoch, 1824-25. 9 v. in 8. 20cm. Continuation of L. M. Chaudon's Dictionnaire universel, historique, critique, et bibliographique (q.v.) A biographical dictionary covering the last 40 years (ca. 1785-ca. 1825)

224   ŌRUI, NOBURU, 1884-
Sekai jimmei jiten. [Tokyo] Tōkyō-do, 1961. 2 v. 19cm. A universal biographical dictionary; ca. 12,300 names listed. An earlier edition was issued in 1952.

225   THE OXFORD CLASSICAL DICTIONARY;
Edited by M. Cary [and others] with the assistance of H. J. Rose, H. P. Harvey [and] A. Souter. Oxford, Clarendon Press, 1949. xx, 971 p. 28cm.

226   PAN-PACIFIC WHO'S WHO;
An international reference work. A biographical encyclopedia of men and women of substantial achievement in the Pan-Pacific area: Alaska, Australia, British Columbia, California, Canal Zone, China, Hawaii, Japan, New Zealand, Oregon, Philippines, Washington. 1940/41- ed. Honolulu, Honolulu star-bulletin, ltd. v. 25cm. Editor: 1940/41- , G. F. M. Nellist. 1940/41 ed. incorporates v. 6 of Men of Hawaii.

227   PANTHÉON BIOGRAPHIQUE;
Revue mensuelle, historique et nécrologique. 1.-3. années; 1849-1851. Paris. 3 v. 8.° Title varies? Some issues

called: Panthéon biographique universelle? Edited by E.
Perraud de Thoury. Biographical pantheon. Universal biography & necrology.

228 PAULY, AUGUST FRIEDRICH VON, 1796-1845.
Der kleine Pauly; Lexikon der Antike. Auf der Grundlage
von Pauly's Realencyklopädie der classischen Altertumwissen-
schaft unter Mitwirkung zahlreicher Fachgelehrter bearb. und
hrsg. von Konrat Ziegler, und Walther Sontheimer. Stuttgart,
A. Druckenmüller, 1964-   v. 23cm. A classical dictionary; abbreviated version of Pauly's Real-Encyclopadie der
classischen Altertumswissenschaft. Contents. --1. Bd.
Aachen bis Dichalkon.

229 PAULY, AUGUST FRIEDRICH VON, 1796-1845.
Real-Encyclopädie der classischen Altertumswissenschaft.
Neue Bearbeitung unter Mitwirkung zahlreicher Fachgenossen
hrsg. von G. Wissowa. Stuttgart, J. B. Metzler, 1894-19
v. in   illus. 25cm. A major classical dictionary with
lengthy bio-bibliographical articles. Vols. 7-18, pt. 1 edited
by Wilhelm Kroll; v. 18, pt. 2, 19-20, pt. 1 by Kroll and Karl
Mittelhaus; v. 18, pt. 3-4, v. 20, pt. 2-   by Kurt Zeigler.

230 ---- ----Supplement. Stuttgart, J. B. Metzler [etc.]
1903-   v. illus. 25cm.

231 ---- ----2. Reihe (R-Z) Stuttgart, J. B. Metzler [etc.]
1914-   v. in   26cm.

232 [PEIGNOT, GABRIEL] 1767-1849.
Dictionnaire géographique et bibliographique portatif des
personnages illustres, célèbres ou fameux de tous les siècles
et de tous les pays du monde, avec les dieux et les héros de
la mythologie. Par L. G. P. Avec une table encyclopédique
et bibliographique, propre à faciliter l'ordre et l'arrangement
des livres dans une bibliothèque. Paris, Hacquart, 1813-15.
3 v. 21cm. A later edition was published 1821-22 under title:
Dictionnaire historique et bibliographique (2 v. in 4)? A universal bio-bibliographical dictionary.

233 A PENNY UNIVERSAL BIOGRAPHY
(Universal biography) Translated, compiled and judicious-
ly condensed from the 'Biographie universelle' and every other authority. London, F. Lawrance [ca. 1830] 10 pts. (320p.)
8.º (The Penny national library, v. 10) No more published?

234 PERSONNALITÉS D'AUJOURD'HUI.
Revue mensuelle internationale de biographie. 1-   ;
1957-   Bruxelles.   v. Personalities of today. A continuation of Célébrités d'aujourd'hui (q. v.)?

235 PHILLIPS, LAWRENCE BARNETT, 1842-1922.
The dictionary of biographical reference, containing over
one hundred thousand names, together with a classed index
of the biographical literature of Europe and America. New
ed. , rev. , corr. and augm. with supplement to date, by

Frank Weitenkampf (Frank Listow White) [3d ed.] London, S. Low, Marston; Philadelphia, Gibbie, 1889. xiii, 1038p. 25cm.

236   PICK, FRED LOMAX, 1898-
The Freemason's pocket reference book, by Fred L. Pick and G. Norman Knight. New York, Philosophical Library [1956] 304p. 18cm. Includes biographical material on leading Freemasons. First published 1955 (London, F. Muller)

237   PIERCE, EDWARD M
The cottage cyclopedia of history and biography. A copious dictionary of memorable persons, events, places, and things, with notices of the present state of the principal countries and nations of the known world, and a chronological view of American history. Hartford, A. S. Hale, 1868. v, 1004p. illus., ports. 25cm. First published 1859?

238   PLATTS, JOHN, 1775-1837.
A new universal biography, containing interesting accounts, critical and historical, of the lives and characters, labours and actions, of eminent persons, arranged in chronological order; showing the progress of men and things, from the beginning of the world to the present time. To which is added an alphabetical index for reference. London, Printed for Sherwood, Jones, 1825-26. 5 v. 24cm. Title varies slightly. Goes up to the 15th-16th centuries. No more published.

239   THE PORTRAIT GALLERY OF DISTINGUISHED POETS,
PHILOSOPHERS, STATESMEN, DIVINES, PAINTERS, ARCHITECTS, PHYSICIANS, AND LAWYERS, since the revival of art; with their biographies. Arr. in chronological order. Originally published by the Society for the Diffusion of Useful Knowledge. London, W. S. Orr, 1853. 3 v. illus., 168 ports. 28cm. The biographical sketches are by Arthur Thomas Malkin. 1st ed. (London, 1833-37) had title: The gallery of portraits: with memoirs.

240   PRUDHOMME, LOUIS MARIE, 1752-1830.
Biographie universelle et historique des femmes célèbres, mortes ou vivants, qui se sont fait remarquer dans toutes les nations, par leurs vertus, leur génie, leur écrits, leurs talens pour les sciences et les arts, par leurs sensibilités, leur courage, leur heroisme, leurs malheurs, leurs erreurs, leurs galanteries, leurs vices, etc., depuis le commencement du monde jusqu'à nos jours, par une société de gens de lettres. Publiée par L. Prudhomme. [2. ed.] Paris, Lebigre, 1830. 4 v. 22cm. Universal biography of famous women of all times. First ed. published in 1826 under title: Répertoire universel, historique, biographique des femmes célèbres, mortes ou vivantes.

241   THE QUARTERLY BIOGRAPHICAL MAGAZINE.
No. 1-2. London, 1828. 2 v. 8.º No more published.

242   RABBE, ALPHONSE, 1786-1830.
Biographie universelle et portative des contemporains;
ou, Dictionnaire historique des hommes vivants et des
hommes morts depuis 1788 jusqu'à nos jours... Publié sous
la direction de MM. Rabbe, Vieilh de Boisjolin et Sainte-
Preuve [pseud.] Paris, F. G. Levrault, 1834. 5 v. An
earlier ed., in 4 v., published in 1830. A universal biographical dictionary for the period 1788-1834.

243   RAPPOPORT, ANGELO SOLOMON, 1871-
Dictionary of socialism. London, T. F. Unwin [1924]
xi, 271p. 23cm. "Who's who in socialism" (p. [131]-223)
contains some 300 biographies.

244   RATHLEF, ERNST LUDWIG, 1709-1768.
Geschichte jetztlebender Gelehrten, als eine Fortsetzung
des Jetztlebenden Gelehrten Europa hrsg. Zelle, J. A.
Deetz, 1740-47. 12 pts. in 3 v. 17cm. Contemporary scho-
lars (1740-1747) Parts 9-12 edited by Johann Christoph
Strodtmann. Continued by Strodtmann's Beyträge zur His-
toire der Gelahrtheit, 1748-1750, and Das neue Gelehrte
Europa, 1752-81.

245   REICHARD, CARL
Moderne Biographien; oder, Kurze Nachrichten von dem
Leben und den Thaten der berühmtesten Menschen welche sich
seit dem Anfange der französischen Revolution bis zu dem
Wiener Frieden... ausgezeichnet haben... Aus dem Fran-
zösischen frey übers und verm. von K. Reichard. Leipzig,
E. Fleischer, 1811. 6 v. ports. 8.º Modern biographies;
or, Brief notes on the life and deeds of the most famous
men... from the beginning of the French Revolution to the
Peace of Vienna (Oct. 14, 1809)

246   ROBINSON, DONALD B   1913-
The 100 most important people in the world today. Boston, Little, Brown [1952] 427p. illus. 18cm.

247   RODALE, JEROME IRVING, 1898-   ed.
The word finder. Compiled and edited by J. I. Rodale
with the collaboration of Kingsbury M. Badger [and others.
New ed.] Emmaus, Pa., Rodale Press [1956, c1947] xxxii,
1317p. 24cm. Nearly one-half of the volume is a "Dictionary
of names," an alphabetical listing which includes fictional
and mythological characters and a large number of actual
persons.

248   ROEDER, WILLIAM S
Dictionary of European history. With an introd. by Harry
Elmer Barnes. New York, Philosophical Library, 1954.
viii, 316p. 24cm. (Midcentury reference library) Several
thousand biographical sketches are included.

249 ROGERS, JOEL AUGUSTUS, 1880-
World's great men of color. New York [1946-47] 2 v.
illus., ports. 24cm.

250 THE ROLL OF HONOR FOR WOMEN;
An annual biographical record of women of the world who
have worked for the public good. [v. 1]-   ; 1906-
London, "The Gentlewoman" Offices.   v. ports. 26cm.

251 ROSE, HUGH JAMES, 1795-1838.
A new general biographical dictionary, projected and
partly arranged by the late Hugh James Rose. London, B.
Fellowes [etc.] 1857. 12 v. 23cm. Vol. 1 edited by Henry
John Rose; v. 2-12 by T. Wright.

252 ROW, AUGUSTUS
Masonic biography and dictionary, comprising the history
of ancient masonry, antiquity of masonry, written and un-
written law, derivations and definition of masonic terms,
biographies of eminent masons, statistics of all the lodges
in the United States, etc. Philadelphia, J. B. Lippincott,
1868. 365p. 20cm.

253 SANDERS, LLOYD CHARLES, 1857-
Celebrities of the century; being a dictionary of men and
women of the nineteenth century. New and rev. ed.   London,
Cassell, 1890. vi, 1077 p.

254 SAXE, CHRISTOPH GOTTLOB, 1714-1806.
Onomasticon literarium; sive, Nomenclator historico-cri-
ticus praestantissimorum omnis aetatis, populi, artiumq.
formulae scriptorum. Item monumentorum maxime illustrium,
ab orbe condito usque ad saeculi, quod vivimus, tempora di-
gestus. E recognitione longe auctiori et emendatiori, ita, ut
non tam editio altera, quam novus omnino liber censeri debeat.
Traiecti ad Rhenum, Apud G. T. à Paddenburg [etc.] 1775-1803.
8 v. 22cm. A general bio-bibliography; includes primarily
the writers of antiquity, but also those up to 1796 who were
concerned with antiquity.

255 SCHAUMBURG, PAUL ERICH BRUNO RICHARD, 1884-
Minerva-Lexikon berühmter Persönlichkeiten aller Zeitalter. Leipzig, R. M. Lippold [1929] 684 p. 26cm. Minerva
dictionary of famous personalities of all times.

256 SCHMIDT, MINNA (MOSCHEROSCH) 1866-   comp.
400 outstanding women of the world and costumology of
their time. Chicago, 1933. xviii, 583 p. illus., ports.
24cm.

257 SCHRÖCKH, JOHANN MATTHIAS, 1733-1808.
Allgemeine Biographie ... Berlin, Mylius, 1767-91. 8 v.
Universal biography.

258 SCHRÖCKH, JOHANN MATTHIAS, 1733-1808.
Lebensbeschreibungen berühmter Gelehrten. Neue umgearb.

33

Ausg. Leipzig, E. B. Schwickert, 1790. 2 v. in 1. ports. 21cm. Lives of famous scholars; universal in scope.

259 [SCIFONI, FELICE]
Dizionario biografico universale, contenente le notizie più importanti sulla vita e sulle opere degli uomini celebri: i nomi di regie e di illustri famiglie; di scismi religiosi; di parti civili; di sette filosofiche, dall'origine del mondo fino a' di nostri. Primo versione dal francese, con molte giunte e correzioni, e con una raccolta di tavole comparative, ora per la prima volta compilate, dimostranti per secoli e per ordini il tesoro di chiari ingegni che può vantare ogni nazione posta a riscontro delle altre, dal principio dell'era volgare all' età presente. Firenze, D. Passigli, 1848-49. 5 v. plates. 26cm. A universal biographical dictionary chiefly compiled from the 'Biographie universelle. '

260 SCOTT, Sir HAROLD RICHARD, 1887- ed.
The concise encyclopedia of crime and criminals. Contributors: J. C. Alderson [and others. 1st ed.] New York, Hawthorn Books [1961] 351 p. plates, ports. 26cm.

261 SECO Y SHELLEY, MANUEL, d. 1877.
La pluma y la espada; apuntes para un diccionario de militares escritores. Madrid, 1877. 1 v. 8.o "The pen and the sword"; annotations for a dictionary of writers on the military arts, chiefly those of Spanish origin.

262 SEKAI JIMMEI JITEN, SEIYÔ HEN.
[Tôkyô, Tôkyôdô, 1952] 892 p. 19cm. World biographical dictionary, Western section.

263 [SEWARD, WILLIAM] 1747-1799.
Anecdotes of distinguished persons, chiefly of the last two and preceding centuries. 5th ed. London, Printed for T. Cadell and W. Davies, 1804. 4 v. illus., ports. 22cm. Sketches universal in scope.

264 [SEWARD, WILLIAM] 1747-1799.
Biographiana. By the compiler of Anecdotes of distinguished persons. London, Printed for J. Johnson, 1799. 2 v. plates, ports. 21cm. Universal biographical sketches.

265 [SIGISMONDO DA VENEZIA] d. 1847.
Bibliografia universale sacra e profana, disposta in ordine cronologico con cenni sugli autori ed illustrazioni sugli scritto loro. Opera originale italiana. Volume unico. Venezia, Tip. di G. B. Merlo, 1842. 998 p. 22cm. Universal [bio-] bibliography, sacred and profane, arranged in chronological order. No more published?

266 SMITH, Sir WILLIAM, 1813-1893.
A classical dictionary of Greek and Roman biography, mythology, and geography, based on the larger dictionaries by the late Sir William Smith. Rev. throughout and in part

rewritten by G. E. Marindin. New York, D. Appleton, 1894. vi, 1018 p. illus. 23cm. Earlier editions issued under title: A classical dictionary of biography, mythology, and geography. Reprinted many times (the latest in 1932?)

267   SMITH, Sir WILLIAM, 1813-1893.
A dictionary of Greek and Roman biography and mythology. London, J. Murray, 1880. 3 v. illus. 25cm.

268   SOCIETY FOR THE DIFFUSION OF USEFUL KNOWLEDGE, London.
The biographical dictionary of the Society for the Diffusion of Useful Knowledge. London, Longmans, 1842-44. 4 v. No more published. Edited by G. Long. A dictionary of universal biography.

269   STEEL, JOHANNES, 1906-
Men behind the war; a "who's who" of our time. New York, Sheridan House, 1943. xviii, 488p. 23cm.

270   [STRODTMANN, JOHANN CHRISTOPH] 1717-1756.
Beyträge zur Historie der Gelahrtheit, worinnen die Geschichte der Gelehrten unserer Zeiten beschrieben werden. Hamburg, C. S. Geissler, 1748-50. 5 v. in 2. 17cm. Biographies of scholars of the 18th century. Continuation of Goetten's Das jetzt-lebende gelehrte Europa, 1735-40; and Rathlef's Geschichte jetztlebender Gelehrten, 1740-47. Continued by Das neue gelehrte Europa, 1752-81.

271   SZYMANOWSKI, WOJCIECH, 1800-1861.
Dykcyonarz biograficzno-powszechny; czyli, Krótkie wspomnienia żywotów ludzi wsławionych cnota, madrościa, przemysłem, meztwem, wynalazkami, bledami. Od poczatku świata do najnowszych czasów. Warszawa, Nakład G. L. Glücksberga, 1884-51. 2 v. At head of title: Wojciech Szymanowski i Leon Rogalski. Universal biographical dictionary.

272   TAILLEMITE, ÉTIENNE
Dictionnaire de la marine. [Paris] Collection Seghers [1962] 380p. illus. 16cm. (Dictionnaire Seghers) Dictionary of the sea, naval affairs; includes biography.

273   T'ANG, CHING-KAO.
Hsien tai wai kuo jên ming tz'ŭ tien. [Shanghai, 1933] 1 v. (various pagings) 19cm. Well-known people of the present day; a universal biographical dictionary.

274   THEVET, ANDRÉ, 1502-1590.
Histoire de plus ilustres et scavans hommes de leur siècles, tant de l'Europe que de l'Asie, Afrique et Amérique... Paris, F. Mauger, 1671. 9 v. ports. Vol. 9 (without t. p. ?) is a collection of portraits. 1st ed. appeared in 1584 under title: Les vrais pourtraits et vies des hommes illustres, grecz, latins, et payens. History of the most illustrious

and learned men of their centuries in Europe, Asia, Africa & America.

275   THOMAS, JOSEPH, 1811-1891.
       Universal pronouncing dictionary of biography and mythology. Philadelphia, Lippincott [c1930] xi, 2550p. 29cm.
       Cover title: Lippincott's pronouncing biographical dictionary.

276   TODA, TEIZO, 1887-1955.
       Shimpen jimmei jiten. [Tôkyô, Kokumin Tosho Kankô-kai, 1953] 808 p. 19cm. Revised biographical dictionary; universal in scope.

277   TOMASINI, JACOPO FILIPPO, 1597-1654.
       Parnassus Euganeus; sive, De scriptoribus ac literatis hujus aevi claris. Accedit index eorum qui elogia considere ac de scriptoribus diversis tractarunt. Patavii, 1647. 1 v. 4.º   The Euganean Parnassus; or, writers & learned men of this age.

278   TOMASINI, JACOPO FILIPPO, 1597-1654.
       Parnassus Euganeus; sive, Museum clariss. virorum, et antiquor. simulacris exornatum. Patavii, 1647. 1 v. ports. 4.º   The Euganean Parnassus; or, Museum of the most famous men, with portraits. Not the same as his Parnassus Euganeus; sive, De scriptoribus ac literatis hujus aevi claris.

279   TSUI HSIN SHIH CHIEH JĚN MING TA TZ'Ŭ TIEN.
       [Taipei, 1964] 1314, 26p. 20cm. Latest world biographical dictionary. Compiled by: Hua wen shu chü pien chi pu.

280   [UNGHERINI, AGLAURO] 1847-
       Manuel de bibliographie biographique et d'iconographie des femmes célèbres... par un vieux bibliophile. Turin, L. Roux, 1892. xi p., 806 columns. 24cm.

281   ---- ----Supplément. Turin, Roux & Viarengo, 1900. x p., 634 columns. 24cm.

282   ---- ----Second et dernier supplément. Rome, Roux & Viarengo, 1905. xiii p., 758 columns. 25cm.
       Bio-bibliography and portraits of famous women & women as authors.

283   UNITED NATIONS INFORMATION OFFICE, New York.
       Who's who; delegates to the United Nations Conference on International Organization, San Francisco, 1945. New York [1945] 106p. 20cm. Cover title.

284   UNITED NATIONS WHO'S WHO IN GOVERNMENT AND IN-
       DUSTRY. [1st]-   year; [1941]-   London, Allied Publications.   v. 19cm.   Title varies: 1941-44, The Who's who of the allied governments and allied trade & industry (varies slightly)

285 U. S. INTERDEPARTMENTAL COMMITTEE FOR ACQUISI-
TION OF FOREIGN PUBLICATIONS.
Abstracts on European and Far Eastern personalities.
no. P-1— Jan. 13, 1945- [Washing-
ton?] v. in 28cm. weekly (irregular) No. 1 has title: Abstracts on personalities.

286 UNIVERSAL BIOGRAPHY.
Containing sketches of prominent persons of the 19th
century. Published by subscription. New York, Hartford
Pub. Co. [187-?] [574] p. ports. 30cm.

287 DIE URNE.
Jahrbuch für allgemeine Nekrologie. 1-2; 1873-74. Leipzig. 2 v. "The Urn." A yearbook of universal necrology,
emphasizing Germany. Edited by Hugo Schramm-Macdonald.

288 VAPEREAU, GUSTAVE, 1819-1906.
Dictionnaire universel des contemporains contenant
toutes les personnes notables de la France et des pays
étrangers... Ouvrage rédige et tenu à jour avec la concours d'écrivains de tous les pays. 6. éd. entièrement refondue et considérablement augm. Paris, Hachette, 1893.
lll, 1629p. 25cm.

289 ---- ----Supplément. Paris, Hachette, 1895. ii, 103p.
25cm.
Universal dictionary of contemporaries (late 19th century),
France & foreign countries.

290 VELASCO, FANOR, 1843?-1907.
Diccionario biográfico moderno. Santiago de Chile, Impr.
Cervantes, 1886. 115 p. 8.⁰ A modern biographical diction-
ary.

291 VELIKIE LIUDI.
Biograficheskaia biblioteka. [St. -Peterburg, "Luch,"
1912-13. 6 v. 8.⁰ Famous people. A [universal] biographical 'library.' Supplement to: Nedielia Viestnika Znaniia.
Edited by W. W. Bittner.

292 VIBERT, PAUL, 1851-1918.
Silhouettes contemporaines. Les hommes de mon temps.
Paris, 1900. 588p. 8.⁰ Contemporary silhouettes; the men
of my time (ca. 1900)

293 VIZETELLY, FRANCIS HORACE, 1864-
Who? When? Where? What? 20,000 facts on makers
of history, art, literature, science, and religion. New York,
Funk & Wagnalls Co. [c1934] 79p. 16 x 9cm. First published 1920.

294 THE VOLUME LIBRARY;
An encyclopedia of practical and cultural information,
brief, concise, clear, topically arranged for ready reference

and home study. 1911- New York, Educators Association
[c1940- v. illus., ports. 29cm. Each volume contains a
biography section with brief data on ca. 3000 persons.

295   WALDAU, GEORG ERNST, 1745-1817.
Thesaurus bio- et bibliographicus. Praefatus est Ioh.
Georg. Meusel. Chemnicii, Apud C. G. Hofmannum [1792]
xxxi, 303 p. 18cm. Bio-bibliographical treasury--universal
in scope.

296   WALTERS, HENRY BEAUCHAMP, 1867-
A classical dictionary of Greek and Roman antiquities,
biography, geography, and mythology. Cambridge [Eng.]
University Press, 1916. x, 1103 p. 23cm.

297   WATKINS, JOHN, fl. 1792-1831?
The universal biographical dictionary... New ed. London,
1821. 1 v. 1st ed. published in 1800 under title: A universal
biographical and historical dictionary.

298   WEBSTER'S BIOGRAPHICAL DICTIONARY;
A dictionary of names of noteworthy persons, with pronunciations and concise biographies. Springfield, Mass., G. &
C. Merriam Co. [c1964] xxxvi, 1697 p. 26cm. First published in 1943(?)

299   WHAT'S WHAT AND WHO'S WHO IN SOME WORLD AFFAIRS.
1st- year; 1938- London, J. Bale, Sons & Curnow.
v. 19cm. Vol. 1- edited by J.A.S. Pooley.

300   THE WHO-WHEN-WHAT BOOK.
Containing five hundred biographical sketches of the world's
most famous and notable men and women. Chicago, Who-
When-What Co., 1900-01. 2v. 28cm. Vol. 2 by William M.
Knox. Title varies slightly; no more published.

301   WHO'S WHO IN FREEMASONRY.
1913-1914- London, Lever Press. v. ports. 26cm.
British Freemasons.

302   WHO'S WHO IN THE UNITED NATIONS.
1st- ed.; 1951- Yonkers-on-Hudson, N. Y., C. E.
Burckel & Associates. v. ports. 23cm.

303   WILSON, HENRY.
Wonderful characters; comprising memoirs and anecdotes
of the most remarkable persons of every age and nation...
London, 1821. 3 v. An American ed. (New York, H. Bill,
1848) was issued in 1 vol. (510 p.)

304   WILSON, W LAWLER ed.
The imperial gallery of portraiture and biographical encyclopaedia. Edition de luxe. London, Iliffe, 1902. 344 p.
fol.

305   WITTE, HENNING, 1634-1696.
Diarium biographicum, in quo scriptores seculi post

natum Christum XVII. praecipui... absque nationis, religionis & professionis discrimine, juxta annum diemque cujusvis
emortualem, concisè descripti magnô adducuntur numerô.
Libro itidem eorum, in ebraica, syriaca, chaldaica [etc.]
aliisque linguis consignati, latiô recensentur idiomate, ut
eruditio praesentis aevi, tanquam in speculo, unô intuitu
cognosci queat, opus, ex variis, tam editis, quàm aliunde ac-
quisitis nomumentis literalis [sic] indefessô studiô ac maximô
labore confectum, ab Henningo Witte. Praemittitur dissertatio de multiplici libri hujus usu acceditq3 demum index, juxta
auctorum cognomina. Gedani, Sumptibus M. Hallervordii,
1688-91. 2 v. in 1. fronts. 21cm. Biographical journal; outstanding writers of the 17th century.

306   THE WOMEN'S WHO'S WHO;
    An annual record of the careers and activities of the lead-
ing women of the day. 1934-5—   London, Shaw
Pub. Co.   v. 22cm.

307   WORLD BIOGRAPHY.
    v. 1; Jan.-Dec. 1947. New York, Institute for Research in
Biography. 1136p. 24cm. monthly. Caption and running title: Who's important in every field in all countries. Biographies of world leaders assembled for the 1948 ed. of World
biography and released before publication.

308   WORLD BIOGRAPHY.
    1st-   ed. New York, Institute for Research in Biogra-
phy [c1940-   v. ports. 24-34cm. Title varies: 1st-3d
ed., 1940-46, Biographical encyclopedia of the World. Beginning in Jan. 1947, material assembled for the annual ed. is
published in a monthly periodical of the same title.

309   WORLD DIPLOMATIC DIRECTORY AND WORLD DIPLOMA-
    TIC BIOGRAPHY. 1st-2d ed.; 1950-51. London. 2 v.
25cm. No more published?

310   ---- ----World diplomatic directory service. Supplement.
no. 1-   1950-   [London]   nos. 22cm. No. 1 only
published?

311   WORLD NOBILITY AND PEERAGE.
    v. [1]-   1843-   London [etc.] Specialized Refer-
ence Pub. Co.   v. coats of arms, ports. 18-20cm.
Vols. for 1849-50 [etc.] are combined issues. Title varies:
1843-48, Annuaire de la pairie et de la noblesse de France,
des maisons souveraines de l'Europe et de la diplomatie (varies slightly). ---1849-50—1891, Annuaire de la noblesse de
France et des maisons souveraines de l'Europe. ---1892-
Annuaire de la noblesse de France.

312   YALE UNIVERSITY.
    Obituary record of graduates of Yale University... pre-
sented at the annual meeting of the alumni. 1.-   ser.;
1859-   New Haven.   v. 21-24cm.

314   ZEITGENOSSEN.
        Ein biographisches Magazin für die Geschichte unserer
        Zeit. 1.-6. Bd., 1816-1821; neue Reihe, 1.-6. Bd, 1821-1827;
        3. Reihe, 1.-6. Bd., 1829-1841. Leipzig [etc.] F. A. Brock-
        haus. 18 v. 20-21cm. Contemporaries; a biographical maga-
        zine for the history of our time. Title varies: [1.]-neue
        Reihe, Zeitgenossen. Biographien und Charakteristiken.

315   ---- ----Alphabetisches Repertorium über den Inhalt der
        Zeitgenossen. Leipzig, F. A. Brockhaus, 1821-41. 3 v. 21cm.

316   ZISCHKA, GERT A
        Allgemeines Gelehrten-Lexikon; biographisches Hand-
        wörterbuch zur Geschichte der Wissenschaften. Stuttgart, A.
        Kröner [1961] viii, 710p. 18cm. (Kröners Taschenausgabe,
        Bd. 306) General dictionary of scholars; biographical hand-
        book for the history of the sciences and learning.

NATIONAL OR AREA BIOGRAPHY

AFRICA

317   THE CENTRAL AND EAST AFRICAN WHO'S WHO FOR 1956:
An official political, social, sporting and commercial
survey of the Rhodesias, Nyasaland, Kenya, Uganda, Tanga-
nyika, Portuguese East Africa and the Belgian Congo.
Salisbury, Southern Rhodesia, Central African Who's Who
(Pvt.) ltd., 1956. 350p.

318   SEGAL, RONALD, 1932-
Political Africa; a who's who of personalities and parties.
In collaboration with Catherine Hoskyns [and] Rosalynde Ains-
lie. New York, Praeger [1961] ix, 475 p. map. 25cm.
(Books that matter)

319   WHO'S WHO IN EAST AFRICA.
1963-64—   [Nairobi, Marco Surveys]   v. illus. 26cm.

320   WHO'S WHO OF RHODESIA, MAURITIUS, CENTRAL AND
EAST AFRICA, 1965. Supplement to the Who's who of
Southern Africa. Johannesburg, Combined Publishers; [New
York, International Publications Service, 1965] 1 v. (various
pagings) illus., ports. 25cm. At head of title: Who's who of
Southern Africa (Rhodesia, Central and East Africa)

321   WHO'S WHO OF THE FEDERATION OF RHODESIA AND
NYASALAND, CENTRAL AND EAST AFRICA, 1959. Johannesburg, K. Donaldson [1959]   196p. illus. Issued as a
supplement to Who's who of southern Africa.

AFRICA, SOUTH

322   DIE AFRIKANER-PERSONEREGISTER.
Johannesburg, Voortrekkerpers [1942] 373p. ports.
Afrikaners (South African "Dutch") living and deceased, in
all walks of life.

323   THE ANGLO-AFRICAN WHO'S WHO AND BIOGRAPHICAL
SKETCH-BOOK. 1905-1910. London, G. Routledge. 6 v.
21 x 17cm. annual. No more published?

324   AUCAMP, GERHARD, ed.
Suid-Afrikaanse heldegalery; gedenkboek van figure in ons
geskiedenis wat deur hulle heldedade, baanbrekerswerk en
selfopoffering in dankbare herinnering behoort te bly.
Kaapstad, Rieck, 1947. x, 238p. ports. South African gallery
of heroes. Includes both English and Afrikaans-speaking
people.

325   MEN OF THE TIMES:
Old colonists of the Cape Colony and Orange River Colony.
Johannesburg, Transvaal Pub. Co., 1906. ix, 645p. illus.

326   MEN OF THE TIMES;
        Pioneers of the Transvaal and glimpses of South Africa.
[Johannesburg] Transvaal Pub. Co., 1905. viii, 390p. illus.

327   NAME WAT LEEF.
        Pretoria, 1946-   v. 8.º Names that live. Biograph-
ical sketches of famous South Africans.

328   NIENABER, PETRUS JOHANNES, 1910-
        Afrikaanse biografiese woordeboek. Johannesburg, L & S
Boek en Kunssentrum, 1947-   v. 22cm. Afrikaans biographical dictionary. South African biography.

329   OLSEN, RIDER FRASER, ed.
        Who's who in Natal, with which is incorporated Women of
Natal. Durban, Knox Print. & Pub. Co., 1933. 294 p. 4.º

330   ROSENTHAL, ERIC, ed.
        Encyclopaedia of Southern Africa. 3d ed. London, New
York, F. Warne [1965] viii, 628p. illus., maps. 21cm.
Includes many biographies.

331   THE SOUTH AFRICAN WOMAN'S WHO'S WHO.
        1938-   Johannesburg, Biographies (Pty.) ltd.   v.
ports. 25cm.

332   VAN ZYL, PAUL HENRIK STEPHANUS, comp.
        Die helde-album van ons vryheidstryd. Verhaal en fotos
van aanvoerders en helde uit ons vryheidstryd. Johannesburg,
Afrikaanse Pers-Boekhandel, 1944. v, 418 p. ports.,
plates, 2 maps. Illustrated biographies of numerous Boer
generals and leaders in the Anglo-Boer War (1899-1902)

333   WHO'S WHO OF SOUTHERN AFRICA.
        1905(?)-   Johannesburg [etc.] K. Donaldson.   v.
illus., ports. 26cm. irregular. Title varies: 1905-   South
African who's who. Absorbed Who's who of the Federation of
Rhodesia and Nyasaland, also Portuguese East Africa in 1959.

334   WIE IS WIE IN SUID-AFRIKA.
        1963(?)-   Johannesburg.   v. illus. 25cm. Who's
who in South Africa. Afrikaans or English.

AMERICAS

335   CORTÉS, JOSÉ DOMINGO, 1839-1884.
        Diccionario biográfico americano. Este volúmen contiene
los nombres, con los datos biográficos; enumeración de las
obras de todas las personas que se han ilustrado en las letras,
las armas, las ciencias, las artes, en el continente americano.
Paris, Tip. Lahure, 1875. xii, 552 p. port. 27cm. Dictionary of biography for the American continent[s]

336   GODOY, JOSE FRANCISCO, 1851-
        Enciclopedia biográfica de contemporáneos. Washington,
Estab. Tip. de T. W. Cadick, 1898. 322 p. illus. 25cm.
Biographical encyclopedia of contemporaries (the Americas)

ARGENTINE REPUBLIC

Anonyms and Pseudonyms

337 CUTOLO, VICENTE OSVALDO
Diccionario de alfónimos y seudónimos de la Argentina,
1800-1930. Buenos Aires, Editorial Elche, 1962. 160 p.
27cm. A dictionary of Argentine pseudonyms used in the
years 1800-1930.

338 DURÁN, LEOPOLDO
Contribución a un diccionario de seudónimos en la Argentina. Noticia prelim. de León Benaros. Buenos Aires,
Librería Huemul [1961] 60 p. illus. 27cm. Contribution
towards a dictionary of Argentine pseudonyms.

General Works

339 BIEDMA, JOSÉ JUAN, 1864-1933.
Diccionario biográfico argentino, por J. J. Biedma y J.
A. Pillado. T. 1: A-Alvarez. Buenos Aires, Impr. de M.
Biedma, 1897. 256p. No more published. Biographical dic-
tionary of the Argentine.

340 DICCIONARIO BIOGRÁFICO DE LA REPÚBLICA ARGENTINA.
1940-   Buenos Aires, A. M. Echevarrieta.   v. 18cm.
Editor: 1940-   Marcelo Echevarrieta. Biographical dictionary of the Argentine Republic.

341 DICCIONARIO HISTÓRICO ARGENTINO,
Publicado bajo la dirección de Ricardo Piccirilli, Francisco
L. Romay [y] Leoncio Gianello. Buenos Aires, Ediciones
Históricas Argentinas, 1953-54. 6 v. 24cm. Biography is
a strong feature of this dictionary of Argentine history.

342 GRAN ENCICLOPEDIA ARGENTINA TODO LO ARGENTINO
ORDENADO ALFABETICAMENTE; geografía e historia,
toponimias, biografías, ciencias, artes, letras, derecho,
economía, industria y comercio, institucións, flora y fauna,
folklore, léxico regional [por] Diego A. de Santillán. Buenos
Aires, Ediar, 1956-   v. illus. 28cm. Vols. 1-4
cover A-Ll. A national, not a general encyclopedia. Biographical entries for Argentinians are numerous.

343 GUTIÉRREZ, JUAN MARÍA, 1809-1878.
Apuntes biográficos de escritores, oradores y hombres
de estado de la República Argentina, con notas y biografías.
Buenos Aires, Impr. de Mayo, 1860. 294 p. 18cm. (Biblioteca americana, t. 7) Biographical sketches for the Argentine Republic.

344 HOMBRES DE LA ARGENTINA;
Diccionario biográfico contemporaneo. 1. -   ed. ;
1945-   Buenos Aires, Veritas. v. ports. 23cm. Title

44

varies: 1945, Diccionario biográfico de hombres de negocios, biografías contemporáneos. Men of affairs in Argentina; contemporary.

345 HOMBRES DEL DÍA, 1917-
El diccionario biográfico argentino en el cual se ha incorporado 'Who's who in Argentina, 1917.' 1.- año. Buenos Aires, Sociedad Inteligencia Sus Americana. v. 21cm. Lettered on cover: Men of the day. Spanish text followed by English.

346 INSTITUTO DE ESTUDIOS BIOGRÁFICOS, Buenos Aires.
Los directores de la República Argentina. Buenos Aires, Distribuidor: Editorial "El Universitario, " 1945. 486p. 21cm. Leaders of the Argentine Republic.

347 [LAMB, WILFRID JOHN] d. 1939.
River Plate personalities; a biographical dictionary. Author and editor: John S. Lamb. Buenos Aires, Sociedad Anónima Impr. Lamb, 1939. 351p. ports. 19cm. Almost 500 biographical sketches of Argentine personalities. 2d and enl. ed. of River Plate personalities, by Wilfrid John Lamb, first published in 1937.

348 LEVILLIER, ROBERTO, 1881-
Biografías de conquistadores de la Argentina en el siglo XVI; Tucumán. Madrid, Impr. de J. Pueyo, 1933. xxiv, 250p. facsims. 25cm. Biographies of Spanish conquistadors in the Argentine of the 16th century.

349 MARRAZZO, JAVIER
Nuevo diccionario geográfico histórico de la República Argentina. Buenos Aires, R. Radaelli, 1921. 550 p. fold. map. 28cm. Chiefly geographical and historical, but it does contain a great number of very brief biographical notices of Argentine historical figures.

350 MOLINA ARROTEA, CARLOS
Diccionario biográfico nacional, que contiene: la vida de todos los hombres de estado, escritores, poetas, militares, etc. (fallecidos) que han figurado en el país desde el descubrimiento hasta nuestros días, por Carlos Molina Arrotea, Servando García y Apolinario C. Casabal. t. 1, entrega [I]-IV: A-Ch. Buenos Aires, Impr. de M. Sanchez, 1877. viii, 279p. 28cm. Published in parts, 1877-1881. No more published. A biographical dictionary for the Argentine Republic.

351 MUZZIO, JULIO A
Diccionario histórico y biográfico de la República Argentina. Buenos Aires, Roldán, 1920. 2 v. An earlier ed. was issued (1896) with title: Diccionario histórico de la República Argentina. Historical and biographical dictionary of the Argentine Republic.

352   PARKER, WILLIAM BELMONT, 1871-1934.
Argentines of to-day.   Buenos Aires, New York, Hispanic
Society of America, 1920.   2 v. (1067 p.) ports. 17cm. (Hispanic notes & monographs, 5)

353   PERSONALIDADES DE LA ARGENTINA;
Diccionario biográfico contemporáneo. 1. -   ed. ;
1945-   Buenos Aires.   v. Argentine personalities; a
contemporary biographical dictionary. Title varies: 1. ed.,
1945, Diccionario biográfico de hombres de negocios; 2. ed.,
1947, Hombres de la Argentina.

354   QUIEN ES QUIEN EN LA ARGENTINA;
Biografías contemporaneas. año 1939-   Buenos Aires,
G. Kraft.   v. plates. 24cm. Who's who in the Argentine
Republic.

355   SCOTTO, JOSÉ ARTURO
Notas biográficas publicadas en la sección Efemérides
americanas de "La Nacion" en los años 1907-[1912. 1.]-2.
sér. Buenos Aires, L. J. Rosso [etc.] 1910-13—   5+v.
1st 4 vols. contain 893 biographies of important figures of the
Argentine.

356   SERVIDORES BENEMÉRITOS DE LA PATRIA.
Buenos Aires, 1909. 91 p. 20cm. 332 short biographical
sketches of Argentine patriots.

357   UDAONDO, ENRIQUE
Diccionario biográfico argentino... Buenos Aires, Casa
Editora "Coni," 1938. viii, 1151p. 28cm. At head of title:
Institución Mitre. Covers the period 1800-1920 in some 3300
biographies of Argentineans.

358   UDAONDO, ENRIQUE
Diccionario biográfico colonial argentino. Obra prologada
por Gregorio Araoz Alfaro. Buenos Aires, Huarpes, 1945.
980p. illus. 27cm. At head of title: Institución Mitre. Biographical dictionary of the Argentine in colonial times (to
1810)

359   YABEN, JACINTO R   1887-
Biografías argentinas y sudamericanas. Introd. del Dr.
Juan B. Terán. Buenos Aires, "Metropolis" [1938-40] 5 v.
ports. 29cm. Argentine & South American biographies. A
large proportion of the subjects of these biographies are military and naval men.

360   ZINNY, ANTONIO, 1821-1890.
Historia de los gobernadores de las provincias argentinas.
Edición reordenada, con un prólogo de Pedro Bonastre. Buenos Aires, Administración General, "Vaccaro," 1920-21. 5v.
23cm. (La Cultura argentina) History of the rulers (governors, etc.) of the Argentine provinces.

ARMENIA

361 GHAZIKEAN, ARSEN GHAZAROS
Hajkakan nor matenagitouthium eu hanragitaran haj keankhi.
Nouvelle bibliographie arménienne et encyclopédie de la vie
arménienne, 1502-1905.   Venedig, 1909-   v.
Bio-bibliographical survey of Armenia.

ASIA

362 THE ASIA WHO'S WHO.
1957-_   Hong Kong, Pan-Asia Newspaper Alliance.   v.
21cm.   1960 (3d ed.) latest?

363 BEALE, THOMAS WILLIAM, d. 1875.
An Oriental biographical dictionary, founded on materials
collected by the late Thomas William Beale.   New ed. , rev.
and enl. by Henry George Keene.   London, W. H. Allen,
1894.   vii, 431 p.   25cm.   Omits Anglo-Indians and Chinese.

364 JAPAN. GAIMUSHŌ. CHOSAKYOKU.
Gendai Tōa jimmei kan. [Tokyo]   Tōhō Kenkyūkai, 1950.
12, 152, 25, 17 p.   Register of persons in contemporary East
Asia.

365 SEKAI JIMMEI JITEN, TÔYÔ-HEN.
[Tôkyô, Tôkyô-dô, 1952]   959p.   19cm.   World biographical dictionary, Oriental section.

366 WHO'S WHO IN THE FAR EAST.
1906/07-1907/08.   Hongkong, China mail [1906-08] 2 v.
19cm.

AUSTRALASIA

367 MENNELL, PHILIP
The dictionary of Australasian biography, comprising notices of eminent colonists from the inauguration of responsible government down to the present time (1855-1892) London,
Hutchinson, 1892.   viii, 542p.   20cm.

AUSTRALIA

369 THE AUSTRALIAN ENCYCLOPAEDIA.
Edited by Arthur Wilberforce Jose and Herbert James Carter with the collaboration of T. G. Tucker.   Sydney, Angus &
Robertson, 1926-27.   2 v.   illus. , maps.   28cm.   Contains
nearly 850 biographies.

370   AUSTRALIAN MEN OF MARK...
Sydney, C. F. Maxwell [1889] 2 v. ports. 4.°

371   THE AUSTRALIAN PORTRAIT GALLERY
And memoirs of representative colonial men. [n. p. ?] 1885.
paging (?) Preface signed: T. S.

372   BOLTON, GEOFFREY CURGENVEN.
The Western Australian Legislature, 1870-1930, by G. C.
Bolton and Ann Mozley. Canberra, Australian National
University, 1961. xxii, 225 p. 21cm. (Australian parliaments:
biographical notes, 2)

373   CANBERRA, AUSTRALIA. NATIONAL LIBRARY.
Parliamentary handbook and record of elections. 1st-
ed. ; 1901-15— Canberra [etc.] v. illus. , ports. 25 cm.
Title varies: 1901-15——1932, Biographical handbook and
record of elections. Vols. for 1901-15——1957-59 issued by
the Library under its earlier name: Commonwealth National
Library.

374   FRED JOHNS'S ANNUAL
... Showing who is who in Australia. 1912 -1914. Adelaide.
3 v. No more published?

375   HEATON, Sir JOHN HENNIKER, bart. , 1848-1914.
Australian dictionary of dates and men of the time; con-
taining the history of Australasia from 1542 to May, 1879.
Sidney, G. Robertson, 1879. 2 pts. in 1 v. 26cm.

376   JOHNS, FRED, 1868-1932.
An Australian biographical dictionary. Melbourne,
Macmillan, 1934. ix, 386p. 22cm. Completed after the
author's death by B. S. Roach.

377   JOHNS, FRED, 1868-1932.
Johns's notable Australians and Who is who in
Australasia; a dictionary of biography containing records of
the careers of men and women of distinction in the Common-
wealth of Australia and the Dominion of New Zealand.
Adelaide, 1908. 366p. 21cm.

378   SERLE, PERCIVAL, 1871-
Dictionary of Australian biography. Sydney, Angus and
Robertson, 1949. 2 v. 26cm. 1030 biographies of people
who died before the end of 1942.

379   WHITINGTON, DON
Ring the bells; a dictionary of Australian federal politics.
Melbourne, Georgian House [1954] viii, 125 p. 23cm.
Some 130 biographies are included in this alphabetical diction-
ary.

380   WHO'S WHO IN AUSTRALIA.
v. [1]-   1922-   Melbourne, The Herald and weekly
times [etc.] v. ports. 19-21cm. Supersedes Fred John's
annual... (incorporating Who is who in Australasia) Title

varies: 1922, Who's who in the Commonwealth of Australia.
Imprint varies.

AUSTRIA
Anonyms and Pseudonyms

381 MARGREITER, HANS, 1873-
Tiroler Anonymen- und Pseudonymen-Lexikon, mit Regis-
ter der Autoren und Monogramme. 2. verm. und verb. Aufl.
Linz an der Donau, Winkler, 1930- v. (Archiv für
Bibliographie, Buch- und Bibliothekswesen, Beiheft 14
Dictionary of Tyrolean anonyms and pseudonymns. 1st ed.,
1912, issued under title: Beiträge zu einem tirolischen Ano-
nymen- und Pseudonymen-Lexikon.

General Works

382 BERMANN, MORITZ, 1823-1895.
Österreichisches biographisches Lexikon; genaue
Lebensbeschreibungen berühmter und denkwürdiger Personen
jedes Standes in der Österreichischen Monarchie von der
frühesten Zeit bis auf unsere Tage. Heft 1-3: A-Babenberger.
Wien, Bermann's Witwe, 1851-52. viii, 348p. Biographical
dictionary for Austria. No more published.

383 EISENBERG, LUDWIG JULIUS, 1858-
Das geistige Wien; Mittheilungen über die in Wien lebenden
Architekten, Bildhauer, Bühnenkünstler, Graphiker,
Journalisten, Maler, Musiker und Schriftsteller, von Ludwig
Eisenberg und Richard Groner. Wien, Brockhausen [etc.] 1889-
93. 5 v. in 6. Vols. 2-[5] (Jahrg. 1-4 & Jahrg. 1893) have
title: Das geistige Wien; Künstler und Schriftsteller-Lexikon.
Mittheilungen... [Vol. 5] (in 2 volumes) may be a 2-volume
edition of the work, combining Jahrg. 1-4, 1889-1892? A biographical dictionary of Viennese architects, sculptors, theatrical persons, drawers, journalists, painters, musicians
& writers.

384 FRÜHLING, MORITZ
Biographisches Handbuch der in der K. K. Österreichisch-
Ungarischen Armee und Kriegsmarine aktiv-gedienten Offiziere, Ärzte, Truppen-Rechnungsführer und sonstigen Mili-
tärbeamten jüdisches Stammes. Wien, 1911. vi, 224p. Biographical handbook of officers, physicians, financial officers
and other military officials of Jewish blood serving in the Imperial Austro-Hungarian Army and Navy.

385 FÜRST, MAX, 1846-
Biographisches Lexikon für das Gebiet zwischen Inn und
Salzach. München, J. J. Lentner, 1901. v, 241 p. 24 cm.
Biographical dictionary for the region between the Inn &
Salzach Rivers, Austria.

386   HANDBUCH DES ÖSTERREICHISCHEN NATIONAL- UND
BUNDESRATES. 1945/46-   Wien, Bilderzeitung. v.
ports. 14cm. Cover title, 1945/46-   Der österreichische
National- und Bundesrat. Includes biographical sketches of
members of the Austrian Parliament.

387   HORMAYR ZU HORTENBURG, JOSEPH, Freiherr von,
d. 1848.
Österreichischer Plutarch; oder, Leben und Bildnisse
aller Regenten und der berühmtesten Feldherren,
Staatsmänner, Gelehrten und Künstler des österreichischen
Kaiserstaates. Wien, 1807-14. 20v. 8.° The Austrian Plutarch; or, Live & portraits of all regents & the most famous
generals, statesmen, scholars & artists of the Austrian Kingdom.

388   INSTITUT FÜR LANDESKUNDE VON OBERÖSTERREICH.
Biographisches Lexikon von Oberösterreich. Bearb. von
Martha Khil. Linz a. d. Donau, Oberösterreichischer
Landesverlag, 1955-   v. (loose-leaf) 22cm. Biogra-
phical dictionary of Upper Austria.

389   KAUZ, CONSTANTIN FRANZ FLORIAN ANTON VON,
1735-1797.
Versuch einer Geschichte der oesterreichischen Gelehrten.
Frankfurt und Leipzig, J. F. Jahn, 1755. 308p. illus. 8.°
History of Austrian scholars.

390   KRACKOWIZER, FERDINAND
Biographisches Lexikon des Landes Österreich ob der
Enns. Gelehrte, Schriftsteller und Künstler Oberösterreichs
seit 1800, von Ferdinand Krackowizer und Franz Berger.
Passau, Institut fur Ostbairische Heimatforschung, 1931.
411 p. port. 19cm. Biographical dictionary of Upper Austria:
scholars, writers and artists since 1800.

391   KUNITSCH, MICHAEL VON, 1765-1835.
Biographien merkwürdiger Männer der Österreichischen
Monarchie. Grätz, 1805-12. 6 v. Biographies of noteworthy
men of the Austrian monarchy.

392   LANNER, ALOIS, ed.
Tiroler Ehrenkranz. Männergestalten aus Tirols letzter
Vergangenheit. Hrsg. unter Beziehung berufener Mitarbeiter
von Alois Lanner. Innsbruck, Verlagsanstalt Tyrolia, 1925.
271p. 8.° Figures from the Tyrol's recent past.

393   LUCA, IGNAZ DE
Das gelehrte Österreich. Ein Versuch. 2. Aufl. mit
einem Anhange. Wien,   1777-78. 1 v. (fascs. 1-12)
Contemporary writers, artists, theatrical personalities of
Austria. Vols. 2-3 (never published) were to cover deceased
authors and artists as well as learned institutions and art
institutes.

394   NEUE ÖSTERREICHISCHE BIOGRAPHIE, 1815-1918.
       Wien, Amalthea-Verlag, 1923-   v. ports. 26cm.
New Austrian biography, 1815-1918.   Vols. 1-9: Erste Abteilung,
Biographien.   Vol. 9 has title: Neue österreichische Biographie ab 1815; v. 10-   : Neue österreichische Biographie ab
1815.   Grosse Österreicher.   Vols. 1-7 edited by A. Bettelheim;
v. 8, by E. Rollett; v. 9-   by H. Studer.

395   --- ----Zweite Abteilung: Bibliographien zur Neuen österreich-
ischen Biographie, unter Mitarbeit von Jaroslav Sutnar und
Julius Stockinger zusammengestellt von Hanns Bohatta.   Wien,
Amalthea-Verlag [1925]   77 p.   26cm.

396   ÖSTERREICH LEXIKON.
       Herausgeber: Richard Bamberger und Franz Maier-Bruck.
Wien, Österreichischer Bundesverlag für Unterricht, Wissenschaft und Kunst [1966-   v. illus. 25cm.   To be in
2 vols. Vol. 1: A-K.   Dictionary of Austria.   Includes a substantial amount of biography.

397   ÖSTERREICHER DER GEGENWART;
       Lexikon schöpferischer und schaffender Zeitgenossen.
[Herausgeber: Österreichisches Institut.   Bearbeitung: Robert
Teichl] Wien, Österreichisches Stattsdruckerei, 1951.   xi,
419 p.   21cm.   Around 250 Austrians of the present.

398   ÖSTERREICHISCHES BIOGRAPHISCHES LEXIKON, 1815-1950.
       Hrsg. von der Österreichischen Akademie der Wissenschaf-
ten unter der Leitung von Leo Santifaller, bearb. von Eva Obermeyer.   Graz, H. Böhlaus Nachf. , 1957 [i. e. 1954]-   v.
24cm.   Austrian biographical dictionary for the years 1815-
1950.   Issued in parts.

399   PARTISCH, HUBERT
       Österreicher aus sudetendeutschem Stamme.   Wien,
1961-   v. 19cm.   (Forschungs- und Kulturstelle der
Österreicher aus dem Donau-, Sudeten- und Karpatenraum.
Wissenschaftliche Reihe, Buch Nr. 5) Austrians of Sudeten
German origin.

400   PEZZL, JOHANN, 1756-1823.
       Oesterreichische Biographien; oder, Lebensbeschreib-
ungen seiner berühmtesten Regenten und Helden.   Wien,
1791. 4 v.   8.º   Austrian biographies; or, Lives of the
country's most famous regents and heroes.

401   REICHL, KURT
       Lexikon der Persönlichkeiten und Unternehmungen:
Steiermark.   Graz, Leykam-Verlag [1955] 558p. illus.
21cm.   Dictionary of personalities and enterprises: Styria,
Austria.

402   SARTORI, FRANZ, 1782-1832.
       Pantheon denkwürdiger Wunderthaten, volksthümlicher
Heroen und furchtbarer Empörer des oesterreichischen

Gesammt-Reiches. Wien, Haas, 1816. 3 v. 8.° Pantheon of memorable deeds, national heroes and formidable warriors of the Austrian Empire.

403. "WER IST WER";

Lexikon österreichischer Zeitgenossen. Wien [Selbstverlag des Biographischen Lexikons "Wer ist wer"] 1937. 419 p. 21cm. Who's who; dictionary of contemporary Austrians. Edited by Robert Teichl and Paul Emödi.

404 WER IST WER IN ÖSTERREICH.

1. - ; 1951- Wien [E. Huttern] v. ports. 30cm. Who's who in Austria.

405 WHO'S WHO IN AUSTRIA.

1954- [Montreal] Intercontinental Book and Pub. Co. [etc.] v. 21cm. Editor: 1954- S. Taylor. Vol. for 1954- published in Zurich.

406 WURZBACH, CONSTANTIN, Ritter von Tannenberg, 1818-1893.

Biographisches Lexikon des Kaiserthums Oesterreich, enthaltend die Lebensskizzen der denkwürdigen Personen, welche seit 1750 in den österreichischen Kronländern geboren wurden oder darin gelebt und gewirkt haben. Wien, L. C. Zamarski [etc.] 1856-91. 60 v. fold. geneal. tables. 22cm.

407 ---- ----Register zu den Nachträgen. Wien, Gilhofer & Ranschburg, 1923. 16p. 23cm. Index to the additions in vols. 9, 11, 14, 22-24, 26 and 28.

Biographical dictionary of the Austrian monarchy, 18th-19th centuries.

BALKAN PENINSULA

408 ENCYCLOPÉDIE BALKANIQUE PERMANENTE.

Publiée sous la direction de Léon Savadjian. Paris, Société générale d'imprimerie et d'édition, 1936- v. maps. 27cm. Each vol. arranged alphabetically as a unit. Includes biography. Covers Albania, Bulgaria, Greece, Rumania, Turkey and Yugoslavia; includes biographical sketches.

409 THE NEAR EAST YEAR BOOK AND WHO'S WHO.

A survey of the affairs political, economical and social of Yugoslavia, Roumania, Bulgaria, Greece and Turkey. 1927- London, The Near East, ltd. v. fold. maps. 22cm. Primarily statistical. At the end is a brief who's who.

BALTIC PROVINCES

410 EESTI BIOGRAAFILINE LEKSIKON.

Toimetus: A. R. Cederberg[et al.] Tartus, K.-ü. Loodus, 1926-29. xviii, 643p. 24cm. (Akadeemilise ajaloo-seltsi toimetused, 2. Academicae Societatis Historicae scripta, 2. Estonia) The Estonian biographical dictionary.

411   FROBEEN, I   G
Rigasche Biographieen, nebst einigen Familien-Nachrichten, Jubiläums-Feiern, etc. Aus den 'Rigaschen Stadt-Blättern' vom Jahre 1810 bis 1879 incl., mit Ergänzungen und Zusätzen, zum Theil aus dem seit dem Jahre 1858 in Riga erscheinenden 'Rigaschen Almanach' bis 1880 incl. Riga, 1881-84. 3 v. Biographies of natives and residents of the city of Riga.

412   GADEBUSCH, FRIEDRICH KONRAD, 1719-1788.
Livländische Bibliothek nach alphabetischer Ordnung. Riga, J. F. Hartknoch, 1777. 3 v. 20cm. J. B. Fischer's Beyträge und Berichtigungen to the above was published as v. 4 of A. W. Hupel's Nordische Miscellanean. Riga, 1872. A bio-bibliography of Livonian personalities (Livonia was a Baltic province of the Russian Empire at this time with a large German-speaking population.)

413   MEYER, WILLIAM
Baltische Studenten in Kiel 1665-1865. Kiel, Druck von Vollbehr & Riepen, 1930. 148p. 23cm. (Mitteilungen der Gesellschaft für Kieler Stadtgeschichte, Nr. 35) Contains 217 biographies of students from the Baltic provinces in Kiel.

414   PHRAGMENIUS, JONAS JOANNES
Riga literata. Rostochii [1699] 1 v. 4.º Literary Riga; writers & scholars in the Baltic city.

415   RECKE, JOHANN FRIEDRICH VON, 1764-1846.
Allgemeines Schriftsteller- und Gelehrten-Lexikon der Provinzen Livland, Esthland und Kurland. Bearb. von Johann Friedrich von Recke und Karl Eduard Napiersky. Mitau, J. F. Steffenhagen, 1827-32. 4 v. 21cm. Author dictionary for the Baltic regions of Livonia, Estonia & Courland.

416   ---- ----Nachträge und Fortsetzungen, unter Mitwirkung von C. E. Napiersky bearb. von Theodor Beise. Mitau, J. F. Steffenhagen, 1859-61. 2 v. 21cm.

417   [SCHULTZ, GEORG JULIUS] 1808-1875.
Dorpats Grössen und Typen vor vierzig Jahren, von Dr. Bertram [pseud.] Dorpat, W. Gläser, 1868. 73 p. 18cm. Dorpat's (or Tartu's) great men and characters of the last 40 years.

BELGIUM

Bibliography, Indexes, Etc.

418   ACADÉMIE ROYALE DES SCIENCES, DES LETTRES ET DES BEAUX-ARTS DE BELGIQUE, BRUSSELS. Annuaire.
(Indexes)
Table des notices biographiques publiées dans l'Annuaire (1835-1914) par Félicien Leuridant. Bruxelles, Hayez, 1919.

55p. 19cm. Additional tables included in the Annuaire for
1915-1919 (81-85 années) and in Complément, 1915-1926.
(Annuaire, 92. année, 1926) etc.   An index to biographical
notices of Belgians appearing in the Annuaire of the Academy.

Anonyms and Pseudonyms

419   DELECOURT, JULES VICTOR, 1835-1906.
Dictionnaire des anonymes et pseudonymes (XVe siècle-
1900) Mis en ordre et enrichi par G. de Le Court.   Bruxelles,
Académie royale de Belgique, 1960-   v. 25cm.   At
head of title: Bibliographie nationale. Dictionary of Belgian
anonyms & pseudonyms (15th century-1900)

420   DELECOURT, JULES VICTOR, 1835-1906.
Essai d'un dictionnaire des ouvrages anonymes et pseudonymes publiées en Belgique au XIXe siècle et principalement
depuis 1830.   Bruxelles, Heusaner, 1863.   iii, 550p.   Belgian anonymous and pseudonymous works.

421   LA MONTAGNE, VICTOR ALEXIS DE.
Vlaamsche pseudoniemen.   Bibliographische opzoekingen.
Roeselare (Roulers) De Seyn-Verhougstraete, 1884.   xiii,
132 p.   8.º   Flemish pseudonyms.

General Works

422   ACADÉMIE ROYALE DES SCIENCES D'OUTRE MER.
Biographie coloniale belge.   Belgische koloniale biografie.
Bruxelles, Falk, 1948-   v. illus., ports. 25cm.
Biographical dictionary of Belgians in the colonies of the
mother country.

423   ACADÉMIE ROYALE DES SCIENCES, DES LETTRES ET DES
BEAUX-ARTS DE BELGIQUE, BRUSSELS.
Biographie nationale.   Bruxelles, H. Thiry-Van
Buggenhoudt [etc.] 1866-19   v. Vols. 29-   are
supplementary volumes. The Belgian national biography.

424   ACADÉMIE ROYALE DES SCIENCES, DES LETTRES ET DES
BEAUX-ARTS DE BELGIQUE, BRUSSELS.
Notices biographiques & bibliographiques concernant les
membres, les correspondants & les associés.   1854-1907/09.
Bruxelles, Hayez, 1854-1909.   5v. 18cm.   Brief biographies,
longer bibliographies.

425   ADER, JEAN JOSEPH, 1796-1859.
Plutarque des Pays-Bas; ou, Vies des hommes illustres
de ce royaume.   Précédé d'une introduction historique.
Bruxelles, Laurent frères, 1828.   3v. 8.º   The Plutarch of
the Low Countries; or, Lives of illustrious men of this kingdom (Belgium & the Netherlands)

426   ALBUM BIOGRAPHIQUE DES BELGES CÉLÈBRES,
dédié à S. A. R. Mgr. le duc de Brabant. Bruxelles,
J. A. Chabannes, 1845. 2 v. plates, ports. 22cm.
Biographical album of celebrated Belgians.

427   BECDELIÈVRE-HAMAL, ANTOINE GABRIEL DE, comte,
1800-1863.
Biographie liégoise; ou, Précis historique et chronologique
de toutes les personnes qui se sont rendues célèbres par leurs
talens, leurs vertus ou leurs actions dans l'ancien diocèse et
pays de Liége, les duchés de Limbourg et de Bouillon, le
pays de Stavelot; et la ville de Maestricht; depuis les temps
les plus reculés jusqu'à nos jours. Bibliographie liégoise.
Liège, Impr. de Jeunehomme frères, 1836-37. 2v. 23cm.
Includes bio-bibliography of the diocese and region around
Liège, the duchy of Limbourg, etc.

428   BEVEL, MAURICE LOUIS
Le dictionnaire colonial (encyclopédie) Explication de plus
de 8.000 noms et expressions se rapportant aux diverses
activités coloniales, depuis l'époque héroique jusqu'aux
temps présents. 3. éd. contenant une carte au 1/4.000.000
et un supplément. Bruxelles, Impr. E. Guyot, 1955. 202,
26p. illus., maps. 23cm. Very brief identifying data for
people connected with colonial activities, especially in the
Belgian Congo.

429   BIOGRAPHIE DES HOMMES REMARQUABLES DE LA
FLANDRE OCCIDENTALE. Bruges, Vandecasteele-
Werbrouck, 1843-49. 4 v. in 2. 22cm. Compiled by C. L.
Carton and others. Famous men of the West Flemish region
of Belgium.

431   DELVENNE, MATHIEU GUILLAUME, 1778-1843.
Biographie du royaume des Pays-Bas, ancienne et moderne;
ou, Histoire agrégée, par ordre alphabétique, de la vie publique et privée des Belges et des Hollandais qui se sont fait
remarquer par leurs écrits, leurs actions, leurs talens, leurs
vertus, ou leurs crimes, extraite d'un grand nombre d'auteurs
anciens et modernes, et augmentée de beaucoup d'articles qui
ne se trouvent rapportés dans aucune biographie. Liege,
Ve, J. Desoer, 1828-29. 2v. 21cm. Biographical dictionary
for the Low Countries (Belgium and Holland)

432   DHONDT, JAN, 1915-
Instruments biographiques pour l'histoire contemporaine
de la Belgique [par] J. Dhondt & S. Vervaeck. 2. éd. Louvain, Éditions Nauwelaerts, 1964. 86p. 24cm. (Centre in-
teruniversitaire d'histoire contemporaine. Cahiers, 13) A

bibliography of Belgian biographical dictionaries & collections.

433   DICTIONNAIRE HISTORIQUE; OU, HISTOIRE ABREGEE DE TOUS LES HOMMES, nés dans les XVII provinces belgiques, qui se sont fait un nom par le génie, les talens...&c. depuis la naissance de J. C. jusqu'à nos jours. Pour servir de supplément aux Délices des Pays-Bays [par J. B. Christyn] Paris, et se trouvent à Anvers, 1786. 2 v. 12. Extracted from François Xavier de Feller's 'Dictionnaire historique,' later entitled 'Biographie universelle.' Cf. British Museum. An historical dictionary; or, Abridged history of all men born in the 17 Belgian provinces who have made a name for themselves through their genius, talents, etc.--after the birth of Christ to the present.

434   DU BUS DE WARNAFFE, CHARLES, vicomte.

Les Congrès national. Biographies des membres du Congrès national et du Gouvernement provisoire, 1830-1831. Par vicomte Du Bus de Warnaffe et Carl Beyaert. Avec une introd. du comte Louis de Lichtervelde. Bruxelles, Van Oest, 1930. 135 p. illus. 4.° Biographies of members of the Belgian National Congress of 1830-1831.

435   FOPPENS, JEAN FRANCOIS, 1689-1761.

Bibliotheca Belgica; sive, Virorum in Belgio vita, scriptisque illustrium catalogus, librorumque nomenclatura; continens scriptores à clariss. viris Valerio Andrea, Auberto Miraeo, Francisco Sweertio, aliisque, recensitos, usque ad annum MDCLXXX. Bruxellis, Per Petrum Foppens, 1739. 2 v. ports. 27 cm. Bio-bibliography of Belgium to the year 1680.

436   GÉLIS, JEAN BAPTISTE

Précis de biographie belge. La Ferté-sous-Jouarre, Impr. de Guédon, 1853. 153 p. An epitome of Belgian biography.

437   HASSELT, ANDRÉ HENRI CONSTANT VAN, 1806-1874.

Biographie nationale; vie des hommes et des femmes illustres de la Belgique, depuis les temps les plus réculés jusqu'à nos jours. Bruxelles [1855?] 2 pts. 4.° General Belgian biography from the earliest times to the present.

438   HAULLEVILLE, PROSPER CHARLES ALEXANDRE, baron de

Portraits et silhouettes. Bruxelles, P. Lacomblez, 1892-93. 2 v. 16.° Biography of famous Belgians.

439   [HENRY, ALBERT] 1870-

La Chambre des représentants en 1894-95. Bruxelles, Société belge de librairie, 1896. 486p. plates, ports. 19cm. Preface signed: Albert Henry, Francois Livrauw. Introd. signed: Alfred de Ridder. Biographies of 152 deputies (Chamber of Representatives of the Belgian Legislative Corps)

440   JANSSENS, ÉDOUARD.
     Les belges au Congo. Notices biographiques, par Édouard
     Janssens et Albert Cateaux. Anvers, Impr. de J. van Hille
     de Backer, 1908-12. 3v. 8.° The Belgians in the Congo;
     biographical notices.

441   LAROIÈRE, LOUIS DE
     Panthéon militaire; ou, Mémorial des généraux belges,
     inspecteurs généraux du service de santé et intendants in
     chief, décédés depuis 1830. Bruges, 1880. 587p. Belgian
     military personnel who died after 1830 (to 1880)

442   LEBROCQUY, GUILLAUME
     Types et profils parlementaires. Paris, Brux, 1873-74.
     2 v. Belgian parliament members and statesmen. Vol. 2
     has imprint: Ixelles, G. Lebrocquy.

443   LECOUVET, FERDINAND F   J
     Tournay littéraire; ou, Recherches sur la vie et les tra-
     vaux d'écrivains appartenant par leur naissance ou leur séjour
     à l'ancienne province de Tournay-Tournesis. 1. ptie. Gand,
     1861. 1 v. Bio-bibliography of the old Belgian province of
     Tournai. No more published? Only 100 copies printed.

444   LIVRAUW, FRANCOIS
     Galérie nationale. Le Parlement belge en 1900-1902. La
     Chambre des représentants. Le Sénat. Ed. nouv., revue et
     mise à jour par François Livrauw. Bruxelles, 1901. 628 p.
     260 biographies of Belgian Parliament members, 1900-1902.

445   LE LIVRE BLEU;
     Recueil biographique. 1950-   Bruxelles, F. Larcier.
     v. 22cm. 1950 vol. the only one published? A who's who
     for Belgium.

446   [MAELEN, PHILIPPE MARIE GUILLAUME VAN DER] 1795-
     1869.
     Dictionnaire des hommes de lettres, des savans, et des
     artistes de la Belgique; presentant l'énumération de leurs
     principaux ouvrages; suivi de la description des principales
     collections que renferme l'Établissement géographique de
     Bruxelles. Bruxelles, Établissement géographique, fondé
     par Ph. Vandermaelen, 1837. iv, [3]-264 p. 25cm. Dic-
     tionary of men of letters, scholars and artists of Belgium.

447   MATTHIEU, ERNEST ANTOINE JOSEPH GHISLAIN, 1851-
     Biographie du Hainaut. Enghien, A. Spinet, 1902-05.
     2 v. 25cm. Biography of the Belgian province of Hainaut.

448   NÉCROLOGE LIÉGEOIS POUR 1852(?) 1855, 1860, 1864(?)
     Liège, 185 -64. 4 v. Necrology for the Province of
     Liege for the years mentioned. Edited by U.C. (i.e. Ulysse
     Capitaine) 4 vols. or only 2 vols. issued? E.g., British
     Museum has vols. for 1855 & 1860 only.

449   LA NOBLESSE BELGE.
        1847-   Bruxelles, A.van Dale [etc.]   v.   illus. , ports.
18-20cm.   Title varies: 1847-1889, Annuaire de la noblesse
Belgique.   The Belgian nobility.   With biographical data.

450   NOS CONTEMPORAINS.
        Portraits et biographies des personnalités belges ou rési-
dant en Belgique, connues par l'oeuvre littéraire, artistique
ou scientifique, ou par l'action politique, par influence morale
ou sociale.   Ixelles-Bruxelles, Impr. économique, A. Breuer,
1904.   500 p.   ports.   28cm.   Issued in parts, 1902-1904, and
edited by A. Breuer and Ch. Donos.   Our contemporaries.
Portraits & biographies of Belgian personalities...

451   LE PARLEMENT BELGE, 1930.
        Préf. de Léon Troclet.   Bruxelles, Kryn [1930]   599 p.
16.°   Biographies of members of the Belgian Parliament in
1930.

452   LE PARLEMENT BELGE.
        Het Belgisch Parlement.   Bruxelles, "Notre temps, " 1938.
2 v.   illus.   24cm.   Biographies of members of the Belgian
legislative body, ca. 1938.

453   PAUWELS DE VIS, JEAN, 1790-1857.
        Dictionnaire biographique des Belges, hommes et femmes,
morts et vivants, qui se sont fait remarquer par les écrits,
leurs actions, leurs talents, leurs vertus et leurs travaux
dans tous les genres, depuis les temps les plus reculés
jusqu'à nos jours.   Suivi d'une notice sur diverses puissances
de l'Europe, avec la chronologie de leurs souverains.
Bruxelles, 1843.   viii, 283p.   8.°   Biographical dictionary of
the Belgians, men & women, dead & living.

454   PAVARD, CAMILLE
        Biographie des liégeois illustres, recueillie dans divers
auteurs anciens et modernes.   Bruxelles, A. Castaigne, 1905.
vii, 388, iv p.   8.°   Biography of famous sons of Liege,
Belgium.

455   PIRON, CONSTANT FIDÈLE AMAND, 1803-1866.
        Algemeene levensbeschryving der mannen en vrouwen van
Belgie welke zich... eenen naem verworven hebben... sedert
de eerste tyden tot den dag van heden. (Byvoegsel, etc.)
Mechelen, 1860-62. 2 v.   4.°   Biographies of men & women
of Belgium, past & present.

456   PRIMS, FLORIS, 1882-
        Biographies anversoises illustrées. Galerie de portraits
anciens anversois. Traduction française sous le contrôle
de l'auteur. Anvers, 1941-   v. ports. Biographies of
renowned citizens of Antwerp.

457 ROGER, PAUL ANDRÉ, 1812-1894.
Biographie générale des Belges morts ou vivants, hommes
politiques, membres des assemblées délibérantes... et gens
de lettres. Bruxelles, 1850. 264p. 4.º General biography
of Belgians, living and dead...

458 SANDERUS, ANTONIUS, 1586-1664.
De Brugensibus eruditionis fama claris libri duo. Antverpiae, Apud Gulielmum a Tongris, 1624. 78 p. 19cm. Bio-
bibliography of learned natives of Bruges, Belgium.

459 SANDERUS, ANTONIUS, 1586-1664.
De Gandavensibus eruditionis fama claris libri tres. Ant-
verpiae, Apud Gulielmum a Tongris, 1624. 127 p. 19cm.
Bio-bibliography of learned men of Ghent, Belgium.

460 SANDERUS, ANTONIUS, 1586-1664.
De scriptoribus Flandriae libri tres. Antverpiae, Apud
Gulielmum a Tongris, 1624. 160, [8] p. 20cm. Bio-bibliog-
raphy of Flemish authors.

461 LE SÉNAT BELGE EN 1894-1898.
Bruxelles, Société belge de librairie, 1897. 557 p. illus.
19cm. (Galerie nationale) The Belgian Senate in 1894-1898.
Introd. by Baron Surmont de Volsberghe; biographies by Louis
Derie and Victor Marchal.

462 SEYN, EUGÈNE DE, 1880-
Dictionnaire biographique des sciences, des lettres et des
arts en Belgique. Bruxelles, Editions L'Avenir, 1935-36.
2 v. illus. 31cm. Biographical dictionary of the sciences,
letters and arts in Belgium.

463 SWEERTS, PIERRE FRANCOIS, 1567-1629.
Athenae Belgicae; sive, Nomenclator Infer. Germaniae
scriptorum, qui disciplinas philologicas, philosophicas,
theologicas, iuridicas, medicas et musicas illustrarunt...
Accessit eodem auct. succincta XVII. eiusdem Inf. Germ.
provinciar. nec non praecipuarum orbis bibliothecarum et
academiarum luculenta descriptio. Antverpiae, Apud
Gulielmum a Tungris, 1628. 708 (i. e. 688), [19] p. 30cm.
Bio-bibliography of Belgian authors--philologists, philosophers, theologians, lawyers, physicians and musicians.

464 [SWERT, PETRUS DE]
Necrologium aliquot utriusque sexus Romano-Catholicorum,
qui, vel scientia, vel pietate, vel zelo, pro communi Ecclesiae bono apud Belgas claruerunt, ab anno 1600 usque 1739.
Insulis Flandrum [i. e. Utrecht] J. B. Brovellio, 1739. ii,
195p. Necrology of Belgian Roman Catholics of both sexes
who had gained renown in learning, piety or zeal, 1600-1739.

465 VIGNERON, HIPPOLYTE
La Belgique militaire; biographies du Roi, des généraux...

et des officiers supérieurs qui ont contribué à fonder l'independance nationale. Bruxelles, 1855-56. 2 v. 8.⁰ Military Belgium; biographies of generals and high-ranking officers who contributed to the establishment of Belgian independence.

466 WHO'S WHO IN BELGIUM AND GRAND DUCHY OF LUXEMBOURG.
[1st]- ed. ; 1957/58- Brussels, Intercontinental Book & Pub. Co. v. 21cm. Title varies: 1957/58, Who's who in Belgium, including the Belgian Congo.

467 WIE IS DAT IN VLAANDEREN?
Biografisch lexicon van bekende tijdgenoten in Vlaams-België op politiek, administratief, rechtskundig, godsdienstig, sociaal, militair, sportief, economisch, wetenschappelijk en artistiek gebied. Brussels, Amsterdam, Elsevier, 1953. 284 p. 23cm. Who's who in Flanders; biographical dictionary of noted contemporaries in Flemish Belgium.

BOLIVIA

468 ASARRUNZ, MOISÉS, 1862-
Hombres célebres de Bolivia. De siglo a siglo. La Paz, González y Medina, 1920. 541p. Celebrated men of Bolivia.

469 PAREDES DE SALAZAR, ELSSA
Diccionario biográfico de la mujer boliviana. [1. ed.] La Paz, Ediciones "Isla" [1965] 309 p. illus. 19cm. Biographical dictionary of Bolivian women.

470 PARKER, WILLIAM BELMONT, 1871-1934.
Bolivians of to-day. 2d ed. , rev. and enl. London, New York, Hispanic Society of America, 1922. xiv, 332 p. ports. 17cm. (Hispanic notes and monographs, 3)

471 QUIEN ES QUIEN EN BOLIVIA.
1942(?)- [La Paz] Editorial Quien es Quien en Bolivia. v. 21cm. Who's who in Bolivia.

BRAZIL
Anonyms and Pseudonyms

472 PAIVA, TANCREDO DE BARROS
Achêgas a um diccionario de pseudonymos, iniciaes, abreviaturas e obras anonymas de auctores brasileiros e de estrangeiros, sobre o Brasil ou no mesmo impressas. Rio de Janeiro, J. Leite, 1929. 248 p. 24cm. Attempt at a dictionary of pseudonyms, initials, abbreviations & anonymous works of Brazilian authors.

473 SIMÕES DOS REIS, ANTONIO, 1899-
Pseudônimos brasileiros, pequenos verbetes para um

dicionario. Rio de Janeiro, Z. Valverde, 1941-   v. 19cm.
Brazilian pseudonyms.

General Works

474   ABRANCHES, DUNSHEE DE, 1868-
Governos e congressos da Republica dos Estados Unidos
do Brazil. Apontamentos biographicos sobre todos os
prezidentes e vice-prezidentes da Republica, ministros de
Estado, e senadores e deputados ao Congresso Nacional.
1889 a 1917. São Paulo, 1918. 2v. 23cm. Governing officials
and legislators of Brazil.

475   BEHAR, ELY, ed.
Vultos do Brasil; diccionario bio-bibliografico brasileiro,
ilustrado. São Paulo, Livraria Exposição do Livro [1963?]
222p. ports. 20cm. Important figures of Brazil; Brazilian
bio-bibliographical dictionary, illustrated.

476   [DIAS DA SILVA, MANUEL FRANCISCO] 1840-
Diccionario biographico de brasileiros celebres nas letras,
artes, politica, philantropia, guerra, diplomacia, industria,
sciencias e caridade, desde o anno 1500 até nossos dias, comp.
por * * * * * . Contendo cento e tres biographias. Rio de
Janeiro, E. & H. Laemmert, 1871. 192, iv p. port. 21cm.
Biographical dictionary of famous Brazilians.

477   GUARANA, ARMINDO
Dicionario bio-bibliografico sergipano. Rio de Janeiro,
Pongetti, 1925. 1 v. A bio-bibliographical dictionary of
the State of Sergipe, Brazil.

478   HENRIQUES LEAL, ANTONIO, 1828-1885.
Pantheon maranhense; ensaios biographicos dos maran-
henses illustres já fallecidos. Lisboa, Imprensa Nacional,
1873-75. 4 v. plates, ports. 22cm. Biographical essays
on famous deceased sons of the State of Maranhão, Brazil.

479   MACEDO, JOAQUIM MANUEL DE, 1820-1882.
Brazilian biographical annual. Rio de Janeiro, Typ. &
Lith. do Imperial Instituto Artistico, 1876. 3 v. 24cm.
Brief biographies of 365 persons, one for each day of the year.
Brazilian ed. (1876. 3 v.) has title: Anno biographico brazileiro.

480   PEREIRA DA COSTA, FRANCISCO AUGUSTO, 1851-
Dicionario biografico de pernambucanos celebres. Recife,
Tip. Universal, 1882. 804p. Biographical dictionary of
Brazilians in the State of Pernambuco.

481   QUEM É QUEM NO BRASIL.
1948-   São Paulo, Sociedad Brasileira de Expansão
Comercial. v. ports. 24cm. Who's who in Brazil.

482   RIBEIRO, JOSÉ JACINTHO, 1846-
Cronologia paulista. São Paulo, 1899. 3 v. illus. In-
cludes biographies of prominent persons in the State of São
Paulo, Brazil.

483   SACRAMENTO BLAKE, AUGUSTO VICTORINO ALVES DO,
1827-
Diccionario bibliographico brazileiro. Rio de Janeiro,
Typographia Nacional, 1883-1902. 7 v. 25cm. A bio-bibliographical dictionary of Brazil.

484   SEGADAS MACHADO-GUIMARÃES, ARGEU DE, 1892-
Diccionario bio-bibliografico brasileiro, de diplomacia,
politica externa e direito internacional. Rio de Janeiro,
1938. 478 p. 26cm. Brazilian bio-bibliographical dictionary
—diplomats & statesmen.

485   SISSON, SEBASTIÃO AUGUSTO, ed. and illus.
Galeria dos Brasileiros ilustres (os contemporâneos)
São Paulo, Livraria Martins [1948] 2 v. ports. 26cm. (Biblioteca historica brasileira, 18) Gallery of illustrious Brazilians (our contemporaries)

486   STUDART, GUILHERME, barão de, 1856.
Dicionario bio-bibliografico cearense. Fortaleza, Tip.
Minerva, 1915. 3 v. Bio-bibliographical dictionary of the
State of Ceara, Brazil.

487   VELHO SOBRINHO, JOÃO FRANCISCO
Dicionario bio-bibliográfico brasileiro. Rio de Janeiro,
Ministerio de Educacão e Saude, 1937-40. 2+v. Brazilian bio-
bibliographical dictionary. Was to be a 16-volume work.
Only 2 vols. published?

BRITISH GUIANA

488   WHO IS WHO IN BRITISH GUIANA.
1937-   Georgetown, The Daily chronicle.   v. ports.
21cm.

BULGARIA

489   SOFIA. INSTITUT PO ISTORIĨA NA BŬLGARSKATA
KOMUNISTICHESKA PARTIĨA.
ĨArki imena v nashata istoriĩa; kratki biografichni spravki.
Sbornik. [Sofiĩa] Bŭlgarska Komunisticheska partiĩa [1955]
237 p. 21cm. Outstanding names in our [Bulgarian Com-
munist] history; short biographical information.

BURMA

490   BURMA TRADE DIRECTORY.
No. 1-   1952-   Rangoon, Burma Commerce. v.
26cm. annual. With a who's who section.

491   WHO'S WHO IN BURMA.
1961-   Rangoon, People's Literature Committee and
House. v. 19cm. triennial.

CAMBODIA

492   BREBION, ANTOINE, 1857-1917.
Livre d'or du Cambodge, de la Cochinchine et de l'Annam, 1625-1910 (biographie) et bibliographie. Saigon, Impr. F. H. Schneider, 1910. 79 p. 23cm. Appeared originally as pt. 4 of the author's Bibliographie des voyages dans l'Indochine française du IXme au XIXme siècle. Biography and bibliography of Cambodia, Cochin China and Annam, 1625-1910, and of Frenchmen in those regions.

493   PERSONNALITÉS DU CAMBODGE.
1. -   éd. ; 1963-   Phnom-Penh [Cambodge] Réalites cambodgiennes.   v. illus., ports. 17cm. annual. Cambodian personalities. Contemporary biography.

CANADA
Bibliography, Indexes, Etc.

494   MATTHEWS, WILLIAM, 1905-
Canadian diaries and autobiographies. Berkeley, University of California Press, 1950. iii, 136p.

Anonyms and Pseudomyms

495   AUDET, FRANCOIS JOSEPH, 1867-
Pseudonymes canadiens [par] Francois-Joseph Audet et Gérard Malchelosse. Préf. de Aegidius Fauteux. Montréal, G. Ducharme, 1936. 189p. 19cm. Canadian pseudonyms.

General Works

496   BIBAUD, MAXIMILIEN, 1824-
Dictionnaire historique des hommes illustres du Canada et l'Amérique. Montréal, Bibaud et Richer, 1857. 389p. 19cm. Historical dictionary of famous men of Canada and America.

497   BIBAUD, MAXIMILIEN, 1824-
Le panthéon canadien; choix de biographies. Nouv. éd., revue, augm. et complétée jusqu'à ce jour, par Adèle et Victoria Bibaud. Montréal, J. M. Valois, 1891. vi, 320p. 23cm. The Canadian Pantheon; a selection of biographies. A biographical dictionary.

498   BIOGRAPHIES CANADIENNES-FRANCAISES.
1. -   année 1920-   Montréal.   v. illus., ports. 20-23cm. Compilers: 1. année, J. A. Fortier; 2. -   année, Raphael Ouimet.

499   LES BIOGRAPHIES FRANCAISES D'AMÉRIQUE.
        [2. éd. Montréal] Journalistes associés, 1950.   913 p.
        ports.   22cm.   Introd. signed: Noel-E. Lanoix.

500   BURPEE, LAURENCE JOHNSTONE, 1873-   ed.
        The Oxford encyclopaedia of Canadian history.   New York,
        Oxford University Press, 1926.   vi, 699 p.   20 cm.   (The
        Makers of Canada series.   Anniversary ed. Vol. 12)   "A far
        more comprehensive work than" his Index and dictionary of
        Canadian history, 1911.   Cf. Introd.

501   THE CANADIAN ALBUM.
        Men of Canada; or, Success by example, in religion, pa-
        triotism, business, law, medicine, education, and agriculture;
        containing portraits of some of Canada's chief business men,
        statesmen, farmers, men of the learned professions, and
        others.   Also, an authentic sketch of their lives.   Edited by
        Wm. Cochrane.   Brantford, Ont. , Bradley, Garretson, 1891-
        96.   5 v.   illus. , ports.   27cm.

502   CANADIAN NEWSPAPER SERVICE , LTD.
        National reference book on Canadian business personalities,
        with other general information for library, newspaper and
        individual use.   [Montreal]   v. ports. 20 cm.   Title varies:
        19   Reference book; biographical reference data and other
        general information

503   THE CANADIAN PARLIAMENTARY GUIDE.
        19   Ottawa.   v. 16cm. 1965 latest edition. Has
        biographies not only of members of the Canadian Parliament
        but also of members of the legislatures of the various provinces
        and the Privy Council.

504   THE CANADIAN WHO'S WHO.
        A handbook of Canadian biography of living characters.
        [v. 1]-   Toronto, Trans-Canada Press, 1910-   v.
        20cm.   Subtitle varies.   Latest vol. : 1961-63.

505   CHARLESWORTH, HECTOR WILLOUGHBY, 1872-
        A cyclopaedia of Canadian biography; brief biographies of
        persons distinguished in the professional, military and political
        life, and the commerce and industry of Canada, in the twentieth
        century.   Toronto, Hunter-Rose Co. , 1919. xii, 303 p. ports.
        27 cm. (National biographical series, 3)

506   DENT, JOHN CHARLES, 1841-1888, ed.
        The Canadian portrait gallery.   By John Charles Dent,
        assisted by a staff of contributors.   Toronto, J. B. Magurn,
        1880-81.   4 v.   col. ports.   28cm.

507   DICTIONARY OF CANADIAN BIOGRAPHY.
        Dictionnaire biographique du Canada.   General editor:
        George W. Brown.   Directeur adjoint: Marcel Trudel.   Sec-
        rétaire général: André Vachon.   Toronto, University of To-
        ronto Press, 1966-   v. Contents. -- v. 1. 1000-1700.

508   THE ENCYCLOPEDIA OF CANADA.
General editor: W. Stewart Wallace. Toronto, University
Associates of Canada, 1935-37. 6 v. illus. 25cm.

509   LE JEUNE, LOUIS MARIE, 1857-1935.
Dictionnaire général de biographie, histoire, littérature,
agriculture, commerce, industrie et des arts, sciences,
moeura, coutumes, institutions, politiques et religieuses du
Canada. [Ottawa] Universite d'Ottawa, 1931. 2 v. illus.
28cm. A general dictionary of Canadian biography, history,
etc.

510   MACHUM, GEORGE C
Canada's V. C. 's; the story of Canadians who have been a
awarded the Victoria Cross. A centenary memorial, 1956.
With a foreword by H. D. G. Crerar. Drawings by Francis M.
L. Barthropp. Toronto, McClelland & Stewart [1956] 208 p.
ports.

511   THE MACMILLAN DICTIONARY OF CANADIAN BIOGRAPHY,
by W. Stewart Wallace. 3d ed. , rev. and enl. London,
Macmillan; New York, St. Martin's Press, 1963. 822 p.
25cm. "Canadians...who died before 1961." Previous
editions published under title: The Dictionary of Canadian
biography.

512   MORGAN, HENRY JAMES, 1842-1913.
The Canadian men and women of the time; a handbook of
Canadian biographies of living characters. [2d ed.] Toronto, Briggs, 1912. xx, 1218p. 2 ports. 23cm. 1st ed. published in 1898. Contains some 7, 960 concise biographies.

513   MORICE, ADRIEN GABRIEL, 1859-
Dictionnaire historique des Canadiens et des Métis français de l'Ouest. Quebec, J. P. Garneau, 1908. xl, 329p.
23cm. Historical dictionary of French-Canadians and Métis
(mixed-bloods) of the Canadian Northwest.

514   NEWFOUNDLAND WHO'S WHO, 1952.
St. John's, Newfoundland Who's Who [1952] 102 p. About
200 persons are included.

515   PROMINENT MEN OF CANADA.
1931/32- Montreal, National Pub. Co. v. 19cm.
Editor: 1931/32- Ross Hamilton.

516   ROSE, GEORGE MACLEAN, 1829-1898, ed.
A cyclopaedia of Canadian biography, being chiefly men
of the time. A collection of persons distinguished in professional and political life, leaders in the commerce and industry of Canada, and successful pioneers. Toronto, Rose Pub.
Co. , 1886-88. 2 v. 24cm. (Rose's national biographical
series, 1-2)

517   A STANDARD DICTIONARY OF CANADIAN BIOGRAPHY;
The Canadian Who was who. Editors: Charles G. D.

Roberts and Arthur L. Tunnell. Toronto, Trans-Canada Press, 1934-38. 2 v. 25cm.

518   VEDETTES 1952;
Le fait français au Canada. 1. éd. Montréal, Société nouvelle de publicité, 1953. xvi, 714p. 24cm. Biographies of French-Canadians — contemporary.

519   WALLACE, WILLIAM STEWART, 1884-
The dictionary of Canadian biography. 2d ed., rev. and enl. Toronto, Macmillan Co. of Canada, 1945. 2 v. (729 p.) 24cm. 1st ed. published in 1926.

520   WHO'S WHO IN AND FROM NEWFOUNDLAND.
Also a chronology of the chief events in the history of the island since its discovery and a review of the principal commercial and industrial enterprises of the country. 19 [St. John's] R. Hibbs. v. illus., ports. 21cm.

521   WHO'S WHO IN BRITISH COLUMBIA.
A record of British Columbia men and women of today. 1931-   Victoria, S. M. Carter. v. ports. 21cm. Subtitle varies slightly.

522   WHO'S WHO IN CANADA.
An illustrated biographical record of men and women of the time. 1911-   Toronto, International Press ltd. v. in ports. 20cm. Issues for   -1915/16 called v. 5-6/7; 1921-   called 15th-year. Title varies: 19   -1921, Who's who and why; a biographical dictionary of men and women of Canada and Newfoundland (subtitle varies) —1922-1945/46, Who's who in Canada, including the British possessions in the Western Hemisphere.

523   WHO'S WHO IN WESTERN CANADA;
A biographical dictionary of notable living men and women of Western Canada. v. 1-   1911-   Vancouver, Portland, Ore. [etc.] Canadian Press Association. v. ports. 20cm.

CENTRAL AMERICA

524   HOMBRES (QUIEN ES QUIEN);
Diccionario biográfico centroamericano. t. 1-
1944-   Guatemala, Editorial Istmo. v. ports. 23cm. Editor: 1944-   J. V. Soto de Avila. Who's who in Central America.

CHILE

Bibliography, Indexes, Etc.

525   ESPEJO, JUAN LUIS, 1888-
Relaciones de méritos y servicios de funcionarios del reino de Chile (siglos XVIII y XIX) Santiago de Chile, Zamorano y Caperán, 1926. 160 p. 27 cm. 335 nos., 215 of which are

reprinted from Medina's Biblioteca hispanochilena. Bibliographical data for Chilean biography.

526   SANTIAGO DE CHILE. BIBLIOTECA NACIONAL.
Bibliografía general de Chile. Por Emilio Vaïsse, jefe de Sección en la Biblioteca Nacional de Chile. Santiago, Impr. Universitaria, 1915-   v. 23cm. Reprinted from Revista de bibliografía chilena y extranjera. Contents. --1. pte. Diccionario de autores y obras (biobibliografía y bibliografía) General bibliography of Chile; part 1: Dictionary of authors and works (bio-bibliography and bibliography)

General Works

527   DICCIONARIO BIOGRÁFICO DE CHILE.
1. -   ed.; 1936-   Santiago, Empresa Periodística "Chile."   v. 27cm. 4th ed., 1942, latest? Biographical dictionary of Chile.

528   DICCIONARIO PERSONAL DE CHILE.
Obra de consulta publicada por la Compañia Editora Whos, Carlos Pinto Duran, directorgerente. Santiago de Chile, Impr. Claret [1921] 224, 224a-224p, 225-226 p. ports. 27cm. "Diccionario personal de Chile. 1924--suplemento 1924" ([16]p.) inserted. Biographical dictionary of Chile.

529   FIGUEROA, PEDRO PABLO, 1857-1909.
Diccionario biográfico de Chile. 4. ed. Santiago, Impr. y Encuadernación Barcelona, 1897-1902. 3 v. ports. 26 cm. 1st ed., 1887; 2d, 1888; 3d, 1891. Earlier editions include names dropped from later editions & later editions add new names. Biographical dictionary of Chile.

530   FIGUEROA, PEDRO PABLO, 1857-1909.
Diccionario biográfico de estranjeros en Chile. Santiago, Impr. Moderna, 1900. 258 p. 27 cm. Biographical dictionary of aliens in Chile.

531   FIGUEROA, VIRGILIO.
Diccionario histórico, biografico y bibliográfico de Chile, por Virgilio Figueroa (Virgilio Talquino) 1800-1931. Santiago, "Balcells," 1925-31. 5 v. in 4. ports. 28 cm. Vol. 1 has title: Diccionario histórico y biográfico de Chile, 1800-1925. Biographical, historical and bibliographical dictionary of Chile.

532   GALERÍA NACIONAL;
O, Colección de biografías y retratos de hombres célebres que han actuado en Chile, escrita por los principales literatos del país, dirijida i publicada por Narciso Desmadryl. Santiago de Chile, Impr. Chilena, 1854-61. 2 v. 65 ports. Biographies and portraits of famous Chileans.

533   MEDINA, JOSÉ TORIBIO, 1852-1930.
Diccionario biográfico colonial de Chile. Santiago, Impr.

Elzeviriana, 1906. 1004p. illus., ports. 31cm. Biographical dictionary of colonial Chile.

534 PARKER, WILLIAM BELMONT, 1871-1934.
Chileans of to-day. New York, Putnam, 1920. xix, 633 p. ports. 17cm. (Hispanic notes and monographs, 4)

535 PRIETO DEL RÍO, LUIS FRANCISCO, 1857-
Muestras de errores y defectos del 'Diccionario biográfico colonial de Chile por José Toribio Medina.' Santiago, Impr. y Encuadernación Chile, 1907. 124p. 19cm. Indications of errors and defects in the Biographical dictionary of colonial Chile of José Toribio Medina.

CHINA (Including Natiʊnalist China)
Bibliography, Indexes

536 CHANG, CH'ÜN
Ku chin t'u shu chi ch'êng chung Ming jên chuan chi so yin. Hongkong, 1963. 222p. 26cm. Index of biographies of the Ming period in "Ku-chin t'u shu chi ch'êng."

537 CHUNG-KUO JEN MING TA TZ'Ŭ TIEN. (INDEXES)
A romanized index to the surnames in the Chinese biographical dictionary Chung-kuo jen-ming ta tz'ŭ-tien, compiled by M. Jean Gates. Washington, Priv. printed, 1942. 32p. 22cm. Cover title.

538 ERH SHIH WU SHIH JEN MING SO YIN.
[Peking] Chung hua shu chü, 1956. 518p. Biographical index to the Twenty-five Dynastic Histories of China. 1st edition issued in 1935.

539 LIANG, CH'I-HSIUNG, 1879-
Nien ssŭ shih chuan mu yin tê. [Shanghai] Chung huo shu chü [1940] 440p. 18cm. Index to the biographies in the Twenty-four histories of China. 1st edition issued in 1936.

540 WU, JUNG-KUANG, 1773-1843, ed.
Li tai ming jên nien p'u. [Ch'ang-sha, 1939] 5 v. 18cm. Bibliography of biographical chronologies of prominent men in Chinese history. Two earlier editions, in 10 v., were issued in 1852 and 1875.

541 WU, WÊN-CHIN
Leaders of twentieth-century China; an annotated bibliography of selected Chinese bibliographical works in the Hoover Library, by Eugene Wu. Stanford, Calif., Stanford University Press, 1956. vii, 106p. 26cm. (Hoover Institute and Library. Bibliographical series, 4)

General Works

542 ASSOCIATION FOR ASIAN STUDIES. MING BIOGRAPHICAL
HISTORY PROJECT.
Draft Ming biographies. New York, 1964-   v. 29cm.

543 BIOGRAPHIES OF MEMBERS OF THE UPPER AND LOWER
HOUSES IN CHINA. 1st ed. Edited by Peking Photo Agency.
[Peking, 1916] 11, 47, 452 p. illus. 31cm. Text in Chinese,
Japanese and English.

544 CH'ÊN, CH'I-T'IEN, comp.
Chung-kuo jên wu chuan hsüan. [Shanghai] Chung hwa shu
chü [1939] 460p. 24cm. Selected Chinese biography.

545 CHEN, I-LIN.
Chung-kuo pai ming jen chuan. [Shanghai] Chung hua shu
chü [1939] 520p. Biographies of 100 famous Chinese.

546 CH'ÊN, NAI-CH'IEN
Ch'ing tai pei chuan wên t'ung chien. [Peking] Chung hua
shu chü, 1959. 1, 1, 3, 410p. Index of epitaph biographies of
the Ch'ing dynasty (1644-1912)

547 CHIA, I-CHÜN
Chung hua min kuo ming jen chuan. [Peiping] Wen hua
hsueh she, 1933. 2 v. (8, 367, 125p.) Biographies of prominent persons of Republican China.

548 CHIANG, LIANG-FU
Li tai jên wu nien li pei chuan tsung piao. [Peking] Chung
hua shu chü [1959] 8, 753, 87 p. First published in 1937 under title: Li tai ming jên nien li pei chuan tsung piao. Another
edition was issued in 1963 in Taipei under title: Li tai jên wu
nien li t'ung p'u (?) Biographical register and index of men
in Chinese history (from tomb biographies)

549 CH'IEN, I-CHI, comp.
Pei chuan chi. [n. p.] Chiang su shu chü, 1893. 60 v.
Collection of epitaph biographies [of notables of the Ch'ing
dynasty]

550 CH'IEN HU TIAO T'U, pseud., comp.
Shang yu lu t'ung pien. [Shanghai] T'ung wen t'u shu
kuan [1916] 16 v. Brief biographies of prominent Chinese
from earliest times to ca. 1875.

551 CHIH, WEI-CH'ENG, comp.
Ch'ing tai p'u hsüeh ta shih lieh chuan. [Shanghai] T'ai
tung t'u shu chü [1928] 2 v. Biographies of Ch'ing dynasty
[1644-1912] (masters of philology?)

552 CHIN-LIANG, ed.
Chin shih jen wu chih. [Taipei] Kuo min ch'u pan she
[1955] 385p. First published in 1934. Biographical references to prominent [Chinese] individuals noted in four famous
diaries of the latter half of the 19th century.

553   THE CHINA WHO'S WHO (FOREIGN)
       A biographical dictionary. 1922 -   Shanghai, Union
       Print. & Service Agency [etc.]   v. ports. 20cm. annual.
       Title varies slightly.

554   CHINA YEARBOOK.
       1937/43 -   Taipeh, China Pub. Co.   v. annual.
       Formerly issued as the China handbook. Imprint varies.
       Includes biographical data on several hundred noteworthy
       Nationalist Chinese. Not to be confused with: The China year
       book (1912-1939) published in Shanghai by the North China
       Daily News & Herald.

555   CHUNG-HUA MIN-KUO JEN SHIH LU.
       [Taipei, Chinese Science Co., 1953] iv, 470p. Who's
       who in the Republic of China.

556   CHOU MO PAO SHE, Hongkong.
       Hsin Chung-kuo jen wu chih. [Hongkong, 1950] 2 v.
       Biographies of persons in New China (the Communist regime)

557   CHU, CHO-TS'UN
       Chung-kuo li tai ming jên chuan. [T'ai-nan, 1959] 3 v.
       (1678p.) 19cm. Biographies of prominent men in Chinese
       history. Facsimile of the 1947 Shanghai edition.

558   CHU, TE-CHÜN, ed.
       Chin tai ming jen chuan chi hsüan. [Shanghai] Wen hsin
       [1948] 158p. Selected biographies of prominent men of mod-
       ern times [in China]

559   CHUNG HUA SHU CHÜ, ed.
       Ch'ing shih lieh chuan. [Shanghai] Chung hua shu chü
       [1928] 80 v. Biographies in the History of the Ch'ing dynasty.

560   CHUNG-KUO JÊN MING TA TZ'Ŭ TIEN.
       [Shanghai, 1933] 1 v. (various pagings) 23cm. Biograph-
       ical dictionary of Chinese names, edited by Tsang Li-ho.

561   CHUNG YANG WEN WU KUNG YING SHE.
       Li tai ming chiang yen hsing lu. [Taipei, 1959] 2 v. Fa-
       mous generals in Chinese history.

562   COULING, SAMUEL, 1859-1922.
       The encyclopedia Sinica. Shanghai, Kelly and Walsh; New
       York, Oxford University Press, 1917. viii, 633 p. 28cm.
       Includes biography.

563   FAN, YIN-NAN
       Tang tai Chung-kuo ming jen lu. [Shanghai, 1931] 11, 460p.
       Biographies of prominent modern Chinese.

564   FU, JEN-HUA, ed.
       Chung-kuo tang tai ming jen chuan. [Shanghai] Shih chieh
       wen wu fu wu she [1948] 310p. Biographies of prominent con-
       temporary Chinese.

565   GENDAI SHINA JIMMEI KAN.
      [Tokyo] Gaimushō, Jōhōbu [1924] 1 v. (various pagings)
      illus. 23cm. Biographical dictionary of modern China.

566   GENDAI SHINA JIMMEI KAN.
      [Tokyo] Tōa Dōbunkai [1928] 4, 69, 957, 10 p. illus.
      23cm. Prominent men in contemporary China. A revised
      edition (?) of a work with the same title published in 1924
      (q. v.) Compiled by: Japan. Gaimushō.

567   GILES, HERBERT ALLEN, 1845-1935.
      A Chinese biographical dictionary. London, B. Quaritch,
      1898. xii,1022 p. 25cm.

568   --- ----Supplementary index to Giles' Chinese biographical
      dictionary, compiled by I. V. Gillis and Yü Ping-yüeh.
      Peiping, 1936. [88] p. 25cm.

569   HAI T'IEN CH'U PAN SHE, ed.
      Hsien tai shih liao. [Shanghai, 1935] 4 v. Historical
      materials on contemporary China (these essays are all bio-
      graphical)

570   HAN-MIN, pseud. , ed.
      Tant tai Chung-kuo jen wu chih. [n. p.] Chung liu shu
      tien [1938] 340p. Biographies of contemporary Chinese.

571   HARA, KANSHŪ, ed.
      Shin Taiwan no jimbutsu... [Taihoku, 1936] 17, 791p.
      illus. 23cm. Men of new Taiwan (i. e. Formosa) At head of
      title: Nanshin Nippon no daiissen mi tatsu shin Taiwan no jim-
      butsu.

572   HARVARD UNIVERSITY. COMMITTEE ON REGIONAL
      STUDIES.
      Biographies of Kuomintang leaders. [Cambridge] 1948.
      3 v. 28cm. Title of the Chinese original (romanized):
      Kuo min tang liu chieh chung wei ko p'ai hsi ming tan.
      Issued by the Publication Information Association of the
      Chinese Communist Party (Shu pao chien hsün shê , Kung
      ch'an tang)

573   HASHIKAWA, TOKIO, 1893-
      Chūgoku bunkakai jimbutsu sōkan. [Peking, 1940]
      4, 82, 815, 28, 12, 8p. ports. 22cm. A who's who of per-
      sonalities in Chinese cultural circles.

574   HIGUCHI, MASANORI, ed.
      Saikin Shina yōjin den. Ōsaka, Asahi shimbun sha [1941]
      1 v. Biographies of important men of recent China.

575   HSIAO, HSIAO, ed.
      Tang tai Chung-kuo ming jen chih. [Shanghai] Shih-chieh
      p'ing lun [1940] 14, 374p. Biographies of prominent men of
      contemporary China. Edited by Hsiao Hsiao and others.

576 HSÜ, LIANG-CHIH, ed.
Chung-kuo jen wu hsin chuan. [Hongkong] Tzu yu ch'u pan she [1954] 166p. New biographies of Chinese.

577 HSÜ, YING
Tang tai Chung-kuo shih yeh jen wu chih. [Shanghai] Chung hua shu chü [1948] 202p. 18cm. (Hsin chung hua ts'ung shu, chuan chi hui k'an chi i) Biographies of modern Chinese industrialists.

578 HUANG, FEN-SHENG.
Pien chiang jen wu chih. Shanghai, Cheng chung, 1946. 10, 89p. Biographies of individuals in the border provinces of China.

579 I, CHÜN-TSO.
Chung-kuo min tsu ying hsiung. [Hongkong] Ya chou [1954] 232p. Biographies of Chinese national heros.

580 JAPAN. GAIMUSHŌ. AJIAKYOKYU.
Gendai Chūgoku Chōsen jimmei kan. [Tokyo, 1953] 28, 50, 313, 6p. Biographical dictionary of contemporary Chinese & Koreans.

581 JAPAN. GAIMUSHŌ. JŌHŌBU.
Gendai Chūkaminkoku Manshūkoku jimmei kan. [Tokyo] Tōa Dōbunkai, 1937. 78, 144, 699p. illus. Who's who of the contemporary Republic of China and of Manchoukuo. An earlier edition (600p.) was issued in 1932 by: Japan. Gaimushō (?)

582 JEN, CHIA-YAO
Tang tai Chung-kuo ming jen tz'u tien. [Shanghai] Tung fang shu tien [1947] 8, 153p. Who's who in contemporary China.

583 KASUMIGASEKI KAI.
Gendai Chūgoku jimmei jiten. [Tokyo, 1962] 5, 2, 116, 789, 6p. 3 fold. charts. 22cm. Biographical dictionary of contemporary China. Issued by: Japan. Gaimushō. Ajiakyokyu.

584 LI, HSI-KENG, ed.
Chung-kuo ming jen tien. [Peking] Li-chih [1949] 78p. Dictionary of prominent Chinese. Edited by Li Hsi-keng and Fang Cheng-hsiang.

585 LI, HUAN, comp.
Kuo ch'ao ch'i hsien lei cheng ch'u pien. [n. p.] Hsiang yin Li shih k'an pen [1884-90] 294 v. Classified biographies of prominent worthies of the Ch'ing dynasty.

586 LIANG, I-CHEN.
Min tsu ying hsiung pai jen chuan. [n. p.] Ch'ing nien [1942] 2 v. Biographies of 100 national heroes of China.

587   LIANG, T'ING-TS'AN.
       Li tai jen ming sheng tsu nien piao. [Shanghai, Commer-
       cial Press, 1933] 26, 33, 279, 15, 5, 6, 4, 38 p. Tables of
       birth & death dates of men in Chinese history.

588   MANSHŪ SHINSHI ROKU.
       [Tokyo] Mammō Shiryo Kyōkai [1943] 61, 1355p. ports.
       22cm. Official register of Japanese and Chinese in Manchukuo
       (4th ed.)

589   MANSHŪKOKU MEISHI ROKU...
       [Tokyo] Jinji Kōshinjo [1934] 17, 218p. 13cm. Eminent
       men of Manchukuo.

590   MAYERS, WILLIAM FREDERICK, 1831-1878.
       The Chinese reader's manual; a handbook of biographical,
       historical, mythological and general literary reference. Re-
       printed from the original ed. [1874] Shanghai, Presbyterian
       Mission Press, 1924. xvi, 444p. 22cm.

591   MIAO, CH'ÜAN-SUN, comp.
       Hsü pei chuan chi. [n. p.] Chiang Ch'u pien i shu chu
       [pref. 1910] 24 v. Continuation to Collection of epitaph biog-
       raphies [of China]

592   MIN, ERH-CH'ANG, comp.
       Pei chuan chi pu. [Peiping] Yenching ta hsüeh kuo hsüeh
       yen chiu so [1932] 24 v. Supplement to Collection of epitaph
       biographies [of China]

593   NELLIST, GEORGE FERGUSON MITCHELL, 1889-
       Men of Shanghai and North China; a standard biographical
       reference work. 1st ed. Shanghai, Oriental Press, 1933.
       516 p. ports. 26cm.

594   PEI CHING FU WU SHE.
       Tsui chin kuan shen li li hui lu. [Peking, 1920] 20, 258p.
       Latest directory of [Chinese] government officials.

595   PERLEBERG, MAX, 1900-
       Who's who in modern China (from the beginning of the Chi-
       nese Republic to the end of 1953) Over 2000 detailed biogra-
       phies of the most important men who took part in the great
       struggle for China... together with a double index in Chinese
       and English and two charts. Hong Kong, Ye Old Printerie,
       1954. xii, 428p. col. illus. , 2 diagrs. 23cm. Title also in
       Chinese.

596   SAWAMURA, YUKIO
       Shina jinshiroku. [Osaka] Mainichi shinbunsha [1929]
       148, 79 p. A 'who's who' of China. Compiled by Sawamura
       Yukio and Ueda Toshio.

597   SCHYNS, JOSEPH, 1899-
       1500 modern Chinese novels & plays by Jos. Schyns &
       others. Present day fiction & drama in China by Su Hsueh-
       lin. Short biographies of authors by Chao Yen-sheng.

Peiping; sole distributors: Catholic University Press, 1948.
iv, lviii, 484 p. 26cm. (Scheut editions. Ser. 1, Critical
and literary studies, v. 3) Ca. 200 biographies of Chinese
writers.

598 SHINA JIMMEI JISHO...
[Tokyo, 1904] 1628, 94, 130, 4 p. facsims. 23cm. Dictionary of famous Chinese [names] Edited by Tsuneo Naniwa.

599 SHINA JIMMEI JISHO.
[Tokyo] Yamagiwara Shoten, 1926. 3 v. Biographical
dictionary of China (4th ed. ?)

600 SHINA KENKYŪKAI, Peking.
Saishin Shina kanshin roku. [Peking, 1918] 1 v. (various
pagings) 23cm. Latest register of Chinese officials.
Another edition issued in the same year (Tokyo, Fuzambo)
with collation: 76, 798, 34 p. (?)

601 SHINA MONDAI JITEN.
[Tokyo] Chūō Kōron Sha [1942] 776, 14, 144 p. 62 articles
on China; includes a biographical dictionary of China.

602 SONODA, IKKI, ed.
Hsin Chung-kuo fen sheng jen wu chih. [Translated by
Huang Hui-chüan and Tiao Ying-hua. Shanghai] Liang yu t'u
shu yin hua kung ssu [1930] 24, 578 p. Biographies of new
China by provinces.

603 SU, CH'I- CH'ANG, ed.
Tang tai jen wu. [Chungking] Ku shih [1947] 247p. Contemporary personalities [of China]

604 T'AN TANG TANG CHAI CHU, pseud. , ed.
Hsien tai Chung-kuo ming jen wai shih. [Peiping] Shih
pao she [1935] 356p. Informal sketches of famous men of
contemporary China.

605 T'ANG, LU-FENG.
Chung-kuo ming jen chuan. [Shanghai] Shih chieh shu
chü [1932] 1 v. Biographies of prominent Chinese.

606 TING, TI-SHENG, ed.
Tzu yu Chung-kuo ming jen chuan. [Taipei] Shih-chieh
wen hua fu wu she [1952] vii, 313p. Biographies of prominent men of Free China.

607 TS'AI, KUAN-LO
Ch'ing tai ch'i pai ming jên chuan. [Hongkong, 1963] 3v.
19cm. Biographies of 700 famous men of the Ch'ing Dynasty.
First published in 1937 (Shanghai, World Book Co.)

608 TZU YU CHUNG-KUO MING JEN SHIH LU
[Taipei, People's Cultural Pub. Co. , 1953] xx, 277p.
Who's who in Free China.

609   U. S. LIBRARY OF CONGRESS. ORIENTALIA DIVISION.
Eminent Chinese of the Ch'ing period (1644-1912) Edited
by Arthur W. Hummel. Washington, U. S. Govt. Print. Off. ,
1043-44. 2 v. 28cm.

610   U. S. OFFICE OF STRATEGIC SERVICES. RESEARCH
AND ANALYSIS BRANCH.
Biographical intelligence on former puppet China. Hono-
lulu, 1945. 262 l. 34cm. (Its R & A 3363)

611   WAN, CHIEH-CH'ING.
Li tai ming jên chuan chi. [Taipei, 1961] 2 v. (4, 4, 804
p.) ports. 25cm. Biographies of famous men in Chinese
history.

612   WANG, CHING
Chung-kuo ming chiang chuan. [Nanking] Chung-kuo wen
hua hsüeh hui [1934] 6, 362p. 18cm. Biographies of famous
Chinese military leaders.

613   WHO'S WHO IN CHINA.
1st-   ed. ; 1918-   Shanghai, China weekly review.
v. ports. 24-26cm. Imprint varies. Subtitle varies; 6th ed.
(1950) without subtitle. Sketches that have appeared previously in the China weekly review.

614   WHO'S WHO IN COMMUNIST CHINA.
Hong Kong, Union Research Institute [1966] v, 754p. 24cm.
1200 biographies.

615   WHO'S WHO OF AMERICAN RETURNED STUDENTS.
Peking, Tsing Hua College, 1917. viii, vi, 215, iv, iv p.
4 folded tables. 24cm. Title and text in English and Chinese.
Editors: G. T. Chao, F. T. Liang and M. Wu.

616   ---- ----Supplement I... Peking, Tsing Hua College, 1918.
63, [4] p. 24cm. Title and text in English and Chinese. No
more published?

617   WHO'S WHO OF THE CHINESE STUDENTS IN AMERICA.
[1921-   Berkeley, Calif. , Lederer, Street & Zeus Co.
v. ports. 23cm. Edited by the Chinese Students' Alliance
in the United States of America to replace the Chinese students directory.

618   WU, CH'ING TI
Hsin hai hsün nan chi. [Tientsin? Privately printed by
Chin-liang, pref. 1935] 250p. Biographies of Chinese Ch'ing
loyalists killed in 1911.

619   WU CH'IU CHUNG TZU, pseud. , ed.
Chin tai ming jen hsiao chuan. [n. p. , 1926] 3 v. Brief
biographies of prominent men of modern China.

620   YANG, CHIA-LO
Min kuo ming jen t'u chien. [Nanking] Nanking tz'u tien
kuan [1937] 2 v. Illustrated 'Who's who' of China's Republican period.

621   YANG, YIN-SHEN, 1898-
Chung-kuo hsüeh shu chia lieh chuan. Shanghai, Kuang
ming, 1948. 10, 504p. Biographies of Chinese scholars.

622   YEH, YÜN-SHÊNG, ed.
Kuang-tung shih jên chih... [Canton] Kai t'ung ch'u pan
she [1946-47] 2 v. ports. 19cm. Current biographies of
Kwangtung Province, China.

623   YÜAN, CH'ING-P'ING
Tang tai tang kuo ming jen chuan. [Canton] Ku chin t'u
shu she, 1936. 24, 524p. Biographies of prominent persons
in the Kuomintang, by Yüan Ch'ing-p'ing and others.

COLOMBIA

624   ACOSTA DE SAMPER, SOLEDAD, 1833-1903.
Biografías de hombres ilustres o notables, relativas a la
época del descubrimiento, conquista y colonización de la parte
de América denominada actualmente Ee. Uu. de Colombia.
Bogotá, Impr. de "La Luz," 1883. 447 p. 33 long biographies
followed by 254 quite brief ones of men of colonial Colombia.

625   ARBOLEDA, GUSTAVO, 1881-1938.
Diccionario biográfico y genealógico del antiguo departamento del Cauca. [3. ed.] Bogotá, Biblioteca Horizontes,
Librería Horizontes, 1962. 488p. 25cm. Biographical and
genealogical dictionary of the department of Cauca, Colombia.

626   LAVERDE AMAYA, ISIDORO
Apuntes sobre bibliografía colombiana, con Muestras es
cogidas en prosa y en verso. Con un apendice que contiene
la lista de las escritoras colombianas, las piezas dramáticas,
novelas, libros de historia y de viajes escritos por colom-
rianos [sic] Bogotá, Impr. de Zalamea Hnos, 1882. ii, viii,
240, [3]-252p. 21cm. "Seudónimos de colombianos": p. 237-
240. Colombian bio-bibliography.

627   LAVERDE AMAYA, ISIDORO.
Bibliografía colombiana. t. 1 (Abadía Méndez-Ovalle)
Bogotá, M. Rivas, 1895. iv, 296p. 24cm. Colombian bio-
bibliography; covers 19th century authors mainly. No more
published.

628   MESA ORTIZ, RAFAEL M   ed.
Colombianos ilustres. Estudios y biografías. Bogotá,
Impr. de "La República"[etc.] 1916-   v. ports. 25cm.
Vols. 1-5 have been published. Distinguished Colombians;
studies and biographies.

629   NIETO CABALLERO, LUIS EDUARDO, 1888-
Colombia joven. 1. ser. Bogotá, Arboleda & Valencia,
1918. 320 p. 20cm. 100 young Colombians; not alphabetically
arranged.

630   OSPINA, JOAQUÍN, 1875-
Diccionario biográfico y bibliográfico de Colombia. Bogotá, Editorial de Cromos, 1927-39. 3 v. ports. 24cm. Vols. 2-3 have imprint: Bogotá, Editorial Aguila. Biographical & bibliographical dictionary of Colombia.

631   OTERO MUÑOZ, GUSTAVO, 1894-
Hombres y ciudades; antología del paisaje, de las letras y de los hombres de Colombia. Bogotá, 1948. xxiii, 710 p. illus. 25cm. Chiefly biography of famous men of Colombia.

632   QUIEN ES QUIEN EN COLOMBIA.
1944-   Bogota, Editorial Kelly. v. illus. 25cm. Who's who in Colombia.

633   RIVAS, RAIMUNDO, 1899-
Los fundadores de Bogotá; estudio presentado por el delegado oficial y presidente de la Academia de historia de Colombia al Segundo Congreso de Historia y Geografía Hispanoamericanas reunido en Sevilla en mayo de 1921. 2. ed., aum. y corr. Bogotá, Editorial Selecta, J. Casís, 1938. 2 v. 23cm. (Biblioteca de historia nacional, v. 57-58) The founders of the City of Bogota, Colombia.

CONGO (Leopoldville)

634   ARTIGUE, PIERRE
Qui sont les leaders congolais? [Éd. 1961] Bruxelles, Éditions Europe-Afrique [1961] 375p. 22cm. (Collection "Carrefours africains") Who are the leaders of the Congo (Leopoldville)?

CUBA
Anonyms and Pseudonyms

635   FIGAROLA-CANEDA, DOMINGO, 1852-1926.
Diccionario cubano de seudónimos. Habana, Impr. "El Siglo XX, " 1922. xvi, 182 p. 26 cm. Dictionary of Cuban pseudonyms.

General Works

636   CALCAGNO, FRANCISCO, 1827-1903.
Diccionario biográfico cubano. Comprende hasta 1878. New-York, N. Ponce de León, 1878 [-86] viii, 727 p. 26 cm. Cuban biographical dictionary.

637   MARTÍNEZ ARANGO, FELIPE
Próceres de Santiago de Cuba, índice biográfico-alfabético. Trabajo presentado al IV Congresso Nacional de Historia. Prólogo de Leonardo Griñán Peralta. Dibujos de Josefina

González de Vilaseca. Habana, 1946. 215 p. illus., ports. 25cm. Worthies of the City of Santiago de Cuba; a biographical-alphabetical index.

638   PARKER, WILLIAM BELMONT, 1871-1934.
Cubans of to-day. New York, Putnam, 1919. xvii, 684 p. ports. 17cm. (Hispanic notes and monographs, 1)

639   PERAZA SARAUSA, FERMÍN, 1907-
Diccionario biográfico cubano. Habana, Ediciones Anuario Bibliográfico Cubano, 1951- v. 27cm. (Biblioteca del bibliotecario, 36 Cuban biografical dictionary.

640   PERAZA SARAUSA, FERMÍN, 1907-
Personalidades cubanas. [2. ed.] Gainesville, Fla., 1964- v. 28cm. (Biblioteca del bibliotecario, 51-56, 58, 73 Cuban personalities. Vol. 8, "Personalidades cubanas (Cuba en el exilio). "

641   TRELLES Y GOVÍN, CARLOS MANUEL, 1866-
Bibliografía cubana del siglo XIX [y XX, 1900-1916] Matanzas, Impr. de Quiros y Estrada, 1911-17. 10 v. 26cm. A continuation of the author's Ensayo de bibliografía cubana de los siglos XVII y XVIII. Includes biographical notes for many of the authors: Cubans of the 19th & early 20th century.

642   TRELLES Y GOVÍN, CARLOS MANUEL, 1866-
Ensayo de bibliografía cubana de los siglos XVII y XVIII. Seguido de unos apuntes para la bibliografía dominicana y portorriquena Matanzas, Impr. "El Escritorio, " 1907. xi, 228, xxviii p. 26cm.

---- ----Suplemento. Matanzas, Impr. "El Escritorio, " 1908. 76p. 27cm.

Includes biographical notes for many of the authors: Cubans of the 17th and 18th centuries.

CYPRUS
643   STEPHANIDES, P   M
Biografikon lexikon Kyprou. Cyprus who's who, 1940. Nicosia [1940] 172p. 8.º

CZECHOSLOVAKIA
Anonyms and Pseudonyms
644   DOLENSKÝ, ANTONÍN, 1884-
Slovník pseudonymů a kryptonymů v československé literatuře... 4. přepracované vydání. Praha, Nakladem vlastním, 1934. xxx,156 p. 25cm. Dictionary of Czech and Slovak pseudonyms.

645   ORMIS, JÁN VLADIMIR, 1903-
Slovník slovenských pseudonymov. [V Turc. Sv. Martine]

Slovenská národná knižnica, 1944.   366 p.   (Knihy slovenskej národnej knižnice v Turčianskom Svätom Martine, sväzok 1) A dictionary of Slovak pseudonyms.

General Works

646   BORN, IGNAZ, Edler von, 1741-1791.
Effigies virorum eruditorum atque artificium Bohemiae et Moraviae. [Prag, 1773-75] 4 v. ports. 8.° Portraits and biographical sketches of learned men and artists of Bohemia and Moravia.

647   ČESKÉ BIOGRAFIE.
Serie 1-   (sešit 1-   ); May 9, 1936-   V Praze, Tiskárna Protektorátu Čechy a Morava [etc.]   v. (loose-leaf) 26cm. Issued every 3 weeks. Title varies: May 9, 1936-Oct. 10, 1938, Ceskoslovensko. Czech biography.

648   GIERACH, ERICH, 1881-   ed.
Sudetendeutsche Lebensbilder. Im Auftrage der Deutschen Gesellschaft der Wissenschaften und Künste für die Tschecho-slowakische Republik hrsg. von Erich Gierach.   Reichenberg, Verlag Gebrüder Stiepel Gesellschaft [1926-34]   3v.   illus., ports. 26cm. Biographies of Germans in the Sudetenland.

649   HELLER, HERMANN
Mährens Männer der Gegenwart.   Biographisches Lexikon. Brünn, Winkler, 1885-92.   5v.   Moravia's men of the time; a biographical dictionary.

650   KALINA VON JÄTHENSTEIN, MATTHIAS, 1772-1848.
Nachrichten über böhmische Schriftsteller und Gelehrte, deren Lebensbeschreibungen bisher nicht bearbeitet sind. Prag, 1818-27. 3v. 9. (Königliche Böhmische Gesellschaft der Wissenschaften. Abhandlungen, Bd. 5-6; n. F., Bd. 1) Notes on Bohemian writers and scholars whose lives have not hitherto been described.

651   KULTURNÍ ADRESÁŘ ČSR.
Biografický slovník žijících kulturních pracovníků a pra-covnic, sestavil Ant. Dolenský. 1.-   ročnik; 1934- Praha, Nakl. J. Zeibrdlich, 1934-   v. illus. 21cm. Cultural directory of the Czechoslovak Republic; biographical dictionary of living cultural workers.

652   PELZEL, FRANZ MARTIN, 1734-1801.
Abbildungen böhmischer und mährischer Gelehrten, nebst kurzen Nachrichten von ihrem Leben und Werken. Prag, 1773-82. 4 v. ports. 8.° Portraits of Bohemian & Moravi-an scholars, with brief notes on their life & works.

653   WOKAUN VON WOKAUNIUS, PETER TOBIAS, RITTER VON, 1741-1805.
Chronologisches Verzeichnis der berühmtesten Männer

Böhmens. Prag, Gerle, 1779. 1 v. Chronological list of the most famous men of Bohemia.

DENMARK

Bibliography, Indexes, Etc.

654 ERICHSEN, BALDER VERMUND AAGE, 1873-
Dansk historisk bibliografi; systematisk fortegnelse over bidrag til Danmarks historie til udgangen af 1912 (i tilslutning til Bibliotheca danica) ved B. Erichsen og Alfr. Krarup. Udg. paa Carlsbergfondets bekostning. København, I kommission hos G. E. C. Gad, 1917-27. 3 v. 24 cm. Reprinted in 1929 with minor additions. Vol. 3 has title: Dansk personal-historisk bibliografi; systematisk fortegnelse over bidrag til Danmarks personalhistorie... An index-type volume with dates of birth and/or death and characterizing phrase. Continued by Dansk tidsskrift-index, 1915- , under the heading: Personal-historie. Useful as a bibliography of Danish biography.

Anonyms and Pseudonyms

655 EHRENCRON-MÜLLER, HOLGER, 1868-
Anonym- og pseudonym-lexikon for Danmark og Island til 1920 og Norge til 1814. København, H. Hagerup, 1940. 391 p. 28 cm. A dictionary of anonyms and pseudonyms for Den-mark and Iceland to 1920, and for Norway to 1814.

General Works

656 BESAETTELSENS HVEM, HVAD, HVOR.
[Redaktion: Jørgen Haestrup, Henning Poulsen og Hjalmar Petersen] København, Politikens forlag, 1965. 488p. illus. , maps. 18cm. (Politikens håndbogsserie) "Biografisk afsnit" (p. 385-476) is a dictionary of persons, chiefly Danish, prominent during the period of World War II in Denmark.

657 BRICKA, CARL FREDERIK, 1845-1903.
Dansk biografisk leksikon, tillige omfattende Norge for tidsrummet 1537-1814. Kjøbenhavn, Gyldendal, 1887-1905. 19 v. port. 23 cm. Danish biographical dictionary, also embracing Norway for the period 1537-1814.

658 DANMARKS ADELS AARBOG.
1884- København. v. illus. 15cm. The Year-book of Danish nobility includes biographical data.

659 DANSK BIOGRAFISK HAANDLEKSIKON.
Redigeret af Svend Dahl og P. Engelstoft. Kjøbenhavn, Gyldendal, 1920-26. 3 v. illus. 24cm. Danish biographical "hand" dictionary.

660 DANSK BIOGRAFISK LEKSIKON.
Grundlagt af C. F. Bricka. Redigeret af Povl Engelstoft

under medvirkning af Svend Dahl. Udg. med støtte af Carls-
bergfondet. København, J. H. Schultz, 1933-44. 27 v. A
revised and enlarged edition of C. F. Bricka's Dansk biografisk leksikon (1887-1905) Danish biographical dictionary.

661 DANSKE I UDLANDET.
1935- [København] I kommission hos R.
Naver. v. 19cm. Danes in foreign countries; with biographical data.

662 HAUCH-FAUSBØLL, THEODOR, 1879-
Slaegthaandbogen. Tillaeg til personalhistoriske
samlinger. Kjøbenhavn, Thieles bogtr., 1900. 480, 7p.
24cm. A [Danish] genealogical handbook, a supplement to
the collections of personal history. Includes biographical
materials.

663 KRAKS BLAA BOG;
Nulevende danske maend og kvinders levnedsløb. 1910-
København, Krak. v. 20cm. Subtitle varies. A Who's
who for Denmark; the careers of Danish men and women now
living.

664 MADSEN, JOHANNES, ed.
Dansk portraetgalleri... København, Dansk portraetgal-
leris forlag, 1904-09. 5 v. ports. 30-31cm. Gallery of
Danish portraits. Contents. --1. Det Kgl. Danske postvaesen.
--2. Danmarks industri- og haandvaerk. --3. Danmarks land-
brug. --4. Danmarks hovedstad. --5. Danmarks kirker.

665 MARQUARD, EMIL, 1873-1950.
Danske gesandter og gesandtskabspersonale indtil 1914.
Udg. af Rigsarkivet. København, I kommission hos Munksgaard, 1952. 493 p. 22cm. Sketches of Danish diplomatic
and consular personnel.

666 NEKROLOGISKE SAMLINGER,
Fjerding aarsskrift for efterretninger om dödsfalt og döde
med andet dertil hörende. Udg. af H. P. Selmer. 1. -2. aarg.;
1848-49. Kjöbenhavn, C. A. Reitzel, 1849-52. 2 v. 22cm.
Necrological collections [for Denmark and Norway] 1848-1849.
Vol. 2 includes the section: Efterretninger om nogle i 1848 og
1849 afdöde normænd. No more published.

667 PERSONALHISTORISK TIDSSKRIFT.
Udg. af Samfundet for dansk-norsk genealogi og personal-
historie. 1. -6. bd. , 1880-85; 2 raekke, 1. -6. bd. , 1886-91;
3. raekke, 1. -6. bd. , 1892-97; 4. raekke, 1. - bd. ; 1898-
Kjøbenhavn, I kommission hos R. Klein [etc.] v. 24cm.
A biographical periodical for Denmark & Norway.

668 RICHTER, VILHELM, 1840-1911.
Dødsfald i Danmark 1761-90, samlede efter "Adressea-
visen. " København, 1907. 127p. Necrology of Denmark,
1761-1790.

669   RICHTER, VILHELM, 1840-1911.
       100 [i. e. Hundrede] aars dødsfald (1791-1890) København
       [etc.] 1901-05.   3 v.   (1230p.)   100 years of [Danish] necrol-
       ogy (1791-1890)

670   STRUNK, ADOLPH, 1816-1888.
       Samlinger til en beskrivende catalog over portraiter af
       Danske, Norske og Holsterne.   København, Trykt hos J. H.
       Schultz, 1865.   740p.   23cm.   Published in 4 parts, 1863-65.
       Collections towards a descriptive catalog of portraits of
       Danes, Norwegians and 'Holsteiners.'

671   THISET, ANDERS, 1850-1917.
       Nyt dansk adelslexikon; fortegnelse over dansk adel i
       fortid og nutid, udg. af Foreningen til udgivelse af Danmarks
       adels aarbog.   [Af] A. Thiset og P. L. Wittrup.   Kjøben-
       havn, V. Tryde, 1904.   siv, 365p.   24cm.   New dictionary of
       the Danish nobility.

672   [TRAP, JENS PETER] 1810-1885.
       Billeder of berømte danske maend og kvinder, der have
       levet i tidsrummet fra Reformationens indførelse indtil Kong
       Frederik VII's død.   Med text af P.   København, C. Steen,
       1867-69.   3 v.   (xvi, 468p.)   130 ports.   30cm.   Portraits &
       biographical sketches of famous Danish men & women who
       lived in the period from the Reformation to the death of Fred-
       erick VII of Denmark (1863)

673   WORM, JENS
       Forsøg til et Lexicon over danske, norske og islandske
       laerde maend, som ved trykte skrifter have giord sig be-
       kiendte, saavelsom andre ustuderede, som noget have skrevet,
       hvorudi deres fødsel, betydeligste levnets omstaendigheder og
       død aarstal kortelig erindres, og deres skrifter, saavidt
       mueligt, fuldstaendig anføres af Jens Worm.   Helsingøer,
       Trykt i det Kong. bogtrykk., 1771-84.   An attempt at a dic-
       tionary of Danish, Norwegian & Icelandic scholars who have
       become well-known through their writings, as well as non-
       scholars who have written something...

DOMINICAN REPUBLIC
Anonyms and Pseudonyms

674   RODRÍGUEZ DEMORIZI, EMILIO, 1908-
       Seudónimos dominicanos.   Ciudad Trujillo, Editorial
       Montalvo, 1956.   280p.   24cm.   Pseudonyms of authors from
       the Dominican Republic.

General Works

675   DAMIRÓN, RAFAEL, 1882-
       Quién es quién en Ciudad Trujillo, directorio diplomático,
       consular, social, oficial, industrial y comercial.   [Ciudad

Trujillo] 1943. 203 p. 23cm. Who's who in Ciudad Trujillo, (now Santo Domingo) capital of the Dominican Republic.

DUTCH GUIANA
See **SURINAM**

DUTCH EAST INDIES
See **INDONESIA**

DUTCH WEST INDIES
See under **WEST INDIES**

ECUADOR

676   ANDRADE, MANUEL DE JESÚS, 1860-
Ecuador. Próceres de la independencia; índice alfabético de sus nombres con algunos bocetos biográficos. Quito, Tip. y Encuadernación de la Escuela de Artes y Oficios, 1909. 418 p. 22cm. Patriots of Ecuador's independence; alphabetical index of their names with some biographical sketches.

677   ARBOLEDA, GUSTAVO, 1881-1938.
Diccionario biográfico de la República del Ecuador, por Gustavo Arboleda R. Quito, Tip. de la Escuela de Artes y Oficios, 1910. 194p. 18cm. Biographical dictionary of the Republic of Ecuador.

678   DESTRUGE, CAMILO, b. 1836.
Album biográfico ecuatoriano. Guayaquil, Tip. El Vigilante, 1903-05. 5 v. ports. 25cm. 310 biographies of Ecuadorians.

679   DESTRUGE, CAMILO, b. 1836.
Diccionario biográfico escolar. Guayaquil, E. A. Uzcátegui, 1917. 95 p. 225 biographies of Ecuadorians. Prepared for use in schools it is an abridgment of Destruge's Album biográfico ecuatoriano.

680   PÉREZ MARCHANT, BRAULIO
Diccionario biográfico del Ecuador. Empresa editora: Editorial Ecuador. Quito, Escuela de Artes y Oficios, 1928. 515p. illus., ports. 30cm. A biographical dictionary for Ecuador.

681   [TORO RUIZ, I   ]
Más próceres de la independencia, otros complementos
y rectificaciones. [Latacunga, Ecuador, 1934] iii, 359p
20cm. More Ecuadorian patriots instrumental in the movement for independence from Spain. Additions to and corrections of 'Ecuador. Próceres de la independencia, ' by M. de
Jesus Andrade (q. v.)

ENGLAND
See GREAT BRITAIN

EUROPE

682   EUROPA.
London, Europa Publications [1939]   3 v.   26 x 21cm.
(Europa service, v. 1-3)   Loose-leaf.   Contents. --1. The
encyclopaedia of Europe. --2. European who's who. --3. European archives.

683   EUROPEAN BIOGRAPHY.
1923-   London, H. Marshall.   v. 8.°   Edited
by Clara L. Thomson.

684   FREHER, PAULUS, 1611-1682.
Theatrum virorum eruditione clarorum. In quo vitae &
scripta theologorum, jureconsultorum, medicorum & philosophorum, tàm in Germania Superiore & Inferiore, quàm in
aliis Europae regionibus, Graecia nempè, Hispania, Italia,
Gallia, Anglia, Polonia, Hungaria, Bohemia, Dania & Suecia
a seculis aliquot, ad haec usque tempora, florentium, secundum annorum emortalium seriem, tanquam variis in scenis
repraesentantur. Opus omnibus eruditis lectu jucundissimum
in quatuor partes divisum quarum I. Theologos varios.
II. Magnates, jurisconsultos & politicos. III. Medicos,
chymicos, botanicos, anatomicos, &c. IV. Philosophis,
philologos, historicos, mathematicus, poetas &c. complecti-
tur. Cum indice locupletissimo. Noribergae, Impensis J.
Hofmanni, & Typis Haeredum Andreae Knorzii, 1688. 1562
(i. e. 1566, 15) p. 82 plates (1312 ports.) 34cm. Each plate
contains 16 portraits. Universal (European) in scope: The
theatre of men famed for their learning.

685   GOETTEN, GABRIEL WILHELM, 1708-1781.
Das jetzt-lebende gelehrte Europa; oder, Nachrichten von

den vornehmsten Lebens-Umständen und Schrifften, jetztlebender europäischen Gelehrten; welche mit Fleiss gesammelt und unpartheyisch aufgesetzet hat Gabriel Wilhelm Götten.
Braunschweig, L. Schröder, 1735-40. 3v. 17cm. Title
varies slightly. E. L. Rathlef wrote most of vol. 3. Continued by Rathlef's Geschichte jetztlebender Gelehrten, 1740-
47, Strodtmann's Beyträge zur Historie der Gelahrtheit, 1748-
50 and Das Neue gelehrte Europa, 1752-81. Contemporary
learned Europe. Bio-bibliographical.

686   DAS NEUE GELEHRTE EUROPA.
       1.-20. Th.   Wolfenbüttel, J. C. Meissner [etc.] 1752-75.
       20 v. in 7. 18cm. New learned Europe; a bio-bibliography.
       Editors: 1752-56 (v. 1-8) J. C. Strodtmann. --1756-75 (v. 1-
       20) F. Stosch.

687   POTTHAST, AUGUST, 1824-1898.
       Bibliotheca historica medii aevi. Wegweiser durch die
       Geschichtswerke des europäischen Mittelalters bis 1500.
       Vollständiges Inhaltsverzeichnis zu 'Acta sanctorum' Boll. —
       Bouquet—Migne—Monum. Germ. hist. —Muratori—Rerum
       Britann. scriptores etc. Anhang: Quellenkunde für die
       Geschichte der europäischen Staaten während des Mittelalters.
       2. verb. und verm. Aufl. Berlin, W. Weber, 1896. 2 v.
       23cm. Bio-bibliography for the Middle Ages and its histo-
       rians.

688   LES PREMIERS EUROPÉENS;
       Annuaire européen illustré. 1. -   année; 1931-
       Paris, U. D. E. [etc.]   v. illus., ports. 14cm. Editor:
       1931-   Lucien Coquet. Outstanding Europeans of the day.

689   RUVIGNY AND RAINEVAL, MELVILLE AMADEUS HENRY
       DOUGLAS HEDDLE DE LA CAILLEMOTTE DE MASSUE
       DE RUVIGNY, 9th marquis of, 1868-1921.
       The nobilities of Europe. London, Melville, 1909-10.
       2 v. illus. 26cm.

690   RUVIGNY AND RAINEVAL, MELVILLE AMADEUS HENRY
       DOUGLAS HEDDLE DE LA CAILLEMOTTE DE MASSUE DE
       RUVIGNY, 9th marquis of, 1868-1921.
       The titled nobility of Europe. An international peerage,
       or "Who's who, " of the sovereigns, princes and nobles of
       Europe. London, Harrison, 1914. 1598p. coats of arms.
       27cm.

691 WHO'S WHO IN CENTRAL AND EAST-EUROPE.
1st- ed. ; 1933-34-- Zurich, Central European
Times Pub. Co. v. 21cm. biennial. Editor: 1933-34-
S. Szabó (under the pseud. Stephen Taylor)

692 WHO'S WHO IN EASTERN EUROPE.
[n. p. , 1962?- 2v. (loose-leaf) ports. 23cm. Cover
title. Contents. --[1] Albania, Bulgaria, Rumania,
Yugoslavia. --[2] Czechoslovakia, East Germany, Hungary,
Poland.

693 WHO'S WHO IN EUROPE.
éd. 1- 1964-65- Bruxelles, Éditions det Feniks.
v. 26cm. Editor: 1964-65- E. A. de Maeyer.

694 WHO'S WHO IN OCCUPIED AND SATELLITE EUROPE,
EXCLUDING FRANCE. [London] 1944. 78p. 25cm.
Cover title.

FINLAND

695 BIOGRAFINEN NIMIKIRJA.
Elämäkertoja Suomen entisiltä ja nykyajoilta toimittanut
Suomen Historiallinen Seura. Helsingissa, 1879-89. 844p.
Biographical register. Biographies of Finns of the past and
present.

696 CARPELAN, TOR, 1867-
Helsingfors universitets studentmatrikel 1828-1852. Hel-
singfors, 1928-30. ix, 245 p. 26 cm. (Skrifter utg. av
Svensk litteratursällskapet i Finland, 203) Issued in 2 parts.
Register of students at the University of Helsingfors (Hel-
sinki) 1828-1852.

697 FINLANDS RIDDERSKAPS OCH ADELS KALENDER.
1897- Helsingfors. v. 17cm. Title varies: Storfurstendömet Finlands ridderskaps och adels kalender. Calendar of Finnish nobility; with biographical material.

698 FINSK BIOGRAFISK HANDBOK;
Under medvärkan af fackmän utgifven af Tor Carpelan.
Helsingfors, G. W. Edlunds forlag, 1903. 2 v. 25cm. Fin-
nish biographical handbook.

699   KUKA KUKIN ON.
       Who's who in Finland.   [1920-   Helsingssä.
       v. 19cm.   Title varies: 1920-1941, Aikalaiskirja.

700   SUOMEN HISTORIALLINEN SEURA.
       Kansallinen elämäkerrasto.   Toimitus: Kaarlo Blomstedt
       [et al.] Porvoo, Söderström [1927-34] 5 v.   ports.   [Fin-
       nish] national biographical reference book.

701   VEM OCH VAD?
       Biografisk handbok.   1920(?)-   Helsingfors, H.
       Schildt.   v. 19cm.   Who and what?   A biographical hand-
       book [of Finland]

FRANCE
Bibliography, Indexes, Etc.

702   LIEUTAUD, SOLIMAN, b. 1795.
       Liste alphabétique de portraits français gravés jusque et y
       compris l'année 1775, faisant le complément de celle de la
       Bibliothèque historique de la France du P. Lelong, cinq vol-
       umes in-folio.   2. éd. , rev. , corr. , et considérablement
       augm.   Paris, 1846.   vi, 105 p.   32cm.   200 copies printed.
       Alphabetical list of engraved French portraits to the year
       1775.

703   LIEUTAUD, SOLIMAN, b. 1795.
       Liste des portraits dessinés, gravés ou lithographiés des
       députés à l'Assemblée nationale de 1789, avec l'indication de
       leur format et le nom des artistes à qui ils sont dus, précédés
       d'une courte notice biographique sur chaque personnage.
       Paris, 1854.   ii, 218 p.   25 x 16cm.   List of portraits, drawn,
       engraved or lithographed, of deputies at the French National
       Assembly of 1789.   Includes a brief biographical note on each
       personage.

Anonyms and Pseudonyms

704   BARBIER, ANTOINE ALEXANDRE, 1765-1825.
       Dictionnaire des ouvrages anonymes.   3. éd. , rev. et
       augm. par Olivier Barbier, René et Paul Billard.   Tome I
       [-IV] Suite de la 2. éd. des Supercheries littéraires dévoilées,
       par J.-M. Quérard, publiée par Gustave Brunet et Pierre
       Jannet.   Tome IV [-VII] Avec une table générale des noms
       réels des écrivains anonymes et pseudonymes cités dans les

deux ouvrages. Paris, P. Daffis, 1872-79. 4 v. 25cm. Issued in 8 parts. 2d ed. issued in 1822-27; 3d ed. reissued in
1882 (Paris, Féchoz et Letouzey) Dictionary of anonymous
[French & Latin] works.

705 BRUNET, GUSTAVE, 1807-1896.
  Dictionnaire des ouvrages anonymes [de Barbier] suivi des
Supercheries littéraires dévoilées [de Quérard] Supplément à
la dernière édition de ces deux ouvrages (Édition Daffis) Avec
les concours des bibliophiles et des bibliographes les plus
distingués. Paris, F. J. Féchoz, 1889. iii p. , 310 columns,
cix p. , 122 columns, xiv p. 25 cm. A supplement to the dictionaries of anonyms and pseudonyms of Barbier & Quérard.

706 COSTON, HENRY
  Dictionnaire des pseudonymes. Paris [Lectures françaises, 1961] 260 p. A dictionary of French pseudonyms.

707 [MANNE, LOUIS CHARLES JOSEPH DE] 1773-1832.
  Nouveau dictionnaire des ouvrages anonymes et pseudonymes
avec les noms des auteurs ou éditeurs, accompagné de notes
historiques et critiques, par E. D. de Manne. 3. éd. rev. ,
corr. et très augm. Lyon, N. Scheuring, 1868. vii, 607 p.
22cm. New dictionary of [French] anonymous and pseudonymous works.

708 [POINSOT, EDMOND ANTOINE] 1833-1902.
  Dictionnaire des pseudonymes, recueillis par Georges
d'Heylli [pseud.] Nouv. éd. , entièrement refondue et augm.
Paris, Dentu, 1887. iii, 559p. 19cm. Dictionary of French
pseudonyms.

709 QUÉRARD, JOSEPH MARIE, 1797-1865.
  Les supercheries littéraires dévoilées. Galerie des
écrivains français de toute l'Europe qui se sont déguisés
sous des anagrammes, des astéronymes, des cryptonymes,
des initialismes, des noms littéraires, des pseudonymes
facétieux ou bizarres, etc. 2. éd. , considérablement augmentée par Gustave Brunet et Pierre Jannet. Édition Daffis.
Paris, Féchoz et Letouzey, 1882. 3 v. 25cm. Dictionary of
French anonyms & pseudonyms. Re-issue of P. Daffis' edition of 1869-70 with new t. p. and half-title: Quérard et Barbier. Les supercheries littéraires et Les ouvrages anonymes.
Tome I-[III] Barbier's Dictionnaire, connected with this edition of Quérard by the phraseology of the half title, was issued separtely. First ed. issued 1847-53 in 5 v.

710   REBOUL, ROBERT MARIE, d. 1905.
Anonymes, pseudonymes et supercheries littéraires de
la Provence ancienne et moderne. Marseille, M. Lebon,
1878. 445p. 25cm. 100 copies printed. Anonyms & pseudonyms of Provence.

General Works

711   ALEMBERT, JEAN LEROND D', 1717-1783.
Histoire des membres de l'Académie francaise morts
depuis 1700 jusqu'en 1771, pour servir de suite aux Eloges
imprimés et lus dans les séances publiques de cette compagnie.
Paris, Moutard, 1785-87. 6v. 18cm. Vol. 1 originally issued
under title:Éloges lus dans les séances publiques de l'Académie
française... History of the members of the Académie
française, Paris, who died in the period 1700-1771.

712   ALHOY, PHILADELPHE MAURICE, 1802-1856.
Biographie parlementaire des représentants du peuple à
l'Assemblée nationale constituante de 1848. Rédigés par une
société de publicistes et d'hommes de lettres, sous la
direction de Maur. Alhoy. Paris, Vve L. Janet [1848]
xxiii, 510p. 8.º Biographies of members of the French
National Constituent Assembly of 1848-1849.

713   ANNUAIRE DIPLOMATIQUE et CONSULAIRE DE LA RÉPUB-
LIQUE FRANCAISE. 1858-   Paris, Impr. nationale.
v. 18-22cm. Brief identifying data for diplomatic and consular officials. Title varies.

714   BABIÉ DE BERCENAY, FRANÇOIS, 1761-1830?
Archives de l'honneur; ou, Notices sur la vie militaire des
généraux de brigade, adjudans-commandans, colonels, majors, chefs de bataillon et d'escadron... capitaines, lieu-
tenans et sous-lieutenans de vaisseaux, frégates et corvettes
de la Marine française, qui par leurs belles actions se sont
illustrés, par F. Babié et J. G. Saint-Sauveur. Paris,
Laurens aîné, 1805-06. 4 v. 8.º The archives of honor, or,
Notices on the military life of French generals... colonels,
majors... and naval captains, lieutenants...

715   BABIÉ DE BERCENAY, FRANCOIS, 1761-1830?
Galerie militaire; ou, Notices historiques sur les généraux
en chef, généraux de division, etc., vice-amiraux, contre-
amiraux, etc., qui ont commandé les armées françaises
depuis le commencement de la Révolution jusqu'à l'an XIII.

Par F. Barbié et L. Beaumont. Paris, Barba, an XIII [1805]
7v. ports. 18cm. Notes on French military and naval commanders.

716   [BESNARD, CR.   ]
       Nouvelle biographie industrielle, commerciale, géogra-
phique, statistique, militaire, historique, biographique,
départementale, arrondissementale, cantonale et communale
de la France. Aigre, Galletaud, 1845. 564p. 8.° Modern
biography of France.

717   BIOGRAPHICAL ANECDOTES OF THE FOUNDERS OF THE
       FRENCH REPUBLIC
       And of other eminent characters who have distinguished
themselves in the progress of the Revolution. London,
printed for Phillips [1798-99; v. 1, 1799] 2 v. front., map.
18cm. Vol. 1: New edition. Erroneously attributed by
Halkett and Laing to John Adolphus. Not alphabetical. An
"Index to the characters" at the front of each volume gives
an alphabetical approach. About 200 persons are listed.

718   BIOGRAPHIE COMPLÈTE DES 750 REPRÉSENTANTS À
       L'ASSEMBLÉE LÉGISLATIVE. Par deux journalistes.
       Nouv. éd. Paris, Pagnerre, 1849. 1 v. 32.° First pub-
lished, in the same year, under title: Biographie des 750
représentants à l'Assemblée législative, élus le 13 mai 1849
(signed E. C., de M.) Complete biography of the 750 representatives at the French National Assembly (1849)

719   BIOGRAPHIE COMPLÈTE DES TROIS CENTS SÉNATEURS,
       précédée d'un résumé historique des origines du Sénat et
du texte des lois constitutionelles. Par trois journalistes.
Paris, E. Dentu, 1876. 2 v. in 1. 17cm. Biographies
of the 300 members of the French Senate, that division of the
National Assembly provided for in the Constitutional law of
Feb. 24, 1875.

720   BIOGRAPHIE DES DÉPUTES COMPOSANT LA REPRÉSENTA-
       TION NATIONALE PENDANT LES SESSIONS DE 1820 à 1822.
       Par P*** P*****   Paris, Plancher, 1822. 1 v. 8.° Biog-
raphies of the membership of the French Chamber of Deputies,
sessions of 1820-1822.

721   BIOGRAPHIE DES FAUX PROPHÈTES VIVANS.
       Par une Société de gens de lettres. Paris, Chez Domère,

1821. 2 v. 21cm. A biographical dictionary with numerous quotations of quondam French Republicans and Bonapartists, the "false prophets" of the compilers who are probably monarchists or Bourbon sympathizers.

722 BIOGRAPHIE DES MEMBRES DU SÉNAT.
Paris, M. Lévy frères, 1852. 320 p. 12.° Members of the upper house of the French legislature as first constituted in 1852 under Louis Napoleon.

723 BIOGRAPHIE DES 900 MEMBRES DE L'ASSEMBLÉE
NATIONALE CONSTITUANTE, par une société de littérateurs et de publicistes. Paris, P.-H. Krabbe, 1849. 432 p. 8.° Biographies of the 900 members of the French National Constituent Assembly of 1848-1849.

724 BIOGRAPHIE DES 900 REPRÉSENTANTS À LA CONSTIT-
UANTE et des 750 représentants à la Législative, session de 1849. Seule éd. contenant l'adresse de tous les représentants dans Paris. Paris, V. Lecou [1849] 888p. 19cm.

725 BIOGRAPHIE DES PRÉFETS DES 86 DÉPARTEMENS DE
FRANCE. Par un sous-préfet. 7. éd., rev., corr. et considérablement augm. Paris, Chez les Marchands de nouveautés, 1826. 155 p. 11cm. Sometimes attributed to E. M. Hilaire and Lamothe-Langon. Prefects of the 86 departments of France as of 1825-1826.

726 BIOGRAPHIE DES REPRÉSENTANTS DU PEUPLE
À l'Assemblée nationale constituante, avec un tableau des députations par départements. Par les rédacteurs de "Notre histoire." Paris, Au Bureau de Notre Histoire, 1848. 378 p. 12.° By L. Girardeau, A. Patin de La Fizelière, W. L. Hughes and R. Kerambrun. Biographies of representatives at the French National Constituent Assembly of 1848-1849.

727 BIOGRAPHIE DES 750 GRANDS HOMMES COMPOSANT
L'ASSEMBLÉE LÉGISLATIVE, 1849-1852. Paris, Impr. de Maistrasse, 1849. 1 v. 32.° The 750 members of the French Legislative Assembly, 1849-1852.

728 BIOGRAPHIE DES 750 REPRÉSENTANTS DU PEUPLE
À l'Assemblée nationale, session de 1849 à 1852. Par un

ancien publiciste. Paris, Renault, 1849. 1 v. 32.º The
750 members of the French National Assembly, session of
1849-1852.

729 BIOGRAPHIE ET GALERIE HISTORIQUE DES CONTEMPOR-
AINS. Ed. complétée sur celle de la Belgique, augmentée
de plus de deux mille articles. Par une société de gens de
lettres francais et étrangers. Paris, P. Barthélemy, éditeur
et l'un des collaborateurs, 1822. 2 v. Goes only up to article
on Brueys. Contemporary Frenchmen.

730 BIOGRAPHIE IMPARTIALE DES REPRÉSENTANTS DU
PEUPLE à l'Assemblée nationale. Seule édition complète
contenant non-seulement les élections des 4 juin et 17 septembre
mais encore celles de l'Algérie et des colonies; publiée par
deux republicains, l'un de la veille, l'autre du lendemain.
Paris, V. Lecou, 1848. 1 v. 12.º Representatives at the
French National Assembly of 1848.

731 BIOGRAPHIE MODERNE; OU, DICTIONNAIRE BIOGRAPHIQUE
DE TOUS LES HOMMES MORTS ET VIVANTS qui ont mar-
qué à la fin du XVIIIe siècle et au commencement de celui-ci
par leurs écrits, leur rang, leurs emplois, leurs talents,
leurs malheurs, leurs vertus, leurs crimes. 2. éd., corr. et
augm. d'un grand nombre d'articles. Breslau, G. T. Korn,
1806. 4 v. Reworking of the Biographie moderne; ou, Dictionnaire historique des hommes...1802, by Beauchamp and
others. Biographical dictionary of Frenchmen prominent in
the French Revolutionary period and the beginning of the 19th
century.

732 BIOGRAPHIE MODERNE.
Lives of remarkable characters, who have distinguished
themselves from the commencement of the French Revolution to the present time. From the French. London, Longman, Hurst, Rees, Orme, and Brown 1811. 3 v. 23cm.
Translated from Biographie moderne; ou, Dictionnaire
historique des hommes qui se sont fait un nom en Europe
depuis 1789 jusqu'en 1802 (par Alphonse de Beauchamp,
Caubrières, Giraud, de Coiffier, et autres) Leipsick (Paris)
1802. Also published in 1814- under title: Lives of remarkable characters... A biographical dictionary of Frenchmen of
the period.

733 BIOGRAPHIE MODERNE; OU, GALERIE HISTORIQUE,
CIVILE, MILITAIRE, POLITIQUE ET JUDICIAIRE, contenant les portraits politiques des Français de l'un et de l'autre

sexe, morts ou vivants, qui se sont rendus plus ou moins célèbres depuis le commencement de la Révolution jusqu'à nos jours. 2. éd., revue, corr., considérablement augm. et ornée de 150 ports. Paris, A. Eymery, 1816. 3 v. Reprinting of the 1806 Breslau ed. of the Biographie moderne; ou, Dictionnaire biographique of Beauchamp [et al.] corrected and augmented with new articles.

734   BIOGRAPHIE NOUVELLE DES CONTEMPORAINS;
      Ou, Dictionnaire historique et raisonné de tous les hommes qui, depuis la Révolution française, ont acquis de la célébrité par leurs actions, leurs écrits, leurs erreurs, ou leurs crimes, soit en France, soit dans les pays étrangers... par A.V. Arnault, A. Jay [et al.] Paris, Librairie historique, 1820-25. 20 v. ports. 21cm. Frenchmen prominent in the early years of the 19th century.

735   BIOGRAPHIE PITTORESQUE DES DÉPUTÉS.
      Portraits, moeurs et costumes. Paris, Delaunay, Pelicier et Ponthieu [etc.] 1820. xviii, 295 p. ports. 21cm. According to Barbier the authors were Henri de Latouche [and others] Sketches of members of the French Chamber of Deputies, 1814-1820.

736   BIOGRAPHIE SPÉCIALE DES PAIRS ET DES DÉPUTÉS DU
      ROYAUME, session de 1818-1819. Paris, Beaucé, 1819-20. 2 v. 8.° Vol. 2 has title: Biographie des pairs... qui ont siégé dans les deux dernières sessions. French political figures and members of the Chamber of Deputies, session of 1818-1819.

737   BIOGRAPHIE STATISTIQUE, PAR ORDRE ALPHABÉTIQUE
      DE DÉPARTEMENTS, de MM. les membres de la Chambre des députés, rédigée sur les documents authentiques de la législature de juillet 1842 à juillet 1846, par deux hommes de lettres. Paris, Dauvin et Fontaine, 1846. 1 v. 8.° Members of the French Chamber of Deputies, 1842-1846.

738   BIOGRAPHIES DES PRINCIPALES PERSONNALITÉS
      FRANÇAIS décédées au cours de l'année. 1956- Paris. v. 22cm. Editor: 1956- H. Temerson. Biographies of the principal French personalities who have died in the course of the year.

739   [BOREL D'HAUTERIVE, ANDRÉ FRANÇOIS JOSEPH] 1812-
      1896, supposed author.
      Les grands corps politiques de l'État. Biographie complète

des membres du Sénat, du Conseil d'État et du Corps legisla-
tif. Par un ancien député. Paris, E. Dentu, 1852. xii, 381 p.
12.° Attributed to A. F. J. Borel, called Borel d'Hauterive,
and also to Charles Baju. Complete biography of the members
of the French Senate, Council of State and Legislative Corps,
ca. 1852.

740   BOURSIN, ELPHÈGE, 1836-1891.
        Dictionnaire de la Révolution française: institutions,
hommes et faits, par E. Boursin et Augustin Challamel.
Paris, Furne, Jouvet, 1893. viii, 935 p. Dictionary of the
French Revolution: institutions, men and facts.

741   BRAUN, J   B   M
        Nouvelle biographie des députés; ou, Statistique de la
Chambre, de 1814 à 1829. Paris, Bechet aîné, 1830. xii,
496 p. 8.° Biographies of members of the French Chamber
of Deputies, 1814-1829.

742   [BRISSOT-THIVARS, LOUIS SATURNIN] d. 1850.
        Le guide électoral; ou, Biographie législative de tous les
députés, depuis 1814 jusques et y compris 1818 à 1819 (et 1819 à
1820) Paris, Librairie constitutionelle, 1819-20. 2 v. 8.°
Electoral guide; or, Legislative biography of all the members
of the French Chamber of Deputies, 1814-1820.

743   CARNOY, HENRY, 1861-   ed.
        Dictionnaire biographique de la haute société et de la no-
blesse. Secrétaire de la rédaction: Émile Maton. Paris,
Impr. de l'Armorial francais [190-] 81 p. illus. 29 cm.
(Collection des grands dictionnaires biographiques) Bound
with (?) or issued with (?) the editor's Dictionnaire biographique international du monde politique. The 2 works have
collective cover title: Dictionnaire biographique international
de la haute société et du monde politique. Bibliographical
dictionary of French high society & nobility.

744   CARNOY, HENRY, 1861-   ed.
        Dictionnaire biographique des grands négociants et indus-
triels. Ouvrage rédigé sous la direction de Henry Junger.
Paris, Impr. de l'Armorial francais [1901] 220 p. illus.
28 cm. (Collection des grands dictionnaires biographiques
internationaux) Edited chiefly by Henry Carnoy. Junger
collaborated only on the first few fascicles. Dictionary of
French businessmen and industrialists.

745   CARNOY, HENRY, 1861-   ed.
Dictionnaire biographique des hommes de l'Est. Paris,
Impr. de l'Armorial francais [1903] 246 p. illus. 29 cm.
(Collection des grands dictionnaires biographiques) Regarded
as Vol. 2 of a sub-series, the other numbers of which have
been issued as follows under Carnoy's editorship (except Vol.
3, edited by P. de Beaurepaire-Froment): [1] Dictionnaire
biographique des hommes du Nord. [3] Dictionnaire biographique des hommes du Midi. [4] Dictionnaire biographique
des hommes du Nord, de l'Est, de l'Ouest et du Midi.
Biographical dictionary of Eastern France.

746   CARNOY, HENRY, 1861-   ed.
Dictionnaire biographique des hommes du Nord, de l'Est,
de l'Ouest et du Midi; notabilités francaises contemporaines.
Tome IV. Paris, Chez l'auteur [1906?] 232 p. illus. 29 cm.
(Collection des grands dictionnaires biographiques inter-
nationaux, t. 15) Vol. 4 of a subseries. See note under
Carnoy, Henry. Dictionnaire biographique des hommes de
l'Est. Biographical dictionary of Northern, Eastern and
Western France & of the Midi; contemporaries.

747   CARNOY, HENRY, 1861-   ed.
Dictionnaire biographique des hommes du Nord. Nord,
Ardennes, Aisne, Somme, Pas-de-Calais & Oise. I. Les
contemporains. Paris, Impr. de l'Armorial francaise [189-]
272 p. illus. 28 cm. [Collection des grands dictionnaires
biographiques] Issued in parts. Regarded as Vol. 1 of a
subseries. See note under Carnoy, Henry. Dictionnaire
biographique des hommes de l'Est. Biographical dictionary
of Northern France.

748   CARNOY, HENRY, 1861-   ed.
Dictionnaire biographique des membres des sociétés
savantes. Paris, Impr. de l'Armorial francais, G. Colombier
[189-] 256 p. illus. 29 cm. (Collection des grands
dictionnaires biographiques) Continued by the editor's
Dictionnaire biographique international des écrivains, des
artistes, des membres des sociétés savantes, du clergé...,
q. v. Biographical dictionary of members of learned societies in France.

749   CARNOY, HENRY, 1861-   ed.
Dictionnaire biographique international du monde politique.
Secrétaire de la rédaction: Émile Maton. Paris, H. Carnoy
[190-] 73 p. illus. 29 cm. (Collection des grands
dictionnaires biographiques) Issued with his Dictionnaire

biographique de la haute société et de la noblesse? The 2
works have collective cover title: Dictionnaire biographique
international de la haute société et du monde politique.
International biographical dictionary of statesmen (chiefly
French)

750 [COIFFIER DE VERSEUX, HENRI LOUIS] 1770-1831?
Dictionnaire biographique et historique des hommes marquans de la fin du XVIII siècle, et plus particulièrement de
ceux qui ont figuré dans la Révolution francaise. Londres,
1800. 3v. 8.° Also attributed to the marquis Louis de La
Maisonfort. Frenchmen of the latter part of the 18th century,
more particularly those important in the Revolution.

751 COLLECTION DE 154 PORTRAITS DES GÉNÉRAUX FRANCAIS
qui ont brillé dans les guerres de 1789 à 1815. Paris,
C. L. F. Panckoucke [18--]   2 v. 8.° French generals
prominent in the wars of 1789 to 1815.

752 [COUAILHAC, LOUIS] 1810-1885.
Sessions 1838-1839. Biographie politique et parlementaire
des députés (Guide des électeurs) Par l'un des rédacteurs du
"Messager." Paris, J. Laisné, 1839. 1v. Political and
parliamentary biography of the French Chamber of Deputies,
1838-1839.

753 COURCELLES, JEAN BAPTISTE PIERRE JULLIEN DE, 1759-
1834.
Dictionnaire historique et biographique des généraux français, depuis le onzième siècle jusqu'en 1820. Paris, L'auteur
[etc.] 1820-23. 9v. 22cm. Historical and biographical dictionary of French generals, 12th century to 1820.

754 COURCELLES, JEAN BAPTISTE PIERRE JULLIEN DE, 1759-
1834.
Dictionnaire universel de la noblesse de France. Paris,
Au Bureau générale de la noblesse de France, 1820-22. 5 v.
plates. 22cm. Universal dictionary of the French nobility.

755 DÉCEMBRE, JOSEPH, 1836-
Dictionnaire de la Révolution française, 1789-1799, par
Décembre-Alonnier. Paris, 1866-68. 2v. A dictionary
of the French Revolution that includes biographical data.

756 DES ESSARTS, ALFRED STANISLAS LANGLOIS, 1811-1893.
Les célébrités françaises. Vies et portraits des rois et
reines, connétables, ministres, chanceliers, magistrats,

généraux, savants, religieux, marins, poetes, écrivains, prédicateurs, philosophes, musiciens, sculpteurs, peintres, etc. Illustré par Hadamard. Paris, J. Vermot, 1862. 588 p. plates. 8.° French celebrities. Lives & portraits of kings, queens, high constables, ministers... judges, generals, scholars [etc., etc.]

757 DICTIONNAIRE BIOGRAPHIQUE DU MOUVEMENT OUVRIER FRANCAIS. Publié sous la direction de Jean Maitron. Paris, Éditions ouvrières [1964-   v. ports. 25cm. Contents. --1. ptie. 1789-1864. De la Révolution francaise à la fondation de la Première Internationale. Biographical dictionary of the French labor movement.

758 DICTIONNAIRE BIOGRAPHIQUE FRANCAIS CONTEMPORAIN. [2. éd.] Paris, Pharos; agent pour les États-Unis: Stechert-Hafner, New York [1954]   708 p. ports. 27cm.

759   --- ----Supplément. [Paris] Pharos.   nos. ports. 27cm.

Contemporary French biographical dictionary.

760 DICTIONNAIRE DE BIOGRAPHIE FRANCAISE, Sous la direction de J. Balteau, M. Barroux [et] M. Prévost, avec le concours de nombreux collaborateurs. Paris, Letouzey et Ané, 1933-   v. 29cm. Issued in parts, 1930- Dictionary of French biography.

761 DICTIONNAIRE DES BRAVES ET DES NON-GIROUETTES. Nomenclature curieuse des francais royalistes, républicains ou bonapartistes. Par une société de non-girouettes. Paris, Levêque, 1816. xvi, 308 p. Edited by F. Babie de Bercenay (?) Dictionary of gallant and honest fellows whether French royalists, republicans or Bonapartists.

762 DICTIONNAIRE DES PARLEMENTAIRES FRANCAIS; Notices biographiques sur les ministres, sénateurs et députés français de 1889 à 1940. Publié sous la direction de Jean Jolly. Paris, Presses universitaires de France, 1960- v. 24cm. A continuation of Dictionnaire des parlementaires français, 1789-1889, by A. Robert and G. Cougny.

763 DICTIONNAIRE DES PROTÉES MODERNES; Ou, Biographie des personnages vivans qui ont figuré dans la Révolution française, depuis le 14 juillet 1789, jusques et compris 1815, par leurs actions, leur conduite ou leurs écrits,

par un homme retiré du monde. Paris, Chez Davi et Locard,
1815. iv, 260 p. 18cm. Biographical dictionary of the French
Revolution.

764   DICTIONNAIRE NATIONAL DES CONTEMPORAINS,
      Contenant les notices des membres de l'Institut de France,
du gouvernement et du Parlement français, de l'Académie de
médecine, et de toutes les personnalités vivantes, françaises
ou demeurant en France, qui se sont fait connaitre par leur
action dans les lettres, les sciences, les arts, la politique,
l'armée, les cultes, l'industrie, l'administration, etc. Ouvrage rédigé et tenu à jour par un groupe d'écrivains, savants,
artistes et hommes politiques, sous en direction de C. -E.
Curinier. Paris, Office général d'édition [1889-1905] 5 v.
28cm. Dictionary of Frenchmen or persons residing in France
(contemporaries, 1899-1905) prominent in all fields.

765   DICTIONNAIRE NATIONAL DES CONTEMPORAINS,
      Dirigé par Nath Imbert. Paris, Éditions Lajeunesse,
1936-39. 3 v. illus. 35cm. A dictionary of 20th century
French biography with the emphasis on 20th century French
literature.

766   DIDIER, ROBERT
      Isographie de l'Académie française; liste alphabétique,
illustrée de 125 fac-similés de signatures, 1906-1963. Paris,
E. de Boccard, 1964. 195 p. facsims. 25cm. Bio-bibliography of deceased members of the Académie Francaise,
1906-1963.

767   DOURILLE, JOSEPH
      Biographie des députés de la nouvelle Chambre septennale,
ornée d'un tableau représentant la salle des séances et indiquant la place que chaque législateur y occupe. Session de
1829. Paris, Chez les Marchands de nouveautés, 1829. ix,
304 p. 8.° Biographies of the members of the French Chamber of Deputies, 1829.

768   DUPORTET, MAURICE
      Répertoire permanent des intellectuels. Néris-les-Bains,
L'auteur, 1947-   v.   Issued in fascicles. A
listing of French intellectuals.

769   [EYMERY, ALEXIS BLAISE] 1774-1854.
      Dictionnaire des girouettes; ou, Nos contemporains peints
d'après euxmêmes; ouvrage dans lequel sont rapportés les

discours, proclamations, chansons, extraits d'ouvrages écrits sous les gouvernemens qui ont eu lieu en France depuis vingt-cinq ans; et les places, faveurs et titres qu'ont obtenus dans les différentes circumstances les hommes d'état, gens de lettres, généraux, artistes, senateurs, chansonniers, évêques, prefets, journalistes, ministres, etc. Par une Société de girouettes. 2. éd., rev., corr., et considérablement augm. Paris, A. Eymery [etc.] 1815. 491 p. 21 cm. Dictionary of 'time-servers'; French personalities of the period 1790-1815.

770   FAURÉ, HONORÉ.
Galerie administrative; ou, Biographie des préfets, depuis l'organisation des préfectures jusqu'à ce jour. Aurillac, P. Picut, 1839. 2 v. in 1. 8.° Biography of French prefects (administrators of the various French departments)

771   FISQUET, HONORÉ JEAN PIERRE, 1818-1883.
Dictionnaire des célébrités de la France; classées par ordre alphabétique et par départements. Paris, A. Le Vasseur [1878] 914p. 26cm. Dictionary of French celebrities, arranged alphabetically and by departments.

772   FORTIA DE PILES, ALPHONSE TOUSSAINT JOSEPH ANDRÉ MARIE MARSEILLE, comte de, 1758-1826.
Préservatif contre la "Biographie nouvelle des contemporains." Paris, Impr. Vve Porthmann, 1822-25. 6 v. Biographies of Frenchmen; critical of the 'Biographie nouvelle des contemporains' (q. v.)

773   FRANQUEVILLE, AMABLE CHARLES FRANQUET, comte de, 1840-1919.
Le premier siècle de l'Institut de France, 25 octobre 1795-25 octobre 1895. Paris, J. Rothschild, 1895-96. 2 v. illus. 28 x 22 cm. Bio-bibliography of members of the Institute of France, Paris.

774   FRENCH WHO'S WHO.
[London, Ministry of Economic Warfare] 1943. 80 p. 25cm. Cover title.

775   --- ----Supplement. [London, Ministry of Economic Warfare] 1944. 21 p. 33cm. Caption title.

776   LA GALERIE DES ÉTATS-GÉNÉRAUX ET DES DAMES FRANCOISES.
[Paris?] 1790. 3 v. in 1. 19cm. Attributed to the Marquis J. P. L. de Luchet, and others. Vol. 3 has title: La

Galerie des dames francoises pour servir de suite à la Galerie des États-Généraux. Par le même auteur. Biographies of deputies to the French Estates-General of 1789 and of some notable women of the period.

777   GALERIE FRANCAISE;
       ou, Collection de portraits des hommes et des femmes qui ont illustré la France dans XVe, XVIIe et XVIIIe siècles; avec des notices et des facsimiles. Précédée d'une introd. qui comprendra les principaux événements qui se sont passés depuis Merovée jusqu'à Louis XII. Par une société d'hommes de lettres et d'artistes. Paris, Impr. de F. Didot, 1821-23. 3 v. ports. 4.° Portraits and biographical notes: notable Frenchmen and Frenchwomen of the 15th, 17th & 18th centuries.

778   GALERIE HISTORIQUE ET BIOGRAPHIQUE DES MEMBRES DU SÉNAT. Par plusieurs publicistes. Vol. 1. Paris, Librairie nouvelle, 1852. 161 p. 8.° No more published. Members of the upper house of the French legislature as first constituted in 1852 under Louis Napoleon.

779   GALLERY OF PORTRAITS OF THE NATIONAL ASSEMBLY, supposed to be written by Count de Mirabeau. Translated from the French. Dublin, H. Chamberlaine and Rice [etc.] 1790. 2 v. in 1. 18cm. The work has been attributed to the Marquis J. P. L. de Luchet, A. de Rivarol, comte de Mirabeau, P. A. F. Choderlos de Laclos, Senac de Meilhan, de Champcenetz and Cérutti---Cf. M. Tourneux, Bibl. de l'hist. de Paris, v. 4, p. 18. Frenchmen influential at the time of the onset of the French Revolution, including members of the Assembly of Notables (?)

780   [GALLOIS, LÉONARD] 1789-1851.
       Biographie de tous les ministres, depuis la constitution de 1791, jusqu'à nos jours. Paris, Chez tous les marchands de nouveautés, 1825. xii, 586 p. 21 cm. Sometimes considered an anonymous work (1948 supplement to LC enters under title) Biographies of French statesmen and government ministers, 1791-1825.

781   [GALLOIS, LEONARD] 1789-1851.
       Biographie des ministres francais, depuis juillet 1789 jusqu'à ce jour. Édition faite sur celle de Paris, corrigée et augm. de 28 articles nouveaux et de notes, par plusieurs hommes de lettres, belges et étrangers. Bruxelles, H. Tarlier, 1826. viii, 318 p. 8.° Belgian ed. of Gallois'

Biographie des tous les ministres... Biographies of French statesmen & government ministers, 1789-1825.

782   [GALLOIS, LEONARD] 1789-1851.
Dictionnaire historique de tous les ministres, depuis la Révolution jusqu'en 1827. Paris, C. Béchet, 1828. xii, 502 p. 8.° Later ed. of Gallois' Biographie de tous les ministres. Biographies of French statesmen & government ministers, 1789-1827.

783   GALTIER-BOISSIÈRE, JEAN, 1888-
Dictionnarie des contemporains, par Jean Galtier-Boissière avec la collaboration de Alexandre (A) [et al. Paris, 1950] 2 v. illus., ports. 32 cm. Special numbers of Le Crapouillot, nouv. sér., no. 8-9. Satirical and humorous biography of contemporary Frenchmen.

784   [GIRARDEAU, LOUIS]
Biographie des 750 représentants du peuple à l'Assemblée nationale législative, par ordre alphabétique, avec un tableau des députations par départements. Par plusieurs journalistes. Paris, A la Librairie rue de Faubourg-Poissonnière, no 25, 1849. 164 p. 8.° By Louis Girardeau, Albert André Patin de La Fizelière and William L. Hughes. Biographical sketches of 750 representatives at the French National Assembly of 1848-1849.

785   GLAESER, ERNEST, 1829-
Biographie nationale des contemporains, redigée par une société de gens de lettres sous la direction de Ernest Glaeser. Paris, Glaeser, 1878. 4,834 p. 28cm. French national biography of the 19th century.

786   GRANGES DE SURGÈRES, ANATOLE, marquis de, 1850-1902.
Les Francaises du XVIIIe siècles, portraits, gravés; avec une préf. de M. le baron Roger Portalis. Ouvrage orné de douze portraits d'après les originaux. Paris, E. Dentu, 1887. xxii, 360 p. 12 ports. 26cm. Frenchmen of the 18th century —a catalog of portraits.

787   GRENIER, ALBERT SYLVAIN, 1848-
Nos députés... Biographies & portraits de MM. les députés... Paris, Berger-Levrault [1893?-1910?] 4v. 32.° Contents. --[1] 1893-1898. --[2] 1898-1902. --[3] 1902-1906. --[4] 1906-1910. Biographies of members of the French Chamber of Deputies, 1893-1910.

788   GRENIER, ALBERT SYLVAIN, 1848-
Nos sénateurs; biographies et portraits de MM. les sénateurs... Paris, E. Flammarion, 1895-1907. 5v. ports.
32. Contents. --[1] 1894-1897. --[2]1897-1900. --[3] 1900-1903.
--[4] 1903-1906. --[5] 1906-1909. Biographies of members of
the French Senate, 1894-1909.

789   GUIFFREY, JULES MARIE JOSEPH, 1840-1918.
Les Conventionnels. Listes par départements et par ordre
alphabétique . . . avec nombreux détails biographiques
inédits. Paris, Société de l'histoire de la Révolution française, 1889. xl, 169 p. 8.° A listing by department and
alphabetically of members of the French Revolutionary
National Convention of 1792-1795.

790   GUILLON, AIMÉ, abbé
Les martyrs de la foi pendant la Révolution française; ou,
Martyrologe des pontifes, prêtres, religieux, religieuses,
laics de l'un et de l'autre sexe qui périrent alors pour la foi.
Paris, G. Mathiot, 1821. 4 v. 8.° Churchmen and laity
who fell victim to the excesses of the French Revolution.

791   HAAG, EUGÈNE, 1808-1868.
La France protestante; ou, Vies des protestants français
qui se sont fait un nom dans l'histoire depuis les premiers
temps de la Réformation jusqu'à la reconnaissance du principe de la liberté des cultes par l'Assemblée nationale... par
Eug. et Ém. Haag. Paris, J. Cherbuliez, 1846-59. 10 v.
24cm. There is a later edition, edited by Henri Bordier,
but only vols. 1-6 (A-Gasparen) were published (Paris, San-
doz, 1877-88) Lives of French Protestants, from the Reformation to the recognition of religious liberty by the National
Assembly during the French Revolution.

792   HENRIQUE-DULUC, LOUIS, 1852-1906.
Nos contemporains; galerie coloniale et diplomatique
[par] Louis Henrique. Paris, Quantin, 1896- v. ports.
19cm. Our contemporaries; gallery of French colonials and
diplomats.

793   IMBERT, JEAN BAPTISTE AUGUSTE, b. 1791.
Biographie des condamnés pour délits politiques depuis
1814 jusqu'en 1828, par Auguste Imbert. Paris, L'Huillier,
1828. iii, 192p. 8.° Incomplete. A-Louvel only. Biography of Frenchmen convicted for political offenses, 1814-
1828.

794   JUNGER, HENRY, ed.
      Dictionnaire biographique des grands commerçants et
industriels. Ouvrage rédigé par un comité de spécialistes
sous la direction de H. Junger. Paris, Impr. de G.
Colombier [1902] vi, 220p. 4.° Biographical dictionary of
the great [French] businessmen and industrialists.

795   KUŚCIŃSKI, AUGUSTE.
      Les députés au Corps législatif, Conseil des Cinq-Cents,
Conseil des anciens, de l'an IV à l'an VII; listes, tableaux et
lois. Paris, Société de l'histoire de la Révolution française,
1905. xix, 419 p. 25cm. Members of France's Corps législatif (Legislative Body) 1795-1798(?)

796   KUŚCIŃSKI, AUGUSTE.
      Les députés de l'Assemblée législative de 1791; listes par
départements et par ordre alphabétique des députés et des
suppléants, avec nombreux détails biographiques inédits.
Paris, Société de l'histoire de la Révolution française, 1900.
v, 171 p. 25cm. Deputies of the French Legislative Assembly
of 1791-92.

797   KUŚCIŃSKI, AUGUSTE.
      Dictionnaire des Conventionnels. Paris, Société de l'his-
toire de la Révolution française, 1917 [cover 1919] iv, 615 p.
25cm. Biographical dictionary of the French Revolution.

798   LACAINE, VICTOR
      Biographies et nécrologies des hommes marquants du XIXe
siècle, par Victor Lacaine et Ch. Laurent. Paris, 1844-66.
12 v. (v. 1-6, 9-14) 8.° Biographies and necrologies of
Frenchmen of the 19th century. Vols. 7-8 never issued, or
missing? Bibliothèque nationale shows only the above.

799   LA CHESNAYE-DESBOIS, FRANCOIS ALEXANDRE AUBERT
      DE, 1699-1784.
      Dictionnaire de la noblesse, contenant les genéalogies,
l'histoire & la chronologie des familles nobles de la France,
l'explication de leurs armes et l'état des grandes terres du
royaume... On a joint à ce dictionnaire le tableau généalo-
gique et historique des maisons souveraines de l'Europe et
une notice des familles étrangères, les plus anciennes, les
plus nobles et les plus illustrés, par La Chenaye-Desbois et
Badier. 3. éd. entièrement refondue... & augm. d'un table
générale de tous les noms de familles, de terres, de fiefs,
d'alliances cités dans le cours de l'ouvrage, ainsi que d'un

Armorial représentant les blasons de maisons dont les généalogies sont comprises dans cette édition. Paris,
Schlesinger frères, 1863-77. 19 v. 28cm. Includes biographical material on the French nobility. Vols. 20-22 and
Armorial were never published.

800   LAGARDE, ALEXIS
       Nouvelle biographie pittoresque des députés de la chambre
       septennale, publiée par M. -A. Lagarde. Paris, Chez les
       Marchands de nouveautés, 1826. Biographies of members of
       the French Chamber of Deputies, ca. 1826.

801   LALANNE, LUDOVIC, 1815-1898.
       Biographie portative universelle, suivie d'une Table
       chronologique et alphabétique ou se trouvent répartis en cin-
       quante-quatre classes les noms mentionnés dans l'ouvrage,
       par Lud. Lalanne [et al.] Paris, Garnier frères, 1852.
       1964 columns. 29cm. Biographical sketches of Frenchmen.

803   LAPIERRE DE CHÂTEAUNEUF, AGRICOL HIPPOLYTE DE,
       1765-1842.
       Cornelius Nepos francais; ou, Notices historiques sur les
       généraux, les marins, les officiers et les soldats qui se sont
       illustrés dans la guerre de la Révolution. Paris, L'editeur
       an XI [1803]-1811. 21 pts. 12.º 5th-11th parts have title: Le
       Nepos francais, par A. -D. [sic] Châteauneuf; 12-21st: His-
       toire des généraux qui se sont illustrés dans la guerre de la
       Révolution. These parts were published separately under the
       titles indicated, but, according to the author's prospectus,
       they were actually or originally intended to be parts of the
       Cornelius Nepos francais.

804   [LARDIER, ALEXANDRE]
       Histoire biographique de la Chambre des pairs, depuis la
       Restauration jusqu'à l'époque actuelle. Précédée d'un essai
       sur l'institution et l'influence de la pairie en France, par C. -
       O. Barbaroux. Paris, Brissot-Thivars, 1829. 2 pts. in 1 v.
       8.º Biographical history of the French Chamber of Senators,
       1814—ca. 1829.

805   LAVALLÉE, JOSEPH, marquis de Bois-Robert, 1747-1816.
Annales nécrologiques de la Légion d'honneur. Paris, F.
Buisson, 1807. xiv, 403p. illus. 20cm. Necrology of the
French Legion of Honor.

806   LERMINA, JULES HIPPOLYTE, 1839-1915.
Dictionnaire universel illustré biographique et bibliographique de la France contemporaine; comprenant, par ordre
alphabétique, la biographie de tous les Francais et Alsaciens-
Lorrains, marquants, de l'époque actuelle, l'analyse des
oeuvres les plus célèbres (théâtre, littérature, sciences) des
auteurs vivants, l'histoire des principaux théâtres et journaux
de Paris et des departements; par une societe de gens de lettres et des savants. Paris, L. Boulanger [etc., 1884]
1397p. illus. 30cm. Bio-bibliographical dictionary of contemporary France.

807   LESAULNIER, C   M
Biographie des neuf cents députés à l'Assemblée nationale,
par ordre alphabétique des départements; tant de ceux qui ont
ete elus le 23 avril aux elections generales, que de ceux qui
ont été nommés le 4 juin aux élections complémentaires.
Avec une table alphabétique. Par une société de gens de
lettres et de publicistes, sous la direction de C.-M. Lesaulnier. Paris, 1848. vi, 551p. 16cm. Biographies of members of the French Chamber of Deputies, 1848.

808   LEVENSBESCHRIJVINGEN VAN DE VOORNAAMSTE
PERSONEN, die, ten tijde der Revolutie, in Vrankrijk,
zijn geguillotineerd geworden. Uit het Fransch en Hoog-
duitsch. La Haye, J. C. Leeuwesteyn, 1802. viii, 294p.
8.º 209 biographical notices of persons guillotined in the
French Revolution. Original French title unknown.

809   LEVOT, PROSPER JEAN, 1801-1878.
Essais de biographie maritime; ou, Notices sur des
hommes distingués de la Marine francais. Brest, Impr. de
C. Le Blois, 1847. ii, 403p. 8.º Remarks on distinguished
men of the French Navy.

810   [LEYMARIE, ACHILLE] 1809-1861.
Profils critiques et biographiques des sénateurs, conseillers d'État et députés... Par un vieil écrivain. Paris,
Garnier frères, 1852. 332p. 8.º Critical and biographical
profiles of contemporary French senators, State councillors,
etc. By A. Leymarie, according to the British Museum.

811   LIÉVYNS, A
      Fastes de la Légion d'honneur; biographie de tous les
décorés, accompagnée de l'histoire législative et réglemen-
taire de l'ordre. Par MM. Liévyns, Verdot et Begat. Paris,
Au Bureau, et chez B. Saint-Edme, redacteur-en-chef, 1842-
47. 5 v. 8.° Biographies of French heroes, possessors of
the Legion of Honor decoration.

812   [LOURDOUEIX, PAUL DE]
      Profils critiques et biographiques des 900 représentants du
peuple, par un vétéran de la presse. Paris, Garnier frères,
1848. 329 p. Critical and biographical profiles of the 900
representatives of the French people --the Legislative Assembly, 1848.

813   [MAGALON, JOSEPH DOMINIQUE]
      Petit dictionnaire ministeriel. Paris, Les Marchands
des nouveautés, 1826. vi, 64p. 32.° Small dictionary of
[French] government officials of the day.

814   MALLET, CHARLES
      Dictionnaire encyclopédique des notabilités contemporaines.
Paris et la Seine. Paris, L'auteur [1894?] 104 p. 4.°
Encyclopedic dictionary of contemporary [French] notables.
The British Museum gives the collation as follows: 192 p. 8.°
--and states that "no more [were] published."

815   MANUEL, PIERRE, 1751-1793.
      L'année francaise; ou, Vies des hommes qui ont honoré la
France ou par leurs talents ou par leurs services, et surtout
par leurs vertus. Paris, Nyon aîné, 1789. 4 v. 12.° Lives
of men who have honored France by their talents [etc.]

816   MARTINIEN, ARISTIDE
      Tableaux, par corps et par batailles, des officiers tués
et blessés pendant les guerres de l'Empire, 1805-1815. Paris,
H. Charles-Lavauzelle [1899] 824 p. 8.° Lists, by corps
and battles, of French officers killed and wounded during the
wars of the Empire, 1805-1815.

817   LE NÉCROLOGE DES HOMMES CÉLÈBRES DE FRANCE,
      Par une société de gens de lettres. 1-17; 1767-1782. Paris,
Impr. de Moreau [etc.] 17 pts. The necrology of celebrated
men of France.

818   NOTICE BIOGRAPHIQUE SUR LES NOUVEAUX PAIRS DE
        FRANCE NOMMÉS PAR L'ORDONNANCE DU 5 MARS 1819.
Paris, E. Gide, 1819. 1 v. 8.° Biographical notes on the
new members of the French Chamber of Senators, 1819.

819   NOUVEAU DICTIONNAIRE HISTORIQUE DES DÉPUTÉS À
        L'ASSEMBLÉE NATIONALE, et de tous les hommes qui
se sont illustrés depuis le commencement de la Révolution par
leurs vertus, leurs talents et leurs erreurs... Paris,
Volland, 1791. 3 v. Deputies at the French Revolutionary
National Constituent Assembly, 1789-1791.

820   ORDRE CHRONOLOGIQUE DES DEUILS DE COUR,
        Avec un précis de la vie et des ouvrages des auteurs qui
sont morts dans le cours de l'année. Paris, Impr. de
Moreau, 1764-66. 3 v. 12.° A necrology of Frenchmen,
with a sketch of the life & works of writers who have died in
the course of the year.

821   LES PARALLÈLES DE NOS JOURS,
        Biographie des législateurs de la République. Les 900 de
la Constituante et les 750 de la Législative. Par plusieurs
journalistes. Paris, À la Librairie rue du Faubourg-Poissonnière, n° 25, 1849. 1v. 8.° Biographies of French legislators, 1848-1849.

822   PETITE BIOGRAPHIE DES CONVENTIONNELS,
        Avec leurs votes dans le procès de Louis XVI; par un
jacobin converti. Paris, Chez les Libraires marchands de
nouveautés, 1826. 1 v. (?) Little biography of the members
of the French Revolutionary National Convention of 1792.

823   PORTRAITS DES HOMMES ILLUSTRES DES DIX-SEPTIÈME
        ET DIX-HUITIÈME SIÈCLES,
        Dessinés d'après nature, et gravés par Édelink, Lubin,
van Schuppen, Duflos et Simond'eux. Paris, C. Volland, 1805.
2 v. in 1. ports. 42cm. Portraits of illustrious Frenchmen
of the 17th & 18th centuries.

824   POSSELT, ERNST LUDWIG
        Lexikon der Französischen Revolution; oder, Sammlung
von Biographien der wichtigsten Männer die sich im Laufe
derselben besonders ausgezeichnet haben. Nuremberg,
Bauer et Mann, 1802. viii, 280p. 8.° Dictionary of the

French Revolution; or, Collection of biographies... First of
a series of volumes; projected to be in several volumes, but
no more were published.

825   PROFILS CRITIQUES ET BIOGRAPHIQUES DE 750 REPRÉ-
        SENTANTS DU PEUPLE À L'ASSEMBLÉE LÉGISLATIVE.
Par trois publicistes. Paris, Garnier frères, 1849. 1 v.
32.º Critical & biographical profiles of 750 representatives
in the French National Legislative Assembly, 1849.

826   [PRUDHOMME, LOUIS MARIE] 1752-1830.
       Histoire générale et impartiale des erreurs, des fautes
et des crimes commis pendant la Révolution française, à
dater du 24 août 1787; contenant le nombre des individus qui
ont péri par la Révolution, de ceux qui ont émigré, et les
intrigues des factions qui pendant ce tems ont désolé la
France. Paris, An V de la République (1796-97) 6 v.
plates. 20cm. Vols. 1-2 have title: Dictionnaire des individus envoyés a la mort judiciairement, révolutionnairement et contre- révolutionnairement pendant la Révolution...
A biographical dictionary of the French Revolution, especially those who perished in its course, or fled abroad.

827   QUÉNARD, PHILIPPE, fl. 1790.
       Portraits des personnages célèbres de la Révolution, avec
tableau historique des notices, par P. Quénard, l'un des
représentants de la commune de Paris, en 1789 et 1790.
Paris, Impr. du Cercle social [etc.] 1796-1802. 4 v. fronts.,
200 ports. 28cm. Vols. 3-4 by F. Bonneville. Title varies
slightly. Portraits of some 200 famous personages of the
French Revolution with [biographical?] notices.

828   QUI EST-CE?
       Ceux dont on parle. Paris, Éditions de la Vie moderne
[1934] 611p. ports. 24cm. A biographical dictionary of
France.

829   QUI ETES-VOUS?
       Annuaire des contemporains; notices biographiques. 1908-
1909/10, 1924. Paris, C. Delagrave [etc.] 3 v. 18-23cm.
A French who's who. Publication suspended from 1911 (?) to
1923 inclusive; ceased with 1924. Sub-title varies.

830   RABAN, LOUIS FRANÇOIS, 1795-1870.
       Petite biographie des deputés, publiée par Raban. 2. éd.,

rev. et corr. Paris, Chez les Marchands de nouveautés,
1826. 108p. 11cm. 1st ed. published in the same year under
title: Petite biographie des pairs (?) Biographical sketches
of members of the French Chamber of Deputies, 1826.

831 [RAUP DE BAPTESTEIN DE MOULIÈRES, ANTOINE
JOSEPH]
Petite biographie conventionnelle; ou, Tableau moral et
raisonné des 749 députés qui composaient l'assemblée dite
de la Convention. 2. éd. Paris, A. Eymery, 1816. viii,
272p. 17cm. 749 deputies at the French Revolutionary National Convention of 1792-1795.

832 RÉVÉREND, ALBERT, vicomte, 1844-1911.
Armorial du Premier Empire; titres, majorats et ar-
moiries coneédés par Napoléon Ier. Paris, Au Bureau de
"L'Annuaire de la noblesse"[etc.] 1894-97. 4 v. in 2. 28cm.
French nobility under Napoleon I.

833 RÉVÉREND, ALBERT, vicomte, 1844-1911.
Titres et confirmations de titres; Monarchie de juillet,
2e République, 2e Empire, 3e République, 1830-1908. Paris,
Chez l'auteur et chez H. Champion, 1909. xi, 352p. 28cm.
At head of title: Les familles titrées et anoblies au XIXe
siècle. Titles and confirmations of titles of the French nobility, 1830-1908.

834 RÉVÉREND, ALBERT, vicomte, 1844-1911.
Titres, anoblissements et pairies de la Restauration, 1814-
1830. Paris, Chez l'auteur et chez H. Champion, 1901-06.
6 v. 29cm. At head of title: Les familles titrées et anoblies
du XIXe siècle. The French nobility in the period 1814-1830.

835 [RION, ADOLPHE]
Biographie nouvelle et complète de la Chambre des députés, contenant les députés nouvellement élus; par l'auteur
de la Nouvelle biographie des pairs (A.R.) Paris, Chez les
Marchands de nouveautés, 1829. xii, 276p. 18.º New and
complete biography of the French Chamber of Deputies
(1829)

836 [RIVAROL, ANTOINE] 1753-1801.
Petit dictionnaire des grands hommes de la Révolution.
Par un citoyen actif, ci-devant rien. [Paris] Au Palais-
royal, de l'Impr. nationale, 1790. xxiv, 119p. 16cm. By

Antoine Rivarol and Louis René Quentin de Richebourg, marquis de Champcenetz. Little dictionary of the great men of the [French] Revolution.

837   ROBERT, ADOLPHE, 1833-
Dictionnaire des parlementaires français, comprenant tous les membres des assemblées françaises et tous les ministres français depuis le Ier mai 1789 jusq'au Ier mai 1889; avec leurs noms, état civil, états de services, actes politiques, votes parlementaires, etc., publié sous la direction de Adolphe Robert, Edgar Bourloton & Gaston Cougny. Paris, Bourloton, 1891. 5 v. illus. 26cm. Continued by Samuel, R. C. L. Les parlementaires français, II. 1900-1914. Dictionary of French parliamentarians (legislators) and statesmen (ministers), 1789-1889.

838   ROBERT, JEAN BAPTISTE MAGLOIRE
Les prisonniers d'État pendant la Révolution, par M. Robert. t. 1. Paris, L'Auteur, 1815. 332p. 8.º No more published? Biographies of people executed during the French Revolution for their loyalty to the Monarchy.

839   ROBINET, JEAN FRANÇOIS EUGÈNE, 1825-1899.
Dictionnaire historique et biographique de la Révolution et de l'Empire. Ouvrage rédigé pour l'histoire générale, par le Dr. Robinet... ; pour la partie descriptive et biographique, par Adolphe Robert... ; pour les matières constitutionnelles et législatives, par J. Le Chaplain. Paris, Librairie historique de la Révolution et de l'Empire [1899] 2 v. 25cm. Historical and biographical dictionary of the French Revolution and Empire.

840   SAINT-ALLAIS, NICOLAS VITON, 1773-1842.
Nobiliaire universel de France; ou, Recueil général des genéalogies historiques des maisons nobles de ce royaume, par MM. de Saint-Allais et de La Chabeaussière. Paris, Au Bureau du Nobiliaire universel de France, reimprimé à la Librairie Bachelin-Deflorrene, 1872[-77] 21 v. The nobility of France; includes biographical data. Vols. 17-18 by J. B. P. J. de Courcelles; v. 21 (supplement) by Ducas. First published in 18 v., 1814-1821.

841   SAINT-EDME, EDME THÉODORE BOURG, known as, 1795-1852.
Biographie des lieutenants généraux, ministres, directeurs généraux, charges d'arrondissements, préfets de la

police en France, et de ses principaux agents, par B. Saint-
Edme. Paris, L'auteur-editeur, 1829. xxxiv, 526p. 21cm.
Biography of French police officials.

842   SAMUEL, RENÉ CLAUDE LOUIS, 1862-1923.
Les parlementaires français. II. 1900-1914. Dictionnaire biographique et bibliographique des sénateurs, députés,
ministres ayant siégé dans les Assemblées législatives de
1900 à 1914, suivi de la liste des groupes politiques par la
rédaction de l'Annuaire du Parlement. [Par] René Samuel et
Géo Bonet-Maury. Paris, G. Roustan, 1914. 479p.
Continuation of Robert's Dictionnaire des parlementaires
français. Volume for 1889-1900 never published. Bio-bibliographical dictionary of French senators, deputies and ministers... 1900-1914.

843   SIX, GEORGES
Dictionnaire biographique des généraux & amiraux français
de la Révolution et de l'Empire (1792-1844) Préf. par André
Lasseray. Paris, G. Saffroy, 1934. 2 v. 26cm. Bio-
graphical dictionary of French generals & admirals of the
Revolution & Empire (1792-1844)

844   SOMAIZE, ANTOINE BAUDEAU DE, b. ca. 1630.
Le dictionnaire des précieuses; par le sieur de Somaize.
Nouv. éd., augm. de divers opuscules du même auteur
rélatifs aux précieuses et d'une clef historique et anecdotique,
par Ch.-L. Livet. Paris, P. Jannet, 1856. 2 v. 16cm.
[Bibliothèque elzevirienne, v. 95-96] The "Clef historique
et anecdotique" of Livet (v. 2, p. [121]-403) is a biographical
dictionary of the Précieuses, a coterie of Frenchmen and women of the 17th century who considered themselves the arbiters
of taste & culture.

845   TARMINI-ALMERTÉ
Petite biographie nationale des contemporains; ou, Dictionnaire historique des Français qui se sont rendus célèbres
ou fameux par leurs vertus ou leurs vices depuis la Révolution jusqu'à nos jours, par Tarmini-Almerté [pseud. ?]
Paris, Bouquin de la Souche, 1825. 352p. 12.º A small national biography of contemporaries; famous Frenchmen who
flourished after the Revolution to ca. 1825.

846   TURPIN, FRANCOIS HENRI, 1709-1799.
La France ilustre; ou, Le Plutarque français, contenant
les eloges historiques des généraux et grands capitaines, des

ministres d'etat, et des principaux magistrats de la nation français, enrichis de leurs portraits. Paris, Des Lauriers, 1780-84. 4 v. ports. 26cm. France illustrious; or, The French Plutarch--generals, the great captains, ministers of state & the chief magistrates, with portraits.

847   U. S. OFFICE OF STRATEGIC SERVICES.
A selected who's who in Vichy, France, June 1940-August 1944. 24 Oct. 1944. [Washington, 1944] 358p. 27cm. At head of title: Restricted. Office of Strategic Services. Research and Analysis Branch. R & A. no. 2344. Reproduced from type-written copy.

848   WALTER, GÉRARD, 1896-
Répertoire de l'histoire de la Révolution française. Travaux publiés de 1800 à 1940. [tome] 1: Personnes. Paris, Bibliothèque nationale, 1941. xii, 573 p. A comprehensive list of participants in the French Revolution, with dates & brief descriptive data, followed by bibliographical references to the lives of the participants.

849   WAROQUIER DE MÉRICOURT DE LA MOTHE DE COMBLES, LOUIS CHARLES, comte.
Tableau historique de la noblesse militaire. tome 1. Paris, Chez l'auteur, 1784. 1 v. 8.° No more published. Historical tableau of the 'military nobility' [of France]; the French nobility in military service.

850   WHO'S WHO IN FRANCE.
1. -   éd. ; 1953-54-   Paris, J. Lafitte. v. 22cm. Title varies slightly. Running title, v. 1: Who's who in Paris. Text in French.

Local

Ain (Dept.)

851   DEPÉRY, JEAN IRENÉE, Bp., 1796-1861.
Biographie des hommes célèbres du département de l'Ain qui se sont distingués par leurs sciences, leurs talents...ou leurs vices. Bourg, P. F. Bottier, 1833-40. 2v. 8.° Biography of the French department of the Ain.

Aisne (Dept.)

852 DICTIONNAIRE BIOGRAPHIQUE, COMPRENANT LA LISTE
ET LES BIOGRAPHIES DES NOTABILITÉS DU DÉPARTE-
MENT DE L'AISNE. Paris, Jouve, 1895. 1 v. (unpaged)
ports. 8.º (Les Dictionnaires départementaux) Biographical
dictionary of the department of the Aisne, France.

Allier (Dept.)

853 DICTIONNAIRE BIOGRAPHIQUE, ANNUAIRE ET ALBUM DE
L'ALLIER, 1898. Paris, Jouve, 1898. 1 v. (unpaged)
ports. 8.º (Les Dictionnaires départementaux) Biographical
dictionary, annual and album of the French department of the
Allier.

Alsace — Lorraine

854 LES ALSACIENS-LORRAINS.
Dictionnaire, annuaire et album. Paris, Jouve, 1896-
v. ports. 8.º (Les Dictionnaires départementaux)
Dictionary, annual and album of Alsace-Lorraine; includes
biographies.

855 CALMET, AUGUSTIN, 1672-1757.
Bibliothèque lorraine; ou, Histoire des hommes illustres
qui ont fleuri en Lorraine, dans les Trois Évêches, dans
l'archevêché de Trèves, dans le duché de Luxembourg...
Nancy, A. Leseure, 1751. xxviii, 1047 p. (with a supplement
of 118 p. and 84 columns) Biographies of famous men of
Lorraine and adjacent areas.

856 CERFBERR DE MÉDELSHEIM, ALPHONSE, 1817-1883.
Biographie alsacienne-lorraine. Paris, A. Lemerre, 1879.
327 p. Biography of famous persons of Alsace-Lorraine.

857 SITZMANN, FR   J   EDUARD
Dictionnaire de biographie des hommes célèbres de l'Alsace, depuis les temps les plus reculés jusqu'à nos jours.
Rixheim, Impr. de F. Mutter, 1909-10. 2 v. 8.º Dictionary of famous men of Alsace, past and present.

858 WINTER, CH
   Les Alsaciens illustres. Portraits en photographie, avec
notices biographiques. Photographies par Ch. Winter.
Strasbourg, 1864-65. 3 fasc. ports. 8.º Illustrious Al-
satians; portraits, with biographical notices.

Ardennes (Dept.)

859 ARDENNES;
   Dictionnaire, annuaire et album. Paris, Jouve, 1897.
vii, 360p. ports. 8.º (Les Dictionnaires départementaux)
Dictionary, annual and album of the department of the
Ardennes, France; includes biographies.

860 BOULLIOT, JEAN BAPTISTE JOSEPH, 1750-1833.
   Biographie ardennaise; ou, Histoire des Ardennais qui se
sont fait remarquer par leurs écrits, leurs actions, leurs
vertus ou leurs erreurs. Paris, Chez l'éditeur, 1830.
2 v. 22 cm. Famous people native to the French department
of the Ardennes.

861 COLIN, HUBERT
   Biographies et chroniques populaires du département des
Ardennes. Vouziers, A. Lapie, 1859-64. 3v.

Aube (Dept.)

862 DICTIONNAIRE BIOGRAPHIQUE DE L'AUBE.
   Paris, Jouve, 1897. vii, 350 p. ports. 8.º (Les Dictionnaires départementaux) Biographical dictionary of the department of the Aube, France.

Auvergne

863 AIGUEPERSE, P G
   Biographie; ou, Dictionnaire historique des personnages
d'Auvergne illustres ou fameux par leurs écrits, leur exploits,
leur vertus, leurs erreurs, leurs crimes ou leur rang.
Clermont-Ferrand, Berthier, 1836. 2v. ports. 22cm.
Historical dictionary of famous persons of the Auvergne
region of France.

864 CHAUMEIL,   abbé
   Biographie des personnes remarquables de la Haute-
Auvergne, formant la totalité du départemente du Cantal et

du diocèse de Saint-Flour, précédée d'un essai sur l'histoire religieuse de cette demi-province. 2. éd. Saint-Flour, Impr. de P. Ribains, 1867. 303 p. Biography of the region of Auvergne, France.

Basses — Alpes (Dept.)

865 [FÉRAUD, JEAN JOSEPH MAXIME]
Biographie des hommes remarquables des Basses-Alpes; ou, Dictionnaire historique de tous les personnages de ce département qui se sont signalés par leur génie, leurs talents... depuis les temps les plus récules jusqu'à nos jours. Par une société de gens de lettres. Digne, Repos, 1850. xix, 376 p. 8.° Biographical dictionary of famous men of the French department of the Basses-Alpes.

Bouches—du—Rhone (Dept.)

866 LES BOUCHES-DU-RHÔNE.
Encyclopédie départementale, publiée par le Conseil général avec le concours de la ville de Marseille et de la Chambre de commerce, sous la direction de Paul Masson. 1. ptie: t. 4, 2. vol.: Dictionnaire biographique: des origines à 1800, par Paul Masson. Marseille, Archives départementales des Bouches-du-Rhône [etc.] 1931. xl, 519p. 4.° Encyclopedia for the French department of Bouches-du-Rhone; pt. 1, v. 4, 2d section is a biographical dictionary for the department up to the year 1800.

Brittany

867 GRANGES DE SURGÈRES, ANATOLE, marquis de, 1850-1902.
Iconographie bretonne; ou, Liste de portraits dessinés, gravés ou lithographiés de personnages nés en Bretagne ou appartenant à l'histoire de cette province, avec notices biographiques. Rennes, J. Plihon et L. Hervé [etc.] 1888-89. 2v. in 1. 29cm. Iconography of Britanny--a list of portraits ... of persons born in Britanny or belonging to the history of this province, with biographical notices.

868 KERVILER, RENÉ POCARD DU COSQUER DE, 1842-1907.
Répertoire général de bio-bibliographie bretonne, par René Kerviler. [Continué par l'abbé Chauffier. Rennes, J. Plihon et L. Hervé, 1886-1908. 17 fascicles. Goes up to

Guépin. No more published. General list of Breton bio-bibliography.

869 LEVOT, PROSPER JEAN, 1801-1878.
Biographie bretonne; recueil de notices sur tous les Bretons qui se sont fait un nom soit par leurs vertus ou leurs crimes, soit dans les arts, dans les sciences, dans les lettres, dans la magistrature, dans la politique, dans la guerre, etc., depuis le commencement de l'ère chrétienne jusqu'à nos jours. Avec la collaboration de MM. Bizeul, Aymar de Blois. Vannes, Cauderan, 1852-57. 2 v. 28cm. Bio-bibliography of Brittany.

870 MIORCEC DE KERDANET, DANIEL LOUIS OLIVIER MARIE, 1793-1857?
Notices chronologiques sur les théologiens, jurisconsultes, philosophes, artistes, littérateurs, poètes, bardes, troubadours et historiens de la Bretagne... Brest, Michel, 1818. iv, 504p. 8.° Chronological notices of theologians, jurists, philosophers [etc.] of Brittany.

Burgundy

871 MUTEAU, CHARLES FRANCOIS THÉRÈSE, 1824-1920.
Galerie bourguignonne, par Ch. Muteau et Joseph Garnier. Dijon, J. Picard [etc.] 1858-60. 3 v. 15cm. Burgundian gallery; biography of Burgundy.

Calvados (Dept.)

872 BOISARD, FRANÇOIS
Notices biographiques, littéraires et critiques sur les hommes du Calvados qui se sont fait remarquer par leurs actions ou par leurs ouvrages. Caen, Impr. de Pagny, 1848. vii, 364 p. 18.° Biographical, literary and critical notes on noted men of the French department of Calvados.

873 DICTIONNAIRE BIOGRAPHIQUE, COMPRENANT LA LISTE ET LES BIOGRAPHIES DES NOTABILITÉS DU DÉPARTEMENT DU CALVADOS. Paris, Jouve, 1894. 1 v. (unpaged) 8.° (Les Dictionnaires départementaux) Biographical dictionary of the department of the Calvados, France.

Champagne

.874 [LETILLOIS, of Mézières]
  Biographie générale des Champenois célèbres, morts et
vivants; précédée des Illustres Champenois, poème lyrique,
et enrichie de plusieurs tables chronologiques. Paris, Bureau des Journal des peintres, 1836. 227p. 8.º General
biography of celebrated natives of Champagne, France, living
and dead.

Charente — Inferieure (Dept.)

875 [FEUILLERET, HENRI] 1817-1879.
  Petite biographie des hommes illustres de la Charente-
Inférieure, suivie d'une notice sur ce département. La
Rochelle, Femeau et Gout, 1853. ii, 117 p. 18.º Biographi-
cal sketches of prominent men of the French department of
Charente-Inférieure.

Cote — d'Or (Dept.)

.876 DICTIONNAIRE BIOGRAPHIQUE, COMPRENANT LA LISTE
  ET LES BIOGRAPHIES DES NOTABILITÉS DU DÉPARTE-
MENT DE LA CÔTE-D'OR. Paris, Jouve, 1895. 1 v. (un-
paged) ports. 8.º (Les Dictionnaires départementaux)
Biographical dictionary of the French department of the Côte-
d'Or.

Cotes — du — Nord (Dept.)

877 DICTIONNAIRE BIOGRAPHIQUE, ANNUAIRE ET ALBUM DES
  CÔTES-DU-NORD, 1899. Paris, Jouve, 1899. 1 v. (unpaged) ports. 8.º (Les Dictionnaires départementaux) Biographical dictionary, annual and album of the department of
the Côtes-du-Nord, France.

Dauphine

878 COLOMB DE BATINES, PAUL, vicomte, 1811-1855.
  Catalogue des Dauphinois dignes de mémoire. [1. ptie:
A-J] Grenoble, Prudhomme, 1840. vii, 92p. 8.º No more

published? Catalog of natives of the French Dauphine worthy of remembrance.

879   ROCHAS, ADOLPHE
       Biographie du Dauphiné, contenant l'histoire des hommes nés dans cette province qui se sont fait remarquer dans les lettres, les sciences, les arts, etc., avec le catalogue de leurs ouvrages et la description de leurs portraits. Paris, Charavay, 1856-60. 2 v. 25cm. Bio-bibliography of the Dauphiné region, France.

880   ROUSSET, HENRY
       Les Dauphinoises célèbres. Grenoble, Impr. générale, 1908. xxiii, 648p. illus., ports. 8.º Famous personages of the Dauphiné region, France.

881   [ROUX, XAVIER] 1850-
       Dictionnaire drolatique des contemporains dauphinois. Grenoble, 1890-91. 3 pts. Published in 14 fascicles. Humorous dictionary of contemporary figures in the Dauphiné region, France.

Doubs (Dept.)

882   DICTIONNAIRE BIOGRAPHIQUE, ANNUAIRE ET ALBUM DU DOUBS, 1898. Paris, Jouve, 1898. 1 v. (unpaged) ports. 8.º (Les Dictionnaires départementaux) Biographical dictionary, annual and album of the department of the Doubs, France.

Drome (Dept.)

883   BRUN-DURAND, JUSTIN, 1836-
       Dictionnaire biographique et biblio-iconographique de la Drôme, contenant des notices sur toutes les personnes de ce département qui se sont fait remarquer par leurs actions ou leurs travaux avec l'indication de leurs ouvrages et de leurs portraits. Grenoble, Librairie Dauphinoise, 1900-01. 2 v. 27 cm. Biographical dictionary of the French department of Drôme.

Eure (Dept.)

884   DICTIONNAIRE BIOGRAPHIQUE, COMPRENANT LA LISTE
ET LES BIOGRAPHIES DES NOTABILITÉS DU DÉPARTE-
MENT DE L'EURE. Paris, Jouve, 1894. 1 v. (unpaged)
ports. 8.⁰ (Les Dictionnaires départementaux) Biographical dictionary of the department of the Eure, France.

Finistere (Dept.)

885   DICTIONNAIRE BIOGRAPHIQUE, ANNUAIRE ET ALBUM DU
FINISTÈRE, 1898. Paris, Jouve, 1898. 1 v. (unpaged)
illus. 8.⁰ (Les Dictionnaires départementaux) Biographical
dictionary, annual and album of the French department of the
Finistère.

Forez

886   BERNARD, AUGUSTE JOSEPH, 1811-1868.
Histoire du Forez. [Biographie et bibliographie
foréziennes, recueillies par l'auteur de l'Histoire du Forez]
Montbrison, Impr. de Bernard aîné, 1835. 2v. 8.⁰ Includes
bio-bibliography for the region of Forez in France.

Franche — Comte

887   DANTÈS, ALFRED LANGUE, 1830-1891.
La Franche-Comté littéraire, scientifique et artistique.
Recueil de notices sur les hommes le plus remarquables du
Jura, du Doubs et de la Haute-Seine. Paris, 1879. 379 p.
19cm. Bio-bibliography of the Franche-Comté, a former pro-
vince of eastern France.

Haute —Garonne (Dept.)

888   DICTIONNAIRE BIOGRAPHIQUE, COMPRENANT LA LISTE
ET LES BIOGRAPHIES DES NOTABILITÉS DE LA HAUTE-
GARONNE. Paris, Jouve, 1895. 1 v. (unpaged) ports. 8.⁰
(Les Dictionnaires départementaux) Biographical dictionary
of the department of the Haute-Garonne, France.

Haute —Vienne (Dept.)

889   PEYROT-MAGENET, FRANCOIS
Biographie contemporaine de la Haute-Vienne. Limoges,
Impr. de Ardillier, 1843. 61p. 8.º Early 19th century biog-
raphy of the department of Haute-Vienne, France.

Hautes — Alpes (Dept.)

890   ALLEMAND, FÉLIX, d. 1918.
Dictionnaire biographique des Hautes-Alpes, avec
bibliographie, armoiries, sceaux & portraits. Gap,
Imprimerie & Librairie Alpines, 1911. vi, 481 p. 23cm.
Biographical dictionary of the department of Hautes-Alpes,
France.

Havre, Le

891   LÉVÉE, JÉRÔME BALTHAZAR
Biographie, ou, Galerie historique des hommes célèbres
du Havre qui se sont fait un nom par leurs écrits, leurs
actions, leurs talens... depuis la fondation de cette ville, en
1516, jusqu'aux premières années du XIXᵉ siècle, suivie d'un
supplément et de la biographie des contemporains... Paris,
C.-J. Trouvé, 1828. 2 pts. in 1 v. 8.º Biography of the city
of Le Havre, France.

Ille—et—Vilaine (Dept.)

892   DICTIONNAIRE BIOGRAPHIQUE D'ILLE-ET-VILAINE.
Paris, Jouve, 1895. vii, 474p. ports. 8.º (Les Dictionnaires départementaux) Biographical dictionary of the French
department of Ille-et-Vilaine.

Indre (Dept.)

893   GRILLON DES CHAPELLES, AMADOR
Esquisses biographiques du département de l'Indre. Paris,
B. Duprat, 1862. 3 v. 19cm. Biographical sketches of the
department of the Indre, France.

Indre—et—Loire (Dept.)

894   CARRÉ DE BUSSEROLLE, JACQUES XAVIER.
Dictionnaire géographique, historique et biographique
d'Indre-et-Loire et de l'ancienne province de Touraine. Tours,
Impr. Rouillé-Ladevèze, 1878-84. 6 v. 25 cm. (Mémoires
de la Société archéologique de Touraine, t. 27-32) Geographical, historical and biographical dictionary of the department of Indre-et-Loire & the old province of Touraine.

895   DICTIONNAIRE BIOGRAPHIQUE, COMPRENANT LA LISTE
ET LES BIOGRAPHIQUES DES NOTABILITÉS DU DÉ-
PARTEMENT D'INDRE-ET-LOIRE. Paris, Jouve, 1895.
1 v. (unpaged) ports. 8.º (Les Dictionnaires département-
aux) Biographical dictionary of the departement of Indre-et-
Loire, France.

Jura (Dept.)

896   MONNIER, DÉSIRÉ
Les Jurassiens recommandables par des bienfaits, des
vertus, des services utiles et par des succès obtenus dans
la pratique des arts et des sciences, pour servir à la statistique morale du Jura et à l'histoire des arts en Franche-
Comté. Lons-Le-Saunier, Impr. F. Gauthier, 1828. x,
530p. 8.º Noteworthy persons from the French department
of the Jura.

897   ROCARD, J
Biographie militaire du Jura, comprenant les généraux
et officiers de toutes armes nés dans la Jura qui se sont
fait remarquer dans les guerres de la République et de
l'Empire, depuis 1791 jusqu'au licenciement de l'armée en
1815. Lons-le-Saunier, A. Courbet, 1845. 2 v. in 1. 8.º
Military biography of the French Jura, comprising generals
and officers born in that region and active in the wars of
1791-1815.

Limousin (Dept.)

898 DU BOYS, AUGUSTE
Biographie des hommes illustres de l'ancienne province du
Limousin, par Auguste Du Boys et l'abbé Arbellot. t. 1.
Limoges, Impr. de Ardillier fils, 1854. 1v. 8.° No more
published. Biographies of illustrious men of the old province
of Limousin, France.

Loire (Dept.)

899 DICTIONNAIRE BIOGRAPHIQUE, ANNUAIRE ET ALBUM DE
LA LOIRE, 1899. Paris, Jouve, 1899. 1 v. (unpaged)
ports. 8.º (Les Dictionnaires départementaux) Biographical dictionary, annual & album of the department of the Loire,
France.

Loire — Inferieure (Dept.)

900 DICTIONNAIRE BIOGRAPHIQUE DE LA LOIRE-INFÉRIEURE.
Paris, Jouve, 1895. vii, 432p. ports. 8.º (Les Dictionnaires départementaux) Biographical dictionary of the old
department of the Loire-Inférieure, France.

Loire Valley

901 TOUCHARD-LAFOSSE, GEORGES, 1780-1847.
La Loire historique, pittoresque et biographique, de la
source de ce fleuve à son embouchure dans l'Océan. Tours,
1851. 5 v. illus. 26cm. The Loire Valley: history, description and biography.

Loiret (Dept.)

902 DICTIONNAIRE BIOGRAPHIQUE, ANNUAIRE ET ALBUM DU
LOIRET, 1898. Paris, Jouve, 1898. 1 v. (unpaged)
illus. 8.º (Les Dictionnaires départementaux) Biographical
dictionary, annual and album of the department of the Loiret,
France.

Lot (Dept.)

903   VIDAILLET, JEAN BAPTISTE
      Biographie des hommes célèbres du département du Lot;
ou, Galérie historique des personnages mémorables auxquels
ce département a donné le jour depuis la conquête des Gaules
jusques à l'année 1827... Gourdon, Impr. de A. Lescure,
1827. 1 v. 8.° Biography of famous men of the department
of Lot, France.

Lot—et—Garonne (Dept.)

904   DICTIONNAIRE BIOGRAPHIQUE, COMPRENANT LA LISTE
      ET LES BIOGRAPHIES DES NOTABILITÉS DU DÉPARTE-
MENT DE LOT-ET-GARONNE. Paris, Jouve, 1894. 1 v.
(unpaged) ports. 8.° (Les Dictionnaires départementaux)
Biographical dictionary of the department of Lot-et-Garonne,
France.

Lyons

905   BRÉGHOT DU LUT, CLAUDE, 1784-1849.
      Biographie lyonnaise; catalogue des Lyonnaise dignes de
mémoire, redigé par MM. Bréghot du Lut et Péricaud aîné.
Paris, Publié par la Société littéraire de Lyon, 1839.
Famous citizens of Lyons, France.

Maine (Dept.)

906   PESCHE, JULIEN RÉMY
      Biographie et bibliographie du Maine et du départment de la
Sarthe... par J.-R. Pesche et N. H. F. Desportes. t.1:
A-Brosset. Le Mans, Monnoyer, 1828. 1 v. 8.° Bio-bibliography of the French departments of Maine & Sarthe. No
more published.

Maine—et—Loire (Dept.)

907   DICTIONNAIRE BIOGRAPHIQUE, COMPRENANT LA LISTE
      ET LES BIOGRAPHIES DES NOTABILITÉS DU DÉPARTE-
MENT DE MAINE-ET-LOIRE. Paris, Jouve, 1894. 1 v.

(unpaged) ports. 8.º (Les Dictionnaires départementaux)
Biographical dictionary of the French department of Maine-
et-Loire.

908   PORT, CÉLESTIN, 1828-1901.
       Dictionnaire historique, géographique et biographique de
       Maine-et-Loire. Paris, J.-B. Dumoulin, 1874-78. 3 v.
       26cm. Historical, geographical & biographical dictionary of
       the department of Maine-et-Loire, France.

Manche (Dept.)

909   DICTIONNAIRE BIOGRAPHIQUE, COMPRENANT LA LISTE
          ET LES BIOGRAPHIES DES NOTABILITÉS DU DÉPARTE-
       MENT DE LA MANCHE. Paris, Jouve, 1894. 1 v. (unpaged)
       ports. 8.º (Les Dictionnaires départementaux) Biographical
       dictionary of the department of the Manche, France.

Marne (Dept.)

910   DICTIONNAIRE BIOGRAPHIQUE, COMPRENANT LA LISTE
          ET LES BIOGRAPHIES DES NOTABILITÉS... DU DÉPARTE-
       MENT DE LA MARNE... Paris, Jouve, 1893. 330p. illus.
       8.º (Les Dictionnaires départementaux) Biographical dic-
       tionary of the department of the Marne, France.

Mayenne (Dept.)

911   ANGOT, ALPHONSE, 1844-
       Dictionnaire historique, topographique et biographique de
       la Mayenne. Laval, A. Goupil, 1900-03. 4v. 26cm.
       Historical, topographical and biographical dictionary of the
       department of Mayenne.

Meurthe—et—Moselle (Dept.)

912   DICTIONNAIRE BIOGRAPHIQUE, ANNUAIRE ET ALBUM DE
          MEURTHE-ET-MOSELLE, 1896. Paris, Jouve, 1896.
       1 v. (unpaged) ports. 8.º (Les Dictionnaires départementaux)
       Biographical dictionary, annual and album of the department
       of Meurthe-et-Moselle, France.

Meuse (Dept.)

913   LES HOMMES REMARQUABLES DE LA MEUSE.
Bar-le-Duc, Laguerre, 1848. 1 v. 8.º Remarkable
men of the department of the Meuse, France.

Moselle (Dept.)

914   BÉGIN, ÉMILE AUGUSTE NICOLAS JULES, 1802-1888.
Biographie de la Moselle; ou, Histoire par ordre
alphabétique de toutes les personnes nées dans ce département,
qui se sont fait remarquer par leurs actions, leurs talens,
leurs ecrits, leurs vertus, ou leurs crimes. Metz, Verro-
nais, 1829-32. 4v. ports. 22cm. Biographical dictionary of
the French department of the Moselle.

915   MICHEL, EMMANUEL
Biographie populaire du département de la Moselle à l'u-
sage des écoles. 1. ptie: Artistes, artisans, industriels et
ouvriers. Metz, Alcan, 1849. 248 p. No more published?
Popular biography of the department of the Moselle.

Nice

916   TOSELLI, JEAN BAPTISTE
Biographie niçoise ancienne et moderne; ou, Dictionnaire
historique de tous les hommes qui se sont fait remarquer...
dans la ville et le comté de Nice... Nice, 1860. 2 v. 8.º
Biography of ancient and modern Nice.

Nivernaise

917   GUENEAU, VICTOR AUGUSTIN, 1835-
Dictionnaire biographique des personnes nées en Nivernais
ou revendiquées par le Nivernais qui ... ont mérité de n'être
pas oubliées. Nevers, Mazeron frères, 1899. 178 p. 28cm.
Biographical dictionary of persons born in Nivernais (the
former French province) or claimed by the people of
Nivernais, who deserve to be remembered.

Nord (Dept.)

918   DICTIONNAIRE BIOGRAPHIQUE, COMPRENANT LA LISTE
ET LES BIOGRAPHIES DES NOTABILITÉS DU DÉPARTE-
MENT DU NORD. Paris, Jouve, 1893. 1 v. (unpaged) ports.
8.º (Les Dictionnaires départementaux) Biographical dictionary of the department of the Nord, France.

Normandy

919   FRONDEVILLE, HENRI DE
Les conseillers du Parlement du Normandie au seizième
siècle, 1499-1594. Recueil genéalogique établi sur la base du
manuscrit Bigot de la Bibliothèque de Rouen. Rouen, A.
Lestringant, 1960. xii, 676 p. illus. 23 cm. (Société de
l'histoire de Normandie. [Publications]) Biography of the
councillors and officials of the Parlement (court of justice)
of Rouen in Normandy.

920   LEBRETON, THÉODORE ÉLOI, 1803-1883.
Biographie normande; recueil de notices biographiques et
bibliographiques sur les personnages célèbres nés en Normandie et sur ceux qui se sont seulement distingués par leurs actions ou par leurs écrits. Rouen, A. Le Brument, 1857-61.
3 v. 23cm. Bio-bibliography of Normandy.

921   OURSEL, Mme. NOÉMI NOIRE, 1847-
Nouvelle biographie normande. Paris, A. Picard, 1886-
88. 2 v. in 1. 26cm. Contains over 6,000 bio-bibliographical notices for Normandy.

922   --- ----Supplément. Paris, A. Picard, 1888. 164 p. 25cm.

Oise (Dept.)

923   DICTIONNAIRE BIOGRAPHIQUE, COMPRENANT LA LISTE
ET LES BIOGRAPHIES DES NOTABILITÉS DU DÉPARTE-
MENT DE L'OISE. Paris, Jouve, 1894. 1 v. (unpaged) 8.º

(Les Dictionnaires départementaux) Biographical dictionary
of the department of the Oise, France.

Orleannais

924   BRAINNE, CHARLES, 1825-1864.
      Les hommes illustres de l'Orléannais; biographie générale
des trois départements du Loiret, d'Eure-et-Loir et de Loir-
et-Cher, par C. Brainne, J. Debarbouiller [et] Ch.-F.
Lapierre. Orléans, A. Gatineau, 1852. 2 v. in 1. 24 cm.
General biography of the three French departments mentioned.

Paris

925   GOURIET, JEAN BAPTISTE, 1774-1855.
      Les charlatans célèbres; ou, Tableau historique des bate-
leurs, des baladins, des jongleurs, des bouffons, des opéra-
teurs, des voltigeurs, des escamoteurs, des filous, des
escrocs, des devins, des tireurs de cartes, des diseurs de
bonne aventure, et généralement de tous les personnages qui
se sont rendus célèbres dans les rues et sur les places publiques de Paris, depuis une haute antiquité jusqu'à nos jours.
2. éd. Paris, Lerouge, 1819. 2v. 8.º Celebrated charlatans ... buffoons ... pickpockets ... fortune-tellers [and
similar types] of Paris.

926   PARIS-NOTABILITÉS.
      Dictionnaire biographique des notabilités parisiennes con-
temporaines —notabilités françaises et notabilités étrangères.
1. sér., 1.-2. ptie. Paris, 1912-13. 2 v. 8.º Noteworthy
people of Paris. A biographical dictionary. No more published.

927   TARDIEU, AMBROISE, 1840-
      Dictionnaire iconographique des Parisiens, c'est-à-dire
liste générale des personnes nées à Paris, dont il existe des
portraits gravés et lithographies, avec une biographie de
chaque nom cité (environ 3000) Ouvrage orné de curieux et
rarissimes portraits par Thomas de Leu, Léonard Gaultier,
etc., reproduits par la photogravure. Herment (Puy-de-
Dome) L'auteur, 1885. iii p., 308 columns. illus., 16 ports.
25cm. Iconographic dictionary of Paris—persons born in
Paris for whom there exist engraved or lithographed portraits with a biography for each name cited (ca. 3000)

Pas—de—Calais (Dept.)

928   DICTIONNAIRE BIOGRAPHIQUE DU PAS-DE-CALAIS.
Paris, Jouve, 1897. 752p. ports. 8.º (Les Dictionnaires départementaux) Biographical dictionary of the department of the Pas-de-Calais, France.

Poitou

929   DREUX DU RADIER, JEAN FRANCOIS, 1714-1780.
Bibliothèque historique, et critique du Poitou, contenant
les vies des savans de cette province, depuis le troisième
siècle jusqu'à présent; une notice de leurs ouvrages, avec des
observations pour en juger... Paris, Ganeau, 1754. 5v.
12.º Bio-bibliography of the province of Poitou, France.

Provence

930   [GUEIDON, ALEXANDRE]
La Plutarque provencal: vies des hommes et des femmes
illustres de la Provence ancienne et moderne, par une Société
des membres de l'Institut, et d'Artistes, recueillies et
publiées par A. G. [Nouv. éd.] Marseille, 1858. 2 v.
ports. 4.º The Provencal Plutarch; lives of famous men
and women of Provence, France, ancient and modern.

931   SÉNÈS, CÉLESTIN, called LA SINSE.
Provencaux: Historiens, philosophes, économistes, artistes,
hommes politiques, savants, soldats et marins ... Notes biographiques. [1.]-2 sér. Toulon, Impr. du Petit var [etc.]
1902-04. 2 v. 8.º Famous men of Provence: historians,
philosophers, economists [etc.]

Rhone (Dept.)

932   DICTIONNAIRE BIOGRAPHIQUE, ANNUAIRE ET ALBUM DU
RHÔNE, 1899. Paris, Jouve, 1899. 1 v. (unpaged) illus.
8.º (Les Dictionnaires départementaux) Biographical dictionary, annual and album of the department of the Rhône,
France.

Roussillon

933 CAPEILLE, JEAN.
   Dictionnaire de biographies roussillonnaises. Perpignan,
   J. Comet, 1914. viii, 724 p. 28 cm. Issued in 5 parts, 1910-
   1912. Dictionary of biography for the French province of
   Roussillon.

Saintonge

934 RAINGUET, PIERRE DAMIEN, b. 1802.
   Biographie saintongeaise; ou, Dictionnaire historique de
   tous les personnages qui se sont illustrés par leurs écrits
   ou leurs actions dans les anciennes provinces de Saintonge
   et d'Aunis, formant aujourd'hui le département de la
   Charente-Inférieure depuis le temps les plus reculés jusqu'à
   nos jours. Saintes, 1851. 642p. port. 19cm. Biographical
   dictionary for the old French provinces of Saintonge and
   Aunis (which were eventually incorporated into the department of Charente-Inférieure)

Saone—et—Loire (Dept.)

935 SAÔNE-ET-LOIRE.
   Dictionnaire, annuaire et album. Paris, Jouve, 1896. 1 v.
   (unpaged) ports. 8.º (Les Dictionnaires départementaux)
   Dictionary, annual and album of the department of Saône-et-
   Loire, France; includes biographies.

Seine—et—Marne (Dept.)

936 DICTIONNAIRE BIOGRAPHIQUE, COMPRENANT LA LISTE
   ET LES BIOGRAPHIES DES NOTABILITÉS DU DÉPARTE-
   MENT DE SEINE-ET-MARNE. Paris, Jouve, 1893. 1 v.
   (unpaged) ports. 8.º (Les Dictionnaires départementaux)
   Biographical dictionary of the department of Seine-et-Marne,
   France.

Seine—et—Oise (Dept.)

937 DANIEL, ERNEST, b. 1795.
   Biographie des hommes remarquables du département de

Seine-et-Oise, depuis le commencement de la monarchie jusqu'à ce jour, par E. et H. Daniel. Rambouillet, Chaignet
[etc.] 1832. 428 p. 22cm. Biographies of prominent men,
past & present, of the French department of Seine-et-Oise.

938 DICTIONNAIRE BIOGRAPHIQUE, COMPRENANT LA LISTE
ET LES BIOGRAPHIES DES NOTABILITÉS DU...DÉPARTE-
MENT DE SEINE-ET-OISE. Paris, Jouve, 1893. vii, 264p.
ports. 8.º (Les Dictionnaires départementaux) Biographical
dictionary of the department of Seine-et-Oise, France.

Seine — Inferieure (Dept.)

939 DICTIONNAIRE BIOGRAPHIQUE, COMPRENANT LA LISTE
ET LES BIOGRAPHIES DES NOTABILITÉS DANS LES
LETTRES, LES SCIENCES ET LES ARTS, DANS LA POLI-
TIQUE, LA MAGISTRATURE, L'ENSEIGNEMENT, L'ARMÉE,
LA NOBLESSE, LE HAUT CLERGÉ, DANS LA GRANDE IN-
DUSTRIE, LE GRAND COMMERCE, L'AGRICULTURE, LA
FINANCE, ETC., DU DÉPARTEMENT DE LA SEINE-
INFÉRIEURE. Paris, Jouve, 1892. vii, 440 p. illus. 8.º
(Les Dictionnaires départementaux) Biographical dictionary
of the old department of the Seine-Inférieure, France.

940 GUILBERT, PHILIPPE JACQUES ÉTIENNE VINCENT
Mémoires biographiques et littéraires, par ordre alphabétique, sur les hommes qui se sont fait remarquer dans le
département de la Seine-Inférieure, par leurs écrits, leurs
actions, leurs talens, leurs vertus, etc. Rouen, F. Mori,
1812. 2 v. fronts. (ports.) 22cm. Biographical and literary memoirs, alphabetically arranged, of distinguished
men of the department of the Seine-Inférieure.

Somme (Dept.)

941 BIOGRAPHIE DES HOMMES CÉLÈBRES,
Des savants, des artistes et des littérateurs...de la Somme.
Amiens, Impr. de R. Machart, 1835-38. 3 v. 8.º Tome 3:
Supplément. Distinguished scholars, artists and men of letters
of the department of the Somme, France.

942 DICTIONNAIRE BIOGRAPHIQUE, COMPRENANT LA LIST
ET LES BIOGRAPHIES DES NOTABILITÉS DU DÉPARTE-
MENT DE LA SOMME. Paris, Jouve, 1893. 1 v. (unpaged)
8.º (Les Dictionnaires départementaux) Biographical dictionary of the department of the Somme, France.

Tarn—et—Garonne (Dept.)

943 FORESTIÉ, ÉMERAND (or ÉMILE?) 1816-1900.
Biographie de Tarn-et-Garonne. Études historiques et
bibliographiques. Publiées par E. Forestié neveu, avec le
concours de plusieurs écrivains. 1. sér. Montauban, Impr.
Forestié neveu, 1860. iv, 524 p. No more published?
Bio-bibliography of the French department of Tarn-et-
Garonne.

944 REY, BERNARD
Galerie biographique des personnages célèbres de Tarn-
et-Garonne. Montauban, Forestié [1857] 322p. plates. 8.°
Biographies of famous persons of the French department of
Tarne-et-Garonne.

Thimerais

945 DREUX DU RADIER, JEAN FRANCOIS, 1714-1780.
Éloges historiques des hommes illustres du Thimerais.
Nouv. éd. Introd. et notes par M. Doublet de Boisthibault.
Chartres, Noury-Coquard, 1859. xxxii,124 p. 18.° The
famous men of Thimerais, France.

Toulouse

946 BIOGRAPHIE TOULOUSAINE;
ou, Dictionnaire historique de personnages de Toulouse,
par une société des gens de lettres. Ouvrage précédé d'un
précis de l'histoire de Toulouse, de tables chronologiques.
Paris, L. G. Michaud, 1823. 2 v. 22cm. By
E. L. baron de Lamothe-Langon, J. T. Laurent-Gousse and
A. L. C. A. Du Mège. Biographical dictionary of personages
of Toulouse, France.

Var (Dept.)

947 DICTIONNAIRE BIOGRAPHIQUE DU DÉPARTEMENT DU VAR.
Paris, Flammarion [1902] vii, 601 p. ports. 8.° (Les
Dictionnaires départementaux) Biographical dictionary of the
department of the Var, France.

Vaucluse (Dept.)

948   AUBERT, AUGUSTE
        Les Vauclusiens; ou, Dictionnaire biographique spécial au
        département de Vaucluse. Avignon, Seguin frères, 1890-92.
        2 v. 16.º A biographical dictionary for the French depart-
        ment of Vaucluse.

949   BARJAVEL, CASIMIR FRANCOIS HENRI, 1803-1868.
        Dictionnaire historique, biographique, et bibliographique
        du département de Vaucluse; ou, Recherches pour servir à
        l'histoire scientifique, littéraire et artistique, ainsi qu'à
        l'histoire religieuse, civil et militaire des villes et arron-
        dissements d'Avignon, de Carpentras, d'Apt et d'Orange.
        Carpentras, Impr. de L. Devillario, 1841. 2 v. 24cm.
        Half title: Bio-bibliographie vauclusienne. Bio-bibliography
        of the department of Vaucluse, France.

Vendee (Dept.)

950   MERLAND, CONSTANT JACQUES, 1808-1885.
        Biographie vendéenne. Nantes, V. Forest et E. Grimaud
        [etc.] 1883. 5 v. 19cm. Biography of the maritime depart-
        ment of the Vendée.

Vendome

951   ROCHAMBEAU, EUGÈNE ACHILLE LACROIX DE VIMEUR,
        comte de, 1836-1897.
        Biographie vendômoise; histoire par ordre alphabétique
        de la vie publique & privée de tous les personnages remarq-
        uables nés dans le Vendomois & de tous ceux qui s'y sont
        signales par leurs services & les travaux. t. 1 [A-D] Paris,
        H. Champion, 1884. 707p. ports. 25cm. No more pub-
        lished. Dictionary of biography of the Vendôme region,
        France.

Vosges (Dept.)

952   DICTIONNAIRE BIOGRAPHIQUE DES VOSGES.
        Paris, Jouve, 1897. 464 p. ports. 8.º (Les Dictionnaires
        départementaux) Biographical dictionary of the French de-
        partment of the Vosges.

953   VUILLEMIN, M   F
      Biographie vosgienne. Nancy, Mlle. Gonet, 1848. 1 v.
8.° Biography of the department of the Vosges, France.

GERMANY
Anonyms and Pseudonyms

954   ERSCH, JOHANN SAMUEL, 1766-1828.
      Verzeichniss aller anonymischen Schriften und Aufsätze
in der vierten Ausgabe des Gelehrten Teutschlands... Nebst
einem Verzeichniss von Uebersetzungen der darin angegeben-
en Schriften in andere Sprachen. Lemgo, 1788-96. 3 v. 8.°
Anonymous writings and essays in the 4th ed. of Gelehrtes
Teutschland.

955   HOLZMANN, MICHAEL, 1860-1930.
      Deutsches Anonymenlexikon, aus den Quellen bearb. von
Michael Holzmann und Hanns Bohatta. Weimar, Gesellschaft
der Bibliophilen, 1902-28. 7 v. 24cm. Supplemented by
'Beiträge zum Deutschen Anonymen-Lexicon, von Alfred
Rosenbaum, published in Zeitschrift fur Bücherfreunde, n.F.,
Leipzig, 1923, 15 Jahrg., p.77-88, 112-128. German anonym-
dictionary.

956   HOLZMANN, MICHAEL, 1860-1930.
      Deutsches Pseudonymen-Lexikon; aus den Quellen bearb.
von Michael Holzmann und Hanns Bohatta. Wien, Akademischer Verlag, 1906. xxiv, 323p. 23cm. German pseudonym-
dictionary.

957   RASSMANN, CHRISTIAN FRIEDRICH, 1772-1831.
      Kurzgefasstes Lexicon deutscher pseudonymer Schrift-
steller, von der ältern bis auf die jüngste Zeit aus allen
Fächern der Wissenschaften. Mit einer Vorrede über die
Sitte der literarischen Verkappung, von J. W. S. Lindner.
Leipzig, W. Nauck, 1830. viii, 248p. 22cm. Concise dic-
tionary of German pseudonymous authors.

958   ROSENBAUM, ALFRED, 1861-
      Beiträge zum Deutschen Anonymenlexikon. (In Zeitschrift
für Bücherfreunde. Leipzig, 1923. Neue Folge, 15. Jahrg.,
p. 77-88, 112-128) Contributions to Holzmann's Deutsches
Anonymen-Lexikon (q. v.)

959   SCHMIDT, ANDREAS GOTTFRIED, 1794-1851.
Gallerie deutscher pseudonymer Schriftsteller vorzüglich
des letzten Jahrhunderts. Ein Beitrag zur neuesten Literar-
geschichte. Grimma, Verlags-Comptoir, 1840. viii, 252 p.
18cm. Gallery of German pseudonymous authors principally
of the last century.

960   SCHNEIDER, MAX, 1859-1939.
Deutsches Titelbuch. Ein Hilfsmittel zum Nachweis von
Verfassern deutscher Literaturwerke. 2., verb. und wesentlich verm. Aufl. Berlin, Haude & Spener, 1927. viii, 799 p.
24cm. First ed. published 1907-1909 under title: Von wem ist
das doch? German 'title-book.' An aid for the identification
of writers of German literary works.

General Works

961   ADAM, MELCHIOR, d. 1622.
Dignorum laude virorum, quos musa vetat mori,
immortalitas, seu Vitae theologorum, jure-consultum &
politicorum, medicorum, atque philosophorum, maximam
partem Germanorum, nonnullam quoque exterorum... Ed. 3,
accurate recensita, ex triplici indice, personarum gemino,
tertio rerum, locupletata. Francofurti ad Moenum, J. M. à
Sande, 1705. 1v. (various pagings) 36cm. A "Gesamtausgabe"
of Adam's earlier Vitae Germanorum theologorum, Vitae
Germanorum medicorum, Vitae Germanorum philosophorum,
Vitae Germanorum jure consultorum et politicorum, &
Decades duae, continentes vitas theologorum exterorum
principuum (issued in 5 vols., 1615-1653(?)) Lives of famous
Germans.

962   ALLGEMEINE DEUTSCHE BIOGRAPHIE.
Hrsg. durch die Historische Commission bei der K.
Akademie der Wissenschaften. Leipzig, Duncker, 1875-1912.
56 v. 24cm. The old German national biography.

963   ANDREAS, WILLY, 1884-   comp.
Die grossen Deutschen; neue deutsche Biographie, hrsg.
von Willy Andreas und Wilhelm von Scholz. Berlin, Propyläen-Verlag [1943-   v. illus., ports. 25cm.
Signed biographies, chronologically arranged. "Neue völlig
durchgesehene Auflage, 1943." First published 1935-
The great Germans; new German biography. In 1956-57 a
work with the same title (in 4 volumes) was published under
the editorship of Theodor Heuss, H. Heimpel and B. Reifenberg.

964   BIOGRAPHISCHE BLÄTTER.
       Jahrbuch für lebensgeschichtliche Kunst und Forschung.
       Unter ständiger Mitwirkung von Michael Bernays [et al.] hrsg.
       von Anton Bettelheim. 1. -2. Bd.   Berlin, E. Hofmann, 1895-
       96. 2 v. ports. 24cm. quarterly. Continued as Biogra-
       phisches Jahrbuch und deutscher Nekrolog. Yearbook for the
       art of biography and biographical research; covers Germany
       only.

965   BIOGRAPHISCHES JAHRBUCH UND DEUTSCHER NEKROLOG;
       Unter ständigen Mitwirkung von Guido Adler [et al.] hrsg.
       von Anton Bettelheim. 1. -18. Bd.; [1896]-1913.   Berlin,
       G. Reimer, 1897-1917. 18 v. ports. 25cm. Supersedes
       Biographische Blätter (1895-1896) Superseded in 1925 by
       Deutsches biographisches Jahrbuch. Yearbook of biography
       for Germany and German necrology.

966   ----Register zu Band I bis X (1896-1905) bearb. von Georg
       Wolff. Berlin, G. Reimer, 1908.   239 columns.   25cm.

967   BRACHVOGEL, ALBERT EMIL, 1824-1878.
       Die Männer der neuen deutschen Zeit.   Eine Sammlung von
       Biographieen unserer Fürsten, Staatsmänner und Helden.
       Hannover, 1873-75. 4 v. 8.º Men of modern Germany;
       biographies of princes, statesmen and heroes.

968   BREDOW, CLAUS VON
       Historische Rang- und Stammliste des deutschen Heeres,
       von Claus von Bredow und Ernst von Wedel. Berlin, A.
       Scherl, 1905. xxi, 1444 p.   Historical ranking list and muster
       roll of the German Army.

969   BRUCKER, JOHANN JAKOB, 1696-1770.
       Ehren-Tempel der deutschen Gelehrsamkeit, in welchem
       die Bildnisse Gelehrter, und um die schönen und philologischen
       Wissenschafften verdienter Manner unter den Deutschen aus
       dem XV., XVI. und ihre Geschichte, Verdienste und Merck-
       würdigkeiten entworfen sind, von Jacob Brucker. In Kupfer
       gebracht von Johann Jacob Haid. Augspurg, J. J. Haid, 1747.
       210 (i. e. 212), [4] p. 50 ports. 25 x 19cm. German scholars
       of the 15th - 17th centuries, with portraits and biographical
       sketches.

970   COLOGNE. UNIVERSITÄT.
       Die Matrikel der Universität Köln, 1389 bis 1559, bearb. von
       Hermann Keussen. Bonn, H. Behrendt [etc.] 1892-1931.   3v.

in 4. 25cm. (Publikationen der Gesellschaft für Rheinische Geschichtskunde, 8) A 2d edition of vol. 1 included the years 1466-1475 which were missing in the first edition of that volume. Rolls of the University of Cologne, 1389-1559.

971 DAS DEUTSCHE FÜHRERLEXIKON 1934/1935.
Berlin, O. Stollberg [c1934] 552, 148 p. ports. 25cm.
Biographical dictionary of leading figures in the Nazi regime.

972 DEUTSCHES BIOGRAPHISCHES JAHRBUCH,
Hrsg. vom Verbande der Deutschen Akademien. Bd. 1-
1914/16- Berlin und Leipzig, Deutsche Verlags-Anstalt
Stuttgart, 1925- v. ports. 25cm. Supersedes Bio-
graphisches Jahrbuch und Deutscher Nekrolog (1896-1913)
Biographical yearbook for Germany.

973 DEUTSCHES GESCHLECHTERBUCH
(Genealogisches Handbuch bürgerlicher Familien) 1. -
Bd. 1889- Charlottenburg, F. Mahler [etc.] v. illus.
15 x 12cm. Title varies: v. 1-10, Genealogisches Handbuch
bürgerlicher Familian [etc.] Imprint varies. Includes biographical material for leading members of German families.

974 DEUTSCHES KOLONIAL-LEXIKON;
Hrsg. von Heinrich Schnee. Leipzig, Quelle und Meyer
[c1920] 3 v. illus., maps. 26cm. Includes biographical
data for prominent persons in the German colonies of the late
19th and early 20th century.

975 DEUTSCHES ZEITGENOSSENLEXIKON.
Biographisches Handbuch deutscher Männer und Frauen der
Gegenwart. Leipzig, Schulze, 1905. 1626 columns. 26cm.
Edited by Franz Neubert. No more published? Dictionary of
contemporary Germans (1905)

976 DEUTSCHLANDS, ÖSTERREICH-UNGARNS UND DER
SCHWEIZ GELEHRTER, KÜNSTLER UND SCHRIFTS-
TELLER IN WORT UND BILD. 3. Ausg. Hannover, A.
Steinhage, 1911. v, 699 p. ports. (Dresslers Verlag für
moderne Literatur) Scholars, artists and writers of Germany,
Austria-Hungary and Switzerland in text and portraits.

977 GANZER, KARL RICHARD, 1909.-
Das deutsche Führergesicht; 200 Bildnisse deutscher
Kämpfer und Wegsucher aus zwei Jahrtausenden. Mit einer

Einführung in der Geist ihrer Zeit. München, J. F. Lehmann [1935] 240 p. ports. , facsims. 25 cm. 200 portraits and biographical sketches of German champions of 2000 years.

978   GENEALOGISCHES HANDBUCH DES ADELS.
1. -   Bd. : 1951-   Glücksburg, Ostsee, C. A. Starke. v. illus. , ports. 17cm. Genealogical handbook of the German nobility; with biographical data.

979   GERMANY (DEMOCRATIC REPUBLIC, 1949-) VOLKS-KAMMER.
Handbuch der Volkskammer der Deutschen Demokratischen Republik. Berlin, Kongress-Verlag, 1957. 536 p. ports. Includes some 500 biographical sketches and portraits of members of the People's Chamber of the German Democratic Republic.

980   GERMANY (FEDERAL REPUBLIC, 1949-) BUNDESMINIS-TERIUM DES INNERN.
Handbuch für die Bundesrepublik Deutschland. 1953-54. Köln-Berlin, C. Heymann. 2 v. 22cm. Issued by the Bundesminister des Innern. Provides facts on government personnel. Absorbed by Die Bundesrepublik. Handbook for the German Federal Republic; provides biographical data for Government personnel.

981   GERMANY (FEDERAL REPUBLIC, 1949-) BUNDESMINIS-TERIUM FÜR GESAMTDEUTSCHE FRAGEN.
SBZ-Biographie; ein biographisches Nachschlagebuch über die sowjetische Besatzungszone Deutschlands, zusammengestellt vom Untersuchungsausschuss Freiheitlicher Juristen, Berlin. [2. Aufl.] Bonn, 1964. 406 p. 21 x 10cm. Biography of Germans in the Soviet zone (i. e. in Eastern Germany or the German Democratic Republic) Completely rev. ed. of Wer ist wer in der SBZ ?

982   DIE GROSSEN DEUTSCHEN:
Deutsche Biographie, hrsg. von Hermann Heimpel, Theodor Heuss [und] Benno Reifenberg. Berlin, Propyläen-Verlag [1956-57] 4 v. illus. 25cm. The great Germans: German biography.

983   HANDBUCH DER DEUTSCHEN WISSENSCHAFT.
1. -   Ausg. ; 1949-   Berlin, F. K. Koetschau.   v. 21cm. Each issue in 2 v. ; vol. 2 contains biographies of contemporary German scholars.

984 HENKELS, WALTER
99 [i. e. Neunundneunzig] Bonner Köpfe. Düsseldorf,
Econ Verlag [1963] 330p. 23cm. 99 important figures in
the German Federal Republic.

985 HENTZEN, ALFRED, 1903-
Die grossen Deutschen im Bild. Hrsg. von Alfred
Hentzen und Niels V. Holst. Mit 460 Abbildungen. Berlin,
Propyläen-Verlag [1936] 487p. ports. 25cm. Portraits:
p. 19-478. Famous Germans in portraiture.

986 HORKENBACH, CUNO, ed.
Das Deutsche Reich von 1918 bis heute. Hrsg. von Cuno
Horkenbach mit sachlicher Unterstützung der Reichsbehörden,
von Parlamentariern und Journalisten, Parteien,
Körperschaften und Verbänden. 1- 1918/30- Berlin,
Verlag für Presse, Wirtschaft und Politik [1931- v.
26cm. The 4th volume of issue is a who's who of leading
persons in German political life.

987 KABISCH, ERNST, 1886-
Die Führer des Reichsheeres, 1921 und 1931; zur Erin-
nerung an die 10-jährige Wiederkehr der Reichsheergründung
vom 1 Januar 1921. Mit 800 Porträts. Stuttgart, Dieck, 1931.
52p. ports. 26 x 33cm. On cover: Eine Bilderreihe.
The leaders of the German Army, 1921 and 1931. With 800
portraits.

988 KNESCHKE, ERNST HEINRICH, 1798-1869.
Neues allgemeines deutsches Adels-Lexicon, im Vereine
mit mehreren Historikern hrsg. Leipzig, Degener, 1929/30.
9 v. 23cm. "Unveränderter Abdruck des... 1859-1870
erschienenen Werkes." A dictionary of the German nobility,
with biographical data.

989 KOSCH, WILHELM, 1879-
Biographisches Staatshandbuch; Lexikon der Politik,
Presse und Publizistik. Bern, Francke, 1959- v.
25cm. A bio-bibliographical dictionary of contemporary
statesmen---German, Swiss and Austrian.

990 KOSCH, WILHELM, 1879-
Das katholische Deutschland; biographisch-bibliographisches Lexikon. Augsburg, Haas & Grabherr, 1933-37. v.
plates, ports. 28cm. Vols. 1-2, A-Rehbach, 16th century

to the present (including living persons) In progress or no
more published? Biographical-bibliographical dictionary of
Catholic Germany.

991   KÜRSCHNERS DEUTSCHER GELEHRTEN-KALENDER.
        1. -   Ausg.; 1925-   Berlin, W. de Gruyter.
        v. ports. 21cm. Calendar of German scholars; contempor-
        ary.

992   LEPORIN, CHRISTIAN POLYCARP, 1689-1747.
        Germania literata vivens; oder; Das jetzt lebende gelehrte
        Deutschland/durch ausführliche Lebens-Beschreibungen vieler
        in Deutschland zu unserer Zeit lebenden gelehrten Männer.
        Quedlinburg, Bey G. E. Struntzen, 1724-25. 2 v. in 1. port.
        18cm. Contemporary littérateurs of Germany; or, Learned
        [men] of Germany now living.

993   LEXIKON SOZIALISTISCHER DEUTSCHER LITERATUR,
        von den Anfängen bis 1945; monographisch-biographische
        Darstellungen. [Redaktionskollegium: Inge Diersen, et al.
        2. Aufl.] Leipzig, Bibliographisches Institut, 1964. 592p.
        22cm. A bio-bibliographical dictionary of socialism in Ger-
        many.

994   MITTELDEUTSCHE KÖPFE;
        Lebensbilder aus einem Jahrtausend. [Hrsg. vom Mittel-
        deutschen Kulturrat e. V., Bonn] Frankfurt am Main, W.
        Weidlich, 1959 [c1958] 239p. 23cm. A biographical diction-
        ary of famous Germans of Berlin, Brandenburg, Saxony,
        Saxony-Anhalt, Thuringia, Pomerania and Mecklenburg.

995   MÜFFLING, WILHELM, Freiherr von
        Wegbereiter und Vorkämpfer für das neue Deutschland.
        Mit 168 Bildnissen von E. Retzlaff (Düsseldorf) und anderen.
        München, J. F. Lehmann, 1933. 64 p. ports. 25cm.
        Portraits of 170 German leaders, with Nazis featured.

996   MUNDT, HERMANN
        Bio-bibliographisches Verzeichnis von Universitäts- und
        Hochschuldrucken (Dissertationen) vom Ausgang des 16. bis
        Ende des 19. Jahrhunderts. Leipzig, E. Carlsohn, 1934-
        v. 26cm. Contains some biographical data; chiefly German
        scholars with a few Dutch & Scandinavians.   Contents. --Bd.
        1. A-Kuhn. --Bd. 2. Kuhn-Ritter.

997   NEKROLOG AUF DAS JAHR 1790[-1800]
Enthaltend Nachrichten von dem Leben merkwürdiger
verstorbener Deutschen. Gesammelt von Friedrich Schlichtegroll. [1.]-11. Jahrg. Gotha, J. Perthes, 1791-1806. Necrology [of Germans] for the years 1790-1800. Continued as Nekrolog der Teutschen für das neunzehnte Jahrhundert.

998   --- ----Supplement-Band für die Jahre 1790, 91, 92 und 93,
rückständige Biographien, Zusätze und Register enthaltend.
Von Friedrich Schlichtegroll. Gotha, J. Perthes, 1798.
444, 238 p. 18cm.

999   NEKROLOG DER TEUTSCHEN FÜR DAS NEUNZEHNTE
JAHRHUNDERT. Hrsg. von Friedrich Schlichtegroll.
1.-5. Bd. Gotha, J. Perthes, 1802-06. 5 v. ports. 16-17cm.
Preceded by: Nekrolog auf das Jahr 1790[-1800] Necrology
of Germans for the 19th century.

1000   NEUE DEUTSCHE BIOGRAPHIE.
Hrsg. von der Historischen Kommission bei der Bayerischen
Akademie der Wissenschaften ... Berlin, Duncker und Humblot, 1953-   v. 26cm. New German biography. Successor to the Allgemeine deutsche Biographie.

1001   NEUER NEKROLOG DER DEUTSCHEN.
1.-30. Jahrg.; 1823-1852. Ilmenau, B. F. Voigt, 1824-34;
Weimar, B. F. Voigt, 1835-54. 60 v. ports. 17-18cm. The
new necrology for Germany, 1823-1852. Editors: 1823-24, F.
A. Schmidt. --1825-52, B. F. Voigt. 2 volumes a year. No
more published.

1002   --- ----Register. Weimar [etc.] B. F. Voigt, 1836-56.
3 v. 17-18cm.

1003   OSTERROTH, FRANZ
Biographisches Lexikon der Sozialismus. Hannover,
Dietz [1960-   v. illus., ports. 21cm. Contents. --
Bd. 1. Verstorbene Persönlichkeiten. Biographical dictionary
of (German) socialists.

1004   PANTALEON, HEINRICH, 1522-1595.
Das erste [-dritte] Theil Teutscher Nation Heldenbuch:
Inn diesem werden aller hochverrümpten teutschen Personen
... Leben unnd namhafftige Thaten ... beschrieben ...
Erstlich ... zu Latein zusammen gezogen ... Jetzmalen aber

von dem ersten Authore selbs verteutschet, gemehret, unnd
gebesseret ... Basel, N. Brylingers Erben, 1567-70. 3 v.
folio. Heroes of the German nation. Translation of Proso-
pographicae heroum atque illustrium virorum totius Germaniae.
The German translation is much more comprehensive in scope
than the original Latin.

1005 PANTALEON, HEINRICH, 1522-1595.
Prosopographiae heroum atque illustrium virorum totius
Germaniae ... a condito mundo (ad ... annum ... millesimum
quingentesimum sexagesimum sextum usque) ... Basileae,
Brylinger, 1565-66. 3 v. folio. Heroes & illustrious men
of Germany from the world's beginning to the year 1566.

1006 PETERSDORFF, HERMANN VON, 1864-
Deutsche Männer und Frauen. Biographische Skizzen
vornehmlich zur Geschichte Preussens in achtzehnten und
neunzehnten Jahrhundert. Berlin, R. Hobbing, 1913. x, 459p.
4.º German men & women. Biographical sketches chiefly
concerned with the history of Prussia in the 18th-19th centuries. Drawn for the most part from the Allgemeine deutsche
Biographie.

1007 REICHSHANDBUCH DER DEUTSCHEN GESELLSCHAFT;
Das Handbuch der Persönlichkeiten in Wort und Bild.
Berlin, Deutscher Wirtschaftsverlag, 1930. 2 v. port.
35cm. No more published? Several thousand biographical
sketches of eminent 'contemporary' Germans. Edited by
Robert Volz.

1008 RÖSSLER, HELLMUTH
Biographisches Wörterbuch zur deutschen Geschichte, von
Hellmuth Rössler und Günther Franz unter Mitarbeit von
Willy Hoppe. München, R. Oldenbourg, 1952 [i. e. 1953]
xlviii, 968p. 24cm. Issued in 8 parts. Covers period from
Roman times to 1933 and includes European figures who have
influenced the historical development of Germany.

1009 SÄNGER, FRITZ, ed.
Handbuch des Deutschen Bundestages. Bearb. von Siegfried Sänger. [3. Aufl.] Stuttgart, J. G. Cotta, 1953. 508p.
ports. 18cm. Includes biographical sketches and portraits
of members of the Bundestag (Diet) of the German Federal
Republic.

1010 SCHMERSAHL, ELIAS FRIEDRICH, 1719-1775.
Neue Nachrichten von jüngstverstorbenen Gelehrten. Nebst
nöthigem Register. Leipzig, Bey Carl Ludwig Jacobi, 1754-
56. 8 pts. in 2 v. 18cm. New notes on the most recently
deceased [German] scholars; bio-bibliographical. Continuation of the author's Zuverlässige Nachrichten von jüngstverstorbenen Gelehrten.

1011 SCHMERSAHL, ELIAS FRIEDRICH, 1719-1775.
Zuverlässige Nachrichten von jüngstverstorbenen Gelehrten.
Zelle, Bei Joachim Andreas Deez, 1748-53. 8 pts. in 2 v.
17cm. Reliable data on [German] scholars who have died most
recently. Continued by the author's Neue Nachrichten von
jüngstverstorbenen Gelehrten.

1012 SELLE, GÖTZ VON, 1893-
Ostdeutsche Biographien; 365 Lebensläufe in Kurzdarstel-
lungen. Hrsg. vom Göttinger Arbeitskreis. Würzburg, Holz-
ner [1955] 1 v. 20cm. (Der Göttinger Arbeitskreis. Ver-
öffentlichung Nr. 131) East German biographies; 365 lives.

1013 WER IST WER?
Das deutsche who's who. [1.]- Ausg.; 1905- Berlin, Arani. v. 22cm. The German who's who. Title
varies: v. 1-9, Wer ist's? Unsere Zeitgenossen (varies slightly)--v. 10, Degeners Wer ist's? Imprint varies. Editor:
v. 1-10, H.A.L. Degener. --v. 11- W. Habel.

1014 WER IST WER?
[1100 Kurzbiographien deutscher Persönlichkeiten aus Politik, Wirtschaft und Kultur] 1. Aufl. Berlin, Arani [1948]
271 p. ports. 21cm. Who's who; 1100 brief biographies of
German personalities in politics, business and culture. No
more published?

1015 WER IST WER IN DER SBZ?
Ein biographisches Handbuch. Berlin-Zehlendorf, Verlag
für Internationalen Kulturaustausch [1958] 307 p. 22cm.
Who's who in the Soviet Zone of Germany? A biographical
handbook. Superseded by: Germany (Federal Republic, 1949-
) Bundesministerium für Gesamtdeutsche Fragen. SBZ-
Biographie, 1961 (q.v.)

1016 WERTHEIMER, FRITZ, 1884-
Von deutschen Parteien und Parteiführern im Ausland.

2., völlig neubearb. Aufl. Berlin, Zentral-Verlag, 1930.
352 p. ports. 26cm. German parties and party leaders in
foreign countries; contains ca. 300 biographical sketches.

1017   WHO'S WHO IN GERMANY.
1956-   Munich, Intercontinental Book and Pub. Co. v.
22cm.

1018   WHO'S WHO IN GERMANY AND AUSTRIA.
[London, British Ministry of Economic Warfare, 1945]
2 pts. 27cm. Cover title. "Fifth edition of... Who's who
in Nazi Germany."

1019   -----Supplement. [London, British Ministry of Economic
Warfare, n. d.] pts. 25cm. Cover title.

1020   WHO'S WHO OF PROMINENT GERMANS IN THE U. S. S. R.
[London, Ministry of Economic Warfare] 1944. 51 l. 21cm.
Cover title.

1021   ---- ----Supplement. no. 1-   [London, Ministry of Economic Warfare] 1944-   v. 21cm.

1022   WILE, FREDERICK WILLIAM, 1873-
"Who's who" in Hunland; a glossary of the persons, issues,
places and things we read about in Germany. London, Simpkin, Marshall, Hamilton, Kent, 1916. 154 p. 19cm.

1023   WINTERBERG, HANS
Die Schüler von Ulrich Zasius. Stuttgart, W. Kohlhammer,
1961. viii, 117 p. 24cm. (Veröffentlichungen der Kommission für Geschichtliche Landeskunde in Baden-Württemberg
[Reihe B: Forschungen] 18. Bd.) An alphabetical list, with
biographical details, of 132 students of Zasius at the University of Freiburg in Breisgau.

1024   ZIEGLER, HIERONYMUS, 1514 (ca.)-1562.
Illustrium Germaniae virorum historiae aliquot singulares...
Ingolstadij, 1562. 1 v. 4.º 104 historical figures, partici-
pants in unusual events in German history.

1025   ZUERL, WALTER, 1911-
Pour le mérite-Flieger; Heldentäten und Erlebnisse unserer Kriegsflieger, unter Mitarbeit der Lebenden und der

Angehörigen der gefallen Flieger gesammelt und hrsg. Mit
einem Vorwort von Friedrich Christiansen. München, C.
Pechstein, 1939. 544p. illus., ports. 22cm. Biographical
sketches of German military aviators (World War I, 1914-
1918, and after)

Local
Altenburg (Duchy)

1026   GOTTER, FRIEDRICH GOTTHILF
       Elogia clarorum virorum qui Altenburgum... tum scriptis
tum egregiis meritis illustrarunt. Accedunt epistolae Reine-
cii, Lambecii... Seckendorfii et C. Sagittarii rem litterariam
illustrantes, et... adhuc nondum editae. Jenae, Apud E. C.
Bailliar, 1713. 101p. 8.º Eulogies of famous men in the
Duchy of Altenburg.

Ansbach

1027   VOCKE, JOHANN AUGUST
       Geburts- und Todten-Almanach Ansbachischer Gelehrten,
Schriftsteller und Künstler. Augsburg, Späth, 1796-97. 2 v.
Almanac of birth and death of scholars, writers and artists
of Ansbach, Germany.

Baden

1028   WEECH, FRIEDRICH OTTO ARISTIDES VON, 1837-1905, ed.
       Badische Biographien. Karlsruhe, G. Braun, 1881-1906.
5 v. in 3. 23cm. Biographical dictionary of Baden, a division of Southwestern Germany. Confined to the 19th century.
Contents. --1. A-K. --2. L-Z und Nachträge. --3-4. Nachträge.
--5. 1891-1901, von F. von Weech und Alb. Krieger.

Bavaria

1029   FINAUER, PETER PAUL, 1732-1788.
       Versuch einer bajerischen Gelehrten Geschichte. München,
Gedruckt bey F. J. Thuille, 1767. 152 p. 19 cm. Attempt at
a history of Bavarian scholars; bio-bibliographical.

1030   GENEALOGISCHES HANDBUCH DES IN BAYERN IMMATRI-
       KULIERTEN ADELS. Bd. 1-   Neustadt an der Aisch
[etc.] Degener, 1950-   v. ports. 15cm. Cover title,
v. 1-   Der in Bayern immatr. Adel. Genealogical handbook of Bavarian nobility; with biographical material.

1031   KOBOLT, ANTON MARIA, 1752-1826.
         Baierisches Gelehrten-Lexicon, worinn alle Gelehrte
         Baierns und der Obern Pfalz, ohne Unterschied der Stände und
         Religion, welche bis auf das XVIII. Jahrhundert und zwar bis
         zum Ausgange des Jahrs 1724 daselbst gelebt und geschrieben
         haben, mit ihren sowohl gedruckten als noch ungedruckten
         Schriften nach alphabetischer Ordnung beschrieben und enthal-
         ten sind. Landshut, M. Hagen, 1795. 806, [15] p. 20cm.

1032   --- ----Ergänzungen und Berichtungen, von Anton Maria
         Kobolt. Nebst Nachträgen von Herrn Gandershofer. Lands-
         hut, F. S. Storno, 1824. 424, [9] p. 20cm. Added t.p.:
         Lexicon baierischer Gelehrten und Schriftsteller.

         A bio-bibliographical dictionary for Bavarian scholars and
         writers.

1033   STUMPF, PLEICKHARD
         Denkwürdige Bayern; kurze Lebensbeschreibungen ver-
         storbener verdienter Männer, die in dem Ländergebiete des
         jetzigen Königreich Bayern geboren oder durch längern
         Aufenthalt ihm angehörig waren. München, Rieger'sche Uni-
         versitäts-Buchhandlung, 1865. xvi, 480p. 8.º Memorable
         Bavarians; short sketches of deceased men...

Berlin

1034   [KONER, WILHELM DAVID] 1817-1887.
         Gelehrtes Berlin im Jahre 1845. Berlin, T. Scherk, 1846.
         xii, 389 p. 21cm. Added t.p.: Verzeichniss im Jahre 1845
         lebender Schriftsteller und ihrer Werke. Bio-bibliography of
         Berlin; scholars and writers living in the year 1845.

1035   MEYER, FERDINAND
         Berühmte Männer Berlins und ihrer Wohnstätten. Nach
         urkundliche Quellen bearb. Berlin, Weile, 1875-77. 3 v.
         Famous men of Berlin & their residences.

Bremen

1036   [IKEN, HEINRICH] 1661-1724.
         Brema literata; virorum qui hoc seculo vixerunt, eruditione
         vel dignitate spectabilium, maximam partem Bremensium,
         tum extraneorum quorundam qui in eorum urbem concesserunt,
         vitas et honores in compendio exhibens. [3. ed.] Bremae,

Literis & Sumptibus H. Braueri, 1726. 156p. 21cm. 3d ed.
rev. and enl. by Hermann von Post. First issued (anonymously) in 1708. Learned Bremen; men of this century (18th) famous for their learning or position, chiefly of Bremen, but
also some 'foreigners' who resided in Bremen.

1037 KÜNSTLERVEREIN, Bremen. HISTORISCHE GESELL-
SCHAFT.
Bremische Biographie des neunzehnten Jahrhunderts. Bremen, G. Winter, 1912. viii, 534 p. 23cm. Bio-bibliography
of 19th century Bremen.

1038 ROTERMUND, HEINRICH WILHELM, 1761-1848.
Lexicon aller Gelehrten, die seit der Reformation in Bremen gelebt haben; nebst Nachrichten von gebohrenen Bremern,
die in andern Ländern Ehrenstellen bekleideten. Bremen, C.
Schünemann, 1818. 3 v. in 2. 20cm. Dictionary of all scholars, who have lived in Bremen since the Reformation...

Coburg

1039 WETZEL, JOHANN CASPAR, 1691-1755.
Das jetzt lebende geehrte und gelehrte Coburg, mit dazu
gehörigen Schrifften, Anmerckungen und Epitaphiis entworffen,
von Antonio Coburgero [pseud.] Itzipoli, 1718. 120 p. 17cm.
Now living honored and learned Coburg, Germany—writings,
notices and epitaphs of famous sons of the city.

Danzig

1040 CHARITIUS, ANDREAS
Commentatio historico literaria de viris eruditis Gedani
ortis, speciatim iis qui scriptis inclaruerunt. Vittembergae
Saxonum, 1715. 138p. 4.° Learned men of Danzig, especially those famed for their writings.

Dresden

1041 KLÄBE, JOHANN GOTTLIEB AUGUST, 1766-1802.
Neuestes gelehrtes Dresden; oder, Nachrichten von jetzt
lebenden Dresdner Gelehrten, Schriftstellern, Künstlern,
Bibliotheken- und Kunstsammlern. Leipzig, Voss, 1796.
200 p. 20cm. Facts about living scholars, writers, artists,
book and art collectors in Dresden.

Frankfurt am Main

1042 HEYDEN, EDUARD
Gallerie berühmter und merkwürdiger Frankfurter. Eine
biographische Sammlung. Frankfurt a. M., H. L. Brönner,
1861. 610p. 13 ports. 22cm. Gallery of famous and noteworthy citizens of Frankfurt am Main.

Friesland, East

1043 TIADEN, ENNO JOHANN HEINRICH, d. 1781.
Das gelehrte Ostfriesland. Aurich, 1785-87. 3 v. 8.⁰
Learned East Friesland; a bio-bibliography.

Hamburg

1044 BEUTHNER, ARNOLD CHRISTIAN, 1689-1742.
Hamburgischer Staats- und Gelehrten-Lexicon, worin die
Namen, das Leben und die Verdienste derjenigen Männer,
geist- und weltlichen Standes, angeführet werden, welche von
der heilsamen Reformation bis auf gegenwärtige Zeit, in
dieser weltberühmten Stadt und derselben Gebiete, ein
ansehnliches Ehren-Amt, oder eine hohe Würde bekleidet,
sich durch Schriften berühmt gemacht, dasselbst geboren
und in der fremde Beförderung erhalten, bereits aber das
Zeitliche gesegnet haben. Hamburg, C. W. Brandt, 1739.
452p. port. 18cm. A dictionary of distinguished natives of
the City of Hamburg, Germany, from the Reformation to 1739.

1045 THIESS, JOHANN OTTO, 1762-1810.
Versuch einer Gelehrtengeschichte von Hamburg, nach
alphabetischer Ordnung mit kritischen und pragmatischen
Bemerkungen. Hamburg, J. L. Schwarz Witwe, 1780. 2 v.
in 1. 20cm. A bio-bibliographical work, alphabetically arranged, on the 'learned' men of Hamburg.

Hanover

1046 ROTERMUND, HEINRICH WILHELM, 1761-1848.
Das gelehrte Hannover; oder, Lexicon von Schriftstellern
und Schriftstellerinnen, Gelehrten, Geschäftsmännern und
Künstlern die seit der Reformation in und ausserhalb den
sämtlichen zum jetzigen Königreich Hannover gehörigen

Provinzen gelebt haben und noch leben, aus den glaubwürdigsten Schriftstellern zusammen getragen. Bremen, C. Schünemann, 1823. 2 v. 20cm. Goes up to Kutscher, with a supplement of 168p. No more published. Learned Hanover; or,
Dictionary of authors, scholars, businessmen [etc.] of that
kingdom who have flourished since the Reformation.

1047   ROTHERT, WILHELM, 1842-
      Allgemeine hannoversche Biographie. Hannover, A.
Sponholtz, 1912-16. 3 v. General biography of Hanover, Germany.

Hesse

1048   GERLAND, OTTO, 1835-
      Grundlage zu einer hessischen Gelehrten-, Schriftsteller-
und Künstler-Geschichte von 1831 bis auf die neueste Zeit.
Kassel, A. Freyschmidt, 1863-68. 2v. in 1. 21cm. (Grundlage zu einer hessischen Gelehrten- und Schriftsteller-
Geschichte seit der Reformation bis auf die gegenwärtige Zeit.
Besorgt von Friedrich Wilhelm Strieder und im Anschlusse
an Karl Wilhelm Justi's gleichnamige Fortsetzung weiter fortgesetzt von Otto Gerland, Bd. 20-21) Bio-bibliography of
Hesse, 1831-ca. 1868.

1049   HAUPT, HERMAN, 1854-1935.
      Hessische Biographien. In Verbindung mit Karl
Esselborn und Georg Lehnert hrsg. von Herman Haupt.
Darmstadt, 1918-34. 3 v. 8.° Hessian biography. Biog-
raphy of prominent persons of Hesse.

1050   JUSTI, KARL WILHELM, 1767-1846.
      Grundlage zu einer hessischen Gelehrten-, Schriftsteller-
und Künstler-Geschichte vom Jahre 1806 bis zum Jahre 1830.
Fortsetzung von Strieder's Hessischer Gelehrten- und
Schriftstellergeschichte und Nachträge zu diesem Werke.
Marburg, C. Garthe, 1831. 22, xii, 852p. 22cm. Basis for
a history of scholars, writers and artists in Hesse from 1806
to 1830.

1051   STRIEDER, FRIEDRICH WILHELM
      Grundlage zu einer hessischen Gelehrten- und Schrift-
steller-Geschichte seit der Reformation bis auf gegenwärtige
Zeiten. Cassel [etc.] Luckhardt [etc.] 1781-1868. 21 v. 8.°
Vol. 16 edited by L. Wachler; v. 17-19 by K. W. Justi; v. 20

by O. Gerland. A bio-bibliographical 'history' of Hessian scholars and writers from the Reformation to the present (1868?)

Königsberg

1052   WEISFERT, JULIUS NICOLAUS
Biographisch-litterarisches Lexikon für die Stadt Königsberg und Ostpreussen. [2. Aufl.] Königsberg, Bon, 1898. 259, v p. 8.° Biographical-literary dictionary for the City of Königsberg and East Prussia.

Leipzig

1053   DAS LITTERARISCHE LEIPZIG.
Illustriertes Handbuch der Schriftsteller- und Gelehrtenwelt, der Presse und des Verlagsbuchhandels in Leipzig. Leipzig, W. Fiedler, 1897. 293, [11] p. ports. 23cm. Literary Leipzig; illustrated handbook of writers, the world of learning, the press and the book trade in Leipzig.

Lübeck

1054   SEELEN, JOHANN HEINRICH VON, 1688-1762.
Athenae Lubecensis; sive, De Athenaei Lubecensis insignibus meritis ... commentarius, praeter gloriosas memorias quorundam Consulum Lubecensium ... multas praestantissimorum theologorum, medicorum ... et philosophorum vitas complectens. Accedit Athenaei Lubecensis historia. Lubecae, Leoburgi, 1720-29. 4 v. 8.° Biography of famous sons of Lubeck: theologians, physicians and philosophers (scholars, etc.)

Lusatia

1055   SCHULZE, JOHANN DANIEL, b. 1777.
Erster Versuch eines vollständigen Verzeichnisses der Niederlausitzer Schriftsteller und Künstler seit der Reformation. Lübben, Gedruckt bei F. Driemel, 1820. 32 p. 18cm. First attempt at a complete listing of the authors and artists of Lower Lusatia since the Reformation. Contains names beginning with letters A-F only.

Mecklenburg

1056 KOPPE, JOHANN CHRISTIAN, 1757-1827.
  Jetztlebendes gelehrtes Mecklenburg. Rostock, 1783-84.
  3 fasc. No more published? Biography of contemporary
  learned men in Mecklenburg.

1057 [MANTZEL, ERNST JOHANN FRIEDRICH] 1699-1768, ed.
  Mecklenburgisches Gelehrten-Lexicon. Rostock, 1729-34.
  8 or 9 fascs. 400 biographies; a dictionary of learned men in
  Mecklenburg.

Nuremberg

1058 WILL, GEORG ANDREAS, 1727-1798.
  Nürnbergisches Gelehrten-Lexicon; oder, Beschreibung
  aller nürnbergischen Gelehrten beyderley Geschlechtes nach
  ihrem Leben, Verdiensten und Schrifften zur Erweiterung der
  gelehrten Geschichts-Kunde und Verbesserung vieler darinnen
  vorgefallenen Fehler, aus den besten Quellen in alphabetischer
  Ordnung verfasset. Nürnberg, L. Schüpfel, 1755-58. 4 v.
  in 2. 20cm.

1059 --- ----Fünfter [-achter] Theil oder erster [-vierter] Supplementband. Fortgesetzt von Christian Conrad Nopitsch. Alt-
  dorf, Beym Herausgeber [etc.] 1802-08. 4 v. 20cm.

  Dictionary of the learned people of Nuremberg of both
  sexes.

Pomerania

1060 BIEDERSTEDT, DIEDERICH HERMANN, 1762-1824.
  Nachrichten von dem Leben und den Schriften neu-vor-
  pommerisch-rügenscher Gelehrten, seit dem Anfang des achtzehenten Jahrhundertes bis zum Jahre 1822. Abt. 1.
  Greifswald, 1824. xiii,144p. No more published. Notes on
  the lives and writings of learned Pomeranians and men of the
  Island of Rügen.

1061 LANGE, EDMUND, 1855-1932.
  Die Greifswalder Sammlung Vitae Pomeranorum. Alphabetisch nach Geschlechtern verzeichnet. Greifswald, J. Abel,

1898. xix, 406p. (Baltische Studien, hrsg. von der Gesellschaft für Pommersche Geschichte und Alterthumskunde.
1. Folge. Ergänzungsband) An alphabetical index (with very
brief biographical notices) of a large collection of printed and
unprinted materials in the care of the Library of the University of Greifswald. Materials cover chiefly Pomeranian family history.

1062   PETRICH, HERMANN, 1845-
         Pommersche Lebens- und Landesbilder. Nach gedruckten
und ungedruckten Quellen entworfen. Hamburg [etc.] 1880-
87. 2 v. 8.º Biography of Pomerania from the time of
Frederick the Great thru' the Wars of Liberation. Also issued successively under the titles: Aus dem Zeitalter
Friedrichs des Grossen and Aus dem Zeitalter der Befreiung.

1063   VANSELOW, AMANDUS KARL, 1699-1769.
         Gelehrtes Pommern; oder, Alphabetisches Verzeichniss
einiger in Pommern Gelehrten, männlichen und weiblichen
Geschlechtes, nach ihren merckwürdigsten Umständen und
verfertigten Schrifften. Stargard, 1728. 151 p. 4.º Learned Pomerania; or, Alphabetical list of Pomeranian scholars
(men & women), their lives and completed writings.

Prussia

1064   BIOGRAPHISCHES LEXIKON ALLER HELDEN UND MILITAIR-
         PERSONEN, welche sich in preussischen Diensten berühmt
gemacht haben. Nebst einer tabellarischen Uebersicht der
Avancements sämtlicher Königl. Preuss. Generalfeldmar-
schalle Generale von der Kavallerie und Infanterie...von 1587
bis 1790. Berlin, 1788-91. 4 v. 8.º Biographical dictionary
of Prussian military notables.

1065   [SCHULTZ, GEORGE PETER]
         Preussischer Todes-Tempel, worin verstorbene Personen
allerhand Standes von den ausserlesensten Sachen der Preussischen, Polnischen, Schwedischen und Brandenburgischen...
Historie...mit einander redende vorgestellet werden. Con-
stantinopel, Leipzig [1740?] 1 v. 4.º Necrology of Prussia
(including Poles, Swedes and Brandenburgers)

Rhine Valley

1066   GESELLSCHAFT FÜR RHEINISCHE GESCHICHTSKUNDE.
Rheinische Lebensbilder. Im Auftrag der Gesellschaft für
Rheinische Geschichtskunde hrsg. von Edmund Strutz. Düsseldorf, Rheinland-Verlag, 1961-   v. illus., fold. map.
24cm. Lives of Germans native to the Rhine Valley.

Rostock

1067   KREY, JOHANN BERNARD, 1771-1826.
Andenken an die Rostock'schen Gelehrten aus den drei
letzten Jahrhunderten. Rostock, Gedruckt bei Adlers Erben,
1816-   v. 21cm.   8 fascicles and a supplement were
issued? Mementos of Rostock's learned men of the last
three centuries.

Saxony

1068   MITTELDEUTSCHE LEBENSBILDER.
Hrsg. von der Historischen Kommission für die Provinz
Sachsen und für Anhalt. Magdeburg, 1926-30. 5 v. Lives of
famous Germans from Saxony and Anhalt.

Saxony, Lower

1069   LINKE, WILHELM, ed.
Niedersächsische Familienkunde; ein biographisches Verzeichnis auf Grund der Leichenpredigten und sonstigen Person-
alschriften der Königlichen Bibliothek zu Hannover und anderer
hannoverschen Sammlungen. Hannover, E. Geibel, 1912.
420 p. 24cm. Family history of Lower Saxony; a biographical
list based on funeral sermons and other personal writings in
the Royal Library at Hanover... In biographical dictionary form.

Schleswig — Holstein

1070   MOLLER, JOHANNES, 1661-1725.
Cimbria literata; sive, Scriptorum ducatus utriusque Sles-
vicensis et Holsatici, quibus et alii vicini quidam accensentur,
historia literaria tripartita... Cum praef. Joannis Grammii.
Havniae, 1744. 3 v. 38cm. Learned Cimbria (the peninsula
of Jutland); or, Writers of Schleswig-Holstein...

Silesia

.1071 BERNER, KARL GUSTAV HEINRICH
Schlesische Landsleute. Ein Gedenkbuch hervorragender,
in Schlesien geborener Männer und Frauen aus der Zeit von
1180 bis zur Gegenwart. Leipzig, P. Schimmelwitz, 1901.
vi, 326p. 24cm. A memorial book for outstanding Silesian
men and women, 1180 to the present.

1072 FUELDENER, JOHANN JACOB VON
Bio- et bibliographia Silesiaca; das ist: Schlesische
Bibliothec und Bücher-Historie, welche eine Erzehlung...
von den gedruckten Scriptoribus rerum Silesiacarum... in
sich fasset... Repositor I. Lauban, 1731. 1 v. 4.º No more
published. Bio-bibliography of Silesia.

1073 HISTORISCHE KOMMISSION FÜR SCHLESIEN.
Schlesische Lebensbilder. [Hrsg. von Friedrich Andreae,
et al.] Breslau, W. G. Korn, 1922-28. 3 v. 8.º A series.
Contents. --Bd. 1. Schlesier des 19. Jahrhunderts. --Bd. 2.
Schlesier des 18. u 19. Jahrhunderts. --Bd. 3. Schlesier
des 17. bis 19. Jahrhunderts. Silesian biographies.

1074 [PEUKER, JOHANN GEORG]
Kurze biographische Nachrichten der vornehmsten schlesischen Gelehrten, die vor dem achtzehnten Jahrhundert ge-
bohren wurden, nebst einer Anzeige ihrer Schriften. Grot-
tkau, 1788. 1 v. 8.º Brief biographical notes on the most
prominent Silesian scholars born before the 18th century as
well as notices on their writings.

Swabia

1075 GEORGII-GEORGENAU, EBERHARD EMIL VON, 1848-
Biographisch-genealogische Blätter aus und über Schwaben.
Stuttgart, E. Müller, 1879. xxix, 1228 p. 22cm. Biographi-
cal-genealogical leaves: Swabia.

1076 PÖLNITZ, GÖTZ, Freiherr von, 1906-   ed.
Lebensbilder aus dem bayerischen Schwaben. München,
M. Hueber, 1952-   v. illus. 21cm. (Schwäbische
Forschungsgemeinschaft bei der Kommission für Bayerische

Landesgeschichte. Veröffentlichungen, Reihe 3) Biographical sketches from Bavarian Swabia. About 20 biographies to a volume. Not alphabetical in arrangement; however there is an index at the end of each vol. and a cumulative alphabetical list of biographees in vol. 8.

Ulm

1077   WEYERMANN, ALBRECHT, 1763-1832.
Nachrichten von Gelehrten, Künstlern und anderen merkwürdigen Personen aus Ulm [und Neue historisch-biobraphisch-artistische Nachrichten von Gelehrten und Künstlern, auch alten und neuen adelichen und bürgerlichen Familien aus der vormaligen Reichsstadt Ulm] Ulm, 1798-1829. 2 v. 8.º Notes on scholars, artists & other noteworthy persons from the City of Ulm, Germany.

Westphalia

1078   HAMELMANN, HERMANN, 1525 or 6-1595.
Geschichtliche Werke. Kritisch neu hrsg. von Heinrich Detmer. Bd. 1: Schriften zur niedersächsisch-westfälischen Gelehrtengeschichte. Münster i. W., Aschendorff, 1902-08. 1 v. in 4 pts. 25cm. (Veröffentlichungen der Historischen Kommission der Provinz Westfalen [5, i. e. 9]) In Latin. Contains a large amount of biographical information about Westphalian-Lower Saxon scholars of the author's period. Alphabetical approach through the comprehensive indexes of names at the end of each part.

1079   SCHULTE, WILHELM, 1891-
Westfälische Köpfe; 300 Lebensbilder bedeutender Westfalen. Biographische Handweiser. Münster, Aschendorff [1963] viii, 444 p. illus. 24cm. 300 biographies of important Westphalians.

Württemburg

1080   HAUG, BALTHASAR, 1731-1792.
Das gelehrte Wirtemberg. Stuttgart, 1790. paging (?) 2684 biographical sketches of learned Württembergers.

1081   WÜRTTEMBERGISCHER NEKROLOG FÜR DIE JAHRE 1913-1916.
Im Auftrage der Württembergischen Kommission für

Landesgeschichte hrsg. von Karl Weller und Viktor Ernst.
Stuttgart, W. Kohlhammer, 1916-20. 4 v. 8.° Necrology
of Württemberg for the years 1913-1916.

Würzburg

1082   [STUMPF, ANDREAS SEBASTIAN] 1772-1820.
Kurze Nachrichten von merkwürdigen Gelehrten des
Hochstifts Wirzburg in den vorigen Jahrhunderten. Frank-
furt, J. J. Stahels Wittwe und Sohn, 1794. 164p. 17cm.
Brief reports on noteworthy scholars of the Diocese (?) of
Würzburg in the preceding centuries.

Wuppertal

1083   WUPPERTALER BIOGRAPHIEN.
Wuppertal, Born-Verlag, 19   v. ports. 19cm.
(Beiträge zur Geschichte und Heimatkunde des Wuppertals,
Bd. 5-7, 11   Biographies of natives of the city of Wupper-
tal, Ger. Series 2-5 (1960-65) contain 49 biographies. Se-
ries 1 not available for examination. A continuing publication.

GREAT BRITAIN

Bibliography, Indexes, Etc.

1084   INDEX SOCIETY, London.
Index of obituary notices, 1880-82. London, Published for
the Index Society, 1882. 84. 3v. 22cm. (Index Society.
Publications, 1881-1883. 9, 12, 14) An index for 1869-1877 was
projected, but apparently never published. No more published.
Indexes for 1878 and 1879 were issued in the appendixes of the
Reports of the 1st-2nd annual neetings of the Index Society
(Publications 4, 7)

1085   INDEX SOCIETY, London.
An index to the biographical and obituary notices in the
Gentleman's magazine, 1731-1780. London, British Record
Society, 1886-91. viii, 677p. 22cm. (Publications of the
British Record Society. Index Society, v. 15) Compiled
by R. H. Farrar.

1086   MATTHEWS, WILLIAM, 1905-
British autobiographies; an annotated bibliography of Brit-

ish autobiographies published or written before 1951. Berkeley, University of California Press, 1955. xiv, 376p. 25cm. Lists 6000 autobiographies.

1087   MATTHEWS, WILLIAM, 1905-
British diaries; an annotated bibliography of British diaries written between 1442 and 1942. London, Cambridge University Press, 1950. xxxiv, 339p. 25cm.

Anonyms and Peudonyms

1088   HALKETT, SAMUEL, 1814-1871.
Dictionary of anonymous and pseudonymous English literature [by] Samuel Halkett and John Laing. New and enl. ed. by James Kennedy, W. A. Smith and A. F. Johnson. Edinburgh, Oliver and Boyd, 1926-[62] 9 v. 27cm.

1089   STONEHILL, CHARLES ARCHIBALD, 1890-
Anonyma and pseudonyma, by Charles A. Stonehill, Jr., Andrew Block and H. Winthrop Stonehill. London, C. A. Stonehill, Jr., 1926-27. 4 v. 21cm. Contains English and American authors.

General Works

1090   THE ANNUAL BIOGRAPHY AND OBITUARY...
v. 1-21; 1817-1837. London, Longman, Hurst, Rees, Orme, and Brown [etc.] 21 v. illus., ports. 22cm. No more published. A yearbook of British biography and necrology.

1091   THE ANNUAL MONITOR;
Or, Obituary of the members of the Society of Friends in Great Britain and Ireland. no. [1]-30, 1813-42; new ser., no. 1-66, 1843-1908; no. 96-   York [etc.]   v. 13-15cm. Title varies.

1092   -----Quaker records; being an index to "The Annual monitor," 1813-1892, containing over twenty thousand obituary notices of members of the Society of Friends, alphabetically & chronologically arr., with references to "The Annual monitor." Edited by Joseph J. Green. London, E. Hicks, Jun., 1894. xv, 458 p. front. 22cm.

1093   BATEMAN, JOHN
The great landowners of Great Britain and Ireland... with

a series of tables by Hon. G. Brodrick. 4th ed., rev. London, Harrison, 1883. xxviii, 533p. 8.°

1094 BIOGRAPHIA BRITANNICA;
Or, The lives of the most eminent persons who have flourished in Great Britain and Ireland, from the earliest ages, to the present times. Collected from the best authorities, printed and manuscript, and digested in the manner of Mr. Bayle's Historical and critical dictionary. The 2d ed., with corrections, enlargements, and the addition of new lives, by Andrew Kippis. With the assistance of other gentlemen. London, Printed by W. & A. Strahan for C. Bathurst [etc,] 1778-93. 5 v. 37cm. 1st ed. (6 v. in 7) published in London 1747-1766.

1095 BOASE, FREDERICK, 1843-1916.
Modern English biography containing many thousand concise memoirs of persons who have died between the years 1851-1900, with an index of the most interesting matter. [2d impression. London] F. Cass, 1965. 6 v. 26cm. 1st ed., published in 1892-1921 in 6 v., had title: Modern English biography... persons who have died since the year 1850. Contents. --v. 1-3. A-Z. --v. 4-6. A-Z. Supplements to v. 1-3.

1096 BRACHER, SAMUEL VEALE
The Herald book of Labour members. London, Labour Pub. Co., 1923-24. 2 pts. 8.° Pt. 2: 1924 supplement. A one-volume ed (vii, 227 p.) was issued in 1923.

1097 BRIEF BIOGRAPHIES OF LEADING LAYMEN.
No. 1-   London, Carey Press [1943-   v. 19cm. Sketches of leading British Baptist laymen.

1098 THE BRITISH PLUTARCH,
Containing the lives of the most eminent statesmen, patriots... and artists of Great Britain and Ireland, from the accession of Henry VIII. to the present time... The 3d ed. rev. and enl. ... London, 1791. 8 v. 12.° Edited by Thomas Mortimer.

1099 BROMLEY, HENRY
A catalogue of engraved British portraits, from Egbert the Great to the present time... With an appendix, containing the portraits of such foreigners, as... may claim a place in the British series... London, T. Payne, 1793. xiv, 479, 56p. ports. 4.°

1100   [BRYDGES, Sir SAMUEL EGERTON] bart., 1762-1837.
        A biographical peerage of the Empire of Great Britain: in
        which are memoirs and characters of the most celebrated
        persons of each family. London, Printed for J. Johnson [etc.]
        1808-17. 4 v. illus. (coats of arms) 15cm.

1101   BUNKER, CAROL, comp.
        Who's who in Parliament. London, St. Botolph Pub. Co.
        [1946] 176 p. 22 cm.

1102   BURKE, JOHN, 1787-1848.
        A genealogical and heraldic history of the extinct and dorm-
        ant baronetcies of England, Ireland and Scotland, by John
        Burke and John Bernard Burke. 2d ed. London, J. R. Smith,
        1844. [London, Burke's Peerage, 1964] 643 p. illus. 25 cm.
        Facsimile of the 1844 reprint of the 1841 ed.

1103   BURKE, Sir JOHN BERNARD, 1814-1892.
        Burke's genealogical and heraldic history of the landed
        gentry. Founded 1836 by John Burke and Sir Bernard Burke.
        Edited by Peter Townsend. 18th ed. London, Burke's
        Peerage, 1965-   v. 28cm.

1104   BURKE, Sir JOHN BERNARD, 1814-1892.
        A genealogical and heraldic dictionary of the colonial
        gentry. London, Harrison [etc.] 1891-95. 2 v. coats of arms.
        28 cm. Vol. 2 edited by Ashworth P. Burke.

1105   BURKE, Sir JOHN BERNARD, 1814-1892.
        Genealogical and heraldic history of the landed gentry of
        Ireland. Edited by L. G. Pine. 4th ed. London, Burke's
        Peerage, 1958. xxxvi, 778 p. coats of arms. 28 cm.

1106   BURKE, Sir JOHN BERNARD, 1814-1892.
        A genealogical history of the dormant, abeyant, forfeited,
        and extinct peerages of the British Empire. New ed. London,
        Harrison, 1883. [London, Burke's Peerage, 1962] ix, 642 p.
        illus. 25 cm.

1107   BURKE'S GENEALOGICAL AND HERALDIC HISTORY OF THE
        PEERAGE, BARONETAGE AND KNIGHTAGE.
        London, Burke's Peerage.   v. illus. 20-28cm.   Title
        varies. Editors: John Burke, J. B. Burke [etc.]

1108   CAMBRIDGE. UNIVERSITY.
     Alumni Cantabrigienses; a biographical list of all known
students, graduates and holders of office at the University of
Cambridge, from the earliest times to 1900, compiled by John
Venn and J. A. Venn. Cambridge, University Press, 1922-
     v. 26 cm.

1109   CAMBRIDGE. UNIVERSITY. PETERHOUSE.
     Admissions to Peterhouse or S. Peter's College in the
University of Cambridge; a biographical register. Being an
exact transcription of the entries in the College admission
books from 1615 to 1887, together with an abstract of the
entries in the academic register from 1887 to October 1, 1911,
and biographical notes, compiled by Thomas Alfred Walker.
Cambridge, University Press, 1912. xi, 760 p. 27 cm.

1110   CAMBRIDGE. UNIVERSITY. PETERHOUSE.
     Admissions to Peterhouse in the University of Cambridge,
October 1911-December 1930; a register consisting of abstracts
from the College historical registers, supplemented by
information from other sources, compiled by E. Ansell. With
a foreword by Field Marshall Lord Birdwood. Cambridge,
University Press, 1939. xxviii, 163 p. 27 cm.

1111   CAMBRIDGE. UNIVERSITY. PETERHOUSE.
     A biographical register of Peterhouse men and of some of
their neighbours from the earliest days (1284) to the commencement (1616) of the first admission book of the College, by
Thomas Alfred Walker. Cambridge, University Press, 1927-
     v. geneal. tables. 27 cm.

1112   THE CATHOLIC WHO'S WHO.
     1908-   London, Burns & Oates.   v. 19cm.   Title
varies: 1908-34, The Catholic who's who & year book. Prominent British Catholics.

1113   THE CELTIC WHO'S WHO:
     Names and addresses of workers who contribute to Celtic
literature, music, or other cultural activities. Kirkcaldy,
Scot., Fifeshire Advertiser ltd., 1921. 170p. 19cm. Compiled by Lachlan Macbean.

1114   CHARNOCK, JOHN, 1756-1807.
     Biographia navalis; or, Impartial memoirs of the lives and
characters of officers of the Navy of Great Britain, from the
year 1660 to the present time; drawn from the most authentic

sources, and disposed in a chronological arrangement. With portraits, and other engravings, by Bartolozzi, & c. London, R. Faulder, 1794-98. 6 v. ports. 21cm.

1115 [COKAYNE, GEORGE EDWARD] 1825-1911.
Biographical list of the members of "The Club of Nobody's Friends" since its foundation 21 June, 1800, to 30 September 1885. London, Privately printed, 1885. xiv, 254p. 8°.

1116 [COKAYNE, GEORGE EDWARD] 1825-1911.
Complete baronetage, edited by G. E. C. [1611-1800] Exeter [Eng.] W. Pollard, 1900-06. 5 v. 25cm.

1117 [COKAYNE, GEORGE EDWARD] 1825-1911.
The complete peerage of England, Scotland, Ireland, Great Britain and the United Kingdom, extant, extinct, or dormant, by G. E. C. New ed., rev. and much enl., edited by the Hon. Vicary Gibbs. London, St. Catherine Press, 1910-59. 13v. in 14. geneal. tables. 30cm. Vols. 6-13 have title: The complete peerage; or, A history of the House of Lords and all its members from the earliest times.

1118 THE COLONIAL OFFICE LIST.
1946- London, H. M. Stationery Off. v. 22cm. annual. Formerly issued in the Dominions Office and Colonial Office list. Includes a biographical section for senior members.

1119 COOPER, CHARLES HENRY, 1808-1866.
Athenae Cantabrigienses, by Charles Henry Cooper and Thompson Cooper. Cambridge [Eng.] Deighton, Bell, 1858-1913. 3v. 23cm. Vol. 3 has imprint: Cambridge [Eng.] Bowes & Bowes. Cambridge University biography.

1120 CREAGH, SIR O'MOORE, 1848-1923, ed.
The V. C. and D. S. O., a complete record of all those officers, non-commissioned officers and men of His Majesty's naval, military and air forces who have been awarded these decorations from the time of their institution... With many biographical and other details... Edited by the late Sir O'Moore Creagh (until 1920) and E. M. Humphris. With a foreword by Earl Beatty, the Earl of Cavan and Sir H. M. Trenchard. With 1748 portrait illustrations. London, Standard Art Book Co. [1924] 3v. illus. (ports.) 29cm.

1121 DEBRETT'S HOUSE OF COMMONS,
And the judicial bench. 1867- London. v.
illus. 22cm. Title varies: 1867- Debrett's illustrated
House of Commons, and the judicial bench.

1122 DEBRETT'S ILLUSTRATED PEERAGE,
And titles of courtesy, of the United Kingdom of Great
Britain and Ireland. 1713- London, Dean [etc.] v.
in illus. 15-20cm. Title varies.

1123 DEBRETT'S PEERAGE, BARONETAGE, KNIGHTAGE, AND
COMPANIONAGE.
London, Odhams Press [etc.] v. coats of arms.
22-26cm. annual. Began circa 1803.

1124 DICTIONARY OF NATIONAL BIOGRAPHY.
Founded in 1882 by George Smith. Edited by Sir Leslie
Stephen and Sir Sidney Lee; from the earliest times to 1900.
London, Oxford University Press [1921-22] 22 v. 24cm.
First published 1885-1901 in 66 vols.

1125 --- ----Supplement[s] 2d- 1901/1911- London,
Oxford University Press [1912- v. 24cm.

1126 DICTIONARY OF NATIONAL BIOGRAPHY.
Edited by Sir Leslie Stephen [and Sidney Lee] v. 1-[63]
Abbadie-[Zuylestein. And Supplement, v. 1-3, Abbott-Wood-
ward] London, Smith, Elder, 1885-1901. 66 v. 24cm.
Another ed. in 22 v. (London, Oxford University Press) pub-
lished in 1921-22 (q. v.)

1127 --- ----Index and epitome. Edited by Sidney Lee. London,
Smith, Elder, 1903. vii, 1456 p. 24cm.

1128 --- ----Errata. London, Smith Elder, 1904. vi, 299 p.
25cm.

1129 --- ----Supplement[s]...2d- London, Smith, Elder
[and Oxford University Press] 1912- v. 24cm.

1130 --- ----Second supplement, index and epitome, edited by Sir
Sidney Lee. London, Smith, Elder, 1913. 129 p. 25cm.

1131 THE DICTIONARY OF NATIONAL BIOGRAPHY,
Founded in 1882 by George Smith. The concise dictionary
...being an epitome of the main work and its Supplement.

London, Oxford University Press [1953-   v. 24cm. Half title: The concise dictionary of national biography. Contents. -- pt. 1. From the beginnings to 1900. --pt. 2. 1901-1950.

1132   DOD'S PARLIAMENTARY COMPANION.
        1833-   London, Whitaker [etc. ?]   Title varies: 1833-1855, The Parliamentary companion, by Charles R. Dod. 1856-1864, The Parliamentary companion, by Robert R. Dod. With biographical sketches of the British Parliament.

1133   DOD'S PEERAGE, BARONETAGE AND KNIGHTAGE OF
        GREAT BRITAIN AND IRELAND. 1841-   London, Dod's Peerage.   v. 18cm.   Title varies: 1841-65, The Peerage, baronetage and knightage of Great Britain and Ireland.

1134   DODWELL, EDWARD
        Alpahbetical list of the officers of the Indian Army; with the dates of their respective promotion, retirement, resignation, or death, 1760 to 1834, corrected to September 30, 1837. By Edward Dodwell and J. S. Miles. London, Mitcham, 1838. 3 v.

1135   DOYLE, JAMES WILLIAM EDMUND, 1822-1892.
        Official baronetage of England, showing the succession, dignities, and offices of every peer from 1066 to 1885.   London, Longmans, Green, 1886. 3v. illus. 25cm.

1136   EMDEN, ALFRED BROTHERSTON, 1888-
        A biographical register of the University of Cambridge to 1500. Cambridge [Eng.] University Press, 1963. xl, 695 p. facsim. 25 cm.

1137   EMDEN, ALFRED BROTHERSTON, 1888-
        A biographical register of the University of Oxford to A. D. 1500. Oxford, Clarendon Press, 1957-59. 3 v. 25 cm.

1138   EMMERT, JOHANN HEINRICH
        The British biography; containing brief accounts of the lives, acts, and writings of the most remarkable persons of the British nation. Göttingen, Dieterich, 1821. 1 v. 8.º

1139   FARBMAN, MICHAEL S   ed.
        Political Britain; parties, policies and politicians. A survey of current British politics, a guide to the new House

of Commons, a directory of political institutions, and a who's
who. London, Europa Publications [1929] 193 p. 19 cm.
(Parchment guides)

1140   THE FOREIGN OFFICE LIST AND DIPLOMATIC AND CONSU-
        LAR YEAR BOOK. London, Harrison. v. 22cm. Title
        varies slightly. Began 1852?; current (1964 latest ed.) In-
        cludes fairly lengthy biographical notices of British Foreign
        Office personnel.

1141   FULLER, THOMAS, 1608-1661.
        The history of the worthies of England. A new ed.,
        containing brief notices of the most celebrated worthies of
        England who have flourished since the time of Fuller. With
        explanatory notes and copious indexes. By P. Austin Nuttall.
        London, T. Tegg, 1840. 3v. port. 23cm. First published
        in 1662.

1142   GILLOW, JOSEPH, 1850-1921.
        A literary and biographical history, or bibliographical dic-
        tionary, of the English Catholics, from the breach with Rome,
        in 1534, to the present time. London, Burns & Oates; New
        York, Catholic Pub. Society Co. [pref. 1885-1902] 5v. 23cm.
        2000 biographies. Useful for names not in the Dictionary of
        national biography.

1143   GORDON-GORMAN, WILLIAM JAMES, 1858-
        Converts to Rome: a biographical list of the more notable
        converts to the Catholic Church in the United Kingdom during
        the last sixty years. New and enl. ed. London [etc.] Sands,
        1910. xvi, 314p. 23cm. First ed. published 1878 under title:
        Rome's recruits. 9 other editions published between 1878-
        1910.

1144   GRANGER, JAMES, 1723-1776.
        A biographical history of England, from Egbert the Great
        to the Revolution: consisting of characters disposed in differ-
        ent classes, and adapted to a methodical catalogue of engraved
        British heads: intended as an essay towards reducing our biog-
        raphy to a system, and a help to the knowledge of portraits:
        interspersed with a variety of anecdotes, and memoirs of a
        great number of persons. With a preface. 5th ed., with up-
        wards of four hundred additional lives. London, W. Baynes,
        1824. 6v. 23cm.

1145   GT. BRIT. ADMIRALTY.
The commissioned sea officers of the Royal Navy, 1660-
1815. [n.p., 1954?] 3v. (1029 1.) 24cm. The work was
begun by David B. Smith, Admiralty librarian, and completed
after his death by the Royal Naval College, Greenwich, in
collaboration with the National Maritime Museum.

1146   GT. BRIT. PARLIAMENT. HOUSE OF COMMONS.
Members of Parliament... London, Printed by H. Han-
sard [1878?] 3v. 34cm. Contents.--pt. 1. Parliaments of
England, 1213-1702.--pt. 2. Parliaments of Great Britain,
1705-1796. Parliaments of the United Kingdom, 1801-1874.
Parliaments and conventions of the Estates of Scotland.--pt. 3.
Index to pt. 1.

1147   --- ----Index to part 2. Parliaments of Great Britain, 1705-
1796. Parliaments of the United Kingdom, 1801-1885. Parliaments and conventions of the Estates of Scotland, 1357-1707.
Parliaments of Ireland, 1559-1800... London, Printed for
H.M. Stationery Off. by the Hansard Pub. Union [1891?] xlv,
300 p. 34cm.

1148   GT. BRIT. WAR OFFICE.
A list of the officers of the Army and of the Corps of Royal
Marines. 1756-   London [etc.]   v. 21-24cm.
Title varies: The Army list [etc.]

1149   [HARDING, EDWARD] 1755-1840.
Naval biography; or, The history and lives of distinguished
characters in the British Navy, from the earliest period of
history to the present time. Illustrated with elegant portraits,
engraved by eminent artists. London, J. Scott, 1805. 2 v.
ports. 22cm.

1150   HISTORICAL PORTRAITS.
The lives by C. R. L. Fletcher. The portraits chosen
by Emery Walker. With an introd. on the history of portraiture in England. Oxford, Clarendon Press, 1909-19.
4 v. ports. 27 x 21cm. Contents.--[1] Richard II to Henry
Wriothesley, 1400-1600.--[2] 1600-1700; the lives by H. B.
Butler and C. R. L. Fletcher.--3. 1700-1800.-- 4. 1800-
1850. Index.

1151   HODSON, VERNON CHARLES PAGET
List of the officers of the Bengal Army, 1758-1834, alpha-

betically arranged and annotated with biographical and genealogical notices. London, Constable, 1927-47. 4 v. 8.º
Vols. 3-4 have imprint: London, Phillimore.

1152   HOLLAND, HENRY, 1583-1650?
        Heroologia Anglica, hoc est, Clarissimorum et doctis-
        simorum aliquot Anglorum qui floruerunt ab anno Cristi MD.
        usq. ad presentem annum MDCXX. vivae effigies, vitae et
        elogiae. [London] Impensis C. Passaei et Jansonii Biblio-
        polae, 1620. 2 v. 65 ports. folio. Famous Englishmen,
        with portraits, who flourished 1500-1620.

1153   HOUBRAKEN, JACOBUS, 1698-1780.
        The heads of illustrious persons of Great Britain, on one
        hundred and eight copper-plates. Engraved by Mr. Houbraken
        and Mr. Vertue. With their lives and characters, by Thomas
        Birch. London, J. Knapton, 1756. 2v. (216 p.) ports. 56cm.

1154   KEELER, MARY FREAR.
        The Long Parliament, 1640-1641; a biographical study of its
        members. Philadelphia, American Philosophical Society,
        1954. ix, 410p. 31cm. (American Philosophical Society.
        Memoirs, v. 36)

1155   KELLY'S HANDBOOK TO THE TITLED, LANDED, &
        OFFICIAL CLASSES. 1875-
        London, Kelly's Directories. v. 19cm. Title varies:
        1875-77, The Upper ten thousand; an alphabetical list of
        noble families. --1878-79, Kelly's handbook of the upper
        [ten thousand?]

1156   KIRK, JOHN, 1760-1851.
        Biographies of English Catholics in the eighteenth century,
        by John Kirk, being part of his projected continuation of
        Dodd's Church history. Edited by John Hungerford Pollen and
        Edwin Burton. London, Burns & Oates, 1909. xvi, 293 p.
        5 ports. 22cm. Includes some names not given in Gillow's
        Literary & biographical history (q.v.)

1157   THE LABOUR WHO'S WHO;
        A biographical directory to the national and local leaders
        in the labour and co-operative movement. 1924-   London,
        Labour Pub. Co. v. 19cm. Vols. for 1924 & 1927 only
        ones published? British labor leaders.

1158   LE NEVE, JOHN, 1679-1741.
Monumenta Anglicana: being inscriptions on the monuments of eminent persons deceased in or since 1600 (to the end of 1718) London, W. Bowyer, 1717-19. 5 v. 8.º

1159   LIVES OF ILLUSTRIOUS SEAMEN...
Including several hundred naval characters... To which is prefixed a brief history of the rise and progress of the British Navy. London, Printed by J. Cundee for T. Hurst [etc.] 1803. xx, 436 p. front., 12 ports. 13cm.

1160   LIVES OF THE MOST REMARKABLE CRIMINALS,
Who have been condemned and executed for murder, high-way robberies, house-breaking, street robberies, coining, or other offences; from the year 1720 to the year 1735. Collected from original papers and authentic memoirs. London, Reeves and Turner, 1874. 2 v. front. 20cm. "A faithful reproduc-tion of the original of 1735." American ed. (New York, Dodd, Mead, 1927) edited by Arthur Lawrence Hayward, has colla-tion: xv, 640 p. front., plates. 26 x 20cm.

1161   LONDON. NATIONAL PORTRAIT GALLERY.
British historical portraits; a selection from the National Portrait Gallery, with biographical notes. Cambridge, Pub-lished for the National Portrait Gallery at the University Press, 1957. 265 p. ports. 22cm.

1162   LOW, SIR SIDNEY JAMES MARK, 1857-1932.
The dictionary of English history, by Sidney J. Low and F. S. Pulling. London, New York, Cassell, 1910. xvi, 1109 (i. e. 1123) p. ports. 23cm. "First edition May 1884... Revised 1896...1910." Includes biographies.

1163   MACKENZIE, DONALD, ed.
Mayors and aldermen of Great Britain and provosts and bailies of Scotland. London, Sir J. Causton, 1935. 1083 p. illus. 29cm. Lists nearly 4000 names of mayors and alder-men in office 1935, with biographies and lists of mayors for the period 1910-1934.

1164   MILLER, WILLIAM, biographer.
Biographical sketches of British characters recently de-ceased: commencing with the accession of George the Fourth... With a list of their engraved portraits. London, 1826. 2 v. ports. 4.º

1165   MUSGRAVE, SIR WILLIAM.
        Obituary prior to 1800 (as far as relates to England, Scotland, and Ireland) compiled by Sir William Musgrave ... and entitled by him "A general nomenclator and obituary, with reference to the books where the persons are mentioned, and where some account of their character is to be found." Edited by Sir George J. Armytage. London, 1899-1901. 6 v. (Publications of the Harleian Society, v. 44-49) Alphabetical, with date of death & sometimes a characterizing word or phrase ...

1166   NOBLE, MARK, 1754-1827.
        A biographical history of England, from the Revolution to the end of George I's reign; being a continuation of the Rev. J. Granger's work: consisting of characters disposed in different classes; and adapted to a methodical catalogue of engraved British heads; interspersed with a variety of anecdotes, and memoirs of a great number of persons. The materials being supplied by the manuscripts left by Mr. Granger, and the collections of the editor. London, W. Richardson, 1806. 3 v. 22cm.

1167   O'BYRNE, WILLIAM RICHARD, 1823-1896.
        A naval biographical dictionary: comprising the life and services of every living officer in Her Majesty's Navy, from the rank of admiral of the fleet to that of lieutenant inclusive. Compiled from authentic and family documents. London, J. Murray, 1849. viii, 1400 p. 26cm.

1168   OXFORD. UNIVERSITY.
        Alumni Oxonienses: the members of the University of Oxford, 1500-1714 [---1715-1886] their parentage, birthplace, and year of birth, with a record of their degrees. Being the matriculation register of the University, alphabetically arr., rev., and annotated by Joseph Foster. Oxford and London, Parker, 1888-92. 8 v. plates. 27cm. Vols. for 1500-1714 called: Early series.

1169   OXFORD. UNIVERSITY. MERTON COLLEGE.
        Merton College register, 1900-1964, with notices of some older surviving members. Oxford, B. Blackwell, 1964. ix, 588 p. 22cm.

1170   PRATT, ALFRED T   CAMDEN, ed.
        People of the period: being a collection of the biographies

of upwards of six thousand living celebrities. London, N.
Beeman, 1897. 2 v. 8.° Biographies of British celebrities.

1171 PUBLIC CHARACTERS.
[v. 1-10]; 1798/99-1809/10. London, R. Phillips [etc.]
1799-1809. 10 v. ports. 21cm. annual. Most of the contents of the first 9 vols. were contributed by Alexander
Stephens. Cf. Dict. Nat. biog. Concerned chiefly with
British biography.

1172 PUGHE, WILLIAM OWEN, 1759-1835.
The Cambrian biography; or, Historical notices of cele-
brated men among the ancient Britons, by William Owen.
London, E. Williams, 1803. vii, 345p. 17cm.

1173 ROTH, ANDREW
The business background of members of Parliament.
Westminster, London, Parliamentary Profile Services [1963]
240p. 21cm. (Parliamentary profiles) Earlier editions issued in 195-(?), 1960, and 1961(?)

1174 RUVIGNY AND RAINEVAL, MELVILLE AMADEUS HENRY
DOUGLAS HEDDLE DE LA CAILLEMOTTE DE MASSUE DE
RUVIGNY, 9th marquis of, 1868-1921, comp.
The roll of honor; a biographical record of all members
of His Majesty's naval and military forces who have fallen in
the war. London, Standard Art Book Co. [1917-   v. 4.°
At least 2 vols. were published.

1175 ST. PETER'S COLLEGE, LONDON.
The record of old Westminsters; a biographical list of all
those who are known to have been educated at Westminster
School from the earliest times to 1927, compiled by G. F.
Russell Barker and Alan H. Stenning. London, Printed at
the Chiswick Press, 1928. 2 v. illus. 26cm.

1176 ---- ----A supplementary volume... comprising part I:
Addenda and corrigenda to the original work. Part II: A
supplement containing a biographical list of all those who
have been admitted to the school from Play term 1919 to Election term 1937... Compiled by J. B. Whitmore and G. R. Y.
Radcliffe. Published by the Elizabethan Club. London, Chiswick Press [1938?]

1177   SMITH-DAMPIER, JOHN LUCIUS.
Carthusian worthies.   Oxford, Printed at the Shakespeare
Head Press, and sold by B. Blackwell, 1940.   xxiv, 366 p.
23cm.   Alumni of Charterhouse (a public preparatory school)
in Godalming, England.

1178   THORPE, ARTHUR WINTON, 1865-   ed.
Burke's handbook to the Most Excellent Order of the British Empire; containing biographies, a full list of persons appointed to the Order, showing their relative precedence, and
coloured plates of the insignia.   London, Burke Pub. Co.,
1921.   703p.   col. illus.   27cm.

1179   THE TIMES, London.
House of Commons, with full results of the polling, biographies of the members and unsuccessful candidates, photographs of all members, and a complete analysis, statistical
tables, and a map of the general election.   London.   v.
illus.   24cm.   Subtitle varies.   Began 1945?

1180   VENN, JOHN, 1834-1923.
Biographical history of Gonville and Caius College, 1349-
1897; containing a list of all known members of the College
from the foundation to the present time, with biographical
notes.   Cambridge [Eng.] University Press [etc.] 1897-
v.   illus.   28cm.

1181   WALFORD'S COUNTY FAMILIES OF THE UNITED KINGDOM;
or, Royal manual of the titled and untitled aristocracy of
England, Wales, Scotland and Ireland...   1st-   annual
publication; 1860-   London, Chatto & Windus [etc.]   v.
26cm.

1182   WARD, THOMAS HUMPHRY, 1845-1926, ed.
Men of the reign; a biographical dictionary of eminent
persons of British and colonial birth who have died during
the reign of Queen Victoria.   London, New York, Routledge,
1885.   iv, 1020 p.   19cm.   Largely compiled from 'Men of
the time.'   Contains some names not in the Dictionary of
national biography nor in Boase: Modern English biography.

1183   WEDGWOOD, JOSIAH CLEMENT WEDGWOOD, baron, 1872-
1943.
History of Parliament...1439-1509.   In collaboration with

Anne D. Holt. London, H. M. Stationery Off., 1936-   v.
illus. 27cm. Contents. --1. Biographies of the members of
the Commons House. --[2] Register of the ministers and of the
members of both Houses, 1439-1509.

1184   WELFORD, RICHARD, 1836-1919.
Men of mark 'twixt Tyne and Tweed. London, W. Scott,
1895. 3 v. 8.° Prominent men in Northern England
(chiefly Northumberland) and Southern Scotland.

1185   WHITAKER'S PEERAGE, BARONETAGE, KNIGHTAGE, AND
COMPANIONAGE... 1897-19   London. v. 19cm.
Title varies: 1897-99, A Directory of titled persons.
1900-06, Whitaker's peerage... being a directory of titled
persons.

1186   WHO WAS WHO.
A companion to Who's who, containing the biographies of
those who died. v. [1]-   1897/1916-   London, A. & C.
Black. v. 22cm. Vol. 1 also in a rev. ed. published in
1935.

1187   WHO'S WHO.
An annual biographical dictionary, with which is
incorporated "Men and women of the time. " 1st-   1849-
London, A. and C. Black [etc.] v. ports. 13-22cm.
Absorbed men and women of the time with v. 53, 1901. Vol.
50, 1898, also called "second year of new issue. " Subtitle
varies; vols. for 1849-98, 1904-12 issued without subtitle.
Imprint varies.

1188   WILSON, JOSHUA, M.A.
A biographical index to the present House of Commons.
Corrected to February, 1808. London, T. Goddard, 1808.
xii, 718 p. 17cm. An earlier edition (corrected to March,
1806) appeared in 1806.

1189   WURTS, JOHN S   1876-
Magna charta. Philadelphia, Brookfield Pub. Co., 1944-
[v. 1, 1945]   v. illus., ports. 24cm. British nobility.

1190   WOOD, ANTHONY A, 1632-1695.
Athenae Oxonienses. An exact history of all the writers

and bishops who have had their education in the University of
Oxford. To which are added the Fasti, or Annals of the said
University. A new ed., with additions, and a continuation by
Philip Bliss. London, Printed for F. C. & J. Rivington [etc.]
1813-20. 5 v. 32cm. Vol. 5 in 2 parts with title: Fasti Ox-
onienses...

Local
Bedforshire

1191   WHO'S WHO IN BEFORDSHIRE AND HUNTINGDONSHIRE.
London, 1936. 156p. 8.° (Who's who in the counties series)

Berkshire

1192   WHO'S WHO IN BERKSHIRE.
London, 1936. 248p. 8.° (Who's who in the counties
series)

Birmingham

1193   THE BIRMINGHAM POST YEAR BOOK AND WHO'S WHO.
1949- Birmingham, Birmingham Post & Mail. v.
illus. 19cm. Formerly the "Cornish's Birmingham year
book." The "Who's who" contains biographies of notable persons of Birmingham, England.

Buckinghamshire

1194   WHO'S WHO IN BUCKINGHAMSHIRE.
London, 1936. 216p. 8.°

Cornwall

1195   BOASE, GEORGE CLEMENT, 1829-1897.
Collectanea Cornubienses; collection of biographical and
topographical notes relating to the County of Cornwall. Truro,
Netherton & Worth, 1890. xi p., 1904 columns.

Fife

1196   CONOLLY, MATTHEW FORSTER, 1789-1877.
Biographical dictionary of eminent men of Fife, of past and

present times, natives of the country, or connected with it by property, residence, office, marriage or otherwise. Cupar-Fife, J. C. Orr [etc.] 1866.   xi, 492 p. 23cm. In double columns.

Glasgow

1197   EYRE-TODD, GEORGE, 1862-
Who's who in Glasgow in 1909. Illustrated with several hundreds of portraits...Glasgow, Gowans & Gray, 1909. 227 p. 4.°

Gloucestershire

1198   STRATFORD, JOSEPH
Gloucestershire biographical notes. Gloucester, "Journal" Office, 1887. xvi, 360p. 23cm.

1199   STRATFORD, JOSEPH
Good and great men of Gloucestershire. A series of biographical sketches, with a brief history of the county. Cirencester, C. H. Savory [etc., 1867] iv, 478p. plates, port. 19cm.

Hertfordshire

1200   WHO'S WHO IN HERTFORDSHIRE.
London, 1936. 227p. 8.° (Who's who in the counties series)

Jersey

1201   BALLEINE, GEORGE REGINALD, 1873-
A biographical dictionary of Jersey. London, Staples Press [1948] 715p. About 300 biographies.

Kent

1202   WHO'S WHO IN KENT, SURREY, AND SUSSEX.
London, 1911. 474p. 8.° (Cox's County series)

Lancashire

1203   HORNYOLD- STRICKLAND, HENRY.
Biographical sketches of the members of Parliament of
Lancashire (1290-1550) [Manchester, Eng.] Chetham Society,
1935. xviii, 134p. 22cm. (Remains historical and literary
connected with the Palatine countries of Lancashire and
Chester, new ser. , v. 93)

Liverpool

1204   IN MEMORIAM; OR, FUNERAL RECORDS OF LIVERPOOL
CELEBRITIES.
Containing many interesting reminiscences of local men.
Liverpool, A. Bowker, 1876. 272p. 22cm.

London

1205   NOTABLE LONDONERS;
An illustrated Who's who of professional and business men.
1st issue: 1921-22.   London, London Pub. Agency [1922]   184 p.
ports. 29cm.   No more published?

Norfolk

1206   NORFOLK, SUFFOLK, AND CAMBRIDGESHIRE:
Who's who in Norfolk, Who's who in Suffolk, Who's who in
Cambridgeshire.   London, 1912.   3 pts. 8.° (Cox's County
who's who series)

Northamptonshire

1207   NORTHAMPTONSHIRE BIOGRAPHICAL NOTICES.
Northampton [Eng.] Taylor [1892-   v. 8.°

Oxfordshire

1208   WHO'S WHO IN OXFORDSHIRE.
London, 1936. 396p. 8.°   (Who's who in the counties
series)

Scotland

1209   ABERDEEN. UNIVERSITY.
Roll of the graduates of the University of Aberdeen, 1901-

1925, with a supplement, 1860-1900, compiled by Theodore
Watt. Aberdeen, Aberdeen University Press, 1935. xx, 952p.
26cm. Continues and supplements William Johnston's Roll of
the graduates of the University of Aberdeen, 1860-1900. Aberdeen, 1906. An earlier list covering the years MVD (1400?)-
1860 is of little biographical value, consisting chiefly of names
with few identifying details.

1210   ANDERSON, WILLIAM, 1805-1866.
        The Scottish nation; or, The surnames, families, litera-
ture, honours, and biographical history of the people of
Scotland. Edinburgh [etc.] A. Fullarton [1859]-63. 3v. in 9.
illus. 27cm.

1211   CHAMBERS, ROBERT, 1802-1871.
        A biographical dictionary of eminent Scotsmen. Originally
edited by Robert Chambers. New ed. , rev. throughout and
continued by Thomas Thomson. London, Blackie, 1870. 3 v.
front. , port. 25 cm. 1855 ed. (New ed.) was in 5 v.

1212   FOSTER, JOSEPH, 1844-1905.
        Members of Parliament, Scotland, including the minor
barons, the commissioners for the shires and the
commissioners for the burghs, 1357-1882. On the basis of the
parliamentary return 1880, with genealogical and biographical
notices. 2d ed. , rev. and corr. London, Priv. print. by
Hazell, Watson & Viney, 1882. xviii, 360 p. 27 cm.

1213   GLASGOW. UNIVERSITY.
        A roll of the graduates of the University of Glasgow from
31st December, 1727 to 31st December, 1897. With short
biographical notes. Compiled by W. Innes Addison. Glasgow,
J. MacLehose, 1898. x, 695 p. 27cm.

1214   IRVING, JOSEPH, 1830-1891.
        The book of Scotsmen eminent for achievements in arms
and arts, church and state, law, legislation, and literature,
commerce, science, travel, and philanthropy. Paisley, A.
Gardner, 1881. ix, 573p. 22 x 17 cm. Running title:
Dictionary of eminent Scotsmen.

1215   JOHNSTON, WILLIAM, 1843-1914.
        Roll of graduates of the University of Aberdeen, 1860-1900.
Aberdeen, University Press, 1906. xvi, 687p. 4.° (Aberdeen University studies, 18)

1216   KAY, JOHN, 1742-1826.
        A series of original portraits and caricature etchings.
        With biographical sketches and illustrative anecdotes.
        Edinburgh, H. Paton, Carver and Gilder, 1837-38. 2v. in 4.
        plates, ports. 28cm. Biographical sketches chiefly by
        James Paterson. See also Paterson's Kay's Edinburgh
        portraits (1885) Scotchmen.

1217   PATERSON, JAMES, 1805-1876
        Kay's Edinburgh portraits; a series of anecdotal biogra-
        phies, chiefly of Scotsmen. Mostly written by James Pater-
        son and edited by James Maidment. [Illus. by J. Kay] Lon-
        don, Hamilton & Adams, 1885. 2 v. illus. 8.º Based on
        or a revision of John Kay's A series of original portraits and
        caricature etchings (1837-38) q. v.

1218   PAUL, Sir JAMES BALFOUR, 1846-1931, ed.
        The Scots peerage; founded on Wood's edition of Sir Robert
        Douglas's peerage of Scotland. Containing an historical and
        genealogical account of the nobility of that kingdom. Edin-
        burgh, D. Douglas, 1904-14. 9 v. plates (coats of arms)
        25cm.

1219   ST. ANDREWS. UNIVERSITY.
        Early records of the graduation roll, 1413-1579, and the
        matriculation roll, 1473-1579. Transcribed and edited by
        James Maitland Anderson. Edinburgh, Printed by T. and A.
        Constable for the Scottish History Society, 1926. xlii, 370p.
        23cm. (Publications of the Scottish History Society, 3d ser.,
        v. 8)

1220   SCOTTISH BIOGRAPHIES, 1938.
        London, E. J. Thurston; Glasgow, Jackson, 1938. xii,
        808 p. 8.º "The first publication of a Who's who in Scotland."
        --Walford, A. J. Guide to reference materials.

Staffordshire

1221.   WHO'S WHO IN STAFFORDSHIRE...
        Worcester [Eng] E. Baylis, 1934. 254p. 8.º

Wales

1222   Y BYWGRAFFIADUR CYMREIG HYD 1940.
        Paratowyd dan nawdd Anrhydeddus Gymdeithas y Cymmro-
dorion.   Llundain, 1953.   liv, 1110 p.   24cm.   Welsh biographical dictionary to 1940.

1223   THE DICTIONARY OF WELSH BIOGRAPHY DOWN TO 1940,
        Under the auspices of the Honourable Society of Cymmro-
dorion.   London, Blackwell, 1959.   lvii, 1157 p.   25cm.
English language ed. of Y Bywgraffiadur Cymreig hyd 1940,
with additions and corrections.

1224   [FOULKES, ISAAC] 1836-1904.
        Geirlyfr bywgraffiadol o enwogion Cymru.   Yn rhyfelwyr,
pregethwyr, beirdd, gwyddonwyr, meddygon... Liverpool, 1870.
iv, 1112 p.   Biographical dictionary of famous men of Wales.

1225   JONES, EDWARD (JEWIN NEWYDD)
        Rhestyr, gyda nodiakau byrion o enwogion Cymrieg o
1700 i 1900.   Rhan I.   Caerdydd, 1908.   xii, 218p.
(National Eisteddfod, Carnarvon, 1906.   Transactions) Fasc.
1 (A-Huxley) only.   No more published.   List, together with
brief notes about famous Welshmen, 1700-1900.

1226   JONES, JOSIAH THOMAS.
        Geiriadur bywgraffyddol o Enwogion Cymru... Aberdâr,
1867-70.   2v.   8.°   Biographical dictionary of famous
Welshmen.

1227   MORGAN, JOHN VYRNWY, 1860-   ed.
        Welsh political and educational leaders in the Victorian
era.   London, J. Nisbet, 1908.   vi, 734p.   8.°

1228   PARRY, JOHN HUMFFREYS, 1786-1825.
        The Cambrian Plutarch: comprising memoirs of some of
the most eminent Welshmen, from the earliest times to the
present, including the substance of all previous researches
into the literary and personal history of Aneurin, Taliesin,
Llywarch Hen, Asser Menevensis, Giraldus Cambrensis,
David ab Gwilym, Humphrey Llwyd, Dr. John David Rys,

Bishop Morgan, and other early Welsh poets and historians.
London, W. Simpkin and R. Marshall, 1824. ix, 385p. 23cm.
Reprinted in 1834.

1229   REES, THOMAS MARDY
Notable Welshmen (1700-1900) With brief notes, in chronological order, and authorities. Also a complete alphabetical
index. Carnarvon, "Herald" Office, 1908. xlii, 474p. 22cm.

1230   ROBERTS, T   R
Eminent Welshmen; a short biographical dictionary of
Welshmen who have attained distinction from the earliest
times to the present, by T. R. Roberts (Asaph) Cardiff,
Educational Pub. Co., 1908. 613p. ports. 26cm. A con-
tinuation of: Williams, Robert. Enwogion Cymru.

1231   ROWLAND, E   H
A biographical dictionary of eminent Welshmen who
flourished from 1700-1900. By E. H. Rowland (Helen Elwy)
[Wrexham] 1907. 295p. 22cm.

1232   WHO'S WHO IN WALES.
1st- ed.; 1921-   v. 21cm. 1st ed., 1921; 2d, 1933; 3d,
1937; no more published?

1233   WILLIAMS, DANIEL
Memoirs and sketches of one hundred and eleven eminent
men, natives of the County of Cardigan. [Cardigan? 1874]
1 v. 8.°

1234   WILLIAMS, ROBERT, 1810-1881.
Enwogion Cymru. A biographical dictionary of eminent
Welshmen, from the earliest times to the present, and includ-
ing every name connected with the ancient history of Wales.
Llandovery, W. Rees [etc.] 1852. 567 p. 23cm.

Warwickshire

1235   COLVILE, FREDERICK LEIGH, 1819-1886.
The worthies of Warwickshire who lived between 1500 and
1800. Warwick, H. T. Cooke; London, J. R. Smith [1870]
iv, 899 p. ports. 22 x 18cm.

1236   WHO'S WHO IN WARWICKSHIRE.
Worcester [Eng.] E. Baylis, 1934. 168p. 8.º

Westmorland

1237   ATKINSON, GEORGE, 1809-1891.
The worthies of Westmorland; or, Notable persons born in
that County since the Reformation. London, J. Robinson,
1849-50. 2v. front. 20cm.

Worcestershire

1238   BROWNE, EDITH OPHELIA, ed.
Short biographies of the worthies of Worcestershire.
Edited by Edith Ophelia Browne and John Richard Burton.
Worcester [Eng.] E. G. Humphreys, 1916. v, 203 p. ports.
26 cm.

1239   CHAMBERS, JOHN, 1780-1839.
Biographical illustrations of Worcestershire: including
lives of persons, natives or residents eminent either for piety
or talent: to which is added, a list of living authors of the
county. Worcester, Printed for W. Walcott, 1820. viii, 608 p.
22 cm.

Yorkshire

1240   HAILSTONE, EDWARD, 1818-1890, ed.
Portraits of Yorkshire worthies. Selected from the National Exhibition of Works of Art at Leeds, 1868. With biographical notices. London, Cundall and Fleming, 1869. 2 v.
200 ports. 26cm. A brief biographical sketch accompanies
each portrait.

1241   ROSS, FREDERICK, 1816-1893.
Celebrities of the Yorkshire Wolds. London, 1878. 1 v.
8.º

1242   WHO'S WHO IN YORKSHIRE—NORTH & EAST RIDING.
[London? 193-?] 1 v. 8.º

GREECE, ANCIENT

1243 KIRCHNER, JOHANNES ERNST, 1859-1940.
Prosopographia Attica. Berolini, Typis et Impensis G.
Reimeri, 1901-03. 2 v. fold. tables. 25cm. Chiefly a
listing, but with biographical data for some of the more important figures of ancient Attica and Athens.

GREECE, MODERN

1244 MEGA HELLĒNIKON BIOGRAPHIKON LEXIKON.
[Athens] "Biomēchanikēs Epitheōrēseos" [1958- v.
ports. 29cm. Biographical dictionary of modern Greece.
Edited by S. A. Bobolinēs and K. A. Bobolinēs.

1245 WHO'S WHO IN GREECE.
19 Athens, Athens news. v. 21cm.

HONG KONG

1246 HONG KONG WHO'S WHO.
1958-60. Hong Kong, R. Luzzatto. v. 22cm. Editor:
1958-60- R. Luzzatto.

HUNGARY

Anonyms and Pseudonyms

1247 GULYÁS, PÁL, 1881-
Magyar írói álnév lexikon; a magyarországi írók álnevei
és egyéb jegyei. Függelék: Néhány száz névtelen munka jeg-
yzéke. Budapest, Akadémiai Kiadó, 1956. 706 p. 21cm.
A dictionary of Hungarian anonyms & pseudonyms.

General Works

1248 GELLÉRT, IMRE
Három évtized története életrajzokban. Szerkesztették
Gellért Imre és Madarász Elemér (Magyarország monografiája
1900-1932) Budapest [1932] 615 p. ports. 8.° Biographies
of Hungarians prominent in the period 1900-1932.

1249   GULYÁS, PÁL, 1881-
Magyar életrajzi lexikon. Szinnyei József Magyar írók
élete és munkái kiegészito sorozata, írja és szerkeszti Gulyás Pál. Budapest, Lantos, 1925-29. 768 columns. Vol.
1, fasc. 1-6 (Aachs-Bacher) No more published. Continues
Szinnyei's Magyar írók élete es munkái...(1891-1914) A bio-
bibliographical dictionary of Hungary and Hungarian literature.

1250   JÁSZNIGI, ALEXANDER, 1861-   ed.
Das geistige Ungarn; biographisches Lexikon. Hrsg.
von Oskar von Krücken[pseud.] und Imre Parlagi. Wien, W.
Braumüller [1918] 2v. 24cm. Intellectual Hungary;
biographical dictionary. Chiefly writers, artists and public
men.

1251   A MAGYAR TÁRSADALOM LEXIKONJA.
2. bőv. kiad. Budapest, A Magyar Tarsadalom Lexikonja
Kiadóvállalat, 1931. 244, 640p. 106 p. of ports. 26cm.
Dictionary of Hungarian 'society' (i.e. people) A biographical dictionary.

1252   MAGYAR ZSIDÓ LEXIKON,
Szerkesztette Ujvári Péter. Budapest, A Magyar zsidó
lexikon kiadása, 1929 [i.e. 1930] 1028 p. 25cm. The dictionary of Hungarian Jews. Originally published in 1929 under
title: Zsidó lexikon.

1253   MIKSZÁTH, KÁLMÁN, 1840-1910.
Az én halottaim; nekrológok. Budapesten, Révai Test-
vérek Irodalmi Intézet, 1914. 240 p. 20cm. (Mikszáth
Kálmán munkái; hátrahagyott iratok, 5. kot.) "My people
(or friends) who died. " A necrology for Hungary.

1254   SZENTMIKLOSSY, GÉZA
A Magyar feltámadás lexikona. A Magyar legujabb kör
története. Budapest, 1930. 1151p. illus. , ports. 4.° A
dictionary of recent Hungarian history with biographical data
included.

1255   WEIDLEIN, JOHANN
Die verlorenen Söhne; Kurzbiograhien grosser Ungarn
deutscher Abstammung. Wien [C. Ueberreuter] 1960-   v.
19cm. (Forschungs- und Kulturstelle der Österreicher aus
dem Donau-, Sudeten- und Karpatenraum. Wissenschaft-

liche Reihe, Nr. 1-   "Lost sons."   Brief biographies
of great Hungarians of German descent.

ICELAND

1256   KRISTJÁNSSON, JÓN, 1884-1918.
Alþingismannatal 1845-1905.   Reykjavik, J. Jóhannesson,
1906.   vi, 76 p.   8.°   Members of the Icelandic parliament.

1257   ÓLASON, PÁLL EGGERT, 1883-
Íslenzkar æviskrár frá landnámstínum til ársloka 1940.
Reykjavík, Birt á kostnad hins Islenzka, 1948-52.   5 v.   Icelandic biographies from the time of the first settlement of the
country to the year 1940.

1258   SIGURÐSSON, JON, 1886-
Alþingismannatal, konungsfulltrúa, landshöfðingja,
ráðherra o. fl. 1845-1930.   Skriftstofa Alþingis gaf út.
Reykjavík, 1930.   xxx, 118 p.   illus.   8.°   At head of title:
Jón Sigurðsson og Helgi Hjörvar.   List of members of the
Icelandic Legislature, royal commissaries, governors,
ministers, etc. in the years 1845-1930.

1259   TOBIASSON, BRYNLEIFUR, 1890-
Alþ ingismannatal, konungsfulltrúa, landshöfðingja,
ráðherra o. fl., 1845-1945.   Reykjavík, Alþingissögunefnd
og Skrifstofa Alþingis, 1952.   222 p.   illus., ports.   25cm.
List of members of the Icelandic Legislature (or Parliament)
royal commissaries, governors, ministers, et al., 1845-1945.

1260   TOBIASSON, BRYNLEIFUR, 1890-
Hver er maðurinn? Íslendingaæevir.   Reykjavík,
Fagurskinna, 1944.   2 v.   "Who is that man?" Biographies
of modern Icelanders—a who's who type dictionary.

INDIA

1261   BĀLA SUBRAHMANYAM
South Indian celebrities.   Madras, Solden & Co., 1934-39.
2v.   8.°

1262   BARQUE, ALI MOHAMMAD, 1915-
Eminent Sikhs of to-day. Assistant editor: T. S. Khosla.
Lahore, Barque & Co., 1942-   v. ports. 19cm.

1263   BHATIA, JAGDISH
Celebrities; a comprehensive biographical thesaurus of
important men and women in India. [1st ed.] New Delhi,
Aeon [1952] 170 p. illus. 25cm.

1264   BUCKLAND, CHARLES EDWARD, 1847-
Dictionary of Indian biography. London, S. Sonnenschein,
1906. 494 p. 21cm. 2600 biographies of English, Indian or
foreign persons noteworthy in India's past (since 1750)

1265   CHITRAO, SIDDHESVARA SHASTRI
Bhāratavarshīya arvāchina-charitra-kosha. Poona, 1946.
xii, 600 p. In Marathi. A dictionary of Indian biography from
1818 to 1945.

1266   CHITRAO, SIDDHESVARA SHASTRI
Bhāratavarshīya-madhyayugina-charitra-kosha. Poona,
1937. xii, 848 p. In Marathi. A biographical dictionary of
ancient and medieval India, 321 B. C. -1818 A. D.

1267   CHITRAO, SIDDHESVARA SHASTRI
Bhāratavarshīya prachina-charitra-kosha. Poona, 1932.
xii, 715 p. In Marathi. Biographical dictionary of ancient
India.

1268   DAS GUPTA, JYOTISH CHANDRA
A national biography for India. Containing biographical
sketches with portraits of all Indian great men and women who
flourished in the nineteenth and twentieth centuries, with an
introduction. Dacca, 1911-19. 10v. 4.°

1269   FIGHTERS FOR FREEDOM:
Who's who. [Editor: S. P. Bhattacharjie] Lucknow, Information Dept., U. P. [1963-   v. 22cm. Contents. --1.
Jhansi Division: Districts Jalaun, Jhansi, Banda, and Hamir-
pur. Biographies of people of India instrumental in India's
independence movement and after.

1270   GUPTA, TANASUKHARĀMA
Bhāratiya-mahāpu-rusha. [Delhi, 1962-   v. 18cm.
In Hindi. Famous men of India.

1271   HIGGINBOTHAM, J   J.
Men whom India has known. 2d ed. , with emendations
and considerable alterations. Madras, Higginbotham & Co. ,
1874. 8pts. 8°.

1272   HINDUSTAN YEAR BOOK AND WHO'S WHO.
1933-   Calcutta, M. C. Sarkar.   v. maps. 19cm.

1273   INDIA (REPUBLIC) PARLIAMENT. HOUSE OF THE PEOPLE.
Who's who. 1st-   ed. ; 1952-   New Delhi, Lok
Sabha Secretariat [etc.]   v. ports. 18cm. Supersedes in
part India (Republic) Parliament. Who's who. Vols. for
1952-   issued by the House under a variant name: Lok
Sabha.

1274   THE INDIA OFFICE AND BURMA OFFICE LIST.
1803-   London, Harrison. v. fold. maps. 17-22cm.
Contains many biographical sketches. Title varies.

1275   INDIAN BIOGRAPHICAL DICTIONARY.
1915-   Madras [1916-   v. 8°. Editors: 1915-
C. Hayavadana Rao.

1276   KHANOLKAR, G   D
Arvācina Marāthī vānmayasevaka. [Bombay] 1949-
v. 19cm. In Marathi. Maratha personalities; each volume
contains anywhere from 40-70 biographies.

1277   LETHBRIDGE, Sir ROPER, 1840-1919.
The Golden book of India; a genealogical and biographical
dictionary of the ruling princes, chiefs, nobles and other personages, titled or decorated, of the Indian Empire, with an
appendix for Ceylon. London, S. Low, Marston, 1900.
xx, 366p. 19cm.

1278   THE MUSLIM YEAR BOOK OF INDIA AND WHO'S WHO,
With complete information on Pakistan, 1948-49. Compiled
by S. M. Jamil with the assistance of Moinuddin Khan. Bombay, Bombay Newspaper Co. [1949?] 1 v. (various pagings)
ports. 23cm.

1279   MYSORE.
History of the ruling family, nobles and leading personages
in Mysore. Bangalore [etc.] 1915-36. 23 pts. (?) 25-30(?)
cm.

1280 NALANDA YEAR-BOOK AND WHO'S WHO IN INDIA AND PAKI-
STAN; an Indian and international annual of current statistics,
events and personalities. 1941/42- Calcutta, Nalanda
Press. v. 18-20cm. Editor: 1941/42- Tarapada Das
Gupta.

1281 NORTHERN INDIA WHO'S WHO.
1st- ed.; 1942- Lahore, Mehta Publicity Corp.,
1942. v. illus., ports. 33cm.

1282 RAJASTHAN YEAR-BOOK & WHO'S WHO.
1961/62- Jaipur, Samriddhi Publication. v. illus.,
ports. 25cm. Editor: 1961/62- M. C. Dandia.

1283 SANYAL, RAM GOPAL
A general biography of Bengal celebrities, both living and
dead. Calcutta, Uma Churn Chuckerbutty, 1889- v.
8.°

1284 SINGH, TRILOCHAN
Indian Parliament (1952-57) ["Personalities"—Series 2]
Authentic, comprehensive and illustrated biographical diction-
ary of members of the two houses of Parliament. New Delhi,
Arunam & Sheel [1954?] xxxviii, [8], 304, [92] p. ports.
26cm.

1285 THE TIMES OF INDIA DIRECTORY AND YEAR BOOK IN-
CLUDING WHO'S WHO. 1914- Bombay, Bennett,
Coleman. v. illus., ports. 20-26cm. Title varies:
1914-47, The Indian year book. -- 1948--1952-53, The Indian
and Pakistan year book and who's who (varies slightly) Issues for 1919-47 include Who's who in India; 1948, Who's who
in India and Pakistan.

1286 WESTERN INDIA STATES.
The ruling princes, chiefs and leading personages in the
Western India States Agency. 2d ed. Delhi, Manager of
Publications, 1935. v, 539 p. fold. map. 26cm.

1287 WHO'S WHO IN INDIA.
Containing lives and portraits of ruling chiefs, notables,
titled personages, and other eminent Indians. Popular ed.
Lucknow, Newul Kishore Press, 1911. [1610] p. ports. 25cm.

1288 -----Supplement, containing lives and photographs of the recipients of honours on 12th December 1911, together with an illustrated account of the visit of their Imperial Majesties the King-Emperor and Queen-Empress to India and the coronation durbar. Popular ed. Lucknow, Newul Kishore Press, 1912. ii, [4], 195, [7], xx p. plates. ports. 25cm. Another supplement was issued in 1914?

1289 WHO'S WHO IN INDIA, BURMA & CEYLON.
   1- [1930?]- Bombay, Who's Who Publishers (India) v. illus., ports. 25cm. Editor: 19 Thos. Peters.

1290 THE WHO'S WHO IN MADRAS.
   A pictorial who's who of distinguished personages, princes, zemindars and noblemen in the Madras Presidency. [1932?- Cochin, Pearl Press. v. 26cm. annual.

1291 WHO'S WHO IN WESTERN INDIA.
   19 Poona, Sun Pub. House. v. ports. 24cm. Editor: 19 Thomas Peters.

1292 WHO'S-WHO— INDIA.
   1927- Calcutta, Tyson & Co. v. 23cm.

1293 THE YEAR BOOK AND WHO'S WHO IN KERALA.
   1950- Calicut [India] Adna Co. v. ports. 26cm.

INDONESIA
(Including former Dutch East Indies)

1294 ENCYCLOPAEDIE VAN NEDERLANDSCH-INDIË.
   2. druk, met medewerking van verschillende geleerden ambtenaren en officieren. 's-Gravenhage, M. Nijhoff, 1917-39. 8 v. 27cm. Vols. 5-8 (suppl. 1-4) issued in 60 parts (xii, 1920 p.) Encyclopedia of the Dutch East Indies, with biographical articles.

1295 --- ----Aanvullingen en wijzigingen; hoofdredacteur: D. G. Stibbe [en] redacteur in Ned.-Indië: F. J. W. H. Sandbergen. Afl. 61-[62] (5. serie) afl. 1-[2] Dec. 1939-[Apr. 1940] 's-Gravenhage, M. Nijhoff, 1939-40. 2 pts. (1921-1984 p.) 27cm. Cover title. No more published?

1296   HARIAN RAKJAT.
Articles on the leaders of the Indonesian Communist Party.
Washington, U. S. Joint Publications Research Service, 1961.
a, 53 1. 28cm. (JPRS: 10971) 62 biographical sketches.

1297   INDONESIA. KEMENTERIAN PENERANGAN.
Kami perkenalkan. . . ! Djakarta [1954?] 158p. illus.
23cm. We introduce. . . ! [Indonesian personalities]

1298   ORANG INDONESIA JANG TERKEMOEKA DI DJAWA.
Tjetakan 1. [Djarkarta?] Gunseikanbu, 2604 [1944]   552 p.
20cm. Prominent Indonesians in Java.

1299   ORANG-ORANG TIONGHOA JANG TERKEMOEKA DI JAVA
(Who's who) Solo, Biographical Pub. Centre [1935]   237 p.
ports. 22cm. Prominent Chinese in Java; a who's who.

IRELAND

1300   CRONE, JOHN SMYTH, 1858-
Concise dictionary of Irish biography.   Rev. and enl. ed.
Dublin, Talbot Press, 1937.   viii, 290 p.   22cm.   First published in 1928.

1301   DUBLIN. UNIVERSITY.
A catalogue of graduates who have proceeded to degrees in
the University of Dublin, from the earliest recorded commencements to July, 1866; with supplement to December 16,
1868.   Dublin, Hodges, Smith, and Foster, 1869.   lxix, 655 p.
23cm.

1302   DUBLIN. UNIVERSITY. TRINITY COLLEGE.
Alumni Dublinenses; a register of the students, graduates,
professors and provosts of Trinity College in the University
of Dublin, 1593-1860. Edited by the late George Dames
Burtchaell and Thomas Ulick Sadleir. New ed. (with supplement) Dublin, A. Thom, 1935.   xix, 905, 148 p.   26cm.

1303   HAYES, RICHARD.
Biographical dictionary of Irishmen in France. Dublin,
M. H. Gill, 1949. 332 p. 22cm. "First appeared serially
in the Irish periodical, Studies. "

1304   KING, JEREMIAH.
County Kerry, past and present... Dublin, Hodges,
Figgis [1931] 2 v. 8? (King's Irish-English dictionary, by
J. King and E. King) Includes a large amount of biography
(in an alphabetical arrangement?)

1305   RYAN, RICHARD, 1796-1849.
Biographia Hibernica; a biographical dictionary of the
worthies of Ireland, from the earliest periods to the present
time. London, E. Ryan [etc.] 1819-21. 2 v. port., plate.
22cm.

1306   THOM'S IRISH WHO'S WHO;
A biographical book of reference of prominent men and
women in Irish life at home and abroad. 1923-   Dublin,
A. Thom. v. front., port. 20cm.

1307   WARE, Sir JAMES, 1594-1666.
The whole works of Sir James Ware concerning Ireland.
Rev. and improved. Containing vol. I. The history of the
bishops of that kingdom... Vol. II. The history and antiquities
of Ireland. Also, The history of the writers of Ireland... with
an account of all the works they published. Written in Latin
by Sir James Ware... newly translated into English, rev. and
improved with many material additions, and continued down
to the beginning of the present century, by Walter Harris.
Dublin, Printed for R. Bell [etc.] 1764. 3 pts. in 2 v. plates,
ports. 33cm. Vol. 1 is a translation of De praesulibus
Hiberniae commentarius, with additions by the editor; vol. 2,
pt., of De scriptoribus Hiberniae "with the addition of near
400 new articles..." First published 1739-46.

1308   WEBB, ALFRED JOHN, 1834-1908.
A compendium of Irish biography; sketches of distinguished
Irishmen and of eminent persons connected with Ireland by
office or by their writings. Dublin, M. H. Gill, 1878. xix,
598 p. 23cm.

ISLAMIC COUNTRIES
(Arabia, Egypt, Near East, Etc.)

1309   AMĪN AHMAD, RĀZĪ, fl. 1594.
Haft-iqlīm. The geographical and biographical
encyclopaedia of Amīn Ahmad Rāzī. Edited by Sir E. Denison

Ross [and others] Calcutta [1918-   v.   (Bibliotheca Indica) Ca. 1,560 Muslim poets, saints, 'ulama, etc.

1310   AL-BITAR, 'ABD AL-RAZZAQ, d. 1916.
Hilyat al-bashar... Damascus [1961-63, i.e. 1962- 64]
3 v. 24cm. (Al-Majma' al-'Ilmī al-'Arabī bi-Dimasq. al-Matbū'āt) 'Ornaments' [of Muslim biography]

1311   AL-DHAHABĪ, MUHAMMAD IBN AHMAD, 1274-1348.
Al-Moschtabih, auctore Schamso'ddín Abu Abdallah Mohammed ibn Ahmed ad -Dhahabī. E codd. mss. editus a P. de Jong. Lugduni Batavorum, E. J. Brill, 1881. xii, 612p. 24cm. Added t. p.: al. Mushtabih fi asmā' al-rijāl.
A dictionary of names and genealogies of [Mohammedan] persons through whom traditions have been handed down.

1312   THE ENCYCLOPAEDIA OF ISLAM;
A dictionary of the geography, ethnography and biography of the Muhammadan peoples, prepared by a number of leading orientalists. Published under the patronage of the International Association of the Academies. Leyden, E. J. Brill, 1913-36. 4 v. illus., maps. 28cm. Also published in French & German.

1313   -----Supplement. Leiden, E. J. Brill, 1938. xvi, 267p. plates. 28cm.

1314   THE ENCYCLOPAEDIA OF ISLAM.
New ed., prepared by a number of leading orientalists. Edited by an editorial committee consisting of H. A. R. Gibb [and others] Leiden, Brill, 1960-   v. illus., maps. 26cm. Issued in fascicles.

1315   FATIMI, GREGORY HAGOP MAMOUR.
Official genealogical directory. The Moslem nobility of the world, 1935 (1353-1354 A.H.) 2d ed. Cairo [Printed by Vosguedar Press, 1935] 175 p. 25 cm.

1316   AL-GHAZZĪ, NAJM AL-DĪN MUHAMMAD IBN MUHAMMAD, 1570-1651.
al-Kawākib al-sā'irah. [Beirut, 1945-59] 3v. 24cm. (American University of Beirut. Publications of the Faculty of Arts and Sciences. Oriental series, no. 18,20,29) Added t. p.: al-Kawākib al-sā'irah bi-a'yān al-mi'ah al-'āshirah, a

biographical dictionary of notable men and women in the Moslem world in the sixteenth Christian century, by Najm-al-Din al-Ghazzi.

1317   HERBELOT DE MOLAINVILLE, BARTHÉLEMY D', 1625-1695.
Bibliothèque orientale; ou, Dictionnaire universel contenant ce qui fait connoître les peuples de l'Orient. Leurs histoires et traditions tant fabuleuses que véritables. Leurs religions et leurs sectes. Leurs gouvernemens, politique, loix, moeurs, coûtumes, et les révolutions de leurs empires. Les arts et les sciences... Les vies de leurs saints, philosophes, docteurs, poëtes, historiens, capitaines, & de tous ceux qui se sont rendus illustres par leur vertu, leur scavoir ou leurs actions. Des jugemens critiques et des extraits de leurs livres, écrits en arabe, persan ou turc sur toutes sortes de matières & de professions. La Haye, J. Neaulme & N. van Daalen, 1777-[82] 4 v. port. 28cm. A new ed., with a supplementary vol. by C. Visdelou [and others] and "Additions" & "Avis aux lecteurs" (signed H. A. Schultens, 1782) The lst ed. appeared in Paris in 1697. A dictionary of Mohammedan & West Asian history & biography.

1318   IBN 'ASĀKIR, 'ALĪ IBN HASAN, 1105-1176.
Tarīkh madīnah Dimashq. Damascus, 1951-   v. In Arabic. Also published under title: al-Ta'rīkh al-kabīr (Damascus, 1911-) A biographical dictionary of the celebrated men of Damascus.

1319   IBN HAJAR AL-'ASQALĀNĪ, AHMAD IBN 'ALĪ, 1372-1449.
Kitāb tahdhīb al-Tahdhīb [Hyderabad, 1907/08-09/10] 12v. in 6. 25cm. Biographical dictionary of Muslim traditionists.

1320   IBN KHALLIKĀN, 1211-1282.
Ibn Khallikan's biographical dictionary. Translated from the Arabic by Bn. Mac Guckin de Slane. Paris, Printed for the Oriental Translation Fund of Great Britain and Ireland, 1842-71. 4v. 32x26cm. (Oriental translation fund, 57) English title preceded by title in Arabic [Kitāb wafajāt al-'ajān]

1321   IBN SA'ĪD, 'ALI IBN MŪSĀ, AL-MAGHRIBĪ, called, 13th cent.
Kitâb al-muġrib fî hulâ al-maġrib. Buch IV: Geschichte der Ihsiden und fustâtensische Biographien. Textausgaben

nach der originalen einzig vorhandenen Handschrift zu Kairo
und deutsche Bearbeitung, mit Anmerkungen und Register.
Nebst einem Auszug aus al-Kindīs Ta'rīh Micr. Von Knut
L. Tallqvist. Leiden, Buchhandlung...vormals E. J. Brill,
1899. 2pts. in lv. 31cm. History of the Ikhshīdid dynasty in
Egypt (935-969) and biographies of Fustāt (or Old Cairo)

1322   AL- KHATĪB, AL-BAGHDĀDĪ, 1002-1071.
          Ta'rīkh Baghdād. [Cairo, 1931-   v.   A
biographical dictionary of the celebrated men of Baghdad,
with an introduction treating of the history and topography of
Baghdad.

1323   KHWĀND AMĪR, GHIYĀS AL-DĪN, d. ca. 1535 or 6.
          Dastūr al-vuzarā. [Teheran, 1938] 23, 514 p.   Biogra-
phies of wazīrs or viziers, Muslim ministers of state or
governing officials.

1324   MAKTAB AL-DIRĀSĀT AL-'ARABIYAH.
          Recueil des archives biographiques permanentes du monde
arabe. 2. éd.   Damas, Bureau des documentations arabes
[1960?-   2 v. (loose-leaf) 33cm.(?)   Biography (contemporary) of the Arab world.

1325   THE MIDDLE EAST;
          A survey and directory of the countries of the Middle
East. 1948-   London, Europa Publications.   v. illus.,
maps. 26cm. Subtitle varies. Includes "Who's who in the
Middle East."

1326   MUHIBB AL-DĪN, AL-DIMASHKĪ, 1651-1699.
          Khulāsat al-Athar fī A'yān al-Karn al-hādī 'ashar.   [Cairo,
1867 or 8?] 4 v.   1,289 biographies of Muslim scholars,
poets, etc., chiefly of the 17th century.

1327   AL-MURĀDĪ, MUHAMMAD KHALĪL IBN 'ALĪ, d. 1791 or 2.
          Kitāb silk al-durar fī a'yān al-qarn al-thānī 'ashar.
[Bulak, 1874-83] 4 v. 25cm. A biographical dictionary of
eminent Muslims of the 12th century A. H.

1328   RONART, STEPHAN
          Concise encyclopaedia of Arab civilization; the Arab East
[by] Stephan and Nandy Ronart. New York, Praeger [1960,
c1959] xiv, 589p. maps. 23cm. (Books that matter) First

published 1959 (Amsterdam, Djambatan) Includes biographical sketches of prominent Moslems.

1329   AL-SAFADI, KHALĪL IBN AYBAK, 1297 (ca.)-1363.
Das biographische Lexikon des Salāhaddīn Halīl ibn Aibak as-Safadi. Istanbul, Staatsdruckerei, 1931-   v. facsims. 25cm. (Bibliotheca Islamica, Bd. 6a-   A biographical dictionary of famous Muslims of the Middle Ages.

1330   AL-SAKHĀWĪ, MUHAMMAD IBN 'ABD AL-RAHMĀN, 1427 or 8-1497.
al-Dau' al-lāmi'. [Cairo, 1934-36] 12 v. in 8. A biographical dictionary of the notable men and women of the ninth century A. H. (after the Hegira); i. e. , Muslim biographies.

1331   AL-SAM'ANI, 'ABD AL-KARIM IBN MUHAMMAD, 1113-1166.
al-Ansāb... [Hyderabad] 1962-   v. 26cm. (al-Silsilah al-jadīdah min al-matbū'āt, 19) Arab 'families'; a book of names and also a biographical dictionary.

1332   WHO'S WHO IN U. A. R. AND THE NEAR EAST.
Cairo.   v. ports. 25cm. annual (irregular) Title varies: 19   -47, Le Mondain égyptien. The Egyptian who's who. --1948-51, Who's who in Egypt and the Middle East.-- 1952-53, 1955-57-58, Who's who in Egypt and the Near East. -- 1954, Le Mondain égyptien et du Proche-Orient. Vols. for have title also in Arabic.

1333   AL-ZIRIKLI, KHAYR AL-DIN, 1893-
al-A'lām. Qāmūs tarājum Li'ashhar al-rijāl wa 'l-nisā' min al-'arab wa al-must'rabīn wa al-mustshriqīn. [Cairo, 1954-59] 10 v. ports. 25cm. A dictionary of bio-bibliography of famous men and women: Arabs and Orientalists.

ISRAEL
See entries under Jews

ITALY
Bibliography, Indexes, Etc.

1334   BONAMICI, DIOMEDE.
Catalogo di opere biografiche e bibliografiche. Lucca, Tip. Giusti, 1893. 228 p. 24cm. A bibliography of Italian biographical and bio-bibliographical literature.

1335   FERRARI, LUIGI, 1878-
        Onomasticon; repertorio biobibliografico degli scrittori
        italiani dal 1501 al 1850. Milano, U. Hoepli, 1947. xlvi, 708 p.
        26 cm. (Bibliotheca veneta, collana di opere erudite) An in-
        dex to Italian bio-bibliographical literature.

1336   PIZZI, FRANCESCO
        Biblioteca di biografia italiana generale; saggio. Padova,
        Tip. Antoniana, 1901. 52p. 8.° Bibliography of Italian bi-
        ography. Superseded by his Italica gens (q. v.) ?

1337   PIZZI, FRANCESCO
        Italica gens; repertori a stampa di biografia generale
        italiana. Pref. di Umberto Monti. Cremona, G. Moschetti,
        1934. 133p. A bibliography of Italian biography.

Anonyms and Pseudonyms

1338   FRATTAROLO, RENZO.
        Anonimi e pseudonimi; repertorio delle bibliografie
        nazionali con un dizionario degli scrittori italiani (1900-1954)
        Caltanissetta, S. Sciascia, 1955. 208 p. 20 cm. Italian
        anonyms and pseudonyms.

1339   LANCETTI, VINCENZO, 1767?-1851.
        Pseudonimia; ovvero, Tavole alfabetiche de' nomi finti o
        supposti degli scrittori con la contrapposizione de' veri, ad
        uso de' bibliofili, degli amatori della storia letteraria e de'
        libraj. Milano, L. di Giacomo Pirola, 1836. L, 449p. 22cm.
        Italian pseudonyms.

1340   [MELZI, GAETANO, conte] 1783-1851.
        Dizionario di opere anonime e pseudonime di scrittori
        italiani, o come che sia aventi relazione all'Italia, di G. M.
        Milano, Coi Torchi di L. di Giacomo Pirola, 1848-59. 3 v.
        25cm. Dictionary of anonymous and pseudonymous works by
        Italian authors. Written in collaboration with Gaetano Zardot-
        ti. Supplemented by G. Passano (Ancona, 1887) and by
        Emmanuele Rocco. Vol. 3 published after author's death,
        edited with preface, corrections, notes and index by his son
        G. A. Melzi.

1341   PASSANO, GIOVANNI BATTISTA
        Dizionario di opere anonime e pseudonime, in supplemento
        a quello di Gaetano Melzi, compilato da Giambattista Passano.
        Ancona, A. G. Morelli, 1887. xi, 517p. 26cm. Supplement-

ed by Emmanuele Rocco, Napoli, 1888. 16p. Dictionary of
[Italian] anonymous works and pseudonyms.

1342 ROCCO, EMMANUELE
Anonimi e pseudonimi italiani. Supplemento al Melzi e al
Passano. Napoli, L. Chiurazzi, 1888. 16p. 24cm. Italian
anonyms and pseudonyms.

1343 ZANGARI, DOMENICO
Anonimi, pseudonimi, eteronimi scrittori calabresi, o di
opere attinente alla storia letteraria della Calabre. Napoli,
Culture calbrese, 1930. viii, 138p. Anonyms & pseudonyms
of Italian writers from Calabria.

General Works

1344 ANNUARIO DELLA NOBILITÀ ITALIANA.
Anno [1]-27; 1879-1905. Pisa, Presso la direzione del
Giornale araldico [etc.] 1878 [-1905] 27 v. illus. 14-15cm.
No more published. Yearbook of Italian nobility, with much
biographical information.

1345 BIOGRAFIA FINANZIARIA ITALIANA.
Roma. v. 25cm. Compiler: E. Lodolini and others.
Biographies of Italian businessmen.

1346 BOZZOLI, GIUSEPPE MARIA.
Studi biografici di rinomati italiani. Serie I-IV. Milano,
Tip. Guglielmini e Radaelli; poi V. Guglielmini, 1842-44.
4 v. in 5. 8.° Biographical studies of renowned Italians.

1347 CAETANI, LEONE, principe di Teano, 1869-
Saggio di un dizionario bio-bibliografico italiano. Roma,
R. Accademia nazionale dei Lincei, Fondazione Caetani, 1924.
880, 144 columns. 34 cm. Comprises only parts of the
letters A and B. An attempt towards an Italian bio-bibliographical dictionary.

1348 CARPI, LEONE, 1815-1898.
Il Risorgimento italiano; biografie storiche-politiche d'illustri italiani contemporanei, per cura di Leone Carpi,
collaboratori i più chiari scrittori italiani. Milano, F.
Vallardi, 1884-88. 4 v. ports. 22 cm. Biographies of leading figures in the Italian Risorgimento.

1349   [CECCHINI, RICCARDO] 1857-
Bio-bibliografia generale italiana, compilata da Paolo
Zincada [pseud.] Aggiuntivi i giudizi di sommi uomini oltre a
quelli della stampa italiana e straniera sulle opere dei vari
autori. Firenze, Coi Tipi della Bio-bibliografia generale
italiana, 1887. xvii, 292 p. ports. 24 cm. Confined to
contemporaries; general Italian bio-bibliography.

1350   CHI È?
Annuario biografico italiano con cenni sommari delle
persone più note del Parlamento, dell'Esercito, dell'Armato,
della magistratura, del clero, delle pubbliche amministra-
zione, dell'insegnamento, della letteratura, dell'arte, dell'
industria e del commercio, compilato a cura di Guido Biagi.
Roma, Romagna, 1908. lxxii, 279, [1], 277-278p. 20cm.
No more published. A later Chi è by A. F. Formiggini
was first issued in 1923. Intended to be an annual biographical dictionary of notable living Italians.

1351   CHI È?
Dizionario biografico degli italiani d'oggi. 1928-
Roma. v. illus. 21-25cm. an earlier Chi è by Guido
Biagi (q. v.) was issued in 1908. Title varies: 1928-1936,
Chi è? Dizionario degli italiani d'oggi. An Italian "who's
who."

1352   CODIGNOLA, ARTURO, 1893-
L'Italia e gli italiani di oggi. Genova, Nuovo mondo,
1947. 751 p. 24cm. A Who's who type of dictionary of
contemporary Italians.

1353   COMO, UGO DA, 1869-
I comizi nazionale in Lione per la costituzione della Repub-
blica Italiana. Vol. III, pt. 2a: Notizie biografiche dei Deputati. Bologna, N. Zanichelli, 1940. [viii],199 p. Biographies of Cisalpine deputies who met in Lyons, France (more
or less at the behest of Napoleon Bonaparte) to form the Cisalpine Republic's successor --the Italian Republic (proclaimed
1802, with Napoleon as president)

1354   DIZIONARIO BIOGRAFICO DEGLI ITALIANI.
[Redazione, direttore: Alberto M. Ghisalberti] Roma,
Istituto della Enciclopedia italiana [1960-   v. 25cm.
Biographical dictionary of Italians.

1355   DIZIONARIO DEL RISORGIMENTO NAZIONALE;
Dalle origini a Roma capitale fatti e persone. Direttore
Michele Rosi. Collaboratori: Agnelli, G. [et al.] Opera con
ilus. intercalate e tavole fuori testo. Milano, F. Vallardi,
1930-37. 4 v. illus. 26cm. (Dizionario dell'unità d'Italia;
il Risorgimento nazionale da Roma capitale ai patti del
Laterano) Contents. -- v.1. I fatti, A-Z. -- v. 2. Le persone,
A-D. -- v. 3. Le Persone, E-Q. -- v. 4. Le persone, R-Z.
Vol. 4 edited by Vittore Giglio and issued without series note.
The last 3 volumes of this dictionary of the Italian Risorgi-
mento are biographical.

1356   ENCICLOPEDIA BIOGRAFICA E BIBLIOGRAFICA "ITALIANA."
Direttore generale: Almerico Ribera. Milano, E.B.B.I.,
Istituto editoriale italiano B.C. Tosi [1936-   v. illus.,
ports. 28cm. To be in 50(?) series, each series devoted to
a special class. Bio-bibliographical encyclopedia of Italians.

1357   FABRONI, ANGELO, 1732-1803.
Elogi di illustri Italiani. Pisa, L. Raffaelli, 1786-89. 2 v.
The 'praises' of illustrious Italians.

1358   FABRONI, ANGELO, 1732-1803.
Vitae Italorum doctrina excellentium qui saeculis XVII. et
XVIII. floruerunt. Pisis, Excudebat C. Ginesius, 1778-1805.
20 v. 21cm. Imprint varies. Contains 154 lives of Italians
of the 17th-18th centuries.

1359   GUBERNATIS, ANGELO DE, conte, 1840-1913.
Piccolo dizionario dei contemporanei italiani. Roma,
Forzani [1895] vii, 989 p. 15cm. Small dictionary of
Italian contemporaries.

1360   LAMI, GIOVANNI, 1797-1770.
Memorabilia Italorum eruditione praestantium, quibus
vertens saeculum gloriatur. Florentiae, Ex Typ. Societatis
ad insigne Centauri, 1742-48. 2 v. in 3. Memorabilia of
learned Italians.

1361   LIBRO D'ORO DELLA NOBILITÀ ITALIANA.
[v.1]- 1910- Roma, Collegio araldico. v. illus.
16cm. annual. Golden book of the Italian nobility; with biographical data.

1362   LITTA, POMPEO, 1781-1852.
      Famiglie celebri italiane. Milano, Presso l'autore (Tip.
della famiglie italiane) 1819-74. 10 v.

1363   --- ----Dispensa 177[-188] Torino, Basadonna, 1875-86.
1 v. (folio)

1364   --- ----Seconda serie, fasc. 1[-76] Napoli, Stab. Tipo-lit.
Richter, 1902-23. 2 v.

      Noted Italian families. Includes biographical material.

1365   LOREDANO, GIOVANNI FRANCESCO, 1606-1661.
      Le glorie de gli incogniti; o vero, Gli huomini illustri
dell'Accademia de' signori Incogniti di Venezia. Venetia, F.
Valvasense, 1647. 432 p. The illustrious members of the
'Academy of Incognito Gentlemen of Venice.'

1366   MEMORIE, IMPRESE, E RITRATTI DE' SIGNORI ACCADE-
      MICI GELATI DI BOLOGNA... Bologna, Per il Manolessi,
1672. 406 p. illus., ports. 4.º Edited by G. Capponi.
Memorials, emblems and portraits of gentlemen of the Academy of the Gelati, Bologna.

1367   MINIERI-RICCIO, CAMILLO, 1813-1882.
      Biografie degli Accademici Alfonsini detti poi Pontaniani
del 1442-1543. Napoli, 1881. viii, 520p. Biographies of
members of the Accademia Alfonsina in Naples.

1368   NOTIZIE ISTORICHE DEGLI ARCADI MORTI.
      Roma, Stamperia di A. de Rossi, 1720-21. 3 v. 8.º
Biographical notes on the members of the Academy of the Arcadi in Rome. Edited by G. M. Crescimbeni.

1369   NOTIZIE LETTERARIE ED ISTORICHE INTORNO AGLI
      UOMINI ILLUSTRI DELLA ACCADEMIA FIORENTINA.
Parte I. Firenze, P. Matini, 1700. xxiv, 378 p. Literary
& historical notes on the illustrious men of the Florentine
Academy (later the Tuscan Academy of Science and Letters in
Florence) No more published. By Jacopo Rilli, Antonio
Magliabecchi, and others.

1370   RUBBI, ANDREA, 1738-1817.
      Elogi italiani. Venezia, P. Marcuzzi, 1782-83. 12 v.
'Italian eulogies'; general biography of Italy.

1371   SALVINI, SLAVINO, 1675-1751.
        Fasti consolari dell'Accademia fiorentina. Firenze,
        Stamperia Tartini e Franchi, 1717. xxxi, 676p. Biography
        of the Florentine Academy (later the Tuscan Academy of
        Science and Letters)

1372   SAN SEVERINO, GIULIO ROBERTO DI
        Les vies des hommes et des femmes illustres d'Italie, de-
        puis le rétablissement des sciences et des beaux-arts. [Tra-
        duit par M. d'Acarq] Paris, Vincent, 1767. 2 v. 12.°
        Other editions published in 1768 (and vol. 1 only, in 1762?)
        The lives of illustrious men and women of Italy after the
        reestablishment of the sciences and the fine arts.

1373   SAVINO, EDOARDO
        La nazione operante; albo d'oro del fascismo, profili et
        figure. 3. ed., riv. e ampliata. Novara, Istituto geografico
        De Agostini, 1937. 784 p. ports. 35cm. 2150 biographies
        of prominent Italian Fascists.

1374   SORGATO, GAETANO
        Memorie funebri antiche e recenti. Padova, Tip. del
        Seminario, 1856-75. 11 v. 8.° Necrology and notes on
        important Italians.

1375   SPRETI, VITTORIO, marchese, 1887-
        Enciclopedia storico-nobiliare italiana; famiglie nobile e
        titolati viventi riconosciute dal R. Governo d'Italia compresi:
        città, mense, vescovili, abazie, parrochie ed enti nobili e
        titolati risconosciuti. Milano, Ed. Enciclopedia storico-
        nobiliare italiana, 1928-35. 8 v. illus. 28cm. Historical
        encyclopedia of the Italian nobility.

1376   TIPALDO, EMILIO DE, 1798-1878.
        Biografia degli Italiani illustri nelle scienze, lettere ed
        arti del secolo XVIII, e de' contemporanei. Compilata da
        letterati italiani di ogni provincia, e pub. per cura del pro-
        fessore Emilio de Tipaldo. Venezia, Tip. di Alvisopoli,
        1834-45. 10 v. 22cm. Imprint varies. Each vol. is sep-
        arately indexed. Ms. index to the complete work at end of
        v. 10.

1377   TOMASINI, JACOPO FILIPPO, 1597-1654.
        Iacobi Philippi Tomasini Patavini Illustrium virorum elo-
        gio iconibus exornata. Patavii, Apud Donatum Pasquardum

& socio, 1630. 373, [50] p. illus., ports. 21cm. Biographical sketches and portraits of famous men [Italians]

1378 VACCARO, GENNARO, ed.
Panorama biografico degli italiani d'oggi. Roma, A. Curcio, 1956. 2 v. (xv, 1648 p.) 25cm. Biographical panorama of Italians of the present day.

1379 VILLANI, CARLO, 1858-
Stelle feminili. Dizionario biobibliografico. Nuova ed. ampliata, riveduta e correta. Napoli, 1915. xiii, 824p. A bio-bibliographical dictionary of outstanding Italian women.

1380 LE VITE DEGLI ARCADI ILLUSTRI SCRITTE DA DIVERSI
AUTORI, e pubblicate d'ordine della generale adunanza da Giov. Mario Crescimbeni. Roma, Stamperia di A. de' Rossi, 1708-51. 5 v. Lives of members of the Arcadia, an academy in Rome founded in 1692 for the purpose of improving taste & literature.

1381 WHO WAS WHO IN FASCIST ITALY.
With an appendix of changes since Mussolini's fall, to 20th August 1943. 4th ed. [london, Ministry of Economic Warfare] 1943. 60p. 25cm. Cover title. "Originally planned as a Who's who in fascist Italy." Earlier editions (e. g., 1942) have title: Who's who in fascist Italy?

1382 -----Who's who in Italy; supplement [to Who was who in fascist Italy. London, Ministry of Economic Warfare] 1943. 31 p. 23cm.

1383 WHO'S WHO IN ITALY.
1957-58— Milano, Intercontinental Book & Publishing. v. 21cm.

Local
Abruzzi and Molise

1384 ALBINO, PASQUALE
Biografie e ritratti degli uomini illustri della provincia di Molise. Campobasso, Tip. Solomone, 1864-66. 3v. 8.°
Biographies and portraits of illustrious men of the province of Molise, Italy (now Abruzzi and Molise)

Basilicata

1385   PEDIO, TOMMASO
La Basilicata nel Risorgimento politico italiano (1700-1870)
Saggio di un dizionario bio-bibliografico, con presentazione
del prof. Ernesto Pontieri. Potenza, Dizionario dei patrioti
lucani, 1962-   v. 26cm. An attempt at a bio-bibliographical dictionary of the Basilicata, a region in southern Italy,
for the period 1700-1870.

Bologna

1386   GARELLI, ANTONIO.
Gli illustri bolognesi; iscrizioni. Bologna, Tip. Cenerelli,
1880. 206 p. 20 cm. Famous persons of Bologna (biographical data from inscriptions)

Calabria

1387   ACCATTATIS, LUIGI
Le biografie degli uomini illustri delle Calabrie. Cosenza,
Tip. Municipale della Redenzione e Migliaccio, 1869-77.
4v. 8.° Biographies of illustrious men of the region of
Calabria in southern Italy.

Como

1388   GIOVIO, GIOVANNI BATTISTA, conte, 1748-1814.
Gli uomini della Comasca diocesi antichi e moderni nelle
arti, e nelle lettere illustri. Dizionario ragionato. Modena,
Società tipographica, 1784. 489 p. The men of the diocese
[and province] of Como, Italy [who have been] illustrious in
the arts and letters.

Ferrara

1389   BAROTTI, GIOVANNI ANDREA, 1701-1772.
Memorie istoriche di letterati ferraresi. Opera postuma
di Giannandrea Barotti. Ferrara, Eredi di G. Rinaldi, 1792-
93. 2v. 28cm. Edited by Lorenzo Barotti. Vol. 1 is a new
ed. (1st appeared 1777)

1390   ----- Continuazione, preceduta da un ragionamento intorno
all'indole e carattere degl'ingegni ferraresi per servire di

illustrazione al quandro istorico, statistico e morale
dell'alta Italia. Ferrara, Bianchi e Negri, 1811. 243p.
31cm. The "Ragionamento" is by Leopoldo Cicognara,
the "Continuazione" by Girolamo Baruffaldi.

Historical memoirs of the cultured men of Ferrara. Bio-
bibliographical.

Florence

1391   MANNI, GIUSEPPE
        Il Senato fiorentino [da Giuseppe Manni]; o sia, Notizia de'
        senatori fiorentini... data in luce da Domenico Maria Manni.
        2. ed. ampliata. Firenze, Per lo Stecchi e il Pagani, 1771.
        xliv, 145 p. illus. 4.° First ed. published in 1722 under
        title: Serie de' senatori fiorentini. Notices of Florentine
        senators.

Liguria

1392   [GRILLO, LUIGI]
        Elogi di Liguri illustri. 2. ed. riordinata, corretta ed
        accresciuta da Luigi Grillo. Genova, Tip. dei Fratelli
        Ponthenier, 1846-47. 4 v. 23cm. In praise of illustrious
        sons of Liguria, a region of Italy.

Milan

1393   ARGELLATI, FILIPPO, 1685-1755.
        Bibliotheca scriptorum Mediolanensium; seu, Acta, et
        elogia virorum omnigena eruditione illustrium qui in metropoli
        Insubriae, oppidisque circumjacentibus orti sunt; additis
        literariis monumentis post eorumdem obitum relictis, aut ab
        aliis memoriae traditis... Mediolani, In Aedibus Palatinis,
        1745. 2v. in 4. illus., port. Library of writers of Milan.

Naples

1394   GATTI, SERAFINO
        Elogi [d'uomini illustri delle provincie Napoletane] Napoli,
        Stamperia del Fibreno, 1832-33. 2 v. Praises of illustrious
        men of the Neapolitan 'provinces.'

1395   [MARTUSCELLI, DOMENICO] ed.
        Biografia degli uomini illustri del Regno di Napoli, or-

nata de' loro rispettivi ritratti, compilata da diversi letterati nazionali. Napoli, Presso N. Gervasi, 1813-30. 15 v.
in 16. ports. 8.º - 4.º   (Ricerche sull'origine, progressi
e de cadimento delle belle arti dell'avvocato G. B. de
Grossi. Biografia de' re di Napoli da N. Morelli di
Gregorio e P. Panvini) Biography of the famous men of the
Kingdom of Naples, with their portraits. First appeared
(1813-15) in 10 v. From 1816-1830 5 more volumes were
added to the original 10.

1396 MORELLI, NICOLÒ
      Biografia dei contemporanei del Regno di Napoli, chiari
per iscienze, lettere... del volgente secolo XIX. Vol. I. :
A-Bia. Napoli, Tramater, 1826. xxviii, 224p. Biography
of contemporaries in the Kingdom of Naples (early 19th century)

1397 TOPPI, NICOLÒ, 1603? - 1681.
      Biblioteca napoletana, et apparato a gli huomini illustri
in lettere di Napoli, e del Regno, delle famiglie, terre,
città, e religioni, che sono nello stesso rego. Dalle loro
origini, per tutto l'anno 1678. Nelle quali vengono molte
famiglie forastiere lodate, e varij autori illustrati, &
emendati. Napoli, Appresso A. Bulifon, 1678. 2 pts. in 1 v.
(400, [56] p.)

1398 ---- ----Addizioni copiose, di Lionardo Nicodemo. Napoli,
Per S. Castaldo, 1683. 250, [4] p. 33cm.

      The Neapolitan library and material on the illustrious men
of letters in the Kingdom of Naples from its beginnings to 1678.

Piacenza

1399 [POGGIALI, CRISTOFORO] 1721-1811.
      Memorie per la storia letteraria di Piacenza. Piacenza,
N. Orcesi, 1789. 2 v. in 1. 27cm. Bio-bibliography for the
city of Piacenza, Italy.

Piedmont

1400 NOVELLIS, CARLO
      Dizionario delle donne celebri piemontesi. Torino, 1853.
x, 307 p.   Dictionary of famous women of the Piedmont, Italy.

1401 PIEMONTESI ILLUSTRI.
      Torino, G. M. Briolo, 1781-87. 5 v. Famous people of
the Italian Piedmont.

1402   TENIVELLI, CARLO
        Biografia piemontese: Decadi I-IV. Torino, G. M.
        Briolo, 1784-92. 4 v. in 5. Biography of the Italian Pied-
        mont.

Sardinia

1403   MARTINI, PIETRO, 1800-1866.
        Biografia sarda ...   Cagliari, Reale stamperia, 1837-
        38.   3 v.   8.°   Biography of Sardinia.

1404   TOLA, PASQUALE, 1800-
        Dizionario biografico degli uomini illustri di Sardegna;
        ossia, Storia della vita pubblica e privata di tutti i Sardi che
        si distinsero per opere, azioni, talenti, virtu' e delitti.
        Torino, Tip. Chirio e Mina, 1837-38. 3 v. 25cm. and port-
        folio (3 plates, 63 ports.) 31cm. Biographical dictionary of
        the famous men of Sardinia. Reprinted in an edition of 200
        copies in 1965 (Bologna, A. Forni)

Sicily

1405   BIOGRAFIA DEGLI UOMINI ILLUSTRI DELLA SICILIA,
        Ornata de loro respettivi ritratti. Napoli, 1817-18. 3 v.
        ports. Biography of the illustrious men of Sicily, with por-
        traits.

1406   BOZZO, GIUSEPPE, b. 1809.
        Le lodi dei più illustri siciliani trapassati ne' primi 45 anni
        del secolo XIX. Palermo, Tip. Clamis e Roberti, 1851. 2 v.
        8.° Praises of the most illustrious Sicilians of the first 45
        years of the 19th century.

1407   CONFEDERAZIONE FASCISTA DEI PROFESSIONISTI E DEGLI
        ARTISTI.
        Dizionario dei Siciliani illustri.   Palermo, F. Ciuni, 1939.
        537 p. 25cm. Dictionary of illustrious Sicilians; a Fascist
        publication.

1408   LINARES, ANTONINO
        Biografie e ritratti d'illustri siciliani morti nel cholera
        l'anno 1837. [Raccolti da Antonio e Vincenzo Linares]
        Palermo, Presso G. Alleva, 1838. ix, 219p. ports. 16.°
        Biographies and portraits of illustrious Sicilians who died in
        the Cholera epidemic of 1837.

1409   MIRA, GIUSEPPE MARIA, b. 1803.
Bibliografia siciliana; ovvero, Gran dizionario bibliografico delle opere edite e inedite, antiche e moderne di autori
siciliani o di argomento siciliano stampate in Sicilia e fuori.
Palermo, G. B. Gaudiano, 1873-81. 2 v. 28cm. Sicilian
bibliography; with some biographical material. Originally
issued in parts; additions & corrections to the letter "A" by
G. Salvocozzo, are to be found in Archivio storico siciliano,
1873-80 (also issued as separate in 1881)

1410   ORTOLANI, GIUSEPPE MARIA
Biografia degli uomini illustri della Sicilia, ornata de' loro
respettivi ritratti, compilata dall'avvocato G. E. Ortolani e
da altri letterati. Napoli, 1817-21. 4 v. 4.º Biography of
the famous men of Sicily.

1411   RAGUSA, GIROLAMO, 1665-1727.
Elogia Siculorum, qui veteri memoriâ literis floruerunt.
Lugduni, Apud Anissonios, Posuel, & Rigaud, 1690. 314,
[30] p. 16cm. Bio-bibliography of Sicily. Reissued in 1700
under title: Siciliae bibliotheca vetus.

Syracuse (Province)

1412   GUBERNALE, APOLLO GAETANO
Dizionario biografico di tutti gli uomini illustri della
provincia di Siracusa. Floridia, S. Cagliola, 1909. 224 p.
Biographical dictionary of all the illustrious men of the
Province of Syracuse in Sicily.

Tuscany

1413   [ALLEGRINI, GIUSEPPE] ed.
Serie di ritratti d'uomini illustri toscani, con gli elogj
istorici dei medesimi. Firenze, G. Allegrini, 1766-73. 4v.
fronts., ports. 47x37cm. A series of portraits of illustrious men of Tuscany.

1414   BROCCHI, FILIPPO
Collezione alfabetica di uomini e donne illustri della
Toscana dagli scorsi secoli fino alla metà del XIX. Firenze,
1852. 218 p. 8.º Alphabetical collection of famous men and
women of Tuscany from past centuries to the 1st half of the
19th century.

1415   ELOGI DEGLI UOMINI ILLUSTRI TOSCANI.   Lucca, 1771-74.
        4 v. Illustrious Italians from Tuscany.

1416   INGHIRAMI, FRANCESCO, 1772-1846.
            Storia della Toscana... Tomo XII-XIV: [Biografia]
        [Fiesole] Poligrafia fiesolana, 1843-44.   3v.   22cm.
        History of Tuscany.   Vols. 12-14 are biographical.

1417   MEMORIE ISTORICHE PER SERVIRE ALLA VITA DI PIÙ
            UOMINI ILLUSTRI DELLA TOSCANA, RACCOLTE DA
        UNA SOCIETÀ DI LETTERATI. Livorno, A. Santini, 1757-
        58. 2 v. Historical memoirs serving to describe the lives of
        the most illustrious men of Tuscany.

Valtellina

1418   GANDOLA, LUIGI
            Albo storico-biografico degli uomini illustri Valtellinesi.
        Sondrio, A. Moro, 1879. 154 p. Historical-biographical al-
        bum of celebrated men of Valtellina, North Italy.

JAMAICA

1419   THE DIPLOMATIC PRESS DIRECTORY OF JAMAICA
            Including trade index and biographical section. 1962-
        London, Diplomatic Press and Pub. Co.   v.   illus., ports.
        29cm.   Cover title, 1962-   Directory of Jamaica including
        trade index and biographical section.

1420   WHO'S WHO IN JAMAICA.
            A biennial biographical record containing careers of
        principal public men and women of Jamaica. 1st-   year of
        issue; 1916-   Kingston, S. A. Hill. v. ports. 23cm.

1421   WHO'S WHO, JAMAICA, BRITISH WEST INDIES.
            An illustrated biographical record of outstanding Jamaicans
        and others connected with the island. 1934/35-   Kingston,
        Jamaica, B. W. I., Who's Who (Jamaica) ltd.   v. ports.
        24cm.   Title varies: -1939/40, Who's who and why in
        Jamaica...

JAPAN

1422   CHOSAKUKEN DAICHO.
[1]-   1951-   [Tokyo] Nippon Chosakuken Kyōgikai.   v.
23cm. annual. Vol. for 1954 not published. A "Who's who in
the cultural world of Japan." Title varies: 1951-53, Bunkajin
meiroku.

1423   DAI NIHON JIMMEI JISHO.
[Tokyo, 1937] 5 v. New revised Japanese biographical
dictionary. Published by Dai Nihon Jimmei Jisho Kankokai
and Tokyo Keizai Zasshi Sha.

1424   DICTIONNAIRE HISTORIQUE DU JAPON.
[Sous la direction de Iwao Seiichi] Tokyo, Librairie Kino-
kuniya [1963-   v. (Publications de la Maison franco-
japonaise) Issued in fascicles. An historical dictionary of
Japan which includes many biographies.

1425   HAGA, YAICHI
Nihon jimmei jiten. [Tokyo] Okura Shōten, 1914. 203,
1174 p. A biographical dictionary of Japan.

1426   IGARASHI, EIKICHI.
Taishō jimmei jiten. [Tokyo] Tōyō Shimpōsha, 1914. 38,
1868, 126 p. Biographical dictionary of the Taisho period,
1912-1926 (in Japan)

1427   INOUE, RAIMEI
Koshitsu jiten. Tokyo, Huzan-bo, 1942. 566p. Japanese
Imperial Household directory (enlarged ed.)

1428   ISEKI, KURO, ed.
Who's who Hakushi in Great Japan. Edited by K. R. Iseki.
Tokyo, Hattensha [1921?-   v. illus. 26cm. English and
Japanese. Vols. 3-   have title: Who's who in "Hakushi"
in Great Japan. Vol. 3, "English version by Umeo Mogami &
Kuro Iseki. "

1429   THE JAPAN BIOGRAPHICAL ENCYCLOPEDIA & WHO'S WHO.
1st-   ed; 1958-   Tokyo, Japan Biographical
Research Dept. , Rengo Press. v. col. maps. 27cm.

1430   JAPAN WHO'S WHO AND BUSINESS DIRECTORY.   1948-
        Tokyo, Tokyo News Service.   v.   19cm.

1431   JINJI KŌSHINROKU.
        1903-   [Tokyo] Kōshinjo.   v.   triennial.   Information
        about people.   A who's who of contemporary Japanese.   Very
        detailed (e. g., 1948 ed. in 2 v. contains over 30,000 sketches)

1432   LANMAN, CHARLES, 1819-1895.
        Leading men of Japan, with an historical summary of the
        empire.   Boston, D. Lothrop [1883]   421p.   port.   20cm.

1433   NIHON JINJI ROKU.
        [1st ed-   1956-   Tokyo] Chūō Tantei Sha.   v.
        Directory of Japanese personages; contains who's who-like
        entries.

1434   NIHON KODAI JIMMEI JITEN.
        [Tokyo] Yoshikawa Kōbunkan, 1958-   v.   Biographical
        dictionary of the Japanese people in olden times.   By
        Takeuchi Rizō and others.

1435   NIHON SHINSHIROKU.
        1889-   [Tokyo] Kōjun Sha.   v.   annual.   Who's who
        in Japan.

1436   ŌKAWA, SHIGEO.
        Kokugakusha denki shūsei [by] Ōkawa Shigeo [and] Minami
        Shigeki.   Tokyo, Dai Nihon Tosho Kankōkai, 1904.   1700, 30p.
        Collection of biographies of Japanese national scholars.   Index
        separately published: Nihon bungaku shiryō kenkyūkai, Kokuga-
        kusha denki shūsei myōgō sōsakuin.   Tokyo Kokuhon shuppansha
        1935.   47 p.

1437   PAPINOT, E
        Historical and geographical dictionary of Japan.   Ann Ar-
        bor, Mich., Overbeck Co., 1948.   842 p.   illus.   Reprint of
        the 1910 ed. (Tokyo, Librairie Sansaisha) Includes many bio-
        graphical sketches.

1438   RAMMING, MARTIN, 1889-   ed.
        Japan-Handbuch; Nachschlagewerk der Japankunde Im
        Auftrage des Japaninstituts Berlin hrsg.   Berlin, Steiniger
        [1941] 740p.   illus.   23cm.   An alphabetical dictionary for
        things Japanese that includes biography.

1439   SANKEI NIHON SHINSHI NENKAN.
1959-   [Tokyo] Sangyō Keizai Shimbun Sha.   v.
31cm. Yearbook [of biography] of 'Japanese gentlemen.'

1440   TAISHŪ JINJIROKU.
1925-   [Tokyo]   v. 26cm. irregular. The popular
who's who [of Japan]

1441   TAKAMURE, ITSUE.
Dai Nihon josei jimmei jisho. Tokyo, Kōseikaku, 1942.
20, 640 p. Biographical dictionary of Japanese women.

1442   TEIKOKU KOSHIN-SHO
Teikoku shin'yo-roku, 1930-1943. [Tokyo] 1930-43. 6 v.
Concise biography of Japanese 'gentlemen,' 1930-1943.

1443   U. S. EMBASSY. JAPAN.
Brief profiles of the members of the House of Representatives. Tokyo, Translation Service Branch, Political Division, American Embassy, 1958. 119p. 34cm. Biographies
of members of the Japanese Diet's House of Representatives.

1444   U. S. EMBASSY. JAPAN.
Profiles of members of the House of Representatives, 1
Sept., 1961. [Edited by] H. P. Smith. Tokyo [1961] 248p.
34cm. Cover title. Sources: Diet and party publications.
Biographies of members of the Japanese Diet's House of
Representatives.

1445   WHO'S WHO IN JAPAN.
1st-   ed.; 1912-   Tokyo, Who's Who in Japan Office.
v. ports. 20cm. annual.

1446   WHO'S WHO IN JAPAN.
no. 1-   ; autumn 1958-   Tokyo, Rengo Press. v.
illus. 26cm. Issued as a companion to the Japan biographical
encyclopedia and who's who.

1447   ZEN NIHON SHINSHI ROKU.
1951-   Tokyo, Jinji Kōshinroku.   v. biennial (since
1953 ed.) Directory of 'gentlemen of Japan.'

JEWS
(Including Palestine and Israel)
Anonyms and Pseudonyms

1448   ZABLOTSKY, MOSES, 1875-1932.
       Ozar ha-psudonimim...[Berdichev, 1902] 32 p. 18cm.
Treasury of [Hebrew] pseudonyms.

General Works

1449   AZULAI, HAYYIM JOSEPH DAVID, 1724-1806.
       Shem ha-gedolin ha-shalem... Shem hagdolim hasholem,
with notes and addenda Ashel hagdolim by Elazer Gartenhaus.
[Brooklyn, 1958] 3 v. 24cm. One of the earliest Jewish biographical dictionaries.

1450   CITRON, SAMUEL LOEB, 1860-1930.
       Leksikon zioni... [Warszawa, S. Sreberk, 1924] 824
columns. ports. 24cm. Dictionary of Zionism. Includes
biographies of Zionists.

1451   EISENSTADT, BENZION, 1873-1951.
       Dor rabanaw we-sofraw... [Warsaw, 1895-1903] 5 v.
ports. 21-23cm. Rabbis and writers contemporary with the
author.

1452   EISENSTADT, BENZION, 1873-1951.
       Sefer Doroth ha-aharonim... [Brooklyn, 1936-41] 3 v.
23-24cm. Book of the latest generation (i.e., modern Jews)

1453   ENCYCLOPAEDIA JUDAICA;
       das Judentum in Geschichte und Gegenwart. Berlin,
Verlag Eschkol [1928-34] 10 v. Vols. 1-10 cover A-Lyra.
No more published. Notable for large number of biographi-
cal sketches of famous Jews.

1454   ENTSIKLOPEDIYAH LA-TSIYONUT...
       [Tel-Aviv, 1946/47-   v. photos. 24cm. Added
t.p.: Encyclopedia of Zionism. Edited by Moses Kleinman.
Includes biographies of Zionists.

1455   ENTSIKLOPEDIYAH LE-TOLDOT GEDOLE YISRAEL...
       [Tel-Aviv, 1946-49/50] 4 v. (1375p) ports. 23cm. Added

t. p. : Encyclopedia of great men in Israel, being a biographical dictionary of Jewish sages and scholars from the 9th to the end of the 18th century. Edited by Mordecai Margulies.

1456   FRANKFURTER, NAFTALI, 1810-1866.
Galerie der ausgezeichneten Israeliten aller Jahrhunderte, von Naphtali Frankfurter und Berthold Auerbach. Stuttgart, 1838. 1 v. Gallery of remarkable Jews of all centuries. Issued in parts, 1834-1838?

1457   FÜNN, SAMUEL JOSEPH, 1818-1890.
Keneseth Yisrael... Varshava, 1886. 704p. 23cm. Only one volume was published. The "congregation" (or gathering) of Israel; biographical sketches of Jewish scholars & rabbis.

1458   GOLOMB, ZEBI NISAN, 1853-1934.
Kol hemdath Yisrael... [Vilna, 1901] 116p. 31cm. Parts 1 to 3 issued 1901-03; no more published. By Z. N. and Emmanuel Golomb. Book [of biography] of famous people of Israel (i. e. Jews in various parts of the world) Pts. 1-3 cover only Jewish scholars.

1459   [GRÄFFER, FRANZ] 1785-1852.
Jüdischer Plutarch; oder, Biographisches Lexicon der markantesten Männer und Frauen jüdischer Abkunft (aller Stände, Zeiten und Länder) mit besonderer Rücksicht auf das österreichische Kaiserthum. Von mehreren jüdischen und nichtjüdischen Schriftstellern. Wien, 1848. 2 v. ports. Biographical dictionary of noted men & women of Jewish ancestry. By Gräffer and Simon Deutsch.

1460   THE JEWISH ENCYCLOPEDIA.
A descriptive record of the history, religion, literature, and customs of the Jewish people from the earliest times to the present day. Prepared under the direction of Cyrus Adler [and others] Isidore Singer, projector and managing editor, assisted by American and foreign boards of consulting editors. New ed. New York, Funk and Wagnalls Co. [c1925] First published in 1916.

1461   THE JEWISH YEAR BOOK.
An annual record of matters Jewish. 5657-   8 Sept. 1896-   London, Greenberg.   v. 19cm.   Has a Who's who of [world] Jewry section which contains ca. 1500 biographies.

1462 JÜDISCHES ATHENAUM.
Gallerie berühmter Männer jüdischer Abstammung und
jüdischen Glaubens, von der letzten Hälfte des achtzehnten,
bis zum Schluss der ersten Hälfte des neunzehnten Jahrhunderts... Grimma & Leipzig, 1851. viii, 253 p. 6 ports.
The Jewish Athenaeum. Gallery of famous men of Jewish
ancestry and the Jewish faith, from the last half of the 18th
century to the close of the first half of the 19th. Sometimes
attributed to Friedrich Korn.

1463 KAYSERLING, MEIER
Gedenkblätter. Hervorragende jüdische Persönlichkeiten
des neunzehnten Jahrhunderts. In kurzen Charakteristiken.
Leipzig, 1892. vii, 92p. Memories; outstanding Jewish personalities of the 19th century, in short character sketches;
alphabetically arranged.

1464 KOHUT, ADOLPH, 1848-1917.
Berühmte israelitische Männer und Frauen in der Kultur-
geschichte der Menschheit; Lebens- und Charakterbilder aus
Vergangenheit und Gegenwart. Ein Handbuch für Haus und
Familie. Mit zahlreichen Porträts und sonstigen Illus.
Leipzig-Reudnitz, A. H. Payne [1900-01] 2 v. illus. 26cm.
Famous Jewish men and women in the cultural history of man-
kind; biographical and character sketches from the past and
present.

1465 LEKSIKON HA-GEVURAH...
[Jerusalem, 1965- v. ports. 25cm. Added t. p. :
Biographical dictionary of Jewish resistance. Edited by
Jechiel Granatsztajn and Moshe Kahanovich. Biographies of
Jewish resistance fighters in World War II. Vol. 1, pt. 1
covers the letters: aleph-yod.

1466 LÖWY, DAVID
Gallerie der verdienstvollsten Juden des XIX. Jahrhunderts
zunächst aus Österreich-Ungarn. Wien, 1882. 2 fascicles.
folio. No more published? Gallery of the most meritorious
Jews of the 19th century.

1468 [OPFERGELDT, FRIEDRICH] 1668-1740.
Aufrichtige Nachricht von den jüdischen Lehrern und

ihren zur Exegesi und Antiquität gehörigen Schriften... Nebst
einer kleinen Bibliotheca Rabbinica. Halle, 1730. 264p. An
honest report on Jewish scholars and their writings which
bear upon exegesis and antiquity.

1470 PHILO-LEXIKON;
Handbuch des jüdischen Wissens. Verm. und verb. Aufl.
Berlin, Philo Verlag, 1936. 830 columns. illus., ports.
19cm. In double columns. A handbook of Jewish learning.
Includes biographies.

1471 REINES, MOSES, 1870-1891.
Dor we-hakhamaw... [Cracovie, 1890] 188 p. ports. 23cm.
Added t. p. : Tableaux historiques; ou, Traités biographiques
et littéraires [sic] sur la vie et les oeuvres des plus eminents
savants juifs contemporains... 1. ptie. No more published.
Bio-bibliography of Jewish scholars of the 19th century.

1472 RUBIN, ELI
140 Jewish marshals, generals & admirals. London, De
Vero Books [1952] 300p. illus. 22cm.

1473 SCHWAB, HERMANN.
Chachme Ashkenaz; a concise record of the life and work
of orthodox Jewish scholars of Germany from the 18th to the
20th century. London, Mitre Press [1964] 131 p. port.
23cm. 96 biographies.

1474 SEFER HA-ISHIM,
Leksikon Erets-Yisraeli ... [Tel-Aviv, 1936/37] 375 p.
illus., ports. 21cm. Edited by David Kalai. Book of famous
people; biographical dictionary of modern Israel.

1475 SOKOLOW, NAHUM, 1859-1936.
Ishim. [Tel-Aviv, 1934/35] 3 v. 21cm. Famous
[Jewish] people.

1476 THE STANDARD JEWISH ENCYCLOPEDIA.
Cecil Roth, editor-in-chief. Garden City, N. Y., Doubleday, 1959. 30, 1978 columns. illus., ports. 27cm. Strong

on brief biographies of Jews (and non-Jews) who have contributed impressively to Jewish history & learning.

1477   STAUFF, PHILIPP, 1876-1923.
Semi-Kürschner; oder, Literarisches Lexikon der
Schriftsteller, Dichter, Bankiers, Geldleute, Ärzte,
Schauspieler, Künstler, Musiker, Offiziere, Rechtsanwalter,
Revolutionäre, Frauenrechterinnen, Sozialdemokraten usw.
jüdischer Rasse und Versippung, die von 1813-1913 in Deutschland tätig oder bekannt waren. Jahrg. 1-   Berlin-Lichter-
felde, 1913-   v. 8.° A work with virulently anti-Semitic
overtones; purports to be a literary dictionary of authors,
bankers, physicians, artists [etc., etc.] of the Jewish race.

1478   UNIVERSAL JEWISH ENCYCLOPEDIA;
An authoritative and popular presentation of Jews and Judaism since the earliest times. Edited by Isaac Landman in
collaboration with... Board of Editors. New York, Universal Jewish Encyclopedia, inc. [1939-43] 10 v. illus., ports.
28cm.

1479   ---- ----A reading guide and index, compiled by Simon Cohen. New York, Universal Jewish Encyclopedia, inc. [1944]
vi, 78 p. 28cm.

Very useful for biography.

1480   WHO'S WHO IN WORLD JEWRY.
1955-   New York.   v. 28cm.

1481   WHO'S WHO ISRAEL.
1945/46-   [Jerusalem, etc.]   v. illus., ports.
25cm. Title varies: 1945/46, The Near and Middle East Who's
who. Vol. 1: Palestine. Trans-Jordan. --1947, Palestine
personalia. —1949, The Near and Middle East who's who. Vol.
2: Israel. Who's who in the State of Israel. Vols. for 1952-
have title also in Hebrew.

1482   WININGER, SALOMON, 1877-
Grosse jüdische National-Biographie, mit mehr als 12,000
Lebensbeschreibungen namhafter jüdischer Männer und Frauen
aller Zeiten und Länder. Ein Nachschlagewerk für das
jüdische Volk und dessen Freunde. Cernauti [etc.] "Arta"
[etc.] 1925-37—   8+(?) v. 25cm. The great Jewish national biography, with more than 12,000 biographies of Jewish
men and women of all times and countries.

1483   WOLF, JOHANN CHRISTOPH, 1683-1739.
       Bibliotheca Hebraea; sive, Notitia tum auctorum Hebr.
cuiuscunque aetatis, tum scriptorum, quae vel Hebraice primum exarata vel ab aliis conversa sunt, ad nostram aetatem
deducta. Accedit in calce Jacobi Gaffarelli Index codicum
cabbalistic. mss. quibus Jo. Picus, Mirandulanus cones,
usus est. Hamburgi [etc.] Impensis C. Liebezeit [etc.] 1715-
33. 4 v. fronts. 21cm. The Hebrew library; or, Notices of
Hebrew authors of all ages and of writers who first wrote in
Hebrew or were translated by others.

1484   WORLD JEWISH REGISTER;
       A biographical compendium of notable Jews in the arts,
sciences and professions. 1955/56-   New York,
Monde.   v. 29cm.

1485   YUNG, PHILIPP, d. 1823.
       Alphabetische Liste aller gelehrten Juden und Jüdinnen,
Patriarchen, Propheten und berühmter Rabbinen, vom Anfange
der Welt bis auf unsere Zeiten, nebst einer kurzen Beschreibung ihres Lebens und ihrer Werke. Leipzig, Kollmann,
1817. xiv, 442p. 8.º Alphabetical list of all learned Jews
and Jewesses, patriarchs, prophets and famous rabbis, from
the beginning of the world to our times, with a brief description of their life and works.

KOREA

1486   CHŌSEN JIMMEI JISHO.
       [Seoul, 1938] 2470 p. Biographical dictionary of Koreans;
includes some 13,000 names. An earlier edition (?) was issued in 1937 (2012 p.)

1487   CHŌSEN JIMMEI JITEN.
       [Keijo] Chōsen Sotoku-hu Chusu-in [1937] 2, 438 p.
Who's who in Korea.

1488   CHŌSEN JIMMEI ROKU.
       [Keijo] Keijō Nippo-sha, 1944. 1 v. (?) Who's who in
Korea.

1489   CHŌSEN KŌBUNSHA, Seoul, Korea.
       Chōsen kokon meiken den. [Seoul, 1923] 2, 22, 495p.
illus., ports. 23cm. Famous Koreans of all periods in history.

1490   CHOSŎN SINSA POGAM. Seoul, Chosŏn ch'ulp'an hyŏphoe,
        1912. 1 v. (?) Mirror of Korean gentlemen.

1491   GENDAI CHŌSEN JIMMEI JITEN.
        [Tokyo, 1962] 509 p. 22cm. Biographical dictionary of
        prominent men in modern Korea. A 1960 ed. was issued by:
        Japan. Gaimushō. Ajiakyoku.

1492   KIM IL-SŎNG CHONGHAP TAEHAK, P'yongyang, Korea.
        YŎKSA YŎN'GUSO.
        Chosŏn ŭi myŏngin. [P'yongyang] 1963. 2 v. illus. 21cm.
        Famous men of Korea.

1493   SON, PO-GI.
        Biographical tables of the Koryŏ period, by Pow-key Sohn.
        Berkeley, East Asia Studies, Institute of International Studies,
        University of California, 1958. v, 179 p. 28cm. Biographi-
        cal dictionary of Korea for the years 935-1392.

LAOS

1494   SITHIBOURN, SITHAT
        Biographies des personnalités du Royaume du Laos. [Ven-
        tiane?] Edition Lao presse, 1960. 1 v. (unpaged) illus.
        24cm. Cover title. Biographies of personalities of the King-
        dom of Laos.

LATIN AMERICA
Bibliographies, Indexes, Etc.

1495   GRISMER, RAYMOND LEONARD
        A reference index to twelve thousand Spanish-American
        authors; a guide to the literature of Spanish America. New
        York, H. W. Wilson Co., 1939. xvi, 150 p. 26cm. (Inter-
        American Bibliographical and Library Association publications.
        Series 3, v. 1) Birth and/or death dates only given.

1496   TORO, JOSEFINA DEL
        A bibliography of the collective biography of Spanish A-
        merica. Rio Piedras, P. R., The University [1938] viii,
        140p. 24cm. (University of Puerto Rico bulletin, ser. 9,
        no. 1, Sept. 1938)

Anonyms and Pseudonyms

1497   MEDINA, JOSÉ TORIBIO, 1852-1930.
       Diccionario de anónimos y suedónimos hispanoamericanos,
       apuntaciones reunidas por José Toribio Medina. Buenos
       Aires, Impr. de la Universidad, 1925. 2 v. in l. 28cm.
       (Buenos Aires. Universidad Nacional. Instituto de Investi-
       gaciones Históricos. Publicaciones, no. 26-27) Spanish-
       American anonyms and pseudonyms.

1498   VICTORICA, RICARDO
       Errores y omisiones del Diccionario de anónimos y seu-
       dónimos hispanoamericanos de José Toribio Medina. Bue-
       nos Aires, Viau & Zona, 1928. 338p. 28cm. Spanish ano-
       nyms & pseudonyms; errors in and omissions from Medina's
       work.

1499   --- ----Verdades que levantan roncha. Belitres enfurecidos.
       (In Gaceta del foro. Buenos Aires. año 15, 11 abril 1930.
       p. 273-278) About 16 colums of "Nuevas adiciones al 'Dic-
       cionario de Medina.' "

1500   VICTORICA, RICARDO.
       Nueva epanortosis al Diccionario de anónimos y seudónimos
       de J. T. Medina. Buenos Aires, L. J. Rosso, 1929.   207 p.
       27cm.   New additions (?) to the Dictionary of [Spanish-Ameri-
       can] anonyms and pseudonyms of José Toribio Medina.

General Works

1501   AZPURÍA, RAMÓN
       Biografías de hombres notables de Hispano-América.
       Obra mandada publicar por el Ejecutivo Nacional de los Esta-
       dos Unidos de Venezuela... Caracas, Impr. Nacional, 1877.
       4v. 23cm.   Biographies of notable men of Spanish America.

1502   BARRIA, J   M
       Hombres de la independencia de América; o sea, El al-
       manach del centenario. Buenos Aires, 1923.   289p.   190 bio-
       graphies of important figures in the Latin American Indepen-
       dence movement; chronological arrangement.

1503   FLOREZ, ADOLFO, d. 1895.
       Estudio cronológico sobre los gobernantes del continente
       americano desde la más remota antiguedad hasta el presente

ano, 1877. [v. 1] Bogotá, Impr. a cargo de F. Pontón, 1888. viii, 335 p. ports. 23 cm. No more published? Chronological study on the rulers of South America, past & present.

1504   MARTIN, MICHAEL, 1917-
    An encyclopedia of Latin American history, by Michael Rheta Martin and Gabriel H. Lovett. Supervisory editor: Henry Bamford Parkes. [New York] Abelard-Schuman [c1956] vi, 392 p. 24cm. Includes brief biographies of famous Latin American historical personages.

1505   MONTOTO DE SEDAS, SANTIAGO, 1890-
    Nobiliario hispano-americano del siglo XVI. Madrid, Compañía Ibero-Americana de Publicaciones [1927?] 403p. coats of arms. 25cm. (Coleccion de documentos inéditos para la historia de Hispano-América, t. 2) Spanish nobility in America in the 16th century.

1506   QUIEN ES QUIEN EN VENEZUELA, PANAMÁ, ECUADOR,
       COLOMBIA.
    June 30, 1952-   Bogotá, O. Perry.   v. ports. 28cm. Who's who in Venezuela, Panama, Ecuador and Colombia.

1507   SCARPETTA, M   LEONIDAS
    Diccionario biográfico de los campeones de la libertad de Nueva Granada, Venezuela, Ecuador i Perú. Que comprende sus servicios, hazañas i virtudes, por M. Leonidas Scarpetta i Saturnino Vergara ... Bogotá, Impr. de Zalamea, por M. Díaz, 1879. 728 p. 26cm. 1,643 short biographical sketches of champions of South American independence: Colombia, Venezuela, Ecuador and Peru.

1508   VALCÁRCEL ESPARZA, CARLOS DANIEL, ed.
    Biografías hispanoamericanas en el Archivo General de Indias. Lima, 1959. 127p. 22cm. Spanish American biographies in the General Archives of the Indies, Seville.

1509   WHO'S WHO IN LATIN AMERICA.
    A biographical dictionary of notable living men and women of Latin America. [1st]-   ed.; 1935-   Stanford University, Calif., Stanford University Press [etc.] v. 24cm. The 3d-   ed. issued in parts. The 1st-2d ed. have subtitle: A biographical dictionary of the outstanding living men and women of Spanish America and Brazil.

LEBANON

1510   WHO'S WHO IN LEBANON.
1. -   éd.; 1963-64- Beyrouth, Éditions Publictec. v.
21cm. biennial. In French.

LUXEMBURG

1511   BIOGRAPHIE NATIONALE DU PAYS DE LUXEMBOURG
Depuis ses origines jusqu'à nos jours; collection présentée
par Jules Mersch. 2. éd., revue et corrigée. Luxembourg,
Impr. de la Cour V. Buck, 1957-   v. ports. 26cm.

1512   NEYEN, AUGUSTE, b. 1809.
Biographie luxembourgeoise; histoire des hommes distingués
originaires de ce pays, considéré à l'époque de sa plus grande
étendue, ou qui se sont rendus recommandables pendant le
séjour qu'ils y ont fait. 2. éd. conforme à la première. Luxembourg, P. Bruck, 1876. 3 v. in 1. 29cm. 1st published
1860. Biography of Luxemburg.

MALAYA

1513   LIN, PO-AI.
Nan yang min jen chi chuan. Penang, 1922. 244 p. Biog-
raphies of famous Chinese in Malaya and Indonesia. By Lin
Po-ai and others.

1514   WHO'S WHO IN MALAYA & MALAYAN YEAR BOOK.
1947/48-   Kuala Lumpur. v. 24cm.

1515   THE WHO'S WHO IN MALAYSIA.
1956-   Kuala Lumpur. v. ports. 27cm. Editor:
1956-   J. V. Morais. Title varies: 1956-1959/60, The
Leaders of Malaya and who's who.

MALTA

1516   MIFSUD, IGNAZIO SAVERIO
Biblioteca maltese. Parte 1, che contiene l'istoria crono-
logica, e la notizia della persona, e delle opere dagli scrit-

tori nati in Malta, e Gozo sino all'anno 1650... Malta, N.
Capaci, 1764. xxiv, 437p. 4.º A bio-bibliography for the
island of Malta.

MAURITIUS

1517   TOUSSAINT, AUGUSTE, ed.
Dictionnaire de biographie mauricienne. Dictionary of
Maruitian biography. Port Louis, Société de l'histoire de
l'Isle Maurice, 1941-   v. Mauritius is an island in the
Indian Ocean, east of Madagascar. Issued in pts. (1-)
Vol. 1, 1941-45 (pts. 1-16) 502p. A-Z & index. 693 entries.
Vol. 2, 1945-   (pts. 17-

MEXICO
Bibliography, Indexes, Etc

1518   IGUÍNIZ, JUAN BAUTISTA, 1881-
Bibliografía biográfica mexicana. México, 1930-
v. 21x16cm. (Monografías bibliográficas mexicanas, núm.
18) Contents. --1. Repertorios biográficos. A bibliography
of Mexican biographical literature.

Anonyms and Pseudonyms

1519   IGUÍNIZ, JUAN BAUTISTA, 1881-
Catálogo de seudónimos, anagramos e iniciales de
escritores mexicanos. París, México, Liberiá de la Viuda de
C. Bouret, 1913. 62p. 23cm. Pseudonyms, anagrams and
initials of Mexican writers.

1520   MANRIQUE DE LARA, JUANA
Seudónimos, anagramas, iniciales, etc., de autores mexicanos y extranjeros, por Juana Manrique de Lara y Guadalupe
Monroy. Mexico, Secretaría de Educación Pública, 1943.
78 p. 23cm. Pseudonyms, anagrams, initials, etc. of Mexican and foreign authors.

General Works

1521   ARRONIZ, MARCOS, d. 1858 or 9.
Manual de biografía mejicana; o, Galería de hombres célebres de Méjico. Paris, Rosa, Bouret; New-York, G. R.
Lockwood, 1857. 317p. 16cm. (Enciclopedia popular mejicana)
80 prominent Mexicans.

1522   BOLIO ONTIVEROS, EDMUNDO.
Diccionario histórico, geográfico y biográfico de Yucatán.
México, I. C. D. , 1944. 250 p. 23cm. Cover dated 1945.
Historical, geographical and biographical dictionary of
Yucatan.

1523   CARRIÓN, ANTONIO
Indios célebres de la República Mexicana; o, Biografiás de
los más notables que ban florecido desde 1521 hasta nuestros
diás. (In Zerecero, Anastasio. Memorias para la historia
de las revoluciones en México. Mexico, 1869. 20 cm. p. 433-
528)   Famous Indians (and Mexicans of Indian ancestry) of
the Mexican Republic.

1524   CASTILLO, JERÓNIMO.
Diccionario histórico, biográfico y monumental de Yucatán.
Desde la conquista hasta el último año de la dominación
española en el país. Tomo I, A-E. Mérida, Impr. de Castillo
y Comp. , 1866. 315 p. 22 cm. No more published. Historical, biographical and monuments dictionary of Yucatan from
the Spanish conquest to the end of Spanish hegemony.

1525   DICCIONARIO PORRUA DE HISTORIA, BIOGRAFÍA Y GEO-
GRAFÍA DE MÉXICO. [1. ed.] México, Editorial
Porrúa [1964] xxix, 1721 p. fold. col. maps. 26cm. Porrua's
dictionary of the history, biography and geography of Mexico.

1526   EGUIARA Y EGUREN, JUAN JOSÉ DE, d. 1763.
Bibliotheca Mexicana; sive, Eruditorum historia virorum,
qui in America Boreali nati, vel alibi geniti, in ipsam
domicilis aut studijs asciti, quavis linguâ scripto aliquid
tradiderunt... Tomus primus... A, B, C. Mexici, Ex Nova
Typ. in Aedibus Authoris Editioni ejusdem Bibliothecae
destinatâ, 1755. 80, 543 p. 30 x 21 cm. No more published.
A bio-bibliography of Mexico in the Colonial period.

1527   GALINDO Y VILLA, JESÚS, 1867-1937.
El Panteón de San Fernando y el futuro panteón nacional.
Notas históricas, biográficas y descriptivas. México, Impr.
del Museo Nacional, 1908. 216 p. illus. 30 cm. 108
biographical sketches of Mexican patriots and national heroes.

1528   GARCIA CUBAS, ANTONIO, 1832-1912.
Diccionario geográfico, histórico y biográfico de los
Estados Unidos Mexicanos. México, Antigua Impr. de

Murguia, 1888-91. 5 v. illus. 31 cm. Vols. 2-5 have imprint: México, Oficina Tip. de la Secretaria de Fomento. In large part taken from F. Sosa's Biografiás de mexicanos. Largely a gazetteer, but a good deal of biography of famous Mexicans is included.

1529   GARCÍA PURÓN, MANUEL
       México y sus gobernantes; biografías. Mexico, Liberĩa de M. Porrua [1964] 244 p. illus. 22 cm. (Biblioteca mexicana, 32) Hombres de México, 1. Mexico and its leaders (including famous Mexicans of Indian extraction)

1530   GARCÍA RIVAS, HERIBERTO
       150 [i. e. Ciento cincuenta] biografías de mexicanos ilustres. Presentadas siguiendo la secuencia de desarrollo histórico, y con un índisce alfabético de biografiados. México, Editorial Diana, 1964. 262 p. 18 cm. (Colección Moderna, 4) 150 biographies of illustrious Mexicans.

1531   JEFES DEL EJÉRCITO MEXICANO EN 1847.
       Biografías de generales de división y de brigada y de coroneles del Ejército Mexicano por fines del año de 1847. Manuscrito anónimo, adicionado en gran parte y precedido de un estudio acerca la participación del Ejército en la vida política de México durante la primera mitad del siglo XIX, con numerosos documentos inéditos, por Alberto M. Carreño. México, Impr. de la Secretaría de Fomento, 1914. cccxxxix, 258p. ports., facsims. 24cm. The editor believes General Gabriel Valencia may be the author of the ms. 137 Mexican generals and colonels of the Army of 1847.

1532   LEDUC, ALBERTO
       Diccionario de geografía, historia y biografía mexicanas, par Alberto Leduc y Luis Lara y Pardo para los artículos históricos y biográficos, y Carlos Roumagnac para los artículos geográficos. México, Vda. de C. Bouret, 1910. viii, 1109p. 18cm. Includes Mexican biography.

1533   LÓPEZ MENA, HECTOR F
       Diccionario geográfico, histórico, biográfico y lingüístico del Estado de Guerrero. 1. ed., con un apéndice. México, Editorial Pluma y Lápiz de México, 1942. 461 p. 23cm. Geographical, historical, biographical and linguistic dictionary of the State of Guerrero, Mexico.

1534   MESTRE GHIGLIAZZA, MANUEL, 1870-
       Efemérides biográficas (defunciones--nacimientos)

Mexico, Antigua Liberı́a Robredo, J. Porrúa, 1945. 347p.
20cm. Biographical sketches of Mexicans who died in the
years 1822-1945.

1535   MORALES DÍAZ, CARLOS
Quien es quien en la nomenclatura de la ciudad de México;
apuntes biográficos de las personas cuyos nombres figuran en
dicha nomenclatura. [México, Impresora Barrie] 1962. ix,
582p. 24cm. Chiefly Mexicans, with a few others, after
whom streets in Mexico City are named.

1536   OSORES Y SOTOMAYOR, FÉLIX, d. 1851.
Noticias bio-bibliográficas de alumnos distinguidos del
Colegio de San Pedro, San Pablo y San Ildefonso de México
(hoy Escuela Nacional Preparatoria) México, Librerı́a de la
Viuda de Ch. Bouret, 1908. 2 v. plates. 21cm. (Documentos
inéditos o muy raros para la historia de México, t. 19-21)
Bio-bibliographical notices of distinguished alumni of the
College of Saint Peter, Saint Paul & Saint Alphonsus (today the
National Preparatory School, Mexico City)

1537   PAVÍA, LÁZARO, 1844-
Ligeros apuntes biográficos de los jefes polı́ticos de los
partidos en los estados de la República Mexicana. México,
Tip. de J. Guerra y Valle, 1891-[92] 2 v. ports. 23cm.
113 biographies of Mexican political party leaders.

1538   PAZ, IRENEO, 1836-1924.
Los hombres prominentes de México. Les hommes éminents du Mexique. The prominent men of Mexico. México,
Impr. y Lit. de "La Patria," 1888. 488, ii p. 208 ports.
39cm. A dubious work based on the payment of a fee for the
right of inclusion. 211 biographies. Spanish, French, and
English in parallel columns.

1539   PAZ, IRENEO, 1836-1924.
México actual. Galerı́a de contemporáneos. México,
Oficina Tip. de "La Patria," 1898. xii, 425p. ports. 24cm.
A work similar in nature to Paz's   Los hombres prominentes
de México (q. v.)

1540   PEÑA Y REYES, ANTONIO DE LA, 1868-1928.
Vidas y tiempos. Diccionario biográfico mexicano. t. l:
A-D. Habana, Impr. "El Renacimiento," 1915. l v. 22cm.
No more published? 249 biographies of famous Mexicans.

1541 PERAL, MIGUEL ANGEL, 1900-
      Diccionario biográfico mexicano. México, Editorial
      P. A. C. [1944] 2 v. 24cm. On spine: De 544 à 1944. Mexi-
      can biographical dictionary.

1542 ---- ----Apéndice. México, Editorial P. A. C. [1944] 465p.
      24cm.

1543 QUIEN ES QUIEN EN LA CIUDAD DE MÉXICO Y DISTRITO
      FEDERAL.
      Biografías breves de hombres de negocios, comerciantes,
      políticos, profesionistas, publicistas, artistas, literatos,
      empleados, etc. , que radican en la Ciudad de México y
      Distrito Federal. (In El Directorio comercial Murguia y
      Guía de la Ciudad de México. México, 1925-26. 30cm.
      p. 1067-1164) Who's who in Mexico City and the Federal Dis-
      trict.

1544 RIVERA CAMBAS, MANUEL
      Los gobernantes de México. Galería de biografías y re-
      tratos de los vireyes, emperodores, presidentes y otros
      gobernantes que ha tenido México, desde don Hernando Cortes
      hasta el C. Benito Juarez. Escrita por Manuel Rivera.
      México, Imp. de J. M. Aguilar Ortiz, 1872-73. 2 v. ports.
      30cm. 123 biographies of Mexican leaders and rulers.

1545 SERRANO DE WILSON, EMILIA, Baronesa de WILSON,
      1843-
      México y sus gobernantes, de 1519 a 1910. Biografías,
      retratos y autógrafos (iconografía completa) Con un reseña
      histórica anterior al descubrimiento y conquista. Barcelona,
      Tip. de la Casa Editorial Maucci [1919] 2 v. ports. 127
      kings and rulers of Mexico in chronological order.

1546 SOSA, FRANCISCO, 1848-1925.
      Anuario biográfico nacional. México, Impr. de la Liber-
      tad, 1884. 923 p. Mexican biographical 'yearbook. ' Biog-
      raphies under each month of the year.

1547 SOSA, FRANCISCO, 1848-1925.
      Biografías de Mexicanos distinguidos. Edición de la Secre-
      taría de Fomento. México, Oficina Tipográfica de la Secre-
      taría de Fomento, 1884. xii, 1115 p. 23cm. Biographies
      of famous Mexicans.

1548   SOSA, FRANCISCO, 1848-1925.
        Efemérides históricas y biográficas. Edición de "El Na-
        cional." México, Tip. de G. A. Esteva, 1883. 2 v. 15cm.
        Historical and biographical 'calendars' [for Mexico]

1549   VILLASEÑOR Y VILLASEÑOR, ALEJANDRO, 1864-1912.
        Biografías de los héroes y caudillos de la Independencia.
        México, Impr. de "El Tiempo" de V. Agüeros, 1910. 2 v.
        illus. 21cm. 85 biographies of Mexican heroes & leaders in
        the struggle for independence.

1550   WRIGHT DE KLEINHANS, LAUREANA
        Mujeres notables mexicanas. México, Tip. Económica,
        1910. 246 (i. e. 546) p. illus., ports. 23cm. 124 biogra-
        phies of famous Mexican women.

MIDDLE EAST
See under ISLAMIC COUNTRIES

NEAR EAST
See under ISLAMIC COUNTRIES

NETHERLANDS
Anonyms and Pseudonyms

1551   DOORNINCK, JAN IZAAK VAN, 1840-1889.
        Vermomde en naamlooze schrijvers opgespoord op het ge-
        bied der Nederlandsche en Vlaamsche letteren. 2. uitg. der
        'Bibliotheek van anonymen en pseudonymen.' Leiden, E. J.
        Brill, 1883-85. 2 pts. in 1 v. 25cm. Dutch & Flemish
        pseudonymous authors.

1552   KEMPENAER, A   DE.
        Vermomde Nederlandsche en Vlaamsche schrijvers;
        vervolg op Mr. J. I. van Doorninck's Vermomde en
        naamlooze schrijvers, opgespoord op het gebied der
        Nederlandsche en Vlaamsche letteren. Leiden, A. W.
        Sijthoff [1928] 690 columns. 25cm. Disguised Dutch and
        Flemish writers--anonyms and pseudonyms.

General Works

1553 AA, ABRAHAM JACOB VAN DER, 1792-1857.
Biographisch woordenboek der Nederlanden, bevattende
levensbeschrijvingen van zoodanige personen, die zich op
eenigerlei wijze in ons vaderland hebben vermaard gemaakt.
Onder medewerking van de heeren: C. M. A. Simon van der
Aa [et al.] Haarlem, J. J. van Brederode, 1852-78. 21v. in
17. 22cm. Biographical dictionary of the Netherlands.

1554 BERKHOF, HENDRIKUS, ed.
Nederlanders van de negentiende eeuw; biografieën.
Onder redactie van H. Berkhof [et al] 's-Gravenhage
[etc.] 1949-53. 3 v. 8.º Biographies of Netherlanders of
the 19th century.

1555 BURMANN, CASPAR , d. 1755
Trajectum eruditum, virorum doctrina illustrium, qui in
urbe Trajecto, et regione Trajectensi nati sunt, sive ibi
habitarunt, vitas, fata et scripta exhibens. Trajecti ad
Rhenum, 1738. 469 p. 4.º Biographical sketches of famous
men of Utrecht & vicinity.

1556 CHALMOT, JACQUES ALEXANDRE DE, 1730 (ca.)-1801.
Biographisch woordenboek der Nederlanden. Van de
oudste tijden af tot heden toe. Deel 1-8 [A-Drebbel] Amsterdam,
J. Allart, 1798-1800. 8 v. ports. 8.º No more published.
A biographical dictionary of the Netherlands.

1557 KOBUS, JAN   CHRISTIAAN, 1793-1881.
Biographisch woordenboek van Nederland, bevattende de
levensbeschrijvingen van personen, die zich in Nederland op
het gebied van kunst, wetenschap en letteren, uitvindingen,
ontdekkingen en belangrijke daden hebben bekend gemaakt.
Onder medewerking van anderen bijeengebracht door J. C.
Kobus en W. de Rivecourt. Nieuwe uitg. Arnhem-Nijmegen,
Gebr. E. & M. Cohen, 1886. 3 v. 19cm. Literal reprint
of the first (1854-1861) ed. which was published under title:
Beknopt biographisch hand-woordenboek van Nederland.
Biographical dictionary of the Netherlands.

1558 MAATSCHAPPIJ TOT NUT VAN'T ALGEMEEN, Amsterdam.
Levensschetsen van vaderlandsche mannen en vrouwen; een

schoolboek. Haarlem, A. Loosjes, 1809. 2 v. in 1. illus.
16cm. First published 1798? Biographical sketches of noted
men and women in the history of the Netherlands.

1559   MANNEN [EN VROUWEN] VAN BETEEKENIS IN ONZE DAGEN.
Haarlem, Kruseman & Tjeenk Willink, 1870-1912. 42 v.
ports. 8.° Men [and women] of importance [in the Nether-
lands] in our day. Edited by H. Tiedeman, D. Beets, J.
Kalff, and others. Began publication under title: Mannen van
beteekenis in onze dagen.

1560   --- ----Nieuwe reeks. Baarn, Hollandia-Drukkerij, 1916-
21. 11 v. ports. 8.°

1562   MOLHUYSEN, PHILIP CHRISTIAAN, 1870-   ed.
Nieuw Nederlandsch biografisch woordenboek, onder redactie van P. C. Molhuysen en P. J. Blok met medewerking
van tal van geleerden. Leiden, A. W. Sijthoff, 1911-37. 10 v.
27cm. A modern Dutch biographical dictionary.

1563   NEDERLAND'S ADELSBOEK.
1907-   's Gravenhage, W. P. van Stockum. v.
ports. 15cm. Netherlands' book of the nobility; includes
biographical data.

1564   NEDERLAND'S PATRICIAAT.
1-   ; 1910-   's- Gravenhage, Centraal Bureau voor
Genealogie en Heraldiek. v. illus., ports. 15cm. Netherlands' patrician families; includes biographical data.

1565   DE NEDERLANDSE ADEL (HISTORISCH GEDEELTE)
1. jaarg., A-2 [en 2. uitg., A-Z] 's Gravenhage, W. P.
van Stockum, 1925-[30] 2 v. 15-16cm. The Dutch nobility
(historical section) Includes biographical data.

1566   [PAQUOT, JEAN NOËL] 1722-1803.
Mémoires pour servir à l'histoire littéraire des dix-sept

provinces des Pays-Bas, de la principauté de Liège, et de
quelques contrées voisines. Louvain, Impr. académique,
1763-70. 18v. 18cm. A folio edition in 3 vols. was issued
in 1765-70. Bio-bibliography for the Netherlands and Belgium
(in part)

1567   PERSOONLIJKHEDEN IN HET KONINKRIJK DER NEDER-
LANDEN IN WOORD EN BEELD.
Nederlandere en hun werk, met een inleiding van H.
Brugmans, mede bevattende de biografieën van de leden van
het Koninklijk huis door N. Japikse. Amsterdam, Van
Holkema & Warendorf, 1938. 1748p. ports. 32cm. About
5000 biographies of Hollanders, with portraits.

1568   R. K. "WIE IST DAT?"
Biografisch lexicon van bekende Nederlandsche Roomsch-
Katholieke tijdgenooten. Leiden, Dieben [1925] 170p. 21cm.
Biographical dictionary of well-known contemporary Dutch
Roman Catholics.

1569   RUE, PIETER DE LA, 1695-1770.
Geletterd Zeeland verdeeld in drie afdeelingen bevattende
in zig de schryvers, geleerden en kunstenaars, uit dien
staat geboortig, met bygevoegd levensverhaal der voornaamst-
en onder dezelve. Saamenvergaderd en in orde geschikt.
Middelburg, M. Schryver, 1734. 21, 354p. 22cm. Learned
Zealand (a province of the Netherlands): writers, scholars
and artists.

1570   SCHELTEMA, JACOBUS, 1767-1835.
Staatkundig Nederland; een woordenboek tot de biographische
kaart van dien naam. Amsterdam, J. Ten Brink, 1805-06.
2 v. in 3. 24cm. Political Netherlands. A dictionary of
Dutch political personages.

1571   SLUIJTERS, HENDRIK
Korte levensschetsen van eenige vermaarde en verdienstelijke Zeeuwen. Middelburg, 1845. 1 v. 8.° Brief sketches
of some renowned and meritorious Zealanders.

1572   WHO'S WHO IN THE NETHERLANDS.
1st-   ed. ; 1962/63-   [Montreal] Intercontinental
Book and Pub. Co.   v. 21cm. Editors: 1962/63-
S. Szabó (under the pseud. Stephen S. Taylor) and M. Spruytenburg.

1573   WIE IS DAT?
1931-   's-Gravenhage, M. Nijhoff.   v.   20cm.   Who
is that?   A who's who for the Netherlands.

NEW CALEDONIA

1574   O'REILLY, PATRICK
Calédoniens; répertoire bio-bibliographique de la Nouvelle-
Calédonie. Illus. de Jean Lebedeff.   Paris, Musée de
l'homme, 1953.   viii, 305 p.   ports.   26cm.   (Publications de
la Société des océanistes, no. 3)   Missionaries, administrators, travellers, etc. as well as the principal native Caledo-
nian chiefs.

NEW HEBRIDES

1575   O'REILLY, PATRICK
Hébridais; répertoire bio-bibliographique des Nouvelles-
Hébrides. Avec des portraits de Jean Lebedeff et des illus.
de Georges Guiraud, Michel Lablais & Roland Mascart.   Paris,
Musée de l'Homme, 1957.   vii, 289 p.   illus., ports.   26cm.
(Société des Oceanistes. Publications, no. 6)   Bio-bibliog-
raphy of the New Hebrides.

NEW ZEALAND

1576   THE CYCLOPEDIA OF NEW ZEALAND.
Wellington, Cyclopedia Co., 1897-1908.   6 v.   4.°   Includes a large number of biographies, most of which were
inserted after payment of a fee.

1577   SCHOLEFIELD, GUY HARDY, 1877-
A dictionary of New Zealand biography.   Wellington, Dept.
of Internal Affairs, New Zealand, 1940.   2 v.   26cm.

1578   WHO'S WHO IN NEW ZEALAND.
1908-   Wellington [etc.]   v.   19-23cm.   "Established
1908."   Title varies: -4th ed., 19   -41, Who's who in New
Zealand and the Western Pacific.   Editor: 19   G. H.
Scholefield.

NIGERIA

1579 WHO'S WHO IN NIGERIA;
A biographical dictionary. [1st ed.] Lagos, Nigerian
Print. and Pub. Co. [1956] 278p. ports. 22cm.

1580 WHO'S WHO [IN THE] WESTERN NIGERIAN LEGISLATURE.
Ibadan, Govt. Printer [1959?] 53p.

NORWAY
Bibliography, Indexes, Etc.

1581 ANDRESEN, HARALD, 1909-
Norsk biografisk oppslagsliteratur; katalog utarbeidet for
Norsk slekthistorisk forening. [Oslo] Cammermeyer [1945]
218p. 23cm. A bibliography of Norwegian biographical reference literature.

1582 DEICHMANSKE BIBLIOTEK, Oslo.
Register til den norske tidskrifter. Kristiana, O. F.
Arnesen, 1908-   v. 23cm. Vol. 2: Norsk biografi
(til 31/12, 1909) lists nearly 15,000 names, giving dates for
each, characterizing phrase & references to biographical
articles. Continued in Norsk tidskriftindex, 1921-1930, under
heading Personalhistorie, and from 1931-1935 in Sommerfeldt
(q. v.) Norwegian biography and a bibliography of Norwegian
biography.

1583 SOMMERFELDT, WILHELM PREUS, 1881-1958.
Biografiske artikler i norske tidssfrifter, 1931-1935.   Oslo,
Fabritius, 1936. 106 p.   (Norsk bibliografisk bibliotek,
bind 2, hft. 3) Biographical articles in Norwegian periodicals, 1931-1935; a bibliography.   Continuation of the "Personalhistorie" in the Norsk tidsskriftindex, 1921-1930.

Anonyms and Pseudonyms

1584 PETTERSEN, HJALMAR MARIUS, 1856-1928.
Norsk anonym- og pseudonym-lexikon. Kristiana, Steen-
ske forlag, 1924. 690 columns, [34] p. 26cm. Added t. p.:
Dictionary of anonyms & pseudonyms in Norwegian literature.
1st ed. , 1890, published under title: Anonymer og pseudonymer i den norske literatur 1678-1890.

1585   SOMMERFELDT, WILHELM PREUS, 1881-1958.
Forfattermerker i norske aviser og tidsskrifter. 2. utg.
Oslo, Fabritius, 1946. 31p. 24cm. (Norsk bibliografisk
bibliotek, bd. 8) Anonyms & pseudonyms in Norwegian newspapers & periodicals.

General Works

1586   HVEM ER HVEM?
1912-   Oslo, Aschehoug. v. 20cm. Who's who [in
Norway]?

1587   ILLUSTRERT BIOGRAFISK LEKSIKON OVER KJENDTE
NORSKE MAEND OG KVINDER.
Redigert av Nanna With. Kristiania, A/S With & co. s
trykkeri [1916-20] 969p. ports. 21cm. At head of title:
Tillaeg til 'Hver 8 dag.' Illustrated biographical dictionary
of noted Norwegian men and women.

1588   NORSK BIOGRAFISK LEKSIKON.
Kristiania, H. Aschehoug, 1923 [i. e. 1921]-   v. 26cm.
Edited by E. Bull, and others. Biographical dictionary for
Norway.

1589   NORSKE KVINDER;
En oversigt over deres stilling og livsvilkaar i hundrede-
aaret, 1814-1914 [--1914-1924] utgit av Marie Høgh under redaktion av Fredrikke Mørck. Kristiania, Berg & Høgh, 1914-
25. 3 v. illus. 25cm. Biography of outstanding Norwegian
women, 1814-1924.

1590   WADSKIAER, CHRISTIAN FREDERIK, 1713-1779.
Aula Norvegiae erudita; seu, De principibus doctis Nor-
vegis. Hafniae, 1776. 1 v. 4.º 'The hall of learned Norway'; or, The chief Norwegian scholars.

PACIFIC ISLANDS

1591   PACIFIC ISLANDS YEAR BOOK AND WHO'S WHO.
[1st]-   ed.; 1932-   Sydney [etc.] Pacific Publications
[etc.]   v. illus., ports. 22cm. Publication suspended
1933-34. Title varies: 1st-8th editions, 1932-59, Pacific Islands year book.

PAKISTAN

1592 ANSARI'S TRADE DIRECTORY OF PAKISTAN AND WHO'S
      WHO. 1950/51-   Karachi, Ansari Pub. House.
      v. 19cm. E.g., 125 biographies included in the 1950/51 ed.

1593 BIOGRAPHICAL ENCYCLOPEDIA OF PAKISTAN.
      1955-56- Lahore, Biographical Research Institute, Pakis-
      tan, for International Publishers (Pakistan)   v. ports.
      25cm. 1st ed., 1955/56; 2d, 1960/61.

1594 GRIFFIN, SIR LEPEL HENRY, 1840-1908.
      The Punjab chiefs. Historical and biographical notices of
      the principal families in the Lahore and Rawalpindi divisions
      of the Punjab. New ed., bringing the histories down to date,
      by Charles Francis Massy. Lahore, Civil and Military Ga-
      zette Press, 1890. 2 v. 25cm.

1595 PAKISTAN TRADE DIRECTORY AND WHO'S WHO.
      1949/50-   Karachi, Barque.   v. ports. 25cm.
      annual. Supersedes All-India trade directory and who's who.
      Editor: 1949/50-   A. M. Barque.

1596 THE PAKISTAN YEAR BOOK & WHO'S WHO.
      1st-   ; 1949-   Karachi, Kitabistan.   v. illus.,
      ports. 22cm.

PALESTINE
See entries under Jews

PANAMA

1597 MEJÍA ROBLEDO, ALFONSO, 1897-
      Quién es quién en Panamá, diccionario biográfico y bibli-
      ográfico de personalidades actuales. 1. ed. Medellín, Co-
      lombia, Editorial Bedout, 1949. 320p. ports. 23cm. Who's
      who in Panama.

1598 VELARDE, MAURICIO
      Semblanzas; figuras políticas, industriales, comerciantes

y profesionales de la República de Panamá. Panama, Impr.
Panamá Tribuna, 1937. 3 v. Biographical sketches of political figures, industrialists, businessmen and professionals
of the Republic of Panama.

PARAGUAY

1599   PARKER, WILLIAM BELMONT, 1871-1934.
     Paraguayans of to-day. London, New York, Hispanic So-
ciety of America, 1921. xv, 317 p. ports. 18cm. (Hispanic
notes and monographs, 6)

1600   QUIEN ES QUIEN EN EL PARAGUAY?
     Ed. ilustrada. 1. -   tomo; 1941-   [Buenos Aires] F.
Monte Domecq.   v. illus., ports. 21-23cm. Who's who
in Paraguay?

1601   ZINNY, ANTONIO, 1821-1890.
     Historia de los gobernantes del Paraguay, 1535-1887. Bue-
nos Aires, Impr. y Librería de Mayo, 1887. xvi, 515, 5 p.
23cm. 99 rulers of Paraguay, 1535-1887.

1602   ZUBIZARRETA, CARLOS
     Cien vidas paraguayas. [Buenos Aires?] Ediciones Nizza,
1961. 201 p. 20cm. 100 Paraguayan lives.

PERU

1603   CHIRINOS SOTO, ENRIQUE
     Actores en el drama del Perú y del mundo. Con prólogo de
Juan Zegarra Russo. Lima, Ediciones de Divulgación Popular, 1961. 253 p. illus. 18cm. 20th century Peruvian and
universal biography.

1604   DICCIONARIO BIOGRÁFICO DEL PERÚ.
     1. ed. 1943-44. [Lima, Escuelas Americanas, 1944] xvi,
977 illus. 25cm. No more published? Edited by Raúl Garbín
Díaz, Raúl Garbín Jr. and Julio Cárdenas Ramírez. Biographical dictionary of Peru.

1605   MENDIBURU, MANUEL DE, 1805-1885.
     Diccionario histórico-biográfico del Perú. 2. ed. con
adiciones y notas bibliográficas publicada por Evaristo San

Cristóval... Lima, Impr. "Enrique Palacios, " 1931-35. 11 v. port. 22cm.

1606 ---- ----Apéndice [por] Evaristo San Cristóval. Lima, Gil, 1935-38. 4 v.

Historical-biographical dictionary of Peru.

1607 PARKER, WILLIAM BELMONT, 1871-1934.
Peruvians of to-day. Lima, Peru [Printed at the Southwell Press] 1919. xvi, 616 p. ports. 17cm. (Hispanic notes and monographs, 2)

1608 PAZ-SOLDÁN, JUAN PEDRO, 1869-   ed.
Diccionario biográfico de peruanos contemporáneos. [Nueva ed. corr. y aumentada] Lima, Gil, 1921. 449p. ports. 24cm. Biographical dictionary of early 20th century Peruvians.

1609 PERU.
Presidentes del Senado, Comisiones directivas y señores senadores, 1829-1960. Lima, Tall. Gráf. del Senado, 1961. 208p. ports. 30cm. 50 portraits and biographical sketches of presidents of the Peruvian Chamber of Senators, followed by a list of all senators from 1829 to 1960. Arranged chronologically.

1610 VARELA Y ORBEGOSO, LUIS, 1878-1930.
Los presidentes de la H. Cámara de Diputados del Perú; apuntes biográficos reunidos, cumpliendo encargo de la H. Comisión de Policía. Lima, Empresa Tipográfica, 1916. 232p. 22cm. The presidents of the Chamber of Deputies of Peru.

PHILIPPINE ISLANDS

1611 GALANG, ZOILO M   ed.
Encyclopedia of the Philippines; the library of Philippine literature, art and science. Manila, P. Vera [1935-   v. ports., illus. 24 cm. Vol. 2: Biography.

1612 KNOW THEM JOURNAL (PHILIPPINE POLITICAL LEADERS)
1st-   ed. ; 1958-   Manila, Public Relations and Allied Services.   v. illus. 23cm.

1613   LLANA, PEDRO DE LA, ed.
The Philippine Commonwealth handbook; a cultural and
economic survey of present-day Philippines with sketches of
outstanding builders of the Commonwealth. Pedro de la Llana,
editor and publisher; F. B. Icasiano, associate editor.
Manila, General Print. Press, 1936. xii, 522 p. 21cm. One
third of the volume is a biographical dictionary.

1614   MANILA'S FOUR HUNDRED;
Social register. Manila, Rojadi Pub. ..., 1935. ca.
500 p. Edited by Roque J. Dizon.

1615   MANUEL, E   ARSENIO, 1909-
Dictionary of Philippine biography. Quezon City, Filipi-
niana Publications, 1955-   v. illus., ports. 25cm.
(Filipiniana Publications biography series)

1616   NELLIST, GEORGE FERGUSON MITCHELL, 1889-
Men of the Philippines; a biographical record of men of
substantial achievement in the Philippine Islands. Manila,
Sugar News Co., 1931-   v. ports. 24cm.

1617   RETIZOS, ISIDRO L
Philippines who's who, by Isidro L. Retizos and D. H.
Soriano. [Manila] Capitol Pub. House [1957?] xxxix, 327p.
ports. 24cm.

1618   ROSENSTOCK'S PRESS REFERENCE LIBRARY.
Philippine ed. Manila, 1913. 180p. ports. 30cm. Ca.
280 brief biographies of Filipinos and Americans in the
Philippines.

1619   TABLEAU;
Encyclopedia of distinguished personalities in the Philip-
pines. v. 1- 1957- Manila, Philippines, National
Souvenir Publications. v. ports. 29cm.

1620   WHO'S WHO IN THE CONSTITUTION CONVENTION [PHILIP-
PINES]
Compiled by Leila M. Poole. [n. p., 193-?] 1 v. (loose-
leaf) ports. Scrapbook type of compilation; alphabetical.

1621   WHO'S WHO IN THE PHILIPPINES.
Compiled by Leila M. Poole. [n. p., 19-?] 1 v. (loose-

leaf) ports. Chiefly government officials. Scrapbook type of
compilation; alphabetical.

1622   WHO'S WHO IN THE PHILIPPINES;
        A biographical dictionary of notable living men of the
        Philippine Islands. v. 1-   1936/37-   Manila, McCul-
        lough Print. Co.   v. ports. 24cm.

1623   WHO'S WHO IN THE PHILIPPINES: WOMEN.
        Compiled by Leila M. Poole. [n.p., 193-?] 1 v. (loose-
        leaf) ports. Loose-leaf scrapbook type of compilation; al-
        phabetical.

POLAND
Bibliography, Indexes, Etc.

1624   MALISZEWSKI, EDWARD, 1875-1928.
        Bibljografja pamietników polskich i Polski dotyczacych
        (druki i rekopisy) Warszawa, Towarzystwo Miłósników
        Historyi, 1928. x, 447 p. 4.° Bibliography of Polish
        memoirs and those relating to Poland (printed books and manu-
        scripts)

Anonyms and Pseudonyms

1625   BAR, ADAM
        Słownik pseudonimów i kryptonimów pisarzy polskich oraz
        Polski dotyczecych, opracował Adam Bar i Tad. God-
        łowskiego... Kraków [Nakł. Krasowskiego koła Zwiezku
        Bibljotekarzy Polskich] 1936-38. 3v. (Prace bibljoteczne
        Krasowskiego koła Zwiezku bibljotekarzy polskich, 7-8)
        Dictionary of pseudonyms and cryptonyms of Polish writers
        and those who write about Poland.

General Works

1627   BERSOHN, MATHIAS, 1823-1908.
        Słownik biograficzny uczonych żydów polskich XVI, XVII

i XVIII wieku... Warszawa, 1905 [wrapper 1906] 81p. 8.°
Biographical dictionary of learned Polish Jews, 16th-18th
centuries.

1628   CHEŁMOŃSKA, MARJA (KORWIN-SZYMANOWSKA) 1859-
      Album biograficzne zasłuzonych Polaków i Polek wieku
XIX, wyd. staraniem i nakładem Maryi Chelmónskiej pod
kierunkiem komitetu redakcyjnego, który składaja: Szymon
Askenazy [i. t. d.] Sekretarz redakcyi Jan Nitowski. Z
prezedmowa Stanisława Krzemińskiego. Warszawa, 1901-
v. illus. , ports. 32 cm. Biographical album of praise-
worthy Poles of the 19th century. At least 2 volumes were
published (v. 1-2, 1901-03)

1629   CHODYNICKI, IGNACY
      Dykcjonarz uczonych Polaków zawierajacy krótkie rysy
ich życia, szczególne wiadomości o pismach i krytyczny roz-
biór wazniejszych dzieł niektórych porzadkiem alfabetcznym
ułozony. Lwów, 1833. 3 v. Dictionary of learned Poles
comprising brief sketches of their lives, particularly information about their writings and critical analysis of some important works, arranged in alphabetical order.

1630   CYRANKIEWICZ, STANISŁAW
      Przewodnik cmentarny Krakowa, Podgórza i Zwierzyńca.
Kraków, 1908. 479 p. 8.° Includes biographical data gathered from epitaphs found in cemeteries of Krakow, Poland and
vicinity.

1631   CZY WIESZ KTO TO JEST ?
      Pod ogólna red. Stanisława Łozy. Warszawa, Wydawn.
Głównej Ksieg. Wojskowej, 1938. 858 p. ports. 25cm.
Polish biography ("Do you know who that is?")

1632   JANOCKI, JAN DANIEL ANDRZEJ, 1720-1786.
      Lexicon derer itzlebende Gelehrten in Polen, von Johann
Daniel Andreas Janozki. Bresslau, J. J. Korn, 1755. 2 v.
8.° Dictionary of contemporary scholars in Poland.

1633   McLEAN, W   MOORE, 1909-
      Notable personages of Polish ancestry (Znamienite oso-
bistości pochodzenia Polskiego) utożył W. Moore McLean
(Bolesław Mak) Detroit, Unique Press, 1938. xvi, 186 p.
24cm.

1634 OLSZEWICZ, BOŁESLAW, 1893-
Lista strat kultury polskiej (1. IX. 1939-1. III. 1946) Warszawa, S. Arct, 1947. xvi, 336 p. 18cm. A register of
Poles who died during or shortly after the 2d World War. Very
brief information.

1635 PERETIATKOWICZ, ANTONI, 1884- ed.
Współczesna kultura polska; nauka, literatura, sztuka:
życiorysy uczonych, literatów i artystów z wyszczególnieniem
ich prac. Poznań, Skład główny: Dom ksiażki polskiej w
Warszawie [etc.] 1932. 319p. 24cm. At head of title: A.
Peretiatkowicz i M. Sobeski. Contemporary Polish culture:
science, literature, art; sketches of scholars, littérateurs
and artists with accounts of their work.

1636 POLSKA AKADEMIA UMIEJETNOŚCI, Krakow.
Polski słownik biograficzny. [Komitet redakcyjny: Wła-
disław Konopczyński, et al.] Krakow, Nakł. Polskiej Akademii Umiejetności, Sklad główny w ksieg. Gebethnera i
Wolffa, 1935- v. 29cm. Vols. 8- issued by Polska Akademia Nauk. The standard Polish biographical dictionary; in progress.

1637 STEKERT, AUGUST
Słownik biograficzno-historyczny polski, ułożony i
wydany przez... t. 1 [A-C] Kraków, 1885. 408 p. At head
of title: August Stekert i Aleksander Stekert. No more published? Polish biographical-historical dictionary.

1638 WÓJCICKI, KAZIMIERZ WŁADYSŁAW, 1807-1879.
Cmentarz Powazkowski pod Warszawa. Litografija M. Fa-
jansa, ryciny A. Matuszkiewicza. Warszawa, W druk. S.
Orgelbranda, 1855-58. 3 v. illus., ports. 26cm. Vol. 3
has title: Cmentarz Powazkowski oraz cmentarze katolickie
i innych wyznań pod Warszawa i w okolicach tegoż miasta.
Biographical data about Poles buried in Powazkowski Ceme-
tery in Warsaw, gathered in large part from epitaphs on tomb-
stones.

PORTUGAL
Anonyms and Pseudonyms

1639 FONSECA, MARTINHO AUGUSTO FERREIRA DA, 1869-
Subsidios para um diccionario de pseudonymos, iniciaes
e obras anonymas de escriptores portuguezes, contribuição

para o estudo da litteratura portugueza. Con poucas palavras
servindo do prologo pelo Theophilo Braga. Lisboa, Academia
Real das Sciencias, 1896. xii, 298 p. 23 cm. Contributions
towards a dictionary of Portuguese pseudonyms, initials &
anonymous works.

General Works

1640 BARBOSA MACHADO, DIOGO, 1682-1772.
Biblioteca lusitana historica, critica e cronológica. 2.
ed. Lisboa, 1930-35. 4v. col. facsims. 28cm. First
published 1741-1759 under title: Bibliotheca Lusitana...
Historical, critical and chronological library of Portugal.
Bio-bibliographical in part.

1641 CAMPOS DE CASTRO DE AZEVEDO SOARES, EDUARDO DE,
1864-
Bibliographia nobiliarchica portugueza, por Eduardo de
Campos de Castro de Azevedo Soares (Carcavellos) Braga,
Typ. Movida a Electricidade de A. Costa & Mattos, 1916-
v. 27 cm. 250 copies printed. Nobility of Portugal; bio-
bibliographical.

1642 LATINO COELHO, JOSÉ MARÍA, 1825-1891.
Galeria de varões illustres de Portugal. Lisboa, 1880-83.
2 nos. 8.º No more published? Gallery of illustrious men
of Portugal.

1643 MARTINS DE CARVALHO, FRANCISCO AUGUSTO, 1844-1921.
Diccionario bibliographico militar portuguez. Lisboa,
Impr. Nacional, 1891. 331 p. 25cm. Bibliographical dic-
tionary of the Portuguese military. Bio-bibliographical.

1644 PINHEIRO CHAGAS, MANUEL, 1842-1895.
Portuguezes illustres. 2. ed. rev., corr. e augm. Lisboa, A. Ferin, 1873. 179p. 16cm. Ca. 120 (?) biographies
of famous Portuguese. 1st ed. (1869) contains 113 biographies.

1645 PINTO DE MATTOS, RICARDO, 1839?-1882.
Manuel bibliographico portuguez de livros raros, classi-
cos e curiosos, revisto e prefaciado por Camillo Castello
Branco. Porto, Livraria Portuense, 1878. xii, 582p. 22cm.
Pages 1-565 are a bio-bibliographical dictionary of Portugal.

1646   QUEM É ALGUÉM (WHO'S WHO IN PORTUGAL)
Dicionário biográfico das personalidades en destaque do
nosso tempo. 1947-   Lisboa, Portugália Editora.   v.
26cm.

1647   [ROUSSADO GORJÃO, JOÃO DAMASIO] 1777-1856.
Galería dos deputados das Cortes geraes extraordinarias
e constituintes da Nação portugueza instauradas em 26 de janeiro de 1821. Epoca I. Lisboa, Typ. Rollandiana, 1822.
372, 108, 346p. 4.º Gallery of the deputies of the Portuguese Cortes (Legislature)

1648   SILVA, THEODORO JOSÉ DA
Miscellanea historico-biographica, extrahida de uma in-
finidade de obras antigas e modernas, contendo mais de 1.200
biographias. Lisboa, F. A. da Silva, 1877. xvi, 346 p.
21cm. Historical-biographical miscellany, extracted from a
large number of old and modern works; containing more than
1200 biographies. Chiefly a dictionary of Portuguese biography, although presumably universal in scope.

PUERTO RICO

1649   FREDERIKSEN, C
The representative men of Porto Rico. [n. p.] F. E. Jackson, 1910. 340 p. illus. , ports. 312 biographies.

1650   HUYKE, JUAN BERNARDO, 1880-
Triunfadores. San Juan, P. R. , Negociado de Materiales,
Imprenta y Transporte, 1926-27. 439p. 21cm. 103(?)
biographies of famous Puerto Ricans.

1651   NEUMANN GANDÍA, EDUARDO
Benefactores y hombres notables de Puerto Rico; bocetos
biográficos-críticos, con un estudio sobre nuestros gobernadores generales. Ponce, Estab. Tip. "La Libertad," 1896-
99. 2 v. illus. , ports. , map. 23cm. Benefactors and notable men of Puerto Rico.

1652   QUIEN ES QUIEN EN PUERTO RICO;
Diccionario biográfico de record personal. 1. -   ed. ;
1933/34-   San Juan, Impreso por Real Hnos.   v.
24cm. Who's who in Puerto Rico.

RHODESIA

1653   YEAR BOOK AND GUIDE OF THE RHODESIAS AND NYASA-
        LAND, WITH BIOGRAPHIES.   19--   Salisbury, Rho-
        desian Publications.   v. 18cm.

ROMAN EMPIRE

1654   PROSOPOGRAPHIA IMPERII ROMANI SAEC. I. II. III.
        Edita consilio et auctoritate Academiae Scientiarum
        Regiae Borussicae. Berolini, Apud G. Reimerum, 1897-98.
        3 v. 27cm. Lists of personalities during the 1st 3 centuries
        of the Roman Empire. A 2d ed. was started in 1933. Only
        2 vols. were published (A-C)?

RUMANIA

1655   CARANFIL, ANDREW G
        Biographical information of members of the Rumanian
        Grand National Assembly. New York, U. S. Joint Publications
        Research Service, 1957. a-d. 103 1. 27 cm. (U. S. Joint
        Publications Research Service. [JPRS/NY] report no. 26)

1656   CORNEL, TH
        Figuri contemporane din România. Dictionar biografic.
        Bucuresti, Socec, 1909.   536 p.   Contemporary figures of
        Rumania; a biographical dictionary.

1657   DICTIONARUL ENCICLOPEDIC ILUSTRAT "CARTEA RO-
        MÂNEASCĂ." Bucuresti, Editura "Cartea Românească
        [1931] xxiv, 1948 p. illus. 25cm. A general encyclopedia,
        but with much biographical material about Rumanians not
        available elsewhere.

1658   SEIVERT, JOHANN, 1735-1785.
        Nachrichten von siebenbürgischen Gelehrten und ihre
        Schriften. Pressburg, Weber und Korabinski, 1785.   xxii,
        519 p. 19cm. Notices of Transylvanian (i.e. Germans in
        Transylvania) scholars and their writings.

RUSSIA
Bibliography, Indexes, Etc.

1659   KAUFMAN, ISAAK MIKHAĬLOVICH.
Russkie biograficheskie i biobibliograficheskie slovari.
Moskva, Gos. izd-vo kul´ turno-prosvetitel´noi lit-ry,
1955. 75lp. 23cm. An earlier edition was issued in 1950
(33lp.) A bibliography of Russian biographical and bio-
bibliographical dictionaries.

1660   MOROZOV, ALEKSEĬ VIKULOVICH, 1857-
Katalog moego sobraniiā gravirovannykh i litografirovannykh portretov.   Moskva, 1912-13. 4 v. (chiefly plates) 37cm.

1661   ---- ---- Alfavitnyi ukazatel´.   Moskva, 1913. 142 columns.
37cm.

Catalog of 'my' collection of engraved and lithographed
portraits [of prominent Russians]

Anonyms and Pseudonyms

1662   [GENNADI, GRIGORIĬ NIKOLAEVICH] 1826-1880.
Spisok russkikh anonimnykh knig s imenami ikh avtorov i
perevodchikov. Dopolnenīe k katalogam russkikh knig Sopikova,
Shtorkha, Plavil´shchikova, Smirdina, Ol´khina, Glazunova i
Bazunova. G. G. S. -Petersburg, 1874. iii, 47 p. 25cm.
List of Russian anonymous works with the names of their au-
thors and translators.

1663   KARTSOV, VASILIĬ SERGEEVICH, 1864-
Opyt slovariā psevdonimov russkikh pisateleĭ.
S. -Peterburg, Tipo-lit. I. A. Efrona, 1891. 158p. 22cm.
Ca. 4700 Russian pseudonyms & initials. At head of title:
V. S. Kartsov i M. N. Mazaev. Supplements appeared in
Bibliograficheskiiā zapiski, 1892, p. 123-126, 370-372, 429-
443, 813-816.

1664   MASANOV, IVAN FILIPPOVICH, 1874-1945.
Slovar´ psevdonimov russkikh pisateleĭ, uchenykh i obshchestvennykh deĩateleĭ; alfavitnyĭ ukazatel´ psevdonimov. Pod-
gotovil k pechati IŪ. I. Masanov. Redaktor B. P. Koz´min.
Moskva, 1956-60. 4 v. port. 27cm. Dictionary of pseudonyms of Russian authors [etc.]

General Works

1665   ADARIÛKOV, VLADIMIR IÂKOVLEVICH, 1863-1932.
Slovar´ russkikh litografirovannykh portretov. Sost.
pri uchastii i pod red. S. P. Vinogradova. T. l[A-D] So 160
fototip. snimkami. Moskva, T-vo tip. A. I. Mamontova,
1916. x, 320p. illus., ports. At head of title: V. IÂ.
Adariûkov, N. A. Obol´ianinov. No more published. Ca.
150 portraits of Russian notables.

1666   AFANAS'EV, NIKOLAĬ IVANOVICH
Sovremenniki. Al'bom biografiĭ. [S.-Peterburg, Tip.
A. S. Suvorina, 1909-10] 2v. illus., ports. 500 biographies.
No more published. Prominent "contemporary" Russians,
i. e., persons active in the last half of the 19th century and
the early years of the 20th.

1667   ALMANAKH SOVREMENNYKH RUSSKIKH GOSUDARSTVEN-
NYKH DIEIATELEĬ. S. - Peterburg, Izd. G. A. Gol'dberga,
1897. 2 v. Almanac of 'contemporary' Russians active in
their government.

1668   ANNUAIRE DE LA NOBLESSE DE RUSSIE. [1889]-
St. Pétersbourg. v. illus. 18-22cm. Yearbook of
the Russian nobility; includes biographical material.

1669   BAKU. INSTITUT ISTORII PARTII.
Aktivnye bortsy za sovetskuiû vlast´ v Azerbaidzhane. Baku, Azerbaidzhanskoe gos. izd-vo, 1957.
410p. ports. 27cm. Fighters for Soviet authority in
Azerbaijan.

1670   BAKUNINA, TAT'IÂNA A
Le répertoire biographique des francs-macons russes
(XVIIIᵉ et XIXᵉ siècles) Bruxelles, Éditions Petropolis,
1940. iv, 655p. 25cm. (Publications de l'Institut de philologie
et d'histoire orientales et slaves de l'Université de Bruxelles.
Sér. slave, no 2) Biographical list of Russian Freemasons
(18th & 19th centuries)

1671   [BANTYSH-KAMENSKIĬ, DMITRIĬ NIKOLAEVICH] 1788-1850.
Biografii rossiiskikh generalissimusov i general-fel´d-
marshalov. Sankt-Peterburg, Tip. Tret´iago departamenta

M-va gos. imushchestv, 1840-41. 4v. in 2. 48 ports. 24cm.
Biographies of Russian generals and field marshalls.

1672   BANTYSH-KAMENSKIĬ, DMITRIĬ NIKOLAEVICH, 1788-1850.
Illustrations de la Russie; ou, Galerie des personnages les
plus remarquables de cet empire, sous le règne de Pierre-
le-Grand. Ouvrage écrit d'après les actes et manuscrits des
archives de Mosgou, par M. Bantisch-Kamensky. Traduit
du russe. 2. éd. Paris, Moutardier, 1829. 408p. ports.
19cm. Illustrations of Russia; or, Gallery of the most remark
able personages during the reign of Peter the Great.

1673   BANTYSH-KAMENSKIĬ, DMITRIĬ NIKOLAEVICH, 1788-1850.
Slovar´ dostopamiatnykh liudei Russkoi zemli. Sankt-
peterburg, 1847. 3v. ports. 23cm. 129 biographies.
Supplementary to the edition of 1836 (q. v.) Dictionary of
memorable people of the Russian land.

1674   BANTYSH-KAMENSKIĬ, DMITRIĬ NIKOLAEVICH, 1788-1850.
Slovar´ dostopamiatnykh liudei Russkoi zemli, soderzhas-
chii v sebie zhizn´ i dieianiia znamenitykh polkovodtsev,
ministrov i muzhei gosudarstvennykh, velikh ierarkhov
Pravoslavnoi tserkvi, otlichnykh litteratorov i uchenykh, iz-
viestnykh po uchastiiu v sobytiiakh otechestvennoi istorii.
Moskva, A. Shiriaev, 1836. 5v. 22cm. 502 biographies.
Dictionary of memorable people of the Russian land... A
3-volume sequel, with same main title, was issued in 1847.

1675   BEKETOV, PLATON PETROVICH, 1776-1836.
Sobranie portretov rossiian, znamenitykh po svoim
dieianiiam, voinskim i grazhdanskim... v khronologicheskom
poriadkie, po godam konchiny, s prilozheniem ikh kratkikh
zhizneopisanii. Ch. I. Moskva, Izdano P. Beketovym, v
Tip. S. Selivanovskago, 1821-24. 292 (i. e. 313)p. ports.
32cm. No more published. A collection of portraits of prominent Russians... in chronological arrangement... with a supplement containing brief biographies. Vol. 1 (only one published) contains 55 portraits and accompanying biographical
sketches.

1676   BOĬOVICH, MILAN MIKHAĬLOVICH
Chleny Gosudarstvennoi Dumy. Portrety i biografii.
Moskva, I. D. Sytin, 1906-07. 2 v. Contents. --[1] 1. sozyv,
1906-1911 g. --[2] 2. sozyv, 1907-1912 g. Portraits and biographies of members of the Russian Government Dumas, 1906-
1912.

1677   BORTSY ZA VLAST' SOVETOV [1919-1959.
Pod red. V. S. Flerova. Tomsk] Tomskoe knizhnoe izd-
vo, 1959 [i. e. 1960-   v. illus. 23cm. Russians prominent in the struggle for the establishment of Soviet authority
in the years 1919-1959.

1678   CHERNOPIATOV, VIKTOR IL'ICH, 1857-
Nekropol' Krymskogo poluostrova. Moskva, Pech. A. I.
Snegirevoi, 1910. 313, vii p. 27 cm. Preprint (?) from
vol. 11 of the Zapiski of the Moskovskii arkheologicheskii
institut (Moscow, 1911) Biographical data from cemeteries
of the Crimea.

1679   CHERNOPIATOV, VIKTOR IL'ICH, 1857-
Nekropol' neskol'kikh mest Kavkaza... Moskva, Tip. A. P.
Pettsman, 1913. iv, 75 p. illus. 25 cm. Biographical data
from the cemeteries of several places in the Caucasus.

1680   CHERNOPIATOV, VIKTOR IL'ICH, 1857-
Russkii nekropol' za granitsei. Moskva, 1908-14. 3 v.
25 cm. Biographical data from Russian cemeteries abroad.

1681   CHLENY I-OI [i. e. PERVOI] GOSUDARSTVENNOI DUMY.
Soderzhanie: biografii, kharakteristiki, politicheskie
vzgliady, obshchestvennaia dieiatel'nost', vybory i prochee...
Moskva, Tip. "Pechat' i graviura," 1906. 79p. ports.
21cm. Members of the 1st Russian Duma, 1906.

1682   DEIATELI REVOLIUTSIONNOGO DVIZHENIIA V ROSSII;
Bio-bibliograficheskii slovar'. Ot predshestvennikov de-
kabristov do padeniia tsarizma. Moskva, 1927-34. 4 v.
ports. 27cm. At head of title: Vsesoiuznoe obshchestvo politicheskikh katorzhan i ssyl'no-poselentsev. Vols. 1, 3-5 only
were published. Various editors. People active in revolutionary movements in Russia; a bio-bibliographical dictionary.

1683   DOLGORUKOI, IVAN MIKHAILOVICH, kniaz', 1764-1823?
Kapishche moego serdtsa; ili, Slovar' vsiekh tiekh lits, s
koimi ia byl v raznykh otnosheniiakh v techenii moei zhizni.
2. izd. Moskva, 1890. 403 p. 25cm. First published in
1874? A dictionary of persons (chiefly Russians) with whom
the author came in contact during the course of his life.
"Stored-up memories of my heart. "

1684   DONTSY XIX VEKA.
Biografii i materialy dlīā biografiǐ donskikh deīateleǐ na poprishche sluzhby voennoǐ, grazhdanskoǐ i obshchestvennoǐ, a takzhe v oblasti nauk, iskusstv, literatury i proch. Novocherkassk, 1907. 476 p. Biographies of 108 outstanding persons in Russia's Don Valley during the 19th century.

1685   DZIDZARIĪA, G   A   ed.
Bortsy za sovetskuĭu vlast´ v Abkhazii. Avtorskiĭ kollektiv: G. A. Dzidzariīā [i dr. Otvetstvennyĭ redaktor G. A. Dzidzariīā] Sukhumi, "Alashara," 1965. 262 p. ports. 23cm. At head of title: Abkhazskoe otdelenie Gruzinskogo nauchnogo obshchestva istorii, arkheologii, etnografii i fol´klora. Glavnoe upravlenie pri Sovete ministrov Abkhazskoǐ ASSR. Biographical sketches (with portraits) of 181 figures prominent in the Russian Revolution of 1917-1921 in Abkhazia (part of the Georgian Soviet Socialist Republic) and its subsequent Sovietization.

1686   FREIMANN, OTTO RUDOLʹFOVICH, 1849-   comp.
Pazhi za 185 (i. e. sto vosem´desīāt pīāt) līet. Biografii i portrety byvshikh pazheĭ s 1711 po 1896 g. Sobral i izdal O. fon Freiman. Fridrikhsgamn, 1897. iii, 952 p. ports. 30 cm. [Russian] boys [and cadets] across 185 years; biographies and portraits, 1711-1896.

1687   GALLEREĪA GOSUDARSTVENNYKH I OBSHCHESTVENNYKH DĪEĪATELEĬ ROSSII I TRETʹĪA GOSUDARSTVENNAĪA DUMA. [n.p. , 1909?] vii, 208 p. ports. 8.° Gallery of persons active in the 3d Russian duma (1907-1912)

1688   GENDAI SOREN JIMMEI JITEN. . .
[Tokyo, 1957] 60, 63, 222, 10 p. 11 tables. 22cm. Dictionary of contemporary Russians. Issued by: Kasumigaseki Kai and Japan. Gaimushō. Ajiakyoku.

1689   GOLOVACHEV, PETR MIKHAĬLOVICH
Dekabristy. 86 portretov, vid Petrovskago zavoda i 2 bytovykh risunka togo vremeni. Poīāsnitelʹnyǐ biograficheskiǐ tekst P. M. Golovacheva. Vstup. statʹīā V. A. Mīākotina. Moskva, M. M. Zenzinov [1906] xx, 294, ii p. plates, ports. 28cm. Portraits and biographies of 86 Decembrists (uprising of 1825 in Russia)

1690   GOSUDARTSVENNAĬA DUMA PERVAGO PRIZYVA.
      Portrety, kratkiĭa biografii i kharakteristiki deputatov.
Moskva, Knigoizd-vo "Vozrozhdenie," 1906. 125 p. ports.
4.° Portraits, brief biographies and characteristics of
deputies to the 1st Russian Government Duma, 1906.

1691   GOSUDARSTVENNYĬ SOVIET.
      St. Petersburg, Tip. "Rossiĭa," 1907. 282 p. plates,
ports. 4.° Preface signed: A. G. i M. L. Biographies of
members of the Russian Council of State which served as an
advisory and deliberative body to the executive branch of the
Russian Imperial Government.

1692   HELBIG, GEORG ADOLF WILHELM VON, d.1813.
      Russische Günstlinge. Unter Benutzung von neuen
Quellenwerken bearb. von M. Bauer. München, G. Müller,
1917. xvi, 468p. 8.° Covers the period 1680-1798. 1st
ed. published anonymously in 1809; 2d ed. in 1883. A chronological arrangement with index of names of Russians. Notables of the period mentioned. Russian 'favorites.'

1693   INSTITUT ZUR ERFORSCHUNG DER UDSSR.
      Biographic directory of the USSR, compiled by the Institute
for the Study of the USSR, Munich, Germany. [General editor:
Wladimir S. Merzalow] New York, Scarecrow Press, 1958.
ix, 782p. 23cm. More than 2000 entries.

1694   IVERSEN, ĬULII BOGDANOVICH, 1823-1900.
      Medali v chest' russkikh gosudarstvennykh dieĭatelei i
chastnykh lits.' Sanktpeterburg, Tip. Imp. Akademii
nauk, 1880-96. 3v. in 2. plates. 31cm. Medals in honor of
Russian statesmen and private citizens.

1695   KOCH, HANS, 1894-   ed.
      5000 [i.e. Fünftausend] Sowjetköpfe: Gliederung und Gesicht
eines Führungskollektivs. Unter Mitwirkung von Otto Böss
und Günter Schäfer hrsg. von Hans Koch. Köln, Deutsche
Industrieverlag, 1959. xiv, 862 p. 18cm. (Bücher der
Deutschen Industrieinstituts) Compiled in the Osteuropa Institut, Munich. 5000 leading figures of Soviet Russia.

1696   KOMMUNISTICHESKAĬA PARTIĬA SOVETSKOGO SOĬUZA.
TSENTRAL' NYĬ KOMITET. OTDEL PO ISTORII OKTĬABR'-
SKOĬ REVOLIŪTSII I VSESOĬUZNOĬ KOMMUNISTICHESKOĬ
PARTII.
      Bratskaĭa mogila. Biograficheskiĭ slovar' umershikh i
pogibshikh chlenov Moskovskoĭ organizatsii RKP (bol'shevikov)

Moskva, Moskovskiĭ rabochiĭ, 1922-23. 2 v. illus., ports.
8.° At head of title: Moskovskoĭ komitet RKP (b.) Gubern-
skoe biŭro Kommissii po istorii Oktiābr´ skoĭ revoliŭtsii i
RKP (Istpart) "A common grave." Biographical dictionary of
deceased members of the Moscow organization of the Communist Party.

1697 KOMMUNISTICHESKAĬĀ PARTIĬĀ SOVETSKOGO SOĬŪZA.
TSENTRAL´ NYĬ KOMITET. OTDEL PO ISTORII OKTĬĀBR´
SKOĬ REVOLIŪTSII I VSESOĬŪZNOĬ KOMMUNISTICHESKOĬ
PARTII.
Pamiātnik borfsam proletarskoĭ revoliŭfsii, pogibshim v
1917-1921 g. g. Sostaviteli: L. Lezhava i G. Rusakov. 3. izd.,
ispr. i dop. Moskva, Gos. izd-vo, 1925. vii, 779 p. illus.,
ports. 24cm. Memorial to fighters of the [Russian] prole-
tarian revolution who fell in the years 1917-1921.

1698 KVADRI, VLADIMIR VIKTOROVICH, 1859-
Imperatorskaiā glavnaiā kvartira... S.-Petersburg, Tip.
N.N. Sobko, 1902-14. 4 v. in 9. illus., ports. 4.° "Imperial Russian [Head]quarters..." Includes sketches of cour-
tiers and military personnel.

1699 LEVENSON, M L ed.
Gosudarstvennyĭ Soviêt. Petrograd, 1915. 148p. Biography of members of the Russian Council of State in the early
years of the First World War.

1700 LEVENSON, M L comp.
Pravitel´stvuiŭshchu senat. St. Petersburg, 1912. 172 p.
Biography of members of the Russian Senat[e] of 1912; at one
time the Senate was a chief administrative organ and judicial
authority. It was abolished in Nov. 1917.

1701 LEWYTZKYI, BORYS
Sowjetische Kurzbiographien, von Borys Lewytzyki und
Kurt Müller. Hannover, Verlag für Literatur und Zeit-
geschehen [1964] 352p. 24cm. (Schriftenreihe des Forsch-
ungsinstituts der Friedrich-Ebert-Stiftung. A. Historisch-
politische Schriften) Short biographies of prominent people
in the Soviet Union.

1702 LUSHEV, ANDREĬ MIKHAĬLOVICH
Istoricheskiĭ al´bom portretov izvestnykh lifs XVI-XVIII vv.,

fotografirovannyĭ i izdannyĭ A. M. Lushevym. Sanktpeterburg, 1870. 64 p. plates, ports. 400 portraits of Russians
of the 16th-18th centuries.

1703 McGRAW-HILL ENCYCLOPEDIA OF RUSSIA AND THE
SOVIET UNION. Editor: Michael T. Florinsky; consultants:
Harry Schwartz [and others. 1st ed.] New York, McGraw-
Hill [1961] xiv, 624 p. illus., maps. 29cm. Includes many
brief biographies.

1704 MANDEL'SHTAM, ROZA SEMENOVNA, 1875-
Bibliografiĭã deĭãteleĭ Urala. Moskva, 1943. 114 p.
345 brief bio-bibliographical references of prominent persons
in the Ural Mountains region of Russia.

1705 MIKHAĬLOVSKIĬ-DANILEVSKIĬ, ALEKSANDR IVANOVICH,
1790-1848.
Imperator Aleksandr I i ego spodvizhniki v 1812, 1813,
1814, 1815 godakh. Voennaĩã gallereĩã Zimnĩago dvortsa...
S.-Peterburg, Tip. K. Kraiĩã, 1845-49. 6 v. ports. 35cm.
Emperor Alexander I and his associates in the years 1812-
1815. Military gallery of the Winter Palace.

1706 MĨUNSTER, ALEKSANDER ERNESTOVICH, b. 1824.
Portretnaĩã galereĩã russkikh dĩeĩãtelei. Galerie de portraits des célébrités russes. S.-Peterburg, 1865-69. 2 v.
ports. folio. 200 portraits of famous Russians, with letter-
press in French, followed by biographical sketches in Russian.

1707 MORDOVTSEV, DANIIL LUKICH, 1830-1905.
Russkiĩã zhenshchiny novago vremeni. Biograficheskie
ocherki iz russkoĭ istorii. S.-Petersburg, A. Cherkesov,
1874. 3 v. 22cm. Biographical sketches of Russian women
of modern times.

1708 MUNICH. OSTEUROPA-INSTITUT.
Sowjetbuch. Herausgeber: Hans Koch unter Mitwirkung
von Alexander Adamczyk [et al. 2. ergänzte Aufl.] Köln,
Deutsche Industrieverlags-GmbH [1958] xii, 687 p. maps.
24cm. (Bücher des Deutschen Industrieinstituts) Contents. --
Sowjetkunde. --Sowjetköpfe. --Sowjetbücher. The section
"Sowjetköpfe" superseded by Koch, Hans: 5000 Sowjetköpfe
(q. v.)? It contains brief biographies of important figures
in Soviet Russia.

1709   NASHI DĪEĪATELI;
       Gallereīa zamīechatel´nykh līudeĭ Rossii v portretakh i bi-
ografiīakh. S.-Peterburg, Izd. A.O. Baumana, 1872-80.
8 v. ports. 24cm. First 4 volumes issued under titles:
Russkie sovremennye deīateli (v. 1, 3-4) and Russkie byvshie
deīateli (v. 2) Our [famous] people; gallery of remarkable
Russians in portraits and biographies.

1710   NEVSKIĬ, VLADIMIR IVANOVICH, 1876-
       Materialy dlīa biograficheskogo slovarīa sofsial-demokratov,
vstupivshikh v rossiĭskoe rabochee dvizhenie za period ot 1880
do 1905 g. Moskva, Gos. izd-vo, 1923. 280 p. 27cm. (Materialy po istorii rabochego dvizheniīa v Rossii, pod red. Vl.
Iv. Nevskogo) Materials for a biographical dictionary of social-
democrats participating in the Russian labor movement, 1880-
1905. No more published. Contents. --vyp. 1. A-D.

1711   NIKOLAĬ MIKHAĬLOVICH, Grand Duke of Russia, 1859-1919.
       Moskovskiĭ nekropol´. [Sostavili V. I. Saitov i B. L.
Modzalevskiĭ po porucheniīu Velikago Knīazīa Nikolaīa Mikhaĭ-
lovicha] S.-Peterburg, Tip. M.M. Stasīulevicha, 1907-08.
3 v. 29cm. "Spravochnyĭ istoricheskiĭ ukazatel´ lifs, zhivshikh v XIV-XX stolīetiīakh v Moskvīe." Persons buried in
Moscow cemeteries. Compiled primarily from monument
inscriptions.

1712   NIKOLAĬ MIKHAĬLOVICH, Grand Duke of Russia, 1859-1919.
       Peterburgskiĭ nekropol´. [Sostavili V. Saitov po poru-
cheniīu Velikago Knīazīa Nikolaīa Mikhaĭlovicha] S.-Peter-
burg, Tip. M. M. Stasīulevicha, 1912-13. 4 v. 29cm. Biographical data from inscriptions in the cemeteries of Leningrad.
"Slovar´ lifs, zhivshikh v XVII-XX stolīetiīakh i pogreben-
nykh na pravoslavnykh i inovīercheskikh kladbishchakh Peter-
burga s nīekotorymi ego okrestnostīami, a takzhe v otdīel´-
nikh fserkvakh." "Peterburgskiĭ nekropol´, napechatannyĭ
... [v 1883 g.] voshel ... v nastoīashchee izdanie."

1713   NIKOLAĬ MIKHAĬLOVICH, Grand Duke of Russia, 1859-1919.
       Russkie portrety XVIII. i XIX. stolīetiĭ. Portraits russes
des XVIIIe et XIXe siècles. S.-Peterburg, Izd. Velikago
knīazīa Nikolaīa Mikhaĭlovicha, 1905-09. 6 v. in 11. plates,
ports. folio. Russian portraits, 18-19th century.

1714   NIKOLAĬ MIKHAĬLOVICH, Grand Duke of Russia, 1859-1919.
       Russkiĭ nekropol´ v chuzhikh kraīakh. Vyp. 1. Parizh i
ego okrestnosti. Petrograd, Tip. M. M. Stasīulevicha, 1915.

xxiii, 101 p. 26cm. Biographical data from inscriptions in
Russian cemeteries on foreign soil. Compiled by V. M. Anderson. No more published?

1715 NIKOLAĬ MIKHAĬLOVICH, Grand Duke of Russia, 1859-1919.
Russkiĭ provinfsial'nyĭ nekropol'. t. 1. Moskva, Tipolit. T-va I. N. Kushnerev, 1914. ix, 1008 p. 29cm. Biographical data from inscriptions in Russian provincial cemeteries. "Obrabotku k pechatanie ... materialov ... Velikiĭ kniaz' Nikolaĭ Mikhaĭlovich soizvolil poruchit' podpisavshemu eti stroki" (signed V. Sheremetevskiĭ)--p. ix. No more published.

1716 OTTO, NIKOLAĬ KARLOVICH
Biograficheskie ocherki lits, izobrazhennykh na pamiatnikie tysiachelietiia Rossii, vozdvignutago v g. Novgorodie 1862 g. Sostavleny N. Otto i I. Kupriianovym. Novgorod, Tip. M. Sukova, 1862. iv, 335p. front. 21cm. Biographical sketches of persons represented on the monument of the 1000th anniversary of Russia, erected in Novgorod in the year 1862.

1717 PANCHULIDZEV, SERGEĬ ALEKSEEVICH, 1855-
Sbornik biografiĭ kavalergardov ... S. -Peterburg, Ekspedifsiia zagotovleniia gos. bumag, 1901-08. 4 v. illus., ports. folio. Collection of biography of [Russian] cavalrymen.

1718 PAVLOVSKIĬ, IVAN FRANTSEVICH, 1851-
Kratkii biograficheskii slovar' uchenykh i pisatelei Poltavskoi gubernii s poloviny XVIII veka... Poltava, Izd. Poltavskoi uchenoi arkhivnoi komissii, 1912. vi, 238p. ports. 433 brief biographies & autobiographies, Poltava Government, Russia, 18th century. Pavlovskii issued a supplement of 85 new biographies in 1913.

1719 PAVLOVSKIĬ, IVAN FRANTSEVICH, 1851-
Poltavtsy. Ierarkhi, gosudarstvennye i obshchestvennye deiateli i blagotvoriteli. Opyt kratkogo biograficheskogo slovaria Poltavskoi gubernii s poloviny XVIII v. Poltava, Izd. Poltavskoi uchenoi arkhivnoi komissii, 1914. xvi, 294p. 182 ports. Short biographical dictionary for Poltava Government, Russia, in the 18th century.

1720 PERVAIA GOSUDARSTVENNAIA DUMA.
Alfavitnyĭ spisok i podrobnyia biografii i kharakteristiki

chlenov Gosudarstvennoĭ Dumy. Moskva, 1906. 158p. The
1st Russian Government Duma; alphabetical list & detailed
biographies... of members .

1721   PORTRÄTS DER UdSSR - PROMINENZ.
München, Institut zur Erforschung der UdSSR, 1960-
1 v. (loose-leaf) ports. 24cm. Biographies & portraits of
prominent persons in Soviet Russia.

1722   PORTRÄTS DER UdSSR—PROMINENZ.
München, Institut zur Erforschung der UdSSR [1965-
v. (loose-leaf) 30cm. Biographies (without the portraits)
of prominent persons in Soviet Russia. Revision of the 1960
ed. Issued in mimeographed fasicles, 1965-

1723   PREEV, ZINOVY N
The Russian Revolution and who's who in Russia. London,
J. Bale, Sons & Danielsson, 1917. 119p. 19cm.

1724   RODOSLOVNAĬA KNIGA KNĬAZEĬ I DVORĬAN ROSSIĬSKIKH
I VYĬEZZHIKH, SODERZHASHCHAĬA V SEBIĔ:
1. Rodoslovnuĭu knigu... kotoraĭa izviĕstna pod nazvaniem
Barkhatnoĭ knigi; 2. Rospis´ alfavitnuĭu... s pokazaniem,
otkudu tiĕ rody proizoshli, ili vyiĕkhali...; 3. Rospis´, v
kotoroĭ vyiĕzzhie rody pokazany vsiĕ vmiĕstiĕ po miestam
ikh vyiĕzda; i 4. Rospis´ alfavitnuĭu... Moskva, V Univ. tip.
u N. Novikova, 1787. 2 v. 21cm. Edited by N. N. Novikov.
Genealogy of Russian princes & noblemen; includes biographical data.

1725   ROVINSKIĬ, DMITRIĬ ALEKSANDROVICH, 1824-1895.
Podrobnyi slovar´ russkikh gravirovannykh portretov.
Izd. s 700 fototipnymi portretami. Sankt-Peterburg, Tip.
Imp. Akademii nauk, 1886-89. 4 v. plates, ports. 4.°
Comprehensive dictionary of Russian engraved portraits; in-
cludes 700 portraits.

1726   ROVINSKIĬ, DMITRIĬ ALEKSANDROVICH, 1824-1895.
Slovar´ russkikh gravirovannykh portretov. Sanktpeter-
burg, Tip. Imp. Akademii nauk, 1872. liv, 236p. 25cm.
Dictionary of engraved Russian portraits.

1727   RUSSIA. GOSUDARSTVENNYĬ SOVET.
Gosudarstvennyĭ soviĕt, 1801-1901. Sostavleno v Gosudar-

stvennŏĭ kantseliării. S.-Peterburg, Gos. tip., 1901. 215,
42p. plates, ports. 36cm. Biography of the Russian Council of State, 1801-1901.

1728   RUSSIA (1923-   U.S.S.R.) VERKHOVNYĬ SOVET.
        Deputaty Verkhovnogo Soveta SSSR. Moskva, Izvestiiă
        Sovetov deputatov trudiăshchikhsiă.   v. ports. 23cm.
        Biographical sketches of deputies of the Supreme Soviet of
        the USSR.

1729   RUSSKAIĂ PORTRETNAIĂ GALLEREIĂ.
        Sobranie portretov zamechatel'nykh russkikh liŭdeĭ, nachi-
        naiă s XVIII stoletiiă, s kratkimi ikh biografiiămi... S.-Pe-
        terburg, Izd. A. S. Suvorina, 1885-87. 19 v. (or numbers or
        fascicles) 112 portraits of famous Russians.

1730   RUSSKIĬ BIOGRAFICHESKIĬ SLOVAR'.
        S.-Peterburg [etc.] Izdanie Imperatorskogo Russkago
        istoricheskago obshchestva, 1896-1918. 25 v. 28cm.
        A major Russian biographical dictionary. No more published.
        Russian letters V, God-Giă, E, M, Nik-Niă, Tk-Tiă, U not
        represented.

1731   RUSSKOE ISTORICHESKOE OBSHCHESTVO.
        Azbuchnyĭ ukazatel' imen russkikh deiătelei dliă Russ-
        kago biograficheskago slovariă. Sankt Peterburg, 1887-88.
        2 v. 27cm. (Sbornik Imp. Russkago istoricheskago
        obshchestva, v. 60, 62) Edited by G. F. Stendman. A pre-
        liminary list of names for inclusion in the Russkii biogra-
        ficheskii slovar' (Russian biographical dictionary) In-
        cludes dates, profession & works.

1732   SEMENOV, P   N   ed.
        Biograficheskie ocherki senatorov po materialam sobran-
        nym P. I. Baranovym. Moskva, Izd. Imperatorskago
        obshchestva istorii i drevnosteĭ rossiĭskikh pri Moskovskom
        universitetĭe, 1866. xii, 229 p. 28cm. Biographical
        sketches of [Russian] 'senators' (statesmen) from materials
        in the collection of P. I. Baranov.

1733   SERIĂKOV, LAVRENTIĬ AVKSENT'EVICH, 1824-1881.
        Russkie deiăteli v portretakh. Izd. red. zhurnala
        "Russkaiă starina." Sankt-Peterburg, Tip. V. S. Bala-
        sheva, 1886-91. 5 v. ports. 24cm. 140 portraits of Rus-
        sian men of action.

1734   SERISEV, INOCENTO
      Album of great, outstanding, and eminent personalities
of Russia, with short biographies. [Sydney, W. C. Penfold]
1945-   v. ports. 29cm. Cover title.

1735   [SKAL'KOVSKII, KONSTANTIN APOLONOVICH] 1843-1906.
      Nashi gosudarstvennye i obshchestvennye dieĭateli. So-
chinenie avtora "Sovremennoĭ Rossii." S.-Petersburg, A.
S. Suvorin, 1891. viii, 586 p. 12.° Russian statesmen and
public figures of the late 19th century. Second edition?

1736   SOVREMENNAIA ROSSIIA V PORTRETAKH I BIOGRAFIIAKH
      VYDAĬUSHCHIKHSIA DEĬATELEI. [Moskva, Tip. IA.
Balĭanskago, 1908?] 208 p. ports. 26 x 36cm. 200 portraits with accompanying biographies of Russians of the turn
of the 20th century. "V pol'zu golodaĭushchikh."

1737   STRAHL, PHILIPP CARL, d. 1840.
      Das gelehrte Russland. Leipzig, F. Fleischer, 1828. xx,
514p. 20cm. Learned Russia. Goes up to the end of the 18th
century. A free and enlarged translation of Metropolitan
Evgenii of Kiev's work (Slovar' istoricheskiĭ o byvshikh v
Rossii pisateliakh dukhovnago china greko-rossiĭskoĭ tserkvi)

1738   TERESHCHENKO, ALEKSANDR VLAS'EVICH, 1806-1865.
      Opyt obozrieniia zhizni sanovnikov, upravliavshikh in-
ostrannymi dielami v Rossii. St. Petersburg, 1837. 3 v. in
1. 23cm. An attempt to review the lives of officials who
managed the foreign affairs of Russia; Russian statesmen.

1739   TOLSTOĬ, DMITRIĬ ANDREEVICH, graf, 1823-1889.
      Liudi ekaterininskogo vremeni. Spravochnaia knizhka k
tsarstvovaniiu Ekateriny II. Sanktpeterburg, Tip. V. S.
Balasheva, 1882. xx, 636p. 318 biographies of Russians and
other Europeans prominent during the reign of Catherine II
of Russia, 1762-1796.

1740   VILENSKIĬ, VLADIMIR DMITRIEVICH, 1888-1932, ed.
      TSentrosibirtsy. Sbornik pamiati pogibshikh chlenov
TSentral'nogo ispolnitel'nogo komiteta sovetov Sibiri 1918
goda... Pod red. V. D. Vilenskogo-Sibiriakova [pseud.]
N. F. Chuzhaka-Nasimovicha i P. F. Shcheloka. Moskva,
Moskovskiĭ rabochiĭ, 1927. 158p. 8.° Central Siberians.
Collection of memoirs of deceased members of the Central
Executive Committee of Soviets, Siberia, 1918.

NATIONAL OR AREA BIOGRAPHY

1741   U. S. S. R. HANDBOOK.
London, V. Gollancz, 1936. 643p. illus. 19cm. A new edition of the "Soviet Union year-book" with additional chapters. Edited by Louis Segal. The Who's who section contains sketches of about 500 persons.

1742   [USHAKOV, SEMEN IVANOVICH]
Dieianiia rossiiskikh polkovodtsev i generalov, oznamenovavshikh sebia v dostopamiatnuiu voinu s Frantsieiu, v 1812, 1813, 1814, i 1815 godakh, s kratkim nachertaniem vsei ikh sluzhby, s samogo nachala vstupleniia v onuiu. S.-Petersburg, Tip. K. Kraiia, 1822. 4 v. ports. 8.° The deeds of Russian captains & generals performed during the war with France, 1812-1815, with brief notes on their service records...

1743   UTECHIN, SERGEJ, 1921-
Everyman's concise encyclopaedia of Russia. London, Dent; New York, Dutton [1961] xxvi, 623p. illus., ports., map. 20cm. (Everyman's reference library) In large part biographical.

1744   VASIL' CHIKOV, ALEKSANDR ALEKSEEVICH, 1832-1890.
Liste alphabétique de portraits russes. Par A. Wassiltchikoff. St.-Peterbourg, Eggers [etc.] 1875. 2 v. 23cm. Alphabetical list of Russian portraits.

1745   VSESOIUZNOE OBSHCHESTVO POLITICHESKIKH KATORZ-HAN I SSYL' NO-POSELENTSEV.
Politicheskaia katorga i ssylka. Biograficheskii spravochnik chlenov Obshchestvo politkatorzhan i ssyl'no-poselentsev. Moskva, Izd. Obshchestva, 1929. 686 p. [Russian] political penal servitude and exile; a biographical reference work for members of the Society of Political Prisoners and Exiles-Deportees.

1746   VSESOIUZNOE OBSHCHESTVO POLITICHESKIKH KATORZ-HAN I SSYL'NO-POSELENTSEV.
Uchastniki russkogo revoliutsionnogo dvizheniia epokhi bor'by s tsarizmom. Biograficheskii ukazatel' chlenov Vsesoiuznogo ob-va politicheskikh katorzhan i ssyl'no-poselentsev. Moskva, 1927. 288 p. 18cm. Participants in Russian revolutionary development during the struggle with Czarism; biographical index of members of the All-Union Society of Political Prisoners & Exiles-Deportees.

1747   WHO'S WHO IN THE USSR.
1961/62-   [Montreal] Intercontinental Book and Pub.
Co. v. 21cm. Vols. for 1961/62-   compiled by the
Institute for the Study of the USSR, Munich.

1748   ZATVORNITSKIĬ, NIKOLAĬ MITROFANOVICH, 1867-
Pamiăt´ o chlenakh Voennago Sovi͡eta; portrety i biograficheskie ocherki... S.-Petersburg, Tip. Tov. M. O. Vol´f,
1907. iv, 781p. ports. 28cm. ([Russia] Voennoe minister-
stvo. Stoli͡etie, t. 3, otd. 4) Recollections of members of
the Russian War Council.

SALVADOR

1749   GARCIA, MIGUEL ÁNGEL, 1862 or 3-1955.
Diccionario histórico-enciclopédico de la República de
El Salvador. San Salvador, Tip. "La Luz, " 1927-   v.
25 cm. Imprint varies. 13 or more vols.; in progress?
Historical-encyclopedic dictionary of the Republic of El Sal-
vador; largely a biographical dictionary.

SANTO DOMINGO
See DOMINICAN REPUBLIC

SARAWAK

1750   SARAWAK. INFORMATION SERVICE.
Sarawak Who's who. [Kuching, 196-] 25 l. 33cm. Cover
title.

SCANDINAVIA
Anonyms and Pseudonyms

1751   COLLIN, EDVARD, 1808-1886.
Anonymer og pseudonymer i den danske, norske og islandske literatur samt i fremmede literaturer, forsaavidt disse
omhandle nordiske forhold, fra de aeldste tider indtil aaret
1860. Kiøbenhavn, J. Lund, 1869. 209 p. 25cm. Anonyms
and pseudonyms in Scandinavian literature (Danish, Norse &
Icelandic)

General Works

1752   VEM ÄR VEM I NORDEN;
Biografisk handbok. Huvudredaktor: Gunnar Sjöstrom.

Stockholm, Bonnier, 1941. 1544p. 25cm. Who's who in Scandinavia; a biographical handbook.

SCOTLAND See Great Britian

SIAM See Thailand

SINGAPORE

1753　WHO'S WHO IN SINGAPORE AND MALAYA.
1947-　Singapore, Oriental Publishers.　v. ports.
28cm.

1754　SHEN, WEI-TSÊ, ed.
Biographies of prominent Chinese in Singapore, compiled under the editorial supervision of Victor Sim. Ed. de luxe in English and Chinese. Singapore, Nan Kok Publication Co. [cover 1950]　i, 111, i, 110 p. (on double leaves) ports. 34cm. 111 biographies, with portraits.

1755　WONG, CHOON-SAN.
The gallery of Chinese kapitans. Singapore, Ministry of Culture, 1963. viii, 114p. illus., 18 plates. 25cm.

SLAVS

1756　KLEINE SLAVISCHE BIOGRAPHIE.
Wiesbaden, O. Harrassowitz, 1958. 832 p. 18cm. Compiled by the Slavisches Seminar, Universität München? Biographies of Slavs.

1757　POLSKA AKADEMIA NAUK. KOMITET SŁOWIANOZNAW-
STWA.
Słownik starożytności słowiańskich; encyklopedyczny zarys kultury słowian od czasów najdawniejszych. Pod red. Władysława Kowalenki, Gerarda Labudy i Tadeusza Lehra-Spławińskiego. Wrocław, Zkład Narodowy im. Ossolinskich, 1961-　v. illus. 31cm. Vols. 1-　have added t. p. : Lexicon antiquitatum Slavicarum. A dictionary of Slavic antiquities. Includes biography.

1758　SLAVONIC ENCYCLOPEDIA.
Edited by Joseph S. Roucek. New York, Philosophical Library, 1949. xi, 1445 p. 25cm. More than half the volume is biographical in nature.

1759　VLAHOVIĆ, VLAHO S
Manual: Slavonic personalities (past and present) New York, Slavonic Press, 1940. 96p. 18cm. Brief identifying data and dates.

SOUTH AFRICA
See Africa, South

SOUTH AMERICA
See Central America; Latin America; Individual
Countries

SPAIN
Bibliography, Indexes, Etc.

1760   FOULCHÉ-DELBOSC, RAYMOND, 1864-1929.
Manuel de l'hispanisant [par] R. Foulche-Delbosc & L.
Barrau-Dihigo. New York, G. P. Putnam, 1920-25. 2 v.
23 cm. Partial contents. --t. 1. [partie] III. Biographies et
bio-bibliographies (p. 41-119) Pt. 3 of vol. 1 contains bibliography of Spanish biographies & bio-bibliographies.

Anonyms and Pseudonyms

1761   HARTZENBUSCH E HIRIART, EUGENIO
Unos cuantos seudónimos de escritores españoles con
sus correspondientes nombres verdaderos. Apuntes recogidos y coleccionados por Maxiriarth [pseud.] con un
prólogo del Sr. D. José Fernández Bremón. Edición corr.
y aum. Madrid, Estab. Tip. Sucesores de Rivadeneyra,
1904. xix, 168p. 18cm. Pseudonyms of Spanish writers with
their corresponding real names.

1762   PONCE DE LEÓN FREYRE, EDUARDO
1. 500 [i. e. Mil quinientos] suedónimos modernos de la
literatura española (1900-1942) recogidos y coleccionados
por Eduardo Ponce de León Freyre y Florentino Zamora Lucas. Madrid, Instituto Nacional del Libro Español, 1942.
126p. 20cm. 1500 pseudonyms of 20th century Spanish literature.

1763   RODERGAS I CALMELL, JOSEP
Els pseudònims usats a Catalunya. Recull de 3. 800.
Barcelona, Editorial Millà, 1951. xv, 408p. 25cm. The
pseudonyms used in Catalonia.

General Works

1764   ALBUM NACIONAL...
[Cartagena] Fenicia [1930-   v. ports. 28cm.
Portraits of Spaniards.

1765   ALMIRANTE, JOSÉ
    Bibliografía militar de España. Madrid, Impr. de Tello,
Librería de Murillo, 1876. cxxx, 988p. 28cm. In double
columns. Bio-bibliographical. Military bibliography of
Spain.

1766   ALONSO CORTÉS, NARCISO, 1875-
    Indice de documentos útiles a la biografía. [Santander]
Boletín de la Biblioteca Menéndez y Pelayo, 1922. 65p. 24cm.
Index of documents useful for biographical data.

1767   ASAMBLEA CONSTITUYENTE DE 1854.
    Biografía de todos los diputados y todos los hombres céle-
bres que han tomado parte en el alzamiento nacional. Por una
sociedad literaria. Madrid, Impr. de Pena, 1854. 509 p. 8.°
Biographies of Spanish deputies (Constituent Assembly of 1854)
and other famous Spaniards of the time.

1768   [BARON,   ]
    Galerie espagnole; ou, Notices biographiques sur les
membres de Cortès et du gouvernement, les généraux en
chef et commandants des guérillas, des armées
constitutionelles et de la Foi, et généralement tous les
hommes, qui ont marqué dans la Péninsule pendant la guerre
de l'Indépendance ou depuis la Révolution de 1820. Bruxelles,
1823. 1 v. 8.° By "Baron" according to Barbier. Biographical notices of important Spaniards of the period (War of Independence against the French, 1808-1814, thru' & including the
revolution of 1820.)

1769   BARRIL, ROBERTO
    Semblanzas de los 340 diputados á Cortés que han fi-
gurado en la Legislatura de 1849 á 1850. Madrid, Impr. de
G. Gil, 1850. 1v. 8.° Biographical sketches of the 340 deputies at the Spanish Cortés who participated in the Legislature
of 1849-1850.

1770   CARRASCO Y SAYZ, ADOLFO, 1830-
    Icono-biografía del generalato español. Madrid, Impr.
del Cuerpo de Artillería San Lorenzo, 1901. xliii, 914 p.
facsims. 23 cm. Iconography-biography of Spanish generals.

1771   CORTES D'ESPAGNE.
    Petite biographie des membres du Congrès espagnol pour
la Législature de 1820 et 1821. Traduit de l'espagnol par Simon

Lefranc. Paris, Renard, 1821. viii, 130 p. Members of
the Spanish Cortes (House of Representatives) 1820-1821.

1772   DIANA, MANUEL JUAN, 1814-1881.
        Cien españoles célebres. Madrid, Impr. de Tejado, 1864.
viii, 247 p. 8.º Arranged chronologically, but with an alphabetical index. 100 famous Spaniards.

1773   DICCIONARIO BIOGRÁFICO ESPAÑOL E HISPANOAMERICANO
        Publicado bajo la direccion de Gaspar Sabater, con la cola-
boración de reputados especialistas españoles e hispanoamericanos. Dirección artística: Gabriel Mateu Mairata. Palma
de Mallorca, Instituto Español de Estudios Biográficos, 1950-
      v. illus., ports. 25cm. Biographical dictionary of
Spain and Spanish America.

1774   DICCIONARIO DE HISTORIA DE ESPAÑA
        Desde sus origenes hasta el fin del reinado de Alfonso XIII.
Madrid, Revista de Occidente [1952] 2 v. maps. 22cm. This
dictionary of Spanish history includes biographical sketches of
noted Spaniards.

1775   DICTIONNAIRE DE CONTEMPORAINS ILLUSTRES.
        I. Espagne. Madrid, Impr. des MM. J. Espinosa et A.
Lamas, 1905. 183p. ports. 23cm. Alternate pages blank.
No more published? Dictionary of famous contemporaries.
Volume 1: Spain.

1776   ESPERABÉ ARTEAGA, ENRIQUE, 1868-
        Diccionario enciclopédico ilustrado y crítico de los hombres
de España. Prólogo del conde de Romanones. [Nueva ed.,
reformada, ampliada y completada] Madrid, Artes Gráficas
Ibarra [1957?] 530 p. ports. 26 cm. A dictionary of Spanish
biography; ca.3000 entries. 1st ed., 1946-47, in 2 v.

1777   FERNÁNDEZ Y SÁNCHEZ, ILDEFONSO.
        Año biográfico español. Hechos, caractéres y producci-
ones de 365 patricios de uno y otro sexo, que han dejado huella
en nuestra historia patria. Barcelona, A. J. Bastinos, 1899.
vi, 512 p. 8.º 'The Spanish biographical year.' 365 Spanish
'patricians.'

1778   FIGURAS DE HOY;
        Enciclopedia biográfica nacional ilustrada de las personali-
dades de la actualidad. 1950-   Madrid, Ediciones Ciencia

y Cultura.   v. illus. 21cm. Cover title: Enciclopedia figuras de hoy. 1956 latest ed. (?) Figures of the day; a national biographical encyclopedia of contemporary Spaniards.

1779   GALERIA MILITAR CONTEMPORANEA;
O sea, Colección de biografías y retratos de los jefes
que más se han distinguido em ambos ejércitos durante la
guerra civil de 1833 a 1840, con inclusion de los hechos de
unos guerrilleros, cuya historia aun no se ha escrito.
Madrid, Impr. de Hortelano, 1845. 2 v. ports. 4.º
Biographies and portraits of military leaders during the
1st Carlist War in Spain.

1780   INSTITUTO INTERNACIONAL DE GENEALOGÍA Y
HERÁLDICA.
Indice nobiliario español. Recopilado y redactado por
Vicente de Cadenas y Vicent [et al.] Madrid, Ediciones
Hidalguía, 1955. 754p. 18cm. (Guía nobiliaria universal.
Sección española) Index of the Spanish nobility; includes bio-
graphical data.

1781   MARTÍNEZ, BENIGNO T
Diccionario biográfico-bibliográfico de escritores antiguos
y modernos nacidos en los países del habla castellana, escrito
en vista de las fuentes mas autorizadas, extractado y tradu-
cido de los diccionarios, revistas, periódicos, catálogos y
otras obras biográficas y bibliográficas publicadas en Europa
y en América. Introducción. Buenos Aires, Impr. de Stiller
y Laass, 1886. 100 p. 28cm. Includes Spanish bio-bibliography for the letter A only. No more published.

1782   OVILO Y OTERO, MANUEL, 1826-1885.
Memorias para formar un catálogo alfabético de los españoles, americanos y extranjeros célebres que más se han señala-
do en España desde el año 1200 [hasta nuestros días, en todas
las carreras] Segovia [etc.] 1854-67. 2 v. Towards an
alphabetical catalog of Spaniards, [Latin-] Americans & aliens
who have distinguished themselves in Spain, 1200-1865 (ca.)
Vol. 2 has title: Diccionario biográfico contemporáneo. Palau
y Dulcet mentions only vol. 1 (477 p.)

1783   PAVÍA Y PAVÍA, FRANCISCO DE PAULA, 1812-1890.
Galería biográfica de los generales de marina, jefes y
personajes notables que figuraron en la misma corporación
desde 1700 á 1868, par Francisco de Paula Pavia. Madrid,
Impr. de J. López y de F. García, 1873-74. 4 v. 22cm.
379 biographies of Spanish naval leaders.

1784   RETRATOS DE LOS ESPAÑOLES ILUSTRES,
       Con un epítome de sus vidas. De orden superior. [Ma-
       drid] En la Impr. Real de Madrid, siendo su regente D.
       Lázaro Gayguer, 1791. [234]p. 114 ports. 45cm. 114 por-
       traits of Spaniards and notes on their lives.

1785   VERA, FRANCISCO, 1888-
       La cultura española medieval; datos bio-bibliográficos
       para su historia. Madrid, V. Suarez, 1933-34—   2+ v.
       illus. 25cm. Medieval Spanish civilization; bio-bibliographi-
       cal data for its history. Only 2 vols. published?

1786   WHO'S WHO IN SPAIN.
       1st-   ed. ; 1963-   [Montreal] Intercontinental Book and
       Pub. Co.   v. 21cm. Editors: 1964-   S. Olives Canals
       and S. Szabó (under the pseud. Stephen Taylor)

Local

Albacete

1787   BAQUERO ALMANSA, ANDRÉS, 1853-1916.
       Hijos ilustres de la provincia de Albacete; estudio bio-
       bibliográfico. Prólogo del Excmo. Sr. marqués de Molins.
       Madrid, Impr. de A. Pérez Dubrull, 1884. xviii, 250p. 17cm.
       Illustrious sons of the province of Albacete, Spain.

Aragon

1788   ARCO, RICARDO DEL, 1888-
       El genio de la raza; figuras aragonesas. 1.-2. ser.
       Zaragoza, Tip. Heraldo de Aragón, 1923-   2v. ports. 18cm.
       No more published?   The genius of the race; Aragon's promi-
       nent figures.

1789   CASTÁN PALOMAR, FERNANDO.
       Aragoneses contemporáneos; diccionario biográfico.
       Zaragoza, Tip. La Académica— F. Martínez, 1934. 619 p.
       ports. 22 cm. At head of title: Ediciones Herrein.   Biogra-
       phical dictionary of contemporary Aragon.

Basque Provinces

1790   AROCENA ARREGUI, FAUSTO
       Diccionario biográfico vasco. San Sebastián, Auñamendi
       [1963-   v. 19cm. (Colección Auñamendi, 32

Contents. --l. Guipúzcoa.   Biographical dictionary of
Spain's Basque Provinces.

Cadiz

1791   CAMBIASO Y VERDES, NICOLÁS MARÍA DE.
Memorias para la biografía y para la bibliografía de la
isla de Cádiz. Madrid, Impr. de D. Leon Amarita, 1929-30.
2 v. 22 cm. Half title: Diccionario de personas célebres de
Cádiz [A dictionary of famous persons of Cadiz, Spain]

1792   MINAÑO, N   N
Diccionario biográfico y bibliográfico de la isla de Cádiz.
Madrid, 1830. 1 v. 8.º Not mentioned in Palau y Dulcet.
Biographical and bibliographical dictionary of the isle of
Cadiz.

Canary Islands

1793   MILLARES TORRES, AGUSTÍN
Hijos ilustres de las Islas Canarias. Biografías de Ca-
narios célebres. 2. ed. considérablement aumentada y
precedida de un estudio sobre los progresos de la civiliza-
ción en el Archipielogo, desde su conquista hasta nuestros
días. Las Palmas de Gran Canaria, Impr. de F. Martín
González, 1878-79. 2 v.   Illustrious sons of the Canary
Islands.

Cordoba

1794   GONZÁLEZ Y SAENZ, FRANCISCO DE PAULA
Biografías cordobesas contemporáneas. Córdoba, Impr.
y Librería del "Diario de Córdoba," 1895.   xxxix,188 p.
Biographies of natives of Cordoba, Spain, flourishing in the
latter part of the 19th century.

1795   PAVÓN, FRANCISCO DE BORJA
Necrologías de varios contemporáneos distinguidos, espe-
cialmente cordobeses, dadas a luz con anterioridad y ahora
coleccionadas por su autor. Córdoba, Estab. Tip. de la
Unión, 1892. vi, 222p. Necrology of various noted Spanish
contemporaries, especially those of Cordoba.

1796   RAMÍREZ DE ARELLANO, RAFAEL, 1854-1921.
Ensayo de un catálogo biográfico de escritores de la provincia y diócesis de Córdoba, con descripción de sus obras.

Madrid, Tip. de la 'Revista de Archivos, Bibliotecas y Museos,' 1921-22. 2 v. facsims. 29cm. Attempt at a biographical catalog for the province & diocese of Cordoba, Spain.

Estremadura

1797   DÍAZ Y PÉREZ, NICOLÁS, 1841-1902.
Diccionario histórico, biográfico, crítico y bibliográfico de autores, artistas y extremenos ilustres. Precedido de un prólogo de Francisco Cañamaque y con noticias del autor por Fernando De-Gabriel y Ruiz de Apodaca. Madrid, Pérez y Boix [1884-88] 2v. in l. ports. 32cm. Largely a bio-bibliographical dictionary for Estremadura, Spain.

Galicia

1798   VESTEIRO TORRES, TEODOSIO
Galería de gallegos illustres. Madrid, 1874-75. 6 v. 8.º   Gallery of famous Gallegans (Galicia, Spain)

Leon

1799   MINGOTE Y TARAZONA, POLICARPIO
Varones ilustres de la provincia de León. León, Estab. Tip. de A. Miñon, 1880. xvi, 337p. 4.º   Illustrious men of the Province of Leon.

Madrid

1800   ÁLVAREZ Y BAENA, JOSÉ ANTONIO, d. 1803.
Hijos de Madrid, ilustres en santidad, dignidades, armas, ciencias y artes. Diccionario histórico... Madrid, 1789-91. 4v. 2lcm. "Sons of Madrid."

1801   BALLESTEROS ROBLES, LUIS
Diccionario biográfico matritense. Editado por el Exemo. Ayuntamiento. Madrid, Impr. Municipal, 1912. xii, 702p. ports. 29cm. Biographical dictionary of Madrid.

Majorca

1802   BOVER DE ROSSELLÓ, JOAQUÍN MARÍA, d. 1865.
Varones ilustres de Mallorca, por J. M. Bover y R. Medel... Palma, Impr. de P. J. Gelabert, 1847-49. 2 v. in l (784) illus. , ports. 24 cm. Illustrious men of Majorca.

Minorca

1803   RAMIS Y RAMIS, JUAN, 1746-1819.
Varones ilustres de Menorca y noticia de los apellidos que
mas se han distinguido en ella. Mahon, Serra, 1817. 272p.
4.º Illustrious men of Minorca.

Santander

1804   ESCAGEDO SALMÓN, MATEO.
Índice de montañeses ilustres de la provincia de Santander.
Cádiz, Impr. de M. Alvarez, 1924. 300 p. 16 cm. Cover
title: Indice de montañeses ilustres: Los montañeses en las
órdenes militares de Santiago, Calatrava, Alcántara y Montesa.
Cover dated 1925. Biography of distinguished natives of the
province of Santander, Spain.

Segovia

1805   VERGARA Y MARTÍN, GABRIEL MARÍA, 1869-
Ensayo de una colección bibliográfico-biográfica de noticias referentes a la provincia de Segovia. Guadalajara,
Tall. Tip. del Colegio de Huérfanos de la Guerra, 1903.
616p. 33cm. Attempt at a bio-bibliographical collection of
notices referring to the Spanish province of Segovia.

Seville

1806   [DÍAZ DE VALDERRAMA, FERNÁNDEZ] d. 1804.
Hijos de Sevilla, ilustres en santidad, letras, armas, artes
o dignidad. Dalos al publico, colocados por orden alfabetico,
D. Fermin Arana de Varflora [pseud. Sevilla] Impr. de Vaz-
quez & Hidalgo, 1791. 4v. in 1. 22cm.

1807   --- ----Adiciones y correcciones, por Justino Matute y
Gaviria... Sevilla, 1886. viii,129 p.

Biographical dictionary of famous sons of Seville.

1808   MATUTE Y GAVIRIA, JUSTINO, fl. 1787.
Hijos de Sevilla señalados en santidad, letras, armas,
artes ó dignidad. Con notas y correcciones. Sevilla, En la

Oficina de "El Orden," 1886-89. 2 v. 23cm. Sons of Seville distinguished in sanctity, letters, arms, arts or nobility.

1809   MÉNDEZ BEJARANO, MARIO, 1857-
Diccionario de escritores, maestros y oradores naturales de Sevilla y su actual provincia. Sevilla, Tip. Gironés, 1922-25. 3 v. 28cm. Dictionary of writers, scholars and orators, natives of Seville and its province.

1810   MÉNDEZ BEJARANO, MARIO, 1857-
Bio-bibliografía hispálica de Ultramar; O, Papeletas bio-bibliográficas de escritores nacidos en la provincia de Sevilla, que han tratado de las tierras y misiones de Ultramar. Madrid, Impr. de Patronato de Huerfanos de Intendencia é Intervención Militares, 1915 [i. e. 1916] 218p. 21cm. (Biblioteca sevillana, 1. ser.) Bio-bibliography of natives of Seville in Spanish America.

Zamora

1811   FERNÁNDEZ DURO, CESÁREO, 1830-1908.
Colección bibliográfico-biográfica de noticias referentes a la provincia de Zamora, o materiales para su historia. Madrid, M. Tello, 1891. 579 p. 28 cm. Bio-bibliographical notices referring to the Spanish province of Zamora.

SPANISH AMERICA
See Central America; Latin America

SUDAN

1812   HILL, RICHARD LESLIE.
A biographical dictionary of the Anglo-Egyptian Sudan. Oxford, Clarendon Press, 1951. xvi, 391p. 23cm. "Over 1900 short notices."

SURINAM

1813   SURINAAMSE HISTORISCHE KRING.
Emancipatie 1863-1963. Biografieën. Paramaribo, Druk. Lionarons, 1964. 198p. fold. maps, ports. 24cm. Includes biographies of figures in Surinam's (Dutch Guiana's) history, 1863-1963.

SWEDEN
Bibliography, Indexes, Etc.

1814   ÅGREN, SVEN, 1887-
Svensk biografisk upplagslitteratur; bibliografisk förteckning. Uppsala, Almqvist & Wiksell, 1929. xiv, 423p. 25cm. (Svenska bibliotekariesamfundets skriftserie, 1) This bibliography of Swedish biographical literature includes material dealing with Finland (to 1809) and other Swedish possessions as well as with Swedes in foreign countries.

Anonyms and Pseudonyms

1815   BYGDÉN, ANDERS LEONARD, 1844-
Svenskt anonym- och pseudonym-lexikon. Bibliografisk förteckning öfver uppdagade anonymer och pseudonymer i den svenska litteraturen. Upsala, Berling, 1898-1915. 2 v. Anonyms and pseudonyms in Swedish literature; a dictionary.

General Works

1816   BIOGRAFISKT LEXICON ÖFVER NAMNKUNNIGE SVENSKE MÄN.
Upsala [etc.] 1835-57. 23 v. in 12. 22cm. Issued in parts. Continued by Svenskt biografiskt lexikon. Ny följd. 1857-1907. Biographical dictionary of noteworthy Swedes.

1817   FRANZÉN, FRANS MICHAEL, Bp., 1772-1847.
Minnesteckninger öfver utmärkte svenske staatsmän, hjeltar, lärde, konströrer och skalder. Stockholm, 1848-60. 3 v. Biographies of distinguished Swedish statesmen, heroes, scholars, artists & poets.

1818   GEZELIUS, GEORG, 1735-1789.
Försök til et biographiskt lexicon öfver namnkundige och lärde svenske män. Stockholm, 1778-87. 4v. 8.° An attempt at a biographical dictionary of famous and learned Swedes.

1819   HOFBERG, HERMANN, 1823-1883.
Svenskt biografiskt handlexikon. Alfabetiskt ordnade lefnadsteckningar af Sveriges namnkunniga män och quinnor från Reformationen till närvarande tid. Efter tryckta källor

och medelst nya bidrag samlade och utarbetade af Herm.
Hofberg. Stockholm, A. Bonnier [1873-76] 2 pts. in 1 v.
23cm. Swedish biographical dictionary; from the Reformation to the present.

1820 LUNDIN, AUGUST HERMAN
Småländska nationen i Lund. Biografiska och genealogiska
anteckningar. Utg. af Smålands nation. Lund, 1882. 420,
33 p. 8.° Biographical and genealogical notes on people from
the Smaland region of Sweden at the University of Lund.

1821 MOLIN, GÖSTA GIDEON
Smolandi Upsalienses. Smålandsstudenter i Upsala på
1500- och 1600-talen; biografier med genealogiska notiser.
Lund, C. Bloms boktr.; [Smålands nation, Uppsala] 1955-
v. 25cm. Biographical notices of students from the
Småland region of Sweden matriculating at the University of
Uppsala.

1822 NETTELBLA, CHRISTIAN, Freiherr von, 1696-1775.
Memoria virorum in Suecia eruditissimorum rediviva; seu,
Semi-Decas 1. [-4.] orationum funebrium... (Adjecta decade
programmatum funebrium) Rostochii & Lipsiae, 1728-31.
4 v. 8.° Memorials of the most learned men of Sweden.

1823 PALMGREN, H
Medlemmar af Gestrike-Helsinge nation i Upsala 1811-1891.
Biografiska notiser. Stockholm, 1892. xi, 166 p. Biographical notices of natives of Gästrikland & Hälsingborg, Sweden,
attending the University of Uppsala in the 19th century.

1824 SCHEFFER, JOHANNES, 1621-1679.
Suecia literata; seu, De scriptis et scriptoribus gentis
Sueciae. Opus postumum, hypomnematis historicis illustra-
tum, a Johanne Mollero, Flensburga Cimbro. Ed. 3. denuo
correcta, & multis modis aucta. Hamburgi, Sumptibus S.
Heylii, 1716. 475 p. port. 17cm. Learned Sweden; or,
About the writings and writers of the people of Sweden [and
Finland]

1825 SJÖSTRÖM, CARL JOHAN, 1851-1918.
Blekingska nationen 1697-1900; biografiska och genealogiska
anteckningar jemte historik. Lund, E. Malmström, 1901.
vi, 496 p. 25cm. Persons from the county of Blekinge,
Sweden, at Lund University (1697-1900); biographical and genealogical notes.

1826   SJÖSTRÖM, CARL JOHAN, 1851-1918.
        Skånska nationen före afdelningarnes tid. Biografiska och
        genealogiska anteckningar.   Lund, Gleerup, 1885-97.   2 v.
        23cm.   Persons from Scania, Sweden, at Lund University in
        the 19th century; biographical & genealogical notes.   Vol. 1
        also published separately (?) under title: Skånska nationen vid
        Lunds universitet 1833-1883.

1827   SVENSKA MÄN OCH KVINNOR;
        Biografisk uppslagsbok.   [Huvudredaktör Nils Bohman]
        Stockholm, A. Bonnier [1942-55]   8 v.   ports.   27cm.   Swed-
        ish men and women; biographical reference book.

1828   SVENSKA SLÄKTKALENDERN.
        Årg. 1-   ; 1912-   Stockholm, A. Bonnier.   v.
        ports.   16cm.   Swedish genealogical calendar; includes bio-
        graphical materials.

1829   SVENSKAR I UTLANDET, 1959.
        Biografiska uppgifter mm. , sammanställda av Utlands-
        svenskarnas föreningen och Riksföreningen for svenskhetens
        bevarande i utlandet.   Stockholm, P. A. Norstedt, 1959.
        241p.   20cm.   Swedes in foreign countries, 1959; biographical
        lists...

1830   SVENSKT BIOGRAFISKT LEXIKON.
        Stockholm, A. Bonnier [1918-   v.   ports.   27cm.
        Swedish biographical dictionary.   Edited by Bertil Boethius
        and others.

1831   SVENSKT BIOGRAFISKT LEXIKON.
        Ny följd.   Örebro, N. M. Linds boktr. , 1857-[1907]   10 v.
        21cm.   Swedish biographical dictionary.   New series.   Im-
        print varies.   Continuation of Biografiskt lexikon öfver
        namnkunnige svenske män, Upsala, 1835-57.

1832   SVENSKT PORTRÄTTGALLERI.
        Stockholm, H. W. Tullberg [1895-1911]   45 v.   illus. ,
        ports.   23cm.   Swedish portrait gallery; covers 20,602 per-
        sons.   Edited by Albin Hildebrand.

1833   ---- ----Generalregister.   Upprättadt af Albin Hildebrand.
        [Stockholm, H. W. Tullberg, 1913]   xi, 867p.   22cm.   On cov-
        er: Biografisk handbok omfattande 20,602 personer.

1834   SVERIGES RIDDERSKAPS OCH ADELS KALENDER.
Årg. 1-   ; 1855-   Stockholm, A. Bonnier.   v.
illus. 16cm. Sweden's nobility; includes biographical mater-

1835   SWALIN, WILHELM
Konungens svenska och norska statsråd 1809-1814-1881.
Biografiska data. Stockholm, J. Haeggstroms boktr., 1881.
194, 64p. 8.º The King's Swedish & Norwegian ministry;
Swedish & Norwegian statesmen, 1809-1881. Biographical
data.

1836   VEM ÄR DET?
Svensk biografisk handbok. 1912-   Stockholm,
Norstedt.   v. 20cm. Who is that? Swedish biographical
handbook.

1837   VEM ÄR VEM I FOLKFRONTEN?
Den angloryska propagandans förgrundsfigurer i Sverige,
en biografisk förteckning. Stockholm, Svea rike, 1943. 375p.
Who's who in the popular fronts? Prominent Swedish figures
in Anglo-Russian propaganda in Sweden.

1838   VEM ÄR VEM INOM HANDEL OCH INDUSTRI?
1944/45-   Stockholm, Jonson & Winter.   v. 22cm.
Who's who in [Swedish] commerce & industry. Editor:
1944/45-   Gunnar Pravitz.

1839   VEM VAR DET?
Biografier över bortgångna svenska män och kvinnor
samt kronologisk förteckning över skilda ämbetens och
tjänsters innehavare. Stockholm, Norstedt [1944] 356p.
20cm. Who was that? Biographies of deceased Swedish men
& women...

1840   VISTRAND, PER GUSTAF, 1852-1912.
Smålands nation i Upsala. Biografiska och genealogiska
anteckningar. 1637-1844. Upsala, 1894-98. 661p. Natives
of Småland, Sweden, in attendance at the University of Upsala, 1637-1844; biographical and genealogical notes.

SWITZERLAND
Bibliography, Indexes, Etc.

1841   BARTH, HANS, 1871-
Repertorium über die in Zeit- und Sammelschriften der

Jahre 1891-1900 enthaltenen Aufsätze und Mitteilungen
schweizergeschichtlichen Inhaltes. Als Fortsetzung zu
Brandstetters Repertorium für die Jahre 1812-1890 hrsg. von
der Allgemeinen Geschichtforschenden Gesellschaft der
Schweiz und in ihrem Auftrag bearb. von Hans Barth. Basel,
Basler Buch- und Antiquariatshandlung, 1906. vii, 359p.
26cm. "Biographien und Nekrologe" (p. 195-327) give full
names and dates of Swiss, living and dead, and bibliographical
references.

1842   BRANDSTETTER, JOSEF LEOPOLD
Repertorium über die in Zeit- und Sammelschriften der
Jahre 1812-1890 enthaltenen Aufsätze und Mitteilungen
schweizergeschichtlichen Inhaltes. Hrsg. von der Allgemeinen
Geschichtforschenden Gesellschaft der Schweiz und in deren
Auftrag bearb. von Josef Leopold Brandstetter. Basel, A.
Geering, 1892. iv, 467 p. 26cm. "Biographien und Necrologe"
(p. 316-428) give full name and dates of Swiss, living and
dead, and bibliographical references.

General Works

1843   BASEL. UNIVERSITÄT.
Die Matrikel der Universität Basel. Im Auftrage der
Universität Basel hrsg. von Hans Georg Wackernagel. Basel,
Universitätsbibliothek, 1951-   v. 25cm. Contents. --Bd.
1. 1460-1529. --Bd. 2. 1532/33-1600/01. Register of the Uni-
versity of Basel.

1844   BIOGRAPHISCHES LEXIKON VERSTORBENER SCHWEIZER.
In memoriam. Zürich, Schweizersiche Industrie-Biblio-
thek, Departement Lexicon, 1947-   v. ports. 30cm.
Biographical dictionary of deceased Swiss.

1845   DICTIONNAIRE HISTORIQUE & BIOGRAPHIQUE DE LA
SUISSE, publié avec la recommandation de la Société générale suisse d'histoire et sous la direction de Marcel Godet,
Henri Turler, Victor Attinger, avec de nombreux collaborateurs de tous cantons... Neuchatel, 1921-34. 7 v. and
supplement (208 p.) illus. , maps. 28cm. Issued in parts.
Issued also in German under title: Historisch-biographisches
Lexikon der Schweiz. Historical and biographical dictionary
of Switzerland.

1846   GENEVA. CONSEIL D'ÉTAT.
Fragmens biographiques et historiques, extraits des
registres du Conseil d'État de la République de Géneve de
1535 à 1792. Geneve, 1815. 1 v. 8.° Biographical & histori-

cal fragments taken from the registers of the Council of
State, Republic of Geneva, 1535-1792. Compiled by F. T. L.
Grenus-Saladin.

1847   HARTMANN, ALFRED, 1814-1897.
Gallerie berühmter Schweizer der Neuzeit. In Bildern
(100 Tafeln) von Fr. und H. Hasler. Mit biographischem
Text von A. Hartmann. Hrsg. von Friedrich Hasler.
Baden im Aargau, F. Hasler, 1868-71. 2 v. in 1. 100 ports.
35cm. French ed. (Zürich, 1867-88. 2 v.) has title:
Galerie nationale. Les Suisses célèbres des temps modernes.
Portraits and biographical sketches of 100 'contemporary'
Swiss.

1848   HAUSER, KASPAR
Der kleine Zürcher Plutarch; oder, Thesaurus der
lebenden Schriftsteller, Künstler und Musiker des Limmat-
Athens. In unparteiischer, alphabetischer Reihenfolge
zusammengestellt. München, M. Steinebach, 1916. 60p.
8.° Dictionary of living writers, artists and musicians of
Zurich.

1849   HISTORISCH-BIOGRAPHISCHES LEXIKON DER SCHWEIZ.
Hrsg. mit der Empfehlung der Allgemeinen Geschichtforschenden Gesellschaft der Schweiz unter der Leitung von
Heinrich Türler, Marcel Godet, Victor Attinger im Verbindung mit zahlreichen Mitarbeitern aus allen Kantonen.
Neuenburg, Administration des Historisch-Biographischen
Lexikons der Schweiz, 1921-34. 7 v. illus. 28cm. Also
issued in French. Vols. 2-7: Deutsche Ausgabe, besorgt
von H. Tribolet.

1850   -----Supplement nebst systematischen Titlelverzeichniss
der vollstaendigen Publikation. Hrsg. unter der Leitung
von Marcel Godet, H. Tribolet, Leon Montandon im Verbindung mit zahlreichen Mitarbeitern aus allen Kantonen.
Neuenburg, V. Attinger, 1934. viii, 205, xiii p. illus. 28cm.

Historical-biographical dictionary of Switzerland.

1851   HISTORISCHE GESELLSCHAFT DES KANTONS AARGAU,
Aarau.
Jubiläumsgabe zum 150jährigen Bestehen des Kantons.
Aarau, Sauerländer, 1953-58. 2 v. ports.   (Its
Argovia, 65, 68-69) Vol. 2 has title: 150 Jahre Kanton
Aargau.   Contents.--[1] Lebensbilder aus dem Aargau,

1803-1953. -- 2. Biographisches Lexikon des Aargaus, 1803-
1957. Vol. 2 is a biographical dictionary of the Swiss canton
of Aargau.

1852   HISTORISCHER VEREIN DES KANTONS BERN. BIOGRAPH-
IEN-KOMMISSION.
Sammlung bernischer Biographien. Bern, J. Dalp'sche
Buchhandlung (K. Schmid) 1887-1906. 5 v. ports. 24cm.
A collection of biographies about people in the Canton of
Bern, Switzerland.

1853   JEANNERET, FRÉDÉRIC ALEXANDRE, 1834-1862.
Biographie neuchâteloise, par F. A. M. Jeanneret et J. H.
Bonhôte... Locle, E. Courvoisier, 1863. 2v. 24cm.
Biography of Neuchatel, Switzerland.

1854   KELLER, WILLY, biographer.
Schweizer biographisches Archiv. Zürich, Verlag
Internationaler Publikationen, 1952-58. 6v. ports. 25cm.
Swiss biographical archives. Alphabetical from A-Z in each
vol. ; v. 6 contains a cumulated index.

1855   LUTZ, MARKUS, 1772-1835.
Moderne Biographien; oder, Kurze Nachrichten von dem
Leben und Wirken interessanter Männer unserer Zeit, welche
sich als Regenten, Feldherren, Staatsbeamte, Gelehrte, und
Künstler, in der Schweiz ausgezeichnet haben. Lichtensteig,
N. Kappler, 1826. iv, 408 p. 21cm. Biographies of out-
standing Swiss of the period (early 19th century)

1856   LUTZ, MARKUS, 1772-1835.
Nekrolog denkwürdiger Schweizer aus dem achtzehnten
Jahrhundert, nach alphabetischer Ordnung. Für Freunde
vaterländischer Kultur und Geschichte. Aarau, H. R. Sauerländer, 1812. 599 p. 21cm. Necrology of memorable Swiss
of the 18th century, in alphabetical order.

1857   MEISTER, LEONHARD, 1741-1811.
Berühmte Züricher... Basel, 1782. 2 v. 8.º Famous
natives of Zürich.

1858   MEISTER, LEONHARD, 1741-1811.
Helvetiens berühmte Männer. In Bildnissen dargestellt
von Heinrich Pfenninger. Nebst kurzen biographischen Nachrichten von Leonhard Meister. Winterthur [etc.] 1782-93.
3 v. ports. Switzerland's famous men. A later (2d) ed.

edited by J. C. Fasi (Zurich, 1799) in 2 vols. (?) with a vol.
3, fasc. 1 issued in 1833 by J. J. Bernet. French ed. (1782-
85, in 2 v.) has title: Hommes célèbres de la Suisse en portraits. Another French ed. issued in 1792 with title: Portraits
des hommes illustres de la Suisse (?) Text of vols. 1-2 issued also alone as: Helvetische Gallerie grösser Männer und
Taten (1786)

1859   MONTET, ALBERT DE, 1845-
Dictionnaire biographique des Genevois et des Vaudois qui
se sont distingués dans leurs pays ou à l'étranger par leurs
talents, leurs actions, leurs oeuvres littéraires ou artis-
tiques, etc. Lausanne, G. Bridel, 1877-78. 2 v. 22cm.
Biographical dictionary of Geneva and the Canton of Vaud.

1860   NEUE SCHWEIZER BIOGRAPHIE.
Nouvelle biographie Suisse. Nuova biografia svizzera.
Chefredaktion, A. Bruckner. Basel, Buchdr. zum Basler
Berichthaus, 1938. 612 p. ports. 35cm. Biographies of
'contemporary' Swiss in French, German, or Italian.

1861   OLDELLI, GIAN ALFONSO, 1733-1821.
Dizionario storico-ragionato degli uomini illustri del canton
Ticino. Lugano, 1807-11. 2 v. (v. 2: Supplemento) Dic-
tionary of famous men of the Swiss Canton of Ticino.

1862   SCHWEIZERISCHE PORTRAIT-GALLERIE.
Zürich, Art. Institut O. Fussli, 1888-1907. 72 nos. in
6 double vols. Portraits of Swiss contemporaries with very
brief biographies.

1863   SCHWEIZERISCHES ZEITGENOSSEN-LEXIKON.
Lexique suisse des contemporains. Lessico svizzero dei
contemporanei. Begründet und redigiert von Hermann Aellen.
2. Ausg. Bern, Gotthelf-Verlag [1932] 1023p. 20cm. Dictionary of contemporary Swiss.

1864   SECRETAN, EUGÈNE, 1839-1921.
Galerie suisse. Biographies nationale, publiés avec le
concours de plusieurs écrivains suisses. Lausanne, 1873-80.
3 v. 23cm. Swiss gallery; national biography. Vol. 3 has
subtitle: Les contemporains.

1865   SENN-BARBIEUX, WALTER, 1844-1913.
Schweizerische Ehrenhalle. Lebensbilder hochverdienter

Eidgenossen. 1.-4. Serie. St. Gallen, Wirth, 1883. 4 pts. in 3 v. The Swiss hall of fame; lives of the most worthy sons of Switzerland.

1866 STÄHELIN, WILHELM RICHARD
Basler Portraits aller Jahrhunderte. Basel, Frobenius, 1919-21. 3 v. ports. Portraits of Basel's worthies accompanied by biographical notices.

1867 VAUCHER, PIERRE, 1833-1898.
Professeurs, historiens & magistrats suisses. Notices biographiques. Genève, 1886. 116p. 8.° Swiss scholars, historians & judges.

1868 WHO'S WHO IN SWITZERLAND, INCLUDING THE PRINCI-
PALITY OF LIECHTENSTEIN. 1950/51- Zurich, Central European Times Pub. Co. v. 21cm.

1869 WOLF, RUDOLF, 1816-1893.
Biographien zur Kulturgeschichte der Schweiz. Zürich, Orell, Füssli, 1858-62. 4 v. ports. 20cm. Biographies for the history of Swiss civilization.

THAILAND

1870 BANGKOK, THAILAND. THAMMASAT MAHAWITTHAYALAI.
KHANA RATTHAPRASASANASAT.
Khrai pen khrai nai Prathet Thai. [Bangkok, 1963] 2v.
Who's who in Thailand. Author: Institute of Public Administration, Thammasat University, Bangkok.

1871 HSÜ, HSIANG-AN.
T'ai kuo hua ch'iao jen wu chih. Bangkok, 1956. 185p. Biographies of Chinese in Thailand.

1872 PRAMUANWIT, pseud.
100 [i.e. Nyng roi] chaofa lae senabọdi. [Bangkok, 1962] [5], 9, 899p. In Thai. 100 Siamese princes and statesmen.

1873 THAI NỌI, pseud.
50 [i.e. Ha sip] khon samkhan khọng Thai. [Bangkok, 1960-61] 2 v. illus. In Siamese. Sub-titles vary. Important people of Thailand; each vol. contains 50 biographies.

TURKEY

1874 ALĪ IBN BĀLĪ, called MANK.
Tasköprüzâde's "es-Saqâ'iq en-no'mânijje" fortgesetzt von
'Alī Miniq unter dem Titel "El-'iqd el-manzûm fī dikr afâdil
er-Rûm, " enthaltend die Biographien der türkischen Gelehrten, Aerzte und Derwis-Seiḫ's von der Regierung des Sultans
Sulaimân b. Selīm bis zu der von Sultan Murad b. Selim. Mit
Zusätzen, Verbesserungen und Anmerkungen nach dem Rand-
druck Cairo 1310 H. und der Hs. Welf' eddīn 2435 übers.
[von O. Rescher] Stuttgart, 1934. 139p. 4.° Only 45 copies
printed. Biographies of Turkish learned men, physicians
and dervishes, 1520-1595 (ca.)

1875 NEBIOǦLU, OSMAN, ed.
Türkiye'de kim kimdir. Yasiyan tanınmıs kimseler ansiklopedisi. [2. baski] Istanbul, Nebioǧlu Yayınevı, 1961-62.
763 p. 24cm. Turkish who's who.

1876 NEBIOǦLU, OSMAN, ed.
Who's who in Turkey. Washington, U. S. Dept. of Commerce,
Office of Technical Services, Joint Publications Research Ser-
vice, 1963. a, 1067 p. 27cm. Cover title. "JPRS: 20, 490."
Translation of Türkiye'de kim kimdir, 2d print. , 1961-1962.

1877 NEBIOǦLU, OSMAN
100 [i. e. Yüz] meshur Türk. [Istanbul] Nebioǧlu [196-?]
121 p. ports. 17cm. (Nebioǧlu cep kitaplari, 7) 100 famous
Turks. Bio-bibliographical.

1878 ṬĀSHKUBRĪZĀDAH, AHMAD IBN MUṢṬAFA, 1495-1561.
eš-Šaqâ'iq en-no'mânijje, von Tašköprüzâde, enthaltend
die Biographien der türkischen und im Osmanischen Reiche
wirkenden Gelehrten, Derwisch-Scheih's und Ärzte von der
Regierung Sultan 'Oṭmân's bis zu der Sülaimân's des Grossen.
Mit Zusaetzen, Verbesserungen und Anmerkungen aus dem
Arabischen uebers. , von O. Rescher. Konstantinopel-
Galata, Buch- und Steindruckerei Phoenix, 1927. iv, 361p.
29cm. Biographies of Turkish and Osmanli scholars, dervishes and physicians, 1290-ca. 1520.

1879 TÜRKIYE TERACIMI AHVAL ANSIKLOPEDISI.
Encyclopédie biographique de Turquie. Who is who in
Turkey. [v. 1- Stamboul, Hamit Matbaasi. v. illus.,

ports. 25cm. Biographical encyclopedia of Turkey (contemporary) Turkish and French in parallel columns. Vol. 3 covers the years 1930/32.

1880   'USHÂQÎZÂDE, fl. 1702.
'Ušâqîzâde's Lebensbeschreibungen berühmter Gelehrter und Gottesmänner des osmanischen Reiches im 17. Jahrhundert (Zeyl-i Šaqâ'iq) Hrsg. und eingeleitet von Hans Joachim Kissling. Wiesbaden, O. Harrassowitz, 1965. lix, 710 p. 25cm. 527 biographical sketches of famous scholars and 'men of God' of the Ottoman Empire in the years 1623-1695. Introduction in German, text in Turkish (Osmanic)

1881   WHO'S WHO IN TURKEY.
[1st]-   ed.; 1958-   Ankara, Cyclopedic Publications.
v.
    29cm.

UNITED ARAB REPUBLIC
See under ISLAMIC COUNTRIES

UNITED STATES
Bibliography, Indexes, Etc.

1882   AMERICAN ANTIQUARIAN SOCIETY, Worcester, Mass.
Index of obituaries in Massachusetts centinel and Columbian centinel, 1784-1840. Boston, G. K. Hall, 1961. 5v.

1883   AMERICAN ANTIQUARIAN SOCIETY, Worcester, Mass.
Index to obituaries in the Boston transcript, 1875-1930. [Worcester, 1938?]-40. 5v. 27cm.

1884   DARGAN, MARION
Guide to American biography. Foreword by Dumas Malone. Alburquerque, University of New Mexico Press, 1949-52. 2v. 23cm.

1885   FULLER, JUANITA BOYKIN.
An annotated bibliography of biographies and autobiographies of negroes, 1839-1961. Atlanta, 1962. iii, 62 1. 28 cm. Thesis (M.S. in L.S.)--Atlanta University. Micro-opaque of typescript. Rochester, N.Y., University of Rochester Press for the Association of College and Research Libraries, 1964. 1 card. 8 x 13 cm. (ACRL microcard series, no. 143)

1886 HAVERFORD COLLEGE. LIBRARY.
   Quaker necrology. Boston, G. K. Hall, 1961. 2 v. 37cm.
   An index to approximately 59, 000 entries from 4 Quaker
   periodicals.

1887 KAPLAN, LOUIS, 1909-
   A bibliography of American autobiographies, compiled by
   Louis Kaplan in association with James Tyler Cook, Clinton
   E. Colby, Jr. [and] Daniel C. Haskell. Madison, University
   of Wisconsin Press, 1961. xii, 372p. 25cm.

1888 MATTHEWS, WILLIAM, 1905-
   American diaries; an annotated bibliography of American
   diaries written prior to the year 1861. Compiled by William
   Matthews with the assistance of Roy Harvey Pearce. Berke-
   ley, University of California Press, 1945. 383p. 24cm.
   (University of California publications in English, v. 16)

1889 U. S. LIBRARY OF CONGRESS. GENERAL REFERENCE
   AND BIBLIOGRAPHY DIVISION.
   Biographical sources for the United States. Compiled by
   Jane Kline. Washington, 1961. v, 58p. 27cm.

Anonyms and Pseudonyms

1890 CUSHING, WILLIAM, 1811-1895.
   Initials and pseudonyms; a dictionary of literary disguises.
   1st [-2d ser.] New York, Crowell[c1885-88] 2v. 26cm.

1891 CUSHING, WILLIAM, 1811-1895.
   Anonyms; a dictionary of revealed authorship. Cambridge
   [Mass.] 1899. 829 p. 26cm.

1892 GAINES, PIERRE WELCH.
   Political works of concealed authorship in the United States,
   1789-1810, with attributions. Rev. and enl. ed. Hamden,
   Conn. , Shoe String Press, 1965. 190 p. facsims. 22 cm.
   1st published in 1959 under title: Political works of concealed
   authorship during the administrations of Washington, Adams,
   and Jefferson, 1789-1809.

General Works

1893 ALLEN, WILLIAM, 1784-1868.
   The American biographical dictionary: containing an

account of the lives, characters and writings of the most
eminent persons deceased in North America from its first
settlement. 3d ed. Boston, J. P. Jewett, 1857. ix, 905p.
27cm. Originally published under title: An American biographical and historical dictionary (1809)

1894   AMERICAN BIOGRAPHIES;
     A genealogical, historical and biographical cyclopedia, com-
piled by the Editorial Press Bureau, inc. Washington [1950-
v. ports. 28cm.

1895   AMERICAN BIOGRAPHY;
     A new cyclopedia. Compiled under the editorial supervision
of a notable advisory board. New York, Published under the
direction of the American Historical Society, 1916-   v.
illus. 28cm. Binder's title: Encyclopedia of American biography. Vol. 1 compiled under the editorial supervision of W.
R. Cutter...assisted by a board of advisory editors. Each vol.
has an index.

1896   THE AMERICAN CATHOLIC WHO'S WHO.
     1911, 1934/35-   St. Louis, B. Herder. v. 23cm.
Imprint varies: 1934/35-   Detroit, W. Romig.

1897   AMERICAN DIRECTORY & WHO'S WHO IN EUROPE.
     New York, A. A. Knopf. v. illus. 19cm.

1898   AMERICAN JEWISH YEAR BOOK,
     5660-Sept. 5, 1899-   Philadelphia, Jewish Publication
Society of America. v. illus., ports. 19cm. Extensive
biographical information and obituaries are included.

1899   AMERICAN JEWS:
     Their lives and achievements; a contemporary biographical
record. 195-   New York, American Jewish Literary Foundation. v. illus. 29cm. Vol. 2 issued in 1958.

1900   THE AMERICAN LABOR WHO'S WHO.
     1925-   New York, Hanford Press. v. No more
published? 1925 vol. only one published? Chiefly American,
but also includes labor leaders of other countries.

1901   AMERICAN MEN IN GOVERNMENT;
     A biographical dictionary and directory of Federal officials.
Edited by Jerome M. Rosow. Lillie Levine and Virginia Mil-

ler, associate editors. [Washington] Public Affairs Press
[1949] xxiii, 472 p. illus. 25cm. 1570 executives in the
Federal service.

1902   AMERICAN PLANNING AND CIVIC ANNUAL;
        A record of recent civic advance. [v. 1]-   ; 1929-
        Washington, American Planning and Civic Association.   v.
        illus. 21cm. Title & subtitle vary. Includes a "Who's who in
        civic achievement" at end of each volume.

1903   AMERICAN UNIVERSITY CLUB OF SHANGHAI.
        American university men in China. Shanghai, Comacrib
        Press, 1936. xii, 233p. plates. 21cm.

1904   AMERICAN WOMEN;
        The official who's who among the women of the nation.
        [v. 1-   1935/36-   Los Angeles, American Publications,
        inc. v. 23cm. biennial. Subtitle varies.

1905   AMERICA'S YOUNG MEN,
        The official who's who among the young men of the nation.
        Edited by Durward Howes. v. 1, 1934-v. 3, 1938/39.
        Los Angeles, American Publications, 1934-38.   3 v.

1906   AMERIKOS LIETUVIU VARDYNAS;
        Jungtinių Amerikos Valstybiu žinomesniu lietuviu biografinės
        žinios. Su K. Pakšto ivadu.   Los Angeles [Lietuvių dienos]
        1953-   v. 24cm.   Vol. 1 (279 p. ; no more pub-
        lished?) contains biographical sketches of about 7000 Lithuani-
        ans living in the U. S.

1907   AMHERST COLLEGE.
        Amherst College biographical record, 1963; biographical
        record of the graduates and non-graduates of the classes of
        1822-1962 inclusive. Amherst, Mass. , Trustees of Amherst
        College, 1963. lxii, 210, 899p. 27cm.

1908   APPLETON'S CYCLOPAEDIA OF AMERICAN BIOGRAPHY.
        Edited by James Grant Wilson and John Fiske. New York,
        D. Appleton, 1887-1900. 7 v. illus. 28cm. Various editions
        have appeared (e. g. , a 6 vol. ed. in 1886-89)

1909   BAIRD, WILLIAM RAIMOND, 1858-1917.
        Betas of achievement; being brief biographical records of

the Beta Theta Pi who have achieved distinction in various
fields of endeavor. Authorized by the Convention of 1913.
New York, Beta Pub. Co. , 1914. 372p. ports. 22cm.

1910   BIOGRAPHIA;
Annuaire pour l'Amérique du Nord des personnalités de
langue francaise et des personnalités américaines ayant des
relations avec la France. Biographia; yearly directory for
North America of French-speaking, Franco-American and
American personalities having relations with France and
other French-speaking countries. 1. éd. -   1929/30-
New York, French Press Bureau.   v. illus. 22cm. Editor: 1929/30-   Georges Bigot.

1911   THE BIOGRAPHICAL CYCLOPAEDIA OF AMERICAN WOMEN.
Vols. 1-2. New York, Halvord Pub. Co. , 1924-25. 2 v.
28cm. No more published?

1912   BIOGRAPHICAL DIRECTORY OF SCHOLARS, ARTISTS,
AND PROFESSIONALS OF CROATIAN DESCENT IN THE
UNITED STATES AND CANADA.
1963-   Chicago.   v. 28cm. Editor: F. H. Eterovich.

1913   BIOGRAPHICAL ENCYCLOPEDIA OF AMERICA.
v. 1-   ; [1940-   New York, Biographical Encyclopedia
of America, inc.   v. ports. 26cm.

1914   THE BIOGRAPHICAL ENCYCLOPEDIA OF THE UNITED
STATES. Chicago, American Biographical Pub. Co. , 1901.
iv, 699 p. ports. 30cm.

1915   A BIOGRAPHICAL RECORD OF AMERICANS OF JAPANESE
ANCESTRY. 1963. [Editor: Blanche L. Kort. Coordinator:
Mitsu Yamato] Honolulu [Stowe & Associates] 1963.   106 p.
illus.

1916   BLAKENEY, JANE, 1898-
Heroes, U. S. Marine Corps, 1861-1955; Armed Forces
awards, flags. Reference book. [1st ed. Washington ? 1957]
xviii, 621 p. illus. , ports. 27cm.

1917   BOATNER, MARK MAYO, 1921-
The Civil War dictionary. Maps and diagrs. by Allen C.
Northrop and Lowell I. Miller. New York, McKay [1959]
947 p. Biographical entries predominate.

1918   BOLTON, CHARLES KNOWLES, 1867-
        The founders; portraits of persons born abroad who came to
        the colonies in North America before the year 1701. With an
        introd. , biographical outlines and commentaries on the
        portraits. [Boston] Boston Athenaeum, 1919-26. 3 v. ports.
        23 cm. (Publications of the Robert Charles Billings Fund,
        issued by the Trustees of the Boston Athenaeum, 6)

1919   BROWN UNIVERSITY.
        Historical catalogue of Brown University. 1764/1894,
        1764/1904, 1924, 1764/1934, 1950-   eds. Providence, 1895-
        19   v. 24-25 cm.

1920   CONCISE DICTIONARY OF AMERICAN BIOGRAPHY.
        Edited by J. E. G. Hopkins. New York, Scribner, 1964.
        1273 p. Includes every article that is in the major work, but
        greatly abbreviated. No people who died later than 1940.

1921   CONGRESSIONAL STAFF DIRECTORY.
        1959-   Indianapolis, Bobbs-Merrill   v.
        24cm. Includes biographical data.

1922   CONTEMPORARY AMERICAN BIOGRAPHY.
        Biographical sketches of representatives of modern thought
        and progress, of the pulpit, the press, the bench and the bar,
        of legislation, invention, and the great industrial interests of
        the country. v. 1-   ; 1895-   New York, Atlantic Pub.
        and Engraving Co.   v. ports.

1923   CROSBY, NATHAN, 1798-1885.
        Annual obituary notices of eminent persons who have died
        in the United States. For 1857 [-1858]   Boston, Phillips,
        Sampson, 1858-59. 2v. ports. 23cm. Compiled largely
        from newspapers.

1924   CULLUM, GEORGE WASHINGTON, 1809-1892.
        Biographical register of the officers and graduates of the
        U. S. Military Academy at West Point, N. Y. , from its es-
        tablishment, in 1802, to 1890; with the early history of the
        United States Military Academy.   3d ed. , rev. and extended.
        Boston, Houghton, Mifflin, 1891. 3v. 25cm.

1925   --- ----Supplement. v. 4-   1890/1900-   [West Point?]
        v. in   25cm. decennial.

1926   THE CYCLOPAEDIA OF AMERICAN BIOGRAPHIES.
        Comprising the men and women of the United States who
        have been identified with the growth of the nation. Edited by
        John Howard Brown. Boston, Cyclopaedia Pub. Co., 1897-
        1903. 7 v. illus. 28cm. Vol. 2-4 published by J. H.
        Lamb Co.; v. 5-7 by Federal Book Co. of Boston. Published
        1900-03 in 7 v. under title: Lamb's biographical dictionary of
        the United States, and in 1904 in 10 v. under title: The Twenti-
        eth century biographical dictionary of notable Americans.

1927   THE CYCLOPAEDIA OF AMERICAN BIOGRAPHY.
        New enl. ed. of Appleton's cyclopaedia of American biogra-
        phy, originally edited by James Grant Wilson and John Fiske;
        revision to 1914 completed under editorial supervision of
        Charles Dick and James E. Homans. New York, Press As-
        sociation Compilers, 1915-31. 12 v. illus. 27cm. No more
        published?

1928   DANNETT, SYLVIA G   L   1909-
        Profiles of Negro womanhood. Illus.: Horace Varela.
        Roll of honor ports.: Tom Feelings. [1st ed.]   Yonkers,
        N. Y., Educational Heritage [1964-   v. illus. 29cm.
        (Negro heritage library)   Contents. --v.1. 1619-1900.

1929   DEXTER, FRANKLIN BOWDITCH, 1842-1920.
        Biographical notices of graduates of Yale College, includ-
        ing those graduated in classes later than 1815, who are not
        commemorated in the annual obituary records. Issued as a
        supplement to the Obituary record. New Haven, 1913. 411 p.
        Covers the years 1815-1884. Kept up-to-date by the Yale Uni-
        versity Obituary record of graduates.

1930   DEXTER, FRANKLIN BOWDITCH, 1842-1920.
        Biographical sketches of the graduates of Yale College,
        with annals of the college history. New York, H. Holt, 1885-
        1912. 6v. 27cm. Covers up to and including 1815. Vol. 6
        has imprint: New Haven, Yale University Press.

1931   DICTIONARY OF AMERICAN BIOGRAPHY.
        Under the auspices of the American Council of Learned
        Societies. New York, C. Scribner, 1928-   v. 26cm.

1932   DIRECTORY OF ITALIAN-AMERICANS IN COMMERCE AND
        PROFESSIONS. Guida italo-americana. [1st-   1937-
        Chicago, Continental Press.   v. illus., ports. 24cm.
        Editor: 1937-   G. F. Arena.

1933   DISTINGUISHED SUCCESSFUL AMERICANS OF OUR DAY;
Containing biographies of prominent Americans now living,
noteworthy as having achieved success in their chosen avoca-
tions... Edited from standard biographical works and original
sources. Chicago, Successful Americans, 1912. 640 p.
23cm.

1934   DRAKE, FRANCIS SAMUEL, 1828-1885.
Dictionary of American biography, including men of the
time; containing nearly ten thousand notices of persons...who
have been remarkable, or prominently connected with the
arts, sciences, literature, politics, or history, of the American continent. Boston, Houghton, Osgood, 1879. x,1019 p.
26cm.

1935   DRAKE, SAMUEL GARDNER, 1798-1875.
Biography and history of the Indians of North America,
from its first discovery...11th ed. Boston, B. B. Mussey,
1851. 720 p. plates, ports. 22cm. 1st ed. (1832) published
under title: Indian biography.

1936   DU PRE, FLINT O
U. S. Air Force biographical dictionary. New York, F.
Watts [1965] x,273 p. 25cm.

1937   EISENSTADT, BENZION, 1873-1951.
Anshe ha-shem... [St. Louis, 1933-   v. 24cm.
Cover title: Anshei hasheim b'arzeis habris. Encyclopedia
containing biographical sketches of all the rabbis, scholars,
writers, authors and other eminent figures in American
Jewry.

1938   ELLET, ELIZABETH FRIES (LUMMIS) 1818-1877.
The women of the American Revolution. With an introd. by
Anne Hollingsworth Wharton. Philadelphia, G. W. Jacobs
[1900] 2 v. ports. 20 cm. An earlier ed. (New York, Baker
& Scribner, 1848-50) was issued in 3 v. Biographies of ca.
140 women.

1939   EMINENT AMERICANS.
1936-   [1st]-   Palo Alto, Calif [etc.] C. W. Taylor.
v. ports. 28-31cm. E. g., 1957 (4th) ed. contains ca.
400 biographies.

1940   ENCYCLOPEDIA OF AMERICAN BIOGRAPHY.
New series. Under the editorial direction of Winfield

Scott Downs in association with a notable advisory board.
New York, American Historical Society, 1934-   v. illus.,
ports. 28cm.

1941   [FRENCH, BENJAMIN FRANKLIN] 1799-1877.
Biographia Americana; or, A historical and critical account
of the lives, actions, and writings of the most distinguished
persons in North America; from the first settlement to the
present time. By a gentleman of Philadelphia. New York,
D. Mallory, 1825. vii, 356 p. port. 23 cm. 181 sketches in
alphabetical arrangement.

1942   GENERALS OF THE ARMY AND THE AIR FORCE AND AD-
MIRALS OF THE NAVY. v. 1-   Feb. 1953-   [Wash-
ington]   v. in   ports. 28cm. monthly. Title varies:
Feb. 1953-Jan. 1954, Generals of the Army. --Feb. 1954-Jan.
1955, Generals of the Army and the Air Force. Editor: 1933-
55, T. M. Dunleavy. Jan. 1956 the last issue?

1943   GRISWOLD, RUFUS WILMOT, 1815-1857.
The biographical annual: containing memoirs of eminent
persons, recently deceased. New York, Linen and Fennell,
1841. 307 p. ports. 19cm. Confined to the United States
of America.

1944   HALL, HENRY, 1845-
America's successful men of affairs. An encyclopedia of
contemporaneous biography. New York, New York Tribune,
1895-96. 2 v. ports. 27cm. Contents. --v.1. The City of
New York. --v.2. The United States at large.

1945   HAMERSLY, LEWIS RANDOLPH, 1847-1910.
The records of living officers of the U.S. Navy and Marine
Corps. 7th ed., rev., with numerous additions. New York,
L.R. Hamersby Co., 1902. 511 p. ports. 27cm.

1946   HARRISON, MITCHELL CHARLES, 1870-
Prominent and progressive Americans; an encyclopaedia
of contemporaneous biography. [New York] New York tribune,
1902-   v. ports. 29cm.

1947   HEITMAN, FRANCES BERNARD, 1838-1926.
Historical register and dictionary of the United States
Army from its organization, Sept. 29, 1789, to March 2,
1903. Published under act of Congress approved March 2,

1903. Washington, Govt. Print. Off., 1903. 2 v. 27cm.
([U.S.] 57th Congress, 2d sess. House doc. no. 446)
Reprinted in 1965 by the University of Illinois   Press.

1948   HEITMAN, FRANCIS BERNARD, 1838-1926.
Historical register of officers of the Continental Army
during the War of the Revolution, April, 1775, to December,
1783. New, rev., and enl. ed. Washington, Rare Book Shop
Pub. Co., 1914. 685p. 26cm.

1949   HERRING, JAMES, 1794-1867, ed.
The national portrait gallery of distinguished Americans;
with biographical sketches by celebrated authors. Philadelphia, Rice, Rutter [c1868] 3 v. ports. 28cm. Several
sketches found in the 1st ed. (edited by Herring and J. B.
Longacre, 1834-39, 4 v.) are replaced in the present ed. by
biographies of Civil War commanders, etc.

1950   HERRINGSHAW, THOMAS WILLIAM, 1858-   ed.
Herringshaw's encyclopedia of American biography of
the nineteenth century. Accurate and succinct biographies
of famous men and women of the United States. Edited and
compiled under the supervision of Thomas William Herringshaw assisted by a corps of well known writers. Chicago,
American Publishers' Association, 1907. cxx, 1046p.
ports. 32cm. 1st published 1898.

1951   HERRINGSHAW, THOMAS WILLIAM, 1858-
Herringshaw's National library of American biography;
contains thirty-five thousand biographies of the acknowledged
leaders of life and thought of the United States... Edited and
compiled under the supervision of Thomas William Herringshaw assisted by a staff of distinguished biographers.
Chicago, American Publishers' Association, 1904-14. 5 v.
ports. 25cm.

1952   HERRINGSHAW'S AMERICAN BLUE BOOK OF BIOGRAPHY;
Prominent Americans of 1912- who have achieved success in the various civil, industrial and commercial lines of
activity. Chicago, American Publishers' Association,
1913-   v. 22-24cm. Title varies: 1912, The American
blue book of biography; men of 1912.   1913: Builders of our
nation... Men of 1913.   1914-   Herringshaw's American
blue book of biography.   Imprint varies.

1953   HOUGH, FRANKLIN BENJAMIN, 1822-1885.
American biographical notes, being short notices of
deceased persons, chiefly those not included in Allen's or in
Drake's biographical dictionaries, gathered from many
sources. Albany, J. Munsell, 1875. iv, 442p. 24cm.
Edition of 130 copies.

1954   ILLUSTRATED AMERICAN BIOGRAPHY.
Containing memoirs, and engravings and etchings of
representative Americans. Issued under the direction of
D. I. Nelke. Chicago, Lewis Pub. Co. [1895-1900] 12pts.
in 4v. illus., ports. 40x30cm.

1955   ITALIAN-AMERICAN WHO'S WHO.
A biographical dictionary of Italian American leaders and
distinguished Italian residents of the United States. v.1-   ;
1935-   New York, Vigo Press. v. 24cm. 1935-
edited by Giovanni Schiavo.

1956   JACKSON (F. E.) & SON.
The makers of the Panama Canal, 1911. Thos. Marine,
photo artist. [New York, c1911] 410p. illus., ports.
24x32cm. Cover title: The makers of the Panama Canal and
representative men of the Panama Republic. 579 biographies
of Americans in Panama and 77 biographies of prominent
Panamanians.

1957   JAMESON, JOHN FRANKLIN, 1859-1937.
Dictionary of United States history: alphabetical,
chronological, statistical, from the earliest explorations
to the present time; based upon the original work prepared
in 1893 by J. Franklin Jameson. Rev. ed. , edited under the
supervision of Albert E. McKinley, 1931. xi, 874p. maps.
24cm. Substantially biographical.

1958   JAMESON, JOHN FRANKLIN, 1859-1937.
Encyclopedic dictionary... Editorial board: Marcus J.
Wright, J. Franklin Jameson [and] J. W. Buel. Limited ed.
Washington, National University Society [1904] 3v. plates,
ports. 23cm. (Analytical reference, v. 1-3) Vols. 1-2 are
an abridged edition of the Dictionary of United States
history, 1st published in 1894; this abridgment appeared in its
present form, in 1900, under the title: Encyclopedic
dictionary of American history, by. J. F. Jameson and J. W.
Buel; also, in the same year, as part of the Library of

American history. Vol. 3 is a supplement to the Encyclopedic dictionary of American history, containing the matter omitted from the 1894 ed., with large additions, chiefly biographical.

1959   JONES, ABNER DUMONT, 1807-1852.
        The American portrait gallery, containing correct portraits and brief notices of the principal actors in American history. From Christopher Columbus down to the present time. The portraits, engraved on wood by J. W. Orr, from original drawings by S. Waller. New York, J. M. Emerson, 1855. iv, 768p. ports. 24cm. 1st issued in 1853 under title: The illustrated American biography.

1960   KAPPA ALPHA.
        Kappa alpha record, 1825-1940; being a record of the members and activities of the Kappa alpha Society. Compiled and published by the Executive Council. [New York] 1941. 568p. illus. 24cm.

1961   KINGSTON, JOHN
        The new American biographic dictionary; or, Memoirs of many of the most eminent persons that have ever lived in this or any other nation. Baltimore, Printed for J. Kingston, and sold at his book and stationary [sic] store, 1810. 303 p. port. 14cm. A 2d ed. (308 p.) was issued in 1811 under title: The new pocket biographical dictionary.

1962   LAMB'S BIOGRAPHICAL DICTIONARY OF THE UNITED STATES. Edited by John Howard Brown. Boston, J. H. Lamb, 1900-03. 7 v. illus. 28cm. Vols. 5-7 have imprint: Boston, Federal Book Co. of Boston. Published 1897-1907 in 7 v. under title: The Cyclopaedia of American biographies; and in 1904 in 10 v. under title: The Twentieth century biographical dictionary of notable Americans.

1963   LANMAN, CHARLES, 1819-1895.
        Biographical annals of the civil government of the United States. From original and official sources. 2d ed., rev., enl. and completed to date, by Joseph M. Morrison. New York, J. M. Morrison, 1887. iv, 568, cviii p. plates, ports. 27cm.

1964   LANMAN, CHARLES, 1819-1895.
        Dictionary of the United States Congress, and the general government. Compiled as a book of reference for the Ameri-

can people. 6th ed. , including the forty-first Congress.
Hartford, T. Belknap and H. E. Goodwin, 1869. 652p. 25cm.
Chiefly a biographical dictionary. 1st published in 1859.

1965 LEVERE, WILLIAM COLLIN, 1872-1927, comp.
Who's who in S. A. E. ; a biographical dictionary of notable
living members of the fraternity. Evanston, Ill. [Evanston
Index Co.] 1912. 291p. 20cm. Who's who in Sigma Alpha
Epsilon fraternity.

1966 LIVINGSTON, JOHN.
Portraits of eminent Americans now living; with biographi-
cal and historical memoirs of their lives and actions. New
York, Cornish, Lamport, 1853-54. 4 v. ports. 23cm.
Originally issued in parts, with cover title: American portrait
gallery, containing portraits of men now living.

1967 MADIGAN, THOMAS F
A biographical index of American public men, classified
and alphabetically arranged; a useful hand-book and check
list for autograph collectors, librarians, etc. New York,
1916. 246 p. 25cm.

1968 MARTIN, MICHAEL, 1917-
Dictionary of American history, with the complete text of
the Constitution of the United States, by Michael Martin and
Leonard Gelber. New student ed. , edited by A. W. Littlefield.
Ames, Iowa, Littlefield, Adams, 1956. vi, 714 p. 21cm.
(Littlefield college outlines) "Originally published as The
new dictionary of American history ... 1952." Includes bio-
graphical sketches.

1969 MEN AND WOMEN OF AMERICA;
A biographical dictionary of contemporaries. New York,
L. R. Hamersly, 1910. 1592p. ports. 22cm. 2d ed. of
'Men of America' (New York, Hamersly, 1908)

1970 MEN OF AMERICA;
A biographical dictionary of contemporaries. Edited by
John W. Leonard. New York, L. R. Hamersly, 1908. 2188p.
22cm. 2d ed. published in 1910 under title: Men and women of
America (q. v.)

1971 MEN OF YALE SERIES.
v. 1- [New Haven?] Yale University, 1962-   v.
illus. 24cm.

1972   MILITARY ORDER OF THE LOYAL LEGION OF THE UNITED
       STATES. ILLINOIS COMMANDERY.
       Memorials of deceased companions of the Commandery of
       the State of Illinois, Military Order of the Loyal Legion of
       the United States. Chicago, 1901-12. 2 v. ports. 24cm.
       Necrology of U. S. Civil War veterans.

1973   MOORE, FRANK, 1828-1904, ed.
       The portrait gallery of the war, civil, military, and naval;
       a biographical record. New York, G. P. Putnam for Derby &
       Miller, 1864. iv, 353p. ports. 26cm. The American Civil
       War in portraits and biographical sketches.

1974   MOORE, FRANK, 1828-1904.
       Women of the war; their heroism and self- sacrifice. Hart-
       ford, Conn. , S. S. Scranton, 1868. 596p. 2 plates, 8 ports.
       23cm.

1975   MORRIS, CHARLES, 1833-1922, ed.
       Men of the century; an historical work giving portraits and
       sketches of eminent citizens of the United States. Philadel-
       phia, L. R. Hamersly, 1896. 326p. ports. 32 x 25cm.

1976   MORRIS, RICHARD BRANDON, 1904-   ed.
       Four hundred notable Americans. Henry Steele Commager,
       chief consultant editor. [1st perennial library ed. , rev. and
       with a new introd.] New York, Harper & Row [1965] 279p.
       19cm. (Perennial library, P 19) "Originally published as the
       biographical section of the Encyclopedia of American history,
       revised and enlarged edition. . . 1961. "

1977   MOTT, ABIGAIL (FIELD) 1766-1851.
       Biographical sketches and interesting anecdotes of persons
       of color. To which is added a selection of pieces in poetry.
       New York, Printed by order of the Trustees of the Residuary
       Estate of Lindley Murray [1839] 408p. 19cm. First published
       in 1826 (192p.)

1978   MOUNT HOLYOKE COLLEGE. ALUMNAE ASSOCIATION.
       One hundred year biographical directory, 1837-1937. South
       Hadley, Mass. , 1937. 713p. 24cm. (Mount Holyoke College.
       Bulletin ser. 30, no. 5)

1979   THE NATIONAL CYCLOPAEDIA OF AMERICAN BIOGRAPHY,
       Being the history of the United States as illustrated in the
       lives of the founders, builders, and defenders of the Republic,

288

and of the men and women who are doing the work and molding the thought of the present time, edited by distinguished biographers, selected from each state, revised and approved by the most eminent historians, scholars, and statesmen of the day ... New York, J. T. White, 1893-19   v. illus., ports. 28cm.

1980 --- ----Current volume A-   New York, J. T. White, 1926- v. illus., ports. 28cm. Loose-leaf.

1981 --- ----A conspectus of American biography, being an analytical summary of American history and biography, containing also the complete indexes of the National cyclopaedia of American biography [v. 1-13]; compiled by George Derby. New York, J. T. White, 1906. 752 p. 28cm.

1982 --- ----White's conspectus of American biography, a tabulated record of American history and biography. 2d ed. A rev. and enl. ed. of A conspectus of American biography. Compiled by the editorial staff of the National cyclopaedia of American biography. New York, J. T. White, 1937. viii, 455 p. 28cm.

1983 --- ----Indexes. Personal and topical indexes to ... the National cyclopaedia of American biography, including the first and revised editions ... New York, J. T. White, 1935. lv. (loose-leaf) 28cm.

1984 --- ----Indexes. Personal and topical indexes to ... the National cyclopaedia of American biography, including the first and revised editions... [3d rev. ed.] New York, J. T. White, 1945-   pts. in v. (loose-leaf) 27cm.

1985 --- ----Indexes. 4th ed. New York, J. T. White, 1959. 3 pts. in 1 v. (loose-leaf) 27cm.

1986 THE NATIONAL CYCLOPEDIA OF THE COLORED RACE. Editor-in-chief: Clement Richardson. Montgomery, Ala., National Pub. Co., 1919-   v. illus., ports. 31cm.

1987 THE NATIONAL REGISTER; Pertinent facts about colored Americans. 1st-   ed.; 1952-   Louisville, Ky., Register Publications.   v. 27cm.

1988 NEGRO YEAR BOOK; An annual encyclopedia of the Negro. 1912-   Tuskegee Institute, Ala., Negro Year Book Pub. Co.   v. illus. 20-

24cm. No editions were published for 1920/21, 1923/24, 1927/28-1929/30. Title varies slightly. Includes biographies of prominent American negroes.

1989   THE NEW TWENTIETH CENTURY CYCLOPAEDIA AND
        DICTIONARY; biography, history, art, science, dictionary
and gazetteer of the world. Edited by A. R. Spofford [and
others. Grand siècle ed.] Chicago, E. R. Du Mont, 1903.
12 v. illus. 23cm. Partial contents. --v. 9-10. Dictionary
of prominent living Americans.

1990   NICANOR, PRECIOSO M
        Profiles of notable Filipinos in the U.S.A. ... Introd. by
Melquiades Gamboa. Foreword by Mauro Baradi. [1st ed.]
New York, Pre-Mer Pub. Co. [c1963-   v. ports, map.
24cm.

1991   OFFICERS OF THE ARMY AND NAVY (REGULAR AND VOLUN-
        TEER) WHO SERVED IN THE CIVIL WAR. Philadelphia,
L. R. Hamersly, 1894. 172 numb. 1., 173-177 p. incl. 838
ports. 32cm.

1993   OUTSTANDING YOUNG MEN OF AMERICA.
        1965-   Montgomery, Ala., Junior Chamber of Com-
merce. v. ports. 27cm. annual.

1994   A PORTRAIT GALLERY, WITH BIOGRAPHICAL SKETCHES
        OF PROMINENT FREEMASONS THROUGHOUT THE
UNITED STATES. [Large paper ed.] New York City, J. C.
Yorston [c1892] 202p. ports. 35cm.

1995   THE PORTRAIT MONTHLY:
        Containing sketches of departed heroes and prominent per-
sonages of the present time, interesting stories, etc. [v. 1-
2; July, 1863-Dec., 1864] New York, T. B. Leggett. 2 v.
in 1. port. 30cm. Americans prominent during the Civil
War.

1996   POWELL, WILLIAM HENRY, 1838-1901.
        List of officers of the Army of the United States from 1779-
        1900, embracing a register of all appointments in the volun-
        teer service during the Civil War and of volunteer officers in
        the service of the United States, June 1, 1900. Compiled from
        the official records. New York, L. R. Hamersly, 1900.
        863p. 24cm.

1997   POWELL, WILLIAM HENRY, 1838-1901.
        Officers of the Army and Navy (regular) who served in
        the Civil War. Edited by William H. Powell and Edward
        Shippin. Philadelphia, Hamersly, 1892. 487p. ports. 32 x
        26cm.

1998   POWELL, WILLIAM HENRY, 1838-1901.
        Officers of the Army and Navy (volunteer) who served in
        the Civil War. Philadelphia, Hamersly, 1893. 419p. ports.
        32cm.

1999   POWELL, WILLIAM HENRY, 1838-1901.
        Records of living officers of the United States Army.
        Philadelphia, L. R. Hamersly, 1890. 689p. 24cm.

2000   PRESTON, WHEELER.
        American biographies. New York, Harper, 1940. viii,
        1147p. 24cm. Concise biographies of 5257 deceased Ameri-
        cans.

2001   PRINCIPAL WOMEN OF AMERICA;
        Being the biographies of American women who stand pre-
        eminent in their country. v. 1-   ; 1930/31-   v. 25cm.
        biennial.

2002   PROMINENT JEWS OF AMERICA;
        A collection of biographical sketches of Jews who have
        distinguished themselves in commercial, professional, and
        religious endeavor. Toledo, Ohio, B. Goodkind, publication
        manager, Hebrew Pub. Co. [c1918] 335, [5] p. ports. 28cm.
        Published also under title: Eminent Jews of America, and as
        vol. 2 of Distinguished Jews of America, edited by J. Pfeffer.

2003   ROGERS, AUGUSTUS C   ed.
        Sketches of representative men, North and South. New
        York, Atlantic Pub. Co., 1872. 612p. ports. 29cm. Ameri-
        can (U. S. A.) biography.

2004   ROGERS, AUGUSTUS C   ed.
United States diplomatic and consular service. Our representatives abroad: biographical sketches of embassadors [sic] ministers, consuls-generals and consuls of the United States in foreign countries; including also a few representative Americans residing abroad in unofficial capacities, and a catalogue of diplomatic, consular, and other officers now in service. New York, Atlantic Pub. Co. , 1874. 469p. 40 ports. 30cm.

2005   ROGERS, THOMAS J   1781-1832.
A new American biographical dictionary; or, Remembrancer of the departed heroes, sages and statesmen of America. Confined exclusively to those who have signalized themselves in either capacity, in the Revolutionary War which obtained the independence of their country. 4th ed. , with important alterations and additions. Philadelphia, S. F. Bradford, 1829. 400p. 18cm. The 3d ed. (Easton, Pa. , 1824) had: 504p. 23cm.

2006   ROSENBLOOM, JOSEPH R
A biographical dictionary of early American Jews, colonial times through 1800. [Lexington] University of Kentucky Press [1960] xii, 175p. 25cm.

2007   SABINE, LORENZO, 1803-1877.
Biographical sketches of Loyalists of the American Revolution, with an historical essay. Boston, Little, Brown, 1864. 2 v. 22cm. A new and enlarged ed. of The American Loyalists.

2008   SCHIAVO, GIOVANNI ERMENEGILDO, 1898-
Italian-American history. New York, Vigo Press, 1947-49. 2 v. ports. 25cm. Partial contents. --v. 1. book 1. Italian music and musicians in America. book. 2. Dictionary of musical biography. book 3. Public officials.

2009   SCHUON, KARL
U. S. Marine Corps biographical dictionary; the Corps' fighting men, what they did, where they served. New York, F. Watts, 1963. vii, 278 p. col. illus. , ports. 25cm.

2010   SCHUON, KARL.
U. S. Navy biographical dictionary. New York, F. Watts [1965, c1964] 277 p. 24cm.

2011   SIBLEY'S HARVARD GRADUATES;
Biographical sketches of those who attended Harvard College... with bibliographical and other notes. v. 1-   1642-58—1721-   Boston, Massachusetts Historical Society, 1873-1942—   6+ v.   illus., ports.   26cm.   Title varies: v. 1-3, Biographical sketches of graduates of Harvard University, in Cambridge, Massachusetts.   Vols. 1-3 by J. L. Sibley; v. 4- by C. K. Shipton.   Imprint varies: v. 1-3, Cambridge, Mass., C. W. Sever; v. 4, Cambridge, Harvard University Press.

2012   SIMMONS, HENRY EUGENE, 1929-
A concise encyclopedia of the Civil War.   New York, A. S. Barnes [1965]   221 p.   22cm.   Includes biographical sketches.

2013   SHOEMAKER, FLOYD CALVIN, 1886-
Missouri and Missourians; land of contrasts and people of achievements.   Chicago, Lewis Pub. Co., 1943.   5 v.   illus., ports.   27cm.   Vols. 3-5, with subtitle "Missouri biography," were written by a special staff of writers.

2014   SIMMONS, WILLIAM J   1849-
Men of mark: eminent, progressive and rising.   With an introductory sketch of the author by Henry M. Turner. Cleveland, G. M. Rewell, 1887.   1138 p.   ports.   24cm. Another issue published in 1891 by Rowell Pub. Co., Cleveland (736 p.   ports.   23cm.)   Biographies of prominent American negroes.

2015   SKETCHES OF MEN OF MARK:
Written by the best talent of the East.   Published by subscription.   New York, New York and Hartford Pub. Co. [1871]   847 p.   ports.   29 x 24cm.   Biographies of Americans.

2016   SKETCHES OF MEN OF PROGRESS.
By James Parton [and others]   Embellished with steel ports. by Ritchie, Perine, and Hall.   [New York] New York and Hartford Pub. Co., 1870-71.   736 p.   50 ports.   29cm.   The larger number of the sketches deal with inhabitants of New York State.

2017   THE SUCCESSFUL AMERICAN.
A magazine devoted to the achievements of and containing biographical and character sketches of representative "successful Americans."   v. 1-   Jan. 1900-   New York,

Press Biographical Co.   v. illus., ports. 28cm. Monthly, Jan. 1900-Apr. 1904; quarterly, July, 1904-

2018   SWISS-AMERICAN HISTORICAL SOCIETY.
Prominent Americans of Swiss origin; a compilation. New
York, J. T. White, 1932-   v. ports. 23cm.

2019   SZY, TIBOR, 1908-   ed.
Hungarians in America; a biographical directory of pro-
fessionals of Hungarian origin in the Americas. New York,
Hungarian University Association, 1963. viii, 606p. 17cm.

2020   THATCHER, BENJAMIN BUSSEY, 1809-1840.
Indian biography; or, An historical account of those individuals who have been distinguished among the North American natives as orators, warriors, statesmen, and other remarkable characters. New York, Harper, 1848. 2 v. 16cm.

2021   THE TWENTIETH CENTURY BIOGRAPHICAL DICTIONARY
OF NOTABLE AMERICANS. Editor-in-chief: Rossiter
Johnson. Managing editor: John Howard Brown. Boston,
Biographical Society, 1904. 10 v. illus., ports. 28cm.
Published in 1900-1903 under title: Lamb's biographical dic-
tionary of the United States (7 v.) and in 1897-1903 under ti-
tle: The cyclopaedia of American biographies (7 v.), both
edited by John Howard Brown.

2022   TWENTIETH CENTURY SUCCESSFUL AMERICANS, LOCAL
AND NATIONAL. United Press Service library. Living
men of America who have attained some prominence in social, industrial, commercial, financial and public affairs.
Compiled from standard biographical publications and original sources. 1st-   ser. [n. p.] Published under the auspices of the United Press Service Bureau [1917?-

2023   U. S. ADJUTANT-GENERAL'S OFFICE.
Official Army register. 1802-   Washington [etc.]
v. 16-24cm. Title varies: Aug. 1913, Register
of the Army of the United States. --Dec. 1813-Jan. 1815, The
Army register of the United States. --May 1815-1817, Army
register. --1948, Official Army and Air Force register. Furnishes data for soldier's place & date of birth, place from
which appointed, education, grade & date of rank, resigna-
tion or discharge from service, etc., & promotion list number.

2024   U. S. AIR FORCE.
Air Force register. 1949-   Washington.   v. 27cm.
annual. The register for 1948 was combined with the Official Army register under title: Official Army and Air Force
register. Contains promotion list number, permanent grade
& date obtained, promotion list service date, date of birth,
temporary grade & date, education, & specialty.

2025   U. S. BUREAU OF NAVAL PERSONNEL.
Medal of Honor, 1861-1949, the Navy. [Washington, 1950?]
ix, 327p. illus., ports. 27cm.

2026   U. S. BUREAU OF NAVAL PERSONNEL.
Register of commissioned and warrant officers of the
United States Naval Reserve. Jan. 1, 1921-
Washington, U. S. Govt. Print. Off.   v. 25-27cm.
Title varies: 1921-49, Register of commissioned and warrant
officers of the United States Naval Reserve and Marine Corps
Reserve. Lists, by means of abbreviations and designator
codes, rank, date of entry into service, decorations and edu-
cation.

2027   U. S. BUREAU OF NAVAL PERSONNEL.
Register of commissioned and warrant officers of the
United States Navy and Marine Corps. 1814-   Washington, U. S. Govt. Print. Off. [etc.]   v. 16-30cm. Title
varies. Presents, by means of abbreviations and designator codes, rank, date of entry into service and seniority,
decorations, education, special qualifications.

2028   U. S. COAST GUARD.
Register of the commissioned and warrant officers and cadets of the United States Coast Guard in the order of precedence. 1915-   Washington, U. S. Govt. Print. Off.   v.
in   24-27cm. annual. Title varies: 1944, List of regular
and reserve commissioned and warrant officers on active
duty... Uses codes & abbreviations to present permanent
rank, present rank, dates of attainment of each, birth date,
year commissioned and special training.

2029   U. S. CONGRESS.
Biographical directory of the American Congress, 1774-
1961: the Continental Congress, September 5, 1774, to October 21, 1788 and the Congress of the United States from the
First to the Eighty-six Congress, March 4, 1789, to January

3, 1961, inclusive. [Rev. ed. Washington] U. S. Govt. Print. Off., 1961. 1863p. illus. 30cm. (85th Cong., 2d sess. House document, no. 442)

2030   U. S. CONGRESS.
Official Congressional directory. Washington, U. S. Govt. Print. Off. [etc.]   v. illus. 15-24cm. Title varies: -49th Cong., Congressional directory. Directories for some sessions issued in revised editions. Includes Directory of Congress, and Department and Congressional directory. Directory for each session of Congress includes biographies of members of the Congress at the time.

2031   U. S. DEPT. OF LABOR.
Biographic register of labor attachés. [Washington] 1959. 24 p. ports. 27cm. Cover title. "Intended to replace the Biographic register... published by the Office of International Labor Affairs... in June 1957."

2032   U. S. DEPT. OF STATE.
Biographic register. Oct. 1, 1870-   Washington, U. S. Govt. Print. Off.   v. fold. maps. 24-26cm. annual (irregular) Title varies: 1870-1942, 1946-48, 1950, Register.

2033   U. S. DEPT. OF THE ARMY. PUBLIC INFORMATION DIVISION.
The Medal of Honor of the United States Army. [Washington, U. S. Govt. Print. Off., 1948] vii, 468p. plates, ports. 30cm.

2034   U. S. MARINE CORPS.
Combined lineal list of officers on active duty in the Marine Corps. [Washington]   v. 26cm. Furnishes officer's specialty, date and manner of entry into service, birth date.

2035   U. S. MARINE CORPS.
Lineal list of commissioned and warrant officers of the Marine Corps Reserve. [Washington]   v. 26cm. triennial. Gives specialites, date & manner of entry into service, birth date.

2036   U. S. NATIONAL GUARD BUREAU.
Air National Guard register. Washington.   v. 26cm. Gives rank, birth date and place, education, military service and decorations.

2037   U. S. NATIONAL GUARD BUREAU.
Official Army National Guard register. 1922-
Washington, U. S. Govt. Print. Off.   v. 23-25cm. Annual, 1922-31; irregular, 1936-   Title varies: 1922-
56, Official National Guard register (Army) Gives rank,
birth date and place, education, military service and decorations.

2038   U. S. NAVAL ACADEMY, Annapolis. ALUMNI ASSOCIA-
TION.
Register of alumni, graduates and former naval cadets
and midshipmen. 1886-   Annapolis [etc.]   v. ports.
24-27cm. Registers for 1897-1900 issued in combined form.
Title varies: 1886-   Annual reunion. --   Annual
reunion and register of graduates. --   Register
of graduates. Vols for 1886-19   issued by the association
under its earlier name: Graduates' Association.

2039   U. S. WEATHER BUREAU.
The cooperative weather observer; who he is and where he
observes, with biographical notes about those whose volunteer
work, for over twenty years of patriotic devotion to the public welfare, has helped their government in the important
job of defining the climates of the United States and its possessions. Washington, U. S. Govt. Print. Off., 1951.
201 p. illus., ports. 26cm.

2040   THE UNITED STATES BIOGRAPHICAL DICTIONARY AND
PORTRAIT GALLERY OF EMINENT AND SELF-MADE
MEN. Chicago, American Biographical Pub. Co., 1876-79.
6 v. ports. 29cm. Contents. -- [1] Illinois volume. 1876
(another issue—augmented?—in 1883). -- [2] Iowa volume. --
[3] Kansas volume. -- [4] Minnesota volume. -- [5] Missouri
volume. -- [6] Wisconsin volume.

2041   VASSAR COLLEGE.
Alumnae biographical register issue. Poughkeepsie, N.
Y., 1939. x, 607p. 26cm. (Bulletin of Vassar College, v.
29, no. 2, Feb. 1939)

2042   VIRKUS, FREDERICK ADAMS, ed.
The abridged compendium of American genealogy; first
families of America. A genealogical encyclopedia of the
United States. Chicago, A. N. Marquis, 1925-42. 7 v.
illus. 26cm. Vols. 4-   have title: The compendium of A-
merican genealogy. Vols. 2- have subtitle: The standard

genealogical encyclopedia of the first families of America.
Vols. 2-3 published by F. A. Virkus; v. 4 by the Virkus Co. ;
v. 5-   by the Institute of American Genealogy.   Vol. 1 edited
by F. A. Virkus under the direction of A. N. Marquis; v. 2 -
by F. A. Virkus.

2043   WARNER, EZRA J
Generals in blue; lives of the Union commanders.   [Baton
Rouge] Louisiana State University Press [1964]   xxiv, 679 p.
ports. 24cm.

2044   WARNER, EZRA J
Generals in gray; lives of the Confederate commanders.
Baton Rouge, Louisiana State University Press [1959]   xxvii,
420 p. ports. 25cm.   425 general officers, 200 of whom
are not in the Dictionary of American biography.

2045   WEST POINT ALUMNI FOUNDATION, INC.
Register of graduates and former cadets, United States
Military Academy. 1802/1946-   New York.   v. ports.
27cm.

2046   WHO KNOWS, AND WHAT, AMONG AUTHORITIES ,
EXPERTS, AND THE SPECIALLY INFORMED.
1st-   ed. ; 1949-   Chicago, A. N. Marquis Co.   v.
28cm. American experts and authorities.

2047   WHO WAS WHO IN AMERICA.
A companion biographical reference work to Who's who in
America. v. 1-   1897-1942-   Chicago, Marquis,   v.
27cm. Subtitle varies.

2048   WHO WAS WHO IN AMERICA.
Historical volume, 1607-1896. A complement volume of
Who's who in American history... Chicago, Marquis, 1963.
670p. 27cm.

2049   WHO'S WHO AMONG ASSOCIATION EXECUTIVES.
1935-   New York, New York Institute for Research
in Biography, inc. v. 21cm. American and Canadian executives.

2050   WHO'S WHO AMONG FINNISH-AMERICANS.
A biographical directory of persons of Finnish descent who
have made noteworthy contributions to the pattern of American
life. Fitchburg, Mass. , Raivaaja Pub. Co. , 1949. iv,
173p. 24cm.

2051   WHO'S WHO AMONG STUDENTS IN AMERICAN HIGH
       SCHOOLS.
        v. 1-   1948-   Louisville, Ky. v. 24cm. annual.

2052   WHO'S WHO AMONG STUDENTS IN AMERICAN UNIVERSITIES
       AND COLLEGES.
        v. 1-   1935-   [Tuscaloosa? etc., Ala.] v. 21cm.
annual. Title varies: 1935-19   Who's who; the official
who's who among students in American universities and
colleges.--19   -1955/56, The Official who's who among
students in American universities and colleges. Cover title,
1935-   Who's who among students in American universities and colleges.

2053   WHO'S WHO AMONG THE BLIND IN THE BUSINESS AND
       PROFESSIONAL WORLD.
        [1st-   ed.; 1950-   Washington, National Society for
the Blind, inc. v. 23cm. annual.

2054   WHO'S WHO IN AMERICA.
        A biographical dictionary of notable living men and women.
v. [1]-   1899-1900—   Chicago, A. N. Marquis Co. [etc.]
v. 20-27cm. biennial. Subtitle varies slightly. Beginning
with v. 28, accompanied by separately paged pt.: Indices and
necrology.

2055   -----Indices to, and vocational analysis of, the living biographees. Chicago, A.N. Marquis Co., 1952. 1 v. (various
pagings) 28cm.

2056   -----The Supplement to Who's who, a current biographical
reference service. Chicago, A. N. Marquis. v. 23-26cm.
Monthly,   -May1956; quarterly, June/Aug. 1956-
Issues for   -Jan. 1950 are called ser. 1-11, no. 1. Title
varies: -Jan. 1942, Who's who in America current biographical reference service (varies)—Feb. 1942-May 1956, The
Monthly supplement, a current biographical reference service (varies) March, June Sept. and Dec. issues for 1940-41
are quarterly cumulations. "Cumulatively indexed."

       INDEXES: 1939-49. 1 v. 28cm.

2057   WHO'S WHO IN AMERICAN JEWRY.
        1926-   New York, Jewish Biographical Bureau, inc.
v. 21cm. biennial. Vol. 3 has subtitle: A biographical
dictionary of living Jews of the United States and Canada.
Imprint varies: 1938-   New York, National News
Associations.

2058   WHO'S WHO IN COLORED AMERICA.
A biographical dictionary of notable living persons of Negro
descent in America. v. 1-   1927-   New York [etc.]
Who's Who in Colored America Corp. v. ports. 28cm.
Subtitle varies slightly.

2059   WHO'S WHO IN GOVERNMENT.
1930-   New York, Biographical Research Bureau, inc.
v. port. 24cm. "Biographies of the outstanding men and
women in every branch of our Federal, state, county and
municipal governments. " - - - -Preface.

2060   - - - - -Supplement. 1931-   New York, Biographical Research Bureau, inc.   v. 25cm.

2061   WHO'S WHO IN LABOR.
The authorized biographies of the men and women who lead
labor in the United States and Canada and of those who deal
with labor. 1946-   ed. New York, Dryden Press. v.
29cm.

2062   WHO'S WHO IN OUR AMERICAN GOVERNMENT.
1935(?)-   Washington.   v. 26cm. On cover: An up-
to-date digest showing intimate facts about government officials—together with Constitution of the United States, with
amendments—and much other vital information.

2063   WHO'S WHO IN PARIS ANGLO-AMERICAN COLONY;
A biographical dictionary of the leading members of the
Anglo-American colony of Paris, 1905. [1st ed.] Founded
and edited by William H. Ingram. Paris, The American register [1905] 176p. ports. 19cm.

2064   WHO'S WHO IN POLISH AMERICA;
A biographical directory of Polish-American leaders and
distinguished Poles resident in the Americas. 19
New York, Harbinger House [etc.]   v. 21-24cm. Edited
by Francis Bolek. 3d ed. issued in 1943.

2065   WHO'S WHO IN THE AIR FORCE;
Biographies of key personnel of the United States Air Force
around the World. 1st-   ed. ; 1954-   Washington, Air
Force Association.   v. 28cm. Supplement to Air Force.

2066   WHO'S WHO IN THE CENTRAL STATES;
A business, professional and social record of men and wo-

men of achievement in the Central States. 1929- Washington, Mayflower Pub. Co. v. 25cm. biennial. Covers Arkansas, Illinois, Indiana, Iowa, Kansas, Michigan, Minnesota, Missouri, Nebraska, North Dakota, Ohio, Oklahoma, South Dakota, Texas, Wisconsin.

2067 WHO'S WHO IN THE LYCEUM.
Edited by A. Augustus Wright. Including A brief history of the lyceum by Anna L. Curtis and How to organize and manage a lyceum course by Laurence Tom Kersey. Philadelphia, Pearson Bros. [1906- v. 23cm.

2068 WHO'S WHO IN THE REGULAR ARMY,
Containing the biographies of all Regular Army officers, by John McD. Thompson. San Antonio, Tex., San Antonio Print. Co. [1925- v. 32cm.

2069 WHO'S WHO IN UNITED STATES POLITICS AND AMERICAN POLITICAL ALMANAC. [1st- ed.] Chicago, Capitol House [1950- v. illus., ports. 29cm.

2070 WHO'S WHO OF AMERICAN WOMEN;
A biographical dictionary of notable living American women. v. 1- 1958-59— Chicago, Marquis - Who's Who. v. 28cm. biennial.

2071 WHO'S WHO OF THE COLORED RACE;
A general biographical dictionary of men and women of African descent. v. 1- 1915- Chicago. v. illus. 20cm. Vol. 1 edited by Frank Lincoln Mather.

2072 WILLARD, FRANCES ELIZABETH, 1839-1898, ed.
A woman of the century; fourteen hundred-seventy biographical sketches accompanied by portraits of leading American women in all walks of life. Edited by Frances E. Willard and Mary A. Livermore, assisted by a corps of able contributors. Buffalo, C. W. Moulton, 1893. 812 p. ports. 28cm.

2073 WOMAN'S WHO'S WHO OF AMERICA;
A biographical dictionary of contemporary women of the United States and Canada. 1914-15— New York, American Commonwealth Co. v. 24cm. Editors: 1914-15- John W. Leonard.

Local

Alabama

2074   GARRETT, WILLIAM, 1809-
Reminiscences of public men in Alabama for thirty years.
With an appendix. Atlanta, Ga. , Plantation Pub. Co. 's Press,
1872. 809 p. 23 cm. A more or less chronological arrangement, with a general alphabetical index to the numerous
sketches of public figures in Alabama, ca. 1840-1870.

2075   WHO'S WHO IN ALABAMA.
v. 1-   1939/40-   Birmingham, DuBose Pub. Co.
v. ports. 29cm.

Alaska

2076   JEFFERY, EDMOND C   ed.
Alaska: who's here, what's doing, who's doing it, 1955.
[1st ed.] Anchorage, 1955. 212p. 24cm. More than 500
biographical sketches.

2077   TEWKESBURY'S WHO'S WHO IN ALASKA AND ALASKA
BUSINESS INDEX. v. 1; 1947. Juneau, Tewkesbury.
1 v. Superseded in part by Tewksbury's Alaska business
directory, travel guide & almanac. No more published?

Arizona

2078   MEN AND WOMEN OF ARIZONA,
Past and present. Phoenix, Pioneer Pub. Co. , 1940.
119p. ports. 29cm.

2079   PORTRAIT AND BIOGRAPHICAL RECORD OF ARIZONA.
Chicago, Chapman Pub. Co. , 1901. 21-1034p. ports.
29 x 24cm.

2080   WHO'S WHO IN ARIZONA IN BUSINESS, PROFESSIONS AND
ARTS.
Authentic biographies of distinguished men and women of
Arizona. v.1-   1938/40-   Phoenix, Arizona Survey
Pub. Co. v. 24cm.

Arkansas

2081   FERGUSON, JOHN LEWIS, 1926-   ed.
Arkansas lives: the Opportunity Land who's who; a reference
edition recording the biographies of contemporary leaders in

Arkansas with special emphasis on their achievements in
making it one of America's greatest States. Written and
prepared under the supervision of John L. Ferguson.
Hopkinsville, Ky. , Historical Record Association, 1965. 631
p. ports. 27 cm.

2082 WHO IS WHO IN ARKANSAS.
   v. 1-   1959- Little Rock. v. ports. 23cm.

Baltimore

2083 WHO'S WHO IN BALTIMORE.
   [Compiled by D. Pittler. Baltimore? 1931] 39 l. 29cm.

Boston

2084 MEN OF BOSTON AND NEW ENGLAND.
   [Boston] The Boston American, 1913. 186p. of ports
(incl. illus.) 28cm.

2085 WHO'S WHO IN BOSTON.
   [Compiled by D. Pittler] Boston [1931] 36 l. 28cm.

California

2086 BANCROFT, HUBERT HOWE, 1832-1918.
   California pioneer register and index, 1542-1848. Includ-
ing Inhabitants of California, 1769-1800, and List of pioneers.
Baltimore, Regional Pub. Co. , 1964. 392p. 23cm.
Extracted from the author's History of California.

2087 CALIFORNIA. SECRETARY OF STATE.
   California blue book; or, State roster, 188- Sacramento.
   v. illus. 23 cm. biennial. Title varies. Includes
biographical sketches of State legislators, officials, etc.

2088 EMINENT CALIFORNIANS. 1953- Palo Alto, Calif. ,
   C. W. Taylor. v. ports. 28 cm.

2089 HUNT, ROCKWELL DENNIS, 1868-
   California's stately hall of fame. Stockton, College of the
Pacific [c1950] xxi, 675p. ports. 24cm. (Publications of
the California History Foundation, no. 2)

2090 A MEMORIAL AND BIOGRAPHICAL HISTORY OF NORTHERN
   CALIFORNIA, ILLUSTRATED.
   Containing a history of this important section of the Pacific
Coast from the earliest period of its occupancy and biogra-

phical mention of many of its most eminent pioneers and also
of prominent citizens of today. Chicago, Lewis Pub. Co.,
1891. 834p. illus., ports, 30cm.

2091   MEN OF CALIFORNIA.
        San Francisco, Pacific Art Co., 1900 to 1902 [c1901]
        12 p.l., 65-440p. ports. 24cm. Edited by Wellington C.
        Wolfe.

2092   MEN OF CALIFORNIA;
        Western personalities and their affiliations, with club
        memberships and civic associations, illustrated record of
        men, with biographs of their activities. San Francisco,
        Western Press Reporter, 1926. 257p. illus., ports. 27cm.
        Edited by W. C. Wolfe in collaboration with assistants.

2093   WHO IS WHO IN CALIFORNIA.
        [1st ed.] Los Angeles, J. M. Moore, 1958. 829p. 24cm.

2094   WHO'S WHO AMONG THE WOMEN OF CALIFORNIA.
        An annual devoted to the representative women of
        California, with an authoritative review of their activities in
        civic, social, philanthropic, art, music, literary and
        dramatic circles, 1922-   San Francisco, Security Pub.
        Co. v. illus., ports. 26cm.

2095   WHO'S WHO EXECUTIVES IN CALIFORNIA.
        1963-   [Los Angeles] A. C. Armstrong. v. ports.
        28cm.

2096   WHO'S WHO IN CALIFORNIA.
        1955/56-   [Los Angeles] v. ports. 28cm.

2097   WHO'S WHO IN CALIFORNIA.
        A biographical directory. Being a history of California
        as illustrated in the lives of the builders and defenders of the
        state, and of the men and women who are doing the work and
        molding the thought of the present time. 1928/29-   San
        Francisco, Who's Who Pub. Co. v. ports. 28cm.

2098   WHO'S WHO IN CALIFORNIA.
        A biographical reference work of notable living men and
        women of California. v.1-   1942/43-   Los Angeles,
        Who's Who Publications Co. v. 24cm. biennial.

2099   WHO'S WHO IN THE PACIFIC SOUTHWEST.
        A compilation of authentic biographical sketches of citizens
        of Southern California and Arizona. Los Angeles, Times-
        Mirror Print. & Binding House, 1913. 410p. 26cm.

Chicago

2100   THE BIOGRAPHICAL DICTIONARY AND PORTRAIT GAL-
        LERY OF REPRESENTATIVE MEN OF CHICAGO, IOWA
        AND THE WORLD'S COLUMBIAN EXPOSITION.
        Chicago, American Biographical Pub. Co., 1893. 744p.
        ports. 30 x 24cm.

2101   THE BIOGRAPHICAL DICTIONARY AND PORTRAIT GAL-
        LERY OF REPRESENTATIVE MEN OF CHICAGO, MINNE-
        SOTA CITIES AND THE WORLD'S COLUMBIAN EXPOSI-
        TION.
        Chicago, American Biographical Pub. Co., 1892. 1033
        (i. e. 1029)p. illus., ports. 30 x 24cm.

2102   THE BIOGRAPHICAL DICTIONARY AND PORTRAIT GAL-
        LERY OF REPRESENTATIVE MEN OF CHICAGO, WISCON-
        SIN AND THE WORLD'S COLUMBIAN EXPOSITION.
        Chicago, American Biographical Publishing Company,
        1895. 609, iv p. ports. 30 x 25cm.

2103   A BIOGRAPHICAL HISTORY, WITH PORTRAITS, OF
        PROMINENT MEN OF THE GREAT WEST. Chicago,
        Manhattan Pub. Co., 1894. 720 p. ports. 36 x 28cm.
        Greater part of the work devoted to Chicago residents.

2104   DROBA, DANIEL D   ed.
        Czech and Slovak leaders in metropolitan Chicago; a bio-
        graphical study of 300 prominent men and women of Czech and
        Slovak descent. [Chicago] Slavonic Club of the University of
        Chicago, 1934. v, 307 p. ports. 22cm.

2105   HERRINGSHAW, CLARK J
        Clark J. Herringshaw's city blue book of current biog-
        raphy; Chicago men of 19   ; an alphabetical record of citi-
        zens prominent in their chosen vocations in Chicago's educa-
        tional, social, civil, industrial and commercial affairs.
        Chicago, American Publishers' Association.   v. 24cm.

2106   NOTABLE MEN OF CHICAGO AND THEIR CITY.
        [Chicago] Chicago daily journal, 1910. 414 p. plates,
        ports. 28cm. The portraits and plates occupy p. 7-406.

2107   WHO'S WHO IN CHICAGO AND ILLINOIS.
[1st]-   ed. ; 1905-   Chicago, A. N. Marquis Co.
[etc.] v. 24cm. irregular. Title varies: 1905-17 (1st-3d ed.) The Book of Chicagoans. —1926-36 (4th-6th ed.) Who's who in Chicago and vicinity: — 1941 (7th ed.) Who's who in Chicago and vicinity, enlarged to include the entire state of Illinois.

Cincinnati

2108   WHO'S WHO IN CINCINNATI.
[Compiled by S. J. Rudkin] Cincinnati [1931] 40 1. 28cm.

Cleveland

2109   WHO'S WHO IN CLEVELAND.
[Compiled by D. Pittler] Cleveland [1931] 43 1. 28cm.

Colorado

2110   CAPITOL'S WHO'S WHO FOR COLORADO;
A triennial reference work. 1941/43-   Portland, Or. , Capitol Pub. Co.   v. 24cm.

2111   PORTRAIT AND BIOGRAPHICAL RECORD OF THE STATE OF COLORADO,
Containing portraits and biographies of many well known citizens of the past and present. Chicago, Chapman Pub. Co. , 1899. [15]-1492p. ports. 29cm.

2112   PROGRESSIVE MEN OF WESTERN COLORADO.
Chicago, A. W. Bowen, 1905. 876p. plates, ports. 28cm.

2113   REPRESENTATIVE MEN OF COLORADO IN THE NINE-TEENTH CENTURY;
A portrait gallery of many of the men who have been instrumental in the upbuilding of Colorado... New York, Denver, Rowell Art Pub. Co. , 1902. xii p. , 272 p. of ports. 24cm.

2114   WHO'S WHO IN COLORADO.
[Editor: Daniel T. Valdes] Centennial anniversary ed. [Denver] Who's Who in Colorado, inc. ; distributed by Sage Books, 1958. 607p. 25cm.

2115   WHO'S WHO IN COLORADO.
A biographical record of Colorado's leaders in business, professional and public life. Compiled by the Colorado Press Association, inc. Boulder, Extension Division, University of Colorado, 1938. 1115p. 24cm.

Connecticut

2116   BIOGRAPHICAL ENCYCLOPAEDIA OF CONNECTICUT AND
RHODE ISLAND of the nineteenth century. New York, Metropolitan Pub. and Engraving Co., 1881. 376 p. 48 ports. 30cm. Edited by H. C. Williams.

2117   ENCYCLOPEDIA OF CONNECTICUT BIOGRAPHY,
GENEALOGICAL-MEMORIAL; representative citizens. Compiled with assistance of the following advisory committee: Samuel Hart [and others] Boston, American Historical Society, 1917. 4 v. illus. 28cm.

2118   MEN OF PROGRESS;
Biographical sketches and portraits of leaders in business and professional life in and of the State of Connecticut. Compiled under the supervision of Richard Herndon. Edited by Richard Burton. Boston, New England magazine, 1898. 480p. ports. 29cm.

2119   REPRESENTATIVE MEN OF CONNECTICUT, 1861-1894.
Everett, Mass., Massachusetts Pub. Co., 1894. 460p. 82 ports. 31cm.

2120   WHO'S WHO AMONG AMERICANS OF ITALIAN DESCENT IN
CONNECTICUT.
[1942-   New Haven, Carlevale Pub. Co. v. 21cm.

2121   WHO'S WHO IN CONNECTICUT.
1933-   New York, Lewis Historical Pub. Co. v. ports. 21cm. Editor: 1933- W. E. Duffy.

Delaware

2122   WHO'S WHO IN DELAWARE.
A biographical dictionary of Delaware's leading men and women. 1932- Philadelphia, National Biographical Society. v. 20cm. Editor: 1932- Seth Harmon.

2123   WHO'S WHO IN DELAWARE.
A biographical dictionary of leading living men and women of the states of Delaware, Pennsylvania, New Jersey, Maryland and West Virginia. v. 1- 1939- Chicago, A. N. Marquis Co. v. 24cm. Published also under titles: Who's who in Maryland; Who's who in New Jersey; Who's who in Pennsylvania; Who's who in West Virginia.

Denver

2124   LANDERS, JOSEPH.
Who's who in the Rockies. Denver, Denver Press Club [1923] [336]p. ports. 23cm. Principally residents of Denver.

2125   PORTRAIT AND BIOGRAPHICAL RECORD OF DENVER AND VICINITY, COLORADO.
Containing portraits and biographies of many well known citizens of the past and present, together with biographies and portraits of all the presidents of the United States. Chicago, Chapman Pub. Co., 1898. 1306p. ports. 29cm.

2126   WHO'S WHO FOR DENVER AND COLORADO.
19-- Denver, Capitol Pub. Co. v. 24cm. Cover title, 19 : Capitol who's who for Denver and Colorado.

Detroit

2127   MARQUIS, ALBERT NELSON, d. 1943, ed.
The book of Detroiters; a biographical dictionary of leading living men of the City of Detroit. 2d ed., rev. and brought down to date 1914. Chicago, A. N. Marquis & Co., 1914. 547 p. 25cm.

2128   WHO'S WHO IN DETROIT.
[Compiled by D. Pittler] Detroit [1931] 46 l. 28cm.

2129   WHO'S WHO IN DETROIT.
A biographical dictionary of representative men and women of metropolitan Detroit. With a complete vocational index. 1935-36- Detroit, W. Romig. v. 22cm.

Eastern States See Northwestern States

Florida

2130   FLORIDA WHO'S WHO.
1953/54- Jacksonville. v. 26cm.

2131   WHO'S WHO AND WHAT TO SEE IN FLORIDA.
A standard biographical reference book of Florida.   Homer
E. Moyer, editor.   St. Petersburg, Current Historical
Company of Florida [1935]   379p.   illus.   24cm.

Georgia

2132   BIOGRAPHICAL SOUVENIR OF THE STATES OF GEORGIA
AND FLORIDA.   Chicago, F. A. Battey, 1889.   880 p.   ports
28 x 22cm.

2133   EMINENT GEORGIANS.
Robert Paul Turbeville, biographical editor.   Atlanta,
Southern Society for Research and History [1937-   v.
ports.   32cm.

2134   GEORGIA.   DEPT. OF ARCHIVES AND HISTORY.
Georgia women of 1926.   Compiled by Ruth Blair, state
historian and director.   [Atlanta?] 1926.   33 p.   23cm.

2135   GEORGIA.   DEPT. OF ARCHIVES AND HISTORY.
Georgia's official register.   1923?-   [Atlanta?]
v.   ports.   24cm.   Includes biographies of all state
officials.

2136   KNIGHT, LUCIAN LAMAR, 1868-   ed.
Encyclopedia of Georgia biography.   Atlanta, A. H. Caw-
ston, 1931-   v.   ports.   28cm.

2137   NORTHEN, WILLIAM J   1835-1913, ed.
Men of mark in Georgia: a complete and elaborate history
of the State from its settlement to the present time, chiefly
told in biographies and autobiographies of the most eminent
men of each period of Georgia's progress and development.
Historical introductory by John Temple Graves, editor.   Atlanta, A. B. Caldwell, 1907-12.   6 v.   ports.   25cm.

2138   TROUP, CORNELIUS V
Distinguished Negro Georgians.   Dallas, Royal Pub. Co.
[1962]   203 p.   21cm.

Hawaii

2139   MEN AND WOMEN OF HAWAII.
[Honolulu] Honolulu Business Consultants.   v.   ports.

25cm. Began 19-- Editor: P. E. Hilleary. "Written by Henry P. Judd. "

Idaho

2140 PROGRESSIVE MEN OF SOUTHERN IDAHO.
Chicago, A. W. Bowen, 1904. 952p. ports. 29cm.

Illinois

2141 BARNET, JAMES, ed.
The martyrs and heroes of Illinois in the Great Rebellion.
Biographical sketches. Chicago, 1865. xvi, 263p.

2142 BIOGRAPHICAL ENCYCLOPAEDIA OF ILLINOIS
Of the nineteenth century. Philadelphia, Galaxy Pub. Co.,
1875. 529 p. ports. 29 x 23cm.

2143 BIOGRAPHIES OF THE STATE OFFICERS AND THIRTY-
THIRD GENERAL ASSEMBLY OF ILLINOIS. Containing
biographical sketches of the governor and other state officers,
and each senator and representative in the Thirty-third General
Assembly. Springfield, Ill., Biographical Pub. Co., 1883.
274 p. illus., ports. 24cm. Sometines attributed to D. L.
Phillips and F. E. Huddle.

2144 ENCYCLOPAEDIA OF BIOGRAPHY OF ILLINOIS.
Chicago, Century Pub. and Engraving Co., 1892-1902.
3 v. ports. 30cm. Vol. 1 edited by H. McGrath, W. J.
Guest and W. James; v. 3 by G. I. Reed and H. G. Cutler.

2145 ILLINOIS BLUE BOOK.
[Springfield] v. illus., ports. 23cm. biennial. Title
varies: 19 -1949/50, Blue book of the State of Illinois.
Issued by the Secretary of State. Includes biographical
sketches of state elective officers, officials, etc.

2146 MEN OF ILLINOIS.
[Chicago, H. Witherspoon, 1902?] 20 p.l., 535p. ports.
28cm.

2147 NOTABLE MEN OF ILLINOIS AND THEIR STATE.
[Chicago] Chicago daily journal, 1912. 428 p. plates,
ports. 28cm.

Indiana

2148   [BENESCH, ADOLPH B   ]
       Men of Indiana in nineteen hundred and one. Indianapolis,
Benesch Pub. Co. , 1901. xiv, 521p. ports. 24cm. Portraits
of the representative men of Indiana.

2149   A BIOGRAPHICAL HISTORY OF EMINENT AND SELF-MADE
       MEN OF THE STATE OF INDIANA. Cincinnati, Western
Biographical Pub. Co. , 1880.   2 v. ports. 29cm.

2150   HEPBURN, WILLIAM MURRAY, 1874-   ed.
       Who's who in Indiana; library of American lives. A refer-
ence edition recording the biographies of contemporary leaders in Indiana, with special emphasis on their achievements
in making the Hoosier State one of America's greatest.
Hopkinsville, Ky. , Historical Record Association [1957]
248p. ports. 27cm.

2151   MEMORIAL RECORD OF NORTHEASTERN INDIANA.
       Chicago, Lewis Pub. Co. , 1896. 895p. plates, 78 ports.
28 x 23cm.

2152   REED, GEORGE IRVING, ed.
       Encyclopedia of biography of Indiana. Chicago, Century
Pub. and Engraving Co. , 1895-[99] 2 v. ports. 30cm.

2153   WOOLLEN, WILLIAM WESLEY, 1828-
       Biographical and historical sketches of early Indiana. In-
dianapolis, Hammond, 1883. viii, 568p. ports. 24cm.

Indianapolis

2154   COMMEMORATIVE BIOGRAPHICAL RECORD OF PROMI-
       NENT AND REPRESENTATIVE MEN OF INDIANAPOLIS
AND VICINITY, containing biographical sketches of business
and professional men and many of the early settled families.
Chicago, J. H. Beers, 1908. x, 1244p. ports. 29cm.

2155   MEMORIAL RECORD OF DISTINGUISHED MEN OF INDIAN-
       APOLIS AND INDIANA.
       Edition de luxe. Jacob Piatt Dunn, associate editor. Chi-
cago, Lewis Pub. Co. , 1912. 504p. ports. 32cm.

Iowa

2156 BIOGRAPHIES AND PORTRAITS OF THE PROGRESSIVE MEN
OF IOWA, leaders in business, politics and the professions:
together with an original and authentic history of the State, by
B. F. Gue. Des Moines, Conaway & Shaw, 1899. 2 v.
ports., maps. 27 x 22cm.

2157 BUSINESS MEN OF IOWA;
A biographical cross-section of commercial, industrial,
professional, agricultural, and public life within the State.
Editor: Edward N. Dodge. Des Moines, Midwest Publications,
1953. 808 p. 29cm.

Kansas

2158 A BIOGRAPHICAL HISTORY OF CENTRAL KANSAS.
New York, Lewis Pub. Co., 1902. 2 v. (1633 p.) illus.,
ports. 28cm.

Kansas City, Missouri

2159 WHO'S WHO IN KANSAS CITY.
[Compiled by Morris Hershman] Kansas City, Mo. [1931]
33 l. 28cm.

2160 WHO'S WHO IN KANSAS CITY.
Biographical sketches of men and women of achievement.
1930- Hebron, Neb., Robert M. Baldwin Corp. v. ports.
28cm. Kansas City, Missouri and Kansas City, Kansas.

Kentucky

2161 BIOGRAPHICAL CYCLOPEDIA OF THE COMMONWEALTH
OF KENTUCKY. Chicago, J. M. Gresham Co., 1896.
631p. ports. 31cm.

2162 THE BIOGRAPHICAL ENCYCLOPAEDIA OF KENTUCKY
Of the dead and living men of the nineteenth century.
Cincinnati, J. M. Armstrong, 1878. 792 p. 70 ports. 29 x
22cm.

2163   MEMORIAL RECORD OF WESTERN KENTUCKY.
      Chicago, Lewis Pub. Co., 1904. 2 v. (805p.) ports.
28cm.

2164   WHO'S WHO IN KENTUCKY.
      [1955] Hopkinsville, Ky., Historical Record Association
[1957?] 378p. ports. 27cm.

2165   WHO'S WHO IN KENTUCKY.
      A biographical assembly of notable Kentuckians, 1936.
Edited by Mary Young Southard. Ernest C. Miller, co-editor.
Louisville, Standard Print. Co. [1936] xv, 582p. ports,
plates. 25cm.

Los Angeles

2166   WHO'S WHO IN LOS ANGELES.
      [19–   [Los Angeles.   v. illus., ports. 28cm.

2167   WHO'S WHO IN LOS ANGELES COUNTY.
      1950/51-   Los Angeles, Who's Who Historical Society.
v. ports. 28cm.

Louisiana

2168   WHO'S WHO IN COLORED LOUISIANA, 1930.
      A. E. Perkins, editor. Baton Rouge, Douglas Loan Co.
[1930] 153p. illus., ports. 21cm.

Louisville, Kentucky

2169   WHO'S WHO IN LOUISVILLE.
      Biographical sketches of Louisville men and women of
achievement. [v. 1-   1926-   Louisville, Standard Print.
Co. v. ports. 24cm.

Maine

2170   BIOGRAPHICAL ENCYCLOPAEDIA OF MAINE
      Of the nineteenth century. Boston, Metropolitan Pub. and
Engraving Co., 1885. 441 p. 50 ports. 30cm. Edited by
H. C. Williams.

2171   BIOGRAPHICAL SKETCHES OF REPRESENTATIVE CITIZENS
      OF THE STATE OF MAINE. Boston, New England Histori-

cal Pub. Co., 1903. 452 p. ports. 29 x 22cm. (American series of popular biographies. Maine ed.)

2172 BRIEF BIOGRAPHIES, MAINE;
A biographical dictionary of Who's who in Maine. Vol. 1-
1926/27- Lewiston, Me., Lewiston Journal Co. v.
20cm. Editor: v. 1- T. R. Hodgkins. "Revised and reissued biennially."

2173 CHASE, HENRY, ed.
Representative men of Maine. A collection of portraits with biographical sketches of residents of the State, who have achieved success... To which is added the portraits and sketches of all the governors since the formation of the State. Portland, Me., Lakeside Press, 1893. 250, liii p. ports.

2174 DAILY KENNEBEC JOURNAL, Augusta, Me.
Biographical sketches of members: 102nd Maine Legislature. Augusta [1965] 62 p. ports. 27cm. Cover title.

2175 MEN OF PROGRESS;
Biographical sketches and portraits of leaders in business and professional life in and of the State of Maine. Compiled under the supervision of Richard Herndon. Edited by Philip W. McIntyre and William F. Blanding. Boston, New England magazine, 1897. 626p. ports. 29cm.

2176 SPENCER, WILBUR DANIEL, 1872-
Maine immortals, including many unique characters in early Maine history. Augusta, Me., 1932. viii, 316 p. 21cm.

Maryland

2177 AGNUS, FELIX, 1839-1925, ed.
The book of Maryland: men and institutions, a work for press reference. Editors: Felix Agnus, editor-in-chief [and others] Baltimore, Maryland Biographical Association, 1920. 350p. illus., ports. 31cm.

2178 THE BIOGRAPHICAL CYCLOPAEDIA OF REPRESENTATIVE MEN OF MARYLAND AND THE DISTRICT OF COLUMBIA. Baltimore, National Biographical Pub. Co., 1879. 716p. 97 ports. 29cm.

2179   BOYLE, ESMERALDA, 1840-
       Biographical sketches of distinguished Marylanders. Bal-
       timore, Kelly, Piet, 1877. 374 p. 19 cm.

2180   MEN OF MARK IN MARYLAND.
       Biographies of leading men of the State. Baltimore, B. F.
       Johnson, 1907-12. 4 v. ports. 24cm. (Johnson's Makers of
       America series)

2181   SPENCER, RICHARD HENRY, 1833-1920.
       Genealogical and memorial encyclopedia of the State of
       Maryland... New York, American Historical Society, 1919.
       2 v. ports. 27cm.

2182   WINCHESTER, PAUL, 1851-1932.
       Men of Maryland since the Civil War; sketches of United
       States Senator Arthur Pue Gorman and his contemporaries and
       successors and their connection with public affairs. Balti-
       more, Maryland County Press Syndicate, 1923-   v. 24cm.

Massachusetts

2183   BIOGRAPHICAL ENCYCLOPEDIA,
       Comprising the lives and records of many of the leading
       professional and business men of the State of Massachusetts.
       Arr. in alphabetical order. Written and compiled expressly
       for Comley's History of the State of Massachusetts. (In
       Comley, W. J. Comley's History of Massachusetts. Bos-
       ton, Comley Bros., 1879. 24cm. [pt. 2] p. 203-462)

2184   BIOGRAPHICAL SKETCHES OF REPRESENTATIVE CITIZENS
       OF THE COMMONWEALTH OF MASSACHUSETTS. Boston,
       Graves & Steinbarger, 1901. 1092 p. ports. 29 x 22cm.
       (American series of popular biographies. Massachusetts ed.)

2185   ELIOT, SAMUEL ATKINS, 1862-   ed.
       Biographical history of Massachusetts; biographies and
       autobiographies of the leading men in the State. Boston,
       Massachusetts Biographical Society, 1911-   v. ports.
       25 cm.

2186   ENCYCLOPEDIA OF MASSACHUSETTS, BIOGRAPHICAL-
       GENEALOGICAL. Compiled with the assistance of the
       following advisory committee: William Richard Cutter [and
       others] New York, American Historical Society, inc., 1916.
       5 v. illus. 28cm.

2187   MEN OF MASSACHUSETTS;
A collection of portraits of representative men in business
and professional life in the Commonwealth of Massachusetts.
Published under the editorial auspices and direction of the
Boston Press Club. Boston, 1903. xxiv p. , 386 p. of ports.
24cm.

2188   MEN OF PROGRESS:
One thousand biographical sketches and portraits of lead-
ers in business and professional life in the Commonwealth of
Massachusetts. Compiled under the supervision of Richard
Herndon. Edited by Edwin M. Bacon. Boston, New England
magazine, 1896. 1027p. ports. 29cm.

2189   RAND, JOHN CLARK, 1842-
One of a thousand; a series of biographical sketches of
one thousand representative men resident in the Commonwealth of Massachusetts, A.D. 1888-'89. Boston, First
National Pub. Co. , 1890. 707p. illus. , ports. 29cm.

2190   REPRESENTATIVE MEN AND OLD FAMILIES OF SOUTH-
EASTERN MASSACHUSETTS,
Containing historical sketches of prominent and representative citizens and genealogical records of many of the
old families. Chicago, J. H. Beers, 1912. 3 v. ports.
28cm.

2191   REPRESENTATIVE MEN OF MASSACHUSETTS, 1890-1900.
The leaders in official business, and professional life of
the Commonwealth. Everett, Mass. , Massachusetts Pub.
Co. , 1898. 491p. port. 4.º

2192   TOOMEY, DANIEL P
Massachusetts of today; a memorial of the State, historical and biographical, issued for the World's Columbian Ex-
position at Chicago. Edited by Thomas C. Quinn. Boston,
Columbia Pub. Co. , 1892. 619p. illus. , ports. 31cm.

2193   WHO'S WHO ALONG THE NORTH SHORE OF
MASSACHUSETTS BAY.
Salem, Mass. , Salem Press Co., 1907-   v. illus.
24cm.

2194   WHO'S WHO IN MASSACHUSETTS.
A volume containing a biographical history of every

important living person in the Commonwealth. v. 1-
1940/41-   Boston. Larkin, Roosevelt & Larkin. v. 24cm.

2195   WHO'S WHO IN STATE POLITICS, 1907.
Boston, Mass., Practical Politics, c1907. 385p. ports.
16 x 10 cm. Massachusetts politicians.

Michigan

2196   AMERICAN BIOGRAPHICAL HISTORY OF EMINENT AND
SELF-MADE MEN. Michigan volume. Cincinnati,
Western Biographical Pub. Co., 1878. 798 p. ports. 28cm.
Preface signed: F. A. B. [i. e. F. A. Barnard] Biographies
of eminent natives of Michigan.

2197   MEMORIAL RECORD OF THE NORTHERN PENINSULA OF
MICHIGAN.
Chicago, Lewis Publishing Company, 1895. 642 (i. e. 632)
p. illus., ports. 28cm.

2198   MEMORIAL SOCIETY OF MICHIGAN, INC.
In memoriam; founders and makers of Michigan. A memo-
rial history of the State's honored men and women. Detroit,
S. J. Clarke Pub. Co. [1933] 544p. ports. 32cm.

2199   MEN OF MICHIGAN;
A collection of the portraits of men prominent in business
and professional life in Michigan. Detroit, Michigan Art Co.,
1904. 24, 24a-24f, 25-394p. ports. 24cm.

2200   MEN OF PROGRESS:
Embracing biographical sketches of representative Mich-
igan men; with an outline history of the State. Detroit,
Evening News Association, 1900. xiv, 528p. ports. 32cm.

2201   MEN WHO HAVE MADE MICHIGAN.
1927-   Detroit, Pipp's magazine. v. ports. 30cm.
Editors: 1927-   E. G. Pipp.

2202   MICHIGAN. DEPT. OF STATE.
Michigan official directory and legislative manual.
1879/80(?)-   Lansing. v. illus., ports. 21-24cm.
Title varies. Includes biographical sketches of State officers, legislators, etc.

2203   MICHIGAN. HISTORICAL COMMISSION.
       Michigan biographies, including members of Congress, elective State officers, justices of the Supreme Court, members of the Michigan Legislature, Board of Regents of the University of Michigan, State Board of Agriculture and State Board of Education. Lansing, 1924. 2 v. 24cm.
A revision of S. D. Bingham's Early history of Michigan, with biographies of State officers... 1888, with additions from the several editions of the Michigan Manual.

2204   THE OFFICIAL WHO'S WHO IN MICHIGAN.
       [v. 1]-   ; 1936-   [Munising, Mich.]   v. 24cm.

2205   PORTRAIT AND BIOGRAPHICAL RECORD OF NORTHERN MICHIGAN.
       Chicago, Record Pub. Co., 1895. 19-551 p. ports. 28 x 22cm.

Middle Western States

2206   WHO'S WHO IN THE CENTRAL STATES,
       A biographical dictionary of leading men and women of the Central States. v. 1. [Limited 1st ed.] Chicago, Larkin, Roosevelt & Larkin, 1947. 1184 p. 24cm. Published also under title: Who's who in Arkansas, Who's who in Illinois, Who's who in Indiana, Who's who in Iowa, Who's who in Kansas, Who's who in Michigan, Who's who in Minnesota, Who's who in Missouri, Who's who in Nebraska, Who's who in Ohio, Who's who in Oklahoma, and Who's who in Wisconsin.

2207   WHO'S WHO IN THE MIDWEST;
       A biographical dictionary of noteworthy men and women of the Central and Midwestern States. 1st-   ed. ; [1949]-
Chicago, A. N. Marquis Co.   v. 24cm.

Milwaukee

2208   WHO'S WHO IN MILWAUKEE.
       [Compiled by D. Pittler] Milwaukee [1931] 32 1. 28cm.

Minnesota

2209   ENCYCLOPEDIA OF BIOGRAPHY OF MINNESOTA.
       History of Minnesota by C. E. Flandrau. Vol. 1. Chicago, Century Pub. and Engraving Co., 1900. 497p. ports. 30cm. No more published?

2210   ILLUSTRATED ALBUM OF BIOGRAPHY OF SOUTHWESTERN
MINNESOTA AND NORTHWESTERN IOWA.
Chicago, Northwest Pub. Co., 1889. xii, 9-1080p. 22
ports. 28cm.

2211   MARQUIS, ALBERT NELSON, d. 1943, ed.
The book of Minnesotans; a biographical dictionary of leading living men of the State of Minnesota. Chicago, A. N.
Marquis & Co., 1907. 572 p. 20cm. On spine: Vol. 1. No
more published.

2212   MEMORIAL RECORD OF SOUTHWESTERN MINNESOTA.
Chicago, Lewis Pub. Co., 1897. 560 p. illus., ports.
30cm.

2213   MEN OF MINNESOTA;
A collection of the portraits of men prominent in business
and professional life in Minnesota. [2d ed.] St. Paul, R. L.
Polk, 1915. 520p. ports. 23cm. 1st ed. published in 1902
(St. Paul, Minnesota Historical Co.)

2214   UPHAM, WARREN, 1850-
Minnesota biographies, 1655-1912, compiled by Warren
Upham and Rose Barteau Dunlap. St. Paul, The Society,
1912. xxviii, 892p. 23cm. (Collections of the Minnesota
Historical Society, v. 14)

2215   WHO'S WHO AMONG MINNESOTA WOMEN.
A history of woman's work in Minnesota from pioneer days
to date, told in biographies, memorials and records of
organizations. Compiled and published by Mary Dillon Foster.
[St. Paul] 1924. 380p. illus., ports. 28cm.

2216   WHO'S WHO IN MINNESOTA.
1941-   Minneapolis, Minneapolis Editorial Association.
v. 28cm.   Editors: 1941-   C. N. Cornwall and Esther
Stutheit.

Mississippi

2217   BIOGRAPHICAL AND HISTORICAL MEMOIRS OF
MISSISSIPPI,
Embracing an authentic and comprehensive account of the
chief events in the history of the state and a record of the
lives of many of the most worthy and illustrious families and

individuals... Chicago, Goodspeed Pub. Co., 1891. 2 v. illus. 31cm.

2218   -----Index to biographical section [by Norman E. Gillis. Baton Rouge? La., 1961] 187p. 28cm.

2219   MISSISSIPPI OFFICIAL AND STATISTICAL REGISTER. 18--   [Jackson]   v. in   illus., ports. 22-24cm. Title varies: 18   -1929/31, Report of the Secretary of State. --1931/33-1945/49, Mississippi blue book. Includes biographical sketches of members of Congress together with briefer notices of members and officers of the State Legislature.

Mississippi Valley

2220   CAMPBELL, JOHN A
A biographical history, with portraits, of prominent men of the Great West. Chicago, Western Biographical and Engraving Co., 1902. 688 p. ports. 31 cm. Covers the Mississippi Valley only.

Missouri (See Item 2013)

Montana

2221   PROGRESSIVE MEN OF THE STATE OF MONTANA. Chicago, A. W. Bowen [190-?] 2 v. ports. 30cm.

Nebraska

2222   A BIOGRAPHICAL AND GENEALOGICAL HISTORY OF SOUTHEASTERN NEBRASKA. Chicago, Lewis Pub. Co., 1904. 2 v. illus. 28cm.

2223   NEBRASKA BLUE BOOK. 18--   [Lincoln, Neb.]   v. illus., ports. 18-24cm. Title varies. Published by the Nebraska Legislative Reference Bureau, 1915-1938; by the Nebraska Legislative Council, 1940-   Includes biographies of State officials, legislators, etc.

2224   WHO'S WHO IN NEBRASKA. [v. 1-   1940-   Lincoln, Nebraska Press Association. v. 29cm. Editor: 1940-   John Faris.

Nevada

2225   WHO'S WHO IN NEVADA.
Brief sketches of men who are making history in the Sage-
brush State. Published by Bessie Beatty. Los Angeles, Home
Print. Co., 1907. 276p. ports. 23cm.

New England

2226   BRADFORD, ALDEN, 1765-1843.
Biographical notices of distinguished men in New England:
statesmen, patriots, physicians, lawyers, clergymen, and
mechanics. Boston, S. G. Simpkins, 1842. 464 p. 19cm.

2227   ELIOT, JOHN, 1754-1813.
A biographical dictionary, containing a brief account of the
first settlers, and other eminent characters among the
magistrates, ministers, literary and worthy men, in New-
England. Salem, Cushing and Appleton, 1809. viii, 511 p.
22 cm.

2228   MEN OF NEW ENGLAND.
Compiled under the personal direction of Winfield Scott
Downs. New York, American Historical Co. [c1941-
v. ports. 28cm.

2229   SAVAGE, JAMES, 1784-1873.
A genealogical dictionary of the first settlers of New En-
gland, showing the three generations of those who came before
May, 1692, on the basis of Farmer's Register. Boston,
Little, Brown, 1860-62. 4 v. 25cm.

2230   --- ----A genealogical cross index of the four volumes of ...
James Savage. By O. P. Dexter. New York, O. Dexter,
1884. 38 p. 25cm.

2231   SHIPTON, CLIFFORD KENYON, 1902-
New England life in the 18th century; representative biographies from Sibley's Harvard graduates. Cambridge, Mass.,
Belknap Press of Harvard University Press, 1963. xxvii,
626 p. ports. 24cm. A selection of biographies from the
volumes of Sibley's Harvard graduates written by Shipton.

2232   WHO'S WHO IN NEW ENGLAND;
A biographical dictionary of leading living men and women
of the states of Maine, New Hampshire, Vermont, Massachusetts, Rhode Island and Connecticut. [1st]-   ed. ;
1909-   Chicago, A. N. Marquis Co.   v. 20-24cm.

New Hampshire

2233   BIOGRAPHICAL SKETCHES OF THE GOVERNOR, COUNCILORS AND MEMBERS OF THE SENATE AND HOUSE OF REPRESENTATIVES OF THE NEW HAMPSHIRE LEGISLATURE for 1881/82 -   v. 1-   Concord, N. H. , A. C. Clark.   v. 24cm.   On cover, 19   The Brown book of the New Hampshire Legislature.

2234   MEN OF PROGRESS;
     Biographical sketches and portraits of leaders in business and professional life in and of the State of New Hampshire. Compiled under the supervision of Richard Herndon.   Edited under the auspices of the Manchester Union.   Boston, New England magazine, 1898.   233p.   illus.   29cm.

2235   NEW HAMPSHIRE NOTABLES;
     Brief biographical sketches of New Hampshire men and women, native or resident, prominent in public, professional, business, educational, fraternal or benevolent work.   Concord, N. H. , Concord Press, 1932.   216 p.   ports.   24cm.

2236   NEW HAMPSHIRE NOTABLES;
     Presenting biographical sketches of men and women who have helped shape the character of New Hampshire and their communities.   Concord, Concord Press, 1955.   211 p.   ports. 25cm.   In double columns.

2237   SKETCHES OF SUCCESSFUL NEW HAMPSHIRE MEN.
     Manchester, N. H. , J. B. Clarke, 1882.   315 p.   ports. 24cm.

New Jersey

2238   THE BIOGRAPHICAL ENCYCLOPAEDIA OF NEW JERSEY
     of the nineteenth century.   Philadelphia, Galaxy Pub. Co. , 1877.   574 p.   84 ports.   29cm.

2239   MEMORIAL CYCLOPEDIA OF NEW JERSEY.
     Under the editorial supervision of Mary Depue Ogden.   Newark, Memorial History Co. , 1915-17.   3 v.   plates, ports. 28cm.   Published also in 1916 under title: Cyclopedia of New Jersey biography.

2240   NEW JERSEY. LEGISLATURE.
     Manual.   18--   Trenton.   v. illus. 17cm.   Title varies slightly.   Includes biographies of State officials and legislators.

New Mexico

2241   HERTZOG, PETER
A directory of New Mexico desperados. [Santa Fe, N. M. ,
Press of the Territorian, 1965] 44 p. 23cm. (Western Americana series, no. 5) Alphabetical list with one to nine lines
identifying a particular desperado and describing his generally violent end.

2242   WHO'S WHO IN NEW MEXICO;
Biographical sketches of contemporary New Mexico.
v. 1-   1937-   Albuquerque, Abousleman Co.   v.
illus. 24cm.

New York (City)

Bibliographies, Indexes, Etc.

2243   BAILEY, ROSALIE FELLOWS, 1908-
Guide to genealogical and biographical sources for New
York City (Manhattan) 1783-1898. With an introd. by John
Ross Delafield. New York [1954] iv, 96p. 23cm. "Revised
from the New England historical and genealogical register,
vol. 106-108 (1952-54). "

General Works

2244   HERRINGSHAW'S CITY BLUE BOOK OF BIOGRAPHY;
New Yorkers of 1917-   Chicago, C. J. Herringshaw.
v. 25cm.

2245   [KING, MOSES] 1853-1909.
Notable New Yorkers of 1896-1899; a companion volume to
King's Handbook of New York City. New York, M. King, 1899.
616 p. ports. 22cm. 2, 336 names and portraits, classified
and indexed.

2246   LEADERS OF THE TWENTIETH CENTURY,
New York City, 1918. New York, Unico News Service
[c1918] 272p. ports. 24cm. Chiefly portraits. On verso of
t. p. : Samuel Mendelson, William Mendelson, editors and
publishers.

2247   NOTABLE NEW YORKERS, 1942.
New York, Empire City Pub. Co. , c1942. 132 p. incl.
ports. plates. 24cm. Portraits: p. 17-132. Prominent
persons in New York City.

2248   WHO'S WHO IN HARLEM.
1st-   ed. ; 1949/50-   New York, Magazine & Period-

ical Print. & Pub. Co. v. illus., ports. 24cm. Compiler:
1949/50 -   B. S. B. Trottman.

2249   WHO'S WHO IN NEW YORK (CITY AND STATE)
        1st-   ed.; 1904-   New York, Who's Who Publica-
        tions, inc.   v. 21-27cm. Subtitle varies. Imprint varies.

2250   WHO'S WHO IN QUEENS.
        1936-   [Jamaica, N. Y.]   v. 21cm.

New York (State)

2251   BIOGRAPHICAL DIRECTORY OF THE STATE OF NEW YORK,
        1900. New York, Biographical Directory Co., 1900. 567p.
        29cm.

2252   FITCH, CHARLES ELLIOTT, 1835-1918.
        Encyclopedia of biography of New York, a life record of
        men and women whose sterling character and energy and
        industry have made them preeminent in their own and many
        other states. Boston, American Historical Society, 1916-
        v. plates, ports. 28 cm. Vols. 1-3 also published under
        title: Memorial encyclopedia of the State of New York. Title
        varies slightly.

2253   GALPIN, WILLIAM FREEMAN, 1890-
        Central New York, an inland empire, comprising Oneida,
        Madison, Onondaga, Cayuga, Tompkins, Cortland, Chenango
        counties and their people. New York, Lewis Historical Pub.
        Co. [1941] 4 v. illus. 28 cm. Vol. 4 contains biographies.

2254   HARLOW, SAMUEL R
        Life sketches of the State officers, senators, and members
        of the Assembly of the State of New York, in 1867 [-1868] by
        S. R. Harlow, H. H. Boone [and S. C. Hutchins] Albany,
        Weed, Parsons, 1867-68. 2 v. fronts. 22cm.

2255   HARRISON, MITCHELL CHARLES, 1870-
        New York State's prominent and progressive men; an en-
        cyclopaedia of contemporaneous biography. [New York]
        New York tribune, 1900-02. 3v. ports. 29cm.

2256   HILLS, FREDERICK SIMON
        New York State men; biographic studies and character
        portraits. Albany, Argus, 1906. 366p. illus. 29cm.
        Ca. 700 portraits and biographical sketches.

2257   MCELROY, WILLIAM HENRY, 1838-   ed.
Life sketches of executive officers and members of the
Legislature of the State of New York for 1873 [-1875] Albany,
Weed, Parsons, printers, 1873-75. 3 v. illus., ports.
21cm. Title varies; vols. for 1874-75 have title: Life sketches
of government officers and members of the Legislature of the
State of New York, by W. H. McElroy and Alex. McBride.

2258   THE MEN OF NEW YORK;
A collection of biographies and portraits of citizens of the
Empire State prominent in business, professional, social,
and political life during the last decade of the nineteenth century. Buffalo, G. E. Matthews, 1898. 2 v. ports. 33cm.

2259   [MORRIS, CHARLES] 1833-1922.
Men of affairs in New York; an historical work giving por-
traits and sketches of the most eminent citizens of New York.
New York, L. R. Hamersly, 1906. 294p. ports. 32cm.
"Practically a second edition of 'The makers of New York
[published 1895]"--Cf. Preface.

2260   MURPHY, WILLIAM D
Biographical sketches of the state officers and members of
the Legislature of the State of New York in 1858 [-1861]   Albany, J. Munsell [etc.] 1858-61.   3 v.   17-19cm.

2261   NOTABLE MEN OF CENTRAL NEW YORK:
Syracuse and vicinity, Utica and vicinity, Auburn, Oswego,
Watertown, Fulton, Rome, Oneida, Little Falls. XIX and XX
centuries. [Syracuse] D. J. Stoddard, 1903.   428 p. ports.
24cm.   A collection of portraits with brief biographical notes.

2262   THE NEW YORK RED BOOK,
Containing latest information relating to the State government. 1895(?)-   Albany, Williams Press [etc.]   v.
illus., ports. 24cm.   With biographies of State elective officers, judges, officials, etc.

2263   REPUBLICANS OF NEW YORK;
A pictorial and concise biographical record of Republicans
of the Empire State at the beginning of the twentieth century.
[New York] Publishing Society of New York [1906]   444 ports.
on 295p. 30cm.

2264   SPENCER, ALFRED
Roster of native sons (and daughters) For each locality
of upstate New York a roster of its eminent sons and daughters,
from earliest settlement to the present time. Bath, N. Y. ,
Courier Press, 1941. ii, 287 p. 24cm.

North Carolina

2265   ASHE, SAMUEL A'COURT, 1840-1938, ed.
Biographical history of North Carolina from colonial times
to the present. [Old North State ed.] Greensboro, N. C. ,
C. L. Van Noppen, 1905-   v. ports. 25cm.

2266   NORTH CAROLINA. SECRETARY OF STATE.
North Carolina manual. 1874-   Raleigh. v. illus.
20-22cm. Title varies: 1874-   The legislative manual and
political register. ---   1911,   A pocket manual for the
use of members of the General Assembly ... --[etc.] Biographical sketches of State elective and appointive officers
included.

North Dakota

2267   WHO'S WHO FOR NORTH DAKOTA.
1955-   Bismarck, H. L. White. v. illus. , ports.
27cm. triennial. Vols. for 1955-   published with the
cooperation of the State Historical Society of North Dakota.

Northeastern States

2268   WHO'S WHO IN THE EAST;
A business, professional and social record of men and wo-
men of achievement in the Eastern States. 1930-   Wash-
ington, Mayflower Pub. Co.   v. 25cm. biennial. Covers
Massachusetts, New Hampshire, Vermont, Connecticut, Rhode
Island, New York, New Jersey, Maryland, Pennsylvania,
Delaware, District of Columbia.

2269   WHO'S WHO IN THE EAST (AND EASTERN CANADA);
A biographical dictionary of noteworthy men and women
of the Middle Atlantic and Northeastern states and Eastern
Canada. 1st-   ed. ; 1942/43-   Chicago, Marquis
Who's Who.   v. 24cm. First ed. published in Boston by
Larkin, Roosevelt & Larkin. Title varies: 1942/43-19
Who's who in the East. Subtitle varies slightly.

Northwest, Pacific

2270   EMINENT MEN OF THE NORTHWEST.
        1955-   Palo Alto, Calif. , C. W. Taylor.   v. ports.
        27cm. The States of Oregon, Washington & Idaho.

2271   ENCYCLOPEDIA OF NORTHWEST BIOGRAPHY.
        Winfield Scott Downs, editor, assisted by a notable
        advisory board. New York, American Historical Co. , 1941.
        515p. plates, ports. 28cm.

2272   WHO'S WHO IN THE NORTHWEST.
        1910-   Portland, Or. , Western Press Association.   v.
        22cm.

Ohio

2273   THE BIOGRAPHICAL ANNALS OF OHIO.
        v. 1-   1902/03- [Springfield, Ohio] v. illus. 25cm.
        Vol. 1 is a revised and enlarged ed. of the Ohio statesmen
        and hundred year book, by William A. Taylor, published in
        1892.

2274   THE BIOGRAPHICAL CYCLOPAEDIA AND PORTRAIT
        GALLERY, with an historical sketch of the State of Ohio.
        Cincinnati, Western Biographical Pub. Co. , 1883 [-95]
        6 v. ports. 32cm.

2275   THE BIOGRAPHICAL ENCYCLOPAEDIA OF OHIO
        Of the nineteenth century. Cincinnati, Galaxy Pub. Co. ,
        1876. 672 p. 99 ports. 29cm. Edited by Charles Robson.

2276   BRENNAN, JOSEPH FLETCHER, ed.
        A biographical cyclopaedia and portrait gallery of
        distinguished men, with an historical sketch, of the State of
        Ohio. Cincinnati, J. C. Yorston, 1879. 504 p. 199 ports. 31
        cm. "Originally begun by Mr. Egbert Cleave in 1873, under
        the title of Cleave's biographical cyclopaedia. "

2277   COMMEMORATIVE BIOGRAPHICAL RECORD OF NORTH-
        WESTERN OHIO, including the counties of Defiance,
        Henry, Williams, and Fulton, containing biographical sketch-

es of prominent and representative citizens, and of many of the early settled families. Chicago, J. H. Beers, 1899. 616p. ports. 29cm.

2278   PROGRESSIVE MEN OF NORTHERN OHIO. Cleveland, Plain Dealer Pub. Co., 1906. 204p. ports. 29cm.

2279   WHO'S WHO IN OHIO; Those who have achieved prominence in their respective lines of endeavor. Cleveland, Biographical Pub. Co., 1930. 263p. 24cm.

Ohio Valley

2280   LEAHY, ETHEL CARTER Who's who on the Ohio River and its tributaries. The Ohio River from the Ice Age to the future: history, biography, statistics. Cincinnati, E. C. Leahy Pub. Co., 1931. xiv, 868p. illus., ports. 24cm.

Oklahoma

2281   HARLOW, REX FRANCIS, 1892- Makers of government in Oklahoma; a descriptive roster of Oklahomans whose influence and activity make them significant in the course of public events in their state. Compiled under the editorial supervision of Victor E. Harlow. Oklahoma City, Harlow Pub. Co., 1930. v, 857p. ports. 27cm.

2282   HARLOW, REX FRANCIS, 1892- Oklahoma leaders; biographical sketches of the foremost living men of Oklahoma. Oklahoma City, Harlow Pub. Co., 1928. 530p. ports. 25cm.

2283   MEN OF AFFAIRS AND REPRESENTATIVE INSTITUTIONS OF OKLAHOMA, 1916; A newspaper reference work. Tulsa, World Pub. Co. [1916] [323] p. illus., ports. 28 x 20cm.

2284   OKLAHOMA BIOGRAPHICAL ASSOCIATION. Oklahomans and their state; a newspaper reference work. Editors: General Roy Hoffman [and others] Oklahoma City, 1919. 116 l. plates, ports. 29cm.

2285 PORTRAIT AND BIOGRAPHICAL RECORD OF OKLAHOMA.
Chicago, Chapman Pub. Co., 1901. 1298p. plates, ports.
29cm.

2286 WHO IS WHO IN THE OKLAHOMA LEGISLATURE.
29th-   Oklahoma City, Oklahoma State Library,
Legislative Reference and Research Division, 1963-   v.
18 x 24cm. biennial.

2287 A WHO'S WHO IN OKLAHOMA.
1964-   [Muskogee, Okla.] Leadership Index.   v.
25 cm.

2288 WHO'S WHO IN OKLAHOMA
(A biographical history of men and women in Oklahoma
life today) By Lyle H. Boren and Dale Boren. Sponsored by
T. H. Reynolds. Guthrie, Okla., Co-operative Pub. Co.,
1935-   v. 23cm.

Omaha

2289 WHO'S WHO IN OMAHA;
Biographical sketches of men and women of achievement.
1928-   Louisville, Ky., R. M. Baldwin Corp.   v. ports.
28cm.

Oregon

2290 CAPITOL'S WHO'S WHO FOR OREGON.
19   Portland, Or., Capital Pub. Co.   v. 24cm.

2291 CORNING, HOWARD MCKINLEY, 1896-   ed.
Dictionary of Oregon history, compiled from the research
files of the former Oregon Writers' Project, with much added
material. Portland, Or., Binfords & Mort [1956]   281 p.
27cm. "A topical and biographical study of Oregon history,
in alphabetical form." --Cf. Foreword

2292 PORTRAIT AND BIOGRAPHICAL RECORD OF WESTERN
OREGON.
Chicago, Chapman Pub. Co., 1904. [21]-1033p. ports.
30cm.

2293 WHO'S WHO IN OREGON;
Biographical dictionary of men and women who are build-

ing a state. v. 1-   1929/30-   Oregon City, Oregon
City enterprise.   v. 24cm.

Pennsylvania

2294   THE BIOGRAPHICAL ENCYCLOPAEDIA OF PENNSYLVANIA
of the nineteenth century. Philadelphia, Galaxy Pub. Co.,
1874. 672 p. ports. 28 x 23cm. Edited by Charles Robson.

2295   BLANCHARD, CHARLES
The progressive men of the Commonwealth of Pennsylvania.
Logansport, Ind., A. W. Bowen, 1900. 2 v. ports. 28cm.

2296   COMMEMORATIVE BIOGRAPHICAL RECORD OF CENTRAL
PENNSYLVANIA, including the counties of Centre, Clinton, Union and Snyder, containing biographical sketches of
prominent and representative citizens, and of many of the
early settled families. Chicago, J. H. Beers, 1898. 1231p.
ports. 30cm.

2297   COMMEMORATIVE BIOGRAPHICAL RECORD OF NORTH-
EASTERN PENNSYLVANIA, including the counties of
Susquehanna, Wayne, Pike and Monroe, containing biographical sketches of prominent and representative citizens, and
many of the early settled families. Chicago, J. H. Beers,
1900. 1852p. ports. 30cm.

2298   ENCYCLOPEDIA OF PENNSYLVANIA BIOGRAPHY.
New York, Lewis Historical Pub. Co., 1914-   v. illus.,
ports. 28cm. Edited by J. W. Jordan and others.

2299   ----Index, v.1-20. New York, Lewis Historical Pub. Co.,
1932. 189p. 28cm.

2300   JORDAN, JOHN WOOLF, 1840-1921, ed.
Colonial and revolutionary families of Pennsylvania;
genealogical and personal memoirs. New York, Lewis Pub.
Co., 1911. 3v. (1706p.) illus. 28cm.

2301   PENNSYLVANIA WHO'S WHO.
1957/58-   Pittsburgh.   v. 28cm.

2302   WHO'S WHO IN PENNSYLVANIA;
Containing authentic biographies of Pennsylvanians who are
leaders and representatives in various departments of worthy

human achievement. 1st-2d ed.; 1904, 1908. New York, L. R. Hamersly Co. [1904-08] 2 v. 22-23cm. 2d ed. (1908) edited by John W. Leonard, has subtitle: A biographical dictionary of contemporaries.

2303 WHO'S WHO IN THE COMMONWEALTH OF PENNSYLVANIA.
Compiled by Jules C. Spiegel. Pittsburgh, Who's Who Pub. Co. of America [1931] 44 l. 32cm.

2304 WILLIAMSON, LELAND M
Prominent and progressive Pennsylvanians of the nineteenth century. A review of their careers. Editors: Leland M. Williamson [and others] Philadelphia, Record Pub. Co., 1898. 2 v. illus., ports. 30cm.

Philadelphia

2305 DIRECTORY OF COLORED BUSINESS AND PROFESSIONAL
WOMEN OF PHILADELPHIA AND VICINITY. 1939-
Philadelphia. v. ports. 23cm. Also published under title: Directory of Negro business and professional women of Philadelphia and vicinity. Editor: 1939, Josephine B. Keene.

2306 MEN OF AMERICA.
A biographical album of the city government of Philadelphia in the bi-centennial year. In which are embraced executive officers, judges of the courts, members of the councils and of the public trusts. Philadelphia, American Biographical Pub. Co., 1883. 208p. front., 52 ports. 28cm. Edited by Solomon Foster and Louis N. Megargee.

2307 SIMPSON, HENRY, 1790-1868.
The lives of eminent Philadelphians, now deceased. Collected from original and authentic sources. Philadelphia, W. Brotherhead, 1859. 993 p. ports. 24cm.

2308 WHO'S WHO IN PHILADELPHIA.
Compiled by Jules C. Spiegel. Pittsburgh, Who's Who Pub. Co. of America [1931] 44 l. 31cm.

Pittsburgh

2309 WHO'S WHO IN PITTSBURGH.
1930- Pittsburgh, Industrial Service Bureau of Pittsburgh. v. 27cm.

Rhode Island

2310 THE BIOGRAPHICAL CYCLOPEDIA OF REPRESENTATIVE
MEN OF RHODE ISLAND. Providence, National
Biographical Pub. Co., 1881. 589p. 132 ports. 29cm.

2311 MEN OF PROGRESS;
Biographical sketches and portraits of leaders in business
and professional life in the State of Rhode Island and Providence Plantations. Compiled under the supervision of Richard
Herndon. Edited by Alfred M. Williams and William F. Blanding. Boston, New England magazine, 1896. 282p. ports.
29cm.

2312 REPRESENTATIVE MEN AND OLD FAMILIES OF RHODE
ISLAND;
Genealogical records and historical sketches of prominent and representative citizens and of many of the old families. Chicago, J. H. Beers, 1908. 3 v. ports. 29cm.

2313 RHODE ISLAND. DEPT. OF STATE.
Manual, with rules and orders, for the use of the General
Assembly of the State of Rhode Island. 1867/68-
Providence. v. plates, ports. 17-20cm. Section: "Bio-
graphical sketches" in 1959-60 vol., e.g., contains data for
State elective officers.

Saint Louis

2314 PORTRAITS OF PROMINENT SAINT LOUISANS IN 1916;
A portrait work of its merchants, manufacturers, bankers,
and professional men... St. Louis, H. Brown [c1916] 235p.
ports. 28 x 24cm.

2315 WHO'S WHO IN ST. LOUIS.
[Compiled by S. J. Rudkin. St. Louis? 1931?] 40 1.
29cm.

2316 WHO'S WHO IN SAINT LOUIS.
1928/29- [St. Louis] Published under auspices Civic Union of St. Louis by the Who's Who Committee. v.
24cm. biennial.

San Diego

2317 WHO'S WHO IN SAN DIEGO.
[1936-   San Diego, Calif., S. Gabriel.   v. 24cm.

South Carolina

2318 HEMPHILL, JAMES CALVIN, 1850-1927, ed.
Men of mark in South Carolina; ideals of American life.
A collection of biographies of leading men of the State.
Washington, Men of Mark Pub. Co., 1907-09. 4 v. ports.
23cm.

2319 WHO'S WHO IN SOUTH CAROLINA;
A dictionary of contemporaries containing biograpical notices of eminent men of South Carolina. Edited by Geddings
Harry Crawford. Columbia, S. C., Printed by McCaw, 1921.
220 p. 24cm.

2320 WHO'S WHO IN SOUTH CAROLINA;
A standard biographical reference book of South Carolina.
1934/35-   Columbia, S. C., Current Historical Association.   v. 24cm.

South Dakota

2321 COURSEY, OSCAR WILLIAM, 1873-
Who's who in South Dakota. v. 1-   ; 1st-   ed.
Mitchell, S. D., Educator School Supply Co. [c1914-
v. ports.

2322 MEMORIAL AND BIOGRAPHICAL RECORD;
An illustrated compendium of biography, including a compendium of local biography, including biographical sketches of
prominent old settlers and representative citizens of South
Dakota with a review of their life work. Also a compendium
of national biography. Chicago, G. A. Ogle, 1898. 11, 1102p.
ports. 28cm. In double columns.

2323 SOUTH DAKOTA. LEGISLATURE.
South Dakota legislative manual. 190-   Pierre.
v. ports. 24cm. Includes biographies of State elective
officers and members of the Legislature.

2324   WHO'S WHO IN SOUTH DAKOTA, 1956;
        A biographical directory. Bernice White, editor. Avis
Person, associate editor. Pierre, S. D., H. L. White
[1956] xxvi, 281p. illus. 27cm.

2325   WHO'S WHO AMONG SOUTH DAKOTANS.
        A biographical directory. v. 1-   1924/25-
Pierre, Statewide Service Co. [etc.] v. 24cm. Title varies:
1924/25, Fox's who's who among South Dakotans.

Southern States

2326   REPRESENTATIVE MEN OF THE SOUTH.
        Philadelphia, C. Robson, 1880. 553p. ports. 29cm.

2327   WHO'S WHO IN THE SOUTH;
        A business, professional and social record of men and wo-
men of achievement in the Southern States. 1927-   Washington, Mayflower Pub. Co.   v. 25cm. biennial.

2328   WHO'S WHO IN THE SOUTH AND SOUTHWEST.
        [1950]-   Chicago, A. N. Marquis Co.   v. 24cm.
Issue for 1950 called 2d ed., but is first under Marquis editorship.

2329   WHO'S WHO IN THE SOUTH AND SOUTHWEST;
        A biographical dictionary of leading men and women of the
Southern and Southwestern States. v. 1. [Limited 1st ed.]
Chicago, Larkin, Roosevelt & Larkin, 1947. 1084p. 24cm.
Published also under titles: Who's who in Alabama, Who's who
in Arizona, Who's who in Florida, Who's who in Georgia,
Who's who in Kentucky, Who's who in Louisiana, Who's who
in Mississippi, Who's who in New Mexico, Who's who in North
Carolina, Who's who in the Northwest, Who's who on the Pa-
cific Coast, Who's who in South Carolina, Who's who in Ten-
nessee, Who's who in Texas, and who's who in Virginia.

Southwest, New

2330   NOTABLE WOMEN OF THE SOUTHWEST;
        A pictorial biographical encyclopedia of the leading women
of Texas, New Mexico, Oklahoma, and Arizona. Dallas, W.
T. Tardy, 1938. vii, 384 p. ports. 24cm.

2331　　PRESS REFERENCE LIBRARY (SOUTHWEST ED.)
　　　　　Notables of the Southwest: being the portraits and biogra-
　　　　phies of progressive men of the Southwest, who have helped
　　　　in the development and history making of this wonderful
　　　　country. Los Angeles, Los Angeles Examiner, 1912. 500p.
　　　　ports. 29cm.

Tennessee

2332　　ALLISON, JOHN, 1845-1920, ed.
　　　　　Notable men of Tennessee. Personal and genealogical,
　　　　with portraits. Atlanta, Southern Historical Association,
　　　　1905. 2v. ports. 27cm.

2333　　MEMORIAL AND BIOGRAPHICAL RECORD;
　　　　　An illustrated compendium of biography, containing a com-
　　　　pendium of local biography, including biographical sketches
　　　　of prominent old settlers and representative citizens of part
　　　　of the Cumberland region of Tennessee, with a review of their
　　　　life work. Also a compendium of national biography. Chicago,
　　　　G. A. Ogle, 1898. 514p. ports. 28cm. In double columns.

2334　　SPEER, WILLIAM S
　　　　　Sketches of prominent Tennesseans... Nashville, A. B.
　　　　Tavel, 1888. vii, 579 p. ports. 30 x 24cm.

2335　　TEMPLE, OLIVER PERRY, 1820-1907.
　　　　　Notable men of Tennessee, from 1833 to 1875, their times
　　　　and their contemporaries, by Oliver P. Temple. Compiled
　　　　and arr. by his daughter, Mary B. Temple. New York, Cos-
　　　　mopolitan Press, 1912. 467p. port. 23cm.

2336　　TENNESSEE BLUE BOOK.
　　　　　19-- 　　Nashville. 　v. illus., ports. 13-23cm. Ti-
　　　　tle varies: 19 　-10, Tennessee pocket manual. --1912-19,
　　　　Tennessee directory and official vote... --1921-27, Tennessee
　　　　handbook and official directory. Includes biographies of
　　　　State elective and appointive officers. Issued by the Secre-
　　　　tary of State.

2337　　WHO'S WHO IN TENNESSEE;
　　　　　A biographical reference book of notable Tennesseans of
　　　　to-day. Memphis, Paul & Douglass Co. , 1911. 670p. 21cm.

2338　　WHO'S WHO IN TENNESSEE;
　　　　　A reference edition recording the biographies of contempo-

rary leaders in Tennessee, with special emphasis on their achievements in making the Volunteer State one of America's greatest. Written and prepared under the supervision of Frank E. Bass. Hopkinsville, Ky., Historical Record Association, 1961. 774p. illus. 27cm.

Texas

2339   BIOGRAPHICAL ENCYCLOPEDIA OF TEXAS.
New York, Southern Pub. Co., 1880.   300 p.   34 ports.
32 x 23cm.

2340   BIOGRAPHICAL SOUVENIR OF THE STATE OF TEXAS,
containing biographical sketches of the representative public, and many early settled families.   Chicago, F. A. Battey, 1889.
950 p.   104 ports.   28 x 20cm.

2341   CROWELL, EVELYN (MILLER) 1899-   ed.
Men of achievement.   Texas ed.   John Moranz, artist.
Dallas, J. Moranz Associates, 1948.   288 p.   ports.   31cm.

2342   THE HANDBOOK OF TEXAS.
Walter Prescott Webb, editor-in-chief.   H. Bailey Carroll, managing editor.   Llerena B. Friend, Mary Joe Carroll [and] Louise Nolen, editorial assistants.   Austin, Texas State Historical Association, 1952.   2 v.   25cm. Includes biography.

2343   MEMORIAL AND GENEALOGICAL RECORD OF SOUTHWEST TEXAS,
Containing biographical histories and genealogical records of many leading men and prominent families.   Chicago, Goodspeed Bros., 1894.   661p.   4 plates, 14 ports, 6 maps.   28cm.

2344   SOUTHWEST TEXANS.
Publisher's ed., rev. San Antonio, Southwest Publications [1952] 1A-72A, 608 p.   illus., ports.   32cm.   1937 edition, edited by Arthur J. Simpson, published under title: The century in southwest Texas.

2345   WRIGHT, MARCUS JOSEPH, 1831-1922.
Texas in the War, 1861-1865.   Edited and notes by Harold B. Simpson. [1st ed. Hillsboro, Tex.] Hill Junior College Press [1965] xx, 246p. ports. 24cm. "Notes and biographical sketches": p. [71]-165 includes 130 portraits and over 140 biographies of prominent Civil War participants from Texas.

2346   YEAR BOOK FOR TEXAS.
        By C. W. Raines. Vol. [1]-2; 1901-[03]   Austin, Gammel-
        Statesman Pub. Co., 1902-03. 2 v. illus., ports. 24cm.
        Includes biographies. No more published.

Utah

2347   SIMMONS, RALPH B
        Utah's distinguished personalities; a biographical directory
        of eminent contemporaneous men and women who are the faith-
        ful builders and defenders of the State. De luxe ed.   Salt Lake
        City, Personality Pub. Co. [1933-   v. ports. 21cm.

Vermont

2348   BIOGRAPHICAL ENCYCLOPEDIA OF VERMONT
        Of the nineteenth century.   Boston, Metropolitan Pub. and
        Engraving Co., 1885. 422 p. 43 ports. 30cm. Edited by
        H. C. Williams.

2349   HILLS, FREDERICK SIMON, comp.
        Men of Vermont State. Individual library ed., with bio-
        graphic studies, character portraits and autographs. Albany,
        N. Y., Albany Argus Art Press, 1925-   v. port. 30cm.

2350   MEN OF PROGRESS;
        Biographical sketches and portraits of leaders in business
        and professional life in and of the State of Vermont. Com-
        piled under the supervision of Richard Herndon. Edited by
        G. Grenville Benedict. Boston, New England magazine, 1898.
        312p. ports. 29cm.

2351   ULLERY, JACOB G   ed.
        Men of Vermont: an illustrated biographical history of
        Vermonters and sons of Vermont. Compiled under the edi-
        torial supervision of Hiram A. Huse. Brattleboro, Tran-
        script Pub. Co., 1894. 3 pts. in 1 v. ports. 29cm.

2352   VERMONT. SECRETARY OF STATE.
        Vermont legislative directory. 1867-   Montpelier.
        v. illus. 17cm. Contains biographical sketches of State
        officials and members of the General Assembly.

Virginia

2353   EMINENT AND REPRESENTATIVE MEN OF VIRGINIA AND
THE DISTRICT OF COLUMBIA in the nineteenth century.
With a concise historical sketch of Virginia, by William Wirt
Henry, and of the District of Columbia, by Ainsworth R.
Spofford. Madison, Wis., Brant & Fuller, 1893. 600p. 55
ports. 30cm.

2354   MEN OF MARK IN VIRGINIA,
Ideals of American life; a collection of biographies of the
leading men in the State. Lyon G. Tyler, editor-in-chief.
Washington, Men of Mark Pub. Co., 1906-09. 5 v. ports.
24cm.

2355   MEN OF MARK IN VIRGINIA.
[2d ser.] Richmond, Men of Mark Pub. Co., 1936-
v. ports. 24cm.

2356   TYLER, LYON GARDINER, 1853-1935, ed.
Encyclopedia of Virginia biography. New York, Lewis
Historical Pub. Co., 1915. 5 v. ports. 23cm.

Washington, D.C.

2357   WHO'S WHO IN THE NATION'S CAPITAL.
1921/22-   Washington, Ransdell inc.   v. 24cm.

Washington (State)

2358   NOTABLE MEN OF WASHINGTON.
Tacoma, Perkins Press, 1912.   65 p. of illus., ports.
28cm.

2359   SKETCHES OF WASHINGTONIANS;
Containing brief histories of men of the State of Washington
engaged in professional and political life, in manufacture, commerce, finance and religion. Seattle, W. C. Wolfe, 1906.
320 p. map. 24cm.

2360   WHO'S WHO IN WASHINGTON STATE:
A compilation of biographical sketches of men and women

prominent in the affairs of Washington State. v. 1-
1927-   Seattle, A. H. Allen.   v. 27cm.

Western States

2361   BARTHOLOMEW, ED ELLSWORTH
The biographical album of western gunfighters; containing
more than 1,000 biographical entries together with over six
hundred rare photographs of the most famous sheriffs, outlaws,
marshalls, and celebrated personalities in the history of the
western frontier. Houston, Frontier Press of Texas [1958]
1v. (unpaged) illus. 35x53cm.

2362   BINHEIM, MAX, ed.
Women of the West; a series of biographical sketches of
living eminent women in the eleven western states of the
United States of America. 1928 ed. Charles A. Elvin,
associate editor. Los Angeles, Publishers Press [c1928]
223p. ports. 24cm.

2363   HAFEN, LE ROY REUBEN, 1893-   ed.
The mountain men and the fur trade of the Far West; biographical sketches of the participants by scholars of the subject and with introductions by the editor. Under the editorial
supervision of LeRoy R. Hafen. Glendale, Calif., A. H.
Clark Co., 1965-   v. illus. 25cm. 6 or more vols.
anticipated which will contain biographies of some 400 mountain men.

2364   NOTABLE MEN OF THE WEST;
Including members of the United States Supreme Court,
supreme courts of the several states, and prominent lawyers
and business men in the western states. Chicago, Inter Ocean
Newspaper Co., 1902. 219 p. of ports. 27 x 21cm.

2365   PRESS REFERENCE LIBRARY (WESTERN ED.)
Notables of the West; being the portraits and biographies
of the progressive men of the West who have helped in the
development and history making of this wonderful country.
New York, International News Service, 1913-15. 2 v. ports.
29 x 22cm. Largely devoted to California and the Southwestern states.

2366   SPEER, WILLIAM S
The encyclopedia of the new West, containing fully authen-
tical information of the agricultural, mercantile, commercial,

manufacturing, mining and grazing industries... Also biographical sketches of... representative men and women.
Hon. John Henry Brown, revising editor. Marshall, Tex.,
United States Biographical Publishing Co., 1881. 1014 p.
89 ports. 31cm. Covers the following states: Texas, Arkansas, Colorado & New Mexico.

2367   STACEY, CLAUDE, firm, publisher.
        Men of the West; a pictorial who's who of the distinguished
men of the West Country. London [1926] xii, 175 p. ports.
4.°

2368   WHO'S WHO IN THE WEST;
        A biographical dictionary of noteworthy men and women of
the Pacific coast and the Western States. 1949-   Chicago,
A. N. Marquis Co.   v. 24cm. Vols. for 1949-   published also under title: Who's who on the Pacific Coast. Supersedes in part Who's who in the South and Southwest, published by Larkin, Roosevelt & Larkin.

2369   WHO'S WHO ON THE PACIFIC COAST;
        A biographical compilation of notable living contemporaries
west of the Rocky Mountains. Edited by Franklin Harper.
Los Angeles, Harper Pub. Co., 1913. 633p. 18cm.

West Virginia

2370   ENCYCLOPAEDIA OF CONTEMPORARY BIOGRAPHY OF
        WEST VIRGINIA. Including reference articles on the
industrial resources of the State, etc., etc... New York,
Atlantic Pub. & Engraving Co., 1894. 293p. ports. 30cm.

2371   MEN OF WEST VIRGINIA.
        Chicago, Biographical Pub. Co., 1903. 2 v. (775p.)
plates, ports. 28cm.

2372   WEST VIRGINIA BLUE BOOK.
        v. [1]-   ; 1916-   Charleston.   v. illus., ports.
24cm. annual. Title varies: 1916-34, West Virginia legislative hand book and manual and official register (1921, Official
register division of the West Virginia legislative hand book
and manual) "Compiled and edited by ... Clerk of the Senate."
No volume was issued for 1932. Includes biographical sketches
of legislators and officials.

Wisconsin

2373   COMMEMORATIVE BIOGRAPHICAL RECORD OF THE
UPPER LAKE REGION, containing biographical sketches
of prominent and representative citizens and many of the
early settled families. Chicago, J. H. Beers, 1905. viii,
554p. ports. 28cm. Covers areas in Wisconsin and Minnesota.

2374   COMMEMORATIVE BIOGRAPHICAL RECORD OF THE
COUNTIES OF ROCK, GREEN, GRANT, IOWA AND
LAFAYETTE, WISCONSIN, containing biographical sketches
of prominent and representative citizens, and of many of the
early settled families. Chicago, J. H. Beers, 1901. 990p.
port. 29cm.

2375   NOTABLE MEN OF WISCONSIN.
Milwaukee, Williams Pub. Co. [1902] 259 p. of ports.
23cm. Text: p. 5-30.

2376   WHO IS WHO IN WISCONSIN.
Los Angeles, Moore's Who is Who Publications, inc.,
1960. 351 p. 24cm.

2377   WISCONSIN. STATE HISTORICAL SOCIETY.
Dictionary of Wisconsin biography. Madison, 1960. xiv,
385p. 28cm. About 1500 persons (deceased) included.

2378   THE WISCONSIN BLUE BOOK.
1862-   [Madison] v. illus., ports. 19-23cm.
Title varies: 1862-78, The Legislative manual of the State of
Wisconsin. --1879-19   The Blue book of the State of Wisconsin. With brief biographical sketches of State elective
officers.

Wyoming

2379   PROGRESSIVE MEN OF THE STATE OF WYOMING.
Chicago, A. W. Bowen, 1903. xvi, 965p. ports. 28cm.

URUGUAY

Anonyms and Pseudonyms

2380   SCARONE, ARTURO, 1885-
Diccionario de seudónimos del Uruguay. Prólogo de
Ariosto D. González. 2. ed., con un apéndice. Montevideo,
C. Garcia, 1942. 632 p. 25cm. A dictionary of Uruguayan
pseudonyms; earlier editions have title: Apuntes para un dic-
cionario de seudónimos y de publicaciones anónimas.

General Works

2381   FERNÁNDEZ SALDAÑA, JOSE MARÍA, 1879-
Diccionario uruguayo de biografías, 1810-1940. Montevideo,
Editorial Amerindia, 1945. 1366 p. 25 cm. Dictionary of
Uruguayan biography for the years 1810-1940.

2382   PARKER, WILLIAM BELMONT, 1871-1934.
Uruguayans of today. London, New York, Hispanic Society
of America, 1921. xvi, 575 p. ports. 17cm. (Hispanic notes
and monographs, 7)

2383   QUIEN ES QUIEN.
1941-   [Montevideo]   v. 26cm. (Libros del Plata)
Who's who (in Uruguay)

2384   SCARONE, ARTURO, 1885-
Uruguayos contemporáneos; nuevo diccionario de datos
biográficos y bibliográficos. Montevideo, Casa Barreiro y
Ramos, 1937. 610, svi p. 26cm. 'Contemporary' Uruguayans; new dictionary of biographical & bibliographical dates.
1st ed. was issued in 1918. The edition above was completely
revised and rewritten. There are 1280 names in the main
alphabet and 71 in the appendix.

VENEZUELA

2385   DÁVILA, VICENTE, 1874-
Diccionario biográfico de ilustres próceres de la independencia suramericana. Caracas, 1924-26. 2v. 24cm. Biographical dictionary of famous persons instrumental in the
Venezuelan and South American independence movement.

2386 DICCIONARIO BIOGRÁFICO DE VENEZUELA.
Editores: Garrido Mezquita y Compañia, publicado bajo la
dirección técnica de Julio Cárdenas Ramirez; director de
recopilaciones Carlos Sáenz de la Calzada. 1. ed. Madrid,
Blass, 1953. li, 1558 p. ports., fold. col. maps. 26cm.
Biographical dictionary of Venezuela.

2387 EDITORIAL BIOGRÁFICA DE VENEZUELA, Caracas.
120 [i. e. Ciento veinte] biografías de próceres e ilustres
venezolanos. Caracas [1963] 275 p. ports. 24 cm. 120
biographies of Venezuelan patriots and worthies.

2388 MAC-PHERSON, TELASCO A
Diccionario histórico, geográfico, estadístico y biográfico
del estado Lara. 2. ed. Caracas, Editorial Elite, 1941.
xii, 558 p. 23cm. 1st published in 1883. Historical, geographical, statistical and biographical dictionary of the Venezuelan state of Lara.

2389 MAC-PHERSON, TELASCO A
Diccionario histórico, geográfico, estadístico y biográfico
del Estado Miranda, República de Venezuela. Caracas, Impr.
de "El Correo de Caracas," 1891. 556 p. Historical, geographical, statistical and biographical dictionary of the State
of Miranda, Venezuela.

2390 SUCRE, LUIS ALBERTO
Gobernadores y capitanes generales de Venezuela. Caracas, Lit. y Tip. del Comercio, 1928. 323p. 25cm. 128
biographies of governors and captain generals of Venezuela.

2391 TEJERA, FELIPE
Perfiles venezolanos; ó, Galería de hombres célebres de
Venezuela en las letras, ciencias y artes. Caracas, Impr.
Sanz, 1881. xviii, 478p. ports. 21cm. 94 Venezuelans.

VIETNAM (Including Old Indochina)

2392 BREBION, ANTOINE, 1857-1917.
Dictionnaire de bio-bibliographie générale, ancienne et
moderne, de l'Indochine française, publié après la mort de
l'auteur par Antoine Cabaton. Paris, Société d'Éditions
geographiques, maritimes et coloniales, 1935. iii, 446 p.
30 cm. (Académie des sciences coloniales. Annales, t. 8)
Dictionary of general bio-bibliography for French Indochina,
ancient and modern.

2393   CAO-VIÊN-TRAI.
        Lê triều lich-khoa tiên-sĩ dể danh bi ký [Chinese characters]
Tâp vǎn bia dể tên tấn sĩ các khoa triều Lê. Nguời dich
Hà-Tĩnh Vô-Oanh [Saigon] Bô Quôc-gia giáo-duc, 1961-62. 3 v.
illus. 24 cm. The book in which are the names of [Vietna-
mese] people who attained the doctoral degree during the Li
period (11th-13th centuries?) of Vietnamese history.

2394   ĐÀO-VĂN-HÔI.
        Danh-nhân nuôc nhà sách nầy dã duôc bô quôc-gia giáo-duc
Viêt-Nam, duyêt khão và nhân làm sách giáo-khoa. Saigon,
Nhà-in Ly-Cong-Quan, 1951. 192 p. 25cm. Notables of the
country [i. e. Vietnam] A textbook of Vietnamese biography.

2395   VIÊT-NAM DANH-NHÂN TU-DIÊN [CỦA] NGUYỄN HUYÊN-
        ANH. [Saigon] Hôi Vǎn-hóa Binh-dân, 1960. xic, 380 p.
21cm. Dictionary of famous Vietnamese (Vietnamese notables)

WALES See Great Britain

WEST INDIES

2396   THE CARIBBEAN WHO, WHAT, WHY.
        1st-   ed.; 1955/56-   [Glasgow, etc.] Printed by
Bell & Bain.   v. ports. 28cm. Title varies: 1st ed.,
1955/56, The British Caribbean who, what, why,

2397   ENCYCLOPAEDIE VAN NEDERLANDSCH WEST-INDIE,
        onder redactie van H. D. Benjamins en Joh. F. Snelleman.
's-Gravenhage, M. Nijhoff [etc.] 1914-17. x, 782p. 18 maps
on 3 fold. plates. 28cm. Published in parts. Encyclopedia of the Dutch West Indies; includes biography.

YUGOSLAVIA

2398   BAŠAGIĆ, SAFVET, 1870-1934.
        Znameniti Hrvati Bošnjaci i Hercegovci u turkskoj carevini.
Zagreb, Izvanredno Izdanje Matice Hrvatske, 1931. 79p.
23cm. Important Croats of Bosnia and Herzegovina during
Turkish rule.

2399   FERRARI-CUPILLI, GIUSEPPE
        Biografie e necrologie d'illustri e benemeriti Dalmati.
Raccolte e pubblicate per cura di Simeone Ferrari-Cupilli.
Zara, Tip. Spiridione Artale, 1874. 91, [7] p. Biography
& necrology of famous natives of Dalmatia.

2400   GAVRILOVIĆ, ANDRA, 1864-   ed.
Znameniti srbi XIX veka. Zagreb, Naklada Srpske shtam-
parije, 1901-04. 3v. ports. 38cm. Famous Serbians of the
19th century.

2401   GLIUBICH, SIMEONE, b. 1822.
Dizionario biografico degli uomini illustri della Dalmazia.
Vienna, R. Lechner, 1856. viii, 325 p. 23cm. Biographical
dictionary of famous men of Dalmatia.

2402   GRLOVIĆ, MILAN, 1852-1915.
Album zaslužnih Hrvata XIX. stoljeća. Sto i pedeset
životopisa, slika i vlastoručnih podpisa. Slike crtao Stjepan
Kovačević. Zagreb, Nakl. Maticevog litografskog zavoda,
1898-1900. 2 v. ports. 32cm. Contents. --[1] Zivotopisi. --
[2] Slike. 150 biographies with portraits of noted Croatians
of the 19th century.

2403   KO JE KO U JUGOSLAVIJI;
Biografski podaci o jugoslovenskim savremenicima. 1. izd.
[Redaktori: Slavko Janković, Mihajlo Milanović] Beograd
[Izd. "Sedme sile"] 1957. 810 p. 23cm. On cover: Ko je ko?
Who's who in Yugoslavia.

2404   MILIĆEVIĆ, MILAN ĐURO, 1831-1908.
Pomenik znamenitih ljudi u srpskog naroda novijega doba.
U Beogradu, U Srpskoj kraljevskoj štampariji, 1888.
svi, 874p. 24cm.

2405   ---- ----Dodatak pomeniku od 1888. Znameniti ljudi y
srpskoga naroda koji su preminuli do kraza 1900 g. U Beogradu, U Srpskoj kraljevskoj štampariji, 1901. iii, 198p.
24cm.

Memoirs of famous Serbians of modern times.

2406   SLOVENSKI BIOGRAFSKI LEKSIKON,
Uredila Izidor Cankar in Franc Ksaver Lukman s sodelo-
vanjem uredniškego odbora. V Ljubljani, Založila Zadružna
gospodarska banka, 1925-52. 2 v. 27cm. Biographical
dictionary of Slovenians. Issued in 8 parts. Vol. 2 edited
by France Kidric and F. K. Lukman. Imprint varies.

2407   STANCOVICH, PIETRO.
Biografia degli uomini distinti dell'Istria. 2. ed. con
saggio di annotazioni. Capodistria, 1888. xxx, 460 p. 8.°

Biography of famous men of the Istrian peninsula (in northern Italy & part of Croatia)

2408   STANOJEVIĆ, STANOJE, 1874-
Narodna enciklopedija srpsko-hravatsko-slovenačka.
Zagreb, Bibliografski zavod D. D. [1925]-   4 + (?) v.
27cm.   Serbo-Croatian-Slovene national encyclopedia; includes much bio-bibliographical material.

2409   ZNAMENITI I ZASLUŽNI HRVATI,
Te pomena vrijedna lica u hrvatskoj provijesti od 925-1925.
Sa pregledom povijesti Hrvatske, Bosne i Istre, hrvatske knjizevnosti i razvitka hrvatskog jezika, te hrv. vladara, hercega, banova i biskupa, kao uvodom. Sa 9 zasebnih slika, te 421 slikom u tekstu. Prigodom proslave 1000-godišnjice hrvatskoga kraljestva izdao: Odbor za izdanje knjige 'Zasluzni i znameniti Hrvati 925-1925.' U Zagrebu, Tisak i oprema Hrvatskog stamparskog zavoda d. d. [1925] xciv, lxxxi-cxxvi, 297p. illus., ports. 37 x 27cm. "Predgovor" signed: Emilij Laszowski. Famous and meritorious Croatians and notices of eminent persons in Croatian history from 925 to 1925.

BIOGRAPHY BY VOCATION

ARTS

Bibliography, Indexes, Artists' Marks, Etc.

2412 BRITISH MUSEUM. DEPT. OF PRINTS AND DRAWINGS.
Index of artists represented in the Department of Prints
and Drawings in the British Museum... London, Longmans,
1893-96. 2 v. 26 cm. No more published?

2413 BRITISH MUSEUM. DEPT. OF PRINTS AND DRAWINGS.
An index of Chinese artists represented in the Sub-department of Oriental Prints and Drawings in the British Museum,
by Arthur Waley... [London] Printed by order of the
Trustees, 1922. xii, 112 p. 22 cm. Supplement was published
by W. Speiser in Ostasiatische Zeitschrift, Mai/Aug. 1931 and
Okt. 1938.

2414 BRULLIOT, FRANZ, 1780-1836.
Dictionnaire des monogrammes, marques figurées, lettres
initiales, noms abrégés, etc., avec lesquels les peintres,
dessinateurs, graveurs et sculpteurs ont désigné leurs noms.
Nouv. éd. rev., corr. et augm. d'um grand nombre d'articles. Munich, J. G. Cotta, 1832-34. 3 v. 30 cm. Dictionary of artists' monograms, marks, etc.

2415 COLUMBIA UNIVERSITY. LIBRARIES. AVERY ARCHITEC-
TURAL LIBRARY.
Avery obituary index of architects and artists. Boston,
G.K. Hall, 1963. 338 p. 37cm.

2416 DUPLESSIS, GEORGES, 1834-1899.
Dictionnaire des marques et monogrammes de graveurs,
par Georges Duplessis et Henri Bouchot. Paris, J. Rouam,
1886-87. 3v. 19cm. (Guides du collectionneur) A dictionary of engravers' marks.

2417 GOLDSTEIN, FRANZ
Monogramm Lexikon; internationales Verzeichnis der Monogramme bildender Künstler seit 1850. Berlin, W. de
Gruyter, 1964. 931 p. 24cm. A dictionary of artists' marks
and monograms.

2418 RIS-PAQUOT, OSCAR EDMOND, 1835-
Dictionnaire encyclopédique des marques et monogrammes,
chiffres, lettres, initiales, signes figuratifs... contenant
12,156 marques... Paris, H. Laurens, 1893. 2 v. illus.
29cm. A dictionary of artists' marks, monograms, etc.

2419 ROYAL INSTITUTE OF BRITISH ARCHITECTS. LIBRARY.
Index of architects of several countries and many periods
(except English medieval) in nearly 60 old and new selected
indexes... London, The Institute, 1956. vii, 66p. 33cm.
"Typewritten script. In progress and expected to appear in

1959, in a limited edition. "--Chamberlain, M. W. Guide to
art reference books.

2420 SMITH, RALPH CLIFTON.
A biographical index of American artists. Baltimore,
Williams and Wilkins, 1930. x, 102 p. 24cm.

General Works

(Including Painting and Engraving, Art Collecting, Etc.)

2422 ACUÑA, LUIS ALBERTO, 1927-
Diccionario biográfico de artistas que trabajaron en el
Nuevo Reino de Granada. Bogotá, Ediciones del Instituto
Colombiano de Cultura Hispánica, 1964. 71p. 40 plates.
23cm. Artists who flourished in the New Kingdom of Gra-
nada (colonial Colombia)

2423 ALCAHALÍ Y DE MOSQUERA, JOSÉ MARÍA RUIZ DE LIHORI
YPARDINES, barón de, d. 1920.
Diccionario biográfico de artistas valencianos. Valencia,
Impr. de F. Domenech, 1897. 443p. 26cm. Biographical
dictionary of artists of Valencia, Spain.

2424 ALIZERI, FEDERIGO
Notizie dei professori del disegno in Liguria dalla
fondazione dell'Accademia. Genova, Tip. L. Sambolino,
1864-66. 3v. plates. 28cm. Artists of the 18th-19th
centuries in Liguria.

2425 ANCONA, PAOLO D', 1878-
Dictionnaire des miniaturistes du moyen âge et de la
renaissance, dans les différentes contrées de l'Europe [par]
Paolo d'Ancona [et] Erhard Aeschlimann. 2. éd., revue et
augm., contenant un index ordonné par epoques, régions,
écoles. Milan, U. Hoepli, 1949. x,239p. illus. 31cm.
Dictionary of miniaturist painters of the Middle Ages and the
Renaissance in the various countries of Europe.

2426 ANDRESEN, ANDREAS, 1828-1871.
Der deutsche peintre-graveur; oder, Die deutschen Maler
als Kupferstecher nach ihrem Leben und ihren Werken, von
dem letzten Drittel des 16. Jahrhunderts bis zum Schluss des
18. Jahrhunderts... Von A. Andresen unter Mitwirkung von
R. Weigel. Leipzig, A. Danz, 1864-78. 5v. 24cm.
The German painter-engraver; or, German painters as engravers, 16th-18th centuries.

2427 AUDIN, MARIUS, 1872-1951.
Dictionnaire des artistes et ouvriers d'art du Lyonnais,

par Marius Audin et Eugène Vidal. Paris, Bibliothèque d'art et d'archéologie, 1918.19. 2v. 26cm. (Publications pour faciliter les études d'art en France) Dictionnaire des artistes et ouvriers d'art de la France par provinces. Limited to artists who died before 1900 in the French region of Lyonnais.

2428 AUERBACH, ERNA.
Tudor artists; a study of painters in the royal service and of portraiture on illuminated documents from the accession of Henry VIII to the death of Elizabeth I. [London] University of London, Athlone Press, 1954. xvi, 222p. 52 plates (part col.) 26cm. Biographical notes are given in the appendices (p. 144-194) and yield brief information on the careers of ca. 400 artists (many of them little known)

2429 BAGLIONE, GIOVANNI, 1571-1644.
Le vite de' pittori, scultori, architetti, ed intagliatori, dal pontificato di Gregorio XIII. del 1572. fino a' tempi di papa Urbano VIII. nel 1642. Con la vita di Salvator Rosa Napoletano, pittore, e poeta, scritta da Gio: Batista Passari, nuovamente aggiunta. Napoli, 1733. 304p. 26cm. First ed., Roma, Fei, 1642; 2d, Roma, Manelfi, 1649. Lives of [Italian] painters, sculptors, architects and engravers from the Pontificate of Gregory XIII to that of Urban VIII (1572-1642)

2430 BALDINUCCI, FILIPPO, 1624?-1696.
Notizie de' professori del disegno da Cimabue in qua, per le quali si dimostra come, e per chi le bell'arti di pittura, scultura, e architettura, lasciata la rozzezza delle maniere greca, e gottica, si siano in questi secoli ridotte all'antica loro perfezione. Edizione accresciuta di annotazione del Sig. Domenico Maria Manni. Firenze, G. B. Stecchi, e A. G. Pagani, 1767-74. 21v. in 10. illus. 23cm. Subtitle varies. First edition, Florence, 1681-1728?

2431 -----Indice del nome, cognome, patria, anni della nascita e morte dei pittori, e scultori, descritti nelle Notizie...; distinta in secoli decennali...Firenze, Presso P. Allegrini, 1813. 63p. 23cm.

Italian masters of artistic design from the time of Cimabue.

2432 BAQUERO ALMANSA, ANDRÉS, 1853-1916.
Catálogo de los profesores de las bellas artes murcianos, con una introducción histórica. Murcia, Nogués, 1913. vi, 500p. port. 23cm. Catalog of the masters of fine arts in Murcia, Spain.

2433 BARTSCH, ADAM VON, 1757-1821.
Le peintre graveur... Nouv. éd. Würzburg, Verlagsdruckerei Würzburg, 1920. 21v. in 18. plates. 23cm.

First published in 1803-1821; reprinted 1854-1876. Famous engravers and their works.

2434 BASAN, PIERRE FRANCOIS, 1723-1797.
Dictionnaire des graveurs anciens et modernes, depuis l'origine de la gravure... 2. éd., mise par ordre alphabé-tique, considérablement augm. et ornée de cinquante estampes par différens artistes célèbres, ou sans aucune, au gré de l'amateur... Paris, L'auteur, 1789. 2v. 50 plates. 22cm. First ed. published in 1767. Dictionary of engravers, ancient and modern.

2435 BEAZLEY, JOHN DAVIDSON, 1885-
Attic black-figure vase-painters. Oxford, Clarendon Press, 1956. xvi, 851p. 24cm.

2436 BEEN, CHARLES ARNOLD, 1869-1914.
Danmarks malerkunst, billeder og biografier...Kapit-lerne indledede af Emil Hannover. København, 1902-03. 2v. in 1. illus. 32cm. Denmark's school of painting; pictures and biographies.

2437 BELLIER DE LA CHAVIGNERIE, ÉMILE, 1821-1871.
Dictionnaire général des artistes de l'école français depuis l'origine des arts du dessin jusqu'à nos jours. Architectes, peintres, sculpteurs, graveurs et lithographes. Ouvrage commencé par Émile Bellier de La Chavignerie, continué par Louis Auvray. Paris, Renouard, 1882-85. 2v. 27cm.

2438 -----Dictionaire général des artistes de l'école francaise depuis l'origine des arts du dessin jusqu'en 1883, par Louis Auvray. Supplément et table topographique. Paris, Renouard, 1887. 266, 80p. 27cm.

General dictionary of French artists, to 1883.

2439 BÉNÉZIT, EMMANUEL, 1854-1920.
Dictionnaire critique et documentaire des peintres, sculpteurs, dessinateurs et graveurs de tous les temps et de tous les pays, par un groupe d'écrivains spécialistes francais et étrangers. Nouv. ed. entièrement refondu, rev. et corr. sous la direction des héritiers de E. Bénézit. Paris, Gründ, 1948-55. 8v. A very important dictionary of artists.

2440 BÉRALDI, HENRI, 1849-
Les graveurs du XIXe siècle; guide de l'amateur d'estampes modernes. Paris, L. Conquet, 1885-92. 12v. in 10. 24cm. Dictionary of engravers of the 19th century.

2441 BÉRARD, ANDRÉ, 1806-1873.
Dictionnaire biographique des artistes francais du XIIe au XVIIe siècle, suivi d'une table chronologique et alphabétique comprenant en vingt classes les arts mentionnés dans l'ouvrage.

Paris, J. B. Dumoulin, 1872. xv p. , 864 columns. 22cm.
In double columns. Biographical dictionary of French artists
of the 12th to the 17th century.

2442 BERCKELAERS, FERDINAND LOUIS, 1901-
A dictionary of abstract painting, preceded by a History of
abstract painting, by Michel Seuphor [pseud.] New York,
Tudor Pub. Co. , 1957. 304p. illus. 22cm. Pages 117-294
contain brief biographical entries for some 500 artists.
English edition issued in London by Methuen, 1957.

2443 BERNT, WALTHER
Die niederländischen Zeichner des 17. Jahrhunderts.
Zwei Bände mit 705 Abbildungen. Mit einem Geleitwort von
J. Q. van Regteren Altena. München, Bruckman [1957-58]
2v. (chiefly illus.) 30cm. Drawings are arranged alphabetically by artists; biographical & bibliographical information
is given for each Dutch artist.

2444 BESSONE-AURELJ, ANTONIETTA MARIA, 1869-
Dizionario dei pittori italiani. 2. ed. ampliata. Milano,
Albrighi, 1928. 678p. 23cm. Dictionary of Italian painters.

2445 THE BLUE BOOK OF PHILATELY;
Who's who in the stamp world. 1st-   ed. ; 1935-   New
York, H. L. Lindquist.   v. ports. 26cm.

2446 BOLTON, THEODORE, 1889-
Early American portrait painters in miniature... New York,
F. F. Sherman, 1921. x, 180 p. ports. 25cm. 300 copies
printed.

2447 [BONAFONS, LOUIS ABEL DE, KNOWN AS ABBÉ DE
FONTENAY] 1737-1806
Dictionnaire des artistes; ou, Notice historique et
raisonnée des architectes, peintres, graveurs, sculpteurs,
musiciens, acteurs et danseurs; imprimeurs, horlogers &
mecha niciens. Ouvrage rédigé par M. l'abbé de Fontenai.
Paris, Vincent, 1776. 2 v. 17cm. A general dictionary of artists

2448 BONNAFFÉ, EDMOND, 1825-1903.
Dictionnaire des amateurs français au XVIIᵉ siècle. Paris,
A. Quantin, 1884. xvi, 353 p. 25cm. Dictionary of French
art collectors of the 17th century.

2449 BRADLEY, JOHN WILLIAM, 1830-1916.
A dictionary of miniaturists, illuminators, calligraphers,
and copyists, with reference to their works and notices of
their patrons, from the establishment of Christianity to the
18th century. Compiled from various sources, many hitherto
unedited. London, B. Quaritch, 1887-89. 3 v. 24 cm.

2450 BRUNE, PAUL, 1862-1920.
Dictionnaire des artistes et ouvriers d'art de la Franche-
Comté... Paris, Bibliothèque d'art et d'archéologie, 1912.

xxviii, 337 p. 26 cm. Dictionary of artists and artisans in the historical region of the Franche-Comté.

2451 BRYAN, MICHAEL, 1757-1821.
Dictionary of painters and engravers. New ed. , rev. and enl. under the supervision of George C. Williamson. Port Washington, N. Y. , Kennikat Press [1964] 5 v. plates. 26 cm. 1st ed. published in 1816 under title: A biographical and critical dictionary of painters and engravers.

2452 BÜNDNERISCHE KULTURELLE ARBEITSGEMEINSCHAFT.
Bündner Maler, Bildhauer, Komponisten und Schriftsteller der Gegenwart. Chur, Bischofberger, 1960. 152 p. ports. 23 cm. Texts in German, Raeto-Romance, or Italian. Summaries in German of the latter two texts. Painters, sculptors, composers and writers of today in the Canton of Grisons.

2453 BULGAKOV, FEDOR IL'ICH, 1852-1908.
Khudozhestvennaia entsiklopediia (Illiustrirovannyĭ slovar' iskusstv i khudozhestv) S. -Peterburg, Izd. A. S. Suvorina [1886-87] 2 v. illus. 24 cm. Covers only A-Okhry. No more published. Encyclopedia of art.

2454 BULGAKOV, FEDOR IL'ICH, 1852-1908.
Nash khudozhniki (zhivopistsy, skul'ptory, mozaichisty, gravery i medal' ery) na akademicheskikh vystavkakh poslednego 25-letiia. Biografii, portrety khudozhnikov i snimki s ikh proizvedenii. V alfavitnom poriadke imen khudozhnikov. S. -Peterburg, Tip. A. S. Suvorina, 1889-99. 2 v. Biographies, portraits, etc. of Russian artists of the latter part of the 19th century.

2455 BUSHNELL, GEORGE HERBERT, 1896-
Scottish engravers; a biographical dictionary of Scottish engravers and of engravers who worked in Scotland to the beginning of the nineteenth century. With a chronological index. London, New York Oxford University Press, 1949. xii, 60 p. 20 cm. 243 engravers.

2456 CAMPORI, GIUSEPPE, marchese, 1821-1887.
Gli artisti italiani e stranieri negli stati Estensi... Modena, Camera, 1855. 537 p. 23 cm. Italian and foreign artists in the States of the House of Este (Modena, Ferrara chiefly)

2457 CAMPORI, GIUSEPPE, marchese, 1821-1887.
Memorie biografiche degli scultori, architetti, pittori, ec. nativi di Carrara e di altri luoghi della provincia di Massa, con cenni relativi agli artisti italiani ed esteri che in essa dimorarono ed operarono, e un saggio bibliografico. Modena, Vincenzi, 1873. xiii, 466 p. 21 cm. Sculptors, architects, painters, etc. of the Province of Massa, Italy.

2458   CÁNOVAS DEL CASTILLO Y VALLEJO, ANTONIO, 1862-
Apuntes para un diccionario de pintores malagueños del
siglo XIX, por A. Cánovas. Madrid, Impr. de A. G. Izquierdo
[1908] 85 p. 16 cm. Sketches for a dictionary of painters
of Malaga, Spain, in the 19th century.

2459   CEÁN BERMÚDEZ, JUAN AGUSTÍN, 1749-1829.
Diccionario histórico de los más ilustres professores de las
bellas artes en España. Publicado por la Real Academia de
S. Fernando. Madrid, En la Impr. de la Viuda de Ibarra, 1800.
6 v. 16 cm. Historical dictionary of the most illustrious
artists in Spain.

2460   CHAMPLIN, JOHN DENISON, 1834-1915, ed.
Cyclopedia of painters and paintings, edited by John Denison
Champlin, Jr. Critical editor, Charles C. Perkins. New York,
C. Scribner, 1887. 4 v. illus. 30 cm. Various reprints
issued in 1892, 1915, etc.

2461   CHENNEVIÈRES-POINTEL, PHILIPPE, marquis de, 1820-
1899.
Recherches sur la vie et les ouvrages de quelques peintres
provinciaux de l'ancienne France. Paris, Dumoulin, 1847-62.
4 v. 4 plates. 22 cm. Provincial painters of Old France.

2462   CLOUZOT, HENRI, 1865-
Dictionnaire des miniaturistes sur émail. [Paris] A.
Morancé [c1924] xix, 241 p. illus. 24cm. (Archives de
l'amateur) Dictionary of enamellists.

2463   COLIN, PAUL, 1890-
La gravure et les graveurs. Bruxelles, G. van Oest, 1916
-18. 2v. (Répertoire des ouvrages à consulter) A bio-bibliography of engravers.

2464   COLNAGHI, SIR DOMINIC ELLIS, 1834-1908.
A dictionary of Florentine painters from the 13th to the 17th
centuries, by Sir Dominic Ellis Colnaghi. Edited by P. G.
Konody and Selwyn Brinton. London, J. Lane [1928] viii,
286 p. 29cm.

2465   COMANDUCCI, AGOSTINO MARIO, 1891-1940.
Dizionario illustrato dei pittori, disegnatori e incisori italiani moderni e contemporani. 3. ed., completamente rifatta
e ampliata da Luigi Pelandi e Luigi Servolini. Milano, L. M.
Patuzzi [1962] 4v. (xv, 2122 p.) illus., col. plates, ports.
31cm. 1st ed. published under title: I pittori italiani dell'-
Ottocento; 2d ed.: Dizionario illustrato dei pittori e incisori
italiani moderni, 1800-1900.

2466   CONNOISSEURS OF THE WORLD;
Being an international biographical dictionary of connoisseurs, collectors, and patrons of art. London, Mitre Press
[1943?] 96 p. 22cm.

2467 CORNA, ANDREA
Dizionario della storia dell'arte in Italia, con duecento illustrazioni. 2. ed. correta ed aumentata. Piacenza, C.
Tarantola [1930] 2 v. illus. 28cm. Dictionary of Italian
art history; includes biographies.

2468 CRAIG, CLIFFORD
The engravers of Van Diemen's Land. [Launceston] Tas-
manian Historical Research Association, 1961. x,172 p.
illus. 26cm.

2469 DARMON, J   E
Dictionnaire des peintres miniaturistes sur vélin, parche-
min, ivoire et écaille... Paris, Morancé [1927] 123 p.
8 plates. 24cm. (Aide-mémoire de l'amateur et du professionnel) Dictionary of miniature painters working on vellum,
parchment, ivory or shells.

2470 DARMON, J   E
Repertoire des estampes japonaises; les artistes et leurs
signatures, les procédés, les oeuvres et leurs prix dans les
ventes, biographies et bibliographies. Paris, Éditions A.
Morancé [1922] 152 p. plates. 25cm. (Aide-mémoire de
l'amateur et du professionel) List of Japanese engravings,
with biographical notes on the engravers.

2471 DEMMIN, AUGUSTE FRÉDÉRIC, 1823?-1898.
Encyclopédie historique, archéologique, biographique,
chronologique et monogrammatique des beaux-arts plastiques,
architecture et mosaïque, céramique, sculpture, peinture et
gravure... Paris, Furne, Jouvet [1873-74] 3v. illus.
26cm. Artists listed under various branches of art.

2472 DESCAMPS, JEAN BAPTISTE, 1706-1791.
La vie des peintres flamands, allemands et hollandois,
avec des portraits gravés en taille-douce, une indication de
leurs principaux ouvrages, & des réflexions sur leurs différentes manières. Paris, C. A. Jombert [etc.] 1753-64. 4v.
ports. 21cm. Lives of Flemish, German & Dutch painters.

2473 DESCAMPS, JEAN BAPTISTE, 1706-1791.
Vie des peintres flamands et hollandais, par Descamps,
réunie à celle des peintres italiens et français, par d'Argenville. Marseille, Impr. J. Barile, 1840-43. 5v. in 2. ports.,
plates. 23cm. Lives of Flemish, Dutch, Italian & French
painters.

2474 DICCIONARIO PICTÓRICO.
Biografías de los hombres que más se han distinguido en la
pintura, dibujo y grabado, desde la más remota antigüedad
hasta nuestros dias. Recopilado por una sociedad de amantes
de las bellas artes. t. 1. Sevilla, J. Moyano, 1875. 350 p.
4.° No more published? Covers letters A-F. A dictionary
of artists, universal.

2475   A DICTIONARY OF ITALIAN PAINTING.
        New York, Tudor Pub. Co. [1965, c1964]   320 p.   illus.
        (part. col.) 22cm.   Ca. 250 painters are represented with
        biographical sketches.

2476   A DICTIONARY OF MODERN PAINTING.
        [Translated from the French by Alan Bird and others]
        General editors: Carlton Lake and Robert Maillard.   New York,
        Tudor Pub. Co. [1956?]   328 p.   illus. 22cm.   Translation
        (or English version) of Dictionnaire de la peinture moderne
        (q. v.)

2477   DICTIONNAIRE DE LA PEINTURE MODERNE.
        [Publié avec la collaboration de Raymond Cogniat, et al.,
        et avec le concours de Robert Maillard]   Paris, F. Hazan
        [1954]   328 p.   illus. 22cm.   Dictionary of modern painting;
        includes biographies of painters.

2478   DICTIONNAIRE DES PEINTRES FRANCAIS.
        [Paris, Seghers, 1961]   378 p.   illus., ports. 17cm.
        (Dictionnaire illustre, 2)   Collection Seghers.   Dictionary of
        French painters.

2479   DICTIONNAIRE DES PEINTRES [NÉS AVANT 1900]
        Par Pierre Vautier [et al.] Pref. de Paul Fierens.
        Bruxelles, Larcier [1951]   694 p. 18cm.   (Petits dictionnaires
        des lettres et des arts en Belgique, 4)

2480   DLABAČ, JAN BOHUMIR, 1758-1820.
        Allgemeines historisches Künstler-Lexikon für Böhmen
        und zum Theil auch für Mähren und Schlesien.   Auf Kosten der
        hochlöblichen Herren Stände Böhmens hrsg.   Prag, Gedruckt
        bei G. Haase, 1815.   3v. in l.   port. 22cm. Dictionary of
        artists in Bohemia, and, in part, in Moravia & Silesia.

2481   DOMINICI, BERNARDO DE'
        Vite de' pittori, scultori, ed architetti napoletani, non mai
        date alla luce da autore alcuno.   Napoli, Nella Stamperia del
        Ricciardi, 1742-44.   3v. 24cm.   Painters, sculptors & ar-
        chitects of Naples.   Presumably this is the 1st large-scale
        treatment of the subject.

2482   DRAKE, WILFRED JAMES, 1879-1948.
        A dictionary of glass-painters and "glasyers" of the tenth
        to the eighteenth centuries.   New York, Metropolitan Museum
        of Art, 1955.   224 p.   illus. 29cm.

2483   DU PELOUX, CHARLES, vicomte.
        Répertoire biographique & bibliographique des artistes du
        XVIIIe siècle français; peintres, dessinateurs, graveurs,
        sculpteurs, ciseleurs, fondeurs, architectes, ébénistes;
        accompagné de notices sur l'art du XVIIIe siècle, les exposi-
        tions, les académies et manufactures royales, les amateurs
        d'art, les ventes publiques et d'une importante bibliographie.

Paris, H. Champion, 1930-41. 2v. 26cm. Subtitle varies.
A dictionary of French artists of the 18th century.

2484 DUSSIEUX, LOUIS ÉTIENNE, 1815-1894.
Les artistes français à l'étranger. 3. éd. Paris, Lecoffre, 1876. 643 p. 24cm. 1st ed., 1852; 2d, 1856. French artists working abroad.

2485 ÉDOUARD-JOSEPH, RENÉ.
Dictionnaire biographique des artistes contemporaine, 1910-1930... Paris, Art & Édition, 1930-34. 3 v. illus. 24 cm.
A supplement appeared in 1936(?)

2486 ELMES, JAMES, 1782-1862.
The arts and artists; or, Anecdotes & relics, of the schools of painting, sculpture & architecture. London, J. Knight & H. Lacey, 1825. 3 v. ports. 17cm.

2487 ENCICLOPEDIA DELL'ARTE ANTICA, CLASSICA E
ORIENTALE. Roma, Istituto della enciclopedia italiana [1958- v. illus. 32cm. A source for biographies of the artists of classical antiquity.

2488 ENCICLOPEDIA DELLA PITTURA ITALIANA
[d'] Ugo Galetti [e] Ettore Camesasca. [Milano] Garzanti [1950] 2 v. illus. 27cm. Encyclopedia of Italian painting.

2489 ENCYCLOPEDIA OF PAINTING:
Painters and painting of the world from prehistoric times to the present day. Bernard S. Myers, editor. Contributing associates: Milton W. Brown [and others] New York, Crown Publishers, 1955. 511p. illus. 29cm.

2490 ENCYCLOPEDIA OF WORLD ART.
New York, McGraw-Hill [1959- v. illus. 31cm.

2491 ERRERA, Mme. ISABELLE, d. 1929.
Dictionnaire répertoire des peintres depuis l'antiquité jusqu'à nos jours. Paris, Hachette, 1913. 716 p. 19 cm.

2492 ----Supplément. Paris, Hachette, 1924. 245 p. 19 cm.

Dictionary of painters, medieval and modern.

2493 FÉLIBIEN, ANDRÉ, sieur des Avaux et de Javercy, 1619-1695.
Entretiens sur les vies et les ouvrages des plus excellens peintres, anciens et modernes; avec la vie des architectes. Nouv. éd., rev., corr. & augm. des Conférences de l'Académie royale de peintre & de sculpture; de l'idée du peintre parfait, des traitez de la miniature, des desseins, des estampes, de la connoissance des tableaux, & du goût des nations; de la description des maisons de campagne de Pline & de celle des Invalides. Trevoux, Impr. de S. A. S., 1725. 6 v. plates. 17 cm. Part of vols. 5 and 6 are by J. F. Félibien.

First published in Paris, 1666-88. Talks on the lives & works of the most eminent painters & architects.

2494 FENAROLI, STEFANO
Dizionario degli artisti bresciani. Bresicia, Tip. Editrice del Pio istituto Pavoni, 1877. 317 p. 20 cm. Dictionary of artists in Brescia, Italy.

2495 FIELDING, MANTLE, 1865-1941.
American engravers upon copper and steel: biographical sketches and check lists of engravings. New York, B. Franklin [1964, c1917] xi, 365 p. plates. 26 cm. (Burt Franklin bibliography and reference series, no. 54) A supplement to D. M. Stauffer's American engravers upon copper and steel.

2496 FIELDING, MANTLE, 1865-1941.
Dictionary of American painters, sculptors & engravers. New York, P. A. Struck, 1945. 433 (i. e. 450) p. illus. 27 cm.

2497 FOSTER, JOSHUA JAMES, 1847-1923.
A dictionary of painters of miniatures (1525-1850) With some account of exhibitions, collections, sales, etc., pertaining to them. Edited by Ethel M. Foster. New York, Macmillan, 1926. 330 p. An amplification of his Miniature painters, British and foreign.

2498 FÜESSLI, JOHANN RUDOLF, 1709-1793.
Allgemeines Künstlerlexicon; oder, Kurze Nachricht von dem Leben und den Werken der Mahler, Bildhauer, Baumeister, Kupferstecher, Kunstgiesser, Stahlschneider u. a., nebst angehängsten Verzeichnissen der Lehrmeister und Schüler; auch der Bildnisse, der in diesem Lexicon enthaltenen Künstler. Zürich, Orell, 1779-1821. 2 v. in 4. 37 cm. 1st published as a one-volume work in Zürich, 1763, with 3 supplements issued in 1767, 1771 and 1777. A general dictionary of artists.

2499 FURÍO, ANTONIO, 1798-1853.
Diccionario histórico de los ilustres profesores de las bellas artes en Mallorca. Palma, Mallorquina, 1946 [i. e. 1947] 337 p. 16 cm. (Biblioteca balear, 10) 1st published in 1841. Historical dictionary of the famous artists of Majorca.

2500 GABET, CHARLES HENRI JOSEPH, 1793-1860.
Dictionnaire des artistes de l'école francaise au XIXe siècle. Peinture, sculpture, architecture, gravure, dessin, lithographie et composition musicale... Orné de vignettes gravées par M. Deschamps. Paris, Vergne, 1831. vi, 709 p. 21 cm. Dictionary of French artists to the 19th century.

2501 GAULT DE SAINT-GERMAIN, PIERRE MARIE, 1754-1842.
Les trois siècles de la peinture en France; ou, Galerie

des peintres français, depuis Francois Ier jusqu'au règne de Napoléon. Paris, Belin, 1808. xiv, 349p. 8.° Three centuries of painting in France; or, Gallery of French painters, after Francis I to the reign of Napoleon I.

2502 GAUNT, WILLIAM, 1900-
Everyman's dictionary of pictorial art. London, Dent; New York, Dutton [1962] 2 v. illus. (part col.) 22 cm. (Everyman's reference library) 1200 artists.

2503 GELSTED, OTTO, 1888-
Kunstner leksikon, med 1100 biografier af danske billedhuggere, malere, grafikere og dekorative kunstnere fra 1900-1942. København, A. Jensen, 1942. 197 p. 24cm. A dictionary of 1100 Danish artists in the period 1900-1942.

2504 GÉRARD, CHARLES, 1814-1877.
Les artistes de l'Alsace pendant le moyen âge. Paris, Berger-Levrault, 1872-73. 2v. 24cm. Alsatian artists during the Middle Ages.

2505 GILBEY, SIR WALTER, 1st bart., 1831-1914.
Animal painters of England from the year 1650; a brief history of their lives and works...illustrated with 28 specimens of their paintings, chiefly from wood engravings by F. Babbage. London, F. Vinton, 1900-11. 3v. plates. 27cm. 97 painters represented.

2506 GIRAUDET, EUGÈNE, 1827-
Les artistes tourangeaux: architectes, armuriers, brodeurs, émailleurs, graveurs, orfèvres, peintres, sculpteurs, tapissiers de haute lisse. Notes et documents inédits... Tours, Rouillé-Ladèveze, 1885. civ, 419 p. facsims. 27cm. Artists of Tours, France.

2507 GNOLI, UMBERTO
Pittori e miniatori nell'Umbria. Spoleto, C. Argentieri [1923] 411 p. plates. 30cm. Painters and miniaturists of the region of Umbria, Italy.

2508 GOOL, JAN VAN, d. 1763.
De nieuwe schouburg der Nederlantsche kunstschilders en schilderessen; waer in de levens- en kunstbedryven der tans levende en reets overledene schilders, die van Houbraken, noch eenig ander schryver, zyn aengeteekend, verhaelt worden. 's-Gravenhage, Gedrukt voor den autheur, 1750-51. 2v. plates. 22cm. The new theater of 'Netherlandish' (Dutch and Belgian) painters (men and women)

2509 GOULD, JOHN, writer on art.
Biographical dictionary of eminent artists: comprising painters, sculptors, engravers, and architects, from the earliest ages to the present time; interspersed with original

anecdotes. To which is prefixed an introduction, containing a brief account of various schools of art. New ed. London, E. Wilson [etc.] 1835. 2v. 17cm. New edition of his A dictionary of painters, sculptors, architects, and engravers (?)

2510 GRANT, MAURICE HAROLD, 1872-
A chronological history of the old English landscape painters (in oil) from the XVIth century to the XIXth century, describing more than 800 painters. [New rev. and enl. ed.] Leigh-on-Sea [Eng.] F. Lewis [1957-   v. plates. 29cm.

2511 GRANT, MAURICE HAROLD, 1872-
A dictionary of British etchers. London, Published for the author by Rockliff, 1952. 232 p. 23cm.

2512 GRANT, MAURICE HAROLD, 1872-
A dictionary of British landscape painters from the 16th century to the early 20th century. Leigh-on-Sea, Eng., F. Lewis [1952] 233 p.

2513 GRASSELLI, GIUSEPPE
Abecedario biografico dei pittori, scultori ed architetti cremonesi... Milano, 1827. 1 v. 12.º Biographical handbook on the painters, sculptors and architects of Cremona, Italy.

2514 GRAVES, ALGERNON.
The British Institution, 1806-1867: a complete dictionary of contributors and their work from the foundation of the Institution. London, G. Bell, & A. Graves, 1908. viii, 617 p. 28cm.

2515 GRAVES, ALGERNON
A dictionary of artists who have exhibited works in the principal London exhibitions from 1760 to 1893. 3d ed., with additions and corrections. London, H. Graves, 1901. xiv, 314 p. 32 x 26cm.

2516 GRAVES, ALGERNON
The Royal Academy of Arts; a complete dictionary of contributors and their work from its foundation in 1769 to 1904. London, H. Graves, 1905-06. 8v. ports. 28cm.

2517 GRAVES, ALGERNON
The Society of Artists of Great Britain, 1760-1791; the Free Society of Artists, 1761-1783; a complete dictionary of contributors and their work from the foundation of the societies to 1791. London, G. Bell, 1907. viii, 354 p. plates. 28cm.

2518 GRIMSCHITZ, BRUNO, 1892-
Austrian painting from Biedermeier to modern times. Wien, Kunstverlag Wolfrum [c1963] 43 p., 124 mounted

plates (part col.) 31cm.   Continuation of The Old Vienna
school of painting.   Brief biographies of 124 painters, with
one example of their work.

2519   GUBERNATIS, ANGELO DE, conte, 1840-1913.
Dizionario degli artisti italiani viventi, pittori, scultori e
architetti.   Firenze, Tipi dei Successori Le Monnier, 1889.
640 p. 25cm.   Gubernatis was assisted by Ugo Matini.
A dictionary of living Italian artists—painters, sculptors
and architects.

2520   GUÉDY, THÉODORE, 1837-
Dictionnaire universel des peintres anciens, modernes
et contemporains...   Paris, L'auteur, Impr. typographique
La Publicité générale, 1892.   450 p. facsims. 26cm.
First published 1882.   Universal dictionary of ancient, mod-
ern and contemporary painters.

2521   HALL, H   VAN
Portretten van nederlandse beeldende kunstenaars. Portraits of Dutch painters and other artists of the Low Countries;
specimen of an iconography. Repertorium door/by H. van Hall.
Amsterdam, Swets en Zeitlinger, 1963.   xii, 419 p. 25cm.

2522   HALL, HENRY CECIL
Artists and sculptors of Nottingham and Nottinghamshire,
1750-1950; a biographical dictionary, containing the names and
dates of over 170 artists and sculptors of the past and present,
with biographical notes of each.   Nottingham, H. Jones, 1953.
95 p. 21cm.

2523   HARPER'S ENCYCLOPEDIA OF ART:
Architecture, sculpture, painting, decorative arts, based
on the work of Louis Hourticq... and translated under the
supervision of Tancred Borenius... Fully rev. under the
supervision of J. Leroy Davidson and Philippa Gerry, with
the assistance of the staff of the Index of Twentieth-Century
Artists, College Art Association, New York City. New York,
Harper, 1937.   2 v. illus. 32cm.   Reprinted in the same
year (1937) under title: New standard encyclopedia of art
(New York, Garden City Pub. Co. 2 v. in 1)

2524   [HEINECKEN, KARL HEINRICH VON] 1706-1791.
Dictionnaire des artistes, dont nous avons des estampes,
avec une notice détaillée de leurs ouvrages gravés. t. 1-4:
A-Diziani. Leipsig, J. G. I. Breitkopf, 1778-90. 4 v. 22cm.
No more published; vol. 4 ends with 'Antonio Diziani.'   Dictionary of artists, some of whose prints we have, with a detailed notice on their engraved works.

2525   HOUBRAKEN, ARNOLD, 1660-1719.
De groote schouburgh der Nederlantsche konstschilders
en schilderessen. Bewerkt door P. T. A. Swillens, met een

inleiding van W. Vogelsang. Maastricht, Leiter-Nypels, 1943-53. 3v. plates, ports. 21cm. First edition published in 1718-1721; a 2d ed. in 1753; a German translation (Bd. 1 only) was issued in 1880. The 'great theater' of Dutch painters.

2526   HUARD, ÉTIENNE.
Vie complète des peintres espagnols et histoire de la peinture espagnole. Paris, Bureau du Journal des artistes, 1839-1941. 2v. 23cm. Complete life of the Spanish painters and history of Spanish painting.

2527   HÜSGEN, HEINRICH SEBASTIAN, 1744-1807.
Nachrichten von Frankfurter Künstlern und Kunst-Sachen, enthaltend das Leben und die Werke aller hiesigen Mahler, Bildhauer, Kupfer- und Pettschier- Stecher...nebst einem Anhang von allen was in ''öffentlichen und Privat -Gebäuden merkwürdiges...ist''...Frankfurt am Main, 1780. xxxii, 378 p. 17cm. Another ed. appeared in 1790 under title: Artistisches Magazin...(xix, 634 p.)? News of artists in Frankfurt...containing the live and works of all painters, sculptors [etc.] of this city.

2528   HUYGHE, RENÉ.
Les contemporains. Nouv. éd. Notices biographiques par Germain Bazin. Paris, Tisné, 1949. 122, [38]p. 164 plates. 34cm. (La Peinture française) The 1st ed. was translated into English (1939) Contemporary French painters.

2529   HYMANS, HENRI SIMON, 1836-1912.
Près de 700 biographies d'artistes belges, parues dans la Biographie nationale, dans L'art flamand et hollandais, dans le Dictionnaire des Drs. Thieme et Becker et dans diverses publications du pays et de l'étranger. 1920. Bruxelles, M. Hayez, 1920. 1v. 29cm. (His Oeuvres, t. 2) Nearly 700 biographies of Belgian artists which have appeared in various publications.

2530   IMMERZEEL, JOHANNES, 1776-1841.
De levens en werken der Hollandsche en Vlaamsche kunst - schilders, beeldhouwers, graveurs en bouwmeesters, van het begin der vijftiende eeuw tot heden...uitg. door C. H. Immerzeel en C. Immerzeel. Amsterdam, Van Kesteren, 1842-43. 3v. ports. 25cm. A 2d ed. issued in 1855 (Amsterdam, Diederich) Lives and works of Dutch and Flemish painters, sculptors, engravers and architects from the beginning of the 15th century to the present day.

2531   THE INDEX OF 20TH CENTURY ARTISTS.
v. 1-4, no. 7; Oct. 1933-Apr. 1937. New York, College Art Association. 4v. 31cm. monthly. Monthly nos. , each of which contains detailed information about one or more artists; 101 artists in all. Publication suspended after April 1937.

2532   INTERNATIONAL ASSOCIATION OF PLASTIC ARTS.
JAPANESE NATIONAL COMMITTEE.
Who's who among Japanese artists. Prepared under the
auspices of Japanese National Commission for Unesco.
[Tokyo] Print. Bureau, Japanese Govt., 1961. 250p. illus.
23cm.

2533   JAHN, JOHANNES, 1892-
Wörterbuch der Kunst. In Verbindung mit Robert Heiden-
reich und Wilhelm von Jenny. 4., durchgesehene und
erweiterte Aufl. Berlin, Akademie-Verlag, 1957. viii,
730p. illus. 19cm. Dictionary of art; includes biographies.

2534   JAMES, RALPH N.
Painters and their works: a dictionary of great artists
who are not now alive, giving their names, lives, and the
prices paid for their works at auctions. London, L. U.
Gill, 1896-97. 3v. plates. 19cm.

2535   KALTENBACH, GUSTAVE ÉMILE.
Dictionary of pronunciation of artists' names, with their
schools and dates; for American readers and students. 2d
ed. [Chicago] Art Institute of Chicago [1938] iv, 74p.
1 illus. 19cm.

2536   KNORR, GEORGE WOLFGANG, 1705-1761.
Allgemeine Künstler-Historie; oder, Berühmter Künstlere
Leben, Werke und Verrichtungen, mit vielen Nachrichten von
raren alten und neuen Kupferstichen beschrieben... Nürn-
berg, Bieling, 1759. 282 p. plates. 21cm. 127 North
European artists, with some material on Italians.

2537   KONDAKOV, S   N
I͡Ubileĭnyĭ spravochnik Imperatorskoĭ Akademii khudozhestv,
1764-1914. [S.-Peterburg, 1914-15] 2 v. illus., ports.
29cm. Contents. --1. Chast' istoricheskai͡a. --2. Chast'
biograficheskai͡a. Jubilee reference book of the Russian Imperial Academy of Arts. Vol. 2 is a biographical dictionary
of Russian painters.

2538   KRAMM, CHRISTIAAN, 1797-1875.
De levens en werken der Hollandsche en Vlaamsche kunstschilders, beeld-houwers, graveurs en bouwmeesters, van
den vroegsten tot op onzen tijd... Amsterdam, Diederichs,
1857-64. 6 pts. & suppl. in 4 v. 25cm. Biographical dictionary, based in part on Immerzeel's work (q.v.) of Dutch
and Flemish artists.

2539   [LACOMBE, JACQUES] 1724-1811.
Dictionnaire portatif des beaux-arts; ou, Abrégé de ce qui
concerne l'architecture, la sculpture, la peinture, la gravure, la poésie et la musique; avec la définition de ces arts,
l'explication des termes et des choses qui leur appartiennent;

ensemble les noms, la date de la naissance et de la mort,
les circonstances les plus remarquables de la vie, et le
genre particulier de talent des personnes qui se sont dis-
tinguées dans ces différens arts parmi les anciens et les modernes, en France et dans les pays étrangers. Par M. L. * *
avocat. Paris, Veuve Estienne, 1752. A fine arts 'pocket'
dictionary that includes notes on artists and musicians.
Later editions have name of author on the t. p.

2540   LECARPENTIER, CHARLES JACQUES FRANCOIS, 1744-1822.
Galerie des peintres célèbres, avec des remarques sur le
genre de chaque maître. Paris [etc.] Chez Treuttel et Wurtz,
1821. 2 v. 21cm. Gallery of celebrated painters.

2541   LENINGRAD. GOSUDARSTVENNYĬ RUSSKIĬ MUZEĬ.
Katalog-putevoditel'. Russkaiā zhivopis' XVIII-XIX vekov.
Leningrad, 1948. 222p. illus. Brief notes on 150 Russian
painters of the 18-19th centuries.

2542   LIRA, PEDRO.
Diccionario biográfico de pintores. Santiago de Chile,
Esmeralda, 1902. viii, 552 p. 24cm. A biographical dictionary of painters, world-wide in scope, but particularly
useful for Chilean artists.

2543   LODOVICI, SERGIO
Storici, teorici e critici delle arti figurativi (1800-1940)
Roma, E. B. B. I., Istituto editoriale italiano B. C. Tosi
[1942] 412 p. ports., facsims. 28cm. (Enciclopedia biografica e bibliografica "Italiana," ser. IV) Arranged in
dictionary form, alphabetical by biographee. Italian art historians and critics.

2544   LÖHNEYSEN, HANS WOLFGANG VON
Die ältere niederländische Malerei; Künstler und Kritiker.
Eisenach, E. Roth [1956] 556 p. plates. 25cm. (Bücher der
Brücke) Artists and critics of early Dutch painting.

2545   LONG, BASIL SOMERSET, 1881-
British miniaturists. London, G. Bles, 1929. xxxiii,
475 p. illus. 32 x 25cm. Covers the period 1520-1860.

2546   MADSEN, HERMAN.
200 [i. e. To hundrede] danske malere og deres vaerker.
København, Pioras, 1946. 2 v. illus. 27cm. 200 Danish
painters and their works.

2547   MAK VAN WAAY, S   J
Lexicon van Nederlandsche schilders en beeldhouwers, 1870-
1940. Amsterdam, N. V. Wereldbibliotheek, 1944. 136 p.
28cm. Dictionary of Dutch painters and sculptors who
flourished 1870-1940.

2548   MALLETT, DANIEL TROWBRIDGE, 1862-
Mallett's Index of artists, international--biographical. In-

cluding painters, sculptors, illustrators, engravers and etchers of the past and the present. New York, R. R. Bowker, 1935. 493 p.

2549 --- ----Supplement. N. Y., R. R. Bowker, 1940. xxxiiii, 319 p. 26cm.

(Both vols. reprinted by P. Smith, New York, 1948)

2550 MALVASIA, CARLO CESARE, conte, 1616-1693.
Felsina pittrice; vite de' pittori bolognesi. Con aggiunte, correzioni e note inedite del medesimo autore, di Giampietro Zanotti e di altri scrittori viventi. Bologna, Tip. Guidi all'Ancora, 1841. 2 v. illus. 25cm. Lives of painters from Bologna. First published in 1678 (to which was added in 1769 Luigi Crespi's Vite de' pittori bolognesi non descritte nella Felsina pittrice)

2551 MARIETTE, PIERRE JEAN, 1694-1774.
Abecedario de P. J. Mariette et autres notes inédites de cet amateur sur les arts et les artistes. Ouvrage publié d'après les manuscrits autographes conservés au Cabinet des estampes de la Bibliothèque impériale, et annoté par Ph. de Chennevières et A. de Montaiglon. Paris, Dumoulin, 1851/53 -1859/60. 6 v. 22cm. (Archives de l'art français, t. 2, 4, 6, 8, 10, 12) A dictionary of art and artists.

2552 MERLINO, ADRIÁN
Diccionario de artistas plásticos de la Argentina, siglos XVIII-XIX-XX. [Buenos Aires, 1954] 433p. illus. 23cm. Dictionary of plastic artists of the Argentine.

2553 MERLO, JOHANN JAKOB, 1810-1890.
Kölnische Künstler in alter und neuer Zeit; Johann Jakob Merlos neu bearb. und erweiterte Nachrichten von dem Leben und den Werken Kölnischer Künstler, hrsg. von Eduard Firmenich-Richartz unter Mitwirkung von Hermann Keussen. Mit zahlreichen bildlichen Beilagen. Düsseldorf, Schwann, 1895. xviii p., 1206 columns. illus., 52 plates. 29cm. (Publikationen der Gesellschaft für Rheinische Geschichtskunde, 9) 1st published 1850. Artists of Cologne in old and modern times.

2554 MEUSEL, JOHANN GEORG, 1743-1820.
Teutsches Künstlerlexikon; oder, Verzeichniss der jetzt-lebenden teutschen Künstler. Nebst einem Verzeichniss sehenswürdiger Bibliotheken, Kunst-, Münz- und Natur-alienkabinete in Teutschland und in der Schweiz. Verfertig von Johann Georg Meusel... 2. umbearb. Ausg. Lemgo, Meyersche Buchhandlung, 1808-14. 3 v. 20cm. Dictionary of German artists now living. 1st ed. published in 1788.

2555   MEYER, JULIUS, 1830-1893, ed.
Allgemeines Künstler-Lexikon. Unter Mitwirkung der namhaftesten Fachgelehrten des In- und Auslandes. 2. gänzlich neubearb. Aufl. von Nagler's Künstler-Lexikon. Leipzig, W. Engelmann, 1872-85. 3 v. 25 :m. A universal dictionary of artists. No more published. Contents. -- 1. Bd. Aa-Andreani. -- 2. Bd. Andreas-Domenico del Barbiere. -- 3. Bd. Giambattista Barbieri-Giuseppe Bezzuoli.

2556   MICHIGAN. STATE LIBRARY , Lansing.
Biographical sketches of American artists. 5th ed. , rev. and enl. Lansing, 1924. 370p. 23cm. Compiled by Helen L. Earle.

2557   MITHOFF, H   WILHELM H
Mittelalterliche Künstler und Werkmeister Niedersachsens und Westfalens, lexikalisch dargestellt. 2. umgearb. und verm. Ausg. Hannover, Helwing, 1885. ix, 462p. 21cm. Dictionary of medieval artists and artisans of Lower Saxony and Westphalia. 1st published 1866.

2558   MOLINIER, EMILE, 1857-1906.
Dictionnaire des émailleurs depuis le moyen âge jusqu'à la fin du XVIIIe siècle. Paris, Rouam, 1885. 113p. illus. 18cm. (Guide du collectionneur) Dictionary of enamelists after the Middle Ages to the end of the 18th century.

2559   MONOD, LUCIEN
Aide-mémoire de l'amateur et du professionnel. Le prix des estampes, anciennes et modernes, prix, atteints dans les ventes, suites et états, biographies et bibliographies. Paris, A. Morance, 1920-[31] 9 v. Dictionary of engravers and their works; brief biographical data.

2560   MÜLLER, HERMANN ALEXANDER, 1814-1894.
Allgemeines Künstler-Lexikon; Leben und Werke der ber berühmtesten bildenden Künstler. 3. umgearb. und bis auf der neueste Zeit ergänzte Aufl. Frankfurt am Main, Rütten & Loening, 1895-1901. 5 v. 24cm. By H. A. Müller and Hans Wolfgang Singer.

2561   --- ----Nachträge und Berichte. Frankfurt am Main, Literarisches Anstalt, Rütten & Loening, 1906. 295, [5] p. 24cm.

A general dictionary of artists.

2562   NAGLER, GEORG KASPAR, 1801-1866.
Die Monogrammisten und diejenigen bekannten und unbekannten Künstler aller Schulen, welche sich zur Bezeichnung ihrer Werke eines figürlichen Zeichens, der Initialen des Namens, der Abbreviatur desselben, &c. bedient haben ... Nachrichten über Maler, Zeichner, Bildhauer, Architekten ... u. s. w.

Ein für sich bestehendes Werk, aber zugleich auch Ergänzung und Abschluss des Neuen allgemeinen Künstlerlexicons, und Supplement zu den bekannten Werken von A. Bartsch [et al.] München, G. Franz, 1858-79. 5 v. facsims. 24cm.

2563 --- ----General-Index. München, G. Hirth, 1920. iv, 109 p. 25cm.
Monogrammists and those artists, known and unknown, of all schools who have used signs, initials, etc. to designate their work.

2564 NAGLER, GEORG KASPAR, 1801-1866.
Neues allgemeines Künstler-Lexikon; oder, Nachrichten von dem Leben und den Werken der Maler, Bildhauer, Baumeister, Kupferstecher, Lithographen, Formschneider, Zeichner, Medailleure, Elfenbeinarbeiter, etc. 3. Aufl. Unveränderter Abdruck der 1. Aufl. 1835-1852. Leipzig, Schwarzenberg & Schumann [1924] 25 v. 23cm. A 2d ed., with title: Allgemeines Künstlerlexikon, and under the editorship of Julius Meyer, appeared in 1872-85, but only 3 vols. (Aa to Bezzuoli) were published. A new general dictionary of artists.

2565 NEUMANN, WILHELM, 1849-
Baltische Maler und Bildhauer des XIX Jahrhunderts. Biographische Skizzen mit dem Bildnissen der Künstler und Reproductionen nach ihren Werke. Riga, Druck A. Grosset, 1902. 178 p. Ca. 90 Baltic painters and sculptors of the 19th century.

2566 NEUMANN, WILHELM, 1849-
Lexikon baltischer Künstler. Riga, Jonck & Poliewsky; Buchdr. des Rigaer Tageblatts, 1908. 172 p. 22cm. Dictionary of Baltic artists.

2567 NEW YORK HISTORICAL SOCIETY.
Dictionary of artists in America, 1564-1860, by George C. Groce and David H. Wallace. New Haven, Yale University Press, 1957. xxvii, 759 p. 25cm. Almost 11,000 names included.

2568 NICOLAS, MICHEL, 1810-1886.
Histoire des artistes peintres, sculpteurs, architectes et musiciens compositeurs nés dans le département du Gard. Nimes, Impr. de Ballivet, 1859. 239 p. 8.° History of the painters, sculptors, architects and composers born in the department of the Garde, France.

2569 NOCQ, HENRY, 1868-
Le poinçon de Paris; répertoire des maîtres-orfèvres de la jurisdiction de Paris depuis le moyen-âge jusqu'à la fin du XVIIIe siècle. Paris, H. Floury, 1926-31. 4 v. illus. 29cm. List of master goldsmiths and silversmiths of Paris, after the

Middle Ages to the end of the 18th century. Supplemented by errata and addenda list (96 p.)

2570 NORWAY. KONTORET FOR KULTURELT SAMKVEN MED UTLANDET.
Norwegian printmakers. Norske grafikere. [Published by the Royal Norwegian Ministry of Foreign Affairs, Office of Cultural Relations in co-operation with "Norske grafikere." Rev. up to autumn 1953] Oslo, 1954. 64 p. illus. 21cm. Brief sketches of 58 Norwegian engravers.

2571 OFFICIAL DIRECTORY, AMERICAN ILLUSTRATORS AND ADVERTISING ARTISTS. [Washington, American Federation of Arts. v. 23cm.

2572 O'NEIL, A
Dictionary of Spanish painters, comprehending simply that part of their biography immediately connected with the arts, from the 14th century to the 18th. London, 1833-34. 2 v. front. , 2 ports. 25cm.

2573 ORLANDI, PELLEGRINO ANTONIO, 1660-1727.
L'abecedario pittorico nel quale compendiosamente sono descritte le patrie, i maestri, ed i tempi, ne' quali fiorirono circa quattro mila professori di pittura, di scultura, e d'architettura diviso in tre parti ... Il tutto disposto in alfabetto per maggior facilità de dilettanti ... In questo edizione corretto e notabilmente di nuove notizie accresciuto da Pietro Guarienti. In Venezia, Appresso G. Pasquali, 1753. 584 p. plates. 4.° A general dictionary of artists. First edition issued in 1704.

2574 OSSORIO Y BERNARD, MANUEL, 1839-1904.
Galería biográfica de artistas españoles del siglo XIX. Continuación del Diccionario de Cean Bermudez hasta el año 1882. Madrid, Impr. de Moreno y Rojas, 1883-84. viii, 749 p. illus., ports. 28cm. In double columns. Ca. 3,000 sketches of Spanish artists of the 19th century.

2575 PADOVANO, ETTORE.
Dizionario degli artisti contemporanei. [Milano] Istituto tip. editoriale [1951] 403 p. illus., col. plates. 25cm. Dictionary of 20th century Italian artists.

2576 PALOMINO DE CASTRO Y VELASCO, ACISCLO ANTONIO, 1653-1726.
El museo pictorico, y escala optica. Madrid, L. A. de Bedmar, [etc.] 1715-24. 3 v. in 2. illus. 31cm. Lives of Spanish artists. Vol. 3 has title: El Parnaso español pintoresco laureado ... Con las vidas de los pintores, y estatuarios eminentes españoles. An abridged ed. of this volume was published separately, London, 1742, under title: Las vidas de los pintores y estatuarios eminentes españoles (q. v.)

2577 PALOMINO DE CASTRO Y VELASCO, ACISCLO ANTONIO, 1653-1726.
Las vidas de los pintores y estatuarios eminentes españoles. Que con sus heroycas obras, han ilustrado la nacion: y de a-quellos estrangeros ilustres, que han concurrido en estas provincias, y las han enriquecido, con sus eminentes obras. Londres, H. Woodfall [etc.] 1742. 325 (i. e. 221) p. 21cm. 227 artists of Spain. An abridged edition of vol. 3 of the author's El museo pictorico, y escala optica (q. v.)

2578 PAMPLONA, FERNANDO DE
Dicionário de pintores e escultores portugueses ou que trabalharam em Portugal. Edicão dirigida e prefaciada por Ricardo do Espírito Santo Silva. [Lisboa, 1954- v. plates. 26cm. Dictionary of Portuguese painters & sculptors.

2579 PARK, ESTHER AILLEEN
Mural painters in America. Pittsburg, Kansas State Teachers College, 1949- v. 27cm. Contents. --pt. 1. A biographical index.

2580 PASCOLI, LIONE, 1674-1744.
Vite de' pittori, scultori, ed architetti moderni... Fac-simile dell' edizione di Roma del MDCCXXX [-MDCCXXVI] Roma, Stab. arti grafiche E. Calzone, 1933. 2 v. port. 25cm. (R. Istituto d'archeologia e storia dell'arte. Opere inedite o rare di storia dell'arte) Lives of 'modern' painters, sculptors & architects [of Italy]

2581 PASSERI, GIOVANNI BATTISTA, 1610?-1679.
Vite de' pittori, scultori ed architetti che hanno laborato in Roma, morti dal 1641 fino al 1673... Romae, G. Settari, 1772. xvi, 492p. 4.º Lives of painters, sculptors & archi-tects who have worked in Rome & died 1641-1673. A German translation was published in 1934 (Leipzig, H. Keller) under title: Die Künstlerbiographien von Giovanni Battista Passeri.

2582 PAVIÈRE, SYDNEY HERBERT, 1891-
A dictionary of flower, fruit and still life painters. Leigh-on-Sea, Eng., F. Lewis [1962- v. in plates. 30cm. Contents. --v. 1. 15th-17th centuries. -- v. 2. 18th century. -- v. 3. pt. 1. 19th century (artists born 1786-1840) pt. 2. 19th century (artists born 1841-1885)

2583 PELLICCIONI, ARMANDO
Dizionario degli artisti incisori italiani (dalle origini al XIX secolo) [Carpi (Modena) Tip. G. Gualdi, 1949] 204p. 22cm. Dictionary of Italian engravers (from the origins of the art to the 19th century)

2584 PELLOQUET, THÉODORE
Dictionnaire de poche des artistes contemporains. Les

peintres. Paris, A. Delahays, 1858. 181p. 16.° Pocket
dictionary of contemporary artists.

2585 PÉREZ COSTANTI, PABLO, 1857-
Diccionario de artistas que florecieron en Galicia durante
los siglos XVI y XVII. Santiago [de Compostela] Seminario
C. Central, 1930. viii, 609p. 25cm. Dictionary of artists
who flourished in Galicia [Spain] during the 16th & 17th centuries.

2586 PILES, ROGER DE, 1635-1709.
Abrégé de la vie des peintres... avec des reflexions sur
leurs ouvrages, et un traité du peintre parfait, de la connoissance des desseins & de l'utilité des estampes... 2. éd.,
rev. par l'auteur; avec un abrégé de sa vie [par C. F.
Fraguier]... Paris, J. Estienne, 1715. 557p. Includes
short sketches of ca. 300 painters. First ed. published 1699;
a "nouvelle édition" was issued in 1767 (Paris. viii, 484p.)
and various English translations were made (e.g. 1706, 1754?)

2587 PILES, ROGER DE, 1635-1700.
The art of painting, with the lives and characters of above
300 of the most eminent painters. Translated from the
French. To which is added, An essay towards an English
school. The 3d ed. : in which is now first inserted the life
of Sir Godfrey Kneller, by the late B. Buckeridge... who
wrote the greatest part of the English school. London,
Printed for T. Payne [1754?] 439p. 22cm. Translation of
Abrégé de la vie des peintres...

2588 PILKINGTON, MATTHEW, 1700?-1784.
A general dictionary of painters; containing memoirs of
the lives and works of the most eminent professors of the
art of painting, from its revival by Cimabue, in the year 1250,
to the present time... With an introd., historical and critical,
by Allan Cunningham. A new ed., corr. and rev. by R. A.
Davenport. London, W. Tegg, 1852. cxii, 623p. port. 23cm.

2589 PILLWEIN, BENEDIKT, 1779-1847.
Biographische Schilderungen; oder, Lexikon salzburgischer theils verstorbener theils lebender Künstler, auch solcher,
welche Kunstwerke für Salzburg lieferten &c. Nach den
zuverlässigsten Quellen, besonders Manuscripten, bearb.
Nebst einem Anhange... Salsburg, Mayr'sche Buchhandlung,
1821. xvi, 356p. 19cm. Biographies of artists, living &
dead, of Salzburg, Austria.

2590 POPOV, PAVLO MYKOLAĬOVYCH, 1890-
Materialy do slovnyka ukrains'kykh graveriv. Kyïv, 1926.
137p. illus. 26cm. 104 notices of Ukranian engravers.

2591 PORT, CÉLESTIN, 1828-1901.
Les artistes angevins, peintres, sculpteurs, maîtres,

d'oeuvre, architectes, graveurs, musiciens, d'après les
archives angevines... Paris, J. Baur [etc.] 1881. xx, 334p.
24cm. (Société de l'histoire de l'art français. [Publications])
French artists & musicians from the old province of Anjou &
the city of Angers, France.

2592   PORTAL, CHARLES LOUIS HENRI FÉLIX ANTOINE, 1862-
      Dictionnaire des artistes et ouvriers d'art du Tarn du
XIIIe au XXe siècle. Albi, Chez l'auteur, 1925. 332p. 25cm.
Dictionary of 1200 artists of the Tarn, France, from the 13th
to the 20th century.

2593   PORTALIS, ROGER, baron, 1841-1912.
      Les dessinateurs d'illustrations au dix-huitième siècle.
Paris, D. Morgand et C. Fatout, 1877. 2 v. 21cm. French
engravers & illustrators of the 18th century.

2594   PORTALIS, ROGER, baron, 1841-1912.
      Les graveurs du dix-huitième siècle, par Roger Portalis
et Henri Béraldi... Paris, D. Morgand et C. Fatout, 1880-
82. 3 v. 23cm. A dictionary of ca. 400 engravers of the
18th century.

2595   POZZO, BARTOLOMEO FR   DAL, conte
      Le vite de' pittori, degli scultori ed architetti veronesi
raccolte da varj autori stampati, e manuscritti, e da altre
particolari memorie. Con la narrativa delle pitture e scul-
ture che s'attrovano nelle chiese, case ed altri luoghi
publici e privati di Verona, e suo territorio... Verona, G.
Berno, 1718. 313p. 24cm.

2596   ---- ----Aggiunta. Verona, Stampa di P. A. Berno, 1718.
42p. 24cm.

      Lives of artists and architects of Verona, Italy.

2597   QUATREMÈRE DE QUINCY, ANTOINE CHRYSOSTOME,
      1755-1849.
      Histoire de la vie et des ouvrages des plus célèbres
architectes du XIe siècle jusqu'à la fin du XVIIIe, accompagnée de la vue du plus remarquable édifice de chacun d'eux.
Paris, J. Renouard, 1830. 2 v. plates. 27cm. Architects' lives. Covers the 11th to the end of the 18th century.

2598   QUILLIET, FRÉDÉRIC.
      Dictionnaire des peintres espagnols. Paris, Chez l'au-
teur, 1816. xxxvii, 407p. 22cm. Dictionary of Spanish
painters. Based for the most part on Ceán Bermúdez's Diccionario histórico de los mas ilustres profesores de las bellas artes en España.

2599   RACZYŃSKI, ATANAZY, hrabia, 1787-1845.
      Dictionnaire historico-artistique de Portugal, pour faire

suite à l'ouvrage ayant pour titre: Les arts en Portugal...
Paris, J. Renouard, 1847. xii, 306p. 23cm. A dictionary
for the history of art in Portugal. Includes biographies of
Portuguese artists.

2600   RAFOLS, JOSÉ F
Diccionario biográfico de artistas de Cataluña desde la
época romana hasta nuestros días. Barcelona, Editorial
Millá, 1951-54. 3 v. illus. 25cm. Biographical dictionary
of Catalan artists.

2601   RAMÍREZ DE ARELLANO, RAFAEL, 1854-1921.
Diccionario biográfico de artistas de la provincia de
Córdoba. Madrid, Perales y Martínez, 1893. 535p. 23cm.
(Colección de documentos inéditos para la historia de España,
t. 107) Biographical dictionary of artists of the province of
Cordoba, Spain.

2602   RASTAWIECKI, EDWARD, baron, 1805-1874.
Słownik malarzów polskich, tudziez obcych w Polsce
osiadłych lub czasowo w niéj przebywajacych. Warszawa,
Nakł. autora, 1850-57. 3 v. ports. 23cm. Dictionary of
Polish painters as well as foreigners residing in Poland or
temporarily staying there.

2603   REDGRAVE, SAMUEL, 1802-1876.
A dictionary of artists of the English school: painters,
sculptors, architects, engravers and ornamentists; with notices of their lives and work... 2d ed. London, G. Bell,
1878. 497p. 22cm. 1st ed. published in 1874.

2604   REES, THOMAS MARDY
Welsh painters, engravers, and sculptors (1527-1911) arranged alphabetically, with thirty portraits... Carnarvon,
[ca. 1912] 188p. ports. 22cm.

2605   RIDOLFI, CARLO, 17th cent.
La maraviglie dell'arte; overo, Le vite de gl'illustri pittori veneti, e dello stato. Ed. 2. ... arricchita d'annotazioni [di G. Vedova] Padova, 1835-37. 2 v. 8.º First ed.
issued 1648; an edition edited by Detlev Freiherr von Hadeln
was issued in 1914-24 (Berlin, G. Grote?) Lives of artists of
Venice.

2606   ROVINSKIĬ, DMITRIĬ ALEKSANDROVICH, 1824-1895.
Podrobnyĭ slovar' russkikh graverov XVI-XIX vv. S. -
Peterburg, Tip. Imp. Akademii nauk, 1895. 2 v. illus.
31cm. Comprehensive dictionary of Russian engravers of
the 16th-19th centuries.

2607   ROVINSKIĬ, DMITRIĬ ALEKSANDROVICH, 1824-1895.
Russkie gravery i ikh proizvedeniia s 1564 goda do osnova-
niia Akademii khudozhestv. Moskva, Izd. grafa Uvarova,

1870. x, 403p. 27cm. and atlas (73 mounted illus.) 90cm.
Russian engravers & their works from 1564 to the founding
of the Academy of Arts.

2608 RUMP, ERNST
Lexikon der bildenden Künstler Hamburgs, Altonas und
der näheren Umgebung. Hamburg, O. Bröcker, 1912. vii,
179p. illus. 4.º Dictionary of artists in Hamburg.

2609 SAMLERENS KUNSTNERLEKSIKON.
Redaktion: Hans Werner... København, Samleren, 1929-
32. 2 v. illus. 19cm. A dictionary of artists, chiefly Danish artists.

2610 SAWADA, AKIRA.
Nihon gaka jiten. Tokyo, Kigensha, 1927. 700p. Dictionary of Japanese painters.

2611 SCHEEN, P   A
Honderd jaren Nederlandsche schilder- en teekenkunst.
De romantiek met voor- en natijd (1750-1850) ... Den Haag,
Uitgevers-Bureau "Boek en Periodiek," 1946. 381, xi p.
417 plates. 25cm. 100 years of Dutch painting and drawing;
includes entries for ca. 3,000 Dutch painters of the Romantic
period (1750-1850)

2612 SCHIDLOF, LÉO R
The miniature in Europe in the 16th, 17th, 18th and 19th
centuries. Graz, Akademische Druck- u. Verlagsanstalt,
1964. 4 v. plates. 28cm. Vols. 1-2 a dictionary of artists;
vols. 3-4 plates.

2613 SCHÜTZ, ALFRED, 1910-   ed.
O mundo artistico do Brazil; enciclopédia biográfica sôbre
todos os setôres da arte brasileira. 1. ed. The artistic
world of Brazil... Rio de Janeiro, Editora Pró-Arte [1954]
402 p. illus., ports. 33cm. A biographical encyclopedia
for all sectors of Brazilian art.

2614 SCHWEIZERISCHER KUNSTVEREIN.
Schweizerisches Künstler-Lexikon. Dictionnaire des
artistes suisses. Redigiert unter Mitwirkung von Fachgenossen von C. Brun. Frauenfeld, Huber, 1905-17. 4 v. 8.º
Dictionary of Swiss artists.

2615 SEGUIER, FREDERICK PETER.
A critical and commercial dictionary of the works of
painters comprising eight thousand eight hundred and fifty
sale notes of pictures and nine hundred and eighty original
notes on the subjects and styles of various artists who have
painted in the schools of Europe between 1250 and 1850. London, Longmans, Green, 1870. xvi, 241 p. 27cm. An appendix to Pilkington and Bryan. Gives birth and death dates

for each painter, prices obtained for his paintings, and some notes on his style.

2616   SERVOLINI, LUIGI, 1906-
Dizionario illustrato degli incisori italiani moderni e contemporanei. Milano, Görlich [c1955] 871 p. illus. 30cm. Illustrated dictionary of modern and contemporary Italian engravers.

2617   SEYN, EUG   M   H   de
Dessinateurs, graveurs et peintres des anciens Pays-Bas; écoles flamande et hollandaise. Turnhout (Belgique) Brepols [1949?] vi, 302 p. ports. 28cm. Early drawers, engravers and painters of the Low Countries: Flemish & Dutch schools.

2618   SIRET, ADOLPHE, 1818-1888.
Dictionnaire historique et raisonné des peintres de toutes les écoles depuis l'origine de la peinture jusqu'à nos jours. 3. éd. originale (considerablement augm.) Berlin, J. Altmann, 1924. 2 v. plates. 27cm. Historical & systematic dictionary of painters of all schools from the origin of painting to our day.

2619   SOBKO, NIKOLAĬ PETROVICH, 1851-1906.
Slovar' russkikh khudozhnikov s drevnĭeĭshikh vremen do nashikh dneĭ (XI-XIX vv.) Na osnovanii lĭetopiseĭ, aktov, arkhivnykh dokumentov, avtobiograficheskikh zamĭetok i pechatnykh materialov. S.-Peterburg, Tip. M.M. Stasĭulevicha, 1893- v. illus. 30cm. Dictionary of Russian artists (11th-19th centuries) Contents.--t. 1. vyp. 1. A. t. 2. vyp. 1. I.   t. 3. vyp. 1. P.

2620   SOPRANI, RAFFAELE, 1612-1672.
Vite de' pittori, scultori, ed architetti genovesi, di Raffaello Soprani. In questa 2. ed. rivedute, accresciute ed arrichite di note da Carlo Giuseppe Ratti. Genova, Nella Stamperia Casamara, 1768-69. 2 v. ports. 27cm. Lives of Genoan painters, sculptors & architects. Vol. 2 by C. G. Ratti.

2621   SPOONER, SHEARJASHUB, 1809-1859.
A biographical history of the fine arts; or, Memoirs of the lives and works of eminent painters, engravers, sculptors, and architects. From the earliest ages to the present time. Alphabetically arr. and condensed from the best authorities. New York, Bouton, 1865. 2 v. plates. 27cm. First published in 1853 under title: A biographical and critical dictionary of painters and engravers.

2622   STAUFFER, DAVID McNEELY, 1845-1913.
American engravers upon copper and steel. New York, Grolier Club of the City of New York, 1907. 2 v. plates,

ports. 25cm. Contents. -- pt. 1. Biographical sketches, illustrated. Index to engravings described, with check-list
numbers and names of engravers and artists. -- pt. 2. Check-
list of the works of the earlier engravers.

2623 STIRLING-MAXWELL, Sir WILLIAM, bart. , 1818-1878.
Annals of the artists of Spain. A new ed. , incorporating
the author's own notes, additions and emendations. London,
J. C. Nimmo, 1891. 4 v. illus. 24cm.

2624 STRICKLAND, WALTER G
A dictionary of Irish artists. Dublin, Maunsel, 1913.
2 v. illus. 26cm.

2625 STRUTT, JOSEPH, 1749-1802.
A biographical dictionary; containing an historical account
of all engravers, from the earliest period of the art of engraving to the present time; and a short list of their most
esteemed works. With cyphers, monograms, and particular
marks... London, Printed by J. Davis for R. Fauldner,
1785-86. 2 v. illus. 27cm.

2626 SUN, TA-KUNG, comp.
Chung-kuo hua chia jen ming ta tz'u tien. [Shanghai] Shen
chou kuo kuang she [1934] 14, 760p. Biographical dictionary
of Chinese painters.

2627 SVENSKA KONSTNÄRER;
Biografisk handbok. 5. uppl. Malmö, Skånetryckeriets
[1955] 438p. 20cm. Swedish artists; biographical handbook;
4000 names included.

2628 SVENSKT KONSTNÄRSLEXIKON;
Tiotusen svenska konstnärers liv och verk. [Redaktion:
Gösta Lilja, Bror Olsson, S. Artur Svensson] Malmö,
Allhems förlag [1952-   v. illus. 29cm. Dictionary of
Swedish artists; life & work of 10, 000 Swedish artists.

2629 SWANENBURG, B   D   ed.
Algemeene kunst encyclopaedie; beknopte samenvatting
der beeldende kunsten. Met medewerking van R. F. P. de
Beaufort [et al.] Utrecht, De Haan, 1950. 453p. illus.
24cm. Encyclopedia of art; includes biographies.

2630 TATE GALLERY, London.
The modern British paintings, drawings and sculpture, by
Mary Chamot, Dennis Farr & Martin Butlin. London, Pub-
lished by the Oldbourne Press by order of the Trustees of
the Tate Gallery, 1964. 2 v. plates (part col.) 25cm.
(Its Catalogues) Contents. -- v. 1. Artists, A-L. --v. 2.
Artists, M-Z. Bio-'bibliographical, ' i. e. , a sketch of the

artist's life followed by a description of his works in the collections of the Tate Gallery. Includes only artists born in or after 1850.

2631 THIEME, ULRICH, 1865-1922, ed.
Allgemeines Lexikon der bildenden Künstler von der Antike bis zur Gegenwart; unter Mitwirkung von 300 Fachgelehrten des In- und Auslandes hrsg. von Ulrich Thieme und Felix Becker. Leipzig, W. Engelmann, 1907-50. 37v. 28cm. Imprint varies. Vols. 14-15 edited by Ulrich Thieme and Fred. C. Willis; v. 16-36 edited by Hans Vollmer. Dictionary of artists; one of the most authoritative works in the field.

2632 TICOZZI, STEFANO, 1762-1836.
Dizionario dei pittori dal rinnovamento delle belle arti fino al 1800. Milano, Tip. di V. Ferrario, 1818. 2 v. plates. 21cm. Dictionary of painters from the Renaissance to 1800.

2633 TOKYO. INSTITUTE OF ART RESEARCH.
Index of Japanese painters. Tokyo, Society of Friends of Eastern Art, Institute of Art Research, 1941. 156p. 19cm. "Brief biographical notes on about 600 Japanese painters."

2634 TICOZZI, STEFANO, 1762-1836.
Dizionario degli architetti, scultori, pittori, intagliatori in rame ed in pietra, coniatori di medaglie, musaicisti, niellatori, intarsiatori d'ogni età e d'ogni nazione. Milano, G. Schiepatti [etc.] 1830-33. 4 v. in 2. port. 22cm. Dictionary of architects, sculptors, painters [etc.] of all ages & nations.

2635 TIROLISCHES KÜNSTLERLEXIKON;
Oder, Kurze Lebensbeschreibung jener Künstler, welche geborne Tiroler waren, oder eine längere Zeit in Tirol sich aufgehalten haben. Von einem Verehrer der Künste [i. e. Joseph von Lemmen?] Innsbruck, Rauch, 1830. 288p. 20cm. Dictionary of Tyrolean artists.

2636 TOMAN, PROKOP, 1872-
Nový slovník československých výtvarných umělcu. S původní litografickou přilohou Maxe Švabinského. [3., značne rozšírené vyd.] V Praze, R. Ryšavý, 1947-50. 2v. ports. 27cm. First ed. published 1936.

2637 ---- ----Dodatky. Prokop Toman [a] Prokop H. Toman. Praha, Státní nakl. krásné literatury, hudby a umění, 1955. 224p. port. 27cm.

New dictionary of Czechoslovak artists.

2638 TUCKERMAN, HENRY THEODORE, 1813-1871.
Book of the artists; American artist life, comprising biographical and critical sketches of American artists: preceded

by an historical account of the rise and progress of art in America. With an appendix containing an account of notable pictures and private collections. New York, G. P. Putnam, 1882. xi, 639p. 25cm. First published 1870.

2639 USPENSKIĬ, ALEKSANDR IVANOVICH, 1873-
Slovar´ patriarshikh ikonopist̃sev. Moskva, Pech A. I. Snegirevoĭ, 1917. 176p. 4.º (Zapiski Moskovskaiã arkheologischeskaiã instituta, izdav. pod red. A. I. Uspenskogo, t. 30) 180 Russian icon-painters.

2640 VARILLE, MATHIEU, 1885-
Les peintres primitifs de Provence. Paris, Rapilly, 1946. 230 p. 17cm. The 'primitive' painters of Provence; covers illuminators, embroiderers and glassmakers, as well as painters.

2641 VASARI, GIORGIO, 1511-1574.
Lives of the most eminent painters, sculptors, and architects. Translated from the Italian with notes and illus. chiefly selected from various commentators by Mrs. Jonathan Foster. London, H. G. Bohn, 1852-59 [v. 5, 1852] 5 v. port. 19cm. First Italian ed. (Le vite de piu eccellenti architetti, pittori, et scultori italiani...) issued in 1550? Many editions in Italian and other languages issued thereafter.

2642 VIAL, HENRI
Les artistes décorateurs du bois; répertoire alphabétique des ébénistes, nenuisiers, sculpteurs, doreurs sur bois, etc., ayant travaillé en France aux XVIIe et XVIIIe siècles, par Henri Vial, Adrien Marcel et André Girodie. Paris, Bibliothèque d'art et d'archéologie, 1912-22. 2 v. 27cm. (Publications pour faciliter les études d'art en France) A dictionary of French artists who worked with wood, 17th-18th centuries.

2643 VIARDOT, LOUIS, 1800-1883.
Notices sur les principaux peintres de l'Espagne; ouvrage servant de texte aux gravures de la Galerie Aguado. Paris, Gavard, 1839. 355p. 26cm. Notes on the chief painters of Spain.

2644 VILLANI, CARLO, 1858-
Scrittori ed artisti pugliesi antichi, moderni e contemporanei. Traní, V. Vecchi, 1904. xiii, 1387p. 25cm.
2645 ---- ----Nuove addizioni. Napoli, A. Morano, 1920. 255p.

Writers & artists of Apulia, ancient, modern & contemporary.

2646 VIÑAZA, CIPRIANO MUÑOZ Y MANZANO, conde de la, 1862-1933.
Adiciones al Diccionario histórico de los más ilustres

profesores de las bellas artes en España de don Juan Agustín
Ceán Bermúdez. Madrid, Tip. de los Huérfanos, 1889-94.
4 v. in 2. 20cm. Additions to Ceán Bermúdez's Dictionary
[of Spanish artists]

2647   VOLLMER, HANS, 1878-   ed.
Allgemeines Lexikon der bildenden Künstler des XX.
Jahrhunderts. Unter Mitwirkung von Fachgelehrten des In-
und Auslandes. Leipzig, E. A. Seemann, 1953-62. 6 v.
27cm. General dictionary of artists of the 20th century. A
continuation of Ulrich Thieme's Allgemeines Lexikon der
bildenden Künstler von der Antike bis zur Gegenwart.

2648   WALLER, FRANCOIS GERARD, 1867-1934.
Biographisch woodenboek van Noord Nederlandsche graveurs, uitg. door beheerders van het Wallerfonds en bewerkt
door W. R. Juynboll. 's-Gravenhage, Nijhoff, 1938. xix,
551 p. illus. 26cm. Biographical dictionary of the engravers
of Northern Netherlands.

2649   WALPOLE, HORACE, Earl or Orford, 1717-1797.
Anecdotes of painting in England: with some account of the
principal artists; and incidental notes on other arts; collected
by the late Mr. George Vertue; and now digested and published
from his original mss. by Mr. Horace Walpole. 3d ed., with
additions. London, Printed for J. Dodsley, 1782. 4 v.
19cm. A new ed., rev. with additional notes by Ralph N.
Wornum was issued in 3 volumes in 1876 (London, Chatto and
Windus)

2650   --- ----Volume the fifth and last. Now digested and published
from [Horace Walpole's] original mss. by Frederick W.
Hilles and Philip B. Daghlian. New Haven, Yale University
Press, 1937. xv, 262 p. facsim. 24cm.

2651   WASTLER, JOSEF
Steirisches Künstler-Lexikon. Graz, Leykam, 1883.
198 p. 23cm. Dictionary of artists in the province of
Styria, Austria.

2652   WATERS, CLARA (ERSKINE) CLEMENT, 1834-1916.
Artists of the nineteenth century and their works. A hand-
book containing two thousand and fifty biographical sketches.
By Clara Erskine Clement and Laurence Hutton. 3d ed. rev.
Boston, J. Osgood, 1885. 2 v. in 1. 20cm.

2653   WATERS, CLARA (ERSKINE) CLEMENT, 1834-1916.
Painters, sculptors, architects, engravers, and their
works; a handbook. By Clara Erskine Clement. Boston,
Houghton, Mifflin [c1901] xlii, 681 p. illus. 20cm. First
published in 1874.

2654   WATERS, CLARA (ERSKINE) CLEMENT, 1834-1916.
Women in the fine arts, from the seventh century B.C. to

the twentieth century A. D. , by Clara Erskine Clement.
Boston, Houghton, Mifflin, 1904. li, 395 p. illus. 20cm.

2655   WEBER, VICTOR FRÉDÉRIC, 1871-
"Ko-ji hô-ten"; dictionnaire à l'usage des amateurs et col-
lectionneurs d'objets d'art japonais et chinois: on y trouvera...
les biographies, les signatures et autres signes particuliers,
des peintres, sculpteurs, ciseleurs, céramistes et autres
artistes et artisans... Paris, L'auteur, 1923. 2 v. illus.
41cm. A dictionary for the use of connoisseurs and collectors of Japanese and Chinese objets d'art. Included in it are
biographies & signatures of Chinese & Japanese artists.

2656   WEILBACH, PHILIP, 1834-1900.
Kunstnerleksikon. Udg. af en komité med støtte af Carls-
bergfondet. Redaktion: Merete Bodelsen og Povl Engelstoft.
[København] Aschehoug, 1947-52. 3 v. illus., ports. 27cm.
A dictionary of [Danish] artists. This is the 3d edition. 1st
ed., 1877-78, under title: Dansk kunstnerlexikon; 2d ed., 1896-
97, under title: Nyt dansk kunstnerlexikon.

2657   WEINWICH, NIELS HENRICH, 1755-1829.
Dansk, norsk og svensk kunstnerlexicon. Kjøbenhavn,
Seidelin, 1829. 197 p. 23cm. Dictionary of Danish, Nor-
wegian and Swedish artists.

2658   WEYERMAN, JACOB CAMPO, 1677-1747.
De levens-beschryvingen der Nederlandsche konst-schilders
en konst-schilderessen, met een uytbreyding over de schilder-
konst der ouden. Verrykt met de konterfeytsels der voornaamste konst-schilders en konst-schilderessen, cierlyk in
koper gesneden door J. Houbraken. 's-Gravenhage, By de
Wed. E. Boucquet [etc.] 1729-69. 4 v. illus., ports. 21cm.
Lives of Dutch painters. Considered by some as a plagiariza-
tion of Houbraken's work (q. v.)

2659   WHO'S WHO IN AMERICAN ART.
1936-37-   New York [etc.] R. R. Bowker. v.
23-26cm. Biennial, 1936-37—1940-41; irregular, 1940-47—
Vols. for 1936-37——1940-47 called v. 1-4. Vols. 1-4
published by the American Federation of Arts. Formerly
published in the American art annual (later American art
directory); v. 4 issued as pt. 2 of v. 36 of the annual.

2660   WHO'S WHO IN ART.
1st-   issue of the directory section of the American
art annual. 19   New York, American Art Annual, inc.
v. ports. 23cm. Bound also with the American art annual.

2661   WHO'S WHO IN ART.
Biographies of leading men and women in the world of art
today ——artists, designers, craftsmen, critics, writers,
teachers, collectors and curators, with appendices of

signatures. 1st-   ed. ; 1927-   London, Art Trade
Press. v. facsims. 19-23cm. Subtitle varies.

2662   WHO'S WHO IN NORTHWEST ART;
A biographical directory of persons in the Pacific Northwest working in the media of painting, sculpture, graphic
arts, illustration, design, and the handicrafts. Marion Brymner Appleton, editor. Seattle, F. McCaffrey, 1941. vii, 87p.
23cm.

2663   WHO'S WHO IN PHILATELY.
[1st-   ed.]; 1914-   London, Philatelic Club.   v.

2664   WHO'S WHO IN PROFESSIONAL PORTRAITURE IN AMERICA.
[Cleveland, Abel Pub. Co. , c1927] [143] p. ports. 38cm.
"Compiled... for the American Institute of Photography by
the Abel Publishing Company of Cleveland, Ohio. "

2665   WITT, Sir ROBERT CLERMONT, 1872-
Catalogue of painters and draughtsmen represented in the
library of reproductions of pictures and drawings formed by
Robert and Mary Witt. London, Priv. print. , 1920. xv,
238p. 25cm.

2666   ---- ----Supplement. [London?] 1925. 238p. 25cm.

Altogether some 13, 000 painters.

2667   WIER, ALBERT ERNEST, 1879-
Thesaurus of the arts: drama, music, radio, painting,
screen, television, literature, sculpture, architecture, ballet.
New York, G. P. Putnam [1943] 690 p. 26cm.

2668   --- ----Appendix. [New York] G.P. Putnam, 1944. 16 p.
25cm.

2669   WINCKELMANN, JOHANN HEINRICH LUDWIG VON
Ludwig von Winckelmanns neues Malerlexikon. 3. umgearb.
Aufl. von J. Heller. Augsburg, 1842. xviii, 353p. 8.º A
dictionary of modern painters.

2670   WURZBACH, ALFRED WOLFGANG, Ritter von Tannenberg,
1879-
Niederländisches Künstler-Lexikon. Auf Grund archival-
ischer Forschungen bis auf die neueste Zeit bearb. Mit
nahezu 3000 Monogrammen. Leipzig, Halm, 1904-11. 3 v.
8.º Dictionary of Dutch artists.

2671   ZANI, PIETRO, 1748-1821?
Enciclopedia metodica critico-ragionata delle belle arti...
Parma, Tip. Ducale, 1817-24. 2 pts. in 28 v. 21cm. An
encyclopedia of the fine arts. First part (19 v.) is an encyclopedia of ca. 400 artists.

2672   ZANNANDREIS, DIEGO
Le vite dei pittori, scultori e architetti veronese...
Giuseppe Biadego, editore. Verona, Franchini, 1891. 559p.

29cm. The lives of the painters, sculptors & architects of Verona, Italy.

2673 ZAPATER Y GÓMEZ, FRANCISCO, d. 1897.
Apuntes histórico-biográficos acerca de la escuela ara-gonesa de pintura. Madrid, Estab. Tip. de T. Fortanet, 1863. 100 p. 24cm. Historical-biographical annotations on the Aragonese school of Spanish painting.

2674 ZÜLCH, WALTER KARL
Frankfurter Künstler, 1223-1700. Frankfurt am Main, M. Diesterweg, 1935. viii, 670 p. 28cm. Artists of Frankfurt am Main, 1223-1700. Chronological arrangement, but with an alphabetical list of artists on p. 629-654.

Architecture

2675 AMERICAN ARCHITECTS DIRECTORY.
1st- 1956- New York, Published under the sponsor-ship of American Institute of Architects by R. R. Bowker.
v. 29cm. Contains several thousand biographical notices.

2676 ARCHITECTURAL PUBLICATION SOCIETY.
The dictionary of architecture. London, T. Richards [1892] 6v. illus. 37cm.

2677 BAUCHAL, CHARLES
Nouveau dictionnaire biographique et critique des architectes francais... Paris, André, Daly, 1887. xvi, 842p. 28cm. New biographical and critical dictionary of French architects.

2678 BEZSONOV, SERGEĬ VASIL′EVICH, 1885-
Krepostnye arkhitektory. 1. Opyt istoricheskogo issledova-niia. 2. Slovar′ krepostnykh arkhitektorov. Moskva, Vsesoĭuznaĭa akademia arkhitektury, 1938. 144p. 142 bio-graphical notices of Russian military architects.

2679 BRITTON, JOHN, 1771-1857.
A dictionary of the architecture and archaeology of the Middle Ages; including words used by ancient and modern authors in treating of architectural and other antiquities... also, biographical notices of ancient architects...Illustrated by numerous engravings by J. Le Keux... London, Longman, Orme, Brown, Green, and Longmans, 1838. xviii, 489 p. 39 plates. 25 cm.

2680 COLVIN, HOWARD MONTAGU, 1886-
A biographical directory of English architects, 1660-1840. Cambridge, Mass., Harvard University Press, 1954. xiv, 821 p. Also published in London by J. Murray.

2681 ENCYCLOPEDIA OF MODERN ARCHITECTURE;
Edited by Wolfgang Pehnt. Contributors: Kyösti Alander

[and others]   New York, H. N. Abrams [1964]   336 p.   illus.,
ports. 27cm. Largely biographical.

2682   HARVEY, JOHN HOOPER
English mediaeval architects, a biographical dictionary
down to 1550, including master masons, carpenters, carvers,
building contractors, and others responsible for design.
With contributions by Arthur Oswald. London, Batsford,
1954. xxiii, 411p. 26cm.

2683   LANCE, ADOLPHE, 1813-1874.
Dictionnaire des architectes français. Paris, Vve. A.
Morel, 1872. 2 v. plates. 25cm. Dictionary of French
architects.

2684   LLAGUNO Y AMÍROLA, EUGENIO, d. 1799.
Noticias de los arquitectos y arquitectura en España desde
su restauración, ilustradas y acrecentadas con notas, adiciones
y documentos por Juan Agustín Ceán-Bermúdez. Madrid,
Impr. Real, 1829. 4 v. in 2. 23cm. Spanish architects &
architecture.

2685   ŁOZA, STANISŁAW, 1888-1956.
Architekci i budowniczowie w Polsce. Warszawa, Budow-
nictwo i Architektura, 1954. 424 p. plates. 25cm. Architects and builders in Poland. A biographical dictionary.
First published in 1917 (2d ed., 1930) under title: Słownik architektów i budowniczych Polaków oraz cudzoziemców w Polsce
pracujacych.

2686   MAYER, LEO ARY, 1895-
Islamic architects and their works. Genève, A. Kundig,
1956. 183p. 26cm.

2687   SOUSA VITERBO, FRANCISCO MARQUES DE, 1845-1910.
Diccionario historico e documental dos architectos, engenheiros e constructores portuguezes, ou a servicio de Portugal. Lisboa, 1899-1922. 3 v. 8.° Historical and documentary dictionary of Portuguese architects, engineers and
builders (or those in the service of Portugal) Vols. 1-2
cover letters A-R. Work completed by someone else?

2688   STURGIS, RUSSELL, 1836-1909.
A dictionary of architecture and building, biographical,
historical, and descriptive, by Russell Sturgis and many
architects, painters, engineers, and other expert writers,
American and foreign. New York, Macmillan, 1901-02. 3 v.
illus. 27cm.

2689   TEMANZA, TOMMASO, 1705-1789.
Vite de' più celebri architetti e scultori veneziani, che
fiorirono nel secolo decimosesto. Venezia, Stamp. di C.
Palese, 1778. xvi, 550p. 4.° Lives of the most celebrated
Venetian architects and sculptors who flourished in the 16th
century.

2690   WASMUTHS LEXIKON DER BAUKUNST...
      Berlin, Wasmuth [c1929-37] 5 v. illus. 30cm. A dictionary of architecture. Many biographies are included.
Edited by Günther Wasmuth.

2691   WHO'S WHO IN ARCHITECTURE.
      1914-   London, Architectural Press. v. 19cm.
Editor: 19   Frederick Chatterton. British architects.
1914, 1923 & 1926 issues only ones published?

2692   WITHEY, HENRY F
      Biographical dictionary of American architects (deceased) by Henry F. Withey & Elsie Rathburn Withey. Los Angeles, New Age Pub. Co. [1956] 678p. 24cm. Ca. 2000 architects who lived 1740-1952.

Sculpture

2693   BAERT, PHILIPPE
      Mémoires sur les sculpteurs et architectes des Pays-Bas ...publiés par M. le baron de Reiffenberg. Bruxelles, Hayez, 1848. 160p. 22cm. "Extrait des Bulletins de la Commission Royale d'Histoire en Belgique." Memorials on the sculptors and architects of the Low Countries.

2694   BESSONE-AURELJ, ANTONIETTA MARIA, 1869-
      Dizionario degli scultori ed architetti italiani. Genova, Società anonima editrice Dante Alighieri, 1947. 523p. 23cm. Dictionary of Italian sculptors and architects.

2695   DICTIONARY OF MODERN SCULPTURE.
      General editor: Robert Maillard. [Translated from the French by Bettina Wadia] New York, Tudor Pub. Co. [1962, c1960] 310 p. illus. 22cm. Translation of Dictionnaire de la sculpture moderne.

2696   GARDNER, ALBERT TEN EYCK
      Yankee stonecutters; the first American school of sculpture, 1800-1850. New York, Published for the Metropolitan Museum of Art by Columbia University Press, 1945. 84 p. 12 plates. 31 cm. "A biographical dictionary; American sculptors born between 1800 and 1830": p. [60]-73.

2697   GIEDION-WELCKER, CAROLA
      Contemporary sculpture; an evolution in volume and space. Selective bibliography by Bernard Karpel: Modern art and sculpture. New York, G. Wittenborn [1955] xxxi, 327 p. (chiefly illus., ports.) 26cm. (Documents of modern art, v.12) 200 artists analyzed thru' biographies. Greatly enl. and rev. ed. of 'Modern plastic art.'

2698   GRANT, MAURICE HAROLD, 1872-
      A dictionary of British sculptors from the XIIIth century to the XXth century. London, Rockliff, 1953. 317 p. 23cm.

2699   GUNNIS, RUPERT.
Dictionary of British sculptors, 1660-1851. London,
Odhams Press, 1953. 514 p. illus. 26cm. American ed.,
1954, by Harvard University Press, Cambridge, Mass.

2700   LAMI, STANISLAS, 1858-
Dictionnaire des sculpteurs de l'antiquité jusqu'au VIe
siècle de notre ère. Paris, E. Perrin, 1884. vii, 147p.
19cm. Ancient Greek sculptors.

2701   LAMI, STANISLAS, 1858-
Dictionnaire des sculpteurs de l'école francaise. Paris,
Champion, 1898-1921. 8 v. 29cm. Contents. --[1] Du moyen
age au règne de Louis XIV. --[2] Sous le règne de Louis
XIV. --[3-4] Au dix-huitieme siècle. --[5-8] Au dix-neuvième
siècle. A dictionary of sculptors of the French school; French
sculptors from the Middle Ages to the 19th century.

2702   WATERS, WILLIAM GEORGE, 1844-1928.
Italian sculptors... 2d ed. enl. London, Methuen; New
York, Doran, 1926. xxi, 285 p. 51 plates. 20cm. 1st ed.,
1911.

Applied Arts

2703   ARMAND, ALFRED, 1805-1888.
Les médailleurs italiens des quinzième et seizième siècles.
2. éd. rev., corr. et considérablement augm. Paris, E.
Plon, 1883-87. 3v. 25cm. First ed., in 1 vol., published
1879. Italian designers & makers of medals of the 15th & 16th
centuries.

2704   BAILLIE, GRANVILLE HUGH
Watchmakers and clockmakers of the world. [2d ed.]
London, N. A. G. Press, 1947. xxv, 388p. maps. 22cm.

2705   BJERKOE, ETHEL HALL
The cabinetmakers of America, by Ethel Hall Bjerkoe and
John Arthur Bjerkoe. Foreword by Russell Kettell. [1st ed.]
Garden City, Doubleday, 1957. xvii, 252 p. illus. 27cm.
A biographical dictionary.

2706   BRITTEN, FREDERICK JAMES, 1843-1913.
Old clocks and watches and their makers; a historical and
descriptive account of the different styles of clocks and watches
of the past in England and abroad, containing a list of nearly
fourteen thousand makers. 7th ed., by G. H. Baillie, C.
Clutton, and C. A. Ilbert, with a front. by L. H. Cresswell
and diagrs by F. Janča. New York, Dutton, 1956. xx, 518 p.
illus. 29 cm. London ed. issued the same year by E. & F.
Spon. "Former clock and watch makers" (p. [319]-505) is
largely a listing, but does contain dates and career material
for some clock and watch makers.

2707   COTTERELL, HOWARD HERSCHEL.
Old pewter: its makers and marks in England, Scotland and Ireland. An account of the old pewterer and his craft, illustrating all known marks and secondary marks of the old pewterers, with a series of plates showing the chief types of their wares. London, B. T. Batsford, 1929. xvi, 432 p. illus. 29cm. On pages 145-344 is an alphabetical list of pewterers.

2708   DREPPERD, CARL WILLIAM, 1898-1956.
American clocks & clockmakers. Enl. [i. e. 2d] ed. Boston, C. T. Branford Co., 1958 [c1947] 312, 52 p. illus. 23cm. A list of American clockmakers: p. 196-293 & p. 3-52 (2d group)

2709   ENSKO, STEPHEN GUERNSEY COOK, 1896-
American silversmiths and their marks. New York, Priv. print., 1927- v. illus. 24 cm. Vol. 3, 1948, the most useful.

2710   FORRER, LEONARD.
Biographical dictionary of medallists: Coin, gem, and seal-engravers, mintmasters, ancient and modern, with references to their works B. C. 500-A. D. 1900. London, Spink, 1902-30. 8 v. ports., illus. 25 cm.

2711   FRENCH, HOLLIS, 1868-
A list of early American silversmiths and their marks, with a silver collectors' glossary. New York, Walpole Society, 1917. 164 p. illus. 25 cm. 200 copies printed.

2712   FRENCH CABINETMAKERS OF THE EIGHTEENTH CENTU-RY. Foreword by Pierre Verlet. [Paris] Hachette [1965] 341 p. illus. 32cm. (Collection Connaissance des arts 'Grands artisans d'autrefois') Completed under the general direction of Claude Frégnac with the cooperation of Connaissance des arts; introductions by Jean Meuvret. "The master cabinetmakers": p. 331-341.

2713   GESTOSO Y PÉREZ, JOSÉ, 1852-1917.
Ensayo de un diccionario de los artífices que florecieron en Sevilla desde el siglo XIII al XVII inclusive. Sevilla, La Andalucía moderna, 1899-1909. 3v. 25cm. Attempt at a dictionary of artisans who flourished in Seville during the 13th-18th centuries.

2714   HEAL, Sir AMBROSE, 1872-
The London furniture makers, from the Restoration to the Victorian era, 1660-1840; a record of 2500 cabinet- makers, upholsterers, carvers and gilders, with their addresses and working dates. With a chapter by R. W. Symonds on the problem of identification of the furniture they produced... London, Batsford, 1953. xx, 276p. illus. 30cm.

2715   HINTZE, ERWIN, 1876-1931.
Die deutschen Zinngieser und ihre Marken. Neudruck

der Ausg. 1921-31. Aalen, O. Zeller, 1964. 7 v. illus. 27cm. German makers of pewter and their marks.

2716 HVEM ER HVEM I DANSK HÅNDVAERK.
Biografisk håndbog over danske håndvaerksmestre. København, Håndvaerksrådets forlag; Håndvaerk og kultur, 1952. 483p. 24cm. Who's who in Danish handicrafts.

2717 IVERSEN, ĬULĬĬ BOGDANOVICH, 1823-1900.
Slovar´ medal´ erov i drugikh lĭts, imena kotorykh vstrechaĭutsĭa na russkikh medalĭakh. S.-Peterburg, Tip. Akademii nauk, 1874. 36p. Dictionary of ca. 90 strikers of medals & other persons whose names are met with on Russian medals.

2718 JACKSON, SIR CHARLES JAMES, 1849-
English goldsmiths and their marks; a history of the goldsmiths and plate workers of England, Scotland, and Ireland; with over thirteen thousand marks reproduced in facsimile from authentic examples of plate, and tables of date-letters and other hallmarks used in the assay offices of the United Kingdom. 2d ed., rev. and enl. London, Macmillan, 1921. xvi, 747p. illus. 31cm.

2719 JERVIS, WILLIAM PERCIVAL, 1850-
The encyclopedia of ceramics, with much original matter now first published. New York [c1902] 673p. illus. 26cm. Includes a large number of biographical sketches.

2720 JONES, BERNARD E   ed.
Cassell's cyclopaedia of photography. London, New York, Cassell, 1911. viii, 572p. illus. 27cm. Includes biographies of deceased photographers.

2721 LAUGHLIN, LEDLIE IRWIN
Pewter in America, its makers and their marks. Boston, Houghton, Mifflin, 1940. 2 v. illus. 33 x 25cm.

2722 LEDOUX-LEBARD, DENISE
Les ébénistes parisiens, 1795-1830; leurs oeuvres et leurs marques. Ouvrage contenant 1500 notices présentées dans l'ordre alphabétique... Paris, Grund [1951] 324p. illus., 55 plates. 28cm. Parisian cabinet-workers, 1795-1830.

2723 LLOYD, HERBERT ALAN
The collector's dictionary of clocks. London, Country Life [1964] 214 p. illus. 32cm. Included in the alphabetical listings are the names of noted clockmakers.

2724 MACQUOID, PERCY, d. 1925.
The dictionary of English furniture, from the Middle Ages to the late Georgian period, by Percy Macquoid and Ralph Edwards. [2d ed.] rev. and enl. by Ralph Edwards. London, Country Life Limited, 1954. 3 v. illus. 39cm. 1st ed., 1924-1927, 3 v. Includes biographical sketches.

2725   MANKOWITZ, WOLF
The concise encyclopedia of English pottery and porcelain, by Wolf Mankowitz and Reginald G. Haggar. London, A. Deutsch [1957] xv, 312 p. illus. 26cm. Includes biographies. American ed. has imprint: New York, Hawthorn Books.

2726   MINGHETTI, AURELIO, 1878-
Ceramisti. Milano, E. B. B. I., Istituto editoriale italiano B. C. Tosi [1939] 451 p. illus., ports. 28cm. (Enciclopedia biografica e bibligrafica "Italiana, " ser. 41) Potters of Italy.

2727   SALVERTE, FRANCOIS DE, comte, d. 1929.
Les ébénistes du XVIIIe siècle, leurs oeuvres et leurs marques; ouvrage contenant un millier de notices présentées dans l'ordre alphabétique. 3. éd., revue, augm. et enrichie de 500 reproductions d'estampiles. Paris, Éditions d'art et d'histoire, 1934. xxiv, 336p. facsims. 29cm. Cabinetworkers of the 18th century.

2728   SMITH, JOHN, clock-maker.
Old Scottish clockmakers from 1453 to 1850. Compiled from original sources, with notes. 2d ed., rev. and enl. Edinburgh, Oliver and Boyd, 1921. xv, 436 p. plates. 24cm.

2729   THUILE, JEAN
Histoire de l'orfèvrerie du Languedoc: généralités de Montpellier et de Toulouse. Répertoire des orfèvres depuis le moyen-âge jusqu'au début du XIXe siècle. Paris, T. & F. Schmied, 1964- v. illus. 28cm. Contents. --[1] A à C. The history of gold and silversmithing and jewellery in Languedoc, France... A [biographical] list of artisans in these crafts from the close of the Middle Ages to the beginning of the 19th century.

2730   TROITSKIĬ, VASILIĬ IVANOVICH, 1868-
Mastera-khudozhniki zolotogo i serebrianogo dela, almazniki i susal'niki, rabotavshie v Moskve pri Patriarshem dvore v XVII veke. Slovar'. Moskva, Pech. A. I. Snegirevoi, 1914. 194p. illus. Alphabetical dictionary—122 Russian goldsmiths, silversmiths, and jewelers working under the Patriarchate of Moscow in the 17th century.

2731   TROITSKIĬ, VASILIĬ IVANOVICH, 1868-
Slovar' Moskovskikh masterov zolotogo, serebrianogo i almaznogo dela XVII veka. vyp. 1-2. Izdal pod nabliudeniem A. V. Oreshnikova. Leningrad, Academia, 1928-30. 2 v. (156 p.) 23cm. At head of title: Gosudarstvennaia oruzheinaia palata. No more published? Dictionary of ca. 460 Muscovite goldsmiths, silversmiths & jewelers of the 17th century.

2732   VERCI, GIOVANNI BATTISTA, 1739-1795.
Notizie intorno alla vita e alle opere de' pittori, scultori

e intagliatori della citta di Bassano. Venezia, E. Gatti,
1775. viii, 328p. front. 18cm. Painters, sculptors and
engravers of the city of Bassano, Italy.

2733   UPMARK, GUSTAF HERMAN FABIAN, 1875-1929.
        Guld- och silversmeder i Sverige, 1520-1850. Stockholm,
Fröleen [1943] 951p. illus. 26cm. First published in 1925.
Swedish goldsmiths & silversmiths, 1520-1850.

2734   VARGAS UGARTE, RUBEN, 1886-
        Ensayo de un diccionario de artífices coloniales de la
América Meridional. [Lima?] Tall. Gráf. A. Baiocco,
1947. 391 p. 24cm.

2735   ---- ----Apéndice. [Lima?] Tall. Gráf. A. Baiocco, 1955.
118p. 24cm.

        Attempt at a dictionary of colonial artisans of South Ameri-
ca.

2736   WHO'S WHO IN AMERICAN PORTRAIT PHOTOGRAPHY.
        Compiled and written for the committee of selection by
Charles Abel. Cleveland, 1943. [300]p. ports. 26cm.

2737   WHO'S WHO IN DESIGNING.
        America's foremost clothing designers, members of
International Association of Clothing Designers. 1949-
New York, F. Kogos Pub. Co. v. ports. 21cm.

2738   WHO'S WHO IN GRAPHIC ART.
        1st-   ed. ; 1962-   Zurich, Amstutz & Herdeg Graphis
Press. v. illus. , ports. 30cm. In English, French, and
German. Editor: 1962-   W. Amstutz.

2739   WHO'S WHO IN PHOTOGRAPHY:
        The focal world register. [Compiled by Ruth Matthews]
London, New York, Focal Press [1951] 340p. 26cm.

Music
Bibliography, Indexes, Etc.

2740   BULL, STORM.
        Index to biographies of contemporary composers.
New York, Scarecrow Press, 1964. 405 p. 22 cm.

2741   COOVER, JAMES B
        Music lexicography, including a study of lacunae in music
lexicography and a bibliography of music dictionaries. Denver, Bibliographical Center for Research, Rocky Mountain
Region, Denver Public Library, 1958. xxx, 126 p. Second
ed. of Bibliography of music dictionaries (1952)

General Works

2742   ABERT, HERMANN JOSEPH, 1871-1927, ed.
        Illustriertes Musik-Lexikon. Mit 503 Bildern auf 72

Tafeln und zahlreichen Notenbeispielen. Stuttgart, J.
Engelhorns Nachf., 1927. 542p. illus.,72 plates. 26cm.
Edited by Abert and others. An illustrated music dictionary
with biography.

2743 AJZENSTADT, DAVID
Algemajner muzik-leksikon. Erszte jidisze populere
muzik-enciklopedje. [Warszawa?] I. M. Alter, 1935. 2v.
By Ajzenstadt and Abram Pragier. A music dictionary, in
Yiddish, with biographies.

2744 ALCAHALÍ Y DE MOSQUERA, JOSÉ MARÍA RUIZ DE LIHORI
Y PARDINES, barón de, d. 1920.
La música en Valencia. Diccionario biográfico y crítico,
por José Ruiz de Lihory barón de Alcahalí. Valencia, Estab.
Tip. Domenech, 1903. xliii,445p. illus. 29cm.
Biographical dictionary of musicians of Valencia, Spain.

2745 ALGEMENE MUZIEKENCYCLOPEDIE;
Onder leiding van A. Corbet en Wouter Paap. Redactie-
secretaris: J. Robijns. Antwerpen, Zuid-Nederlandse Uitg.
[1957-63] 6 v. illus. 24cm. Contents. --deel 1. A-B. --
deel 2. C-F. --deel 3. G-J. --deel 4. K-L-M. --deel 5. M-Q.
--deel 6. R-Z. A general Dutch music dictionary, with bio-
bibliographies.

2746 ALLORTO, RICCARDO
Dizionario di musica [di] Riccardo Allorto e Alberto
Ferrari. Milano, Ceschina [1959] 576p. illus., ports. 24cm.
(Biblioteca italiana di opere di consultazione) A music dic-
tionary, with biographies.

2747 AMERICAN SOCIETY OF COMPOSERS, AUTHORS AND
PUBLISHERS.
The ASCAP biographical dictionary of composers, authors
and publishers. Edited by Daniel I. McNamara. 2d ed. New
York, Crowell [1952] 636p. 22cm.

2748 AMORIM, EUGENIO
Diccionario biográfico de músicos do Norte de Portugal.
[Porto] Edicões Maranus [1935] 110p. Biographical dictionary
of musicians of northern Portugal.

2749 ANGELIS, ALBERTO DE, 1885-
L'Italia musicale d'oggi. Dizionario dei musicisti. 3. ed.,
corredata di una appendice. Roma, Ausonia, 1928. 523,221p.
ports. 20cm. 1st ed., 1918; 2d, 1922. Musical Italy of today;
a dictionary of Italian musicians.

2750 [APELL, DAVID AUGUST VON]
Gallerie der vorzüglichen Tonkünstler und merkwürdigen
Musik-Dilettanten in Cassel, von Anfang des 16ten Jahr-
hunderts bis auf gegenwärtige Zeiten... Cassel, 1806. 63p.
Gallery of the excellent musicians and noteworthy music lovers
in the City of Kassel.

2751   ASCHEHOUGS MUSIKLEKSIKON.
        Under redaktion af Povl Hamburger. [Redaktions-se-
        kretaer og billedred: Inge Henriksen. København] Asche-
        houg, 1957-   v. illus., ports. 24cm. Issued in fas-
        cicles. A music dictionary including biographical sketches.

2752   DAS ATLANTISBUCH DER MUSIK.
        Hrsg. von Fred Hamel und Martin Hürlimann unter Mitar-
        beit zahlreicher Fachgelehrter und Künstler. [9. Ausg.]
        Zürich, Atlantis Verlag [1959] 999 p. illus., ports. 23cm.
        A dictionary of music, with biographical sketches of leading
        musicians.

2753   AUDA, ANTOINE
        La musique et les musiciens de l'ancien pays de Liège.
        Essai bio-bibliographique sur la musique liégeoise depuis ses
        origines jusqu'à la fin de la principauté (1800) Bruxelles,
        Librairie Saint-Georges [1930] 291p. 19 plates. 27cm. The
        music and the musicians of the old territory of Liège, to
        1800.

2754   BACHMANN, ALBERTO ABRAHAM, 1875-
        An encyclopedia of the violin. With an introd. by Eugene
        Ysaÿe. Translated by Frederick H. Martens. Edited by
        Albert E. Wier. New York, D. Appleton, 1925. xiv, 470p.
        illus. 22cm. Includes a biographical dictionary of violinists.

2755   BAKER, THEODORE, 1851-1934.
        Biographical dictionary of musicians. 5th ed., completely
        rev. by Nicolas Slonimsky. New York, G. Schirmer [1958]
        xv, 1855p. 24cm.

2756   ---- ----1965 supplement, by Nicolas Slonimsky. New York,
        G. Schirmer [1965] vii, 143p. 24cm.

2757   BALTZELL, WINTON JAMES, 1864-
        Dictionary of musicians; containing concise biographical
        sketches of musicians of the past and present, with pro-
        nunciation of foreign names. Boston, O. Ditson, c1911.
        [263]p. 22cm.

2758   BAÑAS Y CASTILLO, RAYMUNDO, 1894-
        The music and theater of the Filipino people. Manila,
        The author, 1924. xiii, 131p. ports. 22cm. Partial
        contents. --Filipino musicians (p. 61-113). --Other Filipino
        musicians (p. 114-122).

2759   BAPTIE, DAVID, 1822-1906.
        A handbook of musical biography. London, W. Morley
        [1883] 256p. 19cm.

2760   BAPTIE, DAVID, 1822-1906.
        Musical Scotland, past and present, being a dictionary of
        Scottish musicians from about 1400 till the present time, to

which is added a bibliography of musical publications connected with Scotland from 1611. Paisley, 1894. iv, 219p.

2761 BAPTIE, DAVID, 1822-1906.
Musicians of all times; a concise dictionary of musical
biography. London, 1889. 287p.

2762 BAPTIE, DAVID, 1822-1906.
Sketches of the English glee composers, historical, bio-
graphical and critical (from about 1735-1866) London, W.
Reeves [1896] vii, 235p. 2 ports. 18cm.

2763 BARBÉ, JEAN JULIEN
Dictionnaire des musiciens de la Moselle. Préf. de
René Delaunay. Metz, Impr. du "Messin," 1929. 206p.
ports. 26cm. Dictionary of musicians of the department
of the Moselle, France.

2764 BARNES, EDWIN NINYON CHALONER, 1877-
Who's who in music education. Washington, Music
education, 1925. xiv, 258p. port. 23cm.

2765 BECKER, CARL FERDINAND, 1804-1877.
Systematisch-chronologische Darstellung der
musikalischen Literatur von der frühesten bis auf die neueste
Zeit. Nebst biographischen Notizen über die Verfasser der
darin aufgeführten Schriften, und kritische Andeutungen über
der innern Werth derselben. Leipzig, R. Friese, 1836.
571b (i. e. 572) columns, [572]-605p. 29cm. Classified,
with an index to authors and titles or catchword titles of
anonymous works in musical literature.

2766 -----Anhang: Choralsammlungen aus dem 16. , 17. und 18.
Jahrhundert. Nachtrag. Leipzig, R. Friese, 1839. vi p.,
194 columns. 28cm.

2767 BECKER, GEORG, 1834-1928.
La musique en Suisse depuis les temps les plus reculés
jusqu'a la fin du dix-huitième siècle; notices historiques,
biographiques et bibliographiques. Genève, F. Richard,
1874. 190p. 20cm. Bio-bibliography of Swiss music to the
latter part of the 19th century.

2768 BENNWITZ, HANSPETER
Interpretenlexikon der Instrumentalmusik. Bern, Francke
[1964] 326p. 18cm. (Sammlung Dalp, Bd. 93) A dictionary
of musicians.

2769 BENNWITZ, HANSPETER.
Kleines Musiklexikon. Bern, Francke [1963] 493p. 18cm.
(Sammlung Dalp, Bd. 91) A music dictionary; includes
brief biographies.

2770 BERNANDT, G
Sovetskie kompozitory—laureaty Stalinskoĭ premii;

spravochnik. Moskva, Gos. muzykal´noe izd-vo, 1952.
137p. 20cm. 120 composers of Soviet Russia, winners of
the Stalin Prize.

2771   BERNSDORF, EDUARD, 1825-1901, ed.
Neues Universal-Lexikon der Tonkunst. Unter Mitwirkung
Frz. Liszt [et al.] bearb. und hrsg. von Eduard Bernsdorf.
Dresden, R. Schaefer, 1856-65. 4v. ports. 24cm. Imprint
varies. Preface signed: Julius Schladebach. A music dic-
tionary, with biographies.

2772   BERTINI, GIUSEPPE, d. 1756.
Dizionario storico-critico degli scrittori di musica e de'
piu celebri artisti di tutte le nazioni si antiche che moderne.
Palermo, Tip. reale di guerra, 1814-15. 4v. 20cm.
Musical bio-bibliography, universal in scope.

2773   THE BILLBOARD ENCYCLOPEDIA OF MUSIC.
1939-   Cincinnati.   v. illus., ports. 29 x 35cm.
Annual. Title varies: -3d,   -1941, Talent and tunes on
music machines. --   -5th-   1943-   The Billboard
music year book; the encyclopedia and reference work of the
music industry (5th-   issued without subtitle) Issues for
19   published as a supplement to the Billboard.
Generally includes a "Who's who" section of musicians in the
entertainment world.

2774   BIOGRAFÍA DE NUESTROS ARTISTAS.
[Ascunción? Impr. Trujillo, 1959-   v. illus. 20cm.
(Colección "Ocara Poty Cué mi, " t. 1-   Brief biographies of
Paraguayan musicians.

2776   BISSON, ALEXANDRE CHARLES AUGUSTE, 1848-1912.
Petite encyclopedie musicale, par Alex. Bisson et Th. de
Lajarte. Paris, A. Hennuyer, 1884. 2 v. in 1. illus., ports.
21 cm. Contents. --1. Traité de musique. --2. Histoire
générale de la musique, par A. Bisson, et Biographie des
compositeurs, virtuoses, etc., par Georges Baüdouin.
A music dictionary, with biography included in vol. 2.

2777   BLAZE, FRANCOIS HENRI JOSEPH, called CASTIL-BLAZE,
1784-1857.
Dictionnaire de musique moderne, par Francois Henri-
Joseph Blaze, dit Castil-Blaze. Parìs, A. Egron, 1821.
589 p. Other editions published in 1821 (2 v.), 1825 (2 v.),
1828 (Bruxelles, xvi, 66, 281, 24p.) Dictionary of modern
music; includes biographies.

2778   BLOM, ERIC, 1888-
        Everyman's dictionary of music. Rev. ed. London, Dent;
        New York, Dutton, 1958. xiii, 687 p. 20cm. (Everyman's
        reference library) "The biographical sketches cover many
        composers of secondary interest. " ----Walford. Earlier
        editions appeared in 1946 and 1954.

2779   BOALCH, DONALD HOWARD
        Makers of the harpsichord and clavichord, 1440-1840.
        London, G. Ronald, 1956. xxv, 169 p. 32 plates. 29cm.

2780   BOBILLIER, MARIE, 1858-1918.
        Dictionnaire pratique et historique de la musique, par
        Michel Brenet [pseud.] 510 citations musicales----140 figures.
        Paris, A. Colin, 1926. 487 p. illus. 23 cm. Includes 140
        musical biographies.

2781   BOELZA, IGOR′ FEDOROVICH, 1904-
        Handbook of Soviet musicians. Edited by Alan Bush.
        London, Pilot Press [1943] xiv, 101 p. ports. (Life and
        literature in the Soviet Union)

2782   BONACCORSI, ALFREDO, 1887-
        Nuovo dizionario musicale Curci, con xilografie di Diego
        Pettinelli. Milano, Curci [1954] 556. illus. , ports. 20 cm.
        A music dictionary, with biography included.

2783   BONE, PHILIP JAMES.
        The guitar and mandolin. Biographies of celebrated players
        and composers. [2d ed. , enl.] London, New York, Schott,
        1954. 388 p. ports. , music. 22cm.

2784   BORBA, TOMAS, 1867-1950.
        Dicionário de música, ilustrado [por] Tomas Borba [e]
        Fernando Lopes Graca. Lisboa, Edicões Cosmos, 1956.
        2 v. illus., ports. 24 cm. Dictionary of music; includes
        biography.

2785   BOS, HAN
        Muziekwijzer. Den Haag, Daamen, 1957-60 [v. 5, 1958]
        5 v. 17 cm. (Ooievaar, 35-36, 120-121, 71) Partial contents.
        --1. Beknopte biografieen van Bach tot Bartok. A music hand-
        book; vol. 1 is the biographical volume.

2786   BREMER, FRIEDRICH.
        Handlexikon der Musik. Eine Enzyklopädie der ganzen
        Tonkunst [von] Friedrich Bremer und Bruno Schrader. 6.
        Aufl. der neuen Ausg. Leipzig, P. Reclam Jun. [1929] 551 p.
        (Reclams Universal-Bibliothek, Nr. 1681-1686) A music dic-
        tionary; includes biography.

2787   BROWN, JAMES DUFF, 1862-1914.
        Biographical dictionary of musicians, with a bibliography
        of English writings on music. Paisley [Eng.] A. Gardner,
        1886. vi, 637 p. 22 cm.

2788   BROWN, JAMES DUFF, 1862-1914.
        British musical biography; a dictionary of musical artists,
        authors and composers born in Britain and its colonies, by
        James D. Brown and Stephen S. Stratton. Birmingham [Eng.]
        S. S. Stratton, 1897. 462 p. 24 cm.

2789   BÜCKEN, ERNST, 1884-1949.
        Wörterbuch der Musik. [2. Aufl.] Überarbeitet und ergänzt
        von Fritz Stege. Wiesbaden, Dieterich [1955] 590 p. illus.
        18 cm. (Sammlung Dieterich, Bd. 20) A music dictionary;
        includes biography.

2790   BURTON, JACK.
        The blue book of Tin Pin Alley, a human interest
        encyclopedia American popular music. [Expanded new ed.]
        Watkins Glen, N. Y., Century House [1962-   v. illus.
        24 cm.

2791   CANADIAN BROADCASTING CORPORATION.
        Catalogue of Canadian composers. Edited by Helmut
        Kallmann. Rev. and enl. ed. [Ottawa? 1952?] 254 p. 24 cm.
        1st ed., 1947. "356 composers, of whom 290 are still living."

2792   CANADIAN MUSIC LIBRARY ASSOCIATION.
        A bio-bibliographical finding list of Canadian musicians
        and those who have contributed to music in Canada. Ottawa,
        Canadian Library Association, 1961. v, 53 p.

2793   CANDÉ, ROLAND DE
        Dictionnaire des musiciens. [Paris, Éditions du Seuil
        [1964] 279 p. illus., ports. 18 cm. (Collections Microcosme.
        Dictionnaires, 3)

2794   ČESKOSLOVENSKÝ HUDEBNÍ SLOVNÍ OSOB A INSTITUCÍ.
        [Redaktoři: Gracian Černušák, Bohumír Štědroň,
        Zdenko Nováček. 1 vyd.] Praha, Státni hudební vyda-
        vatelstvi, 1963-   v. illus. 25cm. Czechoslovak music
        dictionary of persons and institutions; Czech musicians.

2795   CHAMPLIN, JOHN DENISON, 1834-1915, ed.
        Cyclopedia of music and musicians. Critical editor:
        William Foster Apthorp. New York, C. Scribner, 1903 [c1888-
        90] 3 v. illus. 30 cm.

2796   CHARTERS, SAMUEL BARCLAY, 1929-
        Jazz: New Orleans, 1885-1963. An index to the Negro
        musicians of New Orleans. Rev. ed. New York, Oak Pub-
        lications [1963] 173p. illus. 22cm.

2797   CHORON, ALEXANDRE ETIENNE, 1771-1834.
        Dictionnaire historique des musiciens, artistes et amateurs,
        morts ou vivans, qui se sont ilustrés en une partie quelconque
        de la musique et des arts qui y sont relatifs. Précédé d'un
        Sommaire de l'histoire de la musique. Par Al. Choron et F.

Fayolle. Paris, Valade, 1810-11. 2 v. music. 21cm. Another edition published 1817 (Paris, Chimont) in 2 v. The work is by Fayolle, with the exception of the introduction and a few of the articles. Dictionary of French musicians, living or dead.

2798 CHYBIŃSKI, ADOLF, 1880-
Słownik muzyków dawnej Polski do roku 1800. Kraków, Polskie Wydawn. Muzyczne [c1949] 163 p. 25cm. Dictionary of Polish musicians to the year 1800.

2799 CLARKE, A   MASON
A biographical dictionary of fiddlers, including performers on the violoncello and double bass. Containing a sketch of their artistic career. Together with notes of their compositions. London, W. Reeves [1895] vii, 360 p. 9 ports. 18cm.

2800 CLÉMENT, FÉLIX, 1822-1885.
Les musiciens célèbres depuis le seizième siècle jusqu'à nos jours. Ouvrage illustré de quarante-cinq portraits gravés à l'eau forte par Masson, Deblois et Massard, et de trois reproductions héliographiques d'anciennes gravures par A. Durand. 4. éd. Paris, Hachette, 1887. 672 p. illus. 27cm. First edition published 1868 (viii, 680 p.)

2801 CLIFFORD, JOHN HERBERT, 1848-   ed.
The musiclover's handbook, containing: (1) A pronouncing dictionary of musical terms and (2) Biographical dictionary of musicians. New York, University Society [c1911] v, 194, 92 p. plates. 19cm.

2802 CLIFFORD, JOHN HERBERT, 1848-   ed.
The standard musical encyclopedia; a comprehensive reference library for musicians and musiclovers, by many eminent contributors, including Reginald De Koven [and others] New York, University Society [c1910] 2 v. illus., ports. 30cm.

2803 COBBETT, WALTER WILLSON
Cobbett's cyclopedic survey of chamber music, compiled and edited by Walter Willson Cobbett, with supplementary material edited by Colin Mason. 2d ed. London, New York, Oxford University Press, 1963. 3 v. illus. 25cm. Includes musical biography.

2804 COEUROY, ANDRÉ, 1891-
Dictionnaire critique de la musique ancienne et moderne. Paris, Payot, 1956. 413 p. 23cm. A music dictionary with biographical sketches.

2805 COOPER, MARTIN, 1910-   ed.
The concise encyclopedia of music and musicians. Contributors: John Barbirolli [and others. 1st ed.] New York, Hawthorn Books [1958] 516 p. illus. 26cm.

2806   CORTE, ANDREA DELLA, 1883-
Dizionario di musica, di A. della Corte e G. M. Gatti.
5. ed. Torino, G. B. Paravia, 1956. vii, 707 p. 22cm.
Spanish ed. , under title: Diccionario de la música, published
1950 (c1949) in Buenos Aires (633 p.) A music dictionary,
with biographical sketches.

2807   COWAN, WILLIAM, 1851-1929.
The music of the church hymnary and the Psalter in metre;
its sources and composers, by William Cowan and James
Love. Edinburgh, New York, H. Frowde, 1901. vi, 259 p.
music. 19cm. Contents.--pt. 1. Historical notices of the
tunes, chants and special settings. --pt. 2. Biographical notices of the composers.

2808   CROWEST, FREDERICK JAMES, 1850-1927.
The dictionary of British musicians, from the earliest
times to the present. London, Jarrold, 1895. 116 p. 19cm.

2809   CROZET, FÉLIX, b. 1800.
Revue de la musique dramatique en France, contenant un
essai abrégé de l'histoire de l'opéra; des notices, par ordre
alphabétique, de tous les opéras...qui ont été représentés en
France...et enfin des notices...des compositeurs dont les
oeuvres ont été représentés en France, avec la liste de tous
leurs ouvrages. Grenoble, Impr. de Prudhomme, 1866.
477 p. 22cm.

2810   --- ----Supplément...contenant des notices...sur les opéras
...représentés à Paris depuis le 31 décembre 1866 jusqu'au 31
décembre 1871. Grenoble, Impr. de Prudhomme, 1872. 39 p.
22cm.

Bio-bibliographical notes on opera composers, foreign and
French.

2811   CUMMINGS, WILLIAM HAYMAN, 1831-1915.
Dictionary of musicians. [New and rev. ed. 1934] London,
Novello; New York, H. W. Gray [1934] 88 p. 22cm. (Novello's music primers and educational series [40]) First
published 1892 under title: Biographical dictionary of musicians.

2812   DAMAŃSKI, JOSEF.
Die Militär-Kapellmeister Österreich-Ungarns. Illu-
striertes biographisches Lexikon. (Schematismus) Leipzig,
Paltur [1904] viii, 144 p. 84 ports. , 22 group ports.
Conductors of military bands in Austria-Hungary.

2813   DASSORI, CARLO.
Opere e operisti (dizionario lirico 1541-1902) Elenco nomi-
nativo universale dei maestri compositori di opere teatrali,
col prospetto cronologico dei loro principali lavori e catalogo
alfabetico generale delle opere serie, semiserie, buffe,

comiche e simili rappresentate. . . dall'origine dell'opera in
musica fino ai di nostri, coll'indicazione di data e di luogo
della prima rappresentazione, avuto speciale riguardo al
repertorio italiano. 3628 autori---Opere 15406. Genova,
Tip. editrice R. Istituto sordomuti, 1903. 977 p. 21cm.
Dictionary of opera composers & operas.

2814 DAVALILLO, MARÍA
Músicos célebres; 90 biografías cortas. Dibujos de J.
Vinyals y E. C. Ricart. [Nueva ed. ampliada a 112 biografías]
Barcelona, Editorial Juventud [1954] 216 p. illus. 22cm.
First ed. published in 1949. 90 short biographies of celebrated
musicians.

2815 DAVIDSON, GLADYS
A treasury of opera biography. New York, Citadel Press
[1955] 352 p. illus. 22cm. English ed. (London, W.
Laurie) has title: Opera biographies.

2816 DE BEKKER, LEANDER JAN, 1872-1931.
The encyclopedia of music and musicians, by Winthrop
Parkhurst and L. J. De Bekker. New York, Crown Publishers [1937] viii, 662 p. illus. 24cm. Previous editions, by
De Bekker, were issued under titles: De Bekker's Music and
musicians (New York, London, 1925); Black's dictionary of
music & musicians (London, 1924); and Stokes' encyclopedia of
music and musicians (1908) An edition of 670 p. was issued
in 1943 (Yonkers, N.Y. , World Pub. Co.)

2817 [DERTHICK, WILBUR M   ]
A manual of music; its history, biography, and literature.
A complete history of music illustrated with chronological
charts. . . A dictionary of technical and proper names with
definitions and simplified pronunciations. Rev. and improved
ed. Chicago, Musical Manual Pub. Co. [c1890] 628 p.

2818 DICCIONARIO DE LA MÚSICA ILUSTRADO.
Director-editor: A. Albert Torrellas. Director técnico:
Jaime Pahissa. Terminología, historia, biografía, bibliografía, organografía, coreografía, iconografía, retratos, autó-
grafos. Barcelona, Central Catalana de Publicaciones [1927-
29] 2 v. illus. , ports. 25cm. An illustrated music dictionary with biography.

2819 DICCIONARIO ENCICLOPÉDICO DE LA MÚSICA.
[Dirección general: A. Albert Torrellas] Barcelona,
Central Catalana de Publicaciones [1947]-52. 4 v. illus. ,
ports. 25cm. Partial contents. --[t.] 2-3. Biografías, bibliografía, monografías, historia, argumentos de operas. Encyclopedic dictionary of music; biographies are included in
vols. 2-3.

2820   A DICTIONARY OF MODERN MUSIC AND MUSICIANS.
London, J. M. Dent; New York, E. P. Dutton, 1924.   xvi,
543 p. illus. 25cm.   General editor: A. Eaglefield-Hull.

2821   DICTIONARY OF ORGANS AND ORGANISTS.
2d ed.   London, G. A. Mate, 1921.   476 p.   8.°   Sometimes attributed to J. H. Burn?   2d ed. of a work previously
edited by Frederick W. Thornsby.   British organists.

2822   DICTIONNAIRE BIOGRAPHIQUE DES MUSICIENS
et un vocabulaire de termes musicaux.   Lachine, 1922.
302 p. ports.   8.°   Biographical dictionary of musicians
and a vocabulary of musical terms.

2823   DICTIONNAIRE PRATIQUE DES COMPOSITEURS ET DES
OEUVRES MUSICALES.   1. -   année.   Paris, Société
francais de diffusion musicale et artistique.   v. 27cm.   At
head of title: Les éditions du journal musical francais.   Editor: 1955-   J. Longchampt.   A music bio-bibliography.

2824   DIZIONARIO RICORDI DELLA MUSICA E DEI MUSICISTI.
[Direttore: Claudio Sartori; redattori: Fausto Broussard,
et al.   Milano] Ricordi [1959]   xii, 1155 p.   geneal. tables.
25cm.   A dictionary of music and musicians.

2825   DOLZHANSKIĬ, A
Kratkiĭ muzykal'nyĭ slovar.́   Izd. 2., peresm. i dop.
Leningrad, Gos. muzykal'noe izd-vo, 1955.   511 p.   illus.
15cm.   A music dictionary; includes biographies.

2826   DUNCAN, EDMONDSTOUNE, 1866-1920.
Reeves' dictionary of musicians.   Biographical accounts
of about 2,500 noteworthy musicians of the past and present,
British and foreign.   Edited and partly re-written by E.
Duncan.   With later additions.   New ed.   London, W. Reeves,
1926.   253 p.   8.°

2827   DUNSTAN, RALPH, 1857-
A cyclopaedic dictionary of music...   4th ed., greatly enl.
and rev.   London, J. Curwen; Philadelphia, Curwen, inc.
[1925]   ix, 632 p.   illus. 22cm.

2828   EBEL, OTTO.
Handbook of music and musicians.   Containing over 3000
musical terms, and biographical notices of more then 1500
prominent composers.   Concisely arr. by Ch. Herman [pseud.
8th ed.] Brooklyn, Chandler-Ebel Music Co. [c1911] xxiii,
246 p. 18 cm.   First published 1893.

2829   EBEL, OTTO.
Women composers; a biographical handbook of woman's
work in music. Brooklyn, F. H. Chandler [1902] viii, 151 p.
16 cm.   French ed. (Paris, 1910) issued under title: Les
femmes compositeurs de musique (xx, 192 p.)?

2830 EGGELING, GEORG.
Tonkünstler-Lexikon. Quedlinburg, Vieweg, 1899. 312 p.
8.° A dictionary of musicians.

2831 EITNER, ROBERT, 1832-1905.
Biographisch-bibliographisches Quellen-Lexikon der Musiker
und Musikgelehrten christlicher Zeitrechnung bis Mitte des
neunzehnten Jahrhunderts. 2. verb. Aufl. Graz, Akademische
Druck- u. Verlagsanstalt, 1959. 11 v. in 6. 26 cm. First
published 1900-04. Dictionary of musicians and music scholars of the Christian era, to the middle of the 19th century.

2832 ELSON, LOUIS CHARLES, 1848-1920.
Elson's pocket music dictionary; the important terms used
in music with pronunciation and concise definition, together
with the elements of notation and a biographical list of over
five hundred noted names in music. Boston, O. Ditson, c1909.
xii, 179 p. music. 16 x 9 cm.

2833 ENCICLOPEDIA DELLA MUSICA.
[Direttore: Claudio Sartori. Redazione: Argia Bertini,
et al. Milano] Ricordi [1963-64] 4 v. illus., music. 30cm.
An Italian encyclopedia of music; includes biographies.

2834 THE ENCYCLOPEDIA OF JAZZ.
1955-   New York, Horizon Press.   v. illus.,
ports. 27cm. 1960 ed. latest? Compiler: 1955-   L.
Feather.

2835 ----[Yearbook] 1956-   New York, Horizon Press.   v.
illus., ports. 27cm.

Each vol. has a distinctive title: 1956, The Encyclopedia
yearbook of jazz --1958. The New yearbook of jazz.
Compiler: 1956-   L. Feather.

2836 ENCYCLOPÉDIE DE LA MUSIQUE.
[Publié sous la direction de Francois Michel en collaboration avec Francois Lesure et Vladimir Féderov et un comité
de redaction composé de Nadia Boulanger [et al.] Paris,
Fasquelle, 1958-61. 3 v. illus. 26cm. A French encyclopedia of music; includes biographies.

2837 ENCYCLOPEDIE VAN DE MUZIEK.
Hoofdredactie: L. M. G. Arntzenius [et al.] Met
bijzondere medwerking van J. Kunst [et al.] Amsterdam,
Elsevier, 1956-57. 2 v. illus. 26cm. A Dutch encyclopedia
of music; includes biographies.

2838 ESCUDIER, LÉON, d. 1881.
Dictionnaire de musique d'après les théoriciens, historiens
et critiques les plus célèbres qui ont écrit sur la musique.
Par MM. Escudier frères. 5. éd., rev., corr., considérablement augm. Paris, E. Dentu, 1872. 4, xxii, 508 p.

19 cm. Two earlier editions (1st, 1854; nouv. éd. , 1858)
issued in 2 v. A music dictionary, with biographies.

2839   EWEN, DAVID, 1907-
        American composers today, a biographical and critical
        guide. New York, H. W. Wilson, 1949. 265 p. ports. 26 cm.
        Includes biographies of major Latin American composers and
        of European composers domiciled in the Western Hemisphere.

2840   EWEN, DAVID, 1907-
        The complete book of classical music. Englewood Cliffs,
        N. J. , Prentice-Hall [1965] xx, 946 p. 26 cm.

2841   EWEN, DAVID, 1907-
        Composers of today; a comprehensive biographical and
        critical guide to modern composers of all nations. 2d ed. New
        York, H. W. Wilson, 1936. xii, 332 p. ports. 26 cm.

2842   EWEN, DAVID, 1907-
        Composers of yesterday; a biographical and critical guide
        to the most important composers of the past. New York, H. W.
        Wilson, 1937. viii, 488 p. ports. 26 cm.

2843   EWEN, DAVID, 1907-
        Encyclopedia of concert music. New York, Hill and Wang
        [1959] ix, 566 p. 22 cm. Includes over 300 biographies.

2844   EWEN, DAVID, 1907-
        Encyclopedia of the opera. New York, A. A. Wyn [1955]
        x, 594 p. 22 cm. Includes more than 1,000 biographies of
        composers, librettists, singers, critics, etc.

2845   EWEN, DAVID, 1907-
        European composers today, a biographical and critical
        guide. New York, H. W. Wilson, 1954. 200 p. ports. 26 cm.
        A companion volume to American composers today. Together,
        these 2 vols. replace Composers of today. . . 1934.

2846   EWEN, DAVID, 1907-
        The lighter classics in music; a comprehensive guide to
        musical masterworks in a lighter vein by 187 composers.
        New York, Arco Pub. Co. [1961] 370 p. 24 cm. Includes
        biographical sketches of the composers.

2847   EWEN, DAVID, 1907-
        Living musicians. New York, H. W. Wilson, 1940. 390 p.
        illus. 26 cm. 500 musicians, with particular emphasis on
        Americans.

2848   ----Supplement. 1st-   New York, H. W. Wilson, 1957-
        v. ports. 26 cm. 150 more musicians in 1st supplement.

2849   EWEN, DAVID, 1907-
        Men of popular music. Chicago, Ziff-Davis Pub. Co.
        [c1944] 4 p.l. , 213 p. illus. 21cm.

2850 EWEN, DAVID, 1907-
The new book of modern composers. 3d ed., rev. and enl.
New York, Knopf, 1961. 491 p. 25 cm. The first two editions
were published under title: The book of modern composers.

2851 EWEN, DAVID, 1907-
Popular American Composers from Revolutionary times to
the present; a biographical and critical guide. New York, H.
W. Wilson, 1962. 217 p. ports. 26 cm.

2852 FALLOUARD, P   J   M
Les musiciens normands. Esquisse biographique comprenant
les noms des artistes musiciens les plus célèbres nés en
Normandie du XIe au XIXe siècle. Honfleur, Impr. de C. de
Baudre, 1857. 127 p. 12.° French musicians from Normandy.

2853 FAVILLI, ENRICO.
Il piccolo Fétis; dizionario biografico dei musicisti e dei
principali fabbricanti di strumenti, dalla musica ai tempi
moderni. 2. ed. Piacenza, Tarantola, 1925. 526 p. 16.°
A dictionary of musicians and makers of musical instruments.

2854 FELL, FREDERICK VICTOR, 1910-   ed.
Who's who in rock'n roll; facts, fotos and fan gossip about
the performers in the world of rock 'n roll. Edited by Vic
Fredericks [pseud.] New York, F. Fell [1958] 96 p. ports.
23 cm. (A Fellco book, 102)

2855 FÉTIS, ÉDOUARD LOUIS FRANCOIS, 1812-1909.
Les musiciens belges. Bruxelles, Jamar [1849] 2 v. illus.
19 cm. (Bibliothèque nationale. Série artistique, 5-6)
Belgian musicians.

2856 FÉTIS, FRANCOIS JOSEPH, 1784-1871.
Biographie universelle des musiciens et bibliographie
générale de la musique. 2. éd. entièrement refondue et
augm. de plus de moitié. Paris, Firmin-Didot, 1875-83.
8 v. 25 cm.

2857 ----Supplément et complément, publiés sous la direction
de Arthur Pougin. Paris, Firmin-Didot, 1878-80. 2 v.
25 cm.

Musical bio-bibliography.

2858 FEY, HERMANN, 1886-
Schleswig-holsteinische Musiker, von den ältesten Zeiten
bis zur Gegenwart; ein Heimatbuch. Hamburg, C. Holler
[1922] xi, 126 p. 22 cm. Musicians of Schleswig-Holstein,
past and present.

2859 FIEDLER, FRANZ.
Handlexikon für Zitherspieler. Biographische Notizen über
hervorragender Musiker, Fabrikanten und Verleger auf dem

Gebiete der Zither. Tölz, Fiedler [ca. 1895] iv, 100 p.
Biographies of zither players and zither makers.

2860 [FISSORE, ROBERT] 1867-
Traité de lutherie ancienne. Les maitres luthiers; nouvelle
Cote des violons, par Robert Fissore. 4. éd. Paris, R.
Dupuich [1900-03?] xix, 147 p. 8.° 1st edition issued in 1894.
Master violin makers.

2861 [FLAMANT, ALEXANDER] 1836-1897.
The realm of tones. Three hundred and two portraits of
the most celebrated European musicians with short biographical
notices. Translated from the German by H. S. F. M. With an
appendix, containing the portraits and biographies of the
principal American musicians. Edited by Frédéric Louis
Ritter. New York, E. Schuberth, c1882. 35 p. ports. 34 x
27 cm. Translation of Das Reich der Töne. Another edition
under title: Celebrated musicians of all nations, published by
E. Schuberth, New York, in 1883?

2862 FLEURY, PAUL DE, comte, 1839-
Dictionnaire biographique des facteurs d'orgues nés ou
ayant travaille en France. Paris, Office général de la
musique, 1926. 197 p. 8.° Biographical dictionary of organ builders born or having worked in France.

2863 FOSS, HUBERT JAMES, 1899-
The concertgoers handbook; [a dictionary of terms and
composers] London, Sylvan Press [1946] 259 p. 22 cm.
A "Pocket book edition" was issued in London, 1951 (6, 310 p.)
A dictionary of musical terms and composers.

2864 GALLI, AMINTORE, 1845-
La musica ed i musicisti dal secolo X sino ai nostri giorni;
ovvero, Biografie cronologiche d'illustri maestri. Milano,
G. Canti, 1871. 111 p. 27 cm. Music and musicians from the
10th century to 1871; or, Chronological biography of famous
masters.

2865 GALLI, AMINTORE, 1845-
Piccolo lessico del musicista; ossia, Dizionario dei termi
tecnici della musica, di biografie di musicisti celebri, della
diverse forme di composizione... Nuova ed. , riv. ed.
ampliata. Milano, G. Ricordi, 1902. 497 p. A music dictionary which includes biographies of famous musicians.

2866 GAMMOND, PETER.
Dictionary of popular music [by] Peter Gammond & Peter
Clayton. New York, Philosophical Library [1961] xi, 274 p.
illus. , ports. 20 cm. London ed. (Phoenix House, 1960)
has title: A guide to popular music.

2867 GARBETT, ARTHUR SELWYN, 1883- comp.
Gallery of distinguished musicians; a collection of portrait-
biographies of the world's foremost composers, singers,

pianists, violinists, organists, and teachers... Philadelphia, T. Presser, 1913. [127] p. ports. 22 cm.

2868 GARDAVSKÝ, ČENĚK
Skladatele dneška. Praha, Panton, 1961. 261 p. illus. 21 cm. (Čtení o hudbě, sv. 15) At head of title: Čeněk Gardavský a kolektiv. Czech composers of the 20th century.

2869 GARRAS, ADOLF
Ruchnoĭ muzykal'nyi slovar', s pribavleniem biografii izvestnykh kompozitorov, artistov i dilletantov, s portretami. Moskva, Tip. A. Semena, 1850. xvi, 180, ii p. illus., ports. A music dictionary with biographies and portraits of musicians .

2870 GEISTLICHER LIEDERBORN;
Oder, 330 Biographien geistlicher Liederdichter, aus dem Porst'schen und Vollhagen'schen Gesangbuch, sowie aus dem Unverfälschten Liedersegen gezogen und chronologisch und geographisch geordnet... Neu-Ruppin, F. W. Bergemann, 1860. 332 p. 12.° 330 biographies of hymn writers.

2871 GERBER, ERNST LUDWIG, 1746-1819.
Historisch-biographisches Lexicon der Tonkünstler, welches Nachrichten von dem Leben und Werken musikalischer Schriftsteller, berühmter Componisten, Sänger... enthält. Leipzig, J.G.I. Breitkopf, 1790-92. 2v. 23cm. Supplemented by the author's Neues historisch-biographisches Lexikon der Tonkünstler (q.v.) Historical-biographical dictionary of musicians.

2872 GERBER, ERNST LUDWIG, 1746-1819.
Neues historisch-biographisches Lexikon der Tonkünstler, welches Nachrichten von dem Leben und den Werken musikalischen Schriftsteller, berühmter Komponisten, Sänger... enthält. Leipzig, A. Kühnel, 1812-14. 4v. illus., ports. 24cm. A supplement to the author's Historisch-biographisches Lexicon der Tonkünstler (q.v.) 1st ed. published 1812-1814 under title: Historisch-biographisches Lexicon der Tonkünstler. A new historical-biographical dictionary of musicians.

2873 GIANELLI, PIETRO
Dizionario della musica sacra e profana, che contiene la spiegazione delle voci e quanto di teoria di reudizione ecc. è spettante alla musica, con alcune notizie di strumenti antichi e moderni; e delle persone che si distinsero in Italia e nei paesi stranieri in quest'arte. 3. ed. corr. ed accresciuta. Venezia, Tip. di G. Picotti, 1830. 7v. A music dictionary, with biographical entries.

2874 GOLLMICK, KARL, 1796-1866.
Handlexicon der Tonkunst. Offenbach a. M., J. André [1857] 2v. in 1. music. 18cm. Vol. 2: Galerie ausgezeichneter Musiker. A music dictionary; includes biography.

2875   LE GRANDE VOCI;
Dizionario critico-biografico dei cantanti, con discografia operistica. Direttore: Rodolfo Celletti. Consulenti per le discografie: Raffaele Vegeto, John B. Richards. Redattore: Luisa Pavolini. Roma, Istituto per la collaborazione culturale [1964] xiv p., 1044 columns. illus., ports. 29cm. (Scenario, 1) Biographical dictionary of singers.

2876   GREEN, STANLEY.
The world of musical comedy; the story of the American musical stage as told through the careers of its foremost composers and lyricists. Foreword by Deems Taylor. New York, Ziff-Davis [1960] xvi, 391 p. illus. 26cm.

2877   GREGOIR, ÉDOUARD GEORGES JACQUES, 1822-1890.
Les artistes-musiciens belges au XVIIIme et XIXme siècle. Bruxelles, Schott, 1885. viii, 486 p. 8.º

2878   --- ----Supplément et complément. Bruxelles, Schott, 1887. 320 p. 8.º

Belgian musicians of the 18th-19th centuries.

2879   GREGOIR, EDOUARD GEORGES JACQUES, 1822-1890.
Biographie des artistes-musiciens néerlandais des XVIIIe et XIXe siècles et des artistes étrangers résidant ou ayant résidé en Néerlande à la même époque. Bruxelles, Schott, 1864. viii, 238 p. 22cm. Bio-bibliography of Dutch musicians of the 18th-19th centuries and foreign artists residing in Holland at that period.

2880   GREGOIR, ÉDOUARD GEORGES JACQUES, 1822-1890.
Galérie biographique des artistes musiciens belges du XVIIIe et du XIXe siècle. Bruxelles, Schott, 1862. 212 p. 8.º Biographical gallery of Belgian musicians of the 18th-19th centuries.

2881   GRIFFITH, FREDERIC, 1867-1917, ed.
Notable Welsh musicians (of today), with portraits, biographies, and a preface on the condition of music in Wales at the present time. 2d ed. London, F. Goodwen, 1896. xvi, 204 p. ports. 23cm.

2882   DAS GROSSE BUCH DER MUSIK;
Mit 20 Beiträgen über Epochen und Gattungen der abendländischen Musik, einem Opern- und Operettenführer mit 280 Inhaltsangaben, 480 Künstlerbiographien, einem kleinen Musiklexikon und 24 Tafeln mit über 100 Abbildungen. [Bearb. von Hanspeter Bennwitz, et al.] Freiburg [i. B.] Herder [1962] 521 p. ports. 23cm. This music encyclopedia includes biographies of 480 musicians.

2883   GROVE, SIR GEORGE, 1820-1900, ed.
Dictionary of music and musicians. 5th ed., edited by Eric

Blom. New York, St. Martin's Press, 1955[cl954] 9 v. illus. 24cm.

2884 --- ----Supplementary volume. Edited by Eric Blom. Associate editor: Denis Stevens. New York, St. Martin's Press, 1961. xxxii, 493 p. illus. 24cm. English ed. by Macmillan (London, 1954)

2885 GURVIN, OLAV, 1893- ed.
Musikkleksikon [av] Gurvin og Anker. [Oslo] Dreyer [cl949] 1350 col. illus., ports. 24cm. A music dictionary, with biography.

2886 HAMMA, FRIDOLIN
Meister deutscher Geigenbaukunst. Stuttgart, Schuler-Verlag, 1948. 70 p. 66 plates, col. port. 30cm. Master German violin-makers.

2887 HÄUSER, JOHANN ERNST, b. 1803.
Musicalisches Lexikon; oder, Erklärung und Verdeutschung der in der Musik vorkommenden Ausdrücke, Benennungen und Fremdwörter, mit Bezeichnung der Aussprache, in alphabetischer Ordnung. Ein unentbehrliches Hand- und Hilfsbuch für Musiklehrer, Organisationen, Cantoren... 2. verb. und sehr verm. Aufl. Meissen, F. W. Goedsche, 1833. 2 v. in 1. music. 20cm. A dictionary of musical terminology that includes biographical data on musicians.

2888 HEMEL, VICTOR VAN
Voorname belgische toonkunstenaars uit de XVIIIe, XIXe en XXe eeuw. Beknopt overzicht van hun leven en hunne werken. Antwerpen, Cupido-Uitgave [1933] 59p. ports. 21cm. Belgian musicians of the 18th, 19th and 20th centuries.

2889 HENLEY, WILLIAM
Universal dictionary of violin and bow makers. [1st ed. Brighton, Sussex, Eng., Amati Pub., ltd., 1959-60] 5 v. 25cm.

2890 HERZFELD, FRIEDRICH, 1897-
Lexikon der Musik. Berlin, Ullstein, 1957. 551p. illus., ports. 25cm. A music dictionary, with biography.

2891 HILLMAN, ADOLF, 1844-
Kammarmusiken och dess mästare intill 1800-talets början, jämte förteckning över kammarmusikkomponister intill nuvarande tid. Stockholm, Wahlström & Widstrand

[1918] 129p. 24cm. Chamber music and its masters until the beginning of the 18th century, together with a list of chamber music composers to the present time.

2892   HISTORICAL RECORDS SURVEY. DISTRICT OF COLUMBIA.
Bio-bibliographical index of musicians in the United States of America since colonial times. 2d ed. Washington, Music Section, Pan American Union, 1956. xxiii, 439p. 28cm. First published in 1941.

2893   HJORTH, ARNE
Danish violins and their makers. [Translated by Johanne Kastor Hansen] Copenhagen, E. Hjorth, 1963. 1 v. (unpaged) plates. 31cm.

2894   HÖIJER, JOHAN LEONARD, 1815-1884.
Musik-lexicon; omfattende dan theoretiska och praktiska tonkunsten, biographier öfver förnamste musikförfattere. Stockholm, 1864. 2 v. in 1 (viii, 560p.)

2895   ----- ----- Supplement—Häfte. Stockholm, 1867. 73, [3]p.

A music dictionary with biographies of the foremost composers.

2896   HÖRNER, OTTO FRIEDRICH, 1746-1781.
Nachrichten von Liederdichtern des Augspurgischen Gesangsbuchs. Nebst einem Liederregister zum Gebrauche der Auswärtigen. 2. , noch so stark verm. Aufl. Schwabach, J. G. Mizler, 1775. 3, 284p. 8.° Facts about hymn writers of the Augsburg hymnary.

2897   HÖWELER, CASPER.
Der Musikführer, Lexikon der Tonkunst; Handbuch für alle Freunde von Konzert, Oper und Rundfunk. München, P. List [1952] 1143 columns. 21 plates, music. 22cm. Translation of the 11th edition of X-Y-Z der muziek. A French translation has also been issued under title: Sommets de la musique (Gand, 1949 and 1951, the latter 2. éd.) A music dictionary; includes biography.

2898   HÖWELER, CASPER.
X-Y-Z der muziek. [Met medewerking von E. Bruning,

et al.] 14. geheel herziene druk. Utrecht, W. de Haan, 1956. 740 columns. illus., ports. 24cm. A Spanish ed. was issued in 1958 (Barcelona, E. Noguer) under title: Enciclopedia de la música (?) A music dictionary; includes biography.

2899   HOFFMANN, CARL JULIUS ADOLF HUGO, b. 1801.
Die Tonkünstler Schlesiens. Ein Beitrag zur Kunst-
geschichte Schlesiens, vom Jahre 960 bis 1830. Enthaltend
biographische Notizen uber schlesische Komponisten, musikalische Schriftsteller und Pädagogen, Virtuosen, Sänger,
Kantoren, Kammermusiker, Instrumentenmacher, so wie
über Beförderer und Liebhaber der Tonkunst. Breslau, In
Kommission bei G. P. Aderholz, 1830. xii, 491p. 20cm.
The musicians and music lovers of Silesia.

2900   HOWARD, JOHN TASKER, 1890-
Our contemporary composers; American music in the
twentieth century [by] John Tasker Howard with the assistance
of Arthur Mendel. New York, T. Y. Crowell, 1941. xv,
447 p. ports. 23cm.

2901   HUBBARD, WILLIAM LINES, 1867 -   ed.
The American history and encyclopedia of music. Toledo,
New York, I. Squire [1908-10] 12v. illus., ports. 25cm.
Vols. 5-6: Musical biographies, by Janet M. Green.

2902   HUGHES, GERVASE.
The Pan book of great composers. London, Pan Books
[1964] 223p. 18cm. (Pan piper [books] XP64)

2903   HUGHES, RUPERT, 1872-1956, ed.
Music lovers' encyclopedia, containing a pronouncing
and defining dictionary of terms, instruments, etc.,
including a key to the pronunciation of sixteen languages,
many charts; an explanation of the construction of music for
the uninitiated; a pronouncing biographical dictionary; the
stories of the operas; and numerous biographical and critical
essays by distinguished authorities. Completely rev. and
newly edited by Deems Taylor and Russell Kerr. Garden
City, N. Y., Garden City Books [c1954] xxv, 897p. illus.
22cm. First published under title: The musical guide.

2904   IL´INSKIĬ, ALEKSANDR ALEKSANDROVICH, 1859-1919, ed.
Biografii kompozitorov s IV-XX viek. Inostrannyĭ i

russkiĭ otdel pod red. A. Il´inskago. Pol´skii otdel pod red.
G. Pakhul´skago. Moskva, K. A. Durnovo, 1904. 2v.
(927p.) ports. 4°. Biographies of composers, 4th-20th
centuries.

2905   ILLING, ROBERT, 1917-
        Pergamon dictionary of musicians and music. Oxford,
Pergamon Press; New York, Macmillan [1963 -   v. 20cm.
(Commonwealth and International library of science,
technology, English and liberal studies. Music division, v. 2
Previously published under title: A dictionary of music
(Penguin Books, 1950 — 318p.)

2906   ILLIUSTRIROVANNYĬ SLOVAR´ SOVREMENNYKH RUSSKIKH
    MUZYKAL'NYKH DEĬATELEĬ.
        Vyp. 1-2. Odessa, "Muzykal'noe samoobrazovanie, "
1907-08. 2v. No more published. Illustrated dictionary of
contemporary Russian musicians.

2907   ILLUSTRIERTER TONKÜNSTLER-KALENDER.
        Biographische Notizen aus allen Zweigen musikalischen
Schaffens, mit 730 Porträts, hrsg. von Josef Seiling sen.
Die wichtigsten Daten aus dem Leben und Wirken aller be-
deutenden Komponisten, Dirigenten, Instrumentalkünstler,
Sänger... usw. der Gegenwart und Vergangenheit, von
urbezw. Erstaufführungen von Opern... Beigefügt: Aphoris-
men und Aussprüche berühmter Männer über Musik.
Leutkirch, J. Bernklau [1909-   ] v.   ports. 24cm.
Illustrated calendar of musicians for 1910-1912; no more
published?

2908   INCORPORATED SOCIETY OF MUSICIANS.
        Handbook and register of members. 1898-   London.
v.   Title varies. "Useful for tracing professional teachers
and musicians. " There is also a classified list of solo
performers — Walford.

2909   THE INTERNATIONAL WHO IS WHO IN MUSIC.
        [1st]-   ed. ; 1927-   Chicago. v. illus. , ports.
29-32cm. Title varies: 1927-41, Who is who in music (varies
slightly) Cover title, 1951: Who is who in music. Editors:
1927, A. V. Frankenstein. —1929, S. Spaeth.—   1951-
J. T. H. Mize.

2910   INTERNATIONAL WHO'S WHO IN MUSIC AND MUSICAL
    GAZETTEER.
        A contemporary biographical dictionary and a record of

the world's musical activity. 1st-   ed.; 1918-
New York, Current Literature Pub. Co. v. 21cm.

2911   JACQUOT, ALBERT, 1853-
Essai de répertoire des artistes lorrains; les facteurs
d'orgues et de clavecins lorrains. Paris, Plon. Nourrit, 1910.
16p. plates. 26cm. List of artists of Lorraine: makers of
organs and pianos.

2912   JACQUOT, ALBERT, 1853-
Essai de répertoire des artistes lorrains: les musiciens,
chanteurs, compositeurs, etc. Paris, Fischbacher, 1904.
69p. ports. 26cm. List of artists of Lorraine; musicians,
singers, composers.

2913   JANSA, FRIEDRICH.
Deutsche Tonkünstler und Musiker in Wort und Bild. 2.
Ausg. Leipzig, 1911. iii, 835p. illus. German musicians
in words and pictures.

2914   JAZZENS HVEM-HVAD-HVOR.
[Redaktører: John Jørgensen og Erik Wiedemann]
København, Politikens forlag, 1962. 391p. ports. 17cm.
Cover title: Musikkens hvem-hvad-hvor jazz. First
published in 1953. Jazz's who, what, where.

2915   JONES, F   O
A handbook of American music and musicians, containing
biographies of American musicians, and histories of the
principal musical institutions, firms and societies.
Canaseraga, N. Y., 1886. 182p. 23cm.

2916   JONES, M   O
Bywgraffiaeth cerddorion Cymreig. Cardiff, 1890. x,
160p. Transactions of the National Eisteddfod, London, 1887,
pt. 2. Biographies of Welsh musicians (and singers & minstrels)

2917   JORDALEN, MARION, 1912-
The who, what and where music series, by Marion
Jordalen [and] Alice J. Eppink. San Francisco, Library
Music Services, 1954-   v. 22cm. Contents. --book 1.
Musicians.

2918   JULIAN, JOHN, 1839-1913.
A Dictionary of hymnology, setting forth the origin and
history of Christian hymns of all ages and nations. Rev. ed.,

with new supplement. London, J. Murray, 1907. xviii,
1768p. 25cm. Reprinted 1915 and 1925, and most recently
in 1957 by Dover Publications, New York (2v.) Includes
biographies of hymn-writers.

2919   KARILA, TAUNO, ed.
      Composers of Finland. [Porvoo?] Suomen Säveltäjät
[1961] 101p. illus. 20cm.

2920   KASTNER, EMERICH, 1847-1916.
      Neuestes und vollständiges Tonkünstler- und Opern-Lexi-
kon, enthaltend ein Verzeichnis aller in der Musikgeschichte
bekannt gewordenen Namen... mit... Aufzählungen aller
grösseren Werke... Namhaftmachung der gesamten
musikalischen Litteratur, nebst biographischen Nachweisen.
1. Bdchn.: Aagesen-Azzoni. Berlin, Brachvogel & Ranft,
1889. vi, 64p. 18cm. No more published. Latest and most
complete dictionary of musicians and opera.

2921   KELLER, GERARD, 1861-   ed.
      Geïllustreerd muzieklexicon, onder redactie van G. Keller
en Philip Kruseman, met medewerking van Sem Dresden
[et al.] 's-Gravenhage, J. P. Kruseman, 1932. 966p.
illus. 25cm. Illustrated music dictionary; includes
biographies.

2922   KISTLER, CYRILL, 1848-1907.
      Volksschullehrer-Tonkünstler-Lexikon. Aufzählung aller
jener Musiker von Bedeutung, welche aus dem Lehrerstande
hervorgegangen sind oder demselben noch angehören. 3.
vollständig umgearb. Aufl. Kissingen, Verlag der Musikalischen Tagesfragen [ca. 1890] 1 v. A dictionary of
musicians for German public schools and teachers.

2923   KLUGE, GOTTLOB, 1715-1771.
      Hymnopoeographia Silesiaca; oder, Historische Leben-
sbeschreibung dererjenigen schlesischen Liederdichter, deren
Leben noch nie, oder doch sehr kurz beschrieben worden.
Breslau, J. J. Korn, 1751-55. 3 pts. in 1 v. 18cm. Silesian
hymn-writers.

2924   KNIPPERS, OTTIS J   1913-
      Who's who among southern singers and composers. Hot
Springs National Park, Ark., Knippers Bros. [1937] 168 p.
ports. 20cm. Singers and composers of the American
South.

2925 KOCH, WILLI AUGUST, 1903-
Musisches Lexikon; Künstler, Kunstwerke und Motive aus
Dichtung, Musik und bildender Kunst. 2., veränderte und
erweiterte Aufl. Stuttgart, A. Kröner [1964] 1250, xxx p.
illus. 24cm. List of musicians, literary works which have
served as musical themes, and figures in art and literature,
fictional and real, who have had some connection with music.

2926 KOMPOZITORY MOLDAVSKOĬ SSR;
Kratkie ocherki zhizni i tvorchestva. [Redaktor Z. L.
Stoliâr] Kishinev, Gos. izd-vo Moldavii, 1955. 179 p. 17cm.
Sketches of the lives and works of composers of Soviet Molda-
via.

2927 KORNMÜLLER, UTTO, 1824-1907.
Lexikon der kirchlichen Tonkunst. 2., verb. und verm.
Aufl. Regensburg, A. Coppenrath, 1891-95. 2 pts. in 1 v.
port. 20cm. Contents. --T. 1. Sachliches. --T. 2. Biographisches. Dictionary of church music; vol. 2 is biographical.

2928 KOSSMALY, KARL, 1812-1893, ed.
Schlesisches Tonkünstler-Lexikon, enthaltend die Biographieen aller schlesischen Tonkünstler, Componisten, Cantoren,
Organisten, Tongelehrten, Textdichter, Orgelbauer, Instrumentenmacher, & c. & c. Nebst genauer Angabe aller schlesischen musikalischen Institute, Vereine, Musikschulen, Lied-
ertafeln, etc., etc. Hrsg. von Kossmaly und Carlo [pseud.]
Breslau, E. Trewendt, 1846-47. 332 p. 23cm. Issued in
4 parts. Dictionary of Silesian musicians.

2929 KUBLITSKIĬ, M   E
Istoriîa opery v luchshikh ee predstaviteliâkh. Kompozitory, pevîsy, pevîsy. Moskva, Pech. S. P. Îakovleva,
1874. xiv, 210, xiv, 211-268, iv p. 150 biographical
sketches of Russian operatic composers and singers.

2930 KÜMMERLE, SALOMON, 1838-1896.
Encyklopädie der evangelischen Kirchen-Musik. Gütersloh, C. Bertelsmann, 1888-95. 4 v. music. 23cm. Issued in 40 parts, 1883-1895. Includes biographies of church
music composers.

2931 KÜRSCHNERS DEUTSCHER MUSIKER-KALENDER, 1954.
2. Ausg. des Deutschen Musiker-Lexikons. Herausgeber:
Hedwig und E. H. Mueller von Asow. Berlin, W. de Gruyter,
1954. xi p., 1702 columns. 21cm. The 1st ed., Deutsches

Musiker-Lexikon, by Erich Hermann Müller, was published in
1929. Approximately 4500 musicians, primarily German,
Swiss & Austrian.

2932   KURTZGEFASSTES MUSICALISCHES LEXICON,
        Worinnen eine nützliche Anleitung und gründlicher Begriff
von der Music enthalten, die Termini technici erkläret, die
Instrumente erläutert und die vornehmsten Musici beschrieben
sind, nebst einer historischen Beschreibung von der Music
Nahmen, Eintheilung, Ursprung, Erfindung, Vermehrung und
Verbesserung. Alles aus derer besten und berühmtesten
Musicorum ihren Schriften mit Fleiss zusammen gesucht.
Neue Aufl. Chemnitz, J. Christoph und J. D. Stössel, 1749.
431 p. 18cm. First published in 1737. Concise musical
dictionary, wherein... the most eminent musicians are
described...

2933   KUTSCH, K   J
        Unvergängliche Stimmen; kleines Sängerlexikon [von] K. J.
Kutsch [und] Leo Riemens. Bern, Francke [1962]   429 p.
18cm. (Sammlung Dalp, Bd. 92)   A biographical dictionary of
singers.

2934   LACÁL, LUISA.
        Diccionario de la música, técnico, histórico, bio-biblio-
gráfico. Madrid, S. F. de Sales, 1899. vii, 600p. port.
32cm. A music dictionary, bio-bibliographical in part.

2935   LANDSHUTH, LESER, 1817-1887.
        'Amude ha-'avodah... [Berolini, 1857-62] 2 v. 22cm.
Added t. p. : Amude ha-aboda (Columnae cultus) onomasticon
auctorum hymnorum Hebraeorum eorumque carminum, cum
notis biographicis et bibliographicis, e frontibus excusis et
mss. A dictionary of authors of Hebrew hyms, with bio-
bibliographical notes.

2936   LANGWILL, LYNDESAY G
        An index of musical wind-instrument makers. 2d and enl.
ed. (illustrated) [Edinburgh?] Scotland [1962] x, 202 p.
illus. 26cm. First edition published 1960.

2937   LAROUSSE DE LA MUSIQUE;
        Publié sous la direction de Norbert Dufourcq avec la col-
laboration de Félix Raugel et Armand Machabey. Paris,
Larousse [1957] 2 v. illus., ports. 27cm. A music dictionary, with biographies.

2938   LAWLESS, RAY McKINLEY, 1896-
Folksingers and folksongs in America; a handbook of biography, bibliography and discography. Illustrated from paintings by Thomas Hart Benton and others, and from designs in Steuben glass. New rev. ed. with special suppl. New York, Duell, Sloan and Pearce [1965] sviii, 750p. illus., ports. 22cm. First ed. published in 1960.

2939   LAWRENCE, JOHN THOMAS
A dictionary of musical biography. London, Simpkin and Marshall, 1892. viii, 129p. 8.°

2940   LEDEBUR, CARL FRIEDRICH HEINRICH WILHELM PHILIPP JUSTUS, Freiherr von, 1806-1872.
Tonkünstler-Lexikon Berlin's von den ältesten Zeiten bis auf die Gegenwart. Berlin, L. Rauh, 1861. iv, 704, iv p. 23cm. A music dictionary centering on Berlin, its music and musicians. Published in 11 parts.

2941   LEIPOLDT, FRIEDRICH, 1900-
Leipoldt-Musik-Lexikon. Hildesheim, F. M. Hörhold [1951-53] 3 v. illus. 12cm. (Miniatur-Bibliothek, Nr. 343/44) Musical biography included in Vol. 2: Musiker-Biographien (252p.)

2942   LETZER, J   H
Muzikaal Nederland, 1850-1910. Bio-bibliographisch woordenboek van Nederlandsche toonkunstenaars en toonkunstenaressen, alsmede van schrijvers en schrijfsters op muziek-literarisch gebied. 2. uitgaaf met aanvullingen en verbeteringen. Utrecht, J. L. Beijers, 1913. 201, 8p. 24cm. A bio-bibliographical dictionary of Dutch music. First published in 1911.

2943   LICHTENTHAL, PETER, 1780-1853.
Dizionario e bibliografia della musica. Milano, A. Fontana, 1826. 4 v. diagrs. 23cm. A dictionary and bibliography of music (including biography) Vols. 3-4 are a translation of Forkel's 'Allgemeine Litteratur der Music,' with additions. A French translation of v. 1-2 appeared in 1839 under title: Dictionnaire de musique.

2944   LIPOWSKY, FELIX JOSEPH, 1764-1844.
Baierisches Musik-Lexikon. Munchen, J. Giel, 1811. x, 338 (i. e. 438) p. port. 21cm. In double columns. Bavarian music dictionary, with biographical sketches of Bavarian musicians.

2945   LISOVSKIĬ, NIKOLAĬ MIKHAĬLOVICH, 1854-1920.
        Slovar' kompozitorov i muzykal'nykh deiatelei v Rossii.
        S.-Peterburg, 1889. 1 v.(?) Dictionary of composers and
        musicians in Russia.

2946   LLOYD'S CHURCH MUSICIANS' DIRECTORY (1910)
        The blue book of church musicians in America. Compiled
        by Frederic E. J. Lloyd. [vol. 1] Chicago, Ritzmann,
        Brookes [1910] 167 p. 24cm. No more published.

2947   LOWE, CLAUDE EGERTON, 1860-
        A chronological cyclopaedia of musicians and musical
        events from A. D. 320 to 1896... London, Weekes, 1896.
        vi, 126 p. 8.°

2948   LÜTGENDORFF, WILLIBALD LEO, Freiherr von, 1856-
        1937.
        Die Geigen- und Lautenmacher vom Mittelalter bis zur
        Gegenwart. 5. u. 6. Aufl. Frankfurt am Main, Frankfurter
        Verlags-Anstalt, 1922. 2 v. illus. 26cm. 1st published
        1904 (xx, 812 p.) Violin and lute makers from the Middle
        Ages to the present.

2949   MCCARTNEY, Mrs. ELIZABETH MYERS.
        Virginia composers, giving a biographical sketch of each
        composer with a list of compositions, published and unpublished,
        together with other interesting data. [n. p.] Virginia Federa-
        tion of Music Clubs, c1935. 60 p. 23cm.

2950   MAGNETTE, PAUL
        Projet de dictionnaire des musiciens wallons. Liège, Impr.
        H. Vaillant-Carmanne [1914] 64 p. An attempt at a dictionary
        of Walloon (Belgian) musicians.

2951   MANFERRARI, UMBERTO.
        Dizionario universale delle opere melodrammatiche. Fi-
        renze, Sansoni, 1954-55. 3 v. 26cm. (Contributi alla Bibli-
        oteca bibliografica italica, 4, 8, 10) Gives dates & place of
        birth and death of composers of operas.

2952   MANGLER, JOYCE ELLEN.
        Rhode Island music and musicians. Detroit, Information
        Service, 1965. xix, 90 p. 23cm. (Detroit studies in music
        bibliography, 7)

2953   MARIZ, VASCO, 1921-
       Diccionario bio-bibliográfico musical (brasileiro e inter-
       nacional) Pref. de Renato Almeida. Rio de Janeiro, Livra-
       ria Kosmos, 1948. 246 p. 25cm. Bio-bibliographical music
       dictionary (Brazil & other countries)

2954   MARTENS, FREDERICK HERMAN, 1874-1932.
       A dictionary-index of musicians, by Frederick H. Martens,
       Mildred W. Cochran and W. Dermot Darby. Books I-II.
       New York, National Society of Music [c1917] 2 v. illus.,
       ports. 24cm. (The Art of music, edited by Daniel Gregory
       Mason, v. 11-12)

2955   MASTRIGLI, LEOPOLDO, 1856-
       Gli uomini illustri nella musica da Guido d'Arezzo fino ai
       contemporanei, cenni storico-biografici; manuale pratico ad
       uso degl'istituti, delle scuole, dei collegi e delle famiglie.
       Torino, G. B. Paravia, 1883. 364p. 19cm. Illustrious mu-
       sicians from Guido d'Arezzo to present times.

2956   MASUTTO, GIOVANNI, 1830-1894.
       I maestri di musica italiana del secolo XIX; notizie
       biografiche raccolte. 3. ed., corr. ed aumentata. Venezia,
       Stab. tip. di G. Cecchini, 1882. 226p. 27cm. In double col-
       umns. The masters of Italian music in the 19th century.

2957   MATTHESON, JOHANN, 1681-1764.
       Grundlage einer Ehren-Pforte, woran der tüchtigsten
       Capellmeister, Componisten, Musikgelehrten, Tonkünstler
       &c. Leben, Wercke, Verdienste &c. erscheinen sollen.
       Zum fernern Ausbau angegeben von Mattheson. Hamburg,
       1740. In Verlegung des Verfassers. Vollständiger, original-
       getreuer Neudruck mit gelegentlichen bibliographischen
       Hinweisen und Mattheson's Nachträgen, hrsg. von Max
       Schneider. Berlin, Kommissionsverlag von L. Liepmanns-
       sohn, 1910. xliv, 428, [16], 51p. coat of arms. 26 x 20cm.
       A reprint of an early biographical lexicon for music, with ad-
       ditional material by the editor.

2958   MAYER-SERRA, OTTO
       Música y músicos de Latinoamérica. México, Atlante;
       Nueva York, W. M. Jackson, 1947. 2 v. (1134p.) illus. 26cm.
       Music and musicians of Latin America.

2959   MAYR, JOHANN SIMON, 1763-1845.
       Biografie di scrittori e artisti musicali Bergamaschi
       nativi od oriundi, raccolte e pubblicate con note dal Prof. Ab.

Antonio Alessandri. Con aggiunte degli Scrittori musicali Bergamaschi del P. Vaerini. Bergamo, Tip. Pagnoncelli, 1875. viii, 190p. 31cm. Biographies of composers and musical artists native to Bergamo.

2960   MAZZA, JOSE, d. 1797.
     Dicionário biográfico de músicos portugueses, com prefácio e notas do P. e Augusto Alegria. [Lisboa, 1945?] 103p. 25cm. Biographical dictionary of Portuguese musicians.

2961   MELCHIOR, EDUARD A
     Wetenschappelijk en biographisch woordenboek der toonkunst. Schiedam, H. A. M. Roclants, 1890. 7 fascicles. 8.° Scholarly and biographical dictionary of music. Was to be complete in 10 fascicles; no more published?

2962   MENDEL, HERMANN, 1834-1876.
     Musikalisches Conversations-Lexikon. Eine Encyklopädie der gesamten musikalischen Wissenschaften. Für Gebildete aller Stände, unter Mitwirkung der Literarischen Commission des Berliner Tonkünstlervereins. Berlin, L. Heimann; New York, J. Schuberth, 1870-79. 11 v. illus., music. 25cm. Title varies slightly. Imprint varies. Vols. 7-11 continued by August Reissmann.

2963   ---- ----Ergänzungsband. Berlin, R. Oppenheim, 1883. iv, 587p. illus., music. 25cm.

     A music dictionary; biographies are included.

2964   [MERSEBURGER, CARL WILHELM] 1816-1885.
     Kurzgefasstes Tonkünstler-Lexikon für Musiker und Freunde der Musik, begründet von Paul Frank [pseud.] Neu bearb. und ergänzt von Wilhelm Altmann. 14., stark erweiterte Aufl. Regensburg, G. Bosse, 1936. 730p. 26cm. 1st published in 1860 under title: Kleines Tonkünstlerlexikon. Concise dictionary of musicians...

2965   METCALF, FRANK JOHNSON, 1865-
     American writers and compilers of sacred music. New York, Abingdon Press [c1925] 373p. ports. 21cm.

2966   MEYERS HANDBUCH ÜBER DIE MUSIK.
     Mannheim, Hrsg. und bearb. von der Fachredaktion Musik des Bibliographischen Instituts [1961] 1064p. illus., ports. 20cm. A music handbook, with biographies.

2967   MICHAELIS, ADOLF ALFRED, 1854-
Frauen als schaffende Tonkünstler; eine biographisches
Lexikon. Stettin, Priedöhl; Leipzig, Michaelis, 1888.
v, 49p. Women as creative musicians; a biographical dictionary.

2968   MILLER, JOSIAH
Our hymns: their authors and origin, being biographical
sketches of nearly 200 of the principal Psalm and hymn writers, with notes on their Psalms and hymns. A companion to
the new Congregational hymn book. London, Jackson, Walford and Hodder, 1866. xvi, 416p.

2969   MILLER, JOSIAH
Singers and songs of the church; being biographical sketches of the hymn-writers in all the principal collections. 2d
ed. London, Longmans, Green, 1869. xviii, 617p. Second
edition of Miller's Our hymns (q. v.)?

2970   MILLER, PAUL EDWARD, 1903-
Miller's Yearbook of popular music. Chicago, PEM Publications, 1943. viii, 195p. 2d edition of Down beat's year-
book of swing (Chicago, 1939) Includes biographies.

2971   MISCELLANEA MUSICAE BIO-BIBLIOGRAPHICA.
Musikgeschichtliche Quellennachweise als Nachträge und
Verbesserungen zu Eitners Quellenlexikon, in Verbindung
mit der Bibliographischen Kommission der Internationalen
Musikgesellschaft hrsg. von Hermann Springer, Max Schneid-
er und Werner Wolffheim. Jahrg. 1-3; 1912-1916. Leipzig,
Breitkopf & Härtel, 1912-16. 3 v. 25cm. quarterly. A mu-
sical bio-bibliography. Publication interrupted by the War of
1914-1918. No more published? Reprinted in 1947 (New York,
Musurgia) with an appendix added and collation: 435p. (?)

2972   MODERN MUSIC AND MUSICIANS.
Editor-in-chief: Louis C. Elson. New York, University
Society [c1912] 6 v. illus., ports. 30cm.

2973   MOFFATT, JAMES, 1870-
Handbook to the Church hymnary, with Supplement, edited
by James Moffatt and Millar Patrick. London, Oxford University Press, 1935. xi, 601, viii, 133p. music. 20cm.

Includes a large section: Biographical and historical notes on authors, composers, sources, etc. First ed. issued in 1927.

2974   MONTEROSSO, RAFFAELLO
Mostra bibliografica dei musicisti Cremonesi. Catalogo storico-critico degli autori. Cremona, Biblioteca governativa e Libreria civica, 1951. xix, 150p., lxxii p. of music. (Annali della Biblioteca governativa e Libreria civica di Cremona, 2) Bibliographical exhibition of the musicians of Cremona, Italy, with an historical-critical catalog of the authors (composers)

2975   MONTEROSSO, RAFFAELLO
Musicisti cremonesi; catalogo storico-critico-bibliografico degli autori e delle opere. Cremona [Biblioteca governativa e Libreria civica di Cremona] 1951. 280p. Musicians of Cremona; historical-critical-bibliographical catalog of composers and their works.

2976   MOORE, FRANK LEDLIE
Crowell's handbook of world opera. Introd. by Darius Milhaud. New York, Crowell [1961] 683p. maps, music. 24cm. (A Crowell reference book) "The people in opera" (p. 184-307) gives short sketches of the best-known singers, authors, conductors, and other people connected with opera.

2977   MOORE, JOHN WEEKS, 1807-1889.
Complete encyclopaedia of music, elementary, technical, historical, biographical, vocal and instrumental. To which is added an appendix, introducing musical events to 1876. Boston, O. Ditson [etc., 1880] 1004, 45p. 25cm.

2978   MOORE, JOHN WEEKS, 1807-1889.
A dictionary of musical information. Containing also a vocabulary of musical terms, and a list of modern musical works published in the U. S. from 1640 to 1875. Boston, O. Ditson, c1876. 211p. 21cm. Includes biographical sketches of musicians.

2979   MORRIS, WILLIAM MEREDITH.
British violin makers; a biographical dictionary of British makers of stringed instruments and bows and a critical description of their work, with introductory chapters, and numerous portraits and illustrations. 2d ed., rev. and enl. London, R. Scott, 1920. xii, 318p. illus., ports. 22cm. 1st ed. published in 1904.

2980   MOSER, HANS JOACHIM, 1889-
        Musik Lexikon. 4., stark erweiterte Aufl. Hamburg, H.
Sikorski, 1955. 2 v. (viii, 1482p.) music. 22cm. A music
dictionary. Includes biography.

2981   DEUTSCHES MUSIKER-LEXIKON,
        Hrsg. von Erich H. Müller. Dresden, W. Limpert,
1929. [12] p., 1644, viii columns. 29cm. A dictionary of
'living' German musicians.

2982   MUSIC AND DANCE IN CALIFORNIA AND THE WEST.
        [1st-   ed.]; 1933-   Hollywood, Calif., Bureau of
Musical Research. v. ports. 29cm. Title varies: 1st
(1933) ed., Who's who in music and dance in Southern California.

2983   MUSIC & DANCE IN NEW YORK STATE.
        Sigmund Spaeth, editor-in-chief. William J. Perlman,
director and associate editor. Joseph A. Bollew, assistant
editor. 1952 ed. New York, Bureau of Musical Research
[1951] 435 p. ports. 24cm. "Personalities of music and
dance": p. [159]-385.

2984   MUSIC AND DANCE IN PENNSYLVANIA, NEW JERSEY, AND
        DELAWARE. Sigmund Spaeth, editor-in-chief. William
J. Perlman, director & managing editor. Philip Ballotta,
assistant editor. Guy Marriner, chairman, Advisory Editorial Board. New York, Bureau of Musical Research [1954]
339 p. ports. 24cm. Biographical section: p. [169]-305.

2985   MUSIC AND DANCE IN TEXAS, OKLAHOMA AND THE SOUTH-
        WEST. Edited by E. Clyde Whitlock and Richard Drake
Saunders. Hollywood, Calif., Bureau of Musical Research
[1950] 256 p. ports. 24cm. LC enters under Whitlock.

2986   MUSIC AND DANCE IN THE CENTRAL STATES.
        Edited by Richard Drake Saunders. Compiled by William
J. Perlman. Hollywood, Calif., Bureau of Musical Research
[c1952] 173 p.   "Personalities of music and dance": p. 67-
162.

2987   MUSIC AND DANCE IN THE NEW ENGLAND STATES,
        Including Maine, New Hampshire, Vermont, Massachusetts,
Rhode Island, and Connecticut. Sigmund Spaeth, editor-in-
chief. William J. Perlman, director & managing editor.
New York, Bureau of Musical Research [1953] 374 p. ports.
24cm. "Biographical section": p. [157]-309.

2988   MUSIC AND DANCE IN THE SOUTHEASTERN STATES,
Including Florida, Georgia, Maryland, North & South Carolina, Virginia & the District of Columbia. Sigmund Spaeth, editor-in-chief. William J. Perlman, director & managing editor. New York, Bureau of Musical Research [1952] 331 p. ports. 24cm. Biographical section: p. [151]-291.

2989   LES MUSICIENS CÉLÈBRES.
[Genève] L. Mazenod [1946] 357 p. illus., ports. 30cm. [La Galerie des hommes célèbres, 1] Edited by Jean Lacroix and others. Celebrated musicians (composers)

2990   MÚSICOS CÉLEBRES.
No. 1-   ; [1942-   [Buenos Aires, Ricordi Americana] v. ports. 19cm. Celebrated musicians.

2991   MUSIIKIN TIETOKIRJA.
Toimituskunta: Toivo Haapanen [et al.] Helsingissä, Kustannusosakeyhtiö Otava [1948] 573 p. ports., music. 21cm. A reference work on music. Includes biographies.

2992   DIE MUSIK IN GESCHICHTE UND GEGENWART;
Allgemeine Enzyklopädie der Musik. Unter Mitarbeit zahlreicher Musikforscher des In- und Auslandes, hrsg. von Friedrich Blume. Kassel, Bärenreiter, 1949-   v. illus., music. 28cm. Music past and present; a general encyclopedia of music with many biographical articles.

2993   MUSIKKENS HVEM HVAD HVOR;
Biografier. [Redigeret af Ludvig Ernst Bramsen, Jr.] København, Politikens forlag, 1961. 2 v. illus., ports. 17cm. (Politikens musikbibliotek) A who, what, where of music; biographies of musicians. Politikens handbøger, nr. 255. An earlier edition was issued in 1950 (in 3v.) under the editorship of Nelly Backhausen and Axel Kjerulf.

2994   MÚSIOL, ROBERT PAUL JOHANN, 1846-1903.
Musiker-Lexikon. Stuttgart, C. Grüninger, 1890. iv, 544 p. 14cm. A dictionary of musicians.

2995   MUZYKA SOVETSKOĬ ESTONII.
[Redakt͡sionnai͡a kollegii͡a: E. Arro i dr.] Tallin, Estonskoe gos. izd-vo, 1956. 260 p. illus. 21cm. Pages [149]-260 contain portraits and biographical sketches of 65 Estonian musicians and musicologists.

2996   DAS NEUE MUSIKLEXIKON,
Nach dem Dictionary of modern music and musicians, hrsg.

von A. Eaglefield-Hull. Übers. und bearb. von Alfred Einstein.
Berlin, M. Hesse, 1926. xxv, 729 p. music. 24cm. Translation of A Dictionary of modern music and musicians, with
additional biographies of Central European musicians.

2997   NIEMANN, WALTER, 1876-
Klavier-Lexikon; Elementarlehre für Klavierspieler, An-
leitung zur Aussprache des Italienischen, Tabelle der Abkürz-
ungen in Wort und Notenschrift, Literaturverzeichnis, aus-
führliches Fremdwörter-, Sach- und Personal-Lexikon. 4.,
völlig umgearb. und reich verm. Aufl. Leipzig, C. F.
Kahnt, 1918. 365 p. music. 17cm. Dictionary of the piano;
includes a 'Personal-Lexikon' or dictionary of pianists, etc.

2998   NORLIND, TOBIAS, 1879-
Allmänt musiklexikon. 2. omarbetade uppl. Stockholm,
Wahlström & Widstrand [1927-28] 2 v. illus., music. 25cm.
A general music dictionary. Includes biographies.

2999   NORTH CAROLINA FEDERATION OF MUSIC CLUBS.
North Carolina musicians; a selective handbook. Chapel
Hill, University of North Carolina Library, 1956. 82 p. 23cm.
(University of North Carolina Extension publication, v. 21,
no. 4)

3000   NOUVEAU MANUEL COMPLET DU FACTEUR D'ORGUES.
Nouv. éd. ... Suivi d'une biographie des principaux facteurs d'orgues français et étrangers, par Joseph Guédon.
Paris, L. Mulo, 1903. xxx, 517 p. illus. 28cm. and atlas
of 43 (i.e. 37) plates. 33cm. (Encyclopédie Roret) Includes
a biographical section for the principal organ-builders, French
and foreign.

3001   OLSÉN, HELGE
Svenska kyrkomusici; biografisk upplagsbok; utg. av Helge
Olsén under redaktionell medverkan av Otto Olsson. [Ny uppl.]
Stockholm, H. Olsén [1936] 506 p. ports. 25cm. First
edition published in 1928. Swedish church musicians.

3002   ONZE MUSICI,
Portretten en biografieen. 3., geheel hernieuwde druk.
Rotterdam, Nijgh & Van Ditmar [1923] 232 p. ports. 14cm.
Our (Dutch) musicians, portraits and biographies.

3003   ORRU, G
Piccolo dizionario biografico dei musicisti che hanno fatto
parte delle orchestre e bande di Cagliari dall'anno 1830 al 95.
2. ed. Firenze, Stab. tip. lit. di G. Passeri, 1897. 186 p.
Biographical dictionary of musicians of Cagliari, Sardinia,
1830-1895. First edition issued in 1896.

3004   PAHLEN, KURT, 1907-
Musiklexikon der Welt. Zürich, Orell Füssli [1956] 370 p.
illus., ports. 24cm. A world music dictionary. Includes
biographies.

3005   PALMER, RUSSELL, 1913-
British music. London, S. Robinson [1948] 283 p. ports.
22cm. A biographical index of British musicians and musical
organizations.

3006   PAN AMERICAN UNION. MUSIC SECTION.
Compositores de América; datos biográficos y catálogos de
sus obras. Composers of the Americas; biographical data and
catalog of their works. [Washington, 1955-   v. ports.
28cm.

3007   PANASSIÉ, HUGUES.
Guide to jazz, by Hugues Panassié and Madeleine Gautier.
Translated by Desmond Flower; edited by A. A. Gurwitch.
Introd. by Louis Armstrong. Boston, Houghton, Mifflin,
1956. viii, 312 p. illus., ports. 22cm. "First published
in Paris, May 1954, under the title Dictionnaire du jazz [and
translated into English under title Dictionary of jazz in Eng-
land] In its present form the book has been brought up to
date and expanded for American publication. "

3008   PANUM, HORTENSE, 1856-1933.
Illustreret musikleksikon. Nyudgave under redaktion af
Poul Hamburger under medvirken af William Behrend, O. M.
Sandvik [og] Jürgen Balzer. København, Aschehoug, 1940.
735 p. illus. 26cm. At head of title: Panum og Behrend.
1st ed., by H. Panum and W. Behrend, was issued in 16 parts,
1924-1926. An illustrated music dictionary. Includes biography.

3009   PARADA Y BARRETO, JOSÉ, 1834-1886.
Diccionario técnico, histórico y biográfico de la música.
Madrid, B. Eslava, 1868. vi, 408 p. 4.° Technical, his-
torical & biographical dictionary of music.

3010   PAUER, ERNST, 1826-1905.
A dictionary of pianists and composers for the pianoforte,
with an appendix of manufacturers of the instrument. London, New York, Novello, Ewer [1896?] v, 159p. 22cm.
(Novello, Ewer and Co. 's music primers and educational
series)

3011 PAUL, OSKAR, 1836-1898.
Handlexikon der Tonkunst. Leipzig, H. Schmidt, 1873.
2 v. in 1. 20cm. A music dictionary. Includes biographies.

3012 PAZDÍRKŮV HUDEBNÍ SLOVNÍK NAUČNÝ.
[Díl] 1-2, sv. 1: A-K. V Brne, Nakl. O. Pazdirka, 1929-
37. 2 v. music. 24cm. A publisher's (Nakl. O. Pazdírka)
dictionary-encyclopedia of music. Includes biographies. At
head of title: S podporou České akademie věd a umění v Praze.
Edited by Gr. Cernušák and Vlad. Helfert. No more published.

3013 PEARCE, JOSEPH
Violins and violin makers. Biographical dictionary of the
great Italian artists, their followers and imitators to the present time. With essays on important subjects connected with
the violin. London, Longman, 1866. 168p. 17cm.

3014 PEDRELL, FELIPE, 1841-1922.
Diccionario biográfico y bibliográfico de músicos y escritores de música españoles, portugueses é hispano-americanos antiguos y modernos, acopio de datos y documentos
para servir a la historia del arte musical en muestra nación.
[Barcelona, Tip. de V. Berdós y Feliu, 1894-97] xix, 715p.
28cm. Vol. 1 (A-F) only one published? Possibly there exists a small portion of vol. 2 (G-Gaz, 88 p.) according to
Palau y Dulcet. Biographical dictionary & bibliography of
musicians & composers of Spanish, Portuguese & Spanish
American music.

3015 PEÑA, JOAQUÍN, 1873-1944.
Diccionario de la música Labor; iniciado por Joaquín Peña,
continuado por Higinio Anglés, con la colaboración de Miguel
Querol y otros distinguidos musicólogos españoles y extranjeros. Barcelona, Labor, 1954. 2 v. (x, 2318p.) illus.,
ports. 26cm. A music dictionary. Includes biography.

3016 PFEIL, HEINRICH, 1835-1899.
Tonkünstler-Merkbüchlein; kleines Lexikon für Musiker
und Musikfreunde. 2., ergänzte, mit einen bis April 1879
fortgeführten Nekrolog versehene Ausg. Leipzig, Pfeil,
1879. xvi, 138p. Musician-notebook... with a necrology to
1879.

3017 PIERRE KEY'S MUSICAL WHO'S WHO;
A biographical survey of contemporary musicians. 1st-
ed. ; 1931-   New York, P. Key, inc.   v. illus., ports.
24cm.

3018   PRATT, WALDO SELDEN, 1857-1939, ed.
American supplement to Grove's dictionary [of music and musicians]; being the sixth volume of the complete work. Charles N. Boyd, associate editor. New ed., with new material. New York, Macmillan, 1928. vii, 438p. ports. 24cm.

3019   PRATT, WALDO SELDEN, 1857-1939.
New encyclopedia of music and musicians. New and rev. ed. New York, Macmillan, 1929. vi, 969p. illus., ports. 24cm. First edition published 1924.

3020   PRAT MARSAL, DOMINGO, 1886-
Diccionario biográfico, bibliográfico, histórico, crítico de guitarras (instrumentos afines) guitarristas (profesores, compositores, concertistas, lahudistas, amateurs) guitarreros (luthiers) Danzas y cantos— terminología. Buenos Aires, Romero y Fernández, 1934. 468p. 32cm. Cover title: Diccionario de guitarristas. Biographical... dictionary for the guitar and its users.

3021   PRIEBERG, FRED K
Lexikon der neuen Musik. Freiburg [i. B.] K. Alber, 1958. x, 494p. illus., ports. 22cm. A dictionary of modern music. Includes biographies.

3022   PROTESTANT EPISCOPAL CHURCH IN THE U. S. A.
The Hymnal 1940 Companion, by the Joint Commission on the Revision of the Hymnal. 3d, rev. ed. New York, Church Pension Fund [1956] xxviii, 741p. illus. 22cm. Over one third of the volume consists of biographies of authors, composers, translators, and arrangers.

3023   PULVER, JEFFREY, 1884-
A biographical dictionary of old English music. London, K. Paul, Trench, Trübner; New York, Dutton, 1927. xii, 537p. port. 24cm.

3024   QUARRY, W   EDMOND
Dictionary of musical compositions and composers, with a copious bibliography. London, Routledge; New York, Dutton [1920] viii, 192p. 20cm.

3025   RANTA, SULHO, 1901-
Suomen säveltäjiä puolentoista vuosisadan ajalta. [Helsinki] Söderström [1945] 76lp. illus., ports. 4.º Finnish composers of all periods.

3026   RASSMANN, CHRISTIAN FRIEDRICH, 1772-1831.
        Pantheon der Tonkünstler. Oder, Gallerie aller bekan-
        nten, verstorbenen und lebenden Tonsetzer, Virtuosen, Mu-
        sikalischen Schriftsteller etc. des In- und Auslandes. Von
        Friedrich Rassmann. Quedlinburg, G. Basse, 1831. x, 284p.
        18cm. Pantheon of musicians, living and dead, of all coun-
        tries.

3027   RECUPITO, MARCO VINICIO, 1910-
        Artisti e musicisti moderni. Cenni storici-critici e bi-
        bliografici, con speciale riguardo alla scuola ed all'esegesi.
        Milano, Editrice La Fiamma, 1933. 316p. ports. 21cm.
        Modern musicians, chiefly Italians.

3028   REFARDT, EDGAR, 1877-
        Historisch-biographisches Musikerlexikon der Schweiz.
        Leipzig-Zürich, Gebr. Hug, 1928. xv, 355p. 26cm. His-
        torical-biographical music dictionary of Switzerland.

3029   REIS, CLAIRE (RAPHAEL)
        Composers in America; biographical sketches of contem-
        porary composers with a record of their works. Rev. and
        enl. ed. New York, Macmillan, 1947. xvi, 399p. 25cm.

3030   REISS, JÓZEF WŁADYSŁAW, 1879-1956.
        Mala encyklopedia muzyki. Pod red. Stefana Śledziń-
        skiego. Warszawa, Panstwowe Wydawn. Naukowe, 1960.
        922p. illus., ports. 20cm. (Biblioteka problemów) A mu-
        sic encyclopedia; includes biographies.

3031   REISS, JÓZEF WŁADYSLAW, 1879-1956.
        Podreczna encyklopedia muzyki. [Zesz. 1-2. Wyd. 1.]
        Kraków, Wiedza, Zawód, Kultura, 1949-50. 320p. music.
        22cm. (Wiedza w alfabecie) No more published. A 'pocket'
        music encyclopedia; includes biography.

3032   REISSMANN, AUGUST, 1825-1903.
        Handlexikon der Tonkunst. Berlin, R. Oppenheim, 1882.
        iv, 632p. 23cm. A music dictionary; includes biographies.
        Abridgment of the Musikalisches Konversationslexikon begun
        by H. Mendel and completed by Reissmann.

3033   RICART MATAS, J
        Diccionario biográfico de la música. [1. ed.] Barcelona,
        Editorial Iberia [1956] 1022p. ports. 28cm. A biographi-
        cal dictionary of musicians.

3034   RIEMANN, HUGO, 1849-1919.
Riemann Musik Lexikon. Personenteil. 12. völlig neu-
bearb. Aufl. Hrsg. von Wilibald Gurlitt. Mainz, B. Schott's
Söhne; New York, Schott Music Corp., 1959-61. 2 v. 27cm.
First published 1882. A dictionary of musicians.

3035   RIEWE, F
Handwörterbuch der Tonkunst, sachlich und biographisch.
Gütersloh, Bertelsmann, 1879. vi, 413p. 8.° Dictionary of
musical terms and musical biography.

3036   ROCK, CHRISTA MARIA (WIESNER) 1896-   ed.
Judentum und Musik, mit dem ABC jüdischer und nicht-
arischer Musikbeflissener, begründet von H. Brückner und
C. M. Rock. 3. Aufl., bearb. und erweitert von Hans
Brückner. Munchen, H. Brückner-Verlag, 1938. 304p.
20cm. Dictionary of Jewish musicians. 3d ed. of Das
musikalische Juden-ABC?

3037   ROCK, CHRISTA MARIA (WIESNER) 1896-
Das musikalische Juden-ABC, unter Benützung authenti-
scher Unterlagen hrsg. ... mit einer Feuilleton-Einleitung
von Christa Maria Rock. München, H. Brückner [1935] 242p.
A dictionary of Jewish musicians.

3038   RÖDER, ERWIN
Geborene Schlesier. Lexikon, enthaltend kurze Biographien in Schlesien geborener Tonkünstler. Bunzlau, G.
Kreuschner, 1890. iv, 58p. 20cm. Native Silesians; dictionary containing short biographies of Silesian musicians.

3039   ROSENTHAL, HAROLD D
Concise Oxford dictionary of opera, by Harold Rosenthal
and John Warrack. New York, Oxford University Press,
1964. xiv, 446p. 19cm.

3040   ROUGNON, PAUL LOUIS, 1846-1934.
Dictionnaire général de l'art musical; les mots: leur
origine, leurs sens... Suivi d'un dictionnaire biographique
des musiciens chefs d'école, créateurs (décédés) Paris,
Delagrave, 1935. 348p. music. 19cm. (Les Manuels pra-
tiques) A general dictionary of the musical art... Followed
by a biographical dictionary of musicians...

3041 RUBETS, ALEKSANDR IVANOVICH, 1837-1913.
Biograficheskii leksikon russkikh kompozitorov i muzykal' nykh deiatelei. S. -Peterburg, Muzikal' nyi magazin
A.Vitnera, 1886. 97p. 23cm. A biographical dictionary;
225 biographical sketches of Russian composers and musicians. New, enlarged ed. of Rubets' work of the same title
issued in 1879 (58p.)?

3042 [SAINSBURY, JOHN S]
A dictionary of musicians, from the earliest ages to the
present time. Comprising the most important biographical
contents of the works of Gerber, Choron, and Fayolle, Count
Orloff, Dr. Burney, Sir John Hawkins, &c. &c. , together
with upwards of a hundred original memoirs of the most eminent living musicians. 2d ed. London, Printed for Sainsbury
and Co. , 1827. 2 v. music. 20cm. First edition issued
1825. Caption title: A biographical dictionary of musicians.

3043 SALDONI Y REMENDO, BALTASAR, 1807-1890.
Diccionario biográfico-bibliográfico de efemérides de músicos españoles... Madrid, Impr. á cargo de A. Pérez Du-
brull, 1868-81. 4 v. 23cm. 1st ed. published 1860 (in 1 vol.)
under title: Efemérides de músicos españoles. Biographical-
bibliographical dictionary (of ephemerides) of Spanish musicians.

3044 SALESKI, GDAL, 1888-
Famous musicians of Jewish origin. New York, Bloch
Pub. Co. , 1949. xvi, 716p. ports. 27cm. 2d edition of
Saleski's Famous musicians of a wandering race (New York,
1927)

3045 [SALVIOLI, GIOVANNI]
Saggio di rettifiche ed aggiunte al supplemento Fetis,
vol. I-II... riferibilmente a maestri italiani e relative opere,
per Luigi Lianovosani [pseud.] Milano, Ricordi [1878]-82.
2 v. (40; 74p.) Bio-bibliography of music, especially Italian
music.

3046 SAMBAMOORTHY, P
A dictionary of South Indian music and musicians. Madras,
Indian Music Pub. House, 1952- v. 25cm.

3047 SAMBAMOORTHY, P
Great composers. 2d ed. , rev. and enl. Madras, Indian

Music Pub. House [1962-   v. illus. 19cm. Not a biographical dictionary; however, the subject--the composers
of India--is unfamiliar to Westerners; the 1st volume has
basic facts about 20 or more composers, and, hopefully, succeeding volumes will include material on a sufficient number
of musicians to make the set a useful biographical reference
tool.

3048   SANDVED, KJELL BLOCH, ed.
The world of music; an illustrated encyclopedia. [1st
American ed.] New York, Abradale Press [1963] 4 v. (1516
p.) illus. 26cm. American edition of Musikkens verden
(Oslo, 1951, c1950) Has also appeared in Danish, English,
Italian and Swedish editions.

3049   SCHACHT, MATTHIAS HENRIKSEN, 1660-1700.
Musicus Danicus; eller, Danske sangmester. Udg. med en
indledning og anmaerkninger af Godtfred Skjerne. Kphenhavn,
H. Hagerup, 1928. 4, xxxii, 400 p. music. 30cm. Danish
music; or, Danish masters of song. A dictionary.

3050   SCHÄFFER, BOGUSŁAW
Leksykon kompozytorów XX wieku. Współpraca: Mieczy-
sława Hanuszewska, Andrzej Trzaskowski, Zygmunt Wacho-
wicz. [Wyd. 1] Kraków, Polskie Wydawn. Muzyczne, 1963-
v. ports. 22cm. Dictionary of composers of the 20th century.
Contents. --1. A-Ł.

3051   SCHILLING, GUSTAV, 1803-1881, ed.
Encyclopädie der gesammten musikalischen Wissenschaft-
en; oder, Universal-Lexicon der Tonkunst. Bearb. von M.
Fink, De la Motte Fouqué [et al.] und dem Redacteur Gustav
Schilling. Stuttgart, F. H. Köhler, 1835-38. 6 v. plates.
24cm.

3052   ---- ----Supplementband. Stuttgart, F. H. Köhler, 1841
[i. e. 1842?] 445, lxxxviiip. 23cm.

An enclyclopedia of musical knowledge; includes biography.

3053   SCHILLING, GUSTAV, 1803-1881.
Das musikalische Europa; oder, Sammlung von durchgehends
authentischen Lebens-Nachrichten über jetzt in Europa lebende
ausgezeichnete Tonkünstler, Musikgelehrte, Componisten,
Virtuosen, Sänger, & c. & c. In alphabetischer Ordnung hrsg.

... Speyer, F. C. Neidhard, 1842. 365 p. 24cm. Musical Europe. A collection of biographical notes on outstanding musicians now living in Europe (ca. 1842)

3054 SCHILLING, GUSTAV, 1803-1881.
Musikalisches Conversations-Hand-Lexikon, enthaltend die vollständige Erklärung aller musikalischen Realien, wie zugleich die Biographien aller um die Tonkunst nur irgend Verdienter, oder sich darin ausgezeichneter Personen, Componisten, Virtuosen, Sänger, u. s.w. 2. Ausg. Augsburg, Schlosser, 1844. 2 v. A musical pocket-dictionary; containing explanations of all musical terms as well as biographies of all those who have served music. First ed. issued in 1840-42 (Mergentheim, Neue Buchhandlung)

3055 SCHILLING, GUSTAV, 1803-1881.
Universal-Lexikon der Tonkunst. Neue Handausg. in einem Bande. Mit Zugrundlegung des grösseres Werkes neu bearb., ergänzt und theilweise verm. von F. S. Gassner. Stuttgart, F. Köhler, 1849. iii, 918 p. 27cm. A universal dictionary of music; includes biographies.

3056 SCHMIDL, CARLO, 1859-
Dizionario universale dei musicisti. Milano, Sonzogno [1928?-29] 2 v. illus. 29cm. 1st published 1887-1890.

3057 --- ----Supplemento. Appendice aggiunte e rettifiche al primo e secondo volume. Milano, Sonzogno [1938] 806 p.

Universal dictionary of musicians.

3058 SCHOENEWERK, L
Le panthéon des musiciens. Tableau chronologique et nécrologique des plus remarquables compositeurs, théoriciens, professeurs ... qui ont vécu depuis le IVme siècle jusqu'à nos jours ... Nice, 1900. 86 p. 8.º The pantheon of musicians; Chronological and necrological tableau of the most remarkable composers, theoreticians, professors, 5th century to the present.

3059 SCHOLES, PERCY ALFRED, 1877-1958.
The Oxford companion to music, self-indexed and with a pronouncing glossary and over 1,100 portraits and pictures. 9th ed., completely rev. and reset and with many additions to text and illustrations. [Reprinted, with corrections, 1960] London, New York, Oxford University Press [1960, c1955]

lx, 1195 p. illus. 25cm. An abridged version of this work was published under title: The Concise Oxford dictionary of music.

3060   SCHUBERTH, JULIUS FERDINAND GEORG, 1804-1875.
Musikalisches Conversations-Lexicon. Ein encyclopädisches Handbuch enthaltend das Wichtigste aus der Musikwissenschaft, die Biographien aller berühmten Komponisten, Virtuosen, Dilettanten, musikal. Schriftsteller und Instrumentenmacher ... Hrsg. von Emil Breslauer. 11. gänzlich umgearb. und bedeutend verm. Aufl. Leipzig, J. Schuberth, 1890. xv, 650 p. 19cm.

3061   --- ----Ergänzungen und Berichtigungen (fortgeführt bis Ende Oktbr. 1894 von Bernh. Vogel) Leipzig, 1894. 651-666 p.

A musical encyclopedia; includes biographies.

3062   SCHUBERTH, JULIUS FERDINAND GEORG, 1804-1875.
Musikalisches Handbuch; eine Encyklopädie für Tonkünstler und Musikfreunde, enthaltend das Wichtigste aus der Elementar-Musikwissenschaft, die Biographie berühmter Componisten, Virtuosen, etc., und Erklärungen aller in Compositionen vorkommenden Fremdwörter. 5. verb. und stark vermehrte Aufl. Leipzig, J. Schuberth, 1860. 319 p. An English translation of an earlier edition was issued in 1859 under title: A musical handbook for musicians and amateurs (xvi, 289 p.) Includes biographies.

3063   SCHUH, WILLI, 1900-   ed.
Schweizer Musikbuch. Unter Mitarbeit von Edmond Appia [et al.] Zürich, Atlantis-Verlag [1939] 2 v. illus. 23cm. Swiss music-book; biographies of Swiss musicians. Vol. 2, with slightly varying title, edited by Schuh and Edgar Refardt.

3064   SCHULZ, WALTHER, 1887-
Reichssänger; Schlüssel zum deutscher Reichsliederbuch. Gotha, P. Ott, 1930. 246 p. German song-writers. Contents. --Die Liederdichter in Einzelbildern nach alphabetischer Rangordnung. --Melodienschöpfer nach alphabetischer Rangordnung.

3065   SCHWARZ-REIFLINGEN, ERWIN, 1891-
Musik ABC. Universal-Lexikon für Musikfreunde und Rundfunkhörer. Musikalisches Wörterbuch, Tonkünstler-Lexikon, Führer durch Oper, Operette und Konzertmusik, nebst Erklärung rundfunktechn. Ausdrücke. Stuttgart, Union Deutsche

Verlagsgesellschaft, 1949. vii p. , 726 columns. illus. 19cm.
A music dictionary, including a dictionary of musicians.
First issued in 1938 (582 p.)

3066   SCHWEIZERISCHER TONKÜNSTLERVEREIN.
Schweizer Musiker-Lexikon, 1964. Dictionnaire des musiciens suisses, 1964. Im Auftrag des Schweizerischen Tonkünstlervereins bearb. von Willi Schuh [et al.] Zürich, Atlantis Verlag [1964] 421 p. 26cm. Dictionary of Swiss musicians, 1964. In German or French.

3067   SHALITA, ISRAEL.
Entsiklopediyah le-musikah. Tel-Aviv, Joshua Chachik [1950] 724 columns. ports. 23cm. Added t. p. : Encyclopedia of music, a biographical dictionary of Jewish & world musicians. Edited by Hanan Steinitz.

3068   SIEGMEISTER, ELIE, 1909-   ed.
The music lover's handbook. New York, W. Morrow, 1943. xiii, 817 p. illus. 22cm. Includes biographical sketches.

3069   SINZIG, PETRUS, Father, 1876-
Dicionário musical. Rio de Janeiro, Livraria Kosmos, 1947. 613 p. illus. , ports. 23cm. A dictionary of music; includes biographies.

3070   SISTERS OF ST. ANN.
Dictionnaire biographique des musiciens canadiens. Lachine, P. Q. , Mont-Sainte-Anne, 1935. 299 p. illus. , ports. 23cm. At head of title: Soeurs de Saint-Anne. First edition published in 1922. Biographical dictionary of Canadian musicians.

3071   SLONIMSKY, NICOLAS, 1894-
Music since 1900. 3d ed. , rev. and enl. New York, Coleman-Ross, 1949. lxiii, 759 p. 23cm. First edition published 1937. Includes a concise biographical dictionary of 20th century musicians.

3072   SLOWNIK MUZYKÓW POLSKICH.
[Redaktor naczelny: Józef Chomiński. Wyd. 1. Kraków] Polskie Wydawn. Muzyczne [1964-   v. 25cm. At head of title, v. 1-   Instytut Sztuki Polskiej Akademii Nauk. Dictionary of Polish music; includes biographies.

3073 SOHLMANS MUSIKLEXIKON;
Nordiskt och allmänt upplagsverk för tonkonst, musikliv
och dans. Redaktion: Gösta Morin, Carl-Allan Moberg [och]
Einar Sundström. Stockholm, Sohlman [1948-52] 4 v. illus.,
ports. 25cm. A dictionary of music, musical biography and
dancing--Scandinavian & universal.

3074 SOĪUZ SOVETSKIKH KOMPOZITOROV SSSR. LENINGRAD-
SKOE OTDELENIE.
Leningradskie kompozitory; kratkie biografii. Pod red.
M. A. Glukha. Leningrad, Gos. muzykal´noe izd-vo, 1950.
133 p. ports. 20cm. Leningrad's composers; brief biog-
raphies.

3075 SOULLIER, CHARLES SIMON PASCAL, 1797-1878.
Nouveau dictionnaire de musique illustré, élémentaire,
théorique, historique, artistique, professionel et complet.
Paris, E. Bazault, 1855. vii, 348, xvi p. illus. 25cm.
A new dictionary of music; includes biographies.

3076 SOUTHEASTERN COMPOSERS' LEAGUE.
Catalogue. [Hattiesburg, Miss., Tritone Press] v.
28cm. "Contains biographies and lists of compositions."

3077 SOVETSKIE KOMPOZITORY ...
[Leningrad] Leningradskaīa filarmoniīa, 1938- v.
ports. 20cm. Soviet (Russian) composers.

3078 SOWIŃSKI, WOJCIECH, 1805-1880.
Les musiciens polonais et slaves, anciens et modernes;
dictionnaire biographique des compositeurs, chanteurs, in-
strumentistes, luthiers, constructeurs d'orgues, poètes
sacrés et lyriques, littérateurs et amateurs de l'art musical.
Précédé d'un résumé de l'histoire de la musique en Pologne
et da la description d'anciens instruments slaves. Notices
sur la bibliographie musicale polonnaise. Fragments de
compositions des grand-maîtres polonais et détails sur les
pèlerinages célèbres en Pologne. Par Albert Sowinski.
Paris, A. Le Clere, 1857. xi, 599 p. 25cm. Biographical dictionary of Polish & Slavic musicians, early and modern.

3079 SOWIŃSKI, WOJCIECH, 1805-1880.
Słownik muzyków polskich dawnych i nowoczesnych kompozytorów wirtuozów, śpiewaków, instrumencistów, lutnistów,
organmistrzów, poetów lirycznych i miłosników sztuki :

muzycznej. Zawierajacy krótki rys historyi muzyki w Polsce,
opisanie obrazów cudownych i dawnych instrumentów z muzyka
i portretem autora przez... Paryż, Nakł. autora, skład
główny w ksieg. Luxemburgskiej, Druk E. Martinet, 1874.
lx, 436 p. illus. Dictionary of Polish music & musicians.
First issued in 1857 in French under title: Les musiciens
polonais et slaves, anciens et modernes(?)

3080   SPEMANN, WILHELM, 1844-1910.
      Spemanns goldenes Buch der Musik; eine Hauskunde für
jedermann. Durchgesehene und ergänzte neue Aufl. hrsg.
unter Mitwirkung von Hermann Abert [et al.] Stuttgart, W.
Spemann, 1912. 4, 973 p. illus., ports. 18cm. (Spemanns'
Hauskunde, 1) First edition published 1900. A music dictionary; includes biography.

3081   STAINER, CECIE.
      A dictionary of violin makers, compiled from the best
authorities. London, Novello; New York, H. W. Gray Co.
[1901?] 102 p. 22cm. (Novello's music primers and educational series [55]) Reissue of work first published in 1896.

3082   STENGEL, THEOPHIL, 1905-
      Lexikon der Juden in der Musik, mit einem Titelverzeich-
nis jüdischer Werke, zusammengestellt im Auftrag der
Reichsleitung der NSDAP, auf Grund behördlicher, partei-
amtlich geprüfter Unterlagen, bearb. von Theo Stengel in
Verbindung mit Herbert Gerigk. Berlin, B. Hahnefeld
[1943] 404 columns. 21cm. (Veröffentlichungen des Instituts der NSDAP zur Erforschung der Judenfrage, Frankfurt
a. M.) Dictionary of Jews in music; an anti-Semitic compilation sponsored by the Nazi party.

3083   STEUER, MAX
      Musikalisches Conversations-Lexicon; ein Handbuch der
Tonkunst, hrsg. zum Gebrauche für Musiker und Musikfreunde. T. 1: Die Lebensbeschreibungen aller berühmten
Musiker, musikalischen Schriftsteller, Instrumentbauer
etc., nebst Angabe der einschlag. Literatur. Berlin,
Schlesinger'sche Buchhandlung, 1881. iv, 196p. No more
published. A music dictionary. The 1st & only volume contains biographies of famous musicians.

3084   STRAETEN, EDMOND VANDER, 1826-1895.
      La musique aux Pays-Bas avant le XIXe siècle. Docu-
ments inédits et annotés. Compositeurs, virtuoses, théoriciens, luthiers; opéras, motets, airs nationaux, académies,

maîtrises, livres, portraits, etc. Bruxelles, G.-A. van Trigt, 1867-68. 8 v. illus. 23cm. Imprint and subtitle vary. Music in the Low Countries before the 19th century... Composers, virtuosos, theorists [etc.]

3085   SUPPAN, WOLFGANG, 1933-
Steirisches Musiklexikon. Im Auftrage des Steirischen Tonkünstlerbundes unter Benutzung der "Sammlung Wamlek" bearb. und hrsg. Graz, Akademische Druck- und Verlagsanstalt, 1962-   p. illus. 24cm. Issued in fascicles, 1962-   The Styrian music dictionary; includes biographies of musicians (chiefly Austrians—from Styria?)

3086   SVENSSON, SVEN ERIC EMMANUEL, 1899-
Bonniers illustrerade musiklexikon. Under medverkan av Erik Noreen. Stockholm, A. Bonnier [1946] 1379p. illus., ports. 22cm. An illustrated dictionary of music; includes biographies.

3087   SZULC, ZDZISŁAW
Słownik lutników polskich. Poznań, Poznańskie Towarzystwo Przyjaciół Nauk, 1953. 264p. illus. 28cm. (Poznańskie Towarzystwo Przyjaciół Nauk. Wydział Historii i Nauk Społecznych. Prace Komisji Historii Sztuki, t. 3) Dictionary of Polish violin makers.

3088   [TERZO, BENVENUTO]
Dizionario dei chitarristi e liutai italiani. Bologna, "La Chitarra," 1937. 286p. Dictionary of Italian guitarists and lutists.

3089   TESTONI, GIAN CARLO
Enciclopedia del jazz [di] Gian Carlo Testoni, Arrigo Polillo [e] Giuseppe Barazzetta. Con la collaborazione di Roberto Leydi e Pino Maffei. Milano, Messaggerie musicali, 1953. 500p. illus., ports. 25cm. A jazz encyclopedia; includes biographies of jazz musicians.

3090   THOMPSON, OSCAR, 1887-1945.
The international cyclopedia of music and musicians. Editor, 9th ed.: Robert Sabin. New York, Dodd, Mead, 1964. 2476p. music, ports. 29cm.

3091   THORNSBY, FREDERICK W   ed.
Dictionary of organs and organists. Bournemouth [Eng.] H. Logan, 1912. 364p. plates. 22cm.

3092 THUNER, OLE ERLAND, 1886-
Danske salme-leksikon; haandbog i dansk salmesang. En
hymnologisk sammenstilling af ord og toner med historiske
og bibliografiskes oplysninger. København, O. Lohse, 1930.
592p. facsims. 24cm.

3093 ---- ----Supplement. København, O. Lohse, 1934. 1 v. (?)

Dictionary of Danish hymns; includes biographies of Danish Lutheran hymn-writers.

3094 TONKONSTEN;
Internationellt musik-lexikon. [Redaktionskommitté:
Natanael Broman, Johannes Norrby, Folke H. Törnblom]
Stockholm, Nordiska upplagsböcker [1955-57] 2 v. illus.,
ports. 22cm. A music dictionary; includes biographies.

3095 UNIVERSITY MUSICAL ENCYCLOPEDIA,
By many eminent editors, experts and special contributors. Chief editor: Louis C. Elson. [New York] University
Society [c1912-14] 12 v. illus. 21cm. An earlier edition was
published in 1911 in 10 v. Partial contents. -- [v. 3-4] Great
composers. -- [v. 6] Vocal music and musicians. -- [v. 9-10]
University dictionary of music and musicians.

3096 URBINO, LEVINA (BUONCUORE)
Biographical sketches of eminent composers. Arranged
in chronological order. Boston, O. Ditson, 1876. 379p.
18cm.

3097 VALABREGA, CESARE
Il piccolo dizionario musicale per tutti. 2. ed., rifatta
e ampliata. Milano, Curci [1952] 295, 16, 256, 44 p. 16cm.
A music dictionary; includes biographies. First ed. published in 1949 (Roma, Editrice Faro)

3098 VALDRIGHI, LUIGI FRANCESCO, conte, 1827-1899.
Ricerche sulla liuteria e violineria modenese antica e
moderna. [Modena, 1878] 48p. 23cm. Caption title.
"Catalogo generale dei liutari e violinari modenesi dal
secolo 16 al 19": p. 19-43. Violin makers of Modena, Italy.

3099 VANNES, RENÉ
Dictionnaire des musiciens (compositeurs) par René
Vannes avec la collaboration de André Souris. Préf. de

Charles van den Borren. Bruxelles, Larcier [1947] 443p. 17cm. (Petits dictionaires des lettres et des arts en Belgique, 4) Dictionary of [Belgian] musicians (composers)

3100   VANNES, RENÉ
Dictionnaire universel des luthiers. Préf. de Giovanni Iviglia. Avertissement de Ernest Closson. Historique de l'Entente internationale des maitres luthiers et archetiers d'art de Émile Francais. 2. éd., rev. et augm. Bruxelles, Les Amis de la musique, 1951. xxi, 408, [165] p. facsims. 29cm. 1st ed. published in 1932 under title: Essai d'un dictionnaire universel des luthiers. A universal dictionary of violin makers.

3101   VASCONCELLOS, JOAQUIM ANTONIO DA FONSECA E, 1849-1936.
Os musicos portuguezes. Biographia-bibliographia. Porto, Impr. Portugueza, 1870. 2 v. 24cm. The Portuguese musicians.

3102   VERCHEVAL, HENRI
Dizionario del violinista, violista e violoncelliste; seguito da un elenco dei violinisti celebri, dei luitai e dei fabbricanti di archetti più conosciuti dall'origine del violini... Corretto ed aumentato di Nella de Angeli. Bologna, C. Sarti, 1924. 248 p. illus. 20cm. Dictionary of violinists, violists, & 'cellists. First published in 1923 in French under title: Dictionnaire du violiniste.

3103   VIDAL, ANTOINE, 1820-1891.
Les instruments à archet; les feseurs, les joueurs d'instruments, leur histoire sur le continent européen, suivi d'un catalogue général de la musique de chambre. Paris, Impr. de J. Claye, 1876-78. 3 v. 122 plates. 27cm. Lists of violinists and 'cellists: v. 2, p. [173]-374. Biographies of chamber music composers: v. 3, p. [33]-160.

3104   VIEIRA, ERNESTO
Diccionario biographico de musicos portuguezes; historia e bibliographia da musica em Portugal. Lisboa, Typ. Moeira & Pinheiro, 1900. 2 v. ports. 24cm. Biographical dictionary of Portuguese musicians.

3105   VILLAR, ROGELIO, 1875-1937.
Músicos españoles. Madrid, Ediciones Mateu [1918-27]

2 v. 19cm. Spanish musicians. Vol. 2 has imprint: Madrid, Hernando. Contents. -- 1. Compositores y directores de orquesta. -- 2. Compositores, directores, concertistas, críticos.

3106   VILLAROSA, CARLO ANTONIO DE ROSA DI, marchese, 1762-1847.
Memorie dei compositori de musica del Regno di Napoli. Napoli, Stamperia reale, 1840. v, xv, 250p. 24cm. Memories of composers of music in the Kingdom of Naples.

3107   VIOTTA, HENRI ANASTASE, 1848-1933.
Lexicon der toonkunst. Met medewerking van de heeren: Peter Benoit, Frans Coenen... enz., enz. Amsterdam, P. N. van Kampen [etc.] 1881-85. 3 v. 25cm. A music dictionary; includes biography.

3108   VODARSKY-SHIRAEFF, ALEXANDRIA, comp.
Russian composers and musicians; a biographical dictionary. New York, H. W. Wilson Co., 1940. 158p. 24cm.

3109   VOLLHARDT, REINHARD, 1858-
Geschichte der Cantoren und Organisten von den Städten im Königreich Sachsen. Berlin, W. Issleib, 1899. xii, 411 p. 25cm. History of the choir masters and organists of the cities in the Kingdom of Saxony.

3110   WARRINER, JOHN, 1858-
National portrait gallery of British musicians. With an introd. by Joseph Bennett. London, S. Low, Marston [1896] x, 75 p., 521 ports. on 35 plates. 26 x 36cm.

3111   WEST, JOHN EBENEZER, 1863-
Cathedral organists past and present. A record of the succession of organists of the cathedrals, chapels royal, and principal collegiate churches of the United Kingdom, from about the period of the Reformation until the present day. With biographical notes, extracts from the chapter books, anecdotes, &c. London, Novello; New York, Novello, Ewer, 1899. xi, 141 p. 23cm.

3112   WESTRUP, JACK ALLAN, 1904-
The new college encyclopedia of music [by] J.A. Westrup [and] F. Ll. Harrison. New York, Norton [1960] xvii, 739 p.

music. 22cm. Published in 1959 (London, Collins) under title: Collins music encyclopedia. Includes biographies.

3113   WETZEL, JOHANN CASPAR, 1691-1755.
        Hymnopoeographia; oder Historische Lebens-Beschreibung der berühmtesten Liederdichter. Herrnstadt, S. Roth-Scholt-zen, 1719-28. 4 v. port. 18cm. The most famous hymn-writers [of Germany] Vols. 2-4 have title: Historische Lebens-Beschreibung der berühmtesten Lieder-Dichter.

3114   WHARTON-WELLS, HARRY
        A handbook of music and musicians. With a supplement of present-day musicians by H. M. Willsher. London, New York, T. Nelson [1930] 328 p. illus. 18cm. First edition published in 1912.

3115   WHELBOURN, HUBERT
        Standard book of celebrated musicians, past and present. De luxe ed. Garden City, N. Y., Garden City Pub. Co. [1937] xiii, 305 p. ports. 24cm. "Revised and enlarged edition" [of Whelbourn's Celebrated musicians, London, 1930] A Spanish edition was issued in Buenos Aires in 1942 under title: Diccionario de músicos célebres del pasado y del presente, and included an appendix compiled by the editors of the Argentine edition.

3116   WHO IS WHO IN MUSIC.
        1941-   ed. A complete presentation of the contemporary musical scene, with a master record catalogue. Chicago, New York, Lee Stern Press.   v. illus., ports. 32cm.

3117   WHO'S WHO IN MUSIC.
        1913-   London, Shaw Pub. Co.   v. 22cm. Suspended publication during the Second World War; resumed 1950.

3118   WHO'S WHO IN MUSIC AND DRAMA,
        Edited by Dixie Hines and Harry Prescott Hanaford; an encyclopedia of biography of notable men and women in music and the drama. 1914. New York, H. P. Hanaford [1914] 560p. ports. 21cm. Advertising matter interspersed. No more published?

3119   WHO'S WHO IN MUSIC AND DRAMATIC ART IN THE TWIN CITIES, MINNEAPOLIS AND SAINT PAUL.
        Compiled by Arthur E. Wascher and Thomas Clayton Ingham. Minneapolis, A. E. Wascher, 1925. 224p. illus.

3120   WHO'S WHO IN MUSIC AND MUSICIANS INTERNATIONAL
        DIRECTORY.
        1935-   New York, Hafner Pub. Co.   v. 26cm.   Ed-
        itor: 19   D. Simmons.

3121   WHO'S WHO IN MUSIC IN CALIFORNIA.
        Los Angeles, The Pacific Coast musician, 1920. 151p.
        ports. 24cm. Edited by W. Francis Gates.

3122   WHO'S WHO TODAY IN THE MUSICAL WORLD;
        A biographical and pictorial record of musicians of today.
        1936/37-   New York, Published by Authors International
        Pub. Co. for Birdsall Publishers.   v. ports. 29cm. Edi-
        tor: 1936/37-   Edna Craig.

3123   WIER, ALBERT ERNEST, 1879-   ed.
        The Macmillan encyclopedia of music and musicians.   New
        York, Macmillan, 1938.   2089 p. 29cm.

3124   WIER, ALBERT ERNEST, 1879-
        The piano: its history, makers, players and music.   New
        York, Longmans, Green, 1940. viii, 467 p. 24cm. "Bio-
        graphical dictionary of pianists": p. 375-417.

3125   WISCONSIN FEDERATION OF MUSIC CLUBS.
        Wisconsin composers. Wisconsin State Centennial, 1848-
        1948. [n. p., 1948] 88p. 23cm.

3126   WYNDHAM, HENRY SAXE, 1867-
        Who's who in music; a biographical record of contemporary
        musicians, compiled and edited by H. Saxe Wyndham and Geof-
        frey l'Epine. 2d ed. , rev. and enl. London, New York, Sir
        I. Pitman, 1915. xxii, 391p. plans. 20cm. First edition
        published in 1913.

3127   THE YEAR IN AMERICAN MUSIC.
        1946/47-   New York, Allen, Towne & Heath.   v.
        24cm. Each volume contains a section on "Composers in
        America, " an alphabetically arranged listing with bio-biblio-
        graphical data.

3128   YOUNG, PERCY MARSHALL, 1912-
        A critical dictionary of composers and their music.   Lon-

don, D. Dobson [1954] 381 p. 23cm. American ed. (New
York, Crowell) has title: Biographical dictionary of composers.

3129 ZAPATA CUENCAR, HERIBERTO
Compositores colombianos. Medellín, Editorial Carpel,
1962. 280p. ports. 24cm. Colombian composers.

3130 ZENEI LEXIKON.
Átdolg. új kiad. Főszerkesztő: Bartha Dénes. Szerkesztő:
Tóth Margit. Budapest, Zeneműkiadó Vállalat, 1965- v.
25cm. Dictionary of music; includes biographies. At head of
title: Szabolcsi Bence, Tóth Aladár. First ed. published 1930-
1931 in 2 v., with a supplementary vol. in 1935. Contents. --
1. kot. A-F. -- 2. kot. G-N.

3131 ZUTH, JOSEF, 1879-
Handbuch der Laute und Gitarre. Wien, Verlag der Zeitschrift für die Gitarre, A. Goll [1926-28] 296p. 26cm.
Handbook of the lute and guitar; includes biographies. Issued
in parts.

Theater
(Including Motion Pictures, Radio and Television)

3132 ABRAHAM, ÉMILE, 1833-
Les acteurs et les actrices de Paris. Biographie
complète. Paris, Chez les éditeurs, 1861. 108p. 12.° First
published 1858. The actors and actresses of Paris.

3133 ADAMS, WILLIAM DAVENPORT, 1851-1904.
A dictionary of the drama; a guide to the plays, playwrights,
players and playhouses of the United Kingdom and America
from the earliest times to the present. Vol. 1:A-G. London,
Chatto & Windus; Philadelphia, Lippincott, 1904. 627p. 23cm.
No more published.

3134 [ALHOY, PHILADELPHE MAURICE] 1802-1856.
Grande biographie dramatique; ou, Silhouette des acteurs,
actrices, chanteurs, cantatrices, danseurs, danseuses, etc,,
de Paris et des départemens. Par l'Ermite du Luxembourg.
Paris, Chez les Marchands de Nouveautés, 1824. iii,315p.
15cm. A "Supplément, suivi des adresses des acteurs et
actrices" was published the same year. Cf. Quérard, France
litt., v. 1, p. 31. French actors and actresses.

3135   ALLGEMEINES THEATER-LEXIKON;
        Oder, Encyklopädie alles Wissenwerthen für Bühnenkünst-
ler, Dilettanten und Theaterfreunde unter Mitwirkung der
sachkundigsten Schriftsteller Deutschlands hrsg. von K.
Herlosssohn, H. Marggraff u. a. Neue Ausg. Altenburg und
Leipzig, Expedition des Theater-Lexikons, 1846. 7 v. in 4.
fold. plates. 17cm. 1st ed. (1839-42) edited by Robert Blum,
Herlosssohn and Marggraff. A dictionary of drama and the
theater which includes biographies.

3136   [BABAULT,   ] b. ca. 1780.
        Annales dramatiques; ou, Dictionnaire général des
théatres... par une société de gens de lettres. Paris, Impr.
de Hénée, chez Babault [etc.] 1808-12. 9v. 21cm. Dramatic
annals; or, General dictionary of the theatres. Includes biographies of actors, chiefly French.

3137   BARTOLI, FRANCESCO SAVERIO, 1745-1806.
        Notizie istoriche de' comici italiani che fiorirono intorno
al anno MDL fino a' giorni presenti. Padova, Per li Con-
zatti, 1782. 2v. 12.º or 16.º No more published. Notes on
Italian actors.

3138   BEFFARA, LOUISE FRANÇOIS
        Dictionnaire alphabétique des acteurs, actrices, danseurs
et danseuses de l'Académie royale de musique. 3 v. manuscript. The above ms. & a whole series of mss. (some 30
vols.) by this author in the Bibliothèque nationale (?) are important sources for compilers of music dictionaries & have
been used by Riemann, Eitner, et al. Cf. Coover, J. B.
Music lexicography, Denver (1958) p. 7. The manuscript
is in the form of a dictionary of actors, actresses, male &
female dancers (of the Royal Academy of Music, Paris)

3139   BENTLEY, GERALD EADES, 1901-
        The Jacobean and Caroline stage. Oxford, Clarendon
Press, 1941-   v. Contents. --v. 1-2. Dramatic companies
and players. --v. 3-5. Plays and playwrights.

3140   THE BEST MOVING PICTURES OF 1922/23-
        Also Who's who in the movies and the Yearbook of the
American screen. Boston, Small, Maynard. v. plates.
20cm.

3141   THE BIOGRAPHY OF THE BRITISH STAGE;
        Being correct narratives of the lives of all the principal

actors and actresses... New-York, Collins and Hannay [etc.]
1824. viii, 267 p. 19cm.

3142 BRITISH FILM AND TELEVISION YEAR BOOK.
[1st]- ed.; 1946- [London, British and American
Press, etc.] v. illus. 22cm. Title varies: 1946- The
British film yearbook. Includes section: Who' who in British
films and television (varies)

3143 CENTRE FRANCAIS DU THÉATRE.
Dictionnaire des hommes de théatre francais contemporain.
Paris, Librairie théatrale [1957- v. 24 cm. Contents.
--t.1. Directeurs, animateurs, historiens, critiques. Dictionary of men of the contemporary French theater.

3144 CHUJOY, ANATOLE, 1894- ed.
The Dance encyclopedia. New York, A.S. Barnes, 1949.
x, 546 p. 25cm. Includes biographies of dancers, choreographers, etc.

3145 DANCER'S ALMANAC AND WHO'S WHO.
1940- New York, Dancer's Almanac and Who's Who. v.
illus., ports. 26cm. Editor: 1940- Ruth E. Howard.

3146 DARTHENAY, V
Les acteurs et les actrices de Paris; biographie complète.
Paris, Chez les éditeurs, 1853. 108 p. 18.° Actors and
actresses in Parisian theatres.

3147 DICTIONARY OF MODERN BALLET.
General editors: Francis Gadan and Robert Maillard.
American editor: Selma Jeanne Cohen. Introd. by John Martin.
[Translated from the French by John Montague and Peggie
Cochrane] New York, Tudor Pub. Co. [1959] 360 p. illus.,
ports. 22cm. Translation of Dictionnaire du ballet moderne.

3148 DICTIONNAIRE DU BALLET MODERNE.
[Publié avec la collaboration de Georges Arout, el al., avec
le concours de Francois Gadan-Pamard & Robert Maillard]
Paris, F. Hazan, 1957. 360 p. illus. 22cm. With biographies of modern dancers, choreographers, etc.

3149 DICTIONNAIRE DU CINÉMA.
[Paris, Seghers, 1962] 388 p. ports. 17cm. (Collection

Seghers)   Cover title: Dictionnaire illustré du cinéma.   Includes biographies of moving-picture actors & actresses,
directors, etc.

3150   EISENBERG, LUDWIG JULIUS, 1858-
        Grosses biographisches Lexikon der deutschen Bühne im
XIX. Jahrhundert. Leipzig, P. List, 1903. 1180 p. port.
26 cm. A biographical dictionary: German actors of the 19th
century.

3151   ENCICLOPEDIA DELLO SPETTACOLO.
        Roma, Casa Editrice Le Maschere [1954-   v. illus.
29cm. Performers, authors, composers, directors, designers, etc., and dramatic themes.

3152   FILM PORTRAITS.
        London, Macdonald [1947-   v. ports. 26cm. "A
short biographical article precedes each group of photographs
and details are given of each star's notable films."----Dust
jacket.

3153   FILM REVIEW.
        1944-   [London] Macdonald. v. illus. ports. 26cm.
annual. Includes much biographical data on movie personalities of all countries, but particularly the U.S. and Great
Britain.

3154   FILMLEXICON DEGLI AUTORI E DELLE OPERE.
        Roma, Bianco e nero [1958-   v. plates. 27cm.
Biographical dictionary of actors, directors, writers for the
screen, and other persons connected with the history of motion pictures; universal in scope.

3155   FUCHS, MAX, 1876-
        Lexique des troupes de comédiens au XVIIIe siècle.   Paris,
E. Droz, 1944. 231 p. (Bibliothèque de la Société des
historiens du théatre, 19)   Dictionary of companies of
[French] actors of the 18th century.

3156   GALERIE BIOGRAPHIQUE DES ARTISTES DRAMATIQUES DE
        PARIS, composée de 100 portraits en pied, dessinés par A.
Lacauchie et gravés sur bois par H. Faxardo. Accompagnés
de 100 biographies par J. Janin [et al.] Paris, Marchant,
1846. 1v. 100 ports. 8.° Biographical gallery of the actors

of Paris; 100 portraits and 100 biographical sketches. An expansion of Galerie des artistes dramatiques de Paris, 2 v., 1841-42 (?)

3157   GALERIE DES ARTISTES DRAMATIQUES DE PARIS.
Portraits en pied dessinés d'après nature par Al. Lacauchie, et accompagnés d'autant de portraits littéraires. Paris, Marchant, 1841-42. 2 v. 80 ports. 31 cm. Issued in parts. Includes 80 biographical sketches to accompany the portraits of actors of Paris.

3158   GALERIE THÉÂTRALE;
Ou, Collection des portraits en pied des principaux acteurs des trois premiers théâtres de la capitale. Gravé par les plus célèbres artistes. Paris, Bance ainé [1812-23] 2 v. illus., ports. 4.° Full-length portraits of the chief actors of the three leading theaters of Paris.

3159   GASCH, SEBASTIÁN
Diccionario del ballet y de la danza. [1. ed.] Barcelona, Argos [1955?] 368 p. illus., ports. 24 cm. Dictionary of ballet and the dance; includes biographical articles.

3160   GRAHAM, PETER JOHN, 1939-
A dictionary of the cinema. London, Tantivy Press; New York, A. S. Barnes [1964] 158p. ports. 16cm. Largely biographical.

3161   THE GREEN ROOM BOOK;
Or, Who's who on the stage. An annual biographical record of the dramatic, musical and variety world. 1906-1909. London, T.S. Clark; New York, F. Warne. 4 v. ports. 19cm. Continued as Who's who in the theatre (q.v.) The British and the American stage.

3162   HALLIWELL, LESLIE
The filmgoer's companion. With a foreword by Alfred Hitchcock. New York, Hill & Wang [c1965] 468p. 22cm. Contains over 3000 entries for directors, actors, composers, writers, cameramen & producers.

3163   HAREL, FRANÇOIS ANTOINE, 1790-1846.
Dictionnaire théâtral; ou, Douze cent trente trois vérités sur les directeurs, régisseurs, acteurs, actrices et employés des divers théâtres. Paris, J. N. Barba, 1824.

318p. 12.° By Harel, P.-M. Alhoy and Aug. Jal. 1233 "truths" about directors, theatrical managers, actors, actresses, etc., of the French theater.

3164   HARTNOLL, PHYLLIS, ed.
The Oxford companion to the theatre. 2d ed. [with illustrated suppl.] London, New York, Oxford University Press, 1957. xi, 887, 32p. illus. 25cm.

3165   INTERNATIONAL MOTION PICTURE ALMANAC.
1929- New York [etc.] Quigley Publications [etc.] v. illus., ports. 24-32cm. Includes sections: Who's who in motion pictures [and TV] Title varies: 1929-1935/36, The Motion picture almanac. --1952/53-55, Motion picture and television almanac.

3166   INTERNATIONAL TELEVISION ALMANAC.
1956- New York, Quigley Pub. Co. v. illus., ports. 24cm. annual. Includes a who's who.

3167   [JACQUELIN, JACQUES ANDRÉ] 1776-1827.
La petite galerie dramatique. Paris, Martinet [18--] 5v. 4.° French actors.

3168   JOANNIDÈS, A 1879-
La Comédie-Française de 1680 à 1900. Dictionnaire général des pièces et des auteurs, avec une préf. de Jules Claretie. Paris, Plon-Nourrit, 1901. xxiii, 136, [274]p. facsims. 26cm. In 1921 Joannidès issued a work: La Comédie-Française de 1680 à 1920; tableau des représentations par auteurs et par pièces (iv, 138p.) Dictionary of plays and their authors at the Comedie-Francaise from 1680 to 1900.

3169   JUNK, VICTOR, 1875-
Handbuch des Tanzes. Stuttgart, 1930. vii, 264p. illus. 26cm. Handbook of the dance; includes biographies.

3170   KOSCH, WILHELM, 1879-
Deutsches Theater-Lexikon; biographisches und bibliographisches Handbuch. Klagenfurt, Kleinmayr, 1951- v. 25cm. Biographical and bibliographical dictionary of the German theater.

3171   KÜRSCHNERS BIOGRAPHISCHES THEATER-HANDBUCH:
        Schauspiel, Oper, Film, Rundfunk. Deutschland, Öster-
        reich, Schweiz, hrsg. von Herbert A. Frenzel und Hans
        Joachim Moser. Berlin, W. de Gruyter, 1956. xii, 840 p.
        21cm. Biographies of German, Austrian and Swiss theatrical,
        film and radio personalities: contemporary.

3172   LEMAZURIER, PIERRE DAVID, 1775-1836.
        Galerie historique des acteurs du Théâtre-Francais, de-
        puis 1600 jusqu'à nos jours. Ouvrage recueilli des mémoires
        du temps et de la tradition. Paris, Chaumerot, 1810. 2 v.
        front. 20cm. French actors at Paris' Théâtre-Francais.

3173   LYONNET, HENRY, 1853-1933.
        Dictionnaire des comédiens français (ceux d'hier): Biogra-
        phie, bibliographie, iconographie. Genève, Bibliothèque de
        la Revue universelle internationale illustrée, 1911-12. 2 v.
        Dictionary of French actors of the past.

3174   MONGRÉDIEN, GEORGES, 1901-
        Dictionnaire biographique des comédiens français du XVIIe
        siècle, suivi d'un inventaire des troupes (1590-1710) d'après
        des documents inédits. Paris, Centre national de la re-
        cherche scientifique, 1961. 239p. 25cm. Biographical dic-
        tionary of French actors of the 17th century.

3175   MOUHY, CHARLES DE FIEUX, chevalier de, 1701-1784.
        Abrégé de l'histoire du théâtre français, depuis son origine
        jusqu'au premier juin de l'année 1780, précédé du dictionnaire
        de toutes les pièces de théâtre jouées et imprimées, du dic-
        tionnaire des auteurs dramatiques et du dictionnaire des ac-
        teurs et actrices. Nouv. éd. Paris, L. Jorry, 1780. 4 v.
        8.º Includes a dictionary of French actors & dramatists to
        1780.

3176   NUNGEZER, EDWIN, 1902-
        A dictionary of actors and of other persons associated with
        the public representation of plays in England before 1642.
        New Haven, Yale University Press, 1929. vi, 438 p. 23cm.
        (Cornell studies in English, 13)

3177   THE OFFICIAL THEATRICAL WORLD OF COLORED ARTISTS,
        National directory and guide; authentic information of mu-
        sicians, concert artists, actors, actresses, performers and
        all others allied with the professions. v. 1, no. 1-   ;
        1928-   New York, Theatrical World Pub. Co.   v. 23cm.
        semiannual.

3178   POIDRAS, HENRI
      Critical & documentary dictionary of violin makers old and modern. Translated by Arnold Sewell. Illus. by A. Chalat. Rouen, Impr. de la Vicomté, 1928-30. 2 v. plates. 24-25cm. Translation of Dictionnaire des luthiers anciens et modernes. Another ed. of the translation was published in 1928 (Reading, Eng., A. Sewell) with collation: 300p.

3179   POIDRAS, HENRI
      Dictionnaire des luthiers anciens et modernes, critique et documentaire... 2. éd. Rouen, Impr. de la Vicomté, 1930. 600p. Dictionary of violin-makers, ancient and modern. First ed. published 1924.

3180   PASCOE, CHARLES EYRE
      The dramatic list; a record of the performances of living actors and actresses of the British stage. Rev. and enl. ed. London, Temple Pub. Co. [1880?] 432p. 19cm. At head of title: Our actors and actresses.

3181   [PEIBA, ABRAHAM] pseud. ?
      Gallerie von teutschen Schauspielern und Schauspielerinnen nebst Johann Friedrich Schinks Zusätzen und Berichtigungen. Mit Einleitung und Anmerkungen hrsg. von Richard Maria Werner. Berlin, Gesellschaft für Theatergeschichte, 1910. lxviii, siv, 401p. 21cm. (Schriften der Gesellschaft für Theatergeschichte, Bd. 13) Gallery of German actors and actresses. Perhaps the work of Johann Jost Anton vom Hagen. Cf. Preface, p. liv-lxi. First published 1783?

3182   PERICAUD, LOUIS, 1835-1909.
      Le panthéon des comédiens; de Molière à Coquelin aîné. Notices biographiques. Préf. de Coquelin aîné. Paris, E. Fasquelle, 1922. vi, 368p. ports. 21cm. At head of title: Tricentenaire de Molière. Biographical sketches, with portraits, of 104 French actors and actresses.

3183   THE PICTUREGOER'S WHO'S WHO AND ENCYCLOPAEDIA OF THE SCREEN TODAY.
      1st ed. Compiled and produced by leading experts in the film industry under the auspices of The Picture-goer weekly. London, Odhams Press [1933] 608p. illus.

3184   POHREN, DONN E
      Lives and legends of flamenco; a biographical history.

[La Mesa, Calif.] Society of Spanish Studies [1964] 357p illus. 22cm. Sequel to the author's The art of flamenco.

3185 RADIO AND TELEVISION WHO'S WHO.
1950/51-   London, Vox Mundi.   v. ports. 25cm.
Radio & TV personnel in Great Britain.

3186 RASI, LUIGI, 1852-
I comici italiani; biografia, bibliografia, inconografia. Firenze, Fratelli Bocca, 1897-1905. 2 v. in 3. illus., ports. 27cm. The Italian actors: biography, bibliography, iconography.

3187 REINERT, CHARLES, ed.
Kleines Filmlexikon: Kunst, Technik, Geschichte, Biographie, Schrifttum. In Verbindung mit. J. P. Brach und P. F. Portmann hrsg. Einsiedeln-Zürich, Benziger [1946] 424p. illus. 19cm. A dictionary of motion pictures; includes biographies.

3188 RIGDON, WALTER, ed.
The biographical encyclopedia & who's who of the American theatre. Introd. by George Freedley. New York, J. H. Heineman [1966, c1965] xiv, 1101p. 29cm.

3189 RUDOLPH, MORITZ, 1843-
Rigaer Theater- und Tonkünstler-Lexikon, nebst Geschichte des Rigaer-Theaters und der Musikalischen Gesellschaft. 1. Th. Rigaer Theater- und Tonkünstler Lexikon. Riga, N. Kymmel, 1890. 282p. 24cm. No more published. A dictionary of the theater and music in Riga; includes biography.

3190 SCHWARZ, HELMUT, 1928-
Regie: Idee und Praxis moderner Theaterarbeit; ein Leitfaden. Bremen, C. Schünemann [1965] 404 p. 19cm. "Regisseure und Wegbereiter des europäischen Sprechtheaters seit der Jahrhundertwende": p. [103]-394. These pages comprise a biographical dictionary of ca. 600 persons prominent as stage directors, producers, etc. of the 20th century European theater.

3191 SHERMAN, ROBERT LOWERY, 1867-
Actors and authors, with composers and managers who helped make them famous; a chronological record and brief biography of theatrical celebrities from 1750 to 1950. Chica-

go [1951]   433 p. 22cm.   Ca. 200 sketches of theatrical personages, primarily American.

3192   SOBEL, BERNARD, ed.
        The theatre handbook and digest of plays. Pref. by George Freedley. [Rev. ed.] New York, Crown Publishers [1948] 897 p. 22cm. Includes quite a large number of biographies scattered through its alphabetical arrangement.

3193   SOUSA BASTOS, ANTONIO, 1844-
        Carteira do artista; apontamentos para a história do theatro portuguez e brazileiro, acompanhados de noticias sobre os principaes artistas, escriptores dramaticos e compositores estrangeiros. Lisboa, J. Bastos, 1898.   866 p. ports. 27cm. A day-by-day, month-by-month arrangement of theatrical events and personalities, chiefly Portuguese and Brazilian. Index gives alphabetical approach to the numerous persons mentioned under the specific dates.

3194   SOUSA BASTOS, ANTONIO, 1844-
        Diccionario do theatro portuguez.   Lisboa, Libanio da Silva, 1908.   380 p. illus. 28cm.   Dictionary of the Portuguese theater; includes biographical notes on actors & musicians.

3195   STUART, RAY, 1899-
        Immortals of the screen.   Los Angeles, Sherbourne Press [1965] 224p. illus. , ports. 29cm. 101 biographical sketches with accompanying portraits and scenes from films (American and British film actors)

3196   SUNDSTRÖM, EINAR, 1885-   ed.
        Svenska konstnärer inom teaterns, musikens och filmens värld. Huvudredaktör, Einar Sundström. För teateravdelningen, Arne Lindenbaum. För musikavdelningen, Åke Vretblad. Stockholm, Mimer [1943] 530p. illus. 28cm. Swedish artists within the worlds of the theater, music and motion pictures; actors and musicians.

3197   TV PERSONALITIES;
        Biographical sketch book. v. 1-   ; 1954-   St. Louis.   v. ports. 21cm.

3198   TEATRAL'NAIĀ ÉNTSIKLOPEDIIĀ.
        Glav. redaktor: S. S. Mokul'skii.   Moskva, Gos. nauch.

449

izd-vo "Sovetskaia entsiklopediia, " 1961-   v. illus.,
ports. 27cm. (Entsiklopedii, slovari, spravochniki) Vols.
2- edited by P. A. Markov. Encyclopedia of the theater;
includes biographies.

3199   THE TELEVISION ANNUAL.
        1950/51-   London, Odhams Press.   v. illus.
        19cm. Includes brief biographies of prominent TV person-
        alities, British and American.

3200   THE THESPIAN DICTIONARY;
        Or, Dramatic biography of the present age; containing
        sketches of the lives, list of productions... of all the prin-
        cipal dramatists, composers, commentators, managers,
        actors, and actresses of the United Kingdom... forming a
        complete modern history of the English stage. 2d ed. , with
        considerable improvements and additions... [London] J.
        Cundee, 1805. iv, [390] p. ports. 19cm.

3201   WHO'S WHO IN BROADCASTING.
        A biographical record of the leading personalities of the
        microphone. 1st-   year. 1933-   London, I. Pitman.
        British radio personalities.

3202   WHO'S WHO IN FILMLAND.
        1922-   New York, National Publishers.   v. ports.
        28cm.

3203   WHO'S WHO IN FILMLAND.
        A biographical year book of . . . men & women of the
        screen. 1st-   ed. ; 1928-   London, Chapman & Hall.
        v. ports. 19cm.

3204   WHO'S WHO IN HOLLYWOOD.
        New York, Dell Pub. Co. v. illus., ports. 28cm.
        Began ca. 1950?

3205   WHO'S WHO IN MOTION PICTURES;
        A biographical work of reference containing sketches of the
        leading actors, actresses, owners, directors and others in
        motion pictures. 1st-   ed. ; 1915-   Chicago, H. A. de
        Masi.   v. 16cm.

3206   WHO'S WHO IN MOVIE LAND.
        [Boston, Standard Press.   v. ports. 15cm. Date of
        first publication unknown. Possibly began in the early 1920's.

3207   WHO'S WHO IN MOVING PICTURES.
       no. 1-   1915-   New York, R. E. Sherwood.   nos.
illus., ports. 26cm. Cover title.

3208   WHO'S WHO IN RADIO.
       Pennsylvania ed. 1927/28/29-   Chicago, W. E.
Johnson Co.   v. illus. 22cm.

3209   WHO'S WHO IN RADIO;
       A review of American broadcasting personalities. 19
New York, Distinctive Radio Publications, inc.   v. illus.,
ports. 28cm.

3210   WHO'S WHO IN SHOW BUSINESS;
       The national directory of show people. 1-   1950-
New York.   v. ports. 36cm. On cover of v. 1: Preview
ed.

3211   WHO'S WHO ON THE STAGE, 1908;
       The dramatic reference book and biographical dictionary
of the theatre, containing [records of the] careers of actors,
actresses, managers and playwrights of the American
stage. Edited by Walter Browne and E. DeRoy Koch. New
York, B. W. Dodge, 1908. 467p. illus. 22cm. No more
published. 1st ed., 1906 (232 p.) was edited by W. Browne
and F. A. Austin.

3212   WHO'S WHO IN THE THEATRE;
       A biographical record of the contemporary stage. [1st]-
ed. London, I. Pitman, 1912-   v. illus. 20cm. At head
of title, 1912-22: The new dramatic list; 1925-   The dramatic list. Supersedes the Green room book. Compiler:
1912-   John Parker.

3213   WHO'S WHO IN TV & RADIO.
       v. 1-   1951-   [New York, Dell Pub. Co.]   v.
ports. 27cm. annual.

3214   WHO'S WHO IN WESTERN STARS.
       1-   1952-   [New York, Dell Pub. Co.]   v. illus.
27cm. annual. Biographies of moving-picture actors.

3215   WILSON, GEORGE BUCKLER LAIRD.
       A dictionary of ballet. Completely rev. ed.   London,

Cassell [1961]   xvii, 312 p.   illus. , ports.   (Belle Sauvage library)   First published 1957 by Penguin Books.

3216   WINCHESTER, CLARENCE, 1892-   ed.
The world film encyclopedia, a universal screen guide. London, Amalgamated Press, 1933.   512 p.   plates, ports. 23cm.   Includes over 1000 film biographies.

3217   WINCHESTER'S SCREEN ENCYCLOPEDIA;
Edited by Maud M. Miller.   London, Winchester Publications [1948]   x, 404 p.   ports.   (part col.)   25cm.

3218   ZYLBERCWEIG, ZALME, 1894-   ed.
Leksikon fun yidishn teater... [New York, etc. , 1931-34] 2 v.   ports.   30cm.   Added t. p. : Lexicon of the Yiddish theatre... Includes biographies of Yiddish actors, etc.   No more published?

ATHLETICS AND GAMES

3219   BASEBALL REGISTER.
[St. Louis] C. C. Spink.   v.   illus. , ports.   23cm.   On cover,   : The game's "400. " Published by the Sporting news (varies slightly) Compilers: J. G. T. Spink and others.

3220   BOROWIK, HANS, 1887-
Wer ist's bei den Olympischen Spielen, 1936.   Kurzbiographien von mehr als 1000 Teilnehmern.   Berlin, Reichssportverlag, 1936.   176 p.   Who's Who at the Olympic Games of 1936; short biographies of more than 1000 participants.

3221   BURKE'S WHO'S WHO IN SPORT AND SPORTING RECORDS, 1922.   London, Burke Pub. Co. , 1922.   381 p.   No more published?   British sportsmen and athletes.

3222   CAPLE, S   CANYNGE.
The cricketer's who's who.   [Completely rev. and brought up to date] Hunstanton [Eng.] Cricket Book Society [1948-   v.   19 cm.   Vol. 1, A-E.   No more published? Not confined to living cricketers.

3223   COSSÍO, JOSÉ MARÍA DE, 1893-
Los toros; tratado técnico e histórico.   Madrid, Espasa-

Calpe, 1960-61.   4v.   Vol. 3 (4. ed. , 1960) is a biographical
dictionary of bull-fighters, banderilleros, picadores, etc.

3224   CRICKET WHO'S WHO.
       1909 -
       London.   v.

3225   DIRECTORY OF HIGH SCHOOL COACHES.
       1963-   [Washington, Athletic Pub. Co.]   v. illus. ,
       ports. 23cm.

3226   DONALDSON, KENNETH MACLEAY, 1864-   ed.
       South African sporting encyclopaedia and who's who.
       [Johannesburg] Donaldson's Publications, 1949.   464 p.   illus.
       8.°

3227   FERNÁNDEZ Y GONZÁLEZ, MANUEL, 1821-1888.
       Las glorias del toreo.   Cuadros biográficos, lances y
       desgracias de los diestros más célebres, desde Francisco
       Romero hasta nuestros modernos lidiadores, con cuantas
       noticias han podido adquirirse acerca de los ilustres campeones
       del redondel.   Madrid, Impr. de D. Pacheco, Liberiá de V.
       Suárez, 1879.   588 p.   plates.   8.° Biographies of Spanish
       bull-fighters.

3228   GALERIE DES CÉLÉBRITÉS DU SPORT EN FRANCE.
       Paris, Impr. de S. Racon [1853]   1 v.   8.°   French sports-
       men and athletes.

3229   THE GOLFER'S HANDBOOK.
       1898-   Edinburgh.   v. 20cm. annual.   Contains a
       Who's who in golf.

3230   THE GUIDE TO CRICKETERS.
       1849-1866.   London.   v.   Edited by F. Lilly-
       white.   Title varies?: 1849-52(?) Fred Lillywhite's guide to
       cricketers.   Absorbed by John Lillywhite's cricketers' com-
       panion.

3231   JOHN LILLYWHITE'S CRICKETERS' COMPANION.
       1865-1885.   London.   v.

3232   LINDNER, KURT, 1906-
       Deutsche Jagdschriftsteller; biographische und bibliograph-

ische Studien. Berlin, W. de Gruyter, 1964- v. illus. 21cm. (Quellen und Studien zur Geschichte der Jagd, 9 Bio-bibliography of German writers on hunting.

3233   POSTAL, BERNARD, 1905-
       Encyclopedia of Jews in sports [by] Bernard Postal, Jesse Silver [and] Roy Silver. Foreword by Abraham Ribicoff. New York, Bloch [c1965] xiii, 526p. illus., ports. 29cm.

3234   SÁNCHEZ DE NEIRA, JOSÉ
       Gran diccionario tauromáquico. Comprende todas las voces técnicas conocidas en el arte ... biografía, semblanzas, bocetos y reseñas de escritores, artistas, lidiadores y otras personas que con sus talentos, influencias ó de cualquiera manera han contribuido al fomento de nuestra fiesta nacional ... Nueva ed., corregida y notablemente aumentada. Madrid, R. Velasco, 1896-[97] xii, 1068 p. illus., ports. 29cm. 1st ed. (1880) issued in 2 v. Dictionary of bullfighting; includes biography.

3235   TURKIN, HY
       The official encyclopedia of baseball, by Hy Turkin and S. C. Thompson. [1st]- ed. New York, Barnes [1951- v. illus., ports., diagrs. 26cm. First ed. called Jubilee edition. Some vols. issued in revised editions. Supplements accompany some volumes. A register of baseball players, with dates of birth and death and records.

3236   WEBBER, ROY.
       Who's who in world cricket. London, Hodder and Stoughton, 1952. 192 p. illus. 22cm.

3237   WHO'S WHO AND ENCYCLOPAEDIA OF BOWLS.
       [Edited by] Godfrey R. Bolsover. Nottingham [Eng.] Rowland Publishers [1959] xxiv, 1298p. illus., ports. 25cm. British bowlers.

3238   WHO'S WHO IN AMERICAN SPORTS.
       Washington, National Biographical Society, inc., 1928. xi, 964p. ports. 28cm. Advertising matter interspersed.

3239   WHO'S WHO IN BATON TWIRLING.
       1950- [Janesville, Wis.] v. ports. 24cm.

3240 WHO'S WHO IN HORSEDOM.
v. [1]- 1948- Lexington, Ky. [etc.] Ransom Pub.
Co. v. illus., ports. 24cm. annual. Title varies: 1948-
54, Who's who and where in horsedom.

3241 WHO'S WHO IN MAJOR LEAGUE BASEBALL.
1933- Chicago, Buxton Pub. Co. v. ports. 29cm.

3242 WHO'S WHO IN MAJOR LEAGUE FOOTBALL.
1935- ed. Chicago, B. E. Callahan. v. ports. 28cm.

3243 WHO'S WHO IN MINNESOTA ATHLETICS.
A compiled record of outstanding athletes and coaches who
have helped to make athletic history. [1941- Minneapolis,
Who's Who in Minnesota Athletics. v. illus., ports.
28cm. Editors: 1941- R. C. Fisher and P. W. DeGrote.

3244 WHO'S WHO IN RACING.
1947- Pinner, Middlesex, Warner's Racing Agency.
v. 23cm. Emphasizes the British horse racing world.

3245 WHO'S WHO IN SMALL COLLEGE BASKETBALL.
1959/60(?)- [n. p.] v. 22cm. Vols. for
prepared by R. L. Streibich.

3246 WHO'S WHO IN SPEEDWAY.
1949- London, Sport-in-Print for Stadium Publications. v. 8.º (A Speedway echo publication) Edited by
Tom Morgan.

3247 WHO'S WHO IN SPORTS.
1950- [New York, Dell Pub. Co.] v. ports. 28cm.
annual. Editor: S. Woodward.

3248 WHO'S WHO IN THE AMERICAN ASSOCIATION.
1947(?)- Minneapolis [etc.] F. P. Hutchinson. v.
ports. 22-27cm. Biographical sketches—American Association of Professional Baseball Clubs.

3249 WHO'S WHO IN THE AMERICAN LEAGUE.
1935 ed. Chicago, B. E. Callahan, c1935. 128p. ports.
23cm. Edited by Harold Johnson. Continued in Who's who in
the major leagues.

3250 WHO'S WHO IN THE BIG LEAGUES.
   v. 1- 1953- [New York, Dell Pub. Co.] v. illus.,
ports. 28cm. annual.

3251 WHO'S WHO IN THE MAJOR LEAGUES.
   1935- [Chicago, B. E. Callahan] v. ports. 24cm.
Half title. Editor: 1935- Harold Johnson. Contains two
books: Who's who in the American league and Who's who in
the National League, each with special t. p. and each also issued separately.

3252 WHO'S WHO IN THE NATIONAL LEAGUE.
   1935 ed. Chicago, B. E. Callahan [c1935] 128p. ports.
23cm. Edited by Harold Johnson. Continued in Who's who in
the major leagues.

3253 WHO'S WHO IN THOROUGHBRED RACING.
   1st- ed.; 1946- Washington, Who's Who in Thoroughbred Racing, inc. v. illus., ports. 28cm.

EDUCATION

3254 AMERICAN ASSOCIATION OF COLLEGIATE SCHOOLS OF
   BUSINESS.
   Faculty personnel; a directory of the instructional staffs
of the member schools. 1925- [v. p.] v. 22-25cm.
Title varies: 1925, Academic histories of faculty members of
associated collegiate schools of business... Contains biographical sketches.

3255 AMERICAN COUNCIL OF LEARNED SOCIETIES DEVOTED
   TO HUMANISTIC STUDIES.
   Recipients of fellowships and grants, 1930-1962; a bio-
graphical directory. [Washington, 1963] 260p. 23cm.
Supersedes the Council's The fellows [of] the American
Council of Learned Societies, 1930-1949 (Washington, 1950)

3256 AMSTERDAM. UNIVERSITEIT.
   Album academicum van het Athenaeum illustre en van de
Universiteit van Amsterdam, bevattende de namen der
curatoren, hoogleeraren en leeraren van 1632 to 1913, der
rectores magnifici en secretarissen van den Senaat der Universiteit van 1877 to 1913, der leden van den Illustrissimus
Senatus Studiosorum Amstelodamensium van 1815 tot 1913, en

der studenten van 1799 to 1913. Uitg. door het Amsterdamsch Studenten-Corps. Amsterdam, R. W. P. de Vries, 1913. xiv, 541p. 14 fold. tables. 29cm. Album of the Athenaeum and University of Amsterdam, comprising the names of professors, rectors, etc. to the year 1913.

3257   ARNIM, MAX, 1889-
Corpus academicum Gottingense (1737-1928); nebst, Verzeichnis der Preisträger der Georgia Augusta (1753-1928) Mit einem Anhang: Kurzgefasstes Repertorium des Universitäts Archivs zu Göttingen, bearb. von Götz v. Selle. Göttingen, Vandenhoeck & Ruprecht, 1930. xii, 346p. 25cm. (Vorarbeiten zur Geschichte der Göttinger Universität und Bibliothek, 7. Heft) Biographical notes on the faculty of the University of Göttingen (1753-1928)

3258   BARDEEN, CHARLES WILLIAM, 1847-1924.
A dictionary of educational biography, giving more than four hundred portraits and sketches of persons prominent in educational work. Syracuse, N. Y. , 1901. iv, 287p. ports. 18x16cm. Published also under title: Note book of the history of education.

3259   BELGIAN AMERICAN EDUCATIONAL FOUNDATION, INC.
Belgian and American C. R. B. fellows, 1920-1950; biographical directory. New York, 1950. xxv, 218p. ports. 24cm. Cover title: Biographical directory; C. R. B. fellows, 1920-1950.

3260   BERLIN. UNIVERSITÄT.
Gesamtverzeichnis des Lehrkörpers der Universität Berlin. Bearb. von Johannes Asen. Leipzig, O. Harrassowitz, 1955-   v. An alphabetical list with birth & death dates, position & biographical references for the teaching staff of the University of Berlin.   Contents. --Bd. 1. 1810-1945.

3261   BRINTON, CLARENCE CRANE, 1898-   ed.
The Society of Fellows. Cambridge, Mass. , Society of Fellows of Harvard University; distributed by Harvard University Press, 1959. v, 268 p. 22cm. "Revised version of a privately printed booklet about the Society...1948... written by George C. Homans and Orville T. Bailey. " Two-thirds of the book is taken up by biographies of 155 Junior Fellows.

3262　COMMONWEALTH FUND. DIVISION OF INTERNATIONAL
FELLOWSHIPS.
Directory of British fellows and continental fellows.
New York.　v. 20-22cm.　Title varies: 19　-25/37,
The Commonwealth Fund fellows. —— 1925/50, Directory of
British fellows.

3263　DIRECTORY OF AMERICAN SCHOLARS;
a biographical directory. [1st]-　ed. ; 1942-　New
York [etc.]　v. 26-29cm.　Editor: 1942-　J. Cattell.

3264　DIRECTORY OF RETURNED FULBRIGHT GRANTEES.
Nov. 1957-　Tokyo, United States Educational Commission in Japan.　v. 15 x 21cm. annual.　Japanese
scholars who were participants in the Fulbright Program.

3265　DIRECTORY OF WOMEN TEACHERS AND OTHER WOMEN
ENGAGED IN HIGHER AND SECONDARY EDUCATION.
1913-　London, Year Book Press.　v. 19cm.　Teachers
in Great Britain.

3266　FIKENSCHER, GEORG WOLFGANG AUGUSTIN, 1773-1813.
Vollständige akademische Gelehrten-Geschichte der
Königlich. Preussischen Friedrich-Alexanders-Universität
zu Erlangen von ihrer Stiftung bis auf gegenwärtige Zeit. Nürnberg, 1806. 3 v. 8.º Biography of scholars at the University of Erlangen.

3267　GESNER, JOHANN MATTHIAS, 1691-1761.
Biographia Academica Goettingensis. Collegit et edidit
J. N. Eyring. Praefatus est Chr. Ad. Koltzius. Halae,
Laue, 1768-79. 3 v. 8.º Vol. 3 has imprint: Gottingae,
Vandenhöck. Biography of the University of Göttingen.

3268　GHENT. RIJKSUNIVERSITEIT.
Liber memorialis, 1913-1960. Uitg. onder de hoofdredactie
van Theo Luykx. Gent, Uitg. van het Rectoraat, 1960.　4v.
ports. 28cm.　Biographies of faculty members, the Royal
University at Ghent.

3269　GÖTTINGEN. UNIVERSITÄT.
Catalogus professorum Gottingensium, 1734-1962. Im Auf-
trage des Senats der Georgia Augusta bearb. und hrsg. von
Wilhelm Ebel. Göttingen, Vandenhoeck & Ruprecht [1962]

222 p. 25cm. A listing by faculty, with dates and disciplines of the professors at the University of Göttingen, 1734-1962.

3270 GÜNTHER, JOHANNES.
Lebensskizzen der Professoren der Universität Jena seit 1558 bis 1858. Eine Festgabe zur dreihundertjährigen Säcularfeier der Universität Jena am 15. , 16. und 17. August 1858. Jena, F. Mauke, 1858. xx, 294 p. 26cm. Sketches of professors at the University of Jena, Germany, 1558-1858.

3271 GUIGUE, ALBERT, 1888-
La Faculté des lettres de l'Université de Paris depuis sa fondation (1808) jusqu'au 1er janvier 1935. Paris, F. Alcan, 1935. 371 p. 24cm. "Personnel de la Faculté (au 1er janvier 1935)": p. 239-360. Biographies of professors in the Faculty of Letters, University of Paris, 1808-1835.

3272 GUNDLACH, FRANZ, 1871-
Catalogus professorum Academiae Marburgensis. Die akademischen Lehrer der Philipps-Universität in Marburg von 1527 bis 1910. Marburg, N.G. Elwert, G. Braun, 1927. xxviii, 606 p. 25cm. (Veröffentlichungen der Historischen Kommission für Hessen und Waldeck, 15) Professors at the University of Marburg, 1527-1910.

3273 GUPTA, K   L   ed.
Educationists in India; an illustrated biographical directory of notable living educationists in India. [1st ed.] Delhi, Tradesman & Men India [1963] viii, 229 p. ports. 23cm.

3274 GUPTA, K   L   ed.
Heads of the educational institutions in India; who's who, an illustrated biographical directory of administrative educationists in India. Edited by K. L. Gupta [and] S. K. Kapoor. Delhi, Tradesman & Men India, 1964. 321 p. ports. 22cm.

3275 [HERZOG, JOHANN WERNER]
Athenae Rauricae; sive, Catalogus professorum Academiae Basiliensis ab anno 1460 ad annum 1778, cum brevi singulorum biographia. Adjecta est recensio omnium Academiae rectorum. Adumbratio eruditorum Basiliensium meritis apud exteros olim hodieque celebrium, adpendicis loco Athenis Rauricis addita. Basiliae, Sumtibus, C. A. Serini, 1778-80. 2 v. in 1. 8.º Professors at the University of Basel, 1460-1778.

3276   HOFSTEAD, JOHN ANDREW, 1885-
        American educators of Norwegian origin; a biographical
        dictionary. Minneapolis, Augsburg Pub. House [c1931]
        316p. 23cm. 860 educators.

3277   IGUÍNIZ, JUAN BAUTISTA, 1881-
        Catálogo bibliográfico de los doctores, licenciados y mae-
        stros de la antigua Universidad de Guadalajara. México,
        Dirección General de Publicaciones, 1963. 313p. illus.
        23cm. At head of title: Universidad Nacional Autónoma de
        México. Instituto de Historia. Bibliographical catalog of the
        doctors, licentiates and teachers of the University of
        Guadalajara; bio-bibliographical.

3278   INDIA (REPUBLIC) MINISTRY OF EDUCATION.
        Who is who. New Delhi, 1962. vi, 40p. 18cm. Brief
        biographical data on the delegates to the 2d Commonwealth
        Education Conference, New Delhi, 1962.

3279   ISAKSEN, ASBJØRN, 1879-
        Norges universitet, professorer, docenter, amanuenser,
        stipendiater, samt øvrige laerere og tjenestemaend 1911,
        kortfattede biografier med 164 portraeter og et gruppebillede
        av det Akademiske kollegium, utg. ved Asbjørn Isaksen og
        Fredrik B. Wallem. Kristiania, Gyldendal, 1911. 123p.
        ports. 24cm. Oslo University's professors and other aca-
        demic personnel in 1911.

3280   KAZAN, RUSSIA (CITY) UNIVERSITET.
        Biograficheskii slovar' professorov i prepodavatelei
        Imperatorskago Kazanskago universiteta (1804-1904). . .
        Pod red. H. P. Zagoskina. Kazan, 1904. 2v. in 1. 26cm.
        Biographical dictionary of professors and instructors of
        Kazan University, 1804-1904.

3281   KHARKOV. UNIVERSITET.
        Istoriko-filologicheskii fakul'tet Kharkovskogo universi-
        teta za pervye 100 let ego sushchestvovaniia (1805-1905)
        1. Istoriia fakul'teta. 2. Biograficheskii slovar' professorov
        i prepodavatelei. Pod red. M. G. Khalanskogo i D. I.
        Bagaleia. [Kharkov] Izd. Universiteta, 1908. viii, 168,
        390, xii p. The history and philology faculty of Kharkov
        University, 1805-1905--its history and biographical
        dictionary of its professors and instructors.

3282   KIEL. UNIVERSITÄT.
      Professoren und Dozenten der Christian-Albrechts-Universität zu Kiel, 1665-1954. Mit Angaben über die sonstigen Lehrkräfte und die Universitäts-Bibliothekare und einem Verzeichnis der Rektoren [von] Friedrich Volbehr [und] Richard Weyl. 4. Aufl. bearb. von Rudolf Bülck; abgeschlossen von Hans-Joachim Neuriger. Kiel, F. Hirt, 1956. ix, 293 p. 25cm. (Veröffentlichungen der Schleswig-Holsteinischen Universitätsgesellschaft, n. F., Nr. 7)   Professors and teachers of the University of Kiel.

3283   KIEV. UNIVERSITET.
      Biograficheskiǐ slovar´ professorov i prepodavateleǐ Imperatorskago universiteta sv. Vladimira (1834-1884) Sostavlen i izdan pod red. V.S. Ikonnikova. Kiev, V Tip. Imp. universiteta sv. Vladimira, 1884. xxxvi, 816, ii p. 26cm. Biographical dictionary of professors and teachers at the University of Kiev.

3284   KRISTJÁNSSON, ÓLAFUR Þ 1903-   ed.
      Kennaratal á Íslandi. Reykjavík, Prentsmiðjan Oddi, 1958-   v. ports. 26cm. A biographical dictionary of teachers in Iceland.

3285   LEADERS IN EDUCATION:
      A biographical directory. 1st-   ed. ; 1932-   Lancaster, Pa. [etc.] Science Press. v. 26cm.

3286   LENINGRAD. UNIVERSITET.
      Biograficheskiĭ slovar´ professorov i prepodavateleĭ Imperatorskago S.-Peterburgskago universiteta za istekshuiŭ tret´iŭ chetvert´ veka ego sushchestvovaniiā, 1869-1894. S.-Peterburg, Tip. i lit. B. M. Vol´fa, 1896-98. 2 v. in 1. 25cm. Biographical dictionary of professors and instructional staff at the University of St. Petersburg (now Leningrad)

3287   LEVITSKIĬ, GRIGORIĬ VASIL´EVICH, 1852-
      Biograficheskiĭ slovar´ professorov i prepodavateleĭ Imperatorskago IUr´evskago, byvshago Derptskago universiteta za sto liēt ego sushchestvovaniiā (1802-1902) IUr´ev, Tip. K. Mattisena, 1902-03. 2 v. 25cm. Biographical dictionary of the professors and teachers at the University of Dorpat, 1802-1902 (now Tartu University)

3288   LEXIKON DER PÄDAGOGIK.
      Im Verein mit Fachmännern und unter besonderer Mit-

wirkung von Otto Willmann hrsg. von Ernst M. Roloff.
Freiburg im Br. , Herder, 1913-17. 5 v. 25cm. Includes
biographies of educators.

3289 LEXIKON DER PÄDAGOGIK.
[Herausgeber und Schriftleiter: Heinrich Kleinert et al.]
Bern, A. Francke [c1950-52] 3 v. illus. 25cm. Vol. 3 in-
cludes a biographical section (Biographien in alphabetischer
Reihenfolge, p. 19-496) with sketches of 1277 educators of
all periods and countries.

3290 LIÈGE. UNIVERSITÉ.
Liber memorialis, l'Université de Liège de 1867 à 1935.
Notices biographiques publiées par les soins de Léon Halkin...
Liège, Rectorat de l'Université, 1936. Memorial book, Uni-
versity of Liège, with biographies. Continuation of Alphonse
Le Roy's Liber memorialis; l'Université de Liège depuis sa
fondation... Liège, 1869.

3291 LOUISIANA. DEPT. OF EDUCATION.
Biographical directory of Louisiana visiting teachers.
[Baton Rouge] v. 23cm. Began publication with 1949
edition. Vols. for issued by the dept. under a variant
name: State Dept. of Education.

3292 MAZZETTI, SERAFINO.
Repertorio di tutti i professori antichi e moderni, della
famosa università, e del celebre istituto delle scienze di
Bologna, con in fine Alcune aggiunte e correzioni alle opere
dell'Alidosi, del Cavazza, del Sarti, del Fantuzzi, e del Tiraboschi, compilate da Serafino Mazzetti Bolognese. Bologna,
Tip. de S. Tommaso d'Aquino, 1848. 379, 94p. 24cm. Professors past and present of the University of Bologna.

3293 MEN OF EDUCATION IN INDIA.
1965- New Delhi, Premier Publishers. v. illus.
25cm. Compiler: 1965- C. L. Khosla.

3294 [MEURS, JOHANNES VAN] 1579-1639.
Illustris Academia Lugd.-Batava: id est Virorum clarissi-
morum icones, elogia ac vitae, qui eam scriptis suis illus-
trarunt. Lvgd.-Bat. , Apud Andreem Cloucquium, C I Ɔ. I Ɔ.
C X I I I. [198]p. ports. 22cm. Bio-bibliography of the
University of Leyden. Dedicatory epistle signed: Andreas
Clovqvius. Afterwards published under titles: Illustrium
Hollandiae et Westfrisiae ordinum alma Acad. Leidensis.

Lugd. Bat., 1614 and Athenae Batavae; seu, De Urbe Leidensi et Academia virisque claris, qui utramque illustrarunt, libri duo. Lugd. - Batav., 1625. Cf. Brunet, J. C. Manuel du libraire. Also ascribed to J. Orlers.

3295 MONROE, PAUL, 1869- ed.
A cyclopedia of education; edited by Paul Monroe with the assistance of departmental editors and more than one thousand individual contributors. New York, Macmillan, 1926-28 [v. 1, 1928] 5 v. in 3. illus., ports. 28cm. First published 1911-13. Includes biographies of educators.

3296 MOSCOW. UNIVERSITET.
Biograficheskii slovar′ professorov i prepodavateleĭ Imperatorskago Moskovskago universiteta, za istekaĭushchee stolětie, so dnĭa uchrezhdenĭiâ iânvarĭâ 12-go 1755 goda, po den′ stolětniâgo iûbileĭâ iânvarĭâ 12-go 1855 goda, sostavlennyĭ trudami professorov i prepodavateleĭ, zanimavshikh kafedry v 1854 godu, i raspolozhennyĭ po azbuchnomu porĭâdku. Moskva, Universitetskaiâ tip., 1855. 2 v. 25cm. 260 biographies of professors and teachers of Moscow University, 1755-1855.

3297 MOSCOW. UNIVERSITET. OBSHCHESTVO LĬUBITELEĬ ROSSIĬSKOĬ SLOVESNOSTI.
Slovar′ chlenov. [Moskva, 1911] 342p. 25cm. At head of title: 1811-1911. Dictionary of members of the Society of Lovers of Russian Literature at Moscow University.

3298 MOTSCHMANN, JUSTUS CHRISTOPH, 1690-1738.
Erfordia literata; oder, Gelehrtes Erffurth. Worinnen so wohl von der Beschaffenheit und Einrichtung der Erffurtheschen Universität als auch von denen gelehrten Leuten, welche sich hieselbst mit Schrifften... bekannt gemacht ausführliche Nachricht ertheilet wird. 1 [-6.] Sammlung nebst einigen Supplementis... Erffurth, 1729-32. 6 v. Continued by Johann Nikolaus Sinnhold and others, 1733-1737, and later? Learned Erfurt. Notices of the faculty at the University of Erfurt.

3299 NIPPON GAKUJUTSU SHINKŌKAI.
Semmonbetsu daigaku kenkyūsha daimoku sōran. Tokyo [1961] 2 v. 26cm. First ed. published in 1956-57 under title: Daigaku kenkyūsha kenkyū daimoku sōran. A listing of Japanese university faculty, with birth dates, specialities and current research projects.

3300 NORLIE, OLAF MORGAN, 1876-
School calendar, 1824-1924. A who's who among teachers in the Norwegian Lutheran synods of America. Minneapolis, Augsburg Pub. House, 1924. 800 p.

3301 OXFORD. UNIVERSITY. RHODES SCHOLARSHIPS.
Register of Rhodes scholars. New York, Oxford University Press, 1950. vii, 290 p. 23cm. 2336 scholars.

3302 PATIN, CHARLES, 1633-1693.
Lyceum Patavinum; sive, Icones et vitae professorum, Patavii, 1682 publice docentium... Patavii, Typis P. M. Frambotti, 1682. 137p. 33 ports. 4.° Portraits & lives of professors at the University of Padua. Contents.--pars 1. Theologos, philosophos et medicos complectens (No more published?)

3303 PEKARSKIĬ, PETR PETROVICH, 1828-1872.
Istoriiā Imperatorskoĭ Akademii nauk v Peterburgiē. Sankt-Peterburg, Izdanie Otd-niiā russkago iāzyka i slovesnosti Imp. Akademii nauk, 1870-73. 2 v. 28cm. Primarily biographies of Russian academicians of the 18th century.

3304 PINNEBERG, GER. BALTIC UNIVERSITY.
Who is who at the Baltic University; biographies of the professors and teachers. [Pinneberg, 1949] 176p. 20cm. Cover title.

3305 PRESIDENTS AND DEANS OF AMERICAN COLLEGES AND UNIVERSITIES.
[v. 1- 1933/34- Nashville, Tenn. [etc.] Who's Who in American Education, inc. [etc.] v. ports. 22-24cm. irregular. Title varies: 1933/34- Presidents of American colleges and universities. -- -1958/59, Trustees, presidents and deans of American colleges and universities.

3306 REICHARD, BARTHOLOMAEUS CHRISTIAN, 1679-1721.
Commentatio de vita et scriptis professorum hodie in Academia Jenensi publice docentium. Jenae, Sumptu Heredum M. Bircknerii, 1710. iv, 120p. 8.° Commentary on the life and writings of today's professors at the Academy (University) of Jena.

3307 RIZZI, FORTUNATO, 1880-
I professori dell'Università di Parma attraverso i secoli;

note indicative bio-bibliografiche. Parma, Tip. Fratelli
Godi [1953] 188p. 25cm. Bio-bibliography of the professors
at the University of Parma across the centuries.

3308 ROSCOE, JAMES ERNEST
The dictionary of educationists. London, Sir I. Pitman
[1914] 337p. 19cm.

3309 SELBY, PAUL OWEN, 1890-
One hundred twenty-three biographies of deceased faculty
members, Northeast Missouri State Teachers College, 1867-
1962. [Kirksville, Mo., Northeast Missouri State Teachers
College] 1963. 80 p. 23cm.

3310 SOLA, SOLMU SALOMON
Helsingin Yliopisto. Opettajat ja virkamiehet vuodesta
1925. Tädennys vuoden 1938 loppuun. Helsinki, Söderstrom,
1940. 2 v. At head of title: Solmu S. Sola, L. O. Th. Tudeu.
Continuation of Tor Carpelan's Helsingfors universitets student matrikel, 1828-1852. Helsingfors (Helsinki) University:
teaching staff and officials (to the?) years 1925-1938.

3311 STAEHELIN, ANDREAS, 1926-   ed.
Professoren der Universität Basel aus fünf Jahrhunderten;
Bildnisse und Würdigungen. Zur Fünfhundertjahrfeier der
Universität und unter Mitarbeit zahlreicher Gelehrter. Basel,
F. Reinhardt [1960] 405 p. ports. 25cm. Professors at
the University of Basel thru' 5 centuries; portraits and ap-
preciations.

3312 [TENGSTRÖM, JOHAN JAKOB] 1787-1858.
Chronologiska förteckningar och anteckningar öfver Finska universitetets fordna procancellerer samt öfver faculte-
ternas medlemmar och adjuncter, från Universitetets
stiftelse inemot dess andra sekularår. Helsingfors, G. O.
Wasenius, 1836 [i. e. 1838] 347p. 21cm. Chronological
lists and notes of the Finnish (Helsinki) University's past
chancellors and faculty members from the establishment of
the University to its 2d secularization.

3313 VRIEMOET, EMO LUCIUS, 1699-1760.
Athenarum Frisiacarum libri duo, quorum alter, praeter
historiam Academiae quae est Franequerae, elogia seren. et
ampl. ephororum, alter cl. professorum, cum serie secre-
tariorum, bibliothecariorum, nec non inspectorum oeconomiae
publicae, a natalibus ejus ad presens aevum usque, complec-

titur. Leovardiae, 1758. 2 v. (?) 4.° A history of & biographical notes on the University at Franeker, Friesland, the
Netherlands; it was in existence from 1585-1810.

3314   WARD, JOHN, 1679?-1758.
    The lives of the professors of Gresham College: to which is
prefixed the life of the founder, Sir Thomas Gresham. With
an appendix, consisting of orations, lectures, and letters,
written by the professors, with other papers serving to illustrate the lives. London, Printed by J. Moore for the author,
1740. xxiv, 338, 156 p. plates, ports. 32cm.

3315   WATSON, FOSTER, 1860-1929, ed.
    The encyclopaedia and dictionary of education; a compre-
hensive, practical and authoritative guide on all matters
connected with education, including educational principles and
practice, various types of teaching institutions, and educational systems throughout the world. With articles by about nine
hundred eminent authorities. London, New York, Sir I.
Pitman, 1921-22. 4 v. illus. 27cm. Issued in 29 parts.
Published also in sections under title: The new educator's
library. Includes a considerable amount of biography.

3316   WHO'S WHO AMONG ADMINISTRATIVE WOMEN IN
        EDUCATION IN VIRGINIA.
    [University, Va., 1928] 64p. 23cm. (University of
Virginia record. Extension series, v. 12, no. 10, April 1928)

3317   WHO'S WHO AT WISCONSIN.
    Prominent faculty members, alumni, students, and
university activities. v. 1-   1916/1921-   Madison,
Published by White Spades. v. 20cm.

3318   WHO'S WHO IN AMERICAN EDUCATION.
    A biographical dictionary of eminent living educators of
the United States. v. 1-   1928-   New York, Who's
Who in American Education. v. ports. 23cm. Imprint
varies. 7th ed., 1935-36, issued also, with slight changes,
under the title: Presidents and professors in American
colleges and universities.

3319   WHO'S WHO IN ASSOCIATION OF UNIVERSITY EVENING
        COLLEGES,
    November 1, 1959. [Edited by Gurth I. Abercrombie.
Boston, Clark-Franklin Press, 1959?] 152p. 23cm.

3320   WHO'S WHO IN EDUCATION.
        A biographical directory of the teaching profession. 1927-
        Greeley, Colo. , Who's Who in Education. v. 24cm. At
        head of title: National directory (United States of America)

3321   WHO'S WHO IN PRACTICAL ARTS AND VOCATIONAL EDU-
            CATION IN NEW YORK STATE. v. 1-   1939/40-
        Oswego, N. Y. , Sequoyah Pub. Co.   v. illus. , ports.
        24cm.

3322   ZEUMER, JOHANN CASPAR
        Vitae professorum theologiae, jurisprudentiae, medicinae
        et philosophiae, qui in illustri Academia Jenensi ab ipsius
        fundatione ad nostra usque tempora vixerunt et adhunc vivunt...
        Praefationem praemisit C. Weissembornius. Jenae, 1711.
        4 v. 8.° Lives of professors of theology, jurisprudence,
        medicine & philosophy at the University of Jena from its be-
        ginnings.

LANGUAGE AND LITERATURE (Including Journalism)
General Works

3323   AUTHOR'S BIOGRAPHICAL MONTHLY SERVICE.
        July 1952-June 1953. Los Angeles, Golden Syndicate
        Pub. Co. 235 p. (in folder) monthly. Edited by Alberta
        Lawrence. No more published?

3324   AUTHOR BIOGRAPHY MASTER INDEX.
        Being compiled by the Gale Research Company for publica-
        tion in 1966 or 1967. The Master Index will be the first
        exhaustive listing of British and American authors from the
        sixth century to the present day, and will bring together in a
        single alphabet about 150,000 references to individual authors
        whose biographical sketches appear in all the volumes being
        reprinted in the "Authors Biography Series", plus references
        to such other standard works as Contemporary Authors,
        Twentieth Century Authors, Who Was Who, and several other
        widely-held sources.

3325   AYRES, HARRY MORGAN, 1881-1948.
        Reader's dictionary of authors. New York, Warren
        Library Co. , 1917. 704p. (In The Warner library (earlier
        published under title: Library of the world's best literature)
        v. 28)

3326   [BEHRISCH, HEINRICH WOLFGANG] 1744-1825.
        Allgemeines Autor- und Litteraturlexikon in alphabeti-
        scher und chronischer Ordnung bis 1778. Hannover, Helwing,
        1778. 912p. 19cm. Many of the notices of non-German
        authors are written in French. Authors also in Meusel's Das
        gelehrte Teutschland are represented by references.   A
        general dictionary of authors and literature to 1778.

3327   BENEDEK, MARCELL, 1885-
        Irodalmi lexikon. Budapest, Győző A. , 1927 [c1926]
        1224 p. 21cm.   A dictionary of world literature that includes
        biographical data.

3328   BENET, WILLIAM ROSE, 1886-1950, ed.
        The reader's encyclopedia. 2d ed. New York, T. Y.
        Crowell [1965]   viii, 1118p. illus. 26cm.

3329   THE BIBLIOPHILE DICTIONARY;
        A biographical record of the great authors, with bibliogra-
        phical notices of their principal works from the beginning of
        history. Published by the International Bibliophile Society,
        1904. [Detroit] Republished by the Gale Research Co. , 1966.
        2 v. in 1. 24cm. (The Bibliophile library of literature, art,
        and rare manuscripts, v. 29-30)

3330   THE BOOK OF CATHOLIC AUTHORS.
        (First-   series) Informal self-portraits of famous
        modern Catholic writers. Edited with pref. and notes by
        Walter Romig. Detroit, W. Romig [1942-   v. ports.
        22cm.

3331   BORNMÜLLER, FRANZ, d. 1888.
        Biographisches Schriftsteller-Lexikon der Gegenwart.
        Unter Mitwirkung namhafter Schriftsteller. Die bekanntesten
        Zeitgenossen Auf dem Gebiet der Nationalliteratur aller
        Völker mit Angabe ihrer Werke. Leipzig, Verlag des
        Bibliographischen Instituts, 1882. vi, 800 p. 20 cm. (Mayers
        Fach-Lexika) Biographical author-dictionary of the present
        (19th century). Universal in scope. Includes anonyms and
        pseudonyms.

3332   BUDDINGH', CORNELIS, 1918-
        Encyclopedie voor de wereldliteratuur. Utrecht, A. W.
        Bruna [1954] 800 p. ports. 24 cm.   An 'encyclopedia' of
        world literature; bio-bibliographical.

3333   CARNOY, HENRY, 1861-   ed.
Dictionnaire international des folkloristes contemporains.
Tome premier. Paris, Impr. de l'Armorial francais, G.
Colombier [1902] 160 p. illus. 28 cm. (Collection des grands
dictionnaires biographiques internationaux) Cover title:
Dictionnaire biographique international des folkloristes, des
voyageurs et géographes. No more published. International
dictionary of contemporary folklorists (chiefly French)

3334   CASSELL'S ENCYCLOPAEDIA OF WORLD LITERATURE.
Editor: S. H. Steinberg. New York, Funk & Wagnalls
[1954, c1953] 2 v. (xxiv, 2086 p.) 25cm. London ed. published in 1953 under title: Cassell's encyclopaedia of literature.
Biographies of authors who died before Aug. 1914 are to be
found on p. 575-1670.

3335   COLUMBIA DICTIONARY OF MODERN EUROPEAN LITERA-
TURE. Horatio Smith, general editor. New York, Columbia University Press, 1947. xiv, 899 p. 24cm. "Including biographical sketches... covering 200 French, 150 German,
100 Russian, 100 Italian, 100 Spanish, 50 Polish, 50 Czech
writers, etc."

3336   CONCISE DICTIONARY OF LITERATURE
[Edited by] I. A. Langnas and J. S. List. New York,
Philosophical Library [1963] 526 p. 22cm.

3337   THE CONCISE ENCYCLOPEDIA OF MODERN WORLD LITER-
ATURE. Edited by Geoffrey Grigson. New York, Hawthorn Books [1963] 512 p. ports. 26cm.

3338   CONTEMPORARY AUTHORS;
The international bio-bibliographical guide to current
authors and their works. v. 1-   Detroit, Gale Research
Co., 1962-   v. 26cm. Vols. 1-10 edited by James M.
Ethridge; vols. 11-   edited by James M. Ethridge and Barbara
Kopala. Over 16,000 listings through the end of 1966.

3339   CRASSO, LORENZO, 17th cent.
Elogii d'huomini letterati. In Venetia, Per Combi, & La
Noù, 1666. 2 v. ports. 17cm. Eulogies for literary per-
sonages, in large part Italian authors.

3340   DICTIONNAIRE BIOGRAPHIQUE DES AUTEURS DE TOUS
LES TEMPS ET DE TOUS LES PAYS [par] Laffont-Bompia-

ni. [1. ed.] Paris, S. E. D. E. [1957-58, c1956] 2 v. illus. 28cm. Contents. --1. A-K. --2. K-Z. Biographical dictionary of authors of all times and countries.

3341 DICTIONNAIRE UNIVERSEL DES LETTRES
[Par] Laffont-Bompiani. Publié sous la direction de Pierre Clarac. Paris, Société d'édition de dictionnaires et encyclopédies [1961] viii, 952 p. illus., ports. 25cm. A universal dictionary of literature; bio-bibliographical in large part.

3342 DIZIONARIO LETTERARIO BOMPIANI
Degli autori di tutti i tempi e di tutte le letterature. Milano, V. Bompiani, 1956-57. 3 v. illus. 22cm. A universal bio-bibliography of literature.

3343 DIZIONARIO UNIVERSALE DELLA LETTERATURA CONTEM-
PORANEA. [Direttore: Alberto Mondadori. Redattore capo: Orlando Bernardi. 1. ed. Milano] A. Mondadori [1959-63] 5 v. 25cm. Dictionary of 20th century literature and writers.

3344 ECKSTEIN, FRIEDRICH AUGUST, 1810-1885.
Nomenclator philologorum. Leipzig, B. G. Teubner, 1871. vii, 656 p. 18 cm. Philologists.

3345 EPPELSHEIMER, HANNS WILHELM, 1890-
Handbuch der Weltliteratur von den Anfängen bis zur Gegenwart. 3. neu bearb. und ergänzte Aufl. Frankfurt a. M., V. Klostermann [1960] xiv, 808 p. 26 cm. A handbook of world literature; bio-bibliographical.

3346 FRONTAURA Y VÁZQUEZ, CARLOS, 1834-1910.
Diccionario biográfico internacional de escritores y artistas del siglo XIX. Publicase bajo la dirección de D. C. Frontaura y D. M. Ossorio y Bernard. t. 1: A-D. Madrid, M. Guijarro, 1890. 918 p. ports. 28 cm. No more published? International biographical dictionary of writers & artists of the 19th century.

3347 GUBERNATIS, ANGELO DE, conte, 1840-1913.
Dictionnaire international des écrivains du jour. Florence, L. Niccolai, 1890-91. 3 v. (2088 p.) 26cm. An international bio-bibliography of contemporary writers, the French edition (greatly extended) of his Dizionario biografico degli scrittori contemporanei (1879)?

3348   GUBERNATIS, ANGELO DE, conte, 1840-1913.
Dictionnaire international des écrivains du monde latin.
Rome, L'auteur, 1905. xii, 1506 p. 25cm.

3349   --- ----Supplément et index. Rome, 1906 [i. e. 1907] 254 p.
26cm. Belgian, French, Italian, Latin-American, Portuguese, Rumanian and Spanish writers of the late 19th and early
20th centuries.

3350   GUBERNATIS, ANGELO DE, conte, 1840-1913.
Dizionario biografico degli scrittori contemporanei.
Firenze, Coi tipi dei Successori Le Monnier, 1879.   xxxii,
1276 p. ports. 25cm. An international bio-bibliography
of contemporary writers.

3351   GUDEMAN, ALFRED, 1862-
Imagines philogorum; 160 Bildnisse aus der Zeit von der
Renaissance bis zur Gegenwart. Leipzig, B.G. Teubner,
1911. viii, 40 p. of ports. 27cm. 160 portraits of philologists, Renaissance to the present.

3352   HAMBERGER, GEORG CHRISTOPH, 1726-1773.
Zuverlässige Nachrichten von den vornehmsten Schriftstellern von Anfang der Welt bis 1500. Mit einer Vorrede des
Herrn Professors Gesner. Lemgo, Meyer, 1756-64. 4 v.
19cm. Reliable facts about the world's leading writers from
its beginning to 1500.

3353   HEDERICH, BENJAMIN, 1675-1748.
Notitia auctorum antiqua et media; oder, Leben,
Schrifften, Editiones und Censuren der biblischen, und
fürnehmsten griechischen und lateinischen Kirchen-schol-
astischen- und Profan-Scribenten, so von Anfange an, bis auf
die Instauration der Studien im Occidente, gelebet... Witten-
berg, G. Zimmermann, 1714. xiv, 1114p. 8.º Notices of
ancient and medieval authors; bio-bibliographical.

3354   HEINZEL, ERWIN
Lexikon der Kulturgeschichte in Literatur, Kunst und
Musik, mit Bibliographie und Ikonographie. Wien, Brüder
Hollinek [1962] xxiv, 493p. 15 plates. 22cm. The diction-
ary of cultural history in literature, art and music, with
bibliography and iconography. Includes biography.

3355   HOEHN, MATTHEW, 1898-   ed.
Catholic authors; contemporary biographical sketches,
1930 - [1952]   Newark, N. J., St. Mary's Abbey, 1948-52.
2 v. ports. 23cm. 994 authors.

3356   HUNGÁRIA IRODALMI LEXIKON.
Szerkesztették: Révay József [és] Kőhalmi Béla.
Függelék: Irodalmi alkotások időrendje. Budapest, Hungária,
1947. 624p. A dictionary of world literature.

3357   INTERNATIONAL ASSOCIATION OF CONFERENCE
INTERPRETERS.
Yearbook. Paris. v. 14cm. Vols. for   published
alternatively in French or English.

3358   THE INTERNATIONAL WHO'S WHO IN POETRY.
v. 1-   1958-   London, Cranbrook Tower Press. v.
22cm.

3359   KINDERMANN, HEINZ, 1894-
Lexikon der Weltliteratur, bearb. von Heinz Kindermann
und Margarete Dietrich. 3. verb. und erweiterte Aufl.
Zürich, Atlantis Verlag [cl951] vi, 1066 p. 18cm. (Sammlung
Die Universität, Bd. 12) Dictionary of world literature; bio-
bibliographical.

3360   KLEINES LITERARISCHES LEXIKON.
3. völlig erneuerte Ausg. bearb. von Albin Eduard Beau
[et al.] Bern, Francke [1961] 2 v. 18cm. (Sammlung Dalp,
Bd. 15-16) Vol. 1 edited by W. Kayser and H. Rüdiger. A
general literary dictionary with bio-bibliographies; emphasis
is on German literature.

3361   KRATKAĨA LITERATURNAĨA ENTSIKLOPEDIĨA.
Glav. redaktor A. A. Surkov. Moskva, Sovetskaĩa
entsiklopediĩa, 1962-   v. illus. (Entsiklopedii,
slovari, spravochniki) A general encyclopedia of literature
that contains much biography.

3362   KUNITZ, STANLEY JASSPON, 1905-   ed.
Authors today and yesterday, a companion volume to Living
authors. Edited by Stanley J. Kunitz, Howard Haycraft, managing editor [and] Wilbur C. Hadden, editorial assistant.
New York, H. W. Wilson Co., 1933. vii, 726 p. ports.
26cm. 320 authors.

3363　KUNITZ, STANLEY JASSPON, 1905-　　ed.
The junior book of authors, edited by Stanley J. Kunitz and
Howard Haycraft. 2d ed., rev. New York, Wilson, 1951.
vii, 309 p. ports. 27cm. (The Authors series) 1st ed.,
1934 (xv, 400 p. ports. 30cm.)

3364　KUNITZ, STANLEY JASSPON, 1905-　　ed.
Living authors, a book of biographies; edited by Dilly Tante
[pseud.] and illustrated with 371 photos. and drawings. New
York, H. W. Wilson Co., 1931. vii, 466 p. ports. 26cm.
371 "living authors."

3365　KUNITZ, STANLEY JASSPON, 1905-　　ed.
Twentieth century authors; a biographical dictionary of
modern literature, edited by Stanley J. Kunitz and Howard
Haycraft. With 1850 biographies and 1700 portraits. New
York, H. W. Wilson Co., 1942. vii, 1577 p. ports. 26cm.
(The Authors series) "Supersedes... Living authors (1931)
and Authors today and yesterday (1933)"

3366　--- ----First supplement. New York, Wilson, 1955 [i.e.
1959, c1955] x, 1123 p. ports. 27cm. (The Authors series)
Second printing, with corrections in text, and a necrology (p.
vii-ix)

3367　KUTZBACH, KARL AUGUST, 1903-
Autorenlexikon der Gegenwart. Bonn, H. Bouvier, 1950
[i.e. 1949]-　　v. 20cm. Each vol. has also special
t.p. Another ed. was published in 1952 under title: Autorenlexikon des XX. Jahrhunderts. Kleine Ausg. Vol. 1. Contents. --[1] Schöne Literatur verfasst in deutscher Sprache;
mit einer Chronik seit 1945. Author dictionary of the present
day [for German literature]

3368　LANCETTI, VINCENZO, 1767?-1851.
Memorie intorno ai poeti laureati d'ogni tempo e d'ogni
nazione... Milano, P. Manzoni, 1839. 689p. ports. 8.º
Distinguished poets of all times and nations.

3369　LENNARTZ, FRANZ
Ausländische Dichter und Schriftsteller unserer Zeit.
Einzeldarstellungen zur schönen Literatur in fremden
Sprachen. 3., erweiterte Aufl. Stuttgart, A. Kröner [1960]
vi, 760p. (Kröners Taschenausgabe, Bd. 217) Foreign (non-
German) poets and writers of our time.

3370   THE LITERARY YEAR-BOOK.
        [1st]-24th vol.; 1897-1923.   London, G. Routledge; New
York, Dutton.   25 v.   ports.   20-26cm.   Publication suspended during 1918-19.   Title varies: 1897-98, 1908-10, The
Literary year-book. --1899-1907, 1911-12, The Literary year-
book and bookman's directory. --1913, The Literary year-book,
illustrators' directory and bookman's guide. --1914-17, The
Literary year-book, authors' who's who and illustrators'
directory. --1920, The Literary who's who.   Imprint varies.
Continued in four separate publications: Who's who in litera-
ture... A continuation of the bibliographical section of the
Literary year-book; What editors and publishers want; The
Librarians' guide; British booksellers.   The Who's who or
Authors section is extensive, often one half of the volume.

3371   LITERATURNAĨA ENŤSIKLOPEDIĨA.
        Redakt͡sionnai͡a kollegii͡a: P. I. Lebedev-Poli͡anskiĭ [i dr.]
Otvetstvennyĭ redaktor V. M. Friche.   [Moskva] Izd-vo
Kommunisticheskoĭ akademii, 1929-   [Ann Arbor, J. W.
Edwards, 1948-   v. illus., ports.   26cm. (American
Council of Learned Societies reprints: Russian series, no. 20)
A general literary encyclopedia, with bio-bibliographies,
especially for Russian literature.

3372   MAGILL, FRANK NORTHEN, 1907-   ed.
        Cyclopedia of world authors.   Associate editor: Dayton
Kohler.   New York, Harper, 1958.   xii, 1198, ii p.   24cm.
Published also under title: Masterplots cyclopedia of world
authors.   Over 750 authors.

3373   MAGNUS, LAURIE, 1872-1933.
        Dictionary of European literature, designed as a companion
to English studies.   2d impression, rev., with addenda.   London, Routledge; New York, Dutton, 1927.   605 p.   27cm.
Includes bio-bibliography.   1st ed. (London, Routledge, 1926)
has collation: xii, 594 p.   27cm.

3374   MELCHINGER, SIEGFRIED
        The concise encyclopedia of modern drama.   Translated
by George Wellwarth.   Edited by Henry Popkin.   Foreword
by Eric Bentley.   New York, Horizon Press [1964] 288p.
illus., ports.   26cm.

3375   [MÉNÉGAULT, A   P   G   ]
        Martyrologe littéraire; ou, Dictionnaire critique de sept
cents auteurs vivants.   Par un hermite qui n'est pas mort.

Paris, G. Mathiot, 1816. 350p. 8.º Literary martyrology;
or, Critical dictionary of 700 living authors [primarily French]

3376   MEYERS HANDBUCH ÜBER DIE LITERATUR;
Hrsg. und bearb. von den Fachredaktionen des Bibliographischen Instituts. Mannheim, Bibliographisches Institut
[1964] 959 p. facsims., ports. 20cm. A literary handbook,
with bio-bibliographies.

3377   MINCHERO VILASARÓ, ANGEL
Diccionario universal de escritores. San Sebastián,
España, EdIdHe, 1957. v. in maps. 25cm. A univer-
sal dictionary of authors. Contents.-- 1. Estados Unidos.--
2. Argentina, Bolivia, Colombia, Costa Rica, Cuba, Chile,
Dominicana.

3378   PERDIGÃO, HENRIQUE
Diccionario universal de literatura (bio-bibliográfico e
cronológico) 2. ed., illustrada. Porto, Lopes da Silva,
1940. xxxv, 1038p. ports. 25cm. Universal dictionary of
literature (bio-bibliographical and chronological)

3379   PERTSCH, JOHANN HEINRICH
Neues allgemeines literarisch-artistisches Lexicon. Coburg [etc.] Sinner (?) 1807. 2 v. 8.º A new general dictionary of literature and art. Includes biographies.

3380   THE READER'S COMPANION TO WORLD LITERATURE.
Editor: Lillian Herlands Hornstein. Co-editor: G. G.
Percy [and others] General editor: Calvin S. Brown. [New
York] New American Library [1956] 493p. 18cm. (A Mentor
book, MD 179) Largely bio-bibliographical.

3381   RONCO, AMADEO
Manual biobibliográfico de escritores, por Amadeo Ronco
y Alfredo O. Conde. Buenos Aires, F. Crespillo, 1938.
460p. 21cm. A general bio-bibliographical manual of the
world's writers.

3382   SÁINZ DE ROBLES, FEDERICO CARLOS, 1899-
Ensayo de un diccionario de la literatura. Madrid,
Aguilar, 1949-50. 3 v. 18cm. Partial contents.-- t. 2.
Escritores españoles e hispanoamericanos.-- t. 3. Escritores
extranjeros. Vols. 2-3 of this dictionary of literature (with
emphasis on Spanish and Spanish-American literature) are
wholly bio-bibliographical.

3383   SHARP, ROBERT FARQUHARSON, 1864-
A short biographical dictionary of foreign literature.
London, J. M. Dent; New York, E. P. Dutton [1933] 302 p.
(Everyman's library. Reference. No. 90) Ca. 550 European (Gt. Brit. excluded) authors.

3384   TARSIS, VENIAMIN IAKOVLEVICH
Sovremennye inostrannye pisateli; bio-bibliograficheskii
spravochnik. Moskva, Gos. Izd-vo, 1930. iv, 204p. 24cm.
At head of title: V. Tarsis, I. Startsev, S. Urban. Title also in French. 20th century alien (non-Russian) writers; a
bio-bibliography.

3385   VAPEREAU, GUSTAVE, 1819-1906.
Dictionnaire universel des littératures, contenant I. Des
notices sur les écrivains de tous les temps et de touts les
pays... l'analyse et l'appréciation des principales oeuvres
individuelles, collectives, nationales, anonymes, etc. II.
La théorie et l'historique des différents genres de poésie et
de prose, les règles essentielles de rhétorique et de prosodie.
III. La bibliographie générale et particulière. Paris, Hachette, 1876. xvi, 2096p. 25cm. A universal dictionary of
literature; pt. I is bio-bibliographical.

3386   WARD, MARTHA E
Authors of books for young people, by Martha E. Ward
and Dorothy A. Marquardt. New York, Scarecrow Press,
1964. 285 p. 22cm. 1030 biographies.

3387   WARNER, CHARLES DUDLEY, 1829-1900, ed.
Biographical dictionary and synopsis of books, ancient and
modern. Hamilton Wright Mabie, Lucia Gilbert Runkle [and]
George Henry Warner, associate editors. [Vol. 1] Biographical dictionary of authors, ancient and modern. Akron,
Ohio, Werner Co. [c1902] Detroit, Gale Research Co., 1965
[i.e. 1966] 619p. 23cm. A reprint of v. 29 of Library of
the world's best literature.

3388   DIE WELTLITERATUR;
Biographisches, literarhistorisches und bibliographisches
Lexikon in Übersichten und Stichwörtern, hrsg. von E. Frauwallner, H. Giebisch und E. Heinzel unter Mitwirkung von K.
Ammer [et al.] Wien, Brüder Hollinek [1951-54] 3 v. 25cm.
World literature; biographical and bibliographical dictionary
and dictionary of literary history.

3389   WHO'S WHO AMONG LIVING AUTHORS OF OLDER NATIONS.
        Covering the literary activities of living authors and writers
        of all countries of the world except the United States of
        America, Canada, Mexico, Alaska, Hawaii, Newfoundland, the
        Philippine[s] , the West Indies and Central America. 1928-
        Los Angeles, Golden Syndicate Pub. Co. v. 21cm. biennial.
        Title varies: 1928, Who's who among authors of older nations.
        Reprinted by Gale Research Co. , 1966.

3390   WHO'S WHO AMONG NORTH AMERICAN AUTHORS.
        1921/22(?)-   Los Angeles, Golden Syndicate Pub. Co.
        v. ports. 25cm. From vol. 2, 1925/26 published biennially.

3391   WHO'S WHO AMONG NORTH AMERICAN ESPERANTISTS.
        Kiu estas kiu inter Nord-Amerikaj Esperantistoj. 1945-
        Little Rock, Ark. , "Espero. " no. ports. 16cm.

3392   WHO'S WHO IN THE COMMON MARKET'S PRESS AND AD-
        VERTISING; a biographical dictionary containing about
        4,000 biographies of prominent people in press and advertis-
        ing in Belgium, France, Germany (West), Italy, Luxembourg
        and the Netherlands. Edited by Helmut von der Heiden [and]
        Stephen S. Taylor. [Montreal] Intercontinental Book and Pub.
        Co. ; [New York] A. Daub, 1965. 557p. 21cm.

3393   WILPERT, GERO VON
        Lexikon der Weltliteratur; biographisch-bibliographisches
        Handwörterbuch nach Autoren und anonymen Werken. Unter
        Mitarbeit zahlreicher Fachgelehrte. Stuttgart, A. Kröner
        [1963] 1471 p. 22cm. Dictionary of world literature; bio-
        graphical-bibliographical handbook to authors and anonymous
        works.

Afrikaans

3394   GROVÉ, A   P
        Letterkundige sakwoordeboek vir Afrikaans. [Kaapstad,
        Nasionale Opvoedkundige Uitgewery, 1964] 104p. 19cm.
        Scattered through this Afrikaans dictionary of literary termi-
        nology are bio-bibliographies of a number of outstanding
        Afrikaans authors.

3395   NIENABER, PETRUS JOHANNES, 1910-
        Hier is ons skrywers; biografiese sketse van Afrikaanse
        skrywers. Johannesburg, Afrikaans Pers-Boekhandel, 1949-

v. ports. 22cm. These are our writers; biographical
sketches of Afrikaans writers.

American

3396 ADAMS, OSCAR FAY, 1855-1919.
A dictionary of American authors. 5th ed., rev. and enl.
Boston, Houghton, Mifflin, 1905. viii, 587p. 22cm.

3397 THE BIOGRAPHICAL DICTIONARY OF CONTEMPORARY
POETS; the who's who of American poets. New York,
Avon House, 1938. 536p. 27cm.

3398 BOWEN, ROBERT O 1920-
Alaska literary directory [by] Robert O. Bowen and Robert
A. Charles. Anchorage, Alaska Methodist University [1964]
91 p. 22 cm.

3399 BRENNI, VITO JOSEPH, 1923-
West Virginia authors: a biobibliography, compiled and
edited by Vito J. Brenni assisted by Andrew Boelcskevy [and
others] Morgantown, West Virginia Library Association, 1957.
73 p. (West Virginia Library Association. Publication no. 2)

3400 BURKE, WILLIAM JEREMIAH, 1902-
American authors and books, 1640 to the present day [by]
W. J. Burke and Will D. Howe. Augm. and rev. by Irving
R. Weiss. New York, Crown Publishers [1962] 834 p. 25cm.
1st ed. published 1943.

3401 COYLE, WILLIAM, ed.
Ohio authors and their books; biographical data and selective bibliographies for Ohio authors, native and resident, 1796-
1950. Prelim. research by Mr. and Mrs. Ernest Wessen.
[1st ed.] Sponsored by the Martha Kinney Cooper Ohioana
Library Association. Cleveland, World Pub. Co. [1962] xxi,
741 p.

3402 DE MENIL, ALEXANDER NICOLAS, 1849-1928.
The St. Louis book authors. St. Louis, W. H. Miner Co.
[etc.] 1925. 69 p. illus., ports. 18cm.

3403 DUYCKINCK, EVERT AUGUSTUS, 1816-1878.
Cyclopaedia of American literature; embracing personal
and critical notices of authors, and selections from their writ-

ings, from the earliest period to the present day... By Evert
A. Duyckinck and George L. Duyckinck. Edited to date by M.
Laird Simons. Philadelphia, T. E. Zell, 1875. 2v. illus.,
ports. 30cm. 1st ed. published in 1855, with a supplement in
1866. Issued in 52 parts, 1873-74. 1875 ed. reprinted by
Gale Research Co., 1965.

3404   FLAGG, MILDRED (BUCHANAN) 1886-
      Notable Boston authors; members of the Boston Authors
Club, 1900-1966. With foreword by Erwin D. Canham. Cambridge, Mass., Dresser, Chapman & Grimes [1965-   v.
ports. 21cm.

3405   HART, JAMES DAVID, 1911-
      The Oxford companion to American literature. 4th ed.
[rev. and enl.] New York, Oxford University Press,
1965. ix, 991p. 25cm.

3406   HARVEY, ALICE H
      Nebraska writers. Rev. [Omaha, Citizens Print. Co.,
1964] 182p. 23cm. First edition issued in 1934. Ca. 80
biographies.

3407   HERRINGSHAW, THOMAS WILLIAM, 1858-   ed.
      Local and national poets of America, with biographical
sketches and choice selections from over one thousand living
American poets. Chicago, American Publishers' Association, 1890. 1036p. ports. 24cm.

3408   HILBERT, RACHEL M   ed.
      Michigan authors. Ann Arbor, Michigan Association of
School Librarians, 1960. 68p. illus., ports. 22cm.

3409   HILBERT, RACHEL M   ed.
      Michigan poets, with supplement to Michigan authors,
1960. Edited by Rachel M. Hilbert. Ann Arbor, Michigan
Association of School Librarians, 1964. vii, 77p. illus.
22cm.

3410   HILL, ROY L
      Who's who in the American negro press. Dallas, Royal
Pub. Co. [1960] 80p. 21cm. 48 sketches.

3411   HINKEL, EDGAR JOSEPH, ed.
      Biographies of California authors and indexes of Cali-
fornia literature. Edgar J. Hinkel, editor [and] William E.

McCann, assistant editor. Oakland, Calif., Published by
the Alameda County Library under the auspices of the Work
Projects Administration, 1942. 2 v. 28cm. Vol. 1 contains
biographies of 2677 authors.

3412   JOINT COMMITTEE ON NORTH CAROLINA LITERATURE
        AND BIBLIOGRAPHY OF THE NORTH CAROLINA ENGLISH
        TEACHERS ASSOCIATION AND THE NORTH CAROLINA
        LIBRARY ASSOCIATION.
           North Carolina authors; a selective handbook. Chapel Hill,
        University of North Carolina Library, 1952. xv, 136p.
        24cm. (The University of North Carolina Library extension
        publication, v. 18, no. 1)

3413   KNIGHT, LUCIAN LAMAR, 1868-
           Biographical dictionary of authors. (In Library of South-
        ern literature. New Orleans, Martin & Hoyt Co., 1910. v.15
        (xii, 487 p.)) 3,800 biographical sketches of writers of the
        American South.

3414   KUNITZ, STANLEY JASSPON, 1905-   ed.
           American authors, 1600-1900; a biographical dictionary of
        American literature, edited by Stanley J. Kunitz and Howard
        Haycraft. With 1300 biographies and 400 portraits. New York,
        H. W. Wilson Co., 1938. vi, 846 p. ports. 26cm.

3415   MAINE WRITERS RESEARCH CLUB.
           Maine writers of fiction for juveniles. Orono, University
        of Maine, 1965. v, 69 p. 23cm. (University of Maine
        studies, 2d ser., no. 81) University of Maine bulletin, v.
        67, no. 20. 67 biographical sketches of authors in an alpha-
        betical arrangement; also included are many names with
        references to biographical sketches for them in such works
        as Twentieth century authors, etc.

3416   MANLY, JOHN MATTHEWS, 1865-1940.
           Contemporary American literature, bibliographies and
        study outlines, by John Matthews Manly and Edith Rickert.
        Introd. and revision by Fred B. Millett. New York, Harcourt,
        Brace [1929] viii, 378 p. 20cm.

3417   MARABLE, Mrs. MARY HAYS
           A handbook of Oklahoma writers, by Mary Hays Marable
        and Elaine Boylan. Norman, University of Oklahoma Press,
        1939. xiii, 308 p. 21cm.

3418   MARPLE, ALICE
Iowa authors and their works; a contribution toward a bibliography. Introd. by Edgar R. Harlan. Des Moines, Historical Dept. of Iowa, 1918. viii, 359 p. 24cm.

3419   MARTIN, DAVID, Brother, 1901-
American Catholic convert authors, a bio-bibliography. Introd. by John Moody. Detroit, W. Romig [1944] 259 p. 22cm.

3420   MILLETT, FRED BENJAMIN, 1890-
Contemporary American authors; a critical survey and 219 bio-bibliographies. New York, Harcourt, Brace, 1940. xiii, 716p. 22cm. Based on Manly's and Rickert's Contemporary American literature.

3421   MINNESOTA. STATEHOOD CENTENNIAL COMMISSION. CENTENNIAL LITERATURE GROUP.
A selected bio-bibliography: Minnesota authors. St. Paul, Minnesota Statehood Centennial Commission, 1958. v, 79p. 23cm. 700 authors represented.

3422   PACIFIC NORTHWEST LIBRARY ASSOCIATION. REFERENCE SECTION.
Who's who among Northwest authors. Edited with a pref. by Hazel E. Mills. [Bozeman, Mont.] 1957. 114 l. 28cm. Circa 185 biographies of authors writing since 1935 (covers Idaho, Montana, Oregon & Washington)

3423   --- ----Supplement. 1st-   [Seattle? 1961-   no. 28cm.

3424   THE READER'S ENCYCLOPEDIA OF AMERICAN LITERATURE, by Max J. Herzberg and the staff of the Thomas Y. Crowell Co. New York, Crowell [1962] x, 1280p. illus., ports. 26cm.

3425   RICHARDS, CARMEN NELSON, ed.
Minnesota writers; a collection of autobiographical stories by Minnesota prose writers, edited by Carmen Nelson Richards and Genevieve Rose Breen. Minneapolis, Lund Press, 1945. xx, 204p. ports. 22cm.

3426   SCALLY, MARY ANTHONY, Sister, 1905-
Negro Catholic writers, 1900-1943, a bio-bibliography. Detroit, W. Romig [1945] 152 p. 22cm.

3427 SCOTT, LORENE LAURA.
Colorado writers. 1st- series; 1939-   [Denver]
Denver Public Library [1939-   v. 23cm.

3428 SHEPHERD, HENRY ELLIOTT, 1844-
The representative authors of Maryland, from the earliest
times to the present day, with biographical notes and comments
upon their work.   New York, Whitehall Pub. Co., 1911.   234
p.   4 ports.   20cm.

3429 SPEECH ASSOCIATION OF AMERICA.
Directory.   Columbia, Mo. [etc.]   v.   17-18cm.
Cover title: National directory of teachers of speech.   In-
cludes some biographical data.

3430 TARDY, Mrs. MARY T   ed.
The living female writers of the South.   Edited by the author of "Southland writers" [Ida Raymond, pseud.] Philadelphia, Claxton, Remsen & Haffelfinger, 1872.   xxx, 568p.
21cm.   Rev. ed. of Southland writers (2 v. 1870)

3431 WALLACE, WILLIAM STEWART, 1884-
A dictionary of North American authors deceased before
1950.   Toronto, Ryerson Press, 1951.   viii, 525 p.   25cm.
More than 25,000 brief entries for U.S. & Canadian authors.

3432 WARFEL, HARRY REDCAY, 1899-
American novelists of today.   New York, American Book
Co. [1951]   vi, 478 p.   ports.   25cm.   575 sketches.

3433 WAUCHOPE, GEORGE ARMSTRONG, 1862-   ed.
The writers of South Carolina; with a critical introd., biographical sketches, and selections in verse and prose.   Columbia, S.C., State Co., 1910.   xi, 420 p.   23cm.

3434 WHO'S WHO COLUMBIA JOURNALISTS.
Edited and compiled by Bernard S. Redmont, editor [and
others] under the direction of Charles P. Cooper.   New York,
Graduate School of Journalism, Columbia University, 1939.
x, 278p.   24cm.

3435 WHO'S WHO IN FOREIGN CORRESPONDENCE.
19   [New York] v.   22cm.   Published by the Overseas
Press Club of America.

3436   WHO'S WHO IN JOURNALISM.
        A biographical directory and reference book of the
        journalistic profession. 1925-   New York, Journalism
        Pub. Co. v. 24cm. At head of title: National directory
        (United States of America and Canada)

Arabic

3437   [ALĪ IBN HUSAIN, ABŪ AL-FARAJ, AL-ISBAHĀNĪ] 897-967.
        The twenty-first volume of the Kitâb al-aghânî, being a
        collection of biographies not contained in the edition of Bûlâq.
        Edited from mss. in the Royal Library of Munich by Rudolph
        E. Brünnow. Part 1. Text. Leyden, E. J. Brill, 1888. 280p.
        28cm. No more published? Biographies of Arab poets and
        musicians.

3438   BROCKELMANN, CARL, 1868-1956.
        Geschichte der arabischen Litteratur. 2. den
        Supplementbänden angepasste Aufl. Leiden, E. J. Brill,
        1943-49. 2 v. 25 cm.

3439   ----Erster [-dritter] Supplementband. Leiden, E. J.
        Brill, 1937-42. 3 v. 25 cm.

        Difficult to use. Chiefly a bio-bibliographical work, but
        in order to get an alphabetical approach by author it is
        necessary to use the author index in the third Supplement-
        band (p. [503]-788). Remains a prime source for data on
        Arabic literature.

3440   DĀGHIR, YŪSUF AS'AD
        Masâdir al-dirāsāt al-adabīyah. Saida, Paris [1951-
        v. 26cm. Cover title: Éléments de bio-bibliographie de la
        littérature arabe, conforme aux programmes officiels de
        l'enseignement: Liban, Syrie, Iraq, Égypte, par Joseph Assad
        Dagher. Bio-bibliography of Arabic literature.

3441   ROSSI, GIOVANNI BERNARDO DE, 1742-1831.
        Dizionario storico degli autori arabi più celebri e delle
        principali loro opere. Parma, Dalla Stamperia Imperiale,
        1807. viii, 198p. Historical dictionary of the most celebra-
        ted Arab authors & their principal works.

3442   SARKIS, JOSEPH ELIAN.
        Dictionnaire encyclopédique de bibliographie arabe, com-
        prenant 1º le nom de tous les ouvrages imprimées, tant en

Orient qu'en Occident et en Amérique, depuis la création de
l'imprimerie jusqu'à 1919 inclusivement. 2° une biographie
succinte de la plupart des auteurs anciens et modernes. 3°
les sources des notes biographiques. Le Caire, 1928-30.
iv p., 2024 columns, 152, 18 p. 33cm. Title from cover.
Bio-bibliography of Arabic literature from the origin of printing to the year 1919. Issued in 11 parts, each with cover titles
in Arabic (Muǧam al-matbū' at al'-arabīja walmu'arraba) and
French. Arabic text paged with Arabic numeral characters.

Belgian (French, Flemish, Walloon)

3443   BIBLIOGRAPHIE NATIONALE.
    Dictionnaire des écrivains belges et catalogue de leurs
publications, 1830-1880. Bruxelles, P. Weissenbruch, 1886-
1910. 4 v. 24cm. Very brief biographical notices (profession, dates and places of birth and death) of Belgian writers.

3444   BIBLIOTHECA BELGICA.
    Bibliographie générale des Pays-Bas, fondée par Ferd.
van der Haeghen et publiée sous sa direction. Gand [etc.]
Vanderpoorten [etc.] 1880-19   v. Bio-bibliographies of
Belgian and Dutch literature. Series 1-2 complete; 3d series
in progress. Each series arranged alphabetically by author,
giving full description of his works and usually accompanied
by a biography and list of works about the author. Last
volume of each series is an index.

3445   CLOSSET, FRANCOIS
    Dictionnaire des littérateurs, par Francois Closset, Ray-
mond Herreman ['et] Étienne Vauthier. Bruxelles, Maison
Larcier [1946?] 158 p. 17cm. (Petits dictionnaires des
lettres et des arts en Belgique, 2) Dictionary of Belgian
littérateurs.

3446   COPPE, PAUL
    Dictionnaire bio-bibliographique des littérateurs d'expres-
sion wallonne, 1622 à 1950 [par] Paul Coppe et Léon Pirsoul.
Gembloux, J. Duculot, 1951. 415 p. 26cm. 1325 sketches of
Walloon authors and their works, 1622-1950.

3448   HANLET, CAMILLE.
Les écrivains belges contemporains de langue francaise,
1800-1946. Liége, H. Dessain, 1946. 2 v. (1302p.) illus.
22cm. Belgian authors, writing in French,1800-1946.

3449   HANLET, CAMILLE.
Publicistes et essayistes chrétiennes de Belgique. Liège,
La Pensée catholique [1950] 96 p. 19cm. (Études religeuses,
no 671) Christian publicists and essayists of Belgium.

3450   SEYN, EUGÈNE DE, 1880-
Dictionnaire des écrivains belges; bio-bibliographie.
Bruges, Editions "Excelsior," 1930-31. 2 v. illus. 27cm.
Dictionary of Belgian writers; bio-bibliography.

3451   SOURIE, LOUIS, 1910-
Vlaams letterkundig lexicon. Komen, 1951. 155 p. 23cm.
Dictionary of Flemish literature.

Bulgarian

3452   KONSTANTINOV, GEORGI.
Bŭlgarski pisateli. Biografski i bibliografski danni.
[Sofia, Khemous] 1947. viii, 454 p. ports. 18cm. Bio-
bibliography of Bulgarian authors.

Catalan

3453   ELÍAS DE MOLINA, ANTONIO, 1850-1909.
Diccionario biográfico y bibliográfico de escritores y
artistas catalanes del siglo XIX (apuntes y datos) Barcelona,
Administración, 1889-[95] 2 v. illus. 28cm. Biographical
& bibliographical dictionary of Catalan writers and artists.

3454   MASSÓ TORRENTS, JAIME, 1863-
Bibliografia dels antics poetes catalans. Barcelona, Institut d'Estudis Catalans, 1914. 284p. 4.º (Institut d'Estudis
Catalans. Anuari, V, 1913-14) Bibliography of early Catalan
poets; bio-bibliographical.

3555   MASSÓ TORRENTS, JAIME, 1863-
        Repertori de l'antiga literatura catalana. Barcelona, Edi-
        torial Alpha, 1932-   v. 28cm. Contents. --[1] La poesia.
        Repertoire of old Catalan literature; bio-bibliographical.

3456   TORRES AMAT, FÉLIX, 1772-1847.
        Memorias para ayudar a formar un diccionario crítico
        de los escritores catalanes, y dar alguna idea de la antigua
        y moderna literatura de Cataluna. Barcelona, Impr. de J.
        Verdaguer, 1836. xliiii, 719p. 21cm. Compiled in collab-
        oration with his brother, Ignacio.

3457   ---- ----Supplemento, por Juan Corminas. Burgos, Impr.
        de Arnaiz, 1849. 368p. 22cm.

        Materials to help in the construction of a dictionary of
        Catalan writers.

Chinese

3458   T'AN, CHENG-PI, comp.
        Chung-kuo wen hsüeh chia ta tz'u tien. [Shanghai] Kuang
        min shu chü [1934] 1746, 55p. Biographical dictionary of
        Chinese men of letters.

3459   YANG, YIN-SHEN, 1898-
        Chung-kuo wên hsüeh chia lieh chuan. [Hongkong] 1962.
        1 v. (various pagings) ports. 21cm. Biographies of Chinese
        men of letters. First published in 1939 (Shanghai) under ti-
        tle: Chung hua shu chü.

Classical

3460   BIOGRAPHIA CLASSICA;
        The lives and characters of all the classic authors, the
        Grecian and Roman poets, historians, orators, and biogra-
        phers. With an account of them and their writings... The
        2d ed., corr. and improv'd... London, D. Browne, 1750.
        2 v. 12.°

3461   BIOGRAPHISCHES JAHRBUCH FÜR ALTERTUMSKUNDE.
        Begründet von Conrad Bursian. 1. -   Jahrg.; 1878-19
        Berlin [etc.] Calvary [etc.]   v. 23cm. (In Jahresbericht
        über die Fortschritte der klassischen Altertumswissenschaft.
        Berlin, 1879-98; Leipzig, 1899-19   ) Contains signed obitua-
        ries of classical philologists. Title varies.

3462   CLASSISCHE BIOGRAPHIE;
oder, Die Leben und Charaktere aller classischen Autoren
... Aus dem Englischen übers., berichtiget und verb. von
Samuel Mursinna. Halle, 1767-68. 2 v. 8.º Translation of
Biographia Classica. The lives and characters of the authors
of classical antiquity.

3463   GADDI, JACOPO
De scriptoribus, non ecclesiasticis, Graecis, Latinis,
Italicis, primorum graduum in quinque theatris, scilicet:
philosophico, poetico, historico, oratorio, critico. Flor-
entiae, Typis Amatoris Massae, 1648-49. 2 v. 31cm.
Largely a bio-bibliographical work for Classical and some
Italian writers.

3464   GESNER, KONRAD, 1516-1565.
Bibliotheca institvta et collecta, primvm a Conrado Gesnero;
deinde in epitomen redacta, & nouorum librorum accessione
locupletata, tertiò recognita, & in duplum post priores editiones
aucta, per Iosiam Simlerum: iam verò postremò aliquot mille,
cùm priorum tùm nouorum authorum opusculis, ex instructis-
sima Viennensi Austriae Imperatoria Bibliotheca amplificata,
per Iohannen Iacobum Frisium. Tigvri, C. Froschovervs,
1583. 835,[40] p. 33cm. An expanded edition of Gesner's
Bibliotheca universalis (1545); a bio-bibliography of Latin,
Greek and Hebrew of writers of the past.

3465   HARVEY, Sir PAUL, 1869-1948.
The Oxford companion to classical literature. Oxford,
Clarendon Press, 1937. xii, 468p. plates, maps,
19cm.

3466   PECK, HARRY THURSTON, 1856-1914, ed.
Harper's dictionary of classical literature and antiquities.
New York, Harper, 1896. xv, 1701p. illus., maps. 27cm.
Reprinted at various intervals (1962 the latest)

3467   PÖKEL, WILHELM
Philologisches Schriftsteller-Lexikon. Leipzig, A.
Krüger, 1882. viii, 328p. 22cm. Dictionary of [classical]
philologists.

3468   STEMPLINGER, EDUARD, 1870-
Griechisch-lateinische Literaturführer von Homer bis auf
unsre Zeit. München, E. Heimeran [c1934] 234p. illus.

18cm. [Tusculum-Schriften] Leading figures in Greek and Latin literature from Homer to our time; bio-bibliographical.

3469 SUIDAS.
Suidae Lexicon, edidit Ada Adler. Lipsiae, In Aedibus B. G. Teubneri, 1928-38. 5 v. 25cm. (Lexicographi graeci recogniti et apparatu critico instructi, v. 1) Also known as the Suda Lexicon. Compiled ca. 1000 A.D. Important for biographical data on Greek classical and Byzantine writers.

3470 TUSCULUM LEXIKON DER GRIECHISCHEN UND LATEINISCHEN LITERATUR VOM ALTERTUM BIS ZUR NEUZEIT. [1. Aufl. München] E. Heimaran [1948] 281p. 18cm. A dictionary of Greek & Latin literature and writers from antiquity to modern times. Based on Eduard Stemplinger's Griechisch-lateinischer Literaturführer vom Homer bis auf unsre Zeit. München [1934]

3471 TUSCULUM-LEXIKON GRIECHISCHER UND LATEINISCHER AUTOREN DES ALTERTUMS UND DES MITTELALTERS. Völlig neu bearb. von Wolfgang Buchwald, Armin Hohlweg [und] Otto Prinz. [Munchen] E. Heimeran [1963] xvi, 544p. 18cm. Dictionary of Greek & Latin authors of antiquity and the Middle Ages. 1st edition (q.v.) was published in 1948 under title: Tusculum Lexikon der griechischen und lateinischen Literatur vom Altertum bis zur Neuzeit.

Czech

3472 BALBIN, BOHUSLAV ALOIS, 1621-1688.
Bohemia docta; opus posthumum editum, notisque illustratum ab Raphaele Ungar. Pragae, Literis Caes. Reg. ad S. Clementem, per I. A. Hagen, 1776-80. 3v. in 2. 19-21cm. Learned Bohemia. Bio-bibliography for Bohemia and Czech literature.

3473 CZIKANN, JOHANN JACOB HEINRICH, 1789-1855.
Die lebenden Schriftsteller Mährens. Brünn, Trassler, 1812. 1 v. 8.° The living authors of Moravia.

3474 KUNC, JAROSLAV
Slovník ceských spisovatelů beletristů, 1945-1956. Praha, Státní pedagogické nakl., 1957. 483 p. 21cm. (Edice Národ-

ni knihovny v Praze, sv. 6) 478 Czech literary figures.
Continues the author's Slovnίk soudobých ceských spisovatelů
...1918-45.

3475 KUNC, JAROSLAV
Slovnίk soudobých českých spisovatelů; krásné písemnictvί
v letech 1918-1945. Praha, Orbis, 1945-46. 2 v. Dictionary
of contemporary Czech writers, 1918-1945.

3476 URBANEK, JOSEF FRANTIŠEK
Bibliografický a biografický slovnik českých spisovatelů.
V Praze, 1910. 2 v. Goes up to Knapp only. No more published. Bibliographical and biographical dictionary of Czech
writers.

Danish

3477 DANSK SKØNLITTERAERT FORFATTERLEKSIKON,
1900-1950. Bibliografisk redaktion: Svend Dahl.
Medredaktører: Ludvig Bramsen og Mogens Haugsted. Biografisk redaktion: Povl Engelstoft. København, Grønholt
Pedersen, 1959-63. 3 v. 25cm. Dictionary of Danish authors,
1900-1950.

3478 EHRENCRON-MÜLLER, HOLGER, 1868-
Forfatterlexikon omfattende Danmark, Norge og Island
indtil 1814. København, Aschehoug, 1924-35. 12 v. 25 cm.
1st supplement bound in at end of vol. 9.

3479 ----Supplement 2. Rettelser, tilaeg og tilføjelser.
København, H. Aschehoug, 1939. 74 p. 25 cm.

Dictionary of authors, embracing Denmark, Norway,
& Iceland up to 1814.

3480 ERSLEW, THOMAS HANSEN, 1803-1870.
Almindeligt forfatter-lexicon for Kongeriget Danmark med
tilhørende bilande, fra 1814 til 1840. Kjøbenhavn, Forlagsforeningens forlag, 1843-53. 3 v. 23 cm.

3481 ----Supplement, indtil udgangen af aaret 1853. Kjøbenhavn,
Forlagsforeningens forlag, 1858-68. 3 v. 23 cm.

General author dictionary for Denmark, 1814-1853.

3482 HVEM SKREV HVAD?
Politikens litteraturhaandbog. [Redaktion: Frederik

Schyberg og Nelly Backhausen. Vignetter af Axel Nygaard]
København, Politikens forlag, 1945 [i. e. 1946] 608p. illus.,
ports. 18cm. Who wrote what? A literary handbook (bio-
bibliographical) of 20th century Danish literature.

3483   HVEM SKREV HVAD?
1945-1951. [Redaktion: Nelly Backhausen] København,
Politikens forlag, 1951. 192p. illus., ports. 17cm. At
head of title: Politikens litteraturhåndbog. Who wrote what?
1945-1951. Bio-bibliography of 20th century Danish
literature in continuation of Hvem skrev hvad? [1946]

3484   MATERIALIER TIL ET DANSK BIOGRAPHISK-LITERARISK
LEXIKON, indeholdende: fortsaettelaer af, tillaeg
til, rettelser i de indtil 1835 udkomne Lexica, om Danske,
Norske og Islaendere. Ved Niels Christian Øst. nr. 1-150,
aarg. 1-4. København, 1835-38. v. 28cm. Materials toward a Danish biographical-literary dictionary.

3485   NYERUP, RASMUS, 1759-1820.
Almindeligt literaturlexicon for Danmark, Norge, og Island;
eller, Fortegnelse over danske, norske og islandske saavel
afdøde som nu levende forfattere, med anførelse af deres vig-
tigste levnets-omstaendigheder og liste over deres skrifter.
Ved R. Nyerup og J. E. Kraft. Kjøbenhavn, Gyldendal, 1820.
viii, 692 p. 25cm. General literary dictionary for Denmark,
Norway & Iceland; or, Register of Danish, Norwegian, and
Icelandic authors, living and dead... Title edition of Nyerup
and Kraft's Dansk-norsk litteraturlexicon (Kjøbenhavn, Gyldendal, 1818-19. 2v.)

3486   VOR TIDS HVEM SKREV HVAD, 1914-1964.
[Udarbejdet af Niels Chr. Lindtner. Redaktion: Else Larsen
og Knud Sandvej] København, Politikens forlag, 1964. 2 v.
illus. 18cm. (Politikens handbøger, nr. 98) The who wrote
what of our time, 1914-1964--a dictionary & bio-bibliography
of 20th century Danish literature. An earlier edition, covering the years 1914-1955, was edited by Henning Fonsmark.
Contents. --bind. 1. Biografier. --bind 2. Titler.

3487   WOEL, CAI MOGENS, 1895-
Dansk forfatterleksikon; 338 biografier over nulevende
danske forfattere. [København] Nordiske landes bogforlag,
1945. viii, 360p. ports. 25cm. Dictionary of Danish authors; 338 biographies of contemporary (20th century) Danish
writers.

Dutch

3488   FREDERIKS, JOHANNES GODEFRIDUS, 1828-1896.
Biographisch woordenboek der Noord- en Zuidnederlandsche
letterkunde, door J. G. Frederiks en F. Jos van den Branden.
2., omgewerkte druk. Amsterdam, L. J. Veen [1888-92] v,
918 p. 23 cm. Biographical dictionary of the literature of
North & South Netherlands.

3489   GEYSBEEK, PIETER GERARDUS WITSEN, 1774-1833.
Biographisch, anthologisch en critisch woordenboek der
Nederduitsche dichters. Amsterdam, C. L. Schleijer, 1821-
27. 6v. 22cm. This work is continued by A. J. van der Aa's
Nieuw biografiesch, anthologiesch en kritiesch woordenboek
van Nederlandsche dichters... Amsterdam, 1864. Biographical, anthological & critical dictionary of Dutch poets.

3490   OTTO, FRIEDRICH
Die Gesammtliteratur Niederlands; oder, Leben und Wirken
der holländischen Schriftsteller seit dem dreizehnten Jahrhundert bis auf unsere Zeit. Für Deutsche bearb. Hildburghaus-
en [etc.] Verlag des Bibliographischen Instituts, 1838. 506
columns. 24cm. A bio-bibliographical dictionary of Dutch
literature, based on N. G. van Kampen's Beknopte geschiedenis
der letteren en wetenschappen in de Nederlanden, Delft, 1821-
1826.

3491   POTTER, FRANS DE, 1834-1904.
Alphabetische lijst van de voorloopig verzamelde namen
der in België geboren Nederlandsche schrijvers, dienende
tot het samenstellen van de biographie der Zuid- Nederlandsche schrijvers. Gent, 1890. 523p. 8.º (Koninklijke
Vlaamse Academie voor Taal- en Letterkunde. Publicaties,
reeks 4, no. 1) Alphabetical list of Dutch authors born in
Belgium useful for the compilation of the biographies of
South Netherland's writers.

English

3492   ADAMS, WILLIAM DAVENPORT, 1851-1904.
Dictionary of English literature, being a comprehensive
guide to English authors and their works. London, New York,
Cassell, Petter & Galpin [1878] 708 p. Reprinted by Gale
Research Co. , Detroit, 1966.

3493   ALLIBONE, SAMUEL AUSTIN, 1816-1889.
      Critical dictionary of English literature and British and
American authors, living and deceased, from the earliest
accounts to the latter half of the nineteenth century. Containing over 46,000 articles (authors) with forty indexes of subjects. Philadelphia, Lippincott, 1858-91. 5 v. Vols. 4-5,
by John Foster Kirk, were published in 1891 as a supplement
to the basic 3-volume work by Allibone. Kirk's 2 volumes
(A-Z) list 37,000 entries which are additional to the 46,000
authors given by Allibone. The whole 5-volume work was reprinted by Gale Research Company in 1965.

3494   THE AUTHOR'S AND WRITER'S WHO'S WHO.
      1934-   London, Shaw Pub. Co.   v.   23cm.   5th ed.,
1963, latest, published by Burke's Peerage Limited.

3495   BAKER, DAVID ERSKINE, 1730-1767.
      Biographia dramatica; or, A companion to the playhouse:
containing historical and critical memoirs, and original
anecdotes, of British and Irish dramatic writers from the
commencement of our theatrical exhibitions, among whom
are some of the most celebrated actors: also an alphabetical
account, and chronological lists, of their work... Originally
compiled to 1764, by David Erskine Baker. Continued thence
to 1782, by Isaac Reed, and brought down to the end of November 1811, with very considerable additions and improvements throughout, by Stephen Jones. London, Longmans,
Hurst, Rees, Orme, and Brown, 1812. 1st ed. published
anonymously in 1764 under title: The companion to the playhouse; the 2d ed., 1782, by Isaac Reed, under the present
title.

3496   BERKENHOUT, JOHN, 1730?-1791.
      Biographia litteraria; or, A biographical history of litera-
ture: containing the lives of English, Scottish, and Irish authors from the dawn of letters in these kingdoms to the present
time, chronologically and classically arranged... Vol. I: From
the beginning of the fifth to the end of the sixteenth century.
London, J. Dodsley, 1777. xxxiv, 537p. 4.° No more published.

3497   A BIOGRAPHICAL DICTIONARY OF THE LIVING AUTHORS
      OF GREAT BRITAIN AND IRELAND; comprising literary
memoirs and anecdotes of their lives; and a chronological
register of their publications... Including notices of some
foreign writers whose works have been occasionally published

in England... London, Printed for Colburn, 1816. viii, 449p.
Presumably written by John Watkins as far as the letter F and
then completed by Frederic Shoberl. The work is sometimes
attributed to William Upcott. Reprinted by Gale Research
Co., 1966.

3498   BOASE, GEORGE CLEMENT, 1829-1897.
      Bibliotheca Cornubiensis: A catalogue of the writings , both
manuscript and printed, of Cornishmen, and of works relating
to the County of Cornwall, with biographical memoranda and
copious literary references. By George Clement Boase and
William Prideaux Courtney. London, Longmans, Green,
Reader and Dyer, 1874-82. 3 v. 29 cm. Imprint varies.

3499   BROWNING, DAVID CLAYTON, 1894-   ed.
      Everyman's dictionary of literary biography, English and
American, compiled after John W. Cousin by D. C. Browning.
[Rev. ed.] London, Dent; New York, Dutton [1962] x, 752 p.
20 cm. (Everyman's reference library) First published in
1910. Supersedes Cousin's Short biographical dictionary
of English literature.

3500   CHAMBERS, ROBERT, 1802-1871.
      Chambers's cyclopaedia of English literature. New ed. by
David Patrick and J. Liddell Geddie. A history, critical and
biographical, of authors in the English tongue from the earliest
times till the present day, with specimens of their writings.
London, W. & R. Chambers [1927-38] 3 v. illus. 28 cm.
American ed. published in 1922-1938 by J. B. Lippincott.

3501   CIBBER, THEOPHILUS, 1703-1758.
      The lives of the poets of Great Britain and Ireland, to the
time of Dean Swift. Compiled from ample materials scattered
in a variety of books, and especially from the ms. notes of
the late ingenious Mr. Coxeter and others, collected for this
design, by Mr. Cibber. London, R. Griffiths, 1753. 5 v.
17cm. Title varies slightly. Compiled mainly by Robert
Shiels, with revisions and additions by T. Cibber.

3502   COUSIN, JOHN W.
      A short biographical dictionary of English literature. Rev.
ed. London, Dent, 1942. 677 p. (Everyman's library.
Reference. no. 449) 1600 names. 1st ed. issued in 1910.

3503   GARVIN, JOHN WILLIAM, 1859-1939, ed.
      Canadian poets. Rev. ed. Toronto, McClelland & Stewart

[1926] xi, 536 p. illus. (ports.) 24 cm. An anthology, but
with bio-bibliographies of the 75 poets represented.

3504   HARVEY, Sir PAUL, 1869-1948, ed.
         The Oxford companion to English literature. 3d ed.
Oxford, Clarendon Press, 1946. viii, 931p. 25cm.
An abridged version of this work was issued under title:
The Concise Oxford dictionary of English literature.

3505   HIGGINSON, ALEXANDER HENRY, 1876-
         British and American sporting authors, their writings
and biographies. With a bibliography by Sidney R. Smith
and foreword by Ernest R. Gee. Berryville, Va., Blue Ridge
Press, 1949. xvii, 443p. ports. 29cm.

3506   INGLIS, RALSTON.
         The dramatic writers of Scotland. Glasgow, G. D.
Mackellar, 1868. 155p. 17cm.

3507   [JACOB, GILES] 1686-1744.
         The poetical register: or, The lives and characters of the
English dramatick poets. With an account of their writings.
London, E. Curll, 1719-20. 2v. ports. 20cm. Dedication
signed: G. J. Vol. 2 has title: An historical account of the
lives and writings of our most considerable English poets,
whether epick, lyrick, elegiack, epigramatists, & c.

3508   JUCHHOFF, RUDOLF, 1894-   comp.
         Sammelkatalog der biographischen und literarkritischen
Werke zu englischen Schriftstellern des 19. und 20.
Jahrhunderts (1830-1958) Verzeichnis der Bestände in
deutschen Bibliotheken. Unter Mitarbeit von Hildegard
Föhl. Krefeld, Scherpe [1959?] 272p. 24cm. Catalog of
the biographical and critical works on English authors of
the 19th and 20th centuries (1830-1958) in German libraries.

3509   KUNITZ, STANLEY JASSPON, 1905-   ed.
         British authors before 1800; a biographical dictionary,
edited by Stanley J. Kunitz and Howard Haycraft. With 650
biographies and 220 portraits. New York, H. W. Wilson Co.,
1952. vi, 584 p. ports. 26cm. (The Authors series)

3510   KUNITZ, STANLEY JASSPON, 1905-   ed.
         British authors of the nineteenth century, edited by Stanley
J. Kunitz. Associate editor: Howard Haycraft. With 1000

biographies and 350 portraits. New York, H. W. Wilson Co.,
1936. 677 p. ports. 26cm.

3511   LANGBAINE, GERARD, 1656-1692.
An account of the English dramatick poets; or, Some observations and remarks on the lives and writings, of all those
that have publish'd either comedies, tragedies, tragi-come-
dies, pastorals, masques, interludes, farces, or opera's in the
the English tongue. Oxford, Printed by L. L. for G. West and
H. Clements, 1691. 556, [31] p. port. 19cm. Based on
Langbaine's 'New catalogue of English plays, London, 1688
[Dec. 1687]' an unauthorized edition of which had appeared a
month earlier under title: Momus triumphans; or, The
plagiaries of the English state. A new edition, revised by
Charles Gildon, appeared 1699 under title: The lives and characters of the English dramatick poets.

3512   LECLAIRE, LUCIEN, 1909-
A general analytical bibliography of the regional novelists
of the British Isles, 1800-1950. Clermont-Ferrand, Impr.
G. de Bussac [1954] 399p. 2 fold. maps. 23cm. Bio-bibliography; topical arrangement, not alphabetical. Also published in French under title: Le roman régionaliste dans les
Iles Britanniques, 1800-1950.

3513   LONG, ROBERT JAMES, 1849-1933.
Novia Scotia authors and their works. A bibliography of
the province. East Orange, N. J., The author, 1918. 312 p.

3514   [MAIDMENT, JAMES] 1795?-1879, ed.
Catalogues of Scottish writers. Edinburg, T. Stevenson,
1833. xxiv, 168 p. 22cm. Partial contents.--A short account
of Scots divines [by L. Charteris].--A catalogue of Scottish
writers.--Account of the learned men and writers of Aberdeen
[by L. Charteris]

3516   MILLER, EDMUND MORRIS, 1881-
Australian literature; a bibligraphy to 1938, extended to

1950. Edited, with a historical outline and descriptive commentaries, by F. T. Macartney. [Rev. ed.] Sydney, Angus & Robertson, 1956. vii, 503p. 26cm. 1st published in 1940 with title: Australian literature, from its beginnings... to 1938. Includes considerable biographical material.

3517 MILLETT, FRED BENJAMIN, 1890-
Contemporary British literature; a critical survey and 232 author-bibliographies. 3d rev. and enl. ed., based on the 2d rev. and enl. ed. by John M. Manly and Edith Rickert. New York, Harcourt, Brace, 1935. xi, 556p. 20cm.

3518 MORGAN, HENRY JAMES, 1842-1913.
Bibliotheca Canadensis; or, A manual of Canadian literature. Ottawa, Printed by G. E. Desbarats, 1867. xiv, 411p. 25cm.

3519 A NEW CATALOGUE OF LIVING ENGLISH AUTHORS:
With complete lists of their publications and biographical and critical memoirs. Vol. I[A-Charlton] London, Printed for C. Clarke, 1799. xvi, 462 p. 22cm. No more published.

3520 THE NEW CENTURY HANDBOOK OF ENGLISH LITERATURE,
Edited by Clarence L. Barnhart, with the assistance of William D. Halsey. New York, Appleton-Century-Crofts [1956] vii, 1167 p. 25cm.

3521 NEW ZEALAND AUTHORS' WEEK COMMITTEE.
Annals of New Zealand literature; being a preliminary list of New Zealand authors and their works, with introductory essays and verses. [n.p.] 1936. 117 p. illus., ports. 24cm. Includes an alphabetical list of New Zealand authors (p. 35-93)

3522 NICHOLS, JOHN, 1745-1826.
Literary anecdotes of the eighteenth century; comprizing biographical memoirs of Wm. Bowyer, printer, and many of his learned friends: an incidental view of the progress of literature in this kingdom during the last century; and biographical anecdotes of a considerable number of eminent writers and ingenious artists: with a very copious index. London, Printed for the author by Nichols and Bentley, 1812-16. 9 v. illus., ports. 23cm. Contains much biographical material, especially of fairly obscure figures; the "copious index" in vol. 7 is the

means of finding a particular person quickly, since there is no alphabetical arrangement within any of the volumes.

3523   O'DONOGHUE, DAVID JAMES, 1866-1917.
The poets of Ireland; a biographical and bibliographical dictionary of Irish writers of English verse. Dublin, Hodges, Figgis, 1912. iv, 504 p. 25cm.

3524   PARKER, WILLIAM MATHIE, 1891-
Modern Scottish writers. Edinburgh, W. Hodge, 1917. 255 p. 8.°

3525   PHILLIPS, EDWARD, 1630-1696?
Theatrum poetarum Anglicarum. Containing the name and characters of all the English poets, from the reign of Henry III. to the close of the reign of Queen Elizabeth. First published in 1675, and now enlarged by additions... from subsequent biographers and critics. Canterbury, Printed by Simmons and Kirkby, for J. White, London, 1800. lxxix, 336, 6 p. 21cm. Edited by Sir Samuel Egerton Brydges.

3526   PITS, JOHN, 1560-1616.
Ioannis Pitsei Angli Relationum historicarum de rebus Anglicis, tonus primus quatuor partes complectens, quorum elenchum pagina sequens indicat. Parisiis, Apud Rolinum Thierry, & Sebastianum Cramoisy, 1619. 990p. 24cm. Edited, with a preface, by William Bishop, after the author's death. No more published. Running title of the second and principal part: De illustribus Angliae scriptoribus (i. e., About illustrious writers of England)

3527   PORTRAITS OF THE BRITISH POETS.
London, W. Walker, 1824. 2 v. in l. 137 ports. 25cm.

3528   PRINCIPAL POETS OF THE WORLD;
Being the biography, detailed bibliography, and a representative poem of... leading poets of the English-speaking countries. London, Mitre Press, 1932-   2 v. 25cm. Editor-in-chief: William K. Fudge. Only 2 vols. published, 1932 & 1938?

3529   REUSS, JEREMIAS DAVID, 1750-1837.
Alphabetical register of all the authors actually living in Great-Britain, Ireland and in the United Provinces of North-

America, with a catalogue of their publications. From the year 1770 to the year 1790. [With supplement and continuation for 1790 to 1803] Berlin, Nicolai, 1791-1804. 3 v. Issued also in German under title: Das gelehrte England; oder, Lexicon der jetzt lebenden Schriftsteller in Grossbritannien.

3530   [RITSON, JOSEPH] 1752-1803.
       Bibliographia poetica; a catalogue of English poets, of the twelfth, thirteenth, fourteenth, fifteenth, and sixteenth, centurys, with a short account of their works. London, Printed by C. Roworth for G. and W. Nicol, 1802. 407 (i. e. 411) p. 19cm. "Poets, natives of Engleland; who wrote in Latin or French": p. [399]- [402]

3531   [RIVERS DAVID]
       Literary memoirs of living authors of Great Britain, arranged according to an alphabetical catalogue of their names; and including a list of their works, with occasional opinions upon their literary character. London, Printed for R. Faulder, 1798. 2 v. 21cm.

3532   RUSSELL, JOSIAH COX
       Dictionary of writers of thirteenth century England. London, New York, Longmans, Green [1936] x, 209p. 25cm. (Bulletin of the Institute of Historical Research. Special supplement, no. 3)

3533   SHARP, ROBERT FARQUHARSON, 1864-
       A dictionary of English authors, biographical and bibliographical. Being a compendious account of the lives and writings of upwards of 800 British and American writers from the year 1400 to the present time. New ed. (rev.) with an appendix bringing the whole up to date and including a large amount of new matter. London, K. Paul, Trench, Trübner, 1904. 363 p. 21cm.

3534   SPENDER, STEPHEN, 1909-   ed.
       The concise encyclopedia of English and American poets and poetry, edited by Stephen Spender and Donald Hall. [1st ed.] New York, Hawthorn Books [1963] 415 p. ports. 26cm.

3535   SUTTON, CHARLES WILLIAM, 1848-
       A list of Lancashire authors, with brief biographical and bibliographical notes. Manchester, A. Heywood, 1876.

vii, 164p. 23cm. (Publications of the Manchester Literary Club, no. 7) Begun by John Howard Nodal and William Edward Armytage Axon.

3536 SYLVESTRE, GUY, ed.
Canadian writers; a biographical dictionary edited by Guy Sylvestre, Brandon Conron [and] Carl F. Klinck. Écrivains canadiens; un dictionnaire biographique. [1st ed.] Toronto, Ryerson Press [1964] xvi, 163p. 25cm. English or French.

3537 TANNER, THOMAS, Bp. of St. Asaph, 1674-1735.
Bibliotheca Brittanico-Hibernica; sive, De scriptoribus, qui in Anglia, Scotia, et Hibernia ad saeculi XVII initium floruerunt, literarum ordine juxta familiarum nomina dispositis commentarius: auctore Thoma Tannero, qui non tantum scriptores quam plurimos, a Lelando, Baleo, Pitseo et aliis praetermissos, e codicibus mss. nunc primum in lucem protulit; sed notis etiam uberioribus, tum omissa supplevit, tum parum fideliter tradita correxit et ilustravit. Opus utilissimum, et XL annorum studio ac industria elaboratum. Praefixa est Davidis Wilkinsii. Praefatio, historiam literariam Britannorum ante Caesaris adventum, bibliothecae hujus schema, Bostonum Buriensem, aliaque scitu no indigna complectens. Tucson, Audax Press, 1963. xlvii, 788p. port. 34cm. Facsimile reproduction of 1748 ed. British-Hibernian library; or, Writers who flourished in England, Scotland and Ireland up to the beginning of the 17th century.

3538 THOMAS, CLARA
Canadian novelists, 1920-1945. Toronto, New York, Longmans, Green [1946] 129p. 21cm. 122 authors represented.

3539 WALPOLE, HORACE, Earl of Orford, 1717-1797.
A catalogue of the royal and noble authors of England, Scotland and Ireland; with lists of their works. Enlarged and continued to the present time by Thomas Park. London, J. Scott, 1806. 5 v. illus. 22cm. The 1st ed., in 2 vols., was printed at Strawberry Hill in 1758.

3540 WATT, HOMER ANDREW, 1884-
A dictionary of English literature; authors, anonymous works, literary terms, versification, chronology, by Homer A. Watt and William W. Watt. New York, Barnes & Noble, 1945. viii, 430 p. 24cm. The 1st of 5 parts is a dictionary of authors (about 900)

3541   WATT, ROBERT, 1774-1819.
Bibliotheca Britannica; or, A general index to British and foreign literature. Edinburgh, A. Constable, 1824. 4 v. 29cm. The first 2 volumes are arranged alphabetically by author, with brief biographical notes.

3542   WHINCOP, THOMAS, d. 1730.
Scanderbeg; or, Love and liberty. A tragedy. To which are added: A list of all the dramatic authors with some account of their lives; and of all the dramatic pieces ever published in the English language, to the year 1747. London, W. Reeve, 1747. xix, 320, [30] p. illus. 21cm. John Mottley is the reputed author of the "Compleat list of all the English dramatic poets" (p. 87-320)

3543   WHO'S WHO IN ENGLISH-SPEAKING POETS.
Los Angeles, National Poetry Association [1958] 140p. 23cm. On spine: English speaking poets.

3544   WHO'S WHO IN LITERATURE
(1924-1934 ed.) A continuance of the bibliographical section of the Literary year book (founded 1897) Liverpool, Literary Year Books Press. llv. 22cm. annual. British authors.

3545   WHO'S WHO IN PRESS, PUBLICITY, PRINTING.
1939-   ed. London, Cosmopolitan Press.   v. 23cm. British journalists, advertising agents and printers.

3546   WRIGHT, WILLIAM HENRY KEARLEY, 1844-1915.
West-Country poets: their lives and works. Being an account of about four hundred verse writers of Devon and Cornwall, with poems and extracts. London, E. Stock, 1896. viii, 488, 4 p. ports. 26cm.

Finno — Ugrian

3547   KUZNETSOVA, A   G
Pisateli Sovetskoĭ Mordovii; bibliograficheskiĭ spravochnik. Saransk, Mordovskoe knizhnoe izd-vo, 1958. 107 p. illus. 21cm. 42 writers of the Mordovskaya A. S. S. R. (Soviet Mordovia)

3548   PISATELI KOMI ASSR.
[Sostavitel' G. I. Torlopov. Syktyvkar] Komi knizhnoe

izd-vo, 1961. 150p. ports. 17cm. Writers of the Komi
ASSR, Russia, in the Syryenian language.

3549 PISATELI SOVETSKOĬ ESTONII.
    Tallinn, Ėstonskoe gos. izd-vo, 1950. 120p. ports. 20cm.
Writers of Soviet Estonia.

3550 PISATELI UDMURTII;
    Biobibliograficheskiĭ spravochnik. [Izhevsk] Udmurtskoe
knizhnoe izd-vo, 1963. 154 p. ports. 17cm. 53 writers in the
Votiak language of the Udmurt Soviet Socialist Republic.

3551 REMMELGAS, L
    Pisateli Sovetskoĭ Estonii; kratkiĭ biograficheskiĭ spra-
vochnik. [Perevod s ėstonskogo] Tallinn, Ėstonskoe gos.
izd-vo, 1956. 268p. ports. 18cm. About 83 writers of
Soviet Estonia.

French

3552 ANSART, LOUIS JOSEPH AUGUSTE, 1748-1823.
    Bibliothèque littéraire du Maine; ou, Traité historique
et critique des auteurs de cette province. Tome premier.
Chalons-sur-Marne, Pavier [etc.] 1784. xv, 404p. 21cm.
Literary library of the department of the Maine. A bio-bibliographical work; only one volume, covering A-B, was published.

3553 ASSOCIATION DES ÉCRIVAINS COMBATTANTS.
    Anthologie des écrivains morts à la guerre, 1914-1918.
Amiens, Malfère, 1924-26. 5v. 22cm. The bio-bibliographical notes include many minor figures in early 20th
century French literature.

3554 ASSOCIATION DES ÉCRIVAINS COMBATTANTS.
    Anthologie des écrivains morts à la guerre, 1939-1945.
Pref. du maréchal Juin. Paris, Michel [1960] viii, 796p.
22cm. Includes biographical sketches and some bibliographies of the authors, Frenchmen who died in World War
II. A companion volume to Anthologie des écrivains morts à
la guerre, 1914-1918.

3555 BARBEAU, VICTOR, 1896-
    La Société des écrivains canadiens: ses règlements, son
action, bio-bibliographie de ses membres. Montréal,
Éditions de la Société des écrivains canadiens, 1944. 117p.

20cm. Includes bio-bibliography of members of the Society of Canadian Authors. French-Canadian littérateurs.

3556 BEUCHOT, ADRIEN JEAN QUENTIN, 1777-1851.
Nouveau nécrologe francais; ou, Liste alphabétique des auteurs nés en France ou qui ont écrit en francais, morts depuis le premier janvier 1800. Paris, Guitel, 1812. 48p. 8.° Necrology of French writers, 1800-1812.

3557 B OISDEFFRE, PIERRE DE, ed.
Dictionnaire de littérature contemporaine, 1900-1962 [par] R. M. Albérès [et al. 1. ed.] Paris, Éditions universitaires [1962] 679 p. ports. 22cm. A dictionary of 20th century French literature.

3558 BRAUN, SIDNEY DAVID, 1912- ed.
Dictionary of French literature. New York, Philosophical Library [1958] xiii, 362 p. ports. 22cm.

3559 CHÉRON, PAUL, 1819-1881.
Catalogue générale de la librairie francaise au XIXe siècle, indiquant, per ordre alphabétique, de noms d'auteurs des ouvrages publiés en France du 1er janvier 1800 au 31 décembre 1855. Paris, Au Bureau de la Propriété littéraire, Courrier de la librairie, et chez P. Jannet, 1856-59. 3 v. 26 cm. Includes brief biographical data. Issued as a premium to subscribers of Courrier de la librairie. Extends only as far as Dubuisson. Bio-bibliographical for French literature, 1801-1855.

3560 CHESNEL, ADOLPHE DE, 1791-1862.
Biographie des femmes auteurs contemporaines francais, avec portraits dessinés d'après nature par J. Boilly, et sous la direction de A. de Montferrand [pseud.] Paris, 1836. 1 v. 8.° and atlas (of ports. ?) in folio. Biography of contemporary Frenchwomen as authors, with portraits.

3561 COOPER, CLARISSA BURNHAM, 1897-
Women poets of the twentieth century in France; a critical bibliography. New York, King's Crown Press, 1943. 317 p.

3562 [CUISIN, J   P   R   ] 1777-ca.1845.
Dictionnaire des gens de lettres vivants. Par un descendant de Rivarol. Paris, Chez les Marchands de nouveautés,

1826. xiii, 285 p. 18.° By Cuisin and G. L. Brismontier according to Quérard. Dictionary of French littérateurs living in 1826.

3563   [DEBRAY, NICOLAS ANTOINE GABRIEL] b. 1756.
    Tablettes biographiques des écrivains francais, depuis la renaissance des lettres, jusqu'à ce jour; le lieu, l'époque, de leur naissance et de leur mort; le genre dans lequel ils se sont distingués, leurs productions marquantes, les éditions estimées et recherchées de leurs oeuvres. Par N. A. G. D. B. Paris, G. A. Debray, 1810. 2 pts. in 1 v. 21cm. Bio-bibliography of French literature, authors living and dead. Pt. 1: Écrivains morts. Pt. 2: Écrivains vivans. 1st published 1809 under title: Tableau des écrivains francais, par E. N. F. D. S. [i. e. Antoine Nicolas Étienne Fantin des Odoars? or E. N. F. de Santeul?] Authorship claimed by Debray in this 2d edition, pt. 2, p. 37.

3564   DESESSARTS, NICOLAS TOUSSAINT LEMOYNE, 1744-1810.
    Les siècles littéraires de la France; ou, Nouveau dictionnaire, historique, critique, et bibliographique de tous les écrivains français, morts et vivans, jusqu'à la fin du XVIIIe siècle. Contenant: 1.° Les principaux traits de la vie des auteurs morts, avec des jugemens sur leurs ouvrages; 2.° Des notices bibliographiques sur les auteurs vivans; 3.° L'indication des différentes éditions qui ont paru de tous les livres français, de l'année où ils ont été publiés, et du lieu où ils ont été imprimés. Par N. -L. -M. Desessarts, et plusieurs biographes. Paris, Chez l'auteur, an VIII (1800)-an XI (1803) 7 v. 21cm. In part a bio-bibliographical dictionary of French literature.

3565   DICTIONNAIRE DES AUTEURS FRANCAIS.
    Nouv. éd. completée. [Paris, Seghers, 1961] 505 p. ports. 16cm. (Dictionnaire Seghers, 1) Collection Seghers. Another (1st?) ed. published in 1961 has collation: 445 p. Dictionary of French authors.

3566   DICTIONNAIRE DES AUTEURS FRANCAIS.
    [Paris, J. Tallandier, 1965] 355 p. 21cm. (Le Trésor des lettres francaises) Dictionary of French authors.

3567   DICTIONNAIRE DES LETTRES FRANCAISES;
    Publié sous la direction de Georges Grente [et al.] Paris, A. Fayard, 1951-   v. in   28cm. A dictionary of French literature and literary biography.

3568   [DINAUX, ARTHUR MARTIN] 1795-1864.
Trouvères, jongleurs et ménestrels du nord de la France
et du midi de la Belgique. [Paris, Téchener, 1837-63] 4v.
illus. 25cm.   Bio-bibliography and anthology of trouvères
(medieval poets) & minstrels of Northern France & Southern
Belgium.

3569   DUJARDIN-SAILLY,
Liste alphabétique des auteurs morts jusqu'en 1805. Paris,
Dujardin-Sailly, 1805. 131p. 8.º Deceased French authors
up to 1805; an alphabetical list.

3570   ERSCH, JOHANN SAMUEL, 1766-1828.
La France littéraire, contenant les auteurs francais de 1771
à 1796. Hambourg, B. G. Hoffmann, 1797-98. 3 v. 21 cm.
Added t. p. : Das gelehrte Frankreich; oder, Lexicon der
französischen Schriftsteller.

3571   ----Supplément, contenant outre les additions et
corrections, les nouveaux articles jusqu'en 1800.
Hambourg, B. G. Hoffmann, 1802. xiii, 600 p. 22 cm.
Added t. p. in German.

3572   ----Second supplément, contenant outre les corrections et
additions au corps de l'ouvrage et au premier supplément
les nouveaux articles jusqu'en 1805. Hambourg, B. G.
Hoffmann, 1806. vi, 592 p. 22 cm. Added t. p. in German.

Dictionary of French authors flourishing 1771-1805.

3573   LA FRANCE LITTÉRAIRE,
Contenant, I. Les académies établies à Paris & dans les
différentes villes du royaume. II. Les auteurs vivans, avec
la liste de leurs ouvrages. III. Les auteurs morts, depuis
l'année 1751 inclusivement, avec la liste de leurs ouvrages.
IV. Le catalogue alphabétique des ouvrages de tous ces auteurs. Paris, Chez la veuve Duchesne, 1769. 2 v. 18cm.
Literary France. Pt. 2—bio-bibliography of living French
authors (18th century) Pt. 3—Deceased authors (after 1751
inclusive) with list of their works.

3574   LA FRANCE LITTÉRAIRE;
Ou, Dictionnaire des auteurs françois vivans. Corr. et
augm. par M. Formey. Berlin, Haude et Spener, 1757.
xiv, 344p. 19cm. Literary France; or, Dictionary of living
French authors (18th century) First edition, by J. de Laporte,
published anonymously in 1756. Supplements were issued in

1760, 1762 and 1764. The whole was incorporated in a work
of the same title published anonymously by J. Hébrail and
Laporte in 1769 (2 v.); supplements issued 1778 and 1784.

3575   GOUJET, CLAUDE PIERRE, 1697-1767.
Bibliothèque françoise; ou, Histoire de la littérature françoise... des livres, publiés en françois, depuis l'origine de
l'imprimerie. Paris, P. J. Mariette [&] H. -L. Guerin,
1741-56. 18 v. 17cm. Bio-bibliographical, in part, for
French literature; books published in French, from the origin of printing. Index for 2 volumes in every other volume.

3576   GUYOT DE FÈRE, FORTUNÉ, 1791-1866.
Biographie et dictionnaire des littérateurs et des savants
francais contemporains, bibliographie, travaux littéraires
et scientifiques. Paris, Au Bureau du Journal des arts, des
sciences et des lettres, 1859-62. 2 v. (?) 4.º No more
published? Bio-bibliography -- French literature of the 19th
century.

3577   GUYOT DE FÈRE, FORTUNÉ, 1791-1866.
Statistique des lettres et des sciences en France... Dic-
tionnaire des hommes de lettres, des savants existant en
France. Paris, 1834-35. 2 v. 8.º Contents. --t. 1.
Paris. --t. 2. Département. Dictionary of contemporary
French littérateurs.

3578   HARVEY, Sir PAUL, 1869-1948, ed.
The Oxford companion to French literature. Compiled
and edited by Sir Paul Harvey and J. E. Heseltine. Oxford,
Clarendon Press, 1959. x, 771p. maps. 24cm.

3579   JOLIETTE, QUEBEC. SÉMINAIRE.
Les anciens du Séminaire: écrivains et artistes.
Joliette [1927] 212, xiv p. 22cm. Alumni of the Seminary at
Joliette, Quebec: writers and artists.

3580   LORENZ, OTTO HENRI, 1831-1895.
Catalogue général de la librairie française. Paris, 1867-
1945. 34 v. 25cm. Covers period 1840-1925. Title varies.
Vols. 1-11 edited by O. Lorenz; v. 12-27 edited by D. Jordell;
v. 28- edited by Henri Stein. Bio-bibliographical. A continuation of J. M. Quérard's La France littéraire... pendant
les XVIIIe et XIXe siècles and Littérature française contemporaine, 1827-1849.

3581   MARTIN, JULES, 1860-
Nos auteurs et compositeurs dramatiques. Portraits et
biographies, suivies d'une notice sur les sociétés d'auteurs,
droits, règlements, statistique et sur les transformations de
l'affiche théâtrale. Préf. par Maurice Donnay. Paris, E.
Flammarion, 1897. 623 p. illus., ports. 14 x 11cm. Bio-
bibliography of French drama.

3582   MONSELET, CHARLES, 1825-1888.
La lorgnette littéraire; dictionnaire des grands et des
petits auteurs de mon temps. Paris, Poulet-Malassis et de
Broisse, 1857. xviii, 240p. 17cm. Dictionary of French authors of the 19th century.

3583   MOURIER, ATHÉNAÏS, 1815-1889.
Notice sur le doctorat és lettres, suivie du catalogue et de
l'analyse des thèses françaises et latines admises par les
facultés des lettres depuis 1810, avec index et table alphabétique des docteurs, par Ath. Mourier et F. Deltour. 4.
éd., corr. et considérablement augm. Paris, Delalain
frères, 1880. xii, 442p. 25cm.

3584   ---- ----Catalogue et analyse des thèses latines et françaises.
Paris, Delalain frères, 1882-1901. 21 v.

Contains very brief biographical data for writers of doctoral
theses in literature at French universities.

3585   PINGAUD, BERNARD, ed.
Écrivains d'aujourd'hui, 1940-1960; dictionnaire antholo-
gique et critique, établi sous la direction de Bernard Pingaud.
Paris, B. Grasset [1960] 535p. ports. 22cm. French
writers, 1940-1960.

3586   PAPILLON, PHILIBERT, 1666-1738.
Bibliothèque des auteurs de Bourgogne. Dijon, F. Des-
venters, 1745. 2 v. port. 38cm. Library of the authors of
Burgundy. A bio-bibliography.

3587   [PIGOREAU, ALEXANDRE NICOLAS] 1765-1851.
Petite bibliographie biographico-romanciere; ou, Dictionnaire des romanciers, tants anciens que modernes, tant
nationaux qu'étrangers; avec un mot sur chacun d'eux, et la
notice des romans qu'ils ont donnés, soit comme auteurs,
soit comme traducteurs... Paris, Pigoreau, 1821. 354p.
21cm.

3588 ---- ----Premier [-vingtième] supplément. Paris, Pigoreau, 1821-31. 29 v. in 1. 21cm.

Brief biographical data are included in this bibliography of French fiction and romances.

3589 QUÉRARD, JOSEPH MARIE, 1797-1865.
La France littéraire; ou, Dictionnaire bibliographique des savants, historiens et gens de lettres de la France, ainsi que des littérateurs étrangers qui ont écrit en français, plus particulièrement pendant les XVIIIᵉ et XIXᵉ siècles. Paris, F. Didot, 1827-64. 12 v. 22cm. Bio-bibliographical dictionary of French literature. Continued by the author's Littérature française contemporaine, 1842-57.

3590 QUÉRARD, JOSEPH MARIE, 1797-1865.
La littérature française contemporaine. XIXe siècle. Le tout accompagné de notes biographiques et littéraires. Paris, Daguin [etc.] 1842-57. 6 v. 22cm. Biographical notes on French authors of the 1st half of the 19th century. Continuation of the author's La France littéraire. Vol. 1 to v. 2, p. 282, by Quérard; the remainder by L. F. Bourquelot: v. 2, p. 282-v. 4, p. 35, with the assistance of C. Louandre; v. 4, p. 369-v. 5, p. 496, with the assistance of F. A. Maurs. Title varies. Vol. 1 first appeared under title: La littérature francaise contemporaine, 1827-1840 [etc.] (Paris, Daguin, 1840)

3591 [RIVAROL, ANTOINE] 1753-1801.
Le petit almanach de nos grands hommes. 1788. [Paris, 1788] 236p. 15cm. By Rivarol and the Marquis de Champcenetz. The little almanac of our great men (i. e. French authors)

3592 [SAINTE-PALAYE, JEAN BAPTISTE DE LA CURNE DE] 1697-1781.
Histoire littéraire des troubadours, contenant leurs vies, les extraits de leurs pieces... Paris, Durand neveu, 1774. 3 v. 12.º Arranged and published anonymously by C. F. X. Millot from materials collected by La Curne de Sainte-Palaye. An [abbreviated] English translation was issued in 1779 under title: The Literary history of the troubadours (xxiv, 495p.) Lives of the troubadours with selections from their works.

3593   SOCIÉTÉ DES ÉCRIVAINS CANADIENS, Montreal.
Répertoire bio-bibliographique, 1954. Montréal [1955]
xviii, 248 p. illus., ports. 20cm. Bio-bibliographical
repertoire [of French-Canadian literature] 1954.

3594   TALVART, HECTOR
Bibliographie des auteurs modernes de langue francaise
(1801-19) par Hector Talvart et Joseph Place. Paris, Éditions de la Chronique des lettres français, 1928-   v.
26cm. Bio-bibliographical; modern authors writing in the
French language, 1801-

3595   THIEME, HUGO PAUL, 1870-1940.
Bibliographie de la littérature française de 1800 à 1930.
Paris, E. Droz, 1933. 3 v. 26cm. A bio-bibliography of
French literature, 1800-1930. A rev. and enl. ed. of the au-
thor's Guide bibliographique de la littérature francaise de
1800 à 1906. Paris, 1907.

3596   LAS VIDAS DELS TROBADORS.
Biographies des troubadours [textes provencaux des XIIIe
et XIVe siècles] By Jean Boutière [and] A.-H. Schutz.
[Limited ed.] Toulouse, E. Privat; [distributed in the U.S.
by Ohio State University, Columbus] 1950 [c1949] xxxii,
451p. 21cm. ([Ohio. State University, Columbus] Contributions in languages and literatures, no. 14. Romance languages [i.e. language] series, 3) Lives of the troubadours in
Provencal texts of the 13th-14th centuries.

Frisian

3597   SUFFRIDUS, PETRUS, 1527-1597.
De scriptoribus Frisiae decades XVI et semis: in quibus
non modo peculiares Frisiae, sed et totius Germaniae com-
munes antiquitates plurimae indicantur, et veterum histori-
corum ac geographorum loci hactenus non intellecti expli-
cantur... Coloniae Agrippinae, 1593. 1 v. 8.° The writers
of Friesland thru' 16 and a half decades.

Gaelic

3598   MACKENZIE, JOHN, 1806-1848.
Sar-obair nam bard gaelach; or, The beauties of Gaelic
poetry, and lives of the Highland bards. With historical and
critical notes, and a comprehensive glossary of provincial

words. With an historical introd. containing an account of the
manners, habits, etc., of the ancient Caledonians, by James
Logan. New ed. Edinburgh, N. Macleod, 1904. viii, lxvi,
408 p. front. 26cm. 1st published 1841.

3599 MACLEAN, DONALD, 1869-
Typographia Scoto-Gadelica; or, Books printed in the Gaelic
of Scotland, from the year 1567 to the year 1914, with bibliographical and biographical notes. Edinburgh, J. Grant, 1915.
x, 372 p. 27cm. Some of the authors listed are identified
in brief notes at the end of the bibliographical data under their
names.

3600 REID, JOHN, 1808-1841?
Bibliotheca Scoto-Celtica; or, An account of all the books
which have been printed in the Gaelic language. With bibliographical and biographical notices. Glasgow, J. Reid, 1832.
lxxii, 178p. 22cm.

Gallegan

3601 COUCEIRO FREIJOMIL, ANTONIO
Diccionario bio-bibliográfico de escritores. Santiago de
Compostela, Editorial de los Bibliófilos Gallegos, 1951-54.
3v. (Enciclopedia Gallega, 1) Bio-bibliographical dictionary
of writers of Galicia, Spain (Gallegan literature)

3602 MURGUÍA, MANUEL, 1833-1923.
Diccionario de escritores gallegos. Vigo, Compañel,
1862. xxxii, 232 p. 4.° A dictionary of Gallegan (Galicia
Spain) writers. Only a few fascicles were published. Goes
up to Freire (Antonio)

German

3603 ALBERTI, EDUARD CHRISTIAN SCHARLAU, 1827-1898.
Lexikon der Schleswig-Holstein-Lauenbergischen und
Eutinischen Schriftsteller. Kiel, C. G. L. v. Maack, 1867-
86. 4v. in 2. 22cm. Forms a continuation to Lübker and
Schröder's Lexicon der Schleswig-Holstein-Lauenbergischen
und Eutinischen Schriftsteller von 1796 bis 1828. Altona,
1829-31. Vol. [2] has imprint: Kiel, K. Biernatzki. Contents.
--[1-2] 1829 bis Mitte 1866.--[3-4] 1866-1882. Dictionary of
authors in Schleswig-Holstein, Lauenberg and Eutin.

3604   ALBRECHT, GÜNTER
Deutsches Schriftstellerlexikon von den Anfängen bis zur
Gegenwart, von Günter Albrecht [et al. Weimar] Volksverlag
Weimar, 1963. xii, 732p. 19cm. Dictionary of German
authors from the oldest period to the present.

3605   BAADER, CLEMENS ALOIS, 1762-1838.
Das gelehrte Baiern; oder, Lexikon aller Schriftsteller,
welche Baiern im achtzehnten Jahrhunderte erzeugte oder
ernährte. Bd. 1: [A-K] Nürnberg, 1804. viii, 658p. 4.°
Scholarly Bavaria; or, Dictionary of all writers that Bavaria
produced or nourished in the 18th century.

3606   BAADER, CLEMENS ALOIS, 1762-1838.
Lexikon verstorbener baierischer Schriftsteller des
achtzehenten und neunzehenten Jahrhunderts. Augsburg, In
der Von Jenisch- und Stage'schen Buchhandlung, 1824-25.
2v. 21cm. Each vol. issued in 2 parts. A 3d vol. was
announced but never published. A dictionary of deceased
Bavarian writers of the 18th and 19th centuries.

3607   [BEHRISCH, HEINRICH WOLFGANG] 1744-1825.
Die Wiener Autoren. Ein Beytrag zum Gelehrten
Deutschland. Wien, Löwe, 1784. 271p. 17cm. Authors of
Vienna. Includes a pseudonymous list.

3608   BIEDERSTEDT, DIEDERICH HERMANN, 1762-1824.
Nachrichten von den jetzt lebenden Schriftstellern in
Neuvorpommern und Rügen. Stralsund, In der Königl.
Regierungs-Buchhandlung, 1822. xii, 168p. 21cm. Notes on
writers now living in Pomerania and Rügen.

3609   BÖCKH, FRANZ HEINRICH.
Wiens lebende Schriftsteller, Künstler und Dilettanten im
Kunstfache. Neue wohlf. Ausg. Wien, Tendler, 1822-23.
2 v. Also published under title: Merkwürdigkeiten der Haupt-
und Residenzstadt Wien und ihrer nächsten Umgebungen, 1823.
2 v.   Authors and artists residing in Vienna in the early years
of the 19th century.

3610   BRUCKER, JOHANN JAKOB, 1696-1770.
Bilder-Sal heutiges Tages lebender und durch Gelahrheit
berühmter Schrift-Steller; in welchem derselbigen nach
wahren Original-Malereyen entworfene Bildnisse in schwarzen
Kunst in natürlicher Aehnlichkeit vorgestellet und ihre Lebens-

Umstände verdienste um die Wissenschafften und Schrifften aus
glaubwürdigen Nachrichten erzählet werden, von Jacob Brucker
und Johann Jacob Haid. Erstes [-zehntes] Zehend. Augspurg,
J. J. Haid, 1741-55. 10 pts. in 2 v. 100 ports. 38 cm. Also
published in Latin, 1741-55 (under title: Pinacotheca scriptorum
nostra aetate literis illustrium?)   A portrait gallery,
with bio-bibliographical data, of famous writers of German
origin.

3611   BRÜMMER, FRANZ, 1836-1923.
        Deutsches Dichter-Lexikon. Biographische und
bibliographische Mittheilungen über deutsche Dichter aller
Zeiten. Unter besonderer Berücksichtigung der Gegenwart,
für Freunde der Literatur zusammengestellt. Eichstätt, H.
Hugendubel, 1876-77. 2 v. 24 cm.

3612   ----Nachtrag. Eichstätt, H. Hugendubel, 1877. 140 p.
        24 cm.

        Dictionary of German authors of all times.

3613   BRÜMMER, FRANZ, 1836-1923.
        Lexikon der deutschen Dichter und Prosaisten vom
Beginn des 19. Jahrhunderts bis zur Gegenwart. 6. völlig
neu bearb. und stark verm. Aufl. Leipzig, P. Reclam Jun.
[1913] 8 v. 15 cm. 9900 German, Austrian & Swiss authors.

3614   BRÜMMER, FRANZ, 1836-1923.
        Lexikon der deutschen Dichter und Prosaisten von den
ältesten Zeiten bis zum Ende des 18. Jahrhunderts. Leipzig,
P. Reclam, Jun. [1884] 612 p. 14 cm. (Reclam's Universal-
Bibliothek, Nr. 1941-1945)   Dictionary of German poets and
prose writers from the oldest times to the end of the 18th
century.

3615   DENINA, CARLO, 1731-1813.
        La Prusse littéraire sous Frédéric II; ou, Histoire abrégée
de la plupart des auteurs, des académiciens et des artistes
qui sont nés ou qui ont vécu dans les États prussiens depuis
MDCCXL jusqu'à MDCCLXXXVI. [Avec Supplément] Berlin,
1790-91. 3 v. 8.° Writers native to or residing in Prussia,
1740-1786.

3616   DEUTSCH-ÖSTERREICHISCHES KÜNSTLER- UND
        SCHRIFTSTELLER-LEXIKON. Wien, Gesellschaft für
Graphische Industrie, 1902-05. 2 v. 23cm. Contents. --

1. Biographien der Wiener Künstler und Schriftsteller. Redigiert von P. G. Rheinhardt auf Grundlage von Ludwig Eisenberg's "Das geistige Wien."--2. Biographien und Bibliographie der deutschen Künstler und Schriftsteller in Österreich-Ungarn ausser Wien. Mit Nachträgen für Wien. Hrsg. von V. A. Reko und Heinr. Bohrmann der Jüngere. Dictionary of German-Austrian artists and writers.

3617 ECKART, RUDOLF, 1861-
Lexikon der niedersächsischen Schriftsteller von den ältesten Zeiten bis zur Gegenwart. Osterwieck, Harz, A. W. Zickfeldt, [1891] 181 p. 27 cm. Covers Hannover, Schleswig-Holstein, Mecklenburg and the bordering small states; dictionary of writers native to these regions of Northern Germany

3618 FIKENSCHER, GEORG WOLFGANG AUGUSTIN, 1773-1813.
Gelehrtes Fürstenthum Baireut; oder, Biographische und literarische Nachrichten von allen Schriftstellern, welche in dem Fürstenthum Baireut geboren sind und in oder ausser demselben gelebet haben und noch leben, in alphabetischer Ordnung. 2., ganz umgearb., verm. und verb. Aufl. Erlangen, In Commission bei I. I. Palm [etc.] 1801-05. 12 v. in 3. 21 cm. Vols. 1-2 only are 2d ed. Biographical dictionary of writers native to the principality of Bayreuth.

3619 FRENZEL, HERBERT ALFRED, 1908-   ed.
Daten deutscher Dichtung; chronologischer Abriss der deutschen Literaturgeschichte von den Anfängen bis zur Gegenwart. Unter Mitarbeit mehrerer Fachgenossen hrsg. von Herbert A. Frenzel. Köln, Kiepenheuer & Witsch [1953] xii, 444 p. 21 cm. Each section preceded by a brief description of the literary history of the period covered and by biographical sketches of the most important German writers of the period.

3620 GEISSLER, MAX, 1868-
Führer durch die deutsche Literatur des zwanzigsten Jahrhunderts. Weimar, A. Duncker, 1913. 755 p. 20cm. Guide thru' 20th century German literature; includes bio-bibliographies.

3621 GERMANY (DEMOCRATIC REPUBLIC, 1949-   ) ZENTRAL-INSTITUT FÜR BIBLIOTHEKSWESEN.
Schriftsteller der Deutschen Demokratischen Republik und ihre Werke; biographisch-bibliographischer Nachweis. [Erarbeitet unter Mitarbeit von Hilde Weise-Standfest] Leipzig,

Verlag für Buch- und Bibliothekswesen [1955] 249 p. 15cm.
Writers of the German Democratic Republic and their works.

3622 GIEBISCH, HANS, 1888-
Bio-bibliographisches Literaturlexikon Österreichs von
den Anfängen bis zur Gegenwart [von] Hans Giebisch [und]
Gustav Gugitz. Wien, Brüder Hollinek [1964] viii, 516 p.
25cm. Bio-bibliographical dictionary of Austrian literature,
past and present.

3623 GIEBISCH, HANS, 1888- ed.
Kleines österreichisches Literaturlexikon, hrsg. von H.
Giebisch, L. Pichler und K. Vancsa. Wien, Hollinek, 1948.
viii, 550 p. 20cm. (Buchreihe "Österreichische Heimat, "
Bd. 8) Dictionary of Austrian literature; bio-bibliographical.

3624 GOEDEKE, KARL, 1814-1887.
Grundriss zur Geschichte der deutschen Dichtung, aus den
Quellen. 2. ganz neu bearb. Aufl. Dresden, L. Ehlermann,
1884-19 14v. 24cm. 1st ed. appeared in 1859-1881 in
3 vols. Vols. 4- continued, with the aid of specialists,
by E. Goetze. Vols. 9- edited by Alfred Rosenbaum.
Includes bio-bibliographical data for German authors.

3625 GOEDEKE, KARL, 1814-1887.
Grundriss zur Geschichte der deutschen Dichtung aus den
Quellen. 3. neu bearb. Aufl. nach dem Tode des Verfassers
in Verbindung mit Fachgelehrten fortgeführt von Edmund
Goetze. Dresden, L. Ehlermann, 1910- v. 25cm.
The 2d ed. (q.v.) is still in progress (at least till 1956) Only
vol. 4 of the 3d ed. has thus far been published. Includes bio-
bibliographical data for German authors.

3626 GOEDEKE, KARL, 1814-1887.
Grundriss zur Geschichte der deutschen Dichtung. Neue
Folge (Fortführung von 1830 bis 1880) Hrsg. von der Deutschen
Akademie der Wissenschaften zu Berlin unter Leitung von
Leopold Magon. Bearb. von Georg Minde-Pouet [und] Eva
Rothe. Berlin, Akademie-Verlag, 1955- v. 24cm.
Includes bio-bibliographical data for German authors.

3627 GRADMANN, JOHANN JACOB, 1750-1817.
Das gelehrte Schwaben; oder, Lexicon der jetzt lebenden
schwäbischen Schriftsteller. Voraus ein Geburtstagalmanach
und hintennach ein Ortsverzeichniss. [Ravensburg] Beym

Verfasser, 1802. xxiv, 872, 30 p. 20cm. Learned Swabia; or, Dictionary of contemporary (1802) authors.

3628 GRÄFE, JULIUS
Bremer Dichter des 19. Jahrhunderts. Auswahl ihrer Gedichte mit biographischen Notizen, unter Mitwirkung von August Freudenthal hrsg. Bremen, Tannen, 1875. vii, 414 p. An anthology with bio-bibliographical notes on the authors, German writers of Bremen in the 19th century.

3629 GROSS, HEINRICH.
Deutsche Dichterinen und Schriftstellerinen. Eine literar-historische Skizze. 2. Ausg. Wien, C. Gerold's Sohn, 1882. iv, 290 p. 23cm. German women as poets and writers.

3630 GROSS, JOHANN, of Oberhausen.
Biographisch.-literarisches Lexikon der deutschen Dichter und Schriftsteller vom 9. bis 20. Jahrhundert. Leipzig, Hillmann, 1922. 285 p. Biographical-literary dictionary of German poets and writers from the 9th to the 20th century.

3631 HAAN, WILHELM, 1801-1884.
Sächsisches Schriftsteller-Lexikon. Alphabetisch geord-nete Zusammenstellung der im Königreich Sachsen gegenwär-tig lebenden Gelehrten, Schriftsteller und Künstler, nebst kurzen biographischen Notizen und Nachweis ihrer im Druck erschienenen Schriften. Leipzig, R. Schaefer, 1875. 391 p. 23cm. Bio-bibliography — Dictionary of authors in Saxony.

3632 HAMBERGER, GEORG CHRISTOPH, 1726-1773.
Alphabetisches Verzeichniss; oder, Lexicon der itzt leben-den schwäbischen Schriftsteller, aus des... Prof. Hamberger Gelehrtem Deutschlande gezogen, mit vielen Zusätzen verme-hret und einer Vorrede begleitet... [von O. F. Hörner] Nördlingen, C. G. Beck, 1771. 78-266p. 8.⁰ Alphabetical list; or, Dictionary of Swabian authors now living, drawn from Hamberger's Gelehrtes Teutschland, with additions, by O. F. Hörner.

3633 HAMBERGER, GEORG CHRISTOPH, 1726-1773.
Das gelehrte Teutschland; oder, Lexikon der jetzt lebenden teutschen Schriftsteller. Fortgesetzt von Johann Georg Meusel. 5. durchaus verm. und verb. Ausg. Lemgo, Meyersche Buchhandlung, 1796-1834. 23 v. in 24. 19cm. Vols. 13-23, by J.G. Meusel, also have title: Das gelehrte Teutschland im neunzehnten Jahrhundert. Complemented by

Meusel's Lexikon der vom Jahr 1750 bis 1800 verstorbenen
teutschen Schriftsteller. Learned Germany; or, Dictionary
of living German writers.

3634   HAYMANN, CHRISTOPH JOHANN GOTTFRIED
Dresdens theils neuerlich verstorbene, theils jetzt lebende
Schriftsteller und Künstler wissenschaftlich classificirt,
nebst einem dreyfachen Register. Dresden, Walther, 1809.
vi, 476p. 8.° Dresden's recently deceased as well as living
writers and artists, classified and with a threefold index.

3635   HINRICHSEN, ADOLF, 1859-
Das literarische Deutschland. Mit einer Einleitung von
C. Beyer. 2. verm. und verb. Aufl. Berlin, C. F.
Steinacker, 1891. xxvi, [736]p. 27cm. Literary Germany;
a bio-bibliographical work.

3636   [HITZIG, JULIUS EDUARD] 1780-1849.
Verzeichniss im Jahre 1825 in Berlin lebender Schriftsteller und ihrer Werke. Aus den von ihnen selbst entworfenen oder revidirten Artikeln zusammengestellt und zu
einem milden Zwecke hrsg. Berlin, F. Dümmler, 1826.
x, 326 p. 22cm. Added t. p.: Gelehrtes Berlin in Jahre
1825. Supplements Schmidt and Mehring's Neuestes gelehrtes
Berlin, 1795. Supplemented by Koner's Gelehrtes Berlin in
Jahre 1845. List of authors (and their works) living in Berlin
in 1825.

3637   JÄCKH, JOACHIM HEINRICH, 1777-1847.
Pantheon der Literaten und Künstler Bambergs. Erlangen,
1812-14. 7 fascicles or nos. Issued also under title: Leben
und Werke der Künstler Bambergs. Pantheon of literary
people and artists of Bamberg.

3638   JÄGER, CAJETAN.
Literarisches Freiburg im Breisgau; oder, Verzeichniss
der gegenwärtig dasselbst lebenden Schriftsteller. Freiburg
[i. B.] 1839. 1v. 8.° Literary Freiburg im Breisgau; or,
List of writers now living there.

3639   JAKSCH, FRIEDRICH, 1894-
Lexikon sudetendeutscher Schriftsteller und ihre Werke
für die Jahre 1900-1929. Mit zwei Anhängen: 1. Die
sudetendeutschen Zeitungen. 2. Die sudetendeutschen
Zeitschriften. Reichenberg, Gebr. Stiepel, 1929. 358p.

17cm. Dictionary of Sudeten German authors and their works for the years 1900-1929.

3640   JEITTELES, IGNAZ, 1814 or 5-1857.
Die Poesie und die Poeten in Österreich im Jahre 1836, von Julius Seidlitz [pseud.] Grimma, Gebhardt, 1837. 2v. 8° Poetry and poets in Austria in the year 1836.

3641   JÖRDENS, KARL HEINRICH, 1757. 1835.
Lexikon deutscher Dichter und Prosaisten. Leipzig, Weidmann, 1806-11. 6v. 22cm. Dictionary of German poets and prose-writers.

3642   JOURNALISTEN-HANDBUCH. 1960.
Wer schreibt worüber? Journalisten, Redakteure, Pressereferenten. 2. Aufl. [Hrsg. vom Deutschen Journalisten-Verband] Wiesbaden, Verlag Chmielorz [1960] 544p. illus. 22cm. Journalists-handbook. Who's writing about what [in Germany]?

3643   KATHOLISCHER LITERATURKALENDER.
Begründet von Heinrich Keiter. Jahrg. 1-15; 1891-1926. Freiburg i. B. [etc.] v. ports. 16-18cm. No issues for 1895-1896, 1898-1901, 1903-1904, 1906, 1908, 1915-1925. Title varies: 1902-14, Keiters katholischer Literatur-Kalender. Catholic literary calendar [for Germany]; includes bio-bibliographies of German Catholic writers.

3644   KEHREIN, JOSEPH, 1808-1876.
Biographisch-literarisches Lexikon der katholischen deutschen Dichter., Volks- und Jugendschriftsteller im 19. Jahrhundert. Zürich, L. Woerl, 1868. 2v. in 1. 24cm. Biographical-literary dictionary of German Catholic authors, popular and juvenile writers in the 19th century.

3645   KESSLIN, CHRISTIAN FRIEDRICH, 1780-
Nachrichten von Schriftstellern und Künstlern der Grafschaft Wernigerode vom Jahre 1074 bis 1855. . . Magdeberg, Commissionsverlag von Gebr. Bänsch, 1856. xii, 312p. 22cm. Notes on writers and artists of the German independency of Wernigerode, 1074-1855.

3646   KINDERMANN, HEINZ, 1894-
Taschenlexikon für deutsche Literatur, von Heinz Kindermann und Margarete Dietrich. Stuttgart, Humboldt-Verlag

[c1953] 192 p. 18cm. (Humboldt Taschenbücher, 3) Pocket dictionary for German literature; includes bio-bibliographies.

3647 KINDERMANN, HEINZ, 1894-
Taschenlexikon der deutschen Literatur. [Neuausgabe, überarbeitet, ergänzt und verm. von Ernst Johann] München, Verlag Lebendiges Wissen [c1958] 233 p. 18cm. (Humboldt Taschenbücher, 74) New edition of Taschenlexikon für deutsche Literatur. A pocket dictionary of German literature; includes biography.

3648 KINDERMANN, HEINZ, 1894-
Wegweiser durch die moderne Literatur in Österreich. Innsbruck, Österreichische Verlagsanstalt [1954] 127 p. illus. 20cm. Austrian authors who write in German; a bio-bibliography.

3649 KOPPE, JOHANN CHRISTIAN, 1757-1827.
Mecklenburgs Schriftsteller von den ältesten Zeiten bis jetzt nach Vor- und Zunahmen, Bedienung und Wohnort in alphabetischer Folge dargestellt. Nebst vorläufiger Abhandlung über Quellen und Bearbeitungs-Plan eines herauszugebenden allgemeinen mecklenburgischen Schriftstellerlexikon. Rostock, Gedruckt bei Adlers Erben, 1816. 95 p. 18cm. Mecklenburg's writers from the earliest times ... alphabetically arranged.

3650 KORDES, BEREND, d. 1823.
Lexikon der jetztlebenden schleswig-holsteinischen und eutinischen Schriftsteller, möglichst vollständig zusammengetragen. Schleswig, J. G. Röhss, 1797. xlviii, 560 p. 20cm. Dictionary of living writers of Schleswig-Holstein and Eutin.

3651 KOSCH, WILHELM, 1879-
Deutsches Literatur-Lexikon; biographisches und bibliographisches Handbuch. 2. vollständig neu bearb. und stark erweiterte Aufl. Bern, A. Francke, 1949 [i. e. 1947]-58. 4 v. 25cm. Issued in 38 parts. A bio-bibliographical dictionary of German literature.

3652 KOSCH, WILHELM, 1879-
Deutsches Literatur-Lexikon. Ausg. in einem Band, bearb. von Bruno Berger. Bern, Francke [1963] 511 p. 25cm. A bio-bibliographical dictionary of German literature. One-volume edition.

3653   KRÜGER, HERMANN ANDERS, 1871-
Deutsches Literatur-Lexikon; biographisches und bibliographisches Handbuch mit Motivübersichten und Quellennach-
weisen. München, Beck, 1914.   vii, 483 p. 24cm. Dictionary of German literature; biographical and bibliographical
handbook. . .

3654   KÜRSCHNERS DEUTSCHER LITERATUR-KALENDER.
Bd. 1-   1879-   Berlin, W. de Gruyter
[etc.]   v. ports. 14-21cm.   Title varies: 1879-82,
Allgemeiner deutscher Literaturkalender.   1883-1902,
Deutscher Litteratur-Kalender.   Publication suspended 1918-
1921, resumed 1922.   Imprint varies.   Calendar of German
literary personalities; contemporary.

3655   KÜRSCHNERS DEUTSCHER LITERATUR-KALENDER.
Nekrolog zu Kürschners Literatur-Kalender, 1901-1935,
hrsg. von Gerhard Lüdtke.   Berlin, W. de Gruyter, 1936.
vi p. , 976 columns.   21cm.   Necrology to Kurschner's literary
calendar (German literature), 1901-1935.

3656   [KÜTNER, KARL AUGUST] 1749-1800.
Charaktere teutscher Dichter und Prosaisten. Von Kaiser
Karl dem Grossen bis aufs Jahr 1780.   Berlin, C. F. Voss,
1781.   2 v. in 1. 16cm.   German poets and prose writers,
from Charlemagne to 1780.

3657   KUNISCH, HERMANN, 1901-   ed.
Handbuch der deutschen Gegenwartsliteratur.   Unter Mitwirkung von Hans Hennecke hrsg. von Hermann Kunisch.
[München] Nymphenburger Verlagshandlung [1965]   781 p.
27cm.   "Autorenartikel A-Z": p. 47-645.   Handbook of contemporary German literature; chiefly bio-bibliographical.

3658   KURZ, HEINRICH, 1805-1873.
Deutsche Dichter und Prosaisten von der Mitte des 15.
Jahrhundert bis auf unsere Zeit, nach ihrem Leben und Wirken
geschildert.   Leipzig, Teubner, 1858-67.   4 v. 8.° Issued
in parts, with F. Paldamus responsible for several of them.
German poets and prose-writers from the middle of the 15th
century to our day.

3659   LANDESMANN, HEINRICH, 1821-1902.
Wieners poetische Schwingen und Federn, von Hieronymus
Lorm [pseud.] Leipzig, Grunow, 1847. 260p. 8.° Covers

Austrian (Viennese) writers of the 1st half of the 19th century from the "Vormärz" democratic standpoint.

3660   LEHMS, GEORG CHRISTIAN, 1684-1717.
Teutschlands galante Poetinnen, mit ihren sinnreichen und netten Proben; nebst einem Anhang ausländischer Dames, so sich gleichfalls durch schöne Poesien bey der curieusen Welt bekannt gemacht, und einer Vorrede. Dass das weibliche Geschlecht so geschickt zum Studieren, als das Männliche. Franckfurt am Mayn, Zu finden bey S. T. Hocker, 1714-15. 2 v. port. 19cm. Germany's women poets, with a glance at some foreign women poets.

3661   LENNARTZ, FRANZ
Dichter und Schriftsteller unserer Zeit; Einzeldarstellungen zur schönen Literatur in deutscher Sprache. 7. Aufl. Stuttgart, A. Kröner [1957] vi, 672p. 18cm. (Kröners Taschenausgabe, Bd. 151) Previous editions published under title: Die Dichter unserer Zeit. [German] poets and writers of our time.

3662   LITERARISCHE SILHOUETTEN;
Deutsche Dichter und Denker und ihre Werke. Ein literarkritisches [Schriftsteller-] Jahrbuch. Ausg. 1907 [-2. -3. Ausg. 1907-1908] Hrsg. und bearb. von Heinz Voss und Bruno Volger. Oetzsch-Leipzig, B. Volger, 1907-08. 3 v. 19-21cm. Literary silhouettes; German writers and thinkers and their works. A literary yearbook.

3663   [LORENZEN, WOLFGANG]
Pantheon berühmter deutscher Dichter, mit einen Verzeichnis ihrer Werke. Coburg, Riemann, 1798. 1 v. (?) Pantheon of famous German poets (or authors?) with a list of their works.

3664   LÜBKER, DETLEV LORENZ, 1773-1852.
Lexikon der Schleswig-Holstein-Lauenburgischen und Eutinischen Schriftsteller, von 1796 bis 1828. Zusammengetragen von D. L. Lübker und H. Schröder. Altona, K. Aue, 1829-30. 2 v. port. 21cm.

3665   --- ----Nachträge und Register... von Hans Schröder. Schleswig, Gedruckt im Königl. Taubstummeninstitut, 1831. vi, [719]-864, 40 p. 21cm.

Continued by Alberti's Lexikon der Schleswig-Holstein-Lauenburgischen und Eutinischen Schriftsteller von 1829 bis

Mitte 1866 and Alberti's Lexikon... von 1866-1882. Dictionary of authors in Schleswig-Holstein & Eutin, 1796-1828.

3666 LUBOS, ARNO
Die schlesische Dichtung im 20. Jahrhundert. München, W. G. Korn [1961] 97 p. Pages 41-97 contain bio-bibliographies of 87 authors native to Silesia.

3667 MEISTER, LEONHARD, 1741-1811.
Charakteristik deutscher Dichter, nach der Zeitordnung gereihet, mit Bildnissen von H. Pfenninger. St. Gallen, 1785-93. 3 v. ports. Vols. 1-2, 3 (fasc. 1-5); no more published? Sketches of German authors, arranged chronologically, with portraits.

3668 MEUSEL, JOHANN GEORG, 1743-1820.
Lexikon der von 1750-1800 verstorbenen teutschen Schriftsteller. Leipzig, G. Fleischer, der Jungere, 1802-16. 15 v. 21cm. Complements Hamberger-Meusel, Das gelehrte Teutschland; oder Lexicon der jetzt lebenden teutschen Schriftsteller, 1796-1834. Dictionary of German authors who died 1750-1800.

3669 MEYER, ANDREAS, 1742-1807.
Biographische und literarische Nachrichten von den Schriftstellern, die gegenwärtig in den Fürstentümern Anspach und Bayreuth leben, in alphabetischer Ordnung. Erlangen, J. J. Palm, 1782. 424, [12] p. 20cm. Biographical and literary notices of the writers who are now living in the principalities of Anspach and Bayreuth. Alphabetical.

3670 MUSCHI, JEAN BERNARD, 1847-   ed.
Das literarische Anhalt. Arbeiten zeitgenössische Schriftsteller. Hrsg. von Jean Bernard Muschi und Herm. Wäschke. 2. Ausg. Dessau, F. Meyer (R. Kahle's Nachfolger) [1889] xxiv, 255 p. 20cm. Literary Anhalt; the works of contemporary writers of the duchy of Anhalt.

3671 NOWACK, KARL GABRIEL
Schlesisches Schriftstellerlexikon; oder, Bio-bibliographisches Verzeichniss der im zweiten Viertel des 19. Jahrhunderts lebenden schlesischen Schriftsteller. Breslau, W. G. Korn, 1836-43. 6 v. in 1. 20cm. Dictionary of Silesian authors of the 2d quarter of the 19th century. No more published.

3672 OTTO, GOTTLIEB FRIEDRICH, 1751-1815.
Lexikon der seit dem fünfzehenden Jahrhunderte verstorbenen
und jetztlebenden oberlausizischen Schriftsteller und Künstler,
aus den glaubwürdigsten Quellen möglichst vollständig zusammengetragen. Görlitz, Bey C. G. Anton [etc.] 1800-03. 3 v.
20cm. Each vol. in 2 parts, with special t. p.

3673 --- ----Supplementband zu J.G. [sic] Otto's Lexikon der
oberlausitzischen Schriftsteller und Künstler, zum theil aus
dem Nachlasse des Verstorbenen, und mit Unterstützung der
Oberlausitzischen Gesellschaft der Wissenschaften und anderer
Gelehrten bearb. von Johann Daniel Schulze. Görlitz und
Leipzig, In Commission bei Zobel, 1821. 624 p. 19cm.

Dictionary of the writers & artists of Lusatia, past &
present.

3674 PATAKY, Frau SOPHIE, 1860-
Lexikon deutscher Frauen der Feder; eine Zusammenstellung der seit dem Jahre 1840 erschienenen Werke weiblicher
Autoren, nebst Biographien der Lebenden und einem Verzeichnis der Pseudonyme. Berlin, C. Pataky, 1898. 2 v.
19cm. Dictionary of German women of the pen: a collection
of the works of women authors that have appeared since 1840
as well as biographies of those living & a list of pseudonyms.

3675 PAULLINI, CHRISTIAN FRANZ, 1643-1711.
Das hoch- und wohlgelahrte teutsche Frauen-Zim̃er.
Nochmahls mit mercklichen Zusatz vorgestellet. Franck-
furth, 1705. 1 v. 8.⁰ An enlarged edition was issued in 1712?
Women in Germany as authors.

3676 PETRY, KARL
Handbuch zur deutschen Literaturgeschichte. Köln, B.
Pick, 1949. 2 v. (1064p.) 21cm. "Titel und Namenregister"
(27p) inserted in v. 2. Chronological arrangement, with a
good deal of bio-bibliographical material in this handbook to
German literary history.

3677 RASSMANN, CHRISTIAN FRIEDRICH, 1772-1831.
Deutscher Dichternekrolog; oder, Gedrängte Uebersicht
der verstorbenen deutschen Dichter, Romanenschriftsteller,
Erzähler und Uebersetzer, nebst genauer Angabe ihrer
Schriften. Nordhausen, G. W. Happach, 1818. xvi, 216p.
18cm. A necrology of German authors.

3678 RASSMANN, CHRISTIAN FRIEDRICH, 1772-1831.
Gallerie der jetzt lebenden deutschen Dichter, Romanenschriftsteller, Erzähler, Uebersetzer aus neuen Sprachen,
Anthologen und Herausgeber belletristischer Schriften,
begleitet zum Theil mit hin und wieder ganz neuen biographischen Notizen. Helmstedt, Fleckeisen, 1818-21. 3 v. A
gallery of living German authors (1818-1821)

3679 RASSMANN, CHRISTIAN FRIEDRICH, 1772-1831.
Literarisches Handwörterbuch der verstorbenen deutschen Dichter und zur schönen Literatur gehörenden Schriftsteller, in acht Zeitabschnitten, von 1137 bis 1824. Leipzig,
1826. 1 v. 8.º Literary pocket-dictionary of deceased
German authors, 1137-1824.

3680 RASSMANN, CHRISTIAN FRIEDRICH, 1772-1831.
Münsterländisches Schriftsteller-Lexicon, ein Beitrag
zur Geschichte der westphälischen Literatur. Angefertigt
von Friedrich Rassmann. Lingen, F. A. Jülicher, 1814.
Issued as a supplement to F. M. Driver's Bibliotheca Mon-
asteriensis, 1799. Author dictionary for the Münsterland.

3681 ---- ----1.-[3] Nachtrag. Lingen [etc.] F. A. Jülicher
[etc.] 1815-24. 3 v. 17-19cm.

3682 RASSMANN, CHRISTIAN FRIEDRICH, 1772-1831.
Pantheon deutscher jetzt lebender Dichter und in die Bel-
letristik eingreifender Schriftsteller; begleitet mit kurzen
biographischen Notizen und der wichtigsten Literatur. Helmstedt, C. G. Fleckeisen, 1823. vi, 426p. 18cm. Pantheon
of contemporary (1823) German authors.

3683 RASSMANN, ERNST
Nachrichten von dem Leben und den Schriften Münster-
ländischer Schriftsteller des achtzehnten und neunzehnten
Jahrhundert. Münster, Coppenrath, 1866. x, 409p. 8.º
Notes on the lives & writings of authors from the
Münsterland, 18th-19th century.

3684 ---- ----Neue Folge. Münster, 1881. viii, 270p. 8.º

3685 RICHTER, GOTTFRIED LEBRECHT, d. 1813.
Allgemeines biographisches Lexikon alter und neuer
geistlicher Liederdichter. Leipzig, G. Martini, 1804. viii,

487p. 22cm. General biographical dictionary of old and modern German religious poets (including members of the clergy)

3686 SARTORI, FRANZ, 1782-1832.
Verzeichnis der gegenwärtig in und um Wien lebenden Schriftsteller, nebst den Wissenschaftsfächern, in welchen sie sich vorzüglichst bemerkbar gemacht haben. Wien, Gerold, 1820. 1 v. List of authors living in and around Vienna, as well as scholars...

3687 SCHADEN, JOHANN NEPOMUK ADOLPH VON, 1791-1840.
Gelehrtes München im Jahre 1834; oder, Verzeichnis mehrerer zur Zeit in Bayerns Hauptstadt lebenden Schriftsteller und ihrer Werke. Aus den von ihnen selbst entworfenen oder revidirten Artikeln zusammengestellt und hrsg. durch Adolph von Schaden. München, Druck von J. Rösl, 1834. ii, 174 p. 22cm. Learned Munich in 1834; or, List of writers living in Bavaria's capital city and their works.

3688 SCHINDEL, CARL WILHELM OTTO AUGUST VON, 1776-1830.
Die deutschen Schriftstellerinnen des neunzehnten Jahrhunderts. Leipzig, F. A. Brockhaus, 1823-25. 3 v. 17cm. German women writers of the 19th century. Supplemented by Pataky's Lexikon deutscher Frauen der Feder, Berlin, 1898.

3689 SCHMID, CHRISTIAN HEINRICH, 1746-1800.
Nekrolog; oder, Nachrichten von dem Leben und den Schriften der vornehmsten verstorbenen teutschen Dichter. Berlin, Mylius, 1785. 2 v. 8.º Necrology; or, news of the life and writings of the most eminent deceased German authors.

3690 SCHMIDT, ANDREAS GOTTFRIED, 1794-1851.
Anhaltisches Schriftsteller-Lexikon; oder, Historisch-literarische Nachrichten über die Schriftsteller, welche in Anhalt geboren sind oder gewirkt haben aus den drei letzten Jahrhunderten, gesammelt und bis auf unsere Zeiten fortgeführt; nebst einem Anhange. Bernburg, F. W. Gröning, 1830. xvii, 567 p. 21cm. Dictionary of the writers of the duchy or territory of Anhalt.

3691 SCHMIDT, VALENTIN HEINRICH
Neuestes gelehrtes Berlin; oder, Literarische Nachrichten von jetztlebenden Berlinischen Schriftstellern und Schriftstellerinnen. Von Valentin Heinrich Schmidt und Daniel Gott-

lieb Mehring. Berlin, Maurer, 1795. 2 v. 8.° Most recent learned Berlin; or, Literary reports on Berlin's authors
of both sexes now living.

3692   SCHOMERUS-WAGNER, JOHANNA, 1918-
Deutsche katholische Dichter der Gegenwart. Nürnberg,
Glock und Lutz, 1950. 197 p. 20cm. German Catholic
authors of the present.

3693   SCHRÖDER, HANS, 1796-1855.
Lexikon der hamburgischen Schriftsteller bis zur Gegenwart. Im Auftrage des Vereins für Hamburgische Geschichte
ausgearb. [Fortgesetzt von F. M. Cropp, R. C. W. Klose
und A. H. Kellinghusen] Hamburg, Auf Kosten des Vereins,
in Kommission bei Perthes-Besser und Mauke, 1851-83. 8 v.
20-22cm. Dictionary of the writers of Hamburg to the present
time.

3694   SCRIBA, HEINRICH FREIDRICH LUDWIG WILHELM EDUARD,
1802-1857.
Biographisch-literarisches Lexikon der Schriftsteller des
Grossherzogtums Hessen im ersten Viertel des 19. Jahrhunderts. Darmstadt, K. W. Leske, 1831-46. 2 v. 20cm. Bio-
bibliographical dictionary of writers of the Grand Duchy of
Hesse in the first quarter of the 19th century.

3695   SPRINGAUF, E   W
Schlesiens Dichter im 19ten Jahrhunderte; oder, Kurzgefasste Nachrichten über die in Schlesien seit 1800 bis 1830
gestorbenen und lebenden Schriftsteller. Breslau, Aderholz,
1831. 1 v. 8.° Silesia's authors in the 19th century (1800-
1830)

3696   STAMMLER, WOLFGANG, 1886-   ed.
Die deutsche Literatur des Mittelalters: Verfasserlexikon.
Unter Mitarbeit zahlreicher Fachgenossen. Berlin, De
Gruyter, 1933 [i.e. 1931-33]-55. 5 v. 25cm. German literature of the Middle Ages: author dictionary. Vols. 1-3 issued
in parts; pts. 1-2 of v. 1 issued under title: Verfasserlexikon
des deutschen Mittelalters. Vols. 4-5 edited by Karl Langosch.

3697   STERN, ADOLF, 1835-1907.
Lexikon der deutschen Nationalliteratur; die deutschen
Dichter und Prosaiker aller Zeiten, mit Berücksichtigung
der hervorragendesten dichterisch behandelten Stoffe und

Motive. Leipzig, Verlag des Bibliographischen Instituts, 1882. vi, 409p. 19cm. Dictionary of German national literature; the German poets & prose writers of all times.

3698 STREIT, KARL KONRAD, 1751-1826.
Alphabetisches Verzeichnis aller im Jahr 1774 in Schlesien lebender Schriftsteller. Breslau, W. G. Korn, 1776. 183p. 20cm. Alpahbetical list of all German writers living in Silesia in the year 1774.

3699 TASCHENBUCH FÜR LITERATUR UND KUNST IM KÖNIGREICH SACHSEN.
Jahrg. 1-2. Dresden, 1825-28. 2 v. 'Pocket book' for literature and art in the Kingdom of Saxony; bio-bibliographical. Edited by J. W. S. Lindner. No more published?

3700 TRAUSCH, JOSEPH FRANZ, 1795-1871.
Schriftsteller-Lexikon, oder biographisch-literarische Denk-Blätter der Siebenburger Deutschen. Kronstadt, J. Gött & Sohn Heinrich, 1868-71 [1876] 3 v. in 2. 24cm. "Eine neue ergänzte Auflage und Fortsetzung von Johann Seiverts Nachrichten von Siebenbürgischen Gelehrten und ihre Schriften [1875]" The 3d vol. was completed after the author's death by Eugen von Trauschenfels in 1876.

3701 ---- ----Schriftsteller-Lexikon der Siebenburger Deutschen. IV. Bd. (Ergänzungsband zu J. Trausch, Schriftstellerlexikon) von Friedrich Schuller. Hermannstadt, W. Krafft, 1902. xi, 575p. 24cm.

Dictionary of German authors in Transylvania.

3702 VETTERLEIN, CHRISTOPH FRIEDRICH RUDOLF
Handbuch der poetischen Literatur der Deutschen; dass ist, Kurze Nachricht von den Leben und Schriften deutscher Dichter. Köthen, Aue 1799. 1 v. Handbook of the poetical literature of Germany; i. e., Brief notes on the lives and works of German poets.

3703 WEIZ, FRIEDRICH AUGUST, 1739-1815.
Das gelehrte Sachsen; oder, Verzeichniss derer in den Churfürstl. Sächs. incorporirten Ländern jetztlebenden Schriftsteller und ihrer Schriften. Leipzig, Bey C. F. Schneidern, 1780. 288 p. 21cm. Learned Saxony; list of authors (and their writings) 'now' living in lands under the jurisdiction of the Electorate of Saxony.

3704   WIENER SCHRIFTSTELLER UND KÜNSTLER LEXIKON;
Oder, Alphabetisches Verzeichniss aller gegenwärtig in
Wien lebender Schrifsteller, Künstler und Künstlerinnen, mit
Angabe ihre Namen, Stände und Werke. Hrsg. von einer
Gesellschaft ihrer Freunde. Wien, 1793. 1 v. Dictionary
of Vienna's writers and artists.

3705   WIENSTEIN, FRIEDRICH
Lexikon der katholischen deutschen Dichter vom Ausgange
des Mittelalters bis zur Gegenwart. Biographisch-literarisch
bearb. Hamm i W., Breer & Thiemann, 1899. iv, 448 p.
8.° Dictionary of German Catholic authors from the end of
the Middle Ages to the present.

3706   WILPERT, GERO VON.
Deutsches Dichterlexikon; biographisch-bibliographisches
Handwörterbuch zur deutscher Literaturgeschichte. Stuttgart,
A. Kröner [1963] xi, 657 p. 18cm. (Kröners Taschenausgabe,
Bd. 288) Dictionary of German authors; biographical-biblio-
graphical handbook to German literary history.

3707   WINCKLERN, JOHANN BAPTIST VON, b. 1768.
Biographische und litterärische Nachrichten von den
Schriftstellern und Künstlern, welche in dem Herzogthum
Steyermark geboren sind, und in oder ausser demselben
gelebt haben und noch leben. Ein Beitrag zur National-Liter-
argeschichte Oesterreich. Grätz, 1810. 1 v. 8.° Biographical and literary news of writers and artists who were born
in the duchy of Styria, Austria, and have lived and worked
there or outside the duchy.

3708   WOLFF, OSKAR LUDWIG BERNHARD, 1799-1851.
Encyclopädie der deutschen National-Literatur; oder,
Biographisch-kritisches Lexikon der deutschen Dichter und
Prosaisten seit den frühesten Zeiten, nebst Proben aus ihren
Werken. 2. Ausg. Leipzig, O. Wigand, 1846-47. 8 v. 30cm.
Encyclopedia of German national literature; or, Biographical-
critical dictionary of German poets and prose-writers from
the earliest times, with examples of their work.

Greek, Modern

3709   SATHAS, KŌNSTANTINOS N   1841-1914.
Neollēnikē filologia. Biographiai tōn en tois grammasi
dialampsantōn Ellēnōn, apo tēs katalyseōs tēs Byzantinōs

autokratorias mechri tēs ellēnikōs ethnegersias (1455-1821)
'En Athēnais, Ek tēs typografias tōn teknōn 'Andreou Koromēla,
1868. 761 p. 22cm.

3710 --- ----Parartēma ... En Athēnais, Tip. A. Koromēla,
1870. 336 p. 22cm.

Modern Greek philology; includes bio-bibliographical material on modern Greek literature.

Hungarian

3711 BOD, PÉTER, felső-csernátoni, 1712-1769.
Magyar Athenas, avagy az Erdélyben es Magyarországon
élt tudós embereknek, nevezetesebben akik valami, világ
eleibe bocsátott írások által esméretesekké lettek, s jo
emélekezeteket fenhagyták, historiájuk. Nagyszeben, 1766.
360 p. Ca. 500 biographical sketches of Transylvanian and
Hungarian writers; alphabetical arrangement.

3712 CZWITTINGER, DAVID, FL. 1700.
Davidis Czvittingeri Specimen Hungariae literatae, virorum
eruditione clarorum natione Hungarorum, Dalmatarum, Croa-
tarum, Slavorum, atque Transylvanorum, vitas, scripta, elogia et censuras ordine alphabetice exhibens. Accedit Bibliotheca scriptorum qui extant de rebus Hungaricis. Francofurti et Lipsiae, J. G. Kohles, 1711. 480, 80 p. 21cm. Biographical sketches of ca. 300 Hungarian writers; alphabetical arrangement.

3713 FÖLDVÁRI, MIHÁLY.
Magyar irodalom zseblexikona. Irodalmi arcképcsarnok.
Köln, Amerikai-Magyar Kiadó, 1954. 110 p. Pocket diction-
ary of Hungarian literature. Literary portraits.

3714 GULYÁS, PÁL, 1881-
Magyar írók élete és munkái. Megindította: id. Szinnyei
József. Uj sorozat. Budapest, Magyar Könyvtárosok és
Levéltárosok Egyesülete, 1939- v. 24cm. Vol. 6
(1944) ends with Dzurányi László. Biographies of Hungarian
authors.

3715 HANER, GEORG JEREMIAS, 1707-1777.
De scriptoribus rerum Hungaricarum et Transylvanicarum saeculi XVIII eorundem antiquioribus ordine chronologico digestis adversaria. [Hermannstadt] 1774-98. 2v.

8.° Bio-bibliography of writers of the 18th century on Hungarian and Transylvanian affairs.

3716 HORÁNYI, ELEK, 1736-1809.
Memoria Hungarorum et provincialium scriptis editis notorum, quam excitat Alexius Horányi. Viennae, Impensis A. Loewii, 1775-77. 3v. 20cm. Imprint varies: v. 3, Posonii, Impensis A. Loewii, 1777. More than a thousand Hungarian writers represented.

3717 HORÁNYI, ELEK, 1736-1809.
Nova memoria Hungarorum et provincialium scriptis editis notorum, quam excitat Alexius Horányi. pars 1 [A-C] Pestini, M. Trattner, 1795. lv. 8.° A projected enlarged edition of Horanyi's Memoria Hungarorum et Provincialium scriptis editis notorum, but which covered only A-C and then ceased.

3718 MONAY, FERENC
Adatok a magyarországi és erdélyi minoriták irodalmi munkásságáról. Roma, Ars-Graf, 1952. 143p. A dictionary of 183 Hungarian and Transylvanian minority writers in Hungary from 1300 to 1952.

3719 SZINNYEI, JÓZSEF, 1830-1913.
Magyar írók élete es munkái, a Magyar Tudományos Akadémia megbizásából irta Szinnyei József. Budapest, Kiadja Hornyánszky V., 1891-1914. 14 v. 23cm. Hungarian literary lives and works.

3720 VÁNYI, FERENC
Magyar irodalmi lexikon. Fóris Miklós és Tóth András közreműködésével szerkesztette: Ványi Ferenc; átnéztek: Dézsi Lajos [és] Pintér Jenő. Budapest, "Studium" [előszó 1926] vi, 880 p. 25cm. Hungarian literary dictionary; includes biographies.

Icelandic (Modern)

3721 HERMANNSON, HALLDØR, 1878-
Icelandic authors of to-day, with an appendix giving a list of works dealing with modern Icelandic literature. Ithaca, N. Y., Cornell University Library, 1913. xiv, 69p. 25cm. (Islandica; an annual relating to Iceland and the Fiske Icelandic Collection in Cornell University Library, v. 6)

Indic

3722 ĀDHUNIKA TELUGU RACAYITALU.
[Madras?] 1962. iv, 138, ix p. 22cm. Added t. p. : Who's
who of Telugu writers. In Telugu; "Index of authors" in English. Issued by the Southern Languages Book Trust.

3723 INNATTE MALAYĀLA SĀHITYAKĀRANMĀR.
[Madras?] 1962. viii, 132p. 22cm. Added t. p. : Who's
who of Malayalam writers. In Malayalam; "Index" in English.
Issued by Southern Languages Book Trust.

3724 RAU, WILHELM
Bilder hundert deutscher Indologen. Wiesbaden, F.
Steiner, 1965. vii, 106p. illus. 25cm. (Verzeichnis der
orientalischen Handschriften in Deutschland. Supplementband 4) Portraits with place & date of birth & place & date
of death of 100 German philologists specializing in Indic studies.

3725 SĀHITYA AKADEMI.
Who's who of Indian writers. New Delhi [1961] 410p.
23cm.

3726 SEN GUPTA, SANKAR
Folklorists of Bengal; life sketches and bibliographical
notes. Foreword by Hiranmay Banerji; introd. by Asok Mitra.
Calcutta, Indian Publications, 1965-   v. ports. 23cm.
(Indian Publications folklore series, no. 2)

3727 SINGH, KAHAN, 1861-1938.
Gurushabada ratanākara. Encyclopaedia of Sikh literature.
[Patiala] 1960. 13, 5, 835, 99 p. illus. 33cm. In Panjabi.
Includes biography.

3728 TAMIL ELUTTĀLAR YĀR-E-VAR.
[Madras? 1962] 140, 7p. 22cm. Added t. p. : Who's who
of Tamil writers. In Tamil; "Index of authors" in English.
Issued by Southern Languages Book Trust.

Indonesian

3729   INDONESIA. DEPARTEMEN PENERANGAN.
Biographie wartawan Indonesia. Djarkarta, Kementerian
Penerangan, Biro Dokumentasi & Research [cover 1958]-
v.   34cm. Biography of Indonesian journalists.

Irish

3730   O'REILLY, EDWARD, d. 1829.
A chronological account of nearly four hundred Irish writers
commencing with the earliest account of Irish history, and
carried down to the year 1750. Dublin, 1820. 1 v.   (Transactions of the Iberno-Celtic Society, 1820, v. 1, pt. 1)

Italian

3731   AFFLITTO, EUSTACHIO D', 1742-1785.
Memorie degli scrittori del regno di Napoli. Tomo I-II
(A-B) Napoli, Stamperia Simoniana, 1782-94. 2v.   No
more published? Recollections of the writers of the Kingdom
of Naples.

3732   AFFÒ, IRENEO
Memorie degli scrittori letterati parmigiani. Parma,
Stamperia Reale, 1789-1833. 7v. in 9. 28cm. Continued by
Angelo Pezzana. Recollections of the littérateurs of Parma.

3733   AGOSTINI, GIOVANNI DEGLI, 1701-1755.
Notizie istorico-critiche intorno la vita e le opere degli
scrittori viniziani. Venezia, S. Occhi, 1752-54. 2v.   31cm.
Covers the years 1074-1591. Lives and works of Venetian
writers.

3734   ALIQUÒ LENZI, LUIGI, 1875-1944.
Gli scrittori calabresi; dizionario bio-bibliografico [di]
Luigi Aliquò Lenzi [e] Filippo Aliquò Taverriti. 2. ed.
Reggio di Calabria, Tip. editrice "Corriere di Reggio," 1955-
v. 1st ed. published in 1913 (448p.) Contents. --v. 1.
A-F. --v. 2. G-M. --v. 3. N-Z. --v. 4. Prima appendice.
Bio-bibliographical dictionary of the writers of Calabria, a
region of southern Italy.

3735 AMBROSI, FRANCESCO
Scrittori ed artisti trentini. 2. ed. notevolmente
accresciuta e corretta. Trento, G. Zippel, 1894. 553p. 8.°
Writers and artists of Trent, Italy.

3736 ANCONA, ALESSANDRO D', 1835-1914.
Manuale della letteratura italiana, compilato dai professori
Alessandro d'Ancona e Orazio Bacci. Nuova ed. interamente
rifatta. Firenze, G. Barberà, 1901-10. 6v. ports. 19cm.
(Collezione scolastica, secondo i programmi governativi) An
anthology & critical work with bio-bibliographical notes
for Italian writers.

3737 ANGIOLGABRIELLO DI SANTA MARIA.
Biblioteca, e storia di quei scrittori cosi della città come
del territorio di Vicenza che pervennero fin' ad ora a notizia
del P.F. Angiolgabriello di Santa Maria. Vicenza, G. B. V.
Mosca, 1772-82. 6v. 27cm. Covers the years 49-1782.
Library, and history of writers of the City and territory of
Vicenza. A bio-bibliography.

3738 ARISI, FRANCESCO, 1756-1743.
Cremona literata; seu, In Cremonenses doctrinis, &
literariis dignitatibus eminentiores chronologicae adnotationes.
Parmae, Typis A. Pazzoni & P. Montii, 1702-05. 2v. 36cm.

3739 -----Cremona literata; seu, In Cremonensis doctrinis, ac
literariis dignitatibus ab anno MDCI. ad MDCCXLI.
adnotationes, et observationes, cum appendicibus. Tomus
tertius. Cremonae, Apud P. Ricchini, 1741. 413p. 36cm.

Literary Cremona. Bio-bibliography.

3740 BIBLIOGRAFIA ROMANA.
Notizie della vita e delle opere degli scrittori romani dal
sec. XI fino ai nostri giorni. Vol. I. Roma, Tip. Eredi
Botta, 1880. clxxiii, 266p. 27 x 19cm. At head of title:
Ministero di agricoltura, industria e commercio. Direzione
di statistica. No more published. 186 sketches of writers
native to or residing in the City of Rome from the 11th century
to the latter half of the 19th century.

3741 CAPUTO, VINCENZO.
I poeti d'Italia en trenta secoli. Milano, Gastaldi [1962]
717 p. 20 cm. (Cultura) Third edition. 1st ed. published
under title: Gli antichi poeti italiani. 2d ed. : I poeti italiani
dall'antichità ad oggi.

3742   ----Appendice. Milano, Gastaldi [1962] 72 p. 19 cm.

The poets of Italy from antiquity to today.

3743   CASATI, GIOVANNI, 1881-
Dizionario degli scrittori d'Italia (dalle origini fino ai
viventi) Milano, R. Ghirlanda [1926-34?] 3 v. 24 cm. To K
only? No more published? Dictionary of the writers of
Italy (from the origins to the present)

3744   CASATI, GIOVANNI, 1881-
Scrittori cattolici italiani viventi; dizionario bio-
bibliografico ed indice analitico delle opere. Con pref. di
Filippo Meda. Milano, R. Ghirlanda, 1928. viii, 128 p.
24 cm. Living Italian Catholic writers; a bio-bibliographical
dictionary.

3745   CHIOCCARELLI , BARTOLOMMEO
De illustribus scriptoribus qui in civitate et regno Neapolis
ab orbe condito ad annum usque MDCXXXXVI floruerunt. t. I.
Neapoli, Ex Officina V. Ursini, 1780. xliv, 351 p. 4.°
Illustrious writers who flourished in the City & Kingdom of
Naples from its foundation to the year 1646.

3746   CINELLI CALVOLI, GIOVANNI, 1625-1706.
Biblioteca volante, continuata dal dottor Dionigi Andrea
Sancassani. Ed. 2. in miglior forma ridotta... Venezia,
Presso G. B. Albrizzi q. Girolamo, 1734-47. 4v. port.
24cm. A bio-bibliography of Italian literature.

3747   CINTI, DECIO.
Dizionario degli scrittori italiani classici, moderni et contemporanei. Milano, Sonzogno, 1939. 253 p. Dictionary
of Italian writers, classic, modern & contemporary.

3748   CODELLI, PIETRO ANTONIO
Gli scrittori friulano-austriaci degli ultimi due secoli. 3.
ed. corr. ed. accresciuta. Gorizia, Tip. G. Tommasini,
1792. [xii], 254 p. 16.° Italian authors of Friuli.

3749   DEROSSI, ONORATO
Scrittori piemontesi, savoiardi, nizzardi registrati nei
cataloghi del vescovo Francesco Agostino della Chiesa, e del
monaco Andrea Rossotto. Nuova compilazione. Torino, 1790.
vii, 220 p. 4.° Bio-bibliography of writers in the Italian
Piedmont, Savoy & Nice.

3750   FANTUZZI, GIOVANNI, 1718-1799.
Notizie degli scrittori bolognesi. Bologna, Stamperia di S.
Tommaso d'Aquino, 1781-94. 9 v. 28 cm. Notices about au-
thors in Bologna, Italy.

3751   FERRI, PIETRO LEOPOLDO, conte, 1786-1847.
Biblioteca femminile italiana. Padova, Tip. Crescini,
1842. 411 p. 26 cm.

3752   ----Aggiunte, compilate dal Dott. Enrico Castreca Brunetti.
In fine alcune lettere di Teresa Bandettini Landucci. Roma,
Tip. delle Belle arti, 1844. 48 p. 22 cm.

Bio-bibliography of Italian women authors.

3753   FUSCO, ENRICO M
Scrittori e idee; dizionario critico della letteratura italiana.
Torino, Società editrice internazionale, 1956. xii, 626 p.
25 cm. Writers & ideas; critical dictionary of Italian literature. Bio-bibliographical.

3754   GALATI, VITO GIUSEPPE, 1893-
Gli scrittori delle Calabrie. Dizionario bio-bibliografico.
Con pref. di Benedetto Croce. Vol. I. Firenze, Vallecchi,
1928. viii, 267 p. 22 cm. (Collezione di studi meridionali)
No more published. The writers of Calabria, Italy; a bio-
bibliographical dictionary.

3755   GAMBA, BARTOLOMMEO, 1776-1841.
Galleria dei letterati ed artisti più illustri delle provincie
Veneziane nel secolo XVIII. Venezia, Tip. di Alvisopoli,
1822-24. 2 v. Gallery of illustrious men of letters and
artists of the province of Venetia (Italy) in the 18th century.

3756   GERINI, EMANUELLE
Memorie storiche d'illustri scrittori e di uomini insigni
dell'antica e moderna Lunigiana. Massa, L. Frediani, 1829.
2v. 23cm. Historical memoirs of famous writers and renowned men of ancien and modern Lunigiana, a mountain district in Tuscany.

3757   GIOVANNI, F
Notizie historico-critiche intorno la vita e le opere degli
scrittori veneziani. Venezia, 1752-54. 2v. Notices of
Venetian writers; bio-bibliography of Venice.

3758 GIUSTINIANI, LORENZO, 1761-1824.
Memorie istoriche degli scrittori legali del Regno di Napoli.
Napoli, Stamperia Simoniana, 1787-88. 3v. Historical mem
ories of the writers on law of the Kingdom of Naples.

3759 GIUSTINIANI, MICHELE, 1612-1680.
Gli scrittori Liguri. Parte I [A-G] Roma, Appresso di
N. A. Tinassi, 1667. 496 p. 22cm. Writers of Liguria,
Italy. Alphabetical by forenames, with index of surnames.
No more published.

3760 GIUSTO, DOMENICO
Dizionario bio-bibliografico degli scrittori Pugliese viventi
e dei morti nel presente secolo. Napoli, L. de Bonis, 1893.
219 p. Bio-bibliographical dictionary of living writers (1893)
of Apulia and of authors who died during the 19th century.

3761 GRECO, OSCAR
Bibliografia femminile italiana del XIX secolo. Venezia,
Presso i principali librai d'Italia, 1875. xxv, 533 p. 22cm.
Bio-bibliography of women authors of Italy, 19th century.

3762 LIRUTI, GIAN GIUSEPPE, 1689-1780.
Notizie delle vite ed opere scritte da' letterati del Friuli.
Venezia, 1760-1830. 4 v. 4.° Notices of the lives and works
written by men of letters of Friuli.

3763 MARTORANA, PIETRO
Notizie biografiche e bibliografiche delgi scrittori del
dialetto napolitano. Napoli, Presso Chiurazzi, 1874. xxiii,
464 p. Biographical and bibliographical notices of writers
in the Neapolitan dialect.

3764 MAZZUCHELLI, GIOVANNI MARIA, conte, 1707-1765.
Gli scrittori d'Italia cioé notizie storiche, e critiche intorno alle vite, e agli scritti dei litterati italiani. Vol. 1,
pte. 1-[v. 2, pte. 4] Brescia, G. Bossini, 1753-63. 2 v. in 6.
35 x 24cm. The writers of Italy. No more published. Goes
only up to BUZ.

3765 MINIERI-RICCIO, CAMILLO, 1813-1882.
Memorie storiche degli scrittori nati nel regno di Napoli.
Napoli, Tip. dell'Aquila di V. Puzziello, 1844. viii, 414p.
24cm. Historical memorials of writers born in the Kingdom
of Naples.

3766   MINIERI-RICCIO, CAMILLO, 1813-1882.
      Notizie biografiche e bibliografiche degli scrittori napole-
tani fioriti nel secoli XVII. Milano, U. Hoepli, 1875-77.
2 v. 27 x 19cm. Biographical and bibliographical notices of
Neapolitan writers flourishing in the 17th century. Designed
as a rev. and enl. ed. of the author's Memorie storiche,
1844. Covers A-B only; work interrupted by author's death.

3767   MONGITORE, ANTONINO, 1663-1743.
      Bibliotheca Sicula; sive, De scriptoribus Siculis qui tum
vetera, tum recentiora saecula illustrarunt, notitiae locu-
pletissimae. Panormi, Ex Typ. Didaci Bua, 1707-14. 2 v.
35cm. The Sicilian library; or, Notices of the old and more
recent writers of Sicily.

3768   NEGRI, GIULIO, 1648-1720.
      Istoria degli scrittori fiorentini, la quale abbraccia intorno
à due mila autori, che negli ultimi cinque secoli hanno illustrata co i loro scritti quella nazione, in qualunque materia, ed in
qualunque lingua, e disciplina: con la distinta nota delle lor'
opere, così manoscritti, che stampate, e degli scrittori, che
di loro hanno con lode parlato, o fatta menzione: opere postuma.
Ferrara, B. Pomatelli, 1722. 557 p. 37 x 24cm. The history of Florentine writers, embracing approximately 200
authors [of Florence] ...

3769   NOTIZIE BIOGRAFICHE E LETTERARIE DEGLI SCRITTORI
      DELLO STATO ESTENSE in continuazione della Biblioteca
modenese del Cav. Ab. Gir. Tiraboschi. Reggio, Tip.
Torreggiani, 1833.37. 5 v. Biographical and literary notes
on the writers of the Este State (chiefly Modena & Ferrara)

3770   ORLANDI, PELLEGRINO ANTONIO, 1660-1727.
      Notizie degli scrittori bolognesi e dell'opere loro stampate
e manoscritte. Bologna, C. Pisarri, 1714. 356 p. 22cm.
The writers of Bologna. Bio-bibliographical. A manuscript
volume (704 p.) of corrections and additions by Count B.A.M.
Carrati, dated 1770, is to be found in the Biblioteca municipale
di Bologna.

3771   PARENTE, GINO
      Dizionario degli scrittori e artisti contemporanei; una
sintesi del panorama dell'arte e della letteratura contemporanea
[di] Gino Parente [e] Guido Massarelli. Campobasso, Il
Pungolo verde, 1949. 121 p. illus. 22cm. Dictionary of
20th century Italian authors and artists.

3772   PICINELLI, FILIPPO, 1604-ca. 1667.
Ateneo dei letterati milanesi. Milano, Stamperia di F.
Vigone, 1670. 520p. Athenaeum of Milanese literati.

3773   REGLI, FRANCESCO, 1804-1866.
Dizionario biografico dei più celebri poeti ed artisti
melodrammatici, tragici e comici, maestri, concertisti,
coreografi, mimi, ballerini, scenografi, giornalisti, im-
presarii, ecc., ecc. che fiorirono in Italia dal 1800 al 1860.
Torino, Coi tipi di E. Dalmazzo, 1860. xv, 592p. 25cm.
Biographical dictionary of the most celebrated poets and
melodramatic artists, tragic & comic, who flourished in
Italy from 1800 to 1860.

3774   ROVITO, TEODORO, 1875-
Letterati e giornalisti italiani contemporanei; dizionario
bio-bibliografico. 2. ed. rifatta ed ampliata. Napoli, T.
Rovito, 1922. 469p. 24cm. First published 1907 as: Dizionario bio-bibliografico dei letterati e giornalisti contemporanei. Contemporary Italian littérateurs and journalists; a
bio-bibliographical dictionary.

3775   RUMOR, SEBASTIANO, 1862-
Gli scrittori vicentini dei secoli decimottavo e decimo-
nono. Venezia, A spese della Società, 1905-09. 3 v. 25cm.
Writers of the 18th-19th centuries in Vicenza, Italy; bio-bibliographical.

3776   RUSSO, LUIGI, 1892-
I narratori. Roma, Fondazione Leonardo per la cultura
italiana, 1923. 214p. 17cm. (Guide bibliografiche [14-15])
Bio-bibliography of Italian fiction writers of the 19th-20th
centuries.

3777   SOPRANI, RAFFAELE, 1612-1672.
Li scrittori della Liguria, e particolarmente della maritima. Genova, P. G. Calenzani, 1667. 300 p. 21cm. The
writers of the region of Liguria, particularly the maritime
part. Alphabetical by forename, with index of surnames.

3778   STERLICH, C   DE, marquis di Cermignano
Opere bibliografiche. Gli scrittori Abruzzesi dai più
remoti tempi sino ad oggi. Pt. A. [n.p.?] 1876. 1 v. No
more published? The writers of Abruzzi, Italy, from the
most remote times to the present.

3779   TAFURI, GIOVANNI BERNARDINO, 1695-1760.
Istoria degli scrittori nati nel Regno di Napoli. Napoli,
Stamperia di F. C. Mosca, per li Severini, 1744-70. 3 v.
in 10. History of writers born in the Kingdom of Naples.

3780   TARTAROTTI, GIACOPO
Saggio della biblioteca tirolese; o sia, Notizie istoriche
degli scrittori della provincia del Tirolo, di Giacopo
Tartarotti e da Domenico Francesco Todeschini... di giunte
e note molto accresciuto. Scanzia prima. Venezia, 1777.
viii, 292p. plate. 8.º Todeschini revised Tartarotti's work
of the same title (1733) and intended it as the first volume of
a series of works. A Tyrolean library; or, Historical notes
on writers of the Tyrol.

3781   TIRABOSCHI, GIROLAMO, 1731-1794.
Biblioteca modenese; o, Notizie della vita e delle opere
degli scrittori natii degli stati del... duca di Modena. Modena, Società tipografica, 1781-86. 6 v. geneal. table.
26cm. Supplemented by "Notizie biografiche e letterarie
degli scrittori dello Stato Estense in continuazione della Biblioteca modenese del cavalier abate Girolamo Tiraboschi."
Reggio, 1833-41. 5 v. "Notizie de' pittori, scultori, incisori, e architetti natii degli stati del... duca di Modena,
con una appendice de' professori di musica": t. 6, p. 217-
607. Bio-bibliography of [Italian] writers born in the jurisdiction of the duchy of Modena.

3782   TRIGGIANI, DOMENICO, 1929-
Dizionario degli scrittori. [1. ed.] Bari, Triggiani editore [1960] 221 p. ports. 17cm. Dictionary of [Italian]
writers of the 20th century.

3783   TURRI, VITTORIO, 1860-1921.
Dizionario storico della letteratura italiana. Nuova [4.]
ed. riv. e aggiornata sul testo originale di Vittorio Turri
[di] Umberto Renda [e] Piero Operti. Torino, G. B. Paravia
[1959] x, 1241p. 24cm. Originally published under the title:
Dizionario storico manuale della letteratura italiana. Chiefly a biobibliographical work with some 1400 entries for deceased and living Italian authors.

3784   VERMIGLIOLI, GIOVANNI BATTISTA, 1769-1848.
Biografia degli scrittori perugini e notizie delle opere
loro. Perugia, Tip. di F. Baduel presso V. Bartelli e G.

Costantini, 1829. 2 v. 28cm. Biographies of the writers of Perugia, Italy & notes on their work.

3785 ZAMBRINI, FRANCESCO SAVERIO, 1810-1887.
Cenni biografici intorno ai letterati illustri italiani; o, Brevi memorie di quello che co' loro scritti illustrarono l'italico idioma... Faenza, Presso Montanari e Marabini, 1837. viii, 238 p. 23cm. In double columns. Biographical notes on famous learned Italians. Brief sketches of those who adorn the Italian language with their writings.

Japanese

3786 JAPAN. MOMBUSHŌ. NIHON YUNESUKO KOKUNAI IINKAI.
Who's who among Japanese writers. [Tokyo, Kasai Pub. & Print. Co. , 1957] 140p.

3787 KYŌDŌ SHUPPANSHA HENSAMBU.
Gendai shuppan bunkajin sōran. [Tokyo] Kyōdō Shuppansha, 1943. 848p. Survey of contemporary Japanese writers.

3788 NIHON SHUPPAN KYŌDŌ KABUSHIKI KAISHA.
Gendai shuppan bunkajin sōran. Tokyo, Nihon Shuppan Kyōdō Kankōkai, 1947. 408p. Survey of present-day writers in Japan. Combines the information found in the Kyōdō Shuppansha's Shoseki nenkan and Zasshi nenkan.

Jewish

3789 BARTOLOCCI, GIULIO, 1613-1687.
Bibliotheca magna rabbinica de scriptoribus, & scriptis Hebraicis, ordine alphabetico Hebraice, & Latine digestis... In qua complures identidem interseruntur dissertationes, et digressiones. Romae, Ex Typ. Sacrae Congregationis de Propaganda Fide, 1675-94. 5 v. illus. 31cm. Title in Hebrew at head of t. p. Vol. 4: "Post eius obitum absoluta, aucta, & in lucem edita a D. C. I. Imbonato." Vol. 5, by C. G. Imbonato, has title: Bibliotheca Latino-Hebraica; sive, De scriptoribus Latinis, qui ex diversis nationibus contra Iudaeos, vel de re Hebraica vtcumque scripaere. Bio-bibliography of Hebrew literature.

3790 LEKSIKON FUN DER NAYER YIDISHER LITERATUR.
[New York, 1956-   v. 29cm. Added t. p. : Biographi-

cal dictionary of modern Yiddish literature. Edited by Samuel
Charney and Jacob Shatzky. In Yiddish.

3791 LIPPE, CHAYIM DAVID, 1823-1900.
Bibliographisches Lexicon der gesammten jüdischen Literatur der Gegenwart und Adress-Anzeiger. Ein lexicalisch
geordnetes Schema mit Adressen von Rabbinen, Predigern,
Lehrern, Cantoren, Schriftstellern, Freunden und Förderern
der jüdischen Literatur. Nebst bibliographisch genauer Angabe
sämmtlicher von jüdischen Autoren der Gegenwart publicirten,
speciell die jüdische Literatur betreffenden Schriftwerke und
Zeitschriften, in chronologischer Anordnung und Reihenfolge
dargestellt. Wien, D. Löwy, 1881-89. 2 v. in 1. 23cm.
Issued in parts, 1879-1889. Only 3 parts of vol. 2 were published. One volume of a new series was published in 1899
under title: Bibliographisches Lexicon der gesammten jüdischen
und theologisch-rabbinischen Literatur der Gegenwart...
Bibliographical dictionary of all Jewish literature of the present and address-directory... of rabbis, cantors [etc.] Bio-
bibliographical.

3792 MORTARA, MARCO
Indice alfabetico dei rabbini e scrittori israeliti di cose
giudaiche in Italia, con richiami bibliografici e note illustrative. Padova, 1886. viii, 73p. 4.º Alphabetical index of
rabbis and Jewish authors in Italy, with biographical references and illustrative notes.

3793 REISEN, ZALMAN, 1887-
Leksikon fun der yidisher literatur, presse un filologie...
[Wilno, B. Kleckin, 1927-29] 4 v. ports. 26cm. Diction-
ary of Yiddish literature, journalism and philology.

3794 ROSSI, GIOVANNI BERNARDO DE, 1742-1831.
Dizionario storico degli autori ebrei e delle loro opere.
Parma, Dalla Reale stamperia, 1802. 2 v. 22cm. Historical dictionary of Jewish authors and their works. A German
translation was published in 1839 (with index, 1846) under title: Historisches Wörterbuch der jüdischen Schriftsteller und
ihrer Werke.

3795 [SOKOLOW, NAHUM] 1859-1936, ed.
Sefer zikaron... [Warschau, 1889] 208 p. 23cm. Cover
title: Sepher zykaron; bio-bibliographisches Lexicon enthaltend
alphabetisch geordnete Biographieen und Autobiographieen jüdischer Schriftsteller der Gegenwart, bearb. von der Redac-

tion des hebr. Jahrbuches "Hassyf" (5-ter Jahrgang) Bio-
bibliographical dictionary of Hebrew literature of the 19th century.

Lettish

3796   PISATELI SOVETSKOĬ LATVII.
Izd. ispr. i dop., pod red. V. Bertše. Riga, Latviĭskoe
gos. izd-vo, 1955. 250p. illus. 15cm. Writers of Soviet
Latvia.

3797   PRANDE, ALBERTS
Latvju rakstniecība portrejās. Literariskās dalas līdz-
strādnieki: A. Birkerts [et al.] Rīgā, Letas izdevums, 1926.
515p. illus. 27cm. Portraits of Lettish authors. With
accompanying biographical sketches.

Lithuanian

3798   BIRŽIŠKA, VACLOVAS, 1884-1956.
Aleksandrynas; senųju lietuvių rašytoju, rasiusiu priež
1865 m., biografijos bibliografijos ir biobibliografijos.
Čikaga, Išleido JAV LB Kultūros fondas, 1960-   v. port.
24cm. At head of title, v. 1- : Lituanistikos institutas.
Vols. 1- have added title pages and pref. in English.
Contents. --1. XVI-XVII amžiai. Older Lithuanian authors
writing before 1865.

3799   BIRŽIŠKA, VACLOVAS, 1884-
Lietuviu rašytoju kalendorius. Tübingen, Patria [1946]
263 p. 21cm. (Mūsu rašytojai ir raštai, 1) A calendar of
Lithuanian writers.

3800   TARYBŲ LIETUVOS RAŠYTOJAI.
Vilnius, Valstybinė grozinės literatūros leidykla, 1957.
572p. ports. 20cm. A collection of autobiographies of
writers of Soviet Lithuania.

Mongolian

3801   PISATELI SOVETSKOĬ BURIATII;
Bio-bibliograficheskii spravochnik. Ulan-Ude, Buriat-
skoe knizhnoe izd-vo, 1959. 185p. ports. 23cm. 58 authors
and critics of Buriat (Mongolian dialect) literature.

Norwegian

3802   HALVORSEN, JENS BRAAGE, 1845-1900.
Norsk forfatter-lexikon, 1814-1880. Paa grundlag af J. E.
Krafts og Chr. Langes "Norsk forfatter-lexikon 1814-1856"
samlet, redigeret og udg. med understøttelse af statskassen af
J. B. Halvorsen. Kristiania, Norske forlagsforening, 1885-
1908. 6 v. 23cm. Vol. 6 "fuldført af Halvdan Koht."
Dictionary of Norwegian writers, 1814-1880.

3803   HYDLE, HALVDAN, 1901-   ed.
Hvem skrev hva i de siste 25 år; Aftenpostens litteratur-
håndbok. [Redaksjon: Halvdan Hydle, Kristian Fikkan og
J. B. Hegna] Oslo, C. Schibsted [1950] 392p. illus.,
ports. 18cm. Who wrote what in the last 25 years; bio-
bibliography of 20th century Norwegian literature.

3804   KRAFT, JENS EDVARD, 1784-1853.
Norsk forfatter-lexikon, 1814-1856. Efter forfatterens død
ordnet, forøget og udgivet af Christian C. A. Lange. Chris-
tiania, J. Dahl, 1863. 728 p. port. 23cm. Published in
6 parts, 1857-63. Incorporated in J. B. Halvorsen's Norsk
forfatter-lexikon, 1814-1880. Dictionary of Norwegian authors,
1814-1856.

3805   SOMMERFELDT, WILHELM PREUS, 1881-1958.
Norsk forfattere, 1811-1920. Personregister. [Oslo,
Universitetsforlaget, 1963] 155 p. 21cm. (Norsk bibliografisk bibliotek. [Publikasjoner] bd. 15) Norwegian authors,
1881-1920. A list that gives birth date, death date (if any) and
occupation of all Norwegian authors who died in the years
1881-1950's or were still active in or born within the years
1881-1920.

Persian

3806   OUSELEY, Sir GORE, bart., 1770-1844.
Biographical notices of Persian poets; with critical and
explanatory remarks. To which is prefixed a memoir of
the late... Sir Gore Ouseley, by James Reynolds. London,
Printed for the Oriental Translation Fund of Great Britain
and Ireland, 1846. ccxxvi, 387p. 22cm. [Oriental Translation Fund. Publications, 61]

3807 STOREY, CHARLES AMBROSE, 1888-
Persian literature; a bio-bibliographical survey. London,
Luzac, 1927-   v. in   22cm.

Polish

3808 DEMBY, STEFAN, 1862-
Album pisarzy polskich. Zebrał i objaśnił S. Demby. Illus-
trował Henryk Piatkowski. Warszawa [1898-99]   2v. illus.
Another volume issued in 1901? (Cf. New York. Public Li-
brary. Slavonic Division. Dictionary catalog of the Slavonic
Collection) An album of Polish writers.

3809 JUSZYŃSKI, MICHAŁ HIERONIM, 1760-1830.
Dykczyonarz poetów Polskich. W Krakowie, 1820. 2 v.
8.° Dictionary of Polish poets.

3810 KORBUT, GABRJEL, 1862-
Literatura polska od poczatków do wojny światowej; ksiażka
podreczna informacyjna dla studjujacych naukowo dzieje
rozwoju pismiennictwa polskiego. Wyd. 2, powiekszone.
Warszawa, Skład główny w Kasie im. Mianowskiego, 1929-
31.   4 v.   26cm.   Polish literature from its beginnings to
the World War (1914-1918); a bio-bibliographical work.

3811 KORZENIEWSKA, EWA, ed.
Słownik współczesnych pisarzy polskich. Opracował
zespół pod red. Ewy Korzeniewskiej. Warszawa, Pánst-
wowe Wydawn. Naukowe, 1963-   v. 25cm. (Instytut
Badań Literackich Polskiej Akademii Nauk. Bibliografia
literatury polskiej. Nowy Korbut) Continuation of Literatura
polska, od poszatków do wojny światowej, by Gabrjel Korbut.
Contents. --t. 1. A-I. --t. 2. J-P.   A dictionary of contemporary Polish writers.

3812 WIERZBOWSKI, TEODOR, 1853-1923.
Materiały do dziejów piśmiennictwa polskiego i biografii
pisarzów polskich. Warszawa, Drukarnia Estetyczna, 1900-
04. 2 v. 4.° Materials for the history of Polish literature
& biographies of Polish writers. Covers the years 1398-1830.
No more published?

Portuguese (Including Brazilian)

3813   CARPEAUX, OTTO MARIA, pseud.
Pequena bibliografia crítica da literatura brasileira.   3. ed.
revista e aumentada.   [Rio de Janeiro] Editora Letras e Artes,
1964.   335 p.   21 cm.   Small critical bibliography of Brazilian
literature.   Bio-bibliographical.

3814   COSTA E SILVA, JOSÉ MARÍA DA, 1788-1854.
Ensaio biographico-critico sobre os melhores poetas portuguezes.   Lisboa, Imprensa Silviana, 1850-55.   10v. in 5.
21cm.   Biographical-critical essay on the major Portuguese
poets.

3815   SALGADO, JOSÉ AUGUSTO, 1807-1855.
Bibliotheca Lusitana escolhida; ou, Catalogo dos escriptores portuguezes de melhor nota, quanto a linguagem, com
a relação de suas principaes obras, colligido de diversos auctores.   Porto, Typ. Commercial Portuense, 1841.   xi, 52p.
8.°   112 bio-bibliographical notices of Portuguese writers.

3816   SILVA, INNOCENCIO FRANCISO DA, 1810-1876.
Dicionário bibliográfico português.   Lisboa, Na Imprensa
Nacional, 1858-1923-- 22+v.   illus.   21cm.   [Bio-]bibliographi-
cal dictionary of Portuguese literature.   Vols. 10-   continued by Brito Aranha and others.

3817   SIMÕES DOS REIS, ANTONIO, 1899-
Poetas do Brasil (bibliografia)   Rio [de Janeiro] Organi-
zacoes Simoes, 1949-   v. 19cm.   (His Bibliografia
brasileira, 3)   A bio-bibliography of Brazilian poets.

Russian

3818   AL'BOM SOVREMENNYKH DEĬATELEĬ ISKUSSTVA I
LITERATURY.
Akrostikhi Z. B. Osetrova.   Sankt-Peterburg, Izd. E.
Tile, 1901.   256, iv p.   ports.   253 Russians of the literary
and artistic world.

3819   ARSEN'EV, ALEKSANDR VASIL'EVICH, 1854-1896.
Slovar' pisatelei drevnego perioda russkoĭ literatury IX-

XVII vĭeka (862-1700) Sostavil A. V. Arsenʹev, pod red. O. F. Millera. S. -Peterburg, Knizhnyĭ magazin "Novago vremeni, " 1882. xxvii, 136p. Dictionary of authors of the early period of Russian literature (862-1700)

3820   ARSENʹEV, ALEKSANDR VASILʹEVICH, 1854-1896.
Slovarʹ pisateleĭ srednego i novogo periodov russkoĭ literatury XVII-XIX vĭeka. (1700-1825g.) Spravochnoe posobie i konspekt russkoĭ literatury. Kratkiĭa biograficheskiĭa dannyĭa... S. -Peterburg, Izd. E. P. Muravʹevoĭ, 1887. xxiv, 243p. Dictionary of authors of the middle & modern period of Russian literature (1700-1825)

3821   DILAKTORSKIĬ, PROKOPIĬ ALEKSANDROVICH, 1868-1904.
Vologzhane-pisateli (Materialy dlĭa slovarĭa pisateleĭ-urozhent͡sev Vologodskoĭ gubernii) Vologda, Tip. Gub. pravl. , 1900. 241 (i. e. 141) p. Ca. 140 writers and scholars of the Vologda Government of Northern Russia.

3822   DOBROLĬUBOV, IOANN VASILʹEVICH, 1838-1905.
Bibliograficheskiĭ slovarʹ pisateleĭ, uchenykh i khudozhnikov, urozhent͡sev (preimushchestvenno) Rĭazanskoĭ gubernii. Sost. I. V. Dobrolĭubovskym i dopoln. S. D. ĬAkhontovym. Izd. Rĭaz. arkhiv. komiss. pod red. S. D. ĬAkhontova. Rĭazanʹ, 1910. 338 p. Ca. 300 bio-bibliographies of writers, scholars & artists in the Ryazan Government, Russia.

3823   DOBRYV, A   P
Biografii russkikh pisateleĭ srednĭago i novago periodov. S alfavitnym ukazatelem proizvedenii pisateleĭ. S. -Peterburg, Stolichnaĭa Tip. , 1900. vi, 534, 49 p. 24cm. 205 biographies of Russian writers of the 18th & 19th centuries.

3824   EVGENIĬ, Metropolitan of Kiev, 1767-1837.
Slovarʹ russkikh svĭetskikh pisateleĭ sootechestvennikov i chuzhestrant͡sev, pisavshikh v Rossii, sochinenie mitropolita Evgeniĭa. Izdanie Moskvitĭanina. Moskva, V Universitetskoĭ tipografii, 1845. 2 v. in 1. 22 cm. I. Snegirev originally published a volume of this dictionary in 1838, containing the letters A-G, with some additions. M. P. Pogodin, editor of the Moskvitĭanin, later acquired the publisher's rights from Snegirev and issued the entire work in the present form following the original manuscript. Dictionary of Russian secular writers inside & outside of Russia.

3825 GENNADI, GRIGORĬĬ NIKOLAEVICH, 1826-1880.
Spravochnyĭ slovarʹ o russkikh pisateliakh i uchenykh,
umershikh v XVIII-XIX stolĕtiĭakh, i spisok russkikh knig s
1725 po 1825 g. Berlin [Tip. Rozentaliá] 1876-1908. 3 v.
25cm. Bio-bibliographical dictionary of Russian writers &
scholars who died in the course of the 18th & early 19th centuries. Vol. 3 has imprint: Moskva, Tip. Shtaba Moskovskago voennago okruga. No more published? Contents. --
T. 1. A-E. -- T. 2. Zh-M. S dopolneniĭami N. Sobko. -- T. 3.
N-R. S predisloviem A. Titova.

3826 GOLITSYN, NIKOLAĬ NIKOLAEVICH, kniazʹ, 1836-1893.
Bibliograficheskiĭ slovarʹ russkikh pisatelʹnits. S. -Peter-
burg, Tip. V. S. Balasheva, 1889. vi, 308 p. 24cm. 1286
Russian women as authors; bio-bibliographical.

3827 HARKINS, WILLIAM EDWARD.
Dictionary of Russian literature. London, Allen & Unwin,
1957. vi, 439p. 24cm. American ed. (New York, Philosophical Library, 1956)

3828 ĬĀZYKOV, DMITRĬĬ DMITRIEVICH, 1850-1918.
Obzor zhizhni i trudov pokoĭnych russkikh pisateleĭ.
S. -Peterburg, Tip. A. S. Suvorina, 1885-1916. 13v. 26cm.
Prime source for Russian writers who died between 1881 &
1893.

3829 IGNATOV, ILʹĬĀ NIKOLAEVICH, 1858-1921.
Gallereiá russkikh pisateleĭ. Moskva, Izd. S. Skirmunta,
1901. vii, 589p. ports. 28cm. 253 biographies, with
portraits, of Russian authors.

3830 LENINGRAD. PUBLICHNAĬĀ BIBLIOTEKA.
Russkie sovetskie pisateli-prozaiki; biobibliograficheskiĭ
ukazatelʹ. [Sostaviteli: V. M. Akimov i dr. Redaktor N. ĬĀ
Morachevskiĭ] Leningrad, 1959- v. 24cm. Soviet
writers: bio-bibliographical.

3831 LIBROWICZ, ZYGMUNT, 1855-1918.
Sto russkikh literatorov. Sto korotenʹkikh biografii i sto
malenʹkikh portretov. Sostavil Viktor Rusakov [pseud.]
Sankt-Peterburg, Izd. T-vo M. O. Volʹf [1895] 208 p.
One hundred Russian men of letters; biographies and por-
traits.

3832   MARTOV, N
        Gallereĭa russkikh pisateleĭ i khudozhnikov (s Pushkinskoĭ
        epokhi do nashikh dneĭ) S 216 portretami, ispolnennymi foto-
        tipograviŭroĭ v artisticheskom atel´e Brendamura v Shtutgarte.
        Sankt-Peterburg, Izd. N. F. Mertsa, 1901. 112 p., 216 ports.
        218 biographical sketches and 216 portraits of Russian authors
        and artists from Pushkin's time to 1901.

3833   MOSCOW. GOSUDARSTVENNAĬA AKADEMIĬA KHUDO-
        ZHESTVENNYKH NAUK. KABINET REVOLIŬTSIONNOĬ
        LITERATURY.
        Pisateli sovremennoĭ epokhi; bio-bibliograficheskiĭ slo-
        var´ russkikh pisatelei XX veka. Tom 1, red. B. P. Koz´-
        min. [Moskva] 1928. 287p. 22cm. (Trudy Gosudarstvennoĭ
        akademii khudozhestvennykh nauk. Sotsiologicheskoe
        otdelenie. Vyp. 1) No more published. Writers of the pre-
        sent epoch; bio-bibliographical dictionary of Russian writers
        of the 20th century.

3834   NEFELOV, K   S
        Russkaĭa literatura v biografiĭakh i obraztsakh; s portretami
        pisateleĭ. Praga, Khutor, 1946.   396 p. ports. 21cm. Rus-
        sian literature in biographies and examples; with portraits of
        the writers.

3835   NIKOL´SKIĬ, V   A
        Sto russkikh pisateleĭ. Portrety, biograficheskie dannye,
        obraztsy proizvedeniĭ. S.-Peterburg, Izd. knizhn. sklada N.
        I. Ignatov [1904] 166 p. 100 Russian writers. Portraits,
        biographical data, specimens of their work.

3836   NOVIKOV, NIKOLAĬ IVANOVICH, 1744-1818.
        Opyt istoricheskogo slovar´o rossiĭskikh pisateliĭakh. [Iz
        raznykh pechatnykh i rukopisnykh knig, soobshchennykh izvestiĭ
        i slovesnykh predaniĭ sobral Nikolaĭ Novikov] S.-Peterburg,
        1772. 264 p. 18cm. Attempt at an historical dictionary of
        Russian authors (317 in all)

3837   OLENIN, K   L   ed.
        Russkie pisateli v portretakh, biografiĭakh i obraztsakh.
        Gallereĭa XIX veka. Peterburg, Odessa, Izd. G. H. Karanta,
        1901.   732 p. illus. 33cm. Russian authors of the 19th
        century in portraits and biographies.

3838   PISATELI SOVETSKOĬ BELORUSSII;
        Kratkii biograficheskii spravochnik. Minsk, Gos. izd-vo

BSSR, 1955. 181p. ports. 21cm. 84 biographies of White Russian authors of today.

3839   [PLETNEV, PETR ALEKSANDROVICH] 1792-1865.
Khronologicheskiĭ spisok russkikh sochiniteleĭ i bibliograficheskie zamechaniia o ikh priozvedeniiakh. [S. -Peterburg, V Tip. Éksped. zagot. gos. bumag, 1836] 164p. 277 Russian authors; a chronological list.

3840   PONOMAREV, STEPAN IVANOVICH, 1832?-1913.
Nashi pisatel′nitsy. Sanktpeterburg, Tip. Imp. Akademii nauk, 1891. 78p. A supplement to Golitsyn's Bibliograficheskii slovar′ russkikh pisatel′nits. 419 Russian women as authors; bio-bibliographical.

3841   ROZANOV, IVAN NIKANOROVICH, 1874-
Putevoditel′ po russkoi literature XIX veka. Moskva, 1927. 340p. 12.° A guide to Russian literature of the 19th century; bio-bibliographical.

3842   RUSSOV, STEPAN VASIL′EVICH, 1768 or 70-1842.
Bibliograficheskiĭ katalog rossiiskim pisatel′nitsam. Sankt-Peterburg, 1826. 46p. 87 women as Russian literary figures. Bio-bibliographical.

3843   SAL′NIKOV, ALEKSANDR NIKOLAEVICH, d. 1909.
Russkie poety za sto let (s Pushkinskoi epokhi do nashikh dnei) v portretakh, biografiiakh i obraztsakh. Sbornik luchshikh liricheskikh proizvedenii russkoi poezii. Sankt-Peterburg, Izd. V. I. Gubinskogo, 1901. xiv, 599p. 123 Russian poets of the 19th century; biographical sketches, portraits & selections.

3844   SEMENNIKOV, VLADIMIR PETROVICH, 1885-
Materialy dlia istorii russkoĭ literatury i dlia slovaria pisateleĭ epokhi Ekateriny II. Na osnovanii dokumentov Arkhiva konferentsii Imperatorskoĭ Akademii nauk. Sankt-Peterburg, 1914. 161 p. illus. 28cm. Materials for the history of Russian literature and for a dictionary of authors of Catherine II's epoch.

3845   SNOW, VALENTINE
Russian writers; a bio-bibliographical dictionary. New York, International Book Service, 1946-   v. 21cm.

Contents. --v. 1. From the age of Catherine II to the October Revolution of 1917. 222 p.

3846 SOVETSKIE PISATELI;
Avtobiografii. [Sostaviteli: B. ÎA. Braĭnina i E. F. Nikitina] Moskva, Gos. izd-vo khudozh. lit-ry, 1959. 2 v. ports. 23cm. 130 autobiographies by Soviet [Russian] writers.

3847 STOZH, M E
Slovar´ sibirskikh pisatelei, poėtov i uchenykh... Izd. 9. ... Irkutsk [1916] 78p. Dictionary of Siberian writers, poets and scholars.

3848 TARSIS, VENIAMIN ÎAKOVLEVICH
Sovremennye russkie pisateli. Pod red. i s dopolneniiami Inn. Oksenova. Leningrad, Izd-vo Pisatelei v Leningrad, 1930. 255p. 12.° Bio-bibliographical; 127 Russian authors of the 20th century.

3849 VENGEROV, SEMEN AFANAS´EVICH, 1855-1920.
Istochniki slovar´ russkikh pisatelei. Sanktpeterburg, Tip. I. Akademii nauk, 1900-17. 4 v. 25cm. Source dictionary of Russian authors. No more published. Contents. -- t. 1. Aaron-Gogol´. -- t. 2. Gogotskaia-Karamzin. -- t. 3. Karamyshev-Lomonosov. -- t. 4. Lonachevskii-Nekrasov.

3850 VENGEROV, SEMEN AFANAS´EVICH, 1855-1920.
Kritiko-biograficheskii slovar´ russkikh pisatelei i uchenykh. (Ot nachala russkoi obrazovannosti do nashikh dnei) S.-Peterburg, Semenovskaia tipo-lit. (I. Efrona) 1889-1904. 6 v. in 5. 26cm. Critical-biographical dictionary of Russian writers & scholars. Vol. 4, pt. 1 extends to the article Bogoiavlenskii; v. 4, pt. 2 has subtitle: Materialy dlia Kritiko-biograficheskago slovar´ russkikh pisatelei i uchenikh; in this and the remaining parts (v. 5 and 6) containing material collected for the continuation of the work, the alphabetical order is disregarded; v. 6 has subtitle: Istoriko-literaturnyi sbornik, and both v. 5 and 6 have inclusive alphabetical indexes. No more published. A 2d ed. was started in 1915 but probably did not progress beyond the 1st volume (?)

3851 VENGEROV, SEMEN AFANAS´EVICH, 1855-1920, ed.
Russkaia literatura XX vieka (1890-1910) Pri uchastii: N. ÎA Abramovicha [i dr.] Moskva, Izdanie T-va "Mir"

[1914-16] 3 v. in 2. illus. 28cm. Russian literature of the 20th century (1890-1910); bio-bibliographical. Consists of 3 parts, issued in 7 numbers and bound in 2 vols. No more published?

3852 ZDOBNOV, NIKOLAĬ VASILʹEVICH, 1888-1942.
Materialy dlía sibirskogo slovaría pisateleĭ (Predvaritelʹ-nyĭ spisok poètov, belletristov, dramaturgov i kritikov) Moskva, 1927. 61 p. 24cm. Materials for a dictionary of Russian authors in Siberia.

3853 ZHEREBTSOV, B I
Sibirskii literaturnyĭ kalendarʹ. Irkutsk, Oblastnoe izdanie, 1940. 168p. Siberian literary calendar; includes bio-bibliography of Russian writers in Siberia.

Serbo—Croatian

3854 ŠPOLJAR, KRSTO, ed.
Književni godišnjak; [pisci jugoslavenskih naroda] Uredili Krsto Špoljar i Miroslav Vaupotić. Zagreb [Lykos] 1961. 336 p. illus., ports. 22cm. Yearbook of literature—Yugoslav authors.

Spanish

3855 AMO, JULIÁN, 1908-
La obra impresa de los intelectuales españoles en América, 1936-1945; bibliografía, compilada por Julián Amo y Charmion Shelby. Prólogo de Alfonso Reyes. Stanford, Stanford University Press, 1950. xiii,145p. 27cm. Imprints of Spanish intellectuals in America. Bio-bibliographical.

3856 ANTONIO, NICOLÁS, 1617-1684.
Bibliotheca Hispana nova; sive, Hispanorum scriptorum qui ab anno MD. ad MDCLXXXIV. floruere notitia. Nunc. primum prodit, recognita emendata aucta ab ipso auctore. [Tomus 1-2.] Matriti, J. de Ibarra, 1783-88. 2v. 36cm. This is the 2d ed., edited by T.A. Sánchez, J.A. Pellicer and R. Casalbón; the lst ed. was published in 1672 as "Bibliotheca Hispana." Second part of a work of which "Bibliotheca Hispano vetus" forms the first part. Bio-bibliographical notes on Spanish authors who flourished 1500-1684.

3857 ANTONIO, NICOLÁS, 1617-1684.
Bibliotheca Hispana vetus; sive, Hispani scritores qui ab

549

Octaviani Augusti aevo ad annum Christi M. D. floruerunt.
Curanta Francisco Perezio Bayerio qui et prologum, &
auctoris vitae epitomen, & notulas adiecit. Matriti, Apud
Viduam et Heredes D. J. Ibarrae, 1788. 2v. illus. 36cm.
The 2d ed. of the 1st part of the work of which the "Bibliotheca Hispana nova" forms the second part. Bio-bibliographical notes on Spanish authors who flourished from the
age of the Emperor Augustus of Rome to 1500.

3858   BAEZA Y GONZÁLEZ, TOMÁS, 1816-1891.
Apuntes biográficos de escritores segovianos. Publicados
por la Sociedad Económica Segoviana de Amigos del Pais.
Segovia, Impr. de la Viuda de Alba y Santiuste, 1877. viii,
366p. 23cm. 107 biographical notices of writers from Segovia
province.

3859   BOVER DE ROSSELLÓ, JOAQUÍN MARÍA, d. 1865.
Biblioteca de escritores baleares. Palma, J. Gelabert,
1868. 2 v. in 1. 26 cm. Library of writers of the Balearic
Islands.

3860   BOVER DE ROSSELLÓ, JOAQUÍN MARÍA, d. 1865.
Memoria biográfica de los mallorquines que se han di-
stinguido en la antigua y moderna literatura. Palma, Impr.
Nacional a cargo de J. Guasp Pascal, 1842. 504 p. front. 4.º
Biographical memoir of those Majorcans who have distin-
guished themselves in ancient and modern literature.

3861   CAMPILLO Y CASAMOR, TORIBIO DEL, 1824-1900.
Indice alfabético de autores para facilitar el uso de las
Bibliotecas antigua y nueva de los escritores aragoneses dadas
á luz el Dr. don Félix de Latassa y Ortín. Madrid, Impr. de
T. Fortanet, 1877. 263 p. 23 cm. 125 copies printed. Al-
phabetical index of authors [in Aragon]

3862   CASCALES Y MUÑOZ, JOSÉ, 1865-
Sevilla intelectual, sus escritores y artistas
contemporáneos. Setenta y cinco biografías de los mejores
ingenios hispalenses, y un apéndice con estudios bibliográficos y críticos acerca de las obras de algunos más que
no han sido biografiados, por José Cascales y Muñoz
(Mathéfilo) Con una carta del Excmo. senor D. Marcelino
Menéndez y Pelayo. Madrid, V. Suárez, 1896. xiv, 562 p.
port. 19 cm. Intellectual Seville, its writers and artists
of today--75 biographies and notes on other writers.

3863   CRIADO Y DOMÍNGUEZ, JUAN PEDRO, 1865-
       Literatas españolas de siglo XIX; apuntes bibliográficos.
       Madrid, Impr. de A. Pérez Dubrull, 1889.   196 p.   23cm.
       Spanish women authors of the 19th century.   Bio-bibliogra-
       phical.

3864   CUENCA BENET, FRANCISCO, 1872-
       Biblioteca de autores andaluces.   Habana, Tip. Moderna,
       1921-25.   2v.   ports.   24cm.   (His Biblioteca de divulgación
       de la cultura andaluza contemporánea, v. 1, 3)   Bio-bibliog-
       raphy of Spanish authors in Andalusia.

3865   DICCIONARIO DE LITERATURA ESPAÑOLA.
       2. ed.   Madrid, Revista de Occidente, 1953.   xiii, 926 p.
       22cm.   1st ed. published in 1949.   Dictionary of Spanish litera-
       ture, with substantial amount of biography.

3866   FUSTER, JUSTO PASTOR, 1761-1835.
       Biblioteca valenciana de los escritores que florecieron
       hasta nuestros días [y de los que aun viven] con adiciones y
       enmiendas a la de D. Vicente Ximeno.   Valencia, J. Ximeno,
       1827-30.   2 v.   30 cm.   Chronological, with author and subject
       indexes.   Library of Valencian authors past and present.

3867   GARCÍA LÓPEZ, JUAN CATALINA, 1845-1911.
       Biblioteca de escritores de la provincia de Guadalajara y
       bibliografía de la misma hasta el siglo XIX.   Madrid, Estab.
       Tip.   Sucesores de Rivadeneyra, 1899.   xii, 799 p.   28 cm.
       280 biographical notices of writers of the province of Guada-
       lajara, Spain.

3868   GARCIA PÉRES, DOMINGO
       Catálogo razonado biográfico y bibliográfico de los autores
       portugueses que escribieron en castellano.   Madrid, Impr. del
       Colegio Nacional de Sordo-Mudos y de Ciegos, 1890.   660 p.
       25 cm.   Biographical & bibliographical catalog of Portuguese
       authors writing in Spanish.

3869   GIRBAL, ENRIQUE CLAUDIO, 1839-1896.
       Escritores gerundenses; o sea, Apuntes biográficos de los
       principales que han florecido desde los primeros siglos hasta
       nuestros días, noticias de sus obras...   Gerona, 1867.   96 p.
       Biographical notes on writers of the province of Gerona,
       Spain who have flourished from the first centuries to our day...

3870 LASSO DE LA VEGA Y ARGÜELLES, ANGEL, 1835-1899.
Historia y juicio crítico de la escuela poética sevillana en
los siglos XVI y XVII. Madrid, Impr. de la Viuda y Hijos de
Galiano, 1871. xx, 352p. 24cm. Spanish poets from the city
of Seville.

3871 LATASSA Y ORTÍN, FÉLIX DE, 1733-1805.
Bibliotecas antigua y nueva de escritores aragoneses;
aumentadas y refundidas en forma de diccionario bibliográ-
fico-biográfico, por Miguel Gómez Uriel. Zaragoza, Impr.
de C. Ariño, 1884-86. 3 v. port. 28cm. A bio-bibliography of Aragonese authors. 1st published in 2 v. in 1796; 6 v.
in 1798-1802 (Pamplona)

3872 MARTÍ GRAJALES, FRANCISCO, 1862-
Ensayo de un diccionario biográfico y bibliográfico de los
poetas que florecieron en el reino de Valencia hasta el ano
1700. Madrid, Tip. de la Revista de archivos, bibliotecas y
museos, 1927. 489 p. 29cm. Edited after the author's
death by Vicente Castañeda y Alcover, with annotations.
Attempt at a bio-bibliographical dictionary of poets in the
Kingdom of Valencia to the year 1700.

3873 MARTÍNEZ AÑIBARRO Y RIVES, MANUEL, 1850-1920.
Intento de un diccionario biográfico y bibliográfico de
autores de la provincia de Burgos. Madrid, M. Tello, 1889.
570 (i. e. 580) p. 28cm. Design for a bio-bibliographical
dictionary of authors for the Spanish province of Burgos.

3874 MARTÍNEZ MORELLÁ, VICENTE
Escritores alicantinos del siglo XX. Alicante, 1963.
108 p. 22cm. Writers of the province of Alicante, Spain
in the 20th century.

3875 MÉNDEZ BEJARANO, MARIO, 1857-
Poetas españoles que vivieron en América; recopilación
de artículos biográfico-críticos. Madrid [1929] 413p. 19cm.
Spanish poets living in Spanish America.

3876 MILLARES CARLO, AGUSTÍN, 1893-
Ensayo de una bio-bibliografía de escritores naturales de
las islas Canarias (siglos XVI, XVII y XVIII) Madrid, Tip.
de Archivos, 1932. 716p. 23cm. An essay towards a bio-
bibliography of writers native to the Canary Islands.

3877   NEWMARK, MAXIM
Dictionary of Spanish literature. New York, Philosophical
Library [1956] vii, 352 p. 22cm. (Midcentury reference
library)

3878   ONÍS Y SÁNCHEZ, FEDERICO DE
Antología de la poesía espanola e hispanoamericana (1882-
1932) Madrid, 1934. xxxv, 1212 p. 20cm. (Publicaciones
de la Revista de filología espanola, v. 10) 160 poets, Spanish
and Spanish-American--selections from their works and bio-
bibliographical material.

3879   OSSORIO Y BERNARD, MANUEL, 1839-1904.
Ensayo de un catálogo de periodistas espanoles del siglo
XIX. Madrid, Impr. y Litografía de J. Palacios, 1903-04.
x, 508 p. port. 25cm. Attempt at a catalog of Spanish
journalists of the 19th century. Issued in 6 parts, 1903-04.

3880   OVILO Y OTERO, MANUEL, 1826-1885.
Manual de biografía y de bibliografía de los escritores
españoles del siglo XIX. Paris, Rosa y Bouret, 1859. 2 v.
17cm. (Enciclopedia popular mexicana) Biography & bibliography of Spanish writers of the 19th century.

3881   PARADA, DIEGO IGNACIO
Escritoras y eruditas españolas; ó, Apuntes y noticias para
servir á una historia del ingenio y cultura literaria de las
mujeres españolas, desde los tiempos mas remotos hasta
nuestros días, con inclusión de diversas escritoras portuguesas
é hispano-americanas. t. 1. Madrid, Impr. de M. Minuesa,
1881. viii, 284 p. 22cm. No more published? Spanish women, past & present, as authors & scholars. A few Portuguese
and Spanish-Americans are included.

3882   RAMÍREZ DE ARELLANO Y GUTIÉRREZ [DE SALAMANCA]
CARLOS
Ensayo de un catálogo biográfico-bibliográfico de escritores que han sido individuos de las cuatro órdenes militares
de España. (In Colección de documentos inéditos para la
historia de España. Madrid, 1894. t. 109, p. 1-244) Attempt at a bio-bibliographical catalog of writers who have
been members of the 4 military orders of Spain.

3883   RENEDO MARTINO, AGUSTÍN, 1870-
Escritores palentinos (datos bio-bibliográficos) Madrid,

Impr. Helénica, 1919-26. 3 v. 25cm. Bio-bibliographical data on writers of the province of Palencia, Spain.

3884　REZABAL Y UGARTE, JOSÉ DE, d. 1800.
Biblioteca de los escritores que han sido individuos de los seis colegios mayores: de San Ildefonso, de la Universidad de Alcalá, de Santa Cruz de la Valladolid, de San Bartolomé de Cuenca, San Salvador de Oviedo, y del Arzobispo de la de Salamanca. Madrid, Impr. de Sancha, 1805. xvi, 472, 54p. 26cm. 325 biographical notices of Spanish writers who were also matriculants of six colleges of Spain, San Ildefonso, etc.

3885　RICO GARCÍA, MANUEL
Ensayo biográfico-bibliográfico de escritores de Alicante y su provincia, por Manuel Rico García y Adalmiro Montero y Pérez. Con una carta-prólogo de Roque Chabás. Alicante, 1888-89. 2 v. 32cm. Bio-bibliographical essay on the writers of Alicante, Spain.

3886　RODRÍGUEZ MARÍN, FRANCISCO, 1855-
Nuevos datos para las biografías de cien escritores de los siglos XVI y XVII. Madrid, Tip. de la Revista de archivos, bibliotecas y museos, 1923. 523p. facsims. 25cm. New data for the biographies of 100 [Spanish] writers of the 16th-17th centuries.

3887　ROGERIO SÁNCHEZ, JOSÉ, 1876-
Autores españoles e hispano-americanos; estudio crítico de sus obras principales. Madrid, Perlado, Páez, 1911. 913p. 21cm. Bio-bibliography of Spanish & Spanish-American authors.

3888　RUIZ, LICINIO, 1872-
Escritores burgaleses, continuación al "Intento de un diccionario bio-bibliográfico de autores de la provincia de Burgos," de Martínez Añibarro y Rives. Por Licinio Ruiz y Julián Sáinz de Baranda. Alcalá de Henares, Impr. de la Escuela de Reforma, 1930. 638, xxxi, 13, [3] p. 22cm. Writers of the province of Burgos, Spain.

3889　SAN VICENTE, FAUSTINA
Diccionario de literatura española. Madrid, Ediciones Boris Bureba [1954] 212 p. illus. 20cm. (Publicación del Colegio Mayor para Menores) Dictionary of Spanish literature.

3890   SERRANO Y SANZ, MANUEL, 1868-1932.
Apuntes para una biblioteca de escritoras españolas desde
el año 1401 al 1883. Madrid, 1903-05. 2 v. ports. 28cm.
Notes for a library of Spanish women authors, 1401-1883.

3891   SUÁREZ, CONSTANTINO, 1890-
Escritores y artistas asturianos; índice bio-bibliográfico.
Madrid, 1936-   v. illus. 25cm. Writers and artists of
the old Spanish province of Asturias.

3892   TEJERA, JOSÉ PÍO, 1846-1902.
Biblioteca del murciano; o, Ensayo de un diccionario biográfico y bibliográfico de la literatura en Murcia, formado,
dispuesto y compilado por José Pío Tejera y R. de Moncada.
Madrid, Tip. de la "Revista de archivos, bibliotecas y museos," 1922-   v. 29cm. An attempt at a bio-bibliographical dictionary of Spanish literature in Murcia province.

3893   VALERA Y ALCALA GALIANO, JUAN, 1824-1905, ed.
Florilegio de poesías castellanas del siglo. Con introd.
y notas biográficas y críticas... Madrid, F. Fé, 1902-03.
5 v. 17cm. Vol. 5 contains biographical and critical notes
on Spanish poets; vols. 1-4 are an anthology of selections
from Spanish poetry.

3894   VELÁZQUEZ BRINGAS, ESPERANZA, 1899-
Índices de escritores [por] Esperanza Velázquez Bringas
y Rafael Heliodoro Valle. México, Herrero Hnos. Sucesores
[1928] 320 p. 19cm. 252 contemporary Spanish-American
authors.

3895   VIDART, LUIS, 1833-1897.
Letras y armas. Breves noticias de algunos literatos y
poetas militares de la edad presente. 2. ed. Sevilla, Impr.
de "El Independiente," 1867. 531p. 8.º Letters & arms;
brief notices on some [Spanish] writers and 'military' poets
of the present age.

3896   XIMENO, VICENTE, d. 1764.
Escritores del reyno de Valencia, chronologicamente
ordenados desde el ano M. CC. XXXVIII. de la christiana
conquista de la misma ciudad, hasta el de M. DCC. XLVII.
Valencia, J. E. Dolz, 1747-49. 2 v. 30cm. Writers of the
Kingdom of Valencia, chronologically arranged, from the

year 1238 (date of the Christian conquest of the city of Valencia) to 1747. Continued and supplemented by Fuster's Biblioteca Valenciana, 1827-30.

Spanish — American

3897 ACADEMIA GUATEMALTECA, GUATEMALA.
Biografías de literatos nacionales. [Guatemala] Estab. Tip. "La Unión," 1889-   v. 25cm. Biographies of Guatemalan littérateurs.

3898 ANUARIO BIBLIOGRÁFICO VENEZOLANO.
1942-   Caracas, Tip. Americana.   v. 24cm. At head of title, 1942-   :Estados Unidos de Venezuela. Biblioteca Nacional, Caracas.

3899 -----Alcance: Escritores venezolanos fallecidos entre 1942 y 1947-   Caracas.   v. 24cm. This supplement to the general bibliographical yearbook for Venezuela contains notices of Venezuelan writers who died between 1942/47-

3900 ARTUCIO FERREIRA, ANTONIA
Parnaso uruguayo, 1905-1922. Barcelona, Casa Editorial Maucci [192-] 336p. port. 19cm. Anthology, with brief bio-bibliographical sketches of 102 Uruguayan poets.

3901 BERISTAIN DE SOUZA, JOSÉ MARIANO, 1756-1817.
Biblioteca hispano-americana setentrional. 2. ed. publícala Fortino Hipolito Vera. Amecameca, Tip. del Colegio Católico. 1883. 3v. 20cm. Includes bio-bibliographical information about 3217 Spanish-American authors. (largely those resident in Mexico) Vol. 4 contains anonyms and additions.

3902 -----Adiciones y correcciones... que á su fallecimiento dejo manuscritas José Fernando Ramírez... México, Impr. de El Tiempo, 1898. xlvii, 662p. port. 18cm.

3903 BOLLO, SARAH
Literatura uruguaya, 1807-1965. Montevideo, 1965. 2 v. 18 cm. Bio-bibliography of the literature of Uruguay, 1807-1965.

3904 CARRASCO PUENTE, RAFAEL, 1902-
Hemerografía de Zacatecas, 1825-1950; con datos biográficos de algunos periodístas zacatecanos. Prólogo de José Mariá González de Mendoza. México, Secretario de

Relaciones Exteriores, Departamento de Información para el Extranjero, 1951. 203 p. illus., ports. 24 cm. (Monografías bibliográficas mexicanas, 2. ser., núm. 4) Second part of the volume gives biographical sketches and portraits of outstanding journalists of Zacatecas.

3905 CORTÉS, JOSÉ DOMINGO, 1839-1884.
Biografía americana; o, Galería de poetas célebres de Chile, Bolivia, Perú, Ecuador, Nueva Granada, Venezuela, Méjico, Uruguay, Argentina. Santiago, Impr. de "El Independiente", 1871. viii,235 p. 26cm. 107 Spanish-American poets.

3906 DÍAZ ARRIETA, HERNÁN, 1891-   ed.
Las cien mejores poesías chilenas; selección de Alone [pseud. 2. ed. Santiago de Chile] Zig-Zag [1949] 213 p. 22cm. (Colección Poesía) Each group of poems is preceded by a biographical sketch of the author and in some instances followed by a bibliography. The 100 major Chilean poets.

3907 FIGUEROA, PEDRO PABLO, 1857-1909.
Prosistas y poetas de América moderna. Bogotá, J. M. Pérez, 1891. 437 p. Modern Spanish American prose-writers and poets.

3908 GRISMER, RAYMOND LEONARD, 1895-
Vida y obras de autores cubanos, por Raymond L. Grismer y Manuel Rodríguez Saavedra. Habana, Editorial "Alfa," 1940-   v. 21cm. The lives and works of Cuban authors.

3909 GRISMER, RAYMOND LEONARD, 1895-
Vida y obras de autores mexicanos, por Raymond L. Grismer y Mary B. MacDonald. La Habana, Editorial "Alfa," 1945-   v. 21cm. [Biografías de autores hispanoamericanos] Ca. 50 bio-bibliographies are contained in the 1st volume of these bio-bibliographical sketches of Mexican writers.

3910 GRISMER, RAYMOND LEONARD, 1895-
Vida y obras de autores puertorriquenos, por Raymond L. Grismer y César Arroyo. Habana, Editorial "Alfa," 1941-   v. 21cm. [Biografías de autores hispanoamericanos] A bio-bibliography of Puerto Rican literature.

3911 GRISMER, Raymond Leonard, 1895-
Vida y obras de autores venezolanos, por Raymond L.

Grismer y George H. Zentz y Hope Housel. La Habana, Editorial "Alfa," 1945- v. 21cm. [Biografía[s] de autores hispanoamericanos, 6] A bio-bibliography of Venezuelan literature.

3912   IGUÍNIZ, JUAN BAUTISTA, 1881-
Bibliografía de novelistas mexicanos. Ensayo biográfico, bibliográfico y crítico, precedido de un estudio histórico de la novela mexicana por Francisco Monterde García Icazbalceta. México [Impr. de la Secretaría de Relaciones Exteriores] 1926. xxxv, 432p. 21cm. (Monografías bibliográficas mexicanas, núm. 3) Bibliography of Mexican novelists; a biographical, bibliographical and critical essay.

3913   ORTEGA TORRES, JOSÉ JOAQUÍN, 1908-
Historia de la literatura colombiana, con prólogos de Antonio Gómez Restrepo y de Daniel Samper Ortega. 2. ed. aumentada. Contiene 568 trozos escogidos de 180 autores. Bogotá, Cromos, 1935. vi, 1214 p. ports. 25cm. The major portion of the work is devoted to biographies and bibliographies of Colombian authors.

3914   PAN AMERICAN UNION. LETTERS SECTION.
Diccionario de la literatura latinoamericana. [Ed. provisional] Washington, Unión Panamericana [1958- v. 25cm. Contents. --[1] Argentina. --[2] Bolivia. A dictionary of Latin American literature and authors.

3915   RIVERA DE ÁLVAREZ, JOSEFINA
Diccionario de literatura puertorriqueña. [Rio Piedras] Universidad de Puerto Rico [1955] xviii, 499p. 24cm. (Ediciones de la Torre. Manuales y tratados) Dictionary of Puerto Rican literature.

3916   ROJAS, JOSÉ MARIA, 1828-
Biblioteca de escritores venezolanos contemporáneos, ordenada con noticias biográficas. Caracas, Rojas Hnos., 1875. xix, 808p. 28cm. Anthology with biographical notices of Venezuelan writers of the 19th century.

3917   SOTELA, ROGELIO, 1894- ed.
Escritores de Costa Rica. San José, Impr. Lehmann, 1942. iv, 876 p. 22cm. An anthology with bio-bibliographical sketches of Costa Rican authors.

3918 TORRES RIOSECO, ARTURO, 1897-
Grandes novelistas de la América Hispana. [2. ed.]
Berkeley, University of California Press, 1949 [c1941-43]
2 v. in 1. 23cm. Ca. 150 novelists of Spanish America.

3919 URIBE MUÑOZ, BERNARDO
Mujeres de América. Medellín, Impr. Official, 1934.
xxi, 460 p. ports. 24cm. 130 prominent women authors of
Spanish America.

Swedish

3920 [HARDT, RICARDUS VON DER] fl. 1702-1711.
Holmia literata. Auctior et emendatior cum appendice de
variis rerum Suecicarum scriptoribus. [Stockholm?] 1707.
5 v. 4.º Literary figures and learned men of Stockholm.

3921 MEIJER, BERNHARD, 1848-1925.
Svenskt literaturlexikon. Stockholm, J. Seligmann [1886]
500p. 19cm. (Samling af myttiga och praktiska upplagsböcker,
3) Dictionary of Swedish literature; with biographies.

3922 RUNNQUIST, ÅKE
Moderna svenska författare. [Stockholm] Forum [1959]
176p. illus. 17cm. (När-var-hur-serien) Modern Swedish
authors.

3923 SVENSKT FÖRFATTERLEXIKON;
Biobibliografisk handbok till Sveriges moderna litteratur.
1900-40-- Stockholm, Rabén & Sjögren. v. in
ports. 26cm. Swedish author-dictionary; bio-bibliographical
handbook to Sweden's modern literature. Editors: 1900-40--
1951-55, B. Åhlen and others.--1956-60-- P. Harnesk and others. Vol. for 1900-40 in 3 v.; vol. for 1951-55 in
2 v., including Register, 1941-55.

3924 SVENSKT LITTERATURLEXIKON.
Lund, C. W. K. Gleerup [1964] 620p. 23cm. Dictionary
of Swedish literature; includes bio-bibliographies.

Swiss (Including French, German, Italian, and Raeto—Romance)

3925 LARESE, DINO
Schweizer Jugendschriftsteller der Gegenwart.

[Amriswil] Amriswiler Bücherei, 1963. 114p. ports. 21cm.
Contemporary writers of Swiss juvenile literature.

3926   MÄGIS, KONRAD, 1814-1885.
Die Schaffhausen Schriftsteller von der Reformation bis zur
Gegenwart, biographisch-bibliographisch dargestellt. Schaffhausen, 1869. 1 v. Writers of the Swiss canton of Schaffhausen from the Reformation to 1869.

3927   SCHUMANN, ALBERT, 1835-1897.
Aargauische Schriftsteller. Aus den Quellen dargestellt.
Lfg. 1. Aarau, 1888. 1 v. 8.° Writers of the Swiss canton
of Aargau. No more published?

3928   SCHWEIZER SCHRIFTSTELLER DER GEGENWART.
Écrivains suisses d'aujourd'hui. Scrittori svizzeri d'oggi.
Scriptuors svizzers da noss dis. Bern, Francke [1962]
200 p. 18cm. Swiss authors of the present.

3929   SCHWEIZERISCHER LITTERATUR-KALENDER AUF DAS
JAHR 1893. Hrsg. von Victor Hardung. 1. Jahrg. Zürich,
Verlags-Magazin, 1893. iv, 260 p. Swiss literary calendar
for 1893; includes biographies. No more published.

3930   SCHWEIZERISCHES SCHRIFTSTELLER-LEXIKON.
Lexique des écrivains suisses. Lessico dei scrittori
svizzeri. Hrsg. von Hermann Aellen. Ausg. 1918. Wein-
felden, 1918. 158 p. 8.° Dictionary of Swiss authors.

3931   TICINO (CANTON) DIPARTIMENTO DELLA PUBBLICA
EDUCAZIONE.
Scrittori della Svizzera italiana; studi critici e brani
scelti. Bellanzona, Istituto editoriale ticinese, 1936. 2 v.
24cm. Writers of the Italian regions of Switzerland; Swiss
writers in Italian.

3932   ZÜRCHER SCHRIFTSTELLERVEREIN.
Zürcher Schrifttum der Gegenwart. Autoren des Zürcher
Schriftstellervereins und ihre Werke. Zürich, O. Fussli
[1961] 205p. illus. 22cm. Swiss writers in German native
to Zurich. Almost 100 authors listed.

Turko — Tataric

3933   ALIMZHANOV, A   ed.
Pisateli Kazakhstana; biograficheskie spravki. [Redaktory:
A. Alimzhanov, S. Mart′ianov. Alma-Ata, Kazakhskoe gos.
izd-vo khudozh. lit-ry, 1958] 219p. illus. 28cm. 71 writers of Kazakhstan.

3934   PISATELI SOVETSKOGO AZERBAĬDZHANA;
Biograficheskiĭ spravochnik. Baku, Azerbaĭdzhanskoe
gos. izd-vo, 1959. 212 p. illus. 17cm. Writers of Soviet
Azerbaijan.

3935   PISATELI SOVETSKOGO UZBEKISTANA.
Tashkent, Gos. izd-vo khudozh. lit-ry UzSSR, 1959. 173p.
illus. 23cm. 76 writers of Soviet Uzbekistan.

3936   SAMAGANOV, DZHENBAĬ, 1915-   ed.
Pisateli Sovetskogo Kirgizstana. Frunze, Kirgizskoe
gos. izd-vo, 1958. 272p. illus. 17cm. Writers of Soviet
Kirghizstan; bio-bibliography of Kirghiz literature.

Ukrainian

3937   KYLYMNYK, O   V   ed.
Pisateli Sovetskoĭ Ukrainy; spravochnik. [Kiev, Radians′-
kiĭ pis′mennik, 1960] 578 p. ports. 21cm. Added t. p. :
Pys′mennyky Radians′koi Ukraĭny. Writers of the Soviet U-
kraine; reference book.

3938   UKRAĬNS′KI PYS′MENNYKY;
Bio-bibliografichnyĭ slovnyk. Redaktsiina kolegiia: O. I.
Bilets′kyĭ [ta in.] Kyïv, Derzh. vyd-vo khudozh. lit-ry,
1960-63. 3 v. 23cm. Bio-bibliographical dictionary of
Ukrainian literature. Contents. -- t.1. Makhnovets′, L. IE.
Davnia ukraïns′ka literatura, XI-XVIII st. st. -- t. 2-3.
Dozhovtnevyĭ period, XIX-XX st. A-IA.

Urdu

3939   MĪR MUHAMMAD KHĀN, d. 1834.
'Umdah-yi muntakhabah... [Delhi, 1961] 19, xxiv, 836p.

26cm. Added t. p. : 'Umdah-i-muntakhabah or Tadhkirah-
i-Sarwar; a biographical anthology of Urdu poets. In Urdu.

LAW

3940 ACADEMIA DE JURISPRUDENCIA Y LEGISLACIÓN, Madrid.
Jurisconsultos españoles; biografías de los ex-presidentes
de la Academia y de los jurisconsultos anteriores al siglo
XX inscritos en sus lápidas. Madrid, Impr. de los Hijos de
M. G. Hernández, 1911-14. 3v. 23cm. Spanish lawyers and
jurists.

3941 THE AMERICAN BAR;
The professional directory of leading lawyers throughout
the world. 1918- Minneapolis, J. C. Fifield. v. illus.
27cm. Subtitle varies: 1918, Contemporary lawyers of the
United States and Canada; 1920-32, A biographical directory
of contemporary lawyers of the United States and Canada;
1933-1951(?), A biographical directory of contemporary lawyers of the United States, Canada, Mexico, South America,
Central America and West Indies.

3942 ATKINSON, GEORGE WESLEY, 1845-1925.
Bench and bar of West Virginia. Charleston, W. Va. ,
Virginian Law Book Co. , 1919. xxvii, 543p. ports. 24cm.

3943 BALL, FRANCIS ELRINGTON, d. 1928.
The judges in Ireland, 1221-1921. New York, E. P. Dutton,
1927. 2v. fronts. 23cm. "A catalogue of the chancellors
and deputy chancellors, keepers of the rolls, justices
itinerant, chief justices [etc.]" appears at the end of major
divisions of the 2 volumes and gives, in many cases, a
substantial amount of detail about the persons mentioned.
The listing in the catalogues is chronological (by date of
appointment to office generally) An index at the end of vol. 2
gives an alphabetical approach to the biographies.

3944 BELL, CHARLES HENRY, 1823-1893.
The bench and bar of New Hampshire, including biographical notices of deceased judges of the highest court, and
lawyers of the Province and State, and a list of names of
those now living. Boston, Houghton, Mifflin, 1894. xv, 795p.
25cm.

3945 BJARNASON, EINAR, 1907-
Lögréttumannatal. Sögufélag gaf út. Reykjavík,
Ísafoldarprentsmiðja, 1952-55. 606 p. (Sögurit, 26)
Biographical dictionary of Icelandic lawyers, law scholars,
etc. Issued in 4 parts, 1952-55.

3946 BROOKS, ULYSSES ROBERT, 1846-1917.
South Carolina bench and bar. Volume I. Columbia, S. C.,
State Co., 1908. vi, 381 p. ports. 24 cm. No more
published.

3947 CALDWELL, JOSHUA WILLIAM, 1856-1909.
Sketches of the bench and bar of Tennessee. Knoxville,
Ogden Bros., 1898. 402 p. ports. 21cm.

3948 DAVIS, WILLIAM THOMAS, 1822-1907.
Bench and bar of the Commonwealth of Massachusetts.
[Boston] Boston History Co., 1895. 2v. ports. 27cm.

3949 DEKKERS, RENÉ
Bibliotheca Belgica juridica. Een bio-bibliographisch overzicht der rechtsgeleerdheid in de Nederlanden van de vroegste
tijden af tot 1800. Bruxelles, Paleis der Academie, 1951.
xix, 236 p. (Verhandelingen van de Koninklijke Vlaamse
Academie voor Wetenschappen, Letteren en Schone Kunsten
van België. Klasse der Letteren, jaarg. 13, no. 14) Bio-
bibliography of law in Belgium.

3950 DIGEST OF WOMEN LAWYERS AND JUDGES;
Biographical sketches and data of women lawyers and
judges of the United States and its possessions. 1st- ed.;
1949- [Louisville, Ky.] Dunne Press. v. ports. 24cm.

3951 DIRECTORY OF LAW TEACHERS
in American Bar Association approved law schools.
1922- St. Paul, West Pub. Co. v. 25cm. annual.
Title varies: 1922-56, Directory of teachers in member
schools. Vols. for 1922-56 issued by the Association of
American Law Schools.

3952 FISCH, EDITH L
Lawyers in industry, by Edith L. Fisch, with Matthew
Foner [and] Albert P. Blaustein. New York, Oceana
Publications [1956] 222p. 22 cm. 11 to 13 or more biographies
in each of 11 sections.

3953   FOSS, EDWARD, 1787-1870.
        Biographia juridica; a biographical dictionary of the judges
of England from the Conquest to the present time, 1066-1870.
London, J. Murray, 1870. 792 p. 24 cm. American ed.
published 1870 by Little, Brown (Boston) See note under Foss's
The judges of England.

3954   FOSS, EDWARD, 1787-1870.
        The judges of England; with sketches of their lives and
miscellaneous notices connected with the courts at
Westminster, from the time of the Conquest. London,
Longman, Brown, Green, and Longmans, 1848-64. 9 v. 22 cm.
Foss's Biographia juridica (q.v.) does not contain the accounts
of the courts, but is more easily consulted for biographical
information.

3955   FOSTER, JOSEPH, 1844-1905.
        Men-at-the-bar; a biographical hand-list of the members
of the various Inns of Court, including Her Majesty's judges,
etc. 2d ed. London, Priv. print. for the author by Hazell,
Watson, and Viney, 1885. xxvi, 528 p. 27 cm.

3956   FRANCE. COUR DE CASSATION.
        Le Tribunal et la Cour de cassation; notices sur le person-
nel (1791-1879) Recueillies et publiées avec l'autorisation de
M. le garde de Sceaux par les soins du Parquet de la Cour.
Paris, Impr. nationale, 1879. lxxvi, 557 p. Introd. signed:
L. de Raynal. Based largely on work begun by A. C.
Renouard.

3957   ----1. [-2.] supplément. Paris, Impr. et librairie
        générale de jurisprudence, Marchal & Billard, 1890-1905.
2 v.

        Notices of French lawyers and judges, connected with the
Court of Cassation.

3958   HISTORY OF THE BENCH AND BAR OF NEW YORK.
        Edited by David McAdam [and others. New York] New
York History Co., 1897-99. 2 v. illus., ports. 27cm.
Vol. 2 is a biographical volume.

3959   THE INTERNATIONAL BAR AND DESKBOOK.
        A manual for the convenience of counsel using the
American bar, the Canadian bar and the International bar.
Minneapolis, R. B. Forster & Associates. v. 19cm.

annual. "The professional directory of ranking international
lawyers. " Editors: R. J. Nelson and B. R. Thornburg.

3960 JONSSON, KLEMENS, 1862-
  Lögfraeðingatal. Stutt aeviágrip þeirra Íslendinga sem
tekið hafa próf i lögfraeði og hagfraeði vid Kaupman-
nahafnarháskola frá 1883 til 1910, og þeirra, sem
fyrin þann tíma höfðu lokið prófi, en voru à lífi 1883.
Svo og skrá yfir alla Íslendinga, sem tekið hafa lagapróf
og hagfraeðispróf fra 1713 til 1910. Sögufjelag gaf út.
Reykjavik, 1910. 73p. (Sögurit, 7) List of lawyers; short
biographical sketches of those Icelanders who have received
degrees in jurisprudence & economics at the University of
Copenhagen from 1883-1910, as well as those who had passed
their examinations before 1883 & were still living in that
year. Also a list of all Icelanders who took degrees in law
& economics.

3961 KOPPE, JOHANN CHRISTIAN, 1757-1827.
  Lexicon der jetzt in Teutschland lebenden juristischen
Schriftsteller und akademischen Lehrer. Bd. l(A-L) Leipzig, Kummer, 1793. xiv, 432 p. No more published. Dictionary of living jurists and law teachers in Germany; bio-
bibliographical.

3962 THE LAW LIST:
  Comprising the judges and officers of the courts of justice;
counsel... notaries, &c. , in England and Wales. 1798-
London, v. 18cm. Title varies: 1798-1802, The New law
list.--1803-1840, Clarke's new law list. Subtitle varies
slightly.

3963 THE LAW LIST OF AUSTRALASIA,
  Comprising the ⎸judges and officers of the different courts
of justice, counsel, attorneys, notaries, &c. , and rules of
the Supreme Courts in Victoria, New South Wales, South Australia, Queensland, Tasmania, New Zealand, Western Australia, Fiji. 1863- Melbourne [etc.] C. F. Maxwell [etc.]
v. 19cm. Title varies slightly.

3964 THE LAWYER'S DIRECTORY...
  Digest of laws for all states and possessions, Canada and
its provinces, principal foreign countries; complete court
calendar for Federal and State courts... and an international
selection of leading lawyers with biographical data. 1883-

Cincinnati, Lawyers Directory, inc. [etc.] v. 18-26cm.
Title varies: 18 -1925, Sharp & Alleman Company's Lawyers
and bankers directory.

3965   LIEBMAN, CHARLES, 1908-   ed.
Directory of American judges, with a table of the Federal
and State courts. Merrie Anne Newman, administrative editor. Chicago, American Directories, 1955. 1 v. (unpaged)
27cm. Includes biographical sketches.

3966   LYNCH, JAMES DANIEL, 1836-
The bench and bar of Mississippi. New York, E. J. Hale,
1881. 539 p. ports. 25cm.

3967   LYNCH, JAMES DANIEL, 1836-
The bench and bar of Texas. Published by the author.
St. Louis, Nixon-Jones Print. Co. , 1885. 610 p. 8 ports.
24cm.

3968   MARTINDALE-HUBBELL LAW DIRECTORY.
Summit, N. J. [etc.]   v. in   26cm. Frequency
varies. Title varies: 18   Martindale's United States law
directory. --18 -1930, Martindale's American law directory.
In 3 vols.: v. 1-2, Lawyers.

3969   MILLER, STEPHEN FRANKS, 1810?-1867.
The bench and bar of Georgia: memoirs and sketches.
With an appendix, containing a court roll from 1790 to 1857,
etc. Philadelphia, Lippincott, 1858. 2 v. 23cm.

3970   MORGAN, HENRY JAMES, 1842-1913.
The Canadian legal directory: a guide to the bench and bar
of the Dominion of Canada. Toronto, R. Carswell, 1878. xii,
279p. 23cm.

3971   MOSER, JOHANN JAKOB, 1701-1785.
Lexicon derer jetztlebenden Rechts-Gelehrten in und um
Teutschland. 2. verm. und verb. Aufl. Züllichau, In Verle-
gung des Waisenhauses, bey G. B. Frommann, 1739. Dictionary of living lawyers in and around Germany.

3972   MOURIK, BERNARDUS
Naamrol der rechtsgeleerde en historische schryvers,
welke over alle rechtzaaken en voorvallen in de rechten in
Holland, by de practizyns gebruikelyk, in't Nederduits gesch-

reeven hebben ... Amsterdam [17--] 472 p. 4.° List of
Dutch legal and historical authors who have written on legal
affairs & cases at law in Holland.

3973 THE NEW AMERICAN LAW LIST,
Including biographical notes; a directory of legal counsel in
the United States, Canada, Great Britain, Ireland, Scotland,
South America, Europe, Australasia, Africa, Asia, &c. 1932/
33- New York. v. 22cm. annual.

3974 NOTABLE LAWYERS OF THE WEST,
Including members of the United States Supreme Court,
Supreme Courts of several states, and prominent lawyers in
the western states. Chicago, Inter Ocean Newspaper Co.,
1902. 186 p. of ports. 27 x 21cm.

3975 O'NEALL, JOHN BELTON, 1793-1863.
Biographical sketches of the bench and bar of South Carolina.
To which is added the original fee bill of 1791, with the signatures in fac-simile [and] the rolls of attorneys admitted to
practice, from the records at Charleston and Columbia, etc.
Charleston, S. C., S. G. Courtenay, 1859. (American culture
series, 213:1) Microfilm copy (positive) made in 1962 by
University Microfilms, Ann Arbor, Mich. Collation of the
original: 2 v. facsims.

3976 THE PORTRAIT GALLERY OF EMINENT LAWYERS.
New York, J. Cockcroft, c1875- v. ports. American
(U. S.) lawyers.

3977 PROCTOR, LUCIEN BROCK, d. 1900.
The bench and bar of New-York. Containing biographical
sketches of eminent judges, and lawyers of the New-York
bar, incidents of the important trials in which they were engaged, and anecdotes connected with their professional, political and judicial career. New-York, Diossy, 1870. viii,
779p. 2 ports. 23cm.

3978 REED, GEORGE IRVING, ed.
Bench and bar of Michigan; a volume of history and biography. Chicago, Century Pub. & Engraving Co., 1897.
vii, 586, xv p. 137 ports. 29cm.

3979 REED, GEORGE IRVING, ed.
Bench and bar of Ohio; a compendium of history and biog-

raphy. Emilius Oviatt Randall and Charles Theodore Greve, associate editors. Chicago, Century Pub. and Engraving Co., 1897. 2 v. ports. 28cm.

3980 REED, PARKER McCOBB, b. 1813.
The bench and bar of Wisconsin. History and biography. Milwaukee, 1882. 542p. ports. 24cm.

3981 REGIS, GIUSEPPE MARIA
Dizionario biografico di magistrati e giureconsulti insigni della monarchia di Savoia. Torino, 1837. 1 v. 8.° Biographical dictionary of magistrates and lawyers of Savoy.

3982 RENO, CONRAD, 1859-1933.
Memoirs of the judiciary and the bar of New England for the mineteenth century with a history of the judicial system of New England; the century's record of the lives of distinguished members of the legal profession, published under the editorial supervision of Leonard A. Jones and Conrad Reno assisted by many eminent New England judges. Boston, Century Memorial Pub. Co., 1900. 2 v. illus., ports. 32cm.

3983 SIGURÐSSON, JON, 1811-1879.
Lögsögumannatal og lögmanna á Íslandi. (In Safn til sögu Íslands. Kaupmannahöfn, 1886. 2 bindi, p. 1-250) The early "law-speakers" (or lawyers) of Iceland.

3984 STEPF, JOHANN HEINRICH, 1758-
Gallerie aller juridischen Autoren von der ältesten bis auf die jetzige Zeit, mit ihren vorzüglichsten Schriften, nach alphabetischer Ordnung aufgestellt. Leipzig, W. Lauffer, 1820-25. 4 v. 21cm. Gallery of all authors of works on law from the oldest times up to our day, with their best writings, arranged in alphabetical order. No more published. Covers A-K only.

3985 STILES, EDWARD HOLCOMB, 1836-
Recollections and sketches of notable lawyers and public men of early Iowa belonging to the first and second generations, with anecdotes and incidents illustrative of their times. Des Moines, Homestead Pub. Co., 1916. 988p. ports. 24cm.

3986 TAISAND, PIERRE, 1644-1715.
Les vies des plus celebres jurisconsultes de toutes des nations, tant anciens que modernes, savoir, latins ou romains,

francois, espagnols, italiens, allemans, anglois, hollandois, &c. Tirées des meilleurs auteurs qui ont écrit, & mises en leur jour par ordre alphabétique. Nouv. éd. Augm. d'un tiers, par M.*** [i. e. C. J. de Ferrière] Paris, Chez Prault pere [etc.] 1737. 762p. 26cm. Biographies of almost 500 jurists of all countries and times. Ferrière's additions are almost entirely drawn from the Mémoires of J. P. Nicéron.

3987   THOMASHOWER, DOROTHY (FISCH) 1923-   ed.
Women lawyers in the United States. Compiled and edited by Dorothy Thomas [pseud. 1st ed.] New York, Scarecrow Press, 1957. xxx, 747p. 23cm. Some 6,000 lawyers.

3988   WEIDLICH, CHRISTOPH, 1713-1794.
Biographische Nachrichten von den jetztlebenden Rechts-Gelehrten in Teutschland. Halle, Hemmerde, 1781-85. 5 v. 18cm. Bio-bibliographical noteces of contemporary German jurists. Incorporates much of the material contained in the author's Geschichte der jetztlebenden Rechtsgelehrten in Teutschland, 1748-49, and in Zuverlässige Nachrichten von denen jetztlebenden Rechtsgelehrten, 1757-61.

3989   WHO'S WHO AMONG WOMEN LAWYERS.
1939-   Boston, Fiona H. Cook. v. 24cm.

3990   WHO'S WHO IN JURISPRUDENCE.
A biographical dictionary of contemporary lawyers and jurists. With a complete geographical index. [1st-   ed.]; 1925-   Brooklyn, John W. Leonard Corp. v. 24cm. American lawyers.

3991   WHO'S WHO IN LAW.
v. 1-   1937-   New York. v. 24cm. Editors: 1937-J. C. Schwarz. American lawyers.

3992   WILLIS, WILLIAM, 1794-1870.
A history of the law, the courts, and the lawyers of Maine, from its first colonization to the early part of the present century. Portland [Me.] Bailey & Noyes, 1863. 712 p. ports. 22cm.

3993   WITTE, HENNING, 1634-1696.
Memoriae jurisconsultorum nostri seculi clarissimorum renovatae decas prima [-quarta] Francofurti, Apud M. Haller-

vord, 1676. 4 v. in 1. 18cm. Recollections of the most famous [German] jurists of the first 4 decades of our century;
bio-bibliographical.

LIBRARY SCIENCE AND BOOK ARTS

3994   AMERICAN ASSOCIATION OF LAW LIBRARIES.
Biographical directory of law librarians in the United
States and Canada. St. Paul, West Pub. Co., 1964. 57 p.
25cm. "Printed for private distribution."

3995   AMES, JOSEPH, 1689-1759.
Typographical antiquities; or, The history of printing in
England, Scotland and Ireland: containing memoirs of our
ancient printers, and a register of books printed by them.
Begun by the late Joseph Ames. Considerably augm, by
William Herbert, and now greatly enl., with copious notes...
Comprehending the history of English literature, and a view
of the progress of the art of engraving in Great Britain, by
Thomas Frognall Dibdin. London, W. Miller, 1810-19.
4v. illus. 29cm. First published 1785-90 in 3v.

3996   ARMANNI, MARIO
Catalogue of Italian publishers and printers of the XVth
century. Introd. by Raffaello Bertieri. Milan, Toscanini,
1930. vii, 398p. 117 plates.

3997   BADER, KARL, 1868-
Lexikon deutscher Bibliothekare im Haupt- und Neben-
amt bei Fürsten, Staaten und Städten. Leipzig, O. Harrassowitz, 1925. vii, 295p. 24cm. (Beiheft zum Zentralblatt
für Bibliothekswesen, 55) Dictionary of German librarians.

4098   BAUDRIER, HENRI LOUIS, 1815-1884.
Bibliographie lyonnaise. Recherches sur les imprimeurs,
libraires, relieurs et fondeurs de lettres de Lyon au XVIe
siècle, publiées et continuées par J. Baudrier. Lyon [etc.]
L. Brun [etc.] 1895-99. 4v. in 3. A bio-bibliography of the
printers, booksellers, bookbinders and type-founders of the
City of Lyons, France.

3999   BENZING, JOSEF, 1904-
Buchdruckerlexikon des 16. Jahrhunderts (Deutsches

Sprachgebiet) Frankfurt am Main, V. Klostermann [1952]
215p. 25cm. Dictionary of printers of the 16th century
(German-speaking areas)

4000   BENZING, JOSEF, 1904-
Die Buchdrucker des 16. und 17. Jahrhunderts im deutschen
Sprachgebiet. Wiesbaden, O. Harrassowitz, 1963. xi, 528p.
26cm. (Beiträge zum Buch- und Bibliothekswesen, Bd. 12)
Printers of the 16th and 17th centuries in German-speaking
countries.

4001   BOLTON, THEODORE, 1889-
American book illustrators, 1845-1955. [New York, 1956]
2 v. in 1. 29 cm. Typescript.

4002   CANADIAN LIBRARY DIRECTORY.
1947/48-   Ottawa, Canadian Library Association.   v.
26cm. annual. (Canadian Library Association. Reference
publication)

4003   ----Supplement. Ottawa, Canadian Library Association.
v. 28cm.

Includes biographical information about members.

4004   COLUMBIA CIVIC LIBRARY ASSOCIATION, Washington,
D. C.
A directory of negro graduates of accredited library
schools, 1900-1936. Compiled... in commemoration of the
fiftieth anniversary of the founding of the first library school.
Washington, 1937. 31 p. 23cm.

4005   COTARELO Y MORI, EMILIO, 1857-1936.
Diccionario biográfico y bibliográfico de calígrafos españoles. Madrid, Tip. de la Revista de arch. , bibl. y museos,
1913-16. 2v. ports. 28cm. Biographical and bibliographical dictionary of Spanish calligraphers.

4006   DAVIES, ROBERT, 1793-1875.
A memoir of the York press, with notices of authors, printers, and stationers, in the sixteenth, seventeenth and
eighteenth centuries. Westminister [Eng.] Nichols, 1868.
vi, 397 p. illus. 23cm. Running title: York printers and
stationers.

4007   DE VINNE, THEODORE LOW, 1828-1914.
        Notable printers of Italy during the fifteenth century, illus-
        trated with facsimiles from early editions and with remarks on
        early and recent printing. New York, Grolier Club of the City
        of New York, 1910. 210 p. facsims. 33cm.

4008   A DICTIONARY OF THE PRINTERS AND BOOKSELLERS WHO
        WERE AT WORK IN ENGLAND, SCOTLAND AND IRELAND
        from 1726 to 1775: those in England, by H. R. Plomer; Scotland,
        by G. H. Bushnell; Ireland, by E. R. McC. Dix. [Oxford]
        Printed for the Bibliographical Society at the Oxford University
        Press, 1932 (for 1930) xxi, 432 p. 23cm. [Bibliographical
        Society, London. Publications] Edited by A. W. Pollard.

4009   DUFF, EDWARD GORDON, 1863-1924.
        A century of the English book trade. Short notices of all
        printers, stationers, book-binders, and others connected with
        it from the issue of the first dated book in 1457 to the incorpor-
        ation of the Company of Stationers in 1557. London, Printed
        for the Bibliographical Society by Blades, East & Blades,
        1905. xxxvi, 200 p. 22cm.

4010   EDMOND, JOHN PHILIP, 1850-1906.
        The Aberdeen printers, Edward Raban to James Nicol,
        1620-1736. Aberdeen, J. & J. P. Edmond & Spark, 1884-86.
        4 v. 2 facsims. 24 cm.

4011   EITNER, ROBERT, 1832-1905.
        Buch- und Musikalienhändler, Buch- und Musikaliendrucker
        nebst Notenstecher, nur die Musik betreffend, nach den
        Originaldrucken verzeichnet. Leipzig, Breitkopf & Härtel,
        1904. 248 p. 25 cm. Music printers and engravers and
        music dealers.

4012   FAELLESREPRAESENTATIONEN FOR DEN DANSKE
        BIBLIOTEKARSTAND.
        Den danske bibliotekarstand. 2. udg. under redaktion af
        Sven Houmøller og Torben Palsbo. København, Bibliotek-
        scentralen, 1963. 330 p. 24 cm. Biographical dictionary of
        Danish librarians.

4013   FINCHAM, HENRY WALTER
        Artists and engravers of British and American book plates,
        a book of reference for book plate and print collectors. London,

572

K. Paul, Trench, Trübner, 1897. xvi, 135 p. plates. 30 cm.
A listing of names with some birth & death dates & biographical
information.

4014 FRATI, CARLO, 1863-1930.
Dizionario bio-bibliografico dei bibliotecari e bibliofili
italiani dal sec. XIV al XIX; raccolto e pubblicato da Albano
Sorbelli. Firenze, L. S. Olschki, 1933. viii, 705 p. 26 cm.
(Biblioteca di bibliografia italiana, 13) Completed by Sorbelli
after the death of Frati.

4015 ----Aggiunte [di] Marino Parenti. Firenze, Sansoni, 1952-
60. 3 v. 25 cm.

Bio-bibliographical dictionary of Italian librarians &
bibliophiles from the 14th to the 19th century.

4016 GRAY, GEORGE JOHN, 1863-
The earlier Cambridge stationers & bookbinders, and the
first Cambridge printer. [Oxford] Printed for the Bibliographical Society at the Oxford University Press, 1904. xvi,
81 p. 29 plates. 29cm. (Illustrated monographs, no. 13)

4017 HEAL, Sir AMBROSE, 1872-
The English writing-masters and their copy-books, 1570-
1800; a biographical dictionary & a bibliography. With an
introduction on the development of handwriting by Stanley
Morison. Cambridge [Eng.] University Press, 1931.
xi, 225p. illus. 33cm. In 2 sections: 1st, Biographies of
the writing-masters; 2d, Bibliographies of the copy-books.

4018 HECKETHORN, CHARLES WILLIAM.
The printers of Basle in the XV. & XVI. centuries; their
biographies, printed books and devices. London, Unwin
Bros., 1897. xiv, 208p. illus. 31cm.

4019 HOPKINSON, CECIL.
A dictionary of Parisian music publishers, 1700-1950.
London, Distributed by G. W. Wheatley, 1954. xiv, 131p.
3 facsims. 29cm.

4020 HUMPHRIES, CHARLES
Music publishing in the British Isles from the earliest
times to the middle of the nineteenth century; a dictionary of
engravers, printers, publishers and music sellers, with a

historical introduction. By Charles Humphries and William
C. Smith. London, Cassell, 1954. ix, 354p. facsims.
26cm.

4021   JONES, IFANO.
A history of printing and printers in Wales to 1810; and of
successive and related printers to 1923. Also a history of
printing and printers in Monmouthshire to 1923. Cardiff, W.
Lewis, 1925. x, 367p. 26cm. Rather difficult to use;
arranged chronologically and by place.

4022   KIDSON, FRANK, 1855-1926.
British music publishers, printers and engravers: London,
provincial, Scottish, and Irish. From Queen Elizabeth's
reign to George the Fourth's, with select bibliographical lists
of musical works printed and published within that period.
London, W. E. Hill [1900] xii, 231 p. 23cm.

4023   LANDAU, THOMAS, ed.
Who's who in librarianship. With a foreword by Robert L.
Collison. [Cambridge, Eng.] Bowes & Bowes [1954] 269p.
26cm. British librarians.

4024   LEPREUX, GEORGES, 1857-1918.
Gallia typographica; ou, Répertoire biographique et chronologique de tous les imprimeurs de France depuis les origines de l'imprimerie jusqu'à la Révolution. Paris, Champion, 1909-14. 5 v. in 6. 25cm. (Revue des bibliothèques.
Supplément 1-3, 5, 7-8, 12   As originally planned the work
was to consist of 20 volumes and a general index. French
printers from the origin of printing to the French Revolution.

4025   LEXIKON DES BUCHWESENS;
Hrsg. von Joachim Kirchner. Stuttgart, Hiersemann,
1952-56. 4 v. illus. 24cm. A dictionary of the book that
includes biography.

4026   LINNSTRÖM, HJALMAR, 1836-1914.
Svenskt boklexikon. Åren 1830-1865. Deel 1: A-L. Stockholm, H. Linnströms förlag, 1883 [i. e. 1867?]-84. Swedish
"book dictionary" with brief biographical data under alphabetical arrangement by authors. Continued by the Svensk bok-
katalog, 1866-

4027   MCKERROW, RONALD BRUNLEES, 1872-1940, ed.
A dictionary of printers and booksellers in England, Scotland and Ireland, and of foreign printers of English books, 1557-1640. By H. G. Aldis [and others] London, Printed for the Bibliographical Society by Blades, East & Blades, 1910. xxiii, 346 p. 23cm. [Bibliographical Society, London. Publications]

4028   MILLER, BERTHA E   (MAHONY)
Illustrators of children's books, 1744-1945, compiled by Bertha E. Mahony, Louise Payson Latimer [and] Beulah Folmsbee. Boston, Horn Book, 1947. xvi, 527p. illus. 28cm.

4029   ---- ----Supplement, 1946-56, compiled by Ruth H. Viguers, Marcia Dalphin [and] Bertha Mahony Miller. Boston, Horn Book, 1958. xvii, 299p. illus. 28cm.

The parent volume and the supplement contain sections with biographical sketches of illustrators.

4030   MOORE, JOHN WEEKS, 1807-1889, ed.
Moore's Historical, biographical, and miscellaneous gatherings, in the form of disconnected notes relative to printers, printing, publishing, and editing of books, newspapers, magazines and other literary productions, such as the early publications of New England, the United States and the world, from the discovery of the art, or from 1420 to 1886, with many brief notices of authors, publishers, editors, printers, and inventors. Concord, N. H., Printed by the Republican Press Association, 1886. 604p. 23cm. Another volume was in preparation but was never published. Index must be used to get at biographical material which is scattered through the volume, but which is extremely valuable for 18th-19th century publishers & printers in the U. S.

4031   NIKOL´SKII, NIKOLAĬ KONSTANTINOVICH, 1863-
Rukopisnaīa knizhnost´ drevnerusskikh bibliotek (XI-XVII vv.) Materialy dlīa slovarīa vladel´tsev rukopiseĭ, pistsov, perevodchikov, spravshchikov i knigokhraniteleĭ. Vyp. I: A-B. [Sankt-Peterburg] Izd. Obshchestva līubiteleĭ drevneĭ pis´mennosti [1914] xliv, 163 p. 4.° (Obshchestvo līubiteleĭ drevneĭ pis´mennosti [Leningrad] Numernyīa izdanīīa, No. 132) Materials for a dictionary of owners of manuscripts, scribes, translators and librarians [in Russia] No more published?

4032   NORDISKT LEXIKON FÖR BOKVÄSEN,
Redigerat av Esli Dansten och Lauritz Nielsen, under medverkan av Harald L. Tveteras och Bengt Ahlén. Köpenhamm,
A. Busck [1946-   v. 27cm.   Issued also with cover
title in Danish.   Scandinavian dictionary for bibliography and
library science.   Includes many biographies of people in the
world of bibliography and books.

4033   PLOMER, HENRY ROBERT, 1856-1928.
Abstracts from the wills of English printers and stationers,
from 1492 to 1630.   London, Printed for the Bibliographical
Society by Blades, East & Blades, 1903. vi, 67p. 22cm.
[Bibliographical Society, London. Publications]

4034   PLOMER, HENRY ROBERT, 1856-1928.
A dictionary of the booksellers and printers who were at
work in England, Scotland and Ireland from 1641 to 1677.
London, Printed for the Bibliographical Society by Blades,
East & Blades, 1907. xxiii, 199p. 22cm. [Bibliographical
Society, London. Publications]

4035   PLOMER, HENRY ROBERT, 1856-1928.
A dictionary of the printers and booksellers who were at
work in England, Scotland and Ireland from 1668 to 1725.
With the help of H. G. Aldis [and others] Edited by Arundell
Esdaile. [Oxford] Printed for the Bibliographical Society at
the Oxford University Press, 1922. xii, 342p. 23cm. [Bib-
liographical Society, London. Publications]

4036   RENOUARD, PHILIPPE, 1862-1934.
Imprimeurs & librairies parisiens du XVIe siècle; ouvrage
publié d'après les manuscrits de Philippe Renouard par le
Service des travaux historiques de la ville de Paris.   Paris,
1964-   v. facsims. 28cm. (Histoire générale de Paris;
collection de documents, publiée sous les auspices de
l'édilité parisienne) Contents. --t. 1. Abada-Avril. Parisian printers and booksellers of the 16th century.

4037   RENOUARD, PHILIPPE, 1862-1934.
Imprimeurs parisiens, libraires, fondeurs de caractères
et correcteurs d'imprimerie, depuis l'introduction de l'imprimerie à Paris (1470) jusqu'à la fin du XVIe siècle. Leurs
addresses, marques, enseignes, dates d'exercice. Notes sur
leurs familles, leurs alliances et leur descendance, d'après
les renseignements bibliographiques et des documents inédits. Paris, Claudin, 1898. xvi, 480p. 20cm. A new ed.,
with considerable additional material and new references to

sources of information, was published in the Revue des bibliothèques, v. 32-44, 1922-1934. Parisian printers, booksellers... 1470 to the end of the 16th century.

4038   REUME, AUGUSTE JOSEPH DE, 1807-1865.
Notices bio-bibliographiques sur quelques imprimeurs,
librairies, correcteurs, compositeurs, fondeurs, lithographes, etc., qui se sont fait connaître à divers titres, principalement comme auteurs; avec indication de leurs portraits,
par A. Dereume. Bruxelles, E. Devroye, 1858. "Première
série." No more published. "Exrrait du tome XIV du Bulletin du bibliophile belge." Bio-bibliographical notices on
Belgians in the book industries and trade.

4039   REUME, AUGUSTE JOSEPH DE, 1807-1865.
Variétés bibliographiques et littéraires. Bruxelles, A.
Dewasme, 1848. 204p. illus. 27cm. Issued in parts, 1847-
49. No more published. Notices of 81 printers and publishers of Belgium, with information on printers' marks.

4040   RICO Y SINOBAS, MANUEL, 1825-1898.
Diccionario de calígrafos españoles. Con un apéndice
sobre los calígrafos más recientes por Rufino Blanco. Pu-
blicalo la Real Academia Española. Madrid, Impr. de J.
Ratés, 1903. viii, 272p. 24cm. Dictionary of Spanish calligraphers.

4041   ROQUET, ANTOINE ERNEST, 1827-1894.
Les relieurs francais. Biographie critique et anecdotique
précédée de l'histoire de la communauté des relieurs et
doreurs des livres de la ville de Paris et d'une étude sur
les styles de reliure, par Ernest Thoinan [pseud.] Paris, E.
Paul, L. Huard, 1893. vii, 416p. illus. 25cm. French
bookbinders; the "Biographie critique" (p. [189]-406) includes
notices of French writers on bookbinding.

4042   SERRANO Y MORALES, JOSÉ ENRIQUE, 1851-1908.
Reseña histórica en forma de diccionario de las imprentas
que han existido en Valencia desde la introducción del arte
tipográfico en España hasta el año 1868, con noticias bio-bibliográficas de los principales impresores. Valencia, Impr.
de F. Domenech, 1898-99. xxviii, 655 p. illus. 27cm.
Historical sketch, in the form of a dictionary, of the printing
establishments in Valencia ... to the year 1868, with bio-
bibliographical notes on the chief printers.

4043   SŁOWNIK BIOGRAFICZNY PRACOWNIKÓW KSIAŻKI
POLSKIEJ; wykaz haseł. [Wyd. 1.] Łodz [Państwowe
Wydawn. Naukowe] 1962. 194 p. 24cm. Biographical dictionary of 'workers' in the field of Polish books; 'catchword' list.

4044   SŁOWNIK BIOGRAFICZNY PRACOWNIKÓW KSIAZKI POL-
SKIEJ; zeszyt próbny. [Red.: Ksawery Świerkowski,
Witold Pawlikowski, Irena Treichel. Wyd. 1.] Łodz, Nakł.
Ministerstwa Szkolnictwa Wyższego, 1958. 135p. 30cm.
Summaries in English, French, German, and Russian. Biographical dictionary of 'workers' in the field of Polish books; tentative part.

4045   TIMPERLEY, CHARLES HENRY.
Encyclopaedia of literary and typographical anecdote; being a chronological digest of the most interesting facts illustrative of the history of literature and printing from the earliest period to the present time. Compiled and condensed from Nichols's Literary anecdotes, and numerous other authorities. 2d ed., to which are added, a continuation to the present time, comprising recent biographies, chiefly of booksellers, and a practical manual of printing. London, H. G. Bohn, 1842. vi, 996p 12p. illus. 25cm. A reissue, with new t. p. and 12 pages of additional matter, of the remainder stock of Timperley's Dictionary of printers and printing (1839) and his Printers' manual (1838)

4046   WHO IS WHO IN PUBLISHING.
1st ed. London, A. P. Wales, 1965.   ix, 277p. "Lists
some 2, 800 men and women throughout the world who "make" books. "--Introduction.

4047   WHO'S WHO IN LIBRARY SERVICE.
1st-   ed; 1933-   New York, H. W. Wilson Co. v.
26cm. 3d ed. (New York, Grolier Society, 1955) has subtitle: A biographical directory of professional librarians of the United States and Canada.

4048   WHO'S WHO IN NEW ZEALAND LIBRARIES.
1951-   Wellington, New Zealand Library Association.
v. 21cm.

4049   WHO'S WHO IN PRINTING IN THE UNITED STATES AND
CANADA, by David Gustafson. [Pittsburgh] The author
[1933-   v. 23cm. (American printing industry bulletin
no. 3-

4050   WHO'S WHO IN PUBLISHING.
        [A biographical dictionary containing 476 biographies of
        publishers attending the 15th Congress of the International
        Publishers' Association at Vienna from May 24th to 30th,
        1959. Vienna, 1959] 85 p.

4051   WORMAN, ERNEST JAMES
        Alien members of the booktrade during the Tudor period.
        Being an index to those whose names occur in the returns of
        aliens, letters of denization, and other documents published
        by the Huguenot Society. With notes. London, Printed for
        the Bibliographical Society by Blades, East & Blades, 1906.
        viii, 73p. 22cm. [Bibliographical Society, London. Publica-
        tions]

4052   YANG, LI-CH'ENG, comp.
        Chung-kuo ts'ang shu chia k'ao lüeh. [Compiled by Yang
        Li-ch'eng and Chin Pu-ying. n. p.] Chekiang sheng li t'u shu
        kuan [1929] 10, 150 l. Biographical notes on Chinese book
        collectors.

MEDICINE

Bibliography, Indexes, Etc.

4053   NEW YORK ACADEMY OF MEDICINE. LIBRARY.
        Catalog of biographies. Boston, G. K. Hall, 1960. 165 p.
        37cm.

4054   NEW YORK ACADEMY OF MEDICINE. LIBRARY.
        Portrait catalog. Boston, G. K. Hall, 1960. 5 v. (4564 p.)
        36cm. "Includes [entries for] the 10,784 separate portraits...
        in the Academy and contains 151,792 entries of portraits
        appearing in books and journals."

General Works

4055   ACADEMY-INTERNATIONAL OF MEDICINE AND DENTISTRY.
        Year book. v.1-   ; 1944-   [Topeka, Kan.] v. 23cm.
        Includes much biographical material. Americans predominate.
        Title varies: 1944, Official roster.

4056   AIKIN, JOHN, 1747-1822.
        Biographical memoirs of medicine in Great Britain from
        the revival of literature to the time of Harvey. London, J.
        Johnson, 1780. xi, 338, [11]p. 22cm.

4057   ALL INDIA MEDICAL DIRECTORY & WHO'S WHO.
        1st/2d-   ed; 1949-50-   Tiruvella, Travancore, A.
        Mathew.   v. ports.   26cm.

4058   AMERICAN ACADEMY OF PEDIATRICS.
        Fellowship list.   Evanston, Ill.   v.   23cm.

4059   AMERICAN COLLEGE OF CHEST PHYSICIANS.
        Membership roster.   19   Chicago.   v.   illus.   24cm.
        Includes biographical data for members.

4060   AMERICAN COLLEGE OF HOSPITAL ADMINISTRATORS.
        Directory.   1938-   Chicago.   v.   26cm.   Provides
        biographical data for members and associates.

4061   AMERICAN COLLEGE OF PHYSICIANS.
        Directory.   1923/24-   Chicago [etc.]   v.   22cm.   biennial
        (irregular)   Provides biographical data.

4062   AMERICAN COLLEGE OF SURGEONS.
        Directory.   1913/14-   Chicago.   v.   illus.   22-24cm.
        Title varies: 19   -50/52, Yearbook.   Provides biographical
        sketches.

4063   AMERICAN DENTAL DIRECTORY.
        1947-   Chicago, American Dental Association.   v.
        illus.   28cm.   Very brief biographical data are provided.

4064   AMERICAN DIRECTORY OF OBSTETRICIANS AND GYN-
        ECOLOGISTS.   1st-   ed. ; 1954/55-   Knoxville, J. T.
        Smith.   v.   28cm.   biennial.   Provides biographical data.

4065   AMERICAN MEDICAL DIRECTORY;
        A register of physicians... of the United States and Canada.
        1st-   ed. ; 1906-   Chicago, American Medical Association.
        v.   30cm.   Subtitle varies.   Very brief biographical data pro-
        vided in the form of abbreviations and symbols.

4066   AMERICAN MEN OF MEDICINE.
        1st-   ed. ; 1945-   New York, Institute for Research
        in Biography, inc.   v. ports.   28cm.   Title varies: 1945-
        52 (1st and 2d ed.)   Who's important in medicine.

4067 AMERICAN PEDIATRIC DIRECTORY.
   1st- 1935- A listing of pediatricians of the United
States, Canada, Hawaii, Philippine Islands & Puerto Rico;
with biographical information. Knoxville, Tenn., American
Pediatric Directory Co. v. 30cm. Provides biographical
data.

4068 AMERICAN PHYSICIANS AND SURGEONS;
   A biographical directory of practicing members of the medical profession in the United States and Canada, including supplements in which are listed and classified the leading hospitals,
sanitariums and health resorts of both countries. Prepared
by James Clark Fifield. Minneapolis, Midwest Co. [c1931]
1737 p. 28cm.

4069 AMERICAN PSYCHIATRIC ASSOCIATION.
   Biographical directory of fellows & members. New York,
R. R. Bowker Co. v. 24-29cm. Began 1941.

4070 AMERICA'S DENTAL LEADERS.
   v. 1- Chicago, Distinction Press, 1953- v. 29cm.

4071 ATKINSON, WILLIAM BIDDLE, 1832-1909, ed.
   A biographical dictionary of contemporary American
physicians and surgeons. Philadelphia, D. G. Brinton, 1880.
747,18p. 26cm. 2d ed. of the Physicians and surgeons of
the United States (Philadelphia, Robson, 1878)

4072 BAILEY, HAMILTON, 1894-
   Notable names in medicine and surgery, by Hamilton
Bailey and W. J. Bishop. [3d ed.] London, H. K. Lewis,
1959. 216p. illus. 23cm. Illustrated biographies of those
whose names are commemorated in medical terminology.

4073 BALDINGER, ERNST GOTTFRIED, 1738-1787.
   Biographien jetzt lebender Aerzte und Naturforscher in
und ausser Deutschland. Bd. 1 (4 Stücke) Jena, Hartung,
1768-72. 4 fascs. in 1v. 8.° No more published. Biographies
of doctors and scientists, German and non-German, active in
the latter part of the 18th century.

4074 BALLAND, JOSEPH ANTOINE FÉLIX, 1845-
   Les pharmaciens militaires francais. Paris, L. Fournier,
1913. [8], 419p. 26cm. French military pharmacists.

4075   BARKER, THOMAS HERBERT, 1814-1865.
Photographs of eminent medical men of all countries, with
brief analytical notices of their works. The photographic
portraits from life by Ernest Edwards. London, J. Churchill,
1867. 2v. plates. 4.°

4076   BARRAUD,
The medical profession in all countries, containing photographic portraits from life by Barraud & Jerrard. London,
1873-75. 4v. ports. 8.°

4077   BAYLE, ANTOINE LAURENT JESSÉ, 1799-1858.
Biographie médicale par ordre chronologique d'après
Daniel Leclerc, Eloy, etc. Mise dans un nouvel ordre,
revue et complétée par Bayle et Thillaye. Paris, A.
Delahaye, 1855. 2v. 8.° First published in 1840? Medical
biography, in chronological arrangement.

4078   BERGHOLM, HJALMAR, 1872-
Suomen lääkärit. Finlands läkare. Biographica, 1927.
Tampere-Tammerfors, 1927. 603p. 24cm. Finnish
physicians.

4079   BERTRAND, THOMAS BERNARD, 1682-1751.
Notice des hommes les plus célèbres de la Faculté de
médecine en l'Université de Paris, depuis 1100, jusqu'en
1750 (inclusivement) extraite (en plus grande partie) du
manuscrit de feu M. Thomas-Bernard Bertrand, communiqué
par M. son fils. Rédigée par Jacques-Albert Hazon... Pour
servir de suite et de complément à l'histoire abrégée de la
Faculté, sous le nom d'Éloge historique, avec des remarques
étendues, imprimée en 1773, chez Butard. Paris, 1778.
xii, 268p. 4.° Biographical notices of members of the Faculty
of Medicine, University of Paris, 1100-1750.

4080   BIOGRAPHISCHES LEXIKON DER HERVORRAGENDEN ÄRZTE
Aller Zeiten und Völker, unter Mitwirkung [von] E. Albert,
A. Anagostakis [et al.] und unter Spezial-Redaktion von E.
Gurlt und A. Wernich, hrsg. von August Hirsch. 2. Aufl.
durchgesehen und ergänzt von F. Hübotter und H. Vierordt.
Berlin, Urban & Schwarzenberg, 1929-34. 5 v. ports. 26cm
Goes up to 1880. Biographical dictionary of outstanding physi-
cians of all times and nations.

4081   ----Ergänzungsband. Nachträge zu den Bänden I-V, bearb.
von W. Haberling und H. Vierordt. Berlin, Urban & Schwarzenberg, 1935. v, 426 p. 26cm.

4082   BISSMARCK, FREDRIK GOTTLIEB, 1862-
        Biografisk matrikel över svenska läkarkåren, 1934.
        Stockholm, H. W. Tullberg, 1934. 875 p. 24cm. Biographi-
        cal material on Swedish physicians, 1934.

4083   BLANC Y BENET, JOSÉ
        Datos para una bibliografía quirúrgica española, donde se
        registran, debidamente ordenados y clasificados, 450 autores
        españoles y más de 1100 obras y artículos sobre cirugía.
        Barcelona, Impr. de la Casa Provincial de Caridad, 1895.
        142, [2] p. 25cm. Bio-bibliography of Spanish surgery.

4084   BLÖNDAL, LÁRUS   H
        Laeknar á Íslandi. Skrifstofa Landlaeknis lét taka saman.
        Sögufélag gaf út. Reykjavík, Isafoldarprentsmiðja, 1944.
        xv, 507 p. ports. At head of title: Lárus H. Blöndal og
        Vilmundur Jónsson. Icelandic physicians.

4085   BLOOM, JAMES HARVEY, 1860-
        Medical practitioners in the diocese of London, licensed
        under the act of 3 Henry VIII, C. II; an annotated list 1529-
        1725, by J. Harvey Bloom and R. Rutson James. Cambridge
        [Eng.] University Press, 1935. vii, 97p. 19cm.

4086   BÖRNER, FRIEDRICH, 1723-1761.
        Nachrichten von den vornehmsten Lebensumständen und
        Schriften jetztlebender berühmter Aerzte und Naturforscher in
        und um Deutschland... Wolfenbüttel, J. C. Meissner, 1749-53.
        3 v. 12.°

4087   ----Herrn Friedrich Börners Nachrichten... ergänzt, von
        E. G. Baldinger. Wolfenbüttel, 1773. paging (?) Includes
        a life of Börner by Baldinger.

        Notes on living physicians in Germany and its neighbors.

4088   BONINO, GIOVANNI GIACOMO.
        Biografia medica piemontese. [Lezione accademiche di
        Prospero Balbo intorno alla storia della Università di Torino]
        Torino, Tip. Bianco, 1824-25. 2 v. ports. 8.° ports.
        Biographies of physicians of the Piedmont, Italy.

4089   BOURDON, JEAN BAPTISTE ISIDORE, 1796-1861.
        Illustres médecins et naturalistes des temps modernes,
        par Isidore Bourdon. Paris, Comptoir des Imprimeurs-unis,
        1844. ix, 467, ii p. 12.° Celebrated physicians and scien-
        tists of modern times.

4090   BRENNSOHN, ISIDORUS, 1854-
        Die Aerzte Estlands vom Beginn der historischen Zeit bis
        zur Gegenwart. Ein biographisches Lexikon nebst einer his-
        torischen Einleitung über das Medizinalwesen Estlands. Riga;
        Druck von L. Schumacher in Berlin, 1922. 552 p. (Der
        Biographien baltischer Aerzte dritter Teil) The physicians
        of Estonia of all times; a biographical dictionary.

4091   BRENNSOHN, ISIDORUS, 1854-
        Die Aerzte Kurlands vom Beginn der herzoglichen Zeit
        bis zur Gegenwart. Ein biographisches Lexikon nebst einer
        historischen Einleitung über das Medizinalwesen Kurlands. 2.,
        wesentlich verm. und erweiterte Ausg. Riga, 1929. 492 p.
        A biographical dictionary of physicians past and present of
        Courland (southwestern Latvia)

4092   BRENNSOHN, ISIDORUS, 1854-
        Die Aerzte Livlands von der ältesten Zeiten bis zur
        Gegenwart. Ein biographisches Lexikon nebst einer
        historischen Einleitung über das Medizinalwesen Livlands.
        Mitau, Gedruckt bei J. Steffenhagen, 1905. 482 p. Biogra-
        phical dictionary of physicians past and present of Livonia
        (an historic region partly in Latvia, partly in Estonia)

4093   BROCKBANK, EDWARD MANSFIELD, 1866-
        Sketches of the lives and work of the honorary medical
        staff of the Manchester Infirmary, from its foundation in
        1752 to 1830, when it became the Royal Infirmary. Manchester
        [Eng.] University Press, 1904. 311, vii p. illus., ports.
        27cm. (Publications of the University of Manchester. Medi-
        cal series, no. 1)

4094   BROCKBANK, WILLIAM
        The honorary medical staff of the Manchester Royal In-
        firmary, 1830-1948. [Manchester, Eng.] Manchester Univer-
        sity Press [1965] xv, 240 p. illus., ports. 22cm. Continua-
        tion of E. M. Brockbank's Sketches of the lives and work of
        the honorary medical staff of the Manchester Infirmary from
        its foundation in 1752 to 1830. Contains sketches and por-
        traits of 101 physicians.

4095   BRÜGGEMANN, AUGUST FERDINAND, 1800-1839.
        Biographie der Aerzte. Aus dem Französischen, mit
        einigen Zusätzen. Bd. 1 [A- Boyle] Halberstadt, 1829. 1v.
        No more published? Biography of physicians. Translated
        from the French [sic] with several additions.

4096 BRUNFELS, OTTO, 1488-1534.
Catalogus illustrium medicorum; sive, De primis medicinae scriptoribus. Argentorati, Apud Ioannem Schottū, 1530.
77p. 4.° Catalog of illustrious physicians; or, About the
first writers of medicine.

4097 BRUZELIUS, ANDERS JOHAN
Svensk läkare-matrikel. Enligt uppdrag af Svenska läkare-
sällskapet. Stockholm, P. A. Norstedt, 1886-95. 6 pts.
(1054, xii + p.) 8.° Forms 3d series of Sveriges läkare-
historia ifrån Konung Gustaf den I:s till närvarande tid.
Register of Swedish physicians, an historical listing.

4098 CALLISEN, ADOLPH CARL PETER, 1787.1866.
Medicinisches Schriftsteller-Lexicon der jetzt lebenden
Aerzte, Wunderärzte, Geburtshelfer, Apotheker, und
Naturforscher aller gebildeten Völker. Copenhagen, Gedruckt
im Königl. Taubstummen Institute zu Schleswig, 1830-45.
33 v. 18 cm. A bio-bibliography for medicine in the 1st half
of the 19th century.

4099 CAMERON, SIR CHARLES ALEXANDER, 1830-
History of the Royal College of Surgeons in Ireland, and of
the Irish schools of medicine; including numerous biographical
sketches: also a medical biography. 2d ed., rev. and enl.
Dublin, Royal College of Surgeons in Ireland, 1916. xiii,
882 p. plates. 8.°

4100 CANADIAN MEDICAL DIRECTORY.
1st- 1955- Toronto, Current Publications, 1955-
v. 24cm. annual. Lists Canadian physicians alphabetically,
giving name, address, school, etc.

4101 CAPPARONI, PIETRO, 1868-
Profili bio-bibliografici di medici e naturalisti celebri
italiani dal sec. XV al sec. XVIII. Roma, Istituto nazionale
medico farmacologico "Serono," 1928-32 [v. 1, 1932] 2 v.
ports. 25 cm. Vol. 1, "con correzioni ed aggiunte."
Bio-bibliographical profiles of famous Italian physicians and
scientists from the 15th to the 18th century.

4102 CARMOLY, ELIAKIM, 1802?-1875.
History of the Jewish physicians. [Translated] from the
French by John R. Dunbar. With notes. Baltimore, Printed
by J. Murphy [1845?] 94, [34] p. illus. 24 cm.

4103   CARNOY, HENRY, 1861-   ed.
Dictionnaire biographique international des médecins et
chirurgiens. Paris, Impr. de l'Armorial francais [1903] 136p.
illus. 29 cm. (Collection des grands dictionnaires biographiques) Issued with (?) or Bound with (?) the editor's
Dictionnaire biographique international des physiciens et
chimistes. International biographical dictionary of medical
men and surgeons.

4104   CARNOY, HENRY, 1861-
Dictionnaire biographique international des physiciens et
chimistes. Paris, Impr. de l'Armorial francais, G.
Colombier [1903?] 57 p. illus. 28 cm. (Collection des grands
Dictionnaires biographiques) Issued (?) or bound (?) with
his Dictionnaire biographique international des médecins et
chirurgiens. International biographical dictionary of physicians
and chemists.

4105   CARRÈRE, JOSEPH BARTHÉLEMY FRANCOIS, 1740-1802.
Bibliothèque littéraire, historique et critique de la
médecine ancienne et moderne. Contenant l'histoire des
médecins de tous les siècles et de celui où nous vivons; celle
des personnes savantes de toutes les nations qui se sont
appliquées à quelque partie de la médecine, ou qui ont concouru
à son avancement; celle des anatomistes, des chirurgiens, des
botanistes, des chimistes... le catalogue et les différentes
éditions de leurs ouvrages... l'origine de la médecine, ses
progrès, ses révolutions, ses sectes, son état chez les différens
peuples. Vol. 1-2 [Æ   Paris, Ruault, 1776. 2 v. 4.°
No more published? In large part a bio-bibliography of
medicine and physicians of all periods.

4106   CASEY, ALBERT EUGENE, 1903-
Biographical encyclopedia of pathologists: Southern United
States of America. Persons trained in pathology before 1937
and resident in the South before the golden anniversary meeting
of the Southern Medical Association, Washington, D. C.,
November 12-15, 1956; and including observations on the
training for research, teaching, and practice in pathology.
Birmingham, Ala. , Published for Memorial Institute of
Pathology by the Amite and Knocknagree Historical Fund, 1963.
xvii, 920 p. ports., diagrs. 29 cm. Pages 377-[806] reduced
in size and photo-reproduced on [105] pages. Bibliography:
p. 917-920.

4107   CASTEELE, PIERRE VAN DE, 1582-1632.
Vitae illustrium medicorum qui toto orbe, ad haec usque
tempora floruerunt. Antverpiae, G. à Tongris, 1617.   255 p.
8.° 184 sketches of famous physicians past and present.

4108   CHÉREAU, ACHILLE, 1817-1885.
Le parnasse médical francais; ou, Dictionnaire des mé-
decins-poëtes de la France, anciens ou modernes, morts ou
vivants. Paris, A. Delahaye, 1874. xxiv, 552 p. 18.°
Dictionary of Frenchmen who were poets as well as physicians.

4109   CHINCHILLA, ANASTASIO, b. 1801.
Anales históricos de la medicina en general, y biográfico-
bibliográficos de la Española en particular. Valencia, Impr.
de López, 1841-46. 8 v. 8.° Collation variously given as 6
to 8 vols. Palau y Dulcet gives 8 v. as collation.   Primarily
a bio-bibliography of Spanish medicine.

4110   CHIOCCO, ANDREA, d. 1624.
De Collegii Veronensis illustribus medicis et philosophis,
qui vel scribendo, vel publice profitendo Collegium, patriam
et bonas literas illustrarunt... Veronae, Typis A. Tami,
1623.   xvi, 171 p. (and appendix of 16 p.) 4.° A new ed. (60
columns, folio) was issued in 1723 (Leyden) About illustrious physicians and philosophers of the 'College' of Verona.

4111   CLARK, JAMES HENRY, 1814-1869.
The medical men of New Jersey, in Essex district, from
1666 to 1866.   Newark, N.J., Published for the author, printed at the Evening Courier Office, 1867.   104 p.   22cm.

4112   CLEAVE, EGBERT.
Biographical cyclopaedia of homoeopathic physicians and
surgeons.   Philadelphia, Galaxy Pub. Co., 1873.   viii, 512 p.
65 ports.   25cm.

4113   COMRIE, JOHN DIXON, 1875-
History of Scottish medicine. 2d ed.   London, Published
for the Wellcome Historical Medical Museum by Baillière,
Tindall & Cox, 1932.   2 v. illus. 24cm.   "Noteworthy for
its illustrations and biographical information." ---Walford.

4114   CONGRESO MÉDICO DOMINICANO.   3d, Ciudad Trujillo,
1944.
Directorio médico dominicano presentado por el Congreso

Médico Dominicano del centenario; compilado por L. F. Thomen. Ciudad Trujillo; [Habana, Impr. Ojeda] 1944. 148 p.
ports. 20cm. Directory of physicians in the Dominican Republic.

4115   CORNELL UNIVERSITY. MEDICAL COLLEGE, NEW YORK.
Directory: Alumni, Cornell University Medical College,
1899-1965 [and] House staff, New York Hospital, 1913-1965.
New York, Published by Cornell University Medical College
and the New York Hospital [pref. 1965] vii, 287 p. 24cm.
A biographical-type directory.

4116   CORTE, BARTOLOMEO, 1666-1738.
Notizie istoriche intorno a' medici scrittori milanesi, e a'
principali ritrovamenti fatti in medicina dagl'Italiani... Milano, Nella Stampa di G. Pandolfo Malatesta, 1718. 311 p.
port. 29cm. Historical notices of writers on medicine in
Milan.

4117   CRAWFORD, DIROM GREY
Roll of the Indian Medical Service, 1615-1930. London,
Thacker [etc.] 1930. li, 711 p.

4118   DEN DANSKE LAEGESTAND.
1832-   København, J. Lund [etc.]   v. ports.
26cm. Began publication in 1832 under title: Fortegnelse over
danske laeger. Issued by the Almindelige danske laegeforening
Danish physicians and graduates of the University of Copenhagen Medical School; largely biographical.

4119   [DEVAUX, JEAN] 1649-1729.
Index funereus chirurgorum Parisiensium ab anno 1315 ad
annum 1714. Accedunt super eorum Societatis positionem, et
praecipuas ejus immutationes, notae historicae; necnon et plu-
rium in arte illustrium compendiosa elogia. Opera M. J. D. V.,
antiquioris Societatis praefecto. Parisiis, 1714. 118 p. 18.°
Mss. additions (in the Bibliothèque nationale) have extended
the coverage to the year 1729. Necrology of Parisian surgeons,
1315-1714.

4120   DEZEIMERIS, JEAN, EUGÈNE, 1799-1852.
Dictionnaire historique de la médecine, ancienne et
moderne; ou, Précis de l'histoire générale, technologique et
littéraire de la médecine, suivi de la bibliographie médicale
du dix-neuvième siècle, et d'un répertoire bibliographique par
ordre de matières. Par MM. Dezeimeris, Ollivier (d'Angers)

et Raige-Delorme. Paris, Béchet jeune [etc.] 1828-39. 4v. in 7. 22cm. A bio-bibliography for medicine.

4121 DICTIONNAIRE DES MÉDECINS, CHIRURGIENS ET PHAR-
MACIENS FRANCAIS, légalement recus avant et depuis la
fondation de la République. Paris, Moreau, 1802. 610 p.
Dictionary of French physicians, surgeons and pharmacists
admitted to practice before and after the founding of the Republic.

4122 DICTIONNAIRE ENCYCLOPÉDIQUE DES SCIENCES MÉDI-
CALES, publié sous la direction de MM. Raige-Delorme
et A. Dechambre, par MM. Axenfeld, Baillarger [et al.]
Paris, P. Asselin, Sr. de Labé, V. Masson, 1864-69. 100 v.
illus. 24cm. In 5 series. Title varies; some vols. have
title: Dictionnaire des sciences médicales. Imprint varies.
Encyclopedic dictionary of medicine; includes biographies.

4123 DIRECTORIO MÉDICO-SOCIAL DE CUBA.
1937-   La Habana. v. illus. 24-26cm. Title varies:
1937-   Anuario médico-social de Cuba (half-title: Directorio médico-social de Cuba)

4124 DIRECTORY OF MEDICAL SPECIALISTS
Holding certification by American Boards. v. [1]-
1939-   Chicago [etc.] Marquis-Who's Who [etc.]
1940-   v. 24cm. Title varies slightly. Published for
and compiled by the Advisory Board for Medical Specialists.

4125 DUBOIS D'AMIENS, FRÉDÉRIC, 1799?-1873.
La Belgique médicale; ou, Notice sur la vie et les écrits
des Belges qui se sont distingués dans les sciences médicales.
Bruxelles, 1836. 1 v. Medical Belgium; or, Notice on the
life & writings of Belgians who have distinguished themselves
in the medical sciences.

4126 ELOY, NICOLAS FRANCOIS JOSEPH, 1714-1778.
Dictionnaire historique de la médecine ancienne et moderne;
ou, Mémoires disposés en ordre alphabétique pour servir à
l'histoire de cette science, et à celle des médecins,
anatomistes, botanistes, chirurgiens et chymistes de toutes
nations. Mons, H. Hoyois, 1778. 4 v. 27 cm. 1st published
in 2 vols. in 1775 under title: Dictionnaire de médecine. A
3-vol. Italian version was published 1761-1763. Dictionary of
medical history, with many biographical articles.

589

4127   ELWERT, JOHANN KASPAR PHILIPP.
Nachrichten von dem Leben und den Schriften jetztlebender
teutscher Aerzte, Wundärzte, Thierärzte, Apotheker und
Naturforscher. 1. Bd. Hildesheim, Gerstenheim, 1799.
1 v. 8.° No more published. Reports and writings of contemporary German doctors, surgeons, veterinarians, pharmacists and scientists.

4128   FAGE, RENÉ, 1848-1929.
Dictionnaire des médecins du Limousin, Corrèze et
Haut-Vienne, jusqu'à la fin du XVIIIe siècle. Tulle, Impr. de
Crauffon, 1895. 205 p. 8.° Dictionary of French physicians
in Limousin to the end of the 18th century.

4129   FEDERIGO, GASPARE, 1769-1840.
Dei meriti dei più celebri professori che nelle mediche
discipline fiorirono nell'Università di Padova nei tre secoli
XIV, XV e XVI. Padova, 1835. 1 v. Physicians at the University of Padua in the 14th-16th centuries.

4130   FISCHER, ISIDOR, 1868-   ed.
Biographisches Lexikon der hervorragenden Ärzte der
letzten fünfzig Jahre. Zugleich Fortsetzung des Biographischen
Lexikon der hervorragenden Ärzte aller Zeiten und Völker.
Berlin, Urban & Schwarzenberg, 1932-33. 2 v. ports. 26 cm.
Biographical dictionary of the outstanding physicians of the
last 50 years (1882-1932)

4131   FISHER, GEORGE JACKSON, 1825-1893.
Biographical sketches of the deceased physicians of
Westchester County, New York... New York, Published by
order of the [Westchester County Medical] Society; Clayton &
Co., printers, 1861. 52 p. 23 cm.

4132   FRANCIS, SAMUEL WARD, 1835-1886.
Biographical sketches of distinguished living New York
physicians. New York, G. P. Putnam, 1867. 228 p. 19 cm.
Reprinted from the Philadelphia medical and surgical reporter.

4133   GARCÍA DEL MQRAL, JOSÉ
Galería de escritores médicos montañeses. Ensayo bio-
bibliográfico. Santander, Impr. Viuda de F. Fons, 1906.
271 p. Gallery of writers on medicine in the province of
Santander, Spain; bio-bibliography.

4134   GOELICKE, ANDREAS OTTOMAR, 1670?-1744?
        Historia medicinae universalis qua celebriorum... quorum-
cunque medicorum qui a primis artis natalibus ad nostra usque
tempora inclaruerunt, vitae, nomina, dogmata singularia...
adcurate pertractantur... Francofurti ad Viadrum, 1718-20.
4v. A history of medicine with the lives of celebrated physicians of all times.

4135   GRIENWALDT, FRANZ JOSEF
        Album Bavariae iatricae; seu, Catalogus celebriorum ali-
quot medicorum, qui suis in Bavaria scriptis medicinam
exornarunt ab anno 1450, quo Boica schola fundata quidem,
at primum anno 1472 publicata fuit, in hodiernam usque lucem,
quantum pro hac yice fieri potuit continuatus, additis ubivis
ferme notatu dignioribus... Monachii, Typis M. M. Riedlin
Viduae, 1733. viii, 148 p. 8.° Album of Bavarian medicine;
or, Catalog of some celebrated physicians who adorned medicine in Bavaria with their writings from the year 1450... to the
present day...

4136   GRIESBACH, HERMANN ADOLF, 1854-
        Medizinisches Wörter- und Nachschlagebuch; ein Hilfsbuch
für Studierende und Ärzte und alle mit der Medizin in Zusam-
menhang stehenden Berufe. Mit Ableitung, Übersetzung und
Erklärung der in der Medizin vorkommenden Fachausdrücke
und mit biographischen und literarischen Angaben. Giessen,
A. Töpelmann, 1927. xxii, 815, 313 p. 16cm. Partial contents. --2. T. Biographische Daten der im 1. Teil genannten
Forscher aus Vergangenheit und Gegenwart. A medical dictionary and reference book which also contains biographical
sketches.

4137   GROSS, SAMUEL DAVID, 1805-1884, ed.
        Lives of eminent American physicians and surgeons of the
nineteenth century. Philadelphia, Lindsay & Blakiston, 1861.
836 p. port. 23cm.

4138   GUIDE MÉDICAL ET PHARMACEUTIQUE ROSENWALD.
        1887-   Paris, Éditions commerciales de France
[etc.]   v. 22-24cm. annual. title varies: -1939,
Guide Rosenwald médical et pharmaceutique. A directory of
French physicians and pharmacists.

4139   HANER, CENGIZ
        Tibbiye sehitleri. Istanbul, Türkiye basimevi, 1940.
55 p. illus., ports. 20cm. Distinguished [Turkish] men of
medicine (contemporary)

4140   HAYMAKER, WEBB, 1902-   ed.
The founders of neurology. One hundred and thirty-three
biographical sketches prepared for the fourth International
Neurological Congress in Paris by eighty-four authors. With
the bibliographical and editorial assistance of Karl A. Baer.
Springfield, Ill., C. C. Thomas, 1953. xxvii, 479p. ports.
24cm.

4141   HENSCHEL, AUGUST WILHELM EDUARD THEODOR, 1790-
1856.
Iatrologiae Silesiae specimen primum, exhibens brevis-
simam medicorum Silesiacorum saeculi XIII. ad XVI.
notitiam... Vratislaviae, Typ. M. Friedlaenderi [1837]
viii, 32p. 4.° The first example of Silesian medicine, giving
a brief report on the physicians of Silesia from the 13th to the
16th century.

4142   HERNÁNDEZ MOREJÓN, ANTONIO, 1733-1836.
Historia bibliográfica de la medicina española. Obra
póstuma. Madrid, 1842-52. 7 v. 20cm. (Biblioteca
escojida de medicina y cirujía) Chiefly bio-bibliographical;
Spanish medicine.

4143   HIRSCHFELD, JOSEF
Gallerie berühmter Kliniker und hervorragender Aerzte
unserer Zeit mit den Biographien, als Beitrag zur Geschichte
der Medicin. Wien, 1875-77. 10 Lieferungen. 4.° No more
published? Gallery of famous clinicians and outstanding physicians of our time.

4144   HUTCHINSON, BENJAMIN
Biographia medica; or, Historical and critical memoirs of
the lives and writings of the most eminent characters that
have existed from the earliest account of time to the present
period; with a catalogue of their literary productions. London,
1799. 2v. 22cm.

4145   INGERSLEV, VILHELM, 1835-
Danmarks laeger og laegevaesen fra de aeldste tider indtil
aar 1800. En fremstilling efter trykte kilder. Kjøbenhavn,
E. Jespersen, 1873. 2v. 21cm. Denmark's physicians and
medicine from the oldest times to the year 1800.

4146   INTERNATIONAL REFUGEE ORGANIZATION. HEALTH
DIVISION.
Professional medical register. Geneva [1948?] 421p.

24cm. Cover title: Displaced persons professional medical register.

4147 INTERNATIONAL WHO'S WHO IN WORLD MEDICINE.
New York, American Universities Medical Research
Publications, 1947. 745p. 25cm. Successor to Who's who in
world medicine, issued by B. U. E. , ltd. , London, 1939.
Emphasis is on American physicians. Does not include birth
date.

4148 IRISH MEDICAL DIRECTORY AND HOSPITAL YEAR BOOK.
193- -
Dublin, Parkside Press. v. 26cm.

4149 JOURDAN, ANTOINE JACQUES LOUIS, 1788-1848.
Biographie médicale. Paris, Panckoucke, 1820-25. 7v.
8.⁰ Reissued 1834 (with a varying title page?) Medical
biography, universal in scope.

4150 KAGAN, SOLOMON ROBERT, 1881-
Jewish contributions to medicine in America, from
colonial times to the present. Foreword by James J. Walsh.
2d ed. , rev. and enl. Boston, Boston Medical Pub. Co. ,
1939. xxxi, 702p. ports. 23cm. First ed. issued in 1934.

4151 KAGAN, SOLOMON ROBERT, 1881-
Jewish medicine. Boston, Medico-Historical Press, 1952.
575p. ports. 24cm.

4152 KELLY, EMERSON CROSBY, 1899-
Enycyclopedia of medical sources. Baltimore, Williams
& Wilkins, 1948. v, 476 p. 24cm. Includes bio-
bibliographical material.

4153 KELLY, HOWARD ATWOOD, 1858-1943.
Dictionary of American medical biography; lives of
eminent physicians of the United States and Canada, from the
earliest times, by Howard A. Kelly and Walter L. Burrage.
New York, D. Appleton, 1928. xxx, 1364p. 27cm. 1st
published 1912 under title: A cyclopedia of American medical
biography; and in 1920 as: American medical biographies.

4154 KESTNER, CHRISTIAN WILHELM, 1694-1747.
Medicinisches Gelehrten-Lexicon. Darinnen die Leben der
berühmtesten Aerzte samt deren wichtigsten Schrifften...

nach alphabetischer Ordnung beschrieben worden. Nebst
einer Vorrede von Gottlieb Stolle. Jena, J. Meyers seel.
Erben, 1740. 940p. 4. Dictionary of learned men of
medicine; lives of the most famous physicians together with
their writings, in alphabetical arrangement.

4155   KIAER, FRANTZ CASPER, 1835-1893.
        Norges laeger i det nittende aarhundrede (1800-1886) 2.
        betydeligt foroegede udg. 1. -2. hefte (A-Capellen) Chris-
        tiania, A. Cammermeyer, 1888-90. 2 v. 25cm. First
        published 1873. Norwegian physicians in the 19th century.

4156   KOBRO, ISAK, 1867-
        Norges laeger, 1800-1908. 3. udg. af F. C. Kiaer: Norges
        laeger i det nittende aarhundrede (1800-1886)... Kristiania,
        A. Cammermeyer, 1915. 2 v. ports. 26cm. Norway's
        physicians, 1880-1908.

4157   KOŚMIŃSKI, STANISŁAW LUBICZ, 1837-1883.
        Słownik lekarzów polskich obejmujacy oprócz krótkich
        zyciorysów lekarzy polaków oraz cudzoziemców w Polsce
        osiadłych, dokładna bibliografia lekarska polska od czasów
        najdawniejszych az do chwili obecnéj. Warszawa, Nakł au-
        tora, 1883-[88] xvii, 665 p. port. 28cm. Cover title.
        Issued in 4 parts. Brought down to 1885 by the author's wife,
        Lucyna Kosminska, with the assistance of J. Peszke. Diction-
        ary of Polish physicians containing short biographies of Polish
        doctors as well as foreigners living in Poland...

4158   KRISTJÁNSSON, JÓN, 1884-1918.
        Laeknatal (1760-1913) Sögufelag gaf út. Reykjavík, 1914.
        vii, 72 p. 8.° (Sögurit, 11) Biographical sketches of Ice-
        landic physicians, 1760-1913.

4159   LAKHTIN, MIKHAIL ĪŪR'EVICH, 1869-1932.
        Kratkiĭ biograficheskiĭ slovar῾znamenitykh vrachei vsekh
        vremen. S.-Peterburg, Meditsinskiĭ zhurnal, " 1902. 103p.
        26cm. Brief biographical dictionary of famous physicians of
        all times.

4160   LENINGRAD. VOENNO-MEDITSINSKAIA AKADEMIIA.
        V pamiat' 25-letiia deiatel' nosti vrachei, okonchivshikh
        kurs Imp. Mediko-Khirurgicheskoĭ akademii v 1873 godu.
        1873. XXV. 1898. S.-Peterburg, Skoropech. A. H. TSepova,
        1898. viii, 76p. Ca. 150 biographies, autobiographies, no-

tices & necrologies of graduates of the Academy of Medicine
and Surgery, St. Petersburg, on the occasion of its 25th anniversary of service.

4161   LENINGRAD. VOENNO-MEDITSINSKAIA AKADEMIIA.
       Sbornik biografii vrachei vypuska 1881 goda imp. Mediko-
Khirurgicheskoi akademii. XXV. (1881-1906) 7 noiabria.
S.-Peterburg, Tip. M-va vnutrennykh del, 1906. 300p.
Ca. 100 biographies & autobiographies of graduates (1881) of
the Academy of Medicine and Surgery (later Academy of Mil-
itary Medicine?) in St. Petersburg.

4162   LEYLAND, JOHN, ed.
       Contemporary medical men and their professional work;
biographies of leading physicians and surgeons, with portraits, from the Provincial medical journal. Edited and extended by John Leyland. Leicester [Eng.] Office of the Provincial Medical Journal, 1888. 2 v. 4.°

4163   LUDEKING, WILLEM ERNST, 1802-1882.
       Levensberigten en lettervruchten van Nederlandsche
geneeskundigen, van de vroegste tijden tot op onze dagen...
Deel 1. Brielle, 1847. 1 v. Lives and writings of Dutch
physicians from earliest times to 1847. No more published?

4164   MANGET, JEAN JACQUES, 1652-1742.
       Bibliotheca scriptorum medicorum veterum et recentiorum,
in qua sub eorum omnium qui a mundi primordiis ad hunc
usque annum vixerunt nominibus, ordine alphabetico adscrip-
tis, vitae compendio enarrantur... sicque historia medica vere
universalis exhibetur... Genevae, Sumptibus Perachon et
Cramer, 1731. 4 v. plates. fol. Library of medical writers
old and new. Bio-bibliographical.

4165   MARTINS BASTOS, FRANCISCO ANTONIO, 1799-1868.
       Nobiliarchia medica. Noticia dos medicos e cirurgiões da
Real Camara, dos physicos mores e cirurgiões mores do
reino, armada, exercito, e ultramarinos etc. desde os tem-
pos mais remotos da monarchia... Lisboa, Imprensa União
Typographica, 1858. xiii, 82 p. 8.° Physicians and surgeons of Portugal, past and present.

4166   MAYER, CLAUDIUS FRANK, 1899-
       Bio-bibliography of XVI century medical authors. Wash-
ington, Govt. Print. Off., 1941. 52p. (In U. S. Surgeon
General's Office. Index catalogue, 4th ser., v. 6)

4167   MAYO CLINIC, Rochester, Minn.
        Physicians of the Mayo Clinic and the Mayo Foundation.
        London, Oxford University Press; Minneapolis, University
        of Minnesota Press, 1937. vi, 1575p. ports. 24cm.

4168   THE MEDICAL DIRECTORY.
        London, provinces, Wales, Scotland, Ireland, abroad,
        Navy, Army & Air Force. 1845-   London, J. & A.
        Churchill. v. 26cm. Title varies: 1845-47, The London
        medical directory. -- 1848-1860, The London and Provincial
        medical directory.

4169   MEDICAL DIRECTORY FOR AUSTRALIA.
        Sydney, Australasian Medical Pub. Co. v. 21cm.
        Includes biographical sketches, etc. Cover title: 19
        Knox's medical directory for Australia.

4170   MEDICAL DIRECTORY OF NEW YORK, NEW JERSEY AND
        CONNECTICUT. New York, Medical Society of the
        State of New York [etc.] v. 19cm.

4171   THE MEDICAL DIRECTORY OF SOUTH AFRICA.
        1st-   1960-   Durban, Knox Pub. Co.   v. 24cm.
        Includes brief biographical data.

4172   THE MEDICAL WHO'S WHO.
        1912-1917/18, 1925-27. London, London & Counties Press
        Association. 9(?) v. 19cm. No more published?

4173   MEDICAL WOMAN'S DIRECTORY.
        1st-   ed.; 1945-   Cincinnati, Elizabeth Press.   v.
        24cm.

4174   MINICUCCI, ATTILIO
        Quadro biografico de' più distinti medici e chirurgi luc-
        chesi. Lucca, 1843. 1 v. The most famous physicians and
        surgeons of Lucca, Italy.

4175   MOEHSEN, JOHANN KARL WILHELM, 1722-1795.
        Verzeichniss einer Sammlung von Bildnissen, grössten-
        theils berühmter Aerzte... Diesem sind verschiedene Nach-
        richten und Anmerkungen vorgesetzt, die sowohl zur
        Geschichte der Arzeneygelahrtheit, als vornehmlich zur
        Geschichte der Künste gehören. Berlin, 1771. 243p. 21cm.

List of a collection of portraits, for the most part of famous physicians. To this are added various notes and observations.

4176 [MOREL DE RUBEMPRÉ, J]
Biographie des médecins français vivants et des professeurs des écoles, par un de leurs confrères. Paris, Chez les Marchands de nouveautés [1826] 160p. 16.º Biography of living French physicians and of professors of medicine.

4177 MOURIK, BERNARDUS
Naamrol der medicinaale, chirurgiale, chimische, natuurkundige schrijvers, welke over alle medicinaale zaaken ... in't Nederduits geschreeven hebben. Amsterdam [1752?] 1 v. 4.º List of authors in medicine, surgery, chemistry & science who have written on medical subjects in Dutch.

4178 OBSHCHESTVO PETERBURGSKIKH VRACHEĬ-NEMTSEV.
Biographisches Album des Vereins St.-Petersburger Aerzte, 1859-1909. Hrsg. zum 50-jährigen Jubiläum des Vereins 31 März 1909. St.-Peterburg, 1909. x, 118 p. Over 400 biographical sketches of members of the Association of Physicians of St. Petersburg.

4179 OEFELE, ANDREAS FELIX VON, 1706-1780.
Ärztebiographien aus dem elenchus quorundam Bavariae medicorum des Münchener Hofbibliothekars Andreas Felix von Oefele. [München] 195 - v. 21cm. A series of doctoral dissertations by various candidates at the University of Munich translating medical biographies from Oefele's manuscript in the Bayerische Staatsbibliothek. The manuscript is a quarto of 767 pages giving 109 lives in alphabetical order.

4180 OLPP, GOTTLIEB, 1872-
Hervorragende Tropenärzte in Wort und Bild. München, Verlag der Ärztlichen Rundschau, O. Gmelin, 1932. vii, 446 p. illus., 71 ports. 25cm. Outstanding practitioners of tropical medicine in word and picture.

4181 PAGEL, JULIUS LEOPOLD, 1851-
Biographisches Lexikon hervorragender Ärzte des neunzehnten Jahrhunderts. Mit einer historischen Einleitung. Mit 669 Bildnissen. Berlin, Urban & Schwarzenberg, 1901. xxxiii p., 1983 columns. illus., ports. 25cm. Biographical dictionary of outstanding doctors of the 19th century. Issued in 5 parts, 190 :901.

4182   PANELLI D'ACQUAVIVA, GIOVANNI
        Memorie degli uomini illustri e chiari in medicina del Pi-
        ceno ossia della Marca d'Ancona.   Ascoli, Per V. Ricci,
        1758. 2 v. 4.º Memorial of famous men of medicine in
        Ancona Province, Italy.

4183   PEISSE, LOUIS, 1803-1880.
        La médecine et les médecins. Philosophie, doctrines,
        institutions, critiques, moeurs et biographies médicales.
        Paris, J. B. Baillière [etc.] 1857. 2 v. 18cm. Includes
        medical biography.

4184   PESCETTO, G   B
        Biografia medica Ligure. Vol. 1-   Genova, Tip. del
        R.-I. Sordomuti, 1846. 1 v. 8.º Medical biography of
        Liguria, Italy. No more published?

4185   PETTIGREW, THOMAS JOSEPH, 1791-1865.
        Medical portrait gallery. Biographical memoirs of the
        most celebrated physicians, surgeons, etc., etc., who have
        contributed to the advancement of medical science. London,
        Fisher [etc., 1838]-40. 4 v. illus., ports. 28cm.

4186   PHILIPPINE MEDICAL DIRECTORY AND THE ALLIED
        PROFESSIONS.
        1st-   ed.; 1948-   Manila, Philmedic Services.   v.
        24cm.

4187   PITTROFF, RAINER, 1939-
        Die Lehrer der Heilkunde der Universität Erlangen 1843-
        1943 und ihr Werdegang. [Erlangen, L. Müller, 1964] 264p.
        21cm. Inaug.-Diss.--Erlangen-Nürnberg. 141 biographical
        sketches of German teachers of medicine at the University of
        Erlangen.

4188   PLARR, VICTOR GUSTAVE, 1863-1920.
        Plarr's lives of the Fellows of the Royal College of Sur-
        geons of England. Rev. by Sir D'Arcy Power with the assist-
        ance of W. G. Spencer and G. E. Gask. Bristol, Printed and
        published for the Royal College of Surgeons by J. Wright,
        1930. 2 v. 26cm.

4189   PLATA Y MARCOS, MIGUEL DE LA, 1837-1885.
        Colección bio-bibliográfica de escritores médicos españ-

oles. Madrid, Impr. de A. Gómez Fuentenebro, 1882.
vii, 339p. 26cm. Bio-bibliographical collection of Spanish
writers on medicine.

4190   POWER, Sir D'ARCY, 1855-1941.
Lives of the Fellows of the Royal College of Surgeons of
England, 1930-1951. Continued by W. R. Le Fanu. London,
The College, 1953. xii, 889p. 25cm. Continues Plarr's
Lives (q. v.)

4191   al-QIFTI, 'ALĪ ibn YŪSUF, 1172 or 3-1248.
Ibn al-Qifti's Ta'rīh al-hukamā' , auf Grund der Vorarbeiten Aug. Müller's hrsg. von Julius Lippert. Leipzig,
Dieterich, 1903. 22, 496p. 26cm. Added t. p. , in Arabic;
text in Arabic. Photocopied in 1960? A history of physicians [chiefly Arabic] A bio-bibliographical work.

4192   THE REGISTER OF VETERINARY SURGEONS.
1884-   London, Royal College of Veterinary Surgeons.
v. 22cm. British veterinarians.

4193   RENAULDIN, LÉOPOLD JOSEPH, 1775-1859.
Études historiques et critiques sur les médecins numismatistes, contenant leur biographie et l'analyse de leurs
écrits. Paris, J. B. Ballière [1851] xvi, 576p. 22cm.
Biographies of 61 physicians who were also interested in numis-
matics and antiquities, and analyses of their writings.

4194   ROSSMÄSSLER, F
Gallerie der vorzüglichsten Aerzte und Naturforscher
Deutschlands, nach neuen Originalzeichnungen gestochen.
Gotha, Perthes, 1831-33. 2 v. & 12 ports. in a folio. Gal-
lery of the best physicians and scientists of Germany.

4195   ROUKEMA, ROELOF, 1669-1743?
Naam-boek der beroemde genees- en heelmeesters van
alle eeuwen. Synde een verkorte beschrijvinge van het leven,
bedrijf en afsterven, der voornaamste namnen in de genees-
en heelkonst; mitsgaders van eenige andere die daar betrek-
lijk toe sijn; voorzien met veele hunner lof en lijkgedigten,
gedenking hunner nagelatene schriften en gevoelens... Amsterdam, J. ten Hoorn, 1706. 387p. 12.º Biographies of
famous doctors and physicians of all times.

4196   ROYAL COLLEGE OF PHYSICIANS OF LONDON.
The roll of the Royal College of Physicians of London,

comprising biographical sketches of all the eminent physicians
whose names are recorded in the Annals... by William Munk.
2d ed., rev. and enl. London, 1878-19   v. 23cm. Vol. 4,
compiled by G. H. Brown, has title: Lives of the fellows...
Contents. -- v. 1. 1518 to 1700. -- v. 2. 1701 to 1800. -- v. 3.
1801 to 1825. -- v. 4. 1826-1925.

4197   SÁ MATTOS, MANOEL DE
        Bibliotheca elementar chirurgico-anatomica; ou, Compen-
        dio historico-critico e chronologico sobre a cirurgia e
        anatomia em geral, que contém os seus principios, incremen-
        tos e ultimo estado, assim em Portugal, como nas mais
        partes cultas do mundo: com a especificacão de seus re-
        spectivos auctores, suas obras, vidas, methodos e inventos,
        desde os primeiros seculos até o presente. Obra dividida
        em trez discursos. Porto, A. A. Ribeiro, 1788. xxiii, 132,
        192, 170p. 8.º   Includes bio-bibliography of surgeons &
        anatomists.

4198   SACHSE, JOHANN DAVID WILHELM, 1772-1860.
        Verzeichniss von Bildnissen von Aerzten und Naturforsch-
        ern seit den ältesten bis zur unsere Zeiten, mit Biographien.
        1. Heft: Petrus de Abano-D'Azzogujoi. Schwerin, Marcus,
        1847. vi, 93p. 8.º Portraits & biographical sketches of
        physicians & scientists of all times. No more published.

4199   SANGIORGIO, PAOLO
        Cenni storici sulle due università di Pavia e di Milano e
        notizie intorno di più celebri medici, chirurghi e speziali di
        Milano dal ritorno delle scienze fino all'anno 1816. Opera
        postuma pubblicata, continuata ed accresciuta delle notizie
        intorno allo stato attuale dell'Università di Pavia, per cura di
        Francesco Longhena. Milano, 1831. 1 v. 8.º   Brief his-
        torical notes on the two universities of Pavia & Milan &
        sketches of the most celebrated physicians, surgeons & spe-
        cialists of Milan from the return of science to the year 1816.

4200   SCHEFFEL, CHRISTIANUS STEPHANUS, 1693-1763.
        Vitae professorum medicinae qui in Academia Gryphiswal-
        densium a primis ejus initiis (1456) usque ad finem anni ipsius
        saecularis tertii vixerunt. Gryphiswaldiae, Typ. Struckianus
        [1756] 324 p. 4.º   Lives of professors of medicine at the
        Academy (University) of Greifswald, 1456-1756.

4201   SCHIVARDI, ANTONIO, 1802-1871.
        Biografia dei medici illustri Bresciani.   Brescia, G. Ven-

turini, 1839-52. 2 v. 8.º Biographies of outstanding physicians of Brescia, Italy.

4202 SCHRADER, G   W
Biographisch-literarisches Lexicon der Thierärzte aller Zeiten und Länder, sowie der Naturforscher, Aerzte, Landwirthe, Stallmeister u. s. w. , welche sich um die Theirheilkunde verdient gemacht haben. Gesammelt von G. W. Schrader. Vervollständigt und hrsg. von Eduard Hering. Stuttgart, Ebner & Seubert, 1863. x, 490 p. Biographical-bibliographical dictionary of the veterinarians of all times and countries.

4203 SERRANO, JOSÉ ANTONIO, 1851-1904.
Il dizionario storico-anatomico de J. A. Serrano. [Trascrizione dal portoghese di] Clodomiro Mancini. Genova, 1961. 107 p.   (Scientia veterum ... 24) The historical-anatomical dictionary. Lives of anatomists, physiologists, etc. Translation of Relação alphabetica dos anatomicos, physiologistas, histologistas, embriologistas, medicos e cirurgiões, cujos nomes figuram na nomenclatura anatomica actual.

4204 STONE, RICHARD FRENCH
Biography of eminent American physicians and surgeons. Indianapolis, Carlon & Hollenbeck, 1894. xxii, 729p. ports. 27cm. A 2d ed. was published in 1898?

4205 STRIKER, CECIL, 1897-   comp.
Famous faces in diabetes. With a foreword by Elliott P. Joslin. Boston, G. K. Hall, 1961. xi, 256p. illus., ports. 27cm. Single page biographies, with portraits.

4206 TALBOT, C   H
The medical practitioners in medieval England; a biographical register, by C. H. Talbot and E. A. Hammond. London, Wellcome Historical Medical Library, 1965. x, 503p. 26cm. (Publications of the Wellcome Historical Medical Library, new ser. , v. 8)

4207 THACHER, JAMES, 1754-1844.
American medical biography; or, Memoirs of eminent physicians who have flourished in America. To which is prefixed a succinct history of medical science in the United States, from the first settlement of the country. Boston, Richardson & Lord [etc.] 1828. 2 v. 15 ports. 21cm.

4208   THIESS, JOHANN OTTO, 1762-1810.
Versuch eines Beitrags zur Biographie hamburgischer
Aerzte. Helmstädt, 1782. 2 v. A contribution to the biog-
raphy of Hamburg's physicians.

4209   TKESHELASHVILI, I   S
Materialy dlia istorii farmatsii v Rossii... biograficheskii
slovar' farmatsevtov, poluchivshikh stepen' magistra farmatsii v imperatorskikh russkikh universitetakh i v Impera-
torskoi Voenno-meditsinskoi akademii s 1845-1901 g. Vyp. 1.
Moskva, Tipo-lit. Russk. t-va pechat. i izdat. dela 1901.
126p. A biographical dictionary of Russian pharmacists.

4210   TONER, JOSEPH MEREDITH, 1825-1896.
The medical men of the Revolution, with a brief history
of the medical department of the Continental Army, containing the names of nearly twelve hundred physicians. An address before the Alumni Association of Jefferson Medical
College, March 11, 1876. Philadelphia, Collins, printer,
1876. 140p. 23cm.

4211   VIGILIIS VON CREUTZENFELD, STEPHANUS HIERONY-
MUS DE
Bibliotheca chirurgica in qua res omnes ad chirurgiam
pertinentes ordine alphabetico, ipsi vero scriptores, quotquot ad annum usque 1779 innotuerunt, ad singulas materias
ordine chronologico exhibentur, adjecto ad libri calcem auctorum indice. Vindobonae, 1781. 2 v. Biography of surgeons, in alphabetical order, and their writings, to 1779.

4212   WADD, WILLIAM, 1776-1829.
Nugae chirurgicae; or, A biographical miscellany illustra-
tive of a collection of professional portraits. London,
Printed by J. Nichols, and sold by Longman, Hurst, Rees,
Orme, Brown, and Green, 1824. ii, 276 p. 22cm. "Trifles"
of surgery; sketches of doctors.

4213   WATSON, IRVING ALLISON, 1849-1918, ed.
Physicians and surgeons of America. A collection of biographical sketches of the regular medical profession. Concord, N. H., Republican Press Association, 1896. iv, 843 p.
ports. 29cm.

4214   WESZPRÉMI, STEPHAN, 1723-1799.
Succincta medicorum Hungariae et Transilvaniae biogra-

phia. Centuria prima excerpta ex adversariis auctoris.
Lipsiae, Ex Off. Sommeria, 1774. 208 p. 8.° Brief
biographies of the earliest Hungarian and Transylvanian
physicians.

4215 WHO'S WHO AMONG INTERNATIONAL MEDICAL WRITERS.
Covering all countries of the world and containing the
biographical and literary data of writers on the subject of
medicine and contributory knowledge. Los Angeles, Golden
Syndicate Pub. Co. v. 21cm. "Revised, enlarged and
published every two years."

4216 WHO'S WHO AMONG PHYSICIANS AND SURGEONS.
v. 1- 1938- New York. v. 24cm. Editor: 1938-
J. C. Schwarz.

4217 WHO'S WHO IN AMERICAN DENTISTRY.
Edited by Alvin J. De Bré. Los Angeles, Dale Dental
Pub. Co., 1963. xi, 198p. 27cm.

4218 WHO'S WHO IN AMERICAN MEDICINE.
1925- N[ew] Y[ork] Who's Who Publications, inc.
v. 21cm.

4219 WHO'S WHO IN DENTISTRY.
Biographical sketches of prominent dentists in the United
States and Canada. v. 1- 1916- New York, Who's
Who Dental Pub. Co. v. 21cm.

4220 WHO'S WHO IN INDUSTRIAL MEDICINE.
Chicago, Industrial Medicine Pub. Co. v. 24cm. biennial.
1948 ed. called 2d ed.

4221 WHO'S WHO IN THE NURSING WORLD,
The nursing profession year-book... containing particulars
of administrative and examining bodies, colleges, the nursing
services, nursing associations, institutions and societies,
nurse training schools, clubs, etc., together with details concerning the nursing careers of the leaders of the nursing profession. 1928- London, H. Edgar Smithers Pub. Co.
v. illus. 17cm. 1929- edition has title: Who's who
in the nursing world; the nursing year book. 1929- edition has imprint: London, Professional Publications, ltd.
British nursing.

4222 WHO'S WHO IN WORLD MEDICINE, 1939.
London, B. U. E. ltd. [1939] 605 p. forms. 26 x 20cm.
First edition. Cf. Foreword.

4223 WICKERSHEIMER, ERNEST, 1880-
Dictionnaire biographique des médecins en France au
moyen âge. Paris, E. Droz, 1936. 2 v. 25cm. Biographical dictionary of physicians in France in the Middle Ages.

4224 WILLIAMS, STEPHEN WEST, 1790-1855.
American medical biography; or, Memoirs of eminent
physicians, embracing principally those who have died since
the publication of Dr. Thacher's work on the same subject.
Greenfield, Mass., L. Merriam, 1895. 664 p. ports. 22cm

4225 [WINSLOW, FORBES BENIGNUS] 1810-1874.
Physic and physicians: a medical sketch-book, exhibiting
the public and private life of the most celebrated medical
men of former days. With memoirs of eminent living London
physicians and surgeons. Philadelphia, 1845. 2 v. in 1.
15cm. (The Home & traveller's library, 10-11) First published in 1839 (London)

4226 WITTE, HENNING, 1634-1696.
Memoriae medicorum nostri saeculi clarissimorum renovatae decas prima. Francofurti, Apud M. Hallervord, 1676.
2 v. in 1. 18cm. Recollections of the most famous [German]
physicians of the 1st decade of our century; bio-bibliographical

4227 WÜSTENFELD, HEINRICH FERDINAND, 1808-1899.
Geschichte der arabischen Aerzte und Naturforscher. Nach
den Quellen bearb. Göttingen, Vandenhoeck und Ruprecht,
1840. xvi, 167, 16p. 22cm. History of Arabic physicians and
scientists; bio-bibliographical.

4228 THE YEAR BOOKS OF PHYSICAL AND NATURAL THERAPY,
Comprising: part I: Who's who in osteopathy; part II: Who's
who in chiropractic; part III: Who's who in naturopathy; part
IV: Who's who in physiotherapy; part V: Who's who in optom-
etry. 1932/33-   New York, Therapeutic Pub. Co.
v. 26cm.

4229 ZMEEV, LEV FEDORVICH, 1832-1901.
Russkie vrachi pisateli. S.-Peterburg, 1886-89. 5 pts. in
1 v. 24cm.

4230   ---- ----Dopolneniia. [S.-Peterburg, 1889?-92] 10, 105p.
24cm.

Caption titles. Russian physician-authors.

PHILOSOPHY AND PSYCHOLOGY

4231   AMERICAN ASSOCIATION FOR APPLIED PSYCHOLOGY.
Directory of applied psychologists, members of the Amer-
ican Association for Applied Psychology. 1941-   Bloomington,
Ind. v. 25cm. Vols. for 1941 & 1943 only ones issued?

4232   AMERICAN PSYCHOLOGICAL ASSOCIATION.
Directory. 1948-   [Washington]   v. 24cm. annual.
Supersedes its Yearbook, 1916-1947. Provides biographical
data.

4233   BIOGRAPHICAL DICTIONARY OF PARAPSYCHOLOGY.
1964-66- New York, Garrett Publications, Helix Press.
v. 25cm. Editors: 1964-66- Helene Pleasants.

4234   [COLLIN DE PLANCY, JACQUES ALBIN SIMON]1794-1881.
Dictionnaire des sciences occultes; ou, Répertoire universel des êtres, des personnages, des livres, des faits et des
choses qui tiennent aux apparitions, aux divinations, à la ma-
gie, au commerce de l'enfer, aux démons, aux sorciers, aux
sciences occultes, et généralement à toutes les fausses
croyances, merveilleuses, suprenantes, mystérieuses ou sur-
naturelles... Publié par M. l'abbé Migné.   Paris, Chez
l'éditeur, 1848-52.   2v. 28cm. (Encyclopédie théologique...
pub. par M. l'abbé Migne, t. 48-49)   Fifth edition of the
author's Dictionnaire infernal, 1818. Includes biographies of
occultists.

4235   DICTIONNAIRE DES PHILOSOPHES.
[Paris, Éditions Seghers, 1962]   376 p. illus., ports.
17cm. (Collection Seghers) A dictionary of philosophers--
Universal.

4236   EISLER, RUDOLF, 1873-1926.
Philosophen-Lexikon; Leben, Werke und Lehren der Denker.
Berlin, E. S. Mittler, 1912. v, 889 p. 24 cm. A dictionary
of philosophers.

4237   ENCICLOPEDIA FILOSOFICA.
        Venezia, Istituto per la collaborazione culturale, 1957-58.
        4 v. illus. 29cm. At head of title: Centro di studi filosofici
        di Gallarate. Many biographical articles are included.

4238   FERRATER MORA, JOSÉ, 1912-
        Diccionario de filosofia. [4. ed.] Buenos Aires, Editorial
        Sudamericana [1958] 1481 p. 26 cm. A dictionary of philo-
        sophy that includes many biographies.

4239   GINZBURG, ISIDOR, 1872-1947.
        Idishe denker un poeten in mitel-alter. [New York] 1918-
        19. 2 v. illus., port. 21cm. Jewish philosphers and writ-
        ers of the Middle Ages.

4240   HARTMANN'S INTERNATIONAL DIRECTORY OF PSYCHIC
        SCIENCE AND SPIRITUALISM;
        Issued under the auspices of the Occult Brotherhood 1930-
        1931. Jamaica, N. Y., Occult Press. 2 v. 24cm. annual.
        No more issued?

4241   HARTMANN'S WHO'S WHO IN OCCULT, PSYCHIC AND
        SPIRITUAL REALMS in the United States and foreign
        countries, compiled and edited by William C. Hartmann.
        To be issued annually, about October first under the auspices
        of the Occult Brotherhood. Jamaica, N. Y., Occult Press
        [c1925-   v. 24cm.

4242   HVEM TÆNKTE HVAD.
        Filosofiens hvem- hvad- hvor [af Henrik Thomsen]
        København, Politikens forlag, 1961. 390p. illus., ports.
        18cm. (Politikens håndbøger, nr. 247) Who thought what.
        Philosophy's who, what, where (or how?) A dictionary of
        philosophers.

4243   KIERNAN, THOMAS P
        Who's who in the history of philosophy. [1st ed.] New
        York, Philosophical Library [1965] vii, 185p. 24cm. Ca.
        400 philosophers listed.

4244   NATIONAL RESEARCH COUNCIL. COMMITTEE ON AN
        INTERNATIONAL DIRECTORY OF PSYCHOLOGISTS.
        International directory of psychologists, exclusive of the
        U.S.A., prepared for the National Academy of Sciences, Na-

tional Research Council by the Committee on an International
Directory of Psychologists, Division of Anthropology and
Psychology. Eugene H. Jacobson, editor. H. C. J. Duijker,
European co-editor. Assen, Netherlands, Royal Van Gorcum,
1958. xxii, 527 p. 21cm. (National Research Council. Pub-
lication 520)

4245 NEW YORK (STATE) UNIVERSITY.
Registered psychologists.   Albany.   v.
23cm. biennial. Period covered by report ends April 30.
Supplements accompany some numbers. Supplement, 1959/60,
and vols. for 1961/63-   issued as the university's Bulletin.

4246 OGAWA, KANDŌ
Kangakusha denki oyobi chojutsu shūran. Tokyo, Seki
Shoin, 1935. 44, 781 p. Biographies of Japanese Confucians,
including their writings.

4247 P'AN, NIEN-CHIH
Ssŭ hsiang chia ta tz'ŭ tien. [Shanghai, World Book Co. of
Shanghai, 1934] 5, 4, 989, 21, 51 p. 20cm. By P'an
Nien-chih and Chang Ts'ai-ling. Biographical dictionary of
thinkers (philosophers)

4248 PHILOSOPHEN-LEXIKON;
Handwörterbuch der Philosophie nach Personen. Unter
Mitwirkung von Gertrud Jung verfasst und hrsg. von Werner
Ziegenfuss. Berlin, W. de Gruyter, 1949-50. 2 v. 25cm.
A dictionary of philosophers planned to take the place of the
earlier Philosophen-Lexikon by Rudolph Eisler (Berlin, 1912)
Six "Lieferungen" (A-Juvalta) were issued in 1937 under the
editorship of Eugen Hauer, Werner Ziegenfuss and Gertrud
Jung.

4249 THE PSYCHOLOGICAL REGISTER;
Edited by Carl Murchison in cooperation with F. C. Bart-
lett [and others] Worcester, Mass. , Clark University Press,
1929-32. v. 24cm. (The International university series
in psychology)

4250 PSYKOLOGISK-PEDAGOGISK UPPSLAGSBOK.
[Huvudredaktion: Gunnar Boalt, et al. ; biträdande redak-
törer: Gösta Harding, et al.] 2. omarb. och utvidgade uppl.
Stockholm, Natur och kultur [1956] 3 v. (1643p.) illus. ,
ports. 27cm. A reference work for educational psychology
& pedagogy that includes biographical materials.

4251   ---- ----Supplement- och registerband, med engelsk-svensk
        ordlista. Stockholm, Natur och kultur [1956] 225p. 27cm.

4252   RIEDL, JOHN O   ed.
        A catalogue of Renaissance philosophers (1300-1650) com-
        piled by Robert A. Baker [and others] under the direction of
        John O. Riedl. Milwaukee, Marquette University Press,
        1940. xi, 179p. illus. 24cm.

4253   ROBBINS, ROSSELL HOPE, 1912-
        The encyclopedia of witchcraft and demonology. New
        York, Crown Publishers [1959] 571p. illus. 26cm. Includes
        biographical sketches of practitioners of the black arts.

4254   SHISO JIMMEI HENSAN-BU
        Shiso jimmei jiten. Tokyo, Daiichi Shuppan K. K., 1951.
        399 p. Biographical dictionary of thinkers.

4255   SOARES, ORRIS
        Dicionario de filosofia. Rio de Janeiro, 1952-   v.
        27cm. At head of title: Ministério da Educacao e Saúde.
        Instituto Nacional do Livro. Dictionary of philosophy, with
        biographical data.

4256   TAKEBAYASHI, KAN'ICHI.
        Kangakusha denki shūsei. [Tokyo] Seki Shoin, 1928. 1381,
        37 p. Collection of biographies of Japanese Confucians.

4257   TAMAKI, HAJIME, 1902-
        Seiyo shiso-ka jiten. [Tokyo] Komeji Shoten, 1952. 294p.
        Dictionary of Western thinkers.

4258   THOMAS, HENRY, 1886-
        Biographical encyclopedia of philosophy. [1st ed.] Gar-
        den City, N. Y., Doubleday, 1965. xii, 273p. 24cm.

4259   URMSON, J   O   ed.
        The concise encyclopedia of Western philosophy and
        philosophers. The contributors: J. L. Ackrill [and others]
        New York, Hawthorn Books [1960] 431 p. illus. 26cm.

4260   VALVERDE TÉLLEZ, EMETERIO, Bp. , 1864-1948.
        Bibliografía filosófica mexicana. 2. ed. notablemente

aumentada. León, Impr. de J. Rodríguez, 1913. 2 v. 25cm. (His Obras, t. 1-2) In part a bio-bibliography of Mexican philosophy.

4261   WEDECK, HARRY EZEKIEL, 1894-
Dictionary of magic. New York, Philosophical Library, 1956. viii, 105 p. 22cm. (Mid-century reference library) With brief sketches of renowned witches, satanists, etc.

4262   WHO'S WHO IN PHILOSOPHY.
Dagobert D. Runes, editor. Lester E. Denonn [and] Ralph B. Winn, associate editors. [New York] Philosophical Library, 1942-   v. 24cm. No more published? Contents. — v. 1. Anglo-American philosophers.

RELIGION
Anonyms and Pseudonyms

4263   LUDOVICI, GOTTFRIED, 1670-1724.
De scriptis anonymis et pseudonymis in caussa religionis a progessu coercendis, exercitationes theologiae. Lipsiae, 1715. 1 v. 8.° Anonymous and pseudonymous religious writers and writings.

4264   SOMMERVOGEL, CARLOS, 1834-1902.
Dictionnaire des ouvrages anonymes et pseudonymes publiés par des religieux de la Compagnie de Jésus, depuis sa fondation jusqu'à nos jours. Paris, Librairie de la Société bibliographique, 1884. iii p., 1398 columns. 25cm. Dictionary of anonymous and pseudonymous works published by the religious of the Society of Jesus (Jesuits) from its foundation to our day. Issued in 2 parts.

4265   URIARTE, JOSÉ EUGENIO DE, 1842-1909.
Catálogo razonado de obras anónimas seudónimas de autores de la Compañía de Jesús pertenecientes á las antigua asistencia española: con un apéndice de otras de los mismos dignas de especial estudio (bibliográfico (28 sept. 1540-16 ag. 1773) Madrid, Estab. Tip. 'Sucesores de Rivadeneyra,' 1904-16. 5 v. 29cm. Vols. 4-5 edited by Mariano Lecina. Anonyms & pseudonyms of Spanish Jesuit authors. Vols. 1-2 contain anonymous works; v. 3, pseudonymous works, v. 4, miscellaneous special classes of works (doubtful, imaginary,

etc.) and supplement to v. 1-3; v. 5, continuation of supplement, additions and corrections to v. 1-5 and indexes to the
complete work.

General Works

4266   ALEXANDER, GEORGE M
        The handbook of Biblical personalities. Greenwich,
        Conn. , Seabury Press, 1962. xv, 299p. 22cm.

4267   DEEN, EDITH
        All of the women of the Bible. New York, Harper [1955]
        xxii, 410p. 25cm. Section I (p. 1-241) contains fairly exten-
        sive sketches of major figures (ca. 50); section 2 (Alphabeti-
        cal listing of named women, p. 243-303) contains brief notes
        on women not included in section 1; section 3 (p. 305-379) is
        a chronological listing of nameless women mentioned in the
        Bible and data about them.

4268   FERM, VERGILIUS TURE ANSELM, 1896-   ed.
        An encyclopedia of religion. New York, Philosophical
        Library [1945] xix, 844 p. 24 cm.

4269   KIMHI, DOV, 1889-
        Entsiklopedyah le-ishim ba-tanakh.   [Tel-Aviv, 196-]
        2 v. 25cm. Added t. p. : Encyclopedia of men and women in
        the Bible, by Dov Kimchi.

4270   LOCKYER, HERBERT
        All the men of the Bible; a portrait gallery and reference
        library of more than 3000 Biblical characters.   Grand Rapids,
        Zondervan [1958]   381 p. 24cm.

4271   MATHEWS, SHAILER, 1863-   ed.
        A dictionary of religion and ethics, edited by Shailer
        Mathews and Gerald Birney Smith. New York, Macmillan,
        1921. vii, 513p. 27cm. Includes many biographies of de-
        ceased figures of all religions.

Buddhism

4272   KAO SENG CHUAN.
        [Nanking] Chin ling k'o ching ch'u [1884-92] 24 v. Con-
        tains (1) Kao seng chuan, by Hui-chiao (497-554); (2) Hsü Kao
        seng chuan, by Tao-hsüan (596-647); (3) Sung Kao seng chuan,

by Tsan-ning (fl. 998); (4) Ming Kao seng chuan, by Ju-hsing (fl. 1617) Biographies of [Chinese] Buddhist monks. Collated by Yang Wen-hui.

4273 WASHIO, JUNKEI
Nihon bukka jimmei jisho. Tokyo, Koyukan, 1911. 1317p.
Biographical dictionary of Japanese Buddhists.

4274 YÜ-CH'IEN
Hsin hsü kao seng chuan ssu chi. [n. p.] Pie yang yin shua chu [1923] 16 v. New supplement to Biographies of Chinese Buddhist monks.

Christianity

4275 ACTA SANCTORUM.
Acta sanctorum quotquot toto orbe coluntur, vel a catholicis scriptoribus celebrantur quae ex Latinis et Graecis, aliarumque gentium antiquis monumentis collegit, digessit, notis illustravit Joannes Bollandus ... servata primigenia scriptorum phrasi. Operam et studium contulit Godefridus Henschenius... Editio novissima curante Joanne Carnandet... Parisiis, V. Palmé; [etc., etc.] 1863-19   v. illus. 40cm. Supplemented by the Analecta Bollandiana, 1885-   A famous collection of lives of the saints, compiled by the Bollandists.

4276 ADAMS, ELEANOR BURNHAM
A bio-bibliography of Franciscan authors in colonial Central America. Washington, Academy of American Franciscan History, 1953. xxi, 97p. 26cm. (Publications of the Academy of American Franciscan History. Bibliographical series, v. 2)

4277 ALBAREDA, ANSELMO MARÍA, 1892-
Bibliografía dels monjos de Montserrat (segle XVI) Montserrat, Monestir de Montserrat, 1928. 301p. illus. 28cm. Bio-bibliographical; monks of the Benedictine abbey of Montserrat in Spain.

4278 ALLAIRE, JEAN BAPTISTE ARTHUR, 1866-
Dictionnaire biographique du clergé canadien-francais. Montréal, Impr. de l'École catholique des sourds-muets, 1908-10. 2v. ports. 24cm. Vol. 2 has imprint: St-Hyacinthe, Impr. de "La Tribune," 1908.

4279   ----Premier supplément. Montréal, Impr. de l'Ecole catholique des sords-muets, 1910. 78p. ports. 24cm.

4280   ----Sécond supplément. Montréal, Impr. du "Devoir," 1911. 98p. ports. 25cm. 2 more supplementary volumes up to 1934?

    Biographical dictionary of the French-Canadian [Catholic] clergy.

4281   ANNUAIRE PONTIFICAL CATHOLIQUE.
1. -   année; 1898-   Paris, Maison de la Bonne presse. v. illus., ports. 19cm. annual. Contains a larg⟨e⟩ amount of biographical data for Roman Catholic Church officia⟨l⟩ and dignitaries.

4282   ANTONINO DE LA ASUNCIÓN, fray.
Diccionario de escritores trinitarios de España y Portugal. Roma, Impr. de F. Kleinbub, 1898-99. 2v. 22cm. Dictionary of Trinitarian writers of Spain and Portugal (the Trinitarian religious order was founded in 1198)

4283   ANTONIO MARIA DI VICENZA
Scriptores Ordinis Minorum strict. observ. reformatorum provinciae S. Antonii Venetiarum. Venetiis, Ex Typ. Aemiliana, 1877. 18⟨6⟩p. 16.° Bio-bibliography of Franciscan⟨s⟩ in the order's province of Venice.

4284   ARMELLINI, MARIANO, 1662-1737.
Bibliotheca Benedictino-Casinensis; sive, Scriptorum Casinensis Congregationis, alias S. Justinae Patavinae qui... ad haec usque tempora floruerunt, operum, ac gestorum notitiae. Assisii, Typ. Pompei Campana, 1731-36. 4v. 4.° Bio-bibliography of Italian Benedictines, chiefly those of Monte Cassino.

4285   ATTWATER, DONALD, 1892-
A dictionary of the Popes, from Peter to Pius XII. London, Catholic Book Club, 1938. vi, 337p. 258 biographies in chronological order.

4286   ATTWATER, DONALD, 1892-   comp.
A dictionary of the saints; being also an index to the rev. ed. of Butler's Lives of the saints. New York, P. S. Kenedy, 1938. vii, 319p. 23cm. Also available in an English ed. (London, Burns, Oates & Washbourne)

4287   ATTWATER, DONALD, 1892-
The Penguin dictionary of saints. Baltimore, Penguin
Books [1965] 362p. 19cm. (Penguin reference books, R30)

4288   BACKER, AUGUSTIN DE, 1809-1873.
Bibliothèque de la Compagnie de Jésus. 1. ptie. : Bib-
liographie, par Augustin et Aloys de Backer. 2. ptie. :
Histoire, par Auguste Carayon. Nouv. éd. par Carlos
Sommervogel. Bruxelles, O. Schepens, 1890-1932. 12v.
33x25cm. No more published. Reprinted in 1960 at Louvain.

4289   -----Corrections et additions. Supplément au "De Backer-
Sommervogel, " par Ernest. -M. Rivière. Toulouse,
L'auteur, 1911-   v. 33 x 25cm.

In large part a bio-bibliography of the Society of Jesus
(Jesuits)

4290   BAPTIST HANDBOOK AND ALMANACK.
1860-   London, Baptist Union Pub. Dept.   v. Has a
ministerial list with brief biographical sketches. Published
1845-1859 under title: The Baptist manual.

4291   BAPTIST WHO'S WHO;
An authoritative reference work and guide to the careers of
ministers and lay officials of the Baptist churches... London,
Shaw Pub. Co. in conjunction with Kingsgate Press, 1933.
195 p.   Baptists in Great Britain.

4292   [BARBIER, HIPPOLYTE]
Biographie populaire du clergé contemporain, par un soli-
taire. Paris, A. Appert, 1840-51. 10 v. ports. 18.° Popular biography of contemporary [French Catholic] clergy.

4293   BARDENHEWER, OTTO, 1851-1935.
Patrology; the lives and works of the Fathers of the Church.
Translated from the 2d ed. by Thomas J. Shahan. Freiburg
i. B. , St. Louis, B. Herder, 1908. xvii, 680p. 24cm.

4294   BARING-GOULD, SABINE, 1834-1924.
The lives of the British saints; the saints of Wales and
Cornwall and such Irish saints as have dedications in Britain,
by S. Baring-Gould and John Fisher. London, For the
Honourable Society of Cymmrodorion by C. J. Clark, 1907-13.
4v. illus. 26cm.

4295   BARING-GOULD, SABINE, 1834-1924.
        The lives of the saints, with introduction and additional
        lives of English martyrs, Cornish, Scottish, and Welsh saints
        and a full index to the entire work. New and rev. ed.
        Edinburgh, Grant, 1914. 16v. illus. 22cm.

4296   BARTOLOMMEO DA S. ANGELO, originally GERONIMO
        BARUTTI, b. 1762.
        Collectio scriptorum Ordinis Carmelitarum excalceatorum
        utriusque congregationis et sexus P. F. Bartholomaei a S.
        Angelo Provinciae Longobardicae opera et solertia exarata.
        Cui accedit Supplementum scriptorum Ordinis qui aut obliti
        fuerunt aut recentius vixerunt, auctore et collectore P. F.
        Henrico M. a SS. Sacramento. Accedunt insuper Catalogus
        episcoporum, index praepositorum generalium et prospectus
        provinciarum et coenobiorum Ordinis. Savonae, Ex. Typ.
        A. Ricci, 1884. 2v. in l. 23cm. With bio-bibliographies
        of Discalced Carmelites in the Province of Lombardy.

4297   BAUDOT, JULES LÉON, 1857-1929.
        Dictionnaire d'hagiographie mis à jour à l'aide des travaux
        les plus récents. Paris, Bloud et Gay, 1925. vii, 662p.
        A dictionary of the saints.

4298   BAUDRILLART, ALFRED, Cardinal, 1859-1942.
        Dictionnaire d'histoire et de géographie ecclésiastiques...
        commencé sous la direction de Mgr. Alfred Baudrillart,
        continué par A. de Meyer et Et. van Cauwenbergh, avec la
        concours d'un grand nombre de collaborateurs. Paris,
        Letouzey et Ané, 1912-   v. illus., maps. 28cm. Only
        up to "F" (1963) Includes many biographical articles on
        figures in church history.

4299   BENEDICTINES IN AUSTRIA.
        Scriptores Ordinis S. Benedicti qui 1750-1880 fuerunt in
        Imperio Austriaco-Hungarico. Vindobonae, Sumptibus Ordi-
        nis in aedibus L. Woerl, 1881. cxix, 600p. 30cm. Bio-
        bibliography of the Benedictine Order in Austria, 1750-1880.

4300   BERNARDUS DE LUTZENBURGO, d. 1535.
        Catalogus haereticorum, omnium penè, qui ad haec usque
        tempora passim literarum monumentis proditi sunt, illorum
        nomina, errores & tempora quibus uixerunt ostendens: à F.
        Bernardo Lutzenbergo conscriptus, in cuius calce & de
        Lutero nõnihil deprehendes. Ed. 2, priore multo emacula-
        tior & locupletior, nempe ab ipso autore nunc aucta & recog-

nita. Anno M. DXXIII, mense nouembri. [Coloniae, Impéndio & ere M. Godefridi Hittorpii, 1523] [248]p. illus. 16cm. Catalog of heresies and heretics; Books 2-4, in alphabetical arrangement, include descriptive notes on heretics and their errors.

4301   BERTRAND, LOUIS.
       Bibliothèque sulpicienne; ou, Histoire littéraire de la Compagnie de Saint-Sulpice. Paris, A. Picard, 1900. 3v. 24cm. Bio-bibliography of the Sulpicians, a 'secular congregation' founded in 1642.

4302   BIBLIOTHECA CARMELITO-LUSITANA, HISTORICA, CRITICA, CHRONOLOGICA.
       P. N. N. carmelitano. Romae, 1754. xxviii, 238p. 4.º Notices of 177 writers of the Carmelite Order in Portugal.

4303   BIBLIOTHECA SANCTORUM.
       [Roma] Istituto Giovanni XXIII nella Pontificia università lateranense [1961-   v. illus. 29cm. A dictionary of saints of the Catholic Church; in Latin.

4304   THE BIOGRAPHICAL AND MARTYROLOGICAL DICTIONARY...
       Including the life... of... Jesus Christ... By a clergyman and others. Newcastle-upon-Tyne, 1790. 1 v.

4305   BIOGRAPHISCH WOORDENBOEK VAN PROTESTANTSCHE GODGELEERDEN IN NEDERLAND; onder redactie van J. P. de Bie en J. Loosjes. 's-Gravenhage, M. Nijhoff, 1919- v. 26cm. "Nieuwe titel-uitgave en voortsetting van L. A. van Langeraad en J. P. de Bie, Het protestantsche Vaderland." Biographical dictionary of Protestant theologians and clergy in the Netherlands.

4306   BOFFITO, GIUSEPPE, 1869-
       Scrittori barnabiti o della Congregazione du chierici regolari di San Pablo (1533-1933) Biografia, bibliografia, iconografia. Collaboratori: Tiberio Abbiati [et al.] Firenze, L. S. Olschki, 1933-37. 4 v. illus., map. 30cm. 240 copies printed. Part of vol. 1, A-Bassi, was also issued separately in 1915 with title: Biblioteca degli scrittori barnabiti. Bio-bibliography of the Barnabites (Clerics Regular of St. Paul) 1533-1933.

4307   BOLLEN, FABIAAN, 1902-
       Bibliographie der Minderbroeders van de Sint-Jozef pro-

vincie in Belgie, 1833-1947 [deur] Fabian Bollen [en] Ladislaus Kerkhove. Malines, 1950. 458 p. Gives date and place of birth, date of entry into the order and date and place of death, Franciscans in the Province of Belgium, 1833-1947.

4308   BONARI, VALDEMIRO.
I cappuccini della provincia milanese dalla sua fondazione (1535) fino a noi. Pt. IIa: Biografie dei più distinti cappuccini. Crema, Tip. S. Pantaleone di L. Meleri, 1898-99. 2 v. (675, lxxv p.) 8.° Biographies of Capuchins of the Province of Milan.

4309   THE BOOK OF SAINTS;
A dictionary of servants of God canonized by the Catholic Church, extracted from the Roman & other martyrologies, compiled by the Benedictine Monks of St. Augustine's Abbey, Ramsgate. 4th ed. rev. and enl. with a calendar of saints. London, Black; New York, Macmillan, 1947. xviii, 708 p. 22cm.

4310   BRASSARD, GÉRARD
Armorial des évèques du Canada; album historico-héraldique contenant les portraits et les armoiries des évêques du Canada depuis Mgr. de Montmorency de Laval jusqu'à date, avec notice biographique pour chacun. [Montréal] Mercury Pub. Co. , 1940] 403 p. illus. , ports. 37 cm. Coats of arms of the bishops of Canada, with portraits and biographical sketches for each bishop.

4311   BREWSTER, H   POMEROY, d. 1906.
Saints and festivals of the Christian Church. New York, F. A. Stokes [1904] xiv, 558 p. illus. 21 cm.

4312   BRUIJN, CASPAR ADAM LAURENS VAN TROOSTENBURG DE, 1830-1903.
Biographisch woordenboek van Oost-Indische predikanten. Nijmegen, P. J. Milborn, 1893. vii, 521 p. 23 cm. Biographical dictionary of Dutch clergymen in the Dutch East Indies.

4313   BUTLER, ALBAN, 1711-1773.
The lives of the saints, originally compiled by Alban Butler, now edited, rev. , and copiously supplemented by Herbert Thurston. London, Burns, Oates & Washbourne, 1926-38. 12 v. 23 cm. Vols. 3, 5-6 edited by Herbert Thurston and Norah Leeson; v. 7-10 by Herbert Thurston and Donald Attwater.

4314   ----Supplementary volume, by Donald Attwater. 1st-
London, Burns, Oates & Washbourne, 1949-   v. 22 cm.

4315   BUTLER, ALBAN, 1711-1773.
Lives of the saints; edited, rev. and supplemented by
Herbert Thurston and Donald Attwater. [London] Burns &
Oates [1956] 4 v. 25 cm. American ed. published by P. J.
Kenedy, 1956.

4317   CAPUCHINS.
Lexicon Capuccinum; promptuarium historico-
bibliographicum Ordinis Fratrum Minorum Capuccinorum
(1525-1950) Romae, Bibliotheca Collegii Internationalis
S. Laurentii Brundusini, 1951. xlvii p. , 1868 columns. illus.
25 cm. Contains many biographies.

4318   CARNOY, HENRY, 1861-
Dictionnaire biographique des membres du clergé
catholique. Paris, Impr. de l'Armorial francais [1903]
156 p. ports. 29 cm. (Collection des grands dictionnaires
biographiques) Biographical dictionary of members of the
Catholic clergy (in France)

4319   CARTER, NATHAN FRANKLIN, 1830-1915.
The native ministry of New Hampshire. Concord, Rumford
Print. Co. , 1906. iv, 1017 p. 24 cm.

4320   CATHCART, WILLIAM, 1826-1908.
The Baptist encyclopaedia. A dictionary of the doctrines,
ordinances, usages, confessions of faith, sufferings, labors,
and successes, and of the general history of the Baptist
denomination in all lands. With numerous biographical sketches of distinguished American and foreign Baptists, and a
supplement. Philadelphia, L. H. Everts, 1881. 1328 p. illus.
28 cm.

4321   THE CATHOLIC ENCYCLOPEDIA;
An international work of reference on the constitution,
doctrine, discipline and history of the Catholic Church.
Edited by Charles G. Herbermann [et al.] assisted by numer-

ous collaborators. New York, R. Appleton Co. [1907-15] 15 v. illus., ports. 28cm. Contains numerous biographies of famous Catholics.

4322 -----Index. New York, Encyclopedic Press (1914] ix, 959p. 28cm.

4323 -----Supplement I. vol. XVII. New York, Encyclopedic Press [1922] 1 v. 26cm. No more published.

4324 CAVE, WILLIAM, 1637-1713.
Scriptorum ecclesiasticorum historia literaria, a Christo nato usque ad saeculum XIV. facili methodo digesta. [Editio novissima, ab auctore recognita & auctior facta] Oxonii, E Theatro Sheldoniano, apud J. Pote, 1740-43. 2 v. 42 cm. Bio-bibliography of ecclesiastical writers from the birth of Christ to the 14th century.

4325 ČERNÍK, BERTHOLD OTTO, 1879-
Die Schriftsteller der noch bestehenden Augustiner-chorherrenstifte Österreichs von 1600 bis auf den heutigen Tag. Von Berthold Otto Černík unter Mitwirkung der Reg. Lat. Chorherren: Johannes Chrysostomus Mitterrutzner [et al.] Wien, H. Kirsch, 1905. xiv, 397 p. 25 cm. The writers of the Augustinian Canons in Austria, 1600-1905.

4326 CERVEAU, RENÉ
Nécrologe des plus célèbres défenseurs et confesseurs de la vérité du dix-septième [et dix-huitième] siècle[s. n. p.] 1760-61. 3 v. 12.º

4327 ---- ----Supplément. [n. p.] 1763. lxxvi, 344p. 12.º

4328 ---- ----Suite du Supplément. [n. p.] 1764. viii, 472p. 12.º

4329 ---- ----Suite du Nécrologe des plus célèbres defenseurs et amis de la vérité, du dix-huitième siècle, depuis 1760 jusqu'à 1767 (et de 1767 jusqu'à 1778) tome VI [-VII. n. p.] 1767-78. 2 v. 12.º

Necrology of the most famous defenders & confessors of the truth (Catholic faith)—17th-18th centuries.

4330 THE CLERGY DIRECTORY AND PARISH GUIDE:
An alphabetical list of the clergy of the Church of England,

with their degree and university, order and date of ordination, benefice and date of induction... London, T. Bosworth, 18 v. 19cm. annual.

4331 THE CLERICAL DIRECTORY OF THE PROTESTANT EPISCOPAL CHURCH IN THE UNITED STATES OF AMERICA. New York [etc.] Published by the Church Hymnal Corporation for the Church Pension Fund [etc.] v. plates, ports. 26cm. triennial. Began publication with issue for 1898. No issue published for 1944. Title varies: Lloyd's clerical directory. --1917-1938/39, Stowe's clerical directory of the American church (varies slightly). --1941-53. Stowe's Clerical directory of the Protestant Episcopal Church in the United States of America. Includes biographical data.

4332 CODE, JOSEPH BERNARD, 1899-
Dictionary of the American hierarchy, 1789-1964. With a pref. by Egidio Vagnozzi. New York, J.F. Wagner [c1964] 452 p. 26cm. An earlier edition covering the years 1790-1940 was published in 1940.

4333 THE CONGREGATIONAL YEAR BOOK.
1846- London, Hodder and Stoughton [etc.] v. illus., ports. 22cm. Includes lists of ministers with brief biographical data and fuller biographies of deceased ministers of the Congregational Union of England and Wales.

4334 CORWIN, CHARLES EDWARD, 1868-
Manual of the Reformed Church in America (formerly Reformed Protestant Dutch Church) 1628-1933. 5th ed., rev. New York, Board of Publication and Bible-School Work of the Reformed Church in America, 1922-33. 782 p. Biographies are to be found on p. 235-606.

4335 COTTON, HENRY, 1789-1879.
Fasti Ecclesiae Hibernicae: the succession of the prelates and members of the cathedral bodies of Ireland. Dublin, Hodges & Smith, 1845-60. 5v.

4336 ----Supplement, containing a continuation of appointments up to the disestablishment of the Church of Ireland, collected with the original diocesan registries by Charles Philip Cotton. Dublin, J. Charles, 1878. ix,141 p.

4337   [COUSIN D'AVALLON, CHARLES YVES COUSIN, called]
1769-1840.
Dictionnaire biographique et bibliographique des prédicateurs et sermonnaires français, depuis le XVIe siècle jusqu'à
nos jours, dont les sermons, prônes, homélies, etc., etc.,
ont été imprimés. Suivi de préceptes sur l'art oratoire, extraits des ouvrages de Laharpe, Marmontel, Maury, etc., par
l'abbé de La P*****; précédé d'un essai historique sur l'élo-
quence de la chaire, par B. de Roquefort. Paris, Persan,
1824. 2 pts. in 1 v. 8.º Biographical and bibliographical
dictionary of French preachers after the 16th century to 1824
(Catholic Church?)

4338   CRESSY, EARL HERBERT, 1883-
City churches in East Asia, and Who's who of city church
pastors. New York, Missionary Research Library, 1955.
32 1. 28cm.

4339   CROCKFORD'S CLERICAL DIRECTORY.
Being a statistical book of reference for facts relating to
the clergy and the church. 1st-   issue; 1858 (?)-
London.   v. illus. 26cm. Subtitle varies slightly.
Includes biographical sketches of Church of England clergy-
men.

4340   DANNHEIMER, WILHELM.
Verzeichnis der im Gebiete der freien Reichsstadt
Rothenburg O. T. von 1544 bis 1803 wirkenden ev.-luth.
Geistlichen. Nürnberg, Kommissionsverlag: Verlag Die
Egge, 1952. 168p. 22cm. (Einzelarbeiten aus der
Kirchengeschichte Bayerns, 27. Bd.) Evangelical-Lutheran
clergymen in and around the city of Rothenburg ob der Tauber,
1544-1803.

4341   DELANEY, JOHN J
Dictionary of Catholic biography, by John J. Delaney and
James Edward Tobin. Garden City, N.Y., Doubleday [1961]
xi,1245 p. 27cm.

4342   DEPÉRY, JEAN IRENÉE, Bp., 1796-1861.
Histoire hagiologique de Belley; ou, Recueil des vies des
saints et des bienheureux nés dans ce diocèse, suivies de
celles de quelques personnages morts en odeur de sainteté
et des actes des martyrs du XVIIIe siècle... Bourg, P.F.
Bottier, 1834-35. 2v. plates. 8.º Lives of saints and near-
saints of the diocese of Belley, France.

4343   DESTOMBES, CYRILLE JEAN
Les vies des saints et des personnes d'une éminente piété des diocèses de Cambrai et d'Arras, d'après leur circonscription ancienne et actuelle. Cambrai, F. Deligne et E. Lesne, 1851-52. 4 v. 12.° Lives of saints & pious persons of the dioceses of Cambrai & Arras, France.

4344   DICTIONNAIRE DE DROIT CANONIQUE,
Contenant tous les termes du droit canonique, avec un sommaire de l'histoire et des institutions et de l'état actuel de la discipline. Commencé sous la direction de A. Villien et E. Magnin; continué sous la direction de A. Amanieu, avec le concours d'un grand nombre de collaborateurs. Paris, Letouzey et Ané, 1935- v. 29cm. Dictionary of canon law; includes many biographies, especially the lives and works of canonists.

4345   DICTIONNAIRE DE SPIRITUALITÉ,
Ascétique et mystique, doctrine et histoire. Publié sous la direction de Marcel Viller assisté de F. Cavallera et J. de Guibert, avec le concours d'un grand nombre de collaborateurs. Paris, G. Beauchesne, 1932- v. 31cm. Dictionary of spirituality; includes many biographies of religious figures.

4346   DICTIONNAIRE DE THÉOLOGIE CATHOLIQUE,
Contenant l'exposé des doctrines de théologie catholique, leurs preuves et leur histoire. Commencé sous la direction de A. Vacant et E. Mangenot, continué sous celle de E. Amann ...avec le concours d'un grand nombre de collaborateurs. Paris, Letouzey et Ané, 1903-50 [i. e. 1899-1950] 15 v. in 23. illus. 28cm. Issued in 150 parts.

4347   --- ----Table analytique. Paris, Letouzey et Ané, 1929-
v. 29cm. Contents. --[1] Tomes I à IX (A à L inclus)

4348   --- ----Tables générales. Paris, Letouzey et Ané, 1951.
v. 28cm.

Useful for scholastic and medieval philosophers.

4349   DICTIONNAIRE HISTORIQUE DES AUTEURS ECCLÉSIAS-
TIQUES; renfermant la vie des pères & des docteurs de l'Église; des meilleurs interpretes de l'Ecriture-Sainte, juifs & chrétiens; des théologiens scholastiques, moraux, mystiques, polémiques, hétérodoxes même qui ont écrit sur des matieres non controversées; des canonistes & des commentateurs des Décretales & du Corps du droit canonique; des historiens,

bibliographes, biographes, & agiographes ecclésiastiques; des orateurs sacrés; des liturgistes, & généralement de tous les auteurs qui ont écrit sur les matieres ecclésiastiques. Avec le catalogue de leurs principaux ouvrages... & l'indication des meilleures éditions de leurs ouvrages... Lyon [i. e. Avignon?] La Veuve Bessiat, 1767. 4 v. 18cm. Written by a "Gascon priest"; L. M. Chaudon wrote the preface and did some editorial work. --Cf. Barbier. An Italian ed. was published in 1768-71 under title: Dizionario storico degli autori ecclesiastici. A bio-bibliographical dictionary of theological writers.

4350   DIONIGI DA GENOVA, Capuchin, d. 1695.
      Bibliotheca scriptorum Ordinis Minorum S. Francisci Capuccinorum, retexta & extensa a F. Bernardo a Bononia... quae prius fuerat a Dionysio Genuensi contexta. Venetiis, Apud S. Coleti, 1747. xx, 322 p. illus. 35cm. 1st ed., 1680(?); 2d, 1691. Bio-bibliography of the Capuchin order.

4351   DIRKS, SERVATIUS, 1825-1887.
      Histoire littéraire et bibliographique des frères Mineurs de l'observance de St. Francois en Belgique et dans les Pays-Bas... Anvers, Typ. van Os-de Wolf [1886] xxiv, 456 p. 22cm. Bio-bibliographies arranged chronologically by date of death, 1473-1886. Franciscans in the Low Countries (Belgium & Holland)

4352   DORCY, MARY JEAN, 1914-
      Saint Dominic's family; lives and legends. Dubuque, Iowa, Priory Press [1964] xxiii, 632 p. 25cm. Chronological arrangement; over 300 biographies.

4353   DÖRING, HEINRICH, 1789-1862.
      Die gelehrten Theologen Deutschlands im 18. und 19. Jahrhundert. Neustadt a. d. Orla, 1831-35. 4v. The learned theologians of Germany in the 18th-19th centuries.

4354   DOWDEN, JOHN, Bp. of Edinburgh, 1840-1910.
      The bishops of Scotland: being notes on the lives of all the bishops, under each of the sees, prior to the Reformation, by the late Right Rev. John Dowden. Edited by J. Maitland Thomson. Glasgow, J. Maclehose, 1912. xxix, 472 p. 23cm.

4355   DUNBAR, AGNES BAILLIE CUNNINGHAME, 1830-1920.
      A dictionary of saintly women. London, Bell, 1904-05. 2v. 24cm.

4356   DUPIN, LOUIS ELLIES, 1657-1719.
        A new history of ecclesiastical writers: containing an ac-
count of the authors of the several books of the Old and New
Testament; and the lives and writings of the primitive fathers;
an abridgment and catalogue of all their works; censures de-
termining the genuine and spurious, a judgment upon their
style and doctrine, and the various editions of their writings:
to which is added, a compendious history of the councils;
and many necessary tables and indexes. Written in French
by Lewis Ellies Du Pin. London, Printed for A. Smalle and
T. Childe [etc.] 1693-99. 13 v. in 4. 32cm. Translation, by
William Wotton, of Nouvelle bibliothèque des auteurs ecclésiastiques. Vols. 7-13 have title: A new ecclesiastical history;
containing... the lives and writings of ecclesiastical authors...
Covers 1st age of the church to the 15th century.

4357   DUPIN, LOUIS ELLIES, 1657-1719.
        Nouvelle bibliothèque des auteurs ecclésiastiques... Paris,
A. Pralard, 1693-1715. 19 v. in 8. 4.º New library of
ecclesiastical (or religious) authors.

4358   EGGS, GEORG JOSEPH, 1663-1755.
        Purpura docta; seu, Vitae, legationes, res gestae, obitus
aliaque scitu ac memoratu digna... S. R. E. cardinalium qui
ingenio, doctrina, eruditione, scriptis... DXL usque ad
aetatem nostram... inclaruere, desumpta ex Alphonso
Ciaconio, Andrea Victorello, Augustino Oldoino, aliisque...
scriptoribus... cum uberrimis notis marginalibus ac triplici
indice authorum, personarum et rerum, digesta et in lucem
edita per Georgium Josephum Eggs. Monachii, Sumptibus,
J. S. Remy, 1714. 3 v. folio. Biographies of cardinals of
the Roman Catholic Church, 1540-1714.

4359   ENCICLOPEDIA CATTOLICA.
        Città del Vaticano, Ente per l'Enciclopedia cattolica e
per il Libro cattolico [1949-54] 12 v. illus., ports. 29cm.
Includes many biographical articles about figures in church
history.

4360   ENCICLOPEDIA ECCLESIASTICA;
        Pubblicata sotto la direzione dell'eccellenza Mons.
Adriano Bernareggi... Milano, F. Vallardi [etc.] 1942-
        v. illus. 26cm. Has a considerable amount of biography
of prominent figures in church history.

4361   ENCYCLOPAEDIE VAN HET KATHOLICISME.
Onder redactie van E. Hendrikx, J. C. Doensen [en] W.
Bocxe. Antwerpen, 't Groeit, 1955-56. 3 v. illus. 25cm.
Includes biography, especially of notable Catholics.

4362   ENDRIZZI, MANSUETO.
Bibliografia Camilliana; ovvero, Brevi memorie degli
scrittori dell'Ordine dei Ministri degl'Infermi (Camilliani)
S. Giuliano-Verona, Tip. Camilliana, 1910. xii, 192 p. Bio-
bibliography of the Camillians, a congregation of priests devoted to care of the sick.

4363   L'ÉPISCOPAT FRANCAIS DEPUIS LE CONCORDAT JUSQU'À
LA SÉPARATION (1802-1905). Ouvrage publié sous la direction de la Société bibliographique, avec le concours de 90
collaborateurs diocésains. Préf. de Mgr. Baunard. Paris,
1907. xvi, 720 p. With biographical sketches of French and
Belgian bishops of the Roman Catholic hierarchy.

4364   EVANGELISCHES KIRCHENLEXIKON;
Kirchlich-theologisches Handwörterbuch. Unter Mitarbeit
von Robert Frick [et. al.] hrsg. von Heinz Brunotte und Otto
Weber. Göttingen, Vandenhoeck & Ruprecht [1956-61] 4 v.
28cm. "Biographischer Anhang" (v. 4, columns 273-924) has
brief biographical notes on persons mentioned in the topical
section of the encyclopedia (1st 3 vols.) with references to
volume[s] and page[s] where their names appear in this Protestant church dictionary.

4365   EVANS, JOSEPH.
Biographical dictionary of ministers and preachers of the
Welsh Calvinistic Methodist body or Presbyterians of Wales.
From the start of the denomination to the close of the year 1850
Carnarvon, D. O'B. Owen, 1907. vii, 338 p. front. (5 ports.)
19 cm.

4366   EVGENIĬ, Metropolitan of Kiev, 1767-1837.
Slovar´ istoricheskii o byvshikh v Rossii pisateliakh
dukhovnago china greko-rossiiskoi tserkvi. Izd. 2., ispr. i
umnozhennoe. Sanktpeterburg, V Tip. I. Glazunova i ego
izhdiveniem, 1827. 2 v. in 1. 22 cm. Bio-bibliographical
dictionary of the Russian Orthodox Eastern Church.

4367   FELDER, FRANZ KARL, 1766-1818.
Gelehrten-Lexikon der katholischen Geistlichkeit Deutsch-

lands und der Schweiz. Landshut, Gedruckt bey J. Thomann, 1817-22. 3 v. 22 cm. Vols. 2-3, by Franz Joseph Waitzenegger, have title: Gelehrten- und Schriftsteller-Lexikon der deutschen katholischen Geistlichkeit. Dictionary of the learned Catholic clergy of Germany & Switzerland.

4368   FELLER, FRANCOIS XAVIER DE, 1753-1802.
Dictionnaire de biographie chrétienne, ouvrage dont le fond, emprunté à Feller, a été corrigé, enrichi d'une foule de notices, et prolongé jusqu'à l'année 1850, par Francois Pérennès. Paris [1851?] 3 v. Issued (as vols. 1-3?) in the series of volumes: Encyclopédie théologique (or Nouvelle encyclopédie théologique) edited by J. P. Migne. British Museum attributes the work to Feller; in the Bibliothèque nationale the work is found under Migne. Encyclopédie théologique. A dictionary of Christian biography.

4369   FORBES, ALEXANDER PENROSE, Bp. of Brechin, 1817-1875.
Kalendars of Scottish saints, with personal notices of those of Alba, Laudonica, and Strathclyde. An attempt to fix the districts of their several missions and the churches where they were chiefly held in remembrance. Edinburgh, Edmonston & Douglas, 1872. lxv, 468 p. 28 cm.

4370   FRANCHINI, GIOVANNI, 1633-1695.
Bibliosofia, e memorie letterarie di scrittori francescani Conventuali ch' hanno scritto dopo l'anno 1585. Modena, Eredi Soliani, 1693. xxxi, 631 p. 25 cm. Bio-bibliography of the Franciscan order (Conventuals) 1586-1693.

4371   [FRANCOIS, JEAN] 1722-1791.
Bibliothèque générale des écrivains de l'Ordre de Saint Benoit, patriarche des moines d'Occident: contenant une notice exacte des ouvrages de tout genre, composés par les religieux des diverses branches, filiations, réformes & congrégations de cet ordre, sous quelque dénomination qu'elles soient connues, avec les dates du temps où ces ouvrages ont paru; & les éclaircissements nécessaires pour en faire connoitre les auteurs. Par un religieux bénédictin de la Congrégation de St. Vannes, membre de plusieurs académies. Bouillon, Société typographique, 1777-78. 4 v. 26 cm. Bio-bibliography of Benedictines.

4372   FRIENDS, SOCIETY OF.
Biographical catalogue, being an account of the lives of Friends and others whose portraits are in the London Friends'

Institute. Also descriptive notices of those of the Friends' schools and institutions of which the gallery contains illustrations, &c. , &c. , &c. London, Friends' Institute, 1888. vi, 878 p. 22 cm.

4373   FUENTES, CELEDONIO
Escritores dominicanos del Reino de Aragón. Zaragoza, Impr. Editorial Gambón, 1932. 330 p. 25 cm. Bio-bibliography of authors of the Dominican order in the Kingdom of Aragon.

4374   FUENTES, CELEDONIO.
Escritores dominicanos del Reino de Valencia. Valencia, Impr. F. Angeles Pitarch, 1930. 375 p. Writers of the Dominican order in the Kingdom of Valencia.

4375   GAMS, PIUS BONIFACIUS, 1816-1892.
Series episcoporum Ecclesiae Catholicae, quotquot innotuerunt a beato Petro apostolo. A multis adjutus edidit Pius Bonifacius Gams. 2. , unveränderte Aufl. Leipzig, K. W. Hiersemann, 1931. xxiv, 963 p. 31 cm.

4376   ----Series episcoporum Ecclesiae Catholicae, qua series, quae apparuit 1873 completur et continuatur ab anno ca. 1870 ad 20. febr. 1885. A plurimis adjutus edidit Pius Bonifacius Gams. 2. , unvëranderte Aufl. Leipzig, K. W. Hiersemann, 1931. iv, 148 p. 31 cm.

Bishops of the Catholic Church to 1885.

4377   GANDOLFO, DOMENICO ANTONIO
Dissertatio historica de ducentis celeberrimis Augustinianis scriptoribus ex illis, qui obierunt post magnam unionem Ordinis Eremitici usque ad finem Tridentini Concilii...Romae, Typis J. F. Buagni, 1704. 416 p. Bio-bibliography of 200 celebrated Augustinian writers who flourished ca. 1256 to the end of the Council of Trent (ca. 1563-1564)

4378   GARÍ Y SIUMELL, JOSÉ ANTONIO, b. 1812.
Biblioteca Mercedaria; o sea, Escritores de la celeste, real y militar Órden de la Merced, redencion de cautivos, con indicacion de sus obras, tanto impresas como manuscritas, su patria, títulos, dignidades, hechos memorables, época y provincia en que florecieron y murieron, y dos copiosos índices, uno de escritores y otro de las obras y escritos. Barcelona, Impr. de los Herederos de la Viuda Pla, 1875.

vii, 395 p. 22 cm. 795 notices; bio-bibliography of the Order of Mercedarians, a group under the Augustinian rule, whose chief purpose was to ransom Christian captives of the Moslems.

4379   GEIGER, MAYNARD J   Father, 1901-
Biographical dictionary of the Franciscans in Spanish Florida and Cuba (1528-1841)   Paterson, N.J., St. Anthony Guild Press, 1940. xii,140 p. 23cm. (Franciscan studies, v. 21)

4380   GIOVANNI CRISOSTOMO DA CITTADELLA
Biblioteca dei Frati Minori Cappuccini della Provincia di Venezia (1535-1939) Padova, Tip. del Seminario, 1944. 303p. Bio-bibliography of the Capuchin order in the province of Venice, covering the years 1535-1939.

4381   GOLUBOVICH, GIROLAMO, 1865-1941.
Biblioteca bio-bibliografica della Terra Santa e dell'Oriente francescano. Quaracchi presso Firenze, Collegio di S. Bonaventura, 1906-27. 5v. illus. 28cm. Bio-bibliography of Franciscans in the Levant.

4382   GOLUBOVICH, GIROLAMO, 1865-1941.
Biblioteca bio-bibliografica della Terra Santa e dell'Oriente francescano. Nuova serie—documente. Quaracchi presso Firenze, Collegio di S. Bonaventura, 1921-39. 14v. illus. 28cm. Bio-bibliography of Franciscans in the Levant (new series)

4383   GOLUBOVICH, GIROLAMO, 1865-1941.
Biblioteca bio-bibliografica della Terra Santa e dell'Oriente francescano. Serie terza—documenti. Quaracchi presso Firenze, Collegio di S. Bonaventura, 1928-   v. fold. map. 28cm. Bio-bibliography of Franciscans in the Levant (and Ethiopia)--third series.

4384   GOOVAERTS, ANDRÉ LÉON, 1840-1916.
Écrivains, artistes et savants de l'ordre de Premontré. Dictionnaire bio-bibliographique. Bruxelles, Société belge de librairie, 1899-[1920] 4v. 27cm. Writers, artists and and scholars of the Premonstratesian order; a bio-bibliographical dictionary.

4385   GOUJET, CLAUDE PIERRE, 1697-1767.
Les vies des saints pour tous les jours de l'année [par les

abbés C. -P. Goujet, Mésenguy et Roussel] avec des instruc-
tions sur les dimanches et les fêtes mobiles... Lyon, Impr.
de A. Vingtrinier, 1866. 2 v. 12.° First published 1730?
Reprinted many times. The lives of the saints for all days of
the year.

4386   GUAITTA, GOTTFRIED
Merckwürdiges Verzeichniss derer von Zeit der Reformation allhier zu Frankfurt am Mayn gestandenen evangelischen
Prediger, an der Zahl 178 ... [Frankfurt am Main?] 1774.
35p. 4.° Noteworthy list of those Protestant preachers
who were in Frankfurt am Main from the time of the Reformation to the present (1774)

4387   GUÉNEBAULT, LOUIS JEAN, 1789-1878.
Dictionnaire iconographique des figures, légendes et actes
des saints, tant de l'ancienne que de la nouvelle loi, et répertoire alphabétique des attributs qui sont donnés le plus ordi-
nairement aux saints par les artistes. Ouvrage suivi 1°,
d'appendices considérables... 2°, d'une table générale et
bibliographique des auteurs cités dans le volume. Publié par
l'abbé Migné. Paris, Chez l'éditeur, 1850. 1232 columns.
illus. 27cm. (Encyclopédic théologique; ou, Série de dictionnaires sur toutes les parties de la science religieuse, t. 45)
A dictionary of saints.

4388   HENGGELER, RUDOLPH, 1890-
Helvetia sacra; Reihenfolge der kirchlichen Obern und
Oberinnen in den schweizerischen Bistümern, Kollegiat-
stiften und Klostern. Hrsg. mit Unterstützung des Schweizerischen Nationalfonds zur Förderung der Wissenschaft-
lichen Forschung. Zug, E. Kalt-Zehnder, 1961-   v.
25cm. Issued in fascicles, 1961- Biography of the Catholic
Church in Switzerland. Alphabetical by bishopric, with
names alphabetically listed thereunder.

4389   HERING, JOHANN GOTTFRIED
Kurzgefasstes Kirchen- und Ketzerlexicon, von J. G. H.
Grösstentheils umgearb., und verm. hrsg. von Johann August
Christoph von Einem. Neue, oder 5. Aufl. Stendal, 1789.
xvi, 532p. 8.° Concise dictionary of the Church and its
heretics; includes biographies. Some earlier editions issued
under title: Compendiöses (or Compendieuses) Kirchen- und
Ketzer-Lexicon (?)

4390   HERZOG, XAVER
Geistlicher Ehrentempel; oder, Pyramide der Unsterb-

lichkeit. Das ist, Lebensbeschreibungen etwelcher
Geistlichen aus dem katholischen Luzernerbiet. Fünf Rei-
henfolgen. Luzern, Gebr. Räber, 1861-68. 5 v. The clergy's temple of honor; or, Pyramids of immortality. That
is, Lives of clergymen from Catholic Lucerne.

4391   [HIBBERT, JULIAN]
A dictionary of modern anti-superstitionists; or, An account, arranged alphabetically, of those, who, whether called
atheists, sceptics, deists, latitudinarians, religious reformers or &c. have, during the last ten centuries, contributed
towards the diminution of superstition. Compiled by a searcher after the truth. London, R. Carlile, 1826. 128p. 8.°
No more published.

4392   HOLWECK, FREDERICK GEORGE, 1856-
A biographical dictionary of the saints, with a general
introduction on hagiology. St. Louis, B. Herder, 1924.
xxix, 1053p. 24cm.

4393   HOOK, WALTER FARQUHAR, 1798-1875.
An ecclesiastical biography, containing the lives of ancient
fathers and modern divines, interspersed with notices of
heretics and schismatics, forming a brief history of the
church in every age. London, F. and J. Rivington [1845]-
52. 8v. 19cm.

4394   HOOK, WALTER FARQUHAR, 1798-1875.
Lives of the archbishops of Canterbury. London,
R. Bentley, 1860-76. 12 v. 22cm.

4395   HORÁNYI, ELEK, 1736-1809.
Scriptores piarum scholarum liberaliumque artium
magistri quorum ingenii monumenta exhibet Alexius Horányi.
Budae, 1808-09. 2 v. 8.° Bio-bibliography of Hungarian
Piarists, a Catholic educational order.

4396   HUNKLER, THÉODORE FRANÇOIS XAVIER.
Vies des saints du diocèse de Paris, enrichies de notes
historiques, critiques, etc. sur les collégiales, monastères
. . . qui ont existé dans cette capitale. Paris, A. Poilleux,
1833. 2v. 8. Lives of the saints of the diocese of Paris.

4397   HURTER, HUGO, 1832-1914.
Nomenclator literarius theologiae catholicae theologos

exhibens aetate, natione, disciplinis distinctos. Ed. 3
emendata et aucta. Oeniponte, Libraria Academica
Wagneriana, 1903-13. 5v. in 6. 24cm. Bio-bibliography;
literary nomenclator of Catholic theology, giving the age,
nationality and disciplines of certain theologians.

4398 ILARINO DA MILANO, Father.
  Biblioteca dei Frati Minori Cappuccini di Lombardia
(1535-1900) Firenze, L. S. Olschki, 1937. xlv, 322p. 30cm.
(Fontes ambrosiani in lucem editi cura et studio Bybliothecae
Ambrosianae, 19) Bio-bibliography of the Capuchin order in
the province of Lombardy.

4399 ITEN, ALBERT, 1891-
  Tugium sacrum; der Weltklerus zugerischer Herkunft und
Wirksamkeit bis 1952. Gendenkbuch zum hundertjährigen
Bestand der Sektion Zug "Zuger Verein für Heimatgeschichte"
des Historischen Vereins der V Orte. Stans, J. von Matt
[1952] xix, 565p. illus. 23cm. (Beiheft Nr. 2 zum
Geschichtsfreund) Chiefly (p. [137]-552) biographical sketches
of the Catholic secular clergy in the Swiss canton of Zug.

4400 IVIMEY, JOSEPH, 1773-1834.
  A history of the English Baptists. London, Printed for the
author, and sold by Burditt, Button, Hamilton, Baynes [etc.]
1811-30. 4v. 22cm. Vol. 2 contains biographical sketches of
"above three hundred ministers. "

4401 JEAN, ARMAND.
  Les évêques et les archévêques de France, depuis 1682
jusqu'à 1801. Paris, A. Picard, 1891. xxv, 544p. 8.°
The bishops and archibishops of France, 1683-1801.

4402 JELENIĆ, JULIJAN, 1877-1931.
  Bio-bibliografija franjevaca Bosne Srebreniĉke. 1. svezak
(Anĉić-Josić) Zagreb, 1925. 1v. No more published.
Bio-bibliography of members of the Franciscan order in
Bosnia-Herzegovina.

4403 KAUFFMAN, DANIEL, Bp. , ed.
  Mennonite cyclopedic dictionary; a compendium of the
doctrines, history, activities, literature, and environments
of the Mennonite Church, especially in America. Scottdale,
Pa. , Mennonite Pub. House, 1937. xi, 443p. maps. 24cm.
Includes biography.

4404   KLEIN, JOHANN SAMUEL
        Nachrichten von den Lebensumständen und Schriften evan-
gelischer Prediger in allen Gemeinen des Königreichs Ungarn.
Leipzig, 1789. 2 v. 8.º Notes on the lives and writings of
Evangelical (Protestant—chiefly Lutheran?) preachers in
all localities of the Kingdom of Hungary.

4405   KLUGE, GOTTLOB, 1715-1771.
        Schlesische Jubelpriester, worin das Leben 100 Jubel-
priester beschrieben ist. Breslau, J. F. Korn, 1763. 1 v.
Silesian clergymen celebrating the 50th (?) year of their con-
secration to the priesthood.

4406   KOCH, LUDWIG, 1878-   ed.
        Jesuiten-Lexikon; die Gesellschaft Jesu einst und jetzt.
Löwen-Heverlee (Belgien) Verlag der Bibliothek S. U., 1962.
2 v. (1875 p.) 28cm.   Reprint of the 1934 (Paderborn) ed.
Jesuit dictionary.

4407   KÜHNER, HANS
        Encyclopedia of the Papacy. [Translated from the German
by Kenneth J. Northcott] New York, Philosophical Library
[1958] 249 p. 22cm.   Translation of Lexikon der Päpste
von Petrus bis Johannes XXIII.

4408   LE CERF DE LA VIÉVILLE, JEAN PHILIPPE
        Bibliot[h]èque historique et critique des auteurs de la Con-
gregation de St. Maur. La Haye, P. Gosse, 1726. x, 492p.
12.º Bio-bibliography of the Maurists, a congregation of
French Benedictine monks noted for scholarship.

4409   LEETE, FREDERICK DE LAND, Bp., 1866-
        Methodist bishops; personal notes and bibliography with
quotations from unpublished writings and reminiscences.
Nashville, Parthenon Press, 1948. 457p. illus., ports.
24cm.   Brief biographical sketches are included.

4410   LE NEVE, JOHN, 1679-1741.
        Fasti Ecclesiae Anglicanae; or, A calendar of the princi-
pal ecclesiastical dignitaries in England and Wales, and of
the chief officers in the Universities of Oxford and Cambridge,
from the earliest times to the year 1715. Corrected and continued to the present time by T. Duffus Hardy. [London?] Oxford University Press, 1854. 3 v. 23cm. Church of England
clergy.

4411   LE NEVE, JOHN, 1679-1741.
The lives and characters, deaths, burials, and epitaphs,
works of piety, charity, and other munificent benefactions of
all the Protestant bishops of the Church of England since the
Reformation, as settled by Queen Elizabeth anno Dom. 1559.
Vol. I. Collected from their several registers, wills in the
prerogative offices, authentick records, and other valuable
ms. collections; and compared with the best accounts hitherto published of this kind. London, Printed by W. Bowyer for
W. and J. Innys, 1720. 1 v. in 2 pts. 20cm. No more published.

4412   LEXIKON FÜR THEOLOGIE UND KIRCHE;
Begründet von Michael Buchberger. 2., völlig neu bearb.
Aufl., unter dem Protektorat von Michael Buchberger und
Eugen Seiterich. Hrsg. von Josef Höfer und Karl Rahner.
Freiburg [i. B.] Herder, 1957-   v. illus. 27cm. 1907-12
ed., entered under Michael Buchberger, has title: Kirchliches
Handlexikon. Dictionary for theology and the church; includes
many biographies.

4413   LINDNER, AUGUST, 1848-
Die Schriftsteller und die um Wissenschaft und Kunst ver-
dienten Mitglieder des Benediktinerordens im heutigen Königreiche Bayern vom Jahre 1750 bis zur Gegenwart. Regensburg, Druck von G. J. Manz, 1880. 2 v. in 1. 25cm.

4414   --- ----Nachträge zum I. und II. Bande. Regensburg, G. J.
Manz, 1884. 89 p. 24cm.

        Members of the Benedictine Order in the Kingdom of Ba-
varia, 1750-1880, active as writers, scholars and artists.

4415   LITTLE, ANDREW GEORGE
Oxford theology and theologians, c. A. D. 1282-1302, by A.
G. Little and F. Pelster. Oxford, Clarendon Press for the
Oxford Historical Society, 1934. xi, 389 p. 22cm. (Oxford
Historical Society. [Publications] v. 96) Includes some
names not in the Dictionary of national biography.

4416   THE LIVES OF THE ENGLISH SAINTS,
Written by various hands at the suggestion of John Henry
Newman. With an introd. by Arthur Wollaston Hutton. Lon-
don, S. T. Freemantle, 1900-01. 6 v. illus. 21cm.

4418   LOBINEAU, GUY ALEXIS, 1666-1727.
Les vies des saints de Bretagne et des personnes d'une
éminente piété qui ont vécu dans cette province. Nouv. éd.,
considérablement augm. par M. l'abbé Tresvaux. Paris,
Méquignon junior, 1836-37. 5 v. 8.° First ed. issued in
1723. The saints of Brittany and other pious persons of that
province.

4419   LONGDEN, HENRY ISHAM
Northamptonshire and Rutland clergy from 1500. Northampton [Eng.] Archer and Goodman, 1938-43. 15 v. 23cm.

4420   LOOSJES, JAKOB, 1874-
Naamlijst van predikanten, hoogleeraren en proponenten
der Luthersche Kerk in Nederland. Biographie en bibliographie.
's-Gravenhage, Nijhoff, 1925. viii, 373 p. 24cm. List of
names of preachers, teachers and postulants of the Lutheran
Church in the Netherlands; biography and bibliography.

4421   LUTHERAN CYCLOPEDIA.
Erwin L. Lueker, editor-in-chief. Saint Louis, Concor-
dia Pub. House [1954] xii, 1160 p. 24cm. Includes biography,
especially of famous Lutherans.

4422   McCABE, JOSEPH, 1867-
A biographical dictionary of ancient, medieval, and modern
freethinkers. Girard, Kan., Haldeman-Julius Publications
[c1945] 96 p. 22cm.

4423   McCABE, JOSEPH, 1867-
A biographical dictionary of modern rationalists. London,
Watts, 1920. xxxii p., 934 columns. 27cm.

4424   MACGREGOR, MALCOLM BLAIR
The sources and literature of Scottish church history.
Glasgow, J. McCallum, 1934. 260 p. 19cm. Includes biographical sketches of outstanding Scotch religious leaders of
all times.

4425   MCINTYRE, WILLARD EZRA, 1852-
Baptist authors; a manual of bibliography, 1500-1914. Mon treal, Industrial and Educational Press [1914-   v. port. 26cm.

4426   MANUEL DE SANTA LUZIA, Brother, d. 1773.
Nobiliarchia trinitaria. Catálogo de varões illustres em lettras, virtudes e nascimento, filhos profissão da Ordem da Sanctissima Trinidade, da Provincia de Portugal. t.1.   Lisboa, Officina de M. Manescal da Costa, 1766.   xvi, 310 p. 8.° No more published? Notable Trinitarians of the Provinc of Portugal.

4427   [MARÉCHAL, PIERRE SYLVAIN] 1750-1803.
Dictionnaire des athées anciens et modernes, par Sylvain M......1.   Paris, Grabit, an VIII [1799/1800]   lxxii, 524 p. 21cm.   Dictionary of atheists, ancient & modern.

4428   MARTIAL DE SAINT-JEAN-BAPTISTE, Father
Bibliotheca scriptorum utriusque Congregationis et Sexus Carmelitarum excalceatorum.   Burdigalae, P. Séjourné, 1730.   xvi, 444 p.   4.°   Bio-bibliography of Discalced Carmelites.

4429   MEDICI, PAOLO SEBASTIANO
Catalogo de' neofiti illustri usciti... dall' Ebraismo e poi rendutisi gloriosi nel Cristianesimo... Firenze, 1701. 1 v.   8.°   Catalogue of converts from Judaism to Christianity.

4430   MEDINA, JOSÉ TORIBIO, 1852-1930.
Noticias bio-bibliográficas de los Jesuitas expulsos de América en 1767. Santiago de Chile, Impr. Elzeviriana, 1914. 327p. illus., ports. 23cm. Bio-bibliographical notes on the Jesuits banished from America in 1767 by decree of Charles III of Spain.

4431   THE MENNONITE ENCYCLOPEDIA;
A comprehensive reference work on the Anabaptist-Mennonite movement. Scottdale, Pa., Mennonite Brethren Pub. House, 1955-   v. 26cm. Includes biographies of Mennonites and Anabaptists.

4432   MENNONITISCHES LEXIKON.
      Hrsg. von Christian Hege und Christian Neff. Frankfurt
am Main 1913-   v. illus. 25cm. A Mennonite encyclopedia that includes many biographies.

4433   MESANZA, ANDRÉS, 1879-
      Bibliografía de la provincia dominicana de Colombia.
Caracas, Editorial Sur-América, 1929. 337p. ports. 23cm.
Bio-bibliography of Dominicans in Colombia.

4434   THE METHODIST WHO'S WHO.
      1910-   London, R. Cully.   v. 20cm. Biographies of
English Methodists (Methodist Episcopal Church)

4435   MEULEMEESTER, MAURICE DE
      Bibliographie générale des écrivains rédemptoristes. Avec
la collaboration de Ern. Collet et Cl. Henze. Louvain, Impr.
Saint-Alphonse [etc.] 1933-39. 3 v. 30cm. Contents.--1.
ptie. Bibliographie de S. Alphonse - M. de Liguori.-- 2. ptie.
Auteurs rédemptoristes, A-Z.-- 3. ptie. Anonymes, péri-
odiques, suppléments, tables. Bio-bibliography of the
religious congregation of Redemptorists.

4436   MEUSEL, KARL HEINRICH, 1837-1902, ed.
      Kirchliches Handlexikon. In Verbindung mit einer Anzahl
ev. - lutherischer Theologen hrsg. von Carl Meusel unter
Mitwirkung von Ernst Haack und B. Lehmann. Leipzig, J.
Naumann, 1877-1902. 7 v. 25cm. Church dictionary; includes biographies.

4437   MIDDLETON, ERASMUS, 1739-1805.
      Evangelical biography; or, An historical account of the
lives & deaths of the most eminent and evangelical authors
or preachers, both British and foreign, in the several denominations of Protestants, from the beginning of the Reformation to the present time. A new ed., illustrated with 51
portraits. London, Printed for W. Baynes, 1816. 4 v.
ports. 22cm. First published in 1779-86 under title: Biographia Evangelica.

4438   MONDO CATTOLICO.
      [1952-   Roma, "Domani."   v. 24cm. Includes a bio-
bibliography of outstanding Catholics.

4439   MORAL, BONIFACIO, b. 1850.
      Catálogo de escritores agustinos españoles, portugueses
y americanos y sus obras por orden alfabético de autores.

2. ed. Valladolid, Colegio de Agustinos Filipinos, 1882-94.
2 v. (or pts?) Supplemented at various intervals in La Ciudad
de Dios, v. 69-76, 1906-1908. Dictionary catalog of Spanish,
Portuguese & Latin American Augustinian authors. Bio-bibliographical.

4440   MORGAN, JOHN VYRNWY, 1860-
Welsh religious leaders in the Victorian era. London,
Nisbet, 1905. xv, 480p.

4441   MORONI, GAETANO, 1802-1883.
Dizionario di erudizione storico-ecclesiastica da S.
Pietro sino ai nostri giorni. Venezia, Tip. Emiliana, 1840-
61. 103 v. in 53 v. 24cm. Title varies slightly. Dictionary
of historical-ecclesiastical learning from St. Peter to our
day; includes much biography.

4442   MOSER, JOHANN JAKOB, 1701-1785.
Beytrag zu einem Lexico der jetztlebender lutherisch- und
reformirten Theologen in und um Teutschland... Züllichau,
Frommann, 1740-41. 2 v. 4.º Contribution towards a dictionary of living Lutheran and Reformed theologians in and
around Germany.

4443   MOTT, AGNES
A dictionary of Hampshire recusants. [n. p.] 1941. 1 v.
4.º Catholics in Hampshire, England who refused to rec-
ognize the authority of the Church of England. Typescript.

4444   MOYER, ELGIN SYLVESTER, 1890-   ed.
Who was who in church history. Chicago, Moody Press,
1962. vi, 452 p. 25cm.

4445   MUÑIZ, ROBERTO
Biblioteca Cisterciense española, en la que se da noticia
de los escritores cistercienses de todas las Congregaciones
de España, y de los de las Ordenes militares que siguen el
mismo Instituto, con la expresion (en la mayor parte) del
lugar de su nacimiento, empleos, honores, y dignidades, y
igualmente que el de sus obras, tanto impresas como m.ss.
Burgos, J. de Navas, 1793.   400 p.   4.º   Bio-bibliography
of the Cisterican Order in Spain.

4446   NEUBAUER, ERNST FRIEDRICH
Nachricht von den itztlebenden Evangelisch-Lutherischen

und Reformirten Theologen in und um Deutschland, welche
entweder die Theologie und heiligen Sprachen öffentlich lehren,
oder sich sonst durch theologische und philologische Schriften
bekannt gemacht haben ... Als eine Fortsetzung, Verbesserung
und Ergänzung des Lexici der itztlebenden Evangelisch-Lutherischen und Reformirten Theologen. Züllichau, Waisenhaus,
1743-46. 2 v. (1148 p.) Information on living Evangelical-
Lutheran and Reformed theologians in and around Germany.

4447   NEW YORK. UNION THEOLOGICAL SEMINARY.
Alumni directory, 1836-1958. New York, Alumni Office,
1958. xxx, 427 p. 24cm.

4448   O'HANLON, JOHN, 1821-1905.
Lives of the Irish saints, with special festivals and the
commemoration of holy persons, compiled from calendars,
martyrologies, and various sources relating to the ancient
church history of Ireland. Dublin, Duffy; New York, Benziger,
1875-[1903] 10 v. (v.1-9 & 7 fascicles of v. 10) No more
published.

4449   OLIVER, GEORGE, 1782-1867.
Collections toward illustrating the biography of the Scotch,
English and Irish members of the Society of Jesus. London,
C. Dolman, 1845. 282 p. 23cm. 2d ed.; 1st ed. published
in Exeter, 1838. 250 copies printed.

4450   OLLARD, SIDNEY LESLIE, 1875-   ed.
A dictionary of English church history. Edited by S. L.
Ollard, Gordon Crosse [and] Maurice F. Bond. New ed.
[i.e. 3d ed. rev.] London, A. R. Mowbray; New York,
Morehouse-Gorham [1948] xx, 698 p. 25cm.

4451   OSSINGER, JOANNES FELIX.
Bibliotheca Augustiniana historica, critica e chronologica
in qva mille quadrigenti Augustiniani Ordinis scriptores,
eorumque opera tam scripta, quam typis edita inveniuntur,
simulque reperitur, quo saeculo uixerint, et de plurimis, quo
anno obierint, nec non cuius nationis, patriae, provinciae, et
coenobii fuerint quos e variis, et plusouam ducentis ac sep-
tuaginta octo scriptoribus tam exteris, quam huius ordinis e
diversis bibliothecis, catalogis, atque manuscriptis collegit,
et in ordinem alphabeticum secundum cognomen, et nomen a
religione impositum redegit Joannes Felix Ossinger. Ingol-
stadii, J. F. X. Craetz, 1768. [Torino, Bottega d'Erasmo,
1963] 1002 p. 25cm. Bio-bibliography of the Augustinian
Order.

4452   THE OXFORD DICTIONARY OF THE CHRISTIAN CHURCH.
Edited by F. L. Cross. London, New York, Oxford University Press, 1957. xix, 1492 p. 25cm.

4453   PATTEN, JAMES ALEXANDER
Lives of the clergy of New York and Brooklyn: embracing two hundred biographies of eminent living men in all denominations. Also, the history of each sect and congregation.
New York, Atlantic Pub. Co., 1874. 635p. ports. 25cm.

4454   PEEL, ALBERT, 1887-
The Congregational two hundred, 1530-1948. London, Independent Press, 1948. 288p. 19cm. "Incorporating A hundred eminent Congregationalists [1927]"

4455   PELZEL, FRANZ MARTIN, 1734-1801.
Boehmische, maehrische und schlesische Gelehrten und Schriftsteller aus dem Orden der Jesuiten von Anfang der Gesellschaft bis auf gegenwärtige Zeit. Prag, 1786. 1 v.
8.° Bohemian, Moravian and Silesian scholars and authors of the Society of Jesus (Jesuits) from the beginning of the Society to the present (1786)

4456   PERINI, DAVIDE AURELIO, 1868-
Bibliographia Augustiniana, cum notis biographis.
Scriptores Itali. Firenze, Tip. Sordomuti [1929-38] 4 v. in 1. Augustinian bibliography with biographical notes--Italian writers.

4457   PETERSON, JOHN, 1879-
A biographical directory of pastors of the Evangelical Lutheran Church, compiled by John Peterson, Olaf Lysnes [and] Gerald Giving. Minneapolis, Augsburg Pub. House [1952] 651p. ports. 24cm.

4458   PETIN, L   M
Dictionnaire hagiographique; ou, Vie des saints et des bienheureux, honorés en tout temps et en tous lieux depuis la naissance du Christianisme jusqu'à nos jours, avec un supplément pour les saints personnages de l'Ancien et du Nouveau testament, et des divers âges de l'Église, auxquels on ne rend aucun culte public, ou dont le jour le fête est inconnu. Paris, Chez l'éditeur, 1850. 2 v. 27cm. (Encyclopédie théologique... pub. par M. l'abbe Migne, v. 40-41)
A dictionary of the saints.

4459   PFISTER, ALOYS, 1833-1891.
Notices biographiques et bibliographiques sur les Jésuites
de l'ancienne mission de Chine, 1552-1773. Par le P. Louis
Pfister. Chang-Hai, Impr. de la Mission catholique, 1932-
34. 2 v. plates. 26cm. (Variétés sinologiques, no. 59-60)
Bio-bibliography of Jesuits in China, 1552-1773.

4460   PHILADELPHIA (MT. AIRY) LUTHERAN THEOLOGICAL
SEMINARY.
The Philadelphia Seminary biographical record, 1864-1923.
Edited by Luther D. Reed. Mt. Airy, Philadelphia, 1923.
271p. illus., ports. 24cm.

4461   PINKERTON, JOHN, 1758-1826.
Pinkerton's lives of the Scottish saints. Rev. and enl. by
W. M. Metcalfe. Paisley [Scot.] A. Gardner, 1889. 2 v.
8.⁰ 1st ed. published in 1789.

4462   PISANI, PAUL, 1852-
Répertoire biographique de l'épiscopat constitutionnel
(1791-1802) Paris, Picard, 1907. xii, 476p. 23cm. Biographical list of the French Revolutionary clergy.

4463   PLACIDO DA PAVULLO, Father
Gli scrittori francescani di Reggio nell'Emilia; note bio-
bibliografiche. Reggio Emilia, "Frate Francesco," 1931.
40p. 8.⁰ A bio-bibliography of Franciscans in Reggio
nell'Emilia, Italy.

4464   PLUQUET, FRANCOIS ANDRÉ ADRIEN, 1716-1790.
Dictionnaire des hérésies, des erreurs et des schismes;
ou, Mémoires pour servir à l'histoire des égarements de
l'esprit humain par rapport à la réligion chrétienne...
Ouvrage augmenté de plus de 400 articles... Continué jusqu'à nos jours pour toutes les matières qui en font le sujet,
comme pour le discours préliminaire, revu et corrigé d'un
bout à l'autre; par J. J. Claris. Suivi 1° d'un dictionnaire
nouveau des jansénistes, contenant un apercu historique de
leur vie... 2° de l'Index des livres défendus par la sacrée
congrégation de ce nom... 3° des propositions condamnées
par l'Église depuis l'an 411 jusqu'à présent: 4° de la liste
complète des ouvrages condamnés par les tribunaux francais...
Paris, J. P. Migné, 1863. 2 v. 29cm. (Première encyclopédie théologique, t. 11-12) Includes biographies of heretics.

4465 PRIETO DEL RÍO, LUIS FRANCISCO, 1857-
Diccionario biográfico del clero secular de Chile, 1535-
1918. Santiago de Chile, Impr. Chile, 1922. 738p. Biographical dictionary of the secular clergy of Chile.

4466 QUÉTIF, JACQUES, 1618-1698.
Scriptores Ordinis Praedicatorum recensiti, notisque
historicis et criticis illustrati, opus quo singulorum vita,
praeclareque gesta referuntur, chronologia insuper, seu-
tempus quo quisque floruit certo statuitur... Inchoavit
Jacobus Quetif, absolvit Jacobus Echard. Lutetiae Parisio-
rum, Apud J.-B.-C. Ballard, et N. Simart, 1719-21. 2 v.
40cm. Title of v. 2 varies slightly. Bio-bibliography of the
Dominican Order. A 2d edition was begun in Paris in 1910
under the editorship of Fr. Remigius Coulon. 5 fascicles
only were published?

4467 RANFT, MICHAEL, 1700-1774.
Leben und Schriften aller Chur-Sächsischen Gottesgelehrten. Leipzig, Deer, 1742. 1453p. Lives & writings of theologians of the Electorate of Saxony.

4468 REBORD, CHARLES M
Dictionnaire du clergé séculier & régulier du diocèse de
Genève-Annecy dès 1535 à nos jours. Par Ch.-M. Rebord
avec la collaboration de A. Gavard. Bourg, Impr. de J.
Dureuil, 1920-21. 2 v. (vii, 803p.) 8.º Dictionary of
the secular & regular clergy of the diocese of Geneva, 1535-
1921.

4469 REES, WILLIAM JENKINS, 1772-1855, ed. and tr.
Lives of the Cambro British saints of the 5th and immed-
iate succeeding centuries, from ancient Welsh & Latin mss.
in the British Museum and elsewhere, with English translations and explanatory notes. Published for the Welsh Manuscripts Society. Llandsvery, W. Rees; London, Longmans,
1853. xxiv, 636, 20p. illus. 26cm. (Society for the Publication of Ancient Welsh Manuscripts, Abergavenny. [Publi-
cations, v. 4]) A continuation of and a companion volume to
the Liber Landavensis.

4470 DIE RELIGION IN GESCHICHTE UND GEGENWART;
Handwörterbuch für Theologie und Religionswissenschaft.
2. völlig neubearb. Aufl., in Verbindung mit Alfred Bertho-
let, Hermann Faber und Horst Stephan hrsg. von Hermann
Gunkel und Leopold Zscharnack. Tübingen, J. C. B. Mohr,

1927-32. 5 v. plates. 27cm. First edition issued 1909-1913.
Includes many biographical articles of religious figures living and dead.

4471　RELIGIOUS LEADERS OF AMERICA.
　　v. 1-　　; 1935/36-　　New York.　v. 22cm.　Title
varies: v. 1, Who's who in the clergy. Editor: v. 1-
J. C. Schwarz. No volumes were published for 1937-1940.

4472　RIVADENEIRA, PEDRO DE, 1527-1611.
　　Bibliotheca scriptorum Societatis Iesu, post excusum anno M. DC. VIII catalogum... nunc hoc nouo apparatu librorum
ad annum reparatae salutis M. DC. XLII. editorum concin-
nati, & illustrium virorum elogiis adornata, a Philippo
Alegambe... Accedit Catalogus religiosorum Societatis Iesu,
qui hactenus pro Catholicâ fide & pietate in variis mundi
plagis interempti sunt. Antverpiae, Apud Ioannem Meursium,
1643. 12, 586p. 32cm. A later famous version with many
additions, etc. by Nathaniel Southwell was published in Rome
in 1676. Bio-bibliography of the Society of Jesus (Jesuits)

4473　RODOSSKIĬ, ALEKSEĬ STEPANOVICH, 1838-
　　Biograficheskiĭ slovar´ studentov pervykh XXVIII kursov
S. -Peterburgskoĭ dukhovnoĭ akademii, 1814-1869 gg. K 100-
letiiu S. -Peterburgskoĭ dukhovnoĭ akademii. S. -Peterburg,
Tip. I. V. Leont´eva, 1907. lxxxiv, 552p. illus. 25cm.
Biographical dictionary of students at the Theological Acad-
emy in St. Petersburg (now Leningrad) 1814-1869.

4474　ROEDER, HELEN, 1909-
　　Saints and their attributes; with a guide to localities and
patronage. London, Longmans, Green, 1955. xxviii, 391p.
illus. 18cm. American ed. published by H. Regnery, Chicago.

4475　ROSELAND, JENS CHRISTIAN, 1859-
　　American Lutheran biographies; or, Historical notices
of over 350 leading men of the American Lutheran Church,
from its establishment to the year 1890. With a historical
introd. By J. C. Jensson. Milwaukee [1890] 901p. ports.
27cm.

4476　RUNKEVICH, STEPAN GRIGOR´EVICH, 1867-
　　Arkhĭerei petrovskoĭ epokhi v ikh perepiskiê s Petrom
Velikim. S. -Peterburg, 1906-　　v. 24cm. Bishops of
the Russian Orthodox Eastern Church in the era of Peter the
Great.

4477   SÁ, MANUEL DE, 1673-1735.
Memorias historicas. Dos illustrissimos arcebispos, bispos e escriptores portuguezes da Ordem de Nossa Senhora do Carmo, reduzidas a catalogo alphabetico. Lisboa, Officina Ferreyriana, 1724. 544p. coats of arms. 23cm. 103 biographies of Portuguese archbishops, bishops and writers of the Order of the Carmelites.

4478   THE SAINTS;
A concise biographical dictionary, edited by John Coulson. With an introd. by C. C. Martindale. London, Burns and Oates, 1958. 496p. plates. 26cm. Over 2200 saints. American edition has imprint: New York, Hawthorn Books.

4479   SALA, TORELLO
Dizionario storico biografico di scrittori, letterati ed artisti dell'Ordine di Vallombrosa. Compilato dal P. abate D. Torello Sala, e pubblicato per le stampe dal P. abate D. Federigo Fedele Tarani. Firenze, 1929-37. 2 v. 8.º Historical-biographical dictionary of writers, littérateurs and artists of the Order of Vallombrosians (living under the Benedictine rule)

4480   SAMARITANI, ANTONIO
I vescovi di Comacchio; fonti, bibliografia, critica. Padova, Tip. Antoniana [1961] xxxi, 193p. illus., ports. 25cm. 80 bishops of the diocese of Comacchio, Italy.

4481   SANTIAGO VELA, GREGORIO DE, 1865-1924.
Ensayo de una biblioteca íbero-americana de la Orden de San Agustín. Obra basada en el catálogo bio-bibliográfico agustiniano del P. Bonifacio Moral ... Madrid, Impr. del Asilo de Huérfanos del S. C. de Jesús, 1913-31. 8 v. illus. 28cm. Bio-bibliography of the Order of Augustinians in Spanish America.

4482   SCHAFF-HERZOG ENCYCLOPEDIA.
Encyclopedia of living divines and Christian workers of all denominations in Europe and America; being a supplement to Schaff-Herzog encyclopedia of religious knowledge. Edited by Philip Schaff and Samuel Macauley Jackson. New York, Funk & Wagnalls, 1887. vi, 271 p. 28cm.

4483   SCHAFF-HERZOG ENCYCLOPEDIA.
The new Schaff-Herzog encyclopedia of religious knowledge, embracing Biblical, historical, doctrinal, and practical theol-

ogy, and Biblical, theological, and ecclesiastical biography
from the earliest times to the present day; based on the 3d ed.
of the Realencyklopädie founded by J. J. Herzog, and edited
by Albert Hauck, prepared by more than six hundred scholars
and specialists under the supervision of Samuel Macauley
Jackson (editor-in-chief) with the assistance of Charles Cole-
brook Sherman and George William Gilmore (associate editors)
and [others] Grand Rapids, Mich., Baker, 1949-50. 13 v.
25cm.

4484   SCHAFF-HERZOG ENCYCLOPEDIA.
Twentieth century encyclopedia of religious knowledge; an
extension of the New Schaff-Herzog encyclopedia of religious
knowledge. Editor-in-chief: Lefferts A. Loetscher.   Grand
Rapids, Baker Book House, 1955.   2 v. (xx, 1205 p.)   25cm.
Includes biographical sketches of religious leaders, living and
dead.

4485   SCOTT, EUGENE CRAMPTON
Ministerial directory of the Presbyterian Church, U.S.,
1861-1941. Rev. and supplemented, 1942-1950. Published by
order of the General Assembly.   Atlanta, Hubbard Print. Co.,
1950.   798 p.

4486   SCOTT, HEW, 1791-1872.
Fasti Ecclesiae Scoticanae; the succession of ministers in
the Church of Scotland from the Reformation.   New ed., rev.
and continued to the present time under the superintendence
of a committee appointed by the General Assembly. Edinburgh,
Oliver and Boyd, 1915-50.   8 v.   Over 15,000 biographies.

4487   SCOTT, WILLIAM J
Biographic etchings of ministers and laymen of the Georgia
Conferences.   Atlanta, Foote & Davies Co., 1895.   iv, 317 p.
20cm. Biography of the Methodist Episcopal Church, South,
in Georgia.

4488   SIGISMONDO DA VENEZIA, d. 1847.
Biografia serafica degli uomini illustri che fiorirono nel
Francescano istituto.   Venezia, Tip. G. B. Merlo, 1846.
956 p.   Biography of the Franciscan order.

4489   SIGURÐSSON, JON, 1811-1879.
Biskupa tal á Íslandi. (In Safn til sögu Íslands. Kaupmannahöfn, 1856. 1. bindi, p. 1-136)   83 Icelandic bishops—1056
to 1846.

4490   SIMON, MATTHIAS
Ansbachisches Pfarrerbuch; die evangelisch-lutherische
Geistlichkeit des Fürstentums Brandenburg-Ansbach 1528-
1806. Nürnberg, Selbstverlag des Vereins für Bayerische
Kirchengeschichte, 1955-57. 30, 759 p. 25cm. (Einzelar-
beiten aus der Kirchengeschichte Bayerns, 28. Bd.) The
Evangelical-Lutheran clergymen of Ansbach (i.e. the princi-
pality of Brandenburg-Ansbach) 1528-1806.

4491   SIMON, MATTHIAS
Bayreuthisches Pfarrerbuch; die evangelisch-lutherische
Geistlichkeit des Fürstentums Kulmbach-Bayreuth (1528/29-
1810) München, C. Kaiser, 1930-31. xxvi, 516 p. 25cm.
(Einzelarbeiten aus der Kirchengeschichte Bayerns, 12. Bd.)
Issued in 3 fascicles, 1930-31. The Evangelical-Lutheran
clergyman of Bayreuth (i.e. the principality of Kulmbach-
Bayreuth, 1528/29-1810)

4492   SIMON, MATTHIAS
Nürnbergisches Pfarrerbuch; die evangelisch-lutherische
Geistlichkeit der Reichsstadt Nürnberg und ihres Gebietes,
1524-1806. Nürnberg, Selbstverlag des Vereins für Bayerisch
Kirchengeschichte, 1965. xx, 359 p. 25cm. (Einzelarbeiten
aus der Kirchengeschichte Bayerns, 41. Bd.) The Evangelical-Lutheran clergymen of Nuremberg, 1524-1806.

4493   SIMON, MATTHIAS, ed.
Pfarrerbuch der Reichsstädte Dinkelsbühl, Schweinfurt,
Weissenburg i.Bay. und Windsheim, sowie der Reichsdörfer
Gochsheim und Sennfeld; die evangelsichen Geistlichen im
Alten Reich, bearb. von Hanns Bauer [et al.] Nürnberg,
Selbstverlag des Vereins für Bayerische Kirchengeschichte,
1962. xii, 124 p. 25cm. (Einzelarbeiten aus der Kirchen-
geschichte Bayerns, 39. Bd.) Clergymen (Evangelical-
Lutheran) of several cities and villages in Franconia.

4494   SMITH, JOSEPH, bookseller.
Bibliotheca anti-Quakeriana; or, A catalogue of books ad-
verse to the Society of Friends, alphabetically arranged.
With biographical notices of the authors, together with the
answers which have been given to some of them by Friends
and others. London, J. Smith, 1873. 474 p. 22cm.

4495   SMITH, JOSEPH, bookseller.
A descriptive catalogue of Friends' books, or books written
by members of the Society of Friends, commonly called Quak-
ers, from their first rise to the present time, interspersed

with critical remarks and biographical notices. London, 1867.
2 v. 22cm.

4496 --- ----Supplement. London, E. Hicks, 1893. 364 p. 23cm.

4497 SMITH, Sir WILLIAM, 1813-1893.
A dictionary of Christian biography, literature, sects, and
doctrines; being a continuation of The dictionary of the Bible.
Edited by William Smith and Henry Wace. London, J. Murray, 1877-87. 4 v. 23cm.

4498 SOLLANA, EMILIO M   DE
Escritores de la Provincia Capuchina de Valencia , Curia
Provincial de Capuchinos, 1963. xxviii, 397 p. 25cm.
Writers of the Order of Capuchins, Province of Valencia,
Spain.

4499 SOUTHERN BAPTIST CONVENTION. FOREIGN MISSION
BOARD.
Missionary album. Compiled by Genevieve Greer. [Rev.
ed.] Nashville, Convention Press [1959, c1954] 210 p. illus.
28cm.

4500 SPARACIO, DOMENICO, 1877-1929.
Frammenti bio-bibliografici di scrittori ed autori minori
conventuali dagli ultimi anni del 600 al 1930... [Assisi] Casa
editrice francescana Assisi, 1931. 232 p. 29cm. Bio-bibliographical fragments on writers and authors, Franciscan
(Conventual) 1600-1930.

4501 SPRAGUE, WILLIAM BUELL, 1795-1876.
Annals of the American pulpit; or, Commemorative notices
of distinguished American clergymen of various denominations
from the early settlement of the country to the close of the
year eighteen hundred and fifty-five. With historical introductions. New York, R. Carter, 1857-[69] 9 v. ports. 24cm.
The volumes for each denomination were issued also separately with special t.p. Contents.--v. 1-2. Trinitarian Congregational.--v. 3-4. Presbyterian.--v. 5. Episcopalian.--v. 6.
Baptist.--v.7. Methodist.--v. 8. Unitarian Congregationalist.
--v. 9. Lutheran. Reformed Dutch. Associate. Associate
Reform. Reformed Presbyterian.

4502 STADLER, JOHANN EVANGELISTA
Vollständiges Heiligen-Lexikon; oder, Lebensgeschichte
aller Heiligen, Seligen, etc., in alphabetischer Ordnung...

Unter Mitwirkung mehrerer Diozesanpriester hrsg. von J. E. Stadler und Franz Joseph Heim. [Fortgesetzt von J. N. Ginal] Augsburg, Schmid, 1858-82. 5 v. 8.° Complete dictionary of the saints.

4503   STANTON, RICHARD
      A menology of England and Wales; or, Brief memorials of the ancient British and English saints, arranged according to the calendar: with the martyrs of the 16th and 17th centuries. London, Burns & Oates, 1887-92. xix, 811 p.

4504   STÖGER, JOHANN .NEPOMUK, 1792-1880.
      Scriptores Provinciae Austriacae Societatis Jesu ab ejus origine ad nostra usque tempora. Viennae, Typis Congregationis Mechitaristicae, G. J. Manz, 1856. 414p. Writers of the Province of Austria of the Jesuits from its origin to our time.

4505   STROEV, PAVEL MIKHAĬLOVICH, 1796-1876.
      Spiski ierarkhov i nastoi͡ateleĭ monastyrei Rossiĭskii͡a t͡serkvi. S.-Petersburg, Izd. Arkheograficheskoĭ kommissii, 1877. x p., 1056, 68 columns. 28cm. Lists of Russian Orthodox hierarchs and abbots.

4506   STURM, CHRISTOPH CHRISTIAN, 1740-1786.
      Handbuch zur Kenntniss der theologischen Schriftsteller unter den Deutschen. 1. Th.: Welcher die Schriftsteller vor dem sechzehnten Jahrhundert in sich begreift. Halle, Swetschke, 1770. 1 v. 8.° Handbook of German theological writers. No more published.

4507   SUMMERS, THOMAS OSMOND, 1812-1882, ed.
      Biographical sketches of eminent itinerant ministers distinguished, for the most part, as pioneers of Methodism within the bounds of the Methodist Episcopal Church, South. Nashville, E. Stevenson & F. A. Owen, agents, for Methodist Episcopal Church, South, 1858. 384p. 24cm.

4508   [TASSIN, RENÉ PROSPER] 1697-1777.
      Histoire littéraire de la Congregation de Saint-Maur, ordre de S. Benoît, où l'on trouve la vie & les travaux des auteurs qu'elle a produits, depuis son origine en 1618, jusqu'à présent: avec les titres, l'énumération, l'analyse, les différentes éditions des livres qu'ils ont donnés au public, & le jugement que les savans en ont porté: ensemble la notice de beaucoup d'ouvrages manuscrits, composés par des Bénédic-

tins du même corps. Bruxelles, Paris, Humblot, 1770. xxviii, 800, [28] p. 27cm. Lives and works of Benedictines of the Congregation of St. Maur, 1618-1770.

4509   TAYLOR, JAMES BENNETT, 1804-1871.
Virginia Baptist ministers. With an introd. by J. B. Jeter. New York, Sheldon, 1860. 2 v. 21cm. First published in 1837 in one vol. under title: Lives of Virginia Baptist ministers.

4510   ÞORSTEINSSON, HANNES, 1860-
Guðfraeðingatal. Stutt aefiágrip þeirra guðfraeðinga íslenzkra, er tekið hafa embaettispróf við Kaupmannahaf-narháskóla 1707-1907. Sögufélag gaf út. Reykjavík, 1907-10. 324 p. (Sögurit, 5) [Icelandic] theologians. Short biographical sketches of those Icelandic theologians who have taken degrees from the University of Copenhagen, 1707-1907.

4511   TORRES SALDAMANDO, ENRIQUE, 1846-1896.
Los antiguos Jesuítas del Perú; biografías y apuntes para su historia. Lima, Impr. Liberal, 1882. 400p. 161 bio-bibliographical notices of Jesuits in Peru.

4512   TORSY, JAKOB, ed.
Lexikon der deutschen Heiligen, Seligen, Ehrwürdigen und Gottseligen. Unter Mitarbeit von Rudolf Lill und Placidus Mittler. Köln, J. P. Bachem, 1959. [23] p. , 578 columns. map. 25cm. Dictionary of German saints and persons of pious and exemplary lives.

4513   TOURON, ANTOINE, 1686-1775.
Histoire des hommes illustres de l'ordre de Saint Dominique... depuis la mort du fondateur, jusqu'au pontificat de Benoît XIII... Paris, Babuty, 1743-49. 6 v. 8.º The history of illustrious men of the Dominican Order, from the death of its founder to the pontificate of Benedict XIII.

4514   TRINIUS, JOHANN ANTON, 1722-1784.
Freydenker-Lexicon; oder, Einleitung in die Geschichte der neuern Freygeister, ihrer Schriften, und deren Widerlegungen. Nebst einem Bey- und Nachtrage zu des seligen Herrn Johann Albert Fabricius Syllabo scriptorum, pro veritate religionis Christianae. Leipzig, C. G. Cörner, 1759. 876p. 18cm. Dictionary of free-thinkers.

4515   UNGARELLI, LUIGI MARIA, 1779-1845.
Bibliotheca scriptorum e Congregatione clerr. regg. S.

Paulli. Vol. I. Romae, Ex Officina J. Salviucci, 1836. xix, 571p. 30cm. No more publiched. A bio-bibliography of the Barnabites or Clerics Regular of St. Paul, ca. 1533-1632.

4516   UNITARIAN AND FREE CHRISTIAN CHURCHES.
Yearbook of the General Assembly... for 1894-
v. 1-   London, Essex Hall [etc.]   v.   Title varies: 1894-1928, Essex Hall year book. With brief biographies for ministers in the British Isles.

4517   UNITED FREE CHURCH OF SCOTLAND.
Fasti, 1900-1929, edited by John Alexander Lamb. Edinburgh, Oliver and Boyd [1956] xi, 639p. 26cm.

4518   U. S. BUREAU OF NAVAL PERSONNEL.
The history of the Chaplain Corps, United States Navy, [compiled by] Clifford Merrill Drury, captain, Chaplain Corps. [Washington, U. S. Govt. Print. Off. , 1948-
v. 3, 1948]   v. illus. , ports. 27cm. Vol. 3 issued without a general title and vol. numbering; vol. 4 compiled by the Chaplain Division of the Bureau of Naval Personnel, Navy Dept. Partial contents. -- [v. 3] United States Navy chaplains, 1778-1945; biographical and service-record sketches of 3,353 chaplains, including 2 who served in the Continental Navy. -- v. 4. United States Navy chaplains, 1946-1952; biographical and service-record sketches of 1,830 chaplains, including corrections and amendments to 1,555 sketches which appeared in United States Navy chaplains, 1778-1945, and sketches of 273 chaplains who had active duty beginning after 1 January 1946.

4519   URIARTE, JOSÉ EUGENIO DE, 1842-1909.
Biblioteca de escritores de la Compañía de Jesús pertenecientes á la antigua asistencia de España desde sus orígines hasta el año de 1773, por José Eug. de Uriarte y Mariano Lecina. Madrid, Impr. de la Viuda de López del Horno, 1925-   v. 29cm. Bio-bibliography of Spanish Jesuits to the year 1773. Contents. -- pt. 1. t. 1. Escritores de quienes se conoce algún trabajo impreso.

4520   VALVERDE TÉLLEZ, EMETERIO, Bp. , 1864-1948.
Bio-bibliografía eclesiástica mexicana (1821-1943) Dirección y prólogo de José Bravo Ugarte. México, Editorial Jus, 1949. 3 v. 25cm. (Colección de estudios históricos) Bio-bibliography of the Mexican clergy (Catholic) 1821-1943.

4521　VANDERPOOL, HERBERT CAMPBELL, 1923-
Twentieth century Baptists; biographies of over one hundred ministers. Also sketches in Enon, Wiseman and Siloan Baptist Associations [and] an additional history of other churches. [By] H. C. Vanderpool [and] W. T. Russell. Tompkinsville, Ky., Printed by Monroe County Press,1962. 322p. illus. 22cm.

4522　VARONES ILUSTRES DE LA COMPAÑIA DE JESÚS.
2. ed. Bilbao, Impr. del Corazón de Jesús, 1887-92. 9 v. 4.º Famous members of the Company of Jesus (Jesuits)—chiefly missionaries.

4523　VIGNAS, TOMMASO
Index bio-bibliographicus CC. RR. PP. Matris Dei Scholarum piarum. Romae, Typ. Vaticana, 1908-11. 3 v. Bio-bibliography of the Piarists, a Catholic educational order.

4524　VILLIERS DE SAINT ETIENNE, COSME DE, 1683-1758.
Bibliotheca Carmelitana, notis criticis et dissertationibus illustrata cura & labore unius è Carmelitis Provinciae Turoniae collecta... 1752... Additis nova praefatione et supplemento... Gabriel Wessels... Romae, Prostat in Aedibus Collegii S. Alberti, 1927. 2 v. in 1.

Bio-bibliography of the Carmelite order.

4525　VISCH, CHARLES DE, 1596 (ca.)-1666.
Bibliotheca scriptorum sacri ordinis Cisterciensis, e-logiis plurimorum maxime illistrium adornata. Editio 2. notabiliter aucta. Coloniae Agrippinae, J. Busaeus, 1656. 432p. Bio-bibliography of the Cistercian order.

4526　VOS, JOACHIM JOSEPH, 1832-
Le clergé du diocèse de Tournai depuis le Concordat de 1801 jusqu'à nos jours. Braine-le-Comte [Belgium] Zech, 1887-93. 5 v. 8.º The Catholic clergy of the diocese of Tournai, Belgium from the Concordat of 1801 to ca. 1893.

4527　WACE, HENRY, 1836-1924, ed.
A dictionary of Christian biography and literature to the end of the sixth century A. D., with an account of the principal sects and heresies. Edited by Henry Wace and William C. Piercy. London, J. Murray, 1911. xi, 1028 p. 24cm. Founded on "the Dictionary of Christian biography, literature,

sects, and doctrines, published under the editorship of Dr.
Wace and the late Dr. Wm. Smith... in four large volumes. "

4528   WHEELER, JOSEPH MAZZINI, 1850-1898.
A biographical dictionary of freethinkers of all ages and
nations. London, Progressive Pub. Co. , 1889.   355 p.
19cm.

4529   WHO'S WHO AMONG PASTORS IN ALL THE NORWEGIAN
LUTHERAN SYNODS OF AMERICA, 1843-1927.
3d ed. of Norsk lutherske prester i Amerika, translated
and rev. by Rasmus Malmin, O. M. Norlie and O. A.
Tingelstad. Minneapolis, Augsburg Pub. House, 1928.   662p.
ports. 24cm.

4530   WHO'S WHO AMONG THE MENNONITES.
1937-   [Newton? Kan.] v. illus. 20cm.

4531   WHO'S WHO IN AMERICAN METHODISM.
v. 1-   1916-   New York, E. B. Treat. v. 21cm.

4532   WHO'S WHO IN BAPTIST AMERICA IN THE NATIONAL
SUNDAY SCHOOL AND BAPTIST TRAINING UNION
CONGRESS.
An illustrated biographical directory of outstanding leaders
and workers in the National Sunday School and Baptist Training Union Congress along with a few of our leading Baptist
institutions. Edited by L. Venchael Booth. Pilot ed.
[Cincinnati, Printed by Western Print. Co.] 1960. 49p.
ports.

4533   WHO'S WHO IN CONGREGATIONALISM.
An authoritative reference work and guide to the careers of
ministers and lay officials of the Congregational churches...
London, Shaw Pub. Co. in conjunction with Independent Press,
1933. 217p. British Congregationalists.

4534   WHO'S WHO IN METHODISM.
Edited under the auspices of the Association of
Methodist Historical Societies, USA, and the International
Methodist Historical Society, an affiliate of the Ecumenical
Conference. Elmer T. Clark, editor-in-chief; T. A.
Stafford, cooperating editor. Chicago, A. N. Marquis Co. ,
1952. x, 860p. 24cm.

4535   WHO'S WHO IN METHODISM.
An encyclopaedia of the personnel and departments,
ministerial and lay, in the United Church of Methodism.
1933-   London, Methodist times and leader (Methodist
Publications ltd.) v. ports. 23cm. British Methodists.

4536   WHO'S WHO IN PAN-METHODISM.
v. 1-   1940/41-   Nashville, Parthenon Press.   v.
illus. , ports. 24cm.

4538   WHO'S WHO IN THE FREE CHURCHES, AND OTHER DE-
NOMINATIONS. 1st-   ed. ; 1951-   London, Shaw Pub.
Co.   v. 22cm.   British clergymen.

4539   WHO'S WHO IN THE PROTESTANT CLERGY.
Encino, Calif. , Nygaard Associates [1957] 264p. 24cm.
American Protestant clergymen.

4540   WIEDEMANN, HANS
Augsburger Pfarrerbuch; die evangelischen Geistlichen der
Reichsstadt Augsburg 1524-1806.   Nürnberg, Selbstverlag des
Vereins für Bayerische Kirchengeschichte, 1962.   viii, 80 p.
25cm. (Einzelarbeiten aus der Kirchengeschichte Bayerns,
38. Bd.)   The Evangelical clergy of Augsburg, 1524-1806.

4541   WILKS, JOHN, d. 1846.
A Christian biographical dictionary, containing an account
of the lives and writings of most distinguished Christians and
theologians. . . in every nation. . .   London, 1821. 1 v. 12.°

4542   WILLIAMS, ETHEL L
Biographical directory of Negro ministers.   New York,
Scarecrow Press, 1965.   xi, 421 p. 22cm.

4543   WINDLE, Sir BERTRAM COGHILL ALAN, 1858-
Who's who of the Oxford movement.   Prefaced by a brief
story of that movement.   New York, Century Co. [c1926]
viii, 251 p. front. 21cm.

4544   WINER, GEORG BENEDIKT, 1789-1858.
Handbuch der theologischen Literatur, hauptsächlich der

protestantischen. Nebst kurzen biographischen Notizen über die theologischen Schriftsteller. 3. sehr erweiterte Aufl. Leipzig, C. H. Reclam, 1838-40. 2 v. 21cm.

4545 ---- ----Erstes Ergänzungsheft zur dritten Auflage. Die Literatur bis zu Ende des Jahres 1841 fortführend. Leipzig, C. H. Reclam, Sen., 1842. viii, 350 columns. 21cm.

Handbook of theological literature, chiefly Protestant, as well as brief biographical notes on the authors.

4546 WORLD CONFERENCE ON FAITH AND ORDER. 2d, Edinburgh, 1937.
Who's who at Edinburgh, 1937. Qui etes-vous? Edimbourg 1937. Wer ist's? Edinburgh 1937. Issued by the Secretariat. Rev. ed. New York, 1937. 107p. 22cm.

4547 WRIGHT, RICHARD ROBERT, 1878-
The bishops of the African Methodist Episcopal Church. [Nashville] Printed by the A. M. E. Sunday School Union, 1963. 389p. illus. 22cm. 79 biographies.

4548 XIBERTA Y ROQUETA, BARTOLOMÉ MARÍA, 1897-
De scriptoribus scholasticis saeculi XIV ex ordine Carmelitarum, disseruit Bartholomaeus Maria Xiberta. Louvain, Bureaux de la Revue [d'histoire ecclésiastique] 1931. 510p. 25cm. (Bibliothèque de la Revue d'histoire ecclésiastique, fasc. 6) Bio-bibliography of Carmelite scholastic philosophers of the 14th century.

4549 ZAMBRANO, FRANCISCO, 1888-
Diccionario bio-bibliográfico de la Compañía de Jesús en México. [1. ed.] México, Editorial Jus, 1961-   v. 24cm Bio-bibliographical dictionary of the Society of Jesus (Jesuits) in Mexico. Contents.--t. 1-2. Siglo XVI (1566-1600)

4550 ZARCO CUEVAS, EUSEBIO JULIÁN, 1887-
Escritores agustinos de el Escorial (1885-1916); catálogo biobibliográfico. Madrid, Impr. Helénica, 1917. xiv, 394p. 20cm. Augustinian writers of the Spanish Escorial; a bio-bibliographical catalog.

4551 ZAWART, ANSCAR
The history of Franciscan preaching and of Franciscan preachers (1209-1927); a bio-bibliographical study. New York, J. F. Wagner, 1928. 241-596p. (Franciscan studies, no. 7, Feb. 1928)

4552   ZIEGELBAUER, MAGNOALD, 1689-1750.
Historia rei literariae Ordinis S. Benedicti, in IV partes
distributa... Ichnographicè adumbratum, recensuit, auxit,
jurisque publici fecit Oliverius Legipontius. Augustae Vind.
& Herbipoli, Sumptibus M. Veith, 1754. 4 v. 38cm. History
of the literary affairs of the Order of Saint Benedict (Benedictines) Vols. 3-4 are biographical and bibliographical respectively.

Islam

4553   ABŪ NU'AIM AHMAD IBN 'ABD ALLĀH, 948-1038.
Hilyat al-awliyā wa-tabakāt al-asfiyā. Cairo, 1932-38.
10v. Accounts of 649 Sufis and their sayings.

4554   AL-ANSARI AL-HARAWI, 'ABD ALLAH IBN MUHAMMAD,
1006-1089.
Tabaqāt al-Sūfiyah... [Kabul, 1962] 2, 48, 738p. facsims.
27cm. (Anjuman-i Tārīkh-i Afghānistān. Nasharāt, 72)
'Levels' of Sufism; biographies of Sufi mystics.

4555   FARĪD AL-DĪN 'ATTĀR, 13th cent.
Parts I [-II] of the Tadhkiratu 'l-awliyā (Memoirs of the
saints) of Faridu 'ddin 'Attār. Edited, with pref. , indices
and variants. . . by Reynold A. Nicholson. With a critical
introduction by Mirzā Muhammad b. 'Abdu 'l- Wahhāb-i
Qazwini. London, 1905-07. 2v. [Persian historical texts,
v. 3, 5] Mohammedan saints.

4556   IBN AL-JAZARĪ, MUHAMMAD IBN MUHAMMAD, 1350-1429.
Das biographische Lexikon der Koranlehrer, von Šamsaddīn
Muhammad ibn al-Ğazarī. Hrsg. von Gotthelf Bergsträsser.
Kairo, Druckerei as-Sa'āda, 1933-35. 2v. 26cm.
(Bibliotheca Islamica, Bd. 8) In Arabic. Biographical dic-
tionary of scholars of the Koran.

4557   IBN SA'D, MUHAMMAD, 784 (ca.)-845.
Biographien Muhammeds, seiner Gefährten und der
späteren Träger des Islams, bis zum Jahre 230 der Flucht.
Im Auftrage der Kgl. Preussischen Akademie der
Wissenschaften, im Verein mit C. Brockelmann [et al.] hrsg.
von Eduard Sachau. Leiden, E. J. Brill, 1904-40 [v.1, pt. 1,
1905] 9v. in 15. 28cm. Added t. p. : al-Tabaqāt... Biographies of Mohammed, his companions and the later standard-
bearers of Islam to the year 230 of the Hegira.

4558 JĀMĪ, 1414-1492.
Nafahāt al-uns min hadarāt al-quds.   [Tehran, 1957]
165, 679p. The lives of the mystics; notices of 567 male
saints, 34 female saints and 13 Sufi poets, chronologically
arranged. The work is a modernized recension of 'Abdallāh
Ansārī's Tabaqāt, which, in turn, was an enlargement of
Muhammad ibn al-Husayn al-Sulamī's Tabaqāt al-Sūfiyya.

4559 NŪR ALLĀH, SHŪSHTARĪ, 1549-1610.
Majālis al-muminīn. [Tehran, 1851 or 2?] collation unknown. Lives of eminent Shiite teachers.

Judaism

4560 BACHER, WILHELM, 1850-1913.
Die Agada der palästinensischen Amoräer. Strassburg,
K. J. Trübner, 1892-99. 3 v. 23cm. and Die Agada der
Tannaiten. Strassburg, K. J. Trübner, 1890-1903. 2 v.
23cm. A series of volumes which record the activities of
early Talmudic scholars (1) The Haggadists (2) the Amoraim-
Palestinian and Babylonian and (3) the Tannaim.

4561 ENTSIKLOPEDIYAH LE-HAKHME HA-TALMUD VEHA-
GEONIM... [Tel-Aviv, 1944/45] 2 v. 23cm. On verso
of t. p. : Encyclopedia of Talmudic and Geonic literature; being
a biographical dictionary of the Tanaim, Amoraim and
Geonim, with the collaboration of prominent scholars. Edited
by Mordechai Margalioth (i. e. Mordecai Margulies)

4562 GOTTLIEB, SAMUEL NOAH
Ohole-Shem... [Pinsk, 1912] xlvi, 560p. 27cm. Biographies of Jewish scholars (rabbis)

4563 HASIDAH, ISRAEL YITZHAK
Ishe ha-tnākh. [Jerusalem, 1964] 432p. 25cm.
Added t. p. : 565 Biblical personalities, as seen by the
sages of the Talmud and Midrash.

4564 KOLATCH, ALFRED J   1916-
Who's who in the Talmud. New York, J. David [1964]
315 p. facsims. 23cm.

4565 LANDSHUTH, LESER, 1817-1887.
Toldot anshe ha-shem... [Berlin, 1884] iv, 123p. 22cm.
Biographies of the rabbis of Berlin, intended to cover the
years 1671-1800. Only one volume was published.

4566   MICHAEL, HEIMANN JOSEPH, 1792-1846.
        Or ha-Hayyim... [Frankfurt a. M., J. Kauffmann, 1891]
        viii, 617p. 23cm. Added t. p. : (Or ha-Chajim) Umfassendes
        bibliografisches und literar-historisches Wörterbuch des
        rabbinischen Schriffthums... Bibliographical and literary-
        historical dictionary of Rabbinical writings.

4567   RAND, OSCAR ZALKA, ed.
        Toldot anshe shem... [New York, 1950-   v. 33cm.
        Biography of well-known people (i. e. rabbis)

4568   STERN, ABRAHAM, rabbi
        Melize esh... [Tyrnau, 193- —   v. 23cm. A collection
        of biographies of famous rabbis.

4569   ZARSKI, SAMUEL ZANVEL
        Anshe shem... [Tel-Aviv, 1939/40-   v. ports. 25cm.
        By S. Z. Zarski and M. D. Schiff. Well-known people (i. e.
        rabbis)

SCIENCE

Bibliography, Indexes, Etc.

4570   IRELAND, NORMA (OLIN) 1907-
        Index to scientists of the world, from ancient to modern
        times: biographies and portraits. Boston, F. W. Faxon Co.,
        1962. xliii, 662p. 24cm. (Useful reference series, no. 90)

General Works

4571   ACADÉMIE DES SCIENCES, PARIS.
        Index biographique des membres et correspondants de
        l'Académie des sciences du 22 décembre 1666 au 15 novembre
        1954. [2. éd.] Paris, Gauthier-Villars, 1954. xi, 534p.
        18cm. 1st ed., 1939, covered 1666-1939.

4572   AKADEMIE DER WISSENSCHAFTEN, BERLIN.
        Biographischer Index der Mitglieder. Bearb. von Kurt R.
        Biermann und Gerhard Dunken. Berlin, Akademie-Verlag,
        1960. xii, 248p. 10 ports. 25cm. A biographical index of
        members of the Academy of Sciences, Berlin.

4573   AKADEMIE DER WISSENSCHAFTEN, GÖTTINGEN.
        Mitglieder-Verzeichnisse der Gesellschaft der
        Wissenschaften zu Göttingen (1751-1927) in ihrem Auftrag

zusammengestellt von Max Arnim. Göttingen, 1928. 234p. 26cm. Membership lists of the Academy of Sciences in Göttingen.

4574 AKADEMIÏA NAUK SSSR.
Materialy dlïa biograficheskago slovarïa dïeïstvitel'-nykh chlenov Imperatorskoï Akademii Nauk. Petrograd, Tip. Rossiskoï akademii nauk, 1915-17. 2v. 4.° (Its Imperator-skaïa Akademiïa nauk, 1899-1914. [t.] 3) Materials for a biographical dictionary of active members of the Russian Imperial Academy of Sciences.

4575 AKADEMIÏA NAUK SSSR.
Spisok chlenov Imperatorskoï Akademii nauk, 1725-1907. Sostavitel B. L. Modzalevskiï. Sanktpeterburg, Tip. Imp. Akademii nauk, 1908. viii, 404p. 16.° Members of the Russian Imperial Academy of Sciences, 1725-1907.

4576 AMERICAN MEN OF SCIENCE.
[1st]- ed. ; 1906- Lancaster, Pa. , Science Press. v. 26cm. Imprint varies:1962- Tempe, Jacques Cattell Press, Annex 15, Arizona State University.

4577 ASIMOV, ISAAC, 1920-
Asimov's biographical encyclopedia of science and technology; the living stories of more than 1000 great scientists from the age of Greece to the space age, chronologically arranged. Garden City, N. Y. , Doubleday, 1964. x, 662p. ports. 25cm.

4578 BOL'SHAÏA SOVETSKAÏA ENTSIKLOPEDIÏA.
Biograficheskiï slovar' deïateleï estestvoznaniïa i tekhniki. Otvetstvennyï redaktor: A. A. Zvorykin. Redaktsionnaïa kollegiïa: N. N. Anichkov [i dr.] Moskva, 1958-59. 2 v. ports 27 cm. At head of title: Glavnaïa redaktsiïa Bol'shoï Sovetskoï entsiklopedii. Institut istorii estestvoznaniïa i tekhniki Akademii nauk SSSR. Biographical dictionary of scientists and technologists.

4579 BONOMI, LINO.
Naturalisti, medici e tecnici trentini (Museo di storia naturale della Venezia Tridentina) Trento, Stab. d'arti grafici A. Scotoni, 1930. iv, 221, [15] p. ports. 8.° Scientists, physicians and technologists of Trent, Italy.

4580 CANTÙ, IGNAZIO.
L'Italia scientifica contemporanea; notizie sugli Italiani

ascritti ai cinque primi congressi, attinte alle fonte più
autentiche ed esposte da Ignazio Cantù. Milano, Vedova di
A. F. Stella e Giacomo figlio, 1844. 320, 172 p. 22cm.
Italian scientists of the 1st half of the 19th century.

4581 ČESKÁ AKADEMIE VĚD A UMĚNÍ, Prague.
[Nekrolog] 1932-   V Praze. nos. ports. Necrology of
the Czech Academy of Sciences.

4582 COHEN, HARRY, 1885-   ed.
Jews in the world of science; a biographical dictionary of
Jews eminent in the natural and social sciences. Edited by
Harry Cohen and Itzhak J. Carmin. Contributing editors: J.
Robert Oppenheimer, Meyer W. Weisgal [and] Louis Gershen-
feld. New York, Monde Publishers [1956] xxiv,264 p.
ports. 29cm.

4583 DALĪL AL-AFRĀD AL-ʿILMIYĪN
Bin al-wizārāt wa al jāmi ʾāt wa al-hayʾāt al-hukūmīyah
bi al-jumhūrīyah al-misrīyah. [Cairo] al-Majlis al-Aʿlā lil
ʾUlūm, 1957. 363p. 25cm. Scientists and engineers in
Egyptian universities and government agencies.

4584 DIRECTORY OF BRITISH SCIENTISTS.
1963-   London, E. Benn. v. 24cm. American ed.
published by St. Martin's Press, New York. Birth dates
are not given.

4585 EGYPT. AL-MARKAZ AL-QAWMĪ LIL-BUHUTH.
Guide to scientific and technical workers in Egypt; classified
subject and name indexes and lists of institutions in Egypt.
Cairo, 1953. xx, 493 p. 25cm. Published by the Institute
under its earlier name: Fouad I National Research Council.

4586 FIGUIER, LOUIS, 1819-1894.
Vies des savants illustres depuis l'antiquité jusqu'au
dix-neuvième siècle. Avec l'appréciation sommaire de leurs
travaux. Paris, Hachette, 1876-81. 5 v. illus., ports. 24
cm. First issued 1866-68 in 3 vols. Lives of famous scholars (chiefly scientists) from antiquity to the 19th century.

4587 FONTENELLE, BERNARD LE BOVIER DE, 1657-1757.
Éloges des académiciens de l'Académie royale des
sciences, morts depuis l'an 1699. Nouv. éd. Paris, Libraires associés, 1766. 2 v. 12.º Academicians of the
Académie des sciences, Paris, who died in the years 1700-
1765.

4588   FRANCE. DÉLÉGATION GÉNÉRALE À LÀ RECHERCHE
SCIENTIFIQUE ET TECHNIQUE.
Répertoire des scientifiques francais. Paris, Office
national des universités et écoles francaises, 1962-   v.
24 cm. Contents. --t. l. Mathématiques pures.   A directory of French scientists.

4589   FUETER, EDUARD, 1908-   ed.
Grosse Schweizer Forscher. Hrsg. im Auftrag der
Fachgruppe Hochschulen und Wissenschaftliche Forschung der
Schweizerischen Landesausstellung 1939 und der Schwei-
zerischen Naturforschenden Gesellschaft unter Mitarbeit
hervorragender Fachleute durch Eduard Fueter. 2. erweiterte
Aufl. Zürich, Atlantis Verlag, 1941. 340 p. ports. 20 cm.
Added title pages in French and Italian: Pionniers suisses de
la science. Pionieri svizzeri della scienza. Text in German,
French, or Italian. Swiss pioneers in the sciences.

4590   GIUCCI, GAETANO
Degli scienzati italiani formanti parte del VII Congresso in
Napoli nell'autunno del 1845. Notizie biografiche raccolte da
G. G. Napoli, Tip. di A. Lebon, 1845.   576 p.   Biographi-
cal notices of Italian scientists participating in a scientific
congress, Naples, 1845.

4591   GRANDJEAN DE FOUCHY, JEAN PAUL
Éloges des académiciens de l'Académie royale des sciences, morts depuis 1744. t. l. Paris, Vve.Brunet, 1761.
1 v. 12.° Academicians of the Académie des sciences, Paris,
who died after 1744 (to 1761) No more published.

4592   HANDWÖRTERBUCH DER NATURWISSENSCHAFTEN.
2. Aufl. hrsg. von R. Dittler [et al.] Jena, G. Fischer,
1931-35. 10 v. illus. 27cm.

4593   -----Sachregister und systematische Inhaltsübersicht.
Jena, G. Fischer, 1935. 242, 16p. 27cm.

A dictionary of the sciences that includes biographies of
deceased scientists.

4594   HOWARD, ARTHUR VYVYAN.
Chambers's dictionary of scientists. New York, Dutton
[1951] vi p. , 500 columns. ports. 23cm. Also published in
London (W. and R. Chambers, 1951)

4595   INDIA (REPUBLIC) COUNCIL OF SCIENTIFIC AND
         INDUSTRIAL RESEARCH.
         National register of scientific and technical personnel in
         India. New Delhi [1950-   v. 28cm. Very brief
         biographical data.

4596   KLUYSKENS, HIPPOLYTE
         Des hommes célèbres dans les sciences et les arts, et
         des médailles qui consacrent leur souvenir. Gand, 1859.
         2 v. 8.° Celebrated scientists and men of the arts and the
         medals that are dedicated to their memory.

4597   KUZNETSOV, I   V   ed.
         Liūdi russkoĭ nauki; ocherki o vydaĭushchikhsĭa deĭateliākh
         estestvoznaniĭa i tekhniki.   Moskva, Gos. izd-vo fiziko-mate-
         maticheskoĭ lit-ry, 1961-65. 4 v. illus., ports. 27cm.   An
         earlier edition (?) in 2 vols. appeared in 1948.   Contents. --
         [1] Matematika, mekhanika, astronomiĭa, fizika, khimiĭa. --[2]
         Geologiĭa, geografiĭa. --[3] Biologiĭa, medeĭsina, sel´ sko-
         khoziāĭstvennye nauki. --[4] Tekhnika.   Biographies of Russian
         scientists, past and present.

4598   LEADERS IN AMERICAN SCIENCE.
             v. 1- 1953/54-   Nashville, Who's Who in American
         Education, inc. v. ports. 24cm. biennial.

4599   LEXIKON DER GESCHICHTE DER NATURWISSENSCHAFTEN;
             Biographien, Sachwörter und Bibliographien. Mit einer
         Einführung "Die Zeitalter der Naturforschung" und einer
         Übersichtstabelle von Josef Mayerhöfer unter Mitwirkung von
         E. Bannerth [et al.] Geleitwort von Josef Stummvoll. Wien,
         Brüder Hollinek [1959-   v. 22cm. Issued in fascicles.
         Dictionary of the history of the sciences; biographies, subjects
         and bibliographies.

4600   MAIRAN, JEAN JACQUES DORTOUS DE, 1678-1771.
             Eloges des académiciens de l'Académie royale des
         sciences, morts dans les années 1741, 1742 et 1743. Paris,
         Durand, 1747. x, 360p. illus. 12.° Praises of academicians
         of the Academy of Sciences, Paris, who died in the years
         1741, 1742 & 1743.

4601   MANGIN, ARTHUR, 1824-1887.
             Les savants illustres de la France. Nouv. éd., entièrement
         refondue et augm. de plusieurs biographies nouvelles, avec un
         appendice, comprenant l'histoire abrégée de la science et des

savants pendant les trois derniers siècles. Ornée de seize
portraits authentiques, dessinés par M. Bocourt. Paris, P.
Durocq [1865] 524 p. ports. 25cm. Distinguished scholars
(scientists) of France.

4602   MEN OF SCIENCES & TECHNOLOGY IN INDIA.
        1964-   New Delhi, Premier Publishers.   v. ports.
        25cm.

4603   MIELI, ALDO, 1879-1950.
        La science arabe et son rôle dans l'évolution scientifique
        mondiale. Avec quelques additions de Henri-Paul-Joseph
        Renaud, Max Meyerhof [et] Julius Ruska. Leiden, E. J.
        Brill, 1938. xix, 388p. 25cm. Bio-bibliographical, in
        part; Arabian science & scientists.

4604   MIELI, ALDO, 1879-1950.
        Gli scienzati italiani dall'inizio del medio evo al nostri
        giorni. Repertorio biobibliografico: dei filosofi, matematici,
        astronomi, fisici, chimici, naturalisti, biologi, medici,
        geografi italiani   Roma, Nardecchia, 1921-23. 2 v. illus.
        27cm. No more published. Italian scientists from the Mid-
        dle Ages to our day.

4605   NATIONAL ASSOCIATION OF SCIENCE WRITERS.
        Membership list. Port Washington, N. Y.   v. 29cm.

4606   NAUKA I NAUCHNYE RABOTNIKI SSSR;
        Spravochnik. 1925(?)-   Leningrad.   v. 22cm.
        Science and scientists in Soviet Russia. Issued by Komissiĩa
        "Nauchnye uchrezhdeniĩa i nauchnye rabotniki SSSR" of the
        Akademiĩa nauk SSSR (Called in 1926 Komissiĩa "Nauka i
        nauchnye rabotniki SSSR")

4607   NEW ZEALAND ASSOCIATION OF SCIENTISTS.
        Directory of New Zealand science. Edited by Lyndon Bas-
        tings. 3d ed. Wellington, H. H. Tombs, 1954. x, 232 p.
        21cm. Very brief biographical sketches. First ed. published
        in 1948 under title: Directory of New Zealand scientists.

4608   PICATOSTE Y RODRÍGUEZ, FELIPE, 1834-1892.
        Apuntes para una biblioteca científica española del siglo
        XVI. Estudios biográficos y bibliográficos de ciencias ex-
        actas, físicas y naturales y sus inmediatas aplicaciones en
        dicho siglo. Madrid, Impr. de M. Tello, 1891. viii, 416p.
        28cm. In double columns. Annotations for a Spanish science

library of the 16th century; biographical & bibliographical
studies of the exact sciences... Bio-bibliography for Spanish
& Portuguese science of the period.

4609   POGGENDORFF, JOHANN CHRISTIAN, 1796-1877.
Biographisch-literarisches Handwörterbuch für Mathematik, Astronomie, Physik, mit Geophysik, Chemie, Kristal-
lographie und verwandte Wissensgebiete. Leipzig, J. A.
Barth, 1863-1904; Leipzig/Berlin, Verlag Chemie, 1926-
v. in   25-26cm. Title varies: 1.-2. Bd. Biographisch-
literarisches Handwörterbuch zur Geschichte der exakten
Wissenschaften... [etc.] A famous bio-bibliography for the
sciences.

4610   ROYAL SOCIETY OF LONDON.
Biographical memoirs of Fellows. v. 1-   ; 1955-
London.   v. 26cm. Supersedes the Society's Obituary
notices of Fellows.

4611   ROYAL SOCIETY OF LONDON.
Obituary notices of Fellows. v. 1-9 (no. 1-[23]);
Dec. 1932-Nov. 1954. London. 9 v. in 10. ports. 25cm.
annual (irregular) Superseded by the Society's Biographical
memoirs of Fellows.

4612   SPAIN. CONSEJO SUPERIOR DE INVESTIGACIONES CIEN-
TÍFICAS.
Colaboradores e investigadores. Madrid, 1956. 442 p.
25cm. (Its Publicaciones generales, 3) Ca. 150 research
scientists of the Spanish Upper Council of Scientific Research
with lists of their publications.

4613   SUCHIER, WOLFRAM
Die Mitglieder der Deutschen Gesellschaft zu Göttingen
von 1738 bis Anfang 1755. Hildesheim, 1916. 87p. 8.º The
members of the German Society at Göttingen (later the Academy of Sciences, Göttingen) from 1738 to the beginning of
1755.

4614   TURKEVICH, JOHN, 1907-
Soviet men of science; academicians and corresponding
members of the Academy of Sciences of the USSR. With editorial assistance of J. Blanshei [and others] Princeton, N. J.,
Van Nostrand [1963] 441 p. 23cm.

4615   UNITED NATIONS EDUCATIONAL, SCIENTIFIC AND CUL-
TURAL ORGANIZATION. MIDDLE EAST SCIENCE CO-
OPERATION OFFICE.
Liste des hommes de science de l'Irak. List of scien-
tists in Iraq. May 1954- Le Caire.   v. 28cm.
Contains brief biographical information.

4616   UNITED NATIONS EDUCATIONAL, SCIENTIFIC AND CUL-
TURAL ORGANIZATION. MIDDLE EAST SCIENCE CO-
OPERATION OFFICE.
Liste des hommes de science de l'Iran. List of scien-
tists in Iran. Jan. 1955- Le Caire.   v. 28cm. Con-
tains brief biographical information.

4617   UNITED NATIONS EDUCATIONAL, SCIENTIFIC AND CUL-
TURAL ORGANIZATION. MIDDLE EAST SCIENCE CO-
OPERATION OFFICE.
Liste des hommes de science du Liban. List of scientists
in Lebanon. Sept. 1952- Le Caire.   v. 28cm. Con-
tains brief biographical information.

4618   UNITED NATIONS EDUCATIONAL, SCIENTIFIC AND CUL-
TURAL ORGANIZATION. SCIENCE COOPERATION OF-
FICE FOR LATIN AMERICA.
Scientific institutions and scientists in Latin America.
[v. p.] 1949- v. 35cm. Published are volumes for Ar-
gentina, Bolivia, Brazil, Chile, Colombia, Cuba, Ecuador,
Mexico, Paraguay, Peru, Puerto Rico (combined with Colom-
bia in 1 v.), Uruguay, Venezuela.

4619   UNITED NATIONS EDUCATIONAL, SCIENTIFIC AND CUL-
TURAL ORGANIZATION. SOUTH ASIA SCIENCE CO-
OPERATION OFFICE.
Scientific institutions and scientists in Pakistan. New
Delhi, 1958. ix, 501p. 28cm. Several hundred brief biog-
raphies included.

4620   VISHER, STEPHEN SARGENT, 1887-
Indiana scientists; a biographical directory and an analysis. With brief sections by F. J. Allen [and others] Indianapolis, Indiana Academy of Science [c1951] viii, 286p.
24cm.

4621   "WER IST WO" IN DER WISSENSCHAFT?
[Berlin, n. d. (19--)] 1 v. (unpaged) Who's who in [Ger-
man] science? At head of title: Notgemeinschaft der Deutschen Wissenschaft (Deutsche Forschungsgemeinschaft) Berlin-
Dahlem.

4622   WHO'S WHO IN BRITISH SCIENCE.
        1953-   London, L. Hill. v. 23cm.

4623   WHO'S WHO IN INDIAN SCIENCE.
        1st-   ed. ; 1964-   Calcutta, Kothari Publications.
        v. 19cm. Editor: 1964-   H. Kothari.

4624   WHO'S WHO IN SCIENCE & RESEARCH.
        Karachi, Bibliographical Information Bureau and Refer-
        ence Centre.   v. 25cm. Compiler: M. I. Khurshid.

4625   WHO'S WHO IN SCIENCE (INTERNATIONAL)
        1912-1914. Edited by H. H. Stephenson. London. J. & A.
        Churchill [1912-14] 3 v. 23cm. American ed. issued by
        Macmillan, New York.

4626   WHO'S WHO IN SOVIET SCIENCE AND TECHNOLOGY.
        Compiled by Ina Telberg. [2d ed. , rev. and enl. by An-
        tonia Dmitriev and V. G. Telberg] New York, Telberg Book
        Co. [1964] vi, 301 l. 28cm. Cover title. Based on Biogra-
        ficheskii slovar′ deiatelei estestvoznaniia i tekhniki, com-
        piled by an editorial board headed by A. A. Zvorykin.

Biology and Geology

4627   AKADEMIIA NAUK SSSR. ZOOLOGICHESKII INSTITUT.
        Handbook of Soviet zoologists. Washington, U. S. Joint
        Publications Research Service, 1962. 443p. "JPRS: 13188.
        CSO: 6810-N. OTS. " Translation of Zoologii Sovetskogo
        Soiuza (q. v.)

4628   AKADEMIIA NAUK SSSR. ZOOLOGICHESKII INSTITUT.
        Zoologi Sovetskogo Soiuza; spravochnik. [Glav. redaktor
        E. N. Pavlovskii] Leningrad, Izd-vo Akademii nauk SSSR
        [Leningr. otd.] 1961. 292p. 21cm. An English translation
        is available under title: Handbook of Soviet zoologists (q. v.)

4629   THE AUK.
        Biographies of members of the American Ornithologists'
        Union, by T. S. Palmer and others. Reprinted from "The
        Auk, " 1884-1954. Washington, 1954. 630p. 24cm.

4630   BOGDANOV, ANATOLII PETROVICH, 1839-1896.
        Materialy dlia istorii nauchnoi i prikladnoi deiatel'nosti v
        Rossii po zoologii i soprikasaiushchimsia s neiu otrasliam

znaniiā, preimushchestvenno za poslednee tridt̂satipīātiletie
(1850-1888) Moskva, 1888-92. 4 v. ports. (Izvestiiā Imp.
O-va līubiteleĭ estestvoznaniiā, antropologii i ėtnografii,
sostoiāshchego pri Imp. Mosk. universitete, t. 55, 57, 70-71)
Trudy Zoologich. otd-niiā Obshchestva, t. 3-4, 6-7. Ca.
400 biographies of Russian zoologists.

4631   BRITTEN, JAMES, 1846-1924, comp.
A biographical index of deceased British and Irish botanists,
compiled by James Britten and George S. Boulger. 2d ed.,
rev. and completed by A. B. Rendle. London, Taylor and
Francis, 1931. xxii, 342 p. 22 cm.

4632   CHRISTENSEN, CARL FREDERIK ALBERT, 1872-
Den danske botaniske litteratur. Bibliographia botanica
Danica, 1912-1939. Med portraetter af 78 danske botanikere...
Kø̸benhavn, E. Munksgaard, 1940. 350 p. ports. 23cm.
Brief biographical sketches are followed by lists of works of
Danish botanists.

4633   COLMEIRO Y PENIDO, MIGUEL, 1816-1901.
La botánica y los botánicos de la peninsula hispano-lusitana.
Estudios bibliográficos y biográficos por Miguel Colmeiro.
Madrid, M. Rivadeneyra, 1858. x, 216 p. 28cm. Spanish &
Portuguese botanists.

4634   DOBSON, JESSIE
Anatomical eponyms: being a biographical dictionary of
those anatomists whose names have become incorporated into
anatomical nomenclature, with definitions of the structures to
which their names have been attached, and references to the
works in which they are described. London, Baillière,
Tindall & Cox, 1946. ix, 240 p. 23cm.

4635   EYCLESHYMER, ALBERT CHAUNCEY, 1867-1925.
Anatomical names, especially the Basle nomina anatomica
("BNA") by Albert Chauncey Eycleshymer assisted by Daniel
Martin Schoemaker. With biographical sketches by Roy Lee
Moodie. New York, W. Wood, 1917. xx, 744 p. illus. 24 cm.
"Biographical sketches, by Roy L. Moodie" (p. 177-354)
contains sketches of some 800 anatomists.

4636   HANSEN, ALFRED, 1925-
Den danske botaniske litteratur; bibliographia botanica
Danica 1940-1959 med tilhø̸rende forfatter-biografier.

København, Munksgaard, 1963. 318p. ports. 24cm.
(Dansk botanisk arkiv, bd. 21, nr. 1) Bio-bibliography of
Danish botanists.

4637   HIATT, ROBERT W   ed.
    Directory of hydrobiological laboratories and personnel in
North America. Edited by Robert W. Hiatt with the cooperation of Arthur D. Hasler [and others] Honolulu, University
of Hawaii Press, 1954. ix, 324p. illus., maps. 22cm.
Includes biographical sketches of over 1, 000 persons. "Prepared under the auspices of the Advisory Committee on
Hydrobiology to the Office of Naval Research [of the] American Institute of Biological Sciences. "

4638   HIRSCH, GOTTWALT CHRISTIAN, 1888-
    Index biologorum; investigatores, laboratoria, periodica.
Editio 1. Berlin, J. Springer, 1928. vi, 545p. 21cm.
Index of biologists.

4639   HORN, WALTHER, 1871-
    Index litteraturae entomologicae. Ser. I: Die Welt-
Literatur über die gesamte Entomologie bis inklusive 1863,
von Walther Horn und Sigm. Schenkling. Berlin-Dahlem,
1928-29. 4v. in 1. fronts. (ports.) 24cm. Bio-
bibliography of entomology.

4640   HSU, YIN-CH'I
    Directory of Chinese biologists. Soochow, Biological
Supply Service, Soochow University, 1934. 162 p. 17cm.
Title also in Chinese. Text in English and Chinese.

4641   INTERNATIONAL MINERALOGICAL ASSOCIATION.
    World directory of mineralogists. Compiled by M. Font-
Altaba with the help of the representatives of the national
mineralogical societies. Barcelona, Published for the
International Mineralogical Association by Editorial Eco,
1962. x, 144p. 22cm.

4642   INTERNATIONAL UNION OF BIOLOGICAL SCIENCES.
    Index des généticiens. Paris, Secrétariat général de
l'U. I. S. B. , 1953. vii, 113p. 22cm. (It's Série C:
[Publications diverses] no. 4) Index of geneticists of
today's world.

4643   INTERNATIONAL UNION OF BIOLOGICAL SCIENCES.
    Index des zoologistes. Paris, Secrétariat général de

l'U. I. S. B. , 1953. viii, 429p. 22cm. (Its Série C:
[Publications diverses] no. 5) Birth date, "present" position
(address) & sometimes a brief bibliography are included in
this index of zoologists of today's world.

4644   LEHMANN, ERNST, 1880-   ed.
Deutsches Biologen-Handbuch. Eine Übersicht über die
deutschen Biologen, die biologischen Institute und Organisationen, von Ernst Lehmann in Gemeinschaft mit Otto Martin.
2. Aufl. München, J. F. Lehmann, 1938. viii, 261p. 21cm.
Handbook of German biology and biologists.

4645   LIPSCHITZ, SERGEĬ ĨŪL' EVICH, 1905-
Russkie botaniki; biografo-bibliograficheskiĭ slovar'.
Otvetstvennyĭ redaktor V. N. Sukachev.   Moskva, Izd-vo
Moskovskogo ob-va ispytateleĭ prirody, 1947-   v. 25cm.
Russian botanists; a bio-bibliographical dictionary.

4646   NEW YORK. BOTANICAL GARDEN. LIBRARY.
Biographical notes upon botanists, maintained in the New
York Botanical Garden Library. Compiled by John Hendley
Barnhart.   Boston, G. K. Hall, 1966.   3 v. 40cm.(?)   A
biographical file on cards. "With each name are included data
on education and professional activities and references to
sources of information. "

4647   OSBORN, HERBERT, 1856-
A brief history of entomology, including time of Demosthene
and Aristotle to modern times, with over 500 portraits.   Co-
lumbus, Ohio, Spahr and Glenn, 1952.   303 p. illus. 24cm.
The historical section is followed by an alphabetical list of
entomologists which yields brief biographical data for each
scientist.

4648   PRAEGER, ROBERT LLOYD, 1865-
Some Irish naturalists: a biographical notebook. Dundalk,
W. Tempest, 1941. 208p. ports. 22cm. Includes brief
notes on over 300 professional and amateur geologists, zoologists and botanists living in the period 12th - 20th century.

4649   PRITZEL, GEORG AUGUST, 1815-1874.
Thesaurus literaturae botanicae omnium gentium, inde a
rerum botanicarum initiis ad nostra usque tempora, quin-
decim milia operum recensens. Ed. novam reformatam
curavit G. A. Pritzel. Milano, Gorlich [1950] 576p. 32cm.
Bio-bibliography of botanists (gives birth & death dates, position or university chair occupied) Reprint of the edition of
1872-1877.

4650   VSESOĬUZNOE BOTANICHESKOE OBSHCHESTVO.
Adresnaĭa kniga botanikov SSSR. Po porucheniĭu Gos.
russkogo botanicheskogo ob-va sostavlena A. E. Zhadovskim.
Leningrad, 1929. 177p. 18cm. Title also in Latin. Address
book of botanists of Soviet Russia. Gives place and date of
birth, specialty, etc.

Chemistry

4651   ADDRESSBUCH DEUTSCHER CHEMIKER.
1950/51- Weinheim, Verlag Chemie. v. 23cm.
Address book of German chemists. Very brief biographical
sketches. Vols. for 1950/51- "gemeinsam herausgegeben
von: Gesellschaft Deutscher Chemiker und Verlag Chemie. "

4652   AMERICAN CHEMICAL SOCIETY. COMMITTEE ON
PROFESSIONAL TRAINING.
Directory of graduate research. 1953-   [Washington]
v. 28cm. Title varies: 1953, Faculties, publications, and
doctoral theses in chemistry and chemical engineering at
United States universities.

4653   ASSOCIATION OF CONSULTING CHEMISTS AND CHEMICAL
ENGINEERS.
Consulting services. New York. v. 28-31cm. annual
(irregular) Title varies: -1941, Directory of association
members. --1942/43-1947, Classified directory. Contains
facts about an individual's position, education, specialty,
professional experience, memberships and publications.

4654   BLOCH, MAKS ABRAMOVICH, 1882-
Biograficheskiĭ spravochnik; vydaĭushchesia khimiki i
uchenye XIX i XX stoletiĭ, rabotavshie v smezhnykh s khimieĭu
oblastiakh nauki. Leningrad, Nauchnoe khimiko-tekhnicheskoe
izd-vo, Nauchno-tekhnicheskoe upravlenie VSNKh, 1929-31.
2 v. ports. 23cm. At head of title: M. A. Blokh. No more
published? Biographical reference book on important chemists
of the 19th and 20th centuries.

4655   CHEMICAL AGE DIRECTORY AND WHO'S WHO.
1923-   London, Benn Bros. v. illus. , ports.
23-32cm. annual. Title varies: 1923-58, The Chemical
age year book (varies slightly) Includes a biographical section (e. g. , 1962 ed. : "Who's who": p. 53-133)

4656   CHEMICAL WHO'S WHO.
[1st]-   1928-   New York [etc.]   Lewis Historical
Pub. Co. [etc.]   v. 25cm. irregular. Title varies: 1928,
Who's who in the chemical and drug industries.

4657   CLARK, GEORGE LINDENBERG, 1892-   ed.
The encyclopedia of chemistry. Editor-in-chief: George L.
Clark. Managing editor: Gessner G. Hawley. Advisory editor: William A. Hamor. New York, Reinhold Pub. Corp.
[1957] xvi,1037 p. illus. 26cm. Includes biographies of
noted chemists.

4658   FARBER, EDUARD, 1892-   ed.
Great chemists. New York, Interscience Publishers, 1961.
1642 p. illus. 25 cm.

4659   GESELLSCHAFT FÜR GESCHICHTE DER PHARMAZIE, Berlin.
Chemisch-pharmazeutisches Bio- und Bibliographikon.
Hrsg. durch Fritz Ferchl. Mittenwald (Bayern) A. Nemayer,
1937. 2v. 26cm. Bio-bibliography of chemistry and pharmacy

4660   GLASGOW. ROYAL TECHNICAL COLLEGE. LIBRARY.
YOUNG COLLECTION.
Bibliotheca chemica; a bibliography of books on alchemy,
chemistry, and pharmaceutics [by] John Ferguson. London,
Derek Verschoyle, 1954-   v. 25cm. (Derek
Verschoyle, Academic and Bibliographical Publications, ltd.
First series, no. 2) Facsimile of the original edition, pub-
lished in 1906 by J. Maclehose, Glasgow. More than a cata-
log. Contains brief biographical accounts of the authors.

4661   INSTITUTE OF CHEMISTRY OF GREAT BRITAIN AND
IRELAND.
A list of official chemical appointments, compiled by
direction of the Council of the Institute of Chemistry and under
the supervision of the Publications Committee. 8th ed. , rev.
and enl. London, 1934. 389p. 22cm.

4662   PROVENZAL, GIULIO, 1872-
Profili bio-bibliografici di chimici italiani sec. XV- sec.
XIX. Roma, Istituto nazionale medico farmacologico
"Serono" [1937] xxiv, 30lp. ports. 25cm. Bio-bibliogra-
phical profiles of Italian chemists, 14-19th centuries.

4663   RÖMPP, HERMANN, 1901-
Chemie Lexikon. 4. völlig neu bearb. Aufl. Stuttgart,
Franckh [1958] 2 v. (5103p.) illus. 26cm. A dictionary of
chemistry that includes 700 biographical sketches of famous
chemists.

4664   SCHAEDLER, KARL, 1843-
Biographisch-litterarisches Handwörterbuch der wissenschaftlich bedeutenden Chemiker. Berlin, R. Friedlaender,
1891. vi, 162 p. 18cm. Half title: Handwörterbuch wissenschaftlich bedeutender Chemiker. Biographical-bibliographical dictionary of important chemists.

4665   SMITH, HENRY MONMOUTH, 1868-
Torchbearers of chemistry; portraits and brief biographies
of scientists who have contributed to the making of modern
chemistry. New York, Academic Press, 1949. 270 p.
illus., ports. 26cm. 223 chemists.

Mathematics

4666   BIERENS DE HAAN, DAVID, 1822-1895.
Bibliographie néerlandaise historique-scientifique des ouvrages importants dont les auteurs sont nés aux 16e , 17e, et
18e siècles, sur les sciences mathématiques et physiques,
avec leurs applications. Rome, Impr. des sciences mathématiques et physiques, 1883. 424p. 30cm. An author alphabet,
with bio-bibliographical notes on Dutch mathematicians and
scientists.

4667   DOPPELMAYR, JOHANN GABRIEL, 1671-1750.
Historische Nachricht von den Nürnbergischen Mathematicis und Künstlern, welche fast von dreyen Seculis her, durch
ihre Schrifften und Kunst-Bemühungen die Mathematic und
mehreste Künste in Nürnberg...befördert...an das Liecht
gestellet, auch mit vielen nützlichen Anmerckungen und ver-
schiedenen Kupffern versehen. Nürnberg, P.C. Monath,
1730. 14,314,[18] p. 15 fold. plates. 38cm. German mathematicians and artists in Nuremberg.

4668   [HOLLENBERG, GEORG HEINRICH] d. 1831.
Nachrichten von dem Leben und den Erfindungen der
berühmtesten Mathematiker, in alphabetischer Ordnung.
Th. 1. Münster, Coppenrath, 1788. 1 v. 8.º No more published? Notes on the life and discoveries of the most famous
mathematicians, alphabetically arranged.

4669   SMITH, DAVID EUGENE, 1860-
        Portraits of eminent mathematicians; with brief biographi-
        cal sketches. New York, Scripta Mathematica, 1936. 2 v.
        illus., ports. 36cm.

4670   TAYLOR, EVA GERMAINE RIMINGTON, 1879-
        The mathematical practitioners of Tudor & Stuart Eng-
        land. Cambridge [Eng., Published] for the Institute of Navi-
        gation at the University Press, 1954. xi, 442p. illus. 23cm.
        Includes short biographical notices of 582 mathematical prac-
        titioners.

Physics

4671   MACPHERSON, HECTOR COPLAND, 1888-
        Biographical dictionary of astronomers.   Edinburgh, 1940.
        82 l. 27cm. Reproduced from type-written copy.

4672   NIPPON BUTSURIGAKKAI.
        Meibo. Tokyo, 1959. 198p. This new membership list of
        the Physical Society of Japan includes very brief biographical
        sketches.

4673   U. S. NATIONAL AERONAUTICS AND SPACE ADMINISTRA-
        TION.
        Space scientists and engineers: selected biographical and
        bibliographical listing, 1957-1961. Washington, For sale by
        the Superintendent of Documents, U. S. Govt. Print. Off.,
        1962. iii, 332p. 26cm. (Its NASA SP-5) 1,107 references.

4674   WHO'S WHO IN ATOMS.
        1959-   London, Vallancey Press. v. 26cm.

4675   WHO'S WHO IN SOVIET NUCLEAR SCIENCE.
        Compiled by Lawrence Ruby and Joan Hurst. Berkeley,
        University of California, Lawrence Radiation Laboratory,
        1960. 120p. 28cm. (UCRL-9173)

4676   WORLD DIRECTORY OF CRYSTALLOGRAPHERS AND OF
        OTHER SCIENTISTS EMPLOYING CRYSTALLOGRAPHIC
        METHODS. [1st]-   ed. ; 1957-   Utrecht, Published
        for the International Union of Crystallography by N. V. A.
        Oosthoek's Uitgeversmaatschappij.   v. 23cm. Vol. for
        1957 published in Irvington-on-Hudson, N. Y., by Philips La-
        boratories as its Contribution no. 115. Title varies slightly.
        Gives academic background and specialties.

SOCIAL SCIENCES
General Works

4677   AMERICAN STATISTICAL ASSOCIATION.
Membership directory. 19   [n. p.]   v. 24cm.
Some issues (e. g. , 1958) give data on a member's positions,
education and special fields of interest.

4678   AMYOT, JACQUES, 1920-   ed.
Directory of the social sciences in Thailand, 1963.
Editors: Jacques Amyot and Robert W. Kickert. Bangkok,
Faculty of Political Science, Chulalongkorn University [1963 ?]
100 1. 28cm. Bio-bibliographical; includes Western scholars
of Thai studies.

4679   DIRECTORY OF STATISTICAL PERSONNEL IN THE AMERI-
CAN NATIONS.
Directorio del personal estadístico en las naciones americanas. Nominata do pessoal estatístico das nacões americanas.
2d- ed. , 1944-   Washington, Inter American Statistical
Institute.   v. 23cm. 1st ed. issued in the Statistical activities of the American nations, 1940 (p. [677]-737) under
title: Biographical directory of statistical personnel.

4680   DIRECTORY OF STATISTICIANS AND OTHERS IN ALLIED
PROFESSIONS.
1961-   Washington, American Statistical Association.
v. 28cm. Includes brief biographies.

4681   ENCICLOPEDIA DI SCIENZE POLITICHE, ECONOMICHE
E SOCIALI. [Capo della redazione: Rodolfo Sommaruga]
Bologna, C. Zuffi, 1956-   v. 29cm. Includes many biog-
raphies of social scientists.

4682   ENCYCLOPAEDIA OF THE SOCIAL SCIENCES.
Editor-in-chief: E. R. A. Seligman. Associate editor: Alvin
Johnson. New York, Macmillan, 1930-35. 15 v. 28cm. Ca.
50 percent of the articles are biographical.

4683   FILLER, LOUIS, 1911-
A dictionary of American social reform. New York,
Philosophical Library [1963] 854 p. 22 cm. Includes
biographies of social scientists, social reformers, statesmen,
etc. connected in some way with social policy in the United
States.

4684   FOREIGN AREA FELLOWSHIP PROGRAM.
Directory [of] foreign area fellows, 1952-1963, of the Joint
Committee of the American Council of Learned Societies and
the Social Science Research Council, 1962-1963; formerly
administered by the Ford Foundation, 1952-1962. [2d ed.]
New York [1964] vi, 301 p. 26 cm. 1st ed. issued in 1959 by
the Ford Foundation.

4685   HANDWÖRTERBUCH DER SOZIALWISSENSCHAFTEN.
Hrsg. von E. V. Beckerath [et al.] Stuttgart, G. Fischer
[1952-   v. illus. 28cm. A dictionary of the social
sciences that includes biographies. "Neuauflage des "Handwörterbuch der Staatswissenschaften." "

4686   INTER-AMERICAN STATISTICAL INSTITUTE.
Directory of constituent members of IASI. Washington,
1962. iv, 57p. 27cm. In English, French, Portuguese, or
Spanish.

4687   INTERNATIONAL DIRECTORY OF OPINION AND ATTITUDE
RESEARCH.
1st-   ed. Mexico, 1948-   v. 23cm. Predominantly
American in emphasis. Includes biographical information.

4688   INTERNATIONALES SOZIOLOGEN LEXIKON.
Unter Mitarbeit zahlreicher Fachleute des In- und Auslandes hrsg. von Wilhelm Bernsdorf in Verbindung mit Horst
Knospe. Stuttgart, F. Enke, 1959. viii, 662p. 22cm. More
than 1000 entries for sociologists of the present.

4689   PR BLUE BOOK AND SUPPLEMENT TO THE INTERNATIONA.
WHO'S WHO IN PUBLIC RELATIONS. 1st-   ed; 1960-
Meriden, N. H. , PR Pub. Co.   v. 24cm.

4690   RUSSKIE LIŪDI;
Zhizneopisaniiá sootechestvennikov, proslavshikhsiá
svoimi dieiánniiami na poprishche nauki dobra i obshchest-
vennoĭ pol´zy... Sanktpeterburg, Izd. knigoprodavtśa i tip.
M. O. Vol´fa, 1866. 2 v. ports. 24cm. No more published?
Russians; biographies of compatriots famed for their work in
the field of social studies and welfare.

4691   SOCIAL SCIENCE RESEARCH COUNCIL.
Fellows of the Social Science Research Council, 1925-1951.
New York, 1951. x, 473 p. 24cm. 1,028 persons.

4692   UNITED NATIONS EDUCATIONAL, SCIENTIFIC AND CUL-
        TURAL ORGANIZATION. SECRETARIAT.
        Social scientists specializing in African studies; directory.
        Africanistes spécialistes de sciences sociales; repertoire.
        Paris [École pratique des hautes études] 1963. 375p. 24cm.
        [Monde d'outre-mer passé et présent. 4 sér. 5. Bibliogra-
        phies et instruments de travail]

4693   WHO'S WHO IN SOVIET SOCIAL SCIENCES, HUMANITIES,
        ART AND GOVERNMENT. Compiled by Ina Telberg.
        [New York, Telberg Book Co. , 1961] v, 147 l. 28cm. "Based
        on the information in the 3rd edition of 'Malaia Sovetskaia
        entsiklopedia' Moscow, 1958-1961. "

Economics and Commerce

4694   ACCOUNTANTS' DIRECTORY AND WHO'S WHO.
        1920-   New York, Forty-First Street Press. v. 20cm.

4695   AMERICAN ECONOMIC ASSOCIATION.
        Handbook. 1938-   [Menasha, Wis. , etc.] v. 23cm.
        Issued irregularly as a supplement to, or number of, the
        American economic review. Title varies: 1938-48, Directory.
        Includes biographical sketches of the majority of the members
        of the Association.

4696   AMERICAN MARKETING ASSOCIATION.
        National roster. Membership directory. 1942-   ...
        [Bloomington, Ind. , etc.] v. 25cm. Includes some
        information about members (employer, job title, educational
        background, teaching experience, activities)

4697   THE BANKERS' WHO'S WHO.
        1st-   ed. New Delhi, Indian Business Publications
        [1964?-   v. ports. 23cm. "The standard biographical
        reference on the world's bankers. "

4698   BOGARDUS, EMORY STEPHEN, 1882-
        Dictionary of cooperation, including encyclopedic materials.
        [3d ed.] Chicago, Cooperative League of the U. S. A. , 1948.
        94 p. 22cm. Brief biographies of living and dead leaders in
        the cooperative movement.

4699   BRAEUER, WALTER.
        Handbuch zur Geschichte der Volkswirtschaftslehre; ein
        bibliographisches Nachschlagewerk. Frankfurt am Main, V.

Klostermann, 1952. 224 p. 25cm. A biobibliography; sketches of important economists.

4700　THE BUILDING SOCIETIES WHO'S WHO; a biographical directory of the home-owning and savings movement throughout the world. London, Franey. v. 22 cm. annual. Issued in Building societies year book, 1925- "Includes brief entries for those no longer living. "

4701　BUSINESS EXECUTIVES OF AMERICA.
[1st]-　ed. ; 1944-　New York, Institute for Research in Biography. v. ports. 19-28cm. Title varies: 1944, Business executives and corporation encyclopedia.

4702　CYCLOPEDIA OF INSURANCE IN THE UNITED STATES.
1st-　ed. 1890-　New York [etc.] Index Pub. Co. v. 19cm. Includes a fairly extensive biographical section at the end of each annual volume. The latest issue has an index to biographical sketches which have appeared in all the earlier issues.

4703　HORTON, BYRNE JOSEPH, 1897-
Dictionary of modern economics, by Byrne Joseph Horton, with Julien Ripley, Jr. and M. B. Schnapper. Washington, Public Affairs Press [1948] ix, 365 p. 24cm. Includes 120 biographies of outstanding economists.

4704　HUNT, FREEMAN, 1804-1858, ed.
Lives of American merchants. New York, Derby and Jackson. . . 1858. 2v. ports. 23cm. Articles written by George R. Russell, and others.

4705　INSURANCE ALMANAC.
Who, what, where and when in insurance; an annual of insurance facts. [1st]-　; 1913-　New York, Underwriter Print. and Pub. Co. v. 22cm. In 1948 a new publication, Who's who in insurance (q. v.) took over the who's who aspect of the almanac. Title varies: 1917-20, The insurance almanac and encyclopedia--1930-32, The insurance almanac and who's who in insurance. Compiled by The Weekly underwriter.

4706　INSURANCE WHO'S WHO.
A biographical dictionary of the principal officials of

British insurance companies and of professional insurance
brokers and claims assessors. 1st-   1924-
London, Insurance news.   v.

4707   INTERNATIONAL WHO'S WHO AMONG HOTEL MEN.
A biographical reference work of the hotel industry. 1924/
1925 - New York, Ahrens Pub. Co. v. ports. 32cm.

4708   MANES, ALFRED, 1877-   ed.
Versicherungslexikon; ein Nachslagewerk für alle Wissensgebiete der gesamten Individual- und Sozial-Versicherung,
unter Mitarbeit von Dr. Apelbaum, Dr. Aurin, Verwaltungsdir.
Beinzger [et al.] Hrsg. von Alfred Manes. 3., wesentlich
erweiterte und umgearb. Aufl. Berlin, Mittler, 1930. 1934 p.
27cm. Includes biographies of deceased persons who were
active in the field of insurance (and social insurance) in Germany.

4709   THE MARKET RESEARCH DIRECTORY.
1st-   ed.; 19 -   Lausanne, J. Anns.   v.
ports. 22cm. Title varies: 1960/61, Who's who in market
research.

4710   MEN OF NOTE IN FINANCE AND COMMERCE, WITH WHICH
IS INCORPORATED MEN OF OFFICE.
A biographical business directory. Edited by Herbert H.
Bassett. 1900-1901. London, E. Wilson [1900] 390p. 20cm.

4711   POOR'S REGISTER OF DIRECTORS AND EXECUTIVES,
United States and Canada. 1928-   New York, Standard
and Poor's Corp.   v. 29-34cm. annual. Title varies.

4712   ---- ----Geographical section. 1935-   New York, Standard & Poor's Corp.   v. 29-31cm. annual.

4713   ---- ----Supplement[s] Mar. 1935-   New York, Standard
& Poor's Corp.

4714   RAND McNALLY INTERNATIONAL BANKERS DIRECTORY.
The bankers blue book. International directory of banks
and bankers. July 1876-   Chicago, Rand McNally.
v. maps. 24-30cm. semiannual. Title varies: 1876-81,
The Bankers' directory of the United States and Canada.
1899-1954, Rand McNally bankers' directory [and list of attorneys, etc.]

4715   SVENSK FÖRSÄKRINGSMATRIKEL.
        1930-   [Stockholm, Svenska försäkringsföreningen]
        v. ports. 25cm. decennial. "Biografisk porträttma-
        trikel over medlemmar i Svenska försäkringsföreningen och
        försäkringssällskapen i Göteborg, Malmö, Östergotland och
        Jönköping." Swedish insurance membership lists; biographi-
        cal sketches.

4716   WAAL, PIETER GERARDUS ADRIANUS DE
        Van Paciolo tot Stevin; een bijdrage tot de leer van het
        boekhouden in de Nederlanden. Roermond, Romen, 1927.
        318 p.   From [Luca?] Pacioli to Simon Stevin; a contribution
        to the study of accountancy in the Netherlands. Includes
        valuable biographical material on early Dutch accountants
        (late 15th?-early 17th centuries)

4717   WENZEL, GEORG
        Deutscher Wirtschaftsführer; Lebensgänge deutscher Wirt-
        schafts-Persönlichkeiten. Ein Nachschlagebuch über 13,000
        Wirtschaftspersönlichkeiten unserer Zeit, bearb. unter För-
        derung wirtschaftlicher Organisationen der Industrie und des
        Handels.   Hamburg, Hanseatische Verlagsanstalt [1929]
        2544 columns. 23cm. Leading German economists... A
        reference work on over 13,000 economists of our times.

4718   WER IST WER IN DER WERBUNG IN EUROPA?
        Ein bio-bibliographisches Handbuch der Werbefachleute.
        Bearb. von der Lexikon-Redaktion. 1. Ausg. Tübingen,
        Demokrit Verlag [1962] 349 p. 22cm. Who's who in adver-
        tising in Europe? A bio-bibliographical handbook.

4719   WER LEITET?
        Die Männer der Wirtschaft und der einschlägigen Verwal-
        tung. 1940-   Berlin, Hoppenstedt.   v. ports. 27cm.
        Editor: 1940-   Paul C. W. Schmidt. Who manages? Men
        of business and pertinent administration in Germany.

4720   WHO IS WHO IN INSURANCE;
        An international biographical dictionary and year book.
        1908-   New York, Singer Co. [etc.]   v. ports. 24cm.

4721   WHO'S WHO IN ADVERTISING.
        1931-   New York, Harper. v. 24cm. A directory of
        American advertising executives.

4722   WHO'S WHO IN ADVERTISING.
        1957-   [London, Buland Pub. Co.]   v. 28cm.
        British advertising biography.

4723   WHO'S WHO IN ADVERTISING.
            1st-   ed.   New York [1963-   v.   24cm.   Editor:
        1963-   E. Peterson.   American advertising biography.

4724   WHO'S WHO IN ADVERTISING AND PUBLIC RELATIONS.
            Jan. 1963-   London, New Homes Press.   v.   23cm.
        Covers Great Britain.

4725   WHO'S WHO IN BRITISH ADVERTISING.
            1924-   London, Gainsborough Pub. Co.   v.   16cm.

4726   WHO'S WHO IN FINANCE, BANKING, AND INSURANCE.
            A biographical dictionary of contemporaries.   1911-
        Brooklyn [etc.] Who's Who in Finance, inc. [etc.]   v.   24-26
        cm.   Title varies: 1911, Who's who in finance. —   1920/22,
        Who's who in finance and banking.   Imprint varies.   American
        and Canadian bankers & financiers.

4727   WHO'S WHO IN HOTELDOM.
            New England ed.   19   Boston, E. D. Kollock.   v.
        ports.   15x9cm.

4728   WHO'S WHO IN INSURANCE.
            1948-   New York, Underwriter Print. and Pub. Co.
        v.   21cm.   A section of the Insurance almanac; formerly issued
        in the Insurance almanac.   Compiled by the Weekly under-
        writer.   American insurance underwriters, etc.

4729   WHO'S WHO IN INSURANCE IN CALIFORNIA.
            [1943-   San Francisco, Pacific insurance magazine.
        v.   ports.   31cm.   Editor: 1943-   Jack Piver.

4730   WHO'S WHO IN INSURANCE IN CANADA.
            A biographical directory of insurance officials of Canada.
        Toronto, Stone & Cox [pref. 1933]   188p.

4731   WHO'S WHO IN INVESTMENT COUNSEL.
            1940-   New York, Who's Who in Investment Counsel,
        inc.   v.   22cm.   Arranged by firm; includes biographical
        sketches of members of the firms.

4732   WHO'S WHO IN PUBLIC RELATIONS, INTERNATIONAL.
            1st-   ed. ; 1959-1960—   Meridan, N. H. , PR
        Pub. Co.   v.   24cm.

4733   WHO'S WHO IN REAL ESTATE AND ALLIED INTERESTS.
[1923-   New York, Biographical Service Bureau.   v.
ports. 21cm.

4734   WHO'S WHO IN THE EXECUTIVE OFFICERS COUNCIL OF
THE NATIONAL ASSOCIATION OF REAL ESTATE BOARD.
19   [Chicago?]   v. 18cm.

4735   WORLD WHO'S WHO IN COMMERCE AND COMMERCE AND
INDUSTRY. [1st]-   ed. ; 1936-   Chicago, Marquis-Who's Who.   v. 21-27cm. biennial (irregular) "The
international business who's who." Title varies: 1936-59,
Who's who in commerce and industry. Vols. for 1940/41,
1947/59 called International edition. Vols. for 1936-38 published in New York by the Institute for Research in Biography.

Geography and Travel

4736   ADELUNG, FRIEDRICH VON, 1768-1843.
Kritiko-literaturnoe obozrienie puteshestvennikov po Rossii do 1700 goda i ikh sochinenii, Fridrikha Adelunga, uvien-
channoe bol' shoiu demidovskoiu nagradoiu. Perevod s
niemetskogo Aleksandra Klevanova. Moskva, Izd. Imp.
obshchestva istorii i drevnostei rossiiskikh pri Moskovskom
universitetie, 1864. 2v. in 1. 28cm. A review of the activities & writings of travelers in Russia during the 18th century.

4737   AMAT DI S. FILIPPO, PIETRO, 1826-1895.
Biografia dei viaggiatori italiani colla bibliografia delle
loro opere. Ed. 2. Roma, Società geografica italiana, 1882.
xi, 742p. maps. 8.° (Studi bibliografici e biografici sulla
storia della geografia in Italia, v. 1) Biography of Italian
travelers with bibliography of their writings.

4738   ASSOCIATION OF AMERICAN GEOGRAPHERS.
Handbook-directory. Washington.   v. 22cm. E. g. ,
1956 ed. has brief biographical notes about 1, 324 of the
1, 922 members at that time.

4739   CARNOY, HENRY, 1861-
Dictionnaire biographique international des voyageurs et
géographes. Paris, Impr. de l'Armorial francais, G.
Colombier [1902] 74 p. illus. 28 cm. (Collection des grands
dictionnaires biographiques) Issued with (?) his Dictionnaire
internationale des folkloristes contemporains. International
biographical dictionary of travelers and geographers.

4740   DONAZZOLO, PIETRO
I viaggiatori Veneti minori. Studio biobibliografico. Roma, Alla sede della Società [1927] 412 p. 25cm. (Memorie della Reale Società geografica italiana, v. 16) Venetian travelers, explorers, navigators. A bio-bibliographical study.

4741   EMBACHER, FRIEDRICH.
Lexikon der Reisen und Entdeckungen. In zwei Abteilungen: I. Die Forschungsreisenden aller Zeiten und Länder. II. Entdeckungsgeschichte der einzelnen Erdteile. Amsterdam, Meridian Pub. Co., 1961. vi, 393 p. 20 cm. Facsimile reproduction of the 1882 Leipzig edition. A dictionary of travels and discoveries that includes biographies.

4742   HARMS, HANS.
Künstler des Kartenbildes; Biographien und Porträts. Oldenburg (Oldb.) E. Völker [1962] 245p. illus., ports., maps. 28cm. Biographies and portraits of cartographers.

4743   LANGNAS, ISAAC A
Dictionary of discoveries. Pref. by J. Salwyn Schapiro. New York, Philosophical Library [1959] v, 201 p. 24cm. Includes biographies of explorers.

4744   LISTER, RAYMOND
How to identify old maps and globes; with a list of cartographers, engravers, publishers and printers concerned with printed maps and globes from c. 1500 to c. 1850. London, G. Bell [1965] 256 p. illus., maps. 26cm. "A list of cartographers..." (p. 117-250) gives birth and/or death dates, or dates when the person flourished, profession or chief activity & occasionally brief bibliographical data.

4745   LYNAM, EDWARD
British maps and map-makers [1250-1935] London, W. Collins, 1944. 47 p. col. plates, maps. 23cm. (Britain in pictures)

4746   NAVARRETE, MARTÍN FERNÁNDEZ DE, 1765-1844.
Biblioteca marítima española. Obra póstuma. Madrid, Impr. de la Viuda de Calero, 1851. 2 v. 25cm. A bio-bibliographical dictionary of Spanish navigators, cosmographers, geographers, sailors, mathematicians, etc.

4747   ORBIS GEOGRAPHICUS.
Adressar géographique du monde. World directory of

geography. Geographisches Weltadressbuch. 1952-
Wiesbaden, F. Steiner. v. 17-18cm. Title varies: 1952,
World directory of geographers. Vol. for 1952 published
in New York by the International Geographical Union. Includes brief biographical data for geographers.

4748 RUSSKIE MOREPLAVATELI.
[Redaktor V. S. Lupach] Moskva, Voenizdat, 1953. xxxii,
671p. illus., ports. 27cm. "Izvestnye russkie moreplavateli (Spravka) Sost. I. I. Magidovich": p. 473-577, contains ca. 500 biographical notices of Russian voyagers and
explorers.

4749 THOMAS, BRADFORD L
A biographical list of cartographers, engravers, and pub-
lishers of the XVI to XIX century maps in the University of
Kansas Library. Lawrence, University of Kansas, Dept. of
Geography, 1961. 29 l. illus. 29cm.

4750 TOOLEY, RONALD VERE, 1898-
A dictionary of mapmakers, including cartographers,
geographers, publishers, engravers, etc., from the earliest times to 1900. London, Map Collectors' Circle,
1965- v. 25cm. (Map Collectors' Circle. Map collectors' series, no. 16) Contents.-- pt. 1. A to Callan.

4751 WIESE, VLADIMIR IUL´EVICH, 1886-
Russkie poliarnye morekhody iz promyshlennykh, torgovykh
i sluzhilykh liudeĭ XVII-XIX vv. Biograficheskiĭ slovar´.
Moskva, Glavsevmorputi, 1948. 71 p. illus., map. 21cm.
Russian polar voyages by commercial and military personages
of the 17th-19th centuries; a biographical dictionary—92 names.

History, Archaeology, Anthropology, Etc.

4752 ALVERNY, MARIE THERESE D'
Répertoire des médiévistes européens [par Marie-Thérèse
d'Alverny, Yvonne Labande-Mailfert et Edmond René Labande.
Poitiers] Université de Poitiers, Centre d'études supérieures
de civilisation médiévale, 1960. 271p. 22cm. (Publications
du C. E. S. C. M., 1) "Supplément aux Cahiers de civilisation
médiévale." Bio-bibliography of medievalists-historians
whose specialty is the Middle Ages.

4753 BIO-BIBLIOGRAFIE DE' SOCI EFFETTIVI DELLA R.
DEPUTAZIONE DI STORIA PATRIA PER LE PROVINCIE
MODENESI. (In Atti e memorie della R. Deputazione di

storia patria per le provincie modenesi. Modena, 1900.
Ser. 4a, v. 10, p. 79-500) Bio-bibliography of those
associated with the Deputation for Local History of the
province of Modena.

4754   DAWSON, WARREN ROYAL, 1888-
Who was who in Egyptology; a biographical index of Egyptologists; of travellers, explorers and excavators in Egypt; of
collectors and dealers in Egyptian antiquities; of consuls, officials, authors and others whose names occur in the literature of Egyptology, from the year 1700 to the present day,
but excluding persons now living. London, Egypt Exploration Society, 1951. x,172 p. 22cm.

4755   [DUPIN, LOUIS ELLIES] 1657-1719.
Bibliotheque universelle des historiens, contenant leurs
vies... et le dénombrement des différentes éditions de leurs
oeuvres, avec des tables chronologiques et géographiques
[par l'abbé de Clairval] Paris, P. Giffart, 1707. 2 v. illus.
8.º Universal library of historians, containing their lives...
various editions of their works...

4756   DUPIN, LOUIS ELLIES, 1657-1719.
The universal library of historians; ⟨viz⟩ the Oriental,
Greek, Latin, French, German, Spanish, Italian, English,
and others: containing an account of their lives; the abridgment, chronology and geography of their histories; with
critical observations on their style and character; and a catalogue of the several editions of their works. Also chronological and geographical tables. Written in French by Lewis
Ellis du Pin, now abbot of Claraval. Done in English from
the Paris edition. [Book I] London, Printed for R. Bonwick
[etc.] 1709. 2 v. 20cm. A translation of Bibliothèque universelle des historiens, of which Book I only was published,
Paris, 1707, 2 v., under the pseudonym 'Abbé de Clairval.'
Cf. Nicéron & Barbier. Book I: Of the historians which
flourish'd before the reign of Alexander the Great.

4757   ELLIOT, Sir HENRY MIERS, 1808-1853.
Bibliographical index to the historians of Muhammedan
India. Vol. 1. Calcutta and London, 1849. 1 v. 8.º No more
published. Bio-bibliographical.

4758   GRASS, NIKOLAUS, ed.
Österreichische Geschichtswissenschaft der Gegenwart in
Selbstdarstellungen. Innsbruck, Wagner, 1950-51. 2v. ports.
24cm. (Schlern-Schriften, 68-69) Bio-bibliography of
Austrian historians.

4759   GUSTAV ADOLFS AKADEMIEN FÖR FOLKLIVSFORSKNING.
        Kungl. Gustav Adolfs akademiens minnesbok, 1932-1942.
        Utg. av Jöran Sahlgren. Uppsala, Almqvist & Wiksell, 1943.
        312 p. ports. 25cm. Memorial book for persons connected
        with the Gustav Adolf Academy for Ethnological Research.

4760   THE HANDBOOK OF AMERICAN GENEALOGY.
        v. 1-   ; 1932-   Chicago, Institute of American
        Genealogy.   v. illus. 24cm. annual. Editor: 1932-
        F. A. Virkus.   Includes an extensive section of "Who's who
        in genealogy. "

4761   INTERNATIONAL DIRECTORY OF ANTHROPOLOGISTS.
        3d ed. Melville J. Herskovits, editor. Barbara Ames
        editorial assistant.   Prepared under the auspices of the
        Committee on International Relations in Anthropology of the
        Division of Anthropology and Psychology, National Research
        Council [and] American Anthropological Association.
        Washington [Division of Anthropology and Psychology, National
        Research Council] 1950. xiv, 210p. 28cm.   2123 biographical
        sketches; "Russian anthropologists omitted, as no information
        was available. "

4762   MACRAY, WILLIAM DUNCAN, 1826-1916.
        A manual of British historians to A. D. 1600: containing a
        chronological account of the early chroniclers and monkish
        writers, their printed works and unpublished mss.   London,
        W. Pickering, 1845. xxiii, 110 p. 23cm.

4763   MARTÍNEZ ALOMIA, GUSTAVO
        Historiadores de Yucatán. Apuntes biográficos y bibliográ-
        ficos de los historiadores de esta península desde su descu-
        brimiento hasta fines del siglo XIX.   Campeche, Tip. "El
        Fénix," 1906. xii, 360 p. 23cm.   Historians of Yucatan;
        biographical and bibliographical annotations.

4764   MOSKOVSKOE ARKHEOLOGICHESKOE OBSHCHESTVO.
        Imp. Moskovskoe arkheologicheskoe obshchestvo v pervoe
        piatidesiatiletie ego sushchestvovaniia (1864-1914 gg.) T. 2:
        Biograficheskii slovar' chlenov Obshchestva. Spisok trudov
        Chlenov Obshchestva, pomeshchennykh v izdaniiakh Obshch-
        estva. Pod red. P. S. Uvarovoi i I. N. Borozdina. Moskva,
        T-vo skoropech. A. A. Levenson, 1915. xxii, 446, 258p.
        ports. Vol. 2 is a biographical dictionary of members of the
        Russian Archaeological Society, 1864-1914, and a bibliography
        of their writings.

4765 PONS BOIGUES, FRANCISCO
Ensayo bio-bibliográfico sobre los historiadores y geógrafos arábigo-españoles. Madrid, Estab. Tip. de San Francisco de Sales, 1898. 514. 28cm. 303 bio-bibliographical notices of Arab-Spanish historians and geographers in Arab-dominated Spain.

4766 SELLIUS, BURCHARD ADAM, d.1746.
Katalog pisatelei, sochineniiami svoimi ob"iasniavshikh grazhdanskuiu i tserkovnuiu rossiiskuiu istoriiu. Pereveden v Vologodskoi seminarii. Moskva, Tip. S. Selivanovskago, 1815. 68 p. 21cm. Bio-bibliographical; 164 Russians and foreigners specializing in Russian political and church history. Alphabetical arrangement. First published in 1736 under title: Schediasma litterarium de scriptoribus, qui historiam politico-ecclesiasticam Rossiae scriptis illustrarunt.

4767 WHO'S WHO IN HISTORY.
General editor: C. R. N. Routh. Oxford, Blackwell, 1960- v. illus., ports., maps. 23cm. Contents. — v.1. British Isles, 55 B. C. to 1485, by W. O. Hassall.

4768 WÜSTENFELD, HEINRICH FERDINAND, 1808-1899.
Die Geschichtschreiber der Araber und ihre Werke. Göttingen, Dieterichsche Verlagsbuchhandlung, 1882. viii, 307p. 27 x 22 cm. The historians of the Arabs and their works; bio-bibliographical.

Political Science

4769 AMERICAN POLITICAL SCIENCE ASSOCIATION.
Biographical directory. 1st- ed. - 1945- Washington. v. 26cm. Title varies: 1945-53, Directory.

4770 DÍAZ DOIN, GUILLERMO
Diccionario político de nuestro tiempo, político-biográfico-económico-sociológico. Buenos Aires, Editorial Mundo Atlántico [1943] 557 p. 22cm. A dictionary of political science (contemporary) with biographical sketches.

4771 DIZIONARIO DI POLITICA;
A cura del Partito nazionale Fascista. Roma, Istituto della Enciclopedia italiana, 1940. 4 v. maps. 31cm. A publication of the Italian Fascist Party which includes biographies of political and social scientists; the majority are Italian.

4772   DUNNER, JOSEPH, ed.
       Dictionary of political science. New York, Philosophical
       Library [1964] xxii, 585 p. 24 cm. Includes biographies of
       political scientists and statesmen.

4773   INTERNATIONAL CITY MANAGERS' ASSOCIATION.
       Membership directory. 3227 members, Nov. 1, 1962.
       Chicago [1962] 41p. 28cm. Includes date of birth, education,
       city managed.

4774   PALGRAVE, Sir. ROBERT HARRY INGLIS, 1827-1919.
       Dictionary of political economy. [New ed.] Edited by
       Henry Higgs. London, Macmillan, 1925-26. 3 v. diagrs.,
       facsims. 23cm. Includes biography. First published 1894-
       99?

4775   VIRGINIA. UNIVERSITY. BUREAU OF PUBLIC ADMINIS-
       TRATION.
       Who's who in public administration research in Virginia.
       Rev. ed. [Charlottesville] Division of Publications of the
       Bureau of Public Administration, University, Virginia, 1940.
       93 p. 28cm. (Its Report. Series A, no. 2) Mimeographed.

TECHNOLOGY AND APPLIED SCIENCE

4776   THE "AEROPLANE" DIRECTORY OF BRITISH AVIATION.
       1928-   London, Published by the English Universities
       Press for Temple Press [etc.] v. 19cm. Vols. for 1928-
       "incorporating 'Who's who in flying,'" 'Who's who in the
       air," and "The Aviation and flying year book." Title varies:
       1928-   Who's who in aviation; 19 -1948, Who's who in
       British aviation. Includes biographical sketches (e. g.,
       1949 ed. has over 1250 entries)

4777   AGRICULTURAL INSTITUTE OF CANADA.
       Who's who in the Agricultural Institute of Canada. Ottawa,
       1948. vi, 226p. 24cm.

4778   AUTOMOTIVE NEWS ALMANAC.
       Detroit, Slocum Pub. Co.   v. Published annually as
       the April issue of Automotive news. "Automotive news family
       album" (e. g., in the 1954 issue) has portraits & biographical
       sketches (in alphabetical arrangement) of automobile executives
       the world over.

4779   THE BLUE BOOK OF AMERICAN AVIATION;
        Who's who in the industry. 1940-   ed. Asheville, N. C.,
    Aviation Statistics Institute of America. v. 24cm.

4780   THE BLUE BOOK OF AVIATION;
        A biographical history of American aviation. 1932-   ed.
    Los Angeles, Hoagland Co. v. illus., ports. 32cm.
    Editor: 1932-   R. W. Hoagland.

4781   CAREY, ARTHUR MERWYN, 1890-
        American firearms makers; when, where, and what they
    made from the Colonial period to the end of the nineteenth
    century. New York, Crowell [1953] xiii, 146 p. illus. 24 cm.

4782   CAREY, ARTHUR MERWYN, 1890-
        English, Irish, and Scottish firearms makers: when, where,
    and what they made, from the middle of the sixteenth century
    to the end of the nineteenth century New York, Crowell [1954]
    xv, 121 p. illus. 24 cm.

4783   COMMONWEALTH AGRICULTURAL BUREAUX. EXECUTIVE
        COUNCIL.
        List of research workers: research workers in agriculture,
    animal health and forestry in the British Commonwealth (includ-
    ing... the Anglo-Egyptian Sudan and the Republic of Ireland)
    19-- Farnham Royal (Bucks.) v. 25cm.

4784   THE CONSULTING ENGINEERS WHO'S WHO & YEAR BOOK.
        London, Princess Press. v. 22cm. Title varies: 19-
    -50, Consulting engineer year book. Beginning with 1951
    "combined with the Association of Consulting Engineers Who's
    who." British engineers.

4785   DEUTSCHE AKADEMIE DER LUFTFAHRTFORSCHUNG.
        Jahrbuch. [1.]-   1937/38-   Berlin. v.
    illus., ports. 25cm. E. g., the volume for 1937/38 con-
    sists chiefly of biographical sketches and bibliographies of
    members of the German Academy for Aeronautical Research.

4786   DIRECTORY OF RESEARCH WORKERS IN AGRICULTURE
        AND ANIMAL HUSBANDRY IN INDIA.
        19   New Delhi, Indian Council of Agricultural
    Research. v. 24cm. Gives academic degrees, positions,
    and specialties.

4787   DUNLAP, ORRIN ELMER, 1896-
Radio's 100 men of science; biographical narratives of
pathfinders in electronics and television.   New York, Harper
[1944]   xx, 294 p.   ports.   22cm.

4788   ELECTRICAL WHO'S WHO.
1950-   London, Electrical Review Publications.   v.
23cm.   Compiled by Electrical review.   Brief biographies
of leading members of the professional and industrial branches
of the British electrical industry.

4789   HAM REGISTER.
1958-   [Indiana, Pa.] Ham Register, inc.   v. 23cm.   With sketches of amateur radio
operators in the U.S., Canada and elsewhere.

4790   HISTORICAL AND BIOGRAPHICAL RECORD OF THE CAT-
TLE INDUSTRY AND THE CATTLEMEN OF TEXAS AND
ADJACENT TERRITORY.
With a new introd. by J. Frank Dobie. [St. Louis, Woodward & Tiernan Print. Co., c1894, 1895] New York, Antiquarian Press, 1959. 2 v. illus. 31cm. Primarily the
work of James Cox. Vol. 2, Biographical (449 sketches)

4791   HVEM ER HVEM I DANSK SØFART.
Kongeriget Danmarks handelsflåde: administration,
institutioner, organisationer og maend. Redaktion: Ove
Nielsen. København, Forlaget Liber, 1954. 694p. ports.
27cm. Who's who in the Danish merchant marine: administration, institutions, organizations and men.

4792   IRE DIRECTORY.
A yearbook containing a radio engineers' directory, a list
of firms and products. 1914-   New York, Institute of Radio
Engineers.   v. in   illus.   23-28cm.   annual.   Title varies:
1914-49, Year book [of] the Institute of Radio Engineers.
Includes (in some issues only?) a section: Biographies of
fellows (as of [date]) in alphabetical arrangement. The membership roster itself gives only occupation and address.

4793   INGENIEROS DE CAMINOS, CANALES Y PUERTOS;
ESCALAFÓN.
Madrid, Revista de obras publicas. v. 12cm. Brief
biographical data for only some of the engineers mentioned
(Spanish builders of roads, canals and harbors)

4794 KOZLOV, A   G
Tvortsy tekhniki na Urale (Kratkii biograficheskii ukazatel')
[Sverdlovsk] 1954. 48 p. 226 biographical notices of Russian
technologists in the Ural Mountains region.

4795 LENINGRAD. INZHENERNO-STROITEL'NYI INSTITUT.
IUbileinyi sbornik sviedienii o dieiatel'nosti byvshikh vospi-
tannikov instituta, 1842-1892. Sostavil, G. V. Baranovskii.
S.-Peterburg, 1893. 400p. illus. Issued by the Institute
under its earlier name: Institut grazhdanskikh inzhenerov.
Russian engineers, graduates of an engineering school in St.
Petersburg (Leningrad)

4796 NIPPON GAKUJUTSU SHINKŌKAI.
Kōgaku kenkyūsha meibo-daigaku kankōritsu kenkyūjo no
bun. Dai 5-6 u. Tokyo, 1959. 745p. Brief biographical
sketches of engineers in educational and other public research
organizations.

4797 NIPPON GAKUJUTSU SHINKŌKAI.
Kōgaku kenkyūsha meibo-kōgyō kaisha, minkan kenkyūjo.
Dai 5-6 u. Tokyo, Nikkan Kōgyō Shimbun Sha, 1961. 349p.
Brief biographical sketches and descriptions of major activi-
ties of engineers in industrial and other private research.

4798 NÚÑEZ OLAECHEA, SAMUEL
Los ferrocarriles del Estado... Santiago de Chile, Impr.
i Encuadernación Chile, 1910. 328 p. port. 26cm. In 3
parts; pt. 3, "Diccionario biográfico" [of figures in the railroad history of Chile]

4799 PROMIS, CARLO, 1808-1872.
Biografie di ingegneri militari italiani dal secolo XIV alla
metà del XVIII. [Torino, Fratelli Bocca, 1874] 858p. 24cm.
(Miscellanea di storia italiana, t. 14) Posthumous publication,
edited by the author's nephew, Vincenzo Promis. Biographies of Italian military engineers of the 14th to the middle
of the 18th century.

4800 PULGAR VIDAL, JAVIER, 1913-
Primer diccionario biográfico profesional de ingenieros
agrónomos en Colombia. Bogotá [Editorial Minagricultura]
1953. 2 v. (xxxiv, 740p.) map. 24cm. (Ministerio de Ag-
ricultura. Fichero Científico Agropecuario. Publicación
no. 2) Cover title. First professional biographical dictionary of agronomy engineers in Colombia.

4801   R. U. S. RURAL UPLOOK SERVICE;
A preliminary attempt to register the rural leadership in
the United States and Canada. [1918-   Ithaca, N. Y.   v.
21cm.   Compiler: 1918-   L. H. Bailey.   1930 ed. (4th issue) has title: R. U. S. ; a biographical register of the rural
leadership in the United States and Canada.

4802   RUBBER RED BOOK;
Directory of the rubber industry.   [1st-   ed.];
1937-   New York, Rubber age.   v. illus. 24cm. biennial.   Includes a section entitled: Who's who in the rubber
industry, i. e. chief executives in the industry.

4803   SATTERLEE, LEROY DEFOREST, 1891-
American gun makers, by L. D. Satterlee and Arcadi
Gluckman.   Buffalo, Ulbrich Co. , 1940.   186 p. 23cm.

4804   SCI-EN-TECH REGISTER AND CLASSIFIED PRODUCTS
LISTING.   2d ed.   Chicago [R. F. Clancy] 1955   460 p.
24cm.   A directory of engineers and scientists in Chicago and
vicinity.

4805   "SHIPPING WORLD" YEAR BOOK.
General maritime information; statutory rules & regula-
tions; classified world directories of shipowners, shipbuilders,
shiprepairers, towing services, marine engine builders, etc. ;
training for the merchant nay.   Who's who in the shipping
world. 1886-   London, The Shipping World.   v. col.
maps. 19-22cm.   Subtitle varies: 18 -1934, A desk manual
in trade, commerce, and navigation; etc.

4806   TECHNISCHER LITERATURKALENDER.
1. -   Ausg. ; 1918-   München, Berlin, R. Oldenbourg.   v. ports. , plates. 22cm.   Bio-bibliography of
German technology and industrial arts.

4807   VESTDAL, JON E
Verkfræðingtal. ÆViágrip íslenzka verkfræðinga og
annarra félagsmanna Verkfræðingafélags Islands...
Reykjavík, Isafoldarprentsmiðja, 1956.   xix, 258 p. ports.
At head of title: Jón E. Vestdal og Stefán Bjarnason.   Dic-
tionary of Icelandic engineers and members of the Icelandic
Society of Engineers.

4808   WHO'S WHO AMONG AUTOMOTIVE EXECUTIVES.
1964-   Detroit, Trends Pub. Co.   v. 23cm.

4809   WHO'S WHO IN AMERICAN AERONAUTICS.
        [1st]-   ed. ; 1922-   New York, Gardner Pub. Co.
[etc.] v. ports. 32cm. On cover, 1925-   : The Blue
book of American airmen. Editors: 1922-   , L. D.
Gardner.

4810   "WHO'S WHO" IN ARMY AVIATION;
        Yearbook. 1954 (?)-   Westport, Conn. , Army
Aviation Publications. v. ports. 22cm.

4811   WHO'S WHO IN AVIATION.
        A directory of living men and women who have contributed
to the growth of aviation in the United States. 1942/43-
Chicago & New York, Ziff-Davis Pub. Co. v. 25cm.
Compiler: 1942/43-   Writers' Program of the Works
Project Administration in the State of Illinois.

4812   WHO'S WHO IN DATA PROCESSING.
        1-   Detroit, American Data Processing [1962 -   v.
29cm.

4813   WHO'S WHO IN ENGINEERING.
        A biographical directory of the engineering profession.
v.1-   1922/23-   New York, Lewis Historical Pub. Co.
v. 25cm. Title varies: 1922-25, Who's who in engineering;
a biographical dictionary of contemporaries. Imprint varies.
American engineers.

4814   WHO'S WHO IN ENGINEERING.
        A directory on the who's who principle of professional
engineers, producing firms, engineering institutions, centres
of technical training, research associations, & c.   1920/21-
London. British engineers.

4815   WHO'S WHO IN ENGINEERING IN PENNSYLVANIA.
        [Philadelphia] v. 30cm. Official publication of the
Engineers Society of Pennsylvania.

4816   WHO'S WHO IN ENGINEERING IN THE DELAWARE VALLEY.
        A directory of engineers. Philadelphia, Engineers' Club
of Philadelphia. v. 23cm. Title varies: Who's who; a
directory of engineers in metropolitan Philadelphia.

4817   WHO'S WHO IN INDIAN ENGINEERING & INDUSTRY.
      1st-   ed. ; 1962-   Calcutta, Kothari Publications.
v. ports. 22cm.

4818   WHO'S WHO IN MINING AND METALLURGY;
      Containing the records of mining engineers and metallur-
gists at home and abroad. Founded by George Safford.
[1908-   London, The mining journal.   v. 21cm.

4819   WHO'S WHO IN PLASTICS IN THE UNITED STATES AND
      CANADA. 1943/44-   New York, Society of the
Plastics Industry.   v. 23cm.

4820   WHO'S WHO IN RAILROADING IN NORTH AMERICA.
      [1st]-   ed. ; 1885-   New York, Simmons-Boardman
Pub. Corp.   v. 23cm. Title varies: 1885-1913: The Biographical directory of the railway officials of America. —
1930, Who's who in railroading, United States, Canada, Mexico, Cuba. Imprint varies.

4821   WHO'S WHO IN THE COMPUTER FIELD, 1956-57.
      3d ed. Newtonville, Mass., Berkeley Enterprises, 1957.
209p. 28cm. Issued as an extra number of Computers and
automation, v. 6, no. El. Previous editions issued as part
of various issues of Computers and automation.

4822   WHO'S WHO IN THE ELECTRONICS INDUSTRY.
      1961/62-   New York, SETI Publishers.   v. 29cm.
Vols. for 1961/62-   edited by the Scientist and Engineer
Technological Institute.

4823   WHO'S WHO IN THE COMPUTER FIELD.
      1963/64-   Newtonville, Mass., Berkeley Enterprises.
      v. 29cm. Three earlier editions appeared in the periodi-
cal Computers and automation: 1st ed. in various issues from
Jan. 1953 to Jan. 1954; 2d ed. in June 1955 issue; 3d ed. as v.
6, no. El, Mar. 1957.

4824   WHO'S WHO IN THE MARITIME INDUSTRY;
      Biographical sketches and illustrations of interest to and
concerning people in the merchant seafaring world. [1946-
      New York, 74 Degrees West Co.   v. illus., ports.
24cm.

4825   WHO'S WHO IN THE MOTOR TRADE [BRITISH];
A biography, alphabetically arranged, of well-known members of the motor trade and prominent motorists. Edited by Percy Peters and H. Thornton Rutter   London, Motor commerce, 1934. xiv, 167p. 8.º

4826   WHO'S WHO IN THE PUBLIC UTILITIES INDUSTRY.
1st-   ed. ; 1942-   Philadelphia, L. Stotz.   v. illus., ports. 23cm. Covers the electric and gas utilities, U.S.A.

4827   WHO'S WHO IN THE RUBBER WORLD.
1914-   London, Exhibition Offices.   v. 19cm.

4828   WHO'S WHO IN TRANSPORTATION AND COMMUNICATION;
A biographical dictionary of important living people in the transportation and communication industries. v. 1-
1942/43-   Boston, Transportation Press in conjunction with Larkin, Roosevelt & Larkin, 1942-   v. 24cm.
American transportation and communication executives.

4829   WJP'S WHO IN WORLD AVIATION AND ASTRONAUTICS.
v. 1-   1955-   Washington, American Aviation Publications.   v. 24cm. Title varies slightly (e. g. : v. 1, 1955, Who's who in world aviation)

AUTHOR INDEX

A

A. G. --SEE: Gueidon, Alexandre
930

A. S. K. B. --SEE: Algemeen Secretariaat voor Katholieke
Boekerijen 180

Aa, Abraham Jacob van der 1553,
3489

Ågren, Sven 1814

Åhlen, Bengt 3923

Abad de Santillán, Diego 342

'Abd al-Karīm ibn Muhammad, al-
Sam'ānī--SEE: al-Sam'ānī,
'Abd al-Karim ibn Muhammad
1331

'Abd Allāh ibn Muhammad al-Ansārī
al-Harawi--SEE: al-Ansārī al-
Harawi, 'Abd Allāh ibn Muhammad 4554

'Abd al-Rahmān, Muhammad ibn,
al-Sakhāwi--SEE: al-Sakhāwi,
Muhammad ibn 'Abd al-Rahmān
1330

'Abd al-Rahmān ibn Ahmad, called
Jāmī--SEE: Jāmī 4458

'Abd al-Razzāq al-Bītār--SEE: al-
Bītār, 'Abd al-Razzāq 1310

A'Beckett, Sir William 40

Abel, Charles 2736

Aberconway, Christabel Mary Melville (Macnaghten) McLaren,
baroness 41

Abercrombie, Gurth I. 3319

Aberdeen. University 1209

Abernethy, J. W. 153

Abert, Hermann Joseph 2742,
3080

Abousleman, Michel D. 2242

Abraham, Émile 3132

Abranches, Dunshee de 474

Abū al-Faraj, al-Isbahānī--SEE:
Alī ibn Husain, Abū al-Faraj,
al-Isbahānī 3437

Abū Nu'aim Ahmad ibn 'Abd Allāh
4553

Academia de Jurisprudencia y
Legislación, Madrid 3940

Academia Guatemalteca, Guatemala 3897

Academia Scientiarum Regiae
Borussicae--SEE: Akademie
der Wissenschaften, Berlin
1654, 3626, 4572

Académie des sciences, Paris
4571

Académie diplomatique internationale 42

Académie royale des sciences co-
loniales--SEE: Académie
royale des sciences d'outre mer
422

Académie royale des sciences, des
lettres et des beaux-arts de
Belgique, Brussels 423-424

Académie royale des sciences, des
lettres et des beaux-arts de
Belgique, Brussels. Annuaire.
(Indexes) 418

Académie royale des sciences
d'outre mer 422

Academy-International of Medicine and Dentistry   4055

Academy of Sciences, Leningrad and Moscow--SEE: Akademiia nauk SSSR   4575-4575

Accattatis, Luigi   1387

Ackrill, J. L.   4259

Acosta de Samper, Soledad   624

Acquaviva, Giovanni Panelli d'. -- SEE: Panelli d'Acquaviva, Giovanni   4182

Acuña, Luis Alberto   2422

Adam, Melchior   961

Adams, Eleanor Burnham   4276

Adams, Henry Gardiner   43

Adams, Oscar Fay   3396

Adams, William Davenport   3133, 3492

Adariukov, Vladimir IAkovlevich   1665

Addison, William Innes   1213

Adelman, Joseph Ferdinand Gottlieb   44

Adelung, Friedrich von   4736

Adelung, Johann Christoph   167

Ader, Jean Joseph   425

Adler, Ada Sara   3469

Adolphus, John   717

Advisory Board for Medical Specialties   4124

Aellen, Hermann   1863, 3930

Aeschlimann, Erardo   2425

Afanas'ev, Nikolaï Ivanovich   1666

Afflitto, Eustachio d'   3731

Affo, Ireneo   3732

Aftenposten, Oslo   3803

Agnus, Felix   2177

Agostini, Giovanni degli   3733

Agramonte y Cortijo, Francisco   45

Agren, Sven--SEE: Ågren, Sven (Å filed Aa)   1814

Agricola, Peter Franz   46

Agricola, Petrus Franciscus--SEE: Agricola, Peter Franz   46

Agricultural Institute of Canada   4777

Ahmad, Rāzī Amīn--SEE: Amīn Ahmad, Rāzī   1309

Ahmad ibn 'Alī ibn Hajar al-'Asqalānī--SEE: Ibn Hajar al-'Asqalānī, Ahmad ibn Alī   1319

Ahmad ibn Mustafā, Tāshkubrīzādah --SEE Tāshkubrīzādah, Ahmad ibn Mustafā   1874, 1878

Aigueperse, P. G.   863

Aikin, John   47, 4056

Air Force. Supplement   2065

Air Force Association   2065

Aizenshtadt, David--SEE:
 Ajzenstadt, David   2743

Ajzenstadt, David   2743

Akademie der Wissenschaften,
 Berlin   1654, 3626, 4572

Akademie der Wissenschaften,
 Berlin. Historische Kommission   962

Akademie der Wissenschaften,
 Göttingen   4573

Akademie der Wissenschaften,
 Munich. Historische Kommission   1000

Akademie der Wissenschaften,
 Vienna   398

Akademiia nauk, Leningrad--SEE:
 Akademiia nauk SSSR   4574-
 4575

Akademiia nauk SSSR   4574-4575

Akademiia nauk SSSR. Institut
 istorii estestvoznaniia i
 tekhniki   4578

Akademiia nauk SSSR. Komissiia
 "Nauchnye uchrezhdeniia i
 nauchnye rabotniki SSSR"
 4606

Akademiia nauk SSSR. Zoologicheskii institut   4627-4628

Akimov, Vladimir Mikhailovich
 3830

Alba, M. Font-. SEE: Font-Alba,
 M.   4641

Albareda, Anselmo María   4277

Albérès, R. M.   3557

Albert Torrellas, A.   2818-2819

Alberti, Eduard Christian
 Scharlau   3603, 3664-3665

Albino, Pasquale   1384

Albrecht, Günter   3604

Alcahalí, José Ruiz de Lihory,
 barón de--SEE: Alcahalí y de
 Mosquera, José María Ruiz de
 Lihori y Pardines, barón de
 2423, 2744

Alcahalí y de Mosquera, José María
 Ruiz de Lihori y Pardines,
 barón de   2423, 2744

Alcalá Galiano, Juan Valera y--SEE:
 Valera y Alcalá Galiano, Juan
 3893

Alcover, Vicente Castañeda y--SEE:
 Castañeda y Alcover, Vicente
 3872

Aldis, Harry Gidney   4027, 4035

Alembert, Jean Lerond d'   711

Alexander, George M.   4266

Algemeen Secretariaat voor Katholieke Boekerijen   180

Alhoy, Philadelphe Maurice   712,
 3134, 3163

Ali ibn Bali, called Mank   1874

'Ali ibn Hasan, called Ibn 'Asā-
 kir--SEE: Ibn 'Asākir 'Ali
 ibn Hasan, 1318

Ali ibn Husain, Abū al-Faraj, al-
 Isbahānī   3437

'Ali ibn Mūsā, al-Maghribī, called
 Ibn Sa'id--SEE: Ibn Sa'id, 'Ali
 ibn Mūsā, al-Maghribī, called
 1321

'Ali ibn Yūsuf, al-Qiftī--SEE: al-Qiftī, 'Ali ibn Yūsuf   4191

'Alī Miniq--SEE: Alī ibn Bālī, called Mank   1874

Alimzhanov, A.   3933

Aliquò Lenzi, Luigi   3734

Aliquò Taverriti, Filippo   3734

Alizeri, Federigo   2424

Allāh, Shūshtarī Nūr--SEE: Nūr Allāh, Shūshtarī   4559

Allaire, Jean Baptiste Arthur 4278-4280

Allegrini, Giuseppe   1413

Allemand, Félix   890

Allen, William   1893, 1953

Allgemeine Geschichtsforschende Gesellschaft der Schweiz, Zürich   1841-1842, 1845, 1849

Allibone, Samuel Austin   3493

Allison, John   2332

Allorto, Riccardo   2746

Almansa, Andrés Baquero--SEE: Baquero Almansa, Andrés 1787, 2432

Almerté, Tarmini-. SEE: Tarmini-Almerté   845

Almindelige danske laegeforening 4118

Almirante, José   1765

Alomia, Gustavo Martínez--SEE Martínez Alomia, Gustavo 4763

Alone, pseud. --SEE: Díaz Arrieta, Hernán   3906

Alonnier, Edmond   755

Alonso Cortés, Narciso   1766

Alten, Georg Karl Friedrich Viktor   49

Altmann, Wilhelm   2964

Álvarez, Josefina Rivera de--SEE: Rivera de Álvarez, Josefina 3915

Álvarez y Baena, José Antonio 1800

Alverny, Marie Thérèse d'   4752

Alves do Sacramento Blake, Augusto Victorino--SEE: Sacramento Blake, Augusto Victorino Alves do   483

Amar du Rivier, Jean Augustin 79

Amat, Félix Torres--SEE: Torres Amat, Félix   3456-3457

Amat, Ignacio Torres--SEE: Torres Amat, Ignacio   3456

Amat di S. Filippo, Pietro   4737

Amaya, Isidro Laverde--SEE: Laverde Amaya, Isidro   626-627

Ambrosi, Francesco   3735

American Academy of Pediatrics 4058

American Anthropological Association   4761

American Antiquarian Society, Worcester, Mass.   1882-1883

American art annual   2659-2660

American Association for Applied
    Psychology   4231

American Association of Colle-
    giate Schools of Business
    3254

American Association of Law Li-
    braries   3994

American Biographical Publishing
    Company   1914, 2040, 2100-
    2102, 2306

American Chemical Society. Com-
    mittee on Professional Train-
    ing   4652

American College of Chest Physi-
    cians   4059

American College of Hospital Ad-
    ministrators   4060

American College of Physicians
    4061

American College of Surgeons
    4062

American Council of Learned So-
    cieties Devoted to Humanistic
    Studies   1931, 3255, 4684

American Data Processing, inc.,
    Detroit   4812

American Dental Association
    4063

American Economic Association
    4695

American Federation of Arts
    2571, 2659

American Historical Company, inc.,
    New York.   1895, 1940, 2117,
    2181, 2186, 2228, 2252, 2271

American Historical Society, New
    York--SEE: American Histori-
    cal Company, inc., New York,
    1895 [etc.]

American Institute of Architects
    2675

American Institute of Photography
    2664

American Jewish Literary Founda-
    tion   1899

American Library Association   1

American Marketing Association
    4696

American Medical Association
    4065

American Political Science Asso-
    ciation   4769

American Psychiatric Association
    4069

American Psychological Associa-
    tion   4232

American Society of Composers,
    Authors and Publishers   2747

American Statistical Association
    4677, 4680

American Universities Medical Re-
    search Publications, inc.
    161, 4147

American University Club of Shang-
    hai   1903

Ames, Joseph   3995

Amherst College   1907

Amiens, Frédéric Dubois d' --SEE:
    Dubois d'Amiens, Frédéric
    4125

Amīn Ahmad, Rāzī   1309

Amírola, Eugenio Llaguno y --SEE:
    Llaguno y Amírola, Eugenio
    2684

Amo, Julián   3855

Amorim, Eugenio   2748

Amory, Cleveland   159

Amsterdam. Universiteit   3256

Amsterdamsch Studenten-Corps
    3256

Amstutz, Walter   2738

Amyot, Jacques   4678

Un Ancien député--SEE: Borel d'
    Hauterive, André François
    Joseph   739

Un Ancien publiciste   728

Ancona, Alessandro d'   3736

Ancona, Paolo d'   2425

Anderson, James Maitland   1219

Anderson, Vladimir Maksimiliano-
    vich   1714

Anderson, William   1210

Andrade, Manuel de Jesús   676,
    681

Andreae, Friedrich   1073

Andreas, Willy   963

Andresen, Andreas   2426

Andresen, Harald   1581

Ángel Garcia, Miguel--SEE: Garcia,
    Miguel Ángel   1749

Angelis, Alberto de   2749

Angiolgabriello di Santa Maria
    3737

Anglés, Higinio   3015

Angot, Alphonse   911

Añibarro y Rives, Manuel Martí-
    nez--SEE: Martínez Añibarro
    y Rives, Manuel   3873, 3888

Anker, Øyvind   2885

Anns, John   4709

al-Ansārī al Harawi, 'Abd Allāh
    ibn Muhammad   4554, 4558

Ansart, Louis Joseph Auguste
    3552

Ansell, Evelyn   1110

Antoine, A., de Saint-Gervais
    52

Antonino de la Asuncion, fray
    4282

Antonio, Nicolás   3856-3857

Antonio Maria di Vicenza   4283

Apell, David August von   2750

Appleton, Marion Brymner   2662

Apthorp, William Foster   2795

Ara, Masato   53

Arango, Felipe Martínez--SEE:
    Martínex Arango, Felipe   637

Aranha, Pedro Wencheslau de Brito
    --SEE: Brito Aranha, Pedro
    Wenceslau de   3816

Arbellot, François   898

Arboleda, Gustavo   625, 677

Arboleda Restrepo, Gustavo--SEE:
    Arboleda, Gustavo   625, 677

Architectural Publication Society
    2676

Archivo General de Indias, Seville--
    SEE: Spain. Archivo General
    de Indias, Seville   1508

Arco, Ricardo del   1788

Arellano, Rafael Ramírez de--SEE:
    Ramírez de Arellano, Rafael
    1796, 2601

Arellano y Gutiérrez de Salamanca,
    Carlos Ramírez de--SEE:
    Ramírez de Arellano y Gutiér-
    rez de Salamanca, Carlos   3882

Arena, Goivanni F.   1932

Argellati, Filippo   1393

Argenville, Antoine Joseph Dezal-
    lier d' --SEE: Dezallier d' Ar-
    genville, Antoine Joseph   2473

Argüelles, Angel Lasso de la Vega
    y --SEE: Lasso de la Vega y
    Argüelles, Angel   3870

Arisi, Francesco   3738-3739

Armand, Alfred   2703

Armanni, Mario   3996

Armellini, Mariano   4284

Armstrong (J. M.) and Company
    2162

Armytage, Sir George John, bart.
    1165

Arnault, Antoine Vincent   734

Arnim, Max   3, 3257, 4573

Arntzenius, Louis Marie George
    2837

Arocena Arregui, Fausto   1790

Arout, Georges   3148

Arregui, Fausto Arocena--SEE:
    Arocena Arregui, Fausto
    1790

Arrieta, Hernán Díaz--SEE: Díaz
    Arrieta, Hernán   3906

Arro, Elmar   2995

Arroniz, Marcos   1521

Arrotea, Carlos Molina--SEE:
    Molina Arrotea, Carlos
    350

Arroyo, César   3910

Arsen'ev, Aleksandr Vasil'evich
    3819-3820

Arteaga, Enrique Esperabé--SEE:
    Esperabé Arteaga, Enrique
    1776

Artigue, Pierre   634

Artucio Ferreira, Antonia   3900

'Asākir, 'Alī ibn Hasan ibn--SEE:
    Ibn 'Asākir, 'Alī ibn Hasan
    1318

Asaph, pseud. --SEE: Roberts, T.
    R.   1230

Asarrunz, Moisés   468

Asen, Johannes   3260

Ashe, Samuel A'Court   2265

Asimov, Isaac   4577

Askenazy, Szymon   1628

Asow, Erich Hermann Mueller von--
SEE: Mueller, Erich Hermann
2931

Asow, Hedwig Mueller von--SEE:
Mueller, Hedwig   2931

al-'Asqalānī, Ahmad ibn 'Alī ibn
Hajar--SEE: Ibn Hajar al-
'Asqalānī, Ahmad ibn 'Alī
1319

Association des écrivains combattants   3553-3554

Association for Asian Studies. Ming
Biographical History Project
542

Association of American Geographers   4738

Association of American Law
Schools   3951

Association of Consulting Chemists
and Chemical Engineers   4653

Association of Consulting Engineers
4784

Association of Methodist Historical
Societies, USA   4534

Association of University Evening
Colleges   3319

Athens news   1245

Atkinson, George   1237

Atkinson, George Wesley   3942

Atkinson, William Biddle   4071

Atlantic Publishing and Engraving
Company, New York   1922,
2003-2004, 2370

Attinger, Victor   1845, 1849

Attwater, Donald   4285-4287,
4313-4315

Aubert, Auguste   948

Aubert de La Chesnaye-Desbois,
François Alexandre--SEE:
La Chesnaye-Desbois, François Alexandre Aubert de
799

Aucamp, Gerhard   324

Auda, Antoine   2753

Audet, François Joseph   495

Audin, Marius   2427

Auerbach, Berthold   1456

Auerbach, Erna   2428

The Auk   4629

Aurelj, Antonietta Maria Bessone-.
SEE Bessone-Aurelj, Anto-
nietta Maria   2444, 2694

Austin, Frederick Arnold   3211

Australia. Commonwealth National
Library, Canberra--SEE:
Canberra, Australia. Nation-
al Library   373

Australia. National Library, Can-
berra--SEE: Canberra, Australia. National Library
373

L'Auteur de la Nouvelle biographie
des pairs (A. R.)--SEE: Rion,
Adolphe   835

The Author of "Southland writers."
--SEE: Tardy, Mrs. Mary T.
3430

Auvray, Louis   2437-2438

Avallon, Charles Yves Cousin,
called Cousin d' --SEE:
Cousin d'Avallon, Charles
Yves Cousin, called   4337

Avery, Catherine B.   211

Aviation Statistics Institute of
America   4779

Avila, J. Víctor Soto de--SEE:
Soto de Avila, J. Víctor   524

À Wood, Anthony--SEE: Wood,
Anthony à   1190

Axon, William Edward Armytage
3535

Ayguals de Izco, Wenceslao   56

Ayres, Harry Morgan   3325

Azevedo Soares, Eduardo de Campos
de Castro de --SEE: Campos
de Castro de Azevedo Soares,
Eduardo de   1641

Azpuría, Ramón   1501

Azulai, Hayyim Joseph David
1449

B

B., A. S. K.--SEE: Algemeen
Secretariaat voor Katholieke
Boekerijen   180

B., N. A. G. D. B. --SEE: Debray, Nicolas Antoine Gabriel
3563

Baader, Clemens Alois   3605-
3606

Babault,   3136

Babié de Bercenay, François
714-715, 761

Bacci, Orazio   3736

Bachelet, Théodore   110

Bacher, Wilhelm   4560

Bachmann, Alberto Abraham
2754

Backer, Aloys de   4288

Backer, Augustin de   4288-4289

Backhausen, Nelly   2993, 3482-
3483

Bacon, Edwin Monroe   2188

Bader, Karl   3997

Badier,   799

Baena, José Antonio Antonio Álvarez y-- SEE: Álvarez y Baena,
José Antonio   1800

Baert, Philippe   2693

Baeza y González, Tomás   3858

Bagaleĭ, Dmitriĭ Ivanovich   3281

al-Baghdādī, al-Khatīb--SEE: al-
Khatīb, al-Baghdādī   1322

Baglione, Giovanni   2429

Bailey, Hamilton   4072

Bailey, Liberty Hyde   4801

Bailey, Orville T.   3261

Bailey, Rosalie Fellows   2243

Baillet, Adrien   30

Baillie, Granville Hugh   2704,
2706

Baird, William Raimond   1909

Baju, Charles   739

Baker, David Erskine   3495

Baker, Robert A.   4252

Baker, Theodore   2755-2756

Baku. Institut istorii partii
  1669

Bakunina, Tat'iana A.   1670

Bāla Subrahmanyam   1261

Balbin, Bohuslav Alois   3472

Baldinger, Ernst Gottfried   4073,
  4087

Baldinucci, Filippo   2430-2431

Baldwin, Charles N.   57

Ball, Frances Elrington   3943

Balland, Joseph Antoine Félix
  4074

Balleine, George Reginald   1201

Ballesteros Robles, Luis   1801

Balteau, J.   760

Baltic University, Pinneberg,
  Ger.--SEE: Pinneberg, Ger.
  Baltic University   3304

Baltzell, Winton James   2757

Bamberger, Richard   396

Bañas y Castillo, Raymundo
  2758

Bancroft, Hubert Howe   2086

Bangkok, Thailand. Thammasāt
  Mahāwitthayālai. Institut of
  Public Administration--SEE:
  Bangkok, Thailand. Thamma-
  sāt Mahawitthayālai. Khana
  Ratthaprasāsanasat   1870

Bangkok, Thailand. Thammasāt
  Mahāwitthayālai. Khana Ratthaprasāsanasat   1870

Bantysh-Kamenskii, Dmitrii
  Nikolaevich   1671-1674

Baptestein de Moulières, Antoine
  Joseph Raup de --SEE: Raup
  de Baptestein de Moulières,
  Antoine Joseph   831

Baptie, David   2759-2762

Baquero Almansa, Andrés   1787,
  2432

Bar, Adam   1625

Baranda, Julián Sáinz de --SEE:
  Sáinz de Baranda, Julián
  3888

Baranov, Platon Ivanovich   1732

Baranovskii, Gavriil Vasil'evich
  4795

Barazzetta, Giuseppe   3089

Barbé, Jean Julien   2763

Barbeau, Victor   3555

Barbier, Antoine Alexandre
  704-705, 709

Barbier, Hippolyte   4292

Barbier, Louis Stanislas H.--SEE:
  Barbier, Hippolyte   4292

Barbieux, Walter Senn-. SEE:
  Seen-Barbieux, Walter   1865

Barbosa Machado, Diogo 1640

Bardeen, Charles William 3258

Bardenhewer, Otto 4293

Baring-Gould, Sabine 4294-4295

Barjavel, Casimir François Henri 949

Barker, George Fisher Russell 1175

Barker, Thomas Herbert 4075

Barnard, F. A. 2196

Barnes, Edwin Ninyon Chaloner 2764

Barnet, James 2141

Barnhart, Clarence Lewis 212, 3520

Barnhart, John Hendley 4646

Baron, 1768

Barotti, Giovanni Andrea 1389-1390

Barque, Ali Mohammad 1262, 1595

Barral, Pierre, abbé 58

Barrau-Dihigo, Louis 1760

Barraud, 4076

Barreto, José Parada y --SEE: Parada y Barreto, José 3009

Barria, J. M. 1502

Barril, Roberto 1769

Barros Paiva, Tancredo de--SEE: Paiva, Tancredo de Barros 472

Barroux, Marius 760

Barth, Hans 1841

Bartholomew, Ed Ellsworth 2361

Bartoli, Francesco Saverio 3137

Bartolocci, Guilio 3789

Bartolommeo da S. Angelo, originally Geronimo Barutti 4296

Bartsch, Adam von 2433, 2562

Barutti, Geronimo--SEE: Bartolommeo da S. Angelo, originally Geronimo Barutti 4296

Bašagić, Safvet 2398

Basan, Pierre François 2434

Basel. Universität 1843

Bass, Frank Embrick 2338

Bassett, Herbert Henry 4710

Bastings, Lyndon 4607

Bastos, Antonio Sousa--SEE: Sousa Bastos, Antonio 3193-3194

Bastos, Francisco Antonio Martins--SEE: Martins Bastos, Francisco Antonio 4165

Bateman, John 1093

Bates, William 59

Batines, Paul, vicomte Colomb de
--SEE: Colomb de Batines,
Paul, vicomte   878

Bauchal, Charles   2677

Baudeau de Somaize, Antoine--
SEE: Somaize, Antoine
Baudeau de   844

Baudot, Jules Léon   4297

Baudrier, Henri Louis   3998

Baudrillart, Alfred, Cardinal
4298

Baur, Samuel   60

Bautier, Pierre   2479

Bayerische Akademie der Wissen-
schaften--SEE: Akademie der
Wissenschaften, Munich
1000

Bayle, Antoine Laurent Jessé
4077

Bayle, Pierre   61-62, 85, 100,
191, 1094

Bazin, Germain   2528

Beale, Thomas William   363

Beard, John Relly   63

Beatty, Bessie   2225

Beau, Albin Eduard   3360

Beauchamp, Alphonse de   731-
733

Beaumont, L.   715

Beauvais, Charles Théodore   79

Beazley, John Davidson   2435

Becdelièvre-Hamal, Antoine
Gabriel de, comte   427

Becker, Carl Ferdinand   2765-
2766

Becker, Felix   2631

Becker, Georg   2767

Beckerath, Erwin   4685

Beckett, Sir William a' --SEE:
A'Beckett, Sir William   40

Been, Charles Arnold   2436

Beers (J. H.) and Company,
Chicago   2154, 2190, 2277,
2296-2297, 2312, 2373-2374

Beeton, Samuel Orchart   64

Beffara, Louise François   3138

Bégat, Pierre   811

Bégin, Émile Auguste Nicolas
Jules   914

Behar, Ely   475

Behrend, William   3008

Behrisch, Heinrich Wolfgang
3326, 3607

Beise, Theodor   416

Bejarano, Mario Méndez--SEE:
Méndez Bejarano, Mario
1809-1810, 3875

Beketov, Platon Petrovich   1675

Bekker, Leander Jan de --SEE:
De Bekker, Leander Jan   2816

Belgian American Educational
Foundation, inc.   3259

Belgium. Académie royale des sciences, des lettres et des beaux-arts de Belgique, Brussels--SEE: Académie royale des sciences, des lettres et des beaux-arts de Belgique, Brussels   423-424

Bell, Charles Henry   3944

Bellchambers, Edmund   65

Bellier de La Chavignerie, Émile   2437-2438

Beltrán y de Torres, Francisco   4

Benedek, Marcell   3327

Benedict, George Grenville   2350

Benedictine Monks of St. Augustine's Abbey, Ramsgate--SEE: St. Augustine's Abbey, Ramsgate   4309

Benedictines in Austria   4299

Benesch, Adolph B.   2148

Benet, Francisco Cuenca--SEE: Cuenca Benet, Francisco   3864

Benet, José Blanc y --SEE: Blanc y Benet, José   4083

Benet, William Rose   3328

Bénézit, Emmanuel   2439

Benjamins, H. D.   2397

Bennwitz, Hanspeter   2768-2769, 2882

Bentley, Gerald Eades   3139

Benzing, Joseph   3999-4000

Béraldi, Henri   2440, 2594

Bérard, André   2441

Berce, Vizbulis   3796

Bercenay, François Babié de -- SEE: Babié de Bercenay, François   714-715, 761

Berckelaers, Ferdinand Louis   2442

Berger, Bruno   3652

Berger, Franz   390

Bergholm, Hjalmar   4078

Bergsträsser, Gotthelf   4556

Berisch, Heinrich Wolfgang--SEE: Behrisch, Heinrich Wolfgang   3326, 3607

Beristain de Souza, José Mariano   3901-3902

Berkenhout, John   3496

Berkhof, Hendrikus   1554

Berlin. Akademie der Wissenschaften--SEE: Akademie der Wissenschaften Berlin   962, 1654, 3626, 4572

Berlin. Deutsche Staatsbibliothek   31

Berlin. Universität   3260

Bermann, Moritz   382

Bermúdez, Juan Agustin Ceán--SEE: Ceán Bermúdez, Juan Agustín   2459, 2574, 2598, 2646, 2684

Bernandt, G.   2770

Bernard, Auguste Jospeh   886

Bernard, John Peter   62

Bernard, Manuel Ossorio y --SEE:
Ossorio y Bernard, Manuel
2574, 3346, 3879

Bernardi, Orlando   3343

Bernardo da Bologna   4350

Bernardus de Lutzenburgo   4300

Bernareggi, Adriano, Bp.   4360

Berner, Karl Gustav Heinrich
1071

Bernsdorf, Eduard   2771

Bernsdorf, Wilhelm   4688

Brent, Walther   2443

Bersohn, Mathias   1627

Bertini, Giuseppe   2772

Bertram, Dr., pseud. --SEE:
Schultz, Georg Julius   417

Bertrand, Antoine Louis--SEE:
Bertrand, Louis   4301

Bertrand, Louis   4301

Bertrand, Thomas Bernard   4079

Bertse, V. --SEE: Bĕrce,
Vizbulis   3796

Besnard, Cr   716

Bessone-Aurelj, Antonietta Maria
2444, 2694

Bessonov, Sergeĭ Vasil'evich--
SEE: Bezsonov, Sergeĭ
Vasil'evich   2678

Bettelheim, Anton   394, 964-965

Beuchot, Adrien Jean Quentin
3556

Beuthner, Arnold Christian
1044

Bevel, Maurice Louis   428

Beyaert, Carl   434

Bezsonov, Sergeĭ Vasil'evich
2678

Bhatia, Jagdish   1263

Biagi, Guido   1350-1351

Bibaud, Adèle   497

Bibaud, Maximilien   496-497

Bibaud, Victoria   497

Bibliographisches Institut A. G.,
Mannheim   2966, 3376

Biblioteca Nacional de Chile,
Santiago--SEE: Santiago de
Chile. Biblioteca Nacional
526

Biblioteca Nacional de Venezuela,
Caracas--SEE: Venezuela.
Biblioteca Nacional, Caracas
3898

Bie, Jan Pieter de   4305

Biederstedt, Diederich Hermann
1060, 3708

Biedma, José Juan   339

Bierens de Haan, David   4666

Biermann, Kurt R.   4572

Bigot, Georges   1910

Bilets´kyi, Oleksandr Ivanovych
    3938

Binet, Jacques Philippe Marie
    (Sainte-Preuve, pseud.)
    242

Bingham, Stephen D.   2203

Binheim, Max   2362

Biographical Directory Company,
    New York   2251

Biographical Publishing Company,
    Chicago   2143, 2279, 2371

Biographical Research Bureau,
    inc.   2059-2060

Biomēchanikē Epitheōrēsus   1244

Birch, Thomas   62, 1153

Biržiška, Vaclovas   3798-3799

Bishop, William   3526

Bishop, William John   4072

Bissmarck, Fredrik Gottlieb   4082

Bisson, Alexandre Charles
    Auguste   2776

al-Bītār, 'Abd al-Razzāq   1310

Bitard, Adolphe Louis Émile   82

Bittner, Wilhelm Wilhelmovich 291

Bjarnason, Einar   3945

Bjarnason, Stefán   4807

Bjerkoe, Ethel Hall   2705

Bjerkoe, John Arthur   2705

Blair, Ruth   2134

Blake, Augusto Victorino Alves
    do Sacramento--SEE: Sacra-
    mento Blake, Augusto Victo-
    rino Alves do   483

Blake, John Lauris   83

Blakeney, Jane   1916

Blanc y Benet, José   4083

Blanchard, Charles   2295

Blanding, William F.   2175,
    2311

Blaze, François Henri Joseph,
    called Castil-Blaze   2777

Bliss, Philip   1190

Bloch, Maks Abramovich   4654

Block, Andrew   1089

Blöndal, Lárus H.   4084

Blok, Petrus Johannes   1562

Blokh, Maks Abramovich--SEE:
    Bloch, Maks Abramovich
    4654

Blom, Eric   2778, 2884

Blomstedt, Kaarlo Viljanti   700

Bloom, James Harvey   4085

Blum, Robert   3135

Blume, Friedrich   2992

Boalch, Donald Howard   2779

Boalt, Gunnar   4250

Boase, Frederick   1095

Boase, George Clement   1195,
    3498

Boatner, Mark Mayo   1917

Bobillier, Marie   2780

Bobolinēs, Kōnstantinos
    Antōniou   1244

Bobolinēs, Spyros Ant.   1244

Bod, Péter   3711

Böckh, Franz Heinrich   3609

Boelza, Igor' Fedorovich   2781

Börner, Friedrich   4086-4087

Boëthius, Bertil   1830

Boffito, Giuseppe   4306

Bogardus, Emory Stephen   4698

Bogdanov, Anatolii Petrovich
    4630

Bohatta, Hanns   395, 955-956

Bohman, Nils Axel Erik   1827

Boigues, Francisco Pons--SEE:
    Pons Boigues, Francisco
    4765

Boiovich, Milan Mikhailovich
    1676

Boisard, François   872

Boisdeffre, Pierre de   205, 3557

Boisjolin, Jacques François Marie
    Vieilh de --SEE: Vieilh de
    Boisjolin, Jacques François
    Marie   242

Bois-Robert, Joseph Lavallée,
    marquis de --SEE: Lavallée,
    Joseph, marquis de Bois-
    Robert   805

Boissière, Jean Galtier-. SEE:
    Galtier-Boissière, Jean
    783

Bolek, Francis   2064

Bolio Ontiveros, Edmundo   1522

Bollandus, Joannes   4275

Bollen, Fabian   4307

Bollo, Sarah   3903

Bolm, August   84

Bol'shaiā Sovetskaiā entsiklopediiā
    4578

Bolsover, Godfrey Rowland   3237

Bolton, Charles Knowles   1918

Bolton, Geoffrey Curgenven   372

Bolton, Theodore   2446, 4001

Bompiani, firm, publishers,
    Milan   3342

Bompiani, Valentino Silvio, conte
    3340-3342

Bonaccorsi, Alfredo   2782

Bonafons, Louis Abel de known as
    Abbé de Fontenay   2447

Bonamici, Diomede   1334

Bonari, Valdemiro   4308

Bond, Maurice F.   4450

Bone, Philip James   2783

Bonhôte, James Henri   1853

Bonino, Giovanni Giacomo   4088

Bonnaffé, Edmond   2448

Bonnegarde, abbé de   85

Bonneville, Frédéric   827

Bonomi, Lino   4579

Boone, H. H.   2254

Booth, Lavaughn Venchael   4532

Borba, Tomas   2784

Bordier, Henri   791

Borel d'Hauterive, André François
   Joseph   739

Boren, Dale   2288

Boren, Lyle H.   2288

Borja Pavón, Francisco de --SEE:
   Pavón, Francisco de Borja
   1795

Born, Ignaz, Edler von   646

Bornemann, Johann Gottfried   86

Bornmüller, Franz   3331

Borowik, Hans   3220

Borozdin, Il'ia Nikolaevich   4764

Bos, Han   2785

Boston, John, of Bury   3537

Boston evening transcript--SEE:
   Boston transcript (i. e. Boston
   evening transcript)   1883

Boston Press Club   2187

Boston transcript (i. e. Boston
   evening transcript)   1883

Botanical Garden, New York--SEE:
   New York. Botanical Garden
   4646

Bouchot, Henri François Xavier
   Marie   2416

Boulger, George Simonds   4631

Boulliot, Jean Baptiste Joseph
   860

Bourdon, Isidore--SEE: Bourdon,
   Jean Baptiste Isidore   4089

Bourdon, Jean Baptiste Isidore
   4089

Bourg, Edme Théodore, known as
   Saint Edme--SEE: Saint-Edme,
   Edme Théodore Bourg, known
   as   841

Bourloton, Edgar   837

Bourquelot, Félix   3590

Boursin, Elphège   740

Boutière, Jean   3596

Bover de Rosselló, Joaquín María
   1802, 3859-3860

Bovier de Fontenelle, Bernard Le--
   SEE: Fontenelle, Bernard Le
   Bovier de   4587

Bowen (A. W.) and Company, Chicago   2112, 2140, 2221, 2295

Bowen, Robert O.   3398

Boyd, Charles Newell   3018

Boylan, Elaine   3417

Boyle, Esmeralda   2179

Boys, Auguste du --SEE: Du Boys, Auguste   898

Bozzo, Giuseppe   1406

Bozzoli, Giuseppe Maria   1346

Bracher, Samuel Veale   1096

Brachvogel, Albert Emil   967

Bradford, Alden   2226

Bradley, John William   2449

Braeuer, Walter   4699

Braĭnina, Berta I͡Akovlevna
3846

Brainne, Charles   924

Bramsen, Ludvig Ernst   2993,
3477

Branden, Franz Jozef Peter van
den   3488

Brandstetter, Josef Leopold
1842

Brant & Fuller, Madison, Wis.
2353

Brassard, Gérard   4310

Braun, J. B. M.   741

Braun, Sidney David   3558

Braunfels, Otto--SEE: Brunfels,
Otto   4096

Brebion, Antoine   492, 2392

Bredow, Claus von   968

Breen, Genevieve Rose   3425

Bréghot du Lut, Claude   905

Bremen. Künstlerverein--SEE:
Künstlerverein, Bremen
1037

Bremer, Friedrich   2786

Brenet, Michel, pseud. --SEE:
Bobillier, Marie   2780

Brennan, Joseph Fletcher   2276

Brenni, Vito Joseph   3399

Brennsohn, Isidorus   4090-4092

Brewer, A.   450

Brewster, H. Pomeroy   4311

Bricka, Carl Frederik   657, 660

Bringas, Esperanza Velázquez--
SEE: Velázquez Bringas,
Esperanza   3894

Brinton, Clarence Crane   3261

Brismontier, G. L.   3562

Brissot-Thivars, Louis Saturnin
742

British Museum. Dept. of Prints
and Drawings   2412-2413

Brito Aranha, Pedro Wenceslau de
3816

Britten, Frederick James   2706

Britten, James   4631

Britton, John   2679

Brocchi, Filippo   1414

Brockbank, Edward Mansfield
4093-4094

Brockbank, William   4094

Brockelmann, Carl   3438-3439

Broman, Natanael   3094

Bromley, Henry   1099

Brooks, Ulysses Robert   3946

Brown, G. H.   4196

Brown, George W.   507

Brown, James Duff   2787-2788

Brown, John Henry   2366

Brown, John Howard   1926,
   1962, 2021

Brown, Stephen James Meredith
   6

Brown University   1919

Browne, Edith Ophelia   1238

Browne, Nina Eliza   1

Browne, Walter   3211

Browning, David Clayton   3499

Bruce, John Edward   87

Bruck, Franz Maier-. SEE: Maier-
   Bruck, Franz   396

Brucker, Jacob--SEE: Brucker,
   Johann Jakob   969, 3610

Brucker, Johann Jakob   969,
   3610

Bruckner, Albert Theophil   1860

Brückner, Hans   3036

Brüggemann, August Ferdinand
   4095

Brümmer, Franz   3611-3614

Brünnow, Rudolf Ernst   3437

Brugmans, Hajo   1567

Bruijn, Caspar Adam Laurens van
   Troostenburg de   4312

Brulliot, Franz   2414

Brun, Carl   2614

Brun-Durand, Justin   883

Brune, Paul   2450

Brunet, Gustave   704-705, 709

Brunetti, Enrico Castreca-. SEE:
   Castreca-Brunetti, Enrico
   3752

Brunfels, Otto   4096

Brunotte, Heinz   4364

Brunsfeld, Othon--SEE: Brunfels,
   Otto   4096

Brussels. Académie royale des
   sciences, des lettres et des
   beaux-arts de Belgique--SEE:
   Académie royale des sciences,
   des lettres et des beaux-arts
   de Belgique, Brussels   423-
   424

Bruxelles--SEE: Brussels

Bruyn, Caspar Adam Laurens van
   Troostenburg de --SEE:
   Bruijn, Caspar Adam Laurens
   van Troostenburg de   4312

Bruzelius, Anders Johan   4097

Bryan, Michael   2451, 2615

Brydges, Sir Samuel Egerton
   1100, 3525

Bucharest. Cartea Românească--
SEE: Cartea Românească,
Bucharest 1657

Buchberger, Michael, Bp. 4412

Buchwald, Wolfgang 3471

Buckeridge, B. 2587

Buckland, Charles Edward 1264

Buddingh', Cornelis 3332

Bücken, Ernst 2789

Buel, James William 1958

Bündnerische Kulturelle Arbeitsgemeinschaft 2452

Buenos Aires. Instituto de Estudios
Biográficos--SEE: Instituto de
Estudios Biográficos, Buenos
Aires. 346

Büsching, Anton Friedrich 89

Bulgakov, Fedor Il'ich 2453-
2454

Bull, Edvard 1588

Bull, Storm 2740

Bullart, Isaac 88

Bunker, Carol 1101

Burckel, Christian E. 302

Bureau des documentations arabes
--SEE: Maktab al-Dirāsāt al-
'Arabīyah 1324

Bureau of Musical Research
2982-2988

Burke, Ashworth Peter 1104

Burke, Bernard--SEE: Burke,
Sir John Bernard 1102-1107

Burke, John 1102-1103, 1107

Burke, Sir John Bernard 1102-
1107

Burke, William Jeremiah 3400

Burman, Caspar--SEE: Burmann,
Caspar 1555

Burmann, Caspar 1555

Burn, John Hervey 2821

Burpee, Laurence Johnstone
500

Burr, N. R. 28

Burrage, Walter Lincoln 4153

Bursian, Konrad 3461

Burtchall, George Dames 1302

Burton, Jack 2790

Burton, John Richard 1238

Burton, Richard 2118

Bus de Warnaffe, Charles, vicomte
du --SEE: Du Bus de Warnaffe,
Charles, vicomte 434

Bushnell, George Herbert 2455,
4008

Busserolle, Jacques Xavier Carré
de --SEE: Carré de Busserolle,
Jacques Xavier 894

Butler, Alban 4286, 4313-4315

Butler, Harold Beresford 1150

Bygdén, Anders Leonard 1815

C

C., E., de M.   718

C., G. E. --SEE: Cokayne,
George Edward   1116-1117

C., U. --SEE: Capitaine, Ulysse
448

C. R. B. Educational Foundation,
inc.--SEE: Belgian American
Educational Foundation, inc.
3259

Caballero, Luis Eduardo Nieto--SEE:
Nieto Caballero, Luis Eduardo
629

Cabany, E. de Saint Maurice--SEE:
Saint Maurice Cabany, E. de
206

Cabany, J. Maurice--SEE: Saint
Maurice Cabany, E. de   206

Cabaton, Antoine   2392

Cadenas y Vicent, Vicente de
1780

Caetani, Leone, principe di Teano
1347

Calcagno, Francisco   636

Caldwell, Joshua William   3947

California. Secretary of State
2087

California. University. Lawrence
Radiation Laboratory, Livermore   4675

Callisen, Adolph Carl Peter
4098

Calmell, Josep Rodergas i --SEE:
Rodergas i Calmell, Josep
1763

Calmet, Augustin   855

Calvoli, Giovanni Cinelli--SEE:
Cinelli Calvoli, Giovanni
3746

Cambas, Manuel Rivera--SEE:
Rivera Cambas, Manuel
1544

Cambiaso y Verdes, Nicolás María
de   1791

Cambridge. University   1108

Cambridge. University. Peterhouse   1109-1111

Camden Pratt, Alfred T. --SEE:
Pratt, Alfred T. Camden
1170

Cameron, Sir Charles Alexander
4099

Camesasca, Ettore   2488

Campbell, John A.   2220

Campillo y Casamor, Toribio del
3861

Campori, Giuseppe   2456-2457

Campos de Castro de Azevedo
Soares, Eduardo de   1641

Canadian Broadcasting Corporation   2791

Canadian Library Association
2792, 4002-4003

Canadian Music Library Association   2792

Canadian Newspaper Service, ltd.
502

Canals, Santiago Olives--SEE:
Olives Canals, Santiago   1786

Canberra, Australia. Common-
wealth National Library--SEE:
Canberra Australia. National
Library   373

Canberra, Australia. National
Library   373

Candé, Roland de   2793

Caneda, Domingo Figarola-. SEE:
Figarola-Caneda, Domingo
635

Cankar, Izidor   2406

Cánovas, Antonio--SEE: Cánovas
del Castillo y Vallejo, Antonio
2458

Cánovas del Castillo y Vallejo,
Antonio   2458

Canseco, Vicente Díez--SEE:
Díez Canseco, Vicente   115

Cantù, Ignazio   4580

Cao-viên-Trai   2393

Capeille, Jean   933

Capitaine, Ulysse   448

Capitol Publishing Company
2110, 2126

Caple, S. Canynge   3222

Capparoni, Pietro   4101

Capponi, Giovanni Battista   1366

Capuchins   4317

Caputo, Vincenzo   3741-3742

Caracas. Biblioteca Nacional--SEE:
Venezuela. Biblioteca Na-
cional, Caracas   3898

Caranfil, Andrew G.   1655

Carayon, Auguste   4288

Carcavellos [pseud. ?] --SEE:
Campos de Castro de Azevedo
Soares, Eduardo de   1641

Cárdenas Ramírez, Julio C.
1604, 2386

Carey, Arthur Merwyn   4781-
4782

Carlevale, Joseph William   2120

Carlo, pseud. --SEE: Herzel, Carl
Heinrich   2928

Carlo, Agustín Millares--SEE:
Millares Carlo, Agustín
3876

Carmin, Itzhak J. --SEE: Karpman,
Itzhak J.   4582

Carmoly, Eliakim   4102

Carnandet, Jean Baptiste   4275

Carnoy, Henry   90, 743-749,
3333, 4103-4104, 4318, 4739

Carpeaux, Otto Maria, pseud.
3813

Carpelan, Tor   696, 698, 3310

Carpi, Leone   1348

Carrasco Puente, Rafael   3904

Carrasco y Sayz, Adolfo   1770

Carré de Busserolle, Jacques
Xavier   894

Carreño, Alberto María   1531

Carrère, Joseph Barthélemy François   4105

Carrión, Antonio   1523

Cartea Românească, Bucharest
1657

Carter, Herbert James   369

Carter, Nathan Franklin   4319

Carter, S. M.   521

Carton, Charles Louis   429

Carvalho, Francisco Augusto Martins de --SEE: Martins de
Carvalho, Francisco Augusto
1643

Cary, Max   225

Casabal, Apolinario C.   350

Casamor, Toribio del Campillo y
--SEE: Campillo y Casamor,
Toribio del   3861

Casati, Giovanni   3743-3744

Cascales y Muñoz, José   3862

Casey, Albert Eugene   4106

Castán Palomar, Fernando   1789

Castañeda y Alcover, Vicente
3872

Casteele, Pierre van de   4107

Castellanus, Petrus--SEE: Casteele,
Pierre van de   4107

Castil-Blaze, François Henri Joseph Blaze, called--SEE:
Blaze, Francois Henri Joseph,
called Castil-Blaze   2777

Castillo, Jerónimo   1524

Castillo, Raymundo Bañas y --SEE:
Bañas y Castillo, Raymundo
2758

Castillo y Vallejo, Antonio Cánovas
del--SEE: Cánovas del Castillo y Vallejo, Antonio   2458

Castreca-Brunetti, Enrico   3752

Castro de Azevedo Soares, Eduardo
de Campos de --SEE: Campos
de Castro de Azevedo Soares,
Eduardo de   1641

Castro y Velasco, Acisclo Antonio
Palomino de --SEE: Palomino
de Castro y Velasco, Acisclo
Antonio   2576-2577

Cateaux, Albert   440

Cates, William Leist Readwin
92

Cathcart, William   4320

Cattell, Jacques   3263, 4576

Caulfield, James   187

Cave, William   4324

Ceán Bermúdez, Juan Agustín
2459, 2574, 2598, 2646, 2684

Cecchini, Riccardo   1349

Cederberg, Arno Rafael   410

Celletti, Rodolfo   2875

Centre français du théatre   3143

Centro di studi filosofici di Gal-
larate   4237

Cerf de la Viéville, Jean Philippe
le--SEE: Le Cerf de la Viéville,
Jean Philippe   4408

Cerfberr de Médelsheim, Alphonse 856

Cermignano, C. de Sterlich, marquis (or marchese) di --SEE: Sterlich, C. de, marquis di Cermignano 3778

Černík, Berthold Otto 4325

Černušák, Gracian 2794, 3012

Cerveau, René 4326-4329

Česká akademie věd a umění, Prague 3012, 4581

Chabannes, J. A., firm, publishers 426

Chabeaussière, Ange Jacques Marie Poissin La --SEE: La Chabeaussière, Ange Jacques Marie Poissin 840

Chagas, Manuel Pinheiro--SEE: Pinheiro Chagas, Manuel 1644

Challamel, Augustin 740

Chalmers, Alexander 97

Chalmot, Jacques Alexandre de 1556

Chaman Lal Khosla--SEE: Khosla, Chaman Lal 3293

Chambers, John 1239

Chambers, Robert 1211, 3500

Chamot, Mary 2630

Champcenetz, Louis René Quentin de Richebourg, marquis de 836, 3591

Champlin, John Denison 2460, 2795

Chang, Ch'ün 536

Chang, Ts'ai-ling 4247

Chao, Kuo-ts'ai

Chao, Yen-sheng 597

Chapelles, Amador Grillon des-- SEE: Grillon des Chapelles, Amador 893

Chaplain, Julien Le --SEE: Le Chaplain, Julien 839

Chapman Publishing Company, Chicago 2079, 2111, 2125, 2285, 2292

Charitius, Andreas 1040

Charles, Robert A. 3398

Charlesworth, Hector Willoughby 505

Charney, Samuel 3790

Charnock, John 1114

Charteris, Lawrence 3514

Charters, Samuel Barclay 2796

Chase, Henry 2173

Châteauneuf, Agricol Hippolyte de Lapierre de --SEE: Lapierre de Châteauneuf, Agricol Hippolyte de 803

Chatterton, Frederick 2691

Chaudon, Louis Mayeul 99, 223, 4349

Chaudru de Raynal, Louis Hector-- SEE: Raynal, Louis Hector Chaudru de 3956

Chauffepié, Jacques Georges de
85, 100

Chaumeil,   abbé   864

Chavignerie, Émile Bellier de la--
SEE: Bellier de La Chavignerie, Émile   2437-2438

Chelmońska, Marja (Korwin-
Szymanowska)   1628

Ch'ên, Ch'i-t'ien   544

Chên, I-lin   545

Ch'ên, Mêng-lei   536

Ch'ên, Nai-ch'ien   546

Chennevières, Philippe de --SEE:
Chennevières-Pointel, Philippe, marquis de   2461,
2561

Chennevieres-Pointel, Philippe,
marquis de   2461, 2561

Chéreau, Achille   4108

Chernopiatov, Viktor Il'ich   1678-
1680

Chéron, Paul   3559

Chesnaye-Desbois, François Alex-
andre Aubert de la--SEE: La
Chesnaye-Desbois, François
Alexandre Aubert de   799

Chesnel, Adolphe de   3560

Chesurolles, Désiré   101

Chevalier, Cyr Ulysse Joseph
102

Chia, I-chün   547

Chiang, Liang-fu   548

Chien, I-chi   549

Ch'ien hu tiao t'u, psued.   550

Chih, Wei-ch'eng   551

Chin, Pu-ying   4052

Chin-liang   552

China weekly review   613

Chinchilla, Anastasio   4109

Chinese Communist Party--SEE:
Chung-kuo kung ch'an tang

Chinese Students' Alliance in the U-
nited States of America   617

Chioccarelli, Bartolommeo   3745

Chiocco, Andrea   4110

Chirinos Soto, Enrique   1603

Chitrao, Siddhesvara Shastri
1265-1267

Chodynicki, Ignacy   1629

Chomiński, Józef   3072

Choron, Alexandre Étienne   2797

Chōsen Kōbunsha, Seoul, Korea
1489

Chou mo pao she, Hongkong   556

Christensen, Carl Frederik A 4632

Christian-Albrechts-Universität,
Kiel--SEE: Kiel. Universität
3282

Chu, Cho-ts'un   557

Chu, Te-chün   558

Chujoy, Anatole   3144

Chung hua shu chü   559

Chung yang wen wu kung ying she
    561

Chuzhak-Nasimovich, N. F. --SEE:
    Nasimovich, Nikolai Fedoro-
    vich   1740

Chybiński, Adolf   2798

Cibber, Theophilus   3501

Cinelli Calvoli, Giovanni   3746

Cinti, Decio   3747

Un Citoyen actif--SEE: Rivarol,
    Antoine   836

Citron, Samuel Loeb   1450

Clairval, abbé de, pseud. --SEE:
    Dupin, Louis Ellies   4755-
    4756

Clarac, Pierre   3341

Clark, Elmer Talmage   4534

Clark, George Lindenberg   4657

Clark, James Henry   4111

Clarke, A. Mason   2799

Clarke, J. B., firm, publisher,
    Manchester, N. H.   2237

Clayton, Peter   2866

Cleave, Egbert   2276, 4112

Clement, Clara (Erskine) -- SEE:
    Waters, Clara (Erskine)
    Clement   2652-2654

Clément, Felix   2800

A Clergyman and others   4304

Clifford, John Herbert   2801-2802

Closset, François   3445

Cloucquius, Andreas   3294

Clouzot, Henri   2462

Club of Nobody's Friends   1115

Cobbett, Walter Willson   2803

Coburgero, Anton, pseud. -- SEE:
    Wetzel, Johann Caspar   1039

Cochran, Mildred W.   2954

Cochrane, William   501

Code, Joseph Bernard   4332

Codelli, Pietro Antonio   3748

Codignola, Arturo   1352

Coelho, José María Latino--SEE:
    Latino Coelho, José María
    1642

Coeuroy, André   2804

Cohen, Harry   4582

Coiffier de Verseux, Henri Louis
    750

Cokayne, George Edward   1115-17

Colin, Hubert   861

Colin, Paul   2463

College Art Association of America
    2523, 2531

Collegio araldico, Rome--SEE:
    Rome (City) Collegio araldico
    1361

Collier, Jeremy   201

Collin, Edvard   1751

Collin de Plancy, Jacques Albin
   Simon   4234

Colmeiro y Penido, Miguel   4633

Colnaghi, Sir Dominic Ellis   2464

Cologne. Universität   970

Colomb de Batines, Paul, vicomte
   878

Colorado Press Association, inc.
   2115

Columbia Civic Library Association, Washington, D. C.
   4004

Columbia University. Libraries.
   Avery Architectural Library
   2415

Columbian centinel   1882

Colvile, Frederick Leigh   1235

Colville, Frederick Leigh--SEE:
   Colvile, Frederick Leigh
   1235

Colvin, Howard Montagu   2680

Comanducci, Agostino Mario   2465

Combles, Louis Charles, comte
   Waroquier de Méricourt de La
   Mothe de --SEE: Waroquier de
   Méricourt de La Mothe de
   Combles, Louis Charles,
   comte   849

Comley, William J.   2183

Commonwealth Agricultural Bureaux.   4783

Commonwealth Fund. Division of
   International Fellowships
   3262

Commonwealth National Library
   of Australia--SEE: Canberra,
   Australia. National Library
   373

Como, Ugo da   1353

Comrie, John Dixon   4113

Conde, Alfredo O.   3381

Confederazione fascista dei professionisti e degli artisti
   1407

Congreso Médico Dominicano.
   3d, Ciudad Trujillo (1944)
   4114

Conjeeveram Hayavadana Rao, rao
   sahib--SEE: Hayavadana, Rao
   Conjeeveram, rao sahib
   1275

Connaissance des arts   2712

Conolly, Matthew Foster   1196

Conron, Brandon   3536

Consejo Superior de Investigaciones Científicas, Spain--SEE:
   Spain. Consejo Superior de
   Investigaciones Científicas
   4612

Cook, Fiona (Hale)   3989

Cooper, Charles Henry   1119

Cooper, Clarissa Burnham   3561

Cooper, Martin   2805

Cooper, Thompson   104, 1119

Coover, James B.   2741

Coppe, Paul   3446

Coquet, Lucien   688

Corbet, August   2745

Corminas y Guell, Juan   3457

Corna, Andrea   2467

Cornel, Th.   1656

Cornell University. Medical College, New York   4115

Corning, Howard McKinley
2291

Cornwall, C. N.   2216

Corte, Andrea della   2806

Corte, Bartolomeo   4116

Cortés, José Domingo   335,
3905

Cortés, Narciso Alonso--SEE:
Alonso Cortés, Narciso
1766

Cortijo, Francisco Agramonte y --
SEE: Agramonte y Cortijo,
Francisco   45

Corwin, Charles Edward   4334

Cossio, José María de   3223

Costa, Francisco Augusto Pereira
da --SEE: Pereira da Costa,
Francisco Augusto   480

Costa e Silva, José María da
3814

Costanti, Pablo Pérez--SEE:
Pérez Costanti, Pablo   2585

Coston, Henry   706

Cotarelo y Mori, Emilio   4005

Cotterell, Howard Herschel
2707

Cotton, Charles Philip   4336

Cotton, Henry   4335-4336

Couailhac, Louis   752

Couceiro Freijomil, Antonio
3601

Cougny, Gaston   762, 837

Couling, Samuel   562

Coulson, John   4478

Cour de cassation, France--SEE:
France. Cour de cassation
3956-3957

Courcelles, Jean Baptiste Pierre
Jullien de   753-754, 840

Courde de Montaiglon, Anatole
de --SEE: Montaiglon, Anatole de Courde de   2551

Coursey, Oscar William   2321

Court, G. de le --SEE: Le Court,
G. de   419

Courtney, William Prideaux 3498

Cousin, Charles Yves, called
Cousin d'Avallon   4337

Cousin, John William   3499,
3502

Cousin d'Avallon, Charles Yves
Cousin, called   4337

Cowan, William   2807

Cox, James   4790

Coxeter, Thomas   3501

Coyle, William   3401

Craig, Clifford   2468

Craig, Edna   3122

Le Crapouillot   783

Crasso, Lorenzo   3339

Crawford, Dirom Grey   4117

Crawford, Geddings Harry
    2319

Creagh, Sir O'Moore   1120

Crescimbeni, Giovanni Mario
    1368, 1380

Crespi, Luigi   2550

Cressy, Earl Herbert   4338

Creutzenfeld, Stephanus Hierony-
    mus de Vigiliis von--SEE:
    Vigiliis von Creutzenfeld,
    Stephanus Hieronymus de
    4211

Criado y Domínguez, Juan Pedro
    3863

Crone, John Smyth   1300

Crosby, Nathan   1923

Cross, Frank Leslie   4452

Crosse, Gordon   4450

Crowell, Evelyn (Miller)   2341

Crowest, Frederick James   2808

Crozet, Félix   2809-2810

Cubas, Antonio Garcia--SEE:
    Garcia Cubas, Antonio
    1528

Cuenca Benet, Francisco   3864

Cuencar, Heriberto Zapata--SEE:
    Zapata Cuencar, Heriberto
    3129

Cuevas, Eusebio Julián Zarco--
    SEE: Zarco Cuevas, Eusebio
    Julián   4550

Cuisin, J. P. R.   3562

Cullum, George Washington
    1924-1925

Cummings, William Hayman
    2811

Cupilli, Giuseppe Ferrari-. SEE:
    Ferrari-Cupilli, Giuseppe
    2399

Curinier, C. E.   764

Cushing, William   1890-1891

Cutolo, Vicente Osvaldo   337

Cutter, William Richard   1895,
    2186

Cymmrodorion Society, London
    1222-1223

Cyrankiewicz, Stanisław   1630

Czikann, Johann Jacob Heinrich
    3473

Czvittinger, David--SEE: Czwit-
    tinger, David   3712

Czwittinger, David   3712

D

D. J. R.   112

D'Acquaviva, Giovanni Panelli--
SEE: Panelli d'Acquaviva,
Giovanni   4182

Da Como, Ugo--SEE: Como, Ugo
da   1353

D'Afflitto, Eustachio--SEE: Afflitto, Eustachio d'   3731

Dagher, Joseph Assad--SEE:
Dāghir, Yūsuf As'ad   3440

Dāghir, Yūsuf As'ad   3440

Dahl, Svend   659-660, 3477

Dahlmann, Peter   32

Dai Nihon Jimmei Jisho Kankōkai
1423

The Daily chronicle, Georgetown,
British Guiana   488

Daily Kennebec journal, Augusta,
Me.   2174

D'Alembert, Jean Lerond--SEE:
Alembert, Jean Lerond d'
711

Dalphin, Marcia   4029

D'Alverny, Marie Thérèse--SEE:
Alverny, Marie Thérèse d'
4752

Damański, Josef   2812

D'Amiens, Frédéric Dubois--SEE:
Dubois d'Amiens, Frédéric
4125

Damirón, Rafael   675

Dampier, John Lucius Smith-.   --
SEE: Smith-Dampier, John
Lucius   1177

D'Ancona, Alessandro--SEE:
Ancona, Alessandro d'
3736

D'Ancona, Paolo--SEE: Ancona,
Paolo d'   2425

Dandia, Milap Chand   1282

Daniel, Ernest   937

Daniel, Hippolyte   937

Daniel de Saint-Anthoine, J. Hip-
polyte--SEE: Daniel, Hip-
polyte   937

Danilevskiĭ, Aleksandr Ivanovich
Mikhaĭlovskiĭ-   --SEE:
Mikhaĭlovskiĭ-Danilevskiĭ,
Aleksandr Ivanovich   1705

Dannett, Sylvia G. L.   1928

Dannheimer, Wilhelm   4340

Dansten, Esli   4032

Dantès, Alfred Langue   107, 887

Đào-văn-Hôi   2394

Darby, William Dermot   2954

Dargan, Marion   1884

D'Argenville, Antoine Joseph
Dezallier--SEE: Dezallier d'
Argenville, Antoine Joseph
2473

Darmon, J. E.   2469-2470

Darsy, Eugène   110

Darthenay, V.   3146

Das Gupta, Jyotish Chandra
1268

Das Gupta, Tarapada   1280

Dassori, Carlo   2813

Davalillo, María   2814

D'Avallon, Charles Yves Cousin,
called Cousin--SEE: Cousin
d'Avallon, Charles Yves
Cousin, called   4337

Davenport, Richard Alfred   108,
138, 2588

Davidson, Gladys   2815

Davidson, J. Leroy   2523

Davies, Robert   4006

Dávila, Vicente   2385

Davis, William Thomas   3948

Dawson, Warren Royal   4754

De Angelis, Alberto--SEE: Angelis, Alberto de   2749

De Backer, Aloys--SEE: Backer,
Aloys de   4288

De Backer, Augustin--SEE: Backer, Augustin de   4288-4289

Debarbouiller, J.   924

De Beauchamp, Alphonse--SEE:
Beauchamp, Alphonse de

De Bekker, Leander, Jan   2816

De Bie, Jan Pieter--SEE: Bie,
Jan Pieter de   4305

De Boisdeffre, Pierre--SEE:
Boisdeffre, Pierre de

Debray, Nicolas Antoine Gabriel
3563

De Bré, Alvin Jack   4217

De Bruijn, Caspar Adam Laurens
van Troostenburg--SEE: Bruijn, Caspar Adam Laurens van
Troostenburg de   4312

Décembre, Joseph   755

De Chalmot, Jacques Alexandre--
SEE Chalmot, Jacques Alexandre de   1556

Dechambre, Amedée   4122

De Chesnel, Adolphe--SEE:
Chesnel, Adelphe de   3560

Deckherr, Johann   33

De Courde de Montaiglon, Anatole
--SEE: Montaiglon, Anatole
de Courde de   2551

Deen, Edith   4267

De Feller, Franz Xavier--SEE:
Feller, Franz Xavier de
121, 433, 4368

De Fère, Fortuné Guyot--SEE:
Guyot de Fère, Fortuné

De Ferrière, Claude Joseph--SEE:
Ferrière, Claude Joseph de

De Fleury, Paul, comte--SEE:
Fleury, Paul de, comte   2862

De Fontenelle, Bernard Le Bovier
--SEE: Fontenelle, Bernard
Le Bovier de   4587

De Fouchy, Jean Paul Grandjean--
SEE: Grandjean de Fouchy,
Jean Paul   4591

De Frondeville, Henri--SEE:
Frondeville, Henri de 919

Degener, Hermann August Ludwig 1013

De Grote, Peter W. 3243

Deichmanske bibliotek, Oslo
1582

De Jong, Pieter--SEE: Jong,
Pieter de 1311

De Kempenaer, A. --SEE:
Kempenaer A. de 1552

De Kerdanet, Daniel Louis Olivier Marie Miorcec--SEE:
Miorcec de Kerdanet, Daniel
Louis Olivier Marie 870

Dekkers, René 3949

De La Chesnaye-Desbois, François Alexandre Aubert--SEE:
La Chesnaye-Desbois, François Alexandre Aubert de 799

De La Montagne, Victor Alexis--
SEE: La Montagne, Victor Alexis de 421

De La Rue, Pieter--SEE: Rue,
Pieter de la 1569

Delaney, John J. 4341

De Laporte, Joseph--SEE: Laporte, Joseph de 3574

Del Arco, Ricardo--SEE: Arco,
Ricardo del 1788

De la Viéville, Jean Philippe Le
Cerf--SEE: Le Cerf de la
Viéville, Jean Philippe 4508

Delbosc, Raymond Foulché- --
SEE: Foulché-Delbosc 1760

Delecourt, Jules Victor 419-
420

Délégation générale a là recherche
scientifique et technique--SEE:
France. Délégation générale
à la recherche scientifique et
technique 4588

Della Corte, Andrea--SEE: Corte,
Andrea della 2806

Delorme, Jacques Raige- --SEE:
Raige-Delorme, Jacques
4120, 4122

Del Río, Luis Francisco Prieto--
SEE: Prieto del Río, Luis
Francisco

Del Toro, Josefina--SEE: Toro,
Josefina del 1496

Deltour, Félix 3583

De Luca, Ignaz--SEE: Luca,
Ignaz de 393

Delvenne, Mathieu Guillaume
431

De Maeyer, Edward Anton--SEE:
Maeyer, Edward Anton de 693

De Mairan, Jean Jacques Dortous--
SEE: Mairan, Jean Jacques
Dortous de 4600

De Manne, Edmond Denis--SEE:
Manne, Edmond Denis de 707

De Manne, Louis Charles Joseph--
SEE: Manne, Louis Charles
Joseph de 707

De Masi, Henri Armand 3205

Demby, Stefan 3808

De Menil, Alexander Nicolas 3402

De Meulemeester, Maurice--SEE:
Meulemeester, Maurice de
4435

Demmin, Auguste Frédéric
2471

De Montaiglon, Anatole de Courde
--SEE: Montaiglon, Anatole
de Courde de   2551

De Montet, Albert--SEE: Montet,
Albert de   1859

Demorizi, Emilio Rodríguez--SEE:
Rodríguez Demorizi, Emilio

Denina, Carlo   3615

Dent, John Charles   506

Denver. Public Library   3427

Denver Press Club   2124

Depéry, Jean Irenée, Bp.   851,
4342

De Piles, Roger--SEE: Piles,
Roger de   2586-2587

De Potter, Frans--SEE: Potter,
Frans de   3491

De Propriac, Catherine Joseph
Ferdinand Girard--SEE:
Girard de Propriac, Catherine
Joseph Ferdinand   136

Deputazione di storia patria per le
provincie modenesi--SEE:
Modena (Province) Deputazione
di storia patria per le provincie
modenesi   4753

De Raillicourt, Dominique Labarre
--SEE: Labarre de Railli-
court, Dominique   174

De Raynal, Louis Hector Chaudru
--SEE: Raynal, Louis Hector
Chaudru de   3956

De Reume, Auguste Joseph--SEE:
Reume, Auguste Joseph de
4038-4039

Derie, Louis   461

Derossi, Onorato   3749

Derthick, Wilbur M.   2817

De Sainte-Palaye, Jean Baptiste
de La Curne--SEE: Sainte-
Palaye, Jean Baptiste de la
Curne   3592

De Salverte, François, comte--
SEE: Salverte, François de,
comte   2727

De Santeul, E. N. F. --SEE:
Santeul, E. N. F. de   3563

Desbois, Francois Alexandre de
La Chesnaye- --SEE: La
Chesnaye-Desbois, Francois
Alexandre Aubert de   799

Descamps, Jean Baptiste   2472-
2473

Un Descendant de Rivarol--SEE:
Cuisin, J. P. R.   3562

Des Essarts, Alfred Stanislas
Langlois   756

Desessarts, Nicolas Toussaint
Lemoyne   756, 3564

De Seyn, Eugène--SEE: Seyn,
Eugène de   462, 3450

Desmadryl, Narciso   532

Des Odoars, Antoine Étienne
Nicolas Fantin--SEE: Fantin
des Odoars, Antoine Étienne
Nicolas   3563

Desplaces, Eugène Ernest   80

Desportes, Narcisse Henri François   906

Destombes, Cyrille Jean   4343

Destruge, Camilo   679-680

Deutsch, Simon   1459

Deutsche Akademie der Luftfahrtforschung   4785

Deutsche Gesellschaft der Wissenschaften und Künste für die
Tschechoslowakische Republik   648

Deutsche Staatsbibliothek, Berlin--
SEE: Berlin. Deutsche
Staatsbibliothek   31

Deutscher Journalisten-Verband
3642

Deux hommes de lettres   737

Deux journalistes   718

Deux republicains   730

Devaux, Jean   4119

De Vinne, Theodore Low   4007

De Vis, Jean Pauwels--SEE: Pauwels de Vis, Jean   453

De Visch, Charles--SEE: Visch,
Charles de   4525

De Volsberghe, Henri Marie
Ghislaine, baron Surmont--

SEE: Surmont de Volsberghe,
Henri Marie Ghislaine, baron
461

De Waal, Pieter Gerardus Adri-
anus--SEE: Waal, Pieter
Gerardus Adrianus de   4716

Dewamin, Émile   109

Dexter, Franklin, Bowditch
1929-1930

Dezallier d'Argenville, Antoine
Joseph   2473

Dezeimeris, Jean Eugène   4120

Dezobry, Louis Charles   110

al-Dhahabī, Muhammad ibn Ahmad   1311

D'Hauterive, André François
Joseph Borel--SEE: Borel d'
Hauterive, André François
Joseph   739

D'Heylli, Georges, pseud.--SEE:
Poinsot, Edmond Antoine
708

Dhondt, Jan   432

Diana, Manuel Juan   1772

Dias da Silva, Manuel Francisco
476

Díaz, Carlos Morales--SEE:
Morales Díaz, Carlos   1535

Díaz, Raúl Garbín--SEE: Garbín
Díaz, Raúl   1604

Díaz Arrieta, Hernán   3906

Díaz de Valderrama, Fernández
1806-1807

Díaz Doin, Guillermo   111,
4770

Díaz y Pérez, Nicolás   1797

Dibdin, Thomas Frognall   3995

Dick, Charles   1927

Didier, Robert   766

Diepenbroick-Grüter, Hans
Dietrich von, firm, Hamburg
7

Diersen, Inge   993

Dietrich, Margarete   3359, 3646

Díez Canseco, Vicente   115

Dihigo, Louis Barrau-   SEE:
Barrau-Dihigo, Louis   1760

Dilaktorskii, Prokopii Aleksandrovich   3821

Dilly Tante, pseud. --SEE: Kunitz,
Stanley Jasspon   3364

al-Dimashki, Muhibb al-Din--SEE:
Muhibb al-Din, al-Dimashki
1326

Dimitriu, Toma (real name of
Cornel, Th (?)) --SEE:
Cornel, Th   1656

Dimpfel, Rudolf A.   8

al-Din, Muhibb, al-Dimashki--
SEE: Muhibb al-Din, al-Dimashki   1326

Dinaux, Arthur Martin   3568

Dionigi da Genova, Capuchin 4350

Dionysius Genuensis--SEE: Dionigi da Genova, Capuchin

Dirks, Servatius   4351

Dix, Ernest Reginald McClintock
4008

Dizon, Roque J.   1614

Dlabač, Jan Bohumir   2480

Dobroliubov, Ioann Vasil'evich
3822

Dobryv, A. P.   3823

Dobson, Jessie   4634

Dod, Charles R.   1132-1133

Dod, Robert R.   1132-1133

Dodge, Edward N.   2157

Dodwell, Edward   1134

Döring, Heinrich   4353

Doin, Guillermo Díaz--SEE: Díaz
Doin, Guillermo   111, 4770

Dolenský, Antonín   644, 651

Dolgorukoi, Ivan Mikhailovich,
kniaz'   1683

Dolgorukov, Ivan Mikhailovich,
kniaz'--SEE: Dolgorukoi,
Ivan Mikhailovich, kniaz'   1683

Dolzhanskii, A.   2825

Domínguez, Juan Pedro Criado y
--SEE: Criado y Domínguez,
Juan Pedro   3863

Dominici, Bernardo de'   2481

Donaldson, Kenneth MacLeay
333, 3326

Donazzolo, Pietro   4740

Donos, Charles   450

Doorninck, Jan Izaak van   1551-1552

Doppelmayr, Johann Gabriel   4667

Dorcy, Mary Jean   4352

Dortous de Mairan, Jean Jacques
--SEE: Mairan, Jean Jacques
Dortous de   4600

Douglas, Sir Robert, bart.   1218

Dourille, Joseph   767

Dowden, John, Bp. of Edinburgh   4354

Downs, Winfield Scott   1940, 2228, 2271

Doyle, James William Edmund   1135

Drake, Francis Samuel   1934, 1953

Drake, Samuel Gardner   1935

Drake, Wilfred James   2482

Drepperd, Carl William   2708

Dreux du Radier, Jean Francois   929, 945

Dreyer, Matthias   37

Droba, Daniel D   2104

Drouet, Étienne François   201

Drugulin, Wilhelm Eduard   9-10

Drury, Clifford Merrill   4518

Dublin. University. Trinity College   1302

Dubois d'Amiens, Frédéric   4125

Du Boys, Auguste   898

Du Bus de Warnaffe, Charles, vicomte   434

Du Chastel, Pierre--SEE: Casteele, Pierre van de   4107

Du Chatel, Pierre--SEE: Casteele, Pierre van de   4107

Duff, Edward Gordon   4009

Duffy, Ward Everett   2121

Dufourcq, Norbert   2937

Dujardin—Sailly   3569

Duluc, Louis Henrique-   SEE: Henrique-Duluc, Louis   792

Du Lut, Claude Bréghot--SEE: Bréghot du Lut, Claude   905

Du Faure de Lajarte, Théodore Édouard--SEE: Lajarte, Théodore Édouard Du Faure de   2776

Du Mège, Alexandre Louis Charles André   946

Dunbar, Agnes Baillie Cunninghame   4355

Duncan, Edmondstoune   2826

Dunkel, Johann Gottlob Wilhelm   117

Dunken, Gerhard   4572

Dunlap, Orrin Elmer   4787

Dunlap, Mrs. Rose Barteau
2214

Dunleavy, Thomas S.   1942

Dunn, Jacob Piatt   2155

Dunner, Joseph   4772

Dunstan, Ralph   2827

Du Peloux, Charles, vicomte
2483

Du Peloux de Saint Romain,
Charles, vicomte--SEE: Du
Peloux, Charles, vicomte
2483

Du Pin, Lewis Ellies--SEE: Dupin, Louis Ellies   4356-
4357, 4755-4756

Dupin, Louis Ellies   4356-4357,
4755-4756

Duplessis, Georges   2416

Duportet, Maurice   768

Du Pre, Flint O.   1936

Du Radier, Jean François Dreux
--SEE: Dreux du Radier,
Jean François   929, 945

Durán, Carlos Pinto--SEE: Pinto Durán, Carlos   528

Durán, Leopoldo   338

Durand, Justin Brun-   SEE:
Brun-Durand, Justin   883

Du Rivier, Jean Augustin Amar
--SEE: Amar du Rivier,
Jean Augustin   79

Duro, Cesáreo Fernández--SEE:
Fernández Duro, Cesáreo

Dussieux, Louis Étienne   2484

Du Verdier, Antoine   118

Duyckinck, Evert Augustus
3403

Duyckinck, George Long   3403

Dyde, Jessie W   13

Dzidzariiã, G. A.   1685

E

E. C., de M.   718

Eadie, John   157

Eaglefield-Hull, Arthur--SEE:
Hull, Arthur Eaglefield
2820, 2996

Earle, Helen L.   2556

Ebel, Otto   2828-2829

Ebel, Wilhelm   3269

Échard, Jacques   4466

Echevarrieta, Marcelo   340

Eckart, Rudolf   3617

Eckstein, Friedrich August   3344

Editorial Biográfica de Venezuela,
Caracas   2387

Editorial Press Bureau, inc.,
Washington   1894

Edmond, John Philip   4010

Édouard-Joseph, René   2485

Edwards, Ernest   4075

Edwards, Ralph   2724

Eggeling, Georg   2830

Eggs, Georg Joseph   4358

Eguiara y Eguren, Juan José de
1526

Eguren, Juan José de Eguiara y
--SEE: Eguiara y Eguren,
Juan José de   1526

Egypt Exploration Society
4754

Egypt. Fouad I National Research Council--SEE: Egypt.
al-Markaz al-Qawmi lil-
Buhuth   4585

Egypt. al-Majlis al-A'lā lil-
'Ulūm   4583

Egypt. al-Markaz al-Qawmi
lil-Buhuth   4585

Ehrencron-Müller, Holger
655, 3478-3479

Einem, Johann August Christoph
von   4389

Einstein, Alfred   2996

Eisenberg, Ludwig Julius   383,
3150, 3616

Eisenstadt, Benzion   1451-1452,
1937

Eisler, Rudolf   4236, 4248

Eitner, Robert   2831, 2971,
4011

Electrical review (London)
4788

Elías de Molina, Antonio   3453

Eliot, John   2227

Eliot, Samuel Atkins   2185

Ellet, Elizabeth Fries (Lummis)
1938

Elliot, Sir Henry Miers   4757

Elliott, Florence   119

Elmes, James   2486

Eloy, Nicolas François Joseph
4126

Elson, Louis Charles   2832,
2972, 3095

Elwert, Johann Kaspar Philipp
4127

Elwy, Helen--SEE: Rowland,
E. H.   1231

Embacher, Friedrich   4741

Emden, Alfred Brotherston
1136-1137

Emmert, Johann Heinrich
1138

Emödi, Paul   403

Endrizzi, Mansueto   4362

Enfield, William   47

Engelstoft, Povl   659-660,
3477

Engineers' Club of Philadelphia
4816

Engineers Society of Pennsylvania   4815

Ensko, Stephen Guernsey Cook
2709

Epine, Geoffrey l'   3126

Eppelsheimer, Hanns Wilhelm
3345

Eppink, Alice J   2917

Erichsen, Balder Vermund Aage
654

L'Ermite du Luxembourg--SEE:
Alhoy, Philadelphe Maurice
3134

Ernesti, Johann Heinrich Martin
151

Ernst, Viktor   1081

Errera, Mme. Isabelle   11,
2491-2492

Ersch, Johann Samuel   954,
3570-3572

Erslew, Thomas Hansen   3480-
3481

Escagedo Salmón, Mateo   1804

Escudier, Léon   2838

Escudier, Marie Pierre Yves
2838

Escuelas Americanas, Lima
1604

Esparza, Carlos Daniel Valcár-
cel--SEE: Valcárcel Esparza, Carlos Daniel   1508

Espejo, Juan Juis   525

Esperabé Arteaga, Enrique 1776

Essarts, Alfred Stanislas Langlois des--SEE: Des Essarts,
Alfred Stanislas Langlois
756

Esselborn, Karl   1049

Eterovich, Francis H   1912

Ethridge, James M.   3338

Europa Publications, ltd.,
London   160, 682

Evans, Joseph   4365

Evening News Association,
Detroit   2200

Evgenii, Metropolitan of Kiev
1737, 3824, 4366

Ewen, David   2839-2851

Eycleshymer, Albert Chauncey
4635

Eymery, Alexis Blaise   769

Eyre-Todd, George   1197

F

Fabroni, Angelo   1357-1358

Faellesrepraesentationen for den
danske bibliotekarstand
4012

Fage, René   4128

Fallouard, P. J. M.   2852

Fan, Yin-nan   563

Fang, Cheng-hsiang   584

Fantin des Odoars, Antoine
Étienne Nicolas   3563

Fantuzzi, Giovanni   3750

Farber, Eduard   4658

Farbman, Michael S.   1139

Farīd al-Dīn 'Attār   4555

Faridu 'ddin 'Attār--SEE: Farīd
al-Dīn 'Attār   4555

Faris, John   2224

Farmer, John   2229

Farrar, Robert Henry   1085

Fasi, J. C.   1858

Fatimi, Gregory Hagop Mamour
1315

Fauré, Honoré   770

Faure de Lajarte, Théodore
Edouard Du--SEE: Lajarte,
Théodore Edouard Du Faure
de   2776

Fausbøll, Theodor Hauch-
SEE: Hauch-Fausbøll, Theodor   662

Favilli, Enrico   2853

Faxardo, H.   3156

Fayolle, François Joseph Marie
2797

Feather, Leonard G.   2834-35

Federigo, Gaspare   4129

Felder, Franz Karl   4367

Félibien, André, sieur des Avaux
et de Javercy   2493

Félibien, Jean François, sieur
des Avaux   2493

Fell, Frederick Victor   2854

Feller, Francois Xavier de
121, 433, 4368

Fenaroli, Stefano   2494

Féraud, Jean Joseph Maxime
865

Ferchl, Fritz   4659

Fère, Fortuné Guyot de--SEE:
Guyot de Fère, Fortuné
3576-3577

Ferguson, John   4660

Ferguson, John Lewis   2081

Ferm, Vergilius Ture Anselm
4268

Fernández de Navarrete, Martín
--SEE: Navarrete, Martín
Fernández de   4746

Fernández Duro, Cesáreo
1811

Fernández Saldaña, José María
2381

Fernández y González, Manuel
3227

Fernández y Sánchez, Ildefonso
1777

Ferrari, Alberto   2746

Ferrari, Luigi   1335

Ferrari-Cupilli, Giuseppe   2399

Ferrater Mora, José   4238

Ferreira, Antonia Artucio--SEE:
Artucio Ferreira, Antonia
3900

Ferreira da Fonseca, Martinho
Augusto--SEE: Fonseca,
Martinho Augusto Ferreira da

Ferri, Pietro Leopoldo, conte
3751-3752

Ferrière, Claude Joseph de
3986

Fétis, Édouard Louis François
2853, 2855-2857, 3045

Feuilleret, Henri   875

Fey, Hermann   2858

Fiedler, Franz   2859

Fielding, Mantle   2495-2496

Fieux, Charles de, chevalier de
Mouhy--SEE: Mouhy,
Charles de Fieux, chevalier
de   3175

Fifield, James Clark   4068

Figarola-Caneda, Domingo
635

Figueroa, Pedro Pablo   529-
530, 3907

Figueroa, Virgilio   531

Figuier, Louis   4568

Fikenscher, George Wolfgang
Augustin   3266, 3618

Fikkan, Kristian   3803

Filler, Louis   4683

Finauer, Peter Paul   1029

Fincham, Henry Walter   4013

Firmin-Didot, firm, publishers,
Paris   220

Fisch, Edith L.   3952

Fischer, Isidore   4130

Fisher, George Jackson   4131

Fisher, John   4294

Fisher, Richard Charles   3243

Fiske, John   1908, 1927

Fisquet, Honoré Jean Pierre
771

Fissore, Robert   2860

Fitch, Charles Elliott   2252

Fitzhugh, Harriet Lloyd Le-
Porte   122

Fitzhugh, Percy Keese   122

Fizelière, Albert de la --SEE:
La Fizelière, Albert de
726, 784

Flagg, Mildred (Buchanan)
3404

Flamant, Alexander   2861

Flandrau, Charles Eugene
2209

Flerov, Vasilii Sergeevich
1677

Fletcher, Charles Robert Leslie   1150

Fleury, Paul de, comte   2862

Flloyd, Thomas   123

Florez, Adolfo   1503

Florinsky, Michael T.   1703

Földvári, Mihály   3713

Folmsbee, Beulah   4028

Fonseca, Martinho Augusto Ferreira da   1639

Fonseca e Vasconcellos, Joaquim Antonio da--SEE: Vasconcellos, Joaquim Antonio da Fonseca e   3101

Fonsmark, Henning B.   3486

Font-Alba, M.   4641

Fontenay, Louis Abel de Bonafons, known as Abbé de--SEE: Bonafons, Louis Abel de, known as Abbé de Fontenay   2447

Fontenelle, Bernard Le Bovier de   4587

Foppens, Jean François   435

Forbes, Alexander Penrose, Bp. of Brechin   4369

Ford Foundation   4684

Foreign Area Fellowship Program   4684

Forestié, Émerand (or Émile?)   943

Formey, Jean Henri Samuel   3574

Forrer, Leonard   2710

Forster (Reginald Bishop) & Associates   3959

Fortia de Piles, Alphonse Toussaint Joseph André Marie Marseille, comte de   772

Fortier, J. A.   498

Foss, Edward   3953-3954

Foss, Hubert James   2863

Foster, Joseph   1168, 1212, 3955

Foster, Joshua James   2497

Foster, Mary Dillon   2215

Foster, Solomon   2306

Fouad I National Research Council--SEE: Egypt. al-Markaz al-Qawmī lil-Buhuth   4585

Fouchy, Jean Paul Grandjean de --SEE: Grandjean de Fouchy, Jean Paul   4591

Foulché-Delbosc, Raymond   1760

Foulkes, Isaac   1224

France. Cour de cassation   3956-3957

France. Délégation générale à la recherche scientifique et technique   4588

Franchini, Giovanni   4370

Francis, Samuel Ward   4132

Francisco da Silva, Innocencio--SEE: Silva, Innocencio Francisco da   3816

François, Jean   4371

Frangulis, A. F. (i. e. Phrangoules, A. P.)   42

Frank, Paul, pseud. --SEE: Merseburger, Carl Wilhelm   2964

Frankenstein, Alfred Victor   2909

Frankfurter, Naftali   1456

Franquet, Amable Charles, comte
de Franqueville--SEE:
Franqueville, Amable Charles
Franquet, comte de   773

Franqueville, Amable Charles
Franquet, comte de   773

Franz, Günther   1008

Franzén, Frans Michael, Bp.
1817

Frati, Carlo   4014-4015

Frattarolo, Renzo   1338

Frauwallner, Erich   3388

Frederiks, Johannes Godefridus
3488

Fredericks, Vic, pseud.--SEE:
Fell, Frederick Victor
2854

Frederiksen, C.   1649

Frégnac, Claude   2712

Freher, Paulus   684

Freijomil, Antonio Couceiro--
SEE: Couceiro Freijomil,
Antonio   3601

Freiman, Otto fon--SEE: Freimann, Otto Rudol'fovich
1686

Freimann, Otto Rudol'fovich
1686

French, Benjamin Franklin
1941

French, Hollis   2711

Frenzel, Herbert Alfred   3171,
3619

Freyre, Eduardo Ponce de León
--SEE: Ponce de León
Freyre, Eduardo   1762

Friche, V. M.   3371

Friends, Society of   1091-1092,
4372

Friends' Institute, London   4372

Fries, Johann Jacob   3464

Frobeen, I. G.   411

Froés Perim, Damiao de, pseud.
--SEE: João de São Pedro,
Brother   165

Frondeville, Henri de   919

Frontaura y Vázquez, Carlos
3346

Frühling, Moritz   384

Fu, Jen-hua   564

Fuchs, Max   3155

Fudge, William Kingston   3528

Füessli, Johann Rudolf   2498

Fueldener, Johann Jacob von,
1072

Fünn, Samuel Joseph   1457

Fuentes, Celedonio   4373-4374

Fürst, Max   385

Fueter, Eduard   4589

Fuller, Juanita Boykin   1885

Fuller, Muriel   124

Fuller, Thomas   1141

Furio, Antonio   2499

Fusco, Enrico M.   3753

Fuster, Justo Pastor   3866, 3896

G

G., A. --SEE: Gueidon, Alexandre   930

G., A. (author (?) of Gosudarstvennyi Soviet)   1691

G., C. W. P.   39

G., G. --SEE: Giucci, Gaetano   4590

G. E. C. --SEE: Cokayne, George Edward   1116-1117

G. Mh. L. y S.   113

Gabet, Charles Henri Joseph   2500

Gadan-Pamard, Francis   3147-3148

Gaddi, Jacopo   3463

Gaddius, Jacobus--SEE: Gaddi, Jacopo   3463

Gadebusch, Friedrich Konrad   412

Gaines, Pierre Welch   1892

Galang, Zoilo M.   1611

Galati, Vito Giuseppe   3754

Galaxy Publishing Company   2142, 2238, 2275, 2294

Gale Research Company   3324, 3329, 3338, 3387, 3389, 3403, 3492-3493, 3497

Galetti, Ugo   2488

Galiano, Juan Valera y Alcalá Galiano--SEE: Valera y Alcalá Galiano, Juan   3893

Galindo y Villa, Jesús   1527

Galli, Amintore   2864-2865

Gallois, Léonard   780-782

Galpin, William Freeman   2253

Galtier-Boissière, Jean   783

Gamba, Bartolommeo   3755

Gammond, Peter   2866

Gams, Pius Bonifacius   4375-4376

Gandershofer, G. Maurus   1032

Gandía, Eduardo Neumann--SEE: Neumann Gandía, Eduardo   1651

Gandola, Luigi   1418

Gandolfo, Domenico Antonio   4377

Ganzer, Karl Richard   977

Garbett, Arthur Selwyn   2867

Garbín Díaz, Raúl   1604

Garbín Montenegro, Raúl (Raúl Garbín Jr.)   1604

García, Manuel Rico--SEE: Rico García, Manuel   3885

García, Miguel Ángel   1749

García, Servando   350

García Cubas, Antonio   1528

García del Moral, José   4133

García López, Juan Catalina
3867

Garcia Péres, Domingo   3868

García Purón, Manuel   1529

García Rivas, Heriberto   1530

Gardavský, Čeněk   2868

Gardner, Albert Ten Eyck
2696

Gardner, Lester Durand   4809

Garelli, Antonio   1386

Gari y Siumell, José Antonio
4378

Garnier, Joseph François   871

Garollo, Gottardo   130

Garras, Adolf   2869

Garrett, William   2074

Garvin, John William   3503

Gasch, Sebastián   3159

A Gascon priest   4349

Gassner, Ferdinand Simon
3055

Gates, Mary Jean   537

Gates, Willey Francis   3121

Gatti, Guido Maria   2806

Gatti, Serafino   1394

Gauhe, Johann Friedrich   131

Gault de Saint-Germain, Pierre
Marie   2501

Gaunt, William   2502

Gautier, Madeleine   3007

Gaviria, Justino Matute y --SEE:
Matute y Gaviria, Justino
1807-1808

Gavrilović, Andra   2400

al-Gazari, Muhammad ibn--SEE:
Ibn al-Jazari, Muhammad ibn
Muhammad   4556

Gazikean, Arsen Ghazaros--SEE:
Ghazikean, Arsen Ghazaros
361

Geddie, John Liddell   3500

Geiger, Maynard J., Father
4379

Geislerus, Fridericus--SEE:
Geissler, Friedrich   34

Geissler, Friedrich   34

Geissler, Max   3620

Gelber, Leonard   1968

Gélis, Jean Baptiste   436

Gellert, Imre   1248

Gelsted, Otto   2503

Geneva. Conseil d'État   1846

Gennadi, Grigorii Nikolaevich
1662, 3825

A Gentleman of Philadelphia--
SEE: French, Benjamin
Franklin   1941

Georgenau, Eberhard Emil von
Georgii- SEE: Georgii-
Georgenau, Eberhard Emil
von 1075

Georgia. Dept. of Archives and
History 2134-2135

Georgia Augusta Universität
Gottingen--SEE: Gottingen.
Universität 3269

Georgii-Georgenau, Eberhard
Emil von 1075

Gérard, Charles 2504

Gerber, Ernst Ludwig 2871-
2872

Gerigk, Herbert 3082

Gerini, Emanuelle 3756

Gerland, Otto 1048, 1051

Germany (Democratic Republic,
1949-) Volkskammer
979

Germany (Democratic Republic,
1949-) Zentralinstitut
für Bibliothekswesen 3621

Germany (Federal Republic, 1949-
) Bundesministerium des
Innern 980

Germany (Federal Republic, 1949-
) Bundesministerium
für Gesamtdeutsche Fragen
981, 1015

Gerrits, Gerrit Engelberts 134

Gerry, Philippa 2523

Gesellschaft der Wissenschaften zu
Göttingen--SEE: Akademie der
Wissenschaften, Göttingen

Gesellschaft Deutscher Chemiker
4651

Gesellschaft für Geschichte der
Pharmazie, Berlin 4659

Gesellschaft für Rheinische
Geschichtskunde 1066

Gesner, Johann Matthias 3267

Gesner, Konrad 3464

Gestoso y Pérez, José 2713

Geysbeek, Pieter Gerardus
Witsen 3489

Gezelius, Georg 1818

Ghazikean, Arsen Ghazaros
361

Al-Ghazzī, Najm al-Dīn Muhammad ibn Muhammad 1316

Ghent. Rijksuniversiteit 3268

Ghigliazza, Manuel Mestre--SEE:
Mestre Ghigliazza, Manuel
1534

Ghisalberti, Alberto Maria
1534

Ghiyās al-Dīn ibn Humām al-Dīn,
Khvānd Amīr--SEE: Khwānd
Amīr, Ghiyās al-Dīn 1323

Gianelli, Pietro 2873

Gibb, Sir Hamilton Alexander
Rosskeen 1314

Gibbs-Smith, Charles Harvard
142

Gidel, Charles Antoine 135

Giebisch, Hans 3388, 3622-23

Giedion-Welcker, Carola 2697

Gierach, Erich 648

Giglio, Vittorio 1355

Gilbey, Sir Walter 2505

Giles, Herbert Allen 567-568

Gillis, Irvin Van Order 568

Gillis, Norman E. 2218

Gillow, Joseph 1142, 1156

Ginzburg, Isidor 4239

Giovanni, F. 3757

Giovanni Crisostomo da Cittadella 4380

Giovio, Giovanni Battista, conte 1388

Girard de Propriac, Catherine Joseph Ferdinand 136

Girardeau, Louis 726, 784

Giraudet, Eugène 2506

Girbal, Enrique Claudio 3869

Girodie, André 2642

Giucci, Gaetano 4590

Giustiniani, Lorenzo 3758

Giustiniani, Michele 3759

Giusto, Domenico 3760

Giving, Gerald Renaas 4457

Glaeser, Ernest 785

Glasgow. Royal Technical College. Library. Young Collection 4660

Glasgow. University 1213

Gleerup, C. W. K., firm, publisher 3924

Gliubich, Simeone 2401

Gluckman, Arcadi 4803

Gluckh, M. A. 3074

Gnoli, Umberto 2507

Godet, Marcel 1845, 1849-1850

Godłowski, Tadeusz 1625

Godoy, José Francisco 336

Godwin, Parke 137

Goedeke, Karl 3624-3626

Goelicke, Andreas Ottomar 4134

Goetten, Gabriel Wilhelm 244, 270, 685

Göttingen. Akademie der Wissenschaften--SEE: Akademie der Wissenschaften, Göttingen 4573

Göttingen. Gesellschaft der Wissenschaften--SEE: Akademie der Wissenschaften, Göttingen 4573

Göttingen. Universität 3269

Goetze, Edmund 3624-3625

Goldstein, Franz 2417

Golitsyn, Nikolaĭ Nikolaevich 3826, 3840

Gollmick, Karl   2874

Golomb, Emmanuel   1458

Golomb, Zebi Nisan   1458

Golovachev, Petr Mikhaĭlovich
    1689

Golubovich, Girolamo   4481-
    4483

Gómez, Francisco Zapater y--
    SEE: Zapater y Gómez,
    Francisco   2673

Gómez Uriel, Miguel   3871

González, Manuel Fernández y--
    SEE: Fernández y González,
    Manuel   3227

González, Tomás Baeza y --SEE:
    Baeza y González, Tomás
    3858

González y Sáenz, Francisco de
    Paula   1794

Goodrich, Samuel Griswold
    138

Goodspeed Brothers, Chicago
    2343

Gool, Jan van   2508

Goovaerts, André Léon   4384

Gopal Sanyal, Ram--SEE: Sanyal,
    Ram Gopal   1283

Gordon, William John   139

Gordon-Gorman, William James
    1143

Gorjão, João Damasio Roussado--
    SEE: Roussado Gorjão, João
    Damasio   1647

Gorman, William James Gordon-
    SEE: Gordon-Gorman, Wil-
    liam James   1143

Gorton, John   140

Gosudarstvennaia akademiia
    khudozhestvennykh nauk,
    Moscow--SEE: Moscow.
    Gosudarstvennaia akademiia
    khudozhestvennykh nauk
    3833

Gosudarstvennoe russkoe bota-
    nicheskoe obshchestvo--SEE:
    Vsesoiuznoe botanicheskoe
    obshchestvo   4650

Gosudarstvennyĭ russkiĭ muzeĭ,
    Leningrad--SEE: Leningrad.
    Gosudarstvennyĭ russkiĭ
    muzeĭ   2541

Gotter, Friedrich Gotthilf   1026

Gottlieb, Samuel Noah   4562

Goujet, Claude Pierre   201,
    3575, 4385

Gould, John, writer on art
    2509

Gould, Sabine Baring-   SEE:
    Baring-Gould, Sabine
    4294-4295

Gouriet, Jean Baptiste   925

Gousse, Jean Théodore Laurent-
    SEE: Laurent-Gousse, Jean
    Théodore   946

Govín, Carlos Manuel Trelles y
    --SEE: Trelles y Govín,
    Carlos Manuel   641-642

Graça, Fernando Lopes--SEE:
    Lopes Graça, Fernando
    2784

Gradmann, Johann Jacob   3627

Gräfe, Julius   3628

Gräffer, Franz   1459

Graham, Peter John   3160

Grajales, Francisco Martí--SEE:
Martí Grajales, Francisco
3872

Granatsztain, Jechiel   1465

Grandjean de Fouchy, Jean Paul
4591

Granger, James   1144, 1166

Granges de Surgères, Anatole,
marquis de   786, 867

Grant, Maurice Harold   2510-
2512, 2698

Grass, Nikolaus   4758

Grasselli, Giuseppe   2513

Grasset de Saint-Sauveur,
Jacques   714

Graves, Algernon   2514-2517

Graves, John Temple   2137

Gray, George John   4016

Gt. Brit. Admiralty   1145

Gt. Brit. Colonial Office   1118

Gt. Brit. Foreign Office   1140

Gt. Brit. Ministry of Economic
Warfare   774-775, 1018-
1021, 1381-1382

Gt. Brit. National Maritime Mu-
seum, Greenwich--SEE:
Greenwich, Eng. National
Maritime Museum   1145

Gt. Brit. Parliament. House of
Commons   1146-1147

Gt. Brit. Royal Naval College,
Greenwich--SEE: Green-
wich, Eng. Royal Naval College   1145

Gt. Brit. War Office   1148

Greco, Oscar   3761

Green, Janet M.   2901

Green, Joseph Joshua   1092

Green, Stanley   2876

Greenwich, Eng. National Maritime Museum   1145

Greenwich, Eng. Royal Naval
College   1145

Greer, Genevieve   4499

Grégoir, Édouard Georges
Jacques   2877-2880

Grégoire, Louis   141

Greifswald. Universität. Bibliothek   1061

Grenier, Albert Sylvain   787-
788

Grente, Georges, Cardinal
3567

Grenus-Saladin, François Théodore Louis, baron   1846

Gresham (John M.) Company
2161

Grienwaldt, Franz Josef   4135

Griesbach, Hermann Adolf
4136

Griffin, Sir Lepel Henry   1594

Griffith, Frederic   2881

Grigson, Geoffrey   142, 3337

Grillo, Luigi   1392

Grillon des Chapelles, Amador
    893

Grimal, Pierre   143

Grimschitz, Bruno   2518

Grismer, Raymond Leonard
    1495, 3908-3911

Griswold, Rufus Wilmot   1943

Grlović, Milan   2402

Groce, George Cuthbert   2567

Gromyko, Andreĭ Andreevich
    116

Groner, Richard   383

Gross, Heinrich   3629

Gross, Johann, of Oberhausen
    3630

Gross, Samuel David   4137

Grové, A. P.   3394

Grove, Sir George   2883-2884,
    3018

Grüter, Hans Dietrich von
    Diepenbroick-   SEE:
    Diepenbroick-Grüter, Hans
    Dietrich von, firm, Hamburg
    7

Guaitta, Gottfried   4386

Guarana, Armindo   477

Guarienti, Pietro   2573

Guatemala. Academia Guate-
    malteca--SEE: Academia
    Guatemalteca, Guatemala
    3897

Gubernale, Apollo Gaetano
    1412

Gubernatis, Angelo de, conte
    1359, 2519, 3347-3350

Gudeman, Alfred   3351

Gue, Benjamin F.   2156

Guédon, Joseph   3000

Guédy, Théodore   2520

Gueidon, Alexandre   930

Guell, Juan Corminas y --SEE:
    Corminas y Guell, Juan
    3457

Gueneau, Victor Augustin   917

Guenebault, Louis Jean   4387

Günther, Johannes   3270

Gugitz, Gustav   3622

Guibaud, Eustache   58

Guiffrey, Jules Marie Joseph
    789

Guigue, Albert   3271

Guilbert, Philippe Jacques
    Étienne Vincent   940

Guillon, Aimé, abbé   790

Guimarães, Argeu de Segadas
    Machado-   SEE: Segadas
    Machado-Guimarães, Argeu
    de   484

Gulyás, Pál   1247, 1249, 3714

Gundlach, Franz   3172

Gunkel, Hermann   4470

Gunn, John   207

Gunnis, Rupert   2699

Gupta, Jyotish Chandra Das--SEE:
Das Gupta, Jyotish Chandra
1268

Gupta, K. L.   3273-3274

Gupta, Sankar Sen--SEE: Sen
Gupta, Sankar   3726

Gupta, Tanasukharāma   1270

Gupta, Tarapada Das--SEE:
Das Gupta, Tarapada
1280

Gurlitt, Wilibald   3034

Gurvin, Olav   2885

Gustafson, David   4049

Gustav Adolfs akademien för
folklivsforskning   4759

Gutiérrez, Juan María   343

Gutiérrez de Salamanca, Carlos
Ramírez de Arellano y --
SEE: Ramírez de Arellano
y Gutiérrez de Salamanca,
Carlos   3882

Guyot de Fère, Fortuné   3576-
3577

H

H., J. G. --SEE: Hering, Johann Gottfried   4389

Haack, Ernst   4436

Haag, Émile   791

Haag, Eugène   791

Haan, David Bierens de--SEE:
Bierens de Haan, David
4666

Haan, Wilhelm   3631

Haapanen, Toivo Elias   2991

Habel, Walter   1013

Haeghen, Ferdinand van der
3444

Haestrup, Jørgen   656

Häuser, Johann Ernst   2887

Hafen, Le Roy Reuben   2363

Haga, Yaichi   1425

Hagen, Johann Jost Anton vom
3181

Haggar, Reginald George   2725

Hai t'ien ch'u pan she   569

Haid, Johann Jacob   3610

Hailstone, Edward   1240

Hale, Sara Josepha (Buell)   144

Halīl ibn Aibak as-Safadī--SEE:
al-Safadī, Khalīl ibn Aybak
1329

Halkett, Samuel   1088

Halkin, Léon Ernest   3290

Hall, Donald   3534

Hall, H. van   2521

Hall, Henry   1944

Hall, Henry Cecil 2522

Halliwell, Leslie 3162

Halvorsen, Jens Braage 3802, 3804

Hamal, Antoine Gabriel de, comte Becdelièvre- SEE: Becdelièvre-Hamal, Antoine Gabriel de, comte 427

Hamberger, Georg Christoph 3352, 3632-3633, 3668

Hamburger, Povl 2751, 3008

Hamel, Fred 2752

Hamelmann, Hermann 1078

Hamersly, Lewis Randolph 1945, 1969-1970, 1975, 1991, 1997-1999, 2259, 2302

Hamilton, Ross 515

Hamma, Fridolin 2886

Hammerton, Sir John Alexander 145

Hammond, E. A. 4206

Hamst, Olphar, Esq. , pseud. -- SEE: Thomas, Ralph 38

Hanaford, Harry Prescott 3118

Haner, Cengiz 4139

Haner, Georg Jeremias 3715

Hanlet, Camille 3448-3449

Han-min, pseud. 570

Hansen, Alfred 4636

Hara, Kanshū 571

al-Harawi, 'Abd Allāh ibn Muhammad al-Ansārī--SEE: al-Ansārī al-Harawi, 'Abd Allāh ibn Muhammad 4554

Hardie, James 146

Harding, Edward 1149

Hardt, Ricardus von der 3920

Hardung, Victor 3929

Hardy, Sir Thomas Duffus 4410

Harel, François Antoine 3163

Harian rakjat 1296

Harkins, William Edward 3827

Harlow, Rex Francis 2281-2282

Harlow, Samuel R. 2254

Harlow, Victor Emmanuel 2281

Harmon, Seth 2122

Harms, Hans 4742

Harnesk, Paul 3923

Harper, Franklin 2369

Harrison, Frank Llewellyn 3112

Harrison, Frederic 147

Harrison, Mitchel Charles 1946, 2255

Hart, James David 3405

Hart, Samuel 2117

Hartmann, Alfred 1847

Hartmann, William C.   4241

Hartnoll, Phyllis   3164

Hartzenbusch e Hiriart, Eugenio
1761

Harvard University. Committee
on International and Regional
Studies--SEE: Harvard University. Committee on Re-
gional Studies   572

Harvard University. Committee
on Regional Studies   572

Harvard University. Society of
Fellows   3261

Harvey, Alice H.   3406

Harvey, John Hooper   2682

Harvey, Sir Paul   3465, 3504,
3578

Hashikawa, Tokio   573

Hasidah, Israel Yitzhak   4563

Hasler, Friedrich   1847

Hasselt, André Henri Constant
van   437

Hà-Tĩnh Võ-Oanh   2393

Hauch-Fausbøll, Theodor   662

Hauer, Eugen   4248

Hauck, Albert   4483

Haug, Balthasar   1080

Haulleville, Prosper Charles
Alexandre, baron de   438

Haupt, Herman   1049

Hauser, Kaspar   1848

Hauterive, André François Joseph Borel d' --SEE: Borel
d'Hauterive, André François
Joseph   739

Haverford College. Library.
1886

Hayavadana Rao, Conjeeveram,
rao sahib   1275

Haycraft, Howard   124, 3362-
3363, 3365-3366, 3414,
3509-3510

Haydn, Joseph Timothy   12

Hayes, Richard   1303

Haymaker, Webb   4140

Haymann, Christoph Johann
Gottfried   3634

Hays, Frances   148

Hazon, Jacques Albert   4079

Heal, Sir Ambrose   2714, 4017

Heaton, Sir John Henniker, bart.
375

Heckethorn, Charles William
4018

Hederich, Benjamin   3353

Hefling, Helen   13

Hege, Christian   4432

Hegna, Johs. B.   3803

Heibon Sha, Tokyo   106, 133

Heiden, Helmut von der   3392

Heilprin, Louis   149

Heim, Franz Joseph   4502

Heimpel, Herman   963, 982

Heinecken, Karl Heinrich von
    2524

Heinzel, Erwin   150, 3354,
    3388

Heitman, Frances Bernard
    1947-1948

Helbig, Georg Adolf Wilhelm
    1692

Helfert, Vladimir   3012

Heller, Hermann   649

Hemel, Victor van   2888

Hemphill, James Calvin   2318

Hendrikx, Ephraem   4361

Henggeler, Rudolf   4388

Henkels, Walter   984

Henley, William   2889

Henrique-Duluc, Louis   792

Henriques Leal, Antonio   478

Henry, Albert   439

Henry, William Wirt   2353

Henschel, August Wilhelm Ed-
    uard Theodor   4141

Henschenius, Godefridus   4275

Hentzen, Alfred   985

Hepburn, William Murray
    2150

Herbelot de Molainville, Barthé-
    lemy d'   1317

Herbert, William   3995

Hering, Johann Gottfried   4389

Herlossohn, Karl   3135

Herman, Ch., pseud. --SEE:
    Ebel, Otto   2828

Hermannson, Halldór   3721

Un Hermite qui n'est pas mort--
    SEE: Ménégault, A. P. G.
    3375

Hernández Morejón, Antonio
    4142

Herndon, Richard   2118, 2175,
    2188, 2234, 2311

Herreman, Raymond   3445

Herring, James   1949

Herringshaw, Clark J.   2105,
    2244

Herringshaw, Thomas William
    1950-1951, 3407

Hershman, Morris   2159

Herskovits, Melville Jean   4761

Hertzog, Peter   2241

Herzberg, Max John   3424

Herzel, Carl Heinrich   2928

Herzfeld, Friedrich   2890

Herzog, Johann Jakob   4483

Herzog, Johann Werner   3275

Herzog, Xaver   4390

Heseltine, Janet E.   3578

Heumann, Christoph August 35-36

Heuss, Theodor, Pres. Ger. Federal Republic 963, 982

Heyden, Eduard 1042

Heylli, Georges d' , pseud. --SEE: Poinsot, Edmond Antoine 708

Hiatt, Robert W. 4637

Hibbert, Julian 4391

Higginbotham, J. J. 1271

Higginson, Alexander Henry 3505

Higgs, Henry 4774

Higuchi, Masanori 574

Hilaire, E. Marc 725

Hilbert, Rachel M. 3408-3409

Hildebrand, Albin 1832-1833

Hill, Richard Leslie 1812

Hill, Roy L. 3410

Hill, Stephen A. 1420

Hilleary, Perry Edward 2139

Hillman, Adolf 2891

Hills, Frederick Simon 2256, 2349

Hines, Dixie 3118

Hinkel, Edgar Joseph 3411

Hinrichsen, Adolf 3635

Hintze, Erwin 2715

Hiriart, Eugenio Hartzenbusch e --SEE: Hartzenbusch e Hiriart, Eugenio 1761

Hirsch, August 4080

Hirsch, Gottwalt Christian 4638

Hirschfeld, Josef 4143

Hirsching, Friedrich Carl Gottlob 151

Historical Record Association 2081, 2150, 2164, 2338

Historical Records Survey. District of Columbia 2892

Historische Gesellschaft des Kantons Aargau, Aarau 1851

Historische Kommission für die Provinz Sachsen 1068

Historische Kommission für Schlesien 1073

Historischer Verein des Kantons Bern. Biographien-Kommission 1852

Hitzig, Julius Eduard 3636

Hjörvar, Helgi 1258

Hjorth, Arne 2893

Hoagland, Roland Waterbury 4780

Hodgkins, Theodore Roosevelt 2172

Hodson, Vernon Charles Paget 1151

Hoefer, Jean Chrétien Ferdinand 220

Høgh, Marie 1589

Hoehn, Matthew   3355

Höijer, Johan Leonard   2894-2895

Hörner, Otto Friedrich   2896, 3632

Höweler, Casper   2897-2898

Hofberg, Hermann   1819

Hoffman, Roy   2284

Hoffmann, Carl Julius Adolf Hugo   2899

Hofstead, John Andrew   3276

Hole, Charles   153

Holland, Henry   1152

Hollenberg, Georg Heinrich   4668

Holst, Niels von   985

Holweck, Frederick George   4392

Holzmann, Michael   955-956

Homans, George Caspar   3261

Homans, James Edward   1927

Un Homme retiré du monde   763

Hongkong. Chou mo pao she--SEE: Chou mo pao she, Hongkong   556

Hongkong. Union Research Institute--SEE: Yu lien yen chiu so, Kowloon   614

Hongkong. Yu lien yen chiu so--SEE: Yu lien yen chiu so, Kowloon   614

Hook, Walter Farquhar   4393-4394

Hoover Institute and Library--SEE: Stanford University. Hoover Institution on War, Revolution and Peace   541

Hoover Institution on War, Revolution and Peace--SEE: Stanford University. Hoover Institution on War, Revolution and Peace   541

Hoover Library--SEE: Stanford University. Hoover Institution on War, Revolution and Peace   541

Hopkins, J. E. G.   1920

Hopkins, John Castell   501

Hopkinson, Cecil   4019

Hoppe, Willy   1008

Horányi, Alexius--SEE: Horányi, Elek   3716-3717, 4395

Horányi, Elek   3716-3717, 4395

Horkenbach, Cuno   986

Hormayr zu Hortenburg, Joseph, Freiherr von   387

Horn, Walther   4639

Hornstein, Lillian Herlands   3380

Hornyold-Strickland, Henry   1203

Hortenburg, Joseph, Freiherr von Hormayr zu--SEE: Hormayr zu Hortenburg, Joseph, Freiherr von   387

Horton, Byrne Joseph   4703

Houbraken, Arnold   2508, 2525, 2658

Houbraken, Jacobus   1153

Hough, Franklin Benjamin   1953

Houmøller, Sven   4012

Hourticq, Louis   2523

Housel, Hope   3911

Howard, Arthur Vyvyan   4594

Howard, John Tasker   2900

Howard, Ruth E.   3145

Howe, Will David   3400

Howes, Durward   1905

Hsiao, Hsiao   575

Hsü, Hsiang-an   1871

Hsü, Liang-chih   576

Hsu, Yin-ch'i   4640

Hsü, Ying   577

Hua wen shu chü pien chi pu   279

Huang, Fen-sheng   578

Huard, Étienne   2526

Hubbard, William Lines   2901

Hubbell, John Henry   3968

Huddle, Freeman E.   2143

Hürlimann, Martin   2752

Hüsgen, Heinrich Sebastian   2527

Hughes, Gervase   2902

Hughes, Rupert   2903

Hughes, William Little   726, 784

Hull, Arthur Eaglefield   2820, 2996

Hummel, Arthur William   609

Humphries, Charles   4020

Humphris, Edith M.   1120

Hunkler, Théodore François Xavier   4396

Hunt, Cecil   154

Hunt, Freeman   4704

Hunt, H. Cecil--SEE: Hunt, Cecil   154

Hunt, Rockwell Dennis   2089

Hurst, Joan   4675

Hurter, Hugo   4397

Huse, Hiram Augustus   2351

Hutchins, Stephen C.   2254

Hutchinson, Benjamin   4144

Hutchinson, Fred Paul   3248

Hutton, Lawrence   2652

Huyghe, René   2528

Huyke, Juan Bernardo   1650

Hyamson, Albert Montefiore   156

Hydle, Halvdan   3803

Hymans, Henri Simon   2529

I

I, Chün-tso   579

ÍAzykov, Dmitriĭ Dmitrievich
3828

Ibn al-Jazarī, Muhammad ibn
Muhammad   4556

Ibn al-Qiftī--SEE al-Qiftī, 'Ali
ibn Yūsuf   4191

Ibn 'Asākir, 'Alī ibn Hasan
1318

Ibn Hajar al-'Asqalānī, Ahmad
ibn 'Alī   1319

Ibn Khallikān   1320

Ibn Sa'd Muhammad   4557

Ibn Sa'īd, 'Ali ibn Mūsā, al-
Maghrībī, called   1321

Icasiano, Francisco B   1613

Igarashi, Eikichi   1426

Ignatov, Il'ía Nikolaevich   3829

Iguíniz, Juan Bautista   1518-
1519, 3277, 3912

Iken, Heinrich   1036

Ikonnikov, Vladimir Stephanovich
3283

Ilarino da Milano, Father   4398

Il'inskiĭ, Aleksandr Aleksandrovich   2904

Illing, Robert   2905

Illinois. Secretary of State
2145

Imbert, Auguste--SEE: Imbert,
Jean Baptiste Auguste   793

Imbert, Jean Baptiste Auguste
793

Imbert, Nath   765

Imbonato, C. G.   3789

Immerzeel, Johannes   2530,
2538

Imperatorskaía Akademiía nauk--
SEE: Akademiía nauk SSSR
4574-4575 [etc.]

Imperatorskaía Mediko- chirur-
gicheskaía akademiía, Lenin-
grad--SEE: Leningrad.
Voenno-meditsinskaía aka-
demiía   4160-4161

Imperatorskii universitet sv.
Vladimira, Kiev--SEE: Kiev.
Universitet.   3283

Imperatorskoe Moskovskoe
arkheologicheskoe obshchest-
vo--SEE: Moskovskoe ar-
kheologicheskoe obshchestvo
4764

Incorporated Society of Musicians
2908

Index Society, London   1084-1085

India. Medical Dept.   4117

India (Republic) Council of Scientific and Industrial Research
4595

India (Republic) Ministry of Education   3278

India (Republic) Parliament
1273

India (Republic) Parliament.
House of the People   1273

India (Republic) Parliament.
Lok Sabha--SEE: India (Republic) Parliament. House
of the People   1273

Indian Council of Agricultural Research   4786

Indonesia. Departemen Penerangan   3729

Indonesia. Kementarian Penerangan   1297

Ingerslev, Vilhelm   4145

Ingham, Thomas Clayton   3119

Inghirami, Francesco   1416

Inglis, Ralston   3506

Ingram, William H.   2063

Inoue, Raimei   1427

Institut für Landeskunde von
Oberösterreich   388

Institut grazhdanskikh inzhenerov,
Leningrad--SEE: Leningrad.
Inzhenerno-stroitel´nyi
institut   4795

Institut istorii partii, Baku--SEE:
Baku. Institut istorii partii
1669

Institut po istoriĩa na Bŭlgarskata
Komunisticheska partiĩa,
Sofia--SEE: Sofia. Institut
po istoriĩa na Bŭlgarskata
Komunisticheska partiĩa   489

Institut royal colonial belge--SEE:
Académie royale des sciences
d'outre mer   422

Institut zur Erforschung der
UdSSR   1693, 1721-1722,
1747

Institute for Research in Biography, inc., New York   307-
308, 4066, 4701, 4735

Institute of American Genealogy
4760

Institute of Art Research, Tokyo--
SEE: Tokyo. Institute of Art
Research   2633

Institute of Chemistry of Great
Britain and Ireland   4661

Institute of Public Administration, Thammasãt University,
Bangkok, Thailand--SEE:
Bangkok, Thailand. Tham-
masãt Mahawitthayalai.
Khana Ratthaprasasanasat
1870

Institute of Radio Engineers
4792

Instituto de Estudios Biográficos,
Buenos Aires   346

Instituto Internacional de Genealogía y Heráldica   1780

Inter American Statistical Institute   4679, 4686

International Association of Conference Interpreters   3357

International Association of Plastic Arts. Japanese National
Committee   2532

International Bibliophile Society
3329

International City Managers' Association   4773

International Geographical Union
4747

International Methodist Historical
Society   4534

International Mineralogical Association   4641

International Music Society   2971

International Refugee Organization. Health Division   4146

International Union of Biological
Sciences   4642-4643

International Union of Crystallog-
raphy   4676

Internationale Musikgesellschaft--
SEE: International Music
Society   2971

Inzhenerno-stroitel'nyï institut,
Leningrad--SEE: Leningrad.
Inzhenerno-stroitel'nyï in-
stitut   4795

Ireland, Norma (Olin)   4570

Irving, Joseph   1214

Isaksen, Asbjørn   3279

al-Isbahānī, Alī ibn Husain, Abū
al-Faraj--SEE: Alī ibn Husain,
Abū al-Faraj, al-Isbahānī
3437

Iseki, Kuro   1428

Istituto Giovanni XXIII nella Ponti-
ficia università lateranense,
Rome--SEE: Rome (City)
Pontificia università lateranense.
Istituto Giovanni XXIII   4303

Istituto per la collaborazione culturale   2875, 4237

Italy. Direzione generale della
statistica   3740

Italy. Parlamento. Camera dei
deputati. Biblioteca   14-17

Iten, Albert   4399

Iversen, IUliï Bogdanovich   1694

Ivimey, Joseph   4400

Iwao, Seiichi   1424

Izco, Wenceslao Ayguals de--SEE:
Ayguals de Izco, Wenceslao
56

J

J., S.   209

J. R., D.   112

Jackson, Sir Charles James
2718

Jackson (F. E.) & Son   1956

Jackson, Samuel Macauley
4482-4483

Jacob, Giles   3507

Un Jacobin converti   822

Jacobson, Eugene Henry   4244

Jacquelin, Jacques André
3167

Jacquot, Albert   2911-2912

Jäckh, Joachim Heinrich   3637

Jäger, Cajetan   3638

Jaetenstein, Matthias Kalina von--
SEE: Kalina von Jäthenstein,
Matthias   650

Jäthenstein, Matthias Kalina von--
SEE: Kalina von Jäthenstein,
Matthias   650

Jagdish Bhatia--SEE: Bhatia,
Jagdish   1263

Jahn, Johannes   2533

Jaksch, Friedrich   3639

Jal, Auguste   164, 3163

James, Ralph N.   2534

James, Robert Rutson   4085

Jameson, John Franklin   1957-
1958

Jāmī   4558

Jamil, S. M.   1278

Jamin, Jules Gabriel   3156

Janisch, Johann Daniel--SEE:
Janocki, Jan Daniel Andrzej
1632

Janković, Slavko   2403

Jannet, Pierre   704, 709

Janocki, Jan Daniel Andrzej
1632

Janotzky, Johann Daniel Andreas--
SEE: Janocki, Jan Daniel
Andrzej   1632

Janozki, Johann Daniel Andreas--
SEE: Janocki, Jan Daniel
Andrzej   1632

Jansa, Friedrich   2913

Janssens, Édouard   440

Japan. Gaimusho   566, 581

Japan. Gaimushō. Ajiakyoku
580, 583, 1491, 1688

Japan. Gaimushō. Chosakyoku
364

Japan. Gaimushō. Jōhōbu   565,
581

Japan. Mombushō. Nihon Yunesuko Kokunai Iinkai   2532,
3786

Japan. National Commission for
UNESCO --SEE: Japan.
Mombushō. Nihon Yunesuko
Kokunai Iinkai   2532

Japanese National Commission for
UNESCO --SEE: Japan.
Mombushō. Nihon Yunesuko
Kokunai Iinkai   2532

Japikse, Nicolaas   1567

Jásznigi, Alexander   1250

al-Jazarī, Muhammad ibn Muhammad ibn --SEE: Ibn al-Jazarī,
Muhammad ibn Muhammad
4556

Jean, Armand   4401

Jeanneret, Frédéric Alexandre
1853

Jeffery, Edmond C.   2076

Jeitteles, Ignaz   3640

Jelenić, Julijan   4402

Jen, Chia-yao   582

Jensson, Jens Christian--SEE:
Roseland, Jens Christian
4475

Jerrard, John   4076

Jervis, William Percival   2719

Jesús Andrade, Manuel de--SEE:
Andrade, Manuel de Jesús
676, 681

Jeune, Louis Marie Le--SEE: Le
Jeune, Louis Marie   509

Jewin, Newydd--SEE: Jones Edward (Jewin Newydd)   1225

Joannidès, A.   3168

João de São Pedro, Brother   165

Jöcher, Christian Gottlieb   117,
166-167, 198

Jördens, Karl Heinrich   3641

Jørgensen, John   2914

Johns, Fred   374, 376-377

Johnson, Alvin Saunders   4682

Johnson, Harold   3249, 3251-
3252

Johnson, Rossiter   2021

Johnson, Stanley Currie   168

Johnston, William   1209, 1215

Joint Committee of the American
Council of Learned Societies
and the Social Sciences Research Council   4684

Joint Committee on North Carolina
Literature and Bibliography of
the North Carolina English
Teachers Association and the
North Carolina Library As-
sociation   3412

Joliette, Quebec. Séminaire
3579

Jolly, Jean   762

Jones, Abner Dumont   1959

Jones, Bernard E.   2720

Jones, Edward (Jewin Newydd)
1225

Jones, F. O.   2915

Jones, Helen Gertrude (Dudenbostel)   28

Jones, Ifano   4021

Jones, Josiah Thomas   1226

Jones, Leonard Augustus   3982

Jones, M. O.   2916

Jones, Stephen   169, 3495

Jong, Pieter de   1311

Jónsson, Klemens   3960

Jónsson, Vilmundur   4084

Jordalen, Marion   2917

Jordan, John Woolf   2298, 2300

Jordell, Daniel   3580

Jose, Arthur Wilberforce   369

Joseph, René Édouard--SEE:
Édouard-Joseph, René   2485

Jourdan, Antoine Jacques Louis
4149

Journalistes associés, Montreal
499

Juchhoff, Rudolf   3508

Judd, Henry Pratt   2139

Julian, John   2918

Jullian, Pierre Louis Pascal de
127

Jung, Gertrud   4248

Junger, Henry   744, 794

Junk, Victor   3169

Justi, Karl Wilhelm   1048,
1050-1051

Juszyński, Michał Hieronim
3809

Juynboll, Willem Rudolf   2648

Jyotish Chandra Das Gupta--SEE:
Das Gupta, Jyotish Chandra
1268

Jyotischandra Dāsa Gupta-- SEE:
Das Gupta, Jyotish Chandra
1268

K

Kabisch, Ernst   987

Kagan, Solomon Robert   4150-
4151

Kahan Singh--SEE: Singh, Kahan
3727

Kahanovich, Moshe   1465

Kalai, David   1474

Kalina von Jäthenstein, Matthias
650

Kallmann, Helmut   2791

Kaltenbach, Gustave Émile
2535

Kamei, Takayoshi   163

Kamenskii, Dmitrii Nikolaevich
Bantysh-   SEE: Bantysh-
Kamenskii, Dmitrii Nikolae-
vich   1671-1674

Kaplan, Louis   1887

Kapoor, S. K.   3274

Kappa alpha   1960

Karila, Tauno   2919

Karpel, Bernard   2697

Karpman, Itzhak J.   4582

Kartsov, Vasilii Sergeevich   1663

Kastner, Emerich   2920

Kasumigaseki Kai   583, 1688

Kauffman, Daniel, Bp.   4403

Kaufman, Isaak Mikhailovich
1659

Kauz, Constantin Franz Florian
Anton von   389

Kay, John   1216-1217

Kayser, Wolfgang Johannes   3360

Kayserling, Meier   1463

Kazan, Russia (City) Universitet
3280

Keeler, Mary Frear   1154

Keene, Henry George   363

Keene, Josephine Bond (Hebron)
2305

Kehrein, Joseph   3644

Keiter, Heinrich   3643

Keitner, Árpâd   170-171

Keller, Gerhard   2921

Keller, Willy, biographer   1854

Kelly, Emerson Crosby   4152

Kelly, Howard Atwood   4153

Kempenaer, A. de   1552

Kennedy, James   1088

Kerambrun, René   726

Kerdanet, Daniel Louis Olivier
    Marie Miorcec de--SEE:
    Miorcec de Kerdanet, Daniel
    Louis Olivier Marie   870

Kerkhove, Ladislaus   4307

Kerr, Russell   2903

Kerviler, René Pocard du Cosquer
    de   868

Kesslin, Christian Friedrich
    3645

Kestner, Christian Wilhelm
    4154

Keussen, Hermann   970

Key, Pierre Van Rensselaer
    3017

Khalanskiĭ, Mikhail Georgievich
    3281

Khalīl ibn Aybak, al-Safadī--SEE:
    al-Safadī, Khalīl ibn Aybak
    1329

Khān, Mīr Muhammad--SEE:
    Mīr Muhammad Khān   3939

Khanolkar, G. D.   1276

Kharkov. Universitet   3281

al-Khatīb, al-Baghdādī   1322

Khautz, Constantin Franz Florian
    Anton von--SEE: Kauz, Con-
    stantin Franz Florian Anton
    von   389

Khayr al-Dīn, al-Ziriklī--SEE:
    al-Zirikli, Khayr al-Dīn
    1333

Khil, Martha   388

Khosla, Chaman Lal   3293

Khurshid, M. I.   4624

Khwānd Amīr, Ghiyās al-Dīn
    1323

Khwāndamīr--SEE: Khwānd Amīr,
    Ghiyas al-Dīn   1323

Kiaer, Frantz Casper   4155-
    4156

Kickert, Robert W.   4678

Kidrič, Franc   2406

Kidson, Frank   4022

Kiel. Universität   3282

Kiernan, Thomas P.   4143

Kiev. Universitet   3283

Kim Il-sŏng Chonghap Taehak,
    P'yongyang, Korea. Yŏksa
    Yŏn'guso   1492

Kimchi, Dov--SEE: Kimhi, Dov

Kimhi, Dov   4269

Kindermann, Heinz   3359, 3646-
    3648

King, Jeremiah   1304

King, Moses   2245

Kingston, John   1961

Kippis, Alexander   1094

Kirchner, Joachim   4025

Kirchner, Johannes Ernst   1243

Kirk, John   1156

Kirk, John Foster   3493

Kissling, Hans Joachim   1880

Kistler, Cyrill   2922

Kjerulf, Axel   2993

Kläbe, Johann Gottlieb August
1041

Klein, Johann Samuel   4404

Kleinert, Heinrich   3289

Kleinhans, Laureana Wright de--
SEE: Wright de Kleinhans,
Laureana   1550

Kleinman, Moses   1454

Kleist, Herbert   171

Klinck, Carl F.   3536

Kline, Jane   1889

Kluge, Gottlob   2923, 4405

Kluyskens, Hippolyte   4596

Knapp, Samuel Lorenzo   172

Kneschke, Ernst Heinrich   988

Knight, Charles   120

Knight, Gilfred Norman   236

Knight, Lucian Lamar   2136,

3413

Knippers, Ottis J.   2924

Knorr, George Wolfgang   2536

Knox, William M.   300

Kobolt, Anton Maria   1031-1032

Kobro, Isak   4156

Kobus, Jan Christiaan   1557

Koch, E. DeRoy   3211

Koch, Hans   1695, 1708

Koch, Ludwig   4406

Koch, Willi August   2925

Kőhalmi, Béla   3356

Köln--SEE: Cologne

Koht, Halvdan   3802

Kohut, Adolph   1464

Kojun Sha   1435

Kokusai Jijo Kenkyūkai   173

Kolatch, Alfred J.   4564

Komissiia "Nauchnye uchrezhdeniia
i nauchnye rabotniki SSSR"--
SEE: Akademiia nauk SSSR.
Komissiia "Nauchnye uchrezh-
deniia i nauchnye rabotniki
SSSR"   4606

Komissiia po istorii Oktiabr´skoi
revoliutsii i Rossiiskoi Kommunisticheskoi partii--SEE:
Kommunisticheskaia partiia
Soyetskogo Soiuza. TSentral´-
nyi Komitet. Otdel po istorii
Oktiabr´skoi revoliutsii i
Vsesoiuznoi Kommunisticheskoi
partii   1696-1697

Kommunisticheskaĭa partiĭa Sovet-
skogo Soĭuza. TSentral'nyĭ
Komitet. Otdel po istorii
Oktĭabr'skoĭ revoliŭtsii i
Vsesoĭuznoĭ Kommunistiches-
koĭ partii   1696-1697

Kondakov, S. N.   2537

Koner, Wilhelm David   1034,
3636

Koninklijk Academie voor Koloniale Wetenschappen--SEE:
Académie royale des sciences
d'outre mer   422

Koninklijk Belgisch Koloniaal In-
stitut--SEE: Académie royale
des sciences d'outre mer
422

Konstantinov, Georgi   3452

Kopala, Barbara   3338

Koppe, Johann Christian   1056,
3649, 3961

Korbut, Gabrjel   3810-3811

Kordes, Berend   3650

Korn, Friedrich   1462

Kornmüller, Utto   2927

Kort, Blanche L.   1915

Korzeniewska, Ewa   3811

Kosch, Wilhelm   989-990, 3170,
3651-3652

Koshinjō, Tokyo   589, 1431

Kosminska, Lucyna   4157

Kosmiński, Stanisław Lubicz
4157

Kossmaly, Karl   2928

Kothari, Henraj   4623

Kowalenko, Władysław   1757

Kowloon. Yu lien yen chiu so--
SEE: Yu lien yen chiu so,
Kowloon   614

Kozlov, A. G.   4794

Koz'min, Boris Pavlovich   1664,
3833

Krackowizer, Ferdinand   390

Kraft, Jens Edvard   3485, 3802,
3804

Kramm, Christiaan   2538

Krarup, Alfred   654

Krey, Johann Bernhard   1067

Krieger, Albert   1028

Kristjánsson, Jón   1256, 4158

Kristjánsson, Ólafur Þ.   3284

Kroll, Wilhelm   229

Krücken, Oskar von, pseud.--SEE:
Jásznigi, Alexander   1250

Krüger, Hermann Anders   3653

Kruseman, Philip   2921

Krzemiński, Stanisław   1628

Kublitskii, M. E.   2929

Kühner, Hans   4407

Kümmerle, Salomon   2930

Künstlerverein Bremen. Historische
Gesellschaft   1037

Kütner, Karl August   3656

Küttner, Karl August--SEE: Kütner, Karl August   3656

Kunc, Jaroslav   3474-3475

Kunisch, Hermann   3657

Kunitsch, Michael von   391

Kunitz, Stanley Jasspon   124,
3362-3366, 3414, 3509-3510

Kupriiânov, Ivan Kipriiânovich
1716

Kurz, Heinrich   3658

Kuśliński Auguste   795-797

Kutsch, K. J.   2933

Kutzbach, Karl August   3367

Kuznetsov, I. V.   4597

Kuznetsova, A. G.   3547

Kvadri, Vladimir Viktorovich
1698

Kylymnyk, O. V.   3937

Kyōdō Shuppansha Hensambu
3787

L

L., M.   1691

L., M. (i. e. Lacombe, monsieur
Jacques)   2539

L. y S., G. Mh.   113

Labande, Edmond René   4752

Labande-Mailfert, Yvonne   4752

Labarre de Raillicourt, Dominique
174

Lacaine, Victor   798

Lacál, Luisa   2934

Lacauchie, Alexandre   3156-
3157

La Chabeaussière, Ange Jacques
Marie Poissin   840

La Chavignerie, Émile Bellier de
--SEE: Bellier de La Cha-
vignerie, Émile   2437-2438

La Chesnaye-Desbois, François
Alexandre Aubert de   799

Lacombe, Jacques   2539

Lacombe de Prezel, Honoré   175

Lacrois, Jean   2989

Lacroix de Vimeur, Eugène A-
chille, comte de Rochambeau
--SEE: Rochambeau, Eugène
Achille Lacroix de Vimeur,
comte de   951

La Curne de Sainte-Palaye, Jean
Baptiste de--SEE: Sainte-
Palaye, Jean Baptiste de La
Curne de   3592

Ladvocat, Jean Baptiste   176

Laffont, Robert Raoul   3340-3341

Lafitte, Jacques   850

La Fizelière, Albert de   726, 784

Lafosse, Georges Touchard-
SEE: Touchard-Lafosse

Lagarde, Alexis   800

Laing, John   1088

Lajarte, Théodore Édouard Du
    Faure de   2776

Lake, Carlton   2476

Lakhtin, Mikhail IŪr'evich   4159

Lalanne, Ludovic   801

Lal Khosla, Chaman--SEE: Khos-
    la, Chaman Lal   3293

La Maisonfort, Louis de   750

Lamb, John Alexander   4517

Lamb, John S.   347

Lamb, Wilfrid John   347

Lami, Giovanni   1360

Lami, Stanislas   2700-2701

La Montagne, Victor Alexis de
    421

La Mothe de Combles, Louis
    Charles, comte Waroquier
    de Méricourt de--SEE:
    Waroquier de Méricourt de La
    Mothe de Combles, Louis
    Charles, comte   849

Lamothe-Langon, Étienne Léon,
    baron de   725, 946

Lance, Adolphe   2683

Lancetti, Vincenzo   1339, 3368

Landais, Napoléon   101

Landau, Thomas   4023

Landers, Joseph   2124

Landesmann, Heinrich   3659

Landman, Isaac   1478

Landshuth, Leser   2935, 4565

Lane, William Coolidge   1

Langbaine, Gerard   3511

Lange, Christian Christoph An-
    dreas   3802, 3804

Lange, Edmund   1061

Langeraad, L. A. van   4305

Langnas, Isaac A.   3336, 4743

Langon, Étienne Léon, baron de
    Lamothe-, SEE: Lamothe-
    Langon, Étienne Léon, baron
    de   725, 946

Langosch, Karl   3696

Langwill, Lyndesay G.   2936

Lanman, Charles   1432, 1963-
    1964

Lanner, Alois   392

Lanoix, Noël E.   499

Lanteires, Jean   177

Lapierre, Charles Ferdinand
    924

Lapierre de Châteauneuf, Agricol
    Hippolyte de   803

La Pipardière, pseud. --SEE: Le
    Cerf de la Viéville, Jean Phi-
    lippe   4408

Laporte, Joseph de   3574

Lara, Juana Manrique de--SEE:
    Manrique de Lara, Juana
    1520

Lara y Pardo, Luis   1532

Lardier, Alexandre   804

Larese, Dino   3925

Larned, Josephus Nelson   178

Laroiere, Louis de   441

Larousse, firm, publishers,
    Paris   2937

La Sinse, Célestin Sénès, called
    --SEE: Sénès, Célestin,
    called La Sinse   931

Lasso de la Vega y Argüelles,
    Angel   3870

Laszowski, Emilije   2409

Latassa y Ortín, Félix de,
    3861, 3871

Latham, Edward   179

Latimer, Louise Payson   4028

Latino Coelho, José María
    1642

Latouche, Henri de   735

Laughlin, Ledlie Irwin   2721

Laurens van Troostenburg de
    Bruijn, Casper Adams--SEE:
    Bruijn, Casper Adams Laurens
    van Troostenburg de   4312

Laurent, Ch. --SEE: Laurent, H.
    Charles   798

Laurent, H. Charles   798

Laurent-Gousse, Jean Théodore
    946

Lavallée, Joseph, marquis de
    Bois-Robert   805

Laverde Amaya, Isidoro   626-
    627

La Viéville, Jean Philippe Le
    Cerf de--SEE: Le Cerf de la
    Viéville Jean Philippe   4408

Lawätz, Heinrich Wilhelm   18

Lawless, Ray McKinley   2938

Lawrence, Alberta (Chamberlain)
    3323

Lawrence, John Thomas   2939

Lawrence Radiation Laboratory,
    Livermore, Calif. --SEE:
    California. University.
    Lawrence Radiation Labora-
    tory, Livermore   4675

Lazikean, Arsen Ghazaros--SEE:
    Ghazikean, Arsen Ghazaros
    361

Leadership Index   2287

Leahy, Ethel Carter   2280

Leal, Antonio Henriques--SEE:
    Henriques Leal, Antonio
    478

Lebard, Denise Ledoux-   SEE:
    Ledoux-Lebard, Denise
    2722

Lebedev-Polianskii, P. I.   3371

Le Bouvier de Fontenelle, Ber-
    nard--SEE: Fontenelle, Ber-
    nard Le Bovier de   4587

Lebreton, Théodore Éloi   920

Lebrocquy, Guillaume   442

Lecarpentier, Charles Jacques
    François   2540

Le Cerf de la Viéville, Jean Philippe   4408

Le Chaplain, Julien   839

Lecina, Mariano   4265, 4519

Leclaire, Lucien   3512

Leclerc, Charles Guillaume
176

Le Court, G. de   419

Lecourt, Jules Victor de--SEE:
Delecourt, Jules Victor
419-420

Lecouvet, Ferdinand, F. J.
443

Ledebur, Carl Friedrich Heinrich
Wilhelm Philipp Justus,
Freiherr von   2940

Ledoux-Lebard, Denise   2722

Leduc, Alberto   1532

Lee, Sir Sidney   1124, 1126-
1127, 1130

Leete, Frederick De Land
4509

Le Fanu, W. R.   4190

Lefranc, Simon   1771

Legipont, Oliver   4552

Lehmann, Ernst   4644

Lehms, Georg Christian   3660

Lehnert, Georg   1049

Leidenfrost, Carl Florentin   181

Leipoldt, Friedrich   2941

Le Jeune, Louis Marie   509

Lelong, Jacques   702

Lemazurier, Pierre David
3172

Lemmen, Joseph von   2635

Lemoine, Henry   187

Lempriere, John   182

Le Neve, Joseph   1158, 4410-
4411

Leningrad. Akademiia nauk SSSR
--SEE: Akademiia nauk SSSR
4574-4575 [etc.]

Leningrad. Gosudarstvennyi russkii muzei   2541

Leningrad. Imperatorskaia
Mediko-khirurgicheskaia a-
kademiia--SEE: Leningrad.
Voenno-meditsinskaia akademiia   4160-4161

Leningrad. Institut grazhdanskikh
inzhenerov--SEE: Leningrad.
Inzhenerno-stroitel'nyi institut   4795

Leningrad. Inzhenerno-stroitel'-
nyi institut   4795

Leningrad. Mediko-khirurgicheskaia akademiia--SEE: Leningrad. Voenno-meditsinskaia
akademiia   4160-4161

Leningrad. Publichnaia biblio-
tela   3830

Leningrad. Universitet   3286

Leningrad. Voenno-meditsinskaia
akademiia   4160-4161

Lennartz, Franz 3369, 3661

Lenzi, Luigi Aliquò--SEE: Aliquò Lenzi, Luigi 3734

León Freyre, Eduardo Ponce de-- SEE: Ponce de León Freyre Eduardo 1762

Leonard, John William 1970, 2073, 2302

L'Epine, Geoffrey--SEE: Epine, Geoffrey l' 3126

Leporin, Christian Polycarp 992

Lepreux, Georges 4024

Lermina, Jules Hippolyte 806

Le Roy, Alphonse 3290

Lesaulnier, C. M. 807

Lethbridge, Sir Roper 1277

Letillois, of Mézières 874

Letzer, J. H. 2942

Leuridant, Félicien 418

Lévée, Jérôme Balthazar 891

Levenson, M. L. 1699-1700

Levere, William Collin 1965

Levillier, Roberto 348

Levitskii, Grigorii Vasil'evich 3287

Levot, Prosper Jean 809, 869

Lewis Publishing Company, Chicago 1954, 2090, 2151, 2155, 2158, 2163, 2197, 2212, 2222, 2300

Lewytzkyi, Borys 1701

Leyland, John 4162

Leymarie. Achille 810

Lezhava, Liudmila 1697

Li, Hsi-keng 584

Li, Huan 585

Liang, Ch'i-hsiung 539

Liang, I-chen 586

Liang, T'ing-ts'an 587

Lianovosani, Luigi, pseud. --SEE: Salvioli, Giovanni 3045

Library of Congress--SEE: U. S. Library of Congress 1, 28, 609, 1889

Librovich, Sigismund Feliksovich --SEE: Librowicz, Zygmunt, 3831

Librowicz, Zygmunt 3831

Lichtenthal, Peter 2943

Liebman, Charles 3965

Liège. Université 3290

Lieutaud, Soliman 702-703

Liévyns, A. 811

Lihori y Pardines, José María Ruiz de, barón de Alcahalí y de Mosquera--SEE: Alcahalí y de Mosquera, José María Ruiz de Lihori y Pardines, barón de 2423, 2744

Lilja, Gösta 2628

Lillywhite, Frederick 3230

Lillywhite, John   3230-3231

Lima. Escuelas Americanas--
    SEE: Escuelas Americanas,
    Lima   1604

Lin, Po-ai   1513

Linares, Antonio   1408

Lindenbaum, Arne   3196

Lindner, August   4413-4414

Lindner, Johann Wilhelm Sigis-
    mund   3699

Lindner, Kurt   3232

Lindtner, Niels Chr.   3486

Linke, Wilhelm   1069

Linnström, Hjalmar   4026

Lipowsky, Felix Joseph   2944

Lippe, Chayim David   3791

Lipschitz, Sergeĭ IUl'evich
    4645

Lira, Pedro   2542

Liruti, Gian Giuseppe   3762

Lisovskiĭ, Nikolaĭ Mikhaĭlovich
    2945

List, Jacob Samuel   3336

Lister, Raymond   4744

Litta, Pompeo   1362-1364

Little, Andrew George   4515

Livermore, Mary Ashton (Rice)
    2072

Livet, Charles Louis   844

Livingston, John   1966

Livrauw, François   439, 444

Ljubić, Sime--SEE: Gliubich,
    Simone   2401

Llaguno y Amírola, Eugenio
    2684

Llana, Pedro de la   1613

Lloyd, Frederic Ebenezer John
    2946

Lloyd, Herbert Alan   2723

Lobineau, Guy Alexis   4418

Lockyer, Herbert   4270

Lodovici, Sergio   2543

Löhneysen, Hans Wolfgang
    2544

Loetscher, Lefferts Augustine
    4484

Löwy, David   1466

Logasa, Hannah   19

Loliée, Frédéric Auguste   135

London. Cymmrodorion Society--
    SEE: Cymmrodorion Society,
    London   1222-1223

London, Friends' Institute--SEE:
    Friends' Institute, London
    4372

London. National Portrait Gallery
    1161

London. Royal College of Physi-
    cians--SEE: Royal College
    of Physicians of London
    4196

London. Royal College of Veterinary Surgeons--SEE: Royal College of Veterinary Surgeons, London 4192

London. Royal Society--SEE: Royal Society of London 4610-4611

London. St. Peter's College-- SEE: St. Peter's College, London 1175-1176

London. Tate Gallery--SEE: Tate Gallery, London 2630

London. Westminster School-- SEE: St. Peter's College, London 1175-1176

Long, Basil Somerset 2545

Long, George 268

Long, Robert James 3513

Longacre, James Barton 1949

Longchampt, Jacques 2823

Longden, Henry Isham 4419

Longhena, Francesco 4199

Loosjes, Jakob 4305, 4420

Lopes Graça, Fernando, 2784

López, Juan Catalina García-- SEE: García López, Juan Catalina 3867

López Mena, Héctor F. 1533

Lord, Eleazar 182

Loredano, Giovanni Francesco 1365

Lorenz, Otto Henri 3580

Lorenzen, Wolfgang 3663

Lorm, Hieronymus, pseud.--SEE: Landesmann, Heinrich 3569

Los Angeles Examiner 2331

Louisiana. Dept. of Education 3291

Lourdoueix, Paul de 812

Love, James 2807

Lovett, Gabriel H 1504

Low, Sir Sidney James Mark 1162

Lowe, Claude Egerton 2947

Łoza, Stanisław 1631, 2685

Lubos, Arno 3666

Luca, Ignaz de 393

Lucas, Florentino Zamora--SEE: Zamora Lucas, Florentino 1762

Luchet, Jean Pierre Louis de la Roche du Maine, marquis de 776, 779

Ludeking, Willem Ernst 4163

Ludovici, Gottfried 4163

Lübker, Detlev Lorenz 3603, 3664-3665

Lüdtke, Gerhard 3655

Lueker, Erwin Louis 4421

Lütgendorff, Willibald Leo, Freiherr von 2948

Lukman, Franc Ksaver 2406

Lundin, August Herman 1820

Lupach, V. S.   4748

Lushev, Andrei Mikhailovich
1702

Lut, Claude Bréghot du--SEE:
Bréghot du Lut, Claude   905

Lutheran Theological Seminary,
Philadelphia--SEE: Phila-
delphia (Mt. Airy) Lutheran
Theological Seminary   4460

Lutz, Markus   1855-1856

Luykx, Theo   3268

Luzzatto, Rola   1246

Lynam, Edward   4745

Lynch, James Daniel   3966-
3967

Lyonnet, Henry   3173

Lysnes, Olaf   4457

M

M., E. C. de   718

M......l, Sylvain--SEE: Maréchal, Pierre Sylvain   4427

Maatschappij Tot Nut van't Algemeen, Amsterdam   1558

McAdam, David   3958

Macbean, Lachlan   1113

McBride, Alexander   2257

McCabe, Joseph   4422-4423

MacCallum, Thomas Watson 188

McCartney, Mrs. Elizabeth
Myers, 2949

Macdonald, Hugo Schramm-
SEE: Schramm-Macdonald,
Hugo   222

MacDonald, Mary B.   3909

Macedo, Joaquim Manuel de
479

McElroy, William Henry   2257

McGrath, Hyland   2144

Macgregor, Malcolm Blair   4424

Mac Guckin de Slane, William,
baron--SEE: Slane, William
Mac Guckin, baron de,   1320

Machado, Diogo Barbosa--SEE:
Barbosa Machado, Diogo
1640

Machado-Guimarães, Argeu de
Segadas--SEE: Segadas
Machado-Guimarães, Argeu
de   484

Machum, George C.   510

McIntyre, Philip Willis   2175

McIntyre, Willard Ezra   4425

Mackenzie, Donald   1163

Mackenzie, John   3598

McKerrow, Ronald Brunlees
4027

Maclean, Donald   3599

McLean, W. Moore   1633

McNamara, Daniel Ignatius
2747

Macpherson, Hector Copland
4671

Mac-Pherson, Telasco A.
2388-2389

Macquoid, Percy   2724

Macray, William Duncan   4762

Madarász, Elemér   1248

Madigan, Thomas F.   1967

Madrid. Academia de Jurisprudencia y Legislación--SEE:
Academia de Jurisprudencia
y Legislación, Madrid
3940

Madsen, Herman   2546

Madsen, Johannes   664

Mägis, Konrad   3926

Maelen, Philippe Marie Guillaume
van der   446

Maeyer, Edward Anton de   693

Magalon, Joseph Dominique   813

Magenet, François Peyrot-
SEE: Peyrot-Magenet, François   889

al-Maghribi, 'Ali ibn Mūsā, called Ibn Sa'īd--SEE: Ibn Sa'īd,
'Ali ibn Mūsā, al-Maghribi,
called   1321

Magill, Frank Northen   3372

Magliabecchi, Antonio   1369

Magnette, Paul   2950

Magnin, Étienne   4344

Magnus, Laurie   3373

Magon, Leopold   3626

Mahony, Bertha E. --SEE: Miller, Bertha E. (Mahony)
4028-4029

Mahul, Alphonse Jacques   51

Maidment, James   1217, 3514

Maier-Bruck, Franz   396

Mailfert, Yvonne Labande-
SEE: Labande-Mailfert,
Yvonne   4752

Maillard, Robert   2476-2477,
2695, 3147-3148

Maine Writers Research Club
3415

Mairan, Jean Jacques Dortous
de   4600

Maisonfort, Louis de la--SEE:
La Maisonfort, Louis de
750

Maitron, Jean   757

al-Majlis al-A'lā lil-'Ulūm--SEE:
Egypt. al-Majlis al-A'lā
lil-'Ulūm   4583

Mak, Bolesław--SEE: McLean,
W. Moore   1633

Mak van Waay, S. J.   2547

Makhnovets', L. IE   3938

Maktab al-Dirāsāt al-'Arabīyah
1324

Malchelosse, Gérard   495

Maliszewski, Edward   1624

Malkin, Arthur Thomas   239

Mallet, Charles   814

Mallett, Daniel Trowbridge
2548-2549

Malmin, Rasmus   4529

Malvasia, Carlo Cesare, conte
2550

Mandel'shtam, Roza Semenovna
1704

Manes, Alfred   4708

Manferrari, Umberto   2951

Mangenot, Eugène   4346

Manget, Jean Jacques   4164

Mangin, Arthur   4601

Mangler, Joyce Ellen   2952

Manhattan Publishing Company,
Chicago   2103

Mank, Alī ibn Bālī, called--SEE:
Alī ibn Bālī, called Mank
1874

Mankowitz, Wolf   2725

Manly, John Matthews   3416,
3420, 3517

Manne, Edmond Denis de   707

Manne, Louis Charles Joseph de
707

Mannheim. Bibliographisches In-
stitut--SEE: Bibliographisches
Institut A. G., Mannheim
2966, 3376

Manni, Domenico Maria   1391,
2430

Manni, Giuseppe   1391

Manrique de Lara, Juana   1520

Mantzel, Ernst Johann Friedrich
1057

Manuel de Sancta Luzia, Brother--
SEE: Manuel de Santa Luzia,
Brother   4426

Manuel de Santa Luzia, Brother
4426

Manuel, E. Arsenio   1615

Manuel, Louis Pierre--SEE:
Manuel, Pierre   815

Manuel, Pierre   815

Manzano, Cipriano Muñoz y, conde
de la Viñaza--SEE: Viñaza,
Cipriano Muñoz y Manzano,
conde de la   2646

Marable, Mrs. Mary Hays   3417

Marcel, Adrien   2642

Marchal, Victor   461

Marchand, Prosper   191

Marchant, Braulio Pérez--SEE: Pérez Marchant, Braulio   680

Marcos, Miguel de la Plata y --SEE:
Plata y Marcos, Miguel de la
4189

Maréchal, Pierre Sylvain   4427

Maréchal, Sylvain--SEE: Maréchal,
Pierre Sylvain   4427

Margalioth, Mordechai--SEE: Margulies, Mordecai   1455, 4561

Marggraff, Hermann   3135

Margreiter, Hans   381

Margulies, Mordecai   1455, 4561

Mariette, Pierre Jean   2551

Marín, Francisco Rodríguez--
SEE: Rodríguez Marín, Francisco   3886

Marindin, George Eden   266

Mariz, Vasco   2953

al-Markaz al-Qawmī lil-Buhuth--
SEE: Egypt. al-Markaz al-
Qawmī lil-Buhuth   4585

Markov, Pavel Aleksandrovich
3198

Marple, Alice   3418

Marquard, Emil   665

Marquardt, Dorothy A.   3386

Marques de Sousa Viterbo, Fran-
cisco--SEE: Sousa Viterbo,
Francisco Marques de   2687

Marquis, Albert Nelson   2042,
2127, 2211

Marrazzo, Javier   349

Marsal, Domingo Prat--SEE:
Prat Marsal, Domingo   3020

Martens, Frederick Herman
2954

Martí Grajales, Francisco
3872

Martial de Saint-Jean-Baptiste,
Father   4428

Martialis a Sancte Joanne Bap-
tista, Father--SEE: Martial
de Saint-Jean-Baptiste, Father
4428

Mart'ianov, Sergeĭ Nikolaevich
3393

Martin, David, Brother   3419

Martin, Frederick   190

Martín, Gabriel María Vergara
y --SEE: Vergara y Martín,
Gabriel María   1805

Martin, Jules   3581

Martin, Michael   1504, 1968

Martin, Michael Rheta--SEE:
Martin, Michael   1504,
1968

Martin, Otto   4644

Martindale, James Boyd   3968

Martínez, Benigno T.   1781

Martínez Alomia, Gustavo
4763

Martínez Añibarro y Rives, Manuel   3873, 3888

Martínez Arango, Felipe   637

Martínez Morellá, Vicente   3874

Martini, Pietro   1403

Martinien, Aristide   816

Martino, Agustín Renedo--SEE:
Renedo Martino, Agustín 3883

Martins Bastos, Francisco Antonio   4165

Martins de Carvalho, Francisco
Augusto   1643

Martorana, Pietro   3763

Martov, N.   3832

Martuscelli, Domenico   1395

Marvin, Francis Sydney   147

Mary Anthony, Sister--SEE:
    Scally, Mary Anthony, Sister,
    3426

Maryland Biographical Associa-
    tion   2177

Masanov, Ivan Filippovich   1664

Masi, Henri Armand de --SEE:
    De Masi, Henri Armand
    3205

Mason, Daniel Gregory   2954

Massachusetts Biographical
    Society   2185

Massachusetts centinel   1882

Massachusetts Publishing Com-
    pany   2119, 2191

Massarelli, Guido   3771

Massó Torrents, Jaime   3454-
    3455

Masson, Paul   866

Massy, Charles Francis   1594

Mastrigli, Leopoldo   2955

Masutto, Giovanni   2956

Matas, J. Ricart--SEE: Ricart
    Matas, J.   3033

Mathéfilo, pseud. --SEE: Cas-
    cales y Muñoz, José   3862

Mather, Frank Lincoln   2071

Mathews, Shailer   4271

Matini, Ugo   2519

Maton, Émile--SEE: Maton, Jo-
    seph Émile   749

Maton, Joseph Émile   749

Mattheson, Johann   2957

Matthews, Ruth   2739

Matthews, William   494, 1086-
    1087, 1888

Matthieu, Ernest Antoine Joseph
    Ghislain   447

Mattos, Manoel de Sá--SEE: Sá
    Mattos, Manoel de   4197

Mattos, Ricardo Pinto de--SEE:
    Pinto de Mattos, Ricardo
    1645

Matute y Gaviria, Justino   1807-
    1808

Maunder, Samuel   192

Maxiriarth, pseud. --SEE: Hart-
    zenbusch e Hiriart, Eugenio
    1761

Maxwell, Sir William Stirling-,
    bart. --SEE: Stirling-Max-
    well, Sir William, bart.   2623

Mayer, Claudius Frank   4166

Mayer, Leo Ary   2686

Mayer-Serra, Otto   2958

Mayerhöfer, Josef   4599

Mayers, William Frederick
    590

Mayo Clinic, Rochester, Minn.
    4167

Mayr, Johann Simon   2959

Mazaev, Mikhail Nikolaevich
1663

Mazza, Jose   2960

Mazzetti, Serafino   3192

Mazzuchelli, Giovanni Maria,
conte   3764

Medel, Ramón   1802

Médelsheim, Alphonse Cerfberr
de--SEE: Cerfberr de
Médelsheim, Alphonse   856

Medical Society of the State of
New York   4170

Medici, Paolo Sebastiano   4429

Mediko-khirurgicheskaiă akademiiă, Leningrad--SEE:
Leningrad. Voenno-meditsin-
skaiă akademiiă   4160-4161

Medina, José Toribio   525, 533,
535, 1497, 4430

Mee, Arthur   193

Megargee, Louis N.   2306

Mège, Alexandre Louis Charles
André du--SEE: Du Mège,
Alexandre Louis Charles
André   946

Mehring, Daniel Gottlieb   3636,
3691

Meijer, Bernhard   3921

Meister, Leonhard   1857-1858,
3667

Mejía Robledo, Alfonso   1597

Melchinger, Siegfried   3374

Melchior, Edward A.   2961

Melzi, Gaetano, conte   1340-
1342

Melzi, Gaetano A.   1340

Memorial History Company, Newark, N. J.   2239

Memorial Society of Michigan,
inc.   2198

Mena, Héctor F. López--SEE:
López Mena, Héctor F.
1533

Mencke, Friedrich Otto   199

Mencke, Johann Burkhard   198-
199

Mendel, Hermann   2962-2963,
3032

Mendelson, Samuel   2246

Mendelson, William   2246

Méndez Bejarano, Mario   1809-
1810, 3875

Mendiburu, Manuel de   1605-
1606

Ménégault, A. P. G.   3375

Menil, Alexander Nicolas de--
SEE: De Menil, Alexander
Nicolas   3402

Mennell, Philip   367

Méricourt de La Mothe de Combles,
Louis Charles, comte Waroquier de--SEE: Waroquier
de Méricourt de La Mothe de
Combles, Louis Charles,
comte   849

Merland, Constant Jacques
950

Merlino, Adrián   2552

Merlo, Johann Jakob   2553

Mersch, Jules   1511

Merseburger, Carl Wilhelm   2964

Mertsalov, V. S.   1693

Merzalow, Wladimir S. --SEE:
    Mertsalov, V. S.   1693

Mesa Ortiz, Rafael M.   628

Mesanza, Andrés   4433

Mésengui, François Philippe   4385

Mésenguy, François Philippe--
    SEE: Mésengui, Francois
    Philippe   4385

Mestre Ghigliazza, Manuel   1534

Metcalf, Frank Johnson   2965

Meulemeester, Maurice de   4435

Meurs, Johannes van   3294

Meursius, Jan (or Joannes)--SEE:
    Meurs, Johannes van   3294

Meusel, Carl--SEE: Meusel,
    Karl Heinrich   4436

Meusel, Johann Georg   2554,
    3633, 3668

Meusel, Karl Heinrich   4436

Meyer, Andreas   3669

Meyer, Ferdinand   1035

Meyer, Julius   2555, 2564

Meyer, William   413

Mh. L. y S., G.   113

Miao, Ch'üan-sun   591

Michael, Heimann Joseph   4566

Michaelis, Adolf Alfred   2967

Michaelis, Alfred--SEE: Mi-
    chaelis, Adolf Alfred   2967

Michaud, Joseph François   78,
    80

Michaud, Louis Gabriel   74, 80

Michel, Emmanuel   915

Michel, François   2836

Michigan. Dept. of State   2202

Michigan. Historical Commis-
    sion   2203

Michigan. State Library, Lan-
    sing   2556

                    of School
)8-3409

Middleton, Erasmus   4437

Mieli, Aldo   4603-4604

Mifsud, Ignazio Saverio   1516

Migne, Jacques Paul   4368

Mikhailovskii-Danilevskii,
    Aleksandr Ivanovich   1705

Mikszáth, Kálmán   1253

Milanović, Mihajlo   2403

Miles, James Samuel   1134

Milićević, Milan Ðuro 2404-2405

Military Order of the Loyal Legion of the United States. Illinois Commandery 1972

Millares Carlo, Agustín 3876

Millares Torres, Agustín 1793

Miller, Bertha E. (Mahony) 4028-4029

Miller, Edmund Morris 3516

Miller, Josiah 2968-2969

Miller, Maude M. 3217

Miller, Paul Edward 2970

Miller, Stephen Franks 3969

Miller, William, biographer 1164

Millett, Fred Benjamin 3416, 3420, 3517

Millot, Claude François Xavier 3592

Mills, Hazel E. 3422

Min, Erh-ch'ang 592

Minami, Shigeki 1436

Minaño, N. N. 1792

Minchero Vilasaró, Angel 3377

Minde-Pouet, Georg 3626

Ming Biographical History Project--SEE: Association for Asian Studies. Ming Biographical History Project 542

Minghetti, Aurelio 2726

Mingote y Tarazona, Policarpio 1799

Minicucci, Attilio 4174

Minieri-Riccio, Camillo 1367, 3765-3766

Minnesota. Statehood Centennial Commission. Centennial Literature Group 3421

Miorcec de Kerdanet, Daniel Louis Olivier Marie 870

Mir Muhammad Khān 3939

Mira, Giuseppe Maria 1409

Mirabeau, Honoré Gabriel Riquetti, comte de 779

Mississippi. Secretary of State 2219

Mithoff, H. Wilhelm H. 2557

Mitteldeutscher Kulturrat e. V. 994

Mittelhaus, Karl 229

Miunster, Aleksandr Ernestovich 1706

Mize, John Townsend Hinton 2909

Moberg, Carl Allan 3073

Modena (Province) Deputazione di storia patria per le provincie modenesi 4753

Modzalevskiĭ, Boris L'vovich 1711, 4575

Moehsen, Johann Karl Wilhelm 4175

Mørck, Fredrikke   1589

Moffatt, James   2973

Mogami, Umeo   1428

Mohammad Barque, Ali--SEE:
    Barque, Ali Mohammad
    1262, 1595

Mokul'skii, Stefan Stefanovich
    3198

Molhuysen, Philip Christiaan
    1562

Molin, Gösta Gideon   1821

Molina, Antonio Elías de--SEE:
    Elías de Molina, Antonio
    3453

Molina Arrotea, Carlos   350

Molinier, Émile   2558

Moller, Johannes   1070, 1824

Monay, Ferenc   3718

Moncada, José Pío Tejera y
    Rodríguez de--SEE: Tejera,
    José Pío   3892

Mondadori, Alberto   3343

Mongitore, Antonio   3767

Mongrédien, Georges   3174

Monnier, Désiré   896

Monod, Lucien   2559

Monroe, Paul   3295

Monroy, Guadalupe   1520

Monselet, Charles   3582

Montagne, Victor Alexis de la--
    SEE: La Montagne, Victor
    Alexis de   421

Montaiglon, Anatole de Courde
    de   2551

Montandon, Leon   1850

Montenegro, Raúl Garbín--SEE:
    Garbín Montenegro, Raúl
    1604

Montero y Pérez, Adalmiro
    3885

Monterosso, Raffaello   2974-
    2975

Montet, Albert de   1859

Montferrand, A. de, pseud. --SEE:
    Chesnel, Adolphe de   3560

Montoto de Sedas, Santiago
    1505

Moodie, Roy Lee   4635

Moore, Frank   1973-1974

Moore, Frank Ledlie   2976

Moore, J. M.   2093

Moore, John Weeks   2977-2978,
    4030

Moore's Who is Who Publications,
    inc.   2376

Mora, José Ferrater--SEE: Fer-
    rater Mora, José   4238

Morachevskii, N. IA.   3830

Morais, J. V.   1515

Moral, Bonifacio   4439, 4481

Moral, José García del--SEE:
García del Moral, José 4133

Moral San Román, Bonifacio del
--SEE: Moral, Bonifacio
4439, 4481

Morales, José Enrique Serrano
y --SEE: Serrano y Morales,
José Enrique 4042

Morales Díaz, Carlos 1535

Moranz, John 2341

Mordovtsev, Daniil Lukich 1707

Morejón, Antonio Hernández--
SEE: Hernández Morejón,
Antonio 4142

Morel de Rubempré, J. 4176

Morellá, Vicente Martínez--SEE:
Martínez Morellá, Vicente
3874

Morelli, Nicolò 1396

Moréri, Louis 201

Morgan, Henry James 512,
3518, 3970

Morgan, John Vyrnwy 1227,
4440

Morgan, Tom 3246

Mori, Emilio Cotarelo y --SEE:
Cotarelo y Mori, Emilio 4005

Morice, Adrien Gabriel 513

Morin, Gösta 3073

Moroni, Gaetano 4441

Morozov, Aleksei Vikulovich
1660-1661

Morris, Charles 202, 1975
2259

Morris, David K. 203

Morris, Richard Brandon 1976

Morris, William Meredith 2979

Morrison, Joseph M. 1963

Mortara, Marco 3792

Mortimer, Thomas 204, 1098

Moscow. Akademiia nauk SSSR--
SEE: Akademiia nauk SSSR
4574-4575 [etc.]

Moscow. Gosudarstvennaia akademiia khudozhestvennykh
nauk. Kabinet revoliutsion-
noi literatury 3833

Moscow. Universitet 3296

Moscow. Universitet. Obshchestvo
liubitelei rossiiskoi slovesnosti 3297, 4031

Moser, Hans Joachim 2980,
3171

Moser, Johann Jakob 3971,
4442

Moskovskoe arkheologicheskoe
obshchestvo 4764

Mosquera, José María Ruiz de
Lihori y Pardines, barón de
Alcahalí y de--SEE: Alca-
halí y de Mosquera, José
María Ruiz de Lihori y Par-
dines, barón de 2423, 2744

Motschmann, Justus Christoph
3298

Mott, Abigail (Field) 1977

Mott, Agnes   4443

Mottley, John   3542

Mouhy, Charles de Fieux, chevalier de   3175

Moulières, Antoine Joseph Raup de Baptestein de--SEE: Raup de Baptestein de Moulières, Antoine Joseph   831

Mount Holyoke College. Alumnae Association   1978

Mourier, Athénaïs   3583-3584

Mourik, Bernardus   3972, 4177

Mourre, Michel   205

Moyer, Elgin Sylvester   4444

Moyer, Homer Edward   2131

Mozley, Ann   372

Müffling, Wilhelm, Freiherr von   995

Mueller, Erich Hermann   2931, 2981

Mueller, Hedwig   2931

Müller, Hermann Alexander   2560-2561

Müller, Holger Ehrencron-SEE: Ehrencron-Müller, Holger   653, 3478-3479

Müller, Kurt   1701

Mueller von Asow, Erich Hermann --SEE: Mueller, Erich Hermann   2931

Mueller von Asow, Hedwig--SEE: Mueller, Hedwig   2931

Muenster, Aleksandr Ernestovich--SEE: Miunster, Aleksandr Ernestovich   1706

Muhammad ibn 'Abd al-Rahmān, al-Sakhāwī--SEE: al-Sakhāwī, Muhammad ibn 'Abd al-Rahmān   1330

Muhammad ibn Ahmad, al-Dhahabī--SEE: al-Dhahabī, Muhammad ibn Ahmad   1311

Muhammad ibn al-Gazarī--SEE: Ibn al-Jazarī, Muhammad ibn Muhammad   4556

Muhammad ibn Ibrāhīm Farīd al-Dīn 'Attār--SEE: Farīd al-Dīn 'Attār   4555

Muhammad ibn Muhammad ibn al-Jazarī--SEE: Ibn al-Jazarī, Muhammad ibn Muhammad   4556

Muhammad ibn Sa'd--SEE: Ibn Sa'd, Muhammad   4557

Muhammad Khalīl ibn 'Alī, al-Murādī--SEE: al-Murādī, Muhammad Khalīl ibn 'Alī   1327

Muhammad Khān, Mīr--SEE: Mīr Muhammad Khān   3939

Muhibb al-Dīn, al-Dimashkī   1326

Mundt, Hermann   996

Munich. Osteuropa Institut   1695, 1708

Munich. Universität. Slavisches Seminar   1756

Muñiz, Roberto   4445

Munk, William   4196

Muñoz, Bernardo Uribe--SEE:
Uribe Muñoz, Bernardo
3919

Muñoz, Gustavo Otero--SEE:
Otero Muñoz, Gustavo
631

Muñoz, José Cascales y --SEE:
Cascales y Muñoz, José
3862

Muñoz y Manzano, Cipriano,
conde de la Viñaza--SEE:
Viñaza, Cipriano Muñoz y
Manzano, conde de la   2646

Munster, Alexandre E. --SEE:
Miunster, Aleksandr Er-
nestovich   1706

al-Murādī, Muhammad Khalīl ibn
'Alī, 1327

Murakami, Masayuki   53

Murchison, Carl Allanmore
4249

Murguía, Manuel   3602

Murphy, William D.   2260

Mursinna, Samuel   3462

Muschi, Jean Bernard   3670

Musgrave, Sir William   1165

Músiol, Robert Paul Johann
2994

Muteau, Charles François Thérèse
871

Muzzio, Julio A.   351

Myers, Bernard S.   2489

Mylius, Johann Christoph   36

Mysore   1279

N

La Nación, Buenos Aires   355

Nagler, George Kaspar   2555,
2562-2564

Najm al-Dīn Muhammad ibn Muhammad, al-Ghazzī--SEE:
al-Ghazzī, Najm al-Dīn Muhammad ibn Muhammad   1316

Naniwa, Tsuneo   598

Napiersky, Karl Eduard   415-
416

Nasimovich, Nikolaĭ Fedorovich
1740

National Aeronautics and Space
Administration--SEE: U. S.
National Aeronautics and
Space Administration   4673

National Association of Real Estate Boards   4734

National Association of Science
Writers   4605

National Biographical Publishing
Company   2178, 2310

National Biographical Society,
inc., Washington   2122,
3238

National Library of Australia--
SEE: Canberra, Australia.
National Library   373

National Maritime Museum,
Greenwich, Eng. --SEE:
Greenwich, Eng. National
Maritime Museum   1145

National Poetry Association
3543

National Portrait Gallery, London--SEE: London. National Portrait Gallery 1161

National Research Council. Committee on an International Directory of Psychologists 4244

National Research Council. Committee on International Relations in Anthropology 4761

National Society for the Blind 2053

National Society for Professional Musicians--SEE: Incorporated Society of Musicians 2908

Navarrete, Martín Fernández de 4746

Nebioǧlu, Osman 1875-1877

Nebraska. Legislative Council 2223

Nebraska. Legislative Reference Bureau 2223

Nebraska Press Association 2224

Nefelov, K. S. 3834

Neff, Christian 4432

Negri, Giulio 3768

Neira, José Sánchez de--SEE: Sánchez de Neira, José 3234

Nelke, David Inman 1954

Nellist, George Ferguson Mitchell 226, 593, 1616

Nelson, Robert J 3959

Nettelbla, Christian, Freiherr von 1822

Nettelbladt, Christian, Freiherr von--SEE: Nettelbla, Christian, Freiherr von 1822

Neubauer, Ernst Friedrich 4446

Neubert, Franz 975

Neumann, Wilhelm 2565-2566

Neumann Gandía, Eduardo 1651

Nevskii, Vladimir Ivanovich 1710

New England Historical Publishing Company, Boston 2171

New Jersey. Legislature 2240

New York. Botanical Garden. Library 4646

New York. Institute for Research in Biography, inc. --SEE: Institute for Research in Biography, inc. , New York 307-308 [etc.]

New York. Union Theological Seminary 4447

New York (State) University 4245

New York Academy of Medicine. Library 4053-4054

New York and Hartford Publishing Company 2015-2016

New York Botanical Garden Library--SEE: New York. Botanical Garden. Library 4646

New York Historical Society
2567

New York Institute for Research
in Biography, inc. 2049

The New York times 195

The New Yorker 24

New Zealand Association of
Scientists 4607

New Zealand Author's Week Committee 3521

New Zealand Library Association
4048

Newman, John Henry, Cardinal
4416

Newmark, Maxim 3877

Neyen, Auguste 1512

Nguyễn-huyên-Anh 2395

Nicanor, Precioso M. 1990

Nicéron, Jean Pierre 213, 3986

Nichols, John 3522, 4045

Nicholson, Reynold A. 4555

Nicodemo, Lionardo 1398

Nicolas, Michel 2568

Nielsen, Lauritz 4032

Nielsen, Ove 4791

Niemann, Walter 2997

Nienaber, Petrus Johannes
328, 3395

Nieto Caballero, Luis Eduardo 629

Nihon Gaikujutsu Shinkōkai--SEE:
Nippon Gakujutsu Shinkōkai
3299, 4796-4797

Nihon Shuppan Kyōdō Kabushiki
Kaisha 3788

Nikitina, Evdoksiiă Fedorovna
3846

Nikolaĭ Mikhailovich, Grand Duke
of Russia 1711-1715

Nikol'skiĭ, Nikolaĭ Konstantinovich 4031

Nikol'skiĭ, V. A. 3835

Nippon Butsurigakkai 4672

Nippon Chosakuken Kyōgikai 1422

Nippon Gakujutsu Shinkōkai 3299,
4796-4797

Nisenson, Samuel 214-216

Nitowski, Jan 1628

Noble, Mark 1166

Nocq, Henry 2569

Nodal, John Howard 3535

Noël, François Joseph Michel
217

Noorthouck, John 218

Nopitsch, Christian Conrad 1059

Nork, Fr., pseud.--SEE: Korn,
Friedrich 1462

Norlie, Olaf Morgan 3300,
4529

Norlind, Tobias 2998

North Carolina. Secretary of State 2266

North Carolina English Teachers Association 3412

North Carolina Federation of Music Clubs 2999

North Carolina Library Association 3412

North Dakota. State Historical Society 2267

Northen, William J. 2137

Northwest Publishing Company, Chicago 2210

Norway. Kontoret for kulturelt samkven med utlandet 2570

Norway. Office of Cultural Relations--SEE: Norway. Kontoret for kulturelt samkven med utlandet 2570

Norwegian Ministry of Foreign Affairs. Office of Cultural Relations--SEE: Norway. Kontoret for kulturelt samkven med utlandet 2570

Notgemeinschaft der Deutschen Wissenschaft 4621

Nováček, Zdenko 2794

Novellis, Carlo 1400

Novikov, Nikolaĭ Ivanovich 1724, 3836

Nowack, Karl Gabriel 3671

Nuñez Olaechea, Samuel 4798

Nungezer, Edwin 3176

Nūr Allāh, Shūshtarī 4559

Nūrī, Nūr Allāh, Shūshtarī, called--SEE: Nūr Allāh Shūshtarī 4559

Nuttall, P. Austin 1141

Nyerup, Rasmus 3485

O

Obermeyer, Eva 398

Obol'ianinov, Nikolaĭ Aleksandrovich 1665

Obshchestvo liubitelei rossiĭskoĭ slovesnosti--SEE: Moscow. Universitet. Obshchestvo liubitelei rossiĭskoĭ slovesnosti 3927, 4031

Obshchestvo peterburgskikh vrachei-nemtsev 4178

Obshchestvo politkatorzhan i ssyl'no-poselentsev--SEE: Vsesoiuznoe obshchestvo politicheskikh katorzhan i ssyl'no-poselentsev 1682, 1745-1746

O'Byrne, William Richard 1167

Odoars, Antoine Étienne Nicolas Fantin des--SEE: Fantin des Odoars, Antoine Étienne Nicolas 3563

O'Donoghue, David James 3523

Oefele, Andreas Felix von 4179

Øst, Niels Christian 3484

Österreichische Akademie der Wissenschaften--SEE: Akademie der Wissenschaften, Vienna 398

Österreichisches Institut, Vienna   397

Oettinger, Eduard Maria   20, 221-222

Ogawa, Kandō   4246

Ogden, Mary Depue   2239

Ogle (George Alden) and Company 2322, 2333

O'Hanlon, John   4448

Ōkawa, Shigeo   1436

Oklahoma. State Library, Oklahoma City. Legislative Reference Division   2286

Oklahoma Biographical Association   2284

Olaechea, Samuel Núñez--SEE: Núñez Olaechea, Samuel 4798

Ólason, Páll Eggert   1257

Oldelli, Gian Alfonso   1861

Olenin, K. L.   3837

Oliver, George   4449

Olives Canals, Santiago   1786

Olivier-Poli, Gioacchino Maria 223

Ollard, Sidney Leslie   4450

Ollivier, Charles Prosper   4120

Olpp, Gottlieb   4180

Olsen, Helge   3001

Olsen, Rider Fraser   329

Olsson, Otto   3001

Olszewicz, Bolesław   1634

O'Neall, John Belton   3975

O'Neil, A.   2572

O'Neill, Edward Hayes   21

Onis y Sánchez, Federico de 3878

Ontiveros, Edmundo Bolio--SEE: Bolio Ontiveros, Edmundo 1522

Operti, Piero   3783

Opfergeldt, Friedrich   1468

Orbegoso, Luis Varela y--SEE: Varela y Orbegoso, Luis 1610

O'Reilly, Edward   3730

O'Reilly, Patrick   1574-1575

Orlandi, Pellegrino Antonio 2573, 3770

Orlers, Jan Jansz   3294

Ormis, Ján Vladimír   645

Orru, G.   3003

Ortega Torres, José Joaquín 3913

Ortín, Félix de Latassa y --SEE: Latassa y Ortín, Félix de 3861, 3871

Ortiz, Rafael M. Mesa--SEE: Mesa Ortiz, Rafael M. 628

Ortolani, Giuseppe Maria   1410

Ōrui, Noburu   224

Osborn, Herbert   4647

Osetrov, Z. B.   3818

Oslo. Deichmanske bibliotek--
SEE: Deichmanske bibliotek,
Oslo   1582

Osores y Sotomayor, Félix
1536

Ospina, Joaquín   630

Ossinger, Joannes Felix   4451

Ossorio y Bernard, Manuel
2574, 3346, 3879

Osterroth, Franz   1003

Osteuropa Institut, Munich--SEE:
Munich. Osteuropa Institut
1695

Otero, Manuel Ovilo y --SEE:
Ovilo y Otero, Manuel 3880

Otero Muñoz, Gustavo   631

Otto, Friedrich   3490

Otto, Gottlieb Friedrich   3672-
3673

Otto, Nikolai Karlovich   1716

Ouimet, Raphael   498

Oursel, Mme. Noémi Noire
921-922

Ouseley, Sir Gore, bart.   3806

Overseas Press Club of America
3435

Ovilo y Otero, Manuel   1782,
3880

Owen, William, afterwards Owen-
Pughe--SEE: Pughe, Wil-
liam Owen   1172

Owen-Pughe, William--SEE:
Pughe, William Owen   1172

Oxford. University   1168

Oxford. University. Merton College   1169

Oxford. University. Rhodes
Scholarships   3301

P

P. --SEE: Trap, Jens Peter
672

P****, P***   720

Paap, Wouter   2745

Pachulski, Henryk   2904

Pacific Northwest Library Association. Reference Sec-
tion   3422-3423

Padovano, Ettore   2575

Pagel, Julius Leopold   4181

Pahissa, Jaime   2818

Pahlen, Kurt   3004

Paiva, Tancredo de Barros   472

Pakhul'skii, G. --SEE: Pachulski, Henryk   2904

Paldamus, Friedrich Christian
3658

Palgrave, Sir Robert Harry
Inglis   4774

Palmer, Russell   3005

Palmer, Theodore Sherman   4629

Palmgren, H.   1823

Palomar, Fernando Castán--SEE:
Castán Palomar, Fernando
1789

Palomino de Castro y Velasco,
Acisclo Antonio   2576-2577

Palsbo, Torben   4012

Pamard, Francis Gadan-   SEE:
Gadan-Pamard, Francis
3147-3148

Pamplona, Fernando de   2578

P'an, Nien-chih   4247

Pan American Union. Letters Section   3914

Pan American Union. Music Section   2892, 3006

Panassié, Hugues   3007

Panchulidzev, Sergeĭ Alekseevich
1717

Panelli, Giovanni--SEE: Panelli d'
Acquaviva, Giovanni   4182

Panelli d'Acquaviva, Giovanni
4182

Pantaleon, Heinrich   1004-1005

Panum, Hortense   3008

Papillon, Philibert   3586

Papinot, E.   1437

Paquot, Jean Noël   1566

Paquot, Oscar Edmond Ris-   SEE:
Ris-Paquot, Oscar Edmond
2418

Parada, Diego Igancio   3881

Parada y Barreto, José   3009

Pardines, José María Ruiz de
Lihori y, barón de Alcahali
y de Mosquera--SEE: Alca-
halí y de Mosquera, José
María Ruiz de Lihori y Pardines, barón de   2423, 2744

Pardo, Luis Lara y --SEE: Lara
y Pardo, Luis   1532

Paredes de Salazar, Elssa
469

Parente, Gino   3771

Parenti, Marino   4015

Paris. Académie des sciences--
SEE: Académie des sciences,
Paris   4571

Paris. Société bibliographique--
SEE: Société bibliographique,
Paris   4363

Park, Esther Ailleen   2579

Park, Thomas   3539

Parker, Alfred   214-216

Parker, John   3212

Parker, William Belmont   352,
470, 534, 638, 1599, 1607,
2382

Parker, William Mathie   3524

Parkhurst, Winthrop   2816

Parlagi, Imre   1250

Parley, Peter, pseud. --SEE:
Goodrich, Samuel Griswold
138

Parry, John Humffreys   1228

Partisch, Hubert   399

Partito nazionale Fascista   4771

Parton, James   2016

Pascallet, E.   71, 75

Pascoe, Charles Eyre   3180

Pascoli, Lione   2580

Passano, Giovanni Battista
1340-1342

Passeri, Giovanni Battista
2581

Pataky, Frau Sophie   3674,
3688

Paterson, James   1216-1217

Patin, Charles   3302

Patin da La Fizelière, Albert--
SEE: La Fizelière, Albert
de   726, 784

Patinus, Carolus--SEE: Patin,
Charles   3302

Patrick, David   3500

Patrick, Millar   2973

Patten, James Alexander   4453

Pauer, Ernst   3010

Paul, Sir James Balfour   1218

Paul, Oskar   3011

Paula González y Sáenz, Francisco de--SEE: González y
Sáenz, Francisco de Paula
1794

Paula Pavía y Pavía, Francisco
de--SEE: Pavía y Pavía,
Francisco de Paula   1783

Paullini, Christian Franz   3675

Pauly, August Friedrich von
228-231

Pauwels de Vis, Jean   453

Pavard, Camille   454

Pavía, Francisco de Paula Pavía
y --SEE: Pavía y Pavía,
Francisco de Paula   1783

Pavía, Lázaro   1537

Pavía y Pavía, Francisco de
Paula   1783

Pavière, Sydney Herbert   2582

Pavlovskii, Evgenii Nikanorovich
4628

Pavlovskii, Ivan Frantsevich
1718-1719

Pavolini, Luisa   2875

Pavón, Francisco de Borja   1795

Pavullo, Placido da, Father--SEE:
Placido da Pavullo, Father
4463

Payne, James Bertrand   12

Paz, Ireneo   1538-1539

Paz-Soldán, Juan Pedro   1608

Pearce, Joseph   3013

Peck, Harry Thruston   3466

Pedio, Tommaso   1385

Pedrell, Felipe   3014

Peel, Albert   4454

Pehnt, Wolfgang   2681

Pei ching Fu wu she   594

Peiba, Abraham, pseud. ?
3181

Peignot, Gabriel   232

Peisse, Louis   4183

Pekarskiĭ, Petr Petrovich
3303

Peking Photo Agency   543

Peking. Tsing Hua College--SEE:
Tsing Hua College, Peking
615-616

Pelandi, Luigi   2465

Pelliccioni, Armando   2583

Pelloquet, Théodore   2584

Peloux, Charles, vicomte du--
SEE: Du Peloux, Charles,
vicomte   2483

Pelster, Franz   4415

Pelzel, Franz Martin   652,
4555

Peña, Joaquín   3015

Peña y Reyes, Antonio de la
1540

Penido, Miguel Colmeiro y--SEE:
Colmeiro y Penido, Miguel
4633

Peral, Miguel Angel   1541-1542

Peraza Sarausa, Fermín   639-
640

Perdigão, Henrique   3378

Pereira da Costa, Francisco
Augusto   480

Pérennes, François Marie
4368

Péres, Domingo Garcia--SEE:
Garcia Péres, Domingo
3868

Peretiatkowicz, Antoni   1635

Pérez, Adalmiro Montero y --
SEE: Montero y Pérez,
Adalmiro   3885

Pérez, José Gestoso y --SEE:
Gestoso y Pérez, José
2713

Pérez, Nicolás Díaz y --SEE:
Díaz y Pérez, Nicolás
1797

Pérez Costanti, Pablo   2585

Pérez Marchant, Braulio   680

Péricaud, Antoine   905

Péricaud, Louis   3182

Péricaud, Marc Antoine--SEE:
Péricaud, Antoine   905

Péricaud aîné--SEE: Péricaud,
Antoine   905

Perim, Damião de Froés, pseud.
--SEE: João de São Pedro,
Brother   165

Perini, Davide Aurelio   4456

Perkins, Archie E.   2168

Perkins, Charles Callahan   2460

Perlebert, Max   595

Perlman, William J.   2983-2984, 2986-2988

Perraud de Thoury, Eugène   227

Pertsch, Heinrich--SEE: Pertsch, Johann Heinrich   3379

Pertsch, Johann Heinrich   3379

Peru   1609

Pescetto, G. B.   4184

Pesche, Julien Rémy   906

Peszke, Józef Emiljan   4157

Peters, Percy   4825

Peters, Thomas   1289, 1291

Petersdorff, Hermann von   1006

Peterson, Eldridge   4723

Peterson, John   4457

Petin, L. M.   4458

Petri Suffridus--SEE: Suffridus, Petrus   3597

Petrich, Hermann   1062

Petrograd--SEE: Leningrad

Petrus Suffridus--SEE: Suffridus, Petrus   3597

Petry, Karl   3676

Pettersen, Hjalmar Marius   1584

Pettigrew, Thomas Joseph   4185

Peuker, Johann Georg   1074

Peurot-Magenet, Francois   889

Pezzana, Angelo   3732

Pezzl, Johann   400

Pfeil, Heinrich   3016

Pfenninger, Heinrich   1858, 3667

Pfister, Aloys   4459

Pfister, Louis--SEE: Pfister, Aloys   4459

Phelps, Robert H   195

Philadelphia (Mt. Airy) Lutheran Theological Seminary   4460

Phillips, David Lyman   2143

Phillips, Edward   3525

Phillips, Lawrence Barnett   235

Phragmenius, Johann Jacob--SEE: Phragmenius, Jonas Joannes

Phragmenius, Jonas Joannes   414

Phrangoules, A. P.   42

Physical Society of Japan--SEE: Nippon Butsurigakkai   4672

Picatoste y Rodríguez, Felipe   4608

Piccirilli, Ricardo   341

Pichler, L.   3623

Picinelli, Filippo   3772

Pick, Fred Lomax   236

The Picturegoer weekly (Periodical)   3183

Pierce, Edward M   237

Piercy, William Coleman   4527

Pietro Amat di S. Filippo--SEE: Amat di S. Filippo, Pietro 4737

Pigoreau, Alexandre Nicolas 3587-3588

Piles, Alphonse Toussaint Joseph André Marie Marseille, comte de Fortia de--SEE: Fortia de Piles, Alphonse Toussaint Joseph André Marie Marseille, comte de 772

Piles, Roger de   2586-2587

Pilkington, Matthew   2588, 2615

Pillado, José Antonio   339

Pillwein, Benedikt   2589

Pin, Lewis Ellis du--SEE: Dupin, Louis Ellies   4356-4357, 4755-4756

Pine, Leslie Gilbert   1105

Pingaud, Bernard   3585

Pinheiro Chagas, Manuel   1644

Pinkerton, John   4461

Pinneberg, Ger. Baltic University   3304

Pinto de Mattos, Ricardo   1645

Pinto Durán, Carlos   528

Pío Tejera y Rodríguez de Moncada, José--SEE: Tejera, José Pío   3892

Pipardière, La, pseud. --SEE: Le Cerf de la Viéville, Jean Philippe   4408

Pipp, Edwin Gustav   2201

Piron, Constant Fidèle Amand 455

Pirsoul, Léon   3446

Pisani, Paul   4462

Pitseus, Ioannes--SEE: Pits, John   3526

Pits, John   3526

Pittler, D.   2083, 2085, 2109, 2128, 2208

Pittroff, Rainer   4187

Piver, Jack   4729

Pizzi, Francesco   1336-1337

Placcius, Vincent   35-37

Place, Joseph   3594

Placido da Pavullo, Father 4463

Plancy, Jacques Albin Simon Collin de--SEE: Collin de Plancy, Jacques Albin Simon 4234

Plarr, Victor Gustave   194, 4188, 4190

Plata y Marcos, Miguel de la 4189

Platts, John   238

Pleasants, Helene   4233

Pletnev, Petr Aleksandrovich
3839

Plomer, Henry Robert   4008,
4033-4035

Pluquet, Francois André Adrien
4464

Plusieurs hommes de lettres,
belges et étrangers   781

Plusieurs publicistes   778

Plusieurs journalistes   821

Pökel, Wilhelm   3467

Pölnitz, Götz, Freiherr von
1076

Poggendorf, Johann Christian
4609

Poggiali, Cristoforo   1399

Pohren, Donn E.   3184

Poidras, Henri   3178-3179

Poinsot, Edmond Antoine   708

Pointel, Philippe, marquis de
Chennevières- SEE: Chen-
nevières-Pointel, Philippe,
marquis de   2461, 2561

Pointel, Phillippe Chennevieres--
SEE: Chennevières-Pointel,
Philippe, marquis de
2456, 2561

Poli, Gioacchino Maria Olivier-
SEE: Olivier-Poli, Gioac-
chino Maria   223

Polianskii, P. I. Lebedev- SEE:
Lebedev-Polianskii, P. I.

Polillo, Arrigo   3089

Pollard, Alfred William   4008

Polska Akademia Nauk   1636

Polska Akademia Nauk. Instytut
Sztuki   3072

Polska Akademia Nauk. Komitet
Słowianoznawstwa   1757

Polska Akademia Umiejetności,
Krakow   1636

Ponce de León Freyre, Eduardo
1762

Ponomarev, Stepan Ivanovich
3840

Pons Boigues, Francisco   4765

Pontificia università lateranense,
Rome--SEE: Rome (City)
Pontificia università latera-
nense   4303

Poole, Leila M.   1620-1621,
1623

Pooley, J. A. Sinclair   299

Popov, Pavel Nikolaevich--SEE:
Popov, Pavlo Mykolaiovych

Popov, Pavlo Mykolaiovych   2590

Port, Célestin   908, 2591

Portal, Charles Louis Henri Félix Antoine   2592

Portalis, Roger, baron   2593-
2594

Posselt, Ernst Ludwig   824

Post, Hermann von   1036

Postal, Bernard   3233

Potter, Frans de   3491

Potter, George   200

Potthast, August   687

Pouet, Georg Minde-   SEE:
   Minde-Pouet, Georg   3626

Pougin, Arthur   2857

Powell, William Henry   1997-
   1999

Power, Sir D'Arcy   4188, 4190

Pozzo, Bartolomeo Fr. dal,
   conte   2595-2596

Praeger, Robert Lloyd   4648

Pragier, Abram   2743

Prague. Česká akademie věd a
   uměni--SEE: Česká akademie
   věd a uměni, Prague   3012,
   4581

Pramūanwit, pseud.   1872

Prande, Alberts   3797

Prat Marsal, Domingo   3020

Pratt, Alfred T. Camden   1170

Pratt, Waldo Selden   3018-3019

Pravitz, Gunnar   1838

Preev, Zinovy N.   1723

Preiss, H.   84

Preston, Wheeler   2000

Prévost, Michel   760

Prezel, Honoré Lacombe de--SEE:
   Lacombe de Prezel, Honoré
   175

Prieberg, Fred K.   3021

Prieto, Luis Francisco--SEE:
   Prieto del Río, Luis Francisco
   535, 4465

Prieto del Río, Luis Francisco
   535, 4465

Prims, Floris   456

Pritzel, Georg August   4649

Proctor, Lucien Brock   3977

Promis, Carlo   4799

Propriac, Catherine Joseph Ferdinand Girard de--SEE: Girard
   de Propriac, Catherine Joseph
   Ferdinand   136

Protestant Episcopal Church in
   the U. S. A.   3022, 4331

Provenzal, Giulio   4662

Provincial medical journal   4162

Prudhomme, Louis Marie   240,
   826

Puente, Rafael Carrasco--SEE:
   Carrasco Puente, Rafael
   3904

Pughe, William Owen   1172

Pulgar Vidal, Javier   4800

Pulling, Frederick Sanders   1162

Pulver, Jeffrey   3023

Purón, Manuel García--SEE:
   García Purón, Manuel   1529

Q

al-Qiftī, 'Ali ibn Yūsuf   4191

Quakers--SEE: Friends, Society
of   1091-1092, 4372

Quarry, W. Edmond   3024

Quatremère de Quincy, Antoine
Chrysostome   2597

Quénard, Philippe   827

Quentin de Richebourg, Louis
René, marquis de Champ-
cenetz--SEE: Champcenetz,
Louis René Quentin de Richebourg, marquis de   836,
3591

Quérard, Joseph Marie   704-705,
709, 3580, 3589-3590

Quétif, Jacques   4466

Quilliet, Frédéric   2598

Quincy, Antoine Chrysostome
Quatremère de--SEE: Quat-
remère de Quincy, Antoine
Chrysostome   2597

Quinn, Thomas Charles   2192

R

R., D. J.   112

Raban, Louis François   830

Rabbe, Alphonse   242

Raczyński, Atanazy, hrabia
2599

Radcliffe, Geoffrey Reynolds Yonge
1176

Radier, Jean François Dreux
du--SEE: Dreux du Radier,
Jean François   929, 945

Rafols, José F.   2600

Ragusa, Girolamo   1411

Raige-Delorme, Jacques
4120, 4122

Raillicourt, Dominique Labarre
de--SEE: Labarre de Ralli-
court, Dominique   174

Raines, Caldwell Walton   2346

Raineval, Melville Amadeus Henry Douglas Heddle de la Caillemotte de Massue de Ruvigny,
9th marquis of Ruvigny and--
SEE: Ruvigny and Raineval,
Melville Amadeus Henry Douglas Heddle de La Caillemotte
de Massue de Ruvigny, 9th
marquis   689-690, 1174

Rainguet, Pierre Damien   934

Ram Gopal Sanyal--SEE: Sanyal,
Ram Gopal   1283

Rāmagopāla Sānnyāla--SEE:
Sanyal, Ram Gopal   1283

Ramírez, José Fernando   3902

Ramírez, Julio C. Cárdenas--
SEE: Cárdenas Ramírez,
Julio C.   1604, 2386

Ramírez de Arellano, Rafael
1796, 2601

Ramírez de Arellano y Gutiérrez
de Salamanca, Carlos   3882

Ramis, Juan Ramis y --SEE:
Ramis y Ramis, Juan   1803

Ramming, Martin   1438

Ramsgate. St. Augustine's Abbey
    --SEE: St. Augustine's Abbey,
    Ramsgate   4309

Rand, John Clark   2189

Rand, Oscar Zalka   4567

Rand, McNally and Company
    4714

Ranft, Michael   4467

Ransom, James Harley   3240

Ranta, Sulho   3025

Rao, Conjeeveram Hayavadana,
    rao sahib--SEE: Hayavadana
    Rao, Conjeeveram, rao sahib
    1275

Rappoport, Angelo Solomon
    243

Rasi, Luigi   3186

Rassmann, Christian Friedrich
    957, 3026, 3677-3682

Rassmann, Ernst   3683-3684

Rassmann, Friedrich--SEE:
    Rassmann, Christian Fried-
    rich   957, 3026, 3677-3682

Rastawiecki, Edward, baron
    2602

Rathlef, Ernst Ludwig   244,
    270, 685

Ratti, Carlo Giuseppe   2620

Rau, Wilhelm   3724

Raup de Baptestein de Moulières,
    Antoine Joseph   831

Raymond, Ida, pseud.--SEE: Tar-
    dy, Mrs. Mary T.   3430

Raynal, Louis Hector Chaudru de
    3956

Rāzī Amīn Ahmad--SEE: Amīn
    Ahmad, Rāzī   1309

Réalités cambodgiennes   493

Rebord, Charles M.   4468

Reboul, Robert Marie   710

Recke, Johann Friedrich von
    415-416

Recupito, Marco Vinicio   3027

Les Redacteurs de "Notre his-
    toire"   726

Redgrave, Samuel   2603

Redmont, Bernard Sidney   3434

Reed, George Irving   2144, 2152,
    3978-3979

Reed, Isaac   3495

Reed, Luther Dotterer   4460

Reed, Parker McCobb   3980

Rees, Thomas Mardy   1229, 2604

Rees, William Jenkins   4469

Refardt, Edgar   3028, 3063

Reformed Church in America
    4334

Regis, Giuseppe Maria   3981

Regli, Francesco   3773

Reichard, Bartholomaeus Chris-
    tian   3306

Reichard, Carl   245

Reichard, Karl--SEE: Reichard, Carl   245

Reichl, Kurt   401

Reid, John   3600

Reifenberg, Benno   963, 982

Reiflingen, Erwin Schwarz-- SEE: Schwarz-Reiflingen, Erwin   3065

Reinert, Charles   3187

Reines, Moses   1471

Reis, Antonio Simões dos--SEE: Simões dos Reis, Antonio   473, 3817

Reis, Claire (Raphael)   3029

Reisen, Zalman   3793

Reiss, Józef Władysław   3030- 3031

Reissmann, August   2962, 3032

Un Religieux bénédictin de la Congrégation de St. Vannes-- SEE: François, Jean   4371

Remendo, Baltasar Saldoni y -- SEE: Saldoni y Remendo, Baltasar   3043

Remmelgas, L.   3551

Renauldin, Léopold Joseph   4193

Renda, Umberto   3783

Renda-Ragusa, Girolamo--SEE: Ragusa, Girolamo   1411

Rendle, Alfred Barton   4631

Renedo Martino, Agustín   3883

Reno, Conrad   3982

Renouard, Augustin Charles   3956

Renouard, Philippe   4036-4037

Rescher, Oskar   1874, 1878

Restrepo, Gustavo Arboleda-- SEE: Arboleda, Gustavo   625, 677

Retizos, Isidro L.   1617

Reume, Auguste Joseph de   4038-4039

Reuss, Jeremias David   3529

Révai, József   3356

Révay, József--SEE: Révai, József   3356

Révérend, Albert, vicomte   832-834

Rey, Bernard   944

Reyes, Antonio de la Peña y -- SEE: Peña y Reyes, Antonio de la   1540

Rezabal y Ugarte, José de   3884

Rhode Island. Dept. of State   2313

Ribadeneyra, Pedro de--SEE: Rivadeneira, Pedro de   4472

Ribeiro, José Jacintho   482

Ribera, Almerico   1356

Ricart Matas, J.   3033

Richard, Bartholomaeus Christian--SEE: Reichard, Bartholomaeus Christian   3306

Riccio, Camillo Minieri-   SEE: Minieri-Riccio, Camillo   1367, 3765-3766

Richards, Carmen Nelson   3425

Richards, Eva   13

Richardson, Clement   1986

Richebourg, Louis René Quentin de, marquis de Champcenetz--SEE: Champcenetz, Louis René Quentin de Richebourg, marquis de   836, 3591

Riches, Phyllis M.   22

Richter, Gottfried Lebrecht   3685

Richter, Vilhelm   668-669

Richert, Edith   3416, 3420, 3517

Rico García, Manuel   3885

Rico y Sinobas, Manuel   4040

Ricordi (G.) e compagnia   2824

Ridder, Alfred de   439

Ridolfi, Carlo   2605

Riedl, John O.   4252

Riemann, Hugo   3034

Riemens, Leo   2933

Riewe, F.   3035

Rigdon, Walter   3188

Rijksuniversiteit Ghent--SEE: Ghent. Rijksuniversiteit   3268

Riksföreningen for svenskhetens bevarande i utlandet   1829

Rilli, Jacopo   1369

Río, Luis Francisco Prieto del--SEE: Prieto del Río, Luis Francisco   535, 4465

Rion, Adolphe   835

Rioseco, Arturo Torres--SEE: Torres Rioseco, Arturo   3918

Ris-Paquot, Oscar Edmond   2418

Ritson, Joseph   3530

Rivadeneira, Pedro de   4472

Rivarol, Antoine   836, 3591

Rivas, Heriberto García--SEE: García Rivas, Heriberto   1530

Rivas, Raimundo   633

Rivecourt, W. de   1557

Rivera, Manuel--SEE: Rivera Cambas, Manuel   1544

Rivera Cambas, Manuel   1544

Rivera de Álvarez, Josefina   3915

Rivers, David   3531

Rives, Manuel Martínez Añibarro y --SEE: Martínez Añibarro y Rives, Manuel   3873, 3888

Rivier, Jean Augustin Amar du--SEE: Amar du Rivier, Jean Augustin   79

Rivière, Ernest M.   4289

Rizzi, Fortunato   3307

Roach, Bertie S.   376

Robbins, Rossell Hope   4253

Robert, Adolphe   762, 837, 839,
    842

Robert, Jean Baptiste Magloire
    838

Robert, M.--SEE: Robert, Jean
    Baptiste Magloire   838

Roberts, Sir Charles George
    Douglas   517

Roberts, T. R.   1230

Robinet, Jean François Eugène
    839

Robinson, Donald B.   246

Robledo, Alfonso Mejía--SEE:
    Mejía Robledo, Alfonso
    1597

Robles, Federico Carlos Sáinz
    de--SEE: Sáinz de Robles,
    Federico Carlos   3382

Robles, Luis Ballesteros--SEE:
    Ballesteros Robles, Luis
    1801

Robson (C.) and Company   2326

Robson, Charles   2326

Rocard, J.   897

Rocco, Emmanuele   1340-1342

Rochambeau, Eugène Achille
    Lacroix de Vimeur, comte
    de   951

Rochas, Adolphe   879

Rochester, Minn. Mayo Clinic--
    SEE: Mayo Clinic, Rochester,
    Minn.   4167

Rock, Christa Maria (Wiesner)
    3036-3037

Rodale, Jerome Irving   247

Rodergas i Calmell, Josep
    1763

Rodosskii, Aleksei Stepanovich
    4473

Rodríguez, Felipe Picatoste y --
    SEE: Picatoste y Rodríguez,
    Felipe   4608

Rodríguez de Moncada, José Pío
    Tejera y --SEE: Tejera,
    José Pío   3892

Rodríguez Demorizi, Emilio
    674

Rodríguez Marín, Francisco
    3886

Rodríguez Saavedra, Manuel
    3908

Röder, Erwin   3038

Roeder, Helen   4474

Roeder, William S.   248

Römpp, Hermann   4663

Rössler, Hellmuth   1008

Rogalski, Leon   271

Roger, Paul André   457

Rogerio Sánchez, José   3887

Rogers, Augustus C.   2003-
    2004

Rogers, Joel Augustus   249

Rogers, Thomas J.   2005

Rojas, José María   4016

Rollett, E.   394

Roloff, Ernst Max   3288

Rome (City) Collegio araldico
    1361

Rome (City) Pontificia università
    lateranense. Istituto Giovanni
    XXIII   4303

Romig, Walter   1896, 2129, 3340

Ronart, Nandy   1328

Ronart, Stephan   1328

Ronco, Amadeo   3381

Roquet, Antoine Ernest   4041

Roqueta, Bartolomé María
    Xiberta y --SEE: Xiberta y
    Roqueta, Bartolomé María
    4548

Rosa di Villarosa, Carlo Antonio
    de, marchese--SEE: Villa-
    rosa, Carlo Antonio de Rosa
    di, marchese   3106

Roscoe, James Ernest   3308

Rose, George Maclean   516

Rose, Henry John   251

Rose, Hugh James   251

Roseland, Jens Christian   4475

Rosenbaum, Alfred   955, 958,
    3624

Rosenbloom, Joseph R.   2006

Rosenthal, Eric   330

Rosenthal, Harold D.   3039

Rosi, Michele   1355

Rosow, Jerome M.   1901

Ross, Frederick   1241

Rosselló, Joaquín María Bover
    de --SEE: Bover de Rosselló,
    Joaquín María   1802, 3859-
    3860

Rossi, Giovanni Bernardo de
    3441, 3794

Rossiĭskaia Akademiia nauk,
    Sankt-Peterburg--SEE: A-
    kademiia nauk SSSR   4574-
    4575 [etc.]

Rossiĭskaia Kommunisticheskaia
    partiia--SEE: Kommuni-
    sticheskaia partiia Sovetskogo
    Soiuza   1696-1697

Rossmässler, F.   4194

Rotermund, Heinrich Wilhelm
    1038, 1046

Roth, Andrew   1173

Roth, Cecil   1476

Rothe, Eva   3626

Rothert, Wilhelm   1047

Roucek, Joseph Slabey   1758

Rougnon, Paul Louis   3040

Roukema, Roelof   4195

Roumagnac, Carlos   1532

Roussado Gorjão, João Damasio
    1647

Roussel, François   4385

Rousset, Henry   880

Routh, Charles Richard Nairne
    4767

Roux, Xavier   881

Rovinskiĭ, Dmitriĭ Aleksandro-
    vich   1724-1725, 2606-2607

Rovito, Teodoro   3774

Row, Augustus   252

Rowell Art Publishing Company
    2113

Rowland, E. H.   1231

Royal College of Physicians of
    London   4196

Royal College of Veterinary Sur-
    geons, London   4192

Royal Commonwealth Society.
    Library   23

Royal Institute of British Archi-
    tects. Library.   2419

Royal Naval College, Greenwich,
    Eng.--SEE: Greenwich, Eng.
    Royal Naval College   1145

Royal Norwegian Ministry of
    Foreign Affairs. Office of
    Cultural Relations--SEE:
    Norway. Kontoret for kul-
    turelt samkven med utlandet
    2570

Royal Society of London   4610-11

Royal Technical College, Glasgow
    SEE: Glasgow. Royal Tech-
    nical College   4660

Rozanov, Ivan Nikanorovich
    3841

Rubbi, Andrea   1370

Rubempré, J. Morel de--SEE:
    Morel de Rubempré, J.
    4176

Rubets, Aleksandr Ivanovich
    3041

Rubin, Eli   1472

Ruby, Lawrence   4675

Rudkin, S. J.   2108, 2315

Rudolph, Moritz   3189

Rue, Pieter de la   1569

Rüdiger, Horst   3360

Ruiz, I. Toro--SEE: Toro Ruiz,
    I.   681

Ruiz, Licinio   3888

Ruiz de Lihori y Pardines, José
    María, barón de Alcahalí y
    de Mosquera--SEE: Alca-
    halí y de Mosquera, José
    María Ruiz de Lihori y
    Pardines, barón de   2423,
    2744

Rumor, Sebastiano   3775

Rump, Ernst   2608

Runes, Dagobert D   4262

Runkevich, Stepan Grigor'evich
    4476

Runnquist, Åke   3922

Rusakov, G.   1697

Rusakov, Viktor, pseud. --SEE:
Librowicz, Zygmunt   3831

Russell, Josiah Cox   3532

Russell, William Thompson
4521

Russia. Gosudarstvennyĭ Sovet
1727

Russia (1923-   U. S. S. R.)
Verkhovnyĭ Sovet   1728

Russkoe botanicheskoe obshchest-
vo--SEE: Vsesoiuznoe botanicheskoe obshchestvo   4650

Russkoe istoricheskoe obshchestvo   1731

Russo, Luigi   3776

Russov, Stepan Vasil'evich 3842

Rutter, H. Thornton   4825

Ruvigny and Raineval, Melville
Amadeus Henry Douglas Heddle de La Caillemotte de
Massue de Ruvigny, 9th
marquis of   689-690, 1174

Ryan, Richard   1305

S

S. , T.   371

Sá, Manuel de   4477

Sá Mattos, Manoel de   4197

Saavedra, Manuel Rodríguez--
SEE: Rodríguez Saavedra,
Manuel   3908

Sabater, Gaspar   1773

Sabin, Robert   3090

Sabine, Lorenzo   2007

Sachau, Eduard   4557

Sachse, Johann David Wilhelm
4198

Sacramento Blake, Augusto Victorino Alves do   483

Sa'd, Muhammad ibn--SEE: Ibn
Sa'd, Muhammad   4557

Sadleir, Thomas Ulick   1302

Sänger, Fritz   1009

Sáenz, Francisco de Paula González y --SEE: González y
Sáenz, Francisco de Paula
1794

Saerchinger, César, ed. --SEE
THE TITLE ENTRY: Inter-
national who's who in music
and musical gazetteer
2910

al-Safadī, Khalīl ibn Aybak
1329

Safford, George Herbert   4818

Sāhitya, Akademi   3725

Sahlgren, Jöran   4759

Sailly,   Dujardin-
SEE: Dujardin-Sailly   3569

Sainsbury, John S.   3042

Saint-Allais, Nicolas Viton   840

St. Andrews. University   1219

Saint-Anthoine, J. Hippolyte
Daniel de--SEE: Daniel,
Hippolyte   937

St. Augustine's Abbey, Ramsgate   4309

Saint-Edme, Edme Théodore Bourg, known as   841

Saint Etienne, Cosme de Villiers de--SEE: Villiers de Saint Etienne, Cosme de   4524

Saint-Germain, Pierre Marie Gault de--SEE: Gault de Saint-Germain, Pierre Marie   2501

Saint-Gervais, A. Antoine de--SEE: Antoine, A., de Saint-Gervais   52

Saint Maurice Cabany, E. de 206

St. Peter's College, London 1175-1176

Saint Romain, Charles du Peloux de, vicomte--SEE: Du Peloux, Charles, vicomte 2483

Saint-Sauveur, Jacques Grasset de--SEE: Grasset de Saint-Sauveur, Jacques   714

Sainte-Palaye, Jean Baptiste de La Curne de   3592

Sainte-Preuve, pseud.--SEE: Binet, Jacques Philippe Marie   242

Sáinz de Baranda, Julián   3888

Sáinz de Robles, Federico Carlos 3382

Saitov, Vladimir Ivanovich 1711-1712

al-Sakhāwī, Muhammad ibn 'Abd al-Rahmān   1330

Sala, Torello   4479

Saladin, François Théodore Louis Grenus-   SEE: Grenus-Saladin, François Théodore Louis, baron   1846

Salāhaddīn Halīl ibn Aibak as-Safadī--SEE: al-Safadī, Khalīl ibn Aybak   1329

Salamanca, Carlos Ramírez de Arellano y Gutiérrez de--SEE: Ramírez de Arellano y Gutiérrez de Salamanca, Carlos   3882

Salazar, Elssa Paredes de--SEE: Paredes de Salazar, Elssa 469

Saldamando, Enrique Torres--SEE: Torres Saldamando, Enrique   4511

Saldaña, José María Fernández--SEE: Fernández Saldaña, José María   2381

Saldoni y Remendo, Baltasar 3043

Saleski, Gdal   3044

Salgado, José Augusto   3815

Sal'nikov, Aleksandr Nikolaevich 3843

Salverte, François de, comte 2727

Salvini, Salvino   1371

Salvioli, Giovanni   3045

Samaganov, Dzhenbai   3936

al-Sam'ānī, 'Abd al-Karīm ibn Muhammad   1331

Samaritani, Antonio   4480

Sambamoorthy, P.   3046-3047

Samfundet for dansk-norsk genealogi og personalhistorie
667

Samper, Soledad Acosta de--SEE:
Acosta de Samper, Soledad
624

Samuel, René Claude Louis
837, 842

San Cristovál, Evaristo   1605-
1606

San Filippo, Pietro Amat di--SEE:
Amat di S. Filippo, Pietro
4737

San Román, Bonifacio del Moral--
SEE: Moral, Bonifacio
4439, 4481

San Severino, Giulio Roberto di
1372

San Vicente, Faustina   3889

Sancassani, Dionigi Andrea 3746

Sánchez, Federico de Onis y --
SEE: Onis y Sánchez, Fed-
erico de   3878

Sánchez, Ildefonso Fernandez y --
SEE: Fernandez y Sánchez,
Ildefonso   1777

Sánchez, José Rogerio--SEE:
Rogerio Sánchez, José 3887

Sánchez de Neira, José   3234

Sancta Luzia, Manuel de, Brother
--SEE: Manuel de Santa Luzia,
Brother   4426

Sanders, Lloyd Charles   253

Sanderus, Antonius   458-460

Sandved, Kjell Bloch   3048

Sangiorgio, Paolo   4199

Sangyō Keizai Shimbun Sha
1439

Sankar Sen Gupta--SEE: Sen
Gupta, Sankar   3726

Sankt-Peterburg--SEE: Leningrad

Santa Luzia, Manuel de, Brother--
SEE: Manuel de Santa Luzia,
Brother   4426

Santa Maria, Angiolgabriello di--
SEE: Angiolgabriello di Santa
Maria   3737

Santeul, E. N. F. de   3563

Santiago de Chile. Biblioteca
Nacional   526

Santiago Vela, Gregorio de
4481

Santifaller, Leo   398

Santillán, Diego Abad de--SEE:
Abad de Santillán, Diego
342

Sanyal, Ram Gopal   1283

Sanz, Manuel Serrano y --SEE:
Serrano y Sanz, Manuel
3890

São Pedro, João de, Brother--SEE:
João de São Pedro, Brother
165

Sarausa, Fermín Peraza--SEE:
Peraza Sarausa, Fermín
639-640

Sarawak. Information Service
1750

Sarkis, Joseph Eliam   3442

Sartori, Claudio   2824, 2833

Sartori, Franz   402, 3686

Sathas, Kōnstantinos N.   3709-
3710

Satterlee, Leroy DeForest,
4803

Saunders, Richard Drake   2985-
2986

Savadjian, Léon   408

Savage, James   2229-2230

Savino, Edoardo   1373

Sawada, Akira   2610

Sawamura, Yukio   596

Saxe, Christoph Gottlob   254

Saxius, Christoph Gottlob--SEE:
Saxe, Christoph Gottlob

Sayz, Adolfo Carrasco y--SEE:
Carrasco y Sayz, Adolfo
1770

Scally, Mary Anthony, Sister
3426

Scarone, Arturo   2380, 2384

Scarpetta, M. Leonidas   1507

Schacht, Matthias Henriksen
3049

Schaden, Adolph von--SEE:
Schaden, Johann Nepomuk
Adolph von   3687

Schaden, Johann Nepomuk Alolph
von   3687

Schaedler, Karl   4664

Schäffer, Bogusław   3050

Schaff, Philip   4482

Schaff-Herzog encyclopedia
4482, 4484

Schaumburg, Paul Erich Bruno
Richard   255

Scheen, P. A.   2611

Scheffel, Christianus Stephanus
4200

Scheffer, Johannes   1824

Scheltema, Jacobus   1570

Schenkling, Sigmund   4639

Schiavo, Giovanni Ermenegildo
1955, 2008

Schidlof, Léo R.   2612

Schiff, Moses David   4569

Schilling, Gustav   3051-3055

Schindel, Carl Wilhelm Otto
August von   3688

Schink, Johann Friedrich   3181

Schivardi, Antonio   4201

Schlichtegroll, Friedrich von
997-999

Schmersahl, Elias Ferdinand
1010-1011

Schmid, Christian Heinrich
3689

Schmidl, Carlo   3056-3057

Schmidt, Andreas Gottfried
959, 3690

Schmidt, Friedrich August
1001

Schmidt, Minna (Moscherosch)
256

Schmidt, Paul C. W.   4719

Schmidt, Valentin Heinrich
3636, 3691

Schnee, Heinrich   974

Schneider, Max   960, 2957,
2971

Schoemaker, Daniel Martin
4635

Schoenewerk, L.   3058

Scholefield, Guy Hardy   1577-
1578

Scholes, Percy Alfred   3059

Scholz, Wilhelm von   963

Schomerus, Johanna--SEE:
Schomerus-Wagner, Johanna

Schomerus-Wagner, Johanna
3692

Schrader, Bruno   2786

Schrader, G. W.   4202

Schramm, Hugo--SEE: Schramm-
Macdonald, Hugo   222

Schramm-Macdonald, Hugo   222

Schröckh, Daniel   34

Schröckh, Johann Matthias
257-258

Schröder, Hans   3603, 3664-
3665, 3693

Schuberth, Julius Ferdinand
Georg   3060-3062

Schütz, Alfred   2613

Schuh, Willi   3063, 3066

Schuller, Friedrich   3701

Schulte, Wilhelm   1079

Schultz, Georg Julius   417

Schultz, George Peter   1065

Schulz, Walther   3064

Schulze, Johann Daniel   1055,
3673

Schumann, Albert   3927

Schuon, Karl   2009-2010

Schutz, Alexander Herman
3596

Schwab, Hermann   1473

Schwarz, Helmut   3190

Schwarz, Julius Caesar   3991,
4216, 4471

Schwarz-Reiflingen, Erwin
3065

Schweizerischer Kunstverein
2614

Schweizerischer Tonkünstlerverein
3066

Schyberg, Frederik   3482

Schyns, Joseph   597

Scientist and Engineer Techno-
    logical Institute   4822

Scifoni, Felice   259

Scott, Eugene Crampton   4485

Scott, Sir Harold Richard   260

Scott, Hew   4486

Scott, Lorene Laura   3427

Scott, William J.   4487^

Scotto, José Arturo   355

Scriba, Heinrich Friedrich Lud-
    wig Wilhelm Eduard   3694

A Searcher after the truth--SEE:
    Hibbert, Julian   4391

Seco y Shelley, Manuel   261

Secretan, Eugène   1864

Sedas, Santiago Montoto de--SEE:
    Montoto de Sedas, Santiago
    1505

Seelen, Johann Heinrich von 1054

Segadas Machado-Guimarães,
    Argeu de   484

Segal, Louis   1741

Segal, Ronald   318

Seguier, Frederick Peter   2615

Seidlitz, Julius, pseud. --SEE:
    Jeitteles, Ignaz   3640

Seiling, Josef   2907

Seivert, Johann   1658, 3700

Selby, Paul Owen   3309

Seligman, Edwin Robert Anderson
    4682

Selle, Götz von   1012, 3257

Sellii, Adam Burkhard--SEE:
    Sellius, Burchard Adam

Sellius, Burchard Adam   4766

Selmer, Hannibal Peter   666

Semennikov, Vladimir Petrovich
    3844

Semenov, P. N.   1732

Sen Gupta, Sankar   3726

Sénès, Célestin, called La Sinse
    931

Senn, Walter--SEE: Senn-Bar-
    bieux, Walter   1865

Senn-Barbeiux, Walter   1865

Seriakov, Lavrentii Avksent'-
    evich   1733

Serisev, Inocento   1734

Serle, Percival   378

Serra, Otto Mayer-   SEE:
    Mayer-Serra, Otto   2958

Serrano, José Antonio   4203

Serrano de Wilson, Emilia,
    baronesa de Wilson   1545

Serrano y Morales, José Enrique
    4042

Serrano y Sanz, Manuel   3890

Servolini, Luigi   2465, 2616

Seuphor, Michel, pseud.--SEE:
    Berckelaers, Ferdinand Louis
    2442

Seville. Archivo General de
    Indias--SEE: Spain. Archivo
    General de Indias, Seville
    1508

Seward, William   263-264

Seyn, Eug. M. H. de   2617

Seyn, Eugène de   462, 3450

Shalita, Israel   3067

Sharp, Robert Farquharson
    3383, 3533

Shatzky, Jacob   3790

Shaw, Thomas Shuler   24

Shchekok, P. F.   1740

Shelby, Charmion Clair   3855

Shelley, Manuel Seco y --SEE:
    Seco y Shelley, Manuel   261

Shen, Wei-tsê   1754

Shepherd, Henry Elliott   3428

Sheremetevskii, Vladimir
    Vladimirovich   1715

Sherman, Robert Lowery   3191

Sherwood, Robert Edmund   3207

Shiells, Robert--SEE: Shiels,
    Robert   3501

Shiels, Robert   3501

Shina Kenkyūkai, Peking   600

Shinoda, Hideo   163

Shippen, Edward   1997

Shipton, Clifford Kenyon   2011,
    2231

Shiraeff, Alexandria Vodarsky-
    SEE: Vodarsky-Shiraeff,
    Alexandria   3108

Shiso Jimmei Hensan-bu   4254

Shoberl, Frederic   3497

Shoemaker, Floyd Calvin   2013

Shore, Thomas Teignmouth   91

Shūshtarī Nūr Allāh--SEE: Nūr
    Allāh, Shūshtarī   4559

Sibley, John Langdon   2011, 2231

Siegmeister, Elie   3068

Sigismondo da Venezia   265, 4488

Sigurdsson, Jón   1258, 3983,
    4489

Silva, Innocencio Francisco da
    3816

Silva, José María da Costa e --
    SEE: Costa e Silva, José
    María da   3814

Silva, Manuel Francisco Dias da--
    SEE: Dias de Silva, Manuel
    Francisco   476

Silva, Theodoro José da   1648

Silver, Jesse   3233

Silver, Roy   3233

Sim, Victor--SEE: Shen, Wei-
    tsê   1754

Simmons, David   3120

Simmons, Henry Eugene   2012

Simmons, Ralph B.   2347

Simmons, William J.   2014

Simões dos Reis, Antonio   473,
3817

Simon, Matthias   4490-4493

Simonin, abbé   121

Simpson, Arthur J.   2344

Simpson, Donald Herbert   23

Simpson, Henry   2307

Singer, Hans Wolfgang   25-26,
2560-2561

Singer Company, New York
4720

Singh, Kahan   3727

Singh, Trilochan   1284

Sinnhold, Johann Nikolaus   3298

Sinobas, Manuel Rico y --SEE:
Rico y Sinobas, Manuel   4040

Sinzig, Petrus, Father   3069

Siret, Adolphe   2618

Sisson, Sebastião Augusto   485

Sisters of St. Ann   3070

Sithat Sithibourn--SEE: Sithibourn,
Sithat   1494

Sithibourn, Sithat   1494

Sitzmann, Fr. J. Éduard   857

Siumell, José Antonio Garí y --
SEE: Garí y Siumell, José
Antonio   4378

Six, Georges   843

Sjöström, Carl Johan   1825-
1826

Sjöström, Gunnar   1752

Skal'kovskii, Konstantin Apollo-
novich   1735

Slane, William Mac Guckin,
baron de   1320

Slavisches Seminar, Universität
München--SEE: Munich.
Universität. Slavisches
Seminar   1756

Śledziński, Stefan   3030

Slonimsky, Nicolas   2755-2756,
3071

Sluijters, Hendrik   1571

Smith, Benjamin Eli   96

Smith, Charles Harvard Gibbs--
SEE: Gibbs-Smith, Charles
Harvard   142

Smith, David Bonner   1145

Smith, David Eugene   4669

Smith, George   1124, 1131

Smith, Gerald Birney   4271

Smith, H. P.   1444

Smith, Henry Monmouth   4665

Smith, Horatio Elwin   3335

Smith, John, clock-maker   2728

Smith, Joseph, bookseller
4494-4496

Smith, Ralph Clifton   2420

Smith, Sir William   266-267,
4497, 4527

Smith, William Charles   4020

Smith-Dampier, John Lucius
1177

Snelleman, Joh. F.   2397

Snow, Valentine   3845

Soares, Eduardo de Campos de
Castro de Azevedo--SEE:
Campos de Castro de Azevedo
Soares, Eduardo de   1641

Soares, Orris   4255

Sobel, Bernard   3192

Sobeski, Michał   1635

Sobko, Nikolaĭ Petrovich   2619,
3825

Sobrinho, João Francisco Velho--
SEE: Velho Sobrinho, João
Francisco   487

Social Science Research Council
4684, 4691

Una Sociedad de amantes de las
bellas artes   2474

Una Sociedad literaria   1767

Una Società di letterati   1417

Société bibliographique, Paris
4363

Une Société de gens de lettres
721, 785, 817, 865, 946

Une Société de gens de lettres
et de publicistes   807

Une Société de gens de lettres
et de savants   806

Une Société de gens de lettres
francais et étrangers   729

Une Société de girouettes   769

Société de l'histoire de l'Île
Maurice   1517

Une Société de littérateurs, de
professeurs et de savants
110

Une Société de littérateurs et de
publicistes   723

Une Société de non-girouettes
761

Une Société de publicistes et
d'hommes de lettres   712

Société des écrivains canadiens,
Montréal   3555, 3593

Une Société des gens de lettres
76, 79

Une Société des gens de lettres
et des savants   78, 80

Une Société des hommes de lettres français et étrangers
71

Une Société des membres de l'Institut, et d'Artistes   930

Une Société d'hommes de lettres
et d'artistes   777

Société générale suisse d'histoire
(Allgemeine Geschicht -
forschende Gesellschaft der
Schweiz)   1845

Society for the Diffusion of Useful Knowledge, London
239, 268

Society of Fellows of Harvard University--SEE: Harvard University. Society of Fellows   3261

Society of Friends--SEE: Friends, Society of   1091-1092, 4372

Society of the Plastics Industry
4819

Soeurs de Saint-Anne--SEE: Sisters of St. Ann   3070

Sofia. Institut po istoriiā na Bŭlgarskata Komunisticheska partiiā   489

Sohn, Pow-key--SEE: Son, Po-gi   1493

Soiūz sovetskikh kompozitorov SSR. Leningradskoe otdelenie   3074

Sokolow, Nahum   1475, 3795

Sola, Solmu Salomon   3310

Soldán, Juan Pedro Paz-   SEE: Paz-Soldán, Juan Pedro 1608

Un Solitaire--SEE: Barbier, Hippolyte   4292

Sollana, Emilio M. de   4498

Somaize, Antoine Baudeau de 844

Sommaruga, Rodolfo   4681

Sommerfeldt, Wilhelm Preus
1582-1583, 1585, 3805

Sommervogel, Carlos   4264, 4288-4289

Son, Po-gi   1493

Sonnenschein, William Swan
27

Sonoda, Ikki   602

Sontheimer, Walther   228

Soprani, Raffaele   2620, 3777

Sorbelli, Albano   4014

Sorgato, Gaetano   1374

Soriano, D. H.   1617

Sosa, Francisco   1528, 1546-1548

Sotela, Rogelio   4017

Soto, Enrique Chirinos--SEE: Chirinos Soto, Enrique
1603

Soto de Avila, J. Víctor   524

Sotomayor, Félix Osores y --SEE: Osores y Sotomayor, Félix
1536

Soullier, Charles Simon Pascal
3075

Sourie, Louis   3451

Souris, André   3099

Un Sous-préfet   725

Sousa Bastos, Antonio   3193-3194

Sousa Viterbo, Francisco Marques de   2687

South Dakota. Legislature   2323

Southard, Mary Young   2165

Southeastern Composers' League
3076

Southern Baptist Convention.
Foreign Mission Board
4499

Southern Languages Book Trust
3722-3723, 3728

Southern Publishing Company,
New York   2339

Southern Society for Research and
History, Atlanta   2133

"Southland writers," The author
of--SEE: Tardy, Mrs. Mary
T.   3430

Southwell, Nathanael   4472

Souza, José Mariano Beristain
de--SEE: Beristain de
Souza, José Mariano   3901-
3902

Sowinski, Albert--SEE: Sowiński,
Wojciech   3078-3079

Sowiński, Wojciech   3078-3079

Spaeth, Sigmund Gottfried
2909, 2983-2984, 2987-2988

Spain.   Archivo General de Indias, Seville   1508

Spain.   Consejo Superior de Investigaciones Cientificas
4612

Sparacio, Domenico   4500

Speech Association of America
3429

Speer, William S.   2334, 2366

Spemann, Wilhelm   3080

Spencer, Alfred   2264

Spencer, Richard Henry   2181

Spencer, Wilbur Daniel   2176

Spender, Stephen   3534

Spiegel, Jules Charles   2303,
2308

Spink, John George Taylor
3219

Spofford, Ainsworth Rand   1989,
2353

Špoljar, Krsto   3854

Spooner, Shearjashub   2621

Sporting news   3219

Sprague, William Buell   4501

Spreti, Vittorio, marchese
1375

Springauf, E. W.   3695

Springer, Hermann Wilhelm
2971

Spruytenburg, Marinus   1572

Stacey, Claude, firm, publisher
2367

Stadler, Johann Evangelista
4502

Staehelin, Andreas   3311

Stähelin, Wilhelm Richard   1866

Stainer, Cecie   3081

Stammler, Wolfgang   3696

Stancovich, Pietro   2407

Standard and Poor's Corporation
4711-4713

Stanford Scholastic Associates
48

Stanford University. Hoover Institution on War, Revolution
and Peace   541

Stanojević, Stanoje   2408

Stanton, Richard   4503

Startsev, Ivan Ivanovich   3384

State Historical Society of North
Dakota--SEE: North Dakota.
State Historical Society
2267

Stauff, Philipp   1477

Stauffer, David McNeely   2622

Štědroň, Bohumír   2794

Steel, Johannes   269

Stege, Fritz   2789

Stein, Henri   3580

Steinberg, Sigfrid Henry   3334

Steinitz, Hanan   3067

Stekert, Aleksander   1637

Stekert, August   1637

Stemplinger, Eduard   3468,
3470

Stendman, Georgii Fedorovich
1731

Stengel, Theophil   3082

Stenning, Alan Herbert   1175

Stepf, Johann Heinrich   3984

Stephanides, P. M.   643

Stephen, Sir Leslie   1124, 1126

Stephens, Alexander   1171

Stephenson, Henry Holder   4625

Sterlich, C. de, marquis di
Cermignano   3778

Stern, Abraham, rabbi   4568

Stern, Adolf   3697

Stern, Lee   3116

Steuer, Max   3083

Stiles, Edward Holcomb   3985

Stirling-Maxwell, Sir William,
bart.   2623

Stöger, Johann Nepomuk   4504

Stoliar, Z. L.   2926

Stone, Richard French   4204

Stonehill, Charles Archibald
1089

Stonehill, H. Winthrop   1089

Storey, Charles Ambrose   3807

Stosch, Ferdinand   686

Stozh, M. E.   3847

Straeten, Edmond vander   3084

Strahl, Philipp Carl   1737

Stratford, Joseph   1198-1199

Stratton, Stephen Samuel   2788

Streibich, Ronald L.   3245

Streit, Karl Konrad   3698

Stribbe, David Gerhard   1295

Strickland, Henry Hornyold-
SEE: Hornyold-Strickland,
Henry   1203

Strickland, Walter G.   2624

Strieder, Friedrich Wilhelm
1048, 1050

Striker, Cecil   4205

Strodtmann, Johann Christoph
244, 270, 685-686

Stroev, Pavel Mikhaĭlovich
4505

Strunk, Adolph   670

Strutt, Joseph   2625

Strutz, Edmund   1067

Stuart, Ray   3195

Studart, Guilherme, barão de
486

Studer, H.   394

Stumpf, Andreas Sebastian
1082

Stumpf, Pleickhard   1033

Sturgis, Russell   2688

Sturm, Christoph Christian 4506

Stutheit, Esther   2216

Su, Ch'i-ch'ang   603

Su, Hsüeh-lin   597

Suárez, Constantino   3891

Subrahmanyam, Bāla--SEE:
Bāla Subrahmanyam   1261

Suchier, Wolfram   4613

Sucre, Luis Alberto   2390

Suffridus, Petrus   3597

Suidas   3469

Summers, Thomas Osmond
4507

Summerskill, Michael   119

Sun, Ta-kung   2626

Sundström, Einar   3073, 3196

Suomen Historiallinen Seura
695, 700

Suppan, Wolfgang   3085

Surgères, Anatole Granges de--
SEE: Granges de Surgères,
Anatole, marquis de   786,
867

Surinaamse Historische Kring
1813

Surkov, Alekseĭ Aleksandrovich
3361

Surmont de Volsberghe, Henri Marie Ghislaine, baron   461

Sutton, Charles William   3535

Svenska försäkringsföreningen
4715

Svensson, Sven Eric Emmanuel
3086

Swalin, Wilhelm   1835

Swanenburg, B. D. 2629

Sweert, François--SEE: Sweerts, Pierre François 463

Sweertius, Franciscus--SEE: Sweerts, Pierre François 463

Sweerts, Pierre François 463

Swert, Petrus de 464

Swert, Pierre de--SEE: Swert, Petrus de 464

Świerkowski, Ksawery 4044

Swinny, Shapland Hugh 147

Swiss-American Historical Society 2018

Sylvestre, Guy 3536

Szabó, Stefan (Stephen (S.) Taylor, pseud.) 188, 405, 691, 1572, 1786

Szabolcsi, Bence 3130

Szentmiklossy, Géza 1254

Szinnyei, Jószef 1249, 3714, 3719

Szulc, Zdzisław 3087

Szy, Tibor 2019

Szymanowski, Wojciech 271

T

T. S. 371

Tafuri, Giovanni Bernardino 3779

Taillemite, Étienne 272

Taisand, Pierre 3986

Takamure, Itsue 1441

Takebayashi, Kan'ichi 4256

Takeuchi, Rizō 1434

Talbot, C. H. 4206

Tallqvist, Knut Leonard 1321

Talquino, Virgilio, pseud.--SEE: Figueroa, Virgilio 531

Talvart, Hector 3594

Tamaki, Hajime 4257

T'an, Cheng-pi 3458

T'an tang tang chai chu, pseud. 604

Tanasukharāma Gupta--SEE: Gupta, Tanasukharāma 1270

T'ang, Ching-kao 273

T'ang, Lu-feng 605

Tanner, Thomas, Bp. of St. Asaph 3537

Tante, Dilly, pseud.--SEE: Kunitz, Stanley Jasspon 3364

Tarapada Das Gupta--SEE: Das Gupta, Tarapada 1280

Tarazona, Policarpio Mingote y -- SEE: Mingote y Tarazona, Policarpio 1799

Tardieu, Ambroise 927

Tardy, Mrs. Mary T. 3430

Tarmini-Almerté 845

Tarsis, Veniamin I͡Akovlevich
3384, 3848

Tartarotti, Giacopo   3780

Tāshkubrīzādah, Ahmad ibn
Mustafā   1874, 1878

Tasköprüzâde--SEE: Tāshkubrīzādah, Ahmad ibn Mustafā
1874, 1878

Tassin, René Prosper   4508

Tate Gallery, London   2630

Taverriti, Filippo Aliquò--SEE:
Aliquò Taverriti, Filippo
3734

Taylor, Charles William   1939,
2088, 2270

Taylor, Deems   2903

Taylor, Eva Germaine Rimington
4670

Taylor, James Bennett   4509

Taylor, Stephen S. , pseud. --SEE:
Szabó, Stefan   188, 405,
691, 1572, 1786, 3392

Taylor, William A.   2273

Teano, Leone Caetani, principe
di--SEE: Caetani, Leone,
principe di Teano   1347

Teichl, Robert   397, 403

Teikoku Koshin-sho   1442

Tejeiro Martínez, Benigno--SEE:
Martínez, Benigno T.   1781

Tejera, Felipe   2391

Tejera, José Pío   3892

Telberg, Ina   4626, 4693

Téllez, Emeterio Valverde, Bp.
--SEE: Valverde Téllez,
Emeterio, Bp.   4260, 4520

Temanza, Tommaso   2689

Temerson, Henri   738

Temple, Oliver Perry   2335

Tengström, Johan Jakob   3312

Tenivelli, Carlo   1402

Tennessee. State Dept.   2336

Tereshchenko, Aleksandr Vlas'-
evich   1738

Terzo, Benvenuto   3088

Testoni, Gian Carlo   3089

Texas State Historical Association   2342

Thacher, James   4207, 4224

Thai Nội, pseud.   1873

Thammasāt University, Bangkok,
Thailand--SEE: Bangkok,
Thailand. Thammasāt Ma-
hawitthayālai   1870

Thatcher, Benjamin Bussey   2020

Thelwall, John   70

Thevet, André   274

Thieme, Hugo Paul   3595

Thieme, Ulrich   2631, 2647

Thiess, Johann Otto   1045, 4208

Thiset, Anders   671

Thivars, Louis Saturnin Brissot-
SEE: Brissot-Thivars, Louis
Saturnin   742

Thoinan, Ernest, pseud. --SEE:
Roquet, Antoine Ernest
4041

Thomas, Bradford L.   4749

Thomas, Clara   3538

Thomas, Dorothy, pseud. --SEE:
Thomashower, Dorothy
(Fisch)   3987

Thomas, Henry   4258

Thomas, Joseph   275

Thomas, Ralph   38

Thomas, S. E.   95

Thomashower, Dorothy (Fisch)
3987

Thomen, Luis Francisco   4114

Thompson, John McDonald   2068

Thompson, Oscar   3090

Thompson, Sherley Clark   3235

Thomsen, Henrik   4242

Thomson, Clara Linklater   152,
683

Thomson, John Maitland   4354

Thomson, Thomas   1211

Thornburg, Betty R.   3959

Thorne, J. O.   98

Thornsby, Frederick W.   2821,
3091

Thorpe, Arthur Winton   1178

Þorsteinsson (i. e. Thorsteins-
son), Hannes   4510

Thoury, Eugène Perraud de--SEE:
Perraud de Thoury, Eugène
227

Thuile, Jean   2729

Thuner, Ole Erland   3092-3093

Thurston, Herbert   4313, 4315

Tiaden, Enno Johann Heinrich
1043

Ticino (Canton) Dipartimento della pubblica educazione   3931

Ticozzi, Stefano   2632, 2634

The Times, London   1179

Timperley, Charles Henry   4045

Ting, Ti-sheng   606

Tingelstad, Oscar Adolf   4529

Tipaldo, Emilio de   1376

Tiraboschi, Girolamo   3769, 3781

Titov, Andreĭ Aleksandrovich
3825

Tjaden, Ernst Johann Heinrich--
SEE: Tiaden, Enno Johann
Heinrich   1043

Tkeshelashvili, I. S.   4209

Tobiasson, Brynleifur   1259-
1260

Tobin, James Edward   4341

Tod, H.   84

Toda, Teizo   276

Todd, George Eyre-   SEE:
Eyre-Todd, George   1197

Todeschini, Domenico Francisco
3780

Tokyo. Heibon Sha--SEE: Heibon
Sha, Tokyo   106, 133

Tokyo. Institute of Art Research
2633

Tokyo. Koshinjō--SEE: Koshinjō,
Tokyo   589, 1431

Tōkyō Keizai Zasshi Sha   1423

Tola, Pasquale   1404

Tolstoĭ, Dmitriĭ Andreevich,
graf   1739

Toman, Prokop   2636-2637

Toman, Prokop H.   2637

Tomasini, Giacomo Filippo, Bp.
of Città Nuova--SEE: Tomasini, Jacopo Filippo   277-
278, 1377

Tomasini, Jacopo Filippo   277-
278, 1377

Tommasini, Giovanni Filippo--
SEE: Tomasini, Jacopo
Filippo   277-278, 1377

Toner, Joseph Meredith   4210

Tooley, Ronald Vere   4750

Toomey, Daniel P.   2192

Toppi, Nicolò   1397-1398

Torlopov, Georgiĭ Ivanovich
3548

Toro, Josefina del   1496

Toro Ruiz, I.   681

Torrellas, A. Albert--SEE: Albert Torrellas, A.   2818-
2819

Torrents, Jaime Massó--SEE:
Massó Torrents, Jaime
3454-3455

Torres, Agustín Millares--SEE:
Millares Torres, Agustín
1793

Torres, Francisco Beltrán y de--
SEE: Beltrán y de Torres,
Francisco   4

Torres, José Joaquín Ortega--
SEE: Ortega Torres, José
Joaquín   3913

Torres, Teodosio Vesteiro--SEE:
Vesteiro Torres, Teodosio
1798

Torres Amat, Félix   3456-3457

Torres Amat, Ignacio   3456

Torres Rioseco, Arturo   3918

Torres Saldamando, Enrique
4511

Torsy, Jakob   4512

Toselli, Jean Baptiste   916

Tóth, Aladár   3130

Touchard-Lafosse, Georges   901

Touron, Antoine   4513

Toussaint, Auguste   1517

Townsend, Peter   1103

Trap, Jens Peter   672

Trausch, Joseph Franz   3700-3701

Trauschenfels, Eugen von   3700

Trelles y Govín, Carlos Manuel   641-642

Tribolet, Hans   1849-1850

Triggiani, Domenico   3782

Trilochan Singh--SEE: Singh, Trilochan   1284

Trinity College, Dublin--SEE: Dublin. University. Trinity College   1302

Trinius, Johann Anton   4514

Troclet, Léon   451

Trois journalistes   719

Trois publicistes   825

Troitskii, Vasilii Ivanovich   2730-2731

Troostenburg de Bruijn, Caspar Adams Laurens van--SEE: Bruijn, Caspar Adams Laurens van Troostenburg de   4312

Trottmann, Beresford Sylvester Briggs   2248

Troup, Cornelius V.   2138

Ts'ai, Kuan-lo   607

Tsang, Li-ho   560

Tsing Hua College, Peking   615-616

Tuckerman, Henry Theodore   2638

Tudeu, L. O. Th.   3310

Türler, Heinrich (Henri Turler)   1845, 1849

Tunnell, Arthur L.   517

Turbeville, Robert Paul   2133

Turkevich, John   4614

Turkin, Hy   3235

Turler, Henri (Heinrich Türler)   1845, 1849

Turpin, François Henri   846

Turri, Vittorio   3783

Tyler, Lyon Gardiner   2354, 2356

U

U. C. --SEE: Capitaine, Ulysse   448

U. D. E.--SEE: Union douanière européene   688

UNESCO--SEE: United Nations Educational, Scientific and Cultural Organization   4615-4619, 4692

Udaondo, Enrique   357-358

Ueda, Toshio   596

Ugarte, José de Rezabal y --SEE: Rezabal y Ugarte, José de   3884

Ugarte, Rubén Vargas--SEE: Vargas Ugarte, Rubén   2734-2735

Ujvári, Péter   1252

Ullery, Jacob G.   2351

Un de leurs confrères (médecins français) --SEE: Morel de Rubempré, J.   4176

Un des redacteurs du "Messager" --SEE: Couailhac, Louis 752

Unesco--SEE: United Nations Educational, Scientific and Cultural Organization 4615-4619, 4692

Ungarelli, Luigi Maria   4515

Ungherini, Aglauro   280-282

Union douanière européenne 688

Union Research Institute--SEE: Yu lien yen chiu so, Kowloon 614

Union Theological Seminary, New York--SEE: New York. Union Theological Seminary 4447

Unitarian and Free Christian Churches   4516

United Free Church of Scotland 4517

United Nations Educational, Scientific and Cultural Organization. Middle East Science Cooperation Office   4615-4617

United Nations Educational, Scientific and Cultural Organization. Science Cooperation Office for Latin America   4618

United Nations Educational, Scientific and Cultural Organization. Secretariat   4692

United Nations Educational, Scientific and Cultural Organization. South Asia Science Cooperation Office   4619

United Nations Information Office, New York   283

United Press Service Bureau 2022

U. S. Adjutant General's Office 2023

U. S. Air Force   2024

U. S. Bureau of International Labor Affairs   2031

U. S. Bureau of Naval Personnel 2025-2027, 4518

U. S. Coast Guard   2028

U. S. Congress   2029-2030

U. S. Dept. of Labor   2031

U. S. Dept. of State   2032

U. S. Dept. of the Army. Public Information Division 2033

U. S. Embassy. Japan   1443-1444

U. S. Interdepartmental Committee for Acquisition of Foreign Publications   285

U. S. Library of Congress   1

U. S. Library of Congress. General Reference and Bibliography Division   28, 1889

U. S. Library of Congress.
Orientalia Division   609

U. S. Marine Corps   2034-
2035

U. S. Military Academy, West
Point. West Point Alumni
Foundation, inc. --SEE:
West Point Alumni Founda-
tion, inc.   2045

U. S. National Aeronautics and
Space Administration   4673

U. S. National Guard Bureau
2036-2037

U. S. Naval Academy, Annapolis.
Alumni Association   2038

U. S. Naval Academy, Annapolis.
Graduates' Association   2038

U. S. Office of Strategic Services
847

U. S. Office of Strategic Services.
Research and Analysis Branch
610, 847

U. S. Weather Bureau   2039

United States Educational Commission in Japan   3264

Universität Basel--SEE: Basel.
Universität   1843

Universität Berlin--SEE: Berlin.
Universität   3260

Universität Göttingen--SEE: Göttingen. Universität   3269

Universität Köln--SEE: Koln.
Universität   970

Universität München--SEE: Munich.
Universität   1756

Université de Liège--SEE:
Liège. Université   3290

University of Aberdeen--SEE:
Aberdeen. University.
1209

University of California--SEE:
California. University.
4675

University of Dublin--SEE: Dublin. University.   1301-
1302

University of Glasgow--SEE:
Glasgow. University.   1213

University of St. Andrews--SEE:
St. Andrews. University.
1219

Untersuchengsausschuss Freiheitlicher Juristen   981

Upcott, William   3497

Upham, Warren   2214

Upmark, Gustaf Herman Fabian
2733

Uppsala. Universitet. Smålands
nation   1840

Urban, S.   3384

Urbanek, Josef František   3476

Urbino, Levina (Buoncuore) 3096

Uriarte, José Eugenio de
4265, 4519

Uribe Muñoz, Bernardo   3919

Uriel, Miguel Gómez--SEE: Gómez Uriel, Miguel   3871

Urmson, J. O.   4259

'Ušâqîzâde--SEE: 'Ushâqîzâde
1880

Ushakov, Semen Ivanovich
1742

'Ushâqîzâde   1880

Uspenskiĭ, Aleksandr Ivanovich
2639

Utechin, Sergej   1743

Uvarov, P. S.   4764

V

Vacant, Alfred   4346

Vaccaro, Gennaro   1378

Vaerini, Barnaba   2959

Vaïsse, Emilio   526

Valabrega, Cesare   3097

Valcárcel Esparza, Carlos Daniel   1508

Valderrama, Fernández Díaz de--
SEE: Díaz de Valderrama,
Fernández   1806-1807

Valdes, Daniel T.   2114

Valdrighi, Luigi Francesco
3098

Valencia, Gabriel   1531

Valera y Alcala Galiano, Juan
3893

Valla, Joseph   58

Valle, Rafael Heliodoro   3894

Vallejo, Antonio Cánovas del
Castillo y --SEE: Cánovas
del Castillo y Vallejo, Antonio   2458

Valverde Téllez, Emeterio, Bp.
4260, 4520

Vancsa, Kurt   3623

Van de Casteele, Pierre--SEE:
Casteele, Pierre van de
4107

Van den Branden, Franz Jozef
Peter--SEE: Branden, Franz
Jozef Peter van den   3488

Van der Aa, Abraham Jacob--SEE:
Aa, Abraham Jacob van der
1553, 3489

Van der Haeghen, Ferdinand--SEE:
Haeghen, Ferdinand van der
3444

Vandermaelen, Philippe--SEE:
Maelen, Philippe Marie
Guillaume van der   446

Vanderpool, Herbert Campbell
4521

Vander Straeten, Edmond--SEE:
Straeten, Edmond vander
3084

Van Doorninck, Jan Izaak--SEE:
Doorninck, Jan Izaak van
1551-1552

Van Gool, Jan--SEE: Gool, Jan
van   2508

Van Hasselt, André Henri Con-
stant--SEE: Hasselt, André
Henri Constant van   437

Van Hemel, Victor--SEE: Hemel,
Victor van   2888

Van Langeraad, L. A. --SEE:
Langeraad, L. A. van
4305

Van Meurs, Johannes--SEE:
Meurs, Johannes van   3294

Vannes, René   3099-3100

Vanselow, Amandus Karl   1063

Van Waay, S. J. Mak--SEE: Mak
van Waay, S. J.   2547

Ványi, Ferenc   3720

Van Zyl, Paul Henrik Stephanus
332

Vapereau, Gustave   288-289,
3385

Varela y Orbegoso, Luis   1610

Vargas Ugarte, Rubén   2734-
2735

Varille, Mathieu   2640

Vasari, Giorgio   2641

Vasconcellos, Joaquim Antonio da
Fonseca e   3101

Vasconcelos, Joaquim de--SEE:
Vasconcellos, Joaquim An-
tonio da Fonseca e   3101

Vasil'chikov, Aleksandr Alekseevich   1744

Vassar College   2041

Vaucher, Pierre   1867

Vaupotić, Miroslav   3854

Vauprivas, Antoine Verdier du--
SEE: Du Verdier, Antoine
118

Vauthier, Étienne   3445

Vautier, Pierre   2479

Vázquez, Carlos Frontaura y --
SEE: Frontaura y Vázquez,
Carlos   3346

Vega y Argüelles, Angel Lasso de
la--SEE: Lasso de la Vega y
Argüelles, Angel   3870

Vela, Gregorio de Santiago--SEE:
Santiago Vela, Gregorio de
4481

Velarde, Mauricio   1598

Velasco, Acisclo Antonio Palo-
mino de Castro y--SEE:
Palomino de Castro y Velasco,
Acisclo Antonio   2576-2577

Velasco, Fanor   290

Velázquez Bringas, Esperanza
3894

Velho Sobrinho, João Francisco
487

Venezuela. Biblioteca Nacional,
Caracas   3898

Vengerov, Semen Afanas'evich
3849-3851

Venn, John   1108, 1180

Venn, John Archibald   1108

Vera, Francisco   1785

Verband der Deutschen Akademien
--SEE: Verband Deutscher
Wissenschaftlicher Körper-
schaften   972

Verband Deutscher Wissenschaftlicher Körperschaften   972

Vercheval, Henri   3102

Verci, Giovanni Battista   2732

Verdes, Nicolás María de Cambiaso y --SEE: Cambiaso y
Verdes, Nicolás María de
1791

Verdier, Antoine du--SEE: Du
Verdier, Antoine   118

Verdier du Vauprivas, Antoine--
SEE: Du Verdier, Antoine
118

Verdot, J. M.   811

Ein Verehrer der Künste   2635

Verein St. -Peterburger Aerzte--
SEE: Obshchestvo peterburgskikh vrachei-nemtsev
4178

Vergara, Saturnino   1507

Vergara y Martín, Gabriel María
1805

Vermiglioli, Giovanni Battista
3784

Vermont. Secretary of State
2352

Verseux, Henri Louis Coiffier
de--SEE: Coiffier de Verseux,
Henri Louis   750

Vertue, George   1153, 2649

Vervaeck, Solange   432

Vestdal, Jón E.   4807

Vesteiro Torres, Teodosio   1798

Un Vétéran de la presse--SEE:
Lourdoueix, Paul de   812

Vetterlein, Christoph Friedrich
Rufolf   3702

Vial, Eugène   2427

Vial, Henri   2642

Viardot, Louis   2643

Vibert, Edmond Célestin Paul--
SEE: Vibert, Paul   292

Vibert, Paul   292

Vicent, Vicente de Cadenas y --
SEE: Cadenas y Vicent, Vicente de   1780

Victorica, Ricardo   1498-1500

Vidaillet, Jean Baptiste   903

Vidal, Antoine   2427, 3103

Vidal, Javier Pulgar--SEE: Pulgar Vidal, Javier   4800

Vidart, Luis   3895

Un Vieil écrivain--SEE: Leymarie,
Achille   810

Vieilh de Boisjolin, Jacques François Marie   242

Vieira, Ernesto   3104

Vienna. Akademie der Wissen-
schaften--SEE: Akademie
der Wissenschaften, Vienna
398

Vienna. Österreichische Akademie
der Wissenschaften--SEE:
Akademie der Wissenschaften,
Vienna   398

Vienna. Österreichisches Institut
--SEE: Österreichisches Institut, Vienna   397

Vierordt, Hermann   4080-
4081

Un Vieux bibliophile--SEE:
Ungherini, Aglauro   280-
282

Viéville, Jean Philippe Le Cerf
de la--SEE: Le Cerf de la
Viéville, Jean Philippe
4408

Vigiliis von Creutzenfeld, Stephanus Hieronymus de   4211

Vignas, Tommaso   4523

Vigneron, Hippolyte   465

Viguers, Ruth Hill   4029

Vilasaró, Angel Minchero--SEE:
Minchero Vilasaró, Angel
3377

Vilenskiĭ, Vladimir Dmitrievich
1740

Vilenskiĭ-Sibiriakov, V. D. pseud.
--SEE: Vilenskiĭ, Vladimir
Dmitrievich   1740

Villa, Jesús Galindo y --SEE:
Galindo y Villa, Jesús   1527

Villani, Carlo   1379, 2644-2645

Villar, Rogelio   3105

Villarosa, Carlo Antonio de Rosa
di, marchese   3106

Villaseñor, Alejandro Villaseñor
y --SEE: Villaseñor y Villaseñor, Alejandro   1549

Villaseñor y Villaseñor, Alejandro
1549

Viller, Marcel   4345

Villien, Antoine   4344

Villiers de Saint Etienne, Cosme
de   4524

Vimeur, Eugène Achille Lacroix
de, comte de Rochambeau--
SEE: Rochambeau, Eugène
Achille Lacroix de Vimeur,
comte de   951

Viñaza, Cipriano Muñoz y Manzano, conde de la   2646

Vinne, Theodore Low de--SEE:
De Vinne, Theodore Low
4007

Viotta, Henri Anastase   3107

Virginia. University. Bureau of
Public Administration   4775

Virginia Federation of Music Clubs
2949

Virkus, Frederick Adams   2042,
4760

Vis, Jean Pauwels de--SEE:
Pauwels de Vis, Jean   453

Visch, Charles de   4525

Visher, Stephen Sargent   4620

Vistrand, Per Gustaf   1840

Viterbo, Francisco Marques de
Sousa--SEE: Sousa Viterbo,
Francisco Marques de
2687

Vize, Vladimir IUl'evich--SEE:
Wiese, Vladimir IUl'evich
4751

Vizetelly, Francis Horace   293

Vlahović, Vlaho S.   1759

AUTHOR INDEX

Vocke, Johann August   1027

Vodarsky-Shiraeff, Alexandria
3108

Voenno-meditsinskaia akademiia,
Leningrad--SEE: Leningrad.
Voenno-meditsinskaia aka-
demiia   4160-4161

Voight, Bernhard Friedrich
1001-1002

Volbehr, Friedrich Ludwig Christian   3282

Volger, Bruno   3662

Vollhardt, Emil Reinhard--SEE:
Vollhardt, Reinhard   3109

Vollhardt, Reinhard   3109

Vollmer, Hans   2631, 2647

Volsberghe, Henri Marie Ghislaine Surmont de, baron--
SEE: Surmont de Volsberghe,
Henri Marie Ghislaine, baron
461

Volz, Robert   1007

Von der Hardt, Ricardus--SEE:
Hardt, Ricardus von der
3920

Von der Heiden, Helmut--SEE:
Heiden, Helmut von der
3392

Von Einem, John August Christoph
--SEE: Einem, Johann Au-
gust Christoph von   4389

Von Lemmen, Joseph--SEE:
Lemmen, Joseph von   2635

Von Oefele, Andreas Felix--SEE:
Oefele, Andreas Felix von
4179

Von Schindel, Carl Wilhelm Otto
August--SEE: Schindel, Carl
Wilhelm Otto August von
3688

Von Seelen, Johann Heinrich--
SEE: Seelen, Johann Hein-
rich von   1054

Von Selle, Götz--SEE: Selle, Götz
von   1012, 3257

Vos, Joachim Joseph   4526

Voss, Heinrich   3662

Vretblad, Åke Patrik   3196

Vriemoet, Enno Lucius   3313

Vsesoiuznoe botanicheskoe
obshchestvo   4650

Vsesoiuznoe obshchestvo politicheskikh katorzhan i ssyl'no-
poselentsev   1682, 1745-46

Vuillemin, M. F.   953

W

Waal, Pieter Gerardus Adrianus
de   4716

Waay, S. J. Mak van--SEE: Mak
van Waay, S. J.   2547

Wace, Henry   4497, 4527

Wackernagel, Hans Georg   1843

Wadd, William   4212

Wadskiaer, Christian Frederik
1590

Wäschke, Hermann   3670

Wagner, Johanna Schomerus-
SEE: Schomerus-Wagner,
Johanna   3692

Waitzenegger, Franz Joseph 4367

Waldau, Georg Ernst   295

Waley, Arthur   2413

Walford, Edward   1181

Walker, Sir Emery   1150

Walker, Thomas Alfred   1109, 1111

Wallace, David H.   2567

Wallace, William Stewart   508, 511, 519, 3431

Wallem, Fredrik Barbe   3279

Waller, François Gerard   2648

Waller, John Francis   157

Walpole, Horace, Earl of Orford 2649-2650, 3539

Walter, Gérard   848

Walters, Henry Beauchamp 296

Wan, Chieh-ch'ing   611

Wang, Ching   612

Ward, John   3314

Ward, Martha E.   3386

Ward,' Thomas Humphrey   1182

Ware, Sir James   1307

Warfel, Harry Redcay   3432

Warnaffe, Charles, vicomte Du Bus de--SEE: Du Bus de War- naffe, Charles, vicomte   434

Warner, Charles Dudley   3387

Warner, Ezra J.   2043-2044

Waroquier de Méricourt de La Mothe de Combles, Louis Charles, comte   849

Warrack, John Hamilton   3039

Warriner, John   3110

Wascher, Arthur E.   3119

Washington, D. C. Columbia Civic Library Association-- SEE: Columbia Civic Li- brary Association, Washing- ton, D. C.   4004

Washio, Junkei   4273

Wasmuth, Günther   2690

Wassiltchikoff, Alexandre--SEE: Vasil'chikov, Aleksandr Alekseevich   1744

Wastler, Josef   2651

Waters, Clara (Erskine) Clement 2652-2654

Waters, William George   2702

Watkins, John   182, 297, 3497

Watson, Foster   3315

Watson, Irving Allison   4213

Watt, Homer Andrew   3540

Watt, Robert   3541

Watt, Theodore   1209

Watt, William Whyte   3540

Wauchope, George Armstrong 3433

Webb, Alfred John   1308

Webb, Walter Prescott   2342

Webber, Roy   3236

Weber, Otto   4364

Weber, Victor Frédéric   2655

Wedeck, Harry Ezekiel   4261

Wedel, Ernst von   968

Wedgwood, Josiah Clement Wedgwood, baron   1183

Weech, Friedrich Otto Aristides von   1028

The Weekly underwriter   4705, 4728

Weidlein, Johann   1255

Weidlich, Christoph   3988

Weilbach, Philip   2656

Weinwich, Niels Henrich   2657

Weisfert, Julius Nicolaus   1052

Weitenkampf, Frank, pseud. -- SEE: White, Frank Listow   235

Weiz, Friedrich August   3703

Welcker, Carola Giedion-   SEE: Giedion-Welcker, Carola   2697

Welford, Richard   1184

Weller, Karl   1081

Wells, Harry Wharton-   SEE: Wharton-Wells, Harry   3114

Wenzel, Georg   4717

Werner, Hans   2609

Werner, Richard Maria   3181

Wertheimer, Fritz   1016

West, John Ebenezer   3111

West Point Alumni Foundation, inc.   2045

West Virginia. Legislature. Senate   2372

Western Biographical Publishing Company, Cincinnati   2149, 2196

Western India States   1286

Western Region of Nigeria. Legislature   1580

Westminster School, London-- SEE: St. Peter's College, London   1175-1176

Westrup, Jack Allan   3112

Weszprémi, Stephan   4214

Wetzel, Johann Caspar   1039, 3113

Weyerman, Jacob Campo   2658

Weyermann, Albrecht   1077

Weyl, Richard   3282

Wharton-Wells, Harry   3114

Wheeler, Joseph Mazzini   4528

Wheeler, William Adolphus   153

Whelbourn, Hubert   3115

Whincop, Thomas   3542

White, Bernice   2324

White, Frank Listow   235

White, Hugh L.   2267, 2324

Whitington, Don   379

Whitlock, Ernest Clyde   2985

Whitmore, John Beach   1176

Whittaker, George Byrom,
    publisher   210

Wickersheimer, Ernest   4223

Wiedemann, Erik   2914

Wiedemann, Hans   4540

Wienstein, Friedrich   3705

Wier, Albert Ernest   2667-
2668, 2754, 3123-3124

Wierzbowski, Teodor   3812

Wiese, Vladimir I͡Ul´evich
4751

Wile, Frederick William   1022

Wilks, John   4541

Will, Georg Andreas   1058-1059

Willard, Frances Elizabeth
2072

Williams, Alfred Mason   2311

Williams, Daniel   1233

Williams, Ethel L.   4542

Williams, Henry Clay   2116,
2170, 2348

Williams, Robert   1230, 1234

Williams, Stephen West   4224

Williamson, Leland M.   2304

Willis, William   3992

Willmann, Otto   3288

Willsher, Harry Martin   3114

Wilpert, Gero von   3393, 3706

Wilson, Emilia Serrano de,
    baronesa de Wilson--SEE:
    Serrano de Wilson, Emilia,
    baronesa de Wilson   1545

Wilson, George Buckley Laird
3215

Wilson, H. W., firm, publishers
5, 105

Wilson, Henry   303

Wilson, James Grant   1908,
1927

Wilson, Joshua, M. A.   1188

Wilson, W. Lawler   304

Winchester, Clarence   3216

Winchester, Paul   2182

Winckelmann, Johann Heinrich
    Ludwig von   2669

Wincklern, Johann Baptist von
3707

Windle, Sir Bertram Coghill
    Alan   4543

Winer, Georg Benedikt   4544-
4545

Wininger, Salomon   1482

Winslow, Forbes Benignus
4225

Winter, Ch.   858

Winterberg, Hans   1023

Wisconsin. State Historical
   Society   2377

Wisconsin Federation of Music
   Clubs   3125

Wisconsin State Historical
   Society--SEE: Wisconsin.
   State Historical Society
   2377

Wissowa, Georg   229

With, Nanna   1587

Witherspoon, Halliday, firm,
   publisher   2146

Withey, Elsie Rathburn   2692

Withey, Henry F.   2692

Witsen Geysbeek, Pieter Gerardus
   --SEE: Geysbeek, Pieter
   Gerardus Witsen   3489

Witt, Mary Helene (Marten)
   2665-2666

Witt, Sir Robert Clermont
   2665-2666

Witte, Henning   305, 3993, 4226

Wittrup, Ludvig Peter Marius
   Christian   671

Woel, Cai Mogens   3487

Wójcicki, Kazimierz Władysław
   1638

Wokaun von Wokaunius, Peter Tobias, Ritter von   653

Wokaunius, Peter Tobias, Ritter
   von Wokaun von--SEE:
   Wokaun von Wokaunius, Peter Tobias, Ritter von   653

Wolf, Johann Christoph   1483

Wolf, Rudolf   1869

Wolfe, Wellington C.   2091-2092

Wolff, Oscar Ludwig Bernhard
   3708

Wolffheim, Werner Joachim   2971

Wong, Choon-san   1755

Wood, Anthony à   1190

Woodward, Stanley   3247

Woollen, William Wesley   2153

Worcester, Mass. American
   Antiquarian Society--SEE:
   American Antiquarian Society,
   Worcester, Mass.   1882-83

World Conference on Faith and
   Order. 2d, Edinburgh
   (1937)   4546

Worm, Jens   673

Worman, Ernest James   4051

Wotton, William   4356

Wright, Alfred Augustus   2067

Wright, Marcus Joseph   2345

Wright, Richard Robert   4547

Wright, Thomas   251

Wright, William Henry Kearley
   3546

Wright de Kleinhans, Laureana
1550

Writers' Program. Illinois 4811

Wu, Ch'ing-ti 618

Wu, Jung-kuang 540

Wu, Wên-chin 541

Wu ch'iu chung tzu, pseud. 619

Württemberg. Kommission für
Landesgeschichte 1081

Wüstenfeld, Heinrich Ferdinand
4227, 4768

Wurts, John S. 1189

Wurzbach, Alfred Wolfgang, Ritter von Tannenberg 2670

Wurzbach, Constantin, Ritter
von Tannenberg 406-407

Wyndham, Henry Saxe 3126

X

Xiberta y Roqueta, Bartolomé
María 4548

Ximeno, Vicente 3866, 3896

Y

Yaben, Jacinto R. 359

Yale University 29, 312, 1929,
1971

Yang, Chia-lo 620

Yang, Li-ch'eng 4052

Yang, Wen-hui 4272

Yang, Yin-shen 621, 3459

Yax, Christoph Gottlob--SEE:
Saxe, Christoph Gottlob
254

Yeh, Yün-shêng 622

Yorston (John C.) and Company
1994

Young, Percy Marshall 3128

Young, Philipp--SEE: Yung,
Philipp 1485

Yü, Ping-yao 568

Yü, Ping-yüeh--SEE: Yü, Ping-
yao 568

Yü-ch'ien 4274

Yu lien yen chiu so, Kowloon
(Union Research Institute)
614

Yüan, Ch'ing-p'ing 623

Yung, Philipp 1485

Z

Zablotsky, Moses 1448

Zagoskin, Nikolaĭ Pavlovich
3280

Zambrano, Francisco 4549

Zambrini, Francesco Saverio
3785

Zamora Lucas, Florentino 1762

Zangari, Domenico 1343

Zani, Pietro 2671

Zannandries, Diego 2672

Zapata Cuencar, Heriberto 3129

Zapater y Gómez, Francisco
2673

Zarco Cuevas, Eusebio Julián
4550

Zardotti, Gaetano   1340

Zarski, Samuel Zanvel   4569

Zatvornitskii, Nikolai Mitrofanovich   1748

Zawart, Anscar   4551

Zdobnov, Nikolai Vasil'evich
3852

Zeigler, Kurt   229

Zentralinstitut für Bibliothekswe-
sen (DDR) --SEE: Germany
(Democratic Republic (1949-
) Zentralinstitut für
Bibliothekswesen   3621

Zentz, George H.   3911

Zeumer, Johann Caspar   3322

Zhadovskii, Anatolii Esperovich
4650

Zherebtsov, B. I.   3853

Ziegelbauer, Magnoald   4552

Ziegenfuss, Werner   4248

Ziegler, Hieronymus   1024

Ziegler, Konrat Julius Fürchte-
gott   228

Zilberzweig, Zalme--SEE: Zylbercweig, Zalme   3218

Zincada, Paolo, pseud--SEE:
Cecchini, Riccardo   1349

Zinny, Antonio   360, 1601

al-Zirikli, Khayr al-Din   1333

Zischka, Gert A.   316

Zitron, Samuel Loeb--SEE: Citron, Samuel Loeb   1450

Zmeev, Lev Fedorovich   4229-
4230

Zscharnack, Leopold   4470

Zubizarreta, Carlos   1602

Zülch, Walter Karl   2674

Zürcher Schriftstellerverein 3932

Zuerl, Walter   1025

Zuth, Josef   3131

Zvorykin, A. A.   4578, 4626

Zyl, Paul Henrik Stephanus van--
SEE: Van Zyl, Paul Henrik
Stephanus   332

Zylbercweig, Zalme   3218

TITLE INDEX

A

A. L. A. portrait index   1

The ASCAP biographical dictionary   2747

Aargauische Schriftsteller   3927

Abbildungen böhmischer und
mährischer Gelehrten   652

Abecedario biografico dei pittori,
scultori ed architetti cremonesi   2513

Abecedario pittorico nel quale
compendiosamente sono
descritte le patrie, i maestri,
ed i tempi, ne' quali fiorirono
circa quattro mila professori
di pittura   2573

The Aberdeen printers   4010

Abrégé de la vie des peintres
2586-2587

Abrégé de l'histoire du théâtre
français   3175

The Abridged compendium of
American genealogy   2042

Abstracts from the wills of English printers and stationers
(from 1492 to 1630)   4033

Abstracts on European and Far
Eastern personalities   285

Abstracts on personalities   285

Academic histories of faculty members of associated collegiate
schools of business   3254

Académie des sciences et des
arts   88

An Account of the English dramatick poets   3511

Accountants' directory and who's
who   4694

Achêgas a um diccionario de
pseudonymos, iniciaes, a-
breviaturas e obras anonymas
de auctores brasileiros e de
estrangeiros   472

Acta sanctorum   4275

Les Acteurs et les actrices de
Paris (Abraham)   3132

Les Acteurs et les actrices de
Paris (Darthenay)   3146

Actores en el drama del Perú y
del mundo   1603

Actors and authors   3191

Adatok a magyarországi és erdélyi
minoriták irodalmi munkásságáról   3718

Ādhunika Telugu racayitalu
3722

Adiciones al Diccionario histórico
de los mas ilustres profesores
de las bellas artes en España
de... Ceán Bermúdez
2646

Admissions to Peterhouse in the
University of Cambridge
1110

Admissions to Peterhouse or S.
Peter's College in the University of Cambridge   1109

Adresnaiā kniga botanikov SSSR
4650

Adressar géographique du monde
4747

Adressbuch deutscher Chemiker
4651

Die Ältere niederländische Malerei
2544

The "Aeroplane" directory of
British aviation   4776

Die Aerzte Estlands   4090

Die Aerzte Kurlands   4091

Die Aerzte Livlands   4092

Africanistes spécialistes de
sciences sociales   4692

Afrikaanse biografiese woorde-
boek   328

Die Afrikaner-personenregister
322

Die Agada der palästinensischen
Amoräer   4560

Die Agada der Tannaiten   4560

Aide-mémoire de l'amateur et du
professionel   2559

Aikalaiskirja   699

Air Force register   2024

Air National Guard register
2036

Aktivnye bortsy za soyetskuiu
vlast' v Azerbaidzhane
1669

al-A'lām   1333

Alaska literary directory   3398

Alaska: who's here, what's doing,
who's doing it (1955)   2076

Albo storico-biografico degli
uomini illustri Valtellinesi
1418

Al'bom sovremennykh deiatelei
iskusstva i literatury   3818

Album academicum van het
Athenaeum illustre en van de
Universiteit van Amsterdam
3256

Album biográfico ecuatoriano
678

Album Bavariae iatricae   4135

Album-biograficzne zasłuzonych
Polaków i Polek wieku XIX
1628

Album biographique des belges
célèbres   426

Album nacional (Spain)   1764

Album of great, outstanding, and
eminent personalities of
Russia   1734

Album pisarzy polskich   3808

Album zaslužnih Hrvata XIX.
stoljeća   2402

Aleksandrynas   3798

Algemajner muzik-leksikon
2743

Algemeene kunst encyclopaedie
2629

Algemeene levensbeschryving der
mannen en vrouwen van
Belgie   455

Algemene muziekencyclopedie
2745

Alien members of the book-trade
during the Tudor period
4051

All India medical directory &
who's who   4057

All-India trade directory and who's
who   1595

All of the women of the Bible
4267

All of the men of the Bible   4270

Allgemeine Biographie (Schröckh)
257

Allgemeine deutsche Biographie
962, 1006

Allgemeine hannoversche Biographie   1047

Allgemeine Künstler-Historie
2536

Allgemeiner Bildniskatalog   25

Allgemeiner deutscher Literaturkalender   3654

Allgemeiner Porträt-Katalog
(Diepenbroick-Grüter)   7

Allgemeiner Portrait-Katalog
(Drugulin)   9-10

Allgemeines Autor- und Litteraturlexikon in alphabetischer
und chronischer Ordnung
(bis 1778)   3326

Allgemeines biographisches Lexikon alter und neuer geistlicher
Liederdichter   3685

Allgemeines Gelehrten-Lexicon
(Jöcher)   166-167

Allgemeines Gelehrten-Lexikon
(Zischka)   316

Allgemeines historisch-biographisches Handwörterbuch merkwürdigen Personen   60

Allgemeines historisches Künstler-Lexikon für Böhmen
2480

Allgemeines Künstlerlexicon
(Fuessli)   2498

Allgemeines Künstler-Lexikon
(Meyer)   2555, 2564

Allgemeines Künstler-Lexikon
(Müller, H. A.)   2560-2561

Allgemeines Lexikon der bildenden
Künstler des XX. Jahrhunderts   2647

Allgemeines Lexikon der bildenden
Künstler von der Antike bis
zur Gegenwart   2631, 2647

Allgemeines Schriftsteller- und
Gelehrten-Lexikon der Provinzen Livland, Estland,
und Kurland   415-416

Allgemeines Theater-Lexikon
3135

Allmänt musiklexikon   2998

An Almanac of current world
leaders   48

Almanakh sovremennykh russkikh
gosudarstvennykh dīeīateleī
1667

Almindeligt forfatter-lexicon for
Kongeriget Danmark   3480-3481

Almindeligt literaturlexicon for
Danmark, Norge, og Island
3485

Alphabetical list of the officers
of the Indian Army   1134

Alphabetical register of all the
authors actually living in
Great Britain, Ireland and
in the United Provinces of
North-America   3529

Alphabetische lijst van de voorloopig verzamelde namen
der in België geboren Nederlandsche schrijvers   3491

Alphabetische Liste aller gelehrten Juden und Jüdinnen
1485

Alphabetisches Verzeichniss; oder,
Lexicon der itzt lebenden
schwäbischen Schriftsteller
3632

Alphabetisches Verzeichnis aller
im Jahr 1774 in Schlesien
lebender Schriftsteller   3698

Les Alsaciens illustres   858

Les Alsaciens-Lorrains   854

Alþingismannatal (Kristjánsson)
1256

Alþingismannatal (Sigurðsson)
1258

Alþingismannatal (Tobiasson)
1259

Alumnae biographical register is-
sur [of Vassar College]
2041

Alumni Cantabrigiensis   1108

Alumni Dublinenses   1302

Alumni Oxonienses   1168

American architects directory
2675

American authors (1600-1900)
3414

American authors and books
3400

American autobiographies (Kaplan)

The American bar   3941

An American biographical and
historical dictionary   1893

The American biographical dictionary   1893

American biographical history of
eminent and self-made men
(Michigan volume)   2169

American biographical notes
1953

American biographies (Preston)
2000

American biographies; a genealogical, historical and biographical cyclopedia   1894

American biography; a new cyclopedia   1895

The American blue book of biography   1952

American Bar Association approved law schools, Directory
of law teachers in   3951

American book illustrators   4001

American Catholic convert authors
3419

The American Catholic Who's
who   1896

American clocks & clockmakers
2708

American composers today
2839

American dental directory   4063

American diaries   1888

American directory & Who's who
in Europe   1897

American directory of obstetricians and gynecologists
4064

American educators of Norwegian
origin   3276

American engravers upon copper
and steel (Fielding)   2495

American engravers upon copper
and steel (Stauffer)   2622

American firearms makers   4781

American gun makers   4803

The American history and encyclopedia of music   2901

American illustrators and advertising artists   2571

American Jewish year book   1898

American Jews   1899

The American labor who's who
1900

The American Loyalists   2007

American Lutheran biographies
4475

American medical biographies
(Kelly)   4153

American medical biography
(Thacher)   4207, 4224

American medical biography
(Williams)   4224

American medical directory
4065

American men in government
1901

American men of medicine
4066

American men of science   4576

American novelists of today
3432

American pediatric directory
4067

American physicians and surgeons
4068

American planning and civic annual   1902

The American portrait gallery
(Jones)   1959

American portrait gallery (Livingston)   1966

American silversmiths and their
marks   2709

American supplement to Grove's
dictionary [of music and mu-
sicians]   3018

American University men in China
1903

American women; the official
who's who...,   1905

American writers and compilers
of sacred music 2965

The Americana... Biographies
50

America's dental leaders 4070

America's successful men of affairs 1944

America's young men 1905

Amerikos lietuviu vardynas
1906

Amherst College biographical
record 1907

'Amude ha-'avodah 2935

Anales históricos de la medicina
en general 4109

Analytical bibliography of universal collected biography 22

Anatomical eponyms 4634

Anatomical names 4635

Les Anciens du Séminaire
[Joliette, Quebec] 3579

Andenken an die Rostok'schen
Gelehrten 1067

Anecdotes of distinguished persons (Seward) 263

Anecdotes of painting in England
2649-2650

The Anglo-African who's who and
biographical sketch-book 323

Anhaltisches Schriftsteller- Lexikon
3690

Animal painters of England 2505

Annales biographiques 51

Annales dramatiques; ou, Dictionnaire général des théatres 3136

Annales nécrologiques de la Légion d'honneur 805

Annals of New Zealand literature
3521

Annals of the American pulpit
4501

Annals of the artists of Spain
2623

L'Année française 815

Anno biographico brazileiro
479

An Annotated bibliography of biographies and autobiographies
of negroes 1885

Annuaire de la noblesse Belgique
449

Annuaire de la noblesse de France
et des maisons souveraines
de l'Europe 311

Annuaire de la noblesse de Russie
1668

Annuaire de la pairie et de la
noblesse de France, des maisons souveraines de l'Europe
... . 311

Annuaire diplomatique et consulaire de la République française 713

Annuaire nécrologique 51

Annuaire pontifical catholique
4281

The Annual biography and obituary   1090

The Annual monitor   1091-1092

Annual obituary notices of eminent persons... United
States   1923

Annual reunion and register of
graduates [U. S. Naval Aca-
demy]   2038

Annuals, directories, who's who,
press guides   2

Annuario della nobilità italiana
1344

Año biográfico español   1777

Anonimi e pseudonimi   1338

Anonimi e pseudonimi italiani
(Rocco)   1342

Anonimi, pseudonimi, eteronimi
scrittori calabresi   1343

Anonym- og pseudonym-lexikon
for Danmark og Island til
1920 og Norge til 1814   655

Anonyma and pseudonyma   1089

Anonymer og pseudonymer i den
danske... literatur   1751

Anonymer og pseudonymer i den
norske literatur (1678-1890)
1584

Anonymes, pseudonymes et supercheries littéraires de la Provence   710

Anonyms (Cushing)   1891

al-Ansāb (al-Sam'ānī)   1331

Ansari's trade directory of Pakistan and who's who   1592

Ansbachisches Pfarrerbuch
4490

Anshe ha-shem (Eisenstadt)
1937

Anshe shem (Zarski)   4569

Anthologie des écrivains morts
à la guerre (1914-1918)
3553

Anthologie des écrivains morts
à la guerre (1939-1945)
3554

Gli Antichi poeti italiani   3741

Los Antiguos Jesuítas del Perú
4511

Antología de la poesía española e
hispanoamericana (1882-1932)
3878

Anuario bibliográfico venezolano
3898-3899

Anuario biográfico nacional [de
México]   1546

Anuario médico-social de Cuba
4123

Appleton's cyclopaedia of American biography   1908
SEE ALSO: The Cyclopaedia
of American biography   1927

Apuntes biográficos de escritores...
de la República Argentina
343

Apuntes biográficos de escritores
segovianos   3858

Apuntes histórico-biográficos
acerca de la escuela arago-
nesa de pintura   2673

Apuntes para un diccionario de
pintores malagueños del
siglo XIX   2458

Apuntes para un diccionario de
seudónimos y de publica-
ciones anónimas   2380

Apuntes para una biblioteca
científica española del siglo
XVI   4608

Apuntes para una biblioteca de
escritoras españolas (desde
el año 1401 al 1883)   3890

Apuntes sobre bibliografía colombiana   626

Aragoneses contemporáneos
1789

Architekci i budowniczowie w
Polsce   2685

Archives biographiques contemporaines   54

Les Archives internationales contemporaines   54-55

Archives de l'honneur   714

Ardennes. Dictionnaire, annuaire et album   859

Argentines of to-day   352

Arkansas lives   2081

Arkhierei petrovskoi epokhi v ikh
perepiskie s Petrom Velikim
4476

Armorial des évêques du Canada
4310

Armorial du Premier Empire
832

The Army list (Gt. Brit.)   1148

The Army register of the United
States   2023

The Art of music   2954

The Art of painting, with the lives
and characters of above 300
of the most eminent painters
2587

Arthur Mee's 1000 heroes   193

Articles on the leaders of the Indonesian Communist Party
1296

Les Artistes angevins   2591

Les Artistes de l'Alsace pendant
le moyen âge   2504

Les Artistes décorateurs des
bois   2642

Les Artistes français à l'étranger
2484

Les Artistes-musiciens belges au
XVIIIme et XIXme siècle
2877-2878

Les Artistes tourangeaux   2506

Artisti e musicisti moderni
3027

Gli Artisti italiani e stranieri
negli stati Estensi   2456

Artistisches Magazin   2527

Artists and engravers of British
and American book plates
4013

Artists and sculptors of Nottingham and Nottinghamshire
2522

Artists of the nineteenth century
and their works   2652

The Arts and artists   2486

Arvācīna Marāthī vāṅmayasevaka
1276

Asamblea Constituyente (de 1854)
1767

Aschehougs musikleksikon   2751

The Asia who's who   362

Ateneo dei letterati milanesi
3772

Athenae Batavae   3294

Athenae Belgicae   463

Athenae Cantabrigienses   1119

Athenae Lubecensis   1054

Athenae Oxonienses   1190

Athenae Rauricae; sive, Catalogus
professorum Academiae
Basiliensis   3275

Athenarum Frisiacarum libri duo
3313

Das Atlantisbuch der Musik   2752

Attic black-figure vase-painters
2435

Aufrichtige Nachricht von den
jüdischen Lehrern und ihren
zur Exegese und Antiquität
gehörigen Schriften   1468

Augsburger Pfarrerbuch   4540

Aula Norvegiae erudita   1590

Ausländische Dichter und Schriftsteller unserer Zeit   3369

An Australian biographical dictionary (Johns)   376

Australian dictionary of dates and
men of the time   375

The Australian encyclopaedia
369

Australian literature   3516

Australian men of mark   370

The Australian portrait gallery
371

Austrian painting from Biedermeier to modern times
2518

Auteurs deguisez   30

Author biography master index
3324

The Author's and writer's who's
who   3494

Author's biographical monthly
service   3323

Authors of books for young people
3386

Authors today and yesterday
3362, 3365

Automotive news almanac   4778

Autorenlexikon der Gegenwart
3367

Autorenlexikon des XX. Jahrhunderts   3367

Autores españoles e hispanoamericanos   3887

Avery obituary index of architects
and artists   2415

The Aviation and flying year
book   4776

Az én halottaim   1253

Azbuchnyĭ ukazatel´ imen russkikh deĭ͡ateleĭ dli͡a Russkago
biograficheskago slovari͡a
1731

B

Badische Biographien   1028

Baierisches Gelehrten-Lexikon
1031-1032

Baierisches Musik-Lexikon
2944

Baltische Maler und Bildhauer
des XIX Jahrhunderts   2565

Baltische Studenten in Kiel   413

The Bankers' directory of the U-
nited States and Canada
4714

The Bankers' who's who   4697

Baptist authors   4425

The Baptist encyclopaedia   4320

Baptist handbook and almanack
4290

The Baptist manual   4290

Baptist who's who   4291

Barkhatnai͡a kniga   1724

Baseball register   3219

La Basilicata nel Risorgimento
politico italiano (1700-1870)
1385

Basler Portraits aller Jahrhunderte   1866

Baton twirling, Who's who in
3239

Bayreuthisches Pfarrerbuch
4491

The Beauties of Gaelic poetry,
and lives of the Highland
bards   3598

Beeton's dictionary of universal
biography   64

Beiträge zu einem tirolischen
Anonymen- und Pseudonymen-
Lexikon   381

Beiträge zum Deutschen Anonymen-
lexikon (Rosenbaum)   955,
958

Beiträge... (See also variant spel-
ling: Beytrag, Beyträge...)

Beknopt biographisch hand-woordenboek van Nederland   1557

Les Belges au Congo   440

Belgian and American C. R. B. fellows (1920-1950)   3259

La Belgique médicale   4125

La Belgique militaire   465

Belgische koloniale biografie   422

The Bench and bar of Georgia
3639

Bench and bar of... Massachusetts   3948

Bench and bar of Michigan 3978

The Bench and bar of Mississippi 3966

The Bench and bar of New Hampshire 3944

The Bench and bar of New York 3977

Bench and bar of Ohio 3979

The Bench and bar of Texas 3967

Bench and bar of West Virginia 3942

The Bench and bar of Wisconsin 3980

Benefactores y hombres notables de Puerto Rico 1651

Berühmte israelitische Männer und Frauen in der Kultur-geschichte der Menschheit 1464

Berühmte Männer Berlins und ihrer Wohnstätten 1035

Berühmte Zürcher 1857

Besaettelsens hvem, hvad, hvor 656

The Best moving pictures of (1922-23-) 3140

Betas of achievement 1909

Beytrag zu einem Lexico der jetztlebender lutherisch- und reformirten Theologen in und um Teutschland 4442, 4446

Beyträge zu der Lebensgeschichte denkwürdiger Personen 89

Beyträge zur Historie der Gelahrtheit 244, 270, 685

Bhāratavarshīya arvāchina-charitra-kosha 1265

Bhāratavarshīya-madhyayugīna-charitra-kosha 1266

Bhāratavarshīya prachina-charitra-kosha 1267

Bhāratīya-mahāpu-rusha 1270

Bibliografía biográfica mexicana 1518

Bibliografia Camilliana 4362

Bibliografía colombiana 627

Bibliografía cubana del siglo XIX [y XX, 1900-1916] 641

Bibliografía de la provincia dominicana de Colombia 4433

Bibliografía de novelistas mexicanos 3912

Bibliografia dels antics poetes catalans 3454

Bibliografía dels monjos de Montserrat 4277

Bibliografia femminile italiana del XIX secolo 3761

Bibliografía filosófica mexicana 4260

Bibliografía general de Chile 526

Bibliografía militar de España 1765

Bibliografia romana 3740

Bibliografia siciliana   1409

Bibliografia universale sacra e
profana   265

Bibliograficheskiĭ katalog rossiiskim pisatel'nitsam
3842

Bibliograficheskiĭ slovar'
pisateleĭ, uchenykh i
khudozhnikov, urozhentsev
... Riazanskoĭ gubernii
3822

Bibliograficheskiĭ slovar' russkikh
pisatel'nits   3826, 3840

Bibliografický a biografický
slovnik českých spisovatelů
3476

Bibliografiiā deiāteleĭ Urala
1704

Bibliographia Augustiniana
4456

Bibliographia nobiliarchica portugueza   1641

Bibliographia poetica   3530

Bibliographical index to the historians of Muhammedan In-
dia   4757

Bibliographie biographique universelle   20

Bibliographie de la littérature
française (de 1800 à 1930)
3595

Bibliographie der Minderbroeders
van de Sint-Jozef provincie
in België   4307

Bibliographie des auteurs modernes
de langue française   3594

Bibliographie générale des écrivains rédemptoristes   4435

Bibliographie lyonnaise   3998

Bibliographie nationale (Belgique)   3443

Bibliographie néerlandaise historique-scientifique   4666

Bibliographisches Lexicon der
gesammten jüdischen Literatur der Gegenwart und Adress-
Anzeiger   3791

A Bibliography of American autobiographies   1887

A Bibliography of history and
historical biography   27

Bibliography of music dictionaries   2741

A Bibliography of the collective
biography of Spanish America   1496

The Bibliophile dictionary   3329

The Bibliophile library of literature, art, and rare manu-
scripts   3329

Bibliosofia, e memorie letterarie
di scrittori francescani Conventuali   4370

Biblioteca Augustiniana historica,
critica e chronologica   4451

Biblioteca bio-bibliográfica
(Beltrán y de Torres)   4

Biblioteca bio-bibliografica della
Terra Santa e dell'Oriente
francescano   4381-4383

Biblioteca Cisterciense española
4445

Biblioteca de autores andaluces
3864

Biblioteca de escritores baleares
3859

Biblioteca de escritores de la
Compañía de Jesús   4519

Biblioteca de escritores de la
provincia de Guadalajara
3867

Biblioteca de escritores venezolanos contemporáneos   4016

Biblioteca de los escritores que
han sido individuos de los
seis colegios mayores: de
San Ildefonso, de la Universidad de Alcalá [etc.]   3884

Biblioteca degli scrittori barnabiti   4306

Biblioteca dei Frati Minori Cappuccini della Provincia di
Venezia (Giovanni Crisostomo da Cittadella)   4380

Biblioteca dei Frati Minori Cappuccini di Lombardia (Ilarimo
da Milano)   4398

Biblioteca del murciano   3892

Biblioteca di biografia italiana
generale   1336

Biblioteca, e storia di quei scrittori... di Vicenza   3737

Biblioteca femminile italiana
3751-3752

Biblioteca hispano-americana
setentrional   3901-3902

Biblioteca hispanochilena   525

Biblioteca lusitana historica,
critica e cronológica   1640

Biblioteca maltese   1516

Biblioteca maritima española
4746

Biblioteca Mercedaria   4378

Biblioteca modenese   3769,
3781

Biblioteca napoletana   1397-
1398

Biblioteca valenciana de los
escritores que florecieron
hasta nuestros días   3866,
3896

Biblioteca volante, continuata
3746

Bibliotecas antigua y nueva de
escritores aragoneses
3871

Bibliotheca anonymorum et pseudonymorum (Mylius)   36

Bibliotheca anti-Quakeriana
4494

Bibliotheca Augustiniana historica
4451

Bibliotheca Belgica (Foppens)
435

Bibliotheca Belgica. Bibliographie générale des Pays-Bays
3444

Bibliotheca Belgica juridica
3949

Bibliotheca Benedictino-Casinensis
4284

Bibliotheca biographica; a synopsis of universal biography 123

Bibliotheca Britannica 3541

Bibliotheca Brittanico-Hibernica 3537

Bibliotheca Canadensis 3518

Bibliotheca Carmelitana 4524

Bibliotheca Carmelito-Lusitana 4302

Bibliotheca chemica 4660

Bibliotheca chirurgica in qua res omnes ad chirurgiam pertinentes ordine alphabetico... innotuerunt 4211

Bibliotheca Cornubiensis 3498

Bibliotheca elementar chirurgico-anatomica 4197

Bibliotheca Hebraea 1483

Bibliotheca Hispana nova 3856

Bibliotheca Hispana vetus 3857

Bibliotheca historica medii aevi 687

Bibliotheca institvta et collecta, primvm a Conrado Gesnero 3464

Bibliotheca Latino-Hebraica 3789

Bibliotheca Lusitana escolhida 3815

Bibliotheca Lusitana historica, crítica e cronólogica 1640

Bibliotheca magna rabbinica de scriptoribus... Hebraicis 3789

Bibliotheca Mexicana 1526

Bibliotheca Sanctorum 4303

Bibliotheca Scoto-Celtica 3600

Bibliotheca scriptorum e Congregatione clerr. regg. S. Paulli 4515

Bibliotheca scriptorum medicorum veterum et recentiorum 4164

Bibliotheca scriptorum Mediolanensium 1393

Bibliotheca scriptorum Ordinis Minorum S. Francisci Capuccinorum 4350

Bibliotheca scriptorum sacri ordinis Cisterciensis 4525

Bibliotheca scriptorum Societatis Iesu 4472

Bibliotheca scriptorum utriusque Congregationis et Sexus Carmelitarum excalceatorum 4428

Bibliotheca Sicula 3767

Bibliotheca universalis (Gesner) 3464

Bibliotheca virorum militia aeque ac scriptis illustrium 199

Bibliotheek van anonymen en pseudonymen 1551

Bibliothèque de la Compagnie de Jesus 4288-4289

Bibliothèque des auteurs de Bourgogne   3586

Bibliothèque française   3575

Bibliothèque générale des écrivains de l'Ordre de Saint
Benoit   4371

Bibliothèque historique et critique
des auteurs de la Congregation de St. Maur   4508

Bibliothèque historique, et critique du Poitu   929

Bibliothèque littéraire du Maine
3552

Bibliothèque littéraire, historique
et critique de la médecine
ancienne et moderne   4105

Bibliothèque lorraine   855

Bibliothèque orientale   1317

Bibliothèque sulpicienne   4301

Bibliothèque universelle des historiens   4755-4756

Bibljografja pamietników polskich
i Polski dotyczacych   1624

The Bijou biography of the world
139

Bilder hundert deutscher Indologen
3724

Bilder-Sal heutiges Tages lebender
... berühmter Schrift-Steller
3610

The Billboard encyclopedia of music   2773

The Billboard music year book
2773

Billeder af berømte danske
maend og kvinder   672

Bio-bibliografía eclesiástica
mexicana (1821-1943)
4520

Bio-bibliografia generale italiana
1349

Bio-bibliografía hispálica de
Ultramar   1810

Bio-bibliografie de' soci effettivi
della R. Deputazione di storia
patria per le provincie
modenesi   4753

Biobibliografiia deiatelei Urala

Bio-bibliografija franjevaca Bosne
Srebreničke   4402

A Bio-bibliographical finding list
of Canadian musicians   2792

Bio-bibliographical index of musicians in the United States
of America since colonial
times   2892

Bio-bibliographie vauclusienne 949

Bio-bibliographisches Literatur-
lexikon Österreichs   3622

Bio-bibliographisches Verzeichnis
von Universitäts- und Hoch-
schuldrucken... ,   996

A Bio-bibliography of Franciscan
authors in colonial Central
America   4276

Bio-bibliography of XVI century
medical authors   4166

Bio- et bibliographia Silesiaca
1072

Biografía americana; o, Galería
de poetas célebres de Chile
[etc.]   3905

Biografía de nuestros artistas
2774

Biografia degli Italiani illustri
nelle scienze, lettere ed arti
del secolo XVIII   1376

Biografia degli scrittori perugini
3784

Biografia degli uomini distinti
dell'Istria   2407

Biografia degli uomini illustri
del Regno di Napoli   1395

Biografia degli uomini illustri
della Sicilia   1410

Biografia dei contemporanei del
Regno di Napoli   1396

Biografia dei medici illustri
Bresciani   4201

Biografia dei viaggiatori italiani
4737

Biografia finanziaria italiana
1345

Biografia medica Ligure   4184

Biografia medica piemontese
4088

Biografia piemontese   1402

Biografia sarda   1403

Biografia serafica degli uomini illustri che fiorirono nel Francescano istituto   4488

Biografia universale antica e
moderna   66

Biografías argentinas y sudamericanas   359

Biografías cordobesas contemporáneos   1794

Biografías de conquistadores de
la Argentina en el siglo XVI;
Tucumán   348

Biografías de hombres ilustres...
de Colombia   624

Biografías de hombres notables
de Hispano-América   1501

Biografías de literatos nacionales
(Guatemala)   3897

Biografías de los héroes y caudil-
los de la Independencia   1549

Biografías de Mexicanos distinguidos   1528, 1547

Biografías hispanoamericanas
en el Archivo General de
Indias   1508

Biograficheskie ocherki senatorov
po materialam sobrannym
P. I. Baranovym   1732

Biograficheskii leksikon russkikh
kompozitorov i muzykal'nykh
deiatelei   3041

Biograficheskii ocherki lits,
izobrazhennykh na pamiatnikie
tysiachelietiia Rossii,
vozdvignutago v g. Novgorodie
1862 g.   1716

Biograficheskii slovar' deiatelei
estestvoznaniia i tekhniki
4578, 4626

Biograficheskii slovar' professorov i prepodavatelei Imperatorskago IUr'evskago, byvsha-
go Derptskago universiteta
3287

Biograficheskiĭ slovar´ professorov i prepodavateleĭ
Imperatorskago Kazanskago
universiteta   3280

Biograficheskiĭ slovar´ professorov i prepodavateleĭ Imperatorskago Moskovskago
universiteta   3296

Biograficheskiĭ slovar´ professorov i prepodavatelei Imperatorskago S. -Peterburg-
skago universiteta   3286

Biograficheskiĭ slovar´ professorov i prepodavatelei Imperatorskago universiteta
sv. Vladimira (1834-1884)
3283

Biograficheskiĭ slovar´ studentov
pervykh XXVIII kursov S. -
Peterburgskoĭ dukhovnoĭ
akademii   4473

Biograficheskiĭ spravochnik;
vydaiūshchesiā khimiki...
4654

Biografie degli Accademici Al-
fonsini detti poi Pontaniani
1367

Le Biografie degli uomini illustri
delle Calabrie   1387

Biografie di ingegneri militari
italiani dal secolo XIV alla
metà del XVIII   4799

Biografie di scrittori e artisti
musicali Bergamaschi nativi
od oriundi   2959

Biografie e necrologie d'illustri e
benemeriti Dalmati   2399

Biografie e ritratti degli uomini
illustri... di Molise   1384

Biografie e ritratti d'illustri siciliani morti nel cholera
(1837)   1408

Biografii kompozitorov s IV-XX
viek [sic]   2904

Biografii rossiiskikh generalis-
simov i general-fel´dmarsha-
lov   1671

Biografii russkikh pisatelei sredni-
ago i novago periodov   3823

Biografije   67

Biografikon lexikon Kyprou   643

Biografinen nimikirja   695

Biografisk handbok omfattande
20, 602 personer   1832-
1833

Biografisk matrikel över svenska
läkarkåren   4082

Biografiske artikler i norske tidsskrifter (1931-1935)   1583

Biografiskt lexicon öfver namnkunnige svenske män   1816,
1831

Le Biographe et l'historien   75

Le Biographe universelle   71

The Biographer (London)   69

The Biographer (New York)   68

The Biographer and review   69

Biographia; annuaire pour l'Amérique du Nord des personnalités de langue française
1910

Biographia; yearly directory for North America of French-speaking... personalities 1910

Biographia Academica Goettingensis 3267

Biographia Americana 1941

Biographia Britannica 1094

Biographia Classica 3460, 3462

Biographia dramatica 3495

Biographia Evangelica 4437

Biographia Hibernica 1305

Biographia juridica 3953-3954

Biographia litteraria 3496

Biographia medica 4144

Biographia navalis 1114

Biographiana (Seward) 264

Biographic directory of the USSR 1693

Biographic etchings of ministers and laymen of the Georgia Conferences 4487

Biographic register of labor attachés 2031

Biographic register of the U. S. Department of State 2032

The Biographical album of western gunfighters 2361

A Biographical and critical dictionary of painters and engravers 2621

A Biographical and genealogical history of southeastern Nebraska 2222

Biographical and historical memoirs of Mississippi 2217-2218

Biographical and historical sketches of early Indiana 2153

The Biographical and Imperial magazine 70

The Biographical and martyrological dictionary... by a clergyman and others 4304

Biographical anecdotes of the founders of the French Republic 717

The Biographical annals of Ohio 2273

Biographical annals of the Civil Government of the United States 1963

The Biographical annual 1943

Biographical catalogue, being an account of the lives of Friends 4372

The Biographical cyclopaedia and portrait gallery... of Ohio 2247

A Biographical cyclopaedia and portrait gallery of distinguished men... of Ohio (Brennan) 2276

The Biographical cyclopaedia of American women 1911

Biographical cyclopaedia of homoeopathic physicians and surgeons 4112

The Biographical cyclopaedia of
representative men of Maryland and the District of Columbia   2178

The Biographical cyclopedia of
representative men of Rhode
Island   2310

Biographical cyclopedia of the
Commonwealth of Kentucky
2161

A Biographical dictionary (Blake)
83

The Biographical dictionary and
portrait gallery of representative men of Chicago, Iowa...
2100

The Biographical dictionary and
portrait gallery of representative men of Chicago, Minnesota cities...   2101

The Biographical dictionary and
portrait gallery of representative men of Chicago, Wisconsin...   2102

Biographical dictionary and synopsis of books   3387

A Biographical dictionary, containing a brief account of the
first settlers... in New-Eng-
land   2227

A Biographical dictionary; containing an historical account
of all engravers   2625

Biographical dictionary of American architects (deceased)
2692

A Biographical dictionary of ancient, medieval, and modern
freethinkers   4422

Biographical dictionary of
astronomers   4671

Biographical dictionary of authors
3413

Biographical dictionary of authors
ancient and modern   3387

Biographical dictionary of composers   3128

A Biographical dictionary of contemporaries (Pennsylvania)
2302

A Biographical dictionary of contemporary American physi-
cians and surgeons   4071

The Biographical dictionary of contemporary poets   3397

A Biographical dictionary of early
American Jews   2006

Biographical dictionary of eminent artists   2509

Biographical dictionary of eminent men of Fife   1196

A Biographical dictionary of eminent Scotsmen   1211

A Biographical dictionary of eminent Welshmen, from the
earliest times to the present
1234

A Biographical dictionary of eminent Welshmen who flourished
from 1700-1900   1231

A Biographical dictionary of fiddlers   2799

A Biographical dictionary of freethinkers of all ages and nations   4528

Biographical dictionary of Irish-men in France   1303

A Biographical dictionary of Jersey   1201

Biographical dictionary of Jewish resistance   1465

Biographical dictionary of medal-lists   2710

Biographical dictionary of minis-ters and preachers of the Welsh Calvinistic Methodist body... ,   4365

A Biographical dictionary of modern rationalists   4423

Biographical dictionary of modern Yiddish literature   3790

Biographical dictionary of musi-cians (Baker)   2755-2756

Biographical dictionary of musi-cians (Brown)   2787

Biographical dictionary of musi-cians (Cummings)   2811

A Biographical dictionary of musi-cians (Sainsbury)   3042

A Biographical dictionary of old English music   3023

Biographical dictionary of para-psychology   4233

A Biographical dictionary of the Anglo-Egyptian Sudan   1812

Biographical dictionary of the Franciscans in Spanish Florida and Cuba   4379

A Biographical dictionary of the living authors of Great Britain and Ireland   3497

A Biographical dictionary of the saints   4392

The Biographical dictionary of the Society for the Diffusion of Useful Knowledge   268

Biographical directory: C. R. B. fellows (1920-1950)   3259

A Biographical directory of Eng-lish architects   2680

Biographical directory of law librarians in the United States and Canada   3994

Biographical directory of Louisiana visiting teachers   3291

Biographical directory of Negro ministers   4542

A Biographical directory of pastors of the Evangelical Lutheran Church   4457

Biographical directory of scholars, artists, and professionals of Croatian descent in the United States and Canada   1912

Biographical directory of the A-merican Congress (1774-1961) 2029

The Biographical directory of the railway officials of America 4820

Biographical directory of the State of New York   2251

Biographical encyclopaedia, com-prising the lives and records of many of the leading profes-sional and business men... of Massachusetts   2183

The Biographical encyclopedia &
who's who of the American
theatre   3188

Biographical encyclopedia of A-
merica   1913

Biographical encyclopaedia of
Connecticut and Rhode Island
2116

Biographical encyclopaedia of Illinois of the nineteenth century
2142

The Biographical encyclopaedia
of Kentucky   2162

Biographical encyclopaedia of
Maine   2170

The Biographical encyclopaedia
of New Jersey   2238

The Biographical encyclopaedia
of Ohio   2275

Biographical encyclopedia of
Pakistan   1593

Biographical encyclopedia of
pathologists: Southern United
States of America   4106

The Biographical encyclopaedia
of Pennsylvania   2294

Biographical encyclopedia of
philosophy   4258

Biographical encyclopedia of
science and technology
4577

Biographical encyclopedia of
Texas   2339

The Biographical encyclopedia of
the United States   1914

Biographical encyclopedia of the
world   308

Biographical encyclopedia of Vermont   2348

Biographical handbook and record
of elections (Australia)   373

Biographical handbook and record
of elections for the Parliament of [Australia]   373

A Biographical history of Central
Kansas   2158

A Biographical history of eminent and self-made men of
the State of Indiana   2149

A Biographical history of England
(Granger)   1144, 1166

A Biographical history of England
(Noble)   1166

Biographical history of Gonville
and Caius College (1349-1897)
1180

Biographical history of Massachusetts   2185

Biographical history of North Carolina from colonial times to
the present   2265

A Biographical history... of
prominent men of the Great
West (1894)   2103

A Biographical history... of
prominent men of the Great
West (Campbell)   2220

A Biographical history of the fine
arts   2621

Biographical illustrations of Worcestershire   1239

A Biographical index of American artists   2420

A Biographical index of American public men   1967

A Biographical index of deceased British and Irish botanists   4631

A Biographical index to the present House of Commons   1188

Biographical information of members of the Rumanian Grand National Assembly   1655

Biographical intelligence on former puppet China   610

A Biographical list of cartographers, engravers, and publishers of the XVI to XIX century maps   4749

Biographical list of the members of "The Club of Nobody's Friends"   1115

The Biographical magazine   72

Biographical memoirs of Fellows [of the Royal Society of London]   4610

Biographical memoirs of medicine in Great Britain   4056

Biographical notes upon botanists, maintained in the New York Botanical Garden Library   4646

Biographical notices of distinguished men in New England   2226

Biographical notices of graduates of Yale College   1929

Biographical notices of Persian poets   3806

A Biographical peerage of the Empire of Great Britain   1100

The Biographical quarterly   73

A Biographical record of Americans of Japanese ancestry   1915

A Biographical register of Peterhouse men   1111

Biographical register of the officers and graduates... West Point   1924-1925

A Biographical register of the University of Cambridge to 1500   1136

A Biographical register of the University of Oxford to A. D. 1500   1137

Biographical sketches and interesting anecdotes of persons of color   1977

Biographical sketches of American artists   2556

Biographical sketches of British characters recently deceased   1164

Biographical sketches of distinguished living New York physicians   4132

Biographical sketches of distinguished Marylanders   2179

Biographical sketches of eminent composers   3096

Biographical sketches of eminent itinerant ministers... pioneers of Methodism   4507

Biographical sketches of graduates of Harvard University 2011, 2231

Biographical sketches of Loyalists of the American Revolution   2007

Biographical sketches of members: 102nd Maine Legislature 2174

Biographical sketches of representative citizens of the Commonwealth of Massachusetts 2184

Biographical sketches of representative citizens of the State of Maine   2171

Biographical sketches of the bench and bar of South Carolina 3975

Biographical sketches of the deceased physicians of Westchester County, New York 4131

Biographical sketches of the governor, councilors and members... of the New Hampshire Legislature   2233

Biographical sketches of the graduates of Yale College   1930

Biographical sketches of the members of Parliament of Lancashire (1290-1550)   1203

Biographical sketches of the state officers and members of the Legislature of the State of New York in 1858 [-1861]   2260

Biographical sources for foreign countries   28

Biographical sources for the United States   1889

Biographical souvenir of the State of Texas   2430

Biographical souvenir of the states of Georgia and Florida 2132

Biographical tables of the Koryŏ period [of Korean history] 1493

The Biographical treasury (Maunder)   192

Biographie; ou, Dictionnaire historique des personnages d' Auvergne illustres   863

Biographie; ou, Galerie historique des hommes célèbres du Havre   891

Biographie alsacienne-lorraine 856

Biographie ardennaise   860

Biographie bretonne   869

Biographie coloniale belge   422

Biographie complète des 750 représentants à l'Assemblée législative   718

Biographie complète des trois cents sénateurs   719

Biographie contemporaine de la Haute-Vienne   889

Biographie de la Moselle   914

Biographie de Tarn-et-Garonne 943

Biographie de tous les ministres, depuis la constitution de 1791, jusqu'à nos jours 780-782

Biographie der Aerzte 4095

Biographie des artistes-musiciens néerlandais des XVIIIe et XIXe siècles 2879

Biographie des condamnés pour délits politiques depuis 1814 jusqu'en 1828 793

Biographie des députés à l'Assemblée nationale 807

Biographie des députés composant la représentation nationale... 720

Biographie des députés de la nouvelle Chambre septennale 767

Biographie des faux prophètes vivans 721

Biographie des femmes auteurs contemporaines français 3560

Biographie des hommes célèbres ... de la Somme 941

Biographie des hommes célèbres du département de l'Ain 851

Biographie des hommes célèbres du département du Lot 903

Biographie des hommes illustres de l'ancienne province du Limousin 898

Biographie des hommes remarquables de la Flandre Occidentale 429

Biographie des hommes remarquables des Basses-Alpes 865

Biographie des hommes remarquables du département de Seine-et-Oise 937

Biographie des hommes vivants 74

Biographie des liégeois illustres 454

Biographie des lieutenants généraux, ministres, directeurs généraux... 841

Biographie des médecins français vivants et des professeurs des écoles 4176

Biographie des membres du Sénat 722

Biographie des ministres français, depuis juillet 1789 jusqu'à ce jour 781

Biographie des neuf cents députés à l'Assemblée nationale 807

Biographie des 900 membres de l'Assemblée nationale constituante 723

Biographie des 900 représentants à la Constituante 724

Biographie des pairs 736

Biographie des personnalités du Royaume du Laos 1494

Biographie des personnes remarquables de la Haute-Auvergne 864

Biographie des préfets des 86 départemens de France 725

Biographie des représentants du peuple à l'Assemblée nationale constituante 726

Biographie des 750 grands hommes composant l'Assemblée législative (1849-1852) 727

Biographie des 750 représentants à l'Assemblée législative 718

Biographie des 750 représentants du peuple à l'Assemblée nationale (session de 1849 à 1852) 728

Biographie des 750 représentants du peuple à l'Assemblée national législative 784

Biographie du Dauphiné 879

Biographie du Hainaut 447

Biographie du royaume des Pays-Bas 431

Biographie et bibliographie du Maine et du département de la Sarthe 906

Biographie et bibliographie foréziennes 886

Biographie et dictionnaire des littérateurs et des savants français contemporains 3576

Biographie et galerie historique des contemporains 729

Biographie étrangère 76

Biographie générale des Belges morts ou vivants, hommes politiques... 457

Biographie générale des Champenois célèbres 874

Biographie impartiale des représentants du peuple à l'Assemblée nationale 730

Biographie législative de tous les députés 742

Biographie liégoise 427

Biographie luxembourgeoise 1512

Biographie lyonnaise 905

Biographie médicale (Jourdan) 4149

Biographie médicale par ordre chronologique 4077

Biographie militaire du Jura 897

Biographie moderne. Lives of remarkable characters... 732

Biographie moderne; ou, Dictionnaire biographique de tous les hommes... 731, 733

Biographie moderne; ou, Dictionnaire historique des hommes 731-732

Biographie moderne; ou, Galerie historique, civil, militaire, politique et judiciaire 733

Biographie nationale [de Belgique] 423

Biographie nationale des contemporains (Glaeser) 785

Biographie nationale du pays de Luxembourg 1511

Biographie nationale; vie des hommes et des femmes illustres de la Belgique 437

Biographie neuchâteloise   1853

Biographie niçoise ancienne et
    moderne   916

Biographie normande   920

Biographie nouvelle des contem-
    porains   734, 772

Biographie nouvelle et complète
    de la Chambre des députés
    835

Biographie parlementaire des re-
    présentants du peuple à l'
    Assemblée nationale constit -
    uante de 1848   712

Biographie pittoresque des députés
    735

Biographie politique du dix-neu-
    vième siècle   77

Biographie politique et parlemen-
    taire des députés (Guide des
    électeurs)   752

Biographie populaire du clergé
    contemporain   4292

Biographie populaire du départe-
    ment de la Moselle   915

Biographie portative universelle
    (Lalanne)   801

Biographie saintongeaise   934

Biographie spéciale des pairs
    736

Biographie statistique   737

Biographie toulousaine   946

Biographie universelle (Feller)
    121, 433

Biographie universelle (Michaud)
    ancienne et moderne   66,
    74, 80

Le Biographie universelle. Revue
    générale biographique et lit-
    téraire   71

Biographie universelle, ancienne
    et moderne   78

Biographie universelle classique
    79

Biographie universelle des musi-
    ciens et bibliographie générale
    de la musique   2853, 2856-
    2857, 3045

Biographie universelle et histo-
    rique des femmes célèbres
    240

Biographie universelle et portative
    des contemporains   242

Biographie vendéenne   950

Biographie vendomoise   951

Biographie vosgienne   953

Biographie wartawan Indonesia
    3729

Biographien jetztlebender Aerzte
    und Naturforscher in und aus-
    ser Deutschland   4073

Biographien merkwürdiger Männer
    der Österreichischen Monar-
    chie   391

Biographien Muhammads, seiner
    Gefährten und der späteren
    Träger des Islams   4557

Biographien zur Kulturgeschichte
    der Schweiz   1869

Biographies and portraits of the progressive men of Iowa 2156

Biographies anversoises illustrées 456

Biographies canadiennes-françaises 498

Biographies des principales personnalités français 738

Biographies des troubadours (Las vidas dels trobadors) 3595

Biographies et chroniques populaires du département des Ardennes 861

Biographies et nécrologies des hommes marquants du XIXe siècle 798

Les Biographies françaises d' Amérique 499

Biographies of California authors and indexes of California literature 3411

Biographies of Kuomintang leaders 572

Biographies of members of the American Ornithologists' Union 4629

Biographies of members of the Upper and Lower Houses in China 543

Biographies of prominent Chinese in Singapore 1754

Biographies of the English Catholics in the eighteenth century 1156

Biographies of the state officers and Thirty-third General Assembly of Illinois 2143

Biographisch, anthologisch en critisch woordenboek der Nederduitsche dichters 3489

Biographisch-bibliographisches Quellen-Lexikon der Musiker und Musikgelehrten 2831, 2971

Biographisch-genealogische Blätter aus und über Schwaben 1075

Biographisch handwoordenboek 134

Biographisch lexicon van bekende Nederlandsche Roomsch-Katholieke tijdgenooten 1568

Biographisch-litterarisches Handwörterbuch der wissenschaftlich bedeutenden Chemiker 4664

Biographisch-literarisches Handwörterbuch für Mathematik, Astronomie, Physik mit Geophysik... und verwandte Wissensgebiete 4609

Biographisch-literarisches Handwörterbuch zur Geschichte der exakten Wissenschaften 4609

Biographisch-literarisches Lexikon der deutschen Dichter und Schriftsteller vom 9. bis 20. Jahrhundert 3630

Biographisch-literarisches Lexikon der katholischen deutscher Dichter... 3644

Biographisch-literarisches Lexikon der Schriftsteller des Grossherzogtums Hessen im ersten Viertel des 19. Jahrhunderts 3694

Biographisch-literarisches Lexicon der Thierärzte aller Zeiten und Länder   4202

Biographisch-litterarisches Lexikon für die Stadt Königsberg und Ostpreussen   1052

Biographisch woordenboek der Nederlanden (Aa)   1553

Biographisch woordenboek der Nederlanden (Chalmot)   1556

Biographisch woordenboek der Noord- en Zuidnederlandsche letterkunde   3488

Biographisch woordenboek van Nederland (Kobus)   1557

Biographisch woordenboek van Noord Nederlandsche graveurs   2648

Biographisch woordenboek van Oost-Indische predikanten   4312

Biographisch woordenboek van protestantsche godgeleerden in Nederland   4305

Biographische Blätter   964-965

Das Biographische Lexikon der Koranlehrer   4556

Das Biographische Lexikon des Salāhaddīn Halīl ibn Aibak as-Safadī   1329

Biographische Nachrichten von den jetztlebenden Rechts-Gelehrten in Teutschland   3988

Biographische Nachschlagwerke Adelslexika, Wappenbücher   8

Biographische Schilderungen; oder, Lexikon salzburgischer ... Künstler   2589

Biographische und literarische Nachrichten von den Schriftstellern, die... in... Anspach und Bayreuth leben   3669

Biographische und litterarische Nachrichten von den Schriftstellern und Künstlern, welche in dem Herzogthum Steyermark geboren sind   3707

Biographischer Index der Mitglieder (Akademie der Wissenschaften, Berlin)   4572

Biographisches Album des Vereins St.-Peterburger Aerzte (1859-1909)   4178

Biographisches Handbuch der in der K.K. Österreichisch-Ungarischen Armee und Kriegsmarine aktiv-gedienten Offiziere... jüdisches Stammes   384

Biographisches Jahrbuch für Altertumskunde   3461

Biographisches Jahrbuch und Deutscher Nekrolog   964-966, 972

Biographisches Lexikon aller Helden und Militairpersonen   1064

Biographisches Lexikon der hervorragenden Ärzte aller Zeiten und Völker   4080-4081, 4130

Biographisches Lexikon der hervorragenden Ärzte der letzten fünfzig Jahre   4130

Biographisches Lexicon der
markantesten Männer und
Frauen jüdischer Abkunft
1459

Biographisches Lexikon der
Sozialismus   1003

Biographisches Lexikon des
Kaiserthums Oesterreich
406-407

Biographisches Lexikon des Landes
Österreich ob der Enns
390

Biographisches Lexikon für das
Gebiet zwischen Inn und
Salzach   385

Biographisches Lexikon hervorragender Ärzte des neunzehnten Jahrhunderts   4181

Biographisches Lexikon verstorbener Schweizer   1844

Biographisches Lexikon von
Oberösterreich   388

Biographisches Schriftsteller-Lexikon der Gegenwart   3331

Biographisches Staatshandbuch
989

Biographisches Theater-Handbuch,
Kürschners   3171

Biographisches Wörterbuch zur
deutschen Geschichte   1008

Biographium faeminum   81

Biography and history of the
Indians of North America 1935

Biography by Americans (1658-
1936)   21

Biography catalogue of the Library
of the Royal Commonwealth
Society   23

Biography in collections   19

Biography index   5

Biography of eminent American
physicians   4204

The Biography of the British stage
3141

The Birmingham post year book
and who's who   1193

The Bishop of Scotland   4354

The Bishops of the African Methodist Church   4547

Biskupa tal á Íslandi   4489

Black's dictionary of music & musicians   2816

Blekingska nationen (1697-1900)
1825

The Blue book of American airmen
4809

The Blue book of American aviation   4779

The Blue book of aviation   4780

The Blue book of philately   2445

Blue book of the State of Illinois
2145

The Blue book of the State of Wisconsin   2378

The Blue book of Tin Pin Alley
2790

Boehmische, maehrische und schlesische Gelehrten und Schriftsteller aus dem Orden der Jesuiten   4555

Bohemia docta   3472

Bolivians of to-day   470

Bonniers illustrerade musiklexikon   3086

The Book of Catholic authors   3340

The Book of Chicagoans   2107

The Book of Detroiters   2127

The Book of Maryland   2177

The Book of Minnesotans   2211

The Book of modern composers   2850

The Book of saints   4309

The Book of Scotsmen eminent for achievements in arms and arts...   1214

Book of the artists; American artist life   2638

Bortsy za sovetskuiu vlast´ v Abkhazii   1685

Bortsy za vlast´ Sovetov   1677

La Botánica y los botánicos de la península hispano-lusitana   4633

Les Bouches-du-Rhône   866

Bratskaia mogila   1696

Brazilian biographical annual   479

Brema literata   1036

Bremer Dichter des 19. Jahrhunderts   3628

Bremische Biographie des neunzehnten Jahrhunderts   1037

A Brief biographical dictionary (Hole)   153

Brief biographies, Maine   2172

Brief biographies of leading laymen   1097

A Brief history of entomology   4647

Brief profiles of the members of the House of Representatives [Japan]   1443

British and American sporting authors   3505

British and Irish botanists   4631

British authors (before 1800)   3509

British authors of the nineteenth century   3510

British autobiographies   1086

The British biography   1138

The British Caribbean who, what, why   2396

British diaries   1087

British film and television year book   3142

The British film yearbook   3142

British historical portraits   1161

The British Institution (1806-
1867)   2514

British maps and map-makers
4745

British miniaturists   2545

British music   3005

British music publishers, painters
and engravers   4022

British musical biography   2788

The British Plutarch   1098

British violin makers   2979

The Brown book of the New Hampshire Legislature   2233

Buch- und Musikalienhändler,
Buch- und Musikaliendrucker
4011

Die Buchdrucker des 16. und 17.
Jahrhunderts im deutschen
Sprachgebiet   4000

Buchdruckerlexikon des 16. Jahrhunderts (Deutsches Sprachgebiet)   3999

Bündner Maler, Bildhauer, Komponisten und Schriftsteller
der Gegenwart   2452

Builders of our nation... Men of
1913   1952

The Building societies who's who
4700

Bŭlgarski pisateli   3452

Bunkajin meiroku   1422

Burke's genealogical and heraldic
history of the landed gentry
1103

Burke's genealogical and heraldic
history of the peerage, baronetage and knightage   1107

Burke's handbook to the Most Excellent Order of the British
Empire   1178

Burke's who's who in sport and
sporting records   3221

Burma trade directory   490

The Business background of members of Parliament   1173

Business executives and corporation encyclopedia   4701

Business executives of America
4701

Business men of Iowa   2157

Y Bywgraffiadur Cymreig hyd
1940   1222-1223

Bywgraffiaeth cerddorion Cymreig   2916

C

The Cabinetmakers of America
2705

Calédoniens   1574

California blue book   2087

Calendars of Scottish saints--SEE:
Kalendars of Scottish saints
4369

California pioneer register and
index (1542-1848)   2087

California's stately hall of fame
2089

The Cambrian biography   1172

The Cambrian Plutarch   1228

Canada's V. C.'s   510

The Canadian album   501

Canadian diaries and autobiographies   494

The Canadian legal directory   3970

Canadian library directory   4002-4003

Canadian medical directory   4100

The Canadian men and women of the time   512

Canadian novelists (1920-1945)   3538

The Canadian parliamentary guide   503

Canadian poets   3503

The Canadian portrait gallery   506

The Canadian who was who   517

The Canadian who's who   504

Canadian writers; a biographical dictionary   3536

Capitol's Who's who for Colorado   2110

Capitol who's who for Denver and Colorado   2126

Capitol's Who's who for Oregon   2290

I Cappuccini della provincia milanese   4308

The Caribbean who, what, why   2396

Carteira do artista   3193

Carthusian worthies   1177

Cassell's biographical dictionary   91

Cassell's cyclopaedia of photography   2720

Cassell's encyclopaedia of literature   3334

Cassell's encyclopaedia of world literature   3334

Cat lovers, A dictionary of   41

Catalog of biographies [of the New York Academy of Medicine]   4053

Catálogo bibliográfico de los doctores, licenciados y maestros de la antigua Universidad de Guadalajara   3277

Catálogo de escritores agustinos españoles, portugueses y americanos   4439, 4481

Catálogo de los profesores de las bellas artes murcianos   2432

Catalogo de' neofiti illustri usciti ... dall' Ebraismo e poi rendutisi glorioso nel Cristianesimo   4429

Catálogo de seudónimos, anagramas e iniciales de escritores mexicanos   1519

Catalogo di opere biografiche e bibliografiche   1324

Catalogo generale dei liutari e violineria modenese   3098

Catalogo metodico degli scritti contenuti nelle pubblicazioni periodiche italiane e straniere 14-17

Catálogo razonado biográfico y bibliográfico de los autores portugueses que escribieron en castellano 3868

Catálogo razonado de obras anónimas seudónimas de autores de la Compañia de Jesús 4265

Catalogue des Dauphinois dignes de mémoire 878

Catalogue général de la librairie française (Lorenz) 3580

Catalogue général de la librairie française au XIXe siècle 3559

Catalogue of Canadian composers 2791

A Catalogue of engraved British portraits, from Egbert the Great to the present time 1099

A Catalogue of graduates... the University of Dublin 1301

Catalogue of Italian publishers and printers of the XVth century 3996

Catalogue of painters and draughtsmen represented in the library of reproductions... formed by Robert and Mary Witt 2665-2666

A Catalogue of Renaissance philosophers 4252

A Catalogue of the royal and noble authors of England, Scotland and Ireland 3539

Catalogues of Scottish writers 3514

Catalogus haereticorum 4300

Catalogus illustrium medicorum 4096

Catalogus professorum Academiae Marburgensis 3272

Catalogus professorum Gottingensium 3269

Cathedral organists past and present 3111

Catholic authors 3355

The Catholic encyclopedia 4321-4323

The Catholic who's who 1112

The Cattlemen of Texas and adjacent territories 4790

Celebrated musicians of all nations 2861

Celebrated musicians, past and present 3115

Célébrités d'aujourd'hui 93, 234

Les Célébrités françaises 756

Celebrities; a comprehensive biographical thesaurus of important men and women in India 1263

Celebrities monthly 94

Celebrities of the century 253

Celebrities of the day: British and foreign   95

Celebrities of the Yorkshire Wolds   1241

The Celtic who's who   1113

Cenni biografici intorno ai letterati illustri italiani   3785

Cenni storici sulle due università di Pavia e di Milano   4199

The Central and East African who's who for 1956   317

Central New York, an inland empire   2253

The Central States, Who's who in   2206

The Century cyclopedia of names   96

The Century in southwest Texas   2344

A Century of the English book trade   4009

Ceramisti   2726

České biografie   647

Československo   647

Československý hudebni·slovní osob a institucí   2794

Chachme Ashkenaz   1473

Chambers's biographical dictionary   98

Chambers's cyclopaedia of English literature   3500

Chambers's dictionary of scientists   4594

La Chambre des représentants (en 1894-95)   439

Charaktere teutscher Dichter und Prosaisten   3656

Charakteristik deutscher Dichter   3667

Les Charlatans célèbres   925

Chemical age directory and who's who   4655

The Chemical age year book   4655

Chemical who's who   4656

Chemie Lexikon   4663

Chemisch- pharmazeutisches Bio- und Bibliographikon   4659

Chi è? Annuario biografico italiano (1908)   1350-1351

Chi è? Dizionario biografico degli italiani d'oggi   1351

Chileans of to-day   534

Chin shi jen wu chih   552

Chin tai ming jen chuan chi hsüan   558

Chin tai ming jen hsiao chuan   619

China handbook   554

The China who's who (foreign)   553

China yearbook (1937-43-   )   554

A Chinese biographical dictionary   567-568

The Chinese reader's manual
590

Chinese students directory 617

Ch'ing shih lieh chuan 559

Ch'ing tai ch'i pai ming jên chuan
607

Ch'ing tai pei chuan wên t'ung
chien 546

Ch'ing tai p'u hsüeh ta shih lieh
chuan 551

Chleny Gosudarstvennoĭ Dumy
1676

Chleny Pervoĭ Gosudarstvennoĭ
Dumy 1681

Chosakuken daichō 1422

Chōsen jimmei jisho 1486

Chōsen jimmei jiten 1487

Chōsen jimmei roku 1488

Chōsen kokon meiken den 1489

Chosŏn sinsa pogam 1490

Chosŏn ŭi myŏngin 1492

A Christian biographical dictionary
4541

A Chronological account of nearly
four hundred Irish writers
3730

A Chronological cyclopaedia of musicians and musical events
(from A. D. 320 to 1896) 2947

A Chronological history of the old
English landscape painters
2510

Chronologisches Verzeichnis der
berühmtesten Männer Böhmens
653

Chronologiska förteckningar och
anteckningar öfver Finska
universitetets fordna
procancellerer... 3312

Chūgoku bunkakai jimbutsu sōkan
573

Chung-hus min-kuo jen shih lu
555

Chung hua min kuo ming jen chuan
547

Chung hua shu chü 3459

Chung-kuo hsüeh shu chia lieh
chuan 621

Chung-kuo hua chia jen ming ta tz'u
tien 2626

Chung-kuo jên ming ta tz'ŭ tien
560

Chung-kuo jên ming ta tz'ŭ tien
(Indexes) 537

Chung-kuo jên wu chuan hsüan
544

Chung-kuo jen wu hsin chuan
576

Chung-kuo li tai ming jên chuan
557

Chung-kuo min tsu ying hsiung
579

Chung-kuo ming chiang chuan
612

Chung-kuo ming jen chuan 605

Chung-kuo ming jen tien 584

Chung-kuo pai ming jen chuan 545

Chung-kuo tang tai ming jen chuan 564

Chung-kuo ts'ang shu chia k'ao lüeh 4052

Chung-kuo wên hsüeh chia lieh chuan 3459

Chung-kuo wen hsüeh chia ta tz'u tien 3458

Cien españoles célebres 1772

Los Cien mejores poesías chilenas 3906

Cien vidas paraguayas 1602

150 [i. e. Ciento cincuenta] biografías de mexicanos ilustres 1530

120 [i. e. Ciento veinte] biografías de próceres e ilustres venezolanos 2387

Cimbria literata 1070

City blue book of biography; New Yorker's (of 1917-) 2244

City blue book of current biography; Chicago men... 2105

City churches in East Asia 4338

The Civil War dictionary 1917

Clark J. Herringshaw's city blue book of current biography; Chicago men... 2105

Clarke's new law list 3962

A Classical dictionary of Greek and Roman antiquities, biography, geography, and mythology 296

A Classical dictionary of Greek and Roman biography (Smith) 266

Classische Biographie 3462

Cleave's biographical cyclopaedia 2276

Le Clergé du diocèse du Tournai 4526

The Clergy directory and parish guide 4330

The Clerical directory of the Protestant Episcopal Church in the U. S. A. 4331

Cmentarz Powazkowski pod Warszawa 1638

Colaboradores e investigadores (Consejo Superior de Investigaciones Científicas, Spain) 4612

Colección bibliográfico-biográfica de noticias referentes a la provincia de Zamora 1811

Colección bio-bibliográfica de escritores médicos españoles 4189

Collectanea Cornubienses 1195

Collectio scriptorum Ordinis Carmelitarum excalceatorum 4296

Collection de 154 portraits des généraux français 751

Collection des grands dictionnaires biographiques internationaux   90, 743-749, 3333,
4318, 4739

Collection encyclopédique des
notabilités du XIXe siècle
109

Collections toward illustrating
the biography of the Scotch,
English and Irish members
of the Society of Jesus   4449

The Collector's dictionary of
clocks   2723

Collezione alfabetica di uomini e
donne illustri della Toscana
1414

Collins music encyclopedia   3112

Colombia joven   629

Colombianos ilustres   628

Colonial and revolutionary families of Pennsylvania   2300

The Colonial Office list   1118

Colorado writers   3427

Columbia dictionary of modern
European literature   3335

Columbia journalists   3434

Combined lineal list of officers
on active duty in the Marine
Corps   2034

La Comédie-Française (de 1680 à
1900)   3168

I Comici italiani   3186

I Comizi nazionale in Lione   1353

Commemorative biographical
record of central Pennsylvania   2296

Commemorative biographical
record of northeastern Pennsylvania   2297

Commemorative biographical
record of northwestern Ohio
2277

Commemorative biographical
record of prominent and
representative men of In-
dianapolis and vicinity   2154

Commemorative biographical
record of the counties of
Rock, Green, Grant, Iowa
and Lafayette, Wisconsin
2374

Commemorative biographical
record of the Upper Lake Region [Wisconsin and Minne-
sota]   2373

Commentatio de vita et scriptis
professorum hodie in Aca-
demia Jenensi publice
docentium   3306

Commentatio historico literaria
de viris eruditis Gedani ortis
1040

The Commissioned sea officers of
the Royal Navy (1660-1815)
1145

The Commonwealth Fund fellows
3262

The Companion to the playhouse
3495

Compendiöses Gelehrten-Lexikon
198

Compendiöses Kirchen- und
Ketzer-Lexicon   4389

The Compendium of American
genealogy   2042

A Compendium of Irish biography
1308

Complete baronetage (Cokayne)
1116

The Complete book of classical
music   2840

Complete encyclopaedia of music
2977

The Complete peerage of England
[etc.]   1117

Composers in America   3029

Composers of Finland   2919

Composers of the Americas
3006

Composers of today   2841

Composers of yesterday   2842

Compositores colombianos
3129

Compositores de América   3006

The Comprehensive dictionary of
biography   103

The Concertgoers handbook
2863

The Concise biographical dictionary of famous men and women
122

Concise dictionary of American
biography   1920

Concise dictionary of Irish biography   1300

Concise dictionary of literature
3336

The Concise dictionary of national
biography   1131

Concise encyclopedia of Arab
civilization   1328

The Concise encyclopedia of crime
and criminals   260

The Concise encyclopedia of English and American poets and
poetry   3534

The Concise encyclopedia of English pottery and procelain
2725

The Concise encyclopedia of
modern drama   3374

The Concise encyclopedia of
modern world literature
3337

The Concise encyclopedia of music
and musicians   2805

A Concise encyclopedia of the
Civil War   2012

Concise encyclopaedia of Russia
1743

The Concise encyclopedia of Western philosophy and philosophers   4259

The Concise Oxford dictionary of
English literature   3504

Concise Oxford dictionary of opera
3039

Concise universal biography   145

The Congregational two hundred (1530-1948)   4454

The Congregational year book   4333

Le Congrès national   434

Congressional directory   2030

Congressional staff directory   1921

Connoisseurs of the world   2466

Les Conseillers du Parlement du Normandie au seizième siècle   919

A Conspectus of American biography   1981-1982

The Consulting engineers who's who & year book   4784

Les Contemporains   2528

Contemporary American authors   3420

Contemporary American biography   1922

Contemporary American literature   3416, 3420

Contemporary authors   3338

Contemporary British literature   3517

Contemporary medical men and their professional work   4162

Contemporary sculpture   2697

Continuazione al Nuovo dizionario istorico degli uomini che si

sono renduti più celebri per talenti, virtù...   223

Contribución a un diccionario de seudónimos en la Argentina   338

Les Conventionnels   789

Converts to Rome   1143

The Cooperative weather observer; who he is and where he serves   2039

Cornelius Nepos français   803

Cornish's Birmingham year book   1193

Corpus academicum Gottingense   3257

Cortes d'Espagne   1771

The Cottage cyclopedia of history and biography   237

County families of the United Kingdom   1181

County Kerry, past and present   1304

Cremona literata   3738-3739

Cricket who's who   3224

The Cricketer's who's who   3222

A Critical and commercial dictionary of the works of painters   2615

Critical & documentary dictionary of violin makers old and modern   3178

A Critical dictionary of composers
and their music   3128

Critical dictionary of English
literature   3493

Crockford's clerical directory
4339

Cronologia paulista   482

Crowell's handbook of world
opera   2976

Cubans of to-day   638

La Cultura española medieval
1785

Current biography   105

Current biography yearbook   105

The Cyclopaedia of American biographies   1926, 1962, 2021

The Cyclopaedia of American biography   1927
SEE ALSO: Appleton's cyclopaedia of American biography
1908

Cyclopaedia of American literature
3403

A Cyclopedia of American medical
biography   4153

The Cyclopaedia of biography   137

A Cyclopaedia of Canadian biography (Charlesworth)   505

A Cyclopaedia of Canadian biography (Rose)   516

A Cyclopedia of education   3295

Cyclopaedia of English literature,
Chambers's   3500

Cyclopaedia of female biography
43

Cyclopedia of insurance in the
United States   4702

Cyclopedia of music and musicians
2795

Cyclopedia of New Jersey biography   2239

The Cyclopedia of New Zealand
1576

Cyclopedia of painters and paintings   2460

Cyclopedia of world authors
3372

A Cyclopaedic dictionary of music
2827

Cyclopedic survey of chamber music   2803

Cyprus who's who   1940

Czech and Slovak leaders in metropolitan Chicago   2104

Czy wiesz kto to jest?   1631

D

Dai Nihon jimmei jisho   1423

Dai Nihon josei jimmei jisho
1441

Daigaku kenkyūsha kenkyū daimoku
sōran   3299

Daijimmei jiten   106

Dalīl al-afrād al-'ilmiyīn bin al-
wizārāt wa al jāmi...   4583

The Dance encyclopedia   3144

Dancer's almanac and who's who
3145

Danh-nhân nuóc chà   2394

Danish violins and their makers
2893

Danmarks adels aarbog   658

Danmarks laeger og laegevaesen
fra de aeldste tider...   4145

Danmarks malerkunst, billeder og
biografier   2436

Danks biografisk haandleksikon
660

Dansk biografisk leksikon (Bricka
& Engelstoft)   660

Dansk biografisk leksikon...
1537-1814 (Bricka)   657

Dansk forfatterleksikon   3487

Dansk historisk bibliografi   654

Dansk kunstnerlexikon   2656

Dansk-norsk litteraturlexicon
3485

Dansk, norsk og svensk kunstnerlexicon   2657

Dansk personalhistorisk bibliografi
654

Dansk portraetgalleri   664

Dansk skønlitteraert forfatterleksikon (1900-1950)   3477

Dansk tidsskrift-index... Personalhistorie   654

Den Danske bibliotekarstand
4012

Den Danske botaniske litteratur
4632, 4636

Danske gesandter og gesandtskabspersonale indtil 1914
665

Danske i udlandet   661

Den Danske laegestand   4118

Danske salme-leksikon   3092-
3093

Dastūr al-vuzarā   1323

Daten deutscher Dichtung   3619

Datos para una bibliografía qui-
rúrgica española   4083

al-Dau' al-lāmi'   1330

Les Dauphinoises célèbres   880

De Bekker's Music and musicians
2816

De Brugensibus eruditionis fama
claris libri duo   458

De Collegii Veronensis illustribus
medicis et philosphis   4110

De Gandavensibus eruditionis fama
claris libri tres   459

De illustribus Angliae scriptoribus
3526

De illustribus scriptoribus qui in
civitate et regno Neapolis...
floruerunt   3745

De libris anonymis ac pseudonymis
schediasma   35

De nominum mutatione et anonymis
scriptoribus   34

De scriptis adespotis, pseudoepigraphis et supposititiis
conjecturae   33

De scriptis anonymis et pseudonymis in caussa religionis...
4263

De scriptoribus Flandriae libri
tres   460

De scriptoribus Frisiae decades
XVI. et semis   3597

De scriptoribus, non ecclesiasticis,
Graecis, Latinis, Italicis
3463

De scriptoribus rerum Hungaricarum et Transylvanicarum
saeculi XVIII   3715

De scriptoribus scholasticis saeculi XIV ex ordine Carmelitarum   4548

Debrett's House of Commons 1121

Debrett's illustrated House of
Commons   1121

Debrett's illustrated peerage
1122

Debrett's peerage, baronetage,
knightage, and companionage
1123

Decades duae, continentes vitas
theologorum exterorum
principuum   961

Degeners Wer ist's?   1013

Degli scienzati italiani formanti
parte del VII Congresso in
Napoli   4590

Dei meriti dei più celebri professori... nell' Università di
Padova   4129

Deîateli revoliûtsionnogo dvizheniîa
v Rossii   1682

Dekabristy   1689

Denkwürdige Bayern   1033

Deputaty Verkhovnogo Soveta SSSR
1728

Les Députés au Corps législatif,
Conseil des Cinq-Cents, Conseil des anciens   795

Les Députés de l'Assemblée législative de 1791   796

Des hommes célèbres dans les
sciences et les arts   4596

A Descriptive catalogue of Friends'
books   4495-4496

Les Dessinateurs d'illustrations
au dix-huitième siècle   2593

Dessinateurs, graveurs et peintres
des anciens Pays-Bas   2617

Deutsch-österreichisches Künstler-
und Schriftsteller-Lexicon
3616

Deutsche Dichter und Prosaisten
von der Mitte des 15. Jahrhundert bis auf unsere Zeit
3658

Deutsche Dichterinnen und Schriftstellerinen   3629

Das Deutsche Führergesicht
977

Das Deutsche Führerlexikon   971

Deutsche Jagdschriftsteller   3232

Deutsche katholische Dichter der
Gegenwart   3692

Die Deutsche Literatur des Mittel-
alters:Verfasserlexikon   3696

TITLE INDEX

Deutsche Männer und Frauen
1006

Der Deutsche peintre-graveur
2426

Das Deutsche Reich von 1918 bis
heute   986

Deutsche Tonkünstler und Musiker
in Wort und Bild   2913

Die Deutschen Schriftstellerinnen
des neunzehnten Jahrhunderts
3688

Die Deutschen Zinngieser und ihre
Marken   2715

Deutscher Dichternekrolog   3677

Deutscher Litteratur-Kalender
3654

Deutscher Musiker-Kalender
2931

Deutscher Wirtschaftsführer
4717

Deutsches Anonymenlexikon   955

Deutsches biographisches Jahrbuch
965, 972

Deutsches Biologen-Handbuch
4644

Deutsches Dichter-Lexikon (Brümmer)   3611-3612

Deutsches Dichterlexikon (Wilpert)   3706

Deutsches Geschlechterbuch   973

Deutsches Kolonial-Lexikon   974

Deutsches Literatur-Lexikon
(Kosch)   3651-3652

Deutsches Literatur-Lexikon
(Krüger)   3653

Deutsches Musiker-Lexikon
2931, 2981

Deutsches Pseudonymen-Lexikon
956

Deutsches Schriftstellerlexikon
von den Anfängen bis zur
Gegenwart   3604

Deutsches Theater-Lexikon
3170

Deutsches Titelbuch   960

Deutsches Zeitgenossenlexikon
975

Deutschlands, Österreich-Ungarns
und der Schweiz Gelehrter...
976

Deutsch-österreichisches Künstler-
und Schriftsteller-Lexikon

Diarium biographicum   305

Diccionario bibliographico brazileiro   483

Diccionario bibliographico militar
portuguez   1643

Diccionario bio-bibliografico brasileiro, de diplomacia, politica externa e direito internacional   484

Diccionario bio-bibliográfico de
escritores   3601

Diccionario bio-bibliográfico de la
Compañia de Jesús en México
4549

Diccionario bio-bibliográfico musical (Brasileiro e internacional)
2953

Diccionario biográfico americano 335

Diccionario biográfico argentino (Biedma and Pillado) 339

Diccionario biográfico argentino (Udaondo) 357

Diccionario biográfico-biblio-gráfico de efemérides de músicos españoles 3043

Diccionario biográfico-bibliográfico de escritores antiguos y modernos nacidos en los países del habla castellana 1781

Diccionario biográfico, bibliográfico, histórico, crítico de guitarras... guitarristas... 3020

Diccionario biográfico colonial argentino 358

Diccionario biográfico colonial de Chile 533, 535

Diccionario biográfico contemporáneo [de los españoles y americanos] 1782

Diccionario biográfico cubano (Calcagno) 636

Diccionario biográfico cubano (Peraza Sarausa) 639

Diccionario biográfico de artistas de Cataluña 2600

Diccionario biográfico de artistas de la provincia de Córdoba 2601

Diccionario biográfico de artistas que trabajaron en el Nuevo Reino de Granada 2422

Diccionario biográfico de artistas valencianos 2423

Diccionario biográfico de Chile 527

Diccionario biográfico de Chile (Figueroa) 529

Diccionario biográfico de estranjeros en Chile 530

Diccionario biográfico de hombres de negocios (Argentina) 344, 353

Diccionario biográfico de ilustres próceres de la independencia suramericana 2385

Diccionario biográfico de la mujer boliviana 469

Diccionario biográfico de la música 3033

Diccionario biográfico de la República Argentina 340

Diccionario biográfico de la República del Ecuador 677

Diccionario biográfico de los campeones de la libertad de Nueva Granada, Venezuela, Ecuador i Perú 1507

Diccionario biográfico de músicos do Norte de Portugal 2748

Diccionario biográfico de peruanos contemporáneos 1608

Diccionario biográfico de pintores 2542

Diccionario biográfico de Venezuela 2386

Diccionario biográfico del clero secular de Chile 4465

Diccionario biográfico del Ecuador 680

Diccionario biográfico del Perú 1604

Diccionario biográfico escolar 679

Diccionario biográfico español e hispanoamericano 1773

Diccionario biográfico internacional de escritores y artistas del siglo XIX 3346

Diccionario biográfico matritense 1801

Diccionario biográfico mexicano (Peña y Reyes) 1540

Diccionario biográfico mexicano (Peral) 1541-1542

Diccionario biográfico moderno 290

Diccionario biográfico nacional (Argentine Republic) 350

Diccionario biográfico profesional de ingenieros agrónomos en Colombia 4800

Diccionario biográfico universal 112

Diccionario biográfico universal de mujeres célebres 115

Diccionario biográfico vasco 1790

Diccionario biográfico y bibliográfico de caligrafos españoles 4005

Diccionario biográfico y bibliográfico de Colombia 630

Diccionario biográfico y bibliográfico de escritores y artistas catalanes del siglo XIX 3453

Diccionario biográfico y bibliográfico de la isla de Cádiz 1792

Diccionario biográfico y bibliográfico de músicos y escritores de música españoles 3014

Diccionario biográfico y genealógico del antiguo departamento del Cauca 625

Diccionario biographico de brasileiros celebres... 476

Diccionario biographico de musicos portuguezes 3104

Diccionario cronológico biográfico universal 45

Diccionario cubano de seudónimos 635

Diccionario de alfónimos y seudónimos de la Argentina 337

Diccionario de anónimos y seudónimos hispanoamericanos 1497

Diccionario de artistas plásticos de la Argentina 2552

Diccionario de artistas que florecieron en Galicia durante los siglos XVI y XVII 2585

Diccionario de caligrafos españoles 4040

Diccionario de escritores gallegos 3602

Diccionario de escritores, maestros y oradores naturales de Sevilla 1809

Diccionario de escritores trinitarios de España y Portugal 4282

Diccionario de filosofia 4238

Diccionario de geografía, historia y biografía mexicanas 1532

Diccionario de guitarristas 3020

Diccionario de historia de España desde sus origenes... 1764

Diccionario de la literatura latinoamericana 3914

Diccionario de la música 2806

Diccionario de la música ilustrado 2818

Diccionario de la música Labor 3015

Diccionario de la música, técnico, histórico, bio-bibliográfico 2934

Diccionario de literatura española (Madrid, 1953) 3865

Diccionario de literatura española (San Vicente, F. Madrid, 1954) 3889

Diccionario de literatura puertorriquena 3915

Diccionario de los artífices que florecieron en Sevilla 2713

Diccionario de músicos célebres del pasado y del presente 3115

Diccionario de personas célebres de Cádiz 1791

Diccionario de seudónimos del Uruguay 2380

Diccionario del ballet y de la danza 3159

Diccionario do theatro portuguez 3194

Diccionario enciclopédico de la música 2819

Diccionario enciclopédico ilustrado y crítico de los hombres de España 1776

Diccionario geográfico, histórico, biográfico y lingüístico del Estado de Guerrero 1533

Diccionario geográfico, histórico y biográfico de los Estados Unidos Mexicanos 1528

Diccionario histórico; o, Biografía universal compendiada 113

Diccionario histórico abreviado 176

Diccionario histórico argentino 341

Diccionario histórico, biográfico, crítico y bibliográfico de autores, artistas y extremenos ilustres 1797

Diccionario histórico-biográfico del Perú 1605

Diccionario histórico, biográfico y bibliográfico de Chile 531

Diccionario histórico, biográfico y monumental de Yucatán 1524

Diccionario histórico de la República Argentina   351

Diccionario histórico de los ilustres profesores de las bellas artes en Mallorca   2499

Diccionario histórico de los mas ilustres professores de las bellas artes en España   2459, 2574, 2598, 2646

Diccionario historico e documental dos architectos, engenheiros e constructores portuguezes   2687

Diccionario histórico-enciclopédico de la República de El Salvador   1749

Diccionario histórico, geográfico, estadístico y biográfico del Estado Lara   2388

Diccionario histórico, geográfico, estadístico y biográfico del Estado Miranda, República de Venezuela   2389

Diccionario histórico, geográfico y biográfico de Yucatán   1522

Diccionario histórico y biográfico de Chile (1800-1925)   531

Diccionario histórico y biográfico de la República Argentina (Muzzio)   351

Diccionario personal de Chile   528

Diccionario pictórico   2474

Diccionario político de nuestro tiempo   4770

Diccionario Porrúa de historia, biografía y geografía de México   1525

Diccionario técnico, histórico y biográfico de la música   3009

Diccionario universal de escritores   3377

Diccionario universal de literatura (bio-bibliográfico e cronológico)   3378

Diccionario uruguayo de biografías (1810-1940)   2381

Dichter und Schriftsteller unserer Zeit   3661

Die Dichter unserer Zeit   3661

Dicionario bibliográfico português   3816

Dicionario bio-bibliográfico brasileiro (Velho Sobrinho)   487

Dicionario bio-bibliográfico cearense   486

Dicionario bio-bibliográfico sergipano   477

Dicionario biográfico de músicos portugueses   2960

Dicionario biografico de pernambucanos celebres   480

Dicionario de filosofia   4255

Dicionário de música   2784

Dicionario de pintores y escultores portugueses   2578

Dicionario musical   3069

Dictionarul enciclopedic ilustrat
"Cartea românească"   1657

A Dictionary-index of musicians
2954

A Dictionary of abstract painting
2442

A Dictionary of actors and of other
persons associated with the
public representation of plays
in England (before 1642)
3176

A Dictionary of American authors
3396

Dictionary of American biography
1931

Dictionary of American biography
(Drake)   1934

Dictionary of American history
(Martin & Gelber)   1968

Dictionary of American medical
biography   4153

Dictionary of American painters,
sculptors & engravers
2496

A Dictionary of American social
reform   4683

Dictionary of anonymous and pseudonymous English literature
1088

Dictionary of anonyms & pseudonyms
in Norwegian literature 1584

The Dictionary of architecture
2676

A Dictionary of architecture and
building, biographical, historical, and descriptive   2668

Dictionary of artists in America
(1564-1860)   2567

A Dictionary of artists of the
English school   2603

A Dictionary of artists who have
exhibited works in the principal London exhibitions   2515

The Dictionary of Australasian
biography   367

Dictionary of Australian biography
(Serle)   378

A Dictionary of ballet   3215

The Dictionary of biographical
reference   235

A Dictionary of biography   108

A Dictionary of British etchers
2511

A Dictionary of British landscape
painters from the 16th century...   2512

The Dictionary of British musicians   2808

Dictionary of British sculptors
(1660-1851)   2699

A Dictionary of British sculptors
from the XIIIth century to the
XXth century   2698

Dictionary of Canadian biography
(1966-   )   507

The Dictionary of Canadian biography (Wallace)   511, 519

A Dictionary of cat lovers   41

Dictionary of Catholic biography
4341

A Dictionary of Christian biography (Smith & Wace)   4497,
4527

A Dictionary of Christian biography
and literature to the end of the
sixth century A. D.   4527

A Dictionary of contemporary
biography   114

Dictionary of cooperation   4698

Dictionary of discoveries   4743

A Dictionary of educational biography   3258

The Dictionary of educationists
3308

Dictionary of eminent Scotsmen
1214

A Dictionary of English authors
3533

A Dictionary of English church
history   4450

The Dictionary of English furniture
2724

The Dictionary of English history
1162

Dictionary of English literature
(Adams)   3492

A Dictionary of English literature
(Watt)   3540

Dictionary of European history
248

Dictionary of European literature
3373

Dictionary of Florentine painters
2464

A Dictionary of flower, fruit, and
still life painters   2582

Dictionary of French literature
3558

A Dictionary of general biography
92

A Dictionary of glass-painters
and "glasyers"   2482

A Dictionary of Greek and Roman
biography and mythology
267

A Dictionary of Hampshire recusants   4443

A Dictionary of hymnology   2918

Dictionary of Indian biography
1264

A Dictionary of Irish artists
2624

Dictionary of jazz   3007

A Dictionary of Italian painting
2475

Dictionary of literary biography,
English and American   3499

Dictionary of magic   4261

A Dictionary of mapmakers, including cartographers...
4750

Dictionary of Mauritian biography
1517

A Dictionary of miniaturists   2449

A Dictionary of modern anti-
superstitionists   4391

Dictionary of modern ballet   3147

Dictionary of modern economists
4703

A Dictionary of modern music
and musicians   2820, 2996

A Dictionary of modern painting
2476

Dictionary of modern sculpture
2695

A Dictionary of music (Illing)
2905

Dictionary of music and musicians (Grove)   2883-2884,
3018

A Dictionary of musical biography
2939

Dictionary of musical compositions and composers   3024

A Dictionary of musical information   2978

Dictionary of musicians (Baltzell)
2757

Dictionary of musicians (Cummings)
2811

Dictionary of musicians (Reeves)
2826

A Dictionary of musicians (Sainsbury)   3042

Dictionary of national biography
1124-1131

A Dictionary of New Zealand
biography   1577

A Dictionary of North American
authors (deceased before
1950)   3431

Dictionary of Oregon history   2291

Dictionary of organs and organists (Thormsby, editor.
Bournemouth, Eng. , 1912)
3091

Dictionary of organs and organists. 2d ed. (London, 1921)
2821

Dictionary of painters and engravers   2451

A Dictionary of painters of miniatures (1525-1850)   2497

A Dictionary of painters, sculptors, architects, and engravers   2509

A Dictionary of Parisian music
publishers   4019

Dictionary of Philippine biography
1615

A Dictionary of pianists and composers for the pianoforte
3010

Dictionary of political economy
4774

Dictionary of political science
4772

A Dictionary of politics   119

Dictionary of popular music   2866

A Dictionary of printers and
booksellers in England,
Scotland and Ireland   4027

Dictionary of printers and printing
4045

Dictionary of pronunciation of
artists' names   2535

A Dictionary of religion and ethics
4271

Dictionary of Russian literature
3827

A Dictionary of saintly women
4355

Dictionary of scientists, Chambers's   4594

A Dictionary of Slavic antiquities
1757

Dictionary of socialism (Rappoport)   243

A Dictionary of South Indian music and musicians   3046

Dictionary of Spanish literature
3877

Dictionary of Spanish painters
2572

Dictionary of the American hierarchy (1789-1964)   4332

A Dictionary of the architecture and archaeology of the Middle Ages   2679

A Dictionary of the artists of the English school   2603

A Dictionary of the booksellers and printers... England, Scotland and Ireland (from 1641 to 1677)   4034

A Dictionary of the cinema   3160

A Dictionary of the drama   3133

A Dictionary of the Popes   4285

A Dictionary of the printers and booksellers... in England, Scotland and Ireland (from 1668 to 1725)   4035

A Dictionary of the printers and booksellers... in England, Scotland and Ireland (from 1726 to 1775)   4008

A Dictionary of the saints   4286

Dictionary of the United States Congress, and the general Government   1964

Dictionary of United States history 1957-1958

Dictionary of universal biography (Beeton)   64

A Dictionary of universal biography of all ages and of all peoples (Hyamson)   156

A Dictionary of violin makers
3081

The Dictionary of Welsh biography down to 1940   1223

Dictionary of Wisconsin biography 2377

A Dictionary of word makers
154

Dictionary of writers of thirteenth century England   3532

Dictionnaire alphabétique des acteurs, actrices, danseurs et danseuses de l'Académie royale de musique   3138

Dictionnaire bio-bibliographique des littérateurs d'expression wallonne   3446

Dictionnaire biographique, annuaire et album de l'Allier 853

Dictionnaire biographique, annuaire et album de la Loire   899

Dictionnaire biographique, annuaire et album de Meurthe-et-Moselle 912

Dictionnaire biographique annuaire et album des Côtes-du-Nord 877

Dictionnaire biographique, annuaire et album du Doubs 882

Dictionnaire biographique, annuaire et album du Finistère 885

Dictionnaire biographique, annuaire et album du Loiret 902

Dictionnaire biographique, annuaire et album du Rhône 932

Dictionnaire biographique, comprenant la liste et les biographies des notabilités du département de l'Aisne 852

Dictionnaire biographique, comprenant la liste et les biographies des notabilités du département de la Côte-d'Or 876

Dictionnaire biographique, comprenant la liste et les biographies des notabilités du département de l'Eure 884

Dictionnaire biographique, comprenant la liste et les biographies des notabilités de la Haute-Garonne 888

Dictionnaire biographique, comprenant la liste et les biographies des notabilités du département de la Manche 909

Dictionnaire biographique, comprenant la liste et les biographies des notabilités... du département de la Marne 910

Dictionnaire biographique, comprenant la liste et les biographies des notabilités du département de l'Oise 923

Dictionnaire biographique, comprenant la liste et les biographies des notabilités... du département de la Seine-Inférieure 939

Dictionnaire biographique, comprenant la liste et les biographies des notabilités du département de la Somme 942

Dictionnaire biographique, comprenant la liste et les biographies des notabilités du département d'Indre-et-Loire 895

Dictionnaire biographique, comprenant la liste et les biographies des notabilités du département de Lot-et-Garonne 904

Dictionnaire biographique, comprenant la liste et les biographies des notabilités du département de Maine-et-Loire 907

Dictionnaire biographique, comprenant la liste et les biographies des notabilités du département de Seine-et-Marne 936

Dictionnaire biographique, comprenant la liste et les biographies des notabilités... du département de Seine-et-Oise 938

Dictionnaire biographique, comprenant la liste et les biographies des notabilités du département du Calvados   873

Dictionnaire biographique, comprenant la liste et les biographies des notabilités du département du Nord   918

Dictionnaire biographique de l'Aube   862

Dictionnaire biographique de la haute société et de la noblesse   743, 749

Dictionnaire biographique de la Loire-Inférieure   900

Dictionnaire biographique des artistes contemporaine (1910-1930)   2485

Dictionnaire biographique des artistes français du XIIe au XVIIe siècle   2441

Dictionnaire biographique des auteurs de tous les temps et de tous les pays   3340

Dictionnaire biographique des Belges   453

Dictionnaire biographique des comédiens français du XVIIe siècle   3174

Dictionnaire biographique des facteurs d'orgue...   2862

Dictionnaire biographique des généraux & amiraux français de la Revolution et de l'Empire (1792-1844)   843

Dictionnaire biographique des Genevois et des Vaudois 1859

Dictionnaire biographique des grands commerçants et industriels   794

Dictionnaire biographique des grands négociants et industriels   744

Dictionnaire biographique des Hautes-Alpes   890

Dictionnaire biographique des hommes de l'Est   745

Dictionnaire biographique des hommes du Midi   745

Dictionnaire biographique des hommes du Nord   745, 747

Dictionnaire biographique des hommes du Nord, de l'Est, de l'Ouest et du Midi   745-746

Dictionnaire biographique des hommes marquans de la fin du XVIIIe siècle   750

Dictionnaire biographique des médecins en France au moyen âge   4223

Dictionnaire biographique des membres des sociétés savantes   748

Dictionnaire biographique des membres du clergé catholique   4318

Dictionnaire biographique des musiciens canadiens   3070

Dictionnaire biographique des musiciens et un vocabulaire de termes musicaux   2822

Dictionnaire biographique des notabilités parisiennes contemporaines   926

Dictionnaire biographique des personnes nées en Nivernais 917

Dictionnaire biographique des sciences, des lettres et des arts en Belgique 462

Dictionnaire biographique d'Ille-et-Vilaine 892

Dictionnaire biographique des Vosges 952

Dictionnaire biographique du Canada 507

Dictionnaire biographique du clergé canadien-français 4278-4280

Dictionnaire biographique du département du Var 947

Dictionnaire biographique du movement ouvrier français 757

Dictionnaire biographique du Pas-de-Calais 928

Dictionnaire biographique et bibliographique... des hommes les plus remarquables 107

Dictionnaire biographique et bibliographique des prédicateurs ... français 4337

Dictionnaire biographique et biblio-iconographique de la Drôme 883

Dictionnaire biographique et historique des hommes marquans de la fin du XVIII siècle 750, 802

Dictionnaire biographique français contemporain 758-59

Dictionnaire biographique international de la haute société et du monde politique 743, 749

Dictionnaire biographique international des écrivains, des artistes, des membres des sociétés savantes... 90, 748

Dictionnaire biographique international des folkloristes 3333

Dictionnaire biographique international des médecins et chirurgiens 4103

Dictionnaire biographique international des physiciens et chimistes 4104

Dictionnaire biographique international des voyageurs et géographes 4739

Dictionnaire biographique international du monde politique 743, 749

Le Dictionnaire colonial (encyclopédie) 428

Dictionnaire critique de biographie et d'histoire (Jal) 164

Dictionnaire critique de la musique ancienne et moderne 2804

Dictionnaire critique et documentaire des peintres... 2439

Dictionnaire de bio-bibliographie générale... de l'Indochine française 2392

Dictionnaire de biographie chrétienne 4368

Dictionnaire de biographie contemporaine français et étrangère   82

Dictionnaire de biographie des hommmes célèbres de l'Alsace   857

Dictionnaire de biographie française   760

Dictionnaire de biographie mauricienne   1517

Dictionnaire de biographies roussillonnaises   933

Dictionnaire de contemporains illustres. I. Espagne   1775

Dictionnaire de droit canonique   4344

Dictionnaire de la marine   272

Dictionnaire de la noblesse   799

Dictionnaire de la peinture moderne   2476-2477

Dictionnaire de la Révolution française (Boursin)   740

Dictionnaire de la Révolution française (Décembre & Alonnier)   755

Dictionnaire de la sculpture moderne   2695

Dictionnaire de littérature contemporaine (1900-1962)   3557

Dictionnaire de médecine   4126

Dictionnaire de musique   2943

Dictionnaire de musique d'après les théoriciens...   2838

Dictionnaire de musique moderne   2777

Dictionnaire de poche des artistes contemporains   2584

Dictionnaire de spiritualité, ascétique et mystique, doctrine et histoire   4345

Dictionnaire de théologie catholique   4346-4348

Dictionnaire des amateurs français au XVIIe siècle   2448

Dictionnaire des anonymes et pseudonymes (XVe siècle - 1900)   419

Dictionnaire des architectes française   2683

Dictionnaire des artistes (Bonafons, L. A. de, known as Abbé de Fontenay)   2447

Dictionnaire des artistes (Heinecken)   2524

Dictionnaire des artistes de l'école française au XIXe siècle   2500

Dictionnaire des artistes et ouvriers d'art de la Franche-Comté   2450

Dictionnaire des artistes et ouvriers d'art du Lyonnais   2427

Dictionnaire des artistes et ouvriers d'art du Tarn   2592

Dictionnaire des artistes suisses   2614

Dictionnaire des athées anciens et modernes   4427

Dictionnaire des auteurs français (Paris, Seghers, 1961) 3565

Dictionnaire des auteurs français (Paris, Tallandier, 1965) 3566

Dictionnaire des biographies 143

Dictionnaire des braves et des non-girouettes 761

Dictionnaire des célébrités de la France 771

Dictionnaire des comédiens français (ceux d'hier) 3173

Dictionnaire des contemporains 783

Dictionnaire des Conventionnels 797

Dictionnaire des écrivains belges (Seyn) 3450

Dictionnaire des écrivains belges et catalogue de leurs publications 3443

Dictionnaire des émailleurs depuis le moyen âge jusqu'à la fin du XVIIIe siècle 2558

Dictionnaire des gens de lettres vivants 3562

Dictionnaire des girouettes 769

Dictionnaire des graveurs anciens et modernes 2434

Dictionnaire des hérésies, des erreurs et des schismes 4464

Dictionnaire des hommes de lettres, des savans et des artistes de la Belgique 446

Dictionnaire des hommes de théatre français contemporain 3143

Dictionnaire des idées contemporaines 205

Dictionnaire des individus envoyés à la mort judiciairement, révolutionnairement et contre-révolutionnairement pendant la Révolution 826

Dictionnaire des lettres françaises 3567

Dictionnaire des littérateurs 3445

Dictionnaire des luthiers anciens et modernes 3178-3179

Dictionnaire des marques et monogrammes de graveurs 2416

Dictionnaire des médecins, chirurgiens et pharmaciens français 4121

Dictionnaire des médecins du Limousin, Corrèze et Haut-Vienne 4128

Dictionnaire des médecins-poetes de la France 4108

Dictionnaire des miniaturistes du moyen âge et de la renaissance 2425

Dictionnaire des miniaturistes sur émail 2462

Dictionnaire des monogrammes 2414

Dictionnaire des musiciens (Candé) 2793

Dictionnaire des musiciens (compositeurs)   3099

Dictionnaire des musiciens de la
Moselle   2763

Dictionnaire des musiciens suisses
(1964)   3066

Dictionnaire des ouvrages anonymes
(Barbier)   704-705, 709

Dictionnaire des ouvrages anonymes
et pseudonymes publié par des
religieux de la Compagnie de
Jésus   4264

Dictionnaire des parlementaires
francais; notices biogra-
phiques sur les ministres,
sénateurs et députés français
de 1889 à 1940   762, 837

Dictionnaire des parlementaires
français, comprenant tous
les membres des assemblées
françaises...   762, 837,
842

Dictionnaire des peintres espagnols   2598

Dictionnaire des peintres français
2478

Dictionnaire des peintres miniaturistes sur vélin...   2469

Dictionnaire des peintres [nés
avant 1900]   2479

Dictionnaire des philosophes 4235

Dictionnaire des portraits historiques, anecdotes et traits
remarquables des hommes
illustres   175

Le Dictionnaire des précieuses 844

Dictionnaire des protées modernes
763

Dictionnaire des pseudonymes
(Coston)   706

Dictionnaire des pseudonymes
(Poinsot)   708

Dictionnaire des romanciers,
tants anciens que modernes
3587-3588

Dictionnaire des sciences médicales   4122

Dictionnaire des sciences occultes
4234

Dictionnaire des sculpteurs de l'
antiquité jusqu'au VIe siècle
de notre ère   2700

Dictionnaire des sculpteurs de l'
école française   2701

Dictionnaire d'hagiographie   4297

Dictionnaire d'histoire et de géographie ecclésiastiques   4298

Dictionnaire diplomatique   42

Dictionnaire drolatique des contemporains dauphinois   881

Dictionnaire du ballet moderne
3147-3148

Dictionnaire du cinéma   3149

s séculier &
se de Genève-
Annecy   4468

Dictionnaire du jazz   3077

Dictionnaire du violiniste   3102

Dictionnaire encyclopédique d'
histoire, de biographie, de
mythologie et de géographie
141

Dictionnaire encyclopédique de
bibliographie arabe   3442

Dictionnaire encyclopédique des
marques et monogrammes
2418

Dictionnaire encyclopédique des
notabilités contemporaines
814

Dictionnaire encyclopédique des
sciences médicales   4122

Dictionnaire général de biographie et d'histoire (Dezobry)
110

Dictionnaire général de biographie,
histoire, littérature... du
Canada   509

Dictionnaire général de l'art musical   3040

Dictionnaire général des artistes
de l'école française   2437-
2438

Dictionnaire général des théatres
3136

Dictionnaire géographique et bibliographique portatif des personnages illustres   232

Dictionnaire géographique, historique et biographique d'
Indre-et-Loire   894

Dictionnaire hagiographique; ou,
Vie des saints...   4458

Dictionnaire historico-artistique
de Portugal   2599

Dictionnaire historique; ou, Histoire abrégée de tous les
hommes, nés dans les XVII
provinces belgiques   433

Dictionnaire historique; ou,
Memoires critiques et littéraires concernant la vie... de
divers personnages distingués
191

Dictionnaire historique, biographique, et bibliographique du
département de Vaucluse
949

Dictionnaire historique de la
jeunesse   52

Dictionnaire historique de la médecine, ancienne et moderne
(Dezeimeris)   4120

Dictionnaire historique de la
médecine ancienne et moderne
(Eloy)   4126

Dictionnaire historique de tous les
ministres, depuis la Révolution jusqu'en 1827   782

Dictionnaire historique des auteurs
ecclésiastiques   4349

Dictionnaire historique des Canadiens et des Métis français
de l'Ouest   513

Dictionnaire historique des hommes
illustres du Canada et l'Amérique   496

Dictionnaire historique des musiciens, artistes et amateurs
2797

Dictionnaire historique des personnages célèbres de l'antiquité
217

Dictionnaire historique des personnages d'Auvergne   863

Dictionnaire historique du Japon 1424

Dictionnaire historique et bibliographique (Ladvocat)   176

Dictionnaire historique et bibliographique (Peignot)   232

Dictionnaire historique... et biographique de la Mayenne 911

Dictionnaire historique et biographique de la Révolution et de l'Empire   839

Dictionnaire historique & biographique de la Suisse   1845

Dictionnaire historique et biographique des généraux français 753

Dictionnaire historique et critique (Bayle)   61

Dictionnaire historique et critique (Bonnegarde)   85

Dictionnaire historique et raisonné des peintres de toutes les écoles   2618

Dictionnaire historique, géographique et biographique de Maine-et-Loire   908

Dictionnaire historique, littéraire et critique   58

Dictionnaire historique portatif 79

Dictionnaire historique portatif des grands hommes   176

Dictionnaire historique, topographique et biographique de la Mayenne   911

Dictionnaire iconographique des figures, légendes et actes des saints   4387

Dictionnaire iconographique des Parisiens   927

Dictionnaire illustré du cinéma 3149

Dictionnaire infernal   4234

Dictionnaire international des écrivains du jour   3347

Dictionnaire international des écrivains du monde latin 3348-3349

Dictionnaire international des folkloristes contemporains 3333

Dictionnaire-manuel-illustré des écrivains et des littératures 135

Dictionnaire national des contemporains (1899-1905)   764

Dictionnaire national des contemporains (1936-39)   765

Dictionnaire portatif des beaux arts   2539

Dictionnaire pratique des compositeurs et des oeuvres musicales 2823

Dictionnaire pratique et historique de la musique   2780

Dictionnaire répertoire des peintres depuis l'antiquité jusqu'à nos jours   2491-2492

Dictionnaire théâtral   3163

Dictionnaire universel de la
noblesse de France   754

Dictionnaire universel des contemporains   288-289

Dictionnaire universel des lettres
3341

Dictionnaire universel des littératures   3385

Dictionnaire universel des luthiers
3100

Dictionnaire universel des peintres
anciennes, modernes et contemporains   2520

Dictionnaire universel, historique,
critique, et bibliographique
(Chaudon)   99

Dictionnaire universel illustré
biographique et bibliographique de la France contemporaine   806

Les Dictionnaires départementaux
852-854, 859, 862, 873, 876-
877, 882, 884-885, 888, 892,
895, 899-900, 902, 904, 907,
909-910, 912, 918, 923, 928,
932, 935-936, 938-939, 942,
947, 952

Dīeīāniīa rossiīskikh polkovodtsev
i generalov   1742

Digest of women lawyers and
judges   3950

Dignorum laude virorum   961

The Diplomatic press directory of
Jamaica   1419

Diplomaticheskii slovar'   116

Los Directores de la República
Argentina   346

Directories, who's who, press
guides and year books   2

Directorio del personal estadístico
en las naciones americanas
4679

Directorio médico dominicano
4114

Directorio médico-social de Cuba
4123

Directory: Alumni, Cornell University Medical College
(1899-1965)   4115

Directory of American judges
3965

Directory of American scholars
3263

Directory of applied psychologists
4231

Directory of British fellows and
continental fellows   3262

Directory of British scientists
4584

Directory of Chinese biologists
4640

Directory of colored business and
professional women of Philadelphia and vicinity   2305

Directory of constituent members
of IASI   4686

Directory [of] foreign area fellows
(1952-1963)   4684

Directory of graduate research
(Chemistry)   4652

Directory of graduate research
[in chemistry]   4652

Directory of high school coaches
3225

Directory of hydrobiological labo-
ratories and personnel in North
America   4637

Directory of Italian-Americans in
commerce and professions
1932

Directory of Jamaica   1419

Directory of law teachers in
American Bar Association approved law schools   3951

Directory of medical specialists
holding certification by American boards   4124

Directory of Negro business and
professional women of Philadelphia and vicinity   2305

A Directory of negro graduates of
accredited library schools
4004

A Directory of New Mexico desperados   2241

Directory of New Zealand science
4607

Directory of New Zealand scientists   4607

Directory of research workers in
agriculture and animal hus-
bandry in India   4786

Directory of returned Fulbright
grantees   3264

Directory of statistical personnel
in the American nations
4679

Directory of statisticians and
others in allied professions
4680

Directory of teachers in member
schools (Association of American Law Schools)   3951

Directory of the social sciences in
Thailand (1963)   4678

A Directory of titled persons
1185

Directory of women teachers and
other women engaged in higher and secondary education
3265

Displaced persons professional
medical register   4146

Dissertatio historica de ducentis
celeberrimis Augustinianis
scriptoribus   4377

Distinguished Jews of America
2002

Distinguished Negro Georgians
2138

Distinguished successful Americans of our day   1933

Dizionario bio-bibliografico degli
scrittori Pugliese   3760

Dizionario bio-bibliografico dei
bibliotecari e bibliofili italiani   4014-4015

Dizionario bio-bibliografico dei
letterati e giornalisti contemporanei   3774

Dizionario biografico degli Italiani
1354

Dizionario biografico degli scrittori contemporanei   3347

Dizionario biografico degli uomini illustri della Dalmatia 2401

Dizionario biografico degli uomini illustri di Sardegna 1404

Dizionario biografico dei più celebri poeti ed artisti melodrammatici, tragici e comici ... che fiorirono in Italia (dal 1800 al 1860) 3773

Dizionario biografico di magistrati e giureconsulti insigni della monarchia di Savoia 3981

Dizionario biografico di tutti gli uomini illustri della provincia di Siracusa 1412

Dizionario biografico universale (Garollo) 130

Dizionario biografico universale (Scifoni) 259

Dizionario degli architetti, scultori, pittori... 2634

Dizionario degli artisti bresciani 2494

Dizionario degli artisti contemporanei 2575

Dizionario degli artisti incisori italiani (dalle origini al XIX secolo) 2583

Dizionario degli artisti italiani viventi, pittori, scultori e architetti 2519

Dizionario degli scrittori d'Italia (Casati) 3743

Dizionario degli scrittori [d'Italia] (Triggiani) 3782

Dizionario degli scrittori e artisti contemporanei 3771

Dizionario degli scrittori italiani classici, moderni i contemporanei 3747

Dizionario degli scultori ed architetti italiani 2694

Dizionario dei chitarristi e liutai italiani 3088

Dizionario dei musicisti 2749

Dizionario dei pittori dal rinovamento delle belle arti (fino al 1800) 2632

Dizionario dei pittori italiani 2444

Dizionario dei Siciliani illustri 1407

Dizionario del Risorgimento nazionale 1355

Dizionario del violinista, violista e violoncelliste 3102

Dizionario della musica sacra e profana 2873

Dizionario della storia dell'arte in Italia 2467

Dizionario delle donne celebri piemontesi 1400

Dizionario di erudizione storico-ecclesiastica da S. Pietro sino ai nostri giorni 4441

Dizionario di musica (Allorto & Ferrari) 2746

Dizionario di musica (Corte & Gatti) 2806

Dizionario di opere anonime e pseudonime di scrittori italiani 1340

Dizionario di opere anonime e
pseudonime in supplemento a
quello di Gaetano Melzi
1341

Dizionario di politica (Partito
nazionale Fascista) 4771

Dizionario e bibliografia della musica 2943

Dizionario illustrato degli incisori
italiani moderni e contemporanei 2616

Dizionario illustrato dei pittori,
disegnatori e incisori italiani
moderni contemporani
2465

Dizionario illustrato dei pittori e
incisori italiani moderni
(1800-1900) 2465

Dizionario letterario Bompiani
degli autori di tutti i tempi
3342

Dizionario Ricordi della musica e
dei musicisti 2824

Il Dizionario storico-anatomico
de J. A. Serrano 4203

Dizionario storico biografico di
scrittori, letterati ed artisti
dell'Ordine di Vallombrosa
4479

Dizionario storico-critico degli
scrittori di musica 2772

Dizionario storico degli autori
arabi più celebri 3441

Dizionario storico degli autori
ebrei e delle loro opere 3794

Dizionario storico degli autori
ecclesiastici 4349

Dizionario storico della letteratura
italiana 3783

Dizionario storico manuale della
letteratura italiana 3783

Dizionario storico-ragionato degli
uomini illustri del canton Ticino 1861

Dizionario universale dei musicisti
3056-3057

Dizionario universale della letteratura contemporanea
3343

Dizionario universale delle opere
melodrammatiche 2951

Dod's parliamentary companion
1132

Dod's peerage, baronetage and
knightage of Great Britain and
Ireland 1133

Dødsfald i Danmark (1761-90)
668

The Dominions Office and Colonial
Office list 1118

Dontsy XIX veka 1684

Dor rabanaw we-sofraw 1451

Dor we-hakhamaw 1471

Doroth ha-aharonim 1452

Dorpats Grössen und Typen vor
vierzig Jahren 417

236 [i. e. Doscientos treintiseis]
biografías sintéticas, políticos
y militares 111

Down beat's yearbook of swing
2970

TITLE INDEX

Draft Ming biographies   542

The Dramatic list   3212

The Dramatic list (Pascoe) 3810

The Dramatic writers of Scotland 3506

Dresdens theils neuerlich verstorbene, theils jetzt lebende Schriftsteller und Künstler 3634

Dykcjonarz uczonych Polaków zawierajacy krótkie rysy ich życia   1629

Dykcyonarz biograficzno-powszechny   271

Dykczyonarz poetów Polskich 3809

E

The Earlier Cambridge stationers & bookbinders   4016

Early American portrait painters in miniature   2446

Early records of the graduation roll, 1413-1579, and the matriculation roll, 1473-1579 [of the University of St. Andrews]   1219

Les Ébénistes du XVIIIe siècle 2727

Les Ébénistes parisiens (1795-1830)   2722

The Eccentric magazine; or, Lives and portraits of remarkable persons   187

An Ecclesiastical biography   4393

Écrivains, artistes et savants de l'ordre de Premontré   4384

Les Écrivains belges contemporains de langue française (1800-1946)   3448

Écrivains canadiens; un dictionnaire biographique   3536

Écrivains d'aujourd'hui (1940-1960)   3585

Écrivains suisses d'aujourd'hui 3928

Ecuador. Próceres de la independencia   676, 681

Edinburgh portraits   1216-1217

Educationists in India   3273

Eesti biograafiline leksikon   410

Efemérides biográficas (defunciones — nacimientos)   1534

Efemérides de músicos españoles 3043

Efemérides históricas y biográficas [de México]   1548

Effigies virorum eruditorum atque artificium Bohemiae et Moraviae   646

The Egyptian who's who   1332

Ehren-Tempel der deutschen Gelehrsamkeit   969

Electrical who's who   4788

Éléments de bio-bibliographie de la littérature arabe   3440

Elenchus quorundam Bavariae medicorum   4179

Éloges des académiciens de l'
Académie royale des sciences
(morts dans les années 1741,
1742 et 1743)   4600

Éloges des académiciens de l'
Académie royale des sciences
(morts depuis l'an 1699)
4587

Éloges des académiciens de l'
Académie royale des sciences
(morts depuis 1744)   4591

Éloges historiques des hommes
illustres du Thimerais   945

Éloges lus dans les séances publiques de l'Académie française
711

Elogi d'uomini illustri delle provincie Napoletane   1394

Elogi degli uomini illustri Toscani
1415

Elogi di illustri Italiani   1357

Elogi di Liguri illustri   1392

Elogi italiani (Rubbi)   1370

Elogia clarorum virorum qui
Altenburgum... tum scriptis
tum egregiis meritis illustrarunt   1026

Elogia Siculorum   1411

Elogii d'huomini letterati   3349

Elson's pocket music dictionary
2832

Emancipatie (1863-1963)   1813

Eminent Americans   1939

Eminent and representative men

of Virginia and the District
of Columbia   2353

Eminent Californians   2088

Eminent Chinese of the Ch'ing
period (1644-1912)   609

Eminent Georgians   2133

Eminent Jews of America   2002

Eminent men of the Northwest
2270

Eminent Sikhs of to-day   1262

Eminent Welshmen (Roberts)
1230

Enciclopedia biográfica de contemporáneos   336

Enciclopedia biografica e bibliografica "Italiana"   1356,
2543

Enciclopedia cattolica   4359

Enciclopedia de la música   2898

Enciclopedia del jazz   3089

Enciclopedia dell'arte antica,
classica e orientale   2487

Enciclopedia della musica   2833

Enciclopedia della pittura italiana
2488

Enciclopedia dello spettacolo
3151

Enciclopedia di scienze politiche,
economiche e sociali   4681

Enciclopedia ecclesiastica   4360

Enciclopedia figuras de hoy   1778

Enciclopedia filosofica   4237

Enciclopedia metodica critico-
ragionata delle belle arti
2671

Enciclopedia storico-nobiliare
italiana   1375

Encyclopaedia Judaica   1453

The Encyclopaedia Sinica   562

Encyclopädie der deutschen National-Literatur   3708

Encyclopädie der gesammten
musikalischen Wissenschaften
3051-3052

Encyclopaedie van het Katholicisme
4361

Encyclopaedie van Nederlandsch-
Indië   1294-1295

Encyclopaedie van Nederlandsch
West-Indië   2397

The Encyclopaedia and dictionary
of education   3415

Encyclopedia of American biography   1895

Encyclopedia of American biography. New series (W. S. Downs,
ed.)   1940

Encyclopedia of American biography of the nineteenth century
1950

Encyclopedia of American history
(Morris)   1976

Encyclopedia of art, Harper's   2523

Encyclopaedia of biography of
Illinois   2144

Encyclopedia of biography of
Indiana   2152

Encyclopedia of biography of Minnesota   2209

Encyclopedia of biography of New
York [State]   2252

The Encyclopedia of Canada   508

The Encyclopedia of ceramics
2719

The Encyclopedia of chemistry
4657

Encyclopedia of concert music
2843

Encyclopedia of Connecticut biography, genealogical-memorial
2117

Encyclopaedia of contemporary biography of West Virginia
2370

Encyclopedia of English and American poets and poetry   3534

Encyclopedia of Georgia biography
2136

Encyclopedia of great men in
Israel   1455

The Encyclopaedia of Islam   1312-
1314

The Encyclopaedia of jazz   2834-
2835

Encyclopedia of Jews in sports   3233

An Encyclopedia of Latin American
history   1504

Encyclopedia of literary and typographical anecdote   4045

Encyclopedia of living divines and Christian workers of all denominations in Europe and America   4482

Encyclopedia of Massachusetts   2186

Encyclopedia of medical sources   4152

Encyclopedia of men and women in the Bible   4269

Encyclopedia of modern architecture   2681

Encyclopedia of music, a biographical dictionary of Jewish & world musicians   3067

The Encyclopedia of music and musicians   2816

Encyclopedia of Northwest biography   2271

Encyclopedia of painting: painters and painting of the world   ...   2489

Encyclopedia of Pennsylvania biography   2298-2299

An Encyclopedia of religion   4268

Encyclopedia of Russia and the Soviet Union   1703

Encyclopaedia of Sikh literature   3727

Encyclopaedia of Southern Africa   330

Encyclopedia of Talmudic and Gaonic literature   4561

The Encyclopedia of the new West   2366

Encyclopedia of the opera   2844

Encyclopedia of the Papacy   4407

Encyclopedia of the Philippines   1611

Encyclopaedia of the social sciences   4682

An Encyclopedia of the violin   2754

Encyclopedia of Virginia biography   2356

The Encyclopedia of witchcraft and demonology   4253

Encyclopedia of world art   2490

Encyclopaedia of world literature   3334

Encyclopedia of Zionism   1454

The Encyclopedia yearbook of jazz   2835

Encyclopedic dictionary (Jameson)   1958

Encyclopedic dictionary of American history   1958

Encyclopédie Balkanique permanente   408

Encyclopédie biographique de Turquie   1879

Encyclopédie de la musique   2836

Encyclopédie historique, archéologique, biographique... des beaux-arts plastiques...   2471

Encyclopedie van de muziek   2837

Encyclopedie voor de wereld
literatuur   3332

Encyklopädie der evangelischen
Kirchen-Musik   2930

The English cyclopaedia
120

The English dramatick poets
3511

The English glee composers
2762

English goldsmiths and their marks
2718

English, Irish, and Scottish firearms makers   4782

English mediaeval architects
2682

English-speaking poets   3543

The English writing-masters and
their copy-books   4017

The Engravers of Van Diemen's
Land   2468

Ensaio biographico-critico sobre
os melhores poetas portuguezes   3814

Ensayo bio-bibliográfico sobre
los historiadores y geógrafos
arábigo-españoles
4765

Ensayo biográfico-bibliográfico de
escritores de Alicante
3885

Ensayo de bibliografía cubana de
los siglos XVII y XVIII
642

Ensayo de un catálogo biográfico-
bibliográfico de escritores
que han sido individuos de las
cuatro órdenes militares de
España   3882

Ensayo de un catálogo biográfico
de escritores de la provincia
y diócesis de Córdoba   1796

Ensayo de un catálogo de periodistas españoles del siglo XIX
3879

Ensayo de un diccionario biográfico-
chronológico de los siglos XV
al XX   45

Ensayo de un diccionario biográfico y bibliográfico de los
poetas... de Valencia   3872

Ensayo de un diccionario de arti-
fices coloniales de la América
Meridional   2734-2735

Ensayo de un diccionario de la
literatura   3382

Ensayo de un diccionario de los
artífices que florecieron en
Sevilla   2713

Ensayo de una biblioteca ibero-
americana de la Orden de
San Agustín   4481

Ensayo de una bio-bibliografía de
escritores naturales de las
islas Canarias   3876

Ensayo de una colección bibliográfico-biográfica de noticias
referentes a la provincia de
Segovia   1805

Entretiens sur les vies et les
ouvrages des plus excellens
peintres   2493

Entsiklopediyah la-tsiyonut   1454

Entsiklopediyah le-hakhme ha-
Talmud veha-geonim   4561

Entsiklopedyah le-ishim ba-
tanakh   4269

Entsiklopediyah le-musikah
3067

Entsiklopediyah le-toldot gedole
Yisrael   1455

Enwogion Cymru   1230, 1234

L'Épiscopat français depuis le
Concordat   4363

Erfordia literata   3298

Erh shih wu shih jen ming so yin
538

Errores y omisiones del Diccionario de anónimos y seudónimos
hispanoamericanos de José
Toribio Medina   1498

Erster Versuch eines vollständigen
Verzeichnisses der Nieder-
lausitzer Schriftsteller und
Künstler   1055

Escritoras y eruditas españolas
3881

Escritores agustinos de el Escorial
(1885-1916)   4550

Escritores alicantinos del siglo
XX   3874

Escritores burgaleses   3888

Escritores de Costa Rica   4017

Escritores de la Provincia Capuchina de Valencia   4498

Escritores del reyno de Valencia
3896

Escritores dominicanos del Reino
de Aragón   4373

Escritores dominicanos del Reino
de Valencia   4374

Escritores gerundenses   3869

Escritores palentinos   3883

Escritores venezolanos fallecidos
entre 1942 y ———   3899

Escritores y artistas asturianos
3891

Esquisses biographiques du département de l'Indre   893

Essai de répertoire des artistes
lorrains   2911-1912

Essai d'un dictionnaire des
ouvrages anonymes et pseudonymes publiées en Belgique
au XIXe siècle   420

Essai d'un dictionnaire universel
des luthiers   3100

Essais de biographie maritime
809

Essex Hall year book   4516

Estudio cronológico sobre los
gobernantes del continente
americano   1503

Etlicher gelehrter Männer gebrauchte Nahmens-Veränder-
ung   39

Études historiques et critiques sur
les médecins numismatistes
4193

Europa   160, 682

European biography   683

European composers today 2845

European Who's who 160

Evangelical biography 4437

Evangelisches Kirchenlexikon 4364

Les Évêques et les archévêques de France 4401

Everyman's concise encyclopaedia of Russia 1743

Everyman's dictionary of literary biography, English and American 3499

Everyman's dictionary of music 2778

Everyman's dictionary of pictorial art 2502

F

Faculties, publications and doctoral theses—chemistry and chemical engineering 4652

Faculty personnel... of the instructional staffs of the member schools [of the American Association of Collegiate Schools of Business] 3254

Famiglie celebri italiane 1362-1364

Les Familles titrées et anoblies au XIXe siècle 833

Les Familles titrées et anoblies du XIXe siècle 834

Famous faces in diabetes 4205

Famous musicians of a wandering race 3044

Famous musicians of Jewish origin 3044

Famous women 44

Fastes de la Légion d'honneur 811

Fasti consolari dell'Accademia fiorentina 1371

Fasti Ecclesiae Anglicanae 4410

Fasti Ecclesiae Hibernicae 4335-4336

Fasti Ecclesiae Scoticanae 4486

Fasti Oxonienses 1190

The Fellows [of] the American Council of Learned Societies (1930-1949) 3255

Fellows of the Social Science Research Council (1925-1951) 4691

Felsina pittrice; vite de' pittori bolognesi 2550

Female biography 172

The Female worthies 81

Les Femmes compositeurs de musique 2829

Los Ferrocarriles del Estado [Chile] 4798

1500 modern Chinese novels & plays 597

Fighters for freedom 1269

Figuras de hoy (1950-   ) 1778

Figuri contemporane din România
1656

Film portraits   3152

Film review   3153

The Filmgoer's companion   3162

Filmlexicon degli autori e delle
opere   3154

Finlands läkare   4078

Finlands ridderskaps och adels
kalender   697

Finsk biografisk handbok   698

565 Biblical personalities, as seen
by the sages of the Talmud
and Midrash   4563

Florida's who's who   2130

Florilegio de poesías castellanas
del siglo   3893

Försök til et biographiskt lexicon
öfver namnkundige och lärde
svenske män   1818

Folklorists of Bengal   3726

Folksingers and folksongs in A-
merica   2938

The Foreign Office list and diplomatic and consular year book
1140

Forfatterlexikon omfattende Danmark, Norge og Island (indtil
1814)   3478-3479

Forfattermerker i norske aviser
og tidsskrifter   1585

Forsøg til et Lexicon over danske,
norske og islandske laerde
maend   673

Fortegnelse over danske laeger
4118

The Founders   1918

Founders and makers of Michigan
2198

The Founders of neurology   4140

Four hundred notable Americans
1976

400 outstanding women of the
world   256

Fox's who's who among South Dakotans   2325

Fragmens biographiques et historiques (Geneva)   1846

Frammenti bio-bibliografici di
scrittori ed autori minori
conventuali   4500

Les Françaises du XVIIIe siècle
786

La France ilustre; ou, Le Plutarque français   846

La France littéraire (Ersch)
3570-3572

La France littéraire; ou, Dictionnaire bibliographique des
savants, historiens et gens
de lettres (Quérard)   3580,
3589

La France littéraire; ou, Dictionnaire des auteurs françois
vivans   3574

La France littéraire, contenant,
I. Les académies établies à
Paris...   3573

La France protestante   791

La Franche-Comté littéraire,
scientifique et artistique
887

Frankfurter Künstler   2674

Frauen als schaffende Tonkünstler
2967

Frauen der Zeit   189

Fred John's annual... showing
who is who in Australia
374, 380

Fred Lillywhite's guide to cricketers   3230

The Free Society of Artists (1761-
1783)   2517

The Freemason's pocket reference
book   236

French cabinetmakers of the
eighteenth century   2712

French who's who   774-775

Freydenker-Lexicon   4514

Die Führer des Reichsheeres
(1921 und 1931)   987

Führer durch die deutsche Literatur des zwanzigsten Jahr-
hunderts   3620

Führerlexikon, Das deutsche
971

5000 [i. e. Fünftausend] Sowetköpfe
1695, 1708

Fulbright grantees, Directory of
returned   3264

Los Fundadores de Bogotá   633

G

Galería biográfica de artistas
españoles del siglo XIX
2574

Galería biográfica de los generales
de marina, jefes y personajes
notables   1783

Galería de gallegos illustres
1798

Galería de varões illustres de
Portugal   1642

Galeria dos Brasileiros ilustres
485

Galería dos deputados das Cortes
geraes extraordinarias
1647

Galería militar contemporánea
1779

Galería nacional; o, Colección de
biografías de hombre célebres
que han actuado en Chile
532

Galería universal de biografías y
retratos de los personas más
distinguidos en política   125

Galerie administrative   770

Galerie biographique des artistes
dramatiques de Paris   3156

Galerie biographique des artistes
musiciens belges du XVIIIe et
du XIXe siècle   2880

Galerie biographique des personnages célèbres de Tarn-et-
Garonne   944

Galerie bourguignonne   871

Galerie choisie d'hommes et de
femmes célèbres de tous les
temps et de toutes les nations   126

Galerie de portraits des célébrités
russes   1706

Galerie der ausgezeichneten
Israeliten aller Jahrhunderte
1456

Galerie des artistes dramatiques
de Paris   3156-3157

Galerie des célébrités du sport en
France   3228

La Galerie des dames françoises
pour servir de suite à la
Galerie des États-Généraux
776

La Galerie des États-Généraux et
des dames françoises   776

Galerie des peintres célèbres
2540

Galerie espagnole; ou, Notices biographiques sur les membres
des Cortès...   1768

Galerie française; ou, Collection
des portraits des hommes et
des femmes qui ont illustré
la France   777

Galerie historique des acteurs du
Théâtre-Français   3172

Galerie historique des contemporains; ou, Nouvelle biographie...   127-128

Galerie historique et biographique
des membres du Sénat   778

Galerie militaire   715

Galerie nationale.   Le Parlement
belge en 1900-1902   444

Galerie nationale.   Les Suisses
célèbres des temps modernes
1847

Galerie suisse   1864

Galerie théâtrale; ou, Collection
des portraits...   3158

Gallereĭa gosudarstvennykh i
obshchestvennykh dieĭatelei
Rossii i tret'ĭa Gosudarstvennaĭa Duma   1687

Gallereĭa russkikh pisatelei
(Ignatov)   3829

Gallereĭa russkikh pisatelei i
khudozhnikov (Martov)   3832

Galleria dei letterati ed artisti più
illustri delle provincie
Veneziane   3755

Gallerie aller juridischen Autoren
von der ältesten bis auf die
jetzige Zeit   3984

Gallerie berühmter Kliniker und
hervorragender Aerzte unserer
Zeit   4143

Gallerie berühmter Schweizer der
Neuzeit   1847

Gallerie berühmter und merkwürdiger Frankfurter   1042

Gallerie der jetzt lebenden
deutschen Dichter, Roman-
enschriftsteller...   3678

Gallerie der verdienstvollsten
Juden des XIX Jahrhunderts
1466

Gallerie der vorzüglichen Tonkünstler und merkwürdigen
Musik-Dilettanten in Cassel
2750

Gallerie der vorzüglichsten Aerzte
und Naturforscher Deutschlands   4194

Gallerie deutscher pseudonymer
Schriftsteller vorzüglich des
letzten Jahrhunderts   959

Gallerie von teutschen Schau-
spielern und Schauspielerin-
nen   3181

The Gallery of celebrities   129

The Gallery of Chinese kapitans
1755

Gallery of distinguished musicians
2867

The Gallery of portaits: with
memoirs   239

Gallery of portraits of the National
Assembly (France)   779

Gallia typographica   4024

Geborene Schlesier... Biographien
in Schlesien geborener
Tonkünstler   3038

Geburts- und Todten-Almanach
Ansbachischer Gelehrten,
Schriftsteller und Künstler
1027

Die Geigen- und Lautenmacher vom
Mittelalter bis zur Gegenwart
2948

Geïllustreerd muzieklexicon   2921

Geiriadur bywgraffyddol o
enwogion Cymru   1226

Geirlyfr bywagraffiadol o enwogion Cymru   1224

Das Geistige Ungarn   1250

Das Geistige Wien   383, 3616

Geistlicher Ehrentempel   4390

Geistlicher Liederborn   2870

Das Gelehrte Baiern   3605

Das Gelehrte England   3529

Das Gelehrte Frankreich   3570

Das Gelehrte Hannover   1046

Das Gelehrte Österreich   393

Das Gelehrte Ostfriesland   1043

Das Gelehrte Russland   1737

Das Gelehrte Sachsen   3703

Das Gelehrte Schwaben   3627

Das Gelehrte Teutschland   954,
3632-3633, 3668

Das Gelehrte Wirtemberg   1080

Gelehrten-Almanach   86

Gelehrten-Lexikon der katholischen
Geistlichkeit Deutschlands
und der Schweiz   4367

Die Gelehrten Theologen Deutschlands im 18. und 19. Jahrhundert   4353

Gelehrten- und Schriftsteller-Lexikon der deutschen katholisch-
en Geistlichkeit   4367

Gelehrtes Berlin (im Jahre 1825)
3636

Gelehrtes Berlin (im Jahre 1845)
1034, 3636

Gelehrtes Fürstenthum Baireut
3618

Gelehrtes München (im Jahre 1834)
3687

Gelehrtes Pommern   1063

Geletterd Zeeland   1569

Gendai Chōsen jimmei jiten   1491

Gendai Chūgoku Chōsen jimmei
kan   580

Gendai Chūgoku jimmei jiten   583

Gendai Chūkaminkoku Manshūkoku
jimmei kan   581

Gendai kokusai jimmei jiten (1937)
173

Gendai kokusai jimmei jiten (1957)
132

Gendai sekai jimmei jiten   133

Gendai Shina jimmei kan (1924)
565

Gendai Shina jimmei kan (1928)
566

Gendai shuppan bunkajin sōran
(Kyōdō Shuppansha Hensambu)
3787

Gendai shuppan bunkajin sōran
(Nihon Shuppan Kyōdō
Kabushiki Kaisha)   3788

Gendai Soren jimmei jiten   1688

Gendai Tōa jimmei kan   364

A Genealogical and heraldic dictionary of the colonial gentry
1104

A Genealogical and heraldic history of the extinct and dormant
baronetcies of England, Ireland and Scotland   1102

Genealogical and heraldic history
of the landed gentry   1103

Genealogical and heraldic history
of the landed gentry of Ireland
1105

Genealogical and heraldic history
of the peerage, baronetage
and knightage   1107

Genealogical and memorial encyclopedia of the State of
Maryland   2181

A Genealogical dictionary of the
first settlers of New England
2229-2230

A Genealogical history of the
dormant, abeyant, forfeited,
and extinct peerages of the
British Empire   1106

Genealogisches Handbuch bürgerlicher Familien   973

Genealogisches Handbuch des
Adels   978

Genealogisches Handbuch des in
Bayern immatrikulierten
Adels   1030

A General analytical bibliography
of the regional novelists of
the British Isles   3512

A General biographical dictionary
(Bellchambers)   65

A General biographical dictionary
(Chalmers)   97

A General biographical dictionary
(Gorton)   140

General biography; or, Lives
critical and historical   47

A General biography of Bengal
celebrities   1283

A General dictionary, historical
and critical   62

A General dictionary of painters
2588

Generals in blue   2043

Generals in gray   2044

Generals of the Army and Air
Force and admirals of the
Navy   1942

El Genio de la raza   1788

The Geographical and biographical
encyclopaedia of Amin Ahmad
Rāzī

Geographisches Weltadressbuch
4747

Georgia women of 1926   2134

Georgia's official register   2135

Germania literata vivens   992

Die Gesammtliteratur Niederlands
3490

Gesamtverzeichnis des Lehrkörpers der Universität Berlin   3260

Geschichte der arabischen Aerzte
und Naturforscher   4227

Geschichte der arabischen Litteratur (Brockelmann)
3438-3439

Geschichte der Cantoren und
Organisten von den Städten
in Königreich Sachsen   3109

Geschichte jetztlebenden Gelehrten
244, 270, 685

Die Geschichtschreiber der Araber
und ihre Werke   4768

Las Glorias del toreo   3227

Le Glorie de gli incogniti   1365

Gloucestershire biographical
notes   1198

Gobernadores y capitanes generales
de Venezuela   2390

Los Gobernantes de México   1544

The Golden book of India   1277

Goldenes Buch der Musik   3080

The Golfer's handbook   3229

Good and great men of Gloucestershire   1199

Gosudarstvennaiā duma pervago
prizyva   1690

Gosudarstvennyĭ Soviet (1801-1901)
1727

Gosudarstvennyĭ Soviet (1907)
1691

Gosudarstvennyĭ Soviet (Levenson,
1915)   1699

Governos e congressos da Republica
dos Estados Unidos do Brazil
474

El Gran diccionario histórico 201

Gran diccionario tauromáquico
3234

Gran enciclopedia Argentina
342

Les Grand dictionnaire historique
201

Grande biographie dramatique
3134

La Grande voci   2875

Grandes novelistas de la
América Hispana   3918

Les Grands corps politiques de
l'État   739

Les Graveurs du dix-huitième
siècle   2594

Les Graveurs du XIXe siècle
2440

La Gravure et les graveurs
2463

Great chemists   4658

Great composers [of India]
3047

The Great historical, geographical and poetical dictionary
201

The Great landowners of Great
Britain and Ireland
1093

The Green Room book   3161,
3212

Die Greifswalder Sammlung Vitae
Pomeranorum   1061

Griechisch-lateinische Literatur-

führer von Homer bis auf
unsre Zeit   3468, 3470

De Groote Schouburgh der Nederlantsche konstschilders en
schilderessen   2525, 2658

Das Grosse Buch der Musik
2882

Grosse jüdische National-Biographie   1482

Grosse Österreicher   394

Grosse Schweizer Forscher
4589

Die Grossen Deutschen (Andreas)
963

Die Grossen Deutschen (Heimpel,
Heuss and Reifenberg)   963,
982

Die Grossen Deutschen: Deutsche
Biographie   982

Die Grossen Deutschen im Bild
985

Grosses biographisches Lexikon
der deutschen Bühne im XIX.
Jahrhundert   3150

Grundlage einer Ehren-Pforte
2957

Grundlage zu einer hessischen
Gelehrten-, Schriftsteller-
und Künstler Geschichte von
1831 bis auf die neueste Zeit
1048

Grundlage zu einer hessischen
Gelehrten-, Schriftsteller-
und Künstler-Geschichte vom
Jahre 1806 bis zum Jahre
1830   1050

Grundlage zu einer hessischen Gelehrten- und Schriftsteller-Geschichte seit der Reformation   1048, 1051

Grundriss zur Geschichte der deutschen Dichtung   3624-3626

Guð fräeð ingatal   4510

Guida italo-americana   1932

Guide bibliographique de la littérature française (de 1800 à 1906)   3595

Le Guide électoral   742

Guide médical et pharmaceutique Rosenwald   4138

Guide Rosenwald médical et pharmaceutique   4138

Guide to American biography   1884

The Guide to cricketers   3230

Guide to genealogical and biographical sources for New York City   2243

Guide to jazz   3007

A Guide to popular music   2866

Guide to scientific and technical workers in Egypt   4585

The Guitar and mandolin   2783

Guld- och silversmeder i Sverige   2733

Gurushabada ratanākara   3727

H

Hā sip khon samkhan khōng Thai   1873

Haft-iqlīm   1309

Hajkakan nor matenagitouthium eu hanragitaran haj keankhi   361

Hakushi, Who's who   1428

Ham register   4789

Hamburgischer Staats- und Gelehrten-Lexicon   1044

The Handbook of American genealogy   4760

A Handbook of American music and musicians   2915

The Handbook of Biblical personalities   4266

Handbook of contemporary biography   190

Handbook of fictitious names   38

Handbook of music and musicians (Ebel)   2828

A Handbook of music and musicians (Wharton-Wells)   3114

A Handbook of musical biography   2759

A Handbook of Oklahoma writers   3417

Handbook of Soviet musicians   2781

Handbook of Soviet zoologists   4627-4628

The Handbook of Texas   2342

Hand-book of universal biography
137

Handbook to the Church hymnary
2973

Handbook to the Most Excellent
Order of the British Empire
1178

Handbuch der deutschen Gegenwartsliteratur   3657

Handbuch der deutschen Wissenschaft   983

Handbuch der Laute und Gitarre
3131

Handbuch der poetischen Literatur
der Deutschen   3702

Handbuch der theologischen Literatur   4544-4545

Handbuch der Volkskammer der
Deutschen Demokratischen
Republik   979

Handbuch der Weltliteratur von
den Anfängen bis zur Gegenwart   3345

Handbuch des Deutschen Bundestages   1009

Handbuch des Österreichischen
National- und Bundesrates 386

Handbuch des Tanzes   3169

Handbuch für die Bundesrepublik
Deutschland   980

Handbuch für Heer und Flotte   49

Handbuch zur deutschen Literaturgeschichte   3676

Handbuch zur Geschichte der
Volkswirtschaftslehre   4699

Handbuch zur Kenntniss der
theologischen Schriftsteller
unter den Deutschen   4506

Handlexikon der Geschichte und
Biographie   84

Handlexikon der Musik   2786

Handlexicon der Tonkunst (Gollmick)   2874

Handlexicon der Tonkunst (Paul)
3011

Handlexikon der Tonkunst (Reissmann)   3032

Handlexikon für Zitherspieler
2859

Handwörterbuch der Naturwissenschaften   4592-4593

Handwörterbuch der Sozialwissenschaften   4685

Handwörterbuch der Staatswissenschaften   4685

Handwörterbuch der Tonkunst,
sachlich und biographisch
3035

Handwörterbuch wissenschaftlich
bedeutender Chemiker
4664

The Handy dictionary of biography
202

Három évtized története
életrajzokban   1248

Harper's dictionary of classical
literature and antiquities
3466

Harper's Encyclopedia of art
2523

Hartmann's international directory
of psychic science and spiritualism   4240

Hartmann's who's who in occult,
psychic and spiritual realms
4241

The Heads of illustrious persons of
Great Britain   1153

Heads of the educational institutions in India   3274

Hébridais   1575

Hefling & Richards' Index to contemporary biography and
criticism   13

Die Helde-album van ons vryheidstryd   332

Helsingfors universitets studentmatrikel   696, 3310

Helsingin Yliopisto. Opettajat ja
virkamiehet vuodesta (1925)
3310

Helvetia sacra   4388

Helvetiens berühmte Männer
1858

Helvetische Gallerie grosser Männer und Taten   1858

Hemerografía de Zacatecas   3904

The Herald book of Labour members
1096

Heroes, U. S. Marine Corps 1916

Heroologia Anglica   1152

Herringshaw's American blue
book of biography   1952

Herringshaw's city blue book of
biography; New Yorker's (of
1917-   )   2244

Herringshaw's encyclopedia of A-
merican biography of the
nineteenth century   1950

Herringshaw's national library of
American biography   1951

Hervorragende Tropenärzte in
Wort und Bild   4180

Hessische Biographien   1049

Hier is ons skrywers   3395

Hijos de Madrid   1800

Hijos de Sevilla, ilustres en santidad, letras, armas, artes
o dignidad (Díaz de Valderrama)   1806-1807

Hijos de Sevilla señalados en santidad, letras, armas, artes
ó dignidad (Matute y Gaviria)
1808

Hijos ilustres de la provincia de
Albacete   1787

Hijos ilustres de las Islas Canarias
1793

Hilyat al-awliyā wa-tabakāt al-
asfiyā   4553

Hilyat al-bashar   1310

Hindustan year book and who's who
1272

Histoire biographique de la
Chambre des pairs   804

Histoire de la vie et des ouvrages
des plus célèbres architectes
du XIe siècle jusqu'à la fin du
XVIIIe   2597

Histoire de l'orfèvrerie du
Languedoc   2729

Histoire de plus ilustres et scavans
hommes de leur siècles
274

Histoire des artistes peintres,
sculpteurs, architectes et musiciens compositeurs nés dans
le département du Gard
2568

Histoire des généraux qui se sont
illustrés dans la guerre de la
Révolution   803

Histoire des hommes illustres de
l'ordre de Saint Dominique
4513

Histoire des membres de l'Académie française morts depuis
1700 jusqu'en 1771   711

Histoire du Forez   886

Histoire générale et impartiale
des erreurs, des fautes et des
crimes commis pendant la
Révolution française   826

Histoire hagiologique de Belley
4342

Histoire littéraire de la Congregation de Saint-Maur   4508

Histoire littéraire des troubadours
3592

Histoire littéraire et bibliographique des frères Mineurs
4351

Historia bibliográfica de la medicina española   4142

Historia de la literatura colombiana   3913

Historia de los gobernadores de
las provincias argentinas
360

Historia de los gobernantes del
Paraguay (1535-1887)   1601

Historia medicinae universalis...
4134

Historia rei literariae Ordinis S.
Benedicti   4552

Historia y juicio crítico de la
escuela poética sevillana 3870

Historiadores de Yucatán   4763

An Historical account of the lives
and writings of our most
considerable English poets
3507

An Historical and biographical
dictionary   176

Historical and biographical record
of the cattle industry... of
Texas   4790

An Historical and classical dictionary   218

Historical and geographical dictionary of Japan   1437

Historical, biographical, and
miscellaneous gatherings...
relative to printers...   4030

Historical biography   152

Historical catalogue of Brown University   1919

Historical portraits [of Great
Britain]   1150

The Historical reference book
(Heilprin)   149

Historical register and dictionary
of the United States Army
1947

Historical register of officers of
the Continental Army   1948

Historisch-biographisches Handwörterbuch der denkwürdigst-
en, berühmtesten und
berüchtigsten Menschen aller
Stande, Zeiten und Nationen 181

Historisch-biographisches Lexikon
der Schweiz   1845, 1849-
1850

Historisch-biographisches Lexikon
der Tonkünstler   2871-2872

Historisch-biographisches Musiker-
lexikon der Schweiz   3028

Historisch-critische Nachrichten
von verstorbenen Gelehrten
...   117

Historisch-literarisches Handbuch
berühmter und denkwürdiger
Personen   151

Historische Lebens-Beschreibung
der berühmtesten Lieder-
Dichter   3113

Historische Nachricht von den
Nürnbergischen Mathematicis
und Künstlern   4667

Historische Rang- und Stammliste
des deutschen Heeres   968

Historisches Helden- und Heldin-
nen- Lexicon   131

Historisches Wörterbuch der
jüdischen Schriftsteller und
ihrer Werke   3794

The History of Franciscan preaching and of Franciscan preachers (1209-1927)   4551

History of Parliament...   1439-1509
(Wedgwood)   1183

A History of printing and printers
in Wales   4021

History of Scottish medicine   4113

History of the bench and bar of New
York (State)   3958

The History of the Chaplain Corps,
United States Navy   4518

A History of the English Baptists
4400

History of the Jewish physicians
4102

A History of the law, the courts,
and the lawyers of Maine
3992

History of the Royal College of
Surgeons in Ireland   4099

History of the ruling family, nobles
and leading personages in
Mysore   1279

The History of the worthies of
England   1141

Das Hoch- und wohlgelahrte
teutsche Frauen-Zimer
3675

Holmia literata   3920

Hombres (quien es quien)   524

Hombres célebres de Bolivia
468

Hombres de la Argentina   344,
353

Hombres de la independencia de
América   1502

Hombres del día (Argentina)
345

Les Hombres prominentes de México   1538-1539

Hombres y ciudades   631

Hommes célèbres de la Suisse en
portraits   1858

Les Hommes eminents du Mexique
1538-1539

Hommes et oeuvres du temps présent   170-171

Les Hommes illustres de l'
Orléannais   924

Les Hommes remarquables de la
Meuse   913

Honderd jaren Nederlandsche
schilder- en teekenkunst
2611

Hong Kong who's who   1246

The Honorary medical staff of the
Manchester Royal Infirmary
(1830-1948)   4094

House of Commons, with full results of the polling, biographies of the members and unsuccessful candidates...
1179

How to identify old maps and
globes   4744

Hsien tai Chung-kuo ming jen wai
shih   604

Hsien tai shih liao   569

Hsien tai wai kuo jên ming tz'ǔ tien
273

Hsin Chung-kuo fen sheng jen wu
chih   602

Hsin Chung-kuo jen wu chih   556

Hsin hai hsün nan chi   618

Hsin hsü kao seng chuan ssu chi
4274

Hsü pei chuan chi   591

A Hundred eminent Congregationalists   4454

100 [i. e. Hundrede] aars dødsfald
(1791-1890)   669

Hungária irodalmi lexikon   3356

Hungarians in America; a biographical directory   2019

Hutchinson's woman's who's who
155

Hvem er hvem?   1586

Hvem er hvem i dansk håndvaerk
2716

Hvem er hvem i dansk søfart
4791

Hvem skrev hva i de siste 25 år
3803

Hvem skrev hvad (1914-1964)
3486

Hvem skrev hvad? (1945-1951)
3483

Hvem skrev hvad? Politikens litteraturhaandbog 3482

Hvem taenkte hvad 4242

Hver er maðurinn? Íslendingaaêvir 1260

The Hymnal 1940 companion (Protestant Episcopal Church in the U. S. A.) 3022

Hymnopoeographia; oder, Historische Lebens-Beschreibung der berühmtesten Liederdichter 3113

Hymnopoeographia Silesiaca 2923

I

IRE directory 4792

ÍArki imena v nashata istoriiâ 489

Iatrologiae Silesiae specimen primum 4141

Icelandic authors of to-day 3721

Icono-biografía del generalato español 1770

Iconographie bretonne 867

Idishe denker un poeten in mitelalter 4239

Illinois blue book 2145

Illiûstrirovannyĭ slovar' iskusstv i khudozhestv 2453

Illiûstrirovannyĭ slovar' sovremennykh russkikh muzykal'nykh deiâteleĭ 2906

Illustrated album of biography of southwestern Minnesota and northwestern Iowa 2210

Illustrated American biography 1954

The Illustrated American biography (Jones) 1959

Illustrations de la Russie 1672

Illustrators of children's books (1744-1945) 4028-4029

Illustrerade musiklexikon Bonniers 3086

Illustreret musikleksikon 3008

Illustrert biografisk leksikon over kjendte norske maend og kvinder 1587

Illustres médecins et naturalistes des temps modernes 4089

Gli Illustri bolognesi 1386

Illustrierter Tonkünstler-Kalender 2907

Illustriertes Musik-Lexikon 2742

Illustris Academia Lugd. -Batava 3294

Illustrium Germaniae virorum historiae aliquot singulares 1024

Illustrium Hollandiae et Westfrisiae ordinum alma Acad. Leidensis 3294

Illustrium virorum elogio iconibus exornata 1377

Imagines philologorum 3351

Immortals of the screen   3195

Imperator Aleksandr I i ego
  spodvizhniki   1705

Imperatorskaia glavnaia kvartira
  1698

The Imperial dictionary of universal biography   157

The Imperial gallery of portraiture
  and biographical encyclopaedia
  304

Imprimeurs & librairies parisiens
  du XVIe siècle   4036

Imprimeurs parisiens, libraires,
  fondeurs de caractères et correcteurs d'imprimerie   4037

Der In Bayern immatr. Adel   1030

In memoriam; founders and makers
  of Michigan   2198

In memoriam; or, Funeral records
  of Liverpool celebrities
  1204

Index and dictionary of Canadian
  history   500

Index bio-bibliographicus CC. RR.
  PP. Matris Dei Scholarum
  piarum   4523

Index biographique des membres
  ... de l'Académie des
  sciences   4571

Index biologorum   4638

Index des généticiens   4642

Index des zoologistes   4643

Index funereus chirurgorum
  Parisiensium   4119

Index litteraturae entomologicae
  4639

Index of architects of several
  counties and many periods
  (except English medieval)...
  2419

Index of artists, international—
  biographical   2548-2549

Index of artists represented in the
  Department of Prints and
  Drawings in the British Mu-
  seum   2412

An Index of Catholic biographies
  6

An Index of Chinese artists represented in the Sub-department
  of Oriental Prints and Drawings... British Museum 2413

Index of Japanese painters   2633

An Index of musical wind-instru-
  ment makers   2936

Index of obituaries in Massachusetts centinel and Columbian
  centinel   1882

Index of obituary notices (1880-82)
  1084

The Index of 20th century artists
  2523, 2531

Index to biographies of contemporary composers   2740

Index to contemporary biography
  and criticism   13

Index to obituaries in the Boston
  transcript   1883

Index to profile sketches in New
  Yorker magazine   24

Index to scientists of the world
4570

An Index to the biographical and
obituary notices in the Gentleman's magazine (1731-1780)
1085

The India Office and Burma Office
list   1274

The Indian and Pakistan year book
and who's who   1285

Indian biographical dictionary
1275

Indian biography (Drake)   1935

Indian biography (Thatcher)
2020

Indian Parliament (1952-57)
1284

The Indian year book   1285

Indiana scientists   4620

Indice alfabético de autores para
facilitar el uso de las Bibliotecas antigua y nueva... 3861

Indice alfabetico dei rabbini e
scrittori israeliti di cose
giudaiche in Italia   3792

Indice de documentos útiles a la
biografía   1766

Indice de montañeses ilustres de
la provincia de Santander
1084

Indice nobiliario español   1780

Índices de escritores   3894

Indios célebres de la República
Mexicana   1523

Ingenieros de caminos, canales y
puertos   4793

Initials and pseudonyms   1890

Innatte Malayāla sāhityakāranmār
3723

Les Instruments à archet   3103

Instruments biographiques pour l'
histoire contemporaine de la
Belgique   432

Insurance almanac; who, what,
where and when in insurance
4705

The Insurance almanac and encyclopedia   4705

The Insurance almanac and who's
who in insurance   4705

Insurance who's who   4706

Intento de un diccionario biográfico
y bibliográfico de autores de
la provincia de Burgos
3873, 3888

International bankers directory
4714

The International bar and deskbook
3959

The International blue book   158

International celebrity register
159

The International cyclopedia of music and musicians   3090

International directory of anthropologists   4761

International directory of banks
and bankers   4714

International directory of opinion and attitude research 4687

International directory of psychic science and spiritualism 4240

International directory of psychologists 4244

International index of Catholic biographies 6

International motion picture almanac 3165

International television almanac 3166

The International who is who in music 2909

The International who's who 160

International who's who among hotel men 4707

International who's who in music and musical gazetteer 2910

The International who's who in poetry 3358

International who's who in public relations 4689

International who's who in world medicine 4147

International world who's who 161

The International year book and statesmen's who's who 162

Internationale Personalbibliographie, 1800-1959 3

Internationales Soziologen Lexikon 4688

Interpretenlexikon der Instrumentalmusik 2768

Iowa authors and their works 3418

El-'iqd el-manzûm fî dikr afâdil er-Rûm 1874

Irish artists 2624

Irish medical directory and hospital year book 4148

Irish naturalists 4648

Irish who's who 1306

Irodalmi lexikon 3327

Ishe ha-tnäkh 4563

Ishim 1475

Islamic architects and their works 2686

Íslenzkar æviskrar frá landnámstínum 1257

Isographie de l'Académie française 766

Istochniki slovar' russkikh pisateleĭ 3849

Istoria degli scrittori fiorentini 3768

Istoria degli scrittori nati nel Regno di Napoli 3779

Istoricheskii al'bom portretov izvestnykh liĭs XVI-XVIII vv. 1702

Istoriiā Imperatorskoĭ Akademii nauk v Peterburgiĕ 3303

Istoriiā opery v luchshikh ee predstaviteliākh 2929

Istoriko-filologicheskiĭ fakul'tet Khar'khovskogo universiteta (1805-1905)   3281

L'Italia e gli italiani di oggi 1352

L'Italia musicale d'oggi   2749

L'Italia scientifica contemporanea 4580

Italian-American history   2008

Italian-American who's who 1955

Italian sculptors   2702

Italica gens   1336-1337

IUbeleĭnyĭ sbornik sviêdiêniĭ o diêiâtel'nosti byvshikh vospitannikov instituta   4795

IUbileĭnyĭ spravochnik Impera-torskoi Akademii khudozhestv (1764-1914)   2537

Iwanami Seiyō jimmei jiten   163

J

The Jacobean and Caroline stage 3139

The Japan biographical encyclo-pedia & who's who   1429, 1446

Japan-Handbuch   1438

Japan who's who and business directory   1430

Jazz: New Orleans, 1885-1963 2796

Jazzens hvem-hvad-hvor   2914

Jefes del Ejército Mexicano (en 1847)   1531

Jesuiten-Lexikon   4406

Das Jetzt lebende geehrte und gelehrte Coburg   1039

Das Jetzt-lebende gelehrte Europa 244, 270, 685

Jetztlebendes gelehrtes Mecklen-burg   1056

Les Jeunes personnes devenues célèbres par leur piété filiale...   52

Jewish contributions to medicine in America   4150

The Jewish encyclopedia   1460

Jewish medicine   4151

Jewish physicians   4102

The Jewish year book   1461

Jews in the world of science 4582

Jinji kōshinroku   1431

John Lillywhite's cricketers' com-panion   3230-3231

John's notable Australians and Who is who in Australasia   377

Journalisten-Handbuch (1960) 3642

Jubiläumsgabe zum 150jährigen Bestehen des Kantons [Aargau]   1851

Judentum und Musik   3036

The Judges in Ireland   3943

The Judges of England   3954

Jüdischer Plutarch 1459

Jüdisches Athenäum 1462

The Junior book of authors 3363

Les Jurassiens recommandables
par des bienfaits, des vertus
... 896

Jurisconsultos españoles 3940

K

Kalendars of Scottish saints
4639

Kami perkenalkan... ! 1297

Kammarmusiken och dess mästare
intill 1800-talets början
2891

Kangakusha denki oyobi chojutsu
shūran 4246

Kangakusha denki shūsei 4256

Kansallinen elämäkerrasto 700

Kao seng chuan 4272

Kapishche moego serdtsa 1683

Kappa alpha record (1825-1940)
1960

Katalog moego sobraniia gravirovannykh i litografirovannykh
portretov 1660-1661

Katalog pisatelei, sochineniiami
svoimi ob"iasniavshikh
grazhdanskuiu i tserkovnuiu
rossiiskuiu istoriiu 4766

Das Katholische Deutschland 990

Katholischer Literaturkalender
3643

al-Kawakib al-sā'irah 1316

Kay's Edinburgh portraits 1216-
1217

Keiters katholischer Literatur-
Kalender 3643

Kelly's handbook of the upper [ten
thousand?] 1155

Kelly's handbook to the titled,
landed, & official classes
1155

Keneseth Yisrael 1457

Kennaratal á Íslandi 3284

Khrai pen khrai nai Prathēt Thai
1870

Khronologicheskii spisok russkikh
sochinitelei 3839

Khudozhestvennaia entsiklopediia
2453

Khulāsat al-Athar fī A'yan al-
Karn al-hādī 'ashar 1326

Kirchliches Handlexikon (Buchberger) 4412

Kirchliches Handlexikon (Meusel)
4436

Kitāb al-aghānī 3437

Kitâb al-muġrib fī hulâ al-magrib
1321

Kitab silk al-durar fī a'yān al-qarn
al-thānī 'ashar 1327

Kitāb tahdhīb al-Tahdhīb 1319

Kiu estas kiu inter Nord-Amerikaj
Esperantistoj 3391

Klavier-Lexikon 2997

Der Kleine Pauly 228

Kleine slavische Biographie 1756

Der Kleine Zürcher Plutarch 1848

Kleines Filmlexikon 3187

Kleines literarisches Lexikon 3360

Kleines Musiklexikon 2769

Kleines österreichisches Literatur-lexikon 3623

Kleines Tonkünstlerlexikon 2964

Književni godišnjak 3854

Know them journal (Philippine political leaders) 1612

Knox's medical directory for Australia 4169

Ko je ko u Jugoslaviji 2403

Kölnische Künstler in alter und neuer Zeit 2553

Kōgaku kenkyūsha meibo-daigaku kankōritsu kenkyūjo no bun 4796

Kōgaku kenkyūsha meibo-kōgyō kaisha, minkan kenkyūjo 4797

Ko-ji hô-ten 2655

Kokugakusha denki shūsei 1436

Kol hemdath Yisrael 1458

Kompozitory Moldavskoĭ SSR 2926

Konungens svenska och norska statsråd (1809—1814—1881) 1835

Korte levensschetsen van eenige vermaarde en verdienstelijke Zeeuwen 1571

Koshitsu jiten 1427

Kraks blaa bog 663

Kratkaia literaturnaia éntsiklopediia 3361

Kratkiĭ biograficheskiĭ slovar' uchenykh i pisateleĭ Poltavskoĭ gubernii 1718

Kratkiĭ biograficheskiĭ slovar' znamenitykh vracheĭ vsekh vremen 4159

Kratkiĭ muzykal'nyĭ slovar' 2825

Krepostnye arkhitektory 2678

Kritiko-biograficheskiĭ slovar' russkikh pisateleĭ i uchenykh 3850

Kritiko-literaturnoe obozrienie puteshestvennikov po Rossii 4736

Ku chin t'u shu chi ch'êng chung Ming jên chuan chi so yin 536

Kuang-tung shih jên chih 622

Künstler des Kartenbildes 4742

Die Künsterbiographien von Giovanni Battista Passeri 2581

Kürschners biographisches Theater-Handbuch 3171

Kürschners deutscher Gelehrten-
Kalender   991

Kürschners deutscher Literatur-
Kalender   3654-3655

Kürschners Deutscher Musiker-
Kalender (1954)   2931

Kuka kukin on   699

Kulturní adresář ČSR   651

Kungl. Gustav Adolfs akademiens
minnesbok (1932-1942)
4759

Kunstner leksikon (Gelsted)
2503

Kunstnerleksikon (Weilbach)
2656

Kuo ch'ao ch'i hsien lei cheng ch'u
pien   585

Kuo min tang liu chieh chung wei
ko p'ai hsi ming tan   572

Kurtzgefasstes musicalisches
Lexicon   2932

Kurze biographische Nachrichten
der vornehmsten schlesischen
Gelehrten   1074

Kurze Nachrichten von merkwürdig-
en Gelehrten des Hochstifts
Wirzburg   1082

Kurzgefasstes Kirchen- und
Ketzerlexicon   4389

Kurzgefasstes Lexicon deutscher
pseudonymer Schriftsteller
957

Kurzgefasstes Tonkünstler-Lexikon
für Musiker und Freunde der
Musik   2964

L

The Labour who's who   1157

The Ladies' court book   155

The Ladies' who's who   155

Laeknar á Íslandi   4084

Laeknatal (1760-1913)   4158

Lamb's biographical dictionary of
the United States   1926,
1962, 2021

Larousse de la musique   2937

Latvju rakstnieciba portrejās
3797

The Law list... England and
Wales   3962

The Law list of Australasia   3963

Lawyers and bankers directory
3964

The Lawyer's directory   3964

Lawyers in industry   3952

Lê Triều lich-khoa tiến-sĩ đề danh
bi ký   2393

Leaders in American science
4598

Leaders in education   3285

The Leaders of Malaya and who's
who   1515

Leaders of the twentieth century,
New York City (1918)   2246

Leaders of twentieth-century
China   541

Leading men of Japan   1432

Leben und Schriften aller Chur-
Sächsischen Gottesgelehrten
4467

Leben und Werke der Künstler
Bambergs 3637

Die Lebenden Schriftsteller
Mährens 3473

Lebensbeschreibungen berühmter
Gelehrten (Schröckh) 258

Lebensbeschreibungen berühmter
Gelehrter und Gottesmänner
des osmanischen Reiches im
17. Jahrhundert 1880

Lebensbilder aus dem bayerischen
Schwaben 1076

Lebensskizzen der Professoren der
Universität Jena 3270

Lectuur-repertorium 180

The Legislative manual and political register [of North Carolina]
2266

The Legislative manual of the
State of Wisconsin 2378

Die Lehrer der Heilkunde der Universität Erlangen (1843-1943)
4187

Leipoldt-Musik-Lexikon 2941

Leksikon fun der nayer yidisher
literatur 3790

Leksikon fun der yidisher literatur,
presse un filologie 3793

Leksikon fun yidishn teater 3218

Leksikon ha-gevurah 1465

Leksikon zioni 1450

Leksykon kompozytorów XX wieku
3050

Leningradskie kompozitory 3074

Lessico dei scrittori svizzeri
3930

Lessico svizzero dei contemporanei 1863

Letras y armas 3895

Letterati e giornalisti italiani contemporanei 3774

Letterkundige sakwoordeboek vir
Afrikaans 3394

De Levens en werken der Hollandsche en Vlaamsche kunst-
schilders (Immerzeel) 2530

De Levens en werken der Hollandsche en Vlaamsche kunst-
schilders (Kramm) 2538

Levensberigten en lettervruchten
van Nederlandsche geneeskundigen 4163

Levensbeschrijvingen van de voornaamste personen, die, ten
tijde der Revolutie, in
Vrankrijk, zijn geguillotineerd
geworden 808

Levensbeschryving van beroemde
en geleerde mannen 183

De Levens-beschryvingen der
Nederlandsche konst-schilders
en konst-schilderessen 2658

Levensschetsen van vaderlandsche
mannen en vrouwen 1558

Lexicon aller Gelehrten, die seit
der Reformation in Bremen
gelebt haben 1038

Lexicon antiquitatum Slavicarum 1757

Lexicon Capuccinum   4317

Lexicon der itzt lebenden schwäbischen Schriftsteller 3632

Lexicon der jetzt in Teutschland lebenden juristischen Schriftsteller und akademischer Lehrer   3961

Lexicon der jetzt lebenden schwäbischen Schriftsteller 3627

Lexicon der toonkunst   3107

Lexicon derer itzlebende Gelehrten in Polen   1632

Lexicon derer jetztlebenden Rechts-Gelehrten in und um Teutschland   3971

Lexicon of the Yiddish theater 3218

Lexicon van Nederlandsche schilders en beeldhouwers (1870-1940) 2547

Lexikon baltischer Künstler 2566

Lexikon der Alten Welt   184

Lexikon der Baukunst   2690

Lexikon der bildenden Künstler Hamburgs, Altonas und der näheren Umgebung   2608

Lexikon der deutschen Dichter und Prosaisten vom Beginn des 19. Jahrhunderts   3613

Lexikon der deutschen Dichter und Prosaisten von den ältesten Zeiten   3614

Lexikon der deutschen Heiligen, Seligen, Ehrwürdigen und Gottseligen   4512

Lexikon der deutschen National-literatur   3697

Lexikon der Französischen Revolution   824

Lexikon der Frau   185

Lexikon der Geschichte der Naturwissenschaften   4599

Lexikon der hamburgischer Schriftsteller bis zur Gegenwart   3693

Lexikon der jetztlebenden schleswig-holsteinischen und eutinischen Schriftsteller 3650

Lexikon der jetztlebenden teutschen Schriftsteller   3633, 3668

Lexikon der Juden in der Musik 3082

Lexikon der katholischen deutschen Dichter vom Ausgange des Mittelalters bis zur Gegenwart   3705

Lexikon der kirchlichen Tonkunst 2927

Lexikon der Kulturgeschichte in Literatur, Kunst und Musik 3354

Lexikon der Musik   2890

Lexikon der neuen Musik   3021

Lexikon der niedersächsischen Schriftsteller   3617

Lexikon der Pädagogik (Kleinert) 3289

Lexikon der Pädagogik (Roloff)
3288

Lexikon der Päpste von Petrus bis
Johannes XXIII   4507

Lexikon der Persönlichkeiten und
Unternehmungen: Steiermark
401

Lexikon der Reisen und Entdeckungen   4741

Lexikon der Schleswig-Holstein-
Lauenburgischen und Eutinischen Schriftsteller   3603,
3664-3665

Lexikon der seit dem fünfzehenden
Jahrhunderts verstorbenen und
jetztlebenden oberlausizischen
Schriftsteller und Künstler
3672-3673

Lexikon der vom Jahr 1750 bis
1800 verstorbenen teutschen
Schriftsteller   3633, 3668

Lexikon der von 1750-1800 vestor-
benen teutschen Schriftsteller
3633, 3668

Lexikon der Weltliteratur (Kindermann und Dietrich)   3359

Lexikon der Weltliteratur (Wilpert)
3393

Lexikon des Buchwesens   4025

Lexikon deutscher Bibliothekare
3997

Lexikon deutscher Dichter und
Prosaisten   3641

Lexikon deutscher Frauen der
Feder   3674, 3688

Lexikon für Theologie und Kirche
4412

Lexikon historischer Ereignisse
und Personen in Kunst,
Literatur und Musik   150

Lexikon sozialistischer deutscher
Literatur, von den Anfängen
(bis 1945)   993

Lexikon sudetendeutscher Schriftsteller und ihre Werke (1900-
1929)   3639

Lexikon verstorbener baierischer
Schriftsteller   3606

Lexique des écrivains suisses
3930

Lexique des troupes de comédiens
au XVIIIe siècle   3155

Lexique suisse des contemporains   1863

Li tai jên wu nien li pei chuan
tsung piao   548

Li tai ming chiang yen hsing lu
561

Li tai ming jên chuan chi   611

Li tai ming jên nien p'u   540

Li tai jen ming sheng tsu nien
piao   587

Liber memorialis, 1913-1960
(Ghent)   3268

Liber memorialis, l'Université
de Liège (de 1867 à 1935)
3290

Libro d'oro della nobilità italiana
1361

Leituviu rašytoju kalendorius
3799

Life sketches of executive officers and members of the Legislature of the State of New York   2257

Life sketches of government officers and members of the Legislature of the State of New York   2257

Life sketches of the State officers, senators, and members of the Assembly of the State of New York   2254

Ligeros apuntes biográficos de los jefes políticos de los partidos... República Mexicana   1537

The Lighter classics in music   2846

The Lincoln library of essential information   186

Lineal list of commissioned and warrant officers of the Marine Corps Reserve   2035

Lippincott's pronouncing biographical dictionary   275

A List of all the dramatic authors with some account of their lives   3542

A List of early American silversmiths and their marks   2711

A List of Lancashire authors   3535

List of officers of the Army of the United States from 1779-1900   1996

A List of official chemical appointments [in Great Britain]   4661

List of regular and reserve commissioned and warrant officers on active duty [U. S. Coast Guard]   2028

List of research workers... in agriculture... in the British Commonwealth   4783

List of scientists in Iran   4616

List of scientists in Iraq   4615

List of scientists in Lebanon   4617

A List of the officers of the Army and of the Corps of Royal Marines   1148

List of the officers of the Bengal Army (1758-1834)   1151

Lista strat kultury polskiej   1634

Liste alphabétique de portraits français   702

Liste alphabétique de portraits russes   1744

Liste alphabétique des auteurs morts (jusqu'en 1805)   3569

Liste des hommes de science de l'Irak   4615

Liste des hommes de science de l'Iran   4616

Liste des hommes de science du Liban   4617

Liste des portraits dessinés, gravés ou lithographiés des députés à l'Assemblée nationale (de 1789)   703

Das Literarische Anhalt   3670

Das Literarische Deutschland 3635

Literarische Silhouetten 3662

Literarisches Freiburg im Breisgau 3638

Literarisches Handwörterbuch der verstorbenen deutschen Dichter 3679

A Literary and biographical history... of the English Catholics 1142, 1156

Literary anecdotes of the eighteenth century 3522, 4045

The Literary history of the troubadours 3592

Literary memoirs of living authors of Great Britain 3531

The Literary Who's who 3370

The Literary year-book 3370, 3544

Literatas españolas de siglo XIX 3863

Literatura polska od poczatków do wojny światowej 3810-3811

Literatura uruguaya 3903

Literaturnaĭa entsiklopediĭa 3371

Das Litterarische Leipzig 1053

La Littérature française contemporaine. XIXe siècle 3580, 3590

Lĭudi ekaterininskogo vremeni 1739

Lĭudi russkoĭ nauki 4597

The Lives and characters, deaths, burials, and epitaphs... of all the Protestant bishops of the Church of England 4411

The Lives and characters of the English dramatick poets 3511

Lives and legends of flamenco 3184

The Lives and portraits of remarkable characters 187

Lives critical and historical, of the most eminent persons of all ages 47

Lives of American merchants 4704

Lives of eminent American physicians and surgeons of the nineteenth century 4137

The Lives of eminent Philadelphians, now deceased 2307

Lives of illustrious seamen 1159

Lives of remarkable characters... 732

Lives of the archbishops of Canterbury 4394

The Lives of the British saints 4294

Lives of the Cambro British saints 4469

Lives of the clergy of New York and Brooklyn 4453

The Lives of the English saints 4416

Lives of the Fellows of the Royal College of Surgeons of England (Plarr) 4188

Lives of the Fellows of the Royal College of Surgeons of England (1930-1951 — Power) 4190

Lives of the Irish saints 4448

Lives of the most eminent painters, sculptors, and architects (Vasari) 2641

Lives of the most remarkable criminals 1160

The Lives of the poets of Great Britain and Ireland, to the time of Dean Swift 3501

The Lives of the professors of Gresham College 3314

The Lives of the saints (Baring-Gould) 4295

The Lives of the saints (Butler, 1926-38) 4313-4314

Lives of the saints (Butler, 1956) 4286, 4315

Lives of the Scottish saints 4461

Lives of Virginia Baptist ministers 4509

Living authors 3362, 3364-3365

The Living female writers of the South 3430

Living musicians 2847-2848

Livländische Bibliothek nach alphabetischer Ordnung 412

Le Livre bleu 445

Livre d'or du Cambodge 492

Lloyd's church musicians' directory 2946

Lloyd's clerical directory 4331

Local and national poets of America 3407

Le Lodi dei più illustri siciliani 1406

Lögfraeðingatal 3960

Lögréttumannatal 3945

Lögsögumannatal og lögmanna á Íslandi 3983

La Loire historique, pittoresque et biographique 901

The London and provincial medical directory 4168

The London furniture makers 2714

The London medical directory 4168

The Long Parliament (1640-1641) 1154

La Lorgnette littéraire 3582

Lutheran cyclopedia 4421

Lyceum Patavinum 3302

M

McGraw-Hill encyclopedia of Russia and the Soviet Union 1703

The Macmillan dictionary of Canadian biography 511

The Macmillan encyclopedia of music and musicians 3123

Mährens Männer der Gegenwart 649

Die Männer der neuen deutschen
Zeit   967

Männer der Zeit   189

I Maestri di musica italiana del
secolo XIX   2956

Magna charta   1189

Magyar Athenas   3711

Magyar életrajzi lexikon   1249

A Magyar feltámadás lexikona
1254

Magyar irodalmi lexikon   3720

Magyar irodalom zseblexikona
3713

Magyar írói álnév lexikon   1247

Magyar írók élete és munkái
(Gulyás)   1249, 3714

Magyar írók élete és munkái
(Szinnyei)   1249, 3719

A Magyar társadalom lexikonja
1251

Magyar zsidó lexikon   1252

Maine immortals   2176

Maine writers of fiction for
juveniles   3415

Les Maîtres luthiers   2860

Mājalis al-muminīn   4559

Makers of government in Oklahoma   2281

The Makers of New York   2259

Makers of the harpsichord and
clavichord   2779

The Makers of the Panama Canal
1956

Mala encyklopedia muzyki   3030

Manila's four hundred   1614

Mannen en vrouwen van beteekenis
in onze dagen   1559-1560

Mannen van beteekenis in onze
dagen   1559

Manshū shinshi roku   588

Manshūkoku meishi roku   589

Manual biobibliográfico de
escritores   3381

Manual de biografía mejicana
1521

Manual de biografía y de bibliografía de los escritores
españoles del siglo   XIX
3880

A Manual of British historians
(to A. D. 1600)   4762

A Manual of music   2817

Manual of the Reformed Church in
America   4334

Manual, with rules and orders,
for the use of the General Assembly of the State of Rhode
Island   2313

Manuale della letteratura italiana
3736

Manuel bibliographico portuguez
de livros raros, classicos e
curiosos   1645

Manuel de bibliographie biographique et d'iconographie des
femmes célèbres   280-282

Manuel de l'hispanisant 1760

La Maraviglie dell'arte 2605

The Market research directory
4709

Martindale-Hubbell law directory
3968

Martindale's American law directory 3968

Martindale's United States law
directory 3968

The Martyrs and heroes of Illinois
in the Great Rebellion 2141

Martyrologe littéraire 3375

Les Martyrs de la foi pendant la
Révolution française 790

Más próceres de la independencia
681

Masādir al-dirāsāt al-adabīyah
3440

Masonic biography and dictionary
252

Massachusetts of today 2192

Mastera-khudozhniki zolotogo i
serebrianogo dela... 2730

Masterplots cyclopedia of world
authors 3372

Materialier til et dansk biographisk-
literarisk lexikon 3484

Materialy dlia biograficheskago
slovaria dieistvitel'nykh
chlenov Imperatorskoi
Akademii Nauk 4574

Materialy dlia biograficheskogo
slovaria sotsial-demokratov
... 1710

Materialy dlia istorii farmatsii v
Rossii 4209

Materialy dlia istorii nauchnoi i
prikladnoi deiatel'nosti v
Rossii po zoologii 4630

Materialy dlia istorii russkoi
literatury i dlia slovaria
pisatelei epokhi Ekateriny II
3844

Materialy dlia sibirskogo slovaria
pisatelei 3852

Materiały do dziejów piśmiennictwa
polskiego i biografii pisarzów
polskich 3812

Materialy do slovnyka ukrains'-
kykh graveriv 2590

The Mathematical practitioners
of Tudor & Stuart England
4760

Die Matrikel der Universität
Basel 1843

Die Matrikel der Universität
Köln 970

Mayors and aldermen of Great
Britain and provosts and
bailies of Scotland 1163

Mecklenburgisches Gelehrten-
Lexicon 1057

Mecklenburgs Schriftsteller von
den ältesten Zeit 3649

Les Médailleurs italiens des
quinzième et seizième
siècle 2703

Medal of Honor, 1861-1949, the
Navy 2025

The Medal of Honor of the United
States Army 2033

Medali v chest´ russkikh gosudarstvennykh dieiätelei i
chastnykh lits´ 1694

La Médecine et les médecins
4183

The Medical directory: London,
provinces, Wales [etc.]
4168

Medical directory for Australia
4169

Medical directory of New York,
New Jersey and Connecticut
4170

The Medical directory of South
Africa 4171

The Medical men of New Jersey,
in Essex district 4111

The Medical men of the Revolution 4210

Medical portrait gallery 4185

The Medical practitioners in
medieval England 4206

Medical practitioners in the diocese of London 4085

The Medical profession in all
countries 4076

The Medical who's who 4172

Medical woman's directory
4173

Medicinisches Gelehrten-Lexikon
4154

Medicinisches Schriftsteller-Lexicon der jetzt lebenden Aerzte
4098

Medizinisches Wörter- und Nachschlagebuch 4136

Medlemmar af Gestrike-Helsinge
nation i Upsala (1811-1891)
1823

Mega Hellenikon biographikon
lexikon 1244

Meister deutscher Geigenbaukunst
2886

Melize esh 4568

Members of Parliament 1146-
1147

Members of Parliament, Scotland
1212

A Memoir of the York Press
4006

Mémoires biographiques et littéraires... sur les hommes
... dans le département de
la Seine-Inférieure 940

Mémoires pour servir à l'histoire
des hommes dans la répub-
lique des lettres 213, 3986

Mémoires pour servir à l'histoire
littéraire des dix-sept provinces des Pays-Bas 1566

Mémoires sur les sculpteurs et
architectes des Pays-Bas
2693

Memoirs and sketches of one hundred and eleven eminent men
... of Cardigan 1233

Memoirs of the judiciary and the
bar of New England for the
nineteenth century 3982

Memoirs of the most illustrious
ladies of all ages and nations 81

Memoirs of the saints [of Islam] 4555

Memorabilia Italorum eruditione praestantium 1360

Memoria biográfica de los mallorquines 3860

Memoria Hungarorum et provincialium scriptis editis notorum 3716

Memoria virorum in Suecia eruditissimorum rediviva 1822

Memoriae jurisconsultorum nostri seculi clarissimorum 3393

Memoriae medicorum nostri saeculi clarissimorum renovatae decas prima 4226

A Memorial and biographical history of northern California 2090

Memorial and biographical record ... Cumberland region of Tennessee 2333

Memorial and biographical record ... South Dakota 2322

Memorial and genealogical record of southwest Texas 2343

Memorial cyclopedia of New Jersey 2239

Memorial encyclopedia of the State of New York 2252

Memorial record of distinguished men of Indianapolis and Indiana 2155

Memorial record of northeastern Indiana 2151

Memorial record of southwestern Minnesota 2212

Memorial record of the Northern Peninsula of Michigan 2197

Memorial record of western Kentucky 2163

Memorials of deceased companions of the Commandery of the State of Illinois, Military Order of the Loyal Legion of the United States 1972

Memorias historicas. Dos illustrissimos arcebispos, bispos e escriptores portuguezes da Ordem de Nossa Senhora do Carmo 4477

Memorias para ayudar a formar un diccionario crítico de los escritores catalanes 3456-3457

Memorias para formar un catálogo alfabético de los españoles, americanos y extranjeros célebres 1782

Memorias para la biografía y para la bibliografía de la isla de Cádiz 1791

Memorie biografiche degli scultori ... nativi di Carrara 2457

Memorie degli scrittori del regno di Napoli 3731

Memorie degli scritti letterati parmigiani 3732

Memorie degli uomini illustri e chiari in medicina del Piceno ossia della Marca d'Ancona 4182

Memorie dei compositori de musica del Regno di Napoli 3106

Memorie funebri antiche e recenti 1374

Memorie, imprese, e ritratti di'
signori Accademici Gelati
di Bologna   1366

Memorie intorno ai poeti laureati
d'ogni tempo e d'ogni na-
zione   3368

Memorie istoriche degli scrittori
legali del Regno di Napoli
3758

Memorie istoriche di letterati
ferraresi   1389-1390

Memorie istoriche per servire
alla vita di più uomini illustri
della Toscana   1417

Memorie per la storia letteraria
di Piacenza   1399

Memorie storiche degli scrittori
nati nel regno di Napoli
3765

Memorie storiche d'illustri scrittori. . . dell'antica e moderna
Lunigiana   3756

Men and women of America; a
biographical dictionary of
contemporaries   1969-1970

Men and women of Arizona, past
and present   2078

Men and women of Hawaii   2139

Men and women of the time   194,
1187

Men-at-the-bar   3955

Men behind the war   269

Men in the news   195

Men of achievement (Texas)
2341

Men of affairs and representative
institutions of Oklahoma (1916)
2283

Men of affairs in New York   2259

Men of America (New York, 1908)
1969-1970

Men of America. A biographical
album of the city government
of Philadelphia (1883)
2306

Men of Boston and New England
2084

Men of California (Wolfe, ed.
1900-1902)   2091

Men of California; western personalities and their affilia-
tions (Wolfe, ed.   1926)
2092

Men of Canada   501

Men of education in India   3293

Men of Hawaii   226

Men of Illinois   2146

Men of Indiana in nineteen hundred
and one   2148

Men of mark: eminent, progressive and rising   2014

Men of mark in Georgia   2137

Men of mark in Maryland   2180

Men of mark in South Carolina
2318

Men of mark in Virginia   2354

Men of mark in Virginia [2d ser.]
2355

Men of mark 'twixt Tyne and Tweed
1184

Men of Maryland since the Civil
War   2182

Men of Massachusetts   2187

Men of Michigan   2199

Men of Minnesota   2213

Men of New England   2228

The Men of New York [State]
2258

Men of note in finance and commerce   4710

Men of office   4710

Men of popular music   2849

Men of progress... Connecticut
2118

Men of progress... Maine   2175

Men of progress... Massachusetts
2188

Men of progress... Michigan
2200

Men of progress... New Hampshire   2234

Men of progress... Rhode Island
2311

Men of progress... Vermont 2350

Men of sciences & technology in
India   4602

Men of Shanghai and North China
593

Men of the century   1975

Men of the day (Argentina)   345

Men of the moment   196

Men of the Philippines   1616

Men of the reign   1182

Men of the time   194, 197, 1182

Men of the times; old colonists of
the Cape Colony...   325

Men of the times; pioneers of the
Transvaal...   326

Men of the West [Country of Eng-
land]   2367

Men of today and their works
170-171

Men of Vermont (Ullery)   2351

Men of Vermont State (Hills)   2349

Men of West Virginia   2371

Men of Yale series   1971

Men who have made Michigan
2201

Men whom India has known   1271

Mennonite cyclopedic dictionary
4403

The Mennonite encyclopedia   4431

Mennonitisches Lexikon   4432

A Menology of England and Wales
4503

Menschen und Menschenwerke
170-171

Merckwürdiges Verzeichniss derer
von Zeit der Reformation allhier zu Frankfurt am Mayn
gestandenen evangelischen
Prediger   4386

Merkwürdigkeiten der Haupt- und Residenzstaat Wien   3609

Merton College register (1900-1964)   1169

Methodist bishops   4409

The Methodist who's who   4434

México actual   1539

México y sus gobernantes; biografías (García Purón)   1529

México y sus gobernantes (de 1519 a 1910)   1545

Meyers Handbuch über die Literatur   3376

Meyers Handbuch über die Musik 2966

Michigan authors   3408

Michigan biographies   2203

Michigan official directory and legislative manual   2202

Michigan poets   3409

The Middle East; a survey and directory   1325

Mil quinientos seudónimos modernos de la literatura española (1900-1942)   1762

Die Militär-Kapellmeister Österreich-Ungarns   2812

Miller's yearbook of popular music   2970

Min kuo ming jen t'u chien   620

Min tsu ying hsiung pai jen chuan 586

Minerva-Lexikon berühmter Persönlichkeiten aller Zeitalter 255

The Miniature in Europe in the 16th, 17th, 18th and 19th centuries   2612

Miniature painters, British and foreign   2497

Ministerial directory of the Presbyterian Church, U. S. (1861-1941)   4485

Minnesota authors   3421

Minnesota biographies   2214

Minnesota writers   3425

Minnesteckninger öfver utmärkte svenske staatsmän...   1817

Minute biographies   214, 216

Miscellanea historico-biographica 1648

Miscellanea musicae bio-bibliographica   2971

Missionary album [of the Southern Baptist Convention]   4499

Mississippi blue book   2219

Mississippi official and statistical register   2219

Missouri and Missourians   2013

Die Mitglieder der Deutschen Gesellschaft zu Göttingen (von 1738 bis Anfang 1755)   4613

Mitglieder-Verzeichnisse der Gesellschaft der Wissenschaften zu Göttingen   4573

Mittelalterliche Künstler und
Werkmeister Niedersachsens
und Westfalens   2557

Mitteldeutsche Köpfe   994

Mitteldeutsche Lebensbilder
1068

The Modern British paintings,
drawings and sculpture
2630

Modern English biography   1095

Modern music and musicians
2972

Modern Scottish writers   3524

Moderna svenska författare
3922

Moderne Biographien (Lutz)
1855

Moderne Biographien (Reichard)
245

Le Mondain égyptien   1332

Le Mondain égyptien et du Proche-
Orient   1332

Mondo cattolico   4438

Moniteur des dates   221-222

Monogramm Lexikon   2417

Die Monogrammisten und diejenigen bekannten und unbekannten Künstler aller Schulen
2562-2563

The Monthly record of eminent
men   200

The Monthly supplement, a current
biographical reference service
2056

Monumenta Anglicana   1158

More junior authors   124

More minute biographies   215

al-Moschtabih   1311

Moskovskiĭ nekropolʹ   1711

The Moslem nobility of the world
(1935)   1315

Mostra bibliografica dei musicisti
cremonesi   2974

The Motion picture almanac
3165

Motion picture and television almanac   3165

The Mountain men and the fur trade
of the Far West   2363

Münsterlandisches Schriftsteller-
Lexicon   3680-3681

Muestras de errores y defectos
del 'Diccionario biográfico
colonial de Chile por José
Toribio Medina'   535

Muǵam al-matbūʹ at al-arabīja
walmu'arraba   3442

Mujeres de América   3919

Mujeres notables mexicanas
1550

O Mundo artistico do Brazil   2613

Mural painters in America   2579

El Museo pictorico, y escala optica   2576-2577

al-Mushtabih fī asmāʹ al-rijāl
1311

Music and dance in California and the West 2982

Music & dance in New York State 2983

Music and dance in Pennsylvania, New Jersey, and Delaware 2984

Music and dance in Texas, Oklahoma and the Southwest 2985

Music and dance in the Central States 2986

Music and dance in the New England States 2987

Music and dance in the Southeastern States 2988

Music and musicians 2816

The Music and theater of the Filipino people 2758

Music lexicography 2741

Music lovers' encyclopedia (Hughes) 2903

The Music lover's handbook (Clifford) 2801

The Music lover's handbook (Siegmeister) 3068

The Music of the church humnary and the Psalter in metre 2807

Music publishing in the British Isles 4020

Music (since 1900) 3071

La Musica ed i musicisti dal secolo X sino ai nostri giorni 2864

La Música en Valencia 2744

Música y músicos de Latinoamérica 2958

The Musical guide 2903

A Musical handbook for musicians and amateurs 3062

Musical Scotland, past and present 2760

Musicalisches Lexikon 2887

Musicians of all times 2761

Les Musiciens belges 2855

Les Musiciens célèbres (1946) 2989

Les Musiciens célèbres depuis le seizième siècle 2800

Les Musiciens normands 2852

Les Musiciens polonais et slaves, anciens et modernes 3078-3079

Musicisti cremonesi 2975

The Musiclover's handbook (Clifford) 2801

Músicos célebres (Buenos Aires, 1942-) 2990

Músicos célebres (Davalillo) 2814

Músicos españoles 3105

Os Musicos portuguezes 3101

Musicus Danicus 3049

Musiikin tietokirja 2991

Musik ABC 3065

Die Musik in Geschichte und Gegenwart 2992

Musik Lexikon (Moser) 2980

Musik Lexikon (Riemann) 3034

Das Musikalische Juden-ABC 3036-3037

Das Musikalische Europa 3053

Musikalisches Conversations-Hand-Lexikon (Schilling) 3054

Musikalisches Conversations-Lexikon (Mendel) 2962-2963, 3032

Musikalisches Conversations-Lexicon (Schuberth) 3060-3061

Musikalisches Conversations-Lexicon (Steuer) 3083

Musikalisches Handbuch 3062

Musiker-Lexikon 2994

Der Musikführer, Lexikon der Tonkunst 2897

Musikgeschichtliche Quellennachweise... 2971

Musikkens hvem hvad hvor 2993

Musikkens hvem-hvad-hvor jazz 2914

Musikkens verden 3048

Musikkleksikon (Gurvin & Anker) 2885

Musik-lexicon (Höijer) 2894-2895

Musik-Lexikon (Leipoldt) 2941

Musiklexikon der Welt 3004

La Musique aux Pays-Bas avant le XIXe siècle 3084

Le Musique en Suisse depuis les temps les plus reculés 2767

La Musique et les musiciens... de Liège 2753

Musisches Lexikon 2925

The Muslim year book of India and who's who 1278

Muziekwijzer 2785

Muzikaal Nederland (1850-1910) 2942

Muzyka Sovetskoi Estonii 2995

N

Naam-boek der beroemde genees-en heelmeesters van alle eeuwen 4195

Naamlijst van predikanten, hoogleeraren en proponenten der Luthersche Kerk in Nederland 4420

Naamrol der medicinaale, chirurgiale, chimische, natuurkundige schrijvers 4177

Naamrol der rechtsgeleerde en historische schryvers... in Holland 3972

Nachricht von den itztlebenden Evangelisch-Lutherischen und Reformirten Theologen in und um Deutschland 4446

Nachrichten über böhmische Schriftsteller und Gelehrte 650

Nachrichten von dem Leben und den Erfindungen der berühmtesten Mathematiker 4668

Nachrichten von dem Leben und den Schriften jetztlebender teutscher Aerzte... 4127

Nachrichten von dem Leben und den Schriften Münsterlandischer Schriftsteller des achtzehnten und neunzehnten Jahrhundert 3683-3684

Nachrichten von dem Leben und den Schriften neu-vor-pommerisch-rügenscher Gelehrten 1060

Nachrichten von den Begebenheiten und Schriften berühmter Gelehrten 213

Nachrichten von den jetzt lebenden Schriftstellern in Neuvorpommern und Rügen 3508

Nachrichten von den Lebensumständen und Schriften evangelischer Prediger in allen Gemeinen des Königreichs Ungarn 4404

Nachrichten von den vornehmsten Lebensumständen... jetztlebender berühmter Aerzte... in und um Deutschland 4086-4087

Nachrichten von Frankfurter Künstlern und Kunst-Sachen 2527

Nachrichten von Gelehrten, Künstlern und anderen merkwürdigen Personen aus Ulm 1077

Nachrichten von Liederdichtern des Augspurgischen Gesangsbuchs 2896

Nachrichten von Schriftstellern und Künstlern der Grafschaft Wernigerode 3645

Nachrichten von siebenbürgischen Gelehrten und ihre Schriften 1658, 3700

Nafahat al-uns min hadarat al-quds 4558

Nalanda year-book and who's who in India and Pakistan 1280

Name wat leef 327

Namenschlüssel, die Verweisungen der Berliner Titeldrucke zu Pseudonymen... 31

Nan yang min jen chi chuan 1513

Nanshin Nippon no daiissen ni tatsu shin Taiwan no jimbutsu 571

Narodna enciklopedija srpsko-hravatsko-slovenačka 2408

I Narratori 3776

Nash khudozhniki (zhivopistsy, skul'ptory, mozaichisty) 2454

Nashi dieiateli 1709

Nashi gosudarstvennye i obshchestvennye dieiateli 1735

Nashi pisatel'nitsy 3840

A National biography for India 1268

The National cyclopaedia of American biography 1979-1985

The National cyclopedia of the colored race 1986

National directory of teachers of speech 3429

National library of American biography 1951

National portrait gallery of
British musicians   3110

The National portrait gallery of
distinguished Americans
1949

National reference book on Canadian business personalities
502

The National register; pertinent
facts about colored Americans   1987

National register of scientific and
technical personnel in India
4595

The Native ministry of New Hampshire   4319

Naturalisti, medici e tecnici
trentini   4579

Nauka i nauchnye rabotniki SSSR
4606

A Naval biographical dictionary
(O'Byrne)   1167

Naval biography (Harding)   1149

La Nazione operante   1373

The Near and Middle East who's
who   1481

The Near East year book and who's
who   409

Nebraska blue book   2223

Nebraska writers   3406

Le Nécrologe des hommes célèbres
de France   817

Nécrologe des plus célèbres défenseurs et confesseurs de la
vérité du dix-septième...
siècle   4326-4329

Nécrologe liégeois pour 1852 (?)
[etc.]   448

Le Nécrologe universel de XIXe
siècle   206

Necrologías de varios contemporáneos distinguidos, especial-
mente cordobeses   1795

Necrologium aliquot utriusque sexus
Romano-Catholicorum   464

Nederlanders van het negentiende
eeuw   1554

Nederland's adelsboek   1563

Nederland's patriciaat   1564

De Nederlandse adel (historisch
gedeelte)   1565

Negro Catholic writers   3426

Negro year book   1988

Nekrolog; oder, Nachrichten von
dem Leben und den Schriften
der vornehmsten verstorbenen
teutschen Dichter   3689

Nekrolog auf das Jahr 1790 [-1800]
997-998

Nekrolog denkwürdiger Schweizer
aus dem achtzehnten Jahr-
hundert   1856

Nekrolog der Teutschen für das
neunzehnte Jahrhundert
997, 999

Nekrolog zu Kürschners Literatur-
Kalender   3655

Nekrologiske samlinger   666

Nekropol' Krymskogo poluostrova
1678

Nekropol' neskol'kikh mest Kavkaza   1679

Nelson's biographical dictionary
207

Neollēnikē filologia   3709-3710

Le Nepos francais   803

Neue deutsche Biographie   1000

Das Neue gelehrte Europa   244,
270, 685-686

Das Neue Musiklexikon   2996

Neue Nachrichten von jüngstverstorbenen Gelehrten   1010-
1011

Neue österreichische Biographie
(1815-1918)   394-395

Neue Schweizer Biographie   1860

Neuer Bildniskatalog   26

Neuer Nekrolog der Deutschen
1001-1002

Neues allgemeines deutsches Adels-
Lexicon   988

Neues allgemeines Künstler-Lexikon   2564

Neues allgemeines literarisch-
artistisches Lexicon   3379

Neues historisch-biographisch-
literarisches Handwörterbuch
60

Neues historisch-biographisches
Lexikon der Tonkünstler
2871-2872

Neues historisches Handlexikon...
bis zu Ende des Jahrs 1810   60

Neues Malerlexikon   2669

Neues Universal-Lexikon der Tonkunst   2771

Neuestes gelehrtes Berlin   3636,
3691

Neuestes gelehrtes Dresden   1041

Neuestes- und vollständiges Ton-
künstler- und Opern-Lexikon
2920

99 [i. e.] Neunundneunzig] Bonner
Köpfe   984

The New American biographic dictionary   1961

A New American biographical dictionary (Rogers)   2005

The New American law list   3973

A New and general biographical
dictionary   208

A New biographical dictionary
(Cooper)   104

A New biographical dictionary
(Jones)   169

A New biographical dictionary; or,
Pocket compendium   209

A New biographical dictionary of
3000 contemporary public
characters, British and foreign   210

The New book of modern composers   2850

New calendar of great men   147

A New catalogue of living English
authors   3519

The New Century classical handbook   211

The New Century cyclopedia of
names   212

The New Century handbook of English literature   3520

The New college encyclopedia of music   3112

The New dictionary of American history   1968

The New dramatic list   3212

A New ecclesiastical history; containing the lives and writings of ecclesiastical authors 4346

The New educator's library   3315

New encyclopedia of music and musicians   3019

New England life in the 18th century   2231

A New general biographical dictionary (Rose)   251

New Hampshire notables (1932) 2235

New Hampshire notables (1955) 2236

A New history of ecclesiastical writers   4356

The New Larned history for ready reference, reading and research   178

The New law list   3962

New Mexico desperados, A directory of   2241

The New pocket biographical dictionary   1961

The New Schaff-Herzog encyclopedia of religious knowledge 4483-4484

New standard encyclopedia of art 2523

The New twentieth century cyclopedia and dictionary   1989

The New universal biographical dictionary, and American remembrancer of departed merit   146

A New universal biography   238

The New yearbook of jazz   2835

The New York red book   2262

New York State men   2256

New York State's prominent and progressive men   2255

Newfoundland who's who (1952) 514

Die Niederländischen Zeichner des 17. Jahrhunderts   2443

Niederländisches Künstler-Lexikon   2670

Niedersächsische Familienkunde 1069

Nien ssŭ shih chuan mu yin tê 539

Nieuw biografiesch, anthologiesch en kritiesch woordenboek van Nederlandsche dichters 3489

Nieuw Nederlandsch biografisch woordenboek   1562

De Nieuw schouburg der Nederlandtsche kunstschilders en schilderessen   2508

Nihon bukka jimmei jisho   4273

Nihon gaka jiten   2610

Nihon jimmei jiten   1425

Nihon jinji roku   1433

Nihon kodai jimmei jiten   1434

Nihon shinshiroku   1435

The Nobel Prize-winners and the Nobel Foundation   188

Nobiliaire universel de France 840

Nobiliarchia medica   4165

Nobiliarchia trinitaria   4426

Nobiliario hispano-americano del siglo XVI   1505

The Nobilities of Europe   689

La Noblesse belge   449

Nomenclator literarius theologiae catholicae theologos exhibens aetate...   4397

Nomenclator philologorum   3344

Nominata do pessoal estatístico das nacões americanas 4679

Nordiskt lexikon för bokväsen 4032

Norfolk, Suffolk and Cambridge-shire   1206

Norges laeger (1800-1908)   4156

Norges laeger i det nittende aar-hundrede (1800-1886)   4155

Norges universitet, professorer, docenter, amanuenser   3279

Norsk anonym- og pseudonym-lexikon   1584

Norsk biografisk leksikon   1588

Norsk biografisk oppslagsliteratur 1581

Norsk forfatter-lexikon (1814-1856)   3802, 3804

Norsk forfatter lexikon (1814-1880)   3802, 3804

Norsk forfattere (1881-1920) 3805

Norsk lutherske prester i Amerika 4529

Norsk tidsskriftindex (1921-1930): Personalhistorie   1582-1583

Norske grafikere   2570

Norske kvinder   1589

North Carolina authors   3412

North Carolina manual   2266

North Carolina musicians   2999

Northamptonshire and Rutland clergy (from 1500)   4419

Northamptonshire biographical notices   1207

Northern India who's who   1281

Norwegian printmakers   2570

Nos auteurs et compositeurs dramatiques   3581

Nos contemporains; galerie colon-iale et diplomatique (France) 792

Nos contemporains. Portraits et biographies des personnalités belges...   450

Nos députés (France)   787

Nos sénateurs (France)   788

Notable Australians and Who is
    who in Australasia   377

Notable Boston authors   3404

Notable lawyers of the West   3974

Notable Londoners   1205

Notable men of central New York
    2261

Notable men of Chicago and their
    city   2106

Notable men of Illinois and their
    state   2147

Notable men of Tennessee (Alli-
    son)   2332

Notable men of Tennessee from
    1833 to 1875 (Temple)   2335

Notable men of the West   2364

Notable men of Washington [State]
    2358

Notable men of Wisconsin   2375

Notable names in medicine and
    surgery   4072

Notable New Yorkers (of 1896-
    1899)   2245

Notable New Yorkers (1942) [New
    York City]   2247

Notable personages of Polish
    ancestry   1633

Notable printers of Italy...   4007

Notable Welsh musicians (of today)
    2881

Notable Welshmen (1700-1900)
    1229

Notable women of affairs   219

Notable women of the Southwest
    2330

Notables of the Southwest   2331

Notables of the West   2365

Notas biográficas publicadas en la
    sección Efemérides america-
    nas de "La Nación"   355

Note book of the history of educa-
    tion   3258

Notes of a thousand men, and some
    things they did   203

Notice biographique sur les nou-
    veaux pairs de France   818

Notice des hommes les plus célè-
    bres de la Faculté de méde-
    cine en l'Université de Paris
    4079

Notice sur le doctorat és lettres
    3583-3584

Notices bio-bibliographiques sur
    quelques imprimeurs,
    librairies, correcteurs...
    4038

Notices biographiques & bibliogra-
    phiques concernant les mem-
    bres... [de l'Académie royale
    ... de Belgique]   424

Notices biographiques et bibliogra-
    phiques sur les Jésuites de l'
    ancienne mission de Chine 4459

Notices biographiques, littéraires
    et critiques sur les hommes
    du Calvados   872

Notices chronologiques sur les théologiens, jurisconsultes [etc.] de la Bretagne   870

Notices sur les principaux peintres de l'Espagne   2643

Noticias bio-bibliográficas de alumnos distinguidos del Colegio de San Pedro, San Pablo y San Ildefonso   1536

Noticias bio-bibliográficos de los Jesuitas expulsos de América (en 1767)   4430

Noticias de los arquitectos y arquitectura en España desde su restauración   2684

Notitia auctorum antiqua et media   3353

Notizie biografiche e bibliografiche degli scrittori del dialetto napolitano   3763

Notizie biografiche e bibliografiche degli scrittori napoletani fioriti nel secoli XVII   3766

Notizie biografiche e letterarie degli scrittori dello Stato Estense   3769, 3781

Notizie de' professori del disegno da Cimabue   2430-2431

Notizie degli scrittori bolognesi (Fantuzzi)   3750

Notizie degli scrittori bolognesi (Orlandi)   3770

Notizie dei professori del disegno in Liguria   2424

Notizie delle vite ed opere scritte da' letterati del Friuli   3762

Notizie historico-critiche intorno la vita... degli scrittori veneziani   3757

Notizie intorno alla vita e alle opere de' pittori, scultori e intagliatori... di Bassano   2732

Notizie istorico-critiche intorno la vita e le opere degli scrittori viniziani   3733

Notizie istoriche de' comici italiani   3137

Notizie istoriche degli Arcadi morti   1368

Notizie istoriche intorno a' medici scrittori milanesi   4116

Notizie letterarie ed istoriche intorno agli uomini illustri della Accademia fiorentina   1369

Nouveau dictionnaire biographique et critique des architectes français   2677

Nouveau dictionnaire de musique illustré, elementaire, théorique, historique, artistique, professionel et complet   3075

Nouveau dictionnaire des biographies françaises et étrangères   174

Nouveau dictionnaire des ouvrages anonymes et pseudonymes   707

Nouveau dictionnaire historique des députés à l'Assemblée nationale   819

Nouveau dictionnaire historique et critique pour servir de supplement... au Dictionnaire historique et critique de Mr. Pierre Bayle 100

Nouveau dictionnaire historique-portatif 99

Nouveau manuel complète du facteur d'orgues 3000

Nouveau nécrologe français 3556

Nouvelle bibliothèque des auteurs ecclésiastiques 4356-4357

Nouvelle biographie des députés 741

Nouvelle biographie générale depuis les temps les plus reculés jusqu'à nos jours 220

Nouvelle biographie industrielle, commerciale, géographique... de la France 716

Nouvelle biographie normande 921-922

Nouvelle biographie pittoresque des députés de la Chambre septennale 800

Nouvelle biographie suisse 1860

Nova memoria Hungarorum et provincialium scriptis editis notorum 3717

Nova Scotia authors and their works 3513

Nový slovník československých výtvarných umelcü 2636-37

Nürnbergisches Gelehrten-Lexicon 1058-1059

Nürnbergisches Pfarrerbuch 4492

Nueva epanortosis al Diccionario de anónimos y seudónimos de J. T. Medina 1500

Nuevo diccionario geográfico histórico de la República Argentina 349

Nuevos datos para las biografías de cien escritores de los siglos XVI y XVII 3886

Nugae chirurgicae 4212

Nung rōi čhaofā lae senābǫdī 1872

Nuova biografia svizzera 1860

Nuovo dizionario musicale Curci 2782

Nyt dansk adelslexikon 671

Nyt dansk kunstnerlexikon 2656

O

Obituary notices of Fellows [of the Royal Society of London] 4611

Obituary prior to 1800 (as far as relates to England, Scotland and Ireland) 1165

Obituary record of graduates of Yale University 312, 1929

La Obra impresa de los intelectuales españoles en América 3855

Obzor zhizni i trudov pokoĭnych russkikh pisateleĭ 3828

Odbor za izdanje knjige 'Zaslužni i znameniti Hrvati 2409

Österreich Lexikon   396

Österreicher aus sudetendeutschen
    Stamme   399

Österreicher der Gegenwart
    397

Oesterreichische Biographien
    (Pezzl)   400

Österreichische Geschichtswissen-
    schaft der Gegenwart in
    Selbstdarstellungen   4758

Der Österreichische National- und
    Bundesrat   386

Österreichischer Plutarch   387

Österreichisches biographisches
    Lexikon (1815-1950)
    398

Osterreichisches biographisches
    Lexikon (Bermann)   382

Officers of the Army and Navy
    (Regular) who served in the
    Civil War   1997

Officers of the Army and Navy
    (Regular and Volunteer) who
    served in the Civil War
    1991

Officers of the Army and Navy
    (Volunteer) who served in the
    Civil War   1998

Official Army and Air Force reg-
    ister   2023-2024

Official Army National Guard
    register   2037

Official Army register (U. S.
    Army)   2023

Official baronetage of England
    1135

Official Congressional directory
    2030

The Official encyclopedia of base-
    ball   3235

Official genealogical directory [of
    the Moslem nobility]   1315

Official directory, American illus-
    trators and advertising artists
    2571

Official National Guard register
    (Army)   2037

The Official theatrical world of
    colored artists   3177

The Official who's who among stu-
    dents in American universities
    and colleges   2052

The Official who's who in Michigan
    2204

Ohio authors and their books
    3401

Ohio statesmen and hundred year
    book   2273

Ohole-Shem   4562

Oklahoma leaders   2282

Oklahoma writers   3417

Oklahomans and their state   2284

Old clocks and watches and their
    makers   2706

Old pewter   2707

Old Scottish clockmakers (from
    1453 to 1850)   2728

140 Jewish marshals, generals & admirals 1472

The 100 most important people in the world today 246

One hundred twenty-three biographies of deceased faculty members, Northeast State Teachers College (1867-1962) 3309

One of a thousand 2189

One thousand five hundred (1500) modern Chinese novels & plays 597

1000 heroes (Mee) 193

Onomasticon; repertorio biobibliografico degli scrittori italiani 1335

Onomasticon literarium 254

Onze musici, portretten en biografieën 3002

Opera biographies 2815

Opere e operisti (dizionario lirico, 1541-1902) 2813

Opyt istoricheskogo slovar′ o rossiiskikh pisateliakh 3836

Opyt obozrieniia zhizni sanovnikov, upravliavshikh inostrannymi dielami v Rossii 1738

Opty slovaria psevdonimov russkikh pisatelei 1663

Or ha-Hayyim 4566

Orang Indonesia jang terkemoeka di Djawa 1298

Orang-orang Tionghoa jang terkemoeka di Java (Who's who) 1299

Orbis geographicus 4747

Ordre chronologique des deuils de cour 820

An Oriental biographical dictionary 363

Ostdeutsche Biographien 1012

Our actors and actresses 3180

Our contemporary composers 2900

Our hymns: their authors and origin 2968

Outstanding young men of America 1993

The Oxford classical dictionary 225

The Oxford companion to American literature 3405

The Oxford companion to classical literature 3465

The Oxford companion to English literature 3504

The Oxford companion to French literature 3578

The Oxford companion to music 3059

The Oxford companion to the theatre 3164

Oxford dictionary of opera 3039

The Oxford dictionary of the Christian church 4452

The Oxford encyclopaedia of Canadian history   500

Oxford theology and theologians (c. A. D. 1282-1302)   4415

Ozar ha-psudonimim   1448

P

PR blue book and supplement to the international Who's who in public relations   4689

Pacific islands year book and who's who   1591

Painters and their works   2534

Painters, sculptors, architects, engravers, and their works 2653

Pakistan trade directory and who's who   1595

The Pakistan year book & who's who   1596

Palestine personalia   1481

Pamiat′ o chlenakh Voennago Sovieta   1748

Pamiatnik bortsam proletarskoi revoliutsii   1697

The Pan book of great composers 2902

Panorama biografico degli italiani d'oggi   1378

Pan-Pacific who's who   226

El Panteón de San Fernando y el futuro panteón nacional 1527

El Panteón universal   56

Pantheon berühmter deutscher Dichter   3663

Panthéon biographique; revue mensuelle, historique et nécrologique   227

Panthéon biographique universelle 227

Le Panthéon canadien   497

Pantheon denkwürdiger Wunderthaten, volksthümlicher Heroen und furchtbarer Empörer des oesterreichischen Gesammt-Reiches   402

Pantheon der Literaten und Künstler Bambergs   3637

Pantheon der Tonkünstler   3026

Le Panthéon des comediens   3182

Le Panthéon des musiciens   3058

Pantheon deutscher jetzt lebender Dichter   3682

Pantheon maranhense   478

Pantheon militaire   441

Paraguayans of to-day   1599

Les Parallèles de nos jours, biographie des législateurs de la République   821

Paris-notabilités   926

Le Parlement belge (1930)   451

Le Parlement belge (1938)   452

Le Parlement belge (en 1900-1902) 444

Les Parlementaires français 837, 842

TITLE INDEX

The Parliamentary companion
1132

Parliamentary handbook and record
of elections (Australia)
373

Parliamentary profiles   1173

El Parnaso español pintoresco
laureado   2576

Parnaso uruguayo (1905-1922)
3900

Le Parnasse médical français
4108

Parnassus Euganeus; sive, De
scriptoribus ac literatis hujus
aevi claris   277

Parnassus Euganeus; sive, Museum
clariss. virorum, et antiquor.
simulacris exornatum   278

Patrology   4293

Pazdírkův hudební slovník naučný
3012

Pazhi za 185 (i. e. sto vosem´desiat
piat) liet   1686

Pediatric directory   4067

The Peerage, baroretage and
knightage of Great Britain and
Ireland   1133

Pei chuan chi   549

Pei chuan chi pu   592

Le Peintre graveur   2433

Les Peintres primitifs de Provence
2640

Penguin dictionary of saints   4287

Pennsylvania who's who   2301

A Penny universal biography
(Universal biography)   233

People; a volume of the good, bad,
great & eccentric   142

People of the period   1170

The People's biographical dictionary   63

Pequena bibliografia crítica da
literatura brasileira   3813

Perfiles venezolanos   2391

Pergamon dictionary of musicians
& music   2905

Persian literature; a bio-bibliographical survey   3807

Personalhistorisk tidsskrift   667

Personalidades cubanas   640

Personalidades de la Argentina
353

Personnalités d'aujourd'hui   234

Personnalités du Cambodge   493

Persoonlijkheden in het Koninkrijk
der Nederlanden in woord en
beeld   1567

Peruvians of to-day   1607

Pervaia Gosudarstvennaia Duma
1720

Peterburgskii nekropol´   1712

Le Petit almanach de nos grands
hommes   3591

Petit dictionnaire biographique 101

Petit dictionnaire des grands hommes de la Révolution   836

Petit dictionnaire ministeriel   813

Petite bibliographie biographico-romancière   3587

Petite biographie conventionnelle; ou, Tableau moral et raisonné des 749 députés...   831

Petite biographie des Conventionnels   822

Petite biographie des députés   830

Petite biographie des hommes illustres de la Charente-Inférieure   875

Petite biographie des pairs   830

Petite biographie nationale des contemporains   845

Petite encyclopédie musicale   2776

La Petite galerie dramatique   3167

Pewter in America   2721

Pfarrerbuch der Reichsstädte Dinkelsbühl, Schweinfurt, Weissenburg i. Bay. und Windsheim   4493

Les Pharmaciens militaires français   4074

The Philadelphia Seminary biographical record (1864-1923)   4460

The Philippine Commonwealth handbook   1613

Philippine medical directory and the allied professions   4186

Philippines who's who   1617

Philo-Lexikon; Handbuch des jüdischen Wissens   1470

Philologisches Schriftsteller-Lexikon   3467

Philosophen-Lexikon (Eisler)   4236, 4248

Philosophen-Lexikon; Handwörterbuch der Philosophie nach Personen   4248

Photographs of eminent medical men of all countries   4075

Physic and physicians   4225

Physicians and surgeons of America   4213

Physicians of the Mayo Clinic and the Mayo Foundation   4167

The Piano: its history, makers, players and music   3224

Piccolo dizionario biografico dei musicisti... Cagliari   3003

Piccolo dizionario dei contemporanei italiani   1359

Il Piccolo dizionario musicale per tutti   3097

Il Piccolo Fétis   2853

Piccolo lessico del musicista   2865

Pictured biographies   216

The Picturegoer's who's who and encyclopaedia of the screen today   3183

Piemontesi illustri   1401

Pien chiang jen wu chih   578

Pierre Key's musical who's who
3017

Pinacotheca scriptorum nostra
aetate literis illustrium
3610

Pionieri svizzeri della scienza
4589

Pionniers suisses de la science
4589

Pisateli Kazakhstana   3933

Pisateli Komi ASSR   3548

Pisateli Sovetskogo Azerbaĭdzhana
3934

Pisateli Sovetskogo Kirgizstana
3936

Pisateli Sovetskogo Uzbekistana
3935

Pisateli Sovetskoĭ Belorussii
3838

Pisateli Sovetskoĭ Burîatii   3801

Pisateli Sovetskoĭ Éstonii (1950)
3549

Pisateli Sovetskoĭ Estonii
(Remmelgas)   3551

Pisateli Sovetskoĭ Latvii   3796

Pisateli Sovetskoĭ Mordovii
3547

Pisateli Sovetskoĭ Ukrainy   3937

Pisateli sovremennoĭ epokhi
3833

Pisateli Udmurtii   3550

Pittori e miniatori nell'Umbria
2507

I Pittori italiani dell'Ottocento
2465

La Pluma y la espada   261

La Plutarque des jeunes demoi-
selles   136

Plutarque des Pays-Bas   425

Le Plutarque français   846

La Plutarque provencal   930

A Pocket manual for the use of
members of the General Assembly [of North Carolina]
2266

Pocket music dictionary   2832

Podreczna encyklopedia muzyki
3031

Podrobnyĭ slovar´ russkikh graverov XVI-XIX vv.   2606

Podrobnyĭ slovar´ russkikh gravirovannykh portretov   1725

Die Poesie und die Poeten in
Österreich (im Jahr 1836) 3640

Poetas do Brasil   3817

Poetas españoles que vivieron en
América   3875

I Poeti d'Italia en trenta secoli
3741-3742

I Poeti italiani dall'antichità ad
oggi   3741

The Poetical register   3507

The Poets of Ireland   3523

Le Poinçon de Paris   2569

Political Africa; a who's who of
personalities and parties
318

Political Britain   1139

Political works of concealed authorship in the United States (1789-
1810)   1892

Politicheskaia katorga i ssylka
1745

Polski słownik biograficzny   1636

Poltavtsy   1719

Pomenik znamenitih ljudi u srpskog
naroda novijega doba   2404-
2405

Pommersche Lebens- und Landes-
bilder   1062

Poor's Register of directors and
executives, United States and
Canada   4711-4713

Popular American composers
2851

Popular biography, by Peter
Parley [pseud.]   138

Porträts der UdSSR-Prominenz
1721-1722

Portrait and biographical record
of Arizona   2078

Portrait and biographical record
of Denver and vicinity, Colorado   2125

Portrait and biographical record
of northern Michigan   2205

Portrait and biographical record
of Oklahoma   2285

Portrait and biographical record
of the State of Colorado   2111

Portrait and biographical record
of western Oregon   2292

Portrait catalog [of the New York
Academy of Medicine]   4054

The Portrait gallery of distinguished poets, philosophers, statesmen, divines, painters...
239

The portrait gallery of eminent
lawyers   3976

The Portrait gallery of the war,
civil, military, and naval
1973

A Portrait gallery, with biographical sketches of prominent Freemasons throughout the United
States   1994

The Portrait monthly: containing
sketches of departed heroes
1995

Portraits des hommes illustres de
la Suisse   1858

Portraits des hommes illustres des
dix-septième et dix-huitième
siècles   823

Portraits des personnages célèbres
de la Révolution   827

Portraits et silhouettes   438

Portraits of Dutch painters and
other artists of the Low
Countries   2521

Portraits of eminent Americans
now living   1966

Portraits of eminent mathematicians   4669

Portraits of prominent Saint Louisans (in 1916)   2314

Portraits of the British poets 3527

Portraits of Yorkshire worthies 1240

Portraits russes des XVIIIe et XIXe siècles   1713

Portretnaiă galereiă russkikh dieĭatelei   1706

Portretten van nederlandse beeldende kunstenaars   2521

Portuguezes illustres   1644

Pour le mérite-Flieger   1025

Pravitel' stvuĭushchu senat 1700

Précis de biographie belge   436

Le Premier siècle de l'Institut de France   773

Les Premiers européens   688

Près de 700 biographies d'artistes belges   2529

Préservatif contre la 'Biographie nouvelle des contemporains' 772

Los Presidentes de la H. Cámara de Diputados del Perú   1610

Presidentes del Senado, Comisiones directivas y señores senadores 1829-1960 (Peru)   1609

Presidents and deans of American colleges and universities 3305

Presidents and professors in American colleges and universities   3318

Presidents of American colleges and universities   3305

Press reference library (Southwest edition)   2331

Press reference library (Western edition)   2365

Preussisher Todes-Tempel 1065

Primer diccionario biográfico profesional de ingenieros agrónomos en Colombia   4800

Principal poets of the world   3528

Principal women of America 2001

4018

Les Prisonniers d'État pendant la Révolution   838

Próceres de la independencia: Ecuador   676

Próceres de Santiago de Cuba 637

Professeurs, historiens & magistrats suisses   1867

Professional medical register [of the International Refugee Organization]   4146

Professoren der Universität Basel aus fünf Jahrhunderten 3311

Professoren und Dozenten der Christian-Albrechts-Universität zu Kiel (1665-1954) 3282

I Professori dell'Università di Parma attraverso i secoli 3307

Profiles of members of the House of Representatives [Japan] (1 Sept. 1961) 1444

Profiles of Negro womanhood 1928

Profiles of notable Filipinos in the U.S.A. 1990

Profili bio-bibliografici di chimici italiani sec. XV-sec. XIX 4662

Profili bio-bibliografici di medici e naturalisti celebri italiani 4101

Profils critiques et biographiques de 750 représentants du peuple à l'Assemblée législative 825

Profils critiques et biographiques des 900 représentants du peuple 812

Profils critiques et biographiques des sénateurs, conseillers d'État et députés 810

Progressive men of northern Ohio 2278

Progressive men of southern Idaho 2140

The Progressive men of the Commonwealth of Pennsylvania 2295

Progressive men of the State of Montana 2221

Progressive men of the State of Wyoming 2379

Progressive men of western Colorado 2112

Projet de dictionnaire des musicians wallons 2950

Prominent Americans (of 1912-) 1952

Prominent Americans of Swiss origin 2018

Prominent and progressive Americans 1946

Prominent and progressive Pennsylvanians of the nineteenth century 2304

Prominent Jews of America 2002

Prominent men of Canada 515

The Prominent men of Mexico 1538-1539

Prosistas y poetas de América moderna 3907

Prosopographia (Du Verdier) 118

Prosopographia Attica 1243

Prosopographiae heroum atque illustrium virorum totius Germaniae 1004-1005

Prosopographia Imperii Romani saec. I. II. III. 1654

Het Protestantsche Vaderland 4305

Provencaux: historiens, philosophes, économistes... 931

La Prusse littéraire sous Frédéric II 3615

Przewodnik cmentarny Krakowa 1630

Pseudonimia 1339

Pseudônimos brasileiros 473

Els Pseudònims usats a Catalunya 1763

Pseudonymes canadiens 495

The Psychological register 4249

Psykologisk-pedagogisk uppslagsbok 4250-4251

Public characters 1171

Publicistes et essayistes chrétiennes de Belgique 3449

The Punjab chiefs 1594

Purpura docta 4358

Putevoditel' po russkoi literature XIX veka 3841

Pys'mennyky Radians'koi Ukrainy 3937

Q

Quadro biografico de' più distinti medici e chirurgi lucchesi 4174

Quaker necrology 1886

Quaker records 1092

The Quarterly biographical magazine 241

Quem é alguém (Who's who in Portugal) 1646

Quem é quem no Brasil 481

Qui est-ce? 828

Qui êtes-vous? 829

Qui sont les leaders congolais? 634

Quien es quien (Uruguay) 2383

Quién es quién en Bolivia? 471

Quién es quién en Ciudad Trujillo 675

Quien es quien en Colombia 632

Quién es quién en el Paraguay? 1600

Quien es quien en la Argentina 354

Quien es quien en la Ciudad de México y Distrito Federal 1543

Quien es quien en la nomenclatura de la ciudad de México 1535

Quién es quién en Panamá 1597

Quien es quien en Puerto Rico 1652

Quien es quien en Venezuela, Panamá, Ecuador, Colombia 1506

R

R. K. "Wie ist dat?" 1568

R. U. S.; a biographical register of rural leadership in the United States and Canada 4801

R. U. S. Rural uplook service... 4801

Radio and television who's who 3185

Radio's 100 men of science
4787

Rajasthan year-book & who's who
1282

Rand McNally bankers' directory
... 4714

Rand McNally international bankers directory 4714

The Rank and talent of our time
114

The Reader's companion to world
literature 3380

Reader's dictionary of authors
3325

The Reader's encyclopedia 3328

The Reader's encyclopedia of American literature 3424

Real-Encyclopädie der classischen
Altertumswissenschaft 228-31

The Realm of tones 2861

Recherches sur la vie... de
quelques peintres provinciaux
de l'ancienne France 2461

Recipients of fellowships and
grants, 1930-1962 [from the
American Council of Learned
Societies] 3255

Recollections and sketches of notable lawyers and public men
of early Iowa 3985

The Record of old Westminsters
1175-1176

The Records of living officers of
the U.S. Navy and Marine
Corps 1945

Records of living officers of the
United States Army 1999

Recueil des archives biographiques
permanentes du monde arabe
1324

Reeves' dictionary of musicians
2826

Reference book; biographical reference data... [Canada] 502

A Reference index to twelve thousand Spanish-American authors 1495

Regie: Idee und Praxis moderner
Theaterarbeit 3190

Register of alumni, graduates and
former naval cadets and midshipmen [U.S. Naval Academy]
2038

Register of commissioned and
warrant officers of the United
States Naval Reserve 2026

Register of commissioned and
warrant officers of the United
States Navy and Marine Corps
2027

Register of graduates and former
cadets, United States Military
Academy 1045

Register of Rhodes Scholars 3301

Register of the Army of the United
States 2023

Register of the commissioned and
warrant officers and cadets
of the United States Coast
Guard 2028

The Register of veterinary surgeons 4192

Register til den norske tidskrifter 1582

Registered psychologists [of New York State] 4245

Das Reich der Töne 2851

Reichshandbuch der deutschen Gesellschaft 1007

Reichssänger 3064

Relação alphabetica dos anatomicos, physiologistas, histologistas, embriologistas, medicos e cirurgiões 4203

Relaciones de méritos y servicios de funcionarios del reino de Chile 525

Les Relieurs français 4041

Die Religion in Geschichte und Gegenwart 4470

Religious leaders of America 4471

Reminiscences of public men in Alabama 2074

Répertoire abrégé d'iconographie 11

Répertoire bio-bibliographique, 1954 (Société des écrivains canadiens) 3593

Répertoire biographique de l'épiscopat constitutionnel (1791-1802) 4462

Le Répertoire biographique des francs-maçons russes 1670

Répertoire biographique & bibliographique des artistes du XVIIIe siècle français 2483

Répertoire de l'histoire de la Révolution française (Walter) 848

Répertoire des estampes japonaises 2470

Répertoire des médiévistes européens 4752

Répertoire des scientifiques français 4588

Répertoire des sources historiques du moyen âge 102

Répertoire général de bio-bibliographie bretonne 868

Répertoire permanent des intellectuels 768

Répertoire universel, historique, biographique des femmes célèbres 240

Repertori de l'antiga literatura catalana 3455

Repertorio di tutti i professori antichi e moderni... di Bologna 3292

Repertorium über die in Zeit- und Sammelschriften der Jahre 1812-1890 enthaltenen Aufsätze... schweizergeschichtliche Inhaltes 1842

Repertorium über die in Zeit- und Sammelschriften der Jahre 1891-1900 enthaltenen Aufsatze... schweizergeschichtlichen Inhaltes 1841

The Representative authors of Maryland 3428

Representative men and old families of Rhode Island 2312

Representative men and old families of southeastern Massachusetts   2190

Representative men of Colorado in the nineteenth century   2113

Representative men of Connecticut (1861-1894)   2119

Representative men of Maine   2173

Representative men of Massachusetts (1890-1900)   2191

The Representative men of Porto Rico   1649

Representative men of the South   2326

Republicans of New York (1906)   2263

Reseña histórica en forma de diccionario de las imprentas ... en Valencia   4042

Retratos de los españoles ilustres   1784

Revue de la musique dramatique en France   2809-2810

Revue générale biographique et littéraire   71

Rheinische Lebensbilder   1066

Rhestyr, gyda nodiadau byrion o enwogion Cymreig (o 1700 i 1900)   1225

Rhode Island music and musicians   2952

Ricerche sulla liuteria e violineria modenese antica e moderna   3098

Riemann Musik Lexikon: Personenteil   3034

Riga literata   414

Rigaer Theater- und Tonkünstler-Lexikon   3189

Rigasche Biographieen   411

Ring the bells; a dictionary of Australian federal politics   379

Il Risorgimento italiano   1348

River Plate personalities   347

Rodoslovnaiã kniga kniãzeĭ i dvoriãn rossiiskikh i vyiẽzzhikh   1724

Roll of graduates of the University of Aberdeen   1209, 1215

The Roll of honor; a biographical record of... His Majesty's naval and military forces...   1174

The Roll of honor for women   250

Roll of the graduates of the University of Aberdeen   1209, 1215

A Roll of the graduates of the University of Glasgow   1213

Roll of the Indian Medical Service   4117

The Roll of the Royal College of Physicians of London   4196

Le Roman régionaliste dans les Iles Britanniques   3512

A Romanized index to the surnames in the Chinese biographical dictionary Chung-kuo
jen-ming ta tz'u-tien   537

Rome's recruits   1143

Rosenstock's press reference
library   1618

Roster of native sons (and daughters) [of upstate New York]
2264

The Royal Academy of Arts; a complete dictionary of contributors   2516

Rubber red book   4802

Ruchnoĭ muzykal′nyĭ slovar′
2869

Rukopisnaiā knizhnost′ drevnerusskikh bibliotek   4031

The Ruling princes, chiefs and
leading personages in the
Western India States Agency
1286

Rural uplook service; a preliminary attempt to register the
rural leadership in the United
States and Canada   4801

Russian composers and musicians   3108

The Russian Revolution and who's
who in Russia   1723

Russian writers; a bio-bibliographical dictionary   3845

Russische Günstlinge   1692

Russkaiā literatura XX vieka
(1890-1910)   3851

Russkaiā literatura v biografiiākh
i obraztsakh   3834

Russkaiā portretnaiā gallereiā.
Sobranie portretov...   1729

Russkaiā zhenshchiny novago
vremeni   1707

Russkie biograficheskie i biobibliograficheskie slovari   1659

Russkie botaniki   4645

Russkie byvshie dieiāteli   1709

Russkie deiāteleĭ v portretakh
1733

Russkie gravery i ikh proizved-
eniiā   2607

Russkie liūdi; zhizneopisaniiā
sootechestvennikov...   4690

Russkie moreplavateli   4748

Russkie pisateli v portretakh biografiiākh i obraztsakh   3837

Russkie poety za sto let   3843

Russkie poliārnye morekhody iz
promyshlennykh, torgovykh
i sluzhilykh liūdeĭ XVII-XIX
vv.   4751

Russkie portrety XVIII. i XIX.
stolietii   1713

Russkie sovetskie pisateli-
prozaiki   3830

Russkie sovremennye dieiāteli
1709

Russkie vrachi pisateli   4229

Russkiĭ biograficheskiĭ slovar′
1730-1731

Russkiĭ nekropol' v chuzhikh
kraiakh   1714

Russkiĭ nekropol' za granitseĭ
1680

Russkiĭ provintsial'nyĭ nekropol'
1715

S

SBZ-Biographie   981, 1015

Sächsisches Schriftsteller-Lexikon
3631

Saeculi XVIII. bibliotheca ecclesiastica authorumque notitiae
biographicae   46

Saggio della biblioteca tirolese
3780

Saggio di rettifiche ed aggiunte al
supplemento Fétis   3045

Saggio di un dizionario bio-bibliografico italiano   1347

Saikin Shina yōjin den   574

Saint Dominic's family   4352

The St. Louis book authors
3402

The Saints; a concise biographical
dictionary   4478

Saints and festivals of the Christian Church   4311

Saints and their attributes   4474

Saishin Shina kanshin roku   600

Samlerens kunstnerleksikon
2609

Samlinger til en beskrivende catalog over portraiter of Danske,
Norske og Holsterne   670

Sammelkatalog der biographischen
und literarkritischen Werke zu
englischen Schriftsteller des
19. und 20. Jahrhunderts
3508

Sammlung bernischer Biographien
1852

Sankei Nihon shinshi nenkan
1439

Saone-et-Loire. Dictionnaire,
annuaire et album   935

es-Saqâ'iq en-no'mânijje   1874,
1878

Sarawak who's who   1750

Sar-obair nam bard gaelach
3598

Les Savants illustres de la France
4601

Sbornik biografii kavalergardov
1717

Sbornik biografii vracheĭ vypuska
1881 goda Imp. Mediko-khir-
urgicheskoĭ akademii   4161

Schaff-Herzog encyclopedia
4482-4484

Die Schaffhausen Schriftsteller
von der Reformation   3926

Schauplatz der masquirten und
demasquirten Gelehrten   32

Schediasma litterarium de scriptoribus, qui historiam politico-
ecclesiasticam Rossiae scriptis illustrarunt   4766

Schlesiens Dichter im 19ten Jahrhunderte   3695

Die Schlesische Dichtung im 20.
Jahrhundert   3666

Schlesische Jubelpriester   4405

Schlesische Landsleute   1071

Schlesische Lebensbilder   1073

Schlesisches Schriftstellerlexikon
3671

Schlesisches Tonkünstler-Lexikon
2928

Schleswig-holsteinische Musiker
2858

School calendar, 1824-1914; a who's
who among teachers in the
Norwegian Lutheran synods of
America   3300

Schriftsteller der Deutschen Demokratischen Republik und ihre
Werke   3621

Die Schriftsteller der noch bestehenden Augustinerchorher-
renstifte Österreichs   4325

Schriftsteller-Lexikon, oder bio-
graphisch-literärische Denk-
Blätter der Siebenburger
Deutschen   3700-3701

Die Schriftsteller und die um Wissenschaft und Kunst verdienter
Mitglieder des Benediktinerordens im heutigen Königreiche
Bayern   4513-4514

Die Schüler von Ulrich Zasius
1023

Schweizer biographisches Archiv
1854

Schweizer Jugendschriftsteller
der Gegenwart   3925

Schweizer Musikbuch   3063

Schweizer Musiker-Lexikon (1964)
3066

Schweizer Schriftsteller der
Gegenwart   3928

Schweizerische Ehrenhalle   1865

Schweizerische Portrait-Gallerie
1862

Schweizerischer Litteratur-Kalender (auf das Jahr 1893)
3929

Schweizerisches Künstler-Lexikon
2614

Schweizerisches Schriftsteller-
Lexikon   3930

Schweizerisches Zeitgenossen-
Lexikon   1863

La Science arabe et son rôle dans
l'évolution scientifique mon-
diale   4603

Sci-en-tech register and classified products listing   4804

Scientific institutions and scientists in Latin America   4618

Scientific institutions and scientists in Pakistan   4619

Gli Scienzati italiani dall'inizio
del medio evo al nostri giorni
4604

The Scots peerage   1218

Scottish biographies (1938)   1220

Scottish engravers   2455

Scottish medicine   4113

The Scottish nation   1210

Scriptores Ordinis Minorum...
     provinciae S. Antonii
     Venetiarum   4283

Scriptores Ordinis Praedicatorum
     recensiti   4466

Scriptores Ordinis S. Benedicti
     qui 1750-1880 fuerunt in Im-
     perio Austriaco-Hungarico
     4299

Scriptores piarum scholarum
     liberaliumque artium magistri
     4395

Scriptores Provinciae Austriacae
     Societatis Jesu   4504

Scriptorum ecclesiasticorum his-
     toria literaria   4324

Scriptuors svizzers da noss dis
     3928

Gli Scrittori abruzzesi dai più re-
     moti tempi sino ad oggi
     3778

Scrittori barnabiti   4306

Gli Scrittori calabresi   3734

Scrittori cattolici italiani viventi
     3744

Gli Scrittori d'Italia   3764

Li Scrittori della Liguria   3777

Scrittori della Svizzera italiana
     3931

Gli Scrittori delle Calabrie   3754

Scrittori e idee   3753

Scrittori ed artisti pugliesi
     2644-2645

Scrittori ed artisti trentini   3735

Gli Scrittori francescani di Reggio
     nell'Emilia   4463

Gli Scrittori friulano-austriaci
     3748

Gli Scrittori Liguri   3759

Scrittori piemontesi, savoiardi
     ...   3749

Scrittori svizzeri d'oggi   3928

Gli Scrittori vicentini dei secoli
     decimottavo e decimonono
     3775

Sefer Doroth ha-aharonim   1452

Sefer ha-ishim, leksikon Erets-
     Yisraeli   1474

Sefer zikaron   3795

Seiyo shiso-ka jiten   4257

Sekai jimmei hyakka jiten   53

Sekai jimmei jiten (Ōrui)   224

Sekai jimmei jiten, Seiyô-hen
     262

Sekai jimmei jiten, Tôyô-hen   365

A Selected bio-bibliography: Min-
     nesota authors   3421

A Selected who's who in Vichy,
     France   847

Semblanzas, figuras políticas, in-
     dustriales, comerciantes y
     profesionales de... Panamá
     1598

Semblanzas de los 340 diputados á
Córtes... 1769

Semi-Kürschner 1477

Semmonbetsu daigaku kenkyūsha
daimoku sōran 3299

Le Sénat belge (en 1894-1898)
461

Il Senato fiorentino 1391

Sepher zykaron 3795

Serie de' senatori fiorentini
1391

Serie di rittratti d'uomini illustri
toscani 1413

Series episcoporum Ecclesiae
Catholicae 4375-4376

A Series of original portraits and
caricature etchings 1216

Servidores beneméritos de la
patria 356

Sessions 1838-1839 (French Chamber of Deputies) 752

Seudónimos, anagramas, iniciales,
etc., de autores mexicanos y
extranjeros 1520

Seudónimos dominicanos 674

Sevilla intellectual 3862

Shang yu lu t'ung pien 550

Sharp and Alleman Company's
Lawyers and bankers directory 3964

Shem ha-gedolim ha-shalem
1449

Shimpen jimmei jiten 276

Shin Taiwan no jimbutsu 571

Shina jimmei jisho (1904) 598

Shina jimmei jisho (1926) 599

Shina jinshiroku 596

Shina mondai jiten 601

Shinsen daijimmei jiten 106

"Shipping world" year book
4805

Shiso jimmei jiten 4254

A Short biographical dictionary of
English literature 3499,
3502

A Short biographical dictionary of
foreign literature 3383

Short biographical sketches of eminent Negro men and women
87

Short biographies of the worthies
of Worcestershire 1238

Shoseki nenkan 3788

Sibirskii literaturnyi kalendar'
3853

Sibley's Harvard graduates 2011

Les Siècles littéraires de la
France 3564

Silhouettes contemporaines (Vibert) 292

Silhouette des acteurs, actrices...
de Paris... 3134

Silk al-durar fi a'yān al-qarn al-
thāni 'ashar 1327

Singers and songs of the church
2969

Skånska nationen före afdelningarnes tid 1826

Sketches of men of mark 2015

Sketches of men of progress 2016

Sketches of prominent Tennesseans 2334

Sketches of representative men, North and South 2003

Sketches of successful New Hampshire men 2237

Sketches of the bench and bar of Tennessee 3947

Sketches of the English glee composers 2762

Sketches of the lives and work of the honorary medical staff of the Manchester Infirmary ... (1752 to 1830) 4093-4094

Sketches of Washingtonians [State of Washington] 2359

Skladatele dneška 2868

Slaegthaandbogen 662

Slavonic encyclopedia 1758

Slavonic personalities (past and present) 1759

Slovar' chlenov [Obshchestva liubitelei rossiiskoi slovesnosti] 3297

Slovar' dostopamiatnykh liudei Russkoi zemli 1673-1674

Slovar' istoricheskii o byvshikh v Rossii pisateliakh dukhovnago china greko-rossiiskoi tserkvi 1737, 4377

Slovar' kompozitorov i muzykal'-nykh deiatelei v Rossii 2945

Slovar' medal'erov i drugikh lits ... 2717

Slovar' Moskovskikh masterov zolotogo, serebrianogo i almaznogo dela XVII veka 2731

Slovar' patriarshikh ikonopistsev 2639

Slovar' pisatelei drevnego perioda russkoi literatury 3819

Slovar' pisatelei srednego i novogo periodov russkoi literatury 3820

Slovar' psevdonimov russkikh pisatelei, uchenykh i obshchestvennykh deiatelei 1664

Slovar' russkikh gravirovannykh portretov 1726

Slovar' russkikh khudozhnikov s drevnieishikh vremen do nashikh dnei 2619

Slovar' russkikh litografirovannykh portretov 1665

Slovar' russkikh svietskikh pisatelei sootechestvennikov i chuzhestrantsev, pisavshikh v Rossii 3824

Slovar' sibirskikh pisatelei, poetov i uchenykh 3847

Slovenski biografski leksikon 2406

Slovník českých spisovatelů beletristů (1945-1956) 3474

Slovník pseudonymů a kryptonymů v československé literatuře 644

Slovník slovenských pseudonymov 645

Slovník soudobých českých spisovatelů 3474-3475

Słownik architektów i budowniczych Polaków 2685

Słownik biograficzno-historyczny polski 1637

Słownik biograficzny pracowników ksiażki polskiej; wykaz haseł 4043

Słownik biograficzny pracowników ksiażki polskiej: zeszyt próbny 4044

Słownik biograficzny uczonych żydow polskich 1627

Słownik lekarzów polskich obejmujacy oprócz krótkich zyciorysów lekarzy polaków... 4157

Słownik lutników polskich 3087

Słownik malarzów polskich 2602

Slownik muzyków dawnej Polski (do roku 1800) 2798

Słownik muzyków polskich (Chomiński, ed.) 3072

Slownik muzyków polskich dawnych i nowoczesnych kompozytorów 3079

Słownik pseudonimów i kryptonimów pisarzy polskich 1625

Słownik starożytności słowiańskich 1757

Słownik współczesnych pisarzy polskich 3811

Smålandska nationen i Lund 1820

Smålands nation i Upsala 1840

Smolandi Upsalienses 1821

Sobranie portretov rossiiam, znamenitykh po svoim dieianiiam... 1675

Social scientists specializing in African studies 4692

The Society of Artists of Great Britain (1760-1791) 2517

The Society of Fellows 3261

Sohlmans musiklexikon 3073

Some Irish naturalists 4648

Sommets de la musique 2897

The Sources and literature of Scottish Church history 4424

South African sporting encyclopaedia and who's who 3226

South African who's who 333

The South African woman's who's who 331

South Carolina bench and bar 3946

South Dakota legislative manual 2323

South Indian celebrities 1261

Southland writers 3430

Southwest Texans   2344

Sovetskie kompozitory (Leningrad, 1938-   )   3077

Sovetskie kompozitory ——— laureaty Stalinskoĭ premii (Bernandt)   2770

Sovetskie pisateli; avtobiografii 3846

Soviet men of science   4614

Soviet Union year-book   1741

Sovremennaiă Rossiiă v portretakh i biografiiăkh vydaiŭshchikh-siă deiăteleĭ   1736

Sovremenniki   1666

Sovremennye inostrannye pisateli 3384

Sovremennye russkie pisateli 3848

Sowjetbuch   1708

Sowjetische Kurzbiographien 1701

Space scientists and engineers 4673

Specimen Hungariae literatae 3712

Spemanns Goldenes Buch der Mu-sik   3080

Spiski ierarkhov i nastoiăteleĭ monastyrei Rossiiskiiă tserkvi 4505

Spisok chlenov Imperatorskoĭ Akademii nauk   4575

Spisok russkikh anonimnykh knig s imenami ikh avtorov i perevod-chikov   1662

Sporting authors   3505

Spravochnyĭ slovar' o russkikh pisateliăkh i uchenykh   3825

Ssŭ hsiang chia ta tz'ŭ tien   4247

Staatkundig Nederland   1570

Standard book of celebrated musi-cians, past and present 3115

A Standard dictionary of Canadian biography   517

The Standard Jewish encyclopedia 1476

The Standard musical encyclopedia 2802

Statistique des lettres et des sciences en France   3577

Steirisches Künstler-Lexikon 2651

Steirisches Musiklexikon   3085

Stelle feminili. Dizionario bio-bibliografico   1379

Sto russkikh literatorov   3831

Sto russkikh pisateleĭ   3835

Stokes' encyclopedia of music & musicians   2816

Storfurstendömet Finlands ridder-skaps och adels kalender 697

Storici, teorici e critici delle arti figurativi (1800-1940)   2543

Stowe's clerical directory of the American church   4331

Stowe's clerical directory of the
Protestant Episcopal Church
in the U. S. A.   4331

The Students' pocket dictionary
204

Studi biografici di rinomati italiani   1346

Subsidios para um diccionario de
pseudonymos...   1639

The Successful American   2017

Successful Americans of our day
1933

Succincta medicorum Hungariae
et Transilvaniae biographia
4214

Suda Lexicon   3469

Sudetendeutsche Lebensbilder
648

Suecia literata   1824

Suid-Afrikaanse heldegalery
324

Suidae Lexicon   3469

Suomen lääkärit   4078

Suomen säveltäjiä puolentoista
vuosisadan ajalta   3025

Les Supercheries littéraires
dévoilées   704-705, 709

Svensk biografisk upplagslitteratur
1814

Svensk försäkringsmatrikel
4715

Svensk läkare-matrikel   4097

Svenska konstnärer; biografisk
handbok   2627

Svenska konstnärer inom teaterns,
musikens och filmens värld
3196

Svenska kyrkomusici   3001

Svenska män och kvinnor; biografisk uppslagsbok   1827

Svenska släktkalendern   1828

Svenskar i utlandet (1959)   1829

Svenskt anonym- och pseudonym-
lexikon   1815

Svenskt biografiskt handlexikon
1819

Svenskt biografiskt lexikon
1830

Svenskt biografiskt lexikon. Ny
följd   1816, 1831

Svenskt boklexikon   4026

Svenskt författerlexikon; bio- bibliografisk handbok till
Sveriges moderna litteratur
3923

Svenskt konstnärslexikon   2628

Svenskt literaturlexikon (Meijer)
3921

Svenskt litteraturlexikon   3924

Svenskt porträttgalleri   1832-
1833

Sveriges ridderskaps och adels
kalender   1834

Systematisch-chronologische
Darstellung der musikalischen
Literatur   2765-2766

T

TV personalities; biographical
sketch book   3197

al-Tabaqāt   4557

Tabaqāt al-Sūfīyah   4554, 4558

Table des notices biographiques
publiées dans l'Annuaire de
l'Académie royale... de Belgique   418

Tableau; encyclopedia of distinguished personalities in the
Philippines   1619

Tableau abrégé de l'antiquité littéraire   177

Tableau des écrivains français
3563

Tableau historique de la noblesse
militaire (France)   849

Tableaux historiques; ou, Traités
biographiques... sur la vie...
des plus éminents savants
juifs contemporains   1471

Tableaux, par corps et par batail-
les, des officiers tués et
blessés pendant les guerres
de l'Empire (1805-1815)   816

Tablettes biographiques des
écrivains français   3563

Tadhkiratu 'l-awliyā   4555

Tagebuch der Geschichte und Biographie   84

Tahdhīb al-Tahdhīb   1319

T'ai kuo jua ch'iao jen wu chih
1871

Taishō jimmei jiten   1426

Taishū jinjiroku   1440

Talent and tunes on music machines
2773

Tamil eluttālar yār-evar   3728

Tang tai Chung-kuo jen wu chih
570

Tang tai Chung-kuo ming jen lu
563

Tang tai Chung-kuo ming jen chih
575

Tang tai Chung-kuo ming jen tz'u
tien   582

Tang tai Chung-kuo shih yeh jen wu
chih   577

Tang tai jen wu   603

Tang tai tang kuo ming jen chuan
623

Ta'rih al-hukamā'   4191

al-Ta'rīkh al-kabīr   1318

Ta'rīkh Baghdād   1322

Tarikh madinah Dimashq   1318

Tarybu Lietuvos rašytojai   3800

Taschenbuch für Literatur und
Kunst im Königreich Sachsen
3699

Taschenlexikon der deutschen Literatur (Kindermann)   3647

Taschenlexikon für deutsche Literatur (Kindermann und Dietrich)   3646-3647

Teatral'naia entsiklopediia   3198

Technischer Literaturkalender
4608

Teikoku shin'yo-roku (1930-1943)
1442

The Television annual   3199

Tennessee blue book   2336

Tennessee directory and official
vote   2336

Tennessee handbook and official
directory   2336

Tennessee pocket manual   2336

Teutscher Nation Heldenbuch, Das
erste [-dritte] Theil   1004

Teutsches Künstlerlexikon   2554

Teutschlands galante Poetinnen
3660

Tewkesbury's Who's who in Alaska and Alaska business index
2077

Texas in the War (1861-1865)
2345

The Theatre handbook and digest
of plays   3192

Theatro heroino   165

Theatrum anonymorum et pseudonymorum   37

Theatrum poetarum Anglicarum
3525

Theatrum virorum eruditione clarorum   684

Thesaurus bio- et bibliographicus
295

Thesaurus literaturae botanicae
omnium gentium   4649

Thesaurus of the arts   2667-2668

The Thespian dictionary   3200

Thom's Irish who's who   1306

Tibbiye sehitleri   4139

The Times of India directory and
year book including who's
who   1285

Tiroler Anonymen- und Pseudonymen-Lexikon   381

Tiroler Ehrenkranz   392

Tirolisches Künstlerlexikon
2635

The Titled nobility of Europe
690

Titres, anoblissements et pairies
de la Restauration (1814-1830)
834

Titres et confirmations de titres
833

200 [i. e. To hundrede] danske
malere og deres vaerker
2546

Toldot anshe ha-shem (Landshuth)
4565

Toldot anshe shem (Rand)   4567

Tonkonsten; internationellt musiklexikon   3094

Tonkünstler-Lexikon (Eggeling)
2830

Tonkünstler-Lexikon Berlin's von
den ältesten Zeiten bis auf
die Gegenwart   2940

Tonkünstler-Merkbüchlein
3016

Die Tonkünstler Schlesiens   2899

Torchbearers of chemistry
4665

Los Toros   3223

Tournay littéraire   443

Traité de lutherie ancienne
2860

Trajectum eruditum   1555

A Treasury of opera biography
2815

Le Tribunal et la Cour de cassation
3956-3957

Triunfadores   1650

Les Trois siècles de la peinture
en France   2501

Trouvères, jongleurs et ménestrels
du nord de la France   3568

Trustees, presidents and deans
of American colleges and universities   3305

TSentrosibirtsy   1740

Tsui chin kuan shen li li hui lu   594

Tsui hsin shih chieh jên ming ta
tz'ŭ tien   279

Tudor artists   2428

Türkiye'de kim kimdir   1875-
1876

Turkiye teracimi ahval ansiklopedisi   1879

Tugium sacrum   4399

Tusculum Lexikon der griechischen
und lateinischen Literatur
vom Altertum bis zur Neuzeit
3470-3471

Tusculum-Lexikon griechischer
und lateinischer Autoren des
Altertums und des Mittel-
alters   3471

Tvortsy tekhniki na Urale   4794

Twentieth century authors
3365-3366

Twentieth century Baptists   4521

The Twentieth century biographical
dictionary of notable Americans   1926, 1962, 2021

Twentieth century encyclopedia of
religious knowledge   4484

Twentieth century successful A-
mericans, local and national
2022

Types et profils parlementaires
442

Typographia Scoto-Gadelica
3599

Typographical antiquities   3995

Tzu yu Chung-kuo ming jen chuan
606

Tzu yu Chung-kuo ming jen shih lu
608

U

U. S.   Air Force biographical
dictionary   1936

U. S.   Marine Corps biographical
dictionary   2009

U. S. Navy biographical dictionary
2010

U.S.S.R.   handbook   1741

Uchastniki russkogo revoliutsionnogo dvizheniiā epokhi bor'by
s tsarizmom   1746

Ukrains'ki pys'mennyky   3938

'Umdah-yi muntakhabah   3939

United Nations who's who in government and industry   284

The United States biographical dictionary and portrait gallery of eminent and self-made men   2040

United States diplomatic and consular service. Our representatives abroad   2004

A Universal biographical and historical dictionary (Watkins)   297

A Universal biographical dictionary (Baldwin)   57

The Universal biographical dictionary (Watkins)   182, 297

A Universal biography (A'Beckett)   40

Universal biography (Lempriere)   182

Universal biography: containing sketches of prominent persons of the 19th century   286

Universal dictionary of violin and bow makers   2889

Universal index of biography   12

Universal Jewish encyclopedia   1478-1479

Universal-Lexikon der Tonkunst   3051-3052, 3055

The Universal library of historians   4756

Universal pronouncing dictionary of biography and mythology   275

University dictionary of music and musicians   3095

University musical encyclopedia   3095

Unos cuantos seudónimos de escritores españoles   1761

Unvergängliche Stimmen   2933

Gli Uomini della Comasca diocesi antichi e moderni   1388

Gli Uomini illustri nella musica da Guido d'Arezzo fino ai contemporanei   2955

The Upper ten thousand   1155

Die Urne; Jahrbuch für allgemeine Nekrologie   287

Uruguayans of to-day   2382

Uruguayos contemporáneos   2384

Utah's distinguished personalities   2347

Utlandssvenskarnas föreningen   1829

V

The V. C. and D. S. O   1120

V pamiat' 25-letiia deiatel'nosti vrachei, okonchivshikh kurs Imp. Mediko-khirurgicheskoi akademii v 1873 godu   4160

Van Paciolo tot Stevin   4716

Variétés bibliographiques et littéraires   4039

Varones ilustres de la Compañía de Jesús   4522

Varones ilustres de la provincia de León   1799

TITLE INDEX

Varones ilustres de Mallorca
1802

Varones ilustres de Menorca
1803

Les Vauclusiens   948

Vedettes 1952; le fait français
au Canada   518

Velikie liudi. Biograficheskaia
biblioteka   291

Vem är det?   1836

Vem är vem i folkfronten?
1837

Vem är vem i Norden   1752

Vem är vem inom handel och industri?   1838

Vem och vad? Biografisk handbok
701

Vem var det?   1839

Verfasserlexikon des deutschen
Mittelalters   3696

Verkfraeðingtal   4807

Die Verlorenen Söhne   1255

Vermomde en naamlooze schrijvers opgespoord op het gebied
der Nederlandsche en Vlaamsche letteren   1551-1552

Vermomde Nederlandsche en Vlaamsche schrijvers   1552

Vermont legislative directory
2352

Versicherungslexikon   4708

Versuch einer bajerischen Gelehrten Geschichte   1029

Versuch einer Gelehrtengeschichte
von Hamburg   1045

Versuch einer Geschichte der
oesterreichischen Gelehrten
389

Versuch eines Beitrags zur Biographie hamburgischer Aerzte
4208

Verzeichnis der gegenwärtig in und
um Wien lebenden Schrift-
steller   3686

Verzeichniss aller anonymischen
Schriften und Aufsätze in der
vierten Ausgabe des Gelehrt-
en Teutschlands   954

Verzeichnis der im Gebiete der
freien Reichstadt Rothen-
burg O. T. ... wirkenden ev.-
luth. Geistlichen   4340

Verzeichniss der vorzüglichsten
Gelehrten alter und neuer
Zeit   86

Verzeichniss einer Sammlung von
Bildnissen, grösstentheils
berühmter Aerzte   4175

Verzeichnis einzelner Lebensbeschreibungen berühmter
Gelehrten und Schriftsteller
älterer und neuerer Zeiten
18

Verzeichniss im Jahre 1825 in
Berlin lebender Schriftsteller
3636

Verzeichniss von Bildnissen von
Aerzten und Naturforschern
...   4198

I Vescovi di Comacchio   4480

I Viaggiatori Veneti minori
4740

Las Vidas de los pintores y estatuarios eminentes españoles 2576-2577

Las Vidas dels trobadors 3596

Vida y obras de autores cubanos 3908

Vida y obras de autores mexicanos 3909

Vida y obras de autores puertor-riqueños 3910

Las Vidas dels trobadors 3596

Vidas y obras de autores vene-zolanos 3911

Vidas y tiempos. Diccionario biográfico mexicano 1540

Vie complète des peintres es-pagnols et histoire de la pein-ture espagnole 2526

La Vie des peintres flamands, allemands et hollandois 2472

Vie des peintres flamands et hollandais 2473

Les Vies des hommes et des fem-mes illustres d'Italie 1372

Les Vies des plus célèbres juris-consultes de toutes les na-tions 3986

Les Vies des saints de Bretagne 4418

Vies des saints du diocèse de Paris 4396

Les Vies des saints et des person-nes... de Cambrai et d'Ar-ras 4343

Les Vies des saints pour tous les jours de l'année 4385

Vies des savants illustres depuis l' antiquité jusqu'au dix-neuvième siècle 4586

Viet-Nam danh-nhân tự-điển 2395

Violins and violin makers 3013

Virginia Baptist ministers 4509

Virginia composers 2949

Virorum eruditorum onomatomor-phosis 39

Vitae Germanorum jureconsultorum et politicorum 961

Vitae Germanorum medicorum 961

Vitae Germanorum philosophorum 961

Vitae Germanorum theologorum 961

Vitae illustrium medicorum 4107

Vitae Italorum doctrina excel-lentium... 1358

Vitae professorum medicinae qui in Academia Gryphiswalden-sium a primis ejus initiis (1456) usque ad finem anni ipsius saecularis tertii vixerunt 4200

Vitae professorum theologiae, juriprudentiae, medicinae et philosophiae, qui in illustri Academia Jenensi... vixer-unt... 3322

Vitae selectorum aliquot virorum, qui doctrina, dignitate aut pietate inclaruere 59

Vite de' pittori bolognesi non descritte nella Felsina pittrice 2550

Le Vite de' pittori, degli scultori ed architetti veronesi 2595-2596

Le Vite de' pittori, scultori, architetti, ed intagliatori 2429

Vite de' pittori, scultori ed architetti che hanno lavorato in Roma... 2581

Vite de' pittori, scultori, ed architetti genovesi 2620

Vite de' pittori, scultori ed architetti moderni 2580

Vite de' pittori, scultori, ed architetti napoletani 2481

Vite de' più celebri architetti e scultori veneziani 2689

Le Vite de più eccellenti architetti, pittori, et scultori italiani (Vasari) 2641

Le Vite degli Arcadi illustri 1380

Le Vite dei pittori, scultori e architetti veronese 2672

Vlaams letterkundig lexicon 3451

Vlaamsche pseudoniemen 421

Volksschulehrer-Tonkünstler-Lexikon 2922

Vollständige akademische Gelehrten-Geschichte der... Universität zu Erlangen 3266

Vollständiges Heiligen-Lexikon 4502

Vologzhane-pisateli 3821

The Volume library 294

Von deutschen Parteien und Parteiführern in Ausland 1016

Von wem ist das doch? 960

Voorname belgische toonkunstenaars uit de XVIIIe, XIXe en XXe eeuw 2888

Vor tids Hvem skrev hvad (1914-1964) 3486

Les Vrais pourtraits et vies des hommes illustres, grecz, latins, et payens 274

Vultos do Brasil 475

W

Walford's County families of the United Kingdom 1181

Warner's dictionary of authors ancient and modern 3387

Wasmuths Lexikon der Baukunst 2690

Watchmakers and clockmakers of the world 2704

Webster's biographical dictionary 298

The Weekly gallery of celebrities 129

Wegbereiter und Vorkämpfer für das neue Deutschland   995

Wegweiser durch die moderne Literatur in Österreich   3648

Welsh painters, engravers, and sculptors (1527-1911)   2604

Welsh political and educational leaders in the Victorian era   1227

Welsh religious leaders in the Victorian era   4440

Die Weltliteratur   3388

Wer ist wer? Das deutsche who's who   1013

Wer ist wer? 1100 Kurzbiographien deutscher Persönlichkeiten aus Politik, Wirtschaft und Kultur   1014

Wer ist wer; Lexikon österreichischer Zeitgenossen   403

Wer ist wer in der SBZ?   981, 1015

Wer ist wer in der Werbung in Europa   4718

Wer ist wer in Österreich   404

Wer ist wo in der Wissenschaft?   4621

Wer ist's? Unsere Zeitgenossen   1013

Wer ist's bei den Olympischen Spielen (1936)   3220

Wer leitet? Die Männer der Wirtschaft...   4719

West-Country poets   3546

West Virginia authors   3399

West Virginia blue book   2372

West Virginia legislative handbook   2372

The Western Australian Legislature   372

Western gunfighters   2361

Westfälische Köpfe   1079

Wetenschappelijk en biographisch woordenboek der toonkunst   2961

What's what and who's who in some world affairs   299

Whitaker's peerage, baronetage, knightage, and companionage   1185

White's conspectus of American biography   1982

Who are they?   168

Who is who at the Baltic University   3304

Who is who [at the 2d Commonwealth Education Conference]   3278

Who is who in Arkansas   2082

Who is who in Australasia   377

Who is who in British Guiana   488

Who is who in California   2093

Who is who in insurance; an international biographical dictionary and year book   4720

Who is who in music (1927-1941) 2909

Who is who in music. A complete presentation of the contemporary music scene 3116

Who is who in publishing 4046

Who is who in the Oklahoma Legislature 2286

Who is who in Turkey 1879

Who is who in Wisconsin 2376

Who is who [of delegates to the 2d Commonwealth Education Conference, New Delhi, 1962] 3278

Who knows, and what, among authorities, experts, and the specially informed 2046

Who was he? 179

Who was who, a companion to Who's who 1186

Who was who in America; a companion biographical reference work to Who's who in America 2047

Who was who in America; historical volume (1607-1896) 2048

Who was who in church history 4444

Who was who in Egyptology 4754

Who was who in Fascist Italy 1381

The Who, what and where of music series 2917

Who, what, where and when in insurance 4705

The Who-when-what book 300

Who? When? Where? What? 293

Who's important in every field in all countries 307

Who's important in medicine 4066

Who's who (India (Republic) Parliament. House of the People) 1273

Who's who; a directory of engineers in metropolitan Philadelphia 4816

Who's who; an annual biographical dictionary 1187

Who's who; delegates to the United Nations Conference on International Organization, San Francisco (1945) 283

Who's who; the official who's who among students in American universities and colleges 2052

Who's who along the north shore of Massachusetts Bay 2193

Who's who among administrative women in education in Virginia 3316

Who's who among Americans of Italian descent in Connecticut 2120

Who's who among association executives 2049

Who's who among authors of older nations 3389

Who's who among automotive
executives   4808

Who's who among Finnish-Americans   2050

Who's who among international
medical writers   4215

Who's who among Japanese artists
2532

Who's who among Japanese writers   3786

Who's who among living authors of
older nations   3389

Who's who among Minnesota women
2215

Who's who among North American
authors   3390

Who's who among North American
Esperantists   3391

Who's who among Northwest
authors   3422-3423

Who's who among pastors in all
the Norwegian Lutheran synods
of America   4529

Who's who among physicians and
surgeons   4216

Who's who among South Dakotans
2325

Who's who among southern singers
and composers   2924

Who's who among students in A-
merican universities and colleges   2052

Who's who among students in A-
merican high schools   2051

Who's who among the blind in the
business and professional
world   2053

Who's who among the Mennonites
4530

Who's who among the women of
California   2094

Who's who among women lawyers
3989

Who's who and encyclopaedia of
bowls   3237

Who's who and encyclopaedia of
the screen today   3183

Who's who and what to see in
Florida   2131

Who's who and where in horsedom
3240

Who's who and why; a biographical
dictionary of men and women
of Canada and Newfoundland
522

Who's who and why in Jamaica
1421

Who's who at Edinburgh (1937)
4546

Who's who at Wisconsin [Universi-
ty]   3317

Who's who Columbia journalists
3434

Who's who executives in California
2095

Who's who for Denver and Colorado   2126

Who's who for North Dakota
2267

Who's who Hakushi in Great
Japan   1428

Who's who in advertising (London,
1957-   )   4722

Who's who in advertising (New
York, 1931-   )   4721

Who's who in advertising (New
York, 1963-   )   4723

Who's who in advertising and public relations   4724

Who's who in Alabama (Birmingham, 1939/40-   )
2075

Who's who in Alabama (Chicago,
Larkin)   2329

Who's who in Alaska and Alaska
business index   2077

Who's who in America   2047,
2054-2056

Who's who in American aeronautics
4809

Who's who in American art   2659

Who's who in American dentistry
4217

Who's who in American education
3318

Who's who in American history
2048

Who's who in American Jewry
2057

Who's who in American medicine
4218

Who's who in American Methodism
4531

Who's who in American portrait
photography   2736

Who's who in American sports
3238

Who's who in and from Newfoundland   520

Who's who in architecture   2691

Who's who in Argentina   345

Who's who in Arizona (Chicago,
Larkin)   2329

Who's who in Arizona in business,
professions and arts   2080

Who's who in Arkansas   2206

Who's who in Army aviation   4810

Who's who in art; biographies of
leading men and women in the
world of art today   2661

Who's who in art. 1st-
issue of the directory section
of the American art annual
2660

Who's who in Association of University Evening Colleges
3319

Who's who in atoms   4674

Who's who in Australia   380

Who's who in Austria   405

Who's who in aviation (Chicago &
New York, 1942/43-   )
4811

Who's who in aviation (London)
4776

Who's who in Baltimore   2083

Who's who in Baptist America
4532

Who's who in baton twirling
3239

Who's who in Bedfordshire and
Huntingdonshire   1191

Who's who in Belgium and Grand
Duchy of Luxembourg   466

Who's who in Belgium, including
the Belgian Congo   466

Who's who in Berkshire   1192

Who's who in Boston   2085

Who's who in British advertising
4725

Who's who in British aviation
4776

Who's who in British Columbia
521

Who's who in British science
4622

Who's who in broadcasting   3201

Who's who in Buckinghamshire
1194

Who's who in Burma   491

Who's who in California (Los
Angeles, 1955/56-   )
2096

Who's who in California; a biographical directory (San Francisco, 1928/29-   )
2097

Who's who in California; a biographical reference work of

notable living men and women
of California (Los Angeles,
1942/43-   )   2098

Who's who in Cambridgeshire
1206

Who's who in Canada   522

Who's who in Central and East
Europe   691

Who's who in Chicago and Illinois   2107

Who's who in Chicago and vicinity
2107

Who's who in China   613

Who's who in Cincinnati   2108

Who's who in Cleveland   2109

Who's who in Colorado (Denver,
1958)   2114

Who's who in Colorado; a biographical record of Colorado's
leaders... (Boulder, 1938)
2115

Who's who in colored America
2058

Who's who in colored Louisiana
2168

Who's who in commerce and industry   4735

Who's who in Communist China
614

Who's who in Congregationalism
4533

Who's who in Connecticut   2121

Who's who in data processing
4812

Who's who in Delaware; a biographical dictionary of Delaware's
leading men and women
2122

Who's who in Delaware; a biographical dictionary of leading
living men and women of the
state of Delaware [etc.]
2123

Who's who in dentistry   4219

Who's who in designing   2737

Who's who in Detroit (Detroit,
1931)   2128

Who's who in Detroit; a biographical dictionary (Detroit,
1935/36-   )   2129

Who's who in East Africa   319

Who's who in Eastern Europe
692

Who's who in education   3320

Who's who in Egypt and the Middle
East   1332

Who's who in Egypt and the Near
East   1332

Who's who in engineering (London,
1920/21-   )   4814

Who's who in engineering (New
York, 1922/23-   )
4813

Who's who in engineering in
Pennsylvania   4815

Who's who in engineering in the
Delaware Valley   4816

Who's who in English-speaking
poets   3543

Who's who in Europe   693

Who's who in Europe, American
directory &
1897

Who's who in Fascist Italy   1381

Who's who in filmland (London)
3203

Who's who in filmland (New York)
3202

Who's who in finance   4726

Who's who in finance and banking
4726

Who's who in finance, banking and
insurance   4726

Who's who in Finland   699

Who's who in Florida (Chicago,
Larkin)   2329

Who's who in flying   4776

Who's who in foreign correspondence   3435

Who's who in France   850

Who's who in Freemasonry   301

Who's who in Georgia (Chicago,
Larkin)   2329

Who's who in Germany   1017

Who's who in Germany and Austria
1018-1019

Who's who in Glasgow (in 1909)
1197

Who's who in government   2059-
2060

Who's who in graphic art   2738

Who's who in Greece   1245

Who's who in "Hakushi" in Great
Japan   1428

Who's who in Harlem   2248

Who's who in Hertfordshire
1200

Who's who in history   4767

Who's who in Hollywood   3204

Who's who in horsedom   3240

Who's who in hoteldom   4727

"Who's who" in Hunland   1022

Who's who in Illinois (Chicago,
Larkin)   2206

Who's who in India   1285, 1287-
1288

Who's who in India and Pakistan
1285

Who's who in India, Burma & Ceylon   1289

Who's who in Indian engineering
& industry   4817

Who's who in Indian science
4623

Who's who in Indiana (Chicago,
Larkin)   2206

Who's who in Indiana: library of A-
merican lives (Hopkinsville,
Ky., 1957)   2150

Who's who in industrial medicine
4220

Who's who in insurance   4705,
4728

Who's who in insurance in California   4729

Who's who in insurance in Canada
4730

Who's who in investment counsel
4731

Who's who in Iowa (Chicago,
Larkin)   2206

Who's who in Italy   1382-1383

Who's who in Jamaica   1420

Who's who in Japan   1445-1446

Who's who in journalism   3436

Who's who in jurisprudence   3990

Who's who in Kansas (Chicago,
Larkin)   2206

Who's who in Kansas City [Mis-
souri] (Kansas City, 1931)
2159

Who's Who in Kansas City [Mis-
souri & Kansas] (Hebron,
Neb., 1930-   )   2160

Who's who in Kent, Surrey, and
Sussex   1202

Who's who in Kentucky (Chicago,
Larkin)   2329

Who's who in Kentucky (Hopkinsville, Ky., 1957?)   2164

Who's who in Kentucky (Louisville, 1936)   2165

Who's who in labor   2061

Who's who in Latin America
1509

Who's who in law   3991

Who's who in Lebanon   1510

Who's who in librarianship
4023

Who's who in library service
4047

Who's who in literature   3370,
3544

Who's who in Los Angeles   2166

Who's who in Los Angeles County
2167

Who's who in Louisiana (Chicago,
Larkin)   2329

Who's who in Louisville   2169

The Who's who in Madras   1290

Who's who in Maine   2172

Who's who in major league baseball   3241

Who's who in major league football   3242

Who's who in Malaya & Malayan
year book   1514

The Who's who in Malaysia   1515

Who's who in market research
4709

Who's who in Maryland (Chicago,
Marquis)   2123

Who's who in Massachusetts   2194

Who's who in Methodism (Chicago,
1952)   4534

Who's who in Methodism (London,
1933-   )   4535

Who's who in Michigan (Chicago,
Larkin)   2206

Who's who in Michigan (Munising,
Mich., 1936-   )   2204

Who's who in Milwaukee   2208

Who's who in mining and metallurgy   4818

Who's who in Minnesota (Chicago,
Larkin)   2206

Who's who in Minnesota (Minneapolis, 1941-   )   2216

Who's who in Minnesota athletics
3243

Who's who in Mississippi (Chicago,
Larkin)   2329

Who's who in Missouri (Chicago,
Larkin)   2206

Who's who in modern China
595

Who's who in motion pictures
3205

Who's who in movie land   3206

Who's who in moving pictures 3207

Who's who in music (London,
Shaw Pub. Co.)   3117

Who's who in music (Wyndham)
3126

Who's who in music and dance in
Southern California   2982

Who's who in music and drama
3118

Who's who in music and dramatic
art in the Twin Cities   3119

Who's who in music and musicians
international directory   3120

Who's who in music education
2764

Who's who in music in California
3121

Who's who in Natal   329

Who's who in Nazi Germany
1018

Who's who in Nebraska (Chicago,
Larkin)   2206

Who's who in Nebraska (Lincoln,
Nebraska Press Association)
2224

Who's who in Nevada   2225

Who's who in New England   2232

Who's who in New Jersey (Chicago,
Marquis)   2123

Who's who in New Mexico (Albuquerque, Abousleman)
2242

Who's who in New Mexico (Chicago,
Larkin)   2329

Who's who in New York (City and
State)   2249

Who's who in New Zealand   1578

Who's who in New Zealand libraries   4047

Who's who in Nigeria   1579

Who's who in Norfolk   1206

Who's who in North Carolina
(Chicago, Larkin)   2329

Who's who in Northwest art
2662

Who's who in occult, psychic and
spiritual realms   4241

Who's who in occupied and satellite Europe   694

Who's who in Ohio (Chicago, Larkin)   2206

Who's who in Ohio (Cleveland,
Biographical Pub. Co.)
2279

Who's who in Oklahoma (Chicago,
Larkin)   2206

Who's who in Oklahoma (Guthrie,
Okla., Co-operative Pub.
Co.)   2288

A Who's who in Oklahoma (Mus-
kogee, Okla., Leadership
Index)   2287

Who's who in Omaha   2289

Who's who in Oregon   2293

Who's who in our American government   2062

Who's who in Oxfordshire   1208

Who's who in pan-Methodism
4536

Who's who in Paris   850

Who's who in Paris Anglo-American colony   2063

Who's who in Parliament   1101

Who's who in Pennsylvania (Chicago, Marquis)   2123

Who's who in Pennsylvania (New York, Hamersly)   2302

Who's who in Philadelphia   2308

Who's who in philately   2663

Who's who in philosophy   4262

Who's who in photography   2739

Who's who in Pittsburgh   2309

Who's who in plastics in the United States and Canada   4819

Who's who in Polish America   2064

Who's who in Portugal   1646

Who's who in practical arts and vocational education in New York State   3321

Who's who in press, publicity, printing   3545

Who's who in printing in the United States and Canada   4049

Who's who in professional portraiture in America   2664

Who's who in public administration research in Virginia   4775

Who's who in public relations. Supplement   4689

Who's who in public relations, international   4689, 4732

Who's who in publishing   4050

Who's who in Queens   2250

Who's who in racing   3244

Who's who in radio (Chicago, W. E. Johnson)   3208

Who's who in radio (New York, Distinctive Radio Publications)   3209

Who's who in railroading in North America   4820

Who's who in railroading, United States, Canada, Mexico, Cuba   4820

Who's who in real estate and allied interests   4733

Who's who in rock 'n roll   2854

Who's who in S. A. E.   1965

Who's who in Saint Louis (1928/29-   )   2316

Who's who in St. Louis (Rudkin, editor —— 1931?)   2315

Who's who in San Diego   2317

Who's who in science (international)   4625

Who's who in science and research   4624

Who's who in show business   3210

Who's who in Singapore and Malaya   1753

Who's who in small college basketball   3245

Who's who in South Carolina (Chicago, Larkin)   2329

Who's who in South Carolina (Columbia, S. C., Current Historical Association)   2320

Who's who in South Carolina (Columbia, S. C. , McCaw) 2319

Who's who in South Dakota (Coursey) 2321

Who's who in South Dakota (Pierre, S. D. , H. L. White) 2324

Who's who in Soviet nuclear science 4675

Who's who in Soviet science and technology 4626

Who's who in Soviet social sciences, humanities, art and government 4693

Who's who in Spain 1786

Who's who in speedway 3246

Who's who in sports 3247

Who's who in Staffordshire 1221

Who's who in State politics, 1907 [Massachusetts] 2195

Who's who in Suffolk 1206

Who's who in Surrey 1202

Who's who in Sussex 1202

Who's who in Switzerland, including the Principality of Liechtenstein 1868

Who's who in TV and radio 3213

Who's who in Tennessee (Chicago, Larkin) 2329

Who's who in Tennessee (Hopkinsville, Ky. , Historical Record Association) 2338

Who's who in Tennessee (Memphis, Paul & Douglass Co.) 2337

Who's who in Texas (Chicago, Larkin) 2329

Who's who in the Agricultural Institute of Canada 4777

Who's who in the air 4776

Who's who in the Air Force 2065

Who's who in the American Association 3248

Who's who in the American League 3249

Who's who in the American negro press 3410

Who's who in the big leagues 3250

Who's who in the Central States (Chicago, Larkin) 2206

Who's who in the Central States (Washington, Mayflower Pub. Co.) 2066

Who's who in the chemical and drug industries 4656

Who's who in the clergy 4471

Who's who in the Common Market's press and advertising 3392

Who's who in the Commonwealth of Australia 380

Who's who in the Commonwealth of Pennsylvania 2303

Who's who in the computer field (1956-57) 4821

Who's who in the computer field (1963/64-   )   4823

Who's who in the Constitution Convention [Philippines] 1620

Who's who in the counties series (England)   1191-1192, 1194(?), 1200, 1202(?), 1206, 1208, 1221(?), 1236(?), 1242(?)

Who's who in the East (Chicago, Marquis)   2269

Who's who in the East (Washington, Mayflower Pub. Co.) 2268

Who's who in the East (and Eastern Canada)   2269

Who's who in the electronics industry   4822

Who's who in the Executive Officers Council of the National Association of Real Estate Boards   4734

Who's who in the Far East   366

Who's who in the Free Churches and other denominations 4538

Who's who in the history of philosophy   4243

Who's who [in the House of the People of the Indian Parliament]   1273

Who's who in the lyceum   2067

Who's who in the major leagues 3249, 3251-3252

Who's who in the maritime industry   4824

Who's who in the Middle East 1325

Who's who in the Midwest   2207

Who's who in the motor trade [British]   4825

Who's who in the movies   3140

Who's who in the National League 3252

Who's who in the nation's capital 2357

Who's who in the Netherlands 1572

Who's who in the Northwest (Chicago)   2329

Who's who in the Northwest (Portland, Or.)   2272

Who's who in the nursing world 4221

Who's who in the Pacific Southwest   2099

Who's who in the Philippines (Poole)   1621

Who's who in the Philippines; a biographical dictionary 1622

Who's who in the Philippines: Women   1623

Who's who in the Protestant clergy   4539

Who's who in the public utilities industry   4826

Who's who in the Regular Army 2068

Who's who in the Rockies   2124

Who's who in the rubber world
4827

Who's who in the South   2327

Who's who in the South and Southwest (Chicago, Larkin)
2329, 2368

Who's who in the South and Southwest (Chicago, Marquis)
2328

Who's who in the stamp world
2445

Who's who in the State of Israel
1481

Who's who in the Talmud   4564

Who's who in the theatre   3161,
3212

Who's who in the United Nations
302

Who's who in the USSR   1747

Who's who in the West   2368

Who's who [in the] Western Nigerian Legislature   1580

Who's who in the world   158

Who's who in thoroughbred racing
3253

Who's who in transportation and
communication   4828

Who's who in Turkey (Ankara,
1958-   )   1881

Who's who in Turkey (Nebioğlu)
1876

Who's who in U. A. R. and the Near
East   1332

Who's who in United States politics and American political
almanac   2069

Who's who in Vichy, France
847

Who's who in Virginia (Chicago,
Larkin)   2329

Who's who in Wales   1232

Who's who in Warwickshire
1236

Who's who in Washington State
2360

Who's who in West Virginia (Chicago, Marquis)   2123

Who's who in Western Canada
523

Who's who in Western India
1291

Who's who in western stars
3214

Who's who in Wisconsin (Chicago,
Larkin)   2206

Who's who in world aviation and
astronautics   4829

Who's who in world cricket   3236

Who's who in world Jewry   1480

Who's who in world medicine
4147, 4222

Who's who in Yorkshire ——
North & East Riding   1242

Who's who —— India   1292

Who's who Israel   1481

Who's who, Jamaica, British West Indies   1421

The Who's who of American poets   3397

Who's who of American returned students   615-616

Who's who of American women   2070

Who's who of city church pastors (East Asia)   4338

Who's who of Indian writers   3725

Who's who of Malayalam writers   3723

Who's who of prominent Germans in the U.S.S.R.   1020-1021

Who's who of Rhodesia, Mauritius, Central and East Africa (1965)   320

Who's who of Southern Africa   320-321, 333

Who's who of Southern Africa (Rhodesia, Central and East Africa)   320

Who's who of Tamil writers   3728

The Who's who of the allied governments and allied trade & industry   284

Who's who of the Chinese students in America   617

Who's who of the colored race   2071

Who's who of the Federation of Rhodesia and Nyasaland, Central and East Africa (1959)   321, 333

Who's who of the Oxford Movement   4543

Who's who on the Ohio River and its tributaries   2280

Who's who on the Pacific Coast (Chicago)   2329, 2368

Who's who on the Pacific Coast (Los Angeles, Harper)   2369

Who's who on the stage; an annual (1906-1909, London & New York)   3161

Who's who on the stage, 1908; the dramatic reference book   3211

Who's who today in the musical world   3122

Who's who: Western Nigerian Legislature--SEE: Who's who [in the] Western Nigerian Legislature   1580

Wie is dat?   1573

Wie is dat in Vlaanderen?   467

Wie is wie in Suid-Afrika   334

Wie ist dat? Biographisch lexicon van bekende Nederlandsche Roomsch-Katholieke tijdgenooten   1568

Die Wiener Autoren   3607

Wiener Schriftsteller und Künstler Lexikon   3704

Wieners poetische Schwingen und Federn   3659

Wiens lebende Schriftsteller, Künstler und Dilettanten im Kunstfache   3609

Winchester's screen encyclopedia 3217

The Wisconsin blue book   2378

Wisconsin composers   3125

Wörterbuch der Kunst   2533

Wörterbuch der Musik   2789

A Woman of the century   2072

Woman's record   144

Woman's who's who   155

Woman's who's who of America 2073

Women composers   2829

Women in the fine arts   2654

Women lawyers   3989

Women lawyers in the United States   3987

Women of Natal   329

The Women of the American Revolution   1938

Women of the day   148

Women of the war   1974

Women of the West   2362

Women poets of the twentieth century in France   3561

The Women's who's who   306

Wonderful characters   303

The Word finder   247

Word makers, A dictionary of 154

World biography   307-308

World diplomatic directory and world diplomatic biography 309-310

World diplomatic directory service 310

World directory of crystallographers and other scientists employing crystallographic methods   4676

World directory of geographers 4747

World directory of geography 4747

World directory of mineralogists 4641

The World film encyclopedia 3216

World Jewish register   1484

World nobility and peerage   311

World notables   158

The World of music   3048

The World of musical comedy 2876

World's great men of color   249

World who's who in commerce and commerce and industry   4735

The Worthies of Warwickshire 1235

The Worthies of Westmorland 1237

The Writers of South Carolina 3433

Współczesna kultura polska; nauka,
literatura, sztuka 1635

Württembergischer Nekrolog für
die Jahre 1913-1916 1081

Wuppertaler Biographien 1083

X

X-Y-Z der muziek 2897-2898

Y

Yale University portrait index
29

Yankee stonecutters 2696

Year book and guide of the Rhodesias and Nyasaland 1653

The Year book and who's who in
Kerala 1293

Year book for Texas 2346

Yearbook of popular music
2970

Yearbook of the American screen
3140

The Year books of physical and
natural therapy 4228

The Year in American music
3127

York printers and stationers
4006

Yüz meshur Türk 1877

Z

Zasluzni i znameniti Hrvati
2409

Zasshi nenkan 3788

Zeitgenossen 314-315

Zen Nihon shinshi roku 1447

Zenei lexikon 3130

Zeyl-i Saqâ'iq 1880

Znameniti Hrvati Bošnjaci i
Hercegovci 2398

Znameniti i zaslužni Hrvati
2409

Znameniti srbi XIX veka 2400

Znamienite osobistości pochodzenia Polskiego 1633

Zoologi Sovetskogo Soiuza 4627-
4628

Zsidó lexikon 1252

Zürcher Schrifttum der Gegenwart
3932

Zuverlässige Nachrichten von den
vornehmsten Schriftstellern
3352

Zuverlässige Nachrichten von
jüngstverstorbenen Gelehrten
1011

SUBJECT INDEX

A

Aargau   1851, 3927

Aberdeen, Scot.   3514, 4010

Aberdeen, Scot.   University
    1209, 1215

Abkhazia   1685

Abruzzi and Molise   1384, 3778

Academia Lugd. -Batava--SEE:
    Leyden. Rijksuniversiteit

Académie des sciences, Paris
    4571, 4587, 4591, 4600

Académie française, Paris
    711, 766

Académie royale des sciences,
    des lettres et des beaux-arts
    de Belgique, Brussels   424

Accademia Alfonsina, Naples
    1367

Accademia de' signori incogniti,
    Venice   1365

Accademia degli Arcadi, Rome
    1368, 1380

Accademia dei Gelati, Bologna
    1366

Accademia fiorentina--SEE: Ac-
    cademia toscana di scienze
    e lettere La Colombaria,
    Florence

Accademia toscana di scienze e
    lettere La Colombaria,
    Florence   1369, 1371

Accountants   4694, 4716

Actors and actresses   3136,
    3191   SEE ALSO: Moving-
    pictures, Radio entertainers,
    Television entertainers,
    Theater

Actors and actresses
    France   3132, 3134, 3136,
    3138, 3146, 3155- 3158,
    3167-3168, 3172-3175, 3182

    Germany   3150, 3181

    Great Britain   3139, 3141,
    3176, 3180, 3495

    Italy   3137, 3186, 3773

    Latvia   3189

    Portugal   3193-3194

    Sweden   3196

    United States   3118, 3177,
    3188, 3191

Actors and actresses, Jewish
    3218

Actors and actresses, Negro--
    SEE: Negro actors and
    actresses

Advertising   3392, 3545, 4718,
    4722, 4723-4725

Aeronautics   1025, 1936, 1942,
    2024, 2065, 4776, 4779-4780,
    4785, 4809-4811, 4829

Africa   317-334

    Central   317, 320-321

    East   317, 319-321, 333

    Portuguese East   333

    South   322-334, 3226, 4171

African Methodist Episcopal
Church   4547

Africanists   4692

Afrikaans authors--SEE: Authors,
Afrikaans

Aggada   4560-4561

Agriculturists   4777, 4783,
4786, 4800-4801

Ain, France (Dept.)   851

Aisne, France (Dept.)   852

Akademie der Wissenschaften,
Berlin   4572

Akademie der Wissenschaften,
Göttingen   4573, 4613

Akademiia khudozhestv, Leningrad
2537

Akademiia nauk SSSR   3303,
4574-4575, 4614

Alabama   2074-2075

Alaska   2076-2077, 3398

Albacete, Spain   1787

Alchemists   4660

Alicante, Spain (Province)   3874,
3885

Allier, France (Dept.)   853

Alpes, Basses-, France (Dept.)
865

Alpes, Hautes-, France (Dept.)
890

Alsace-Lorraine   854-858,
2504, 2912

Altenburg (Duchy)   1026

America   146, 335-336, 496,
3006, 4430, 4679, 4686

American anonyms and pseudo-
nyms--SEE: Anonyms and
pseudonyms, American

American Association of Professional Baseball Clubs   3248

American authors--SEE: Authors,
American

American League of Professional
Baseball Clubs   3249

American novelists--SEE:
Novelists, American

American poets--SEE: Poets,
American

Americans in China   1903

Americans in Europe   1897

Americans in France   2063

Americans in Panama   1956

Americans in Paris   2063

Americans in the Philippine Islands   1618

Amherst College   1907

Amoraim   4560-4561

Amsterdam. Universiteit   3256

Anabaptists   4431

Anatomists   4197, 4203, 4634-
4635

Ancona, Italy   4182

Andalusia   3864

Angers, France   2591

Anglican Church--SEE: Church
   of England

Anglo-Egyptian Sudan--SEE:
   Sudan

Anhalt   1068, 3670, 3690

Animal painters   2505

Anjou, France   2591

Annam   492

Anonyms and pseudonyms   30-
   39, 180, 4263-4265

   American   1089, 1890-1892

   Argentine   337-338

   Austrian   381

   Belgian   419-421

   Brazilian   472-473

   Canadian   495

   Catalan   1763

   Colombian   626

   Cuban   635

   Czech   644

   Danish   655, 1751

   Dominican   674

   Dutch   1551-1552

   English   1088-1089

   Flemish   421, 1551-1552

   French   704-710

Anonyms and pseudonyms (cont'd)

   German   954-960

   Hebrew--SEE: Anonyms and
   pseudonyms, Jewish

   Hungarian   1247

   Icelandic   1751

   Italian   1338-1343

   Jesuit   4264-4265

   Jewish   1448

   Latin   704

   Latin-American--SEE: Anonyms and pseudonyms, Brazilian; and Anonyms and
   pseudonyms, Spanish-American

   Mexican   1519-1520

   Norwegian   1584-1585,
   1751

   Polish   1625

   Portuguese   1639

   Provençal   710

   Russian   1662-1664

   Scandinavian   1751

   Slovak   645

   Spanish   1761-1763

   Spanish-American   1497-
   1500, 3901-3902

   Swedish   1815

   Tyrolese   381

Anonyms and pseudonyms (cont'd)

   Uruguayan   2380

Ansbach   1027, 3669, 4490

Anthropologists   4761

Antwerp   456

Apulia   2644-2645, 3760

Arabic authors--SEE: Authors,
   Arabic

Arabic physicians--SEE: Physicians, Arabic

Arabic scientists--SEE: Scientists, Arabic

Arabs--SEE: Muslim biography

Aragon   1788-1789, 2763, 3861,
   3871, 4373

Arcadia, Rome   1368, 1380

Archaeologists   4764

Archbishops of Canterbury--SEE:
   Bishops--Great Britain

Architects   2493, 2597, 2675-
   2692

Architects--Bibliography, indexes,
   etc.   2415, 2419

Architects

   Belgium   2693

   France   2677, 2683

   Great Britain   2680, 2682,
   2691

   Islamic countries   2686

   Italy   2689, 2694

Architects (cont'd)

   Netherlands   2693

   Poland   2685

   Portugal   2687

   Russia   2678

   Spain   2684

   United States   2675, 2692

Ardennes, France (Dept.)
   859-861

Argentine anonyms and pseudo-
   nyms--SEE: Anonyms and
   pseudonyms, Argentine

Argentine Republic   339-360,
   2552

Arizona   2078-2080, 2099

Arkansas   2081-2082

Armenia   361

Arras, France (Diocese)   4343

Art collectors   2448, 2466

Art critics   2543-2544

Art dealers   2466

Art historians   2543-2544

Artisans

   Denmark   2716

   France   2427, 2450, 2729

   Germany   4806

   Latin America   2734-2735

   Spain   2713

Artists   2412-2739, 3346, 3379,
4596

Argentina   2552

Austria   2589, 2635, 2651,
3616, 3707

Baltic Provinces   2566

Belgium   2529-2530, 2538,
2617

Bohemia   646, 2480

Brazil   2613

Canada   2662

Catalonia   2600

China   2413, 2655

Colombia   2422

Czechoslovakia   2636-2637
SEE ALSO: Artists--Bohemia;
Artists--Moravia

Denmark   2436, 2503, 2609,
2656

Flanders   2530, 2538, 2617

France   2427, 2437-2438,
2441, 2450, 2483, 2500, 2504,
2506, 2568, 2591-2592, 2640
2642

Germany   1027, 1048, 1050,
2426, 2527, 2553-2554, 2557,
2608, 2674, 3616, 3634, 3637

Great Britain   2514-2517,
2522, 2603-2604, 2630

Hungary   1250

Ireland   2624

Artists (cont'd)

Italy   2424, 2429-2431, 2456-
2457, 2465, 2467, 2481, 2494,
2513, 2519, 2575, 2580-2581,
2595-2596, 2605, 2620, 2644-
2645, 2672, 2732, 3771

Japan   2532, 2655

Lusatia   1055, 3672-3673

Moravia   646, 2480

Netherlands   2443, 2521,
2530, 2538, 2617, 2670

Portugal   2599

Russia   2454, 2619

Saxony   2557

Scandinavia   2657

Silesia   2480

Spain   2423, 2432, 2459,
2574, 2576-2577, 2585, 2600-
2601, 2623, 2646, 2673, 2699,
3991

Sweden   2627-2628

Switzerland   2452, 2614

Tyrol   2635

United States   2556, 2567,
2571, 2638, 2659-2660, 2662

Wales   2604

Artists--Bibliography, indexes,
    etc.   2412-2413, 2415,
    2419-2420, 2548-2549

Artists, Ancient   2487

Artists, Women   2654

Artists' marks   2414, 2416-2418,
   2562-2563, 2707, 2709, 2711,
   2715, 2718, 2721-2722, 2727

Asia   285, 362-366

Astronautics   4673, 4829

Astronomers   4671

Asturias   3991

Atheists   4427

Athens   1243

Athletes   3220-3221, 3226, 3228,
   3233, 3238, 3243

Attica, Greece   1243

Aube, France (Dept.)   862

Augsburg   4540

Augustinians   4325, 4377, 4439,
   4451, 4456, 4481, 4450

Aunis, France   934

Australasia   367, 377, 3963

Australia   369-380, 3516, 4169

Australia, Western--SEE: Western Australia

Austria   382-407, 976, 1018-
   1019, 2518, 2812, 3171, 3607,
   3609, 3622-3623, 3648, 4299,
   4504, 4758

   Upper   388, 390

Austrian anonyms and pseudo-
   nyms--SEE: Anonyms and
   pseudonyms, Austrian

Austrian authors--SEE: Authors,
   Austrian

Authors   135, 191, 199, 213,
   254, 261, 277-278, 305, 3323-
   3939
   SEE ALSO: Educators and
   scholars; etc.

Authors--Bibliography, indexes,
   etc.   3324

Authors

   Afrikaans   3394-3395

   American   3330, 3396-3436,
   3493, 3505, 3529, 3533-3534,
   4605

      Alaska   3398

      Boston   3404

      California   3411

      Colorado   3427

      Iowa   3418

      Maine   3415

      Maryland   3428

      Massachusetts   3404

      Michigan   3408-3409

      Minnesota   3421, 3425

      Missouri   3402

      Nebraska   3406

      North Carolina   3412

      Northwest   3422-3423

      Ohio   3401

      St. Louis   3402

      South Carolina   3433

Authors (cont'd)

American

    Southern States   3413,
3430

    West Virginia   3399

Arabic   3437-3442

Australian   3516

Austrian   976, 3607, 3609,
3613, 3616, 3622-3623, 3640,
3648, 3659, 3686, 3704, 3707

Azerbaijani   3934

Belgian   443, 460, 3443-
3451, 3568

Bengali   3726

Bohemian--SEE: Authors,
Czech

Brazilian   3813, 3817

Bulgarian   3452

Buriat   3801

Byzantine--SEE: Authors,
Greek (Medieval)

Canadian   3431, 3503, 3513,
3518, 3536, 3538

Catalan   3453-3457, 3866,
3872

Catholic--SEE: Catholic
authors

Celtic   1113

Children's--SEE: Children's
authors

Chilean   3906

Authors (cont'd)

Chinese   597, 3458-3459

Classical   254, 3353, 3460-
3471

Colombian   626-627, 3913

Costa Rican   3917

Cuban   3908

Czech   650, 3472-3476

Danish   3477-3487

Dutch   3444, 3488-3491

Early Christian   4293,
4356-4357

English   3370, 3492-3546

    Australia--SEE: Authors,
    Australian

    Canada--SEE: Authors,
    Canadian

    Cornwall   3498, 3546

    Devon   3546

    Ireland--SEE: Authors,
    Irish (English)

    Lancashire   3535

    New Zealand--SEE: Au-
    thors, New Zealand

    Scotland--SEE: Authors,
    Scottish

    Worcestershire   1239

English (Middle English)
3530, 3532

Estonian   3549, 3551

Authors (cont'd)

Finnish   1824

Finno-Ugrian   3547-3551

Flemish   460, 3451

French   765, 820, 3375,
3552-3596

    Belgium   3443-3445,
    3448-3450, 3568

    Burgundy   3586

    Canada--SEE: Authors,
    French-Canadian

    Maine (Dept.)   3552

    Normandy   920

    Vaucluse (Dept.)   949

French-Canadian   3536,
3555, 3579, 3593

Frisian   3597

Gaelic   3598-3600

Gallegan   3601-3602

German   976, 992, 3367,
3603-3708

    Anhalt   3670, 3690

    Ansbach   1027, 3669

    Austria--SEE: Authors,
    Austrian

    Bamberg   3637

    Bavaria   1031-1032,
    3605-3606, 3687

    Bayreuth   3618, 3669

Authors (cont'd)

German

    Berlin   1034, 3636,
    3691

    Bremen   3628

    Dresden   3634

    Eutin   3603, 3650,
    3664-3665

    Freiburg im Breisgau
    3638

    Hamburg   3693

    Hesse   1048, 1050-1051,
    3694

    Königsberg   1052

    Leipzig   1053

    Lusatia   1055, 3672-
    3673

    Mecklenburg   3649

    Münsterland   3680-3681,
    3683-3684

    Munich   3687

    Pomerania   1060, 1063,
    3608

    Prussia   3615

    Prussia, East   1052

    Rügen (Island)   3608

    Saxony   3631, 3699,
    3703

    Schleswig-Holstein
    1070, 3603, 3650, 3664-65

Authors (cont'd)

German

Silesia   3666, 3671,
3695, 3698

Styria, Austria   3707

Sudetenland   3639

Swabia   3627, 3632

Switzerland   3613
SEE ALSO: Authors,
Swiss

Transylvania   3700-3701

Vienna   3607, 3609,
3659, 3686, 3704

Wernigerode   3645

German (Low German)   3617

German (Middle High German)
3696

German (Old High German)
3696

Greek   3649   SEE ALSO:
Authors, Classical

Greek (Medieval)   3469

Greek (Modern)   3709-3710

Guatemalan   3897

Hebrew--SEE: Authors, Jewish

Hungarian   1249-1250, 3711-
3720

Icelandic   3478-3479, 3485,
3721

Indic   3722-3728

Authors (cont'd)

Irish   1307, 3730

Irish (English)   1307, 3496-
3497, 3501, 3523, 3529, 3537,
3539

Italian   2644-2645, 3339,
3463, 3731-3785

Abruzzi   3778

Apulia   2644-2645, 3760

Bologna   3750, 3770

Calabria   3734, 3754

Cremona   3738-3739

Dalmatia   2401

Ferrara   3769

Florence   3768

Friuli   3748, 3762

Liguria   3759, 3777

Lunigiana   3756

Milan   3772

Modena   3679, 3781

Naples   3731, 3745,
3758, 3763, 3765-3766,
3779

Nice   3749

Parma   3732

Perugia   3784

Piedmont   3749

Rome (City)   3740

Authors (cont'd)

   Italian

      Savoy   3749

      Sicily   3767

      Switzerland   3931

      Trent   3735

      Tyrol   3780

      Venetia   3733, 3755

      Venice   3757

      Vicenza   3736, 3775

   Japanese   3786-3788

   Jewish   1451, 1483, 3789-3795, 4239

   Kazakh   3933

   Kirghiz   3936

   Latin   3460, 3464, 3468, 3470-3471
SEE ALSO: Authors, Classical

   Latin (Medieval and modern) 3470-3471

   Latin-American--SEE: Authors, Brazilian; Authors, Spanish American; etc.

   Lettish   3796-3797

   Lithuanian   3798-3800

   Malayalam   3723

   Marathi   1276

   Medieval   3353, 4356-4357

Authors (cont'd)

   Mexican   3909, 3912

   Mordvinian   3547

   Negro   3426

   New Zealand   3521

   North American   3390

   Norwegian   3478-3479, 3485, 3802-3805

   Persian   3806-3807

   Polish   3808-3812

   Portuguese   3813-3817

   Provençal   710, 3592, 3596

   Puerto Rican   3910, 3915

   Russian   3818-3853

      Poltava (Government) 1718

      Ryazan (Government) 3822

      Siberia   3847, 3852-3853

      Ural Mountains region 1704

      Vologda (Government) 3821

   Scandinavian--SEE: Authors, Danish; Authors, Norwegian; etc.

   Scottish   3496, 3506, 3514, 3524, 3537, 3539
FOR WRITERS IN GAELIC SEE: Authors, Gaelic

Authors (cont'd)

Serbian--SEE: Authors, Yugoslav

Spanish   261, 1781, 3382, 3855-3896
SEE ALSO: Authors, Catalan; Authors, Gallegan; Authors, Spanish-American

Alicante (Province) 3874, 3885

Andalusia   3864

Aragon   3861, 3871

Asturias   3991

Balearic Islands   3859

Burgos (Province) 3873, 3888

Cadiz   1791

Canary Islands   3876

Cordoba   1796

Gerona (Province) 3869

Guadalajara (Province) 3867

Majorca   3860

Murcia   3892

Palencia (Province) 3883

Segovia (Province) 3858

Seville   3862, 3870

Valencia   3866, 3872, 3896

Authors (cont'd)

Spanish-American   1495, 3382, 3878, 3887, 3894, 3897-3919
SEE ALSO: Authors, Colombian; etc.

Swedish   1824, 3920-3924, 4026

Swiss   976, 3613, 3925-3932

Syryenian   3548

Tamil   3728

Telugu   3722

Ukrainian   3937-3938

Urdu   3939

Uruguayan   3900, 3903

Uzbek   3935

Venezuelan   3898-3899, 3911, 3916

Votiak   3350

Walloon   3446

White Russian   3838

Yiddish   3790, 3793

Yugoslav   3854

Autobiographies--Bibliography, indexes, etc.   494, 1086-1087, 1887-1888

Automobile industry and trade 4778, 4808, 4825

Automobile racing   3246

Auvergne   863-864

Aviators--SEE: Aeronautics

Azerbaijan   1669, 3934

Azerbaijani authors--SEE: Authors, Azerbaijani

B

Baden   1028

Baghdad   1322

Baireuth--SEE: Bayreuth

Balearic Islands   3859

Balkan Peninsula   408-409

Ballet--SEE: Dancers

Baltic Provinces   410-417, 2565-2566

Baltic University, Pinneberg, Ger. --SEE: Pinneberg, Ger. Baltic University

Baltimore   2083

Bamberg, Ger.   3637

Bankers   4697, 4714, 4726

Baptist missionaries--SEE: Missionaries, Baptist

Baptists   1097, 4290-4291, 4320, 4400, 4425, 4499, 4509, 4521

Barnabites   4306, 4515

Baronetage (Gt. Brit.)   1102, 1107, 1116, 1123, 1133, 1135, 1155, 1185

Baseball   3219, 3235, 3241, 3248-3252

Basel   1866, 4018

Basel. Universität   1843, 3275, 3311

Basilicata, Italy   1385

Basketball   3245

Basque Provinces   1790

Bassano, Italy   2732

Bavaria   1029-1033, 2944, 3605-3606, 4135, 4179, 4413-4414

Basses-Alpes, France (Dept.)-- SEE: Alpes, Basses-, France (Dept)

Baton twirling   3239

Bayreuth   3618, 3669, 4491

Bedfordshire, Eng.   1191

Belgian anonyms and pseudonyms --SEE: Anonyms and pseudonyms, Belgian

Belgian authors--SEE: Authors, Belgian

Belgian Congo--SEE: Congo, Belgian

Belgium   418-467, 4279, 2508, 2529, 2693, 2855, 2877-2878, 2880, 2888, 2950, 3084, 3099, 3259, 3268, 3290, 3443-3451, 3949, 4038-4039, 4125, 4307, 4351, 4363

Armée   441, 465

Congrès national (1830-1831) 434

Corps législatif   439

Corps législatif. Sénat 461

Belgium (cont'd)

Parlement   442, 444, 451

Belgium--Bibliography, indexes,
etc.   418, 432

Belley, France (Diocese)   4342

Benedictines   4277, 4284, 4299,
4371, 4413-4414, 4552

Benedictines. Congrégation de
Saint Maur   4408, 4508

Bengal   1283, 3726

Army   1151

Bengali authors--SEE: Authors,
Bengali

Bergamo, Italy   2959

Berkshire, Eng.   1192

Berlin   1034-1035, 2940, 3636,
3691, 4565

Akademie der Wissenschaften
--SEE: Akademie der Wis-
senschaften, Berlin

Universität   3260

Bern (Canton)   1852

Beta Theta Pi   1909

Bible--Biography   4266-4267,
4269-4270, 4563

Bibliophiles--SEE: Book collectors

Bio-bibliography (general)   82,
107, 117, 124, 135, 166-167,
170, 180, 198, 205, 229-232,
254, 265, 270, 274, 277-278,
280-282, 295, 305, 316

Bio-bibliography--Bibliography,
indexes, etc.   3-4, 8, 20

Biography (general)   40-316

Biography--Bibliography, indexes,
etc.   2-6, 8, 12-24, 27-28,
156, 221-222, 235

Biography

Ancient period--SEE: Biography, Classical

Middle Ages   102

17th century   263, 305

18th century   46, 74, 127-
128, 151, 223, 242, 244-245,
264, 270

19th century   74, 77, 82,
94-95, 109, 114, 125, 127-128,
189-190, 194, 197, 200, 206,
210, 223, 227, 242, 245, 253,
286-289, 292, 314-315

20th century   48, 54-55,
93, 105, 111, 132-133, 158-
162, 170-171, 173, 188, 195-
196, 205, 226, 234, 250, 269,
273, 283-285, 299, 306-311

Biography, Classical--SEE: Classical biography

Biography, Military--SEE: Military biography

Biography, Naval--SEE: Naval
biography

Biologists   4637-4638, 4640,
4644, 4648

Biologists, Marine--SEE: Marine
biologists

Birmingham, Eng.   1193

Bishops   4375-4376, 4409

Belgium   4363

Canada   4310

Comacchio, Italy (Diocese) 4480

France   4363, 4401

Great Britain   4394, 4411

Iceland   4489

Russia   4476

Scotland   4354

United States   4547

Blekinge, Sweden (County)   1825

Blind   2053

Boer War (1899-1902)   324, 332

Bogotá   633

Bohemia   646, 650, 652-653, 2480, 3472, 4455

Bohemian authors--SEE: Authors, Czech

Bolivia   468-471

Bologna   1366, 1386, 2550, 3750, 3770

Accademia dei Gelati--SEE: Accademia dei Gelati, Bologna

Università   3292

Bombay (State)   1276

Book collectors   4014-4015, 4052

Book illustrators   124, 4001, 4028-4029

Book industries and trade   4025, 4030, 4032, 4045

Belgium   4038-4039

France   3998, 4036-4037

Germany   1053

Great Britain   4008-4009, 4027, 4033-4035, 4051

Poland   4043-4044

Russia   4031

Sweden   4026

United States   4030

Bookbinders   3998, 4016, 4041

Booksellers--SEE: Book industries

Bosnia and Herzegovina   2398, 4402

Boston   2084-2085, 3404

Boston Authors Club   3404

Botanists   4631-4633, 4636, 4645-4646, 4649-4650

Bouches-du-Rhone, France (Dept.) 866

Bowling   3237

Brandenburg   1065

Brazil   472-487, 2613, 3193, 3813, 3817

Brazilian anonyms and pseudonyms --SEE: Anonyms and pseudonyms, Brazilian

Brazilian authora--SEE: Authors, Brazilian

Bremen   1036-1038, 3628

Brescia, Italy   2494, 4201

British authors--SEE: Authors, Celtic; Authors, English; Authors, Gaelic; Authors, Irish; Authors, Scottish

British Columbia   521, 2662

British Guiana   488

British in Burma   1274

British in France   2063

British in India   1274

British in Paris   2063

Brittany   867-870, 4418

Brooklyn, N. Y.   4453

Brown University   1919

Bruges, Belgium   458

Buckinghamshire, Eng.   1194

Buddhists   4272-4274

Building and loan associations 4700

Bulgaria   489

Bulgarian authors--SEE: Authors, Bulgarian

Bull-fighters   3223, 3227, 3234

Burgos, Spain (Province)   3873, 3888

Burgundy   871, 3586

Buriat authors--SEE: Authors, Buriat

Buriat-Mongolia   3801

Burma   490-491, 1274, 1289

Business teachers   3254

Businessmen   4735

Burma   490

Canada   502, 2049, 4711- 4713, 4726

China   577

France   744, 794

Germany   4719

Great Britain   4710

Italy   1345

Sweden   1838

United States   2049, 2095, 2118, 4701, 4704, 4711-4713, 4726

Byzantine authors--SEE: Authors, Greek (Medieval)

C

Cabinet-workers   2705, 2712, 2714, 2722, 2724, 2727

Cadiz, Spain   1791-1792

Cagliari, Sardinia   3003

Calabria   1387, 3734, 3754

California   2086-2099, 2166-2167, 2317, 2982, 3121, 3411, 4729

California, Southern   2099, 2982

Calligraphers   2449, 4005,
4017, 4040

Calvados, France (Dept.)   872-
873

Cambodia   492-493

Cambrai, France (Diocese)
4343

Cambridge, Eng.   4016

University   1108-1111, 1119,
1136, 1180

Cambridgeshire, Eng.   1206

Camillians   4362

Canada   494-523, 2269, 2791-
2792, 3070, 3503, 3513, 3518,
3536, 3538, 3555, 3579, 3593,
3964, 3970, 3994, 4002-4003,
4047, 4049, 4065, 4100, 4216,
4278-4280, 4310, 4711-4713,
4726, 4730, 4777, 4801

Parliament   503

Canada--Bibliography, indexes,
etc.   494

Canada, Western   523

Canadian anonyms and pseudonyms
--SEE: Anonyms and pseudonyms, Canadian

Canadian authors--SEE: Authors,
Canadian

Canadian Northwest--SEE: Northwest, Canadian

Canadian novelists--SEE: Novelists, Canadian

Canadian poets--SEE: Poets,
Canadian

Canary Islands   1793, 3876

Canonists   4344

Capitalists and financiers--SEE:
Businessmen

Capuchins   4308, 4317, 4350,
4380, 4398, 4498

Cardiganshire, Wales   1233

Cardinals   4358

Caribbean area   2396-2397

Carmelites   4296, 4302, 4428,
4477, 4524, 4548

Cartographers   4742, 4744-4745,
4749-4750

Cassel, Ger. --SEE: Kassel, Ger.

Catalan anonyms and pseudonyms
--SEE: Anonyms and pseudonyms, Catalan

Catalan authors--SEE: Authors,
Catalan

Catalan poets--SEE: Poets, Catalan

Catalonia   2600, 3453-3457

Catholic authors   3330, 3355,
3418, 3426, 3643-3644, 3692,
3705, 3744

Catholics   4281, 4285, 4321-
4323, 4326-4329, 4341, 4344-
4349, 4358-4361, 4375-4376,
4389, 4397, 4407, 4438

Belgium   464, 4526

Canada   4278-4280, 4310

Chile   4465

Catholics (cont'd)

France   4292, 4318, 4342

Geneva (Diocese)   4468

Germany   990

Great Britain   1112, 1142-1143, 1156, 4415, 4443

Lucerne (Canton)   4390

Mexico   4520

Netherlands   1568

Switzerland   4388, 4390, 4399, 4468

Tournai, Belgium (Diocese) 4526

United States   1896, 4332

Zug (Canton)   4399

Cattle breeders   4790

Cauca, Colombia (Dept.)   625

Caucasus   1679

Ceara, Brazil (State)   486

Celtic authors--SEE: Authors, Celtic

Celtic musicians--SEE: Musicians, Celtic

Celts   1113, 1172

Central Africa--SEE: Africa, Central

Central America   524, 4276

Central Europe--SEE: Europe, Central

Ceramics   2719, 2725

Česká akademie věd a umění, Prague   4581

Chambre des députés (France)-- SEE: France. Chambre des députés

Champagne   874

Chaplains, Military   4518

Charente-Inférieure, France (Dept)   875, 934

Charterhouse School, Godalming, Eng.   1177

Chemical engineers   4652

Chemists   4104, 4651-4665

Chicago   2100-2107, 4804

Children's authors   124, 3363, 3386

American   3415

German   3644

Swiss   3925

Chile   525-535, 3906, 4465, 4798

Chile--Bibliography, indexes, etc.   525-526

Chilean authors--SEE: Authors, Chilean

Chilean poets--SEE: Poets, Chilean

China   536-623, 2413, 2626, 2655, 3458-3459, 4052, 4272, 4274, 4640

China--Bibliography, indexes, etc.   536-541

Chinese authors--SEE: Authors, Chinese

Chinese in Indonesia   1299, 1513

Chinese in Java   1299

Chinese in Malaya   1513

Chinese in Singapore   1754-1755

Chinese in Thailand   1871

Chiropractors   4228

Christian authors, Early--SEE: Authors, Early Christian

Christian biography   4275-4552

Church Fathers--SEE: Fathers of the Church

Church musicians   2807, 2870, 2896, 2918, 2923, 2927, 2930, 2935, 2946, 2965, 2968-2969, 2973, 3001, 3022, 3092-3093, 3113

Church of England   4330, 4339, 4394, 4410-4411, 4543

Church of Ireland   4335-4336

Church of Scotland   4486, 4517

Cincinnati   2108

Cistercians   4445, 4525

City managers   4773

City planners   1902

Ciudad Trujillo--SEE: Santo Domingo (City)

Civil engineers   4793

Classical authors--SEE: Authors, Classical

Classical biography   177, 184, 211, 217, 225, 228-231, 266-267, 296, 1243, 1654, 3460-3471

Clergy

Asia   4338

Belgium   4526

Canada   4278-4280

Chile   4465

France   4292, 4318, 4337, 4462

Georgia   4487

Germany   4340, 4367, 4386, 4405, 4490-4493, 4540

Great Britain   4330, 4339, 4410-4411, 4419, 4516, 4533, 4535, 4538

Hungary   4404

Indonesia   4312

Ireland   4335-4336

Mexico   4520

Netherlands   4305, 4312, 4420

New Hampshire   4319

New York (City)   4453

Russia   4366, 4505

Scotland   3514, 4424, 4486, 4517

Clergy (cont'd)

Southern States (U. S.)
4507

Switzerland   4367, 4390,
4399, 4468

United States   4319, 4331-
4332, 4334, 4447, 4453, 4471,
4485, 4487, 4501, 4507, 4509,
4518, 4529, 4531, 4533-4534,
4536, 4539

Virginia   4509

Wales   4333, 4365, 4440

Clergy, Negro--SEE: Negro clergy

Cleveland   2109

Clock and watch makers   2704,
2706, 2708, 2723, 2728

Clothing designers--SEE: Costume
designers

Club of Nobody's Friends   1115

Coaches (Athletics)   3225

Coburg (City)   1039

Cochin China   492

Cologne   2553

Universität   970

Colombia   624-633, 1506-1507,
2422, 3129, 3913, 4433, 4800

Colombian anonyms and pseudo-
nyms--SEE: Anonyms and
pseudonyms, Colombian

Colombian authors--SEE: Authors,
Colombian

Colorado   2110-2115, 2124-2126,
3427

Columbia University. Graduate
School of Journalism   3434

Comacchio, Italy (Diocese)   4480

Commonwealth of Nations   3278,
4783

Communication and traffic   4828

Communist Party of Indonesia--
SEE: Partai Komunis Indonesia

Como, Italy (Province)   1388

Composers   2809-2810, 2813,
2823, 2829, 2841-2842, 2844-
2846, 2863, 2891, 2902, 2904,
2951, 2989, 3010, 3024, 3050,
3096, 3103, 3128

America   3006

Belgium   3099

Canada   2791

Colombia   3129

Czechoslovakia   2868

Europe   2845

Finland   2919, 3025

France   2809-2810

Great Britain   2762

India   3047

Italy   2959, 2974-
2975, 3106

Latin America   3014

Portugal   3014

Composers (cont'd)

Russia 2770, 2926, 2929, 2945, 3041, 3074, 3077, 3108

Southern States (U.S.) 2924, 3076

Spain 3014

United States 2839, 2851, 2876, 2900, 2924, 2949, 3029, 3076, 3125, 3127

Virginia 2949

Wisconsin 3125

Conductors 2812

Confederate States of America 2044

Confucians 4246, 4256

Congo (Leopoldville) 634

Congo, Belgian 422, 428, 440, 466

Congregational Churches 4333, 4454, 4533

Congregational Union of England and Wales 4333

Congressional Medal of Honor-- SEE: Medal of Honor (U.S.)

Connecticut 2116-2121

Consejo Superior de Investigaciones Científicas--SEE: Spain. Consejo Superior ...

Converts 1143, 4429

Cooperative movement 4698

Copenhagen. Universitet 4118, 4510

Copyists 2449

Cordoba, Spain 1794-1796, 2601

Cornell University. Medical College, New York 4115

Cornwall 1195, 3498, 3546

Costa Rica 3917

Costa Rican authors--SEE: Authors, Costa Rican

Costume designers 2737

Côte-d'Or, France (Dept.) 876

Côtes-du-Nord, France (Dept.) 877

Courland 415-416, 4091

Cremona 2513, 2974-2975, 3738-3739

Cricket 3222, 3224, 3230-3231, 3236

Crime and criminals 260

France 925

Great Britain 1160

New Mexico 2241

Paris 925

United States 2241, 2361

The West (U.S.) 2361

Crimea 1678

Critics (Literature) 3583-3584

Croatia   2398-2399, 2401-2402,
2407, 2409

Croats in Canada   1912

Croats in the U. S.   1912

Crystallographers   6

Cuba   635-642, 3908, 4123, 4379

Cuban anonyms and pseudonyms--
SEE: Anonyms and pseudo-
nyms, Cuban

Cuban authors--SEE: Authors,
Cuban

Cyprus   643

Czech anonyms and pseudonyms--
SEE: Anonyms and pseudo-
nyms, Czech

Czech authors--SEE: Authors,
Czech

Czechoslovakia   644-653, 2636-
2637, 2794, 2868, 3472-3476,
4581

Czechs in Chicago   2104

D

Dalmatia   2399, 2401

Damascus   1318

Dancers   2982-2988, 3138, 3144-
3145, 3147-3148, 3159, 3169,
3184, 3215

Danes in foreign countries   661

Danes in the U. S.   661

Danish anonyms and pseudonyms--
SEE: Anonyms and pseudo-
nyms, Danish

Danish authors--SEE: Authors,
Danish

Danzig   1040

Data processing, Electronic--SEE:
Electronic data processing

Dauphiné   878-881

Decembrists   1689

Delaware   2122-2123, 2984

Delaware Valley   4816

Demonology   4253, 4261

Denmark,   654-673, 2436, 2503,
2546, 2656, 2716, 2893, 3049,
3092-3093, 3477-3487, 4012,
4118, 4145, 4632, 4636, 4791

Denmark--Bibliography, indexes,
etc.   654

Denmark--Portraits   664, 670

Dentists   4055, 4063, 4070,
4217, 4219-4220

Denver   2124-2126

Detroit   2127-2129

Deutsche Gesellschaft zu Göttingen
--SEE: Akademie der Wissenschaften, Göttingen

Devon, Eng.   3546

Diplomats   42, 116, 309-310

    Brazil   484

    Denmark   665

    France   713, 792

    Great Britain   1140

Diplomats (cont'd)

United States   2004

Distinguished Service Order
1120

District of Columbia--SEE: Washington, D. C.

Doctors--SEE: Physicians

Dominican anonyms and pseudo-
nyms--SEE: Anonyms and
pseudonyms, Dominican

Dominican Republic   674-675,
4114

Dominicans   4352, 4374, 4433,
4466, 4513

Don River and Valley   1684

Dorpat--SEE: Tartu

Doubs, France (Dept.)   882

Dramatists   3374

  English   3139, 3495

  French   3175, 3581

  Scottish   3506

Dresden   1041, 3634

Drôme, France (Dept.)   883

Drum majors   3239

Dublin

  Royal College of Surgeons in
  Ireland   4099

  University   1301-1302

Dutch anonyms and pseudonyms--

SEE: Anonyms and pseudo-
nyms, Dutch

Dutch authors--SEE: Authors,
Dutch

Dutch Guiana--SEE: Surinam

Dutch in Indonesia   1294-1295,
4312

Dutch missionaries--SEE: Missionaries, Dutch

Dutch poets--SEE: Poets, Dutch

Dutch West Indies--SEE: West
Indies, Dutch

E

Early Christian authors--SEE:
Authors, Early Christian

The East--SEE: Asia; East (Far
East); etc.

East (Far East)   285, 364, 366,
4338

East Africa--SEE: Africa, East

East Africa, Portuguese--SEE:
Africa, Portuguese East

East Friesland--SEE: Friesland,
East

East Prussia--SEE: Prussia, East

Eastern Europe--SEE: Europe,
Eastern

Eccentrics and eccentricities   187

Economists   4695, 4699, 4703,
4717, 4774

Ecuador   676-681, 1506-1507

Edinburgh   1217

Educators and scholars   86, 117,
166-167, 244, 258, 270, 274,
277-278, 316, 684-686, 3258,
3288-3289, 3295, 3304, 3308,
3315, 4250-4251

Austria   389, 393, 976

Belgium   424, 3268

Bohemia   646, 650, 652

China   551, 615-617, 621

Commonwealth of Nations
3278

Denmark   673

Finland   3310, 3312

France   748, 3271

Germany   969, 976, 983,
991-992, 996, 1010-1011, 1027,
1029, 1031-1032, 1034, 1036,
1038-1041, 1043, 1045, 1048,
1050-1051, 1053, 1056-1060,
1063, 1067, 1074, 1078, 1080,
1082, 3257, 3260, 3266-3267,
3269-3270, 3272, 3282, 3298,
3306, 3322

Great Britain   1227, 3265,
3314

Iceland   673, 3284

India   3273-3274, 3293

Italy   1360, 3292, 3302,
3307

Japan   1436, 3299

Mexico   3277

Moravia   646, 652

Netherlands   3294, 3313

Educators and scholars (cont'd)

Norway   673, 1590, 3279

Poland   1629, 1632

Russia   3280-3281, 3283,
3286-3287, 3296

Switzerland   976, 3275, 3311

United States   3254-3255,
3263, 3276, 3285, 3291, 3300,
3305, 3309, 3316-3321, 3429

Virginia   3316

Wales   1227

Wisconsin   3317

Educators and scholars, Jewish
1457-1458, 1468, 1470-1471,
1473

Educators and scholars, Muslim
1326

Educators and scholars, Women
3265, 3316

Egypt   1321, 1332, 4583, 4585
SEE ALSO: United Arab Re-
public

Egyptologists   4754

Electrical engineers   4788

Electronic data processing
4812, 4821, 4823

Electronics industries   4822

Enamelists   2462, 2558

Engineers

Egypt   4583

Great Britain   4784

Engineers (cont'd)

   Iceland   4807

   India   4817

   Italy   4799

   Japan   4796-4797

   Portugal   2687

   Russia   4795

   Spain   4793

   United States   1956, 4804,
   4813, 4815-4816

Engineers, Electrical--SEE:
   Electrical engineers

England--SEE: Great Britain

English anonyms and pseudonyms--
   SEE: Anonyms and pseudonyms, English

English authors--SEE: Authors,
   English

English poets--SEE: Poets, English

Engravers   2426, 2433-2434,
   2440, 2451, 2455, 2463, 2468,
   2470, 2495, 2511, 2559, 2570,
   2583, 2590, 2593-2594, 2621,
   2625

   France   2593

   Germany   2426

   Great Britain   2511, 4013

   Italy   2583, 2616

   Japan   2470

   Netherlands   2648

Engravers (cont'd)

   Norway   2570

   Russia   2590, 2606-2607

   Scotland   2455

   Tasmania   2468

   Ukraine   2590

   United States   2495, 2622,
   4013

Engravers' marks   2414, 2416,
   2625

Entomologists   4639, 4647

Erfurt. Universität   3298

Erlangen. Universität   3266,
   4187

Esperantists   3391

Essex Co., N. J.   4111

Estonia   410, 415-417, 2995,
   3549, 3551, 4090

Estonian authors--SEE: Authors,
   Estonian

Estremadura   1797

Etchers   2511

Ethnologists   4759

Eure, France (Dept.)   884

Eure-et-Loir, France (Dept.)
   924

Europe   248, 270, 285, 311, 682-
   694, 2845, 2861, 3053, 4718

Europe, Central   691

Europe, Eastern   691-692

European War (1914-1918)   1022,
1174, 3553

Eutin   3603, 3650, 3664-3665

Evangelical-Lutheran churches
4340, 4446, 4457, 4490-4493

Explorers   4740-4741, 4743,
4748, 4751

F

Far East--SEE: East (Far East)

Fathers of the Church   4293,
4356-4357

Felinophiles   41

Ferrara   1389-1390, 3769

Fife, Scot.   1196

Filipinos in the U. S.   1990

Financiers--SEE: Bankers;
Businessmen

Finistère, France (Dept.)   885

Finland   695-701, 2919, 3025,
3310, 3312, 4078

Finnish authors--SEE: Authors,
Finnish

Finns in the U. S.   2050

Firearms industry and trade--SEE:
Gunsmiths

Flamenco   3184

Flanders   429, 460, 467, 2472-
2473, 2530, 2538, 2617, 3451

Flanders, West   429

Flemish anonyms and pseudonyms
--SEE: Anonyms and pseudonyms, Flemish

Flemish artists--SEE: Artists
Flanders

Flemish authors--SEE: Authors,
Flemish

Flemish painters--SEE: Painters--
Flanders

Florence   1369, 1371, 1391,
2464, 3768

Florence. Accademia toscana di
scienze e lettere La Colom-
baria--SEE: Accademia
toscana di scienze e lettere
La Colombaria, Florence

Florida   2130-2132, 4379

Folklorists   3333, 4759

Football   3242

Foreign correspondents--SEE:
Journalists

Forestry   4783

Forez, France   886

Formosa   555, 571, 606, 608

France   52, 174, 220, 311, 702-
953, 2437-2438, 2441, 2448,
2461, 2483-2484, 2500-2501,
2528, 2593, 2642, 2677, 2683,
2701, 2712, 2797, 2809-2810,
2862, 3134, 3138, 3155-3158,
3163, 3167-3168, 3172-3175,
3182, 3228, 3552-3596, 3956-
3957, 4024, 4036-4037, 4041,
4074, 4079, 4108, 4119, 4121,
4138, 4176, 4223, 4292, 4318,
4337, 4363, 4401, 4571, 4587-
4588, 4591, 4600-4601

France (cont'd)

Armée   714-715, 751, 753,
803, 816, 843, 849, 897

Assemblée législative (1848-
1851)   718, 727, 812, 821,
825

Assemblée nationale (1789-
1791)   779, 819

Assemblee nationale (1848-
1852)   728, 730, 784, 807

Assemblée nationale (1871-
1942)   842

Assemblée nationale (1871-
1942) Chambre des députés
787, 842

Assemblée nationale (1871-
1942) Sénat   719, 788,
837, 842

Assemblée national constituante (1848-1851)   712, 724,
726, 821

Assemblée nationale législative (1791-1792)   796

Chambre des députés (1814-
1849)   720, 735-737, 741-
742, 752, 767, 800, 804, 810,
818, 830, 835, 837

Convention nationale (1792-
1795)   789, 797, 822, 831

Corps législatif (1795-1814)
795

Etats-Généraux   776

Légion d'honneur   805, 811

Marine   809, 843

Parlement (Rouen)   919

France (cont'd)

Sénat (1852-1870)   722,
778, 810

France--Colonies   792

France--Portraits   702-703,
786, 823, 827, 867, 927

France--Revolution and Empire
717, 731-734, 740, 750-751,
755, 761, 763, 769, 779, 790,
795-797, 803, 808, 819, 822,
824, 826-827, 832, 836, 838-
839, 843, 845, 848, 4462

Franche-Comté   887, 2450

Franciscans   4276, 4282-4283,
4307, 4351, 4370, 4379, 4381-
4383, 4402, 4463, 4488, 4500,
4551

Franconia   4493

Franeker, Netherlands. Universiteit   3313

Frankfurt am Main   1042, 2527,
2674, 4386

Freemasons   236, 252, 301,
1670, 1994

Freethinkers--SEE: Rationalists

Freiburg im Breisgau   3638

Universität   1023

French anonyms and pseudonyms
--SEE: Anonyms and pseudonyms, French

French authors--SEE: Authors,
French

French-Canadian authors--SEE:
Authors, French-Canadian

French-Canadians   498-499,
513, 518, 1910, 4278-4280

French dramatists--SEE: Dramatists, French

French in the United States   1910

French Indochina--SEE: Indochina,
French

French poets--SEE: Poets, French

Friends, Society of   1091-1092,
1886, 4372, 4494-4496

Friends, Society of--Bibliography,
indexes, etc.   1886

Friesland, East   1043

Frisian authors--SEE: Authors,
Frisian

Frisian Islands   3313, 3597

Friuli   3748, 3762

Furniture makers--SEE: Cabinet-
workers

G

Gaelic authors--SEE: Authors,
Gaelic

Gaelic poets--SEE: Poets, Gaelic

Gästrikland, Sweden   1823

Galicia, Spain   1798, 2585,
3601- 3602

Gallegan authors--SEE: Authors,
Gallegan

Garde, France (Dept.)   2568

Genealogists   4760

Geneticists   4642

Geneva   1846, 1859, 4468

Genoa   2620

Gentry (Great Britain)   1103-
1105, 1155, 1181

Geographers   4738-4739, 4747,
4765

Geologists   4648

Geonim   4561

Georgia   2132-2138, 3969,
4487

German anonyms and pseudonyms
--SEE: Anonyms and pseudonyms, German

German authors--SEE: Authors,
German

German poets--SEE: Poets, German

Germans in Czechoslovakia
648, 3639

Germans in foreign countries
1016

Germans in Hungary   1255

Germans in Russia   1020-1021

Germans in Sudetenland   648,
3639

Germans in Transylvania   1658,
3700-3701

Germany   287, 954-1083, 2426,
2554, 2715, 2913, 2981, 3064,
3113, 3150, 3170-3171, 3181,
3257, 3260, 3266-3267, 3269-
3270, 3272, 3282, 3298, 3306,
3322, 3603-3708, 3724, 3961,
3971, 3988, 3993, 3997, 4073,
4086-4087, 4127, 4194, 4200,

Germany (cont'd)

4226, 4353, 4367, 4442,
4446, 4506, 4512, 4572-
4573, 4613, 4621, 4644,
4651, 4708, 4717, 4719,
4785, 4806

Heer (Army)   968,
987

Germany--Colonies   974

Germany--Portraits   969, 977,
985, 987, 3610, 3724

Germany (Democratic Republic,
1949-   )   979, 981,
1015, 3621

Germany (Federal Republic,
1949-   )   980, 984, 1009,

Bundestag   1009

Germany, Eastern   979, 981,
1012, 1015

Gerona, Spain (Province)   3869

Ghent   459

Rijksuniversiteit   3268

Glasgow   1197

University   1213

Glass painters and stainers
2482

Glossators   4344

Gloucestershire, Eng.   1198-
1199

Göttingen. Universität   3257,
3267, 3269

Goldsmiths

France   2569, 2729

Great Britain   2718

Russia   2730-2731

Sweden   2733

Golf   3229

Gosudarstvennyĭ Sovet--SEE:
Russia. Gosudarstvennyĭ
Sovet

Great Britain   73, 97, 104, 129,
208, 210, 1084-1242, 2428,
2510-2512, 2514-2517, 2545,
2603, 2630, 2649-2650, 2680,
2682, 2691, 2698-2699, 2707,
2718, 2724-2725, 2762, 2788,
2808, 2821, 2979, 3005, 3023,
3110, 3117, 3133, 3139, 3141,
3176, 3180, 3200-3201, 3221,
3262, 3265, 3314, 3492-3546,
3953-3955, 3962, 3995, 4008-
4009, 4017, 4022-4023, 4027,
4033-4035, 4056, 4162, 4168,
4172, 4188, 4190, 4192, 4196,
4206, 4221, 4262, 4294, 4330,
4333, 4339, 4394, 4400, 4410-
4411, 4416, 4434, 4449-4450,
4454, 4503, 4516, 4533, 4535,
4538, 4543, 4585, 4611, 4622,
4631, 4655, 4661, 4670, 4706,
4710, 4722, 4724-4725, 4745,
4762, 4776, 4782, 4784, 4788,
4814, 4818, 4825

Armed Forces   1120, 1174

Army   1134, 1148, 1151,
1171

Navy   1114, 1145, 1149,
1159, 1167, 1174

Parliament   1132, 1183

Great Britain (cont'd)

   Parliament (1640-1641) 1154

   Parliament. House of Commons 1096, 1101, 1121, 1139, 1146-1147, 1173, 1179, 1183, 1188

   Royal Marine Forces 1148

Great Britain--Bibliography, indexes, etc. 1084-1087

Great Britain--Colonies 1118

Great Britain--Portraits 1099, 1150, 1153, 1161, 1205, 3527

Greece, Ancient 1243, 2435, 2700

Greece, Modern 1244-1245, 3709-3710

Greek authors--SEE: Authors, Greek

Greifswald. Universität 4200

Gresham College, London 3314

Grisons, Switzerland 2452

Guadalajara, Mexico. Universidad 3277

Guadalajara, Spain (Province) 3687

Guatemala 3897

Guatemalan authors--SEE: Authors, Guatemalan

Guerrero, Mexico (State) 1533

Guiana, British--SEE: British Guiana

Guiana, Dutch--SEE: Surinam

Guitarists 2783, 3020, 3088, 3131

Gunsmiths 4781-4782, 4803

Gynecologists 4064

H

Hadith--Authorities 1319

Hälsingborg, Sweden 1823

Haggadists--SEE: Aggada

Hainaut, Belgium 447

Hamburg 1044-1045, 2608, 3693, 4208

Hampshire, Eng. 4443

Hanover, Ger. 1046-1047

Harlem, New York (City) 2248

Harpsichord makers 2779

Harvard University 2011, 2231, 3261

   Society of Fellows 3261

Haute-Garonne, France (Dept.) 888

Haute-Vienne, France (Dept.)--SEE: Vienne, Haute-, France (Dept.)

Hautes-Alpes, France (Dept.)--SEE: Alpes, Hautes-, France (Dept.)

Havre, Le 891

Hawaii 2139

Hebrew anonyms and pseudonyms
--SEE: Anonyms and pseudonyms, Jewish

Hebrew authors--SEE: Authors,
Jewish

Helsingfors. Universitet 696,
3310, 3312

Helsinki--SEE: Helsingfors

Heretics 4300, 4389, 4464

Hertfordshire, Eng. 1200

Herzegovina--SEE: Bosnia and
Herzegovina

Hesse 1048-1051, 3694

Historians 687, 1867, 4752-
4753, 4755-4758, 4762-4763,
4765-4768

Historians, Military--SEE: Military historians

Holstein--SEE: Schleswig-Holstein

Homeopathy 4112

Hongkong 1246

Horsemen 3240, 3244, 3253

Hospital administrators 4060

Hotel managers, etc. 4707,
4727

Huguenots 791

Hungarian anonyms and pseudo-
nyms--SEE: Anonyms and
pseudonyms, Hungarian

Hungarian authors--SEE: Authors,
Hungarian

Hungarians in the U. S. 2019

Hungary 1247-1255, 3711-3720,
4214, 4395, 4404

Hunting 3232

Huntingdonshire, Eng. 1191

Hymn writers 2807, 2870,
2896, 2918, 2923, 2935
2695, 2968-2969, 2973, 3022,
3092-3093, 3113, 3685

I

Iceland 673, 1256-1260, 3284,
3478-3479, 3485, 3721, 3945,
3960, 3983, 4084, 4158, 4489,
4510, 4807

Alþing 1256, 1258-1259

Icelandic anonyms and pseudo-
nyms--SEE: Anonyms and
pseudonyms, Icelandic

Icelandic authors--SEE: Authors,
Icelandic

Idaho 2140

Ille-et-Vilaine, France (Dept.)
892

Illinois 1972, 2100-2107, 2141-
2147

Illustrators 124, 2571, 2593,
4101
SEE ALSO: Book illustrators

Imperatorskaiă Akademiiă nauk--
SEE: Akademiiă nauk SSSR

India 1261-1293, 3047, 3273-
3274, 3293, 3722-3728, 4057,
4117, 4595, 4602, 4623, 4787,
4817

Army 1134

India (Republic)

   Parliament   1284

   Parliament. House of the
   People   1273

   Parliament. Lok Sabha--SEE:
   India (Republic) Parliament.
   House of the People

Indiana   2148-2155, 4620

Indianapolis   2154-2155

Indians of Mexico   1523

Indians of North America   1935,
2020

Indic authors--SEE: Authors,
Indic

Indochina, French   2392, 492

Indonesia   1294-1299, 3729,
4312

Indonesian Communist Party--
SEE: Partai Komunis Indo-
nesia

Indonesian journalists--SEE:
Journalists--Indonesia

Indre, France (Dept.)   893

Indre-et-Loire, France (Dept.)
894-895

Industrialists--SEE: Businessmen

Institut de France, Paris   773

Insurance   4702, 4705-4706,
4708, 4715, 4721, 4726,
4728-4730

Intellectuals   768

Interpreters--SEE: Translators

Investment counsellors   4731

Iowa   2100, 2156-2157, 3418,
3985

Irak--SEE: Iraq

Iran   3806-3807, 4616

Iraq   4615

Ireland   1093, 1105, 1300-1308,
2624, 3495-3497, 3501, 3523,
3730, 3943, 4099, 4148, 4335-
4336, 4448, 4631, 4648, 4782

Irish authors--SEE: Authors, Irish

Irish in France   1303

Irish poets--SEE: Poets, Irish
(English)

Islamic architects--SEE: Archi-
tects--Islamic countries

Islamic biography--SEE: Muslim
biography

Islamic countries   1309-1333,
3437-3442, 4603, 4768
SEE ALSO: Muslim biography

Israel   1474, 1481

Istanbul. Üniversite. Tip fakül-
tesi   4139

Istria   2407

Italian anonyms and pseudonyms--
SEE: Anonyms and pseudo-
nyms, Italian

Italian authors--SEE: Authors,
Italian

Italians in Connecticut   2120

Italians in the United States
1932, 1955, 2008, 2120

Italy   1334-1418, 2429-2431,
2444, 2465, 2467, 2475, 2488,
2519, 2575, 2580-2581, 2583,
2616, 2694, 2702-2703, 2749,
2956, 3013, 3027, 3045, 3137,
3186, 3292, 3302, 3307, 3731-
3785, 3996, 4407, 4014-4015
4101, 4199, 4284, 4456, 4580,
4590, 4604, 4662, 4737, 4771,
4799

Italy--Bibliography, indexes, etc.
1334-1337

Italy--Portraits   1413

J

Jamaica   1419-1421

Japan   1422-1447, 2470, 2532,
2610, 2633, 2655, 3264, 3299,
4246, 4256, 4273, 4672, 4796-
4797

Diet--SEE: Japan. Teikoku
Gikai

Teikoku Gikai. House of
Representatives--SEE: Japan.
Teikoku Gikai. Shūgiin

Teikoku Gikai. Shūgiin
1443-1444

Japanese authors--SEE: Authors,
Japanese

Japanese in Formosa   571

Japanese in Hawaii   1915

Japanese in Manchuria   588-589

Japanese in the U.S.   1915

Java   1298-1299

Jazz musicians   2796, 2834-
2835, 2914, 3007, 3089

Jena. Universität   3270, 3306,
3322

Jersey   1201

Jesuit anonyms and pseudonyms--
SEE: Anonyms and pseudo-
nyms, Jesuit

Jesuit missionaries--SEE: Missionaries, Jesuit

Jesuits   4288-4289, 4406, 4430,
4449, 4455, 4472, 4519,
4522

America   4430

Austria   4504

China   4459

Great Britain   4449

Mexico   4549

Peru   4511

Jewelers   2729-2731

Jewish actors--SEE: Actors and
actresses, Jewish

Jewish anonyms and pseudonyms--
SEE: Anonyms and pseudo-
nyms, Jewish

Jewish authors--SEE: Authors,
Jewish

Jewish educators and scholars--
SEE: Educators and scholars,
Jewish

Jewish military biography--SEE:
Military biography, Jewish

Jewish musicians--SEE: Musicians, Jewish

Jewish naval biography--SEE: Naval biography, Jewish

Jewish physicians--SEE: Physicians, Jewish

Jewish poets--SEE: Poets, Jewish

Jewish scholars--SEE: Educators and scholars, Jewish

Jewish scientists--SEE: Scientists, Jewish

Jews   1448-1485, 2935, 3036-3037, 3044, 3067, 3082, 3218, 3233, 3789-3795, 4102, 4150-4151, 4239, 4429, 4560-4569, 4582

Jews in Austria   384

Jews in Berlin   4565

Jews in Germany   1473

Jews in Hungary   1252

Jews in Italy   3792

Jews in Poland   1627

Jews in the U. S.   1899, 1937, 2002, 2006, 2057

Journalists

    Canada   3436

    Europe   3392

    Germany   3642

    Great Britain   3545

    Indonesia   3729

Journalists (cont'd)

    Italy   3774

    Mexico   3904

    Spain   3879

    United States   3410, 3434-36

Judges

    Australasia   3963

    Canada   3970

    France   3956-3957

    Georgia   3969

    Great Britain   1121, 3953-3954, 3962

    Ireland   3943

    Massachusetts   3948

    Michigan   3978

    Mississippi   3966

    New England   3982

    New Hampshire   3944

    New York (State)   3958, 3977

    Ohio   3979

    Savoy (Duchy)   3981

    South Carolina   3946, 3975

    Switzerland   1867

    Tennessee   3947

    Texas   3967

Judges (cont'd)

   United States   3950, 3965
   SEE ALSO VARIOUS STATES

   Wales   3962

   West Virginia   3942

   Wisconsin   3980

Jura, France (Dept.)   896-897

K

Kansas   2158, 2160

Kansas City, Kan.   2160

Kansas City, Mo.   2159-2160

Kappa Alpha   1960

Kassel, Ger.   2750

Kazakh authors--SEE: Authors,
   Kazakh

Kazakhstan   3933

Kazan, Russia (City) Universitet
   3280

Kent, Eng.   1202

Kentucky   2161-2165, 2169

Kerala   1293

Kerry Co. , Ireland   1304

Kharkov. Universitet   3281

Kiel. Universität   413, 3282

Kiev. Universitet   3283

Kirghiz authors--SEE: Authors,
   Kirghiz

Kirghizstan   3936

Knights and knighthood (Great
   Britain)   1107, 1123, 1133,
   1185

Köln--SEE: Cologne

Königsberg   1052

Komi A. S. S. R.   3548

Kommunisticheskaiā partiiā
   Sovetskogo Soiūza   1696-
   1697

Kongo, Belgian--SEE: Congo,
   Belgian

Korea   580, 1486-1493

Krakow   1630

Kwangtung,   China (Province)
   622

L

Labor and laboring classes

   France   757

   Great Britain   1157

   United States   1900, 2061

Labour Party (Gt. Brit.)   1096,
   1157

Lancashire, Eng.   1203, 3535

Landscape painters   2510, 2512

Languedoc   2729

Laos   1494

Lara, Venezuela   2388

Latin America   335-336, 359,
1495-1509, 1773, 1782, 2734-
2735, 2958, 3014, 3894, 3897-
3919, 4481, 4618

Latin America--Bibliography, indexes, etc.   1495-1496

Latin American anonyms and
pseudonyms--SEE: Anonyms
and pseudonyms, Brazilian;
and Anonyms and pseudonyms,
Spanish-American

Latin American authors--SEE:
Authors, Brazilian; Authors,
Spanish-American

Latin American poets--SEE:
Poets, Brazilian; Poets,
Spanish-American

Latin anonyms and pseudonyms--
SEE: Anonyms and pseudo-
nyms, Latin

Latvia   411, 414-416, 3796-3797

Latvian authors--SEE: Authors,
Lettish

Law librarians   3994

Law teachers   3951, 3961

Lawyers   3940-3993
SEE ALSO: Judges

Australia   3963

Belgium   3949

Canada   3964, 3970

France   3956-3957

Georgia   3969

Germany   3961, 3971, 3988,
3993

Lawyers (cont'd)

Great Britain   3955, 3962

Iceland   3945, 3960, 3983

Iowa   3985

Maine   3992

Massachusetts   3948

Michigan   3978

Mississippi   3966

Netherlands   3972

New England   3982

New Hampshire   3944

New York (State)   3958,
3977

Ohio   3979

Savoy (Duchy)   3981

South Carolina   3946, 3975

Spain   3940

Tennessee   3947

Texas   3967

United States   3941, 3950-
3952, 3964, 3968, 3976, 3987,
3989-3991, 4731
SEE ALSO VARIOUS STATES

Wales   3962

The West (U. S.)   3974

West Virginia   3942

Wisconsin   3980

Lebanon   1510, 4617

Légion d'honneur--SEE: France.
  Légion d'honneur

Le Havre--SEE: Havre, Le

Leiden--SEE: Leyden

Leipzig   1053

Leningrad   1712, 3074

  Akademiia nauk SSSR--SEE:
  Akademiia nauk SSSR

  Akademiia khudozhestv--SEE:
  Akademiia khudozhestv,
  Leningrad

  Universitet   3286

Leon, Spain (Province)   1799

Lettish authors--SEE: Authors,
  Lettish

Leyden. Rijksuniversiteit   3294

Librarians

  Canada   3994, 4002-4003,
  4047

  Denmark   4012

  Germany   3997

  Great Britain   4023

  Italy   4014-4015

  New Zealand   4048

  United States   3994, 4004,
  4047

Librarians, Negro--SEE: Negro
  librarians

Librettists   2876

Liechtenstein   1868

Liège   427, 448, 454, 2753

  Université   3290

Liguria   1392, 2424, 3759,
  3777, 4184

Limburg, Belgium (Duchy)
  427

Limousin, France   898, 4128

Literary critics--see: Critics
  (Literature)

Literature--SEE: Authors;
  Authors, Afrikaans; etc.,
  etc.

Lithuania   3798-3800

Lithuanians in Germany   3304

Lithuanians in the U. S.   1906

Liverpool   1204

Livonia   412, 415-416, 4092

Loir-et-Cher, France (Dept.)
  924

Loire, France (Dept.)   899

Loire-Inférieure, France (Dept.)
  900

Loire Valley   901

Loiret, France (Dept.)   902,
  924

Lombardy   4296, 4398

London   1205, 2714, 4085

London (cont'd)

    Gresham College--SEE:
    Gresham College, London

    Royal College of Physicians--
    SEE: Royal College of Phy-
    sicians of London

    Royal College of Surgeons
    4188, 4190

    St. Peter's College--SEE: St.
    Peter's College, London

    Westminster School--SEE:
    St. Peter's College, London

"Long Parliament" --SEE: Gt.
    Brit. Parliament (1640-1641)

Lorraine--SEE: Alsace-Lorraine

Los Angeles   2166-2167

Lot, France (Dept.)   903

Lot-et-Garonne, France (Dept.)
    904

Louisiana   2168

Louisville, Ky.   2169

Lower Saxony--SEE: Saxony,
    Lower

Loyalists, American--SEE: A-
    merican Loyalists

Lucca, Italy   4174

Lucerne (Canton)   4390

Lübeck   1054

Lund. Universitet   1820, 1825-
    1826

Lunigiana   3756

Lusatia   1055, 3672-3673

Lutheran Church   4421, 4442,
    4446

Lutheran Church in Germany
    4340, 4442, 4446

Lutheran Church in the Nether-
    lands   4420

Lutheran Church in the United
    States   3300, 4460, 4475,
    4529

Lutists   3088, 3131

Luxemburg   466, 1511-1512

Lyonnais   2427

Lyons   905, 3998

M

Madras   1290

Madrid   1800-1801

Maine   2170-2176, 3415, 3992

Maine, France (Dept.)   906,
    3552

Maine-et-Loire, France (Dept.)
    907-908

Majorca   1802, 3860

Malaga, Spain   2458

Malaya   1513-1515, 1753

Malaysia   1515

Mallorca--SEE: Majorca

Malta   1516

Manche, France (Dept.)   909

Manchester, Eng.   4093-4094

Manchester, Eng.   Royal In-
    firmary   4093-4094

Manchukuo--SEE: Manchuria

Manchuria   581, 588-589

Mandolinists   2783

Manila   1614

Maranhão, Brazil (State)   478

Marathi authors --SEE: Authors,
    Marathi

Marburg. Universität   3272

Marine biologists   4637

Marketing   4696, 4709

Marks, Artists' --SEE: Artists'
    marks

Marne, France (Dept.)   910

Martyrs   4304

Maryland   2083, 2123, 2177-2182,
    3428

Massa, Italy (Province)   2457

Massachusetts   2084-2085, 2183-
    2195, 3948

Mathematicians   4666-4670

Maurists--SEE: Benedictines.
    Congrégation de Saint Maur

Mauritius   320, 1517

Mayenne, France (Dept.)   911

Mayors (Great Britain)   1163

Mecklenburg   1056-1057, 3649

Medal of Honor (U. S.)   2025,
    2033

Medallists   2703, 2710, 2717

Medicine --SEE: Physicians;
    Surgeons; and similar head-
    ings

Mennonites   4403, 4431-4432,
    4530

Menorca--SEE: Minorca

Mercedarians   4378

Merchant marine   4791, 4805,
    4824

Merchants--SEE: Businessmen

Metallurgists   4818

Meteorologists, Amateur   2039

Methodist Church   4409, 4531,
    4534, 4535-4536

Methodist Episcopal Church
    4434

Methodist Episcopal Church, South
    4487, 4507

Meurthe-et-Moselle, France
    (Dept.)   912

Meuse, France (Dept.)   913

Mexican anonyms and pseudo-
    nyms--SEE: Anonyms and
    pseudonyms, Mexican

Mexican authors--SEE: Authors,
    Mexican

Mexican novelists--SEE: Novel-
    ists, Mexican

Mexico   1518-1550, 3277, 3909,
3912, 4260, 4520, 4549, 4763

Mexico--Bibliography, indexes,
etc.   1518

Mexico (City)   1543

Real Colegio de San Pedro,
San Pablo y San Ildefonso
1536

Michigan   2127-2129, 2196-2205,
3408-3409, 3978

Middle East--SEE VARIOUS
ITEMS UNDER ISLAMIC
COUNTRIES

Middle Western States   2066,
2206-2207, 2986

Milan   1393, 3772, 4116, 4308

Università   4199

Military biography   49, 199

Austria   384

Belgium   441, 465

China   561, 612

France   714-715, 751, 753,
803, 816, 843, 849, 897

Germany   968, 987, 1025,
1064

Great Britain   1120, 1134,
1148, 1151, 1174

Italy   4799

Mexico   1531

Portugal   1643

Prussia   1064

Military biography (cont'd)

Russia   1671, 1698, 1705,
1717, 1742, 1748, 2678

Spain   1765, 1770, 1779

United States   1924-1925,
1942, 1947-1948, 1991, 1996-
1999, 2023, 2033, 2043-2044,
2068, 4810

Military biography, Jewish
384, 1472

Military historians   261

Milwaukee   2208

Mineralogists   4641

Miniature painters   2425, 2449,
2469, 2497, 2507, 2545, 2612

Mining engineers   4818

Ministers (Clergymen)--SEE:
Clergy

Minneapolis   3119

Minnesota   2101, 2209-2216,
3243, 3421, 3425

Minorca   1803

Miranda, Venezuela   2389

Missionaries, Baptist   4499

Missionaries, Dutch   4312

Missionaries, Jesuit   4522

Mississippi   2217-2219, 3966

Mississippi Valley   2220

Missouri   2013, 2314-2316, 3309

Missouri. Northeast Missouri State Teachers College, Kirksville 3309

Modena 3769, 3781, 4753

Mohammedan biography--SEE: Muslim biography

Mohammedan Empire--SEE VARIOUS ITEMS UNDER IS-LAMIC COUNTRIES

Mohammedans--SEE HEADINGS BEGINNING WITH "ISLAMIC" OR "MUSLIM"

Moldavia 2926

Molise--SEE: Abruzzi and Molise

Monograms 2414, 2416-2418, 2563, 2670

Montana 2221

Monte Cassino (Benedictine abbey) 4284

Montserrat (Benedictine abbey) 4277

Moravia 646, 649, 652, 2480, 3473, 4455

Mordovia 3547

Mordvinian authors--SEE: Au-thors, Mordvinian

Moscow 1711, 2730-2731

Akademiiā nauk SSSR--SEE: Akademiiā nauk SSSR

Universitet 3296-3297

Moselle, France (Dept.) 914-915, 2763

Moslems--SEE: Muslims

Motion pictures--SEE: Moving-pictures

Mount Holyoke College 1978

Moving-pictures 3140, 3142, 3149, 3152-3154, 3160, 3162, 3165, 3171, 3183, 3187, 3195-3196, 3202-3207, 3214, 3216-3217

Münsterland, Ger. 3680-3681, 3683-3684

Munich 3687

Municipal officials 4773

Murcia, Spain 2432, 3892

Music printers 4011, 4019-4020, 4022

Music teachers 2764

Musicians 2740-3131

America 3006

Austria 2812, 2931, 3085

Bavaria 2944

Belgium 2753, 2855, 2877-2878, 2880, 2888, 2950, 3084, 3099

Berlin 2940

Brazil 2953

California 2982, 3121

Canada 2791-2792, 3070

Colombia 3129

Czechoslovakia 2794, 2868

Musicians (cont'd)

Delaware   2984

Denmark   3049, 3092-3093

Estonia   2995

Europe   2845, 2861, 3053

Finland   2919

France   2591, 2763, 2797,
2809-2810, 2852

Germany   2750, 2858, 2899,
2913, 2928, 2931, 2940, 2944,
2981, 3038, 3064, 3109, 3113

Great Britain   2760, 2762,
2788, 2808, 2881, 2908, 2916,
3005, 3023, 3110, 3117

India   3047

Italy   2749, 2956, 2959,
2974-2975, 3003, 3027, 3045

Latin America   2958, 3014

Latvia   3189

Middle West   2986, 3119

Moldavia   2926

Netherlands   2879, 2942,
3002, 3084

New England   2987

New Jersey   2984

New Orleans   2796

New York (State)   2983

North Carolina   2999

Oklahoma   2985

Musicians (cont'd)

Paraguay   2774

Pennsylvania   2984

Philippine Islands   2758

Poland   2798, 3072, 3078-
3079

Portugal   2748, 2960, 3014,
3101, 3104

Rhode Island   2952

Russia   2770, 2781, 2906,
2926, 2945, 3041, 3074,
3077, 3108

Sardinia   3003

Saxony   3109

Schleswig-Holstein   2858

Scotland   2760

Silesia   2899, 2928, 3038

Southern States (U.S.)   2924,
2988, 3076

Southwestern States (U.S.)
2985

Spain   2744, 3014, 3043,
3105

Sweden   3001, 3196

Switzerland   2767, 2931,
3028, 3063, 3066

Texas   2985

United States   2008, 2790,
2796, 2839, 2847-2848, 2851,
2876, 2892, 2900, 2915, 2924,
2938, 2946, 2949, 2952, 2965,

Musicians (cont'd)

United States (cont'd)
2982-2988, 2999, 3029, 3076,
3116, 3118-3119, 3121-3122,
3125, 3127
SEE ALSO VARIOUS STATES
AND CITIES

Virginia   2949

Wales   2881, 2916

Wisconsin   3125

Musicians--Bibliography, indexes,
etc.   2740-2741, 2765-2766,
2892

Musicians, Arabic   3437

Musicians, Celtic   1113

Musicians, Jewish   2935, 3036-
3037, 3044, 3067, 3082

Musicians, Negro--SEE: Negro
musicians

Musicians, Slavic   3078

Musicians, Women   2829, 2967

Musicologists   2995

Muslim biography   1309-1333,
2686, 3437-3442, 3866, 4191,
4227, 4553-4559, 4603, 4757,
4765, 4768
SEE ALSO: Islamic countries

Muslim educators and scholars--
SEE: Educators and scholars,
Muslim

Muslim saints--SEE: Saints,
Muslim

Muslim scholars--SEE: Educators
and scholars, Muslim

Muslims in India   1278, 4757

Mysore   1279

N

Naples   1367, 1394-1398, 2481,
3106, 3731, 3745, 3758, 3763,
3765-3766, 3779

Accademia Alfonsina--SEE:
Accademia Alfonsina, Naples

Natal   329

Nationalsozialistische Deutsche
Arbeiter-Partei   971, 995,
1018-1019

Naturalists   4648
SEE ALSO: Biologists; Botanists; etc.

Naval biography   49, 272, 4740-
4741, 4746, 4748, 4751

Austria   384

France   809, 843

Great Britain   1114, 1145,
1149, 1159, 1167, 1174

Spain   1783

United States   1942, 1945,
1997-1998, 2010, 2025-2027,
2038

Naval biography, Jewish   1472

Nazis--SEE: Nationalsozialistische
Deutsche Arbeiter-Partei

Near East--SEE VARIOUS ITEMS
UNDER ISLAMIC COUNTRIES

Nebraska   2222-2224, 3406,
2289

Negro actors and actresses   3177

Negro authors--SEE: Authors, Negro

Negro clergy   4542, 4547

Negro journalists   3410

Negro librarians   4004

Negro musicians   2796

Negroes   87, 249, 1928, 1977, 1986-1988, 2014, 2058, 2071, 2138, 2168, 2305, 3410, 4004, 4542

Georgia   2138

Louisiana   2168

Negroes--Bibliography, indexes, etc.   1885

Netherlands   180, 183, 431, 1551-1573, 2443, 2472-2473, 2508, 2525, 2530, 2538, 2547, 2611, 2617, 2648, 2658, 2670, 2693, 2879, 2942, 3002, 3084, 3256, 3294, 3313, 3488-3491, 3972, 4163, 4177, 4305, 4351, 4420, 4666, 4716

Netherlands West Indies--SEE: West Indies, Dutch

Neuchâtel   1853

Neurologists   4140

Nevada   2225

New Caledonia   1574

New England   2084, 2226-2232, 2987, 3982

New Hampshire   2233-2237, 3944, 4319

New Hebrides   1574

New Jersey   2123, 2238-2240, 2984, 4111

New Mexico   2241-2242

New Southwest--SEE: Southwest, New

New York (City)   1944, 2243-2250, 2259, 4115, 4132, 4453

Union Theological Seminary   4447

New York (City)--Bibliography, indexes, etc.   2243

New York (State)   2016, 2243-2264, 2983, 3958, 3977, 4245

New Zealand   377, 1576-1578, 3521, 4048, 4607

New Zealand authors--SEE: Authors, New Zealand

Newfoundland   514, 520

Nice   916, 3749

Niedersachsen--SEE: Saxony, Lower

Nigeria   1579-1580

Nigeria, Western Region of--SEE: Western Region of Nigeria

Nivernais, France   917

Nobel Prize winners   188

Nobility   311

Bavaria   1030

Belgium   449

Denmark   658, 671

Egypt   1315

Nobility (cont'd)

    Europe   689-690

    Finland   697

    France   743, 754, 799,
    833-834, 840, 849

    Germany   978, 988, 1030

    Great Britain   1106-1107,
    1117, 1122-1123, 1133, 1135,
    1155, 1181, 1185, 1189, 1218

    Italy   1344, 1361, 1375

    Netherlands   1563-1565

    Portugal   1641

    Russia   1668, 1724

    Scotland   1218

    Spain   1505, 1780

    Sweden   1834

Nord, France (Dept.)   918

Norfolk, Eng.   1206

Normandy   919-922, 2852

North America   3390-3391, 4637,
4820

North Carolina   2265-2266, 2999,
3412

North Dakota   2267

Northamptonshire, Eng.   1207,
4419

Northeast Missouri State Teachers
College, Kirksville--SEE:
Missouri. Northeast Missouri
State Teachers College

Northeastern States   2268-2269,
4170

Northumberland   1184

Northwest, Canadian   513

Northwest, Pacific   2270-2272,
2662, 3422-3423

Norway   667, 670, 673, 1581-
1590, 1835, 2570, 3279, 3478-
3479, 3485, 3802-3805, 4156

Norway--Bibliography, indexes,
    etc.   1581-1583

Norwegian anonyms and pseudo-
nyms--SEE: Anonyms and
pseudonyms, Norwegian

Norwegian authors--SEE: Authors,
Norwegian

Norwegians in the U. S.   3276,
3300, 4529

Nottinghamshire   2522

Nova Scotia   3513

Novelists

    American   3432

    Canadian   3538

    English   3512

    Mexican   3912

    Spanish-American   3918

Nuclear physicists--SEE:
Physicists

Nürnberg--SEE: Nuremberg

Numismatists   4193

Nuremberg   1058-1059, 4492,
4667

Nurses and nursing   4221

Nyasaland   321, 333, 1653

O

Oberösterreich--SEE: Austria,
Upper

Obstetricians   4064

Occult sciences   4234, 4240-
4241, 4253, 4261

Oceanica   1591

Ohio   2108-2109, 2273-2279,
3979

Ohio Valley   2280

Oise, France (Dept.)   923

Oklahoma   2281-2288, 2985,
3147

Olympic Games, Berlin (1936) 3220

Omaha   2289

Opera   2809-2810, 2813, 2815,
2844, 2929, 2951, 2976, 3039

Optometrists   4228

Order of the British Empire   1178

Order of Vallombrosians--SEE:
Vallombrosians

Ordine di Vallombrosa--SEE:
Vallombrosians

Oregon   2290-2293

Organ builders   2862, 2911, 3000

Organists   2821, 3091, 3109,
3111

Orientalists   1333

Orleannais   924

Ornithologists   4629

Orthodox Eastern Church, Russian
4366, 4476, 4505

Oslo. Universitet   3279

Osteopaths   4228

Ostfriesland--SEE: Friesland,
East

Ostpreussen--SEE: Prussia,
East

Oxford. University   1137,
1168-1169, 1190, 4415

Oxford Movement   4543

Oxfordshire, Eng.   1208

P

Pacific area   226, 1591

Pacific Northwest--SEE: Northwest, Pacific

Padua. Università   3302, 4129,
4199

Painters   2425, 2442, 2449,
2451, 2460, 2469, 2476-2477,
2489, 2491-2493, 2497, 2520,
2534, 2540, 2542, 2582, 2584,
2586-2588, 2612, 2615, 2618,
2621, 2632, 2665-2666, 2669

Austria   2518

Baltic Provinces   2565-2566

Painters (cont'd)

Belgium   2472-2473, 2479, 2508

Bologna   2550

Chile   2542

China   2626

Denmark   2436, 2546

Flanders   2472-2473

Florence   2464

France   2461, 2478, 2501, 2528, 2640

Germany   2426, 2472

Great Britain   2428, 2505, 2510, 2512, 2545, 2649-2650

Greece, Ancient   2435

Italy   2444, 2464, 2475, 2488, 2507, 2550, 2605

Japan   2610, 2633

Netherlands   2472-2473, 2508, 2525, 2547, 2611, 2658

Poland   2602

Portugal   2578

Provence   2640

Russia   2537, 2541, 2639

Spain   2458, 2526, 2572, 2598, 2643

United States   2446, 2579

Venice   2605

Pakistan   1278, 1280, 1285, 1592-1596, 3939, 4619, 4624

Palencia, Spain (Province)   3883

Palestine   1474, 1481
SEE ALSO: Israel; Jews

Panama   1506, 1597-1598, 1956

Paraguay   1599-1602, 2774

Paris   925-927, 2063, 2569, 2722, 3132, 3146, 3156-3158, 4019, 4036-4037, 4119, 4396

Académie des sciences--SEE:
Académie des sciences, Paris

Académie française--SEE:
Académie française, Paris

Université. Faculté de méde-cine   4079

Université. Faculté des let-tres   3271

Parma   3732

Università   3307

Partai Komunis Indonesia   1296

Pas-de-Calais, France (Dept.)   928

Pathologists   4106

Peace officers (The Western United States)   2361

Pediatricians   4058, 4067

Peerage--SEE: Nobility

Pennsylvania   2123, 2294-2309, 2984, 4815

Pernambuco, Brazil (State)   480

Persia--SEE: Iran

Persian authors--SEE: Authors,
Persian

Persian poets--SEE: Poets,
Persian

Peru   1507, 1603-1610, 4511

Perugia, Italy   3784

Pewter makers   2707, 2715,
2721

Pharmacists   4074, 4121, 4138,
4209, 4659

Philadelphia   2305-2308

Philatelists   2445, 2663

Philippine Islands   1611-1623,
2758, 4186

Philipps-Universität in Marburg--
SEE: Marburg. Universität

Philologists   3344, 3351, 3461,
3467, 3724

Philosophers   205, 4235-4239,
4242-4243, 4246-4248, 4252,
4254-4260, 4262, 4548

Photographers   2664, 2720, 2736,
2739

Physicians   4053-4230

    Africa, South   4171

    Australia   4169

    Bavaria   4135, 4179

    Belgium   4125

    Canada   4065, 4100, 4124,
    4216

Physicians (cont'd)

    Courland   4091

    Cuba   4123

    Denmark   4118, 4145

    Dominican Republic   4114

    Estonia   4090

    Finland   4078

    France   4079, 4108, 4119,
    4121, 4128, 4138, 4176, 4223

    Germany   4073, 4086-4087,
    4127, 4135, 4141, 4179, 4187,
    4194, 4200, 4208, 4226

    Great Britain   4056, 4085,
    4093-4094, 4113, 4162, 4168,
    4172, 4188, 4190, 4196, 4206

    Hungary   4214

    Iceland   4084, 4158

    India   4057, 4117

    Ireland   4099, 4148

    Italy   4088, 4101, 4110,
    4116, 4129, 4174, 4182, 4184,
    4199, 4201, 4579

    Livonia   4092

    London   4085

    Netherlands   4163, 4177

    New Jersey   4111

    New York (City)   4115, 4132

    New York (State)   4131

    Northeastern States (U.S.)   4170

Physicians (cont'd)

   Norway   4155

   Philippine Islands   4186

   Poland   4157

   Portugal   4165

   Russia   4160-4161, 4178,
   4229-4230

   Scotland   4113

   Silesia   4141

   Southern States (U. S.)   4106

   Spain   4083, 4109, 4133,
   4142, 4189

   Sweden   4082, 4097

   Transylvania   4214

   Turkey   4139

   United States   4058-4059,
   4061-4062, 4064-4069, 4071,
   4106, 4111, 4115, 4124, 4137,
   4147, 4153, 4167, 4173, 4204,
   4207, 4210, 4213, 4216, 4218,
   4220, 4224

Physicians--Bibliography, indexes,
etc.   4053-4054

Physicians--Portraits--Catalogs
4175, 4054

Physicians, Arabic   4191, 4227

Physicians, Jewish   4102, 4150-
4151

Physicians, Women--SEE: Women
as physicians

Physicists   4671-4676

Physiotherapists   4228

Piacenza, Italy   1399

Pianists   2997, 3010, 3124

Piano makers   2779, 2911, 3124

Piarists   4495, 4523

Piedmont, Italy   1400-1402,
3749, 4088

Pinneberg, Ger. Baltic University
3304

Pittsburgh   2309

Piyutim   2935

Plastics industry   4819

Poets   3358, 3368

   American   3358, 3397, 3407
   3409, 3534, 3543

   Arabic   3437

   Austrian   3640

   Brazilian   3817

   Canadian   3503

   Catalan   3454, 3872

   Chilean   3906

   Dutch   3489

   English   3358, 3506, 3511,
   3525, 3527-3528, 3530, 3534,
   3542-3543, 3546

   French   3561, 3568, 4108

   Gaelic   3598

   German   3640-3641, 3656,
   3660-3661, 3685, 3702

Poets (cont'd)

Irish (English)   3523

Italian   3741-3742, 3773

Jewish   4239

Pakistani--SEE: Poets, Urdu

Persian   3806

Polish   3809

Portuguese   3814, 3817

Russian   3843

Spanish   3870, 3872, 3875,
3878, 3893

Spanish-American   3878,
3905

Urdu   3939

Uruguayan   3900

Poitou   929

Poland   1624-1638, 2602, 2685,
2798, 3072, 3078-3079, 3808-
3812, 4043-4044, 4157

Poland--Bibliography, indexes,
etc.   1624

Poles in Prussia   1065

Poles in the U. S.   1633, 2064

Police--France   841

Polish anonyms and pseudonyms--
SEE: Anonyms and pseudo-
nyms, Polish

Polish authors--SEE: Authors,
Polish

Political scientists   4769-4775

Poltava, Russia (Government)
1718-1719

Pomerania   1060-1063, 3608

Popes   4285, 4407

Porto Rico--SEE: Puerto Rico

Portrait painters   2428, 2446

Portraits   94, 239
SEE ALSO: Portraits under
names of countries: e. g. ,
Great Britain--Portraits,
and under certain subjects;
e. g. , Physicians--Portraits

Portraits--Catalogs, indexes,
etc.   1, 7, 9-11, 25-26,
29, 280-282, 2491-2492, 2498,
2521

Portugal   165, 1639-1648, 2578,
2599, 2687, 2748, 2960, 3014,
3101, 3104, 3193-3194, 3814-
3816, 4165, 4282, 4302, 4426,
4608, 4633

Portuguese anonyms and pseudo-
nyms--SEE: Anonyms and
pseudonyms, Portuguese

Portuguese authors--SEE: Authors,
Portuguese

Portuguese East Africa--SEE:
Africa, Portuguese East

Portuguese poets--SEE: Poets,
Portuguese

Potters--SEE: Ceramics

Précieuses   844

Premonstratensians   4384

Presbyterian Church   4485

Press--SEE: Journalists

Preussische Friedrich-Alexanders-
Universität zu Erlangen--
SEE: Erlangen. Universität

Printers   3995-3996, 3998-
4000, 4006-4011, 4016, 4018-
4022, 4024, 4027, 4030, 4033-
4039, 4042, 4045, 4049

Belgium   4038-4039

Canada   4049

France   4024, 4036-4037

Germany   3999-4000

Great Britain   3545, 3995,
4006, 4008-4009, 4016, 4027,
4033-4035

Ireland   3995, 4008, 4027,
4034-4035

Italy   3996, 4007

Paris   4036-4037

Scotland   3995, 4008, 4010,
4027, 4034-4035

Spain   4042

Switzerland   4018

United States   4030

Wales   4021

Printers' marks   4039

Protestant Churches   791, 4305,
4364, 4437, 4544-4546
SEE ALSO: Denominations,
e.g.: Baptists; etc.; Clergy;
Theologians; etc.

Protestant Episcopal Church in
the U. S. A.   4331

Provençal anonyms and pseudo-
nyms--SEE: Anonyms and
pseudonyms, Provençal

Provençal authors--SEE: Authors,
Provençal

Provence   930-931, 2640, 3592,
3596

Prussia   1064-1065, 3615

Prussia, East   1052

Pseudonyms--SEE: Anonyms and
pseudonyms

Psychiatrists   4069

Physical research   4233, 4240-
4241

Psychologists   4231-4233, 4244-
4245, 4249-4251, 4687

Public relations consultants
4289, 4724, 4732

Public utilities   4826

Publishers   4046, 4050

France   4019

Great Britain   4020, 4022

Italy   3996

United States   4030

Puerto Rico   1649-1652, 3910,
3915

Punjab   1594

Q

Quebec   3579

Queens, New York City (Borough)
2250

R

Rabbis   1451, 1457, 3789, 3791-
3792, 4562, 4565-4569

Radio engineers, etc.   4787,
4789, 4792

Radio entertainers   3171, 3185,
3201, 3208-3209, 3213

Railroad engineers, etc.   4798,
4820

Rajputana   1282

Rationalists   4391, 4422-4423,
4514, 4528

Real Colegio de San Pedro, San
Pablo y San Ildefonso, Mexico
City--SEE: Mexico (City)
Real Colegio de San Pedro,
San Pablo y San Ildefonso

Real estate business   4733-4734

Redemptorists   4435

Reformed Church   4334, 4442,
4446

Refugees   4146

Reggio nell'Emilia, Italy   4463

Religious biography   4263-4569
SEE ALSO: Buddhists;
Christian biography; etc.

Rhine Valley   1066

Rhode Island   2116, 2310-2313,
2952

Rhodes scholars   3301

Rhodesia   320-321, 1653

Rhodesia and Nyasaland   321,
333, 1653

Rhône, France (Dept.)   932

Riga   411, 414, 3189

Roman Catholic Church--SEE:
Catholics

Roman Empire   1654

Rome (City)   1368, 1380, 2581,
3740

   Accademia degli Arcadi--
   SEE: Accademia degli
   Arcadi, Rome

Rossiĭskaiā akademiiā nauk--SEE:
Akademiiā nauk SSSR

Rostock   1067

Rothenburg ob der Tauber   4340

Roussillon, France (Province)
933

Royal College of Physicians of
London   4196

Royal College of Surgeons, Lon-
don--SEE: London. Royal
College of Surgeons

Royal College of Surgeons in
Ireland, Dublin--SEE: Dublin. Royal College of Surgeons in Ireland

Royal Infirmary, Manchester,
Eng.--SEE: Manchester,
Eng. Royal Infirmary

Royal Society of London   4611

Rubber industry   4802, 4827

Rügen (Island)   1060, 3608

Rumania   1655-1658

Russia   1659-1748, 2454, 2537,
  2541, 2606-2607, 2619, 2639,
  2678, 2717, 2730-2731, 2770,
  2781, 2906, 2929, 2945, 3041,
  3077, 3108, 3280-3281, 3283,
  3286-3287, 3296-3297, 3303,
  3818-3853, 4160-4161, 4178,
  4209, 4229-4230, 4476, 4505,
  4574-4575, 4597, 4606, 4614,
  4626-4628, 4630, 4645, 4650,
  4675, 4690, 4693, 4736, 4748,
  4751, 4764, 4766, 4794-4795

Armiia̐   1671, 1698, 1705,
  1717, 1742

Gosudarstvennaia̐ duma (1st,
  1906)   1676, 1681, 1690,
  1720

Gosudarstvennaia̐ duma (3d,
  1907-1912)   1676, 1687

Gosudarstvennyĭ Sovet   1691,
  1699, 1727

Senat   1700

Voennyĭ sovet   1748

Russia--Bibliography, indexes,
  etc.   1659

Russia--Portraits   1660-1661,
  1675, 1687, 1690, 1702, 1724-
  1725, 1729, 1733-1734, 1736,
  1744, 3882

Russia--Revolution (1917-1921)
  1669, 1677, 1685, 1697, 1723,
  1740

Russia (1923-   U.S.S.R.) Verkhovnyĭ Sovet   1728

Russian anonyms and pseudonyms
  --SEE: Anonyms and pseudonyms, Russian

Russian authors--SEE: Authors,
  Russian

Russian Orthodox Eastern Church
  --SEE: Orthodox Eastern
  Church, Russian

Russians in foreign countries
  1680, 1714

Rutland, Eng.   4419

Ryazan, Russia (Government) 3822

S

St. Andrews, Scot. University
  1219

St. Louis   2314-2316, 3402

Saint Paul, Minn.   3119

St. Peter's College, London
  1175-1176

St. Petersburg--SEE: Leningrad

Saintonge, France   934

Saints   4275, 4286-4287, 4295,
  4297, 4303, 4309, 4311, 4313-
  4315, 4355, 4385, 4387, 4395,
  4458, 4474, 4478, 4502

France   4342-4343, 4396,
  4418

Germany   4512

Great Britain   4294, 4416,
  4469, 4503

Ireland   4448

Scotland   4369, 4461

Saints (cont'd)

    Wales   4469, 4503

Saints, Muslim   4555, 4558

Saints, Women   4355

Salvador   1749

Salzburg, Austria (Province)
    385, 2589

San Diego, Calif.   2317

Sankt-Peterburg--SEE: Leningrad

Santander, Spain (Province)
    1804, 4133

Santiago de Cuba   637

Santo Domingo (City)   675

Santo Domingo (Republic)--SEE:
    Dominican Republic

São Paulo, Brazil (State)   482

Saone-et-Loire, France (Dept.)
    936

Sarawak   1750

Sardinia   1403-1404, 3003

Sarthe, France (Dept.)   906

Savoy (Duchy)   3794, 3981

Saxony   1068-1069, 1078, 2557,
    3109, 3631, 3699, 3703, 4467

Saxony, Lower   1069, 1078, 2557

Scandinavia   1751-1752, 2657

Scandinavian anonyms and pseudo-
    nyms--SEE: Anonyms and
    pseudonyms, Scandinavian

Scandinavian authors--SEE: Au-
    thors, Danish; Authors, Nor-
    wegian; etc.

Scania, Sweden   1826

Schaffhausen (Canton)   3926

Schleswig-Holstein   670, 1070,
    2858, 3603, 3650, 3664-3665

Scholars--SEE: Educators and
    scholars

Scientists   4073, 4089, 4198,
    4570-4676

    Czechoslovakia   4581

    Egypt   4583, 4585

    France   4571, 4587-4588,
    4591, 4600-4601

    Germany   4073, 4194, 4572-
    4573, 4613, 4621

    Great Britain   4584, 4611,
    4622

    India   4595, 4602, 4623

    Indiana   4620

    Iran   4616

    Iraq   4615

    Italy   4101, 4579-4580,
    4590, 4604

    Japan   4672

    Latin America   4618

    Lebanon   4617

    Netherlands   4177

    New Zealand   4607

Scientists (cont'd)

    Pakistan   4619, 4624

    Portugal   4608

    Russia   4574-4575, 4597,
4606, 4614, 4626

    Spain   4608, 4612

    Switzerland   4589

    United States   4576, 4598,
4605, 4620, 4804

Scientists, Arabic   4227, 4603

Scientists, Jewish   4582

Scientists--Bibliography, indexes,
    etc.   4570

Scotland   1184, 1209-1220, 2455,
2760, 3506, 3514, 3524, 3598-
3600, 4113, 4354, 4369, 4424,
4461, 4486, 4517

    Parliament   1212

Scotland--Portraits   1216-1217

Scottish authors--SEE: Authors,
    Scottish

Sculptors   2693-2702

    Baltic Provinces   2565

    Belgium   2693

    France   2701

    Great Britain   2698-2699

    Greece, Ancient   2700

    Italy   2689, 2694, 2702

    Netherlands   2547, 2693

Sculptors (cont'd)

    Portugal   2578

    United States   2696

Segovia, Spain   1805, 3858

Seine-et-Marne, France (Dept.)
936

Siene-et-Oise, France (Dept.)
937-938

Seine-Inférieure, France (Dept.)
939-940

Serbia   2400, 2404-2405

Serbian authors--SEE: Authors,
    Yugoslav

Sergipe, Brazil (State)   477

Seville   1806-1810, 2713, 3862,
3870

Shanghai   593

Shiites   4559

Shipping and ship-building--SEE:
    Merchant marine

Siam--SEE: Thailand

Siberia   1740, 3847, 3852-3853

Sicily   1406-1411, 3767

Sigma Alpha Epsilon   1965

Sikhs   1262, 3727

Silesia   1071-1074, 2480, 2899,
    2923, 2928, 3038, 3666, 3671,
    3695, 3698, 4141, 4405, 4455

Silversmiths

    France   2659, 2729

Silversmiths (cont'd)

    Great Britain   2718

    Russia   2730-2731

    Sweden   2733

    United States   2709, 2711

Singapore   1753-1755

Singers   2815, 2844, 2875, 2916,
2924, 2929, 2933, 2938

Slavic musicians--SEE: Musicians,
Slavic

Slavs   1756-1759, 3079

Slovak anonyms and pseudonyms--
SEE: Anonyms and pseudo-
nyms, Slovak

Slovaks in Chicago   2104

Slovenia   2406

Småland, Sweden   1820-1821,
1840

Social psychologists   4687

Social reformers   4683

Social scientists   4582, 4677-
4693, 4771

Socialists   243, 993, 1003, 1710

Society of Fellows of Harvard Uni-
versity--SEE: Harvard University. Society of Fellows

Society of Friends--SEE: Friends,
Society of

Sociologists   4688

Somme, France (Dept.)   941-942

Song-writers   3064

South Africa--SEE: Africa, South

South America   359, 2385, 2734-
2735
    SEE ALSO: Latin America

South Carolina   2318-2320, 3433,
3946, 3975

South Dakota   2321-2325

Southern California--SEE: California, Southern

Southern States   2326-2329, 2924,
2988, 3076, 3413, 3430, 4106,
4499, 4507

Southwest, New   2328-2331, 2985

Space scientists--SEE: Astronautics

Spain   125, 348, 360, 1760-1811,
2459, 2526, 2572, 2574, 2576-
2577, 2598, 2623, 2643, 2646,
2684, 3014, 3043, 3105, 3223,
3227, 3234, 3855-3896, 3940,
4005, 4040, 4083, 4109, 4142,
4189, 4277, 4282, 4445, 4519,
4608, 4612, 4633, 4746, 4765,
4793

    Armada (Navy)   1783

    Asamblea Constituyente (1854)
1767

    Consejo Superior de Investi-
gaciones Cientíticas   4612

    Cortés   1767-1769, 1771

    Ejército (Army)   1765,
1770, 1779

Spain--Bibliography, indexes, etc.
1760, 1766

Spain--Portraits   1764, 1784

Spaniards in America   3855,
3875

Spanish America--SEE: Latin A-
merica

Spanish-American anonyms and
pseudonyms--SEE: Anonyms
and pseudonyms, Spanish-
American

Spanish American authors--SEE:
Authors, Spanish-American

Spanish-American poets--SEE:
Poets, Spanish-American

Spanish anonyms and pseudonyms
--SEE: Anonyms and pseudonyms, Spanish

Spanish authors--SEE: Authors,
Spanish

Spanish poets--SEE: Poets, Spanish

Speech teachers   3429

Spiritualism   4240-4241

Sports   3221, 3228, 3233, 3238,
3247, 3505
SEE ALSO: Athletes; particular sports, e. g. : Baseball

Staffordshire, Eng.   1221

Stamp-collectors--SEE:
Philatelists

Statisticians   4677, 4679-4680,
4686

Stockholm   3920

Students, American   2051-2052

Students, Chinese   615-617

Styria   401, 2651, 3085, 3707

Sudan   1812

Sudetenland   648, 3639

Suffolk, Eng.   1206

Sufis   4553-4554, 4558

Sulpicians   4301

Surgeons   4072, 4103, 4112,
4197, 4211-4212

    Canada   4216

    France   4119, 4121

    Great Britain   4188, 4190

    Ireland   4099

    Portugal   4165

    Spain   4083

    United States   4062, 4068,
4071, 4204, 4213, 4216, 4218,
4220

Surinam   1813

Surrey, Eng.   1202

Sussex, Eng.   1202

Swabia   1075-1076, 3627, 3632

Sweden   1814-1840, 2627-2628,
2733, 3196, 3920-3924, 4026,
4082, 4097, 4715, 4759

Sweden--Bibliography, indexes,
etc.   1814

Swedes in foreign countries   1829

Swedes in Prussia   1065

Swedish anonyms and pseudonyms
--SEE: Anonyms and pseudonyms, Swedish

Swedish authors--SEE: Authors,
Swedish

Swiss authors--SEE: Authors,
Swiss

Swiss in the U. S.   2018

Switzerland   976, 1841-1869,
2614, 2767, 3028, 3063, 3066,
3171, 3275, 3311, 3925-3932,
4367, 4388, 4589

Switzerland-- Bibliography,
etc.   1841

Switzerland--Portraits   1847

Syracuse, Sicily (Province)
1412

Syryenian authors--SEE: Authors,
Syryenian

T

Taiwan--SEE: Formosa

Talmud   4564

Tamil authors--SEE: Authors,
Tamil

Tannaim   4560-4561

Tarn, France   2592

Tarn-et-Garonne, France (Dept.)
943-944

Tartu   417

Ülikool   3287

Tasmania   2468

Teachers--SEE: Educators and
the headings: Business
teachers; Speech teachers;
Visiting teachers; etc.

Technologists   4577-4578

Egypt   4583, 4585

Germany   4806

India   4595, 4602

Italy   4579

Russia   4597, 4626, 4797

Television engineers, etc.   4787

Television entertainers   3142,
3166, 3185, 3197, 3199, 3213

Telugu authors--SEE: Authors,
Telugu

Tennessee   2332-2338, 3947,
4521

Texas   2339-2346, 2985, 3967,
4790

Thailand   1870-1873, 4678

Theater   3135-3136, 3151, 3164,
3190-3193, 3198, 3210
SEE ALSO: Actors and
actresses

Austria   3171

Brazil   3193

France   3143, 3163

Germany   3170-3171

Great Britain   3133, 3161,
3200, 3212

Italy   3773

Theater (cont'd)

Portugal   3193-3194

Sweden   3196

Switzerland   3171

United States   3133, 3161,
3177, 3191, 3211-3212

Theologians   46, 4346-4349,
4397, 4412, 4441-4442, 4446,
4470, 4544-4545

Germany   4353, 4442, 4446,
4467, 4506

Great Britain   3514, 4415

Iceland   4510

Netherlands   4305

Russia   4473

Scotland   3514

United States   4447

Therapists, Physical--SEE:
Physiotherapists

Thimerais, France   945

Ticino (Canton)   1861

Toulouse   946

Touraine   894

Tournai, Belgium   443, 4526

Tours, France   2506

Translators   3357

Transvaal   326

Transylvania   1658, 3700-3701,
3711, 3715, 3718, 4214

Travelers   4736-4737, 4739-
4741

Trent, Italy   3735, 4579

Trinitarians   4282, 4426

Troubadours   3592, 3596

Trouvères   3568

Tucumán, Argentina (Gobernación)
348

Turkey   1874-1881, 4139

Tuscany   1413-1417

Tyrol   392, 2635, 3780

Tyrolese anonyms and pseudonyms
--SEE: Anonyms and pseudonyms, Tyrolese

U

Udmurt A. S. S. R.   3550

Ukraine   2590, 3937-3938

Ukrainian authors--SEE: Authors,
Ukrainian

Ulm   1077

Umbria, Italy   2507

Union Theological Seminary, New
York--SEE: New York.
Union Theological Seminary

Unitarian and Free Christian
Churches   4516

United Arab Republic   1324,
1332

United Nations   283, 302

United States   83, 146, 158,
1633, 1882-2379, 2446, 2495-
2496, 2556, 2567, 2571, 2579,
2622, 2638, 2659-2660, 2662,
2664, 2675, 2692, 2696, 2705,
2708-2709, 2711, 2721, 2736-
2737, 2790, 2839, 2847-2848,
2851, 2876, 2892, 2900, 2915,
2938, 2965, 3029, 3116, 3118,
3122, 3127, 3133, 3140, 3188,
3209-3214, 3238, 3247, 3254-
3255, 3259, 3263, 3276, 3285,
3291, 3300, 3305, 3309, 3317-
3321, 3396-3436, 3493, 3941,
3950-3952, 3964-3965, 3968,
3976, 3987, 3989-3991, 3994,
4001, 4047, 4049, 4058-4071,
4124, 4137, 4153, 4167, 4204,
4207, 4210, 4213, 4216-4220,
4224, 4231-4232, 4262, 4331-
4332, 4334, 4457, 4471, 4475,
4485, 4501, 4518, 4529, 4531-
4532, 4534, 4536, 4539, 4542,
4547, 4576, 4598, 4605, 4629,
4652-4653, 4656, 4673, 4677,
4680, 4683, 4691, 4694-4696,
4701-4702, 4704-4705, 4711-
4713, 4721, 4723, 4726-4728,
4731, 4733-4734, 4738, 4760,
4769, 4779-4781, 4790, 4792,
4801, 4808-4813, 4815-4816,
4821-4824, 4826, 4828

Air Force   1936, 1942,
2024, 2065

Air National Guard   2036

Army   1924-1925, 1942,
1947-1948, 1991, 1996-1999,
2023, 2033, 2043, 2068

Coast Guard   2028

Congress   1921, 1964, 2029-
2030

Dept. of Labor   2031

Dept. of State   2031-2032

United States (cont'd)

Marine Corps   1916, 2009,
2027, 2034-2035

Marine Corps Reserve   2035

Military Academy, West
Point   1924-1925, 2045

Naval Academy, Annapolis
2038

Naval Reserve   2026

Navy   1942, 1945, 1997-1998,
2010, 2025-2027, 4518

United States--Armed Forces
1942

United States--Bibliography, indexes, etc.   1882-1889,
1967

United States--Civil War   1917,
1972-1974, 1991, 1995, 1997-
1998, 2012, 2043-2044, 2345

United States--Colonial period
1918

United States--Militia   2037

United States--Officials and
employees   1901

United States--Portraits   29,
1991, 2106, 2113, 2147, 2245,
2247, 2261, 2314, 2358, 2364,
2375, 3974

United States--Revolution   1938,
1948, 2007, 4210

Universal biography--SEE: Biography (general)

Universität Jena--SEE: Jena.
Universität

SUBJECT INDEX

Universität Köln--SEE: Cologne. Universität

Université de Liège--SEE: Liège. Université

Université de Paris--SEE: Paris. Université

University of Aberdeen--SEE: Aberdeen. University

University of Glasgow--SEE: Glasgow. University

Upper Austria--SEE: Austria, Upper

Uppsala. Universitet 1821, 1823, 1840

Ural Mountains region 1704

Urdu authors--SEE: Authors, Urdu

Urdu poets--SEE: Poets, Urdu

Uruguay 2380-2384, 3900, 3903

Uruguayan anonyms and pseudonyms--SEE: Anonyms and pseudonyms, Uruguayan

Uruguayan poets--SEE: Poets, Uruguayan

Utah 2347

Utrecht 1555

Uzbek authors--SEE: Authors, Uzbek

Uzbekistan 3935

V

Valencia 2423, 2744, 3866, 3872, 3896, 4042, 4374, 4498

Vallombrosians 4479

Valtellina, Italy 1418

Var, France (Dept.) 947

Vase painters 2435

Vassar College 2041

Vaucluse, France (Dept.) 948-949

Vaud (Canton) 1859

Vendée 950

Vendôme, France 951

Venetia 3733, 3755

Venezuela 1506-1507, 2385-2391, 3898-3899, 3911, 3916

Venezuelan authors--SEE: Authors, Venezuelan

Venice 1365, 2605, 2689, 3757, 4283, 4380, 4740

Accademia de' signori incogniti--SEE: Accademia de' signori incogniti, Venice

Vermont 2348-2352

Verona 2595-2596, 2672, 4110

Veterinarians 4192, 4202, 4783

Vicenza 3737, 3775

Victoria Cross 510, 1120

Vienna 383, 3607, 3609, 3659, 3686, 3704

Vienne, Haute-, France (Dept. 889

Vietnam   2392-2395

Violin makers   2860, 2886,
2889, 2893, 2948, 2979, 3013,
3081, 3087, 3098, 3100, 3178-
3179

Violinists   2754, 2799, 3102

Violoncellists   2799

Virginia   2949, 3316, 4509,
4775

Visiting teachers   3291

Vologda, Russia (Government)
3821

Vosges, France (Dept.)   952-953

Votiak authors--SEE: Authors,
Votiak

W

Wales   1222-1234, 2604, 2881,
2916, 3962, 4021, 4365, 4440,
4469, 4503

Walloon authors--SEE: Authors,
Walloon

Warsaw   1638

Warwickshire, Eng.   1235-1236

Washington (State)   2358-2360

Washington, D. C.   2178, 2357

Watch makers--SEE: Clock and
watch makers

Weather observers   2039

Welsh Calvinistic Methodist
Church   4365

Wernigerode   3645

West Flanders--SEE: Flanders,
West

West Indies   2396-2397

West Indies, Dutch   2397

West Point Military Academy--
SEE: U. S. Military Academy,
West Point

West Virginia   2123, 2370-2372,
3399, 3942

Westchester Co. , N. Y.   4131

Western Australia   372

Western India States   1286,
1291

Western Region of Nigeria   1580

Western States (U. S.)   2361-
2369, 3974

Westminster School, London--
SEE: St. Peter's College,
London

Westmorland   1237

Westphalia   1078-1079, 2557

White Russia   3838

White Russian authors--SEE: Authors, White Russian

Wind instrument makers   2936

Wisconsin   2102, 2208, 2373-
2378, 3125, 3980

University   3317

Witchcraft   4253, 4261

Women   43-44, 81, 115, 136,
144, 148, 155, 165, 172,
185, 219, 240, 250, 256,
280-282, 306, 2654, 2829,
2967, 4355

Africa, South   331

Bolivia   469

California   2094

Canada   512, 521-523

France   776

Georgia   2134

Germany   1006

Great Britain   3265

Italy   1379, 1400

Japan   1441

Latin America   1509

Mexico   1550

Minnesota   2215

Natal   329

Norway   1589

Philadelphia   2305

Philippine Islands   1623

Portugal   165

Russia   1707

Southwestern States (U. S.)
2330

Women (cont'd)

United States   1904, 1911,
1928, 1938, 1974, 2001, 2070,
2072-2073, 2094, 2134, 2215,
2305, 2330, 2362, 3950, 3987,
3989, 4173

The West (U. S.)   2362

Women as artists--SEE: Artists,
Women

Women as authors   280-282

France   3560-3561

Germany   3629, 3660,
3674-3675, 3688

Italy   3751-3752, 3761

Latin America   3919

Russia   3826, 3840, 3842

Southern States (U. S.)
3430

Spain   3863, 3881, 3890

United States   3430

Women as educators--SEE: Educators and scholars, Women

Women as lawyers   3950, 3987, 3989

Women as physicians   4173

Women educators and scholars--
SEE: Educators and scholars,
Women

Women in the Bible   4267

Women musicians--SEE: Musicians, Women

Women saints--SEE: Saints, Women

Women scholars--SEE: Educators and scholars, Women

Worcestershire, Eng. 1238-1239

World biography--SEE: Biograph (general)

World War (1914-1918)--SEE: European War (1914-1918)

World War (1939-1945) 269, 656, 694, 774-775, 847, 1018-1021, 1381-1382, 1465, 1634, 3554

Württemberg 1080-1081

Würzburg 1082

Wuppertal 1083

Wyoming 2379

Y

Yale University 312, 1929-1930, 1971

Yiddish authors--SEE: Authors, Yiddish

York, Eng. 4006

Yorkshire, Eng. 1240-1242

Young people 52, 1905, 1993

Yucatan 1522, 1524, 4763

Yugoslav authors--SEE: Authors, Yugoslav

Yugoslavia 2398-2409, 3854

Z

Zacatecas, Mexico 3904

Zamora, Spain (Province) 1811

Zealand, Netherlands 1571

Zionists 1450, 1454

Zither makers 2859

Zither players 2859

Zoologists 4627-4630, 4643

Zürich--SEE: Zurich

Zug (Canton) 4399

Zurich 1848, 1857, 3932